THE (

This volume presents students and scholars with a comprehensive overview of the fascinating world of the occult. It explores the history of Western occultism, from ancient and medieval sources via the Renaissance, right up to the nineteenth and twentieth centuries and contemporary occultism. Written by a distinguished team of contributors, the essays consider key figures, beliefs and practices as well as popular culture.

Christopher Partridge is Professor of Religious Studies in the Department of Politics, Philosophy and Religion at Lancaster University, UK. His research and writing focuses on alternative spiritual currents, countercultures and popular music.

THE ROUTLEDGE WORLDS

THE CELTIC WORLD
Edited by Miranda Green

THE GREEK WORLD
Edited by Anton Powell

THE REFORMATION WORLD
Edited by Andrew Pettegree

THE EARLY CHRISTIAN WORLD
Edited by Philip F. Esler

THE ROMAN WORLD
Edited by John Wacher

THE MEDIEVAL WORLD
Edited by Peter Linehan and Janet L. Nelson

THE BIBLICAL WORLD
Edited by John Barton

THE HINDU WORLD
Edited by Sushil Mittal and Gene Thursby

THE ENLIGHTENMENT WORLD
Edited by Martin Fitzpatrick

THE WORLD OF POMPEII
Edited by Pedar W. Foss and John J. Dobbins

THE BABYLONIAN WORLD
Edited by Gwendolyn Leick

THE RENAISSANCE WORLD
Edited by John Jeffries Martin

THE EGYPTIAN WORLD
Edited by Toby Wilkinson

THE ISLAMIC WORLD
Edited by Andrew Rippin

THE VIKING WORLD
Edited by Stefan Brink and Neil Price

THE BYZANTINE WORLD
Edited by Paul Stephenson

THE ELIZABETHAN WORLD
Edited by Susan Doran and Norman Jones

THE WORLD OF THE AMERICAN WEST
Edited by Gordon Morris Bakken

THE OTTOMAN WORLD
Edited by Christine Woodhead

THE VICTORIAN WORLD
Edited by Martin Hewitt

THE ORTHODOX CHRISTIAN WORLD
Edited by Augustine Casiday

THE SUMERIAN WORLD
Edited by Harriet Crawford

THE ETRUSCAN WORLD
Edited by Jean MacIntosh Turfa

THE GOTHIC WORLD
Edited by Glennis Byron and Dale Townshend

THE WORLD OF THE REVOLUTIONARY AMERICAN REPUBLIC
Edited by Andrew Shankman

THE WORLD OF INDIGENOUS NORTH AMERICA
Edited by Robert Warrior

THE FIN-DE-SIÈCLE WORLD
Edited by Michael Saler

THE OCCULT WORLD
Edited by Christopher Partridge

Forthcoming:

THE ATLANTIC WORLD
Edited by D'Maris Coffman, Adrian Leonard, William O'Reilly

THE MODERNIST WORLD
Edited by Andrew Lindgren and Stephen Ross

THE WORLD OF IONIA
Edited by Alan Greaves

THE BUDDHIST WORLD
Edited by John Powers

THE CRUSADER WORLD
Edited by Adrian Boas

THE POSTCOLONIAL WORLD
Edited by Jyotsna Singh and David Kim

THE WORLD OF FORMATIVE EUROPE
Edited by Martin Carver and Madeleine Hummler

THE OCCULT WORLD

Edited by

Christopher Partridge

LONDON AND NEW YORK

First published in 2015
by Routledge
2 Park Square, Milton Park, Abingdon, Oxfordshire OX14 4RN

Simultaneously published in the USA and Canada
by Routledge
711 Third Avenue, New York, NY 10017

First issued in paperback 2016

Routledge is an imprint of the Taylor & Francis Group, an informa business

British Library Cataloguing in Publication Data
A catalogue record for this book is available from the British Library

Library of Congress Cataloging in Publication Data
A catalog record has been requested for this book

ISBN 13: 978-1-138-21925-0 (pbk)
ISBN 13: 978-0-415-69596-1 (hbk)

Typeset in Sabon
by Saxon Graphics Ltd, Derby

CONTENTS

NOTES ON CONTRIBUTORS

Deborah Allison is a London-based cinema programmer and Associate Research Fellow at De Montfort University's Cinema and Television History Research Centre. She is the author of *The Cinema of Michael Winterbottom* (2012), co-author of *The Phoenix Picturehouse: 100 Years of Oxford Cinema Memories* (2013), and has also contributed to more than a dozen books and journals, including *Film International*, *Film Quarterly*, *Senses of Cinema*, *Screen*, *Scope*, and *The Schirmer Encyclopaedia of Film*.

Egil Asprem is a postdoctoral scholar at the University of California Santa Barbara, specializing in the history of Western esotericism. He is the author of *Arguing with Angels: Enochian Magic and Modern Occulture* (2012) and *The Problem of Disenchantment* (2014), and co-editor of *Contemporary Esotericism* (2013).

Brian Baker has worked at Glyndwr University and the University of Chester, and is currently Lecturer in English at Lancaster University, UK. He is the author of *Masculinities in Fiction and Film* (2006) and *Iain Sinclair* (2007), and is completing the *Reader's Guide to Essential Criticism in Science Fiction* (for Palgrave Macmillan) and *Contemporary Masculinities in Fiction, Film and Television* (for Bloomsbury Academic). He has contributed to numerous books and journals, often on science fiction. He is also currently working on science fictions of the 1960s: a critical monograph on the decade, and a critical/creative work on experimental science fiction. He teaches American literature, film, and genre fiction.

Phil Baker is the author of a number of books, including *The Devil is a Gentleman: The Life and Times of Dennis Wheatley* (2009) and *Austin Osman Spare: The Life and Legend of London's Lost Artist* (2011), which Alan Moore has described as 'little short of marvellous.' He has also written a study of Samuel Beckett, a cultural history of absinthe, and a short critical biography of William S. Burroughs, as well as co-editing (with Antony Clayton) *Lord of Strange Deaths: The Fiendish World of Sax Rohmer* (2014).

Michael Barkun is Professor Emeritus of Political Science in the Maxwell School at Syracuse University. His books include *Chasing Phantoms: Reality, Imagination, and*

Homeland Security Since 9/11 (2011); *A Culture of Conspiracy: Apocalyptic Visions in Contemporary America* (2003); and *Religion and the Racist Right: The Origins of the Christian Identity Movement* (1997).

Tessel M. Bauduin is an art historian, specializing in art and culture of the late nineteenth and early twentieth centuries. Her Ph.D. from the University of Amsterdam, 'The Occultation of Surrealism,' which explored the relationship between the Surrealism of André Breton and occultism, is published by Amsterdam University Press/Chicago University Press (2014). She is currently working on a postdoctoral research project on medievalism in Surrealism and other avant-gardes, as well as teaching courses in art history and cultural studies at both Radboud University, Nijmegen and the University of Amsterdam. She has published several articles and reviews, and guest-edited (with Nina Kokkinen) a special issue of the journal *Aries* on 'Occulture and Modern Art.'

Henrik Bogdan is Associate Professor in History of Religions at the University of Gothenburg. His main areas of research are Western Esotericism, New Religious Movements, and Freemasonry. He is the author of *Western Esotericism and Rituals of Initiation* (2007), editor of *Brother Curwen, Brother Crowley: A Correspondence* (2010), and co-editor of *Aleister Crowley and Western Esotericism* (2012), *Occultism in a Global Perspective* (2013), *Sexuality and New Religious Movements* (2014), and *The Brill Handbook on Freemasonry* (2014).

Dylan M. Burns is Research Associate at Universität Leipzig, Germany. His work addresses a diversity of topics in Early Christianity, Gnosticism, and Neoplatonism. In addition to numerous scholarly articles, he is the author of *Apocalypse of the Alien God: Platonism and the Exile of Sethian Gnosticism* (2014) and a contributing editor to *Gnosticism, Platonism, and the Late Ancient World: Essays in Honour of John D. Turner* (2013).

Alison Butler holds a postdoctoral research fellowship with the Social Sciences and Humanities Research Council of Canada in the Department of Philosophy at Memorial University of Newfoundland, Canada. Her publications include *Victorian Occultism and the Making of Modern Magic: Invoking Tradition* (2011).

Nicholas Campion is Senior Lecturer in the School of Archaeology, History and Anthropology at the University of Wales Trinity Saint David. His research interests include the history of astrology and astronomy as well as the place of both disciplines in contemporary culture. He also researches millenarian and apocalyptic belief, magic, New Age and Pagan ideas and practices, the sociology of new religious movements and the nature of belief in general. His most recent book is a major, two-volume *History of Western Astrology* (2009).

Douglas E. Cowan is Professor of Religious Studies and Social Development Studies at Renison University College in the University of Waterloo, Waterloo, Canada. The author of numerous books and articles, his recent works include *Sacred Terror: Religion and Horror on the Silver Screen* (2008) and *Sacred Space: The Quest for Transcendence in Science Fiction Film and Television* (2010). He is currently working on two books, one on atheism and scepticism, the other on the social construction of pornography.

Adam Crabtree is on the faculty of the Centre for Training in Psychotherapy in Toronto. He has written books in the field of dissociative phenomena and the history of hypnotism and psychotherapy, including *Irreducible Mind: Toward a Psychology for the 21st Century* (2007), *Trance Zero: The Psychology of Maximum Experience* (1999) and *From Mesmer to Freud: Magnetic Sleep and the Roots of Psychological Healing* (1993).

Owen Davies is Professor of Social History at the University of Hertfordshire. He has published widely on the history of magic, witchcraft, ghosts and popular medicine.

Erik Davis writes and speaks regularly on media, counterculture, and spirituality (www.techgnosis.com). He is the author of *Techgnosis: Myth, Magic, and Mysticism in the Age of Information* (1998), *Led Zeppelin IV* (2005) and, most recently, *Nomad Codes: Adventures in Modern Esoterica* (2010). He has taught and lectured widely at universities and festivals, hosts the weekly Internet radio show 'Expanding Mind', and is currently pursuing a Ph.D. in Religious Studies at Rice University, Houston, US.

Colin Duggan holds M.A. degrees in both Philosophy and Religious Studies from the National University of Ireland, Galway and the University of Amsterdam, respectively. He is a doctoral researcher in the Study of Religions Department, University College Cork, Ireland and is working on a dissertation entitled 'The Theosophical Society: Esoteric Discourse and Politics in Early 20th Century Ireland.' He has previously published on Chaos Magick.

Florian Ebeling is a lecturer and researcher in the Department of Egyptology at the University of Heidelberg. He has written a number of articles and books, including *The Secret History of Hermes Trismegistus: Hermeticism from Ancient to Modern Times* (2007) and (with Jan Assmann) *Ägyptische Mysterien. Reisen in die Unterwelt in Aufklärung und Romantik* (2011).

Helen Farley is a Senior Research Fellow within the School of History, Philosophy, Religion and Classics at the University of Queensland. She is also a Senior Lecturer at the Australian Digital Futures Institute at the University of Southern Queensland. Her research is diverse, ranging from the cultural history of various esoteric traditions to religion in virtual worlds.

Peter J. Forshaw is Senior Lecturer in History of Western Esotericism in the Early Modern Period at the Center for History of Hermetic Philosophy and Related Currents, University of Amsterdam. He researches the intellectual and cultural history of learned magic and its relation to religion, science and medicine in early modern Europe. He is editor-in-chief of *Aries: Journal for the Study of Western Esotericism.*

Robert A. Gilbert is a retired antiquarian bookseller and writer, who is the author or editor of many books on the 'occult revival' of the nineteenth century and on the many movements and individual involved in it. Dr. Gilbert has also written and lectured extensively on the history and philosophy of Freemasonry and on various areas of Christian Spirituality. His books include *A.E. Waite: Magician of Many Parts* (1987), *Elements of Mysticism* (1991), *Gnosis and Gnosticism: An Introduction* (2012) and a critical edition of A. E. Waite and Arthur Machen's *The House of the*

Hidden Light (2003). He is a former editor of the masonic research journal, *Ars Quatuor Coronatorum* and currently edits the journal, *The Christian Parapsychologist.*

Christian Giudice studied at St. Hugh's College Oxford University, following which he researched Kenneth Grant and post-Crowleyan magic at Exeter University's Centre for the Study of Esotericism. His interests include French and Italian occultism, occult influences in cinema, the history of Thelema after Aleister Crowley, and Traditionalism. He is currently studying at Gothenburg University, writing a Ph.D. on Arturo Reghini and occultism under the Fascist regime in Italy.

Kennet Granholm is Docent in Comparative Religion at Åbo Akademi University. He has published extensively on contemporary esotericism, esotericism and popular culture, and method and theory. He is the author of *Dark Enlightenment: The Historical, Sociological, and Discursive Contexts of Contemporary Esoteric Magic* (2014) and the co-editor of *Contemporary Esotericism* (2013).

Christian Greer is currently engaged in doctoral studies at the University of Amsterdam. His research interests include the interface between anti-authoritarianism and esotericism, the Beat Generation writers, underground publishing, and cyberpunk literature.

Cathy Gutierrez is a Professor of Religion at Sweet Briar College, Virginia, US. Her primary research interests are nineteenth-century Spiritualism and the history of esotericism, particularly where they intersect with ideas of consciousness. She has published on the Free Love movement in America, Theosophy, millennialism, and the Freemasons. Her monograph, *Plato's Ghost: Spiritualism in the American Renaissance* (2009), examines the American legacy of Neoplatonism in popular religious expression and she is the editor of the *Handbook of Spiritualism and Channeling* (2014).

Olav Hammer is Professor of the Study of Religions at the University of Southern Denmark. He has published extensively on religious innovation in Europe, New Age religiosity, and new religious movements, especially in the Theosophical tradition. Most recently, he has edited *Alternative Christs* (2009) and co-edited (with Mikael Rothstein) *The Cambridge Companion to New Religious Movements* (2012) and *The Handbook of the Theosophical Current* (2013).

Wouter J. Hanegraaff is Professor of History of Hermetic Philosophy and Related Currents at the University of Amsterdam, the Netherlands, and a member of the Royal Dutch Academy of Arts and Sciences. Alongside numerous articles, he is the author of *New Age Religion and Western Culture: Esotericism in the Mirror of Secular Thought* (1996 and 1998); *Lodovico Lazzarelli (1447–1500): The Hermetic Writings and Related Documents* (2005); *Swedenborg, Oetinger, Kant: Three Perspectives on the Secrets of Heaven* (2007); *Esotericism and the Academy: Rejected Knowledge in Western Culture* (2012); and *Western Esotericism: A Guide for the Perplexed* (2013). He has also edited and co-edited seven volumes, including *Dictionary of Gnosis and Western Esotericism* (2005) and *Hidden Intercourse: Eros and Sexuality in the History of Western Esotericism* (2011).

Graham Harvey is Reader and Head of the Department of Religious Studies at the Open University. His research and publications largely focus on Paganisms and indigenous religions. Most recently he published *Food, Sex and Strangers: Understanding Religion as Everyday Life* (2013) and *The Handbook of Contemporary Animism* (2013).

Georgiana D. Hedesan is a Wellcome Trust Fellow in Medical Humanities at the University of Oxford, researching the topic of universal medicine in seventeenth-century alchemy. In 2013, she was a Frances A. Yates Fellow at the Warburg Institute, London, and a Cantemir Junior Fellow at the University of Oxford. Her Ph.D. thesis, submitted in 2012 to the University of Exeter is entitled: '"Christian Philosophy": Medical Alchemy and Christian Thought in the Work of Jan Baptista Van Helmont (1579–1644).' She has published several chapters and articles in scholarly journals, such as *Medical History* and *Ambix*.

Jay Johnston is Senior Lecturer in the Department of Studies in Religion, University of Sydney, Australia, and co-convenor of the Religion, Science, and Philosophy Research Cluster, at the Centre for Religion, Conflict and the Public Domain, University of Groningen, Netherlands. Her research projects include: 'The Function of Images in Magical Papyri and Artefacts of Ritual Power from Late Antiquity' funded by the Australian Research Council and a monograph *Stag and Stone: Archaeology, Religion and Esoteric Aesthetics* (2014). Previous publications include *Angels of Desire: Esoteric Bodies, Aesthetics and Ethics* (2008) and, co-edited with Geoffrey Samuel, *Religion and the Subtle Body in Asia and the West: Between Mind and Body* (2013).

Peter King is Reader in Social Thought in the Department of Politics and Public Policy at De Montfort University, Leicester. He has written a number of books and articles, including *Reaction: Against the Modern World* (2012) and *The Antimodern Condition* (2014), both of which make extensive use of Guénon and Traditionalist ideas. His blog can be found at http://antimoderncondition.our.dmu.ac.uk.

Jeffrey J. Kripal holds the J. Newton Rayzor Chair in Philosophy and Religious Thought at Rice University, where he chaired the Department of Religious Studies for eight years and helped create the GEM Program, a doctoral concentration in the study of Gnosticism, Esotericism and Mysticism that is among the largest programs of its kind in the world. He is the author of seven books, including *Comparing Religions: Coming to Terms* (2014), *Mutants and Mystics: Science Fiction, Superhero Comics, and the Paranormal* (2011), and *Authors of the Impossible: The Paranormal and the Sacred* (2010).

Roderick Main is Professor at the Centre for Psychoanalytic Studies, University of Essex, UK. He is the author of *The Rupture of Time: Synchronicity and Jung's Critique of Modern Western Culture* (2004) and *Revelations of Chance: Synchronicity as Spiritual Experience* (2007), the editor of *Jung on Synchronicity and the Paranormal* (1997), and the co-editor of *Myth, Literature, and the Unconscious* (2013).

Christopher A. McIntosh is a writer and historian whose books include *Eliphas Lévi and the French Occult Revival* (latest edition, 2011), a biography of King Ludwig II of Bavaria, a study of sacred and symbolic gardens, and works on Rosicrucianism and other esoteric traditions of the West. Earlier in his life he worked in publishing in London and subsequently for the United Nations in New York and UNESCO in Hamburg and has travelled throughout the world. He was for several years on the teaching faculty of the Centre for the Study of Esotericism at Exeter University. He lives in Bremen, Germany.

Dan Merkur is a psychoanalyst in private practice in Toronto, Canada. He is on the teaching faculty at both the Toronto Institute for Contemporary Psychoanalysis and the Living Institute, which trains transpersonal psychotherapists in Toronto. Currently also a Visiting Scholar at the Department for the Study of Religion at the University of Toronto, he has taught religious studies at five universities in Canada and the United States, and published fourteen books and over fifty articles.

Andreas Önnerfors is Reader in the History of Sciences and Ideas and currently holds a teaching position at the University of Malmö, Sweden in the field of Global Political Studies. His principal research focus is on people, media, mobility, and encounters from a transgressive, predominantly early modern perspective. He has specialized in the European dimensions of press history, translation, and organized sociability, in particular Swedish and European freemasonry.

Glyn Parry is Professor of Early Modern History at the University of Roehampton, London. He is the author of *The Arch-Conjuror of England: John Dee* (2012), which was runner-up for the Longman/History Today Prize 2013. He has published articles on Dee in *The Historical Journal* and *Studies in the History and Philosophy of Science*, and articles on sixteenth-century magic and other topics in leading journals including *Reformation: The Journal of the Tyndale Society*, *The Journal of Ecclesiastical History*, *The English Historical Review*, and *History of Science*. He continues his research on Elizabethan magic and is also investigating Shakespeare's biographical background.

Christopher Partridge is Professor of Religious Studies in the Department of Politics, Philosophy and Religion at Lancaster University, UK. His research and writing focus on alternative spiritual currents, countercultures, and popular music.

Jesper Aagaard Petersen is Associate Professor at the Norwegian University of Science and Technology, Trondheim, Norway. He has published extensively on modern Satanism and contemporary esotericism. He has edited *Contemporary Religious Satanism: An Anthology* (2009) and co-edited (with Per Faxneld) *The Devil's Party: Satanism in Modernity* (2013).

Jeremy Rapport is a faculty member in the Department of Religious Studies at the College of Wooster. His teaching and research focus on American religious history with a special interest in New Thought, Christian Science, and other forms of alternative Christianity.

George J. Sieg received his doctorate in Western Esotericism from the Centre for the Study of Esotericism, Exeter University, in 2010. His thesis on occult war traced the origin and development of occult warfare beliefs from prehistoric Iranian dualism into the contemporary period. His research into dualist world-views has extended into studies of radicalism and extremism in religion and in politicized esotericism.

His articles on this and related subjects include 'Angular Momentum: From Traditional to Progressive Satanism in the Order of Nine Angles,' *International Journal for the Study of New Religious Movements* (2014). He is currently an adjunct professor at the University of New Mexico teaching religion, psychology, philosophy, and history.

Francisco Santos Silva has a doctorate in Religious Studies from the University of Manchester on 'MacGregor' Mathers. He specializes in Early Modern and Contemporary Esotericism and is now carrying out postdoctoral research in 'Occult Properties in Early Modern Medicine' and lecturing in the Philosophy of Religion at Universidade Nova in his home city of Lisbon.

Jan A. M. Snoek is attached to the Institute for the Sciences of Religions at the University of Heidelberg (Germany) as a specialist in ritual studies. He has published widely on the development of masonic rituals. With Jens Kreinath and Michael Stausberg he published *Theorizing Rituals*, two vols (2006, 2007), and with Alexandra Heidle, *Women's Agency and Rituals in Mixed and Female Masonic Orders* (2008). He is also the author of *Einführung in die Westliche Esoterik, für Freimaurer* (*Introduction to Western Esotericism for Freemasons*) (2011) and *Initiating Women in Freemasonry. The Adoption Rite* (2012)/*Le Rite d'Adoption et l'initiation des femmes en franc-maçonnerie, des Lumières à nos jours* (2012).

Julian Strube has studied History and the Study of Religions at the University of Heidelberg, Germany. He specializes in the relationship between religion, science, philosophy and politics in the nineteenth and twentieth centuries. In his first monograph, he reconstructed the genealogy of the fictitious energy 'Vril' in that context. He is currently completing doctoral research into occultism and socialism in nineteenth-century France.

György E. Szönyi is Professor of English at the University of Szeged, Hungary, and Professor of Cultural and Intellectual History at the Central European University, Budapest. His interests include cultural theory, the Renaissance, the Western Esoteric traditions and conventions of symbolization – early modern and (post)modern. His recent monographs include: *Pictura and Scriptura. Twentieth Century Theories of Cultural Representations* (in Hungarian, 2004); *Gli angeli di John Dee* (2004); *John Dee's Occultism* (2004). He is currently working on *The Enoch Readers. A Cultural History of Angels, Magic, and Ascension on High*.

Hereward Tilton has taught the history of Western esotericism at the University of Amsterdam and the Ludwig-Maximilians-Universität in Munich, where he was a fellow of the Alexander von Humboldt Foundation. He has published work on Rosicrucianism, alchemy and magic in early modern Germany, and has been teaching units on Rosicrucianism, Christian Cabala and Carl Gustav Jung's *Red Book* at the University of Exeter since 2010. His research currently concerns high-grade manuscripts of the Gold-und Rosenkreuz and the employment of entheogens in early modern theurgy.

Hugh Urban is Professor of Religious Studies and South Asian Studies at Ohio State University. He is the author of seven books, including *Magia Sexualis: Sex, Magic and Liberation in Modern Western Esotericism* (2005), *The Power of Tantra:*

Religion, Sexuality and the Politics of South Asian Studies (2010), and *The Church of Scientology: A History of a New Religion* (2011).

Jeffrey S. Victor holds a Ph.D. in Sociology. He has published extensively about satanic cult rumours and false accusations of crime. His book on the topic has been used in many court cases. He is a retired Professor from State University of New York, Jamestown College.

Angela Voss teaches at Canterbury Christ Church University. Her interests focus on the nature of symbolic interpretation and the role of the creative imagination in Western esoteric traditions. She has published extensively on the Renaissance magus Marsilio Ficino. Her website is www.angelavoss.org.

Andrew Weeks, Professor of German and Comparative Literature at Illinois State University has published intellectual biographies of Paracelsus, Jacob Boehme and Valentin Weigel and translated their works.

Jane Williams-Hogan is a Professor of Sociology and Co-Director of a Master of Arts in Religious Studies program at Bryn Athyn College, Pennsylvania. She has explored the connections of Emanuel Swedenborg to many different currents, including Western esotericism, Kabbalah, and Spiritualism. She is currently writing a biography of Emanuel Swedenborg.

INTRODUCTION

Christopher Partridge

Throughout Western history, from late antiquity to the present, there have been a number of related theological and philosophical currents that have been rejected as profane within some religious cultures and as regressive or irrational within certain secular discourses. However, following the rediscovery of ancient texts during the Renaissance, which led to the scholarly revival of occult subjects in the West, not only did aspects of these intellectual and spiritual currents become widely accepted, but they have been deceptively influential within the history of ideas. Moreover, as a result of the erosion of Christianity's hegemonic position in Western societies, the modern turn to the self, and the questioning of deference to traditional authorities, many of the 'fields of discourse' (Stuckrad, 2005: 7) generated by the 'occult sciences' have survived into late-modernity. Not only that, but, having experienced a significant revival in the nineteenth century, they have been subsequently adopted and developed in ways that can hardly be ignored by contemporary scholarship. 'The occult', broadly defined, haunts the twenty-first century imagination, permeates popular culture, and contributes to new spiritual trajectories.

Drawing together the work of a distinguished team of international scholars, the aim of the present volume is to provide an accessible, but scholarly overview of these currents, focusing particularly on their influence since the occult revival of the nineteenth century. Although, of course, any comprehensive treatment of the history of occult thought would run to many volumes, and although readers will, no doubt, bemoan the omission of favourite theorists, practitioners, authors, artists, traditions, texts and practices, it is hoped that this collection of essays reflects enough of the occult world, past and present, to indicate its significance as an important area of research.

I

The claim that the occult has been significant in Western history usually meets with a raised eyebrow from colleagues in the academic community who simply assume, often with uninformed contempt, that it has little to do with very much that has been formative in our culture. Indeed, there are many who simply reject the very suggestion that the study of the occult has anything to do with what passes for serious scholarship and are bemused by the notion that intelligent, sane people might be interested in studying it. To some extent, this is, of course, understandable. Certainly, it has to be recognized that, in everyday cultures, the word 'occult' has become an unhelpfully broad umbrella term, under which is collected a constantly recycled hodgepodge of spiritual, paranormal and transgressive beliefs and practices, many of which are widely dismissed as perverse, profane, ephemeral, irrational, or childish. Central to the construction of this understanding has been a number of 'occulturally' influential books published since the 1960s, the most significant being probably Colin Wilson's trilogy, *The Occult* (1971), *Mysteries: An Investigation Into the Occult, the Paranormal, and the Supernatural* (1978), and *Beyond the Occult* (1988), each of which discusses a wide range of subjects, from Spiritualism to UFOs (see also Freedland, 1972). Needless to say, widely held assumptions informed by such literature hardly provide a propitious starting point for those wanting to argue that occultism is a subject deserving of respectable intellectual scrutiny.

In order to help the reader towards an appreciation of the significance of the subject, perhaps the best place to begin is with the terminology itself, which, over the last couple of centuries, has become 'tainted' in a way that its sister term 'esotericism' has not (see Hanegraaff, 2012: 153–91). Certainly, the latter term, which lacks the peculiarly profane signification of 'the occult' in Western popular culture, does not elicit the same emotional response. This may, I suspect, be an underlying reason for abandoning the terminology of 'occultism' in much academic discourse. It carries too much unhelpful/embarrassing baggage. That is to say, over the last couple of decades, efforts have been made by a number of scholars to establish some degree of terminological coherence and consistency, the result of which has been the adoption of 'Western esotericism' as the general category, rather than 'occultism'.

The term 'occult', of course, simply refers to that which is 'hidden' or 'concealed'. For example, in astronomy, 'stellar occultation' refers to the passing of an object before a distant star, thereby partially obscuring it. Again, within religion, for Shī'a Islam, occultation (*ghaybah*) refers to the hidden state of the twelfth Imam, a messianic figure whose eschatological return is anticipated by the faithful. However, 'occult', as it is used in this volume, has acquired a particular set of meanings related to gnosis, mystical experience, ancient wisdom, and the secrets of antiquity. Derived from the Latin *occultus* ('hidden', 'concealed', 'secret')—from *celare* ('to hide')—the word 'occult' first appeared in French (*occulte*) in 1120 in the *Psautier d'Oxford* and then in other European languages during the sixteenth century, when we see it beginning to refer to spheres of knowledge beyond everyday understanding, such as the mysterious operations of God. As the sixteenth century progressed, it began to be used for a specialized sphere of knowledge relating to the hidden properties of the natural world. During the Italian Renaissance, *occolto* was used in a related sense in the philosophical work of the Dominican friar Giordano Bruno (1548–1600), having previously been used by Henry Cornelius Agrippa (1486–1535) in his seminal work *De occulta philosophia libri tres* (1533). Hence, by 1593, the English scholar Gabriel Harvey (*c.* 1552–1631) was able to freely speak of 'the greatest empirics, spagyrics, cabbalists, alchemists, magicians, and occult philosophers' (1593: 71). However, by 1842, when the noun 'occultism' was coined in a dictionary article by A. de Lestrange and then quickly taken up by Éliphas Lévi in 1856, the signification had shifted.

'Occultism' now represented a particular construction of a coherent countercultural wisdom tradition, following a linear pattern, rather than a dynamic complex of rhizomatic currents. Indeed, it is this construction of 'the occult' as a linear, countercultural tradition that informs contemporary popular understandings. It is a construction that was initially articulated by Protestant and Enlightenment thinkers who sought to establish their own identities over against the opposing Other of irrational *superstitio*; it was then developed by occultists themselves seeking the intellectual and theological respectability of a specific identity and an ancient tradition. These nineteenth- and twentieth-century articulations of 'occultism' and the subsequent development of the terminology within 'occulture' (see below) have led some scholars to limit its application to developments within the last 150 years or so. In other words, in current scholarly usage, the term 'occultism' is often restricted to nineteenth-century developments and succeeding esoteric trajectories, including fields of discourse related to spiritualism, Theosophy, magical initiatory orders (such as the Hermetic Order of the Golden Dawn), and the New Age. 'Occultism in this sense', notes Wouter Hanegraaff, 'has its pioneers in 18th-century authors such as, notably, Emanuel Swedenborg and Franz Anton Mesmer, and covers the great majority of esoteric currents from at least the mid-nineteenth century on' (2006: 888). 'Esotericism', on the other hand, a term coined in 1828 by the historian Jacques Matter in his work on early Christian Gnosticism, *Histoire critique du gnosticisme et de son influence*, originated within academia. Consequently, 'Western esotericism' became the term preferred by academics—particularly in France (*'l'ésotérisme occidental'*). Hence, *The Occult World* is, nowadays, a rather controversial title for an academic volume that begins its survey in late antiquity, rather than in the nineteenth century.

Having said that, although we should be careful not to read back contemporary popular understandings of 'the occult' into pre- and early modern texts, it is significant that the terminology is used in those texts. Not only does it have an interesting history stretching back to the medieval reception of Aristotelian natural philosophy, but it has been, certainly since the publication of the first volume of Agrippa's *De occulta philosophia* in 1531, the preferred terminology of many of the principal architects of occult thought. Indeed, the same is true of the previous generation of scholars, such as Francis Yates, who did much to establish the occult as a field of academic research. They used the terminology with which they had become familiar in their studies of Renaissance and early modern magic. Less controversially, perhaps, the title of the present volume can also be defended on the grounds that, although it spans the history of occult thought, it is deliberately focused on the modern period, from the nineteenth century on. As such, it follows the current convention of limiting the terminology to this period, with the earlier chapters functioning as important historical material. That said, again, 'occult' is widely used prior to the nineteenth century and attending to the history of the idea, rather than attempting to be too prescriptive, can be instructive.

II

'The occult' may have been both common sense and ubiquitous in early modern Europe, but attitudes towards the study of it were often ambiguous. There was a sense that the study of the occult constituted 'edgework', it being a transgressive discipline that operated at the boundaries of the sacred and the profane. Consequently, the occult sciences were not without risk. For example, not only were angelic and demonic entities believed to be themselves adept occultists, but, in a Christian, biblically circumscribed culture, 'Satan himself masquerades as an angel of light' (2 Corinthians 11:14). In other words, because the Devil is the 'father of lies' (John 8:44) who has significant expertise and power in the field, any foray into the occult world could become treacherous: 'do not believe every spirit, but test the spirits to see whether they are from God, because many false prophets have gone out into the world' (1 John 4:1). It is not surprising, therefore, that in his influential *Daemonologie*, James VI of Scotland (later James I of England), who had been troubled by the North Berwick witch trials, warned of those spiritual beings which are 'farre cunninger then man in the knowledge of all the occult properties of nature' (1597: 44). Likewise, a few years later Sir Walter Raleigh reminded his readers (not that they needed reminding) that 'the Devill from the beginning hath sought to thrust himself into the same employment among the ministers and servants of God, changing himself for that purpose into an Angell of light' (1614: 205). As such, says Raleigh, 'he hath led men into Idolatrie as a doctrine of religion; he hath thrust in his Prophets among those of the true God; he hath corrupted the Art of *Astrologie*, by giving a divine power to the Starrs, teaching men to esteeme them as Gods, and not as instruments' (Raleigh, 1614: 205). It's not that astrology is considered to be profane, but rather that the study of astrology could be guided by malign spiritual entities. Consequently, as Lauren Kassell comments of the early modern period, 'great learning and suspicion of its demonic sources are inseparable' (2006: 109). In a society, genuinely concerned about the possibility of demonic interference, any sense that the sources of one's learning might be profane could lead to serious social and religious consequences (see, Briggs, 1996; Johnstone, 2006; Russell, 1986). That is to say, because these were societies in which individuals imagined themselves to be embroiled in spiritual warfare, in which neutrality was not an option, demonstrating that one was on the right side was of the utmost importance. Unfortunately, of course, the very nature of the occult made determining this difficult, both for occultists themselves and for those observers who might, at any moment, condemn them as pagan servants of the Devil – an accusation that scholars were wise to avoid in early modern societies.

Consequently, during this period, a discussion of the occult often included an apologia, which distinguished between the angelic and the demonic, the sacred and the profane. For example, Giambattista della Porta makes a clear distinction between 'two sorts of Magick; the one is infamous...because it hath to do with soul spirits and...Inchantments...and is called Sorcery...The other Magick is natural...The most noble Philosophers...call this knowledge the very...perfection of the natural Sciences' (quoted in Copenhaver, 2008: 454). This difference between knowledge gained through natural magic – the source of which is God – and that acquired through demonic agency is conspicuous in the work of Raleigh, who is keen to rescue the occultist, the *magus*, from accusations of witchcraft: 'It is true that many men abhorre the very name and word (*Magus*) because of *Simon Magus* [see Acts 8: 9–25]: who being indeede, not *Magus*, but...familiar with evill spirits, usurped that title. For *Magicke*, Conjuring, and Witcherie are farre differing arts...*Magus* is a Persian word primitively, whereby is exprest such a one as is altogether conversant in things divine. And...the art of *Magicke* is the art of worshipping God' (1614: 205). Hence, in a response to James VI's 'first booke of *Demonologie*', he encourages his readers to remember 'that under the name of *Magicke* all other unlawful arts are comprehended... For the *Magicke* which *His Majestie* condemneth is of that kinde whereof the Devill is a partie' (1614: 201). His point is simple. While one ought to beware of 'corruptions, which have made odious the very name of *Magicke*' (1614: 202), in actual fact the study of the occult is a sacred vocation with significant utilitarian value. For example, '*Astrologie*' is useful 'to sowing and planting, and all kinds of agriculture and husbandry', which is, he says, 'a knowledge of the motions and influences of the Starres into those lower elements' (1614: 202). More importantly, the biblical patriarch Abraham discovered astrology to be a helpful tool in the pursuit of the 'knowledge of the true God' (1614: 202). In the final analysis, '*Magicke* containeth the whole Philosophie of nature...that which bringeth to light the inmost vertues, and draweth them out of natures hidden bosome to human use, *Virtutes in centro centrilatentes, Vertues hidden in the center of the center*, according to the *Chymists* [chemists]. Of this sort were *Albertus* [Magnus], *Arnoldus de villanova, Raymond* [Lull], and [Roger] *Bacon*, and many others' (1614: 202). In short, 'a *Magician*...is no other then *divinorum cultor & interpres, A studious observer and expounder of divine things*' (1614: 205), his overall point being that '*the good knowledge in the ancient Magicke is not to be condemned: though the Devill here as in other kinds hath sought to obtrude evill things under the name and colour of good things*' (1614: 205).

Again, the above highlights the perennial problem for 'the occult'. It has been constructed as theologically ambiguous in a Christian culture. Although, in premodern societies, the occult sciences were theologically justified along the lines of attending to God's general revelation in nature, which had significant instrumental value, there was always the problem that, as James VI had warned, 'the Devill (who knoweth more than any man) doth also teach Witches and Poysoners the harmefull parts of hearbs, druggs, minerals, and excrements' (1614: 205). However, as we will see later, once empirical science had distanced itself from the occult, dismissing it as *superstitio* (i.e. irrational), the earlier apologetic responses of such as Raleigh no longer appeared credible and, slipping into the sphere of the amateur enthusiast, it became, irredeemably, the profane Other.

That this was so accounts, to some extent, for the fact that the same concerns about 'sorcery', 'Black Magic', 'the dark arts', and the 'left-hand path' continued into modern occultism. For example, as well as those within the Christian community whose scholarship sought to expose and combat diabolism in the world, such as, most famously, the Catholic priest Montague Summers, influential occultists of the period, such as Éliphas Lévi and Helena Blavatsky, also warned of the dangers awaiting the 'student of the *Divina Sapientia*' (Blavatsky, 1939: 13). In Blavatsky's discussion of 'the conditions under which alone the study of Divine Wisdom can be pursued with safety, that is without danger that Divine [Magic] will give place to Black Magic', she insists that 'it is the motive, *and the motive alone*, which makes any exercise of power become black, malignant, or white, beneficent Magic' (1939: 12; cf. Lévi, 1923: 167–69).

Hence, while we should be careful to avoid anachronism, understanding the dualistic Christian cultural context of occultism helps toward an understanding of its sacred–profane ambiguity. Whether the occult was explicitly developed with reference to its Christian theological context – as in the case of some early discussions of *qualitates occultae* or, later, in New Thought – or whether it was demonized as the profane Other and vice versa, or whether it was articulated as an interpretation of particular Christian theological ideas – as in Annie Besant's *Esoteric Christianity or the Lesser Mysteries* (1905), Alice Bailey's *The Reappearance of the Christ* (1947), Levi H. Dowling's *The Aquarian Gospel of Jesus the Christ* (1964) and Anthony Duncan's *The Christ, Psychotherapy and Magic* (1969) and Dion Fortune's *Esoteric Orders and Their Work* (2000) – it is difficult to understand its construction in the West without reference to Christian religion and culture. Even Aleister Crowley, one of the most influential and creative occultists of the modern period, needs to be understood in relation to his Christian context. The explicit rejection of his upbringing within the Plymouth Brethren, the not infrequent references to Christian theological ideas (e.g. Crowley, 1977: 11–13), the enthusiastic embrace of discourses of profanation made available to him by Christian demonology – most notably, his identification as 'Master Therion', 'the Great Beast, 666' (Greek: θηρίον, therion, beast), taken from the biblical Book of Revelation (e.g. Crowley, 1996: 75) – and his 'profound respect for Christ as an individual who had attained enlightenment' (Bogdan, 2012: 100), are all important for understanding the development of his thought.

III

While much discussion in *The Occult World* focuses on the spiritual and the metaphysical, its constructive relationship with early modern science should not be forgotten. Despite attempts by some scholars, such as Brian Vickers (1984), to reject any significant continuity between Renaissance occultism and the emergence of the new science, the boundaries between the two were in fact porous and the relationship conspicuous. Hence, although there have been anachronistic attempts to demonize pre-modern occultism over against the rigorous logic of modern science, in reality there were significant areas of overlap between core fields of discourse. It is not surprising, therefore, that the intellectual and moral status of the occult found support in authoritative early modern texts. As Copenhaver discusses, 'practical interest in astrology, alchemy, and other departments of the occultist tradition ran strong throughout the early modern period among serious thinkers in many disciplines...' (2008: 455). This concord, however, was not to last.

As occult ideas were typically embedded within religious and mythological narratives, it wasn't too long before the relationship between the occult sciences and the new empirical sciences became strained. As Hanegraaff notes of Blaise de Vigenère (1523–96) – possibly the first person to refer to 'the occult sciences' – he situates occultism 'within a more general context entirely dominated by the ancient wisdom narrative' (2012: 182). This link between the occult and theories of ancient universal wisdom is important. The 'occult sciences' were occupied with the formulation of rigorous methods for understanding the secrets of nature, informed by a unifying notion of ancient wisdom. Hence, whereas, 'seen merely "from the outside", the domains of magic, astrology, kabbalah, and alchemy might look like relatively distinct disciplines', as Hanegraaff comments, 'referring to them as "occult sciences" carried the deliberate suggestion that they were unified at a deeper level, because they reflected one and the same, comprehensive, hidden, but universal knowledge about the true nature of reality' (2012: 183). Occultism thus emerged as a specialist field devoted to the excavation of knowledge about the underlying unity of the cosmos and the energies and agencies with which it was animated. Its aim was to access truths that had been 'hidden from the vulgar, but revealed to the wise as "higher knowledge"' (Hanegraaff, 2012: 182).

As the early modern period progressed, however, it was increasingly difficult for such notions to avoid conflict with the new ideas of the scientific revolution. Although there were, of course, interests and areas of enquiry that overlapped with new scientific thinking, the study of the occult was becoming theoretically and methodologically distinct. Of course, initially, there was some ambivalence about the scientific validity of occult ideas, just as there was about their theological validity. For example, while, on the one hand, many early modern theorists, such as Gottfried Leibniz (1646–1716) and Isaac Newton (1643–1727), failed to detach themselves entirely from the influence of esoteric ideas (see Coudert, 1995; Dobbs, 1991), on the other hand, it is revealing that, for example, Leibniz dismissed Newton's theory of gravity as the reintroduction of the *qualitates occultae*, which, he insisted, René Descartes had so successfully trounced (see, Hall, 1980: 146–67). In other words, 'the occult' was slowly becoming a derogatory term, used to indicate, not profanity as such, but irrationality. In the early modern scientific milieu, it mattered less that occult ideas transgressed Christian constructions of the sacred, and more that they transgressed objective, rational, scientific thought. In a climate in which ideas about nature were shifting towards increasingly secularized notions of a deterministic system governed by natural laws, a system in which observation, empirical evidence, and logic were paramount, any theories that seemed to rest on *qualitates occultae* were dismissed.

Thinkers such as Newton are, therefore, peculiarly interesting. As John Maynard Keynes described him, he is 'not the first of the age of reason', but rather 'the last of the magicians, the last of the Babylonians and Sumerians, the last great mind which looked out on the visible and intellectual world with the same eyes as those who began to build our intellectual inheritance rather less than 10,000 years ago' (1947: 27). Indeed, although a major influence on the development of modern science, Newton spent at least 20 years studying Hermetic materials and over two-thirds of his writings discuss ideas relating to alchemy and to religion (see, Dobbs, 1991). For Newton, physics and magic were generally understood to be part of the same natural philosophy (see, McGuire & Rattansi, 1966; Webster, 1982). Even Leibniz, who Keynes might have considered a more likely candidate for 'the first of the age of reason', was, nevertheless, 'not willing to pay the high price of eliminating mind, spirit, or soul from his scientific world picture' (Coudert, 1995: 123).

The times, however, were changing. As the modern period progressed, the idea that science might be rooted in magic was an increasingly uneasy one. As Randall Styers notes, while, in the seventeenth century, 'there was no clear line of demarcation between occultism, philosophy, religion and science', by the mid-eighteenth century, the situation had fundamentally changed, in that 'natural magic was abandoned, and all forms of demonic and occult causation were effectively expelled from the natural world. Moreover, the natural and the supernatural realms were clearly differentiated, and the role of the supernatural was severely constrained' (2004: 50). Eventually, 'magic's erasure from the philosophical agenda of the Enlightenment was so complete as to conceal its significance in earlier periods. Just as Fontenelle found Newton's early curiosity about astrology too embarrassing to mention in his obituary, so later historians of philosophy seldom bothered to ask whether the elders of their profession were interested in topics so contemptible' (Copenhaver, 2008: 503).

This, of course, is not to argue that scientific and occultic fields of discourse never again overlapped. They did. As well as scientists with a keen interest in the occult, such as Jack Parsons (1914–52), there have been more subtle moments of cross-fertilization. For example, as Mark Morrisson has argued, not only was the alchemical revival in the nineteenth century shaped by the emerging science of radioactivity, but it informed it. 'Stunning landmarks of atomic science occurred alongside an efflorescence of occultism that ascribed deep significance to questions about the nature of matter and energy. And perhaps more surprising, the broad alchemical revival had an impact on the way some scientists understood and portrayed their research programs' (Morrisson, 2007: 5).

IV

The assessment of the occult as irrational, along with the sacred–profane ambiguity that made it vulnerable to accusations of heresy, hindered its progress as an academic discipline in Christian societies. 'The occult is *rejected knowledge*' (Webb, 1974: 191). Although there is little doubt that occult subjects were researched and taught in some early modern European universities (see, Feingold, 1984), because the study of religion in academia had been dominated by Christian theology since the Middle Ages, any objective analysis of that which the Church suspected as 'pagan' was culturally and theologically problematic. This position was further exacerbated as the modern period progressed. When it was eventually abandoned as irrational, resistance to the occult hardened on both fronts – theological and scientific. As a result, during the eighteenth century, the study of the occult became the domain of the amateur enthusiast. This led to a final parting of the ways. The mainstream discourses of both science and theology othered the occult. As such, there emerged a popular perception of it as an unsafe, profane, spiritual culture. Added to this, in some quarters during the twentieth century, the occult became associated with far-right totalitarian discourses, which added to its reputation as irrational and dangerous. For example, the influential Marxist philosopher Theodor Adorno was particularly concerned about the malign influence of the irrational in Western societies. As a Jewish intellectual during the Second World War, he was understandably concerned about tendencies towards totalitarianism and barbarism. He associated occultism with a regression toward barbarism, in that it seemed to constitute resistance to reason, progress and the whole Enlightenment project: 'the tendency to occultism is a symptom of the regression in consciousness' (Adorno, 1994: 128). Occultism is, in short, antithetical to modernity and the future of Western civilization. Interestingly, one of the first to make this connection was George Orwell. In an essay on William Butler Yeats, he sought to establish a direct relationship between his interest in the occult and his fascist sympathies (1946: 115–19; see also Pasi, 2009: 59–62). It should be noted, however, that these discussions are somewhat naïve and, although it is not difficult to find examples of the confluence of occultism and far right politics in the modern world, the two are not necessarily related. Moreover, recent scholarship has shown that occultism did not always represent 'a flight from reason', as James Webb famously summed up the occult (1974: 5). As discussed in several of the following chapters, during the modern period there has often been dialogue and negotiation between occult and scientific fields of discourse. Nevertheless, the point here is that such associations have tainted the reception of 'the occult' in the West and biased scholarship in the area.

In more recent years, however, for a number of intellectual and cultural reasons, the fortunes of the occult in the academy have changed. As modernity has progressed, so there has emerged a climate in which Christian theology itself has had to struggle for legitimacy as an academic discipline. Within this climate, any defence of theology in secular universities must be careful to avoid the suspicion of special pleading. Christianity is simply one expression of a universal human phenomenon. As such, it is difficult to exclude other expressions, such as those of occultism. Moreover, within the humanities and social sciences, there is now a wealth of research demonstrating the importance of the quotidian and the value of understanding those experiences and ideas that shape everyday lives. This has led to a broadening of the scholarly gaze to include commitments to the occult and the paranormal (see Bader, Mencken & Baker, 2010; Jenzen & Munt, 2013; Partridge, 2013b; 2005; 2004).

In particular, during the twentieth century historical scholarship led to a revision of the occult's significance in Western history (Broek & Hanegraaff, 1998; Faivre, 1994). Historians of antiquity and the Renaissance began to discover a rich heritage of Neoplatonic and Hermetic thought and practice. Important studies, most of which were initially produced by scholars at London University's Warburg Institute, such as Edgar Wind, Ernst Cassirer, Daniel Pickering Walker, and Frances Yates, led to renewed thinking. Walker's *Spiritual and Demonic Magic: From Ficino to Campanella* (1958) and particularly Yates's *Giordano Bruno and the Hermetic Tradition* (1964), *The Art of Memory* (1966), *The Rosicrucian Enlightenment* (1972), and *The Occult Philosophy in the Elizabethan Age* (1979), pioneered a history of ideas in which the influence of the occult was central. Further careful historical work by scholars such as Keith Thomas in his *Religion and the Decline of Magic* (1971) revealed the widespread influence of popular occultism. Although, of course, nowadays, we might not agree with all of their conclusions, this scholarship, followed by that of other scholars such as Henry Corbin and Antoine Faivre (who established 'Western esotericism' as a field of interdisciplinary scholarship), did important work. For example, if demonstrated that, not only did the Gnostic, Hermetic, and Neoplatonic ideas of late antiquity survive into the Middle Ages (as a result of their relationship with the Abrahamic religions), but, having been significantly developed during the Renaissance, they have continued to have an influence on the formation of Western religion and culture. This research has continued apace. It is now relatively well established that, whether we consider the important role occultism played in the development of science and philosophy, or its shaping of modern religious traditions, such as Mormonism, or its contribution to National Socialist ideology, or its significance in the work of influential writers, artists, musicians and poets, from W. B. Yeats and André Breton to Kenneth Anger, Jimmy Page and Alan Moore, it is difficult to deny its cultural significance.

In the countercultural embrace of 'the Other' over the last century or so, and particularly since the 1960s, the occult as a signifier of the profane and the irrational has become dominant. In a way quite distinct from earlier periods, the profane nature of the occult has been articulated as a systematic challenge to hegemonic religion, culture, morality, and rationality. Again, this reification of the occult as a profane discourse that challenges hegemonic constructions of reality has its roots in the rhetoric of Christian demonology, which has since been developed and recycled in popular culture. Central to this discourse is the notion that the occult is a hidden, malign influence within Western culture, a distillation of the profane, a threat to all that a society holds sacred. As such, it functions as the perfect foil for Christian morality and modern rationality. Within literature, for example, the novels of Joris-Karl Huysmans (1848–1907), not only reflect his deep Roman Catholic convictions, but also a fascination with the Other, *fin-de-siècle* occultism. *Là-Bas* (1891), in particular, betrays the influence of his friend, Abbé Joseph-Antoine Boullan, a Roman Catholic priest whose occult interests led to accusations of Satanism. The protagonist of *Là-Bas* discovers that, far from Christianity and science expelling occultism from the modern world, they have merely driven it underground, where black masses and exotic rituals thrive. Similarly, in the 1930s, the fiction of Dennis Wheatley (1897–1977) became central to the construction of the popular image of occultism in Britain. Influenced by Montague Summers (1880–1948) – another clergyman with occult interests – Wheatley's work is conspiratorial, arguing that, not far beneath the thin veneer of Christian culture, occultists manipulate dark forces which threaten the very fabric of Western civilization. Respected members of society, particularly the powerful and wealthy, are ritually giving themselves to dark occult forces. Through some ritualized contractual arrangement with a demonic entity, often Satan, in which an occultist's soul may be exchanged and obedience secured, *gnosis* is imparted and, with it, access to power. These are common and influential themes within 'occulture'.

V

What is 'occulture'? Several years ago, I began trying to make sense of a social and cultural environment within which there seemed to be a meaningful confluence of competing spiritual and paranormal discourses, many of which appeared to be related in some way to everyday life through popular culture and the media. On the one hand, it was difficult to ignore the force of the sociological arguments and the evidence marshaled in support of widespread secularization driven by the currents of modernization. It is, for example, irrefutably the case that traditional forms of institutional Christianity in Western liberal democracies (particularly in Europe) are experiencing a significant decline in power, popularity and prestige. Institutional religion may be flourishing beyond the West and it may still occupy a place of significance in the public life of the United States, but, generally speaking, the evidence seems to support a narrative of secularization. On the other hand, within this progressively secular environment, where modernization appeared to be highly corrosive of religion, there is a conspicuous, widespread, and vibrant interest in the paranormal, the pursuit of experiences of transcendence, the acquisition of occult knowledge, and the development of some form of mysticism or inner-life spirituality.

While many of these ideas and interests may seem bizarre and exotic to the majority of our contemporaries, many, it would seem, do not. Occulture is often imperceptibly viral. As John Wilcock pointed out in 1976, in his popular *Guide to Occult Britain*, 'you start by studying the zodiac and sooner or later you're going to be a pushover for ESP, telepathy, telekinesis, spiritual messengers, mystic visions, witchcraft, psychometry, and any of the hundreds and thousands of other magical themes. So, astrology (or any of the other subjects I've mentioned) is an introduction, if you want to look at it that way, to a whole new vision of life' (1976: 12). In particular, occult and paranormal ideas have become everyday and ordinary, thanks largely to the media and popular culture. From the advertising of products that claim to promote wellbeing to the ubiquity of musical and visual cultures fascinated with occultism and experiences of the paranormal, discourses antagonistic to secularization are being circulated within everyday life. Furthermore, there is evidence for a two-way relationship between, on the one hand, underground ideas emanating from what the sociologist Colin Campbell had identified as the 'cultic milieu' (1972) and, on the other hand, the wellbeing claims for beauty products, the themes of popular television series, the growth of interest in mind–body–spirit products, cyber-spirituality on the Internet, and yoga classes in the local village hall. In short, there is evidence for an influential culture of enchantment, which encompasses the marginal and the mainstream, the deviant and the conventional, and which circulates ideas, creates synergies, and forms new trajectories, all of which are driven by wider cultural forces, particularly those of popular culture and the media (Partridge, 2013a).

The point is that, although late-modern societies are different in many ways from their premodern antecedents, it would be unwise to claim an absolute distinction. Just as early modern Christian societies were host to a rich mixture of alternative ideas and practices, Christianity itself being shaped by a number of overlapping fields of discourse, so today there is a thriving occulture that shapes the contours of everyday life. Particularly during the nineteenth century, there emerged a common trade in stock occultural elements, which, primarily through the arts, began to shape the Western imagination: 'the mist-shrouded castle, the villain sworn to the Devil, ghosts, spectres, sorcerers and witches, a flirting with the weird, the uncanny, the bizarre, with sado-masochistic sexuality – and, underpinning all, the Burkeian obsession with dread and the infinite unknown. Supernatural elements like spectralization triggered new sexual frissons; the old demonological themes of possession, incubi and succubi were eroticized...Such disciplines as alchemy, astrology and animal magnetism, and the fringes of physiognomy and phrenology evidently enjoyed a certain vogue' (Porter, 1999: 249–50). Although these elements have, many times, been rebranded and transformed within occulture as a result of the influence of other fields of discourse, they continue to retain their power to enchant the everyday. Hence, while often rejected and marginalized by society's religious and intellectual gatekeepers, the esoteric ideas that are generated, articulated and disseminated within occulture are deceptively significant.

In summary much of the thinking discussed in the following pages has, in some way or another, contributed both to the history of ideas and to contemporary occulture. As such, some understanding of it is necessary for an informed appreciation of the social and cultural worlds that shape us. It is hoped that this volume will facilitate that understanding.

REFERENCES AND FURTHER READING

Adorno, T.W. (1994) 'Theses Against Occultism', in T.W. Adorno, *The Stars Down to Earth and Other Essays on the Irrational*, ed. by S. Crook. London: Routledge, 128–34.

Bader, C.D., F.C. Mencken and J.O. Baker (2010) *Paranormal America: Ghost Encounters, UFO Sightings, Bigfoot Hunts, and Other Curiosities in Religion and Culture*. New York: New York University Press.

Bailey, A. (1947) *The Reappearance of the Christ*. London: Lucis Press.

Besant, A. (1905) *Esoteric Christianity or the Lesser Mysteries*. London: The Theosophical Publishing Society.

Blavatsky, H.P. (1939) *Practical Occultism and Occultism Versus the Occult Arts*. Adyar: Theosophical Publishing House.

Bogdan, H. (2012) 'Envisioning the Birth of a New Aeon: Dispensationalism and Millenarianism in the Thelemic Tradition', in H. Bogdan & M.P. Starr, eds., *Aleister Crowley and Western Esotericism*. New York: Oxford University Press, 89–106.

Breslaw, E.P., ed. (2000) *Witches of the Atlantic World: A Historical Reader and Primary Sourcebook*. New York: New York University Press.

Briggs, R. (1996) *Witches and Neighbours: The Social and Cultural Context of European Witchcraft*. London: HarperCollins.

Broek, R. van den, & W.J. Hanegraaff, eds. (1998) *Gnosis and Hermeticism from Antiquity to Modern Times*. Albany: State University of New York Press.

Campbell, C. (1972) 'The Cult, the Cultic Milieu and Secularization', in M. Hill, ed., *Sociological Yearbook of Religion in Britain 5*. London: SCM, 119–36.

Copenhaver, B. (2008) 'The Occultist Tradition and Its Critics', in D. Garber & M. Ayers, eds., *The Cambridge History of Seventeenth-Century Philosophy*, Vol. 1. Cambridge: Cambridge University Press, 454–512.

Coudert, A.P. (1995) *Leibniz and the Kabbalah*. Dordrecht: Kluwer Acaemic Publishers.

Crowley, A.E. (1977) *777 and Other Qabalistic Writings of Aleister Crowley*. Edited by I. Regardie. Boston: Red Wheel/Weiser.

——(1996) *Magical Diaries of Aleister Crowley: Tunisia 1923*. Edited by S. Skinner. Boston: Red Wheel/Weiser.

Dobbs, B.J.T. (1991) *The Janus Faces of Genius: The Role of Alchemy in Newton's Thought*. Cambridge: Cambridge University Press.

Dowling, Levi H. (Levi) (1964) *The Aquarian Gospel of Jesus the Christ*. London: L.N. Fowler & Co.

Duncan, A.D. (1969) *The Christ, Psychotherapy and Magic: A Christian Appreciation of Occultism*. London: George Allen & Unwin.

Faivre, A. (1994) *Access to Western Esotericism*. Albany: State University of New York Press.

——(2010) *Western Esotericism: A Concise History*. Trans. Christine Rhone. Albany: State University of New York Press.

Feingold, M. (1984) 'The Occult Tradition in the English Universities of the Renaissance: A Reassessment', in B. Vickers, ed., *Occult Scientific Mentalities in the Renaissance*. Cambridge: Cambridge University Press, 73–94.

Fortune, D. (2000) *Esoteric Orders and Their Work*. York Beach: Samuel Weiser.

Freedland, N. (1972) *The Occult Explosion*. London: Michael Joseph.

Gilbert, R.A. (2004) 'Western Esotericism', in C. Partridge, ed., *Encyclopedia of New Religions*. Oxford: Lion Publishing/New York: Oxford University Press, 304–8.

Goodrick-Clarke, N. (2008) *The Western Esoteric Traditions: A Historical Introduction*. New York: Oxford University Press.

Granholm, K., & E. Asprem, eds. (2013) *Contemporary Esotericism*. Sheffield: Equinox.

Hall, R.A. (1980) *Philosophers at War: The Quarrel Between Newton and Leibniz*. Cambridge: Cambridge University Press.

Hammer, O., & M. Rothstein, eds. (2013) *Handbook of the Theosophical Current*. Leiden: Brill.

Hanegraaff, W.J. (2006) 'Occult/Occultism', in W.J. Hanegraaff, ed., *Dictionary of Gnosis and Western Esotericism*. Leiden: Brill, 884–9.

——(2008) 'The Study of Western Esotericism: New Approaches to Christian and Secular Culture', in P. Antes, A.W. Geertz & R.R. Warne, eds., *New Approaches to the Study of Religion: Regional, Critical, and Historical Approaches*. Berlin: Walter de Gruyter, 489–519.

——(2012) *Esotericism and the Academy: Rejected Knowledge in Western Culture*. Cambridge: Cambridge University Press.

Harvey, G. (1593) *Pierce's Supererogation, or A New Praise of the Old Ass*. London: John Wolfe.

Huysmans, J.-K. (1891) *Là-Bas*. Paris: Tresse et Stock.

James VI (1597) *Daemonologie, in Forme of a Dialogue, Diuided into Three Bookes*. Edinburgh: Robert Walde-graue, printer to the Kings Maiestie.

Jenzen, O., & S. Munt, eds. (2013) *Research Companion to Paranormal Cultures*. Farnham: Ashgate.

Johnstone, N. (2006) *The Devil and Demonism in Early Modern England*. Cambridge: Cambridge University Press.

Kassell, L. (2006) '"All was this land full fill'd of faerie," or Magic and the Past in Early Modern England', *Journal of the History of Ideas* 67, 107–22.

Keynes, J.M. (1947) 'Newton, the Man', in The Royal Society, *Newton Tercentenary Celebrations, 15–19 July, 1946*. Cambridge: Cambridge University Press, 27–34.

Laurant, J.-P. (1993), 'The Primitive Characteristics of Nineteenth-Century Esotericism', in A. Faivre & J. Needleman, eds., *Modern Esoteric Spirituality*. London: SCM Press, 277–87.

Lévi, E. (1923) *Transcendental Magic: Its Doctrine and Ritual*. Trans. A.E. Waite. London: William Rider & Son.

McGuire, J. E., & P. M. Rattansi (1966) 'Newton and the Pipes of Pan', *Notes and Records of the Royal Society* 21: 108–43.

Morrisson, M. (2007) *Modern Alchemy: Occultism and the Emergence of Atomic Theory*. New York: Oxford University Press.

Orwell, G. (1946) *Critical Essays*. London: Secker & Warburg.

Owen, A. (2004) *The Place of Enchantment: British Occultism and the Culture of the Modern*. Chicago: University of Chicago Press.

Partridge, C. (2004) *The Re-Enchantment of the West: Alternative Spiritualities, Sacralization, Popular Culture and Occulture*, vol. 1. London: T&T Clark/Continuum.

——(2005) *The Re-Enchantment of the West: Alternative Spiritualities, Sacralization, Popular Culture and Occulture*, vol. 2. London: T&T Clark/Continuum.

——(2013a) 'Occulture is Ordinary', in K. Granholm & E. Asprem, eds., *Contemporary Esotericism*. Sheffield: Equinox, 113–33.

——(2013b) 'Haunted Culture: The Persistence of Belief in the Paranormal', in O. Jenzen & S. Munt, eds., *Research Companion to Paranormal Cultures*. Farnham: Ashgate, 39–50.

Pasi, M. (2009) 'The Modernity of Occultism: Reflections on Some Crucial Aspects', in W. Hanegraaff & J. Pijnenburg, eds., *Hermes in the Academy: Ten Years Study of Western Esotericism at the University of Amsterdam*. Amsterdam: Amsterdam University Press, 59–74.

Porter, R. (1999) 'Witchcraft and Magic in Enlightenment, Romantic and Liberal Thought', in B. Ankarloo and S. Clark, eds., *Witchcraft and Magic in Europe: The Eighteenth and Nineteenth Centuries*. Philadelphia: University of Pennsylvania Press, 191–274.

Raleigh, W. (1614) *The Historie of the World*. London: Walter Burre.

Russell, J.B. (1986) *Mephistopheles: The Devil in the Modern World*. Ithaca: Cornell University Press.

Stuckrad, Kocku von (2005) *Western Esotericism: A Brief History of Secret Knowledge*. Trans. N. Goodrick-Clarke. London: Equinox.
Styers, R. (2004) *Making Magic: Religion, Magic, and Science in the Modern World*. New York: Oxford University Press.
Thomas, K. (1971) *Religion and the Decline of Magic*. London: Weidenfeld & Nicholson.
Treitel, C. (2004) *A Science for the Soul: Occultism and the Genesis of the German Modern*. Baltimore: Johns Hopkins University Press.
Vickers, B. (1984) 'Introduction', in B. Vickers, ed., *Occult Scientific Mentalities in the Renaissance*. Cambridge: Cambridge University Press, 1–56.
Walker, D.P. (1958) *Spiritual and Demonic Magic: From Ficino to Campanella*. Studies of the Warburg Institute, vol. 22. London: The Warburg Institute.
Webb, J. (1974) *The Occult Underground*. La Salle: Open Court.
——(1976) *The Occult Establishment*. La Salle: Open Court.
Webster, C. (1982) *From Paracelsus to Newton: Magic and the Making of Modern Science*. Cambridge: Cambridge University Press.
Wilcock, J. (1976) *Guide to Occult Britain: The Quest for Magic in Pagan Britain*. London: Sidgwick & Jackson.
Wilson, C. (1971) *The Occult*. London: Hodder & Stoughton.
——(1978) *Mysteries: An Investigation Into the Occult, the Paranormal, and the Supernatural*. London: Hodder & Stoughton.
——(1988) *Beyond the Occult*. New York: Bantam Press.
Yates, F. (1964) *Giordano Bruno and the Hermetic Tradition*. London: Routledge & Kegan Paul.
——(1966) *The Art of Memory*. London: Routledge & Kegan Paul.
——(1972) *The Rosicrucian Enlightenment*. London: Routledge & Kegan Paul.
——(1979) *The Occult Philosophy in the Elizabethan Age*. London: Routledge & Kegan Paul.

PART I

ANCIENT AND MEDIEVAL SOURCES

CHAPTER ONE

ANCIENT ESOTERIC TRADITIONS
Mystery, Revelation, Gnosis

Dylan M. Burns

Gar das antike Leben! Was versteht man von dem,
wenn man die Lust an der Maske,
das gute Gewissen alles Maskenhaften nicht versteht!
Hier ist das Bad und die Erholung des antiken Geistes.
(F. Nietzsche, *Die fröhliche Wissenschaft*, §77)

INTRODUCTION

Ancient esoteric tradition is a modern scholarly term useful for designating currents in Hellenistic and Late Antique Mediterranean culture that are concerned with the mediation of some kind of absolute knowledge via a dialectic of secrecy, concealment, and revelation (cf. 'esotericism'—von Stuckrad 2010: xi; for a different approach, see Hanegraaff 2012). These currents often occupy the fault-lines between ancient 'magic', 'philosophy', and 'religion'. It is efficacious to use the second-order, etic word 'esoteric' to describe these myriad literary and ritual elements of ancient religious life, such as Graeco-Oriental mystery-cults, Neoplatonic theurgy, Christian mysticism and Gnosticism, Jewish apocalyptic and Merkavah literature, and more. While the contours of esoteric discourse in the Renaissance, Modern, and contemporary eras are to a large extent defined by their marginalization in mainstream religious and academic institutions, many (although certainly not all) esoteric traditions occupied central, respected and publicly acknowledged places in ancient life.

ANCIENT MYSTERY-CULTS, PYTHAGOREANISM, AND ORPHISM

Esoteric discourse has always played a role in religious life in the West (taken here to extend to the Mediterranean basin, including Egypt, Israel/Palestine, and Syria, regions deeply Hellenized following the conquests of Alexander the Great and afterwards usually ruled or contested by Greeks or Romans through the end of antiquity). Priests in ancient Mesopotamian and Egyptian religion were highly trained specialists who formed their own elite scribal culture; the disparity between their education and that of the rest of society lent them and their craft an aura of mystery, enhancing their sense of power. The iconographic nature of their alphabets was highly regarded as mysterious, powerful and even dangerous (Lenzi 2008). Egyptian mythology also offered its own analogue to the later, transcendent God of the Platonists with its descriptions of a god 'whose name is hidden' and paradoxically unbegotten, although his shroud of secrecy was not bound to his role as source of divinity and unity until the later second millennium BCE (Assmann 1998: 12–25). Greco-Roman philosophers would later enshrine 'barbarian' speech, script and emphasis on the transcendence of the deity as 'oriental' wisdoms contributing to Greek wisdom, often phrased as secret, 'esoteric' doctrine.

Greco-Roman religious life, meanwhile, was full of traditions inundated with and governed by secrecy (Martin 1995). Primary amongst these were, of course, the 'mystery cults', which were widespread and diverse. Nonetheless, one can distinguish general features usually found amongst them (Burkert 1987; Johnston 2004). These cults enforced secrecy of one's experience(s) in their rites, which (ostensibly) had positive effects upon one's existence—both during and following life—through eliciting a special encounter with a deity. They did not challenge everyday civic religion as much as supplement it, and, since they were usually open to individuals of any class, ethnicity, age or gender, they occupied a significant and public role in ancient life.

Moreover, despite the injunctions to keep the rites secret, the content of the rites themselves appears to have been something of a public secret; divulging them was not itself illegal as much as was the 'impiety' of profaning them in public (Heraclid. Pont. Frag. 170; Thuc. 6.28, 6.61; Martin 1995: 109). Certainly the myths connected to them were usually well-known: the Eleusinian mysteries, for instance, appear to recreate for initiates the experience of Demeter's reactions to Hades' kidnapping of Persephone—descent into the underworld, grief, fasting, and eventual recovery, culminating in the presentation of a symbol of life to the initiates (Hipp. *Haer.* 5.8.39ff Marcovich), who obtained a 'password' to a happy afterlife. These transformative rites resemble more than anything what anthropologists term 'rites of passage', practices whose performance changes a child into an adult. Such rites are strangely absent from Greco-Roman life, so perhaps mystery-cults filled this gap (Johnston 2004: 106).

In themselves the Eleusinian mysteries (like those of Mithras, Isis, the 'Great Mother', etc.) are of little importance for the history of 'Western Esotericism', because their institutions and myths perished along with other Greco-Roman cults during the rise of Christianity. The same is true of their religious competitors, Orphism and Pythagoreanism. Plato's Socrates refers to cryptic 'books', associated with the primaeval musician Orpheus, invoked by wandering soothsayers to support their exhortations to a life governed by ritual purity and vegetarianism (*Resp.* II 364a ff). Much later, the 'Neoplatonists'—a movement of systematizing readers of Plato, starting with Plotinus (mid-third century CE)—would quote cosmogonic poetry referred to as 'Orphic', the oldest body of which could go back to the sixth century BCE (West 1983). Modern reconstructions of this poetry portray an 'Orphic' mystery-religion whose initiates came to learn of a secret myth concerning the dismemberment of Dionysus and the birth of humankind from the blood of the evil Titans. However, the same evidence may rather indicate a family of disparate but related myths that were marketed by itinerant ritual specialists (Brisson 1995; Radcliffe 1999).

Nonetheless, even in antiquity the adjective 'Orphic' connoted secret teachings about salvific knowledge regarding the cosmos and human life. Archaeologists have unearthed funerary texts that interpret Orphic poetry in the context of the afterlife, or even provide instructions for successful descent into the underworld—the *Derveni Papyrus* and 'Orphic' *Golden Tablets* (Betegh 2004; Radcliffe 2011). Yet most cosmological poetry associated with Orpheus would not have survived but for the importance placed upon them by the Neoplatonists, who adopted him as one of their Hellenic culture-heroes. The same is true of thinkers who devoted themselves to the teachings of the mathematician Pythagoras, adopting vegetarianism, communal life, and a vow of silence (Cic. *Nat. d.* 1.74; Burkert 1972: 178ff). While few of their writings survive, their teachings about geometry and lifestyle exerted enormous influence over the Neoplatonists, who even composed hagiographies of Pythagoras. The incorporation of Orpheus and Pythagoras into the ranks of the Platonic authorities, not any particular 'esoteric' teaching, made them attractive to admirers of the Greeks in later eras. Similarly, the content and rites of the 'mysteries' themselves may have been lost, but the accounts of their salvific importance and esoteric trappings provided ample fodder for later, 'esoteric' thinkers who sought to 'revive' what they thought ancient, Pagan wisdom to be.

MAGIA, SUPERSTITIO, THEURGIA

The concept of 'magic', too, obtained part of its 'esoteric' valence in the modern world by virtue of its association with 'Paganism', yet some forms of ancient private ritual life can be aptly described as 'esoteric' in the same sense as the secret rites of salvation we find in the mystery-cults. Private ritual practices aimed at alleviating disease, cursing enemies, or obtaining one's desires by supernatural means were commonplace in the ancient world. However, thanks to the rise of new ways of organizing knowledge (like 'philosophy' and 'medicine') in the sixth century BCE, Greeks began to use the set of terminology that we would commonly translate today as 'magic' (*magia, goeteia,* etc.) to denote and distance these competing ritual specialists (Graf 1995). Meanwhile, Greek 'religion' was largely a public, civic affair. Rituals were usually carried out as part of greater festivals that reinforced the bonds between a local municipality, its greater political sphere, and the gods. Even at home, worship remained decidedly exoteric—a public custom shared with the community. This religious exotericism was based in part upon the depth of belief in supernatural powers: prayers and rites that were uttered or conducted in secret were assumed to be motivated by selfish, or even anti-social concerns.

The subversive nature of 'magic' was twofold, insofar as it appeared to come from the east and to reside in the private, and therefore potentially criminal, sphere—indeed, 'magia' is a Persian word, and 'goetia' initially referred to Persian funerary laments, which were imagined by the Greeks to possess necromantic efficacy (Aesch. *Pers.* 684–88). Thanks to Greek influence, the Romans, too, stigmatized private ritual practice. While the mystery-cults were generally not seen as magical sects, they could be targeted when it was politically convenient, as with the crackdown (186 BCE) on a cult of Bacchus in Rome, on charges of secret orgies, cannibalism, magic, and conspiracy against the state (Liv. *Hist.* 39.8–19). In the following century, Romans began using the term *superstitio* to denote foreign or private religions in Rome, in juxtaposition to the civic cult (Martin 2004: 130ff), replicating the double stigma of magic in Greek culture as alien and secret. One of these was Christianity, a barbarous 'superstition' shrouded in the mystery of its closed meetings in house churches (Plin. *Ep.* 10.96). Christians would be accused of secret, conspiratorial activity in charges recalling those leveled against the Bacchants of Cicero's day (ibid.; Min. Fel. *Oct.* 8; Orig. *Cels.* 1.1, 1.3). Apologists replied that the Christian churches were innocent political clubs (*collegia*)—private, but safe (Ter. *Apol.* 39).

Nonetheless, mystery-cults grew in popularity under the Roman Empire, as worship of 'oriental' deities—most famously, Isis, the 'Great Mother', and Mithras—spread far and wide. Our knowledge of these mysteries is slight, but the paradigm of a ritual drama plunging the initiate into darkness before a restoration to new, greater life, as we saw at Eleusis, held enough currency to be used by Apuleius of Madaura in our only first-person (albeit fictional) description of (Isiaic) initiation (*Metam.* 11). Nor did private ritual specialists cease operations; some went corporate, as when an Egyptian priest accompanied Emperor Marcus Aurelius on a German campaign (Cass. Dio 72.8.4).

The sands of Egypt have preserved spells used during the Hellenistic and Roman periods which offer a window into the ancient marketplace of private ritual life (Betz 1992; Meyer/Smith 1994). Many charms possessed an esoteric force through their use of the medium of the written word. While estimates of the degree of ancient literacy in everyday society vary widely (anywhere from .5 per cent through 10 per cent, before allowing for the 'semi-literate'—Humphrey 1991), the culture of writing, largely limited to the aristocratic and priestly strata of society, possessed an iconographic beauty and mystery to the unlearned. The allure of letters was particularly intense in Egypt and Mesopotamia, where scribal culture was doubly sacred and whose alphabets were seen as unintelligible but potent symbols even to educated Greeks and Romans (e.g. Plot. *Enn.* 5.8.6). The efficacy of many spells is therefore premised upon the power of decorative arrangements of letters in shapes, strings of vowels to be chanted (Dornseiff 1925), and especially so-called *nomina barbara* (PGM III.1–164, IV.3007–86)—foreign or nonsensical words simulating the powerful holy tongues of Egypt, Syria and Israel (*Corp. herm.* 16.1–2). Other spells could be regarded as 'esoteric' insofar as they do not grant practical benefits, as much as abstract knowledge of or a mystical confrontation with the transcendent God (PGM IV.1115–66, VII.756–94; Betz 1995), which can even bestow immortality (as in the so-called 'Mithras Liturgy'—PGM IV.475–829).

The Neoplatonists drew from this wellspring of Graeco-Egyptian magic and the fetish of 'oriental' wisdom in formulating a ritual culture premised on the practice of 'divine works (theurgy)'. Iamblichus of Chalcis (ca. 300 CE) theorized these practices aimed at facilitating the ascent of the soul by adopting the pose of an Egyptian priest in an exchange of letters with his elder contemporary, Porphyry of Tyre (Shaw 1995; Clarke et al. 2003). Porphyry, following his teacher Plotinus, believed that the soul communed with the divine intellect, and therefore needed to avoid engagement with the world in order to practice contemplation; Iamblichus responded that the soul had fully descended into matter, and must navigate and master the cosmos by means of proper symbolic manipulation of objects (Iamb. *An.* 6–7; Damasc. *Comm. Phaedo*

105). His admixture of Neoplatonic metaphysics, valorization of Hellenic culture (particularly Pythagoreanism and Orphism), and 'orientalizing' ritual trappings (drawn from the Middle Platonic hexameter poetry of the *Chaldean Oracles*) proved to be popular and effective at a time when Hellenic philosophers sought to define themselves against Christianity. Julian the Apostate (361–63 CE) attempted to institutionalize theurgic cult during his brief reign (O'Meara 2003: 120–24), and the Neoplatonic school persisted in rituals like the animation of statues up through its closing by the Emperor Justinian in 529 CE (Proc. *Comm. Tim.* 3.155.18–22). Yet all Neoplatonists, Plotinian and theurgic, Hellenic and Christian, agreed on the importance of meditative contemplation of God (The One) as negotiated by the esoteric wordplay of 'negative theology' (Mortley 1986).

Iamblichus distinguished 'theurgy' from 'magic,' although it was clearly a product of contemporary private ritual culture. Porphyry charged that the use of *nomina barbara* to subdue demons was superstitious and barbaric; no true philosopher would claim, like a 'sorcerer' (*goēs*), to have power over the gods (*Aneb.* 2.10). Iamblichus replied that theurgic power belonged not to the theurgist, but the providential divine activity which raises humanity to heaven (*Myst.* 1.12). The *Chaldean Oracles* excoriate popular divination (frag. 107). While Iamblichus' adoption of theurgy was motivated by philosophical concerns and remained relevant thanks to anti-Christian polemics, it also marked a turn to esotericism in the Platonic tradition. 'Theurgy' as equated with 'magic' (Iamblichus' protestations notwithstanding), would later take on the status of a forbidden system of absolute, oriental knowledge passed on by ancient heathens. Yet the theurgic tradition also exemplified a particular blend of Platonic metaphysics, heathen mythologoumena, and esoteric pedagogy that flourished in the second–fifth centuries CE (Lewy 2011).

THE PLATONIC UNDERWORLD, ORIENTALISM, AND HERMETISM

A textbook on ancient philosophy includes an appendix concerning an 'Underworld of Platonism': literature that discusses elaborate Platonic metaphysics, but describes the universe through 'mythologizing' soteriological schemata that feature the ascent of soul (a divine 'spark') out of evil, material existence (Dillon 1977: 384; Majercik 1989: 4–5). These texts include the aforementioned *Chaldean Oracles*, the Hermetica, and Gnostic literature. This grouping oversimplifies much (e.g., the 'spark' is hardly the most common metaphor for the fallen soul during this period), but also presents a fundamental insight into one 'Pagan intellectual milieu' (Fowden 1986: 114), a Platonic worldview emphasizing divine transcendence and a cognate epistemology struggling to know the unknowable, while embracing a diversity of Greco-Roman and 'oriental' mythologoumena. Our conceptualization of the range (Greek, Persian, Egyptian) and function (philosophical, theurgic, polemical) of myth and symbolism in these circles, and how important they were for articulating the social reality behind the texts, remains controversial.

The Platonic corpus itself contains no 'secret' doctrine; references to oral tradition address the deficiency of textual production and exalt personal dialectic, rather than esotericism per se (*Phaedrus* 276a), although a spurious letter (*Ep.* 2 314b-c) does describe a secret theology orally transmitted at the Academy. This epistle is commonly regarded to be a forgery stemming from the revival (first century CE) of the thought of Pythagoras; indeed, another 'Neopythagorean', Numenius of Apamea (second century CE), would have agreed with modern critic Leo Strauss that Plato, recalling the execution of Socrates, had employed an esoteric 'art of writing' to conceal his more controversial thoughts while providing clues for careful readers (Num. frag. 23 des Places; Strauss 1952). Part of Plato's brilliance is that many of his narratives *can* be read as esoteric puzzles which, properly unlocked, yield radically unexpected readings; the Neoplatonists followed Numenius in holding that these readings concerned ideas about cosmogony and theology synthesized from the dialogues, Pythagorean teaching, and allegorical readings of 'Orphic' poetry, but which agreed with their conception of the *prisci theologi* (Lat., 'ancient theologians'), the great teachers of the Orient. Numenius appeals to the authority of 'the justifiably famous nations...the Brahmins, Jews, Magi, and Egyptians', thanks to their elder stature, rich ritual tradition, and, most importantly, their concordance with Plato's theology (frag. 1a). Although such notions of the superiority of the ancient wisdom of the east go back to Plato himself (Baltes 2005), this 'Platonic Orientalism' became, with Numenius, typical in Platonic circles, even through the medieval period and beyond (Burns 2006).

The content of these Platonic systems naturally varies, but the general paradigm is the same (Dillon 1977): in the first century CE, Platonists became interested in fusing the concept of the transcendence and unknowability of the first principle—'The One' (or 'monad') as discussed in Plato's dialogue *Parmenides*—with the concept, drawn from the *Timaeus*, of the cosmos as created by a divine craftsman ('demiurge'), occasionally identified with the divine creative intellect. The ambiguity in the latter text regarding the material with which this craftsman worked begat speculations on a separate, passive, occasionally evil principle of matter, often termed 'The Dyad.' The objective of the human mind and soul is to go beyond the material principle and reunite, whether in mystical contemplation in this life or in post-mortem release, with their source, God.

Platonists thus (mostly) agreed upon the basic schema of the cosmos and the role of humanity in it, upon the identity of human and divine with respect to soul and intellect, and upon the ultimate unknowability of The One, God. While accepting the importance of contemplation, they disagreed about the character of other means to access this divinity—clearly one kind of 'absolute knowledge'—and the relative value of the authorities that claimed to possess it. Although he championed the goal of union with The One, Plotinus, for instance, staunchly defended the tradition of exoteric Greek education as the best road there, particularly against the Gnostics (*Enn.* 2.9.6, 9–10).

Hermetic dialogues like *Poimandres*, perhaps the ancient esoteric text *par excellence*, also offered Platonized accounts of cosmogony and salvation, but as transmitted by Hermes Trismegistus, a semi-divine culture-hero of Hellenistic Egypt vested with the authority of Thoth (the Egyptian god of writing) but employing a particularly Greek idiom (Festugière 1950–54; Fowden 1986; Copenhaver 1995). While some 'Hermetica' are fairly dry philosophical discourses, others deal with practical 'occult' techniques (such as magic or astrology); still others portray Hermes leading an interlocutor to acquire an indescribable vision of the divine, even in an out-of-body experience (*Corp. Herm.* 13.11–13). The Hermetica sometimes describe the experience as the acquisition of 'knowledge (*gnōsis*)' or 'mystery' (ibid., 10.5–6), although the terminology varies widely (e.g., NHC VI, 6.3–25: 'contemplative vision…wisdom (*theōria…sophia*)'; cf. Hanegraaff 2008). Like the *Chaldean Oracles*—whose content and even mythologoumena is largely Greek notwithstanding (its God is 'Mind'; its prime intermediary, 'Hecate')—the Hermetica 'auto-orientalize', authorizing their Platonism by clothing themselves in the garb of the hoary ancient east.

The theurgic Neoplatonists, like Numenius and other 'Orientalizing' Hellenes (mentioned by Diog. Laer. 1.1–3), ultimately saw the Greeks and Plato as first amongst equals; they respected Trismegistus and considered the *Oracles* fully valid revelations (Fowden 1986: 201–5; Mar. *Vit. Proc.* 916–19), yet their authoritative texts claimed usually Greek heritage: Pythagorean, Orphic, Platonic. Their teaching revolved around an esoteric hermeneutics of the Platonic dialogues that would disclose total understanding of material and metaphysical reality, beginning with ethics, proceeding to (meta)physics, and culminating in allegorical interpretations of Orphic myths as describing the matters of high theology (Proc. *Theo. Plat.* 1.5ff). As with the *Oracles* and Hermetica, the presence of myth alone does not denote esotericism; rather, it is the assignment of authoritative, urgent content to the myths, and their mediation through secrecy and disclosure (revelation or, in this case, allegory). Moreover, the theurgists were themselves ambivalent auto-orientalizers, brandishing the wisdom of Hellas above all others. 'Chaldean' and 'Egyptian' Platonism appeared safe, because Greeks traditionally regarded these nations as authoritative. In later times, the association of Persia and Egypt with 'magic' would tar these 'Orientalizing' Neoplatonists with the brush of sorcery. In their own day, meanwhile, they were consumed by the threat of Christianity.

MYSTERY, ESOTERICISM, AND REVELATION IN EARLY CHRISTIANITY

Early Christian literature and rituals are replete with esoteric discourse, sometimes dominant, sometimes coexisting with an exoteric *kerygma* (Christian message). The latter current is commonly associated with 'proto-orthodox' groups, although they also traded in esoteric leanings in Scripture, popular use of the language of 'mysteries', and mysticism. The Gospel of Mark is undergirded by the so-called 'Messianic Secret' (Jesus' concealment of his identity—Wrede 1901) and emphasizes the esotericism of the parables (Mk 4:3–34). The Gospel of John, too, makes wide use of parables and riddling language (Dunderberg 2011). Yet both texts, like the other canonical gospels, are centered upon the exoteric theophany of the Son of God, his death, and resurrection. The bizarre symbolism of The Revelation to John appears decidedly esoteric but actually trades in popular cryptography (such as *gematria*—coding words with numbers, e.g., '666' = '(Emperor) Nero', widely feared amongst Christians) to express reaction to crisis. The apostle Paul deals particularly often with esoteric language. He combats his opponents' claims to esoteric authority in favor of the exoteric gospel of love (esp. 1 Cor 13), while invoking his own heavenly journey (2 Cor 12:1–10) and making wide use of the term *mystērion* to describe the allure of Christian experience and initiation (Bultmann 1933: 709; Morray-Jones 1995; Pearson 2011). This 'mystery-language' was widespread in the Apostolic Era, and while it could have roots in both Jewish and Hellenic culture (cf. Stroumsa 1996: 156), early modern Protestant polemics opted for the latter, hoping to marginalize a supposed 'Paganized' esoteric Hellenism of the early Church (Smith 1990: 54ff).

One thesis holds that 'esoteric' language of divine mysteries and 'secrets' (*arrēta*) in early Christianity disappeared in the fourth century with the downfall of Gnosticism. The terms became more common, but referred no longer to 'secret doctrine', as much as the ineffable knowledge negotiated by mystics (Stroumsa 1996: 147–68). In the fourth century and beyond, there is indeed a very public (e.g., exoteric) and 'orthodox' emphasis on divine ineffability, as in Constantine's remarks on the mystery of the Trinity (Eus. *Vit. Const.* 2.69), the Neoplatonic mysticism of the Cappadocian Fathers (Greg. Naz. *Or.* 28.5), or the Miaphysite contention that the single, divine nature of the Incarnation is *arrēton* (Cyr. Alex. *Ep.* 4 [PG 77.44–50]). Yet 'esoteric' Christianity was hardly limited to or even chiefly associated with Gnosticism. Anti-Gnostic teachers like Clement and Origen focused on divine ineffability, but also developed Greek allegory for enlightened exegetes of Scripture (Pépin 1958), an esoteric hermeneutics that would become commonplace in the Church. In other literature, like the pedagogical letters of the Platonist monk Evagrius of Pontus (Brakke 2011), one can hardly distinguish between 'esotericism' and 'mysticism', and the Neoplatonism of Pseudo-Dionysius the Areopagite draws on not just the contemplative language but the esoteric pedagogy of the theurgists (Burns 2004). Early Christian esotericism is therefore not to be strictly identified with Gnosticism, whose communities and practices were often no less exoteric than their proto-orthodox contemporaries (De Jong 2006: 1052).

Perhaps most importantly, the identification of 'esotericism' and 'Gnosticism' misleadingly implies that any non-orthodox revelation is 'Gnostic' by virtue of its esotericism. This is particularly acute in the case of clashes about authority and canonicity between the proto-orthodox and groups who were authorized by a different 'revelation' (Gk. *apokalupsis*, 'uncovering': the acquisition of divine knowledge completely altering one's understanding). The Hellenistic and Roman eras saw a proliferation of revelatory texts in Judaism and eventually Christianity that used the genre 'apocalypse'—pseudepigraphic accounts of revelations transmitted by a supernatural mediator to a seer (Collins 1979; Charlesworth 1985). Such texts and their readers directly challenged the proto-orthodox claim to authority transmitted instead via apostolic succession. The proto-orthodox thus opposed groups who held different views based upon different revelatory authority, such as the Syrian baptists known as the Elchasaites. They sharply distinguished the canon from the worthless 'secret books' (*apocrypha*—Athan. *Ep. Fest.* 39) like the apocalypses, and opposed new prophecies, such as the ecstatic millenarianism of Montanism. Elchasaism, the apocrypha, and Montanism each have relationship (or lack thereof) to Gnosticism, yet each also possesses an esoteric flair, by virtue of association with 'heretical', revelatory, knowledge of secret things (Hipp. *Haer.* 9.13.2ff; *1 En.* 37:2-5; Ter. *An.* 9). Yet while every revelation was once a secret—and conversely, esotericism is nothing more than the promise of revelation—not every revelation is 'Gnostic', for 'Gnosticism' is not just about *gnōsis*, but creation.

GNOSTICISM, MANICHAEISM, AND THOMASINE MYSTICISM

'Gnosticism' is a modern term used by scholars to denote groups known in antiquity as 'Gnostics' (*gnostikoi*, 'knowers') and related individuals sharing a distinctive mythography that distinguishes God from an imperfect creator-deity, identifies the human essence with the Godhead, and holds salvation to be 'knowledge' (*gnōsis*) of God and one's divine origins (Brakke 2010). 'Gnostic' literature and thought is of particular importance for the understanding of 'esotericism'. Since Gnosticism became regarded as heresy, information about it survived into the modern era, until recently, only through the writing of its orthodox opponents. Its focus on salvation via knowledge and its wide use of Platonic thought (in the form common to the 'Platonic Underworld') led to its association with 'Pagan' Neoplatonism, 'Hermetism,' 'magic,' and 'theurgy,' leading both exponents and detractors to identify these disparate ancient religious discourses under a variety of terms, such as an 'underworld', *l'ésoterisme*, or, as often in German scholarship, *die Gnosis*. Yet the 1945 discovery of a cache of ancient literature—much of it Gnostic—preserved in the Coptic language at Nag Hammadi (Egypt) offers us a rare glimpse, unclouded by the heresiographers, into this supposedly 'esoteric' Christianity (Layton 1987; Meyer 2007).

Chief amongst the Gnostic teachers was Valentinus (ca. 150 CE), whose theology appears to revise earlier, 'Classic Gnostic' myths in light of Platonic-Pythagorean thought (Layton 1987). Students such as Ptolemy or Theodotus developed his thought into a potent rival to 'proto-orthodox' churches. Irenaeus of Lyons (late-second century CE) claims that Valentinian communities employed an esoteric soteriology which divided up humanity into nonbelievers, learners (other Christians), and elite individuals (Valentinians) who were already saved (Ir. *Haer.* 1.6). The criterion for membership in the elect was 'initiation' into the Gnostic 'mystery' of the production of the cosmos and humanity through the fall of divine Wisdom (Gk. *Sophia*) from heaven, underlying the Christian message found in various New Testament writings, often expressed through the esoteric hermeneutics of allegory. Indeed, some Valentinian exoteric literature—such as the *Epistle of Ptolemy to Flora* or the *Gospel of Truth* (NHC I, 3)—only make oblique, vague references to the story of the Fall of Sophia, so perhaps Irenaeus was correct to identify the Gnostic myth as 'secret knowledge' only granted to the 'initiates' in Valentinian communities. A version of the myth by another teacher, 'Justin the Gnostic', begins with an injunction to keep its contents secret (Hipp. *Haer.* 5.27).

Nag Hammadi revealed two other major Gnostic literary traditions, Ophitism and Sethianism, together commonly referred to as 'Classic Gnosticism'; the paradigmatic 'Gnostic' text, the *Apocryphon of John*, blends both traditions. Ophite thought focuses on the serpent (Gk. *ophis*) in the Garden of Eden, regards Adam and Eve's eating of the apple from the Tree of Knowledge as positive, and employs a distinctive set of mythologoumena, chiefly comprised of beastly demons (Rasimus 2009). Sethianism, meanwhile, is uninterested in the Garden-narrative and deals with the incarnations of Seth (the third child of Adam and Eve), drawing widely on the Jewish apocalypses (particularly Enochic traditions) in forming its own mythologoumena of the divine world and the revelators and saviors that descend from it. Some Sethian texts weld apocalyptic genre and literary motifs to the contemplative praxis of

Neoplatonism, producing *sui generis* apocalypses whose revealers discuss technical metaphysics (Turner 2001; Burns 2014). Christian 'heretics' circulated these texts in the school of Plotinus in Rome, producing controversy over revelatory authority (Plato vs. Seth et al.) and estranging themselves from the philosophers (Porph. *Vit. Plot.* 16). The Sethian literature thus presents a particularly strong conjunction of ancient esoteric traditions (Gnostic apocalypse vs. Neoplatonism) and furnishes a case-study of the breakup (into Christian and Hellenic parties) of an 'interconfessional' circle (Wasserstrom 2000) once united by shared interest in these esoteric traditions.

Sethian thought appears to have grown out of a Syrian baptismal circle like the Elchasaites, deeply influenced by Jewish pseudepigrapha but regarding Jesus of Nazareth as one of many salvific figures (Burns 2012). Elchasaism also birthed the prophet Mani (mid-third century CE), who synthesized a religion which, like Gnosticism, regarded the material world as a negative creation, but differed in viewing its creator as a good being appointed by heaven (Gardner/Lieu 2004). Manichaean use of mystery-language is entirely consonant with contemporary Christian language, and its pedagogy, lifestyle, and missionary activity (extending to East Asia) were decisively exoteric (Pedersen 2011; De Jong 2006: 1052). At the same time, Manichaeism popularized esoteric traditions from Gnostic and apocalyptic literature. For instance, Manichaean salvation-history is traced by a line of *prisci theologi* who transmit revelation (e.g., Adam, Enoch, Jesus, the Buddha, et al.), a development independent of the 'Oriental wisdom' esteemed by the Platonists but derived rather from (Elchasaite) Christian speculation about multiple descents of the savior (Burns 2012: 388ff).

Mani was also influenced by Thomasine literature. The *Gospel of Thomas* (NHC II, 2; early second century CE), like the famous *Hymn of the Pearl* (embedded in the *Acts of Thomas*, chs. 105–8) strongly affirms that one can be saved by the secret knowledge that one is in fact divine (*Gos. Thom.* log. 3) and thus escape the trappings of the body. Thomasine traditions say nothing about the creator of the world or the fall of Sophia, but they emphasize salvation by knowledge, a secret revealed by a certain favored apostle: Jesus' divine twin, Judas Didymus Thomas (Aram., *tā'mā*; Gk. *didumos*, cf. John 11:16). We do not know if there was a 'school' of St. Thomas; like Sethianism and Ophitism, Thomasine Christianity is a literary tradition that, unlike Valentinianism and Manichaeism, cannot be traced to any ancient community known to scholarship. Nonetheless, despite its lack of Gnostic myth, the *Gospel of Thomas* has been marketed and received as the most popular 'Gnostic' text recovered from Nag Hammadi, generating controversy and commentary amongst churchgoers, scholars, and even New Age exegetes alike, who 'find' in it what they 'seek' (Burns 2007).

JEWISH 'GNOSTICISM' AND 'THEURGY' FROM QUMRAN TO THE HEKHALOT

The literary frame of Jesus secretly passing on esoteric knowledge to one of his disciples was a common tool of self-authorization in early Christian pseudepigrapha, viciously opposed by the proto-orthodox (e.g., Ir. *Haer.* 1.25.5). Scholars once referred to such texts as comprising their own genre—the '(Gnostic) revelation dialogue'—although they are really apocalypses, 'revelations' granted on this world (by Jesus) rather than during a heavenly journey (Collins 1979). Literary traditions of the Jewish apocalypses deeply influenced early Christian literature, particularly in

Gnosticism, which drew on apocalyptic topics (ranging from wild cosmological speculation to the 'historical eschatology' of the end of days) as well as popular motifs (a seer's ascent to heaven via cloud or assimilation to angelhood). The apocalypses' strong claims to revelatory authority made them controversial in proto-orthodox circles but popular amongst Gnostics.

The ascent traditions of the apocalypses survived into the so-called 'Hekhalot' or 'Merkavah' literature, sometimes argued to be the earliest instance of Jewish esotericism. These texts, whose manuscripts go back to the early medieval period, provide information about visionary ascent to the celestial palaces (*hekhalot*), culminating in worship before God's chariot-throne (*merkavah* – Davila 2013). The ascent is said to be difficult and potentially fatal (Schäfer 1981: ch. 259); the texts paradoxically call it a 'descent', and its practitioners 'descenders to the chariot'. The merkavah-vision follows upon long and prolix descriptions of the heavenly gates, their angelic guards, and rivers of fire, all of which must be carefully navigated using the correct passwords and keys. A famous passage describes how visionaries made their 'journeys' through what appears to have been an ecstatic, out-of-body experience, 'like going up and down a ladder in a house' (Schäfer 1981: ch. 199; cf. 225ff, 560). Useful comparison to some methods and goals of ascent in Gnostic and magical literature once led scholarship to dub the Hekhalot-texts 'Jewish Gnosticism' (Scholem 1960), misleadingly implying a direct historical relationship between these disparate textual traditions. Similarly misleading is the unfortunate designation (common in Judaic studies) of such practices as 'theurgy'; as noted earlier, *theourgia* in ancient sources denotes not just any visionary or self-deifying practice, but a specific body of spiritual techniques used in the later Neoplatonic school and derived from the culture of 'Orientalizing' Hellenism.

Gnostic, apocalyptic, and Merkavah literature each probably drew separately upon a common well of scribal and/or priestly traditions developed in Israel during the Second Temple Period (Alexander 2006: 135). Ezekiel's vision of the *merkavah* (Ezek 1) was the cornerstone of these speculations, which developed into various accounts of the heavenly palaces, ranging from participation in the celestial liturgy (as in the *Songs of the Sabbath Sacrifice* discovered amongst the Dead Sea Scrolls—García Martínez/Tigchelaar 2000) to the culmination of Enoch's flight to heaven in pursuit of cosmological secrets (*1 En.* 14). In many apocalypses, sages are transformed into angels, or even the celestial vice-regent, Metatron (*3 En.* 4ff). The Rabbis frowned on such dangerous practices, without forbidding them outright (m. Hag. 2.1). Merkavah-speculations appear to have been a kind of open secret, since the texts themselves never describe their contents as esoteric. Kabbalah sprang from these variegated traditions, which, together, thus form crucial opening chapters in the history of Jewish mysticism (Schäfer 2009).

GNOSIS, REVELATION, ESOTERICISM

These ancient esoteric traditions emerged from distinct socio-cultural backgrounds: Greco-Roman and Egyptian mystery-religion, private magical practice, Pythagorean and Orphic revival, Hellenic (but 'orientalizing') Platonists, early Christian initiation, theology, and apocrypha, Gnostic literature, and the development of Jewish mysticism. These traditions employed secrecy, concealment, and revelation about absolute knowledge for very different and even conflicting ends. Most importantly, the content of their 'absolute knowledge' was in no way identical. Why, then, group these highly disparate ancient traditions under a single moniker, 'esoteric'? Certainly scholars have long recognized that an emphasis on revelatory or secret knowledge is a marked feature of religious life in the Hellenistic and Late Antique periods (e.g., Hengel 1996: 1.210–18); they have simply disagreed on how best to term it.

For instance, a recent reference work discusses 'esotericism' in ancient religions, but is unable to define the term, or the rubric under which various Egyptian, Neoplatonic, Jewish, and Gnostic trends fall into the same chapter (Johnston, ed., 2004: 640–56). Older scholarship, meanwhile, has often opted for the language of *gnōsis*. Most often, 'gnosis' designates any tradition that considers knowledge of God the key to salvation (Festugière 1954: 4.ix; Majercik 1989: 4; Markschies 2000: 1045; Hanegraaff 2012: 12). However, scholars disagree about the *object* of this knowledge: 'gnosis' can thus refer to knowledge whose knowledge is of itself (Filoramo 2000: 1043), elite secret knowledge (Scholem 1960: 1), knowledge opposed to mere faith (Rudolph 1987: 55–56), experiential knowledge of the divine (Jonas 2001 [1958]: 286; Hanegraaff 2004: 492, 510; Hanegraaff 2008; DeConick 2006: 7), or knowledge of divine origins (van den Broek 2006: 404–5).

Each of these definitions is unsatisfying. First, none of the primary sources testify to a 'gnosis' which has no specific content outside of itself; a classic example (*Corp. Herm.* 1.27–29) does state that 'gnosis' is salvific without defining its content, but the rest of the tractate makes clear that it is 'knowledge' of divine origins. Second, the charge of 'elitism' fails to capture the goal of many esoteric claims, which is namely to become revealed (exoteric); Hermetic or apocalyptic literature, for example, is replete with the themes not just of secret knowledge but paraenesis and even mission (*Corp. Herm.* 1.29; 2 *En.* 39). Third, the juxtaposition of 'gnosis' and 'faith' encodes a juxtaposition between proto-orthodox Christians (identified with 'faith'—Matt 10:32; Acts 2:44, 4:32) and their 'Gnostic' opponents, clumsily grouping 'gnosis' with any and all Christian heresy. Yet ancient religious literature, Christian or not, often equates 'knowing' (*gnōsis*) with 'believing' (*pistis*—e.g., Just. Mart. *Dial.* 69.1; Athan. *Vit. Anth.* 77; *Corp. Herm.* 4.4; Porph. *Marc.* 21–24). Fourth, 'experience' is a category whose hermeneutic utility is questionable (for a critical discussion, see Sharf 1998), particularly in antiquity, and in any case, the use of the term 'gnosis' for it misleadingly implies that 'Gnosticism' was the mystical tradition of Late Aniquity *par excellence*.

Salvation through 'gnosis' of 'divine origins' is a stronger definition with wide textual evidence in Gnosticism and Hermetism (Clem. Alex. *Exc. Theod.* 78.2; Hipp. *Haer.* 5.10.2). It has nothing to do with secrecy and thus is not necessarily esoteric (van den Broek 2006: 406), but is predicated upon the axiom of the identity between the human and the divine; knowledge of this identity elicits—indeed itself is—access to the divine (Filoramo 2000: 1044; Markschies 2000: 1045; Hanegraaff 2012: 372). The objection to this approach is twofold: 'gnosis' is a misleading term for such knowledge, and the lack of emphasis on 'secrecy' hides the importance of the concept of 'revelation', which is in turn tied to concealment.

Ancient literature used various terms to designate what modern scholars would like 'gnosis' to describe. For instance, the fifth-century Neoplatonist Proclus calls the 'theurgic virtue' associated with mystical experience produced by negative theology 'faith' (Gk. *pistis*), not *gnōsis* (*Theo. Plat.* 1.25). A seminal Sethian Gnostic text uses the term *gnōsis* for salvific knowledge in general, but 'primary revelation' for esoteric, intimate knowledge of the Great Invisible Spirit (*Allogenes* NHC XI, 3.53.8, 60.37–61.1). Conversely, early Christians commonly used the word 'gnosis' without a 'Gnostic' sense (Brakke 2010: 30–31 re: *1 Clem.* 36:2; *Ep. Bar.* 19:1; etc.). Moreover, modern coining of the term 'gnosis' implies an association with Gnosticism, which is both historically misleading (e.g., the Hermetic literature commonly considered representative of 'gnosis' was produced by circles distinct from the *gnostikoi* known to Irenaeus and Plotinus) and plays into the hands of the heresiologists, who preferred to group a variety of heretics under the umbrella of 'gnosis falsely-so-called' (Ir. *Haer.* Pref.).

The exclusive focus on the language of gnosis in the ancient traditions addressed here thus masks the variety of terms in the sources themselves and shuts us off from other, useful comparisons (e.g., between Gnosticism and the apocalypses) which could be governed by another term. The language of 'esotericism' is useful precisely because it addresses the importance of revelation (and in turn concealment) that is central to these traditions. Indeed, the same currents have often been described as a spike of interest in 'revelation' in antiquity, and studies of 'gnosis' often remark on its 'revelatory' character (Bultmann 1933: 693, 702; Rudolph 1987: 55; Markschies 2000: 1051; van den Broek 2006: 403). Regardless, any revelation, whether it became mainstream or not, must have seemed strange and esoteric when first proclaimed, and thus employed secrecy in the interests of both security and allure (King 2011: 82ff). Thus 'esoteric' tendencies are integral to revealed religion.

Yet the term 'esoteric' is useful in the ancient context for the particular traditions surveyed above because of the role they played in the flowering of 'Esotericism'—Renaissance Platonism, Hermeticism, alchemy, occultism, theosophy, etc. These esoteric discourses developed out of the reception-history, beginning in the Renaissance, of precisely the materials addressed in this essay—Hermetic texts, Neoplatonism and its association with the mysteries of Orpheus and Pythagoras, theurgy and ancient magic, Kabbalah and its ancestry in the apocalypses and Merkavah-speculation, and, sometimes thanks to their heretical reputation, the thought of the Gnostics themselves. Because the term 'esotericism' (like 'occultism') does not appear until the eighteenth century and after, and is used today to denote these relatively recent historical developments, it would perhaps be anachronistic to speak of 'ancient esotericism' per se. At the same time, recalling the debt of 'esotericism' and 'occultism' to the secret revelations of the Hellenistic and Late Antique worlds, one might speak of 'ancient esoteric traditions'.

NOTE

This article was written under the auspices of a postdoctoral research fellowship from Copenhagen University (the Faculty of Theology), to which I express my gratitude.

REFERENCES AND FURTHER READING

Primary Sources

While much of the ancient evidence is scattered, there are some 'classics' which will illuminate students of antiquity as well as those of more recent eras. Other primary sources are presented in the above chapter using the abbreviations found in the *SBL Handbook of Style* (1999), and the *Oxford Classical Dictionary* (2003).

Betz, H.D., ed. (1992) *The Greek Magical Papyri in Translation*, Chicago/London: University of Chicago Press.

Charlesworth, J., ed. (1985) *Old Testament Pseudepigrapha*, 2 vols. New York: Doubleday.

Clarke, E.C., J.M. Dillon and J.P. Hershbell, ed. and tr. (2003) *Iamblichus of Chalcis. On the Mysteries*, Atlanta: Society of Biblical Literature (SBLWGRW 4).

Copenhaver, B., tr. (1995) *Hermetica*, Cambridge: Cambridge University Press.

Davila, J., tr. (2013) *Hekhalot Literature in Translation*, Leiden: E.J. Brill (JJTPSup 20).

García Martínez, F. and E.J.C. Tigchelaar, ed. and tr. (2000) *The Dead Sea Scrolls: Study Edition*. 2 vols., Leiden: E.J. Brill.

Gardner, I. and S. Lieu, eds. (2004) *Manichaean Texts from the Roman Empire*, Cambridge: Cambridge University Press.

Layton, B., tr. (1987) *The Gnostic Scriptures*, New York: Doubleday (Anchor Bible Reference Library).

Majercik, R., ed. and tr. (1989) *The Chaldean Oracles. Text, Translation, and Commentary*, Leiden: E.J. Brill (SGRR 5).

Meyer, M., ed. (2007) *The Nag Hammadi Scriptures: the International Edition*, New York: HarperOne.

Meyer, M. and R. Smith, eds. (1994) *Ancient Christian Magic. Coptic Texts of Ritual Power*, San Francisco: HarperSanFrancisco.

Schäfer, P., ed. (1981) *Synopse zur Hekhalot-Literatur*, Tübingen: JCB Mohr.

Secondary Sources

Alexander, P. (2006) *Mystical Texts. Songs of the Sabbath Sacrifice and Related Manuscripts*, London: T&T Clark International (Library of Second Temple Studies 61).

Assmann, J. (1998) 'Ägyptische Geheimnisse: Arcanum und Mysterium in der ägyptischen Religion', in A. Assmann and J. Assmann (with T. Sundermeier), eds., *Schleier und Schwelle: Geheimnis und Offenbarung*, München: Wilhelm Fink (Archäologie der literarischen Kommunikation 5), 15–42.

Baltes, M. (2005) 'Der Platonismus und die Weisheit der Barbaren', in M. Baltes, *EPINOĒMATA. Kleine Schriften zur antiken Philosophie und homerischen Dichtung, Marie-Luise Lakmann. München/Leipzig: K.G. Saur* (Beiträge zur Altertumskunde), 1–26.

Betegh, G. (2004) *The Derveni Papyrus: Cosmology, Theology, and Interpretation*, Cambridge: Cambridge University Press.

Betz, H.D. (1995) 'Secrecy in the Greek Magical Papyri', in Kippenberg and Stroumsa, eds., *Secrecy and Concealment*, 153–76.

Brakke, D. (2010) *The Gnostics. Myth, Ritual, and Diversity in Early Christianity*, Cambridge: Harvard University Press.

——(2011) 'Mystery and Secrecy in the Egyptian Desert: Esotericism and Evagrius of Pontus', in C.H. Bull et al., eds., *Mystery and Secrecy in the Nag Hammadi Collection and other Ancient Literature*, 205–20.

Brisson, L. (1995) *Orphée et l'Orphisme dans l'Antiquité gréco-romaine*, Ashgate: Aldershot (VCS 476).

Bull, C.H., L.I. Lied and J.D. Turner, eds. (2011) *Mystery and Secrecy in the Nag Hammadi Collection and other Ancient Literature: Ideas and Practices. Studies for Einar Thomassen at Sixty*, Leiden: E.J. Brill (NHMS 76).

Bultmann, R. (1933) 'Gignōskō, Gnōsis, etc.' *TWNT* 1, 688–719.

Burkert, W. (1972) *Lore and Science in Ancient Pythagoreanism*, Cambridge: Harvard University Press.

——(1987) *Ancient Mystery Cults*, Cambridge: Harvard University Press.

Burns, D.M. (2004) 'Proclus and the Theurgic Liturgy of Pseudo-Dionysius', *Dionysius* 18, 111–32.

——(2006) '*The Chaldean Oracles of Zoroaster*, Hekate's Couch, and Platonic Orientalism in Psellos and Plethon', *Aries* 6:2, 158–79.

——(2007) 'Seeking Ancient Wisdom in the New Age: New Age and Neo-Gnostic Commentators on the *Gospel of Thomas*', in K. von Stuckrad and O. Hammer, eds., *Polemical Encounters: Esoteric Discourse and its Others*, Leiden: E.J. Brill (Aries Book Series 6), 252–89.

——(2012) 'Jesus' Reincarnations Revisited in Jewish Christianity, Sethian Gnosticism, and Mani', in S.E. Meyers, ed., *Portraits of Jesus: Studies in Christology*, Tübingen: Mohr Siebeck (WUNT 321), 371–92.

——(2014) *Apocalypse of the Alien God: Platonism and the Exile of Sethian Gnosticism*, Philadelphia: University of Pennsylvania Press (Divinations).

Collins, J.J. (1979) 'Morphology of a Genre', *Semeia* 14, 1–19.

DeConick, A.D. (2006) 'What is Early Jewish and Christian Mysticism?' in A.D. DeConick, ed., *Paradise Now: Essays on Early Jewish and Christian Mysticism*, Leiden: E.J. Brill, 1–26.

De Jong, A. (2006) 'Secrecy I: Antiquity', in Hanegraaff et al., eds., *Dictionary of Gnosis and Western Esotericism*, 1050–54.

Dillon, J. (1977) *The Middle Platonists*, London: Duckworth.

Dornseiff, F. (1925) *Das Alphabet in Mystik und Magie*, Leipzig: Teubner.

Dunderberg, I. (2011) 'Secrecy in the Gospel of John', in C.H. Bull et al., eds., *Mystery and Secrecy in the Nag Hammadi Collection and other Ancient Literature*, 221–43.

Festugière, A.-J. (1950–54) *La révélation d'Hermès Trismégiste*, 4 vols, Paris: Gabalda.

Filoramo, G. (2000) 'Gnosis/Gnostizismus, I. Religionswissenschaftlich', *RGG*[4] 3: cols. 1043–44.

Fowden, G. (1986) *The Egyptian Hermes. A Historical Approach to the Late Pagan Mind*, Cambridge: Cambridge University Press.

Graf, F. (1995) 'Excluding the Charming', in M. Meyer and P. Mirecki, eds., *Ancient Magic and Ritual Power*, Leiden: E.J. Brill (Religions of the Graeco-Roman World 129), 29–42.

Hanegraaff, W.J. (2004) 'The Study of Western Esotericism: New Approaches to Christian and Secular Culture', in P. Antes, A.W. Geertz, and R.R. Warne, eds., *New Approaches to the Study of Religion. Volume 1: Religion, Critical, and Historical Approaches*, Berlin/New York: Walter de Gruyter (Religion and Reason 42), 489–519.

——(2008) 'Altered States of Knowledge: The Attainment of Gnōsis in the Hermetica', *International Journal of the Platonic Tradition* 2, 128–63.

——(2012) *Esotericism and the Academy: Rejected Knowledge in Western Culture*, Cambridge: Cambridge University Press.

Hanegraaff, W.J., et al., eds. (2006) *Dictionary of Gnosis and Western Esotericism*, Leiden: E.J. Brill.

Hengel, M. (1996) *Judaism and Hellenism. Studies in Their Encounter in Palestine During the Early Hellenistic Period*, tr. J. Bowden, 2 vols., Philadelphia: Fortress Press.

Humphrey, J.A., ed. (1991) *Literacy in the Roman World*, Ann Arbor: University of Michigan Press (Journal of Roman Archaeology Supplementary Series 3).

Johnston, S.I. (2004) 'Mysteries', in S.I. Johnston, ed., *Religions of the Ancient World*, 99–111.

——, ed. (2004) *Religions of the Ancient World: A Guide*, Cambridge: Harvard University Press.

Jonas, H. (2001 [1958]) *The Gnostic Religion: The Message of the Alien God and the Beginnings of Christianity*, Boston: Beacon Press.

King, K.L. (2011) 'Mystery and Secrecy in *The Secret Revelation of John*', in C.H. Bull et al., eds., *Mystery and Secrecy in the Nag Hammadi Collection and other Ancient Literature*, 61–86.

Kippenberg, H. and G.G. Stroumsa, eds. (1995) *Secrecy and Concealment: Studies in the History of Mediterranean and Near Eastern Religions*, Leiden: E.J. Brill (Numen Book Series 65).

Lamberton, R. (1995) 'The *Aporrhētos Theoria* and the Roles of Secrecy in the History of Platonism', in Kippenberg and Stroumsa, eds., *Secrecy and Concealment*, 139–52.

Lenzi, A. (2008) *Secrecy and the Gods: Secret Knowledge in Ancient Mesopotamia and Biblical Israel*, Helsinki (State Archives of Assyria Studies, volume 19): The Neo-Assyrian Text Corpus Project.

Lewy, H. (2011) *Chaldaean Oracles and Theurgy. Troisème édition par Michel Tardieu avec un supplément «Les Oracles chaldaïques 1891–2001»*, Paris: Institut d'Études Augustiniennes (Collection des Études Augustiniennes, Série Antiquité 77).

Markschies, C. (2000) 'Gnosis/Gnostizismus, II. Christentum', *RGG*[4] 3: cols.1045–53.

Martin, L.H. (1995) 'Secrecy in Hellenistic Religious Communities', in Kippenberg and Stroumsa, eds., *Secrecy and Concealment*, 101–21.

Martin, D. (2004) *Inventing Superstition: From the Hippocratics to the Christians*, Cambridge: Harvard University Press.

Morray-Jones, C.R.A. (1995) 'Paul and the Beginning of Jewish Mysticism', in J.J. Collins and M. Fishbane, eds., *Death, Ecstasy, and Otherworldly Journeys*, Albany: State University of New York Press, 95–121.

Mortley, R. (1986) *From Word to Silence. The Way of Negation, Christian and Greek*, 2 vols., Bonn: Peter Hanstein.

O'Meara, D.J. (2003) *Platonopolis: Platonic Political Philosophy in Late Antiquity*, Oxford: Oxford University Press.

Pearson, B. (2011) 'Mystery and Secrecy in Paul', in C.H. Bull et al., eds., *Mystery and Secrecy in the Nag Hammadi Collection and other Ancient Literature*, 287–302.

Pedersen, N.A. (2011) 'The Term MYSTĒRION in Coptic-Manichaean Texts', in C.H. Bull et al., eds., *Mystery and Secrecy in the Nag Hammadi Collection and other Ancient Literature*, 133–43.

Pépin, J. (1958) *Mythe et Allégorie. Les origines grecques et les contestations judéo-chrétiennes*, Aubier: Éditions Montaigne.

Radcliffe, E.G. (1999) 'Tearing Apart the Zagreus Myth: A Few Disparaging Remarks on Orphism and Original Sin', *Classical Antiquity* 18.1, 35–73.

——, ed. (2011) *The 'Orphic' Golden Tablets: Further Along the Path*, Cambridge: Cambridge University Press.

Rasimus, T. (2009) *Paradise Reconsidered in Gnostic Mythmaking. Rethinking Sethianism in Light of the Ophite Evidence*, Leiden: E.J. Brill (NHMS 68).

Rudolph, K. (1987) *Gnosis: The Nature and History of Gnosticism*, tr. R. McL. Wilson, San Francisco: HarperSanFrancisco.

Schäfer, P. (2009) *The Origins of Jewish Mysticism*, Tübingen: Mohr Siebeck.

Scholem, G. (1960) *Jewish Gnosticism, Merkabah Mysticism, and Talmudic Tradition*, New York: Jewish Theological Seminary of America.

Sharf, R.H. (1998) 'Experience', in M.C. Taylor, ed., *Critical Terms for Religious Studies*, Chicago: University of Chicago Press, 94–116.

Shaw, G. (1995) *Theurgy and the Soul: the Neoplatonism of Iamblichus*, University Park: Pennsylvania University Press.

Smith, J.Z. (1990) *Drudgery Divine: On the Comparison of Early Christianities and the Religions of Late Antiquity*, Chicago: University of Chicago Press.

Strauss, L. (1952) *Persecution and the Art of Writing*, Westport: Greenwood Press.

Stroumsa, G.G. (1996) *Hidden Wisdom: Esoteric Traditions and the Roots of Christian Mysticism*, Leiden: E.J. Brill (Numen Studies in the History of Religions 70).

Turner, J. D. (2001) *Sethian Gnosticism and the Platonic Tradition*, Louvain/Paris: Peeters (BCNH Section 'Études' 6).

van den Broek, R. (2006) 'Gnosis I (Gnostic Religion)', in Hanegraaff et al., eds., *Dictionary of Gnosis and Western Esotericism*, 403–15.

von Stuckrad, K. (2010) *Locations of Knowledge in Medieval and Early Modern Europe: Esoteric Discourse and Western Identities*, Leiden: E.J. Brill (Brill's Studies in Intellectual History 186).

Wasserstrom, S. (2000) 'Jewish-Muslim Relations in the Context of Andalusian Emigration', in M.D. Meyerson, E.D. English, eds., *Christians, Muslims and Jews in Medieval and Early Modern Spain*, Notre Dame: University of Notre Dame Press, 69–87.

West, M.L. (1983) *The Orphic Poems*, Oxford: Clarendon Press.

Wrede, W. (1901) *Das Messiasgeheimnis in den Evangelien. Zugleich ein Beitrag zum Verständnis des Markusevangeliums*, Göttingen: Vandenhoeck & Ruprecht.

CHAPTER TWO

THE OCCULT MIDDLE AGES

Peter J. Forshaw

This chapter introduces some of the arts and sciences generally subsumed under the notion of occult thought during the Christian Middle Ages, roughly defined as the period from 500 to 1500 CE. As a working definition, 'occult' is understood as that which is hidden, secret or concealed, but also that which is insensible, not directly perceptible, indeed at times incomprehensible to the human intellect (Kwa 2011, 104). This encompasses the concept of 'occult qualities' (*virtutes occultae*) in nature, as a way of accounting for qualities in an object that were not explicable by knowledge of their manifest physical qualities (e.g., light, heat, motion, taste, colour, odour). Occult qualities at times appeared to be incompatible with the general expectations people had about the normal behaviour of the four elements on which Aristotelian scholastic philosophy was based. Some properties could not be explained in those terms. A popular example was the power of loadstones to attract iron, a property visible to the eye, but its cause occult because magnetic virtue did not result from the specific mixture of the four elements. Other examples were the belief in influences emanating from the planets, the sympathies and antipathies believed to exist between animals, vegetables and minerals, the wondrous (electrical) rays of the torpedo fish, or the occult, i.e., 'interior' properties of alchemical substances (Eamon 1994, 24; Newman 1996).

Nature, then, was a repository of occult powers and the studies involved in discovering and harnessing them came to be known as the 'occult sciences', knowledge kept secret from the uninitiated and profane. While the list of occult sciences can extend into the many divinatory arts, there are generally three main representatives: astrology, alchemy and magic. The gifted practitioner of these occult sciences, capable of recognizing nature's secrets, could manipulate them in order to produce wonders surpassing the abilities of his less informed peers.

During the ninth and tenth centuries much Greek material relating to these arts and sciences was translated into Arabic, followed by a flood of translation from Arabic into Latin in the twelfth and thirteenth centuries. The transmission of Arabic learning to the West, through, for example, the scriptorium of King Alfonso X of Castile (1221–84), introduced scholars to new conceptions of the occult sciences and an impressive new corpus of works on astrology, alchemy and magic (Garcia Avilés

1997; Dominguez Rodriguez 2007; Fernández Fernández 2013). The impact of Arabic knowledge on the West is particularly apparent from the eleventh to the thirteenth centuries, during the High Middle Ages, and was to have a profound influence on the learned Christian West, indeed the impact of this material was so widespread that European scholars had to 'undertake fundamental reconsideration of their views on magic' (Kieckhefer 1989, 18).

While much could be said about the presence of occult theories and practices in the Greek, Arabic and Jewish worlds, the main focus of this essay will be on occult thought in the Latin Christian West: the terrestrial and celestial 'occult sciences', alchemy and astrology, and the broad category of learned magic, with the aim of introducing important figures, significant works, and outlining influential themes that were to be of continuing influence in the Renaissance.

ASTROLOGY IN THE MIDDLE AGES

In the Early Middle Ages, there were few developed textbooks on either astronomy or astrology in the Christian West; indeed detailed observations of the heavens appear to have been rare in Europe until the twelfth century (Tester 1987, Chapter 5; Flint 1990). What knowledge there was of classical astrology existed in two main sources, the *Consolatio philosophiae – Consolation of Philosophy* (c. 523) of the Roman Christian and Platonic philosopher Boethius (480–524) and the encyclopedic *Etymologiarum libri XX – 20 Volumes of Etymologies* of Isidore, Bishop of Seville (c. 570–636) (Von Stuckrad 2007, 187–88). These two works were major conduits of late antique thought for medieval Christian scholarship. Isidore's distinction between *astrologia superstitiosa* and *astrologia naturalis* became the standard argument for medieval scholars to justify 'licit' astrology. 'Superstitious' astrology makes use of horoscopes and seeks to predict the character and the fate of an individual; 'Natural' astrology, on the other hand, concerns itself with meteorological predictions, for instance of flood or drought and includes iatromathematics, or astrological medicine (Tester 1987, 124–26). Isidore's assertion, in keeping with the classical medical authorities Hippocrates (c. 460–370 BC) and Galen (129–99/217 CE), that every physician ought to be familiar with astrology, which indicates the appropriate times for purgations, venesections, and the preparation and administering of medicine, retained an influence in Christian culture right into early modern times (Prioreschi 2003, 64). A common manifestation of this influence, in medieval manuscripts of astrological medicine, is the presence of the *melothesia*, the image of the astrological man, whose body parts are governed by the signs of the zodiac, from the head ruled by the first sign, Aries, down to the feet ruled by the last sign, Pisces (Clark 1982).

It was only, however, with the twelfth-century translation of Arabic treatises into Latin that Christian thinkers gained access to essential reading for more sophisticated practice of astrology. This became possible with the Latin translations of the *Almagest* and the *Tetrabiblos*, two of the most famous classical textbooks of astronomy and astrology by the second-century Greco-Roman astrologer Claudius Ptolemy (90–168). The *Tetrabiblos* was translated in 1138 and became one of the most popular astrological manuals of the Middle Ages (Barton 1994; Tester 1987, Chapter 4). There, in addition to Ptolemy's philosophical arguments in support of astrology, the novice astrologer learned of the powers of the seven planets of the Ptolemaic cosmos (Saturn, Jupiter, Mars, Sun, Venus, Mercury, Moon), the twelve constellations of the Zodiac, and the essentials of both mundane and judicial astrology (on these, see Page 2001).

This boom in translation did not just provide the West with copies of classical Greek and Roman material preserved in Arabic, but also opened up a wealth of knowledge from medieval Islamic culture, with works that introduced new genres of astrology, such as the doctrine of 'Revolutions'. A key proponent of this theory was the Persian philosopher Abu Mashar (Latin Albumasar, 787–886), whose encyclopedic treatment of all aspects of astrological theory and practice in his *Introduction to Astrological Prediction* (known in the West as *Liber Introductorius maior*) appeared in Latin in 1133 (Albumasar 1997). His *De magnis coniunctionibus – On the Great Conjunctions*, was an elaborate treatise on mundane astrology with special regard to the conjunctions of the outermost planets of the Ptolemaic cosmos, Jupiter and Saturn. In this work Abu Mashar set forth his chronosophical theory of the impact that the coming together of these two most slow-moving planets exerted on major natural, political and religious terrestrial events, from the growth and decline of religions and empires to the outbreak of wars, plagues and floods (Albumasar 2000). These ideas were taken up by both Christians and Jews in order to calculate, respectively, the return of Christ or the beginning of the messianic era (Boudet 2005, 61). Whereas the casting of horoscopes of individuals underwent periods of condemnation by the church due to concerns about the question of free will, influential medieval theologians like Thomas Aquinas, Roger Bacon and Bonaventure considered this form of astrology legitimate, arguing that it was in fact easier and more accurate to predict such 'universal' events (Zambelli 1986, 21–22).

By the end of the twelfth century, astrology was prevalent in almost all monasteries, and interest began to spread from the clergy to the court, and other layers of society. It attracted the attention of influential thinkers. The Platonist philosopher Bernardus Silvestris's *Cosmographia* (1147–48), with its two parts, Megacosmus and Microcosmus, concerning respectively the greater world and the creation of man, became one of the most important works of the High Middle Ages for its adaptation of Abu Mashar's ideas to a Christian context (Silvestris 1990). In the *Liber introductorius – Introductory Book*, Michael Scot (fl. 1217–35) presents his readers with a history of astrology stretching back to the first magician, Zoroaster, and instructs them with a great deal of medieval star lore. One of the most famous astrologers of his time, the Italian Guido Bonatti (d.c. 1297) wrote a comprehensive textbook, the *Liber astronomicus*, described as 'the most important astrological work produced in Latin in the thirteenth century' (Thorndike 1929, 826). By the mid-thirteenth century, astrology had been incorporated into the standard philosophical curriculum of Western universities, as part of the quadrivium with mathematics, music and geometry; and was firmly allied with medicine by the fifteenth century (Kusukawa 1993, 34).

ALCHEMY IN THE MIDDLE AGES

Two early Latin references to the 'science of alchemy' can be found in the works of the scholastic philosophers Dominicus Gundissalinus (fl. 1150) and Daniel of Morley (c.1140–1210). In *De divisione Philosophie – On the Division of Philosophy*,

Gundissalinus introduces the 'sciencia de alquimia' as one of the eight parts of natural science, while in Morley's *Liber de naturis inferiorum et superiorum – Book on the Natures of Lower and Upper Things* we discover that the 'scientia de alckimia' is, apparently, one of the eight parts of astrology (Forshaw 2013, 147).

The West's initiation into the mysteries of alchemy begins in 1144 with Robert of Chester's *Liber de compositione alchemiae – Book on the Composition of Alchemy*, a translation of instructions on how to make the Philosophers' Stone, allegedly given by the Christian monk Morienus Romanus to the Umayyad prince Khalid ibn-Yazid (Principe 2013, 51f). The work is presented in at times highly allegorical language, which leaves open the possibility that there are various levels of interpretation at play in the text, particularly with the presence of such assertions as that the matter needed for the work 'comes from you, who are yourself its source', alongside discussions of alchemical terms and procedures (Morienus 1974, 27).

Another early alchemical work to become available to Western readers in the twelfth century was the short enigmatic text known as the *Tabula Smaradgina* or *Emerald Tablet*, attributed to the legendary Hermes Trismegistus, alleged author of hundreds of treatises on astrology, magic and alchemy. There the reader is introduced to the classic Hermetic formulation 'What is below is like what is above; and what is above is like what is below', to the notion that the sought-for goal of the alchemical 'operation of the sun', be that the elixir or the Philosophers' Stone, has, for example, the sun as its father, the moon as its mother, and the earth as its nurse (Principe 2013, 32; Kahn 1994; Ruska 1926). Such opaque, poetic language was to represent a major style of transmission of the occult science of alchemy for the rest of the Middle Ages and into the Renaissance. Although some alchemical writers chose to express themselves in down-to-earth language, alchemical forms of communication in many medieval works can be particularly 'occult', in the sense that their authors made use of cover-names to conceal the identity of the substances and processes employed in the Great Work from the profane. Hence, rather than discuss work with quicksilver, an alchemist would write about the 'dragon', or simply speak of the necessary 'water'; instead of advising the use of volatile salts, an author would speak of eagles with bows in their talons. Colour changes would be implied by the mention of black ravens, white swans, multicoloured peacocks, and golden eagles, much to the puzzlement of the uninitiated (Ferrario 2009; Read 1995, Chapter 4). Given the highly visual nature of alchemical metaphor, it was only a matter of time before the emergence of a new genre of alchemical images in the Late Middle Ages, one of the earliest examples being Constantine of Pisa's *Book of the Secrets of Alchemy* (c. 1257), succeeded by far more elaborate image sequences in such fifteenth-century manuscript works as the *Aurora consurgens – The Rising Dawn* and *Buch der heiligen Dreifaltigkeit – Book of the Holy Trinity* (Constantine of Pisa 1990; Obrist 1982; Gabriele 1997). The occultation, as it were, of alchemical communication was deepened by the substitution of signs for substances and processes. The alchemical symbols for the seven metals (gold, silver, copper, etc.), were shared with the astrological signs for the planets (sun, moon, Venus, etc.), but other signs or 'hieroglyphs', such as those for minerals like antimony, sulphur and cinnabar were specific to alchemy. A further method contributing to the concealment of knowledge was 'dispersa intentio' (dispersion of knowledge), when instructions for an alchemical operation would be written in the wrong order, some parts only fragmentary, sometimes with the full process distributed in different books. A major exponent of this approach is the medieval author Geber, who in his *Summa perfectionis magisterii – Summation of the Perfection of the Magistery* (c. 1300), generally agreed to be the most influential medieval work of practical transmutational alchemy, writes of scattering information here and there in different chapters of his work and has 'hidden it where we have spoken most openly' (Newman 1991, 784f; Principe 2013, 45).

GOALS OF MEDIEVAL ALCHEMY

There have been many different interpretations of the *Emerald Tablet*, ranging from readings of it as a text of *Chrysopoeia* (Gold-Making), *Chymiatria* (Chemical Medicine), or indeed Spiritual Alchemy. The first of these represents the major form of alchemical endeavour in the Middle Ages, the amelioration of base-metals with the aim of their ultimate transmutation into gold. Most medieval practitioners were concerned with this *Opus Magnum* (Great Work), the production of precious metals through the art of transmutation by means of a series of laboratory processes, involving, for example, calcination, dissolution, sublimation, coagulation, fixation, and projection, and the quest for the *Lapis Philosophorum* (Philosophers' Stone) and the *Elixir*, for the healing of either 'sick' metals or human beings. These ideas were taken up by Pseudo-Lull, whose *Testamentum* (c. 1330) spoke of metallic transmutation, the enhancement of human health, and the production of artificial stones and precious stones (Principe 2013, 47, 72; Pereira & Spaggiari 1999). In his *Liber de consideratione quintae essentiae omnium rerum – Book on the Consideration of the Quintessence of All Things* (1351–52), the Franciscan John of Rupescissa (c. 1310–c. 1362) described the distillation of quintessences of various things, including the preparation of alcohol distilled from wine, to produce the paradoxical 'fiery water' of the alchemists. Rupescissa's popular work is one of the most widespread of the Middle Ages (DeVun 2009). Lest anyone think, however, that alchemy was always considered purely natural, it is worth mentioning that Petrus Bonus, the author of another popular work, the fourteenth-century *Pretiosa margarita novella – New Pearl of Great Price* (1330), claimed that alchemy was natural, supernatural and divine, and that a knowledge of the generation of the Philosophers' Stone enabled pagan philosophers to predict the virgin birth of Christ (Crisciani 1973; Principe 2013, 68).

MAGIC IN THE MIDDLE AGES

The Latin West inherited a rich tradition of magical literature from antiquity. Although far less documentary evidence survives from the early Middle Ages, some important early classifications of magic are available. In Isidore of Seville's *Etymologies*, for example, we read that mankind learned the magical arts from bad angels. Despite his overall negative attitude towards magic, Isidore's entry on 'magi' contains a catalogue of magical arts that would remain a standard topos in medieval writings: necromancy, the forms of divination linked with the four elements (hydromancy, pyromancy, aeromancy, geomancy), well-known methods of classical divination, including observation of the flight of birds (augury), the entrails of sacrificial animals (haruspicy), and the positions of stars and planets (astrology) (Kieckhefer 1989, 11).

As with astrology and alchemy, magical literature was profoundly influenced by the influx of new learning in the twelfth and thirteenth centuries. The Arabic philosophical and astrological corpus provided Western scholars with a theoretical framework well suited to supporting numerous forms of magical practice. The focus of the following sections will be on the diversity of learned magic in the Middle Ages, an introduction to the most important genres: natural magic, astral magic and ritual magic.

NATURAL MAGIC

Despite the opposition of theologians like Hugh of St Victor (c.1096–1141) to the idea that any type of magic should be included in the curriculum of legitimate learning (Eamon 1994, 59), the influence of newly translated Arabic treatises in the domain of natural philosophy almost inevitably introduced the concept of a new branch of science, 'natural magic', to learned discourse. Rather than simply rejecting all magic as demonic, after the manner of Saint Augustine (354–430), some writers argued for a distinction between a licit form of natural magic and an illicit demonic magic. Natural magic enabled human beings to know and make use of the occult virtues of natural things, the properties of stones, metals, plants, and animals, the sympathies and antipathies existing in the whole of nature, without the assistance of or manipulation by demons. Not only could discerning scholars know about these natural virtues, and offer naturalistic explanations for the phenomena, but they could apply the knowledge for the benefit of mankind through a practical magic that made use of the things of nature (Lang 2008, 51–78; Page 2013, 31–48).

An influential voice in this natural magic worldview was the theologian William of Auvergne (c. 1180–1249). In *De Legibus – On the Laws* (1228–30), William introduced the term 'natural magic' as the eleventh part of natural philosophy, justifying its inclusion by arguing that it operates merely through natural virtues, inherent in the objects of nature. In the slightly later *De Universo – On the Universe* (1231–36), he discussed *experimenta* related to these occult powers and the notion of magical correspondences, implying an underlying network of secret relationships between the three kingdoms of nature (animal, vegetable and mineral), celestial configurations and the parts of the human body (Lang 2008, 25). The Dominican theologian and natural philosopher Albertus Magnus (ca. 1193–1280) similarly acknowledged the possibility of natural magic in philosophical writings, such as *De animalibus – On Animals*, though in his theological work he was cautious about distinguishing it from the demonic kind (Thorndike 1929, Chapter LIX, esp. 548–60). Probably the most widespread medieval treatise on natural magic was the *Experimenta*, frequently, if falsely, attributed to Albertus, and later known as the *Liber aggregationis seu secretorum de virtutibus herbarum, lapidum et animalium – Book of Collection or of Secrets of the Virtues of Plants, Stones and Animals*. Another pseudo-Albertan work, *De mirabilibus mundi – On the World's Marvels*, likewise contributed to an interest in the hidden properties of nature. Indeed, a whole culture of popular books of secrets developed, containing collections of *secreta*, *experimenta* and recipes, predominantly concerned with practical recipes for producing cosmetics or dyeing textiles, preparing drugs or brewing beer. The *Liber Secretum Secretorum – Book of the Secret of Secrets*, pseudonymously attributed to Aristotle, a work that has been called 'the most popular book in the Middle Ages' (Thorndike 1929, 267), its full translation dating from the mid-thirteenth century, is filled with material from the occult sciences, on alchemy, information from lapidaries and herbals, medical astrology and the fabrication of talismans (Eamon 1994, 45ff; Williams 2003).

ASTRAL MAGIC

With this reference to talismans we enter the domain of one of the most important new categories of learned magic introduced into the Christian West from mainly Arabic sources during the twelfth and thirteenth centuries, a genre that has been variously termed astral, astrological, celestial, or image magic, a set of practices that occupy a midpoint between tolerated natural and illicit demonic magic.

The ninth-century works of the Iraqi mathematician, physician and 'first philosopher of the Islamic world', Abu Yusuf Ya-qub ibn Ishaq al-Kindi (d. c. 870), in particular his influential combination of Platonism and Aristotelianism in *De radiis stellarum – On the Rays of the Stars*, were to have a profound impact on Western theories of occult influence (Al-Kindi 1974). In *De radiis*, which circulated widely in Latin translation from the thirteenth century through to the Renaissance, Al-Kindi promotes the theory that not only do all material things in the natural world, the stars included, send out rays, but so too do words and actions, such that ritual, prayer and sacrifice can all be powerful magical ways of influencing the cosmos (Travaglia 1999). Here astral magic is presented as working through a cosmic harmony of interconnected rays, with the informed practitioner having the ability to direct the virtues of the celestial bodies (planets, constellations, fixed stars) down into terrestrial objects for magical purposes, on a natural rather than supernatural basis.

Al-Kindi's theoretical work on magic was complemented by another ninth-century work, *De imaginibus astrologicis – On Astrological Images* by the Sabian scholar and philosopher Thabit ibn Qurra (826–901). By 'Astrological Images', Thabit means 'talismans' (hence the frequent reference to this genre as 'Image Magic') and his book is a work dealing with the practical issues of creating astral magical talismans, an activity that Thabit declares is the height and summit of the science of the stars. In Al-Kindi, there is no suggestion of rituals directed to planetary spirits, but instead an emphasis on the creator of talismans drawing down celestial virtue. Such is the case, too, if the reader consults the Latin translation by 'Magister John of Seville'; if, however, the reader possesses the translation by Adelard of Bath, made slightly earlier in the twelfth century, there one finds prayers to spirits (Burnett 1996, 6). Here, then, we have slightly ambiguous instructions for rituals to be performed over a three-dimensional object (image, talisman or statue) in order to induce a spirit or heavenly body to imbue it with power under well-defined astrological circumstances. Some argued that these were purely natural talismans, incorporating the combined power of a star, stone, herb and character; others, however, were more dubious.

Although, following Al-Kindi, image magic ostensibly depended on occult powers in nature, especially those of celestial origin, 'many of its sources of power – words, characters, images and spirits – were more controversial' and astral magical techniques and practices could also be identified with far more subversive genres such as necromantic texts and manuals, creating affinities between astral magic and the invocation of demons (Page 2013, 48). Such was certainly the case with the most complex work of astral magic available to the West, the Arabic compendium drawn from 224 magical sources, the *Ghayat al-Hakim* or *Goal of the Wise*, composed in Spain in the eleventh century. This work, better known in the Christian West in its Latin translation as the *Picatrix*, introduces itself as a book of necromancy and includes far more dangerous practices, including animal sacrifices directed to spirits and rituals using human blood, although the translator omits certain passages, such as one for creating a divinatory head from a decapitated prisoner (Boudet et al. 2011, 156).

One of the most important medieval works on astrology, the *Speculum astronomiae – Mirror of Astronomy* (1255–60), usually attributed to Albertus Magnus, contributed to learned interest in astral magic with its survey of newly translated Greek and Arab astronomical and astrological practices (Zambelli 1992; Paravicini Bagliani 2001). The author's primary interest is in establishing the philosophical legitimacy of astrology, in accordance with both Aristotelianism and Christianity. In the process he differentiates between useful and innocent astrological texts and dangerous necromantic works concerning images, characters and seals (Zambelli 1992, 241ff; Lang 2008, 27). The *Speculum*'s eleventh chapter, devoted to the *Scientia Imaginum* (Science of Images) distinguishes three categories of texts, respectively 'abominable' Hermetic images, 'detestable' Solomonic images, and acceptable astrological images. The first group, represented by such Hermetic works as the *Liber praestigiorum – Book of Talismans* and the *Liber Lunae – Book of the Moon*, constitutes the most dangerous category, being idolatrous, including rites that require suffumigations and invocations to spirits. The second group, including *De quatuor annuli Salomonis – On the Four Rings of Solomon* and the *Almandal of Solomon*, is 'less unsuitable', avoiding ceremonies, but nonetheless encouraging the use of unknown characters of dubious origin, and performed by inscribing characters and the use of demonic seals, which are to be exorcized by certain names (Véronèse 2012). What remains is a third group of two acceptable works: Thabit's *De imaginibus* and Pseudo-Ptolemy's *Opus imaginum – Work of Images*, works that provide practical information about fashioning images at a suitable astrological moment, concerned (according to the author of the *Speculum*) solely with utilizing stellar influxes without any suggestion of resorting to idolatrous rituals, suffumigations or invocations, exorcism or inscription of characters.

A decade or so later, similar concerns about discriminating between licit and illicit forms of talismanic magic were discussed by Thomas Aquinas (1225–74). In *De occultis operibus naturae – On the Occult Works of Nature*, Aquinas conceded that some bodies, such as magnets, have workings that cannot be caused by the powers of the elements and their actions must be traced to higher principles (either to heavenly bodies or to separated intellectual substances). In *Summa contra gentiles* (esp. Book 3, Chapters 104 & 105), he appears to accept that some power from celestial bodies may be present in natural, unfashioned amulets; he rejects talismans that include signs, figures or images, for they receive their efficacy from an intelligent being to whom the communication is addressed, and that being is most likely demonic (Thorndike 1929, 602ff; Walker 2003, 43; Skemer 2006, 63f).

RITUAL MAGIC IN THE LATE MIDDLE AGES

The later middle ages was witness to increasing numbers of a new kind of work, manuals of ritual magic, concerned with the conjuring of spirits, be that the summoning of infernal demons or the invocation of celestial angels. The reliance on spiritual, demonic, or angelic assistance and the magicians' use of prayers and conjurations as means of communicating with these supernatural powers clearly differentiates this genre of magic from its more licit natural and astral forms. The boundaries between these various genres, however, are permeable, indeed it is extremely common to find ritual magicians, busy with their angelic, theurgic or demonic operations, incorporating astrological practices, ranging from simple attention to specific planetary days and hours, or the transits of the moon through the zodiac, to more sophisticated calculations of planetary events; likewise, a knowledge of the *materia magica* of natural magic was essential both for the sacrifices employed in certain forms of necromantic ritual and for the fabrication of the at times elaborate instruments and weapons employed in some ceremonies.

While these texts of ritual magic, like those of other forms, clearly show the influence of earlier Greek, Arabic Neo-Platonic, and Jewish traditions, the extant manuscripts draw for the most part on Christian biblical and liturgical texts and practices, most notably exorcism, for their structure and justification. In contrast to many of the practices of natural and astral magic, one identifying characteristic of this genre is that the rituals are often long and complex, sometimes taking months to complete (Fanger 1998 a, vii–ix; Lang 2008, 162–88).

Ritual magic manifests in two fundamental forms, along the lines of classical distinctions between *theurgia* and *goetia*, namely, a magic concerned with angelic powers and another involving angelic and demonic powers.

The first form of ritual magic, angelic or theurgic, described rituals concerned with revelation, techniques for inducing dreams and visions, for speaking to spirits, for a direct infusion of knowledge and experience of the celestial realm, for the development of the practitioner's memory, eloquence and understanding, with the ultimate aim of improving the practitioner's chances of salvation. This normally involved intensive and extensive rituals for the purification of the practitioner's soul, preparations in the form of fasting, confession, periods of silence and meditation, lengthy prayers to the Holy Trinity and accompanying angels (Page 2011; Page 2013, 93–129; Klaassen 2013, 89–113).

Although the word 'magic' is not found in the text, one of the most important representatives of this angel magic is the *Ars notoria* – *Notory Art*, with its claim to enable the solitary practitioner, the student intent on bettering himself in his studies or the monk earnestly hoping for visionary experience, to acquire spiritual and intellectual gifts from the Holy Spirit by means of angelic intermediaries. According to the *Ars notoria* it is a set of holy prayers revealed to Solomon by an angel in order for the successful practitioner to become the beneficiary of a divine infusion of knowledge of the liberal arts, philosophy, theology, medical and divinatory knowledge. This involves the recitation of prayers, some recognizably orthodox, others containing mysterious *verba ignota*, purificatory rituals, contemplative exercises involving the inspection of *notae* – complex figures composed of words, shapes and magical characters – drinking of special decoctions, and so forth, extending over a four-month period (Véronèse 2007; Camille 1998). The earliest version of the *Ars notoria* probably originates in Northern Italy and dates from the latter half of the twelfth century; its influence can be seen in the fourteenth-century *Liber visionum – Book of Visions* of John of Morigny (Fanger 1998 b, 216–49), as well as other forms of Christianized magic, like the *Anacrisis* and the *Ars crucifixi – Art of the Crucifix*, both attributed to the Majorcan hermit Pelagius (d. 1480). The latter text, for example, in a combination of magic technique and pious devotion, provides a ritual of dream incubation in order to grant the earnest practitioner a vision of Christ during sleep (Gilly & van Heertum 2002, vol. 1, 288–89; Véronèse 2006). In general, these manuals of Christian ritual magic are so orthodox in tone that manuscripts of the *Ars notoria* and its derivatives have been mistaken for prayer formularies.

The same could not be said, however, of another influential treatise of angel magic, the *Liber sacer sive iuratus Honorii – The Holy or Sworn Book of Honorius*, an original composition in Latin dating from probably fourteenth-century southern France. This work claims to provide a twenty-eight day ritual that will result in no less than the Beatific Vision (Hedegård 2002; Mesler 1998); the complete Honorius ritual, however, requires seventy-two days! In the prologue to the *Liber iuratus*, we learn of a general council of eighty-nine Masters of Magic from Naples, Athens and Toledo, who defend the magical art and reject the unjust charges of misguided bishops and prelates who have been led astray by demons (despite the fact that the magic in question is one of binding and loosing spirits). Their argument is that such spirits are constrained only by pure men, not the wicked. What follows is a detailed set of instructions for fashioning a *Sigillum Dei* (Seal of God), directions for the rituals of consecration (involving blood of a mole, dove, bat or hoopoe), and the requisite prayers and invocation of a set of around one hundred divine names, so that the operator can conjure angels and demons for various purposes, the highest activity being the *opus visionis divine*, an operation leading to the radical transformation of the practitioner with a vision of God, while still in mortal frame (Mathiesen 1998). Subsequent parts of the manual include further rituals for conjuring planetary, aerial and terrestrial spirits, the construction of a magic circle, use of magical equipment, such as a hazel wand, swords, a whistle, use of *voces magicae* and so forth. Significant parts of this material are also found in the impressive fourteenth-century compendium of magic, the *Summa sacre magice*, by the Spanish scholar Berengarius Ganellus, which similarly assures the operator that the use of the *Sigillum Dei* will grant a vision of God, knowledge of God's power, the absolution of sins, sanctification, and dignification over all spirits (Veenstra 2012; Klaassen 2013, 102).

The other, potentially far more subversive form of ritual magic, frequently accused of idolatry, is most often referred to as necromancy, literally translating as 'divination by the dead', but generally understood as the conjuring of demonic beings, through practices inspired by religious rites of exorcism, in order to constrain them to do the operator's will. The aims of necromantic practitioners range from the relatively anodyne goals of locating hidden treasure and stolen goods (or the thief), or discovering secret information, through gaining invisibility, creating illusions, to the more malign desires to manipulate human emotions, cause physical or mental harm, dominating others to gratify sexual desires (Klaassen 2013, 115–55; Kieckhefer 1989, 151–75).

The early history of necromancy, however, is fragmentary and the earliest surviving British dedicated manuscript collections date from the fifteenth century (Klaassen 2013, 123). As with angelic magic, necromantic rituals are also derived from the liturgy, with multiple invocations of God, the Virgin Mary, the saints and angels. The operations, loosely based upon exorcism, conjure and bind demons through the power of the Christian operator, who has ritualistically prepared himself through a strict regimen of abstinence, prayer, confession, communication, and penance. The fifteenth-century *Liber Consecrationum*, for example, advises fasting and prayer, providing many pages of prayers replete with divine names and words of power, to be said over periods of weeks. These are followed by pages of adjurations and conjurations of Satan, details on how to obtain knowledge from a magical mirror, lists of demons, and detailed instructions for conjuring spirits (Kieckhefer 1997). Far more visible, moreover, in these goetic rites, is the use of suffumigations, creation of magic circles with pentagrams, astrological characters, demonic seals, and the inclusion of an impressive array of *instrumenta magica*: the rings, mirrors, wands, swords, knives, lances and so forth found in works like the *Clavicula Salomonis – Key of Solomon*, of which few copies survive from the middle ages, but which was to become the most popular magical manuscript in Europe from the eighteenth century onwards.

CONCLUSION

The Middle Ages received a wealth of occult material from antiquity, particularly so due to the industrious programme of translation of Arabic texts, although it should be said that texts translated into Latin in the twelfth century and initially seen as repositories of valuable new knowledge and useful practical arts were already being treated with suspicion by the end of the thirteenth century. The Dominicans issued condemnations of alchemy in 1272, 1287, 1289, and 1323 (Newman 1989, 439). In 1312, all members of the Franciscan order were forbidden to possess occult books of any kind, or to engage in alchemy, necromancy, or the invocation of demons, or face the consequences of prison or excommunication. Just five years later, in 1317, a papal Bull banned the practice of alchemy (Page 2013, 30).

Fortunately, a great deal of manuscript material survives in the archives, many of the treatises from these different occult currents (astrological, alchemical and magical) can be found bound together, although some genres, such as the conjurations of ritual magic, tend to follow their own separate stream of transmission. This being said, many of these occult practices were clearly interrelated, sometimes in an obvious way: for example, a fashioner of talismans would doubtless benefit from the products of the alchemical laboratory; likewise at least some alchemists paid attention to the specifics of correct astrological timing, seeking the most propitious celestial moment for their 'lower astronomy'. At other times the connections are less obvious: many historians of alchemy would be surprised to discover that the necromantic *Picatrix* provides insights into some of the enigmatic terms in the *Emerald Tablet*. All this material was waiting for the next stage of assimilation when, in the Renaissance, it was finally dignified with the name 'Occult Philosophy'.

REFERENCES AND FURTHER READING

Al-Kindi 1974, *De radiis*, edited by d'Alverny, M-Th & Hudry, F, *Archives d'histoire doctrinale et littéraire du Moyen Age* 41, 139–260.

Albumasar 1997, *The Abbreviation of the Introduction to Astrology*, edited and translated by C Burnett, Arhat Publications, Reston, VA.

——2000, *On Historical Astrology: The Book of Religions and Dynasties (On the Great Conjunctions)*, edited and translated by K Yamamoto & C Burnett, 2 vols, Brill, Leiden.

Bakhouche, B, Fauquier, F & Pérez-Jean, B (trans.) 2003, *Picatrix: Un traité de magie médiéval*, Brepols, Turnhout.

Barton, TS 1994, *Power and Knowledge: Astrology, Physiognomics, and Medicine under the Roman Empire*, University of Michigan Press, Ann Arbor.

Berthelot, M (ed.) 1967, *La Chimie au moyen* âge, 3 vols., Paris 1893; repr. Otto Xeller, Osnabrück/Philo Press, Amsterdam.

Blume, D 2000, *Regenten des Himmels. Astrologische Bilder in Mittelalter und Renaissance*, Akademie Verlag, Berlin.

Boudet, J-P 2005, 'Astrology,' in *Medieval Science, Technology, and Medicine: An Encyclopedia*, edited by TF Glick, S Livesey, & F Wallis, Routledge, New York.

——2006, *Entre science et nigromance: Astrologie, divination et magie dans l'Occident médiéval (XIIe-XVe siècle)*, Publications de la Sorbonne, Paris.

Boudet, J-P, Caiozzo, A, & Weill-Parot, N (eds) 2011, *Images et Magie: Picatrix entre Orient et Occident*, Honoré Champion, Paris

Burnett, C 1996, 'Talismans: magic as science? Necromancy among the Seven Liberal Arts', in C Burnett, *Magic and Divination in the Middle Ages: Texts and Techniques in the Islamic and Christian Worlds*, Variorum Collected Studies Series, Aldershot.

Burnett, C & Ryan WF (eds) 2006, *Magic and the Classical Tradition*, Warburg Institute, London.

Camille, M 1998, 'Visual Art in Two Manuscripts of the *Ars Notoria*', in C Fanger (ed.), *Conjuring Spirits: Texts and Traditions of Medieval Ritual Magic*, Sutton Publishing, Stroud.

Clark, C 1982, 'The Zodiac Man in Medieval Medical Astrology,' *Journal of the Rocky Mountain Medieval and Renaissance Association* 3, 13–38.

Constantine of Pisa 1990, *The Book of the Secrets of Alchemy*, edited and translated by B Obrist, Brill, Leiden.

Crisciani, C 1973, 'The Conception of Alchemy as Expressed in the »Pretiosa Margarita Novella« of Petrus Bonus of Ferrara', *Ambix* 20, 165–81.

——2002, *Il Papa e l'alchimia: Felice V, Guglielmo Fabri e l'elixir*, Viella, Rome.

Crisciani, C & Paravicini Bagliani, A (eds) 2003, *Alchimia e medicina nel Medioevo* (Collana 'Micrologus' Library'), Sismel-Edizioni del Galluzzo, Florence.

DeVun, L 2009, *Prophecy, Alchemy, and the End of Time: John of Rupescissa in the Late Middle Ages*, Columbia University Press, New York.

Dominguez Rodriguez, A 2007, *Astrología y Arte en el* Lapidario *de Alfonso X El Sabio*, Edición de la Real Academia Alfonso X el Sabio, Murcia.

Eamon, W 1994, *Science and the Secrets of Nature: Books of Secrets in Medieval and Early Modern Culture*, Princeton University Press, Princeton.

Fanger, C 1998 a, 'Medieval Ritual Magic: What it is and Why We Need to Know More About it', in C Fanger (ed.), *Conjuring Spirits: Texts and Traditions of Medieval Ritual Magic*, Sutton Publishing, Stroud.

——1998 b, 'Plundering the Egyptian Treasure: John the Monk's *Book of Visions* and its Relation to the Ars Notoria of Solomon', in C Fanger (ed.), *Conjuring Spirits: Texts and Traditions of Medieval Ritual Magic*, Sutton Publishing, Stroud.

Fanger, C (ed.) 2012, *Invoking Angels: Theurgic Ideas and Practices, Thirteenth to Sixteenth Centuries*, Pennsylvania State University Press, University Park.

Fernández Fernández, L 2013, *Arte y Ciencia en el* scriptorium *de Alfonso X el Sabio*, El Puerto de Santa María, Cádiz.

Ferrario, G 2009, 'Understanding the Language of Alchemy: The Medieval Arabic Alchemical Lexicon in Berlin, Staatsbibliothek, Ms Sprenger 1908', *Digital Proceedings of the Lawrence J. Schoenberg Symposium on Manuscript Studies in the Digital Age*, Vol. 1, Issue 1, 1–14.

Flint, VIJ 1990, 'The Transmission of Astrology in the Early Middle Ages,' *Viator* 21, 1–28.

——1991, *The Rise of Magic in Early Medieval Europe*, Princeton University Press, Princeton.

Forshaw, PJ 2013, '"Chemistry, that Starry Science": Early Modern Conjunctions of Astrology and Alchemy,' in N Campion & E Greene (eds), *Sky and Symbol*, Sophia Centre Press, Lampeter.

Gabriele, M 1997, *Alchimia e Iconologia*, Forum, Udine.

Garcia Avilés, A 1997, 'Alfonso X y el *Liber Razielis*: Imágenes de la magia astral judia en el scriptorium alfonsi,' *Bulletin of Hispanic Studies* 74, 21–39.

Ganzenmüller, W 1939, 'Das Buch der heiligen Dreifaltigkeit. Eine deutsche Alchemie aus dem Anfang des 15. Jahrhunderts,' *Archiv für Kulturgeschichte* 29, 93–146.

Gilly, C & van Heertum, C (eds) 2002, *Magia, alchimia, scienza dal '400 al '700: l'influsso di Ermete Trismegisto*, 2 vols. Centro Di, Florence.

Hanegraaff, WJ 2012, *Esotericism and the Academy: Rejected Knowledge in Western Culture*, Cambridge University Press, Cambridge.

Hedegård, G 2002, *Liber Iuratus Honorii: A Critical Edition of the Latin Version of the Sworn Book of Honorius*. Almqvist & Wiksell International, Stockholm.

Henry, J 1986, 'Occult Qualities and the Experimental Philosophy: Active Principles in Pre-Newtonian Matter Theory', *History of Science* 24, 335–81.

Isidore of Seville 2006, *The Etymologies of Isidore of Seville*, translated, with Introduction and Notes, by SA Barney, WJ Lewis, JA Beach, & O Berghof, Cambridge University Press, Cambridge.

Kahn, D 1994, *La table d'émeraude et sa tradition alchimique*, Les Belle Lettres, Paris.

Kieckhefer, R 1989, *Magic in the Middle Ages*, Cambridge University Press, Cambridge.

——1994, 'The Specific Rationality of Medieval Magic,' *American Historical Review* 99, 813–36.

——1997, *Forbidden Rites: A Necromancer's Manual of the Fifteenth Century*, Sutton Publishing, Stroud.

Klaassen, F 1998, 'English Manuscripts of Magic, 1300–1500: A Preliminary Survey,' in C Fanger (ed.), *Conjuring Spirits: Texts and Traditions of Medieval Ritual Magic*, Sutton Publishing, Stroud.

——2013, *The Transformations of Magic: Illicit Learned Magic in the Later Middle Ages and Renaissance*, Pennsylvania State University Press, University Park.

Kusukawa, S 1993, 'Aspectio divinorum operum: Melanchthon and Astrology for Lutheran Medics,' in OP Grell & A Cunningham (eds), *Medicine and the Reformation*, Routledge, London & New York.

Kwa, C 2011, *Styles of Knowing: A New History of Science from Ancient Times to the Present*, University of Pittsburgh Press, Pittsburgh.

Lang, B 2008, *Unlocked Books: Manuscripts of Learned Magic in the Medieval Libraries of Central Europe*, Pennsylvania State University Press, University Park.

Lucas, JS 2003, *Astrology and Numerology in Medieval and Early Modern Catalonia: The Tractat de prenostication de la vida natural dels hòmens*, Brill, Leiden.

Magdalino, M & Mavroudi, MV (eds) 2006, *The Occult Sciences in Byzantium*, Éditions de la Pomme d'Or, Geneva.

Mathiesen, R 1998, 'A Thirteenth-Century Ritual to Attain the Beatific Vision from the Sworn Book of Honorius of Thebes,' in C Fanger (ed.), *Conjuring Spirits: Texts and Traditions of Medieval Ritual Magic*, Sutton Publishing, Stroud.

Maxwell-Stuart, PG 2005, *The Occult in Medieval Europe* 500–1500, Palgrave Macmillan, London.

Mesler, K 1998, 'The *Liber iuratus Honorii* and the Christian Reception of Angel Magic,' in C Fanger (ed.), *Conjuring Spirits: Texts and Traditions of Medieval Ritual Magic*, Sutton Publishing, Stroud.

Morienus 1974, *A Testament of Alchemy being the Revelations of Morienus, Ancient Adept and Hermit of Jerusalem to Khalid ibn Yazid ibn Mu'Awiyya, King of the Arabs of the Divine Secrets of the Magisterium and Accomplishment of the Alchemical Art*, edited and translated by L Stavenhagen, University Press of New England/Brandweis University Press, Hanover, NH.

Newman, WR 1989, 'Technology and Alchemical Debate in the Late Middle Ages,' *Isis* 80, 423–45.

——1991, *The 'Summa perfectionis' of Pseudo-Geber: A Critical Edition, Translation and Study*, Brill, Leiden.

——1996, 'The Occult and the Manifest among the Alchemists', in FJ Ragep & SP Ragep (eds), *Tradition, Transmission, Transformation*, Brill, Leiden.

Newman, WR & Grafton, A 2001, 'Introduction: The Problematic Status of Astrology and Alchemy in Premodern Europe', in WR Newman & A Grafton (eds), *Secrets of Nature: Astrology and Alchemy in Early Modern Europe*, The MIT Press, Cambridge, MA & London.

Obrist, B 1982, *Les Débuts de l'Imagerie Alchimique (XIVe-XVe siècles)*, Éditions le Sycomore, Paris.

——1993, 'Cosmology and Alchemy in an illustrated 13th-Century Alchemical Tract: Constantine of Pisa, "The Book of the Secrets of Alchemy"', *Micrologus* 1, 115–60.

——2003, 'Visualisation in Medieval Alchemy', *HYLE: International Journal for Philosophy of Chemistry* 9, 131–70.

Page S 2001, 'Richard Trewythian and the Uses of Astrology in Late Medieval England', *Journal of the Warburg and Courtauld Institutes* 64, 193–228.

——2002, *Astrology in Medieval Manuscripts*, British Library, London.

——2004, *Magic in Medieval Manuscripts*, British Library, London.

——2011, 'Speaking with Spirits in Medieval Magic Texts', in J Raymond (ed.), *Conversations with Angels: Essays Towards a History of Spiritual Communication, 1100–1700*, Palgrave Macmillan, London.

——2013, *Magic in the Cloister: Pious Motives, Illicit Interests, and Occult Approaches to the Medieval Universe*, Pennsylvania State University Press, University Park.

Paravicini Bagliani, A 2001, *Le* Speculum Astronomiae, *une énigme? Enquête sur les manuscrits*, SISMEL, Edizioni del Galluzo, Florence.

Pereira, M 1989, *The Alchemical Corpus attributed to Raymond Lull*, Warburg Institute, London.

Pereira, M & Spaggiari, B (eds) 1999, Pseudo-Ramon Lull, *Il 'Testamentum' alchemico attribuito a Raimondo Lullo*, SISMEL, Edizioni del Galluzo, Florence.

Pingree, D 1987, 'The Diffusion of Arabic Magical Texts in Western Europe,' in B Scarcia Amoretti (ed.), *La diffusione delle scienze islamiche nel Medio Evo europeo*, Accademia Nazionale dei Lincei, Rome.

Pingree, D (ed.) 1986, *Picatrix: The Latin Version of the Ghayat al-Hakim*, Warburg Institute, London.

Principe, L 2013, *The Secrets of Alchemy*, University of Chicago Press, Chicago & London.

Prioreschi, P 2003, *Medieval Medicine*, Horatius Press, Omaha, NE.

Rampling, JM 2013, 'Depicting the Medieval Alchemical Cosmos: George Ripley's *Wheel* of Inferior Astronomy', *Early Science and Medicine* 18, 45–86.

Read, J 1995, *From Alchemy to Chemistry*; reprint of *Through Alchemy to Chemistry*, 1957, Dover Publications, New York.

Ruska, J 1926, *Tabula Smaragdina. Ein Beitrag zur Geschichte der hermetischen Literatur*, Winter, Heidelberg.

Silvestris, B 1990, *The Cosmographia of Bernardus Silvestris*, translated with an Introduction and Notes by W Wetherbee, Columbia University Press, New York.

Skemer, DC 2006, *Binding Words: Textual Amulets in the Middle Ages*, Pennsylvania State University Press, University Park.

Tester, SJ 1987, *A History of Western Astrology*, The Boydell Press, Woodbridge.

Thorndike, L 1929, *A History of Magic and Experimental Science*. vol. 2 of 8, Columbia University Press, New York.

Travaglia, P 1999, *Magic, Causality and Intentionality: The Doctrine of Rays in al-Kindi*, Sismel-Edizioni del Galluzzo, Florence.

Vescovini, GF 2011, *Le Moyen* Âge *magique. La magie entre religion et science aux XIIIe et XIVe siècles*, Vrin, Paris.

Veenstra, JR 2002, 'The Holy Almandal: Angels and the Intellectual Aims of Magic', in JN Bremmer & JR Veenstra (eds), *The Metamorphosis of Magic from Late Antiquity to the Early Modern Period*, Peeters, Leuven.

——2012, 'Honorius and the Sigil of God: The *Liber iuratus* in Berengario Ganell's *Summa sacre magice*', in C Fanger (ed.), *Invoking Angels: Theurgic Ideas and Practices, Thirteenth to Sixteenth Centuries*, Pennsylvania State University Press, University Park.

Véronèse, J 2006, 'La notion d'"auteur-magicien" à la fin du Moyen Âge: Le cas de l'ermite Pelagius de Majorque († v. 1480)', *Médiévales* 51, 119–38.

——2007, *L'*Ars notoria *au Moyen* Âge. *Introduction et* édition *critique*, SISMEL, Edizioni del Galluzzo, Florence.

——2012, *L'*Almandal *et l'*Almadel *latins au Moyen* Âge. *Introduction et éditions critiques*, SISMEL, Edizioni del Galluzzo, Florence.

Von Stuckrad, K 2007, *Geschichte der Astrologie: Von den Anfängen bis zur Gegenwart*, C.H. Beck Verlag, Munich.

Walker, DP 2003, *Spiritual and Demonic Magic: From Ficino to Campanella*, Pennsylvania State University Press, University Park.

Weill-Parot, N 2002, *Les 'images astrologiques' au Moyen* Âge *et à la Renaissance: Spéculations intellectuelles et pratiques magiques (XIIe–XVe siècle)*, Honoré Champion, Paris.

Williams, SJ 2003, *The Secret of Secrets: The Scholarly Career of a Pseudo-Aristotelian Text in the Latin Middle Ages*, University of Michigan Press, Ann Arbor.

Zambelli, P (ed.) 1986, *'Astrologi hallucinati': Stars and the End of the World in Luther's Time*, Walter de Gruyter, Berlin.

——1992, *The Speculum Astronomiae and Its Enigma: Astrology, Theology and Science in Albertus Magnus and his Contemporaries*, Kluwer Academic Publishers, Dordrecht & London.

PART II
THE RENAISSANCE

CHAPTER THREE

THE HERMETIC REVIVAL IN ITALY

György E. Szönyi

TWO MISCONCEPTUALIZATIONS WITH SIGNIFICANT CONSEQUENCES

Ironically, the hermetic revival in Italy, which proved to be so important in the ensuing history of the European Renaissance, started with a misunderstanding. Further adding to this irony, the modern historiographical appreciation of this hermetic revival also included a great deal of misconceptualization, which, nevertheless, also exercised a great influence on Renaissance research, from intellectual history and the history of science, to the appreciation of magic, and a new understanding of some of the roots of Western esotericism. It is thus particularly appropriate to start the present survey with the recollection of this double misconceptualization, one in recent scholarship, the other in fifteenth-century Italy.

In 1964 the Warburg Institute scholar, Frances Yates, who had already been well established among Renaissance researchers, but was little known outside those circles, published a large monograph entitled, *Giordano Bruno and the Hermetic Tradition*. The book, which was built on the scholarship of P.O. Kristeller, Eugenio Garin, D.P. Walker, and other Renaissance scholars, offered such an idiosyncratic and challenging interpretation of some Renaissance texts that it soon became a scholarly bestseller. It not only called for a completely new understanding of Giordano Bruno, up to then the hero of the proto-Enlightenment and the martyr of scientific investigation sent to the stake by the Catholic Inquisition, but also suggested a then bold rethinking of the origins of the scientific revolution, looking for its roots in Renaissance hermeticism and magic. In a later article Yates defined hermeticism as follows:

> When treated as straight philosophy, Renaissance Neoplatonism may dissolve into rather vague eclecticism. But the new work on Ficino and his sources has demonstrated that the core of the movement was hermetic, involving a view of the cosmos as a network of magical forces with which man can operate. The Renaissance magus had his roots in the Hermetic core of Renaissance Neoplatonism, and it is the Renaissance magus, I believe, who exemplifies that

> changed attitude of man to the cosmos which was the necessary preliminary to the rise of science.
>
> (Yates 1967 in Yates 1984, 228)

It is clear that her reevaluation of Bruno was closely connected with her reconceptualization of Ficino's Neoplatonism and her enthusiasm about this 'new, magical' Ficino can be compared to Ficino's own enthusiasm about the rediscovery of the *Corpus Hermeticum.*

Ficino Rediscovers and Recycles the Corpus Hermeticum

As is well known, around 1460 a Greek manuscript was delivered to Cosimo de' Medici from Macedonia, containing the mysterious tracts, attributed to the exalted mystic, Hermes Trismegistus, who had supposedly gained his wisdom and knowledge directly from the divine Nous, Pimander, and who later himself became deified. The aging and weak Cosimo became so excited about the apparent occult profundity of these treatises that he directed Ficino to suspend the translation of Plato, which he had been engaged with, and translate the *Corpus* into Latin prior to his death. The excitement of Ficino and the Florentine Neoplatonists, however, was based on a misconception. According to their conviction (relying on Lactantius and other classical Christian Fathers as well as on various medieval speculations) Hermes Trismegistus was a historical figure who had lived at the time of Moses, and while the Hebrew patriarch received from God a public teaching summarized in the ten commandments, Hermes became the immediate recipient of a secret, occult lore. In his introduction to the Latin translation, Ficino set up a genealogy of this ancient theology (*prisca theologia*): '*Primus igitur theologie apellatus est auctor*' (Ficino 1576, 1836) – Trismegistus is identified as the first theologian who was followed by Orpheus, then Aglaophemus, then Pythagoras, who was the master of our divine Plato.

In reality – as later proved by Isaac Casaubon in 1614 – the hermetic texts were much more recent, dating from the late-Hellenistic period, contemporaneous to the philosophy of Plotinus. However, this was not known to the Florentine Neoplatonists and as they saw certain convergences among the Christian doctrines, the teachings of Plato, and hermetic lore, they were inspired to forge a syncretic philosophy in which the ancient elements were not only precursors of Christian truth, but in many ways contained a shortcut to the deepest mysteries of the anthropological standing of humans in the great work of creation (Vasoli 2010; Walker 1958).

Ficino and his colleagues were greatly impressed by Plato's doctrine of divine frenzy that could catapult humans from the prison of matter back to the divine spheres. On countless occasions Ficino expressed his high esteem about this exalted state of mind. Even in his letters he comments that

> Plato considers, as Pythagoras, Empedocles and Heraclitus maintained earlier, that our soul, before it descended into our bodies, dwelt in the abodes of heaven where it was nourished and rejoiced in the contemplation of the truth. Those philosophers I have just mentioned had learnt from Mercurius Trismegistus, the wisest of all the Egyptians, that God is the supreme source and light within whom shine the models of all things, which they call ideas...But souls are

> depressed into bodies through thinking about and desiring earthly things...They do not fly back to heaven, whence they fell by weight of their earthly thoughts, until they begin to contemplate once more those divine natures which they have forgotten.
>
> (Letter 7 to Peregrino Agli *On Divine Frenzy*, in Ficino 1975, 43)

In another letter he elaborated on the process, discussing how the soul could regain its lost, originally perfect state, even before physically leaving the body upon death:

> By certain natural instruments [Philosophy] raises the soul from the depth, through all that is compounded of the four elements, and guides it through the elements themselves to heaven. Then step-by-step on the ladder of mathematics the soul accomplishes the sublime ascent to the topmost orbs of Heaven. At length, what is more wonderful than words can tell, on the wings of metaphysics it soars beyond the vault of heaven to the creator of heaven and earth Himself. There, through the gift of Philosophy, not only is the soul filled with happiness but since in a sense it becomes God, it also becomes that very happiness.
>
> (Letter 123 to Bernardo Bembo, *Oratorical, moral, dialectical and theological praise of Philosophy*. In Ficino 1975, 189)

Strictly speaking, this concept, which is part of a contemplative theological philosophy, is, on the one hand, pure Platonism and, on the other, a syncretic Christian theory of *unio mystica*. But the Florentine philosophers were not fully contented with such a rather passive, meditative technique. The acknowledgement of a more active willpower on the part of the human host of the soul needed a theological anthropology somewhat bolder than the biblical concept of the creation and fall of man and its medieval Christian interpretation. This bold encouragement could be derived from the *Corpus Hermeticum*, which offered an alternative creation myth with a much more dignified First Man than the failing Adam. In the initial act of Creation, the Mind-God (Nous-Theos) manifested itself as a cosmos, then by speaking gave birth to a second, Craftsman-Mind (Demiurge) who then created the seven Governors, 'which encompass the sensible world in circles and their government is called fate' – here one encounters the idea of astrological determination over the material existence (CH I.8–9, see Copenhaver 1995, 2). Later the Mind-God once again creates, this time the first human who will be beautiful, delighting all the ranks of existence, and will be allowed to become himself a creator god:

> Mind, the father of all, who is life and light, gave birth to a man like himself whom he loved as his own child. The man was most fair: he had the father's image...And after the man had observed what the craftsman (Demiurge) had created with the father's help, he also wished to make some craftwork and the father agreed to this...Having all authority over the cosmos of mortals and unreasoning animals, the man broke through the vault and stooped to look through the cosmic framework thus displaying to lower nature the fair form of god. Nature smiled for love when she saw him whose fairness brings no surfeit and who holds in himself all the energy of the governors and the form of god.
>
> (CH I.12–14, Copenhaver 1995, 3)

The treatises in the *Corpus Hermeticum* reconfirmed in various ways this dignified image of humans as well as encouraging belief in the possibility of reverse emanation, the *exaltatio* of the soul. In the longest tract, the *Asclepius*, which survived in its entirety only in Latin, one finds the famous sentence that became one of the most oft-quoted commonplaces of Renaissance philosophy and anthropology: '[O] Asclepius, a human being is a great wonder, a living thing to be worshipped and honored: for he changes his nature into a god's, as if he were a god; he knows the demonic kind inasmuch as he recognizes that he originated among them' (*Asclepius* 6 in Copenhaver 1995, 69). The notion of human dignity is even intensified and suggests magical capabilities when Trismegistus reminds Asclepius about the man-made statues of gods, which are 'ensouled and conscious, filled with spirit and doing great deeds; statues that foreknow the future and predict it by lots, by prophecy, by dreams and by many other means; statues that make people ill and cure them, bringing them pain and pleasure as each deserves' (*Asclepius* 24, Copenhaver 1995, 81). Taking into consideration the above passages from the *Corpus Hermeticum* and adding those which could not be recalled here, one should not be surprised at registering the enthusiasm Ficino and his scholarly friends felt while recognizing the potential the Hermetic ingredient catalyzing Plato's teachings could release for the true Christian philosopher. And the mistaken understanding according to which the *Hermetica* was to be as old as the books of Moses, only increased their reverence and admiration for these texts.

Frances Yates Rediscovers and Recycles Ficino's Hermeticism

Frances Yates, studying Ficino's enthusiasm for the Hermetic teachings and registering the significant influence these ideas exercised on generations of Renaissance thinkers from Pico della Mirandola, through Cornelius Agrippa and Paracelsus, to Giordano Bruno and beyond, became equally enthusiastic about these ideas, but this feeling also led her to some misconceptions. In her papers and books following her 1964 monograph, *Giordano Bruno and the Hermetic Tradition*, she increasingly tried to explain many intellectual developments of the Renaissance, especially major achievements of the scientific revolution, in terms of the impact of Renaissance intellectual magic, specifically the Hermetic teachings. As Paolo Rossi in the so-called 'Hermeticism debate' has remarked, 'to explain the genesis – which is not only complicated but often confused – of some modern ideas is quite different from believing that one can offer a complete explanation of these ideas by describing their genesis' (1975, 257). Frances Yates and her followers definitely opened up new vistas and contributed to doing away with looking at Western esotericism as a residue of murky medieval superstition. On the other hand, the conclusions based on this discovery were misguided, to some extent, by concentrating almost entirely on a rewriting of science history. No doubt, Hermeticism had some impact on the new scientific ideas, but it also had an important influence on the understanding of humanity, on the nature of artistic expression, and, last but not least, on theological thinking, especially that of mysticism, pietism, and some other radical, often countercultural trends of religiosity.

Furthermore, when examining the origins of the Italian Hermetic revival, Yates also had a narrow lens, focusing primarily on the *Corpus Hermeticum*. More recently, scholarship has established that Hermeticism was only one trend within a complex syncretic development. To understand what happened in Italy after 1460, one has to take into consideration the prominent authors of the later Neoplatonic schools as well as the great variety of medieval magical theories and practices, including, amongst much else, the following: technical Hermetica; certain trajectories springing from Jewish merkabah mysticism and the Kabbalah; the Arabic works of magic which were translated into Latin during the scholastic period; and popular magical practices of the 'clerical underground'. Finally, one should not forget about the changing sociocultural contexts, such as the following: the crisis of the medieval universities; the free, sometimes subversive spirit of the private academies and the rise of humanism with its increased interest in Antiquity; and those socio-psychological changes which produced an early modern occulture, leading to the new, Faustian type of Western hero emerging in the sixteenth century. The following survey of the Italian Hermetic revival is intended to pay attention, even if in a hopelessly concise way, to all these factors outlined above.

THE KEY FIGURES OF THE HERMETIC REVIVAL: FICINO AND PICO

If we approach the title phenomenon from a traditional angle, two towering figures overshadow a lot of minor, but also important issues: these are Marsilio Ficino (1433–99), founder of the Florentine Neoplatonic Academy (on the historical and mythical aspects of the Academy see della Torre 1902 and Field 1988), and his younger friend, to some extent a disciple, but no less a severe critic, who at the same time also inspired the older philosopher, Giovanni Pico della Mirandola (1463–94), the aristocrat who during his short life first became a herald of the new, human-centred Renaissance philosophy, then a convert to Savonarola, the ascetic theocrat of Florence (1494–98).

Ficino was a native of Florence, son of a physician close to the circle of the town's untitled ruler, Cosimo de' Medici. In 1439 Cosimo managed to invite the Ecumenical Council to Florence and the city witnessed the visit of many outstanding Greek scholars, among them Gemisthos Pletho, who was considered a direct heir of the 'divine Plato'. Cosimo, who was not only a merchant and politician, but a humanist himself, desired to boost Greek studies in order to promote the cult of Plato in his surroundings. The task was accomplished by young Marsilio, whose Humanist tuition was sponsored by the Medici lord (on the role of Cosimo in patronizing Ficino's programme of Neoplatonic revival, see Field 2002). When Marsilio's great talents in Greek and philosophy became manifest, Cosimo acknowledged this by addressing his father as follows: 'You, Ficino, have been sent to us to heal bodies, but your Marsilio here has been sent down from heaven to heal souls' (Giovanni Corsi, *The Life of Marsilio Ficino*, quoted from Ficino 1981, 138). Ficino himself commented on this situation later. In the dedication to Lorenzo de' Medici of his *Three Books on Life*, he recalled, 'I had two fathers, Ficino the doctor and Cosimo de' Medici. From the former I was born, from the latter reborn. The former commended me to Galen as both a doctor and Platonist; the latter consecrated me to the divine Plato. And both the one and the other alike dedicated Marsilio to a doctor – Galen, doctor of the body, and Plato, doctor of the soul' (Ficino 1989, 103). The chronology of Ficino's translations and his own works display a constant oscillation between Christian theology, Platonism, Hermetic esotericism, and again Platonized Christianity. Among his early works, the translation and commentary of the *Corpus Hermeticum* (1463) stands out, together with his translations of Plato, Alcinous, Xenocrates, and a treatise on love that comments on Plato's *Symposium* (1469). In 1473, Ficino was ordained a priest, and declared that, from a pagan, he had become a soldier of Christ (Corsi, *Life of Ficino*, in Ficino 1981, 140). This turn resulted in his treatise *On the Christian Religion* (1476) and his work on the *Platonic Theology*, which was printed in 1482 (see Ficino 2001–6). Two years later he published his complete translations and some commentaries on Plato, while he was working with full energy on translating further Neoplatonists, some of them also magically imbued: Iamblichus, Porphyry, Proclus, Psellus, and, above all, Plotinus – apparently encouraged and urged by the young Pico (Farmer 1998, 12 n.35). The complete Plotinus was published in 1492, preceded and followed by his own works, *Three Books on Life* (1489) and *On the Sun and Light* (1493).

In 1496, he published his translation of *The Mystic Theology* and *Divine Names* of Pseudo-Dionysius and, a year later, he collected in one volume all his translations that can be considered as an 'anthologia esoterica' (see below). His last work was a commentary on the Epistles of St. Paul, which he left unfinished at his death. (The chronology of Ficino's works can be found in Ficino 2009, 95–96; important editions are: Ficino 1989; 2001–6; and his letters published between 1975–2009. Key studies include: Allen 1995; Allen and Rees 2002; Canziani 2001; Clucas, Forshaw, and Rees 2011; Raffini 1998.)

Giovanni Corsi, in his near-contemporary biography of Ficino, has an interesting remark: 'Here is something not to be left out: he had a unique and divine skill in magic, driving out evil demons and spirits from very many places and putting them to flight. Always a very keen defender of religion, he was extremely hostile to superstition' (Corsi in Ficino 1981, 145). How does one reconcile these apparently contradictory statements? This will lead us to the evaluation of Ficino's esotericism according to thematic issues, but first something needs to be said about his compatriot, Pico.

Without wanting to be tautologous, Giovanni Pico della Mirandola was a genuine Renaissance man. According to Eugenio Garin, if one desires to examine just one of his works, the *Commentary on a Canzone of Benivieni,* he will have to be well versed in poetry, mythology, the figurative arts, religion and philosophy, as well as being conversant in Tuscan vernacular, Latin, Greek, Arabic, and ancient Hebrew (Garin 1995, cited by Borghesi 2008, 203). Furthermore, Pico was a child prodigy, already, at the age of ten, receiving a title of apostolic protonotary and starting his studies of canon law at the age of fourteen. His early studies in Bologna, Ferrara and Padua led him to the study of Aristotle and his early acquaintance with some Arabo-Judaic philosophers, such as Elia del Medigo, who directed him to the Arabic commentators of Aristotle.

Around 1480, he befriended Angelo Poliziano, a member of Ficino's humanist circle in Florence, at the same time an admirer of Savonarola, who then was a Franciscan preacher in Ferrara. Through Poliziano, Pico asked for Ficino's *Theologia Platonica* and thus he also entered the circle of Italian Neoplatonists. But Pico never took sides in the rivalry between the followers of Plato and Aristotle. Having said that, his aim was to reconcile the two classical thinkers and, furthermore, to found a syncretic philosophy by which all knowledge and even the wildest ambitions of humans could be realized. In 1484, Pico moved to Florence and stayed near Ficino to study Plato and Plotinus with him. At the same time, he entered into a warm friendship with the magnanimous patron, Lorenzo de' Medici. In spite of his great reverence for Ficino, Pico remained an independent intellectual, who was ready to absorb other fields of intellectual thinking, from the poetry of Dante to the mysteries of the Jewish Kabbalah and the *Zohar*. He had Jewish teachers at his side, notably Elia del Medigo, then the converted Guglielmo Raimondo de Moncada – also known as Flavius Mithridates – and later on the learned Rabbi Yohanan Alemanno (for his knowledge of Hebrew and Judaica, see Wirszubski 1989). As well as the Hebrew and Aramaic, Pico learned from these scholars, he also studied Arabic. Fascinated by the esoteric aspects of these eastern philosophies, he became the first Western European representative of what later became known as the 'Christian Cabala' (in Christian contexts, it is more helpful to follow Pico's spelling as opposed to the common Hebrew transcription 'Kabbalah').

After a brief stay at the Sorbonne in Paris, in 1485, he decided to collect the common essentials of all philosophies in 900 theses and discuss them in a synod of scholars invited, at his own expense, to Rome (being an aristocrat with freshly inherited estates this was feasible), in front of the Pope. He came back to Florence and embarked upon an 'extraordinary year' in 1486 (Borghesi 2008, 212). First, he wrote the already mentioned complex commentary on the *Canzone* of his friend, Benivieni, then became involved in the abduction of a woman – the wife of a relative of Lorenzo de' Medici. Thanks to the benevolence of his patron, he got away without punishment and spent the following months quietly learning Hebrew and writing his *Conclusiones* and the preface to them, later entitled the *Oration on the Dignity of Man* (*Oratio de hominis dignitate*). Later that year he moved to Rome and had his *900 theses* published.

The outcome, however, turned out to be troublesome. Certain theologians became frustrated with some of these theses and Pope Innocent VIII decided to cancel the conference. In early 1487, Pico was tried by the inquisitorial committee set up by the Pope, who brushed aside Pico's hastily drafted *Apologia* and found thirteen of his theses outright heretical, resulting in the papal order of all the printed copies to be burned. Pico managed to flee to France and, although he was arrested there, thanks to the protection of the French king, he was released soon after, returning to Florence in April 1488. There he wrote some important and influential works: a commentary on the six days of creation in seven sessions (*Heptaplus*), a treatise *On Being and the One* (*De ente et uno*), and an enormous *Disputation Against Judicial Astrology* (*Disputationes adversus astrologiam divinatricem*) which was eventually posthumously completed by his nephew, Gianfrancesco.

In 1489 he became instrumental in persuading Lorenzo to invite the ascetic preacher, Savonarola, to Florence. In his last years he was in close friendship with Savonarola who was on his deathbed in 1494, the same day that Charles VIII entered Florence and shortly before Savonarola established his theocracy in the city (on Pico's life and work, see Pico 1971; 1998; 2004; Bacchelli 2001; Bori 2000; Blum 2008a; Dougherty 2008; Farmer 1998; Rabin 2008; Roulier 1989; Still 2008; etc.).

Both Ficino and Pico were instrumental in the Renaissance Hermetic revival in Italy. However, although Pico is generally considered to have been Ficino's faithful disciple, they represented different trends and ambitions in developing an occult philosophy and advocating, at least in theory, some magical practices (on Pico's disputes with Ficino, see Aasdalen 2011; Blum 2008b; Farmer 1998, 12–13, 118–19). The next section deals with the main issues in their esotericism as well as with the most important differences.

THEMATIC ISSUES

To gauge the nature of Ficino's and Pico's esoteric ideas, we have to examine quite a large corpus of texts. Concerning Ficino, key texts include his Neoplatonic translations and commentaries, the *Corpus Hermeticum* translation and commentaries, many of his letters, and, above all, his most magical work, the third part of *De vita*, entitled *On Obtaining Life from the Heavens* (*De vita coelitus comparanda*). In the case of Pico one has to deal with practically his entire oeuvre, except perhaps the last part of his *Disputations*, which is particularly anti-magical and anti-astrological. That said, concerning the latter, there are reasons to think that his original thoughts were edited by Savonarola and his nephew Gianfrancesco (Farmer 1998, 154–59; Rabin 2008, 168–73). What remains is the *Commentary on Benivieni*, the *Oration on the Dignity of Man*, the *900 Conclusions*, and the *Heptaplus*. Taking all these into consideration, one can see that, although their schooling was different, they both shared a general world picture and the image of the medieval cosmos. The most important difference manifests itself between their horizon of orientation concerning authorities: Ficino was fully saturated with Plato and the Neoplatonists and could become thrilled by only those occult sources that were offsprings, or closely connected, to Neoplatonism, such as the *Orphic hymns*, the *Corpus Hermeticum*, the Egyptian mysteries of Iamblichus, and the demon-lore of Porphyry, Proclus, or Psellus. His attention to this latter group, actually, was drawn by Pico, who was proud of announcing his priority in distilling the magical contents of the Orphic hymns as well as the late Neoplatonist philosophers (Farmer 1998, 129 and annotations to p. 505). Beyond these, Pico was also examining Aristotle and the scholastics, Arabic and oriental philosophers, Jewish kabbalistic teachers. But the common ground between their approaches was an esoterically open world picture, based on the ideas of the Great Chain of Being, the analogical correspondences among the layers of the universe, and the image of man as microcosm, a mirror of the great cosmos. Furthermore, they also shared a desire to catapult the soul and reverse it along the Plotinian emanation to an exalted state and union with the divine. For this they needed an anthropological foundation that would not exclude the mobilization of occult willpower either. Last, but not least, both of them were devout Christians who, by the help of syncretic auxiliary means, only desired a better understanding and experiencing of the truth, incarnated in Jesus.

The Occult World Picture and the Doctrine of Exaltatio

The best concise description of the medieval cosmos and the Great Chain of Being can be found in Pico's Second Proem of his *Heptaplus*:

> Antiquity imagined three worlds. Highest of all is that ultramundane one, which theologians call the angelic and philosophers the intelligible, and, of which, Plato

> says in the *Phaedrus*, no one has worthily sung. Next to this comes the celestial world, and last of all, this sublunary one which we inhabit. This is the world of darkness; that the world of light; the [celestial] heavens are compounded light and darkness...Here there is an alternation of life and death; there, eternal life and unchanging activity; in the [celestial] heavens, stability of life and change of activity and position...The third is moved by the second; the second is governed by the first.
>
> (Pico 1998, 75–76)

At this point Pico compares the three worlds to the three parts of the Ark of the Covenant and has interesting things to say about the nature of allegorical expression, elaborating on the medieval semiotics of Augustine and Aquinas. Then he continues with the correspondences:

> Truly, whatever is in the lower world is also in the higher ones, but of better stamp; likewise, whatever is in the higher ones is also seen in the lowest, but in a degenerate condition and with a nature one might call adulterated...In the first world, God, the primal unity, presides over nine orders of angels as if over as many spheres. In the middle world, that is, the celestial, the empyrean heaven likewise presides like the commander of an army over nine heavenly spheres, each of which revolves with an unceasing motion. There are also in the elemental world, after the prime matter which is its foundation, nine spheres of corruptible forms.
>
> (Pico 1998, 77–78)

And, finally, he arrives at the human microcosm and his being related to the three worlds:

> There is, moreover, besides the three that we have mentioned, a fourth world in which are found all those things that are in the rest. This is man himself, who is, as the Catholic doctors say, referred to in the Gospel by the name of every creature. [...] It is a commonplace that man is a lesser world, in which are seen, a body compounded from the elements, and a heavenly spirit, and the vegetative soul of plants, and the sense of brutes, and reason, and the angelic mind, and the likeness of God.
>
> (Pico 1998, 79)

A few years earlier, in the *Oratio*, Pico outlined a compelling myth about the creation of humans, which concluded with them gaining an undetermined, changeable nature with unlimited possibilities. According to this myth, while creating humans after the creation of the world had been finished, God found that he had run out of archetypes to give to his new creatures, so he decided 'that this creature, to whom He could give nothing wholly his own, should have a share in the particular endowment of every other creature. Taking man, therefore, this creature of indeterminate image, He set him in the middle of the world and thus spoke to him' with the following words:

> 'We have given you, O Adam, no visage proper to yourself, nor endowment properly your own, in order that whatever place, whatever form, whatever gifts

> you may select, these same you may have and possess through your own judgement and decision…We have made you a creature neither of heaven nor of earth, neither mortal nor immortal, in order that you may, as the free and proud shaper of your own being, fashion yourself in the form you may prefer. It will be in your power to descend to the lower, brutish forms of life; you will be able, through your own decision, to rise again to the superior orders whose life is divine.'
>
> (Pico 1964, section 6 – Richard Hooker's translation)

This indeterminate nature makes it possible for humans to move up or down the Great Chain of Being and to shape their own fate by free will. Later on, Pico makes it clear in a Platonist manner, that the ultimate goal of free will cannot be anything else but the mystical union with God, a mystical union which is not reserved for the afterlife, but can be experienced as part of earthly existence! 'Let us…hasten to that court beyond the world, closest to the most exalted Godhead. There, as the sacred mysteries tell us, the Seraphim, Cherubim and Thrones occupy the first places; but, unable to yield to them, and impatient of any second place, let us emulate their dignity and glory. And, if we will it, we shall be inferior to them in nothing' (1964, section 10). Since man is not lower than the angels, humans should imitate the Cherubim, who, according to Dionysius, go through the process of purification, illumination, and perfection.

> We, therefore, imitating the life of the Cherubim here on earth, by refraining the impulses of our passions through moral science, by dissipating the darkness of reason by dialectic may likewise purify our souls, so that the passions may never run rampant, nor reason, lacking restraint, range beyond its natural limits…Who would not long to be admitted to such mysteries? Who would not desire, putting all human concerns behind him, holding the goods of fortune in contempt and little minding the goods of the body, thus to become, while still a denizen of earth, a guest at the table of the gods, and, drunk with the nectar of eternity, receive, while still a mortal, the gift of immortality?
>
> (Ibid. sections 13 and 18)

If we try to define the place of magic within the system of esotericism, we have to relate it to mysticism and occult knowledge. One should imagine concentric circles. The largest is *mysticism*: the opening up of a special way, an altered state of consciousness, a kind of illumination, epiphany, *unio mystica*. This happens more or less independently of the experiencing subject as a gift, like when in epiphany the divine suddenly becomes manifest. *Occult knowledge* comprises a mystical, secret lore by the help of which illumination can be catalyzed or brought about by the human will. *Magic* is the smallest circle, mobilizing the active will of humans to manipulate, by means of occult knowledge, nature and the supernatural; it also employs procedures to elevate the human to divine exaltation.

The texts of Ficino and Pico so far quoted point to the first two categories: mysticism and occult knowledge. And Quattrocento Hermeticism mostly focused on these areas. Nevertheless, both these Florentine Neoplatonists were also touched and intrigued by certain possibilities of magical agency: Ficino at least partially, because of his having been trained as a physician, Pico rather inspired by his studies of Eastern esotericism and the Jewish Kabbalah.

Magic in Ficino and Pico

As Sheila Rabin has recently reminded us, while astrology was an integral part of university curricula, integrated with mathematics, philosophy, and medicine, magic was not an official subject. It was, however, much discussed, classified, and used in various ways both among the university wits as well as the clerical underworld (see, Rabin 2008; Kieckhefer 1989). In the thirteenth century, Bishop William of Auvergne and the mysterious author of the famous *Speculum astronomiae* offered typologies of magic, talking about *magia naturalis*, which was to be considered legitimate; *image* or *talismanic magic*, the legitimacy of which was debated, but principally condemned; and *demonic* or *ceremonial magic*, which was to be avoided outright, because, as Jean Gerson of the Sorbonne a century later summarized, 'demons cannot be compelled by magic arts; they only pretend that they are compelled so that they will be adored like gods, and will be able to deceive their invokers' (quoted by Láng 2008, 22).

It seems that Ficino's adventures into the field of secret arts aimed at the middle category, namely, talismanic or image magic. Being close to the medical profession, he was surely confronted with the questions of talismans used for healing, and as a bibliophile Humanist, he could hardly avoid the voluminous medieval literature on the subject. Inspired thus, in the middle of his career he decided to temporarily turn from pure philosophy towards this kind of practical magic. His important work, *On Obtaining Life from the Heavens*, forms the third part of his larger medical philosophical work, *Three Books on Life* (*De vita triplici*, 1489).

The first part (*De vita sana*) is devoted to the question of how to maintain your health if you are a scholar under the shadow of Saturnian melancholy. On the one hand, he argues that the melancholic black bile is a requisite for being a genius, and, on the other hand, he gives tips on how to fight 'occupational hazards such as insomnia, headaches, and the dimness of vision' ('Introduction' in Ficino 1989, 4). The second part (*De vita longa*) is devoted to the task of preserving life. Here one finds advice relating to lifestyle, hygiene and medicaments. The third part concerns itself with the relationship between the body and the radiation of the stars, a field of study closely related to both medicine and astrology. And this is where Ficino's theory about talismanic magic is expanded. Since he also alludes here to ceremonies (quasi-religious singing, dancing, suffumigations) in order to get in touch with the *Anima Mundi*, which is behind the strength of the personal stars, at this point his magic verges on the border of the 'demonic'. Needless to say, the author fervently rejected any such accusations and maintained that his theory was entirely based on natural principles. In 1489, he had become aware of the misfortunes of Pico with his magical propositions of 1486, and, indeed, Ficino also felt compelled to write an 'Apology, Dealing with Medicine, Astrology, the Life of the World, and the Magi Who Greeted the Christ Child at his Birth' (published in Ficino 1989, 394–405). In it he anticipated the charges he expected to receive (since Marsilio was an ordained priest by that time): 'What business do priests have with medicine or, again with astrology?' and 'What does a Christian have to do with magic or images?' (Ficino 1989, 395). His answer consists of the following arguments: (1) In antiquity medicine and priesthood had always been connected with each other, as is known about the Chaldeans, the Persians and the Egyptians. (2) Furthermore, he denied approving of demonic magic and claimed to have dealt with it only as much as his book formed part of his commentary on Plotinus. What he approves in the Apology is only natural magic, which 'must be granted to minds which use it legitimately, as medicine and agriculture are justly granted' (Ficino 1989, 397).

An interesting personal reason behind writing *De vita* may have been the fact that Ficino had a very unfavourable horoscope. He was a Saturnian and described himself as a deeply melancholic man, only little helped by Venus in Libra at his birth. Because of this apparent fatalism, he swung between the rejection of astrology altogether and the utilizing of its effects within certain limits.

The assumptions on which Renaissance astral magic was based were elegantly summarized in Cornelius Agrippa's *Three Books of Occult Philosophy*:

> Magicians teach that Celestial gifts may through inferiors being conformable to superiors be drawn down by opportune influencies of the Heaven; and so also by these Celestial, the Celestial Angels, as they are servants of the Stars. Jamblichus, Proclus, and Synesius, with the whole School of Platonists confirm, that not only Celestiall, and vitall, but also certain Intellectuall, Angelicall, and divine gifts may be received from above by some certain matters, having a naturall power of divinity (i.e.) which have a naturall correspondency with the superiors, being rightly received, and opportunely gathered together according to the rules of Naturall Philosophy, and Astronomy...For this is the harmony of the world, that things supercelestiall be drawn down by the Celestiall, and super-naturall by naturall, because there is one operative vertue that is diffused through all kinds of things; so a Magician doth make use of things manifest, to draw forth things that are occult, viz. through the rays of the Stars, through fumes, lights, sounds, and naturall things.
>
> (1.38, Agrippa 1651, 76)

As Agrippa had emphasized the Neo/Platonic origin of this kind of magic, so it became embedded in Ficino's Neoplatonism. The latter summed up his natural principles as follows: 'Heaven, the husband of earth, does not touch the earth, as is the common opinion. It does not have intercourse with its wife; but by rays of its stars alone as if with the rays of its eyes, It illuminates her on all sides; it fertilizes her by its illumination and procreates living things' ('Apology,' Ficino 1989, 401).

Scholars have been examining and debating the origins and components of Ficino's astral magic. Brian Copenhaver has emphasized the importance of the 'Neoplatonici': Porphyry, Iamblichus, Proclus, Psellus and their notions of the World Soul as well as their doctrines of daemons (1986, 1988). Others, such as Frances Yates, David Pingree and Carol Kaske have highlighted another, murkier inspiration, which was only indirectly acknowledged by Ficino, namely Arabic astrology and magic, especially *On the Stellar Rays* by the ninth-century philosopher, Al-Kindi (*De radiis*), as well as the influential medieval grimoire, the *Picatrix*.

The latter, an anonymous compendium demonstrating Arabic interest in Hermeticism, was translated into Spanish, then into Latin around the middle of the thirteenth century, and is proof that parallel to the dominant scholastic philosophy,

Neoplatonic esotericism could be reinterpreted from an Arabic perspective (see the Latin and English editions: *Picatrix* 1986 and 2010). The *Picatrix* is the largest and most coherent medieval magical handbook and, according to the English editors, the single most important work between Iamablichus's *De mysteriis* and Agrippa's *De occulta philosophia* (*Picatrix* 2010, 12). It discusses at length sympathetic magic, astrology, image magic, and pays particular attention to the spirits and demons of the universe. The cornerstone of magic in the *Picatrix* is the assumption that the material world is full of occult sympathies drawn from the corresponding stars and planets. With the appropriate skills, the scholar can access and use these energies; the magus can interpret the zodiacal decans and contact the demons of the planets by using magical talismans as mediators (see Szönyi 2004, 73–78; also Garin 1983, 46–55; and Yates 1964, 49–57, 70–82).

Ficino certainly knew the *Picatrix*, although he did not mention it in print, only in one of his private letters, in which he advised his friend and patron, Filippo Valori, not to read it because it was, for the most part, heretical, deserving of condemnation by the Church. Instead, he should read his *De vita coelitus comparanda*, into which all valuable material from the Arabic book had been incorporated ('Introduction,' in Ficino 1989, 45).

Ficino began his book by referring to the correspondences of the macro- and microcosms, stating that the human soul is capable of absorbing the strength of the World Soul through the rays of the planets (Szönyi 2004, 81–89). In Chapter 13 he introduces the concept of talismanic magic: 'On the power acquired from the heavens both in images, according to the Ancients, and in medicines', in his explanation of how the talismans work, he tried to keep to materialistic reasoning, pointing out how 'the flames without light' penetrate the metals and gems, 'imprinting in them wonderful gifts' (Ficino 1989, 323). After giving general guidance on how to construct 'powerful images' in talismans, Chapter 19 advises how one might construct a universal sign, representing the whole cosmos, thus preparing the way for John Dee's famous hieroglyphic monad eighty years later.

Beginning in Chapter 21, Ficino discusses the use of words of power, incantations and magical prayers, thus moving in the direction of ceremonial magic. Chapter 26, the closing chapter, returns to the theoretical plane and offers an encomium of magical practices: '*Subicit Magus terrena coelestibus*. The Magus subjects earthly things to celestial, lower things everywhere to higher, just as particular females everywhere are subjected to males appropriate to them for impregnation, as iron to a magnet to get magnetized, as camphor to hot air for absorption, as crystal to the Sun for illumination…' (Ficino 1989, 387).

Ficino's magical lore drew directly on his Platonic ideas concerning love, which he took as the greatest magical force of the universe (see Allen 1995). As he wrote in his commentary on Plato's *Symposium*, 'Why do we think love is a sorcerer? Because in love there is all the power of enchantment. The work of enchantment is the attraction of one thing by another because of a certain similarity of their nature' (Ficino 1944, 91, 199). His magic basically seeks to capture and manipulate supernatural forces in order to free the soul and intellect from the burden of the material world. For this he relied on material/'natural' intermediaries. That said, his Platonic concepts of Supreme Good, creative Nous, and transmitting demons can easily be associated with Christian theological ideas relating to God, angels and the human soul. As he reminds his readers in the *Symposium* commentary, 'the good daemons, our protectors, Dionysius the Areopagite is accustomed to call by the proper names, Angels, [are] the governors of the lower world, and this differs very little from the interpretation of Plato' (Ficino 1944, 79, 186).

Next to Neoplatonism, other influences, especially Arabic magic can also be detected in Ficino's works. S.A. Farmer ascribes this influence to the younger Pico, who, on several occasions, bemoaned the 'limited scope' of esoteric scholarship and had already, in his early writings, offered a perplexingly broad 'syncretism in the West' (see Farmer 1998). Last, but not least, one should not forget the traditions of medieval scholastic astrology and its radical exponents, such as Pietro d'Abano, the early fourteenth-century author on magic and the study of the stars, who also exercised some influence on the Florentine philosopher (Seller 2009, 95, 104).

Christian Cabala

Apart from being a more eclectic syncretist, Pico went beyond Ficino's relatively cautious magic in three respects: he professed the doctrine of the dignity of man in a more radical way than his master; he openly advocated magic as a direct means to ascension on high (*exaltatio*); and he pioneered in amalgamating Classical and Christian esotericism with Jewish mysticism, the Kabbalah.

In the *Oration on the Dignity of Man*, Pico created a poetically elevated expression of the programme of *exaltatio* (see quotations above), founding his argument on an idiosyncratic interpretation of the macrocosm–microcosm theories, asserting the indeterminate nature of man. The actual processes of divine frenzy and ascension were described using the terminology of Neoplatonic Hermeticism, but the practice itself utilized kabbalistic techniques, thereby directing his contemporaries to the as yet unexplored riches of Jewish esotericism. This he explained by subverting the central tenet of the Ficinian *prisca theologia*, which imagined two traditions of 'the Truth', the public Mosaic and the occult Hermetic. Pico claimed that, in the books of Moses, one can also find a secret, esoteric lore. 'Not famous Hebrew teachers alone, but, from among those of our own persuasion, Esdras, Hilary and Origen all write that Moses, in addition to the law of the five books which he handed down to posterity, when on the mount, received from God a more secret [occult] and true explanation of the law' (Pico 1964, section 33).

The complexities of Pico's magic can be inferred from his *900 theses* (noted above). He composed the theses as follows: 402 theses were extracted from the works of various schools, or philosophical 'sects' (*gentes*), such as the Latins, the Arabs, the Greek Peripatetics, the Platonists, Pythagorean mathematicians, Chaldean theologians, Mercury Trismegistus the Egyptian, and Hebrew Kabbalists; following this, he added 498 theses, which he described as 'conclusions', among which, there were 131 'dissenting from the common philosophy' and 'introducing new doctrines in philosophy' (*philosophia nova*); there were also separate groups of conclusions concerning numerology, Zoroaster, magic, the Orphic Hymns, and the Cabala, the last exclusively used for confirming the Christian religion.

The conclusions have led to various interpretations since Pico's time, but the most detailed, analytical study appeared only in 1998 by Stephen Farmer. One of his most important points is that the first part constitutes a summary of various philosophical schools as Pico understood them. However, this by no means suggests that he adhered to all of them. So, when one looks for the true character of Pico's occultism, his own theses deserve particular attention.

As much as one can generalize about a manifold and syncretistic system, Farmer uses a contemporary definition of magic to approach Pico's programme. Petrus Garcias in 1489 published an attack on Pico's theses in which he defined magic as follows: '*Magia secundum communiter loquientes est ars cognoscendi et divinandi occulta faciendique magna et mirificia in natura*' – 'Magic according to common language is the art of knowing occult things and divining, as well as making great and miraculous things in nature' (quoted by Farmer 1998, 129; my altered translation). From this it follows that magic is either natural or intellectual, the latter involving divination, addressing supernatural beings for illumination, or prophecy.

Both Farmer and Rabin emphasize that Pico's system included a variety of magic. In this respect the twenty-six magical conclusions are of particular importance. Natural magic is praised without reservation: 'Magic is the practical part of natural science' (9 > 3) and 'Magic is the noblest part of natural science' (9 > 4, see Farmer 1998, 495); but all this has to come from God, who endows the occult powers on 'the contemplative men of good will' (9 > 6). What has to be excluded from magic is the deliberate turn to wicked demons: 'All magic that is in use among the moderns, and which the Church justly exterminates, has no firmness, no foundation, no truth, because it depends on the enemies of the first truth, those *powers of darkness*, which pour the darkness of falsehood over poorly disposed intellects' (9 > 1).

The magical conclusions are permeated with references to the Kabbalah, that complex Jewish system of meditation and divination, which ultimately aimed at a mystical deification, an ascension on high (see Idel 1988a; 2005). Pico's praise of the Kabbalah is not restricted to his Christian cabalistic conclusions, but connects the conclusions on the Orphic Hymns, on Zoroaster, and on magic, all of which reaches a climax in the notorious 9 > 9: 'There is no science that assures us more of the divinity of Christ than magic and the Cabala.'

This is the kind of orientation that has led Farmer to propose that Pico's magic was primarily intellectual, aimed at the deification of the Magus by means of meditative and contemplative techniques (1998, 128–30). Ultimately, this philosophy of magic was directed toward a specific religious programme, an improved and intensified *unio mystica*.

THE SYNCRETIC THEOLOGY OF LAZZARELLI AND THE CURIOUS CASE OF GIOVANNI DA CORREGGIO

Among the so-called Italian Hermeticists, two more persons require brief discussion. Lodovico Lazzarelli (1447–1500) was one of those eccentric wandering humanists who were in possession of impressive philological knowledge about ancient languages and philosophies, whilst concurrently exploring syncretic and esoteric ideas of religious enthusiasm and magical *exaltatio*. These people travelled the roads of Europe from court to court, looking for prospective patrons, and not infrequently suffering incarceration as a result of dissatisfied princes or the Inquisition. While, as a Neoplatonist philosopher, Lazzarelli is less known than Ficino or Pico, from the perspective of Hermeticism, he is an important thinker.

Lazzarelli started his career in the humanist circles of northern Italy, later becoming an apostle of the Hermetic tradition. This conversion was significantly influenced by a certain Giovanni Mercurio da Correggio, who, in 1481, appeared in Rome and roamed the streets wearing a crown of thorns and preaching a mystical interpretation of Christianity. Lazzarelli commemorated this encounter in a work, written in the form of a letter by Enoch, in which he called himself 'Lodovicus Enoch Lazarellus Septempedanus, once a poet but now by new rebirth the son of true wisdom' (Thorndike 1923–58, 5:438). Thus, it seems, Lazzarelli believed himself to be a reincarnation of Enoch by means of a Hermetic rebirth, referring to Giovanni da Correggio as 'the Second Mercury' after Hermes Trismegistus (see Lazzarelli 2005).

Lazzarelli acquired several tracts of the *Corpus Hermeticum*, which had been unknown to Ficino, translated these and prepared a full edition of the *Hermetica*, the manuscript of which he dedicated and presented to Giovanni da Correggio. From the editor's three prefaces we know that by 1482, Correggio regarded himself as 'Hermes' spiritual son.' The mendicant prophet returned to Rome on Palm Sunday, 1484, and marched to the high altar of St. Peter's and declared himself to be the true Messiah. He carried a plate which bore the inscription, 'This is my servant Pimander, whom I have chosen...to cast out demons and proclaim my judgement and truth to the heathen.' This scandalous event resulted in Correggio being imprisoned repeatedly in Rome, Bologna and Florence, and the ways of the two illuminati parted. Lazzarelli settled down at the Naples court of King Ferdinand I (also known as Don Ferrante). The king tried to maintain an intellectual circle, similar to the Platonic Academy of the Florentine Medicis. His main Humanist scholar was Giovanni Pontano (1426–1503), who had enjoyed a spectacular career in the south – arriving there as a penniless scholar, he soon became the tutor of the son and grandson of Alfonso I and was eventually invited to be military advisor and chancellor to Ferdinand I. Lazzarelli had no such fortune. His private correspondence reveals a man embittered by the disinterest of the king and Pontano (Saci 1999, 89).

In this environment, soon after 1490, Lazzarelli wrote his mystical Hermetic-Platonic dialogue, under the title *Crater Hermetis*, or *The Mixing Bowl of Hermes*. The participants of the conversations are Ferdinand, Pontano and the author himself. The subject matter of the dialogues concerns the paths towards spiritual rebirth and the attainment of *gnosis*. The instruction culminates in the supreme mystery of the 'making of gods', echoing the Hermetic *Asclepius* (see, Hanegraaff 2005, 57–96).

The *Crater Hermetis* begins with Lazzarelli's announcement, according to which he had been transfigured by the divine Pimander and thus received authorization to become a spiritual teacher. In this capacity he reveals great mysteries to his audience, the king and his chancellor. The dialogues are dominated by the presence of Hermes Trismegistus, however the gnostic teachings are mixed with meditations on some biblical questions, such as 'The Meaning of Paradise Trees', 'The Meaning of the Woman in Proverbs', 'The Spiritual Meaning of Myths', and 'The Meaning of the "Daughters of Men"'. Five hymns are also inserted into the work, expressing with strong poetical beauty the author's rapturous understanding of self-knowledge, contemplation and divine generation.

The subtitle of the work is 'A Dialogue on the Supreme Dignity of Man', and its tone echoes Pico's elevated claims about human potentials: 'Thus you will come to understand the excellence of your own essence...[and] will rise up out of the body, ascending absolutely and purely, to fly to that transcendent and most shining darkness where God dwells, to take your place among the number of the Powers; and having been received among the Powers you shall enjoy God, and henceforth begetting a divine offspring...' (*Crater* 21.4, Lazzarelli 2005, 231). The king is increasingly impressed by the lofty philosophy, but consistently urges the narrator to unpack the practical implications of the work, namely how one might reach that exalted state of the self. Lazzarelli leads the treatise towards its climax by inserting a hymn to 'Divine Generation'. At its start the poem recalls the biblical Enoch, the predecessor-archetype of the narrator: 'Where do you transport me, Father? Is this not the place where pious aged Enoch went[?]' (27.1). The place is a place of magic and by the end of the hymn we return to the god-making act of the *Asclepius*:

> This is certainly the newest novelty of novelties
> and a miracle far greater than all others,
> that man has discovered the nature of God
> and knows how to make it...
> That is why the Begetter has given man
> a mind like his own, and speech,
> that he, like the gods, may bring forth gods,
> fulfilling the decrees of the Father.
> (27.1, Lazzarelli 2005, 253–55)

Sections 28–29 discuss the themes of the supernatural abilities of man in a way that fuses Enoch, Hermes and the most mystical Kabbalistic book, the *Sefer Yetzira* (*The Book of Creation*). Because Lazzarelli was not familiar with the original, he incorporated a motif which could only to be found in a commentary written by the thirteenth-century Jewish mystic, Eleazar of Worms. Nevertheless, the point is that this allusion to Hebrew folklore asserts that an artificial being, a Golem, can be created from 'red and virgin earth', from inanimate matter. This thesis is supported by citing Hermes, Plato, Philo Judaeus and the example of Christ, in that, parabolically speaking, 'Adama, the red and virgin earth, is the mind of the wise itself, that has been made virginal by the wine of the Messiah, that germinates virgins. A new man having been created in this manner' (29.5, ibid., 259).

No matter how inquisitive the king is, at this point, Lazzarelli decides to postpone the teachings and closes his work with a hymn addressed to the 'Light of the Father, radiant Word, Pimander', whom he finally identifies with Christ.

What sort of esotericism can be thus inferred from the *Crater Hermetis*? The discussion about the origins and components of Renaissance Hermeticism, as well as the actual standpoints of its Italian representatives is an ongoing scholarly process. Accordingly, Lazzarelli has been associated with Platonism, Hermeticism, Jewish mysticism and any combination of the three. Undoubtedly, along with Ficino, Lazzarelli shared an enthusiasm for the mystical teachings of Hermes and, like Pico, he learned Hebrew and became deeply influenced by the teachings of the Hebrew scholars.

Daniel P. Walker and Moshe Idel interpreted the soul-creating motive as if Lazzarelli promised by a magical act to create a spirit to enliven the ailing king (Walker 1958, 70–71; Idel 1988b, 68–69). According to Walker, the *Crater Hermetis* thus moves from the god-making of *Asclepius*, which argued that a demon or spirit had to be drawn to a lifeless statue, to the kabbalistic creation of a soul, by which a wise man creates, by the power of his words, something of the same substance as his own, similarly to the creative generation of God himself (1958, 67). Alternatively, according to Hanegraaff, soul-creation is a symbol to refer to perfect *gnosis*, a non-magical, but mystical illumination by which the practitioner becomes equal with God (Hanegraaff 2005, 92). This argument is developed according to Idel's reading of Pico's teacher (and Lazzarelli's probable acquaintance), Yohanan Alemanno, who, quoting Abraham Abulafia in his *Collectanaea*, claimed that the Kabbalah was more of an ecstatic and prophetic exercise than a practice of magic: 'Since God made man perfect, in the image of God...this is why every learned person is obliged to make souls...this being the way a man can imitate the Creator' (Abulafia, quoted via Idel 1988b, 70; see also Hanegraaff 2005).

The most recent voice in the debate, that of Hanegraaff, has proposed that Lazzarelli represents the purest form 'Christian Hermetism' (the distinction between 'Hermetism' and 'Hermeticism' is discussed in Hanegraaff 2005). Because he rejected the questionable astral magic of the *Corpus Hermeticum* and of Ficino, being, instead, influenced by allegorical interpretations of the *Sefer Yetzirah* and other kabbalistic works, he developed a purely spiritual, meditative and transformative *generatio mentis*. Contrary to Idel, Walker and Yates, Hanegraaff holds that, for Lazzarelli, the making of the Golem did not mean any kind of magical procedure, but should rather be understood figuratively, as a description of the process of *exaltatio*.

Having said that, Hanegraaff has noted the importance of considering the cultural background, which was as complex as that of Ficino or Pico. This occultural complexity led such Renaissance thinkers to believe that there could be many roads leading to the ultimate goal of rapturous transportation to God. A good example of this kind of occultural syncretism is Ficino's 'anthologia esoterica' (briefly noted above). In 1497 Ficino decided to collect his translations of esoteric sources and publish them in one volume. Here one finds such texts that were not even included in his *Opera omnia* of 1561. The beautiful Aldus print did not have a proper title page, being referred to in catalogues as the *Index eorum, quae hoc in libro habentur*. Indeed, it is often associated with Iamblichus's *On the Egyptian Mysteries*, which is the opening piece of the collection. Here one also finds the 'Platonici': Proclus and Porphyry on daemons, sacrifices and magia; Synesius on dreams; Psellus on daemons; further commentaries on Pythagorean numerology; and, the *Corpus Hermeticum* with commentaries. The volume is completed by Ficino's own esoterical-magical works, the complete *De vita* plus a few smaller treatises.

As for Lazzarelli, once again, one should not forget about his alchemical tracts, written quite soon after the *Crater*. Hanegraaff claims, that it was his new interest, inspired by his acquaintance with a Flemish alchemist, Joannes Rigaud, around 1495. In that year Lazzarelli compiled a collection of traditional alchemical texts principally by Lull and one by Rigaud (*Vade mecum*), which he prefaced with a prologue. This short tract nevertheless has important theoretical bearings, as Chiara Crisciani describes: 'Lazzarelli's alchemical interests and readings are thus not the result of occasional curiosity, but act as ingredients, albeit less important than his cabalistic interests, but nonetheless specific, which are operative in the construction of his highly syncretistic repertoire of texts, terms and, above all, images' (2000, 155).

Crisciani further demonstrates that Lazzarelli in his preface, when he describes the three types of natural, celestial and divine magic (*magia sacerdotalis*) puts as great a stress on the first two, as did Ficino in his *De vita*. Last but not least, the opening sentences of the prologue explicitly bring together magic and Hermetic ecstasy by referencing the *Tabula Smaragdina*, the Pseudo-Aristotelian *Secretum secretorum*, and the *Picatrix*. Hermes is mentioned here as the one who is the father of Theologians, Magicians and Alchemists. According to Crisciani, 'Lazzarelli specifies that the tria arcana and the three sciences are actually three modes, three declinations of one single field, namely magic' (2000, 152).

Hanegraaff, together with Farmer, also discredited that concept of the Yates thesis, according to which Hermeticism fermented the germs of the scientific revolution. Farmer in fact sarcastically argues, why should the Quattrocento Neoplatonists have been bothered with material progress, when they were looking for the mystical-magical shortcut to achieve those goals science might not even be able to lead to (1998, 131). But this statement is as much a sweeping generalization as its opposite by Yates. Apparently, Ficino in a letter to Paul of Middelburg praised 'the Golden Age in Florence' with the following words, paying enough attention to technical inventions:

> For this century, like a golden age, has restored to light the liberal arts, which were almost extinct: grammar, poetry, rhetoric, painting, sculpture, architecture, music, the ancient singing of songs to the Orphyc lyre, and all this is in Florence... The age has joined wisdom with eloquence, and prudence with the military art... In you, my dear Paul, this century appears to have perfected in astronomy; in Germany in our times have been invented the instruments for printing books, and those tables in which in a single hour the whole face of the heavens for an entire century is revealed, and one may mention also the Florentine machine which shows the daily motion of the heavens.
>
> ('Laudes seculi nostri tanquam aurei' (Letter to Paul of Middelburg), 1492, Ficino 1576, 944. English tr. quoted from Ross and McLaughlin 1968, 79–80)

EPILOGUE

The given limits of this essay do not allow further excursions. Consequently, there is no way to examine those complexities and contexts that would provide the full backdrop to those leading thinkers of the Hermetic revival in Renaissance Italy. Nor is there a chance to look at the wider social settings of Quattrocento Italy, in which the new type of intellectuals, the humanists, were moving around, still deeply rooted in medieval customs, habits, religious, scientific, and popular beliefs, urban settings, and the most mundane realities of life. All these contributed to their disposition toward magic and the occult. No doubt, the rediscovery of the writings under the name of Hermes Trismegistus provided a great intellectual challenge, inspiring 'Renaissance Hermetism' which soon developed into a much more diffuse and hazy complex of attitudes, beliefs and practices. The latter, as Hanegraaff also proposed, could be called 'Hermeticism' and already at its genesis, as we could see, produced such different proponents, as Ficino, Pico or Lazzarelli.

Regrettably, there is also no space to talk about the medieval survival of Hermes, the importance of which has been realized relatively recently (see the *Hermes Latinus* series under publication by Brepols, general editor Paolo Lucentini). Nor could we discuss the popular utilizations of love magic about which the Neoplatonists spoke with such lofty words. Historical research has revealed much less noble and purified practices, too (for the former see Canziani 2001; for the latter Duni 2007 and Ruggiero 1993).

Last, but not least, a word about the cultural heritage of the Quattrocento Hermetists and Hermeticists. If we only look at Italy, we see a growing variety of Western esotericism during the sixteenth century, enough to mention such well-known representatives as Leone Ebreo, who reformed the Neoplatonist concept of love combining it with his Hebrew heritage; Giovanni della Porta, who practiced natural magic and turned it into engineering; Girolamo Cardano who applied astrology and contributed to the development of psychology; Giordano Bruno, who developed a new cosmology from his admiration for the Egyptian mysteries; or Tommaso Campanella who again fused old and new, utopia, religion and science.

The Christian Cabalist movement started by Pico also brought about important fruits. The appreciation of Jewish culture and the Hebrew language was internationalized by Johann Reuchlin and he set a trend which grew well into the seventeenth century. Paolo Rossi (1975, 259–61) as well as Sheila Rabin (2008, 176–78) provided a long list of early modern scientists, who were in one way or another touched by Hermeticism and the Cabala. If not in the purist sense of Hanegraaff's cited definitions, but in a more widely interpreted framework of esotericism, Hermes Trismegistus was so influential between the fifteenth and the eighteenth centuries, that the Biblioteca Nazionale Marciana in Venice and the Bibliotheca Philosophica Hermetica in Amsterdam took the trouble to produce two fat folio volumes in which a team of international experts, under the leadership of Carlos Gilly, demonstrated the lure and long-lasting effect: *Magic, Alchemy, and Science – 15th-18th Centuries – The Influence of Hermes Trismegistus* (Gilly and van Heertum 2002). Among recent publications one could also mention the twenty-fifth volume of the *Storia d'Italia* (*History of Italy*), which, edited by Gian Mario Cazzaniga (2010), devotes 781 pages to the topic of 'esoterismo' in which key articles deal with the period covered in the present chapter, too (Brach; Perrone Compagni; Vasoli).

Although still not an entirely settled picture, the account of the Renaissance Italian Hermetic revival remains a particularly important chapter in the book of the 'World of the Occult'.

REFERENCES AND FURTHER READING

Aasdalen, Unn Irene (2011) 'The First Pico–Ficino Controversy', in S. Clucas, P.J. Forshaw, and V. Rees, ed., *Laus Platonici Philosophi. Marsilio Ficino and His Influence*, Leiden: Brill (Studies in Intellectual History 198), 67–89.

Allen, Michael J.B. (1995) *Plato's Third Eye. Studies in Marsilio Ficino's Metaphysics and its Sources*, Aldershot: Ashgate Variorum.

Allen, Michael J.B. and Valery Rees, eds. (2002) *Marsilio Ficino: His Theology, His Philosophy, His Legacy*, Leiden: Brill (Studies in Intellectual History 108).

Bacchelli, Franco (2001) *Giovanni Pico e Pier Leone da Spoleto. Tra filosofia dell'amore e tradizione cabalistica*, Firenze: Leo S. Olschki.

Blum, Paul Richard (2008a) 'Pico, Theology, and the Church', in M.V. Dougherty, ed., *Pico della Mirandola: New Essays*, Cambridge University Press, 37–61.

——(2008b) 'On Popular Platonism: Giovanni Pico with Elia del Medigo against Marsilio Ficino', in Sabrina Ebbersmeyer et al., eds. *Sol et Homo. Mensch und Natur in der Renaissance.* Festschrift zum 70. Geburtstag für Eckhard Kessler, München: Wilhelm Fink, 421–31.

Borghesi, Francesco (2008) '[Pico] A Life in Works', in M.V. Dougherty, ed., *Pico della Mirandola: New Essays*, Cambridge: Cambridge University Press, 202–19.

Bori, Pier Cesare (2000) *Pluralità delle vie. Alle origini del Discorso sulla dignità umana di Pico della Mirandola.* Testo latino, versione italiana, apparato testuale a cura di Severino Marchignoli. Milano: Feltrinelli.

Brach, Jean-Pierre (2010) 'Umanesimo e correnti esoteriche in Italia: l'esempio della "qabbalah Cristiana"', in G. M. Cazzaniga, ed., *Storia d'Italia. Annali 25: Esoterismo*, Torino: Giulio Eidnaudi, 257–88.

Canziani, Guido (2001) *Le metamorfosi dell'amore. Ficino, Pico e 'I fuori' di Bruno*, Milano: CUEM.

Cazzaniga, Gian Mario, ed. (2010) *Storia d'Italia. Annali 25: Esoterismo*, Torino: Giulio Eidnaudi.

Clucas, Stephen, Peter J. Forshaw, and Valery Rees, eds. (2011) *Laus Platonici Philosophi. Marsilio Ficino and His Influence*, Leiden: Brill (Studies in Intellectual History 198).

Copenhaver, Brian P. (1986) 'Renaissance Magic and Neoplatonic Philosophy: *Ennead* 4.3–5 in Ficino's *De vita coelitus comparanda*', in Giancarlo Garfagnini ed. *Marsilio Ficino e il ritorno di Platone* (2 vols), Firenze: Leo S. Olschki.

——(1988) 'Hermes Trismegistus, Proclus, and the Question of a Philosophy of Magic in the Renaissance', in I. Merkel & Allen G. Debus, eds. (1988) *Hermeticism and the Renaissance. Intellectual History and the Occult in Early Modern Europe*, Washington, DC / London: Folger Shakespeare Library/Associated University Presses, 79–110.

——ed. (1995) 'Introduction', *Hermetica. The Greek Corpus Hermeticum and the Latin Asclepius in a New English Translation* (first edition 1992). Cambridge: Cambridge University Press.

Crisciani, Chiara (2000) 'Hermeticism and Alchemy: The Case of Ludovico Lazzarelli.' *Early Science and Medicine* 5.2: 145–59.

Della Torre, Arnaldo (1902) *Storia dell' accademia platonica di Firenze.* Firenze: G. Garnesecchi.

Dougherty, M.V., ed. (2008) *Pico della Mirandola: New Essays*, Cambridge: Cambridge University Press.

Duni, Matteo (2007) *Witches, Sorcerers, and the Inquisition in Renaissance Italy.* Florence: Syracuse University in Florence.

Farmer, S.A. (1998) *Syncretism in the West: Pico's 900 Theses (1486). With Text, Translation, and Commentary.* Tempe, AZ: Medieval & Renaissance Texts & Studies.

Ficino, Marsilio (1516) *Index eorum, quae hoc in libro habentur. Iamblichus, de mysteriis Aegyptiorum*...Venice: Aldus (reprint of the 1497 edition).

——(1576) *Opera omnia* (2 vols, consecutively numbered). Basel: Henricpetri. First edition: 1561.

——(1944) *Commentary on Plato's 'Symposium' on Love (1475).* Tr. Sears Jayne. Columbia: University of Missouri Press.

——(1975) *The Letters*, Volume I. Tr. and ed. by the Fellowship of the School of Economic Science, London. London: Shepheard-Walwyn.

——(1981) *The Letters*, Volume III. Tr. and ed. by the Fellowship of the School of Economic Science, London. London: Shepheard-Walwyn.

——(1989) *Three Books on Life*. A Critical Edition and Translation with Introduction and Notes by Carol V. Caske and John R. Clark. Binghamton, NY: The Renaissance Society of America (Medieval & Renaissance Texts & Studies).

——(2001–6) *Platonic Theology*. Tr. and ed. Michael J.B. Allen and James Hankins. 6 vols. Cambridge, MA: Harvard UP (I Tatti Renaissance Library).

——(2009) *The Letters*, Volume VIII. Tr. and ed. by the Fellowship of the School of Economic Science, London. London: Shepheard-Walwyn.

Field, Arthur (1988) *The Origins of the Platonic Academy in Florence*. Princeton: Princeton University Press.

——(2002) 'The Platonic Academy of Florence', in Allen and Rees eds. 2002, 359–76.

Garin, Eugenio (1983). *Astrology in the Renaissance. The Zodiac of Life* (first Italian ed. 1976). London: Routledge and Kegan Paul.

——(1995) 'Ricordando Giovanni e Gianfrancesco Pico della Mirandola.' *Giornale critico della filosofia italiana* 74.1: 5–19.

Gilly, Carlos and Cis van Heertum, eds. (2002) *Magic, Alchemy, and Science – 15th-18th Centuries – The Influence of Hermes Trismegistus*. Venice / Amsterdam: Biblioteca Nazionale Marciana / Bibliotheca Philosophica Hermetica.

Hanegraaff, Wouter J. (2005) 'Lodovico Lazzarelli and the Hermetic Christ: At the Sources of Renaissance Hermetism', in Lazzarelli 2005, 1–151.

Idel, Moshe (1988a) *Kabbalah*. New Haven: Yale University Press.

——(1988b) 'Hermeticism and Judaism', in Merkel and Debus eds. 1988, 59–77.

——(2005) *Ascension on High in Jewish Mysticism: Pillars, Lines, Ladders*, Budapest / New York: Central European University Press (Pasts Incorporated 2).

Kieckhefer, Richard (1989) *Magic in the Middle Ages*, Cambridge: Cambridge University Press.

Láng, Benedek (2008) *Unlocked Books. Manuscripts of Learned Magic in the Medieval Libraries of Central Europe*, University Park, PA: University of Pennsylvania Press.

Lazzarelli, Lodovico (2005) *The Hermetic Writings and Related Documents*, ed. Wouter J. Hanegraaff and Ruud M. Bouthoorn, Tempe, AZ: Arizona Center for Medieval and Renaissance Studies.

Merkel, Ingrid and Allen G. Debus, eds. (1988) *Hermeticism and the Renaissance. Intellectual History and the Occult in Early Modern Europe*, Washington, DC / London: Folger Shakespeare Library / Associated University Presses.

Perrone Compagni, Vittoria (2010) 'Ermete nel Medievo cristiano', in G. M. Cazzaniga, ed., *Storia d'Italia. Annali 25: Esoterismo*, Torino: Giulio Eidnaudi, 149–74.

Picatrix: the Latin Version of the Ghayat al-Hakim (1986), ed., David E. Pingree, London: The Warburg Institute.

The Picatrix (2010) ed. and tr. John M. Greer and Christopher Warnock, Phoenix, AZ: Adocentyn Press.

Pico della Mirandola, Giovanni (1964) *Oration on the Dignity of Man*. Tr. Richard Hooker, in P.O. Kristeller ed. *Eight Philosophers of the Italian Renaissance*, Stanford: Stanford University Press, 1964. Online: http://cscs.umich.edu/~crshalizi/Mirandola/ (accessed 20 July 2012)

——(1971) *Opera omnia*, Torino: Bottega d'Erasmo. (Facsimile of the Basel, Henricpetri, 1572 edition with an introduction by Eugenio Garin.)

——(1998) *On the Dignity of Man; On Being and the One; Heptaplus*, ed., Paul J.W. Miller. Indianopolis: Hackett (reprint with new bibliography of the 1965 edition).

——(2000) *Oratio / Discorso* [Latin / Italian]. See, Pier Cesare Bori (2000) *Pluralità delle vie. Alle origini del Discorso sulla dignità umana di Pico della Mirandola*. Testo latino, versione italiana, apparato testuale a cura di Severino Marchignoli. Milano: Feltrinelli.

——(2004) *De Hominis dignitate e sritti varii; Disputationes adversus astrologiam divinatricem*, ed. Eugenio Garin, amended Franco Bacchelli, 3 vols (reprint), Turin: Nino Argano Editore.

Rabin, Sheila J. (2008) 'Pico on Magic and Astrology', in M.V. Dougherty, ed., *Pico della Mirandola: New Essays*, Cambridge: Cambridge University Press, 152–79.

Raffini, Christine (1998) *Marsilio Ficino, Pietro Bembo, Baldassare Castiglione. Philosophical, Aesthetic, and Political Approaches in Renaissance Platonism*, New York: Peter Lang.

Ross, James Bruce and Mary Martin McLaughlin, eds. (1968) *The Portable Renaissance Reader*, London: Penguin.

Rossi, Paolo (1975) 'Hermeticism, Rationality and the Scientific Revolution', in M.L. Righini Bonelli and William R. Shea, eds., *Reason, Experiment, and Mysticism in the Scientific Revolution*, New York: Science History Publications, 247–75.

Roulier, Fernand (1989) *Jean Pic de la Mirandole, humaniste, philosophe et théologien*, Genève: Slatkine.

Ruggiero, Guido (1993) *Binding Passions. Tales of Magic, Marriage, and Power at the End of the Renaissance*, Oxford: Oxford University Press.

Saci, Maria Paola (1999) *Ludovico Lazzarelli: Da Elicona a Sion*, Roma: Bulzoni.

Seller, Fabio (2009) *Scientia Astrorum. La fondazione epistemologica dell'astrologia in Pietro d'Abano*, Naples: Giannini Editore.

Still, Carl N. (2008) 'Pico's Quest for All Knowledge', in M.V. Dougherty, ed., *Pico della Mirandola: New Essays*, Cambridge: Cambridge University Press, 179–202.

Szönyi, György E. (2004) *John Dee's Occultism. Magical Exaltation through Powerful Signs*, Albany, NY: SUNY Press.

Thorndike, Lynn (1923–58) *History of Magic and Experimental Science*. 8 vols., New York: Columbia University Press.

Vasoli, Cesare (2010) '*Prisca theologia* e scienze occulte nell'umanesimo fiorentino', in G. M. Cazzaniga, ed., *Storia d'Italia. Annali 25: Esoterismo*, Torino: Giulio Eidnaudi, 175–205.

Walker, D.P. (1958) *Spiritual and Demonic Magic from Ficino to Campanella*. London: The Warburg Institute. Reprint: Pennsylvania State University Press, 2000.

Wirszubski, Chaim (1989) *Pico della Mirandola's Encounter with Jewish Mysticism*, Cambridge MA: Harvard University Press.

Yates, Frances A. (1964) *Giordano Bruno and the Hermetic Tradition*, London: Routledge & Kegan Paul.

——(1967) 'The Hermetic Tradition in Renaissance Science', in Charles S. Singleton, ed., *Art, Science, and History in the Renaissance*, Baltimore: Johns Hopkins University Press, 255–74.

——(1984) *Ideas and Ideals in the North European Renaissance. Collected Essays III*, London: Routledge & Kegan Paul.

CHAPTER FOUR

ALCHEMICAL HERMETICISM

Florian Ebeling

The definition of Hermeticism or the 'hermetic tradition' is controversial. Some scholars refer to special figures of thought who are related to Hermes Trismegistos, the eponym of this tradition, others to the history of editions and commentaries of the *Corpus Hermeticum*. In this discussion all the texts that are treated as part of the hermetic tradition, are those ascribed explicitly or implicitly to the authorship of Hermes.

Commonly, the hermetic tradition is used as a collective singular. As it deals with writings ascribed to the legendary Egyptian Hermes Trismegistos this term seems to be reasonable. On closer investigation, the tradition appears very complex, not to say heterogenic in parts. I propose to distinguish two different traditions of Hermeticism. One is focused on the *Corpus Hermeticum* and the *Asclepius*, their emergence in Antiquity, their rediscovery in Renaissance Italy, their relevance in Renaissance philosophy and the scholarly disputations about their dating and authenticity (see the article by György Szonyi). The other tradition is in many instances connected to and interwoven with the first, but, to some extent, develops its own path. This tradition begins with magical, alchemical and astrological texts in late Antiquity, proceeds in the Arabic literature and their Latin translations during the Middle Ages and has a climax in the German speaking world in the sixteenth and seventeenth century. Within this tradition the *Tabula Smaragdina* (*Emerald Table*) is regarded as the most important text by Hermes and as the 'alchemical bible' (Birkholz 1779: 28).

While the traditions have inspired each other in multiple ways and were blended in some instances, they can also be sharply distinguished from each other. However, for heuristic reasons alone, it seems sensible not to deal with just one Hermetic tradition, but rather to explore each and the ways in which they are mingled.

Hermeticism in its different forms is an important part of Western culture. While not as relevant as Platonism or Christianity, the understanding of it is indispensable for the comprehension of many chapters within the history of ideas, literature, philosophy, theology and art. Particularly detailed studies are required to understand the specific role of Hermeticism in the European cultural history. This is not the purpose of this discussion, which is simply to sketch the profile and history of the form of alchemical Hermeticism.

Hermeticism generally in its concept of itself does not have any substantial development. The followers of Hermes believe themselves to be part of a supratemporal and immemorial tradition first articulated in ancient Egypt. They believed the most ancient wisdom to be the most perfect. This has meant that Hermetists struggled to preserve the primordial knowledge of Hermes and not to improve it. In fact, many of the texts believed to be written by Hermes are treated as canonical writings. Notwithstanding the self-concept, we find remarkable developments in the commentaries of the *Corpus Hermeticum* or the *Tabula Smaragdina*, and in the prefaces of the different hermetic writings outlining the relevance of Hermeticism in the special sociohistorical framework.

In many instances Hermetism is an important part of the image formed of Egypt in the Western world. From late Antiquity to the seventeenth century, the discussion of Egyptian religion and wisdom was also one of Hermeticism. It was regarded as the essence of the ancient Egyptian mystery cult, up to the point when the Hermetic writings lost their reputation as being from time immemorial. From then onwards it was common to form a concept of Egyptian religion without much consideration of the hermetic writings, for within academia Hermeticism lost its relevance to the study of ancient Egypt (Mulsow 2002).

The early close alliance of Egypt and Hermetism, however, had some implications concerning the history of the ideas connected to it. With Middle Platonic philosophy Egypt was regarded as a culture of symbolic forms par excellence. Plutarch stated that the deeper and the more esoteric, rather than the obvious is the essence of Egyptian culture and shows its true character. Apuleius dramatized the mysteries of Isis in the novel *Metamorphoses* or *The Golden Ass* and made Egypt the culture of mysteries which was strongly connected to Platonic teachings. The hieroglyphs seemed to fit this pattern, because they were not described as a combination of logographic, alphabetical and ideographic elements but primarily as symbols used by the priests to veil their knowledge (Assmann 2003: 27–35). Jamblichos (in his book known as *The Egyptian Mysteries* in Ficino's translation) read the Egyptian symbolism as an articulation of Neoplatonic philosophy; his identification of Egyptian religion with Hermeticism provided a widely accepted Neoplatonic interpretation of Hermeticism, especially when it was regarded as the oldest Egyptian wisdom.

The heuristic value of the distinction between a more philosophically and theologically focused discussion in connection with the *Corpus Hermeticum* and a more alchemically and practically focused discussion (likewise with strong theological and philosophical implications) in connection with the *Tabula Smaragdina* is quite controversial. Some scholars use this distinction and try to elaborate on the ways in which they differ from each other and where there are interactions or amalgams, others deny the plausibility of this distinction in all (Alt and Wels 2010).

Without any question there are prominent cases where we can find both traditions. The Jesuit Athanasius Kircher (1602–80) describes the *Corpus Hermeticum* and the *Tabula Smaragdina* in his *Oedipus Aegyptiacus* in 1652/54. The same is true for the alchemists Michael Maier (1569–1622) and Heinrich Khunrath (1560–1605) or some of the most prominent followers of Paracelsus. Nevertheless, there are a lot of writings solely referring to just one tradition.

Even though the hermetic tradition focused on the *Tabula Smaragdina* had its most prominent articulation in Germany during the late sixteenth and seventeenth century and is widely connected to the Paracelsian movement, I will refer to it as 'alchemical Hermeticism' as the discussion of alchemy seems to be the basic movement (cf. Law 2010: 60–62). Alchemy was widely known in the West under the name of Hermes Trismegistos, as an 'ars hermetica (hermetic art)' (Telle 1978: 199f.).

HERMETIC WRITINGS IN ANTIQUITY AND THE PLAUSIBILITY OF THE DIFFERENTIATION BETWEEN PHILOSOPHICAL AND TECHNICAL HERMETICA

As early as Antiquity and late Antiquity hermetic writings were an elusive conglomerate of writings. Under the name of its supposed author, Hermes Trismegistos, very different kinds of texts were circulating. The most well-known texts were collected in a Byzantine edition and came to fame as the *Corpus Hermeticum* in conjunction with the *Asclepius*, which survived in Latin, Coptic and Greek versions. The excerpts of Stobaeos date from the fifth century. All these texts, very different in detail, offer philosophical and theological teachings without being systematized: the polarity between mind/spirit and matter, the deliverance of the soul from animal instincts and the boundaries of the body, as well as the idea of the body as a divine organ or the interdependence of the body and the planets. It is a holistic model which combines god, human being and nature in a hierarchic cosmos focused on theology, philosophy of nature and ethics treated as belonging together.

In addition, we find the so-called 'technical Hermetica' (Fowden 1986). They share similar theological and ontological paradigms, but they are focused on their utilizations in astrology, magic and alchemy, which are treated by the other hermetical texts just *en passant*. In the name of Hermes, we find detailed spells of love or evil, magical medications or iatromathematical writings, describing the use of astronomy for medicine. Likewise, there is the idea of the special cosmic relationship between the human being as the microcosmos with the cosmic sphere as the macrocosmos. In alchemy, Hermes is cited by the first nameable alchemist, Zosimos of Panopolis (Akhmin in Upper Egypt) because of his spiritual alchemy, that does not care above all for the transmutation of metals but for the transformation of the humans into a spiritual being.

Festugière divides the hermetic writings into two groups: (1) the 'Hermétisme savant' by which he refers to the *Corpus Hermeticum*, the *Asclepius* or the excerpts by Stobaeus; and (2) the 'Hermétisme populaire' by which he means the alchemical, astrological or magical treaties (Festugière 1944–54). Two separated groups for two different types of readers. Garth Fowden tries to avoid any pejorative connotation for the second group and speaks about 'technical Hermetica'. Indeed, he assumes that the two groups, though apparently different, belong to one hermetic curriculum. Likewise, recent research stresses the nexus between the two groups. A categorical separation of these two groups seems to be implausible because they refer to the same cosmological or anthropological principles and the boundaries seem to be not as distinct after a second view: within the *Corpus Hermeticum* there are astrological passages and within the hermetic excerpts by Stobaeus, belonging to the philosophical Hermetica, there is a teaching on deans. In the library of Nag Hammadi, discovered in 1945, there is the philosophical *Asclepius* next to Hermetica using a magical name of god. Were there hermetic communities that used the texts for cultic practice or just as reading matter? We still do not know enough for an understanding of the *sitz im leben* of the different hermetic texts. Most scholars differentiate between the 'technical' and the 'philosophical' Hermetica, while also assuming that they belong together.

ARABIC AND LATIN HERMETICA FROM THE MIDDLE AGES TO THE RENAISSANCE

A rediscovery of Hermes in the Renaissance was not necessary as there were many writings ascribed to him during the Middle Ages. Augustine condemned Hermetic teachings as demonic magic but Lactantius justified them as an overture to Christianity. The hermetic *Asclepius* was handed down in the Latin Middle Ages in more than eighty manuscripts, even though often under the name of Apuleius. Scholars like Petrus Abaelardus, Thierry of Chartres or Berthold of Moosburg cited it. Moreover there emerged Latin writings ascribed to Hermes Trismegistus. Many hermetic writings were translated from the Arabic into Latin maintaining the image of Hermes as saviour of a legendary antediluvian wisdom affiliated with astronomy, alchemy and magic.

The image of Hermes in the Arabic occult science is of utmost importance for the alchemical Hermeticism. The legend of the three sages named Hermes is especially famous (van Bladel 2009: 121–63). The first Hermes lived before the Flood, invented astrology and medicine and worshipped god in temples. In order to prevent his knowledge from disappearing, he erected the temple of Akhmin and engraved his ideas on the walls. The second Hermes lived after the Flood, he was the teacher of Pythagoras and revived the antediluvian wisdom in philosophy, maths and medicine. Finally, the third Hermes was the teacher of Asclepius and wrote a book on alchemy.

The histories of discoveries, already known from Antiquity, have been widely disseminated (Speyer 1970). The frame narrative of the book of Crates the sage, which dates to the ninth century, tells how the author achieved his knowledge. Crates was enraptured to heaven where he 'wandered with the sun and the moon' (Speyer 1970: 74–75). There he saw the 'venerable old man' Hermes, clad in white, sitting on a throne with a radiant tablet in his hand. According to this narrative, the book claims to be of supernatural origin and special dignity. These texts, translated into Latin and, later, into German and other vernaculars remained valid for some followers of Hermes even into the eighteenth century. The famous freemason Ignaz von Born (1742–91) referred to it in his *On the Mysteries of the Egyptians* (1784) and Christoph Martin Wieland (1733–1813) satirized the legendary discovery of the hermetic wisdom in his fairy tale *The Philosopher's Stone* (Assmann and Ebeling 2011: 141–61).

In the *Treasure of Alexander the Great*, the frame narrative lends a special dignity to magical, alchemical and medical texts. Caliph al-Mutasim found a chest that Antiochius I had hidden in a monastery wall at the behest of Alexander the Great. In this chest he found a golden book in which Aristoteles informs Alexander that he was found worthy of receiving the heavenly and antediluvian wisdom of king Hermes in this book (Ruska 1926: 68–107). This supposedly age-old knowledge was unfolded in ten books of alchemo-medical content, with technical instructions, fundamental principles of natural philosophy and also information about magic and the effectiveness of talismans.

As the frame narratives stress, hermetic knowledge was of divine origin. It had been lost but now had emerged once again into history, and it could lead mankind to a new happiness that was the one of the golden past.

In the *Mystery of Creation* of Balinus (pseudo-Apolonius of Tyana) we read that Balinus was digging at the feet of a statue of Hermes and discovered a vault. Exhausted by his vain attempts to enter, Balinus fell asleep and in his dream he received a revelation about the right way to enter the vault. There he saw an old man on a golden throne who held in his hands an emerald table entitled 'Representation of Nature' and at his feet lay the book entitled 'Mystery of Creation'. Following the chronology of the history of creation, the origin and material essence of the world are described according to the Aristotelian doctrine of the elements. The principle of the unity and coherence of the cosmos is primordial matter, which is the substrate of all natural bodies. Using the analogy between heaven and earth, as we already know it from the Hermetica from late Antiquity, what exists above always remains the cause of what is below in this ontological order: the course of the planets determines the three natural kingdoms of animals, plants and stones (Weisser 1980: 74–88). The final part of this book is the *Tabula Smaragdina*:

> True it is, without falsehood, certain and most true. That which is above is like to that which is below, and that which is below is like to that which is above, to accomplish the miracles of one thing.
>
> And as all things were by contemplation of one, so all things arose from this one thing by a single act of adaption.
>
> The father thereof is the Sun, the mother the Moon.
>
> The wind carried it in its womb, the earth is the nurse thereof.
>
> It is the father of all works of wonder throughout the whole world.
>
> The power thereof is perfect.
>
> If it be cast on to earth, it will separate the element of earth from that of fire, the subtle from the gross.
>
> With great sagacity it doth ascend gently from earth to heaven.
>
> Again it doth descend to earth, and uniteth in itself the force from things superior and things inferior.
>
> Thus thou wilt possess the glory of the brightness of the whole world, and all obscurity will fly far from thee.
>
> This thing is the strong fortitude of all strength, for it overcometh every subtle thing and doth penetrate every solid substance.
>
> Thus was this world created.
>
> Hence will there be marvellous adaptations achieved, of which the manner is this.

> For this reason I am called Hermes Trismegistus, because I hold three parts of the wisdom of the whole world.
>
> That which I had to say about the operation of Sol is completed.
>
> (Linden 2010: 28)

The *Tabula Smaragdina* was translated by Hugo of Santalla in the twelfth century into Latin and was widely spread in numerous manuscripts in the West during the Middle Ages (Telle 1995). It was for instance part of the 'long version' of the *Secreta Secretorum*, preserved in about 350 copies in the late Middle Ages (Heiduk 2010: 57).

Beside the *Tabula Smaragdina* a lot of other hermetic writings were translated from Arabic into Latin: The *Treasure of Alexander the Great* was translated in 1144 by Robert of Chester (Castrensis) into Latin. Titled *Liber de Compositione Alchemiae* it was in print in the West not later than 1559 and the alchemist Michael Maier drew on it as a source for his description of the figure of Hermes. In the Preface by Robert of Chester we find the narrative of the three sages named Hermes. This legend we can find in at least two more Latin books: in the Preface of the translator of the *Septem Tractatus Hermetis* and in the Preface of the *Liber Hermetis Mercurii Triplicis de sex rerum principiis* (Burnett 1976).

In the twelfth and thirteenth centuries there were a lot of examples of 'technical Hermetica' available in the West. Another example of Arabic Hermetica translated into Latin is the *Centiloquium Hermetis*, which consists of a hundred sentences about astrology which Stephen of Messina compiled from Arabic sources in the middle of the thirteenth century.

These hermetic writings with Arabic origin have been widely discussed in the Latin West. The *Tabula Smaragdina* was interpreted and popularized in many commentaries. The most influential one was that by Hortulanus, who read the *Tabula Smaragdina* as an allegory of the Philosopher's Stone. Bernardus Trevisanus, who lived during the fifteenth century, reports that Hermes came to the valley of Hebron where he found the tablet, which was decorated with the knowledge of the seven liberal arts. By the virtue of their alchemical wisdom the Egyptians became rich and Hermes recorded this wisdom in the *Tabula Smaragdina*. These prefaces and commentaries were printed frequently till the eighteenth century.

Besides the Hermetic writings being translated from Arabic into Latin there are also some Latin Hermetica without Arabic or Greek templates – at least the templates are not known so far. The most prominent one is the *Book of the Twenty-four Philosophers* with twenty-four definitions concerning the essence of God. It was often ascribed to Hermes and many important philosophers like Meister Eckhart, Bonaventure, Nicolas of Cusa, Giordano Bruno or Leibniz cited Hermes-dicta from it (Flasch 2011).

Many alchemical, magical and astrological Hermetica, but also philosophical texts were known to the Latin West. Nevertheless, the discovery of the *Corpus Hermeticum* caused a sensation in the world of letters.

HERMETICISM IN THE GERMAN-SPEAKING WORLD OF THE FIFTEENTH AND SIXTEENTH CENTURY

The discovery, translations and commentaries of the *Corpus Hermeticum* initialized a new enthusiasm for Hermeticism in Europe, likewise in the German-speaking parts. Basel was a very important place of printing but there are also editions printed in Mainz or Hamburg.

A very interesting example of reception of the *Corpus Hermeticum* in Germany can be found in the works of Sebastian Franck (1499–1543). In his *Guldin Arch*, Franck refers to Hermes as a teacher of all knowledge necessary for salvation. God is not just part of one limited revelation but a universal God of reason and ethics. Hermes had heralded him just as Plato, Plotin, Orpheus and some others had done. With his reading of the *Corpus Hermeticum* Franck limited the claim to truth of Christianity in favour of a religio-philosophical universalism. He derived his image of Hermes largely from Ficino but he explained the relevance of Hermeticism much more radically by deeming the hermetic writings as a sufficient substitute for Christianity and the Jewish-Christian revelation. The hermetic writings are not just considered to be a precursor of the truth totally revealed in the Bible but as being as good as the writings of Moses. Franck is not a professing hermeticist and does not have any preference for Hermes. He was simply focused on the 'inner word' (Hannak 2010: 297–322) and the condemnation of any dogmatic teaching. The *Corpus Hermeticum* served to show that there are many options and to argue the case for religious tolerance. Nevertheless, Franck must have had a great fascination for the *Corpus Hermeticum* as he translated it into German during his final year of his life, a translation that has not yet been printed.

Aside from this form of Hermeticism in Germany, we also find the tradition of the alchemical Hermeticism. The *Tabula Smaragdina* was printed in many editions throughout Europe, but especially Germany was now regarded as being the new home of alchemical Hermeticism. Jacob Friederich Reimmann (1668–1743) included a treatment of 'literary Hermeticism' in his history of German literature. A new physics had been invented in Germany and this hermetic science derived its name from and had its origin in Hermes Trismegistos. It had been handed down from the Egyptians to the Greeks and from the Greeks to the Arabs and finally to the Germans. It had been known in Germany since the fourteenth century, until it was later displaced by 'scholastic and Aristotelian philosophy', and it had first been resuscitated by Paracelsus. How did it happen that this linear filiation from Egypt to Paracelsus was constructed, incorporating the late Middle Ages without the Hermeticism of the Italian Renaissance?

PARACELSUS AS GERMAN HERMES IN THE SIXTEENTH AND SEVENTEENTH CENTURY

Since the second half of the sixteenth century some followers of Paracelsus referred emphatically to Hermes Trismegistus and adored Paracelsus as his true heir (Kühlmann and Telle 2004: 27–33). A good example is a writing published in 1603 in the appendix of an edition of the works of Theophrast of Hohenheim alias Paracelsus: *Apocalypsis Hermetis ab illustrissimo viro, Aureolo Helvetico, qui fuit Hermes Secundus* or as it was entitled in the 1608 edition, *Apocalypsis Des*

Hocherleuchten Aegyptischen Königs und Philosophi, Hermetis Trismegisti; von unserm Teutschen Hermete, dem Edlen, Hochthewren Monarchen und Philosopho Trismegisto, A[ureolo] Ph[ilippo] Theophrasto Paracelso [...] Verdolmetschet. The title announces a revelation of Hermes, translated by Paracelsus who is revered as the second or the German Hermes.

The first edition of this book was neither published under the name of Hermes nor under that of Paracelsus. In fact, the Venetian Giovanni Battista Agnello first published the *Apocalypsis spiritus secreti* in 1566 in London together with some commentaries. It consists of compilations of different dicta from many alchemical texts. Arnold of Villanova, Johannes de Rupescissa, Raimundus Lullus or Aristotle are cited together with some dicta by Hermes Trismegistos, while Paracelsus is not even mentioned! However, just a few years after the first edition Paracelsus was declared to be its author. In 1570, the first person narrator Paracelsus claims in the pseudo-paracelsian *Tinctura Physicorum*, that he has written an 'Apocalypsis Hermetis'. All editions after 1570 are associated with Paracelsus. The relevance of this nexus between Paracelsus and Hermes is explained in many texts. In the Foreword to the 1608 edition, the publisher, Benedictus Figulus (Telle 1987: 303–26), described it in a narrative history of the development of Hermetic knowledge. This history is embedded in an autobiographical account of the author's conversion.

According to this account, Figulus was first instructed in Aristotelian philosophy. Through reading the works of Paracelsus, Roger Bacon and Isaac Hollandus, he had an experience of philosophical awaking. As a result, he understood Aristotelianism to be a false teaching inspired by Satan. The alchemical teaching impressed him and he resolved to search for the Philosopher's Stone. He thus declared himself to be a disciple of the Hermetic science, which in his view comprised astronomy, alchemy, magic and cabala. Then Figulus related the history of the development of this true, divine knowledge.

The continuation of Adam's universal knowledge was endangered by the Flood, but it survived in Egypt in the Hermetic tradition. Here in Egypt, Moses was initiated in this wisdom and in this regard Hermeticism and the biblical tradition are consistent. Later on the 'idolatrous and superstitious' Greeks broke away from this knowledge and established a tradition which consisted of a mixture of falsehood, unbelief, Satan's work and conceited rationalism. This they passed on to Roman philosophy. Figulus believed that this mixture of profane, false knowledge still influenced the thinking in the academies and universities everywhere in Europe at his time. Using Aristotelian philosophy, Satan had duped the whole of Christendom. Figulus, however, was convinced that following hermetic philosophy is the way to salvation. It is only this philosophy that is able to guide Christendom back on a path to its original theology and philosophy. This history of the hermetic philosophy served to justify a sharp distinction between true and false knowledge, between knowledge received from revelation and knowledge derived from human reason. Within this model, it was Paracelsus who was understood to have instigated the renaissance of Hermeticism, bringing the light of Hermetic knowledge into the darkened world of Aristotelian reason. For such hermetists, Paracelsus is rightly called the 'second Hermes', the 'German Hermes' or 'Trismegistus Germanus' (Gilly 2010).

Looking at the *Aurora philosophorum* (Redl 2008), known as a manuscript from 1569 and first printed in 1577, helps us towards understanding what the reason is behind the harsh anti-Aristotelian attitude. In its opening chapters, the semiosis of hermetic writings is legitimized by citing the history of Hermetic knowledge. The primeval knowledge was written down by Adam's sons on two tablets of stone, 'in which they engraved the natural sciences with secret and veiled characters, which they called hieroglyphs'. After the Flood, a large part of this knowledge managed to survive in Egypt, but it was also passed along by Moses to 'the children of Israel'. Hermes was the wisest of all Egyptians, and also the one mankind is indebted to for the transmission of the primeval Adamic knowledge through his writings.

In this regard, for the hermetic wisdom, the 'how' rather than the 'what' of knowledge, is important. In order for divine wisdom to spread, it is necessary, according to the author of the *Aurora Philosophorum*, to understand the symbolic representation by means of which that wisdom had been handed down from Egypt. Egyptian wisdom was expressed in symbols and enigmas and was adopted in this form by a number of Greeks, such as Homer and Pythagoras.

The hermetic tradition is not seen as consisting of a positive, but of a symbolic knowledge and epistemology. The crucial point here is the distinction between the superficial and the profound, and a recognition that essential truth is hidden beneath mere names and appearances. It is precisely at this point – the recognition of a deep structure behind mere appearance – that Aristotelian philosophy is found wanting.

Even though Aristotle and his philosophy played an important role in the theory of alchemy, he was widely stigmatized in the alchemical Hermeticism of the sixteenth and seventeenth centuries. Within the history of philosophy, this attitude can be understood in Platonic terms, by distinguishing between idea and appearance. The Platonic tradition had systematized the ancient concept that a common, enduring principle is the fundamental basis for various superficial manifestations. Thus all Western thinkers to whom a symbolic doctrine was attributed or who could be understood as adherents of a Platonic philosophy could be integrated into this tradition formed by Adam and Egyptian Hermeticism. And the Aristotelian philosophy, by rejecting the Platonic doctrine of ideas and maintaining the dictum that the essence of things lies only within themselves, did not conform to the hermetic-symbolic semiosis and, accordingly, was little appreciated in the legends intended to legitimize this Hermeticism.

These legitimation legends of Hermeticism can be found in numerous books (Ebeling 2007; Law 2010). They hardly even refer to the *Corpus Hermeticum* as can be seen in the book *Kurtzer/ deutlicher und warer Unterricht/ von der geheimen und verborgenen Kunst Chymia* published by Christoph Balduff in 1609. Hermes is praised as the first philosopher to have written about alchemy. Balduff refers to the statements of classical authors on Hermes, such as Augustine and Lactantius, statements that led to the enthusiasm for the *Corpus Hermeticum* in the Italian renaissance. Nothing of this is mentioned. Balduff is only aware of the *Tabula Smaragdina* and the *Tractatus Septem de Lapide Philosophico* as authentic writings by Hermes.

Even if the majority of alchemical writings just mention these texts and ignore the *Corpus Hermeticum*, we find some remarkable books referring to both traditions. In the *Occulta Philosophia* from 1603, there is a quotation of the *Pimander* introducing the *Tabula Smaragdina*. And in one of Heinrich Khunrath's famous copperplates printed in *Amphitheatrum Sapientiae Aeternae* from 1595 and 1610 we find the

Tabula Smaragdina depicted together with a passage from the 'philosophical' *Corpus Hermeticum* and the 'alchemical' *Septem Tractatus* (Gilly 2010: 129).

ALCHEMICAL HERMETICISM BETWEEN RELIGION AND SCIENCE

Some scholars have understood alchemy as the basis for modern chemistry, with even Newton studying alchemical texts and providing a translation of the *Tabula Smaragdina* (Dobbs 1988). Indeed, the Renaissance magus, using the hidden powers of nature to bring the obscure to light, is often regarded as a prototype of the modern scientist (Westman and McGuire 1977). This corresponds to the fact that alchemical Hermeticism often claims the status of a special form of science for itself.

For a long time alchemy conformed to the scientific standards of its time, and in some instances alchemy seems even to be compatible with modern science. However, alchemical Hermeticism, which refers emphatically to Hermes, is hardly compatible with a positivistic concept of science and nature. Often it insisted on an ethical and religious foundation of their science: 'A true philosopher leaps only heavenwards, derides that which the world derides in him' (Petraeus 1730: 6). The critics were advised against 'rashly [running] into the *sacrarium naturae* or the sanctuary of alchemy with unwashed hands' (S. 3). Only those who believed in God and understood the divine essence of nature could be true philosophers. The point is that this thinking is indicative of religion, rather than that of the modern scientific worldview. Hermetic science rejected the notion that human reason alone was qualified to investigate the physical universe. Rather, in this form of alchemical Hermeticism, we find a concept of revealed knowledge which is handed down in mysteries. In a kind of spiritual-mystery the reader of the alchemical texts relies on receiving a divine revelation by studying the classical alchemical texts. These revelations will only be granted to the faithful, who will then be able to understand the books properly and be in a position to decode the symbols and enigmas. If he fails to prepare the Philosopher's Stone this will only show that he is not qualified as regards religion or intellect. The books ascribed to the old sages themselves retained the aura of undisputable truth. The 'mystery of the text' corresponds to the 'mystery of nature'. Both of them veil the essence and truth at a first glance until a proper allegorical interpretation brings the deeper structures and truth to light. For this purpose the human intellect needs to be guided by the divine spirit according to these alchemical Hermetica.

This model of revelation and reading mysteries often has a theological connotation. Due to secrecy and mysteries the salutary properties of the Philosopher's Stone are inaccessible to the selfish man. Only after leading a godly life in charity and studying the books of divine inspiration will the seeker be able to achieve all the fruits the Philosopher's Stone promises (Ebeling 2001).

The scientific revolution of the seventeenth century consisted of, among other things, change in the criteria of rationality. Impelled by an anti-authoritarianism, directed against the monopoly on interpretation exercised by church and university scholasticism, it understood the search for truth not as a question of interpretation of a tradition and its normative texts, but rather as work on nature. Observations, experiments, quantification, and mathematical interpretation, methods leading to knowledge of the laws describing natural processes, were the credo of the new science.

The study of nature was no longer the matter of reconstructing some long-forgotten knowledge but of collecting and increasing new knowledge. The idea of the 'hidden' thus lost its dignity, instead of a 'mystery of nature' that needed to be uncovered, now it was nature itself that became the object for research. This way the scientific revolution brought with it a shift of emphasis from the visible and the invisible (Meinel 1992). Surface phenomena were understood to be the objects of research, and, in documenting observations of nature, methods of classification and quantification were systematized.

This concept of science is hardly compatible with the *Ars Hermetica* described above. Hermetic researchers sought for the '*interna rerum*', the hidden effective causes of nature, and, for this purpose they believed it is necessary to penetrate the surface of natural phenomena and explore their depths. Thus they reproached the superficialities of Aristotelians.

THE DISPUTE ON THE LEGITIMACY OF THE ALCHEMICAL HERMETICISM

Through the use of philological criticism, Isaac Casaubon was able to show in 1614 that the *Corpus Hermeticum* is not an ancient text, the origins of which were lost in the mists of time, but rather a conglomerate of Christian and platonic teachings written in the first centuries (Grafton 1991). Within the academic world, Hermeticism had declined in respectability and popularity (Mulsow 2002). That said, initially, Casaubon's failure to discuss the *Tabula Smaragdina* and the alchemical Hermetica did not have much of an impact on the hermetical tradition itself. This situation, however, fundamentally changed in 1648 when Hermann Conring, a professor of medicine at Helmstedt University, published a book on the ancient hermetic medicine of the Egyptians and the new hermetic medicine of the Paracelsists. Entitled *De hermetica Aegyptiorum vetere et Paracelsicorum nova medicina liber unus*, the volume challenged the validity of alchemo-Paracelsism and its hermetic legitimation legends. Conring's aim was to investigate whether the 'school of Paracelsus' could refer to a hermetic tradition. In a source analysis of the Hermetic literature – mainly texts from classical and late classical antiquity – he concurs with Casaubon, affirming that all books that laid claim to being written by Hermes Trismegistus were forgeries. He contended that there had never been a man with this name and, moreover, that the legendary cultural innovations of the Egyptians did not amount to much. For him, the medicine of the Egyptians was pure superstition, far surpassed by that of the Greeks; the same was true of mathematics, physics and philosophy. Conring suspected that the Paracelsists were abusing the traditional esteem for Hermes Trismegistus to create prestige for their own doctrines, although Theophrast of Hohenheim and his earliest and most important adherents had never declared themselves supporters of Hermes. The similarity of ancient Egyptian and modern Paracelsian Hermeticism amounted to nothing more than self-aggrandizing and a theologically false understanding of the concept of revelation: both traditions believed that they received direct divine revelation that was being handed down through their texts. For Conring Hermeticism was the tradition of the *Corpus Hermeticum* first of all; he also mentioned the *Tabula Smaragdina* and the alchemical Hermetica, but just en passant without discussing them.

In 1674, Oluf Borch published *Hermetis Aegyptiorum et Chemicorum Sapientia* (*The Wisdom of Hermes, the Egyptians and the Chemists*) in direct opposition to Conring's invective against Paracelsism and Hermeticism. In the work, he attempts to demonstrate their superiority and dignity and affirms that the Paracelsists, in contrast to Conring's assertion, stood in a single Hermetic tradition with the Ancient Egyptians. Paracelsus and his adherents cultivated a science that was not only ancient and venerable with a direct link to Hermes Trismegistus, but also rational. Borch cited Conring's invectives, seeking to demonstrate how the latter had erred in his judgements. In Borch's effort to point out the dignity of Hermes Trismegistus, his book grew into a compendium of ancient Hermetic citations. In defending Hermeticism he did not respond to the redating of the *Corpus Hermeticum*. This lack of response is rather surprising, because, although Borch disagreed with nearly all of Conring's theses, he overlooked his adversary's detailed discussion of the *Corpus Hermeticum* (Ebeling 2007: 97–100).

This dispute between the Aristotelian and the Hermetist shows an interesting continuity between the two hermetic traditions, as well as a striking discontinuity: Conring borrowed Casaubon's critique of the *Corpus Hermeticum* and turned it against the alchemical Hermetica without discussing the texts in detail. In doing so, he treated these Hermetic traditions as one. Similarly, Borch also did not insist on the fact that the critique of the *Corpus Hermeticum* did not necessarily mean that the alchemical Hermetic texts had lost their dignity too. Each scholar was focused on a mutually distinct part of the Hermetic tradition, but both were equally focused on Hermes Trismegistus as the author of all texts ascribed to him and missed the opportunity to differentiate in order to strengthen their position.

Subsequently, Paracelsism could be identified with Hermeticism in general and all forms of Hermeticism could be regarded as parts of one tradition. The loss of reputation for the *Corpus Hermeticum* fed the anti-paracelsian and anti-hermetical polemics. The orthodox Lutheran scholar Ehrgott Daniel Colberg (1659–98) stated in *Das Platonisch-Hermetisches Christenthum* (*Platonic-Hermetic Christianity*) in 1690, that the Paracelsists, Rosicrucians, Quakers and Böhmists all appealed to Hermes Trismegistos as their spiritual father. These fanatics, he claimed, erroneously believed that Hermes was the vehicle of a primeval, Adamic wisdom. Instead, all the Hermetic books are pseudepigraphical and the hermetic legend of the Paracelsists lacks any historical substance. In his critique of the Paracelsists' image of Hermes, Colberg, along with Pierre Gassendi, relied primarily on Hermann Conring and Isaac Casaubon. The Paracelsistic texts contained no ancient Egyptian teachings but rather Platonic and Christian doctrines, combined in an illegitimate way. Colberg thought he had detected a diabolic infiltration of Christianity in the platonic-hermetic tradition.

This image of Hermeticism as a gateway for pagan and demonic teachings can also be found in the disputes over the historical foundations of pietism (Lehmann-Brauns 2004). The pietists were accused by their opponents of having adopted, together with Platonic and Hermetic doctrines, ungodly teachings from the ancient Egyptians (Bücher 1699; Bücher 1705). The pietists had little interest in the image of ancient Egypt or Hermeticism and rejected the notion that they were part of an Egyptian-Hermetic tradition. They explained that, any analogies between the hermetic teachings and pietist doctrines were the result of Joseph's teaching of ancient biblical truth to the Egyptians, who, in turn, corrupted it with idolatry and zoolatry. In the hermetic books one can find the echo of the beneficent work of Joseph in Egypt. Everything true and holy in the Hermetic writings is owed to Joseph and not to the Egyptians (Köpke 1700).

ALCHEMICAL HERMETICISM IN EIGHTEENTH-CENTURY GERMANY

During the seventeenth century Hermeticism and its eponymous founder lost much of their prestige. In fact, in the eighteenth century even the disputes formerly carried out cease to take place.

In Zedler's *Universallexikon* Hermes Trismegistos is regarded as nothing more than a legend and the texts ascribed to him as pseudepigraphical (Zedler 1735: 1736). Although no longer meeting the scientific standards of the time, the '*Ars Hermetica*' continued to enjoy enormous publishing success in the eighteenth century. Jean-Jacques Magnet's *Bibliotheca Chemica Curiosa* from 1702, Friedrich Roth-Scholtz's *Deutsches theatrum chemicum* from 1728–30, and the *Hermetisches A.B.C. derer ächten Weisen alter und neuer Zeiten vom Stein der Weisen* from 1778 included much alchemical Hermetica and cultivated the image of Hermes as a primordial Egyptian sage. In the circles of the readers of these books, Conring's and Casaubon's criticism was ignored. However, few new hermetic books were published, so the image of Hermes remained as portrayed in the older writings.

A further amalgamation of the two hermetic traditions took place in the first German edition of the *Corpus Hermeticum*, printed in 1706. Referring to Oluf Borch, Hermes is praised in the preface as the legendary Egyptian sage and the *Tabula Smaragdina* is printed as a part of the preface to the *Corpus Hermeticum* (Alethophilo 1706). Nevertheless, the hermetic tradition focused on the *Corpus Hermeticum* and that focused on the *Tabula Smaragdina* were not merged entirely. The reception of alchemical Hermeticism had a further peak with the Gold- and Rosicrucians (McIntosh 2011; Geffarth 2007).

Of the twelve addresses published in *Freymäurerische Versammlungsreden der Gold-und Rosenkreuzer des alten Systems (Freemasonic Addresses to the Assembly of the Gold- and Rosicrucians of the Ancient System)* in 1779, the ninth is devoted to Hermes Trismegistos: 'Address to the assembled brothers regarding the Hermetic philosophy, its antiquity, excellence, and usefulness.' The address is introduced by a poem by Otto Tachenius alias Crassellame, a seventeenth-century alchemist, praising the 'divine Hermes' as the author of the *Tabula Smaragdina* and the founder of alchemy.

The image of Hermes in this book is a traditional one. He is acclaimed as the rescuer of the primeval and symbolic hidden knowledge, whose overwhelming importance could be seen in his *Tabula Smaragdina*, the only authentically hermetic writing, because it is in perfect congruence with the natural philosophy of the patriarchs. The Greeks betrayed this hermetic and biblical wisdom because they did not conceptualize the world as God's creation. In contrast to the older tradition a clear distinction is made between Hermeticism and Platonism to make the alchemical Hermeticism consistent with the theology and philosophy of biblical creation.

In the name of Hermes these freemasons understood themselves in this account to be a part of a long chain, one that passed along revealed knowledge and combatted emanationist, deistic and atheistic tendencies which were associated in this time with Neoplatonism. They rejected the concept of the Enlightenment of autonomous reason.

Soon after, another book articulating a similar concept of Hermeticism was published by the community of Gold und Rosenkreuzer (Golden and Rosy Cross). The *Compaß der Weisen* (Birkholz 1779) discusses three sages named Hermes (see above). The author recommends the engagement with the triad of mercury (quicksilver), salt, and sulphur (S. 17). This Paracelsist doctrine of three principles is regarded as the ideal path to the understanding of the self, nature and God. Again the *Tabula Smaragdina* is mentioned as an example of this hermetic philosophy, but not the *Corpus Hermeticum*.

Hermeticism is thus understood as a synonym for alchemy or the paracelsian medicine. In the era of the Enlightenment, the concept of a divine, immutable philosophy also clearly assumed characteristics of counter-Enlightenment. In the name of Hermes, some members of the Gold und Rosenkreuzer tried to shield themselves from the challenges of the modern period, from the emancipatory concepts of religion, reason, and science.

In his influential history of freemasonry, James Anderson referred to Egypt, but not to Hermes (Anderson 1723, 5f.). How difficult it was for the members of the Gold und Rosenkreuzer to maintain their position between the values of Enlightenment and Hermeticism is evident in the case of the Lodge of the 'Afrikanische Bauherren' (Gerlach 1996). Karl Friedrich Köppen (1734–97), the *spiritus rector* and author of the legitimation legend, interpreted the lodge as the true heir to the Rosicrucians of the seventeenth century and tried to reject the claim of the Gold und Rosenkreuzer (Köppen s.l.). Although he affiliated the lodge to the ancient Egyptians, Köppen simply mentioned Thoth as the founder, but not Hermes Trismegistos, thereby attempting to avoid any association with Hermeticism (Ebeling 2011). In other words, Köppen sought to establish a lodge, which was, on the one hand, related to ancient Egypt and spiritual alchemy and, on the other hand, drew on aspects of Enlightenment thinking. Hence, at this point it seems clear that Hermeticism was considered a tradition to avoid – possibly because it was too closely connected with reactionary freemasonry and counter-rationalist tendencies.

TRANSFORMATIONS AND TRANSITIONS

At the end of the eighteenth century Hermeticism appeared within the literary motive of the 'Egyptian mysteries'. Christoph Martin Wieland (1733–1813) satirized the belief in magic and supernatural powers in his fairy tale *The Philosopher's Stone* (Assmann and Ebeling 2011, 141–61). In this story the mysterious Misfragmutosiris introduces himself as the 'heir to the great Trismegistus' and states that he was introduced a thousand years ago within the great Pyramid in Memphis into the highest degree of the hermetic order. With this hermetic knowledge he is able to prepare the Philosopher's Stone, but at the end of the story he turns out to be a fraud who cunningly utilized the desire of man for eternal health and riches.

With this story Wieland alluded to the notorious fraud Giuseppe Balsamo who, under the pseudonym Cagliostro (1743–95), used the aura of Hermeticism for self-dramatization. He was revered as a sage, alchemist and faith healer who generously helped the poor and had a special relationship to divinity. Using this mystical reputation he instituted the 'Rite de la Haute Maçonnerie Egyptienne' (Assmann and Ebeling 2011: 147–54).

Although Hermeticism was widely discredited during Enlightenment it had a revival within the Romantic movement. Karl von Eckartshausen (1752–1803) referred to Egypt as the homeland of mystical theosophy and to Hermes as the sage experienced in the occult sciences and having lived long before Moses. Later in the nineteenth century, Egypt and Hermeticism had another success story in the 'rite of Memphis-Misraim', the 'Theosophical society' or the 'Hermetic Order of the Golden Dawn'.

This esoteric imaginary which referred to Egypt and Hermeticism became wholly isolated from mainstream scholarly activity. In 1822, Champollion succeeded in deciphering the hieroglyphs and, gradually, throughout the nineteenth century Egyptology emerged as an academic discipline. As Egyptologists found no hermetic teachings in hieroglyphic texts, the study of Hermeticism became the preserve of classical philology and the history of religion. Despite this detachment from Egyptology and the undermining of many of its presuppositions, it has continued within the belief systems of many people with a penchant for ancient wisdom and the occult.

REFERENCES AND FURTHER READING

Alethophilo [ps.] (ed) (1706) *Hermetis Trismegisti Erkäntnüß der Natur und des darin sich offenbarenden Gottes*, Hamburg: Heyl und Liebezeit.

Alt, Peter-André and Wels, Volkhard (2010) *Konzepte des Hermetismus in der Literatur der Frühen Neuzeit*, Göttingen V&R unipress.

Anderson, James (1723) *The Constitutions of the Free-Masons. Containing the History, Charges, Regulations etc. of the most Ancient and Right Worshipful Fraternity. For the Use of the Lodges*, London: Senex.

Anonymus (1603) Apocalypsis Hermetis ab illustrissimo viro, Aureolo Helvetico, qui fuit Hermes Secundus, in Paracelsus *Opera* II, Straßburg: Zetzner, 668–71.

Assmann, Jan (2003) 'Antike Äußerungen zur ägyptischen Schrift' in Aleida Assmann and Jan Assmann (eds) *Hieroglyphen, Stationen einer anderen abendländischen Grammatologie*, 27–35, München: Fink.

Assmann, Jan and Ebeling, Florian (2011) Ägyptische Mysterien. *Reisen in die Unterwelt in Aufklärung und Romantik*, München: C. H. Beck.

Balduff, Christoph (1610) Kurtzer/ deutlicher und warer Unterricht/ von der geheimten und verborgenen Kunst Chymia, in Joachim Tancke, *Promptuarium Alchemiae*, Leipzig: Groß.

Borch, Oluf (1674) *Hermetis Aegyptiorum et Chemicorum Sapientia*, Copenhagen: Haubold.

Bücher, Christian Friedrich (1699) *Plato Mysticus In Pietista redivivus, Das ist: Pietistische Uebereinstimmung mit der Heydnischen Philosophia Platonis Und seiner Nachfolger*, Danzig: Reiniger.

——(1705–6), *Menses pietistici, die Tieffe des Sathans in dem Hermetisch-Zoroastrisch-Pythagorisch-Platonisch-Cabbalistischen Christentum der Pietisten*, Wittenberg: Ludwig.

Burnett, Charles S. F. (1976) 'The legend of the three Hermes and Abu Ma'shar's Kitab Al-Uluf in the Latin Middle-Ages', *Journal of the Warburg and Courtauld Institutes* XXXIX, 231–34.

Colberg, Ehrgott Daniel (1690) *Das Platonisch-Hermetisches Christenthum, begreiffend die historische Erzehlung vom Ursprung und vielerley Secten der heutigen fanatischen*

Theologie, unterm Namen der Paracelsisten, Weigelianer, Rosencreutzer, Quäcker, Böhmisten, Wiedertäuffer, Bourignisten, Labadisten und Qietisten, Erfurt: Weidmann und Köhler.

Conring, Hermann (1648) *De hermetica Aegyptiorum vetere et Paracelsicorum nova medicina*, Helmstedt: Muller.

Dobbs, Betty Jo Teeter (1988) 'Newton's Commentary on the Emerald Tablet of Hermes Trismegistus' in Ingrid Merkel and Allen G. Debus (eds) *Hermeticism and the Renaissance*, 182–91, Washington: Folger.

[Ecker und Eckhoffen, Hans Heinrich Freiherr von] (1779) *Freymäurerische Versammlungsreden der Gold- und Rosenkreuzer des alten Systems*, Amsterdam [i.e. Hof].

Ebeling, Florian (2001) '"Geheimnis" und "Geheimhaltung" in den Hermetica der Frühen Neuzeit' in: Ann-Charlott Trepp and Hartmut Lehmann (ed) *Antike Weisheit und kulturelle Praxis. Hermetismus in der Frühen Neuzeit*, 63–80, Göttingen V&R.

——(2007) *The secret history of Hermes Trismegistus; Hermeticism from Ancient to Modern Times*. Ithaca: Cornell UP.

——(2011) 'Zum Hermetismus in der Freimaurerei des 18. Jahrhunderts' *Quatuor Coronati Jahrbuch für Freimaurerforschung* XLVIII, 55–71.

Festugière, André-Jean (1944–54) *La révélation d'Hermès Trismégiste* (4 volumes), Paris: Les Belles Lettres.

Figulus, Benedictus (ed.) (1608) *Apocalypsis Des Hocherleuchten Aegyptischen Königs und Philosophi, Hermetis Trismegisti; von unserm Teutschen Hermete, dem Edlen, Hochthewren Monarchen und Philosopho Trismegisto, A[ureolo] Ph[ilippo] Theophrasto Paracelso [...] Verdolmetschet*, Straßburg: Zetzener.

Flasch, Kurt (2011) *Was ist Gott? Das Buch der 24 Philosophen*, München: C.H. Beck.

Fowden, Garth (1986) *The Egyptian Hermes. A Historical Approach to the Late Pagan Mind*, Cambridge: Cambridge University Press.

Geffarth, Renko D. (2007) *Religion und arkane Hierarchie: der Orden der Gold-und Rosenkreuzer als geheime Kirche im 18. Jahrhundert*, Leiden: Brill.

Gerlach, Karlheinz (1996) 'Die Afrikanischen Bauherren. Die Bauherrenloge der Verschwiegenheit der Freunde freier Künste und schönen Wissenschaften 1765–75 in Berlin', *Quatuor Coronati Jahrbuch* XXXIII, 61–90.

Gilly, Carlos (2010) 'Vom ägyptischen Hermes zum Trismegistus Germanus. Wandlungen des Hermetismus in der paracelsistischen und rosenkreuzerischen Literatur' (Alt and Wels 2010) 71–131.

Grafton, Anthony (1991) 'Protestant versus Prophet: Isaac Casaubon on Hermes Trismegistus' in Anthony Grafton, *Defenders of the Text. The tradition of scholarship in an age of science, 1450–1800*, 145–61.

Hanegraaff, Wouter Jacubus (ed) (2006) *Dictionary of Gnosis & Western Esotericism*, Leiden: Brill.

Hannak, Kristine (2010) 'Pymander als inneres Wort. Sebastian Francks Übersetzung des "Corpus Hermeticum" in der Tradition mittelalterlicher Logos-Mystik' (Alt and Wels 2010) 297–322.

Heiduk, Matthias (2010) 'Gewachsene Tradition' in Andreas B. Kilcher, *Construction Tradition. Means and Myths of Transmission in Western Esotericism*, Leiden: Brill, 47–70.

Ketmia Vere [i.e. Adam Michael Birkholz] (1779) *Der Compaß der Weisen, von einem Mitverwandten der innern Verfassung der ächten und rechten Freymäurerey beschrieben [...] in welcher die Geschichte dieses erlauchten Ordens, von Anfang seiner Stiftung an, deutlich, und treulich vorgetragen*, Berlin: Ringmacher.

Köpke, Balthasar (1700) *Sapientia Dei in Mysterio Crucis Christi Abscondita. Die wahre Theologia Mystica oder Ascetica. [...] Entgegen gesetzt der falschen aus der heydnischen Philosophia Platonis und seiner Nachfolger*, Halle: Wäyser-Haus.

Köppen, Karl Friedrich (s.a.), *Geschichte des Ordens nach dem afrikanischen System* (s.l.)

Kühlmann, Wilhelm and Telle, Joachim (2001–4) *Corpus Paracelsisticum. Dokumente frühneuzeitlicher Naturphilosophie in Deutschland*. Tübingen: Niemeyer.

Law, Esteban (2010) 'Die Hermetische Tradition' (Alt and Wels 2010) 23–70.

Lehmann-Brauns, Sicco (2004) *Weisheit in der Weltgeschichte. Philosophiegeschichte zwschen Barock und Aufklärung*, Tübingen: Niemeyer.

Leinkauf, Thomas (1993) *Mundus Combinatus. Studien zur Struktur der barocken Universalwissenschaft am Beispiel Athanasius Kirchers SJ (1602–1680)*, Berlin: Akademie Verlag.

——(2001) 'Interpretation und Analogie. Rationale Strukturen im Hermetismus der Frühen Neuzeit', (Trepp and Lehmann 2001), 41–61, Göttingen V&R.

Linden, Stanton J. (2010) *The Alchemy Reader*, Cambridge: Cambridge University Press

Lucentini, Paolo and Compagni, Vittoria Perrone (2006) 'Hermetic Literature II, Latin Middle Ages' (Hanegraaff 2006) 499–529.

McIntosh, Christopher (2011) *The Rose Cross and the Age of Reason*, New York: SUNY Press.

Meier-Oeser, Stephan (2001) 'Die hermetisch-platonische Naturphilosophie' in: Helmut Holzhey (ed.) *Grundriss der Geschichte der Philosophie. Die Philosophie des 17. Jahrhunderts. Band 4: Das Heilige Römische Reich Deutscher Nation. Nord-und Ostmitteleuropa*. Basel: Schwabe.

Mulsow, Martin (2002) *Das Ende des Hermetismus. Historische Kritik und neue Naturphilosophie in der Spätrenaissance*, Tübingen: Mohr Siebeck.

Meinel, Christoph (1992) 'Okkulte und exakte Wissenschaften' in: August Buck (ed) *Die occulten Wissenschaften in der Renaissance*, 21–43, Wiesbaden Harrassowitz.

[Paracelsus, presumably wrongly attributed] (1570) De Tinctura Physicorum in: Paracelus *Archidoxa*, Straßburg: Riehel.

[Paracelsus, presumably wrongly attributed] (1577) *Aurora thesaurusque philosophorum*, Basel 1577

Petraeus, Benedictus Nicolaus (1730) Critique über die Alchymistischen Schriften/ Und deren Scribenten/ ihren neuen Projections-Historien, wie auch von der Materia Prima Philosophica und andern Dingen mehr, handelnd; in Friedrich Roth-Scholtz: *Deutsches Theatrum Chemicum II*, Nürnberg: Felßecker.

Redl, Philipp (2008) 'Aurora Philosophorum. Zur Überlieferung eines pseudo-paracelsischen Textes aus dem 16. Jahrhundert', *Daphnis* XXXVII, 689–712.

Reimmann, Jacob Friederich (1709) *Versuch einer Einleitung in die Historiam literariam derer Teutschen, vol. 3,1*, Halle: Renger.

Ruska, Julius (1924) *Rabische Alchemisten I*. Heidelberg: Winter.

——(1926) *Tabula Smaragdina. Ein Beitrag zur Geschichte der hermetischen Literatur*. Heidelberg: Winter.

Schmidt-Biggemann, Wilhelm (2004) *Philosophia perennis: Historical Outlines of Western Spirituality in Ancient, Medieval and Early Modern Thought*, Dordrecht: Springer.

Schönberger, Rolf (2011) *Repertorium edierter Texte des Mittelalters aus dem Bereich der Philosophie und angrenzender Gebiete*, Berlin: Akademie-Verlag.

Speyer, Wolfgang (1970) *Bücherfunde in der Glaubenswerbung der Antike*. Göttingen V&R.

Stolzenberg, Daniel (2013) *Egyptian Oedipus: Athanasius Kircher and the secrets of Antiquity*. Chicago: Chicago University Press.

Telle, Joachim (1978) 'Alchemie' *TRE* II, 199–227, Berlin de Gruyter.

——(1987) 'Benedictus Figulus. Zu Leben und Werk eines deutschen Paracelsisten' *Medizinhistorisches Journal* XXII, 303–26.

——(1995) 'Tabula Smaragdina', in Burghart Wachinger (ed), *Die deutsche Literatur des Mittelalters: Verfasserlexikon. Bd. 9*, Berlin: de Gruyter.

van Bladel, Kevin (2009) *The Arabic Hermes. From Pagan Sage to Prophet of Science*, Oxford: Oxford University Press.

Weisser, Ursula (1980) *Das 'Buch über das Geheimnis der Schöpfung' von Pseudo-Apollonius von Tyana*, Berlin: de Gruyter.

Westman, Robert S. and McGuire, James E. (1977) *Hermeticism and the Scientific Revolution.* Los Angeles: University of California.

Zedler, Johann Heinrich (ed) (1735) *Universal Lexikon, vol. 35*, Halle und Leipzig: Zedler.

CHAPTER FIVE

HEINRICH CORNELIUS AGRIPPA

Wouter J. Hanegraaff

In the opening scene of Johann Wolfgang von Goethe's *Faust* tragedy, we meet a scholar in despair. The aging Johannes Faust has spent his life studying philosophy, law, medicine, 'and theology too, unfortunately' – but sitting now in his study surrounded by dusty books, he must admit that it has been all in vain. None of the human arts and sciences has brought him the knowledge and certainty he has been looking for. 'So now there I stand, poor fool that I am – still as ignorant as before.' Finally, as a last resort, he decides to try magic, hoping that perhaps some spirit may reveal to him the secrets of existence: 'that I may learn the innermost power that holds the world together, behold its active powers and seeds, and no longer need to babble mere words.' He proceeds to evoke the Spirit of the Earth, but with doubtful result: the spirit does appear, but treats him as an ignorant earthworm and departs in contempt. Eventually, however, there comes an answer to Faust's desperate attempts at contacting the mysterious realm of the occult. During a walk through the fields he is approached by a black poodle who follows him back to his study, where he transforms into his true shape: Mephistopheles, the Devil, who proceeds to offer Faust what he wants in return for his soul.

Among the most obvious models that were used by Goethe to create his Faust figure is the German Humanist intellectual Heinrich Cornelius Agrippa (1486–1535/36). Agrippa's *On the Uncertainty and Vanity of the Human Arts and Sciences, and the excellence of God's Word* (1529) is a work of thorough philosophical scepticism about the vain pretences of mere human scholarship and learning: as Goethe's Faust discovers, after a lifetime of study, none of it can give us true certainty and knowledge. But Agrippa is most famous for his other major work, his *summa* of all the traditional magical arts known as *Three Books of Occult Philosophy* (1533): could it be – as Faust hopes – that where mere book-learning fails, magic can provide the answers? In fact, Agrippa did not consider his three books on Occult Philosophy as a reaction or an antidote to the intellectual scepticism of his previous work, as some later commentators have assumed; but they certainly established his doubtful reputation of a master of magic who might well be in league with the Devil. Agrippa actually owned a dog, a black poodle whom he fondly named *Monsieur*, and already during his lifetime this gave rise to rumours that his closest companion was a familiar, a demon in animal shape.

Clearly, then, the Agrippa of the imagination must be distinguished from the real Agrippa. If the latter is the object of properly historical research, the former belongs to the domain of mnemohistory, that is to say, the history of how we *remember* the past. Mnemohistorical narratives are subject to continuous change and are often factually incorrect – entire generations have 'remembered' Agrippa as a black magician in league with the Devil – but their power can be so overwhelming as to make us lose sight entirely of the historical figures hidden behind the screen of our collective imagination. In the rest of this contribution we will try to dispel the myth as best as we can: who was the real Agrippa?

He was born in Nettesheim, near Cologne, in a family belonging to the middle nobility. From 1499 on he studied a humanist curriculum, first in Cologne and then in Paris, after which he embarked on years of travel and adventures of all kinds. During his early life Agrippa served in the army of the Holy Roman Emperor Maximilian I, but he kept studying and in 1509 gave his first academic lectures, at the University of Dôle in Burgundy. His topic was the first large book by Johannes Reuchlin, the great authority of Christian kabbalah. In this important work, *De verbo mirifico* (*The Word that Creates Wonders*, 1494), Reuchlin divided the 'miraculous arts' of the occult into three categories: physical practices concerned with the sublunar world; celestial and mathematical practices (especially number symbolism and astrology) concerned with the world above the sphere of the moon but below the fixed stars; and religious or ceremonial practices concerned with demonic, angelic, and divine realities above the stars. Reuchlin used the term magic (*magia*) only for this third and highest level, and added a subdivision of superstitious *goetia* and religious *theurgia*. Henceforth, Agrippa would adopt the same scheme, but he decided to use *magia* as the umbrella term for all three levels or 'worlds'. Right afterwards, in the winter of 1509–10, Agrippa visited the Abbot Johannes Trithemius, a famous authority on cryptography and demonology. The two men seem to have agreed that it was time to restore the ancient reputation of magic as a divine art, and Agrippa set himself to the task of making the argument. In the same year 1510, he produced the first draft (still in only one volume) of *De occulta philosophia*, dedicated to Trithemius. It remained unpublished for the time being.

From 1511 to 1518 Agrippa lived in Italy, the homeland of Renaissance culture, where famous authors such as Marsilio Ficino and Giovanni Pico della Mirandola had created an intellectual revolution grounded in what may be called 'Platonic Orientalism'. This modern term refers to the widespread conviction that Plato and the later Platonists represented an extremely ancient tradition of supreme spiritual (and not just rational–philosophical) wisdom that had originated not in Greece but somewhere in the Orient. Like his predecessor in this regard, the Byzantine philosopher Gemistos Plethon, Ficino himself thought that the ancient wisdom tradition had originated in Persia with Zoroaster, the chief of the *magi* and supposed author of the mysterious *Chaldaean Oracles*. Giovanni Pico della Mirandola had a different opinion: the supreme wisdom could not have originated with a pagan sage such as Zoroaster but must be found among the Hebrews. He claimed that at Mount Sinai, Moses himself had received not just the Tables of the Law, but also a secret revelation intended for the priestly elites. This tradition was known as the Kabbalah, had been preserved by the Jews, and had now been rediscovered by Pico himself, who claimed that its basic tenets came directly from God himself and therefore had to be Christian in essence. But next to these 'Zoroastrian' and 'Mosaic' interpretations of Platonic Orientalism, there was yet a third option, which pointed to the legendary Egyptian sage Hermes Trismegistus as the ultimate source of wisdom. The most explicit exponent of this third, 'Hermetic' variant was a little known Italian humanist and poet, Lodovico Lazzarelli. Next to the Bible, his basic reference was a collection of Greek texts known today as the *Corpus Hermeticum*, fourteen of which had been translated into Latin by Ficino (first published in 1471) while three additional ones had been translated by Lazzarelli himself (first published by Symphorien Champier in 1507).

These backgrounds are crucial for understanding Agrippa's lifelong project of restoring the 'occult philosophy' grounded in the ancient 'magical' disciplines. In 1515 he was lecturing in Pavia, about Ficino's famous *Pimander* (his 1471 translation of *Corpus Hermeticum* I-XIV, named after the divine figure Poimandres who appears in *Corpus Hermeticum* I); and although the lectures themselves are lost, we still have Agrippa's Introduction. One year later, in 1516, he wrote a dialogue *On Man* (*De homine*), only the first part of which has been preserved, and, finally, a complete text known as *On the Three Ways of Knowing God* (*De triplici ratione cognoscendi Deum*). All these texts are permeated with references not just to the Hermetic writings, but, more specifically, to Lazzarelli's ideas about the profound unity and harmony between Hermetism and Christian faith. Agrippa knew Ficino's *Pimander*, of course, but the truth is that this famous translation is not very helpful if one wishes to understand the religious message of the Hermetica: Ficino simply does not seem to have understood it all too well, and therefore it must have been puzzling to Agrippa as well. Lazzarelli, however, did understand what the *Corpus Hermeticum* was all about, probably better than anyone of his generation. Next to his translation of the final three treatises, he had written a beautiful neo-Hermetic dialogue known as the *Crater Hermetis* (*The Mixing-Bowl of Hermes*), and this text leaves no doubt about Lazzarelli's profound knowledge and understanding of the message of spiritual salvation that is central to Hermetic writings. It was published for the first time in an abridged version by the French Humanist Jacques Lefèvre d'Étaples in 1505, and this is how Agrippa knew about it.

Lazzarelli's *Crater Hermetis*, in Lefèvre's 1505 edition, may well be the key to Agrippa's worldview. His Italian writings, listed above, show that he read the Hermetica entirely through a Lazzarellian lens; and when his *Three Books of Occult Philosophy* were published almost two decades later, they still contained the same essential message. At first sight though, it might seem as though this famous work is little more than an erudite but derivative compendium of traditional 'magical' lore. Its overall framework is the classic Aristotelean cosmos, with the earth at the center, the moon and the other planets circling around it, and the stars and constellations fixed on the interior side of the cosmic sphere. Beyond that sphere are the angels and divine realities. Since the four elements that constitute the earth are supposed to be inert, the active powers responsible for movement and life must come from above; and hence it is entirely logical to assume that higher powers or virtues from the stars or even higher entities can be 'drawn down' by means of magical techniques, such as invocations or the use of amulets and talismans. Essentially, what Agrippa is doing in his *Three Books of Occult Philosophy* is going through all the levels and realities that exist in the cosmos, while discussing in considerable detail what the ancient authorities tell us about their nature and powers. He does so by starting down below in our world of the four elements, and working his way upwards to the world of the angels and God himself. This procedure is chosen not just for didactic reasons but has a spiritual dimension as well: the downward movement of 'magical' powers or virtues that can be attracted from above finds its complement in a 'mystical' upward movement through which the human soul distances itself from the world of matter and the senses and draws ever closer to its divine origin.

So, how did we get separated from that origin in the first place? For both Lazzarelli and Agrippa the answer was obvious. It was because of the Fall of Man as narrated in Genesis. In itself this opinion may sound traditional enough, but under the direct influence of Lazzarelli's *Crater Hermetis*, Agrippa went far beyond current theological views in highlighting the original *divinity* of prelapsarian man. Before the Fall, man was literally (and not just metaphorically) the image of God himself. As a perfect microsmic reflection of the macrosm, he embraced in his own being the full plenitude of all natures and substances that exist in the whole universe. Although his body was made of 'discordant and contrary elements', making it mortal at least in theory, God had made sure that it would never have to fall apart: it was inhabited by the divine light itself, which continually 'imposed peace upon the elements' (that is to say, kept them in a state of harmony and balance) and thereby insured eternal life. But all of that changed due to man's transgression, which in Agrippa's view consisted quite literally in the sexual act. Offended by this carnal behaviour, the divine light withdrew, the harmony was disrupted, and the body became subject to illnesses and decay, finally leading to death. Echoeing Lazzarelli's formulations, Agrippa says quite literally that 'because he embraced the body' man fell 'from the luminous sphere of contemplation into the sphere of carnal lust and darkness'.

So this is why we find ourselves living in mortal bodies in a material world, forgetful of our original divinity and immortality. It all happened because man chose the path of 'carnal generation', that is to say, sexual reproduction. The tragedy, according to both Lazzarelli and Agrippa, is that he thereby lost his divine powers of *spiritual* generation, a superior alternative to sexual reproduction that results in the creation not of bodies but of *souls*. And this, they claim, is precisely what the process of spiritual ascent is all about. While human beings are capable of 'drawing down' divine virtues on all levels of the cosmos, their ultimate goal must be, rather, to 'rise up' from the things of the body to the things of the spirit, thereby reversing the effects of the Fall and regaining their original status as divine beings who will be 'procreating for God and not for themselves'. The underlying idea is that only God can create souls, and therefore if human beings gain that ability, this proves they have become re-united with their divine essence. Once having done so, they have in fact gained unlimited 'superpowers': they are gods capable of creating new gods, and there is literally nothing they cannot accomplish. This perspective is central to Agrippa's third book of Occult Philosophy, but he must have been well aware that such an extreme doctrine of human *deification* was quite problematic from orthodox theological perspectives. He therefore presents it in a rather enigmatic fashion that is hard to understand unless one can read the 'coded' references to Lazzarelli's Christian–Hermetic message of divine/spiritual versus merely human/sexual 'generation' (reproduction). He begins with a hymn that is copy-pasted from Lazzarelli's *Crater Hermetis* (in Lefèvre's edition) and then moves into a prose passage by Agrippa himself:

> Therefore the Begetter [i.e. God] gave man a mind quite like his own, and speech, that, having also been given consciousness, he would bring forth gods that are truly like gods....They overcome the trials of fate and chase away destructive illness, they give prophetic dreams, they offer help in man's need, they punish the godless, and splendidly reward the pious. Thus they fulfill the command of God the Father. These are the disciples, these are the sons of God who are born not from the will of the flesh, nor from the will of a man or of a menstruating woman, but from God. But it is a literal generation in which the son is like the father in all manner of similitude, and in which the begotten is the same in species as the begetter. And this is the power, given form by the mind, of the Word rightly received in a well-disposed subject, like semen in the womb for generation and giving birth....And these things belong to the most recondite secrets of nature, which should not be publicly discussed any further.

In short, Agrippa here lifts a tip of the veil that covers his true doctrine, but suggests that these are deep secrets that can be understood only by a spiritual elite.

It will not come as a surprise, then, that most people with whom Agrippa came into contact failed to understand his true intentions, to his increasing frustration. A typical example of the wandering Renaissance intellectual – a model, next to similar figures such as Paracelsus, for Marguerite Yourcenar's famous novel *L'oeuvre au noir* – Agrippa essentially spent his whole life looking for wealthy patrons, but never with lasting success. At the time when he started out as a university lecturer in Dôle in 1509 (see above) he tried to win the favour of Margaret of Austria with a text *On the Nobility and Preeminence of the Female Sex* that has earned him the reputation of an early feminist (among other things, he blames Adam and not Eve for eating the apple in paradise and causing the Fall). Due to attacks by the Franciscan prior Jean Catilinet, who accused him of Judaizing heresy, he was forced to leave Dôle, and eventually ended up in London, where he wrote a work on Reuchlin to defend himself against Catilinet and prove that learning from the Jews does not invalidate one's Christian commitments. In London, he began studying the Epistles of St. Paul, which became an important influence on his subsequent thought; and after a stay in his home-town Cologne he went on to Italy, where he absorbed much of the new Platonic, Hermetic, and Christian-kabbalistic culture. He lectured at the university of Pavia, on Plato's *Symposium* as well as Ficino's *Pimander*, as we have seen; and having married his first (Italian) wife, he enjoyed one of the happiest periods of his life here. When the French armies invaded the area in 1515, Agrippa was forced to leave and move on to Casale. Here he wrote his treatise on *The Three Ways of Knowing God*, which is extremely critical of scholastic philosophy and highlights faith rather than reason as the exclusive way to attaining certain knowledge: a conviction that would remain a red thread in his thinking, culminating in his great book on the uncertainty and vanity of all human knowledge. His last lectures in a university context were given in Turin in 1516, about the Epistles of Paul.

In 1518 we find Agrippa in Metz, working as a public advocate and defense lawyer. At this time he was following the arguments of the Reformers with great interest and much sympathy, but would never make the step of converting to the new faith. It is in this same year that he published his text *On Original Sin*, with the claim that it had consisted in the sexual act. Still in Metz, he showed considerable courage (especially given his known interest in the occult philosophy) by defending a woman accused of witchcraft. While he succeeded in saving her life, his conflicts with the Dominican authorities forced him to leave the city and move back to Cologne with his wife and child. His wife died during their travel to Geneva, where Agrippa found work as a physician and remarried just a few months later, with a woman who would bear him six further children. Having moved on to Fribourg in 1523, Agrippa continued his medical practice; but one year later he made the mistake of accepting a position of physician to Louise of Savoy, Queen Mother of France, in Lyon. To his disappointment, the queen made him write astrological prognostications but refused to pay his salary, and her courtiers were making fun of Agrippa behind his back. His humiliating experiences in Lyon, next to the fact that his wife was suffering from illness, seem to have contributed to the pessimist outlook in his great book of scepticism *On the Uncertainty and Vanity*, finished in 1526 and first published in 1529.

Things began to look better for Agrippa in 1528, when he found employment in Antwerp as advisor and historiographer of Margaret of Austria. Here he also attracted more and more students, including Johannes Weyer (Wier), who would later become famous through his pioneering witchcraft tract *On the Tricks of Demons* (1563). During the period of relative quiet and happiness, Agrippa was able to devote himself to studying the ancient sciences, and in 1529 he published a collection of theological writings, later expanded with texts on such topics as monasticism and relics. That same year, however, the plague hit Antwerp, killing his wife and causing the official town physicians to flee the city. Again showing considerable courage, Agrippa stayed to care for the sick – only to be accused of unlicensed practice by his colleagues after the plague was over! Even more problematic for Agrippa, his sponsor Margaret of Austria was suspicious of *On the Uncertainty and Vanity* and ordered it to be evaluated by the Theological Faculty of Louvain; the Emperor Charles V was warned against it by his brother Ferdinand; and it was attacked by the theologians of the Sorbonne as well. All this hostility endangered Agrippa's position at the court. He was no longer paid, and he spent a brief time in prison for debt in 1531. Agrippa's first book *On Occult Philosophy* was finally published in the same year, and evoked considerable hostility as well; the complete *Three Books of Occult Philosophy* finally appeared in 1533, just two years before his death. Agrippa's final years seem to have been difficult. He married for the third time, but his wife betrayed him; he was briefly imprisoned by King Francis in Lyon; and he died while traveling to Grenoble.

What can we conclude from the above? The Agrippa of history was a devout Christian, who sincerely believed in the compatibility of the biblical revelation and Hermetic wisdom, saw faith in Jesus Christ as the only way towards true and certain knowledge, and defended an inclusive understanding of Christianity as the culmination of an ancient wisdom tradition inspired by the divine Logos and originating in very ancient times. The Agrippa of mnemohistory, however, looks quite different: already during his lifetime he was suspected and accused of heterodoxy and trafficking with demons, and this is how later generations have mainly perceived him. His reputation of a black magician in league with the Devil was strongly enhanced by the publication in mid-century of a spurious *Fourth Book of Occult Philosophy*. It is fair to say that while countless authors with occult interests have plundered his *Three Books of Occult Philosophy* for useful information about the magical arts and related topics – perhaps the most notorious example being Francis Barrett's extensive plagiarisms in his volume *The Magus* (1801), a major influence on the occult revival of the nineteenth century, very few of them have understood his actual beliefs or shown any real interest in them. In this sense, it must be said that the history of the reception and appropriation of Agrippa's works dwarfs the history of his influence.

REFERENCES AND FURTHER READING

Hanegraaff, W.J. (2009) 'Better than Magic: Cornelius Agrippa and Lazzarellian Hermetism', *Magic, Ritual, and Witchcraft* 4:1, 1–25.

Lehrich, Christopher (2003) *The Language of Demons and Angels: Cornelius Agrippa's Occult Philosophy*, Leiden/Boston: Brill.

Nauert, C.G. (1965) *Agrippa and the Crisis of Renaissance Thought*, Urbana: University of Illinois Press.

Poel, M. van der (1997) *Cornelius Agrippa: The Humanist Theologian and his Declamations*, Leiden/Boston: Brill.

Prost, A. (1882) *Corneille Agrippa: Sa Vie et ses Oeuvres*, Paris: Champion; facs. Reprint Cambridge University Press 2011.

Valente, M. (2005) 'Agrippa, Heinrich Cornelius', in W.J. Hanegraaff (ed.) in collaboration with Antoine Faivre, Roelof van den Broek, and Jean-Pierre Brach, *Dictionary of Gnosis and Western Esotericism*, Leiden/Boston: Brill, 4–8.

CHAPTER SIX

PARACELSUS

Andrew Weeks

Born Theophrastus Bombastus von Hohenheim in 1493 or early 1494 in Einsiedeln, Switzerland, to a physician father from Southwestern Germany and a Swiss mother of plebeian descent, raised in Carynthia, Austria, schooled in monastic circles, and educated in medicine at the University of Ferrara, the author we know as Paracelsus professes to have spent early adult years wandering through Europe as a military surgeon or itinerant physician, thereby acquiring the knowledge and critical view of tradition embodied in his work. His career as a writer begins, as far as we know, in the mid-1520s in Salzburg. His work is further stimulated by an abortive teaching role at the University of Basel during ten months in the summer and fall of 1527 and early 1528. His writing activity extends roughly to his death in Salzburg in 1541. His profile has been dominated longest by his fame as a physician and by his aspirations as a philosopher of nature. More recently, his no less imposing engagement as a dissenting author on matters of scripture, doctrine, and the practices of faith, rivalling in volume his medicine and philosophy, has come to light as a result of the belated critical editions of his religious writings by Kurt Goldammer, Hartmut Rudolph, Urs Leo Gantenbein and others.

To the medical theorist, nature philosopher, alchemist and religious dissenter must be added the oracle on occult topics, magic, natural marvels and superstitions. The recently rekindled, still contested, evaluation of his status in intellectual history will be decided in part by our assessment of preoccupations manifest throughout his work that appear to grow in its course. The importance of the occult in Paracelsus is only contested because the medical historian Karl Sudhoff chose either to ignore or to reject the prevalence of his occult concerns. Without evidence or compelling argument, Sudhoff branded as spurious a number of writings that have come down to us under the name of Paracelsus. Set in contrasting type and designated as *Spuria*, these writings were excised from the canon. Muddying the waters even further, Wilhelm Kuhlmann and Joachim Telle have recently adopted the designation 'deutero-Paracelsian' for writings to which a non-canonical status is to be ascribed. This has created an unsustainable gap in their compilation of a sequenced *Corpus Paracelsisticum* documenting his impact on posterity. For either the excised writings are authentic, in which case the center of gravity in Paracelsus' work shifts toward the occult; or they were written by others under his influence, in which case they belong in the *Corpus Paracelsisticum* and pose the question: are there then elements in the undisputed work of Paracelsus that encouraged the occult writings ascribed to him? Such elements are in fact legion.

The disputed *De philosophia occulta* and the undisputed *De causis morborum invisibilium* (*On the Invisible Diseases*, composed in German by Paracelsus in Sankt Gallen in 1531) share so much in common that nearly every theme of the former is found either in the latter or in Paracelsus' *Philosophia magna*. These writings offer evidence of a knowledge of, though not a systematic response to, Agrippa von Nettesheim's Latin *De occulta philosophia* (which appeared in ten editions prior to 1535), suggesting that Paracelsus took part in the controversy over magic catalyzed by the Humanist (Weeks 2013). Paracelsus' occult interests became intertwined with his medical and religious pursuits. A comparison of his writings on syphilis of 1529 with the attempted system he elaborated in Sankt Gallen in 1530–31 or the *Vita beata* writings of the early 1530s, the Munich 'mantic fragment', or the large-scale, unfinished *Astronomia magna* (*Philosophia sagax*) among his final efforts, indicates how the occult gradually gained in prominence until his preoccupation with the supernatural subsumed his medical naturalism and dissenting theology. From the start, the boundary between the natural and the supernatural and between magic and religion was fluid. The disputed writings and their interrelation with his work in its entirety are a field left fallow by ideological prejudice and disciplinary constraint.

Paracelsus' occult themes include image magic, the power of the imagination, the ceremonial magic of incantations, consecrations, and ceremonies, the realm of spirits, and the necromancy, sorcery, and witches that he eschews. His notions of natural magic are interesting but hard to isolate as such for several reasons. The invisible powers of God extend throughout nature. The naturalism of what might be called Paracelsian natural magic is as much an acknowledgement of religious tenets as a deviation from them. Sacramental powers strengthen the credibility of natural magic. Even the most physically oriented work on surgery includes in its venue the treatment of wounds inflicted by magic (Sudhoff 1922, 10: 229). Unlike Agrippa or Pico, Paracelsian magic in its variants rests not on cited ancient sources but on the *ad hoc* authority of experience and hearsay. Since he develops his views unsystematically, we do well to discuss their evolving pattern as it appears in key works.

The *Volumen Paramirum*, a fragmentary draft devoted to the five *Entia* or causes of disease, is regarded as one of his earliest medical works – an assumption encouraged more by its draft status than by external evidence. Its final two causes are *ens spiritale* (or *characterale*) and *ens deale*. *Ens spiritale* is a disease with a spiritual rather than a material cause. It is neither the work of God nor of the devil. The natural human volition engenders an invisible, intangible spirit that inflicts diseases on others. What is said of *ens spiritale* calls to mind either the psychosomatic disorder of the individual, or the hysteria or sociopathic mass psychology of the crowd. Yet the 'spiritual' aetiology is an occult causality. Animosity, dreams and the voodoo-like use of objects or waxen images can inflict injury or illness without material agency. The author states that, as in necromancy, a spirit-engendering malevolence can conjure things absent and inflict harm on humans and animals. Spiritual causation also makes use of 'characters': it inherits ancient or medieval uses of amulets, signs or images and is compatible with the livestock-afflicting sorcery of witches. The author is reluctant to ascribe it directly to the devil, as does the devil literature of the later sixteenth century (cf. *Theatrum diabolorum*, Frankfurt am Main, 1569, 1575, 1587).

On the Invisible Diseases (1531), written as the last in his sequence of *Para*-prefixed works in an attempt to provide a comprehensive response to his detractors in Basel and Nuremberg, is a thematic linchpin tying Paracelsus' theories of the occult to the full sweep of his medical and theological evolution. Since 2008, the works of 1530–31 have been available in a scholarly translation, juxtaposed with the authoritative text from Johann Huser with cross-references to the entire oeuvre and commentary based on external contemporaneous or modern sources. *On the Invisible Diseases* addresses ailments of the spirit. Paracelsus re-claims ground neglected by traditional Galenic medicine. He accords supreme importance to the invisible phenomenalism of the diseases. On the one hand, their status repeats his subclassification into material and immaterial diseases. On the other, it elevates their status by placing them in a hierarchy ascending from the visible to the invisible: 'I will proceed onward into a realm that extends from the visible into the invisible' (Weeks 2008, 723). This would make little sense if the devout reader were not expected to recall the Apostle Paul's assurance that the invisible powers of God are revealed through the visible things of the creation (Romans 1: 20). The spirit possessions recall Jesus' healing miracles of those afflicted by devils.

Paracelsus' notions of the occult form a broad circle of phenomena that overlaps with the circles of his medical and theological topics. Within the broad circle, the divine or beneficent occult is putatively distinct but hard to distinguish from the evil or diabolical occult. All magic is natural and supernatural. No power is intelligible without reference to God's omnipotence. His assertion that the power of faith is, in Jesus' words, like the tiny mustard seed that overshadows all (Mt 17: 20), not only affirms Bible-based doctrine; it reconfirms the non-material occult powers of the spirit (Weeks 2008, 739). The divine power of faith extolled by Luther overlaps with the occult powers of the imagination (Weeks 2008, 748). The powers of saints and religious images, despised by Paracelsus and Luther, cannot be wholly denied. Such powers are therefore relegated to a contested zone of occult spirit magic. Their sanctity, though not their efficacy, depends on whether they are infused with a proper faith in God. The discourse of the occult plays out in dialog with theological controversies. This interaction extends not only to his condemnation of Catholic rites as equivalent to occult ceremonies, but also to sects or doctrinal controversies disputed around 1531. The Anabaptists' forbidden repetition of the sacrament of baptism is compared to the occult practice of incantatory repetition (Weeks 2008: 783, 785).

In the realm of phenomena that we might recognize as psychosomatic, the occult powers of the imagination are pertinent to the epidemic of St. Vitus' dance, to St. Valentine's illness (epilepsy), and to the convulsions of St. Anthony's fire, which are now understood to have had a physical cause in ergotism (Weeks 2008: 772, 776, 778). Occult forces come into play in conception as well as in the then commonly acknowledged prodigy of frogs falling from the sky like rain (Weeks 2008: 808–11). Most sinister of all is the occult agency that foments epidemics when a woman is dying in childbirth. Her 'envy and hatred' inflict cosmic reverberations that issue in mass death (Weeks 2008: 820). We might prefer Paracelsus' recognition that evil inflicted on women leads to a magnified evil inflicted on all to crude recriminations against witches; but *On the Invisible Diseases* also associates women's unwholesome sexuality with the allegations of a witches' convention at Höwberg Mountain (Weeks 2008: 930–31). Any inclination to segregate such lore and traditions of magic from Renaissance science and orthodox theology encounters obstacles, insofar as Paracelsus' acceptance of giants, monsters, and the invisible night spirits of *incubi* and *succubi* harks back to St. Augustine and the Bible (Weeks 2008: 826, 830). His *Vita beata* writings, edited by Gantenbein, incorporate magic into theology. In the *Liber de religione perpetua*, the question is not whether magic is effective but whether its practitioners acknowledge God as the ultimate agent. True *magi* do so, *malefici* do not (Gantenbein 2008: 309). Like Agrippa von Nettesheim, Paracelsus recognized that God's powers were the highest and purest magic.

Theology reconceived as magic lent its benefits to medicine more readily than did the medieval saints' cults, pilgrimages and healing miracles, which were rejected by Paracelsus and noxious to many in the early Reformation. The older faith-based modes of healing were under the control of the Church – a serious economic rival and challenger to the reforming healer. After his systematic academic medical program of 1530–31 failed to replace the medieval medical faculties, he projected faculties of the occult which would overshadow or subsume the medical and surgical disciplines by insinuating his authority in all fields of learning. These efforts approached fruition in the lengthy, magisterial, yet unfinished work *Astronomia magna, oder die ganze Philosophia sagax der großen und kleinen Welt* (1537–38; Sudhoff 1922, 12). Certain scholars have preferred to ignore or exclude its massive supernaturalization of knowledge as untypical of an author ranked alongside Copernicus and Vesalius in the mainstream of Renaissance natural science. But *Astronomia magna* had been anticipated by a fragment that Huser edited from a manuscript in Paracelsus' own hand: the Munich 'Mantischer Entwurf', so called by Sudhoff who inserted it in the interval between *On the Invisible Diseases* and *Astronomia magna*. The mantic fragment refers to 'die ganze astronomie' and subdivides the magic arts into 'faculties' in the manner of the larger subsequent treatise (Sudhoff 1922, 10: 637–59).

Astronomia magna begins by subordinating the knowledge of the astronomer to that of the theologian. However, the two are not so much separate disciplines as distinct aspects of the human being. Any certainty in the natural sciences derives from the presence of the creator in nature. As soon as the exposition moves to the sciences in chapter three, the forms of magic dominate the scope of learning. Under the heading, 'Interpretation of *magica* and its species; what *magica* and *magus* signify', and with frequent references to the Bible, the author observes that the stars can only be comprehended by the *magi* who practice *insignis magica* (Sudhoff 1922, 10: 83). A second biblical species, *magica transfigurativa*, concerns the transformation or transfiguration of bodies (83–84). A third called *characteralis* teaches how to fashion names that possess powers imparted by the heavens to herbs (84). A fourth teaches how to manufacture gems of magical potency. A fifth is concerned with magical images (84). A sixth called, quite misleadingly, *ars cabalistica* makes it possible to discern another's voice at an immense distance (85). Classification overshadows explanation: *nigromantia* can be subdivided into five species of its own (85). Their common denominator is the recognition that after death the human being is survived not only by the soul but also by a spirit born of the stars. The physician's ways of knowing and interacting with this spirit constitute the species of *nigromantia* (86).

When it comes to *nectromantia*, which concerns visions, the subdivisions are 14 in number (87). As the exposition progresses on to *astrologia*, *signatum*, *artes incertae*, *sortilelegium*, *geomantia*, *pyromantia*, *hydromantia*, *chaomantia*, and so on, the reader begins to suspect that a kind of Hogwarts principle is at work: the elaboration of disciplines and specializations serves to make the details and practices appear more convincing than they might be on their particular merits. When it comes to the occult subdivision of *mathematica* – named after a discipline of great importance in Paracelsus's day but of scant real presence in his work – it is apparent that his reclamation of occult knowledge is a way of bolstering the author's authority while preempting rival claims to such (99).

The short treatises that Sudhoff relegated to the back of volume 10 or to the final volumes of his edition (while casting as many aspersions on their authenticity as circumstances would allow) are the most revealing of Paracelsus' understanding of the occult, the supernatural, and the marvelous. Among these shorter works, the clearest is the *Liber de imaginibus* (Sudhoff 1922, 13: 361–86), which, significantly, the medical historian did not attempt to discredit. Here, Paracelsus treats the theme of the magical power of images by drawing on biblical lore, doing so with contemporary controversies over iconoclasm in mind. Good and evil image magic are prefigured in the Bible. Their source is the magical art of the heathens and Babylonians, perverted into idolatry, yet still bearing out a capacity to serve useful purposes (361). For, as long as they are not worshiped, images can serve to remind us of important antecedent events and persons such as the Passion of Christ (363). Taking his point of departure from this bit of refreshing common sense, the author immediately slides from the power of images for reminding and instructing us to assertions of their occult powers. After all, images found in the Old Testament prefigure events and persons in the new: a 'magical prophecy' (364) that occurs also in dreams. The adept arts and alchemical source tracts rely on images (365). Astral and planetary influences occur by way of their manifestations in the form of similitudes, images, figures and colors (369), as do the elements and metals (370, 371). As the exposition extends to all sorts of natural and cultural phenomena, a guiding principle of Paracelsus' theory of nature comes to light. The causal or meaningful relations between the objects of knowledge are manifest in their outer appearances. What they look like, or can be construed to resemble, is the key to their relations with other objects. The font of these relations, however, resides in their occult powers which have their ultimate wellspring in God. The marriage of theology and the study of nature yields a kind of magical empiricism with medieval roots. The rediscovery of forgotten heathen or Christian images is interpreted, not as an expression of independent cultures, but solely as the confirmation or refutation of current articles of faith. Yet alongside this historical ethnocentrism, the author also recognizes that 'through faith and through our powerful imagination', we can inject the human spirit into an image, thereby exponentially intensifying its potency (380), an assertion that subjects the central doctrinal preoccupation with faith of his time to psychological re-contextualization.

The 23 tracts compiled under the heading of *Philosophia magna, de divinis operibus et secretis naturae (volumen primum)* in Sudhoff's self-demoting final volume provide a clear and topical guide to Paracelsus' engagement with the occult themes of his time, their roots in medieval and religious tradition, and their interpenetration of his medical and natural philosophical work as a whole. The topic of witches is placed on a biblical foundation and contextualized with a pious regard for nature: witchcraft is possible because its practioners circumvent the true creator of nature, placing their faith in 'ceremonies' (Sudhoff 1922, 14: 11). Its lurid features in Paracelsus are in conformity with the contemporary demonization of witches (24–27). The topic of demonic possession draws heavily on Gospel sources (35ff.). That of lunatics is stretched to incorporate John the Baptist's denunciation of the Pharisees, as well as other passages from Matthew (50ff.). More fanciful occult phenomena, including those of the elemental spirits, giants, sprites, and their sort, are taken up with regard to the doctrines of creation, salvation, and resurrection. It appears that the supernatural or prodigious offered a desirable corroboration of faith in a time when many of its established articles were being challenged. Yet the corroboration took on a life of its own. Prophecy and divination could claim a biblical pedigree. Yet once licensed, they extended their legitimacy to all sorts of occult applications some of which were quite blasphemous.

Even the most practical of topics, the skills of craftsmen admired by Paracelsus, are tinged with the occult insofar as the author discerns their wellspring in divine or supernatural wisdom and knowledge. Everything comes from God (252). Living in an age when faith and with it the spirit veritably moved mountains, and in full awareness of the intellectual revolution taking place in the realm of Bible scholarship, Paracelsus endeavored to flesh out the consequences of the *zeitgeist*. He discovered pretexts of medieval provenance in popular lore. His topics adumbrate a realm in which ghosts or spirits of the dead are compatible with the occult power of an imagination that imprints itself upon the unborn quite as naturally as the sun affects the colors and qualities of earthly things (310–11); in which the attraction of lust is of a piece with the power of the magnet or the influences of the stars. Just as spirits, divorced from the body yet not identical with the soul, can survive death, human corpse flesh possesses innate powers embodied in a medicinal *mumia* that can heal the ailments of the living, an agency rendered all the more plausible by the parallel, though distinct, salvific powers of the altar sacrament, the flesh and blood of Christ (307–8). For all its religious underpinnings, this sort of speculation opened the door to themes that appeared blasphemous then and are luridly fascinating now, whether the project of creating the *homunculus*, an artifical humanoid (325–36), or the scenario of the women abandoned to die in childbirth whose *menstruum* acts in conjunction with malevolent will to wreak pestilence and death (315).

In evaluating the large and in many instances influential body of writings classified as spurious by Sudhoff, we would be well served by setting aside unanswerable questions of authenticity and asking instead what, if anything in these writings, cannot be found in the undisputed ones. If the answer is little or nothing, then the next step is to inquire how the authentic *themes* of the *disputed* writings magnify and clarify the thematic evolution of the main body of work. We should bear in mind that those presumed to have either edited or amended Paracelsus did so on the basis of a grasp of his relevance which, though unfamiliar now, would have been shared with contemporaries. Finally, whether authentic or not, the body of Paracelsian writings of the sixteenth century can reveal much about the cultural currents of the age. Recent decades have seen great advances in our understanding of such topics as witchcraft hysteria, madness and anticlericalism in the sixteenth century. New material is now becoming available on the Protestant 'wonder books' and on the doctrinal polemics of the period. Much is already available on the compendious literature of the devil. Gantenbein has shed light on the affinities of Paracelsus with the legendary and historical figure of Dr. Faustus (van der Laan and Weeks 2013, 93ff.). What is still poorly understood is the development of Paracelsian ideas by the religious dissenters, mystics, and precursors of Pietism, most notably, Valentin Weigel, Jacob Boehme, and Johann Arndt, by the Baroque poets and spiritual outsiders who wrote in a similar vein.

To free a mental space for incorporating the neglected Paracelsian or pseudo-Paracelsian writings in volume 14 of Sudhoff's edition, we need to rethink the dominions of church history (with its traditional tendency to apply standards of orthodoxy and to neglect whatever does not meet them) and Renaissance studies (which have often been more eager to countenance the high hermetic magic of a Giordano Bruno or Pico della Mirandola than the low, unlearned, superstitious varieties with their obscure origins and contaminating lay piety). It is precisely the neglected fields of weedlike supernaturalism that offer an opportunity to reintegrate our disparate visions of the Renaissance and Reformation which, despite the advances of Keith Thomas, Carlo Ginzburg or Emmanuel Le Roy Ladurie, are still accessed via separate portals within the academy. When the popular anticlerical revolt climaxed in the early Reformation and the common people launched their assault on the medieval church and its monopolies of learning, their popular usurpation not only took the Bible into its own hands, interpreting it to suit its purposes. Unsurprisingly, the anticlerical appropriation of authority encompassed magical lore and practices as well, illicitly combining them with popular theology. Paracelsus – the lay theologian and rebel against humanism, the church, and the universities; the itinerant, Bible-citing physician who claimed to learn from women, gypsies, executioners, and conjurers – allows us to study the dispersion and integration of various magical notions and practices in the early modern period.

REFERENCES AND FURTHER READING

Gantenbein, Urs L., ed. (2008) *Paracelsus: Theologische Werke I (Vita beate – Vom glückseligen Leben), Neue Paracelsus Edition*, Berlin: de Gruyter.

Goldammer, K. (1986) 'Magie bei Paracelsus,' in *Paracelsus in neuen Horizonten. Kurt Goldammers gesammelte Aufsätze*. Salzburger Beiträge zur Paracelsusforschung 24, Vienna: Verband der wissenschaftlichen Gesellschaften Österreichs.

——(1991), *Der göttliche Magier und die Magierin Natur*, Stuttgart: Steiner.

——ed. (1955ff.) *Sämtliche Schriften. Abteilung II: theologische und religionsphilosophische Schriften*, Stuttgart: Steiner.

Kühlmann, W. and J. Telle, eds. (2001, 2004) *Corpus Paracelsisticum*, I, *Der Frühparacelsismus*, parts I and II, Tübingen: Niemeyer.

Pachter, H. M. (1951) *Paracelsus: Magic into Science*, New York: Henry Schuman.

Pagel, W. (1982) *Paracelsus: An Introduction to Philosophical Medicine in the Era of the Renaissance*, Basel: Karger.

Schott, H. (1998) 'Magie – Glaube – Aberglaube: zur *Philosophia Magna* des Paracelsus,' in *Paracelsus und seine internationale Rezeption in der frühen Neuzeit. Beiträge zur Geschichte des Paracelsismus*, ed. Schott, H. and Zinguer, I., Leiden: Brill.

Scribner, R. W. (1987) *Popular Culture and Popular Movements in Reformation Germany*, London: Hambledon Press.

——(2001) *Religion and Culture in Germany (1400–1800)*, ed. Lyndal Roper, in *Studies in Medieval and Reformation Thought*, Leiden: Brill.

Sudhoff, K., ed. (1922ff.) *Sämtliche Werke*, 14 vols., *Abteilung I: medizinische, naturwissenschaftliche und philosophische Schriften*, Munich (Berlin): Barth (Oldenbourg).

van der Laan, J. and A. Weeks, eds. (2013) *The Faustian Century: German Literature and Culture in the Age of Luther and Faustus*, Rochester: Camden House.

Weeks, A., ed. (1997) *Paracelsus: Speculative Theory and the Crisis of the Early Reformation*, Albany: State University of New York Press.

——(2008) *Paracelsus (Theophrastus Bombastus von Hohenheim, 1493–1541): Essential Theoretical Writings*, Leiden: Brill.

——(2013) 'Paracelsus and the Idea of the Renaissance,' in Helmut Koopmann and Frank Baron (eds.) *Die Wiederkehr der Renaissance im 19. und 20. Jahrhundert*, Münster: Mentis Verlag.

——(2014) 'The Invisible Diseases of Paracelsus and the Cosmic Reformation,' in A. Classen (ed.) *Health, Spirituality, and Religion in the Middle Ages and Early Modern Age*, Berlin (Boston): De Gruyter.

CHAPTER SEVEN

JOHN DEE

Glyn Parry

John Dee's life demonstrates how occult beliefs were not just deeply woven into the everyday life of Tudor England, but also central to its intellectual culture, its educational institutions, its social hierarchy, its religious environment, and even its politics. Dee's Court career in particular reveals that a profound belief in astrology, apocalyptic alchemy, angel magic, and other forms of occult divination, distinguished Elizabeth I, her great minister Lord Burghley, the Earl of Leicester, and many lesser figures. In the right political circumstances occult philosophy could shape policy-making, the central preoccupation of government.

Born on 13 July 1527 in the London parish of St Dunstan-in-the-East, to Roland and Jane Dee, John grew up in the last years of English Catholic society, a culture resonating with magical forces. The rituals surrounding his baptism, like the annual cycle of Church festivals and ceremonies, were believed to ward off those invisible demonic enemies who provoked discord in a society that valued community, and mental illness in individuals. Fifty years after he received the 'holy oil' in his baptism, John used it in a futile attempt to exorcise demons from his servant, Anne Frank.

Catholicism in the 1540s still incorporated the laity's magical beliefs. Only gradually would 'elite' Catholic clergy tacitly accept Protestant criticisms and purge Church ceremonies of their magical associations. Dee's later 'conjuring' reputation partly reflects his attachment to traditional magical prayers and rituals, including Rogationtide processions to drive the Devil from the parish and restore neighbourly unity. Sixty years later he led processions that beat the boundaries of Manchester parish to pacify tithe disputes (Parry 2012, 2–3).

The wealthy parishioners richly decorated St Dunstan's, including 'the Great Cross with Beryl', a huge sparkling crystal at its centre (The National Archives, E117/4/1). Whenever in after years Dee crossed himself, a Catholic practice frowned on by devout Protestants, he would pause in the middle of his chest in memory of that profound junction, where in his *Monas Hieroglyphica* (1564), he would place the philosopher's stone. Like other magicians Dee frequently crossed himself and recited psalms from the Latin Vulgate Bible in his ritual invocation of angels with Edward Kelley, whose revelations included recipes for making the philosopher's stone (Casaubon 1659, 387–93).

Dee matriculated at St John's College, Cambridge, in November 1542. All the tutors he later thanked belonged to the conservative, Catholic faction in the deeply divided college. The university and college curricula ostensibly omitted occult philosophy, but Aristotelian natural philosophy encouraged belief in transmutation, and Dee's Cambridge predecessors, Thomas Smith, William Cecil and Richard Eden had avidly pursued the philosopher's stone (Feingold 1984, 80–81; Kitching 1971, 308–15; Gwyn 1984, 13–34). Dee alluded to his Cambridge alchemical studies in his 'Mathematical Preface' of 1570 (Dee 1975, sig. b3v).

Dee's mathematical studies included perspective, which laid the groundwork for his later summoning of angels into crystals through light rays, and underpinned astrology, alchemy and magical 'Catoptric,' or divination, using light from polished surfaces. He befriended John Hatcher, a Fellow of St John's who practised angel magic, and sought out works by Roger Bacon, who had taught that conjured spirits revealed the hidden secrets of Nature (Parry 2012, 10).

Increasing Protestant criticism of conjuring as 'sorcery' helps explain why the growing Protestant faction at St John's refused to make Dee a Fellow. Instead, Henry VIII appointed him a founding Fellow of Trinity College in December 1546, along with five other resolute Catholics from St John's (Gillow 1885–1902, i, 486). To deceive his critics, in 1570 Dee tried to attribute his conjuring reputation to 'vain reports' about his stage illusions for a production of Aristophanes's *Peace* at Trinity College. In fact his pulleys and mirrors derived from rediscovered classical treatises. Precisely because he could explain these illusions naturally, he used them to distract attention from his 'conjuring' magic on behalf of Princess Elizabeth in 1555, the real source of his scandalous reputation (Parry 2012, 11–12).

In 1547 influential Catholic patrons at Trinity College enabled Dee to pursue advanced astronomy and astrology with Gerardus Mercator at Louvain, recently savagely purged by the Inquisition. Dee returned to Louvain in the summer of 1548 following the collapse of his father's political career, and chose to matriculate, swearing allegiance to papal authority he had recently foresworn at Cambridge. He now studied Mercator's precise measurement of the 'rays of celestial virtue', which influenced the weather, but more controversially human fates, depending on the celestial influences prevailing at conception and birth. Therefore, the method could be applied to medicine, as demonstrated in 'Doctor' Dee's mis-named 'Diary', an ephemerides by which he could correlate celestial influences with the weather, his patients' health and occurrences.

In Paris in July 1550, Dee met the eccentric, deeply learned Guillaume Postel, just returned from studying Semitic languages in the Near East. Dee accepted Postel's kabbalistic theories about the construction of Hebrew letters from 'points, lines, and surfaces', a method which Dee used to construct his profound talisman, the Hieroglyphic Monad, which combined the influences of all the planets (Parry 2012, 20–21).

Dee returned impoverished to his meagre Trinity Fellowship in October 1551. Despite his hopes of reward from John Dudley, Duke of Northumberland, who now dominated Edward VI's government, he became merely an occasional intellectual consultant to the Court, and servant to the Earl of Pembroke on 28 February 1552. From Pedro Nunez he had learned to construct a 'paradoxal compass', a polar chart to solve English difficulties navigating in high latitudes. Dee sold this idea to the

Muscovy Company as his own, attributing mystical significance to the fact that a ship following a fixed compass bearing will create a 'loxodrome' spiralling into the pole the further it sailed towards it (Heilbron 1975, 29–31). Edward's meagre reward was a legally dubious presentation to the Rectory of Upton-upon-Severn, over the furious protests of the firebrand Protestant bishop, John Hooper. Keeping the income from this living would cost Dee much money and stress (Parry 2012, 25–26).

More immediately, his father's arrest and financial destruction for supporting Northumberland's abortive coup against Mary Tudor, followed by Pembroke's defeat of the Wyatt rebellion in early February 1554, left Dee needing to prove his loyalty to Mary's increasingly orthodox regime. Therefore, encouraged by Pembroke, he hurriedly became a Catholic priest on 17 February 1554, defying the canon law by exploiting his friendship with Edmund Bonner, Bishop of London, to whom he now became chaplain (Parry 2012, 29).

In April 1555, probably recruited by her Dudley supporters, Dee began magical divination to forecast the political future for Princess Elizabeth at Woodstock. Queen Mary believed herself to be pregnant, but at thirty-eight she and her child might die in childbirth, expected in late May. This would destroy Philip II's power in England, unless he planned to seize the throne. Elizabeth had to be forewarned to resist him, and after Mary ordered her to Hampton Court on 17 April, Dee continued his divination in Oxfordshire and London. His methods may have included the mathematical 'genethlialogy' taught at Louvain. Beyond conventional general horoscopes, destinary horoscopes calculated from times of conception, and questionary horoscopes about princes held political dangers (Means 1992, 376–85). Two rivals denounced Dee and his accomplices in Elizabeth's household to the Privy Council. By 5 June they had confessed to 'lewd and vain practices of calculing', but more ominous accusations of 'conjuring or witchcraft', allegedly including wax image magic, followed two days later (Dasent 1890–1964, v, 137, 139, 143, 145; Parry 2012, 32–34). Dee had probably performed 'Archemastry' to summon spirits, using light focussed by crystals and constantly reflected from highly polished surfaces, which sent the virgin soul into a self-reflexive spiral of religious rapture, inducing visions. Adepts believed that spirits travelled along the light beams, could be trapped in the crystals by spells, and interrogated about the future. Catholic priests were often associated with summoning and controlling spirits, and Dee dropped hints about 'Archemastry' in his 'Mathematical Preface' just after indignantly denying accusations, persisting since 1555, that he was a 'Conjuror of wicked and damned Spirits' (Clulee 1984, 57–71; Parry 2012, 35–36; Dee 1975, sigs. A1v-2r).

Under the threat or reality of torture Dee cracked, and returned to Bonner's household by early July. By early August even Philip had stopped believing in Mary's phantom pregnancy, and to purge Elizabeth's reputation as heir-apparent, the Privy Council formally cleared all the conjurors. However, Dee's inept performance the following November, with Bonner's other chaplains interrogating the prominent martyr Archdeacon John Philpot, helped to perpetuate the scandal. John Foxe's *Acts and Monuments* (1563, 1570) identified Dee as a 'conjuror' when recounting Philpot's sufferings from the anonymous *Examination of John Philpot* (1559). In 1563 Foxe added an unsigned letter, purportedly from a friend of Philpot, which Dee blamed for all later slanders about 'Dr Dee the great Conjuror'. Vincent Murphyn had forged the letter as indirect revenge against Sir William Cecil, Dee's patron. Cecil had persecuted

Murphyn's brother-in-law John Prestall, part of his campaign to smear Catholicism with magical associations and ensure the passage of the Witchcraft Act of 1563 (Foxe 1563, 1444–45; Parry 2012, 64–66). Murphyn forged other letters, allegedly from Dee, supporting his own low-level conjuring practice in London. They boosted his energetic spreading of slanders against Dee, which Dee denied, until his 1577 *Memorials Pertaining to the Perfect Art of Navigation* admitted that his forecasting for Elizabeth in 1555 had prompted this 'very Injurious Report...Spread and Credited' that he was 'The Great Conjuror: and so, (as some would say), *The Arch-Conjuror*, of this whole kingdom' (Dee 1577, sig. [delta] 3v; Parry 2012, 66–67).

In Bonner's household Dee began building the largest occult library in Elizabethan England, by late 1555 already numbering several hundred books and manuscripts on astronomy and astrology, angel magic, optics, geography, alchemy, and some Neoplatonic philosophy. Sixty-eight books and eight manuscripts from this period survive. His collecting prompted Dee to petition Queen Mary to finance a Royal Library, effectively a Royal Occult Institute where manuscripts from all branches of occult philosophy would be copied, and some printed. Nothing daunted when Mary ignored him, Dee began borrowing and copying Cambridge and Oxford manuscripts of occult philosophy, and methods of divination including branches of 'Archemastry' (Parry 2012, 40–42).

In July 1556 Dee began reading intensively in alchemy, like Roger Bacon connecting it with optics, the measurement of the celestial and occult rays controlling the sublunary world. The adept could harness the creative power of light through talismans, and Dee began pondering his Monad, a universal symbol uniting all the planetary influences. The structure of the Monad also encapsulated his religious contemplation, inspired by Postell, of the geometrical Kabbalah hidden in alphabets (Parry 2012, 42–43). First, however, he applied his Louvain training, with ideas drawn from Bacon and al-Kindi's treatise *On Rays*, to vindicate astrology by systematically measuring the intersecting occult influences from all celestial bodies. This theory produced *Propaedeumata aphoristica* (1558), a staggeringly complex programme of geometric optics that became hopelessly involved, but which he largely plagiarized from the twelfth-century doctor Urso of Salerno, unless we believe his claim that both wrote under divine inspiration (Parry 2012, 44–45, 110).

To supplement his meagre income from Upton, Dee worked as a jobbing mathematician and astrologer, later claiming to have written several treatises with practical applications. At Elizabeth's accession Pembroke and Lord Robert Dudley recruited him for a more important task. The French, still at war with England, publicized Nostradamus' predictions of catastrophe for Elizabeth's projected religious changes, stirring up popular anxiety and unsettling an infant regime bogged down in an unpopular war, confronting a sluggish economy and an empty treasury. Moreover, mere days after Mary's death on 17 November, the Privy Council arrested a group of Catholics who had used the services of one John Prestall for a 'lewd conjuror's conference with the Devil, how long the Queen's highnesses government and this [Protestant] religion should endure' (Dasent 1890–1964, vii, 5, 7, 22; Norton, 1569, sig. H3r). To counter these dire predictions Dee calculated an encouraging electionary horoscope for Elizabeth's Coronation Day, 15 January 1559. He never made the claim, beloved of later historians, that he chose the actual day. However, some Catholics, encouraged by the predictions of Elizabeth's imminent death, and appalled by the religious changes grinding through Parliament, conspired to rebel by early March 1559. The Spanish Ambassador in London urged Philip II, residing at Brussels, to support them, who sent £5,000 with the promise of £10,000 more. The projected rebellion fizzled out, and that April and May the Court witnessed the official response, in a 'Masque of the Astronomers', complete with props of celestial globes and astrolabes, which doubtless predicted a glorious reign. Probably on one of these occasions Dudley presented Elizabeth with a beautiful astrolabe made by Thomas Gemini, now 'Queen Elizabeth's Astrolabe' in the Oxford Museum of the History of Science (Parker 1998, 86–87; Feuillerat 1908, 97–98).

Dee's first astrological service for Elizabeth received a typically meagre reward, the Rectory of distant Long Leadenham, Lincolnshire. Dee even found it necessary to reside there for the next few years, until he embarked on a scholarly tour of Europe from January 1562 to June 1564 (Parry, 2012, 49). He headed first for Louvain and Antwerp, to acquire books on the Kabbalah. A year later he squeezed more time (and money) from Cecil, by announcing the stupendous discovery of 'Steganographia', Johannes Trithemius' manuscript describing how to invoke spirit messengers to convey instant messages. Trithemius' long-established reputation for trafficking with evil spirits, including demons named in this text, did not deter Dee, who never realized that the incantations contained encrypted instructions for concealing messages inside gibberish or inoffensive 'plain text' (Reeds, 1998, 291–317; Ernst 1998, 318–41).

On his travels Dee shaped his exalted theory of the Monad, which had decorated the title-page of *Propaedeumata aphoristica*. He acquired kabbalistic books arguing that semitic languages, particularly Syriac, concealed profound meanings in the very shapes of their letters, which supported Dee's belief that hieroglyphs concentrated celestial powers (Parry 2012, 50–51; Wilkinson 2007, 11–13). However, Dee surpassed Postel in his lost 'Compendious Table of the Hebrew Kabbalah' written at Paris in 1562, which by kabbalistic geometry derived the 'real' Kabbalah's 'signs and characters' from visible and invisible things in Nature, not just alphabets. This encouraged Dee to describe himself, like Postel, as a 'Cosmopolite', a citizen of no country but Christ's imminent kingdom, a word his *Monas hieroglyphica* used when foreseeing Maximilian II's apocalyptic empire, and later Elizabeth's.

After visiting Rome, where his Catholic priesthood opened doors, Dee arrived at Bratislava for Maximilian of Habsburg's coronation as King of Hungary in September 1563. For eight centuries Europeans had cherished prophecies of an heroic Last World Emperor, who would destroy Islam and reign from Jerusalem over global peace and true religion before ushering in the Second Coming of Christ. Many hoped Maximilian would prove such an imperial 'cosmopolite', and back in Antwerp in January 1564 Dee hurriedly wrote *Monas hieroglyphica*, as 'cosmopolitical theories' to usher in this 'fourth, great, and truly metaphysical revolution'. Dee claimed his *Monas* uncovered the divine language of things hidden in the world at Creation. From the basic geometry of 'points, straight lines and circles', by which he created his Monad, Dee derived not just all alphabets and numbers but all forms of knowledge, including his favourite Paracelsian alchemy. Therefore the hieroglyphic Monad concealed at its centre the philosopher's stone, which Dee offered to Maximilian to ensure his success as the cosmopolitan Last World Emperor (Parry 2012, 52–59; Dee 1964, 117–21, 127, 123; Clulee 1988, 77–142; Clulee 2005, 197–215).

Dee's play for patronage – the Monad combined Habsburg symbols representing the Sun, the Moon, the Cross and Aries – failed, and he returned to England in July 1564. By then Murphyn had successfully embellished Dee's reputation as a persecuting Catholic 'conjuror', because Cecil had exploited carefully watched Catholic plots using magic against Elizabeth to push the 1563 Witchcraft Act through a legislative log-jam in Parliament (Parry 2012, 60–67). The plotters included Murphyn's relative Prestall, whose magical rivalry with Dee would obstruct Dee's career. Therefore Elizabeth had to defend *Monas* against 'Strange and undue speeches...of that Hieroglyphical writing' as a form of conjuring. This highlights Elizabeth's interest in the alchemical 'secrets of that book', which helped to suppress criticism after her 'little perusal of the same with me' (Dee 1726, 507, 519). Yet even this backfired on Dee, for his alchemical Theorem XXI in *Monas* promised the 'great secret' of the stone would please the *Voarchadumicus*, an allusion to Joannes Pantheus' book of that name. Within months Cornelius de Lannoy wrote to Cecil from Bruges offering Elizabeth his thirty years' experience in the art of 'Boarchadamia' and she royally entertained him for some years in a vain attempt at transmutation. Unable to match such extravagant claims, in 1565 Dee married Katheryn Constable, a respectable City matron and widow of Thomas Constable, a general trader closely associated with Roland Dee's business and parish careers (Parry 2012, 69–79).

Dee's career was going nowhere. In January 1567 Pembroke secured Prestall's release from the Tower after he promised to transmute silver into gold. In response Dee translated his *Monas* into German and sent the manuscript to Maximilian. When that failed to attract attention, later that year he revised his *Propaedeumata aphoristica*, inserting new material addressing the Court's vogue for alchemy, linking that study to the measurement of celestial influences. Though he presented copies to Cecil and, via Pembroke, to Elizabeth, the failure of de Lannoy's promises had temporarily dampened Elizabeth's interest in alchemy (Parry 2012, 78–80).

For the next few years Dee maintained himself in his mother's house at Mortlake by teaching students the construction of sundials, Paracelsian alchemy, astrology, geometry, navigation, map-making, and mathematics, courses of instruction that only encouraged the contemporary confusion of the latter with magic. In February 1570 he advertised these services, and applied mathematics to both terrestrial and celestial purposes, including 'Archemastry', or angelic magic using crystals, in his 'Mathematical Preface' to Billingsley's edition of Euclid. There he again used his stage effects at Trinity to deflect Murphyn's renewed accusations of conjuring evil spirits. Later that year he helped write Humphrey Gilbert's plan for 'Queen Elizabeth's Academy' to train young nobles in requisite studies, including not just applied mathematics but alchemy. The alchemical teachers would annually report on their experiments 'without Equivocations or Enigmaticall phrases', recording both successes and failures to guide successors (British Library, Manuscript: Lansdowne 98, fos. 1r–7r). Dee's only surviving notebook of alchemical experiments, from July to October 1581, follows precisely this method, eschewing enigmatic metaphors for quantified and clearly named substances, exact timings to measure astrological influences, and explanations for failure (Bodleian Library, Manuscript: Rawlinson D. 241).

This proposal brought Dee notice from noble patrons, especially Mary Dudley Sidney and her husband Sir Henry Sidney, who had beggared himself as Elizabeth's Lord Deputy in Ireland. With Elizabeth they sponsored Dee's journey to Lorraine in

1571 to purchase many alchemical vessels, though his dangerous illness on his return may explain why no evidence about his alchemical work survives. Complicated rivalry amongst alchemists for patronage in the 1570s explains why Murphyn redoubled his accusations against Dee, accusing him of involvement in treasonous conspiracies against Elizabeth, funded by alchemical gold, and forging documents to prove it. Dee therefore had to prosecute Murphyn for slander at Guildhall in September–October 1580, eventually convincing a reluctant jury of his good name, but never receiving his damages (Parry 2012, 86–87, 138–41; Bodleian Library, Manuscript: Ashmole 487, October 1580).

By then Dee had greatly bolstered his reputation at Court by writing treatises encouraging Elizabeth to recover King Arthur's 'British Empire' in both Europe and the Americas, which implicitly supported the Earl of Leicester's policy of militarily supporting the Protestant Dutch against Philip II. Underpinning his *General and Rare Memorials Pertayning to the Perfect Art of Navigation* (1577), and three manuscript treatises written the next year, was Dee's belief in prophecies of the Last World Emperor, and his conviction that the 1572 supernova, for him in the orbit of Venus, foreshadowed that Elizabeth would produce the philosopher's stone in 1577, to recreate the 'British Empire'. Dee's occult philosophy enabled Leicester to procure him audiences with Elizabeth from November 1577, when he reassured courtiers 'of no small account' that that month's great comet would not harm the Queen. Dee spent three days closeted with Elizabeth, engaged in magical and alchemical practices, after which she promised to defend him against attacks on 'any my rare studies and Philosophical exercises'. Like other occult writers, Dee's 'imperial' treatises addressed hidden topics, and his patrons also intended that his audience would advance the 'Protestant Cause', both in England, and in foreign policy towards the Netherlands (Parry 2012, 94–99; Dee 1726, 521).

Dee's *Memorials* included his own 'commonwealth' agenda, begging Elizabeth to clean up the Thames and preserve its fisheries from the well-connected. His occult philosophy enabled him to pursue this agenda in the autumn of 1578. Amidst Protestant anxiety about Elizabeth's marriage negotiations with the French Catholic Duke of Anjou, in late August three wax images were found under a dunghill in London, one figure richly clothed with 'Elizabeth' scratched into it. These were sent to the Court, on Progress at Norwich. The Privy Council brought Dee to perform unspecified magic at Norwich, which directed the Council to a nest of Catholics subsequently tortured into naming further accomplices, including Murphyn and Prestall. Dee's stock at Court never stood higher, and the Council pressured the City of London into restoring the Thames as Dee's *Memorials* had suggested. Since the City had encouraged Dee to write this section, they happily obliged. However, though Leicester attempted to exploit the magic plot to smear the Catholics at Court and prevent the Anjou marriage, it transpired that the wax images were merely love magic by a conjuror, Thomas Elkes. Leicester's patronage had persuaded John Foxe to remove the identification of Dee as the 'Arch-Conjuror' from the 1576 *Acts and Monuments*. Dee also utilized his increased influence to marry his second wife, Jane Fromoundes, in February 1578, overcoming the resistance of her Catholic father, Bartholomew, who omitted her from his will (Parry 2012, chaps 11, 12).

However, Dee's Court career nose-dived again when Leicester changed his policy towards France and abruptly dropped Dee in late 1580. Soon afterwards Dee's longstanding angel magic with several 'scryers' took a new direction. From March 1582 he relied on Edward Kelley to 'scry' angelic revelations. Kelley's deep reading in scriptural prophecy and Dee's occult library soon made Dee dependent on his increasingly apocalyptic 'revelations', particularly about dramatic changes predicted for Eastern Europe in November 1583. This gave added impetus to Dee's reform of the Calendar, which Burghley agreed must be done before November 'for a secret reason'. Dee pointed out that for political reasons Pope Gregory XIII had removed only ten days, not the correct eleven, but Elizabeth pushed Dee to complete a new almanac and 'Queen Elizabeth's Calendar', omitting only ten. Walsingham covertly scuttled the scheme, by sending Dee to dictate the new ecclesiastical calendar to his old foes, the bishops. For once Grindal's bitter protests succeeded, and Dee reappeared in Foxe's *Acts and Monuments* that year as 'conjuring' (Parry 2012, chap. 14; Foxe 1583, 1577–78, 1581–87).

The increasingly apocalyptic angelic revelations also reveal Dee and Kelley's long experience in traditional *grimoires*. Dee expected Kelley to trap spirits in crystals, burn the names of evil spirits with brimstone, use magic circles, ritual spells, and a commonplace 'Solomon's Ring', as well as the elaborate paraphernalia Kelley delineated at angelic command (Casaubon 1659, 168–71, 177–85). These procedures attracted Albrecht Laski, a Polish nobleman who arrived in London in May 1583 and soon acquired a dubious reputation. He began to make much of his alleged English royal blood, and Kelley foolishly identified him as a potential Last World Emperor. This alienated Dee's former patrons, and in September 1583, after solemnly covenanting with Laski as God's chosen instrument, the entire Dee household decamped for eastern Europe, relying on angelic assurances that Dee would be the prophet of the Last Days. This only emphasized the disturbed Kelley's political ineptness, manifested in their chilly reception by Stephen Bathory, King of Poland, and the Emperor Rudolf II in Prague. The angels began slowly dictating God's original creative language to reveal the hidden secrets of Nature, including transmutation. This attracted a following at Rudolf's Court, and therefore the enmity of the papal Nuncio. Pope Sixtus V had published the Bull *Coeli et terrae* in April 1586, condemning all forms of divination, including Dee's ritual invocation of spirits into crystals. Dee and Kelley had formally reconciled with Catholicism, but Sixtus' Nuncio, Filippo Strega, having failed to induce them to visit Rome, where doubtless Sixtus waited to condemn them under the Bull, persuaded Rudolf II to ban them from imperial lands in May (Parry 2012, 179–93; Maxwell-Stuart 1999, 58–59).

Readmitted in August with Dee, Kelley abandoned apocalyptic revelations about Nature for the greater rewards of the philosopher's stone, soon establishing a European reputation for transmutation. Rudolf II richly rewarded him, but insisted Dee leave Habsburg territory. He settled near Bremen, on the most direct route to England, realizing that he needed Kelley's alchemy to succeed at Elizabeth's Court. However, he eventually returned in December 1589, depending on his relationship with Kelley to bargain for patronage. Elizabeth hoped to entice Kelley back by treating Dee generously and engaging in alchemy with him in 1590, and Burghley tried direct appeals in the spring of 1591. Whenever Kelley intimated his return Dee's stock rose, but John Whitgift, Grindal's successor as Archbishop of Canterbury, combined with Sir Christopher Hatton both to denigrate Kelley's alleged transmutation and the entire alchemical enterprise, blocking Dee's promotion as part of a reactionary campaign to marginalize magic from Court and politics (Parry 2012, chap. 18). Only after Hatton's death on 20 November 1591 could Cecil counter-attack, using Dee's prediction that the Spanish would conquer England in 1592 to panic Elizabeth into reversing her support of Whitgift's authoritarian ecclesiastical policies. By November 1592 Cecil had capitalized on Dee's prophecy to rescue leading presbyterians from Whitgift's persecution and finally purge Catholics from the commissions of the peace. Having done so, he abandoned Dee to Whitgift's revenge (Parry 2012, chap. 19). For the next two years, though Dee developed patronage relationships with influential courtiers by his alchemical teaching, Whitgift prevented his promotion. In early 1595 he intrigued to head off Dee's imminent installation as Chancellor of St Paul's Cathedral, instead lumbering him with the Wardenship of the financially ruined Christ's College, Manchester. There Dee endured eight tumultuous years, at religious and financial odds with the Fellows, while attempting to contact the angels, to create the philosopher's stone, teach pupils, and earn a little money by conjuring for lost goods. Whitgift and his followers continued their attacks, using Dee's notoriety as the 'Arch-Conjuror' to discredit the Presbyterian John Darrell, whose spectacular public exorcisms of the demonically possessed in Manchester and elsewhere gathered support for ecclesiastical reform. Despite initial Presbyterian denials, the conservatives established that Dee had called Darrell to Manchester (Parry 2012, chaps. 20, 21).

In 1604 Dee petitioned King James I for justice against his public defamation as a devil-conjuror. Amongst Catholics he had been reviled since 1592 as the 'conjuror to the Privy Council' who had assisted Cecil by his invasion prediction. His involvement in exorcisms in London and Manchester further tarnished his reputation amongst Protestants. Following the death of his wife and several children in the 1605 plague epidemic, which destroyed Manchester's social order, he retired to London, where he continued his angel magic, alchemy, conjuring for buried treasure and lost property, and casting medical horoscopes. In 1608, aged eighty-one, he hoped for some appointment in Germany, at the newly opened alchemical college of Marburg University, but ill-health intervened. After receiving charity from the Mercers, his family's London livery company, in January 1609, he died on 26 March in the house of his student and friend John Pontois in Bishopsgate Street, London, a frail, white-haired figure of eighty-one, surrounded by the remnants of his library and scientific instruments (Parry 2012, chaps 22–23).

REFERENCES AND FURTHER READING

Bodleian Library, Manuscript: Ashmole 487.

Bodleian Library, Manuscript: Rawlinson D. 241.

British Library, Manuscript: Lansdowne 98, fos. 1r-7r.

Casaubon, M (1659) *A True and Faithful Relation of What Passed for Many Yeers Between Dr John Dee and some spirits* (London).

Clulee, N (1984) 'At the Crossroads of Magic and Science: John Dee's *Archemastrie*,' in *Occult and Scientific Mentalities in the Renaissance*, ed. B. Vickers (Cambridge), 57–71.

——(1988) *John Dee's Natural Philosophy: Between Science and Religion* (London and New York).

——(2005) 'The *Monas hieroglyphica* and the Alchemical Thread of John Dee's Career', *Ambix*, 52, 3, 197–215.

Dasent, J (1890–1964) *Acts of the Privy Council of England*. New series, 46 vols (London).

Dee, J (1577) *General and Rare Memorials Pertayning to the Perfect Art of Navigation* (London).
——(1726) 'The Compendious Rehearsal of John Dee' in *Johannis, confratris et monachi Glastoniensis, chronica sive historia de rebus Glastoniensibus*, ed. T. Hearne, 2 vols (Oxford).
——(1964) C. H. Josten, 'A Translation of John Dee's *Monas hieroglyphica* with an Introduction and Annotations,' *Ambix* 12, 84–221.
——(1975) *John Dee: The Mathematical Preface to the Elements of Geometrie of Euclid of Megara (1570)* with an introduction by Allen G. Debus (New York).
Ernst, T (1998) 'The Numerical-Astrological Ciphers in the third book of Trithemius's Steganographia,' *Cryptologia*, 22, 4, 318–41.
Feingold, M (1984) 'The Occult Tradition in the English Universities of the Renaissance: A Reassessment,' in *Occult and Scientific Mentalities in the Renaissance*, ed. B. Vickers (Cambridge), 73–94.
Feuillerat, A (1908) *Documents relating to the Office of the Revels in the time of Queen Elizabeth* (Louvain).
Foxe, J (1563, 1583) *Actes and monuments of these latter and perillous dayes touching matters of the Church* (London).
Gillow, Joseph (1885–1902) *A literary and biographical history, or bibliographical dictionary of the English Catholics: From the breach with Rome in 1534 to the present time*, 5 vols (London).
Gwyn, D. (1984) 'Richard Eden: Cosmographer and Alchemist,' *The Sixteenth-Century Journal*, 15, 13–34.
Heilbron, J (1975) *John Dee on Astronomy. Propaedeumata Aphoristica (1558 and 1568), Latin and English*, ed. and trans. W. Shumaker, intro. by J. L. Heilbron (Berkeley, Los Angeles and London).
Kitching, C (1971) 'Alchemy in the Reign of Edward VI: an Episode in the Careers of Richard Whalley and Richard Eden,' *Bulletin of the Institute of Historical Research*, 44, 308–15.
Maxwell-Stuart, P (1999) *The occult in early modern Europe: a documentary history* (Basingstoke).
Means, L (1992) 'Electionary, Lunary, Destinary, and Questionary: Toward Defining Categories of Middle English Prognostic Material,' *Studies in Philology*, LXXXIX, no. 4, 367–403.
National Archives, Kew, London, Manuscript: E117/4/1.
Norton, T (1569) *A Warning Against the Dangerous Practices of Papistes* (London).
Parker, G (1998) *The Grand Strategy of Philip II* (New Haven).
Parry, G (2012) *The Arch-Conjuror of England: John Dee* (New Haven and London).
Reeds, J (1998) 'Solved: The Ciphers in Book III of Trithemius's *Steganographia*,' *Cryptologia*, 22, 4, 291–317.
Wilkinson, R (2007) 'Immanuel Tremellius' 1569 Edition of the Syriac New Testament,' *Journal of Ecclesiastical History*, 58(i), Jan. 2007, 9–25.

PART III

SEVENTEENTH CENTURY AND EIGHTEENTH CENTURY

CHAPTER EIGHT

JACOB BÖHME AND CHRISTIAN THEOSOPHY

Wouter J. Hanegraaff

The relation between Protestantism and esotericism is quite peculiar. On the one hand, there can be no doubt that due to their insistence on strict biblicism and the absolute exclusivity of the Christian revelation, Protestants have often been far more extreme in their rejection of 'pagan heresies' and the alleged dangers of 'the occult' than their Roman Catholic counterparts. But on the other hand, it is precisely in Protestant – more precisely, Lutheran – contexts that the most creative innovations in Western esotericism during the early modern period have taken place. There are reasons for this. Roman Catholics tended to think in terms of 'Tradition': the venerable truths of Christianity had already been anticipated in the inspired writings of 'pagan' sages far before the birth of Christ, and even during the earliest periods of history, before the Flood, profound mysteries of nature had been discovered and passed on to later generations. To get access to these truths, one therefore needed to travel back far in time and study the texts of ancient authorities with an attitude of humble piety and respect. As a result, much of early modern esotericism in Catholic context takes the form of learned commentaries on ancient texts, rather than of original speculations. For Protestants, however, such an essentially conservative approach had become highly problematic, because the very authority of 'Tradition' as a source of true knowledge had been called into question by the events of the Reformation. The true Christian message had been corrupted at least since the institution of the Papacy, and many Protestants believed that the Roman Catholic Church and its entire hierarchical system had in fact become the vehicle of anti-Christ and his demonic helpers. How could the true religion have been 'handed down' (viz. the literal meaning of 'tradition') by the members of such an utterly corrupt institution? How could one possibly maintain belief in what its representatives presented as ancient, absolute, universal truth and wisdom? But if so, what to do? If the very Tradition of Christianity had lost its authority for Christians, and its self-appointed custodians had been unmasked as deceivers leading the deceived, then where should one look for the truth instead? There could be only one answer: one needed to turn to God himself.

One way of doing so was by focusing on the Bible. Whereas Roman Catholics were used to having Scripture interpreted for them by the cumulative Tradition of the

Church and its priesthood, Protestant believers tried to bypass those mediators and increasingly began to read God's Word directly, either in translation or (if they could) in the original language. This process reached a point of culmination in the early seventeenth century. This new focus on the Biblical text, read directly by each individual believer, is a first key to understanding the phenomenon of Protestant esotericism. Potentially at least, every reader now became an interpreter of the Bible in his own right, instead of just a passive recipient of the Church's time-honoured interpretations; and as more and more readers began to draw their own conclusions from what they were reading, it was inevitable that some of them would come up with highly innovative 'heterodox' conclusions.

A second way one could listen to God directly was through personal religious experience. One should not underestimate the levels of emotional involvement of which Protestant Bible-readers were capable. Luther's God was an awe-inspiring, even terrifying presence: the Creator of the Universe had absolute sovereignty and power over his creatures, including human beings, and demanded unconditional submission to his will. Since the salvation of one's eternal soul depended on a correct understanding of God's demands, it was natural for Bible-reading to be combined with a practice of intense and anxious prayer for enlightenment. Many Protestants experienced their spiritual life as a prolonged struggle for understanding what it was that God wanted of them, and some of them reported that their prayers had been answered in the form of life-changing experiences of divine 'illumination' or 'interior (re)birth'.

A third way towards knowing God's will is particularly typical of those Lutheran currents that we nowadays tend to associate with esotericism. Inspired by alchemical models and particularly by the legacy of Paracelsus, the 'Book of Nature' came to be seen as a major source of knowledge next to the other book, the Bible. God revealed himself not only through the Old and New Testament Scriptures, but also through a mysterious language of 'signatures' inscribed in the natural world. This meant that natural science or philosophy could be seen as a pious pursuit in harmony with religion or theology: the Bible should be read by the 'light of faith', while the 'light of nature' guided students of the natural world. In this context, alchemical traditions became particularly important.

The great Christian theosopher and Protestant visionary Jacob Böhme (1575–1624) exemplifies all these three avenues towards knowledge of God: the Bible, personal religious experience, and the Book of Nature read according to alchemical/Paracelsian models. As probably the most powerful and creative thinker of all Lutheran Theosophers, his oeuvre laid the foundations for one of the most important esoteric currents to emerge since the Renaissance. It is very different from the largely Platonic models of esotericism most typical for the Roman Catholic context, with their emphasis on a venerable Tradition known as *prisca theologia/philosophia perennis*. Böhme's worldview is not Platonic but essentially alchemical, focusing on arduous processes of transmutation, a struggle 'from darkness to light', rather than on celebrating the beauty of a harmonious and hierarchical universe.

Böhme was born in a prosperous Lutheran peasant family in Alt-Seidenberg, and spent most of his life in nearby Görlitz, a charming town presently located on the border between Germany and Poland. Having received a quite solid education, he became a shoemaker and acquired the rights of citizenship as a master shoemaker in

1599. Having bought a house and married the daughter of a prosperous butcher, the first of his four children was born one year later. Böhme thus seemed to have embarked upon a perfectly ordinary existence as a respected citizen and family man. However, he took his Christian faith much more seriously than most, and was tormented by questions about the presence of suffering and evil in the world. How could the frightening, wrathful God of the Old Testament be reconciled with the New Testament message of a God of Love? Why was there evil as well as good in the world, not just among human beings but even among unreasoning creatures in the natural world? And what role did the 'little spark of man' play in the great drama of creation?

Such questions caused Böhme to sink into a state of melancholy and depression, 'and the devil often inspired heathenish thoughts in me, about which I will be silent here' (*Aurora*, ch. 19). He compares himself to his namesake Jacob, who struggled with God and refused to let go unless he be blessed (Gen. 32:22–32). And so the blessing finally came: Böhme's prayers for understanding and illumination were answered in the form of an ecstatic vision, presumably triggered by the sight of a beam of light reflected in a tin or pewter vessel standing on his table. His description of this event has become famous, and deserves to be quoted in full:

> But as I, in my determination, stormed hard against God and against all the gates of hell…, after several hard attempts, finally my spirit has broken through the gates of hell and all the way into the innermost birth of the Godhead, and was received there with love, the way a groom receives his dear bride.
>
> But this triumph in the spirit I cannot express by the written or spoken word; indeed it cannot be compared with anything but with the birth of life in the midst of death, and with the resurrection of the dead.
>
> In this light, my spirit has right away seen through everything, and in all creatures, even in herbs and grass, it has seen God: who he is, how he is, and what his will is. And right away, in this light, my will has grown with a great desire to describe the essence of God.
>
> (*Aurora*, ch. 19)

This is a classic example of theosophical illumination: grounded in intense reading of the Bible and a prolonged practice of anxious prayer, culminating in a profound religious experience through which the whole of Nature became transparent and was transformed into a book whose mysterious contents could now be read and deciphered by the visionary. From 1600 to 1612 (and further inspired by a second illumination in 1610), Böhme worked on what would become his first great book: a 400-page manuscript entitled *Morgen Röte im auffgang* ('Breaking Dawn'), best known under the equivalent title *Aurora*. It quickly began to be copied and circulated, leading immediately to discussion and controversy. Eventually it came into the hands of the Lutheran chief pastor of Görlitz, Gregor Richter, who was appalled by its heretical contents and severely reprimanded Böhme. He was ordered to stop writing, and for the next six years he seems to have obeyed. But in 1618, coinciding with the start of the Thirty-Year War, Böhme resumed his writing activity, and this time he continued in spite of Richter's warnings and attacks, until his early death in 1624.

Among the most important titles of Böhme's prodigious oeuvre are his *Description of the Three Principles of Divine Being* (1618), *On the Threefold Life of Man* (1620),

Forty Questions about the Soul (1620), *On How Jesus became Man* (1620), *On Six Theosophical Points* (1620), *The Signature of All Things* (1622), *The Great Mystery* (1623), and *The Way to Christ* (1624). As well as all these thousands of pages, Böhme has also left a long correspondence, his *Theosophical Letters* (1618–1624) along with other texts, such as a *Speech of Defense against Gregor Richter* (1624). His enemy Richter died in 1624, followed by Böhme himself.

Summarizing Böhme's system is not easy – in fact, it might well be impossible. He is an unsystematic writer, capable of impressive literary power and visionary brilliance, but also of great obscurity. Looking for strict rational consistency is a sure recipe for missing his point, for Böhme is not a philosopher but a visionary theosopher: he uses symbolic language, mythical imagery, and analogical reasoning to convey mystical insights that ultimately resist discursive speech. One sees him continually struggling with the limitations of verbal expression, grasping for ways of expressing the unspeakable, and coming up with quite some creative solutions in German. And last but not least, not only is his worldview highly unusual and extremely complicated, it also keeps changing and evolving from book to book. Therefore any short synthesis cannot be much more than a rough approximation: what follows is a deliberate didactic simplification that might suggest much more clarity and consistency than one will ever find in Böhme's own writings.

Everything begins with Böhme's concept of the *Ungrund* (Un-Ground). This deliberately paradoxical term is meant to refer to the mysterious essence of an Absolute Reality that is, however, perceived as the Absolute Nothing from any human perspective. It is impossible for human beings to have any actual relation with the radical alterity and absolute transcendence of the *Ungrund*, or to make any correct statements about it at all – and this includes any statement by which the *Ungrund* is identified with God. For Böhme, only a God who reveals himself to human beings can properly be called 'God', and because the *Ungrund* cannot be known – neither by man, nor even by the *Ungrund* himself, one is forced to conclude that God is absent in the *Ungrund*.

The central topic of Böhme's Theosophy is God's revelation, which must be understood quite literally as the *birth of God* out of this original state of non-being. 'In the beginning' (but even this formulation is inadequate, for time does not yet exist, and hence there cannot really be a 'before' or an 'after'), the *Ungrund* is stirred by a movement of *desire*. The Nothing desires to know Itself, but searches in vain for 'something'. Böhme speaks of an original roving 'eye', a kind of 'pure seeing' that fails to see anything due to the absence of an object. However, this birth of desire triggers a process that will eventually lead to the birth of God. For the *Ungrund* as 'Nothing', the self-manifestation of God is like a mirror in which it perceives itself. However, the *ultimate* subject of perception – and hence, the completion of the process of revelation – is not the *Ungrund* but *Man*: the fulfillment of revelation will consist in Man's perfect knowledge of God. This is why the birth of God out of the *Ungrund* will eventually be mirrored by the 'second birth' of God that must take place inside each and every human being.

God reveals himself by being born in a *body*, which Böhme refers to as 'eternal nature' or the 'eternal soul' (and this is no contradiction, for in fact Böhme conceives of the soul as a subtle body: see Deghaye 1985, 31). This must not be understood as a form of pantheism, at least in the strict monistic sense, for two reasons. First, at this stage we are still dealing with an archetypal reality, a *pleroma* that should not be confused with our own world. And second, while God does need a body to manifest himself, as a spiritual entity he is ultimately more than his body alone. However, Böhme does claim that God never manifests himself without a body, and hence we can speak of pan*en*theism (not just on this archetypal level, but eventually also on the level of our own world, on which more below). Böhme's remarkably strong concern with *corporeality* is also reflected in his consistent emphasis on sensations or sense experiences: God is 'an all-powerful, all-wise, all-knowing, all-seeing, all-hearing, all-smelling, all-feeling, all-tasting God' (*Aurora* 3.11). Although Böhme would become a significant influence on philosophers such as Schelling and Hegel, he is definitely not an idealist.

God's incarnation as 'eternal nature' is described as taking place in seven stages, but again, it is ultimately misleading to conceive of Böhme's intention in terms of 'succession'. As limited human beings we just cannot help thinking of any 'process' as taking place in a temporal sequence, but Böhme is still speaking about something that 'happens' before the emergence of time itself: what he really has in mind might be described as the original *archetype of time* as we know it from our own material world. From the perspective of the completed sevenfold cycle – i.e. from that of its final stage – all seven steps are one. Hence the 'succession' of the first six stages is meant to be a prefiguration of time, and the completion of the 'process' in the seventh stage is meant to be a prefiguration of eternity. In short, time is not a primary category but a secondary derivate from a more original reality that cannot be reduced to or understood in terms of those derivates. It is therefore misleading to refer to Böhme's sevenfold process in terms of 'evolution'.

The seven stages in which God is born as a perfectly manifested body, 'Eternal Nature', are referred to in terms of seven *qualities* (*Qualitäten*, also known as seven *Formen*, *Gestalten*, *Eigenschaften*, *Geister*, or *Quell-Geister*). Böhme is thinking of the 'seven spirits' mentioned in the Book of Revelation (1:4, 3:1, 4:5, 5:6) but also associates them analogically with the seven days of creation and the seven planets. From the perspective of the completed cycle, all seven are one, and they mutually participate in one another. To understand the peculiar names that Böhme gives to these qualities, we must once again stress his emphasis on corporeality and sensual experience: rather than describing the qualities in abstract terms, he tries to convey to his reader what a quality 'feels' like, or even what it 'tastes' like!

The birth of God begins with '*die herbe Qualität*', that is to say, with a quality of roughness, sourness, or acidity. Böhme means to convey a sensation of extreme *contraction*: a potentially infinite 'inward movement' caused by the initial impulse of desire that fails to find anything external to itself and can therefore only turn inward upon itself. The final result of this movement is petrification, that is to say, corporeality in its most extreme form: everything turns to stone. In Böhme's *Aurora*, this first quality is associated with Saturn, probably because this planet was seen as symbolizing the *nigredo*, the black initial stage of the alchemical *magnum opus*. Hence the 'birth of God' begins under a very grim and dark sign: 'Saturn, the cold, sharp and severe, rough Ruler...has dominion over the chamber of death, and dries up all powers, resulting in corporeality' (*Aurora* 26.1).

The second quality takes the form of a counter-movement against the unlimited movements of contraction and petrification. Next to the primal desire, and against it, a 'second will' emerges: the wish to break through the wall of stone that has trapped and imprisoned the emerging soul due to its own inward movement. Böhme speaks of '*die bittere Qualität*', and also refers to it as 'gall', 'poison' or 'sting'. Although Böhme associates this second quality with (among other things) the 'angel of death', it must also be seen as a very first announcement of life and movement, as opposed to the deathly rigour and immobility resulting from the first quality.

In the third quality we have a situation where the two contrary impulses or forces are engaged in mortal combat. The impulse towards contraction and petrification struggles with the impulse towards movement and liberation, but none of them can win: quite literally, we have a situation here of the irresistable force meeting the immovable object. Böhme describes this no-escape situation as an insanely whirling 'wheel', or as a 'chamber of fear': it is a domain of terror and a literal prefiguration of hell. In Böhme's analogical thinking, this third quality corresponds with the existential fear of the man who walks in darkness and searches for God in vain.

It is clear that in these first three qualities, we are dealing with a dark, hellish world of fear and terror. We will see that the fourth quality marks the turning point, leading to the final three qualities that represent the positive counterpart of the first three. Now the dark 'world' of the first three qualities, extending into the fourth, is referred to as *the First Principle*; and the 'world' of the final three qualities, initiated by the fourth, is called *the Second Principle*. The First Principle stands under the sign of Wrath (associated with God the Father), the Second Principle under the sign of Love (associated with God's Son). In other words, it is in the Second Principle that the Love of the Son vanquishes the Wrath of the Father: the dark God is reborn as a God of Light. Finally, we will see that our own material world, where Love and Wrath are struggling with one another, is *the Third Principle*.

The fourth quality marks the decisive moment in which light is born from darkness. In describing this event, Böhme uses fire-symbolism. In the first Principle, God's wrath is raging as a destructive, 'devouring fire'. In the hell of terror of the third quality, this fire gives neither warmth nor light: it is a 'dark' fire, cold like the fire of fever. This changes in the fourth quality: in the dark world of the First Principle, a *Blitz* (Flash) emerges. The destructive lightning-bolt is a potent symbol of God's wrath, but as a light that shines in the darkness, it simultaneously represents the first appearance of Love. The same fire that devours and destroys everything as 'Wrath' turns out to be capable of giving warmth and light when it manifests as 'Love'. Hence the 'Flash' functions as the pivotal event in Böhme's sevenfold cycle, through which darkness turns to light, and wrath to love.

The fifth quality is actually described as that of 'Love', but also as 'Light' or 'Joy'. It is important to emphasize that, in Böhme's thinking, this positive quality does *not* abolish, destroy, or take the place of its negative counterpart (with the implication that the Son would replace the Father, or the New Testament would abolish the Old). On the contrary, the ultimate unity of God consists in the fact that the forces of love and light temper, reconcile, or redeem the forces of wrath and darkness, rendering them harmless without annihilating them. Hence God's wrath does not vanish: it merely becomes latent or invisible. The sixth quality is described with reference to hearing rather than sight, as 'Sound' or 'the Word'. Among other things, Böhme seems to think here of divine 'harmony'. It is clear that we have now entered a 'heavenly' world of light in which the darkness and fear of the first beginning are forgotten as their opposites have come to prevail. Hell has turned into heaven. This heavenly reality finally finds its completion in the seventh quality, described as the perfect *Corpus* (Body). Böhme means to refer here to the divine fullness in which all the previous qualities turn out to be one.

God's birth has now been completed. The result is a perfect, luminous body of light, similar to the gnostic *pleroma* or divine plenitude, and referred to by Böhme as 'eternal nature'. Now the lightworld of the perfect Corpus is also described as the divine incarnation of 'God's thoughts', personified as *angels*. In other words, the entire world of eternal nature consists of angelic communities: it is filled with perfect light-beings. The head of the angels, who in some sense encompasses or represents the entire community, is Lucifer. This supreme angelic being has never known darkness: he has been born as light and has a perfect bodily constitution. But he is not satisfied: he wants to become even more perfect, and believes he can achieve this through a 'second birth' modeled after the birth of God himself. However, he overlooks a crucial difference. God has been *born as light out of darkness*, but because Lucifer stands already at the pinnacle of perfection, he can only move 'downwards' (so to speak), plunging himself back into the dark source of being: he will be *born as darkness out of light*. The results are destructive. We might visualize what happens by imagining how, somewhere in the perfect universe of luminous substance that is God's body, a tiny blot of darkness appears, which then begins to spread and infect the whole of Eternal Nature. Lucifer's fall leads to the fatal disintegration of God's body, and the 'fire of wrath' that had been hidden and rendered harmless becomes manifest again as a separate Principle set against the Principle of Light. The result is a situation that had never existed before: two *separate* and independent worlds, one of darkness and one of light. In the dark world, Lucifer is 'reborn' indeed, as the Prince of Darkness. Hence the First Principle, the darkness of which had made it possible for the Light to be born, has now become a wholly negative, anti-divine world, the world of realized evil, or hell. The Second Principle is damaged and weakened by Lucifer's fall, and has lost its original integrity and wholeness; but because Light is indestructible, it continues to exist next to the dark world. And moreover, as a direct result of Lucifer's fall, a *Third Principle* comes into existence: our own material world in time and space, the realm of 'temporal' instead of 'eternal' Nature. In this fallen world, the two principles of Light and Darkness, Love and Wrath, are engaged in mortal combat as independent forces struggling for dominion; and it is only now that they can literally be characterized as Good versus Evil. Unfortunately, the wrathful forces of evil and darkness seem to be dominant, and hence our world resembles the 'wheel of fear' of the third quality: we are living in the midst of a dark world of terror, that can only be redeemed and saved through the Light of the second birth.

Human beings are small microcosmic reflections of God's body, and they find themselves in a world of darkness, terror and suffering rather similar to the first stages of God's own birth. From this dark and frightening beginning, they must struggle towards salvation, which can come only through the miraculous birth of light and love in their own hearts. In short, Böhme says that our task as human beings is to replicate the birth of God, thereby transforming ourselves into the perfect divine beings of light and love that we were originally meant to be. This transformation, or transmutation, may begin here on earth but finds its fulfilment after death, when we leave the coarse material body behind and continue our existence in a more subtle, purified, luminous body. By achieving this new birth, we are not just reaching salvation for ourselves alone: rather, we are contributing to the redemption or reintegration of Eternal Nature, God's own body. Through this process, Lucifer's Fall will finally be reversed and its destructive results will be repaired.

It must be repeated that such a short summary of Böhme's system can never be more than a rough approximation or simplification. Countless details, such as the Fall of Adam and Eve (next to Lucifer's Fall) have not even been mentioned. Already during Böhme's own lifetime, the great complexity and frequent obscurity of his writings led to a great variety of different interpretations, for instance about the question of whether or not all beings, even the demons, will ultimately be saved ('apocatastasis'). With due mention of forerunners such as Valentin Weigel, Heinrich Khunrath and Johann Arndt, Böhme is usually seen as the originator of 'Christian theosophy' (not to be confused, of course, with the nineteenth-century Theosophy of Mme Blavatsky: representatives of the latter are usually referred to as 'Theoso*phists*', while thinkers in the line of Böhme are referred as as 'Theoso*phers*').

During the later seventeenth century, Christian theosophical ideas became central to a range of spiritual communities known for the prominence of ecstatic or trance-like states among their membership. The German Theosopher Johann Georg Gichtel (1638–1710) became the centre of a community in Amsterdam that would eventually come to be known as the 'Angelic Brethren', and emphasized practices of ecstatic union with Sophia (Wisdom) as the feminine manifestation of the divine. In England, the 'Philadelphian Society' around John Pordage (1607/08–1681) and Jane Leade (1623–1704) is marked by its communal lifestyle with a woman in a role of leadership. These and other Theosophical communities are particularly fascinating for their systematic focus on gender in the context of religious practice. An extreme case was the group around 'mother' Eva von Buttlar (1670–1721), which seems to have gone as far as practicing a ritual of sacramental sex between the male members of the group and Eva herself, symbolic of the union between spiritual man and Sophia.

Apart from such communities, Böhme's theosophical ideas also spread through international dissemination of his writings and translations into other languages. During the first half of the eighteenth century, Christian theosophy largely returned from a current of fervent religious activity to one of pious reading and commentary. The most central representative in this period was Friedrich Christoph Oetinger (1702–82). In the decades around 1800, the theosophical current entered its 'second golden age' in the context of Illuminism and German Romanticism. Louis-Claude de Saint-Martin (1743–1803) and Franz von Baader (1765–1841) are perhaps the most central figures here, surrounded by a wide international correspondence network of 'hommes de désir' (men of desire) who found in Böhme a religious alternative both to the dogmatism of the established churches and the dominant trends of rationalization. The question of how important the Böhme-Renaissance of this period has been to German Romanticism and Idealism remains somewhat controversial to the present day. In any case, one must beware of distorting the specificity of Böhme's worldview by anachronistically reading Romantic and Idealist philosophical tenets back into his writings. For instance, it is easy for us to put an evolutionist spin on his dialectics of darkness and light and read those dynamical 'processes' through the lenses of Hegelian philosophy; in fact, however, Böhme did not think of them in terms of temporality and historicity, and hence it is incorrect to see the 'birth of God' as a process of evolution taking place in our universe of time and space. To understand Böhme, we need to forget a whole range of worldviews and unlearn a whole set of assumptions that have become so natural to us that we find it hard to think otherwise, and try as best as we can to meet this visionary genius on his own terms, in his own time and place.

REFERENCES AND FURTHER READING

Deghaye, Pierre (1985) *La naissance de Dieu, ou la doctrine de Jacob Böhme*, Paris: Albin Michel.

——(1992) 'Jacob Böhme and his Followers', in Antoine Faivre and Jacob Needleman, eds., *Modern Esoteric Spirituality*, New York: Crossroad, 210–47.

Faivre, Antoine (2005) 'Christian Theosophy', in W.J. Hanegraaff, ed. (in collaboration with Antoine Faivre, Roelof van den Broek, and Jean-Pierre Brach), *Dictionary of Gnosis and Western Esotericism*, Leiden: Brill, 258–67.

Gibbons, B.J. (1996) *Gender in Mystical and Occult Thought: Behmenism and its Development in England*, Cambridge: Cambridge University Press.

Harmsen, Theodor (2007) *Jacob Böhmes Weg in die Welt: Zur Geschichte der Handschriftensammlung,* Übersetzungen *und Editionen von Abraham Willemsz van Beyerland*, Amsterdam: In de Pelikaan.

Koyré, Alexandre (1929) *La philosophie de Jacob Böhme*, Paris: Vrin.

Temme, Willi (1998) *Krise der Leiblichkeit: Die Sozietät der Mutter Eva (Buttlarsche Rotte) und der Radikale Pietismus um 1700*, Göttingen: Vandenhoeck & Ruprecht.

Versluis, Arthur (1999) *Wisdom's Children: A Christian Esoteric Tradition*, Albany: State University of New York Press.

Viatte, August (1927) *Les sources occultes du Romantisme: Illuminisme, Théosophie 1770–1820*, Paris: Honoré Champion.

Weeks, Andrew (1991) *Böhme: An Intellectual Biography of the Seventeenth-Century Philosopher and Mystic*, Albany: State University of New York Press.

CHAPTER NINE

THE ROSICRUCIAN MANIFESTOS AND EARLY ROSICRUCIANISM

Hereward Tilton

INTRODUCTION

Four hundred years ago the dawn of Rosicrucianism was heralded across Germany by the publication of the anonymous *Rumour of the Fraternity* (*Fama fraternitatis*, 1614). This short tract described the opening of the tomb of 'Brother C. R.' (Christian Rosenkreuz), the founder of a fraternity of learned monks dedicated to establishing a universal reformation. Within the tomb were books containing the primeval wisdom (*prisca sapientia*) granted by God to Adam, Enoch, Moses and Solomon – alchemy, Kabbalah and magic. These were the fruits of Brother C. R.'s journey to Arabia and Morocco, and their rediscovery was said to presage a new age of the knowledge of God and nature in which 'it shall not be said, this is true according to philosophy, but false according to theology'. Rather, this 'double truth' of Scholastic Aristotelianism will be overthrown and the essential unity of Biblical teachings and pagan philosophy will be established (*Fama fraternitatis*, 1615: 46–47). In the following year a second manifesto appeared, the *Confession of the Fraternity* (*Confessio fraternitatis*, 1615), which gave the year of Christian Rosenkreuz's birth as 1378, and claimed that he had lived for 106 years (by implication due to his possession of the life-imparting Philosophers' Stone). As the *Rumour of the Fraternity* states that his tomb remained undisturbed for 120 years, the time of its opening may be calculated as 1604 – the year a supernova appeared in the constellation of Serpentarius. In the *Confessio fraternitatis* this 'new star' is described as a divine seal, such as are found imprinted in the Bible and throughout all creation. The brethren of the rosy cross have created a new magical language based upon these 'occult signs', and thus they are able to predict the coming eclipse in ecclesiastical affairs as surely as an astronomer predicts a celestial eclipse (*Confessio fraternitatis*, 1615a: 71–73).

In the centuries since the first appearance of this ingenious amalgam of legend and historical events, the Rosicrucian mantle has been assumed by a motley group of initiates, both real and imaginary: purely fictional characters inhabiting novels, the polemical caricatures of propaganda tracts, real apologists for wholly virtual fraternities, and even the members of historically verifiable esoteric societies legitimating their authority with as many pseudo-historical myths of origin. Despite this diversity, one central motif lies at the heart of the Rosicrucian phenomenon across the four centuries of its existence: the notion of a conspiratorial cabal of transfigured beings intervening, unseen, in the course of human history. Transfiguration is the metamorphosis of the human body into that spiritualized condition described by St. Paul in his account of the body of the resurrection (1 Corinthians 15); and with transfiguration the Rosicrucian achieves gnosis, a knowledge of the mind of God reserved for that select few privy to the mysteries of Christ (1 Corinthians 2; Origen, 1980: 169). Within the history of Rosicrucianism this quasi-divine condition has been attained in a variety of ways, above all alchemically through ingestion of the Philosophers' Stone and magically through the Christian Cabalistic heavenly ascent. These paths to transfiguration and gnosis are depicted in the earliest Rosicrucian texts, which provoked both hope and fear in early modern Europe with their portrayal of an invisible brotherhood ushering in a new age of justice, peace and divine knowledge.

INSPIRATIONISM, MAGIC AND THE AMBIGUITY OF THE ROSICRUCIAN MANIFESTOS

Notwithstanding this central underlying motif, early Rosicrucianism was anything but ideologically unified, and cannot be described as a unitary 'movement' or 'culture' (e.g. Yates, 1978: ix, xiii). This is true of the early reception of the manifestos' message within the storm of sympathetic apologies and opposing polemical tracts (*Kampfschriften*) that broke upon their publication, as diverse confessional voices advanced their own visions of the true fraternity within the virtual arena opened up by the manifestos. Yet it is also true of the manifestos themselves, which evince two conflicting doctrinal tendencies. This tension within the texts reflects a broader struggle to define religious orthodoxy within a Christendom left ideologically splintered by the Reformation.

The Holy Roman Empire during the Counter-Reformation was a fragmented patchwork of Catholic, Lutheran and Calvinist states, and within them all there existed a super-confessional religious orientation that Carlos Gilly – borrowing a term coined by the Rosicrucian apologist Adam Haslmayr – has named the *Theophrastia sancta* (Holy Theophrastia) (Gilly, 1994b: 450). This orientation drew its inspiration from the theological works of Paracelsus (1493–1541, chapter six), which circulated in manuscript form among his followers in the sixteenth and seventeenth centuries. Paracelsus advocated the revival of an early Christian community reflecting Christ's injunctions to the apostles (Luke 9.1–6, 10.1–9) and founded upon selfless love, collective property and obedience to divine rather than secular or ecclesiastical authority (Paracelsus, 2008: 159, 279; Goldammer, 1952: 62–64). Indeed, in the early 1530s Paracelsus gathered a small community of peasants around himself in the Appenzell region of Switzerland, and the majority of his theological writings stem from this period of lay preaching. Although he had been involved in the peasant and miners' revolt in Salzburg (1525–26), Paracelsus was an avowed pacifist (Sudhoff, 1936: 16). In his view, the bloodletting by Catholics, Lutherans, Zwingliites and Anabaptists alike could only be the work of 'false Christians', i.e. adherents of the 'walled churches' (*Mauerkirchen*) under the sway of corrupt worldly powers, a notion he derived from the medieval Franciscans

(Gantenbein, 2008: 33–34). In their stead Paracelsus promoted a church of the 'inner man', its scattered congregation united in the Holy Spirit and ongoing divine revelation. While God is the source of a light of nature penetrating all Creation and revealing its hidden (occult) powers, through faith the Christian receives another eternal light, termed the light of grace in the work of Valentin Weigel (1533–88); from this second light proceed prophecy and the highest knowledge of theology.

The *Theophrastia sancta* is a current of Reformation inspirationism or 'spiritualism', a term referring in this historical context to an anti-institutional tendency asserting the primacy of direct inspiration through the Holy Spirit. The influence of the inspirationist ideals of Paracelsus and his followers upon the Rosicrucian manifestos is unmistakeable. That the primitive apostolic Church constitutes a model for the brotherhood is evident in its first law, which enjoins the brethren to dedicate their lives to the curing of the sick and forbids them to accept money for their services (*Fama fraternitatis*, 1615: 28–29). The brotherhood's meeting place is the 'house of the Holy Spirit', and the *Confessio fraternitatis* invites all mortals impelled by the spirit of God to join the fraternity there (*Confessio fraternitatis*, 1615b: I2 *recto*). Understood symbolically, these words lend themselves to an inspirationist interpretation – the fraternity's dwelling is not a sectarian *Mauerkirche* belonging to this or that warring confession, but rather a church that is to be found wherever good Christians are united in the Holy Spirit (Figure 9.1).

The Augustinian notion of an inner 'invisible Church' is also to be found in the early writings of Luther, who wrote of a 'hidden, invisible and spiritual' Christian community of which the 'corporeal, visible, external' Church is only a sign (Luther, 1520b: Bi *verso*). Nevertheless, Luther insisted upon the indispensability of Scripture and sacrament as mediators of inspiration, and his plea for the support of the princes gave rise to a Lutheran territorial church intimately tied to worldly power (Luther, 1520a: ix *verso*). Furthermore, in the wake of the Reformation inspirationist theological currents influentially merged with Christian Cabalistic and magical traditions, which advanced esoteric techniques for addressing non-human beings, such as angels (i.e. 'addressative' magical practices; Weill-Parot, 2002: 169). Such recourse to supernatural magic was condemned by Luther, who condoned only the purely natural magic of the Persian magi and King Solomon: by the manipulation of the occult forces inhering in herbs, minerals and metals, the magus and the doctor alike may achieve seemingly miraculous results just as alchemists transmute copper into gold (Luther, 1547: 169 *verso*).

Yet addressative magic is depicted in both the *Fama fraternitatis* and the *Confessio fraternitatis*. Thus the *Confessio fraternitatis* refers to the control of spirits and 'mighty princes of the world' through Orphic singing (*Confessio fraternitatis*, 1615a: 62), and states that the knowledge possessed by Christian Rosenkreuz has been gained through communication with angels and spirits (*Confessio fraternitatis*, 1615a: 59–60). Interaction with angels alone was a problematic subject for Protestant theologians struggling to define orthodoxy, given the post-biblical cessation of prophetic revelation (cf. Hunnius, 1619: Diii *verso*-Div *recto*) and the well-attested custom of demons to disguise themselves as God's messengers (Augustine, 2002: 931); yet here it is implied the brethren are able to communicate with undefined 'spirits'. On this matter the *Fama fraternitatis* is no more orthodox than the *Confessio fraternitatis*, as the floor of the tomb of Christian Rosenkreuz depicts a demonic

Figure 9.1 The house of the Holy Spirit, as depicted by Matthäus Merian in Daniel Mögling's *Mirror of Rosicrucian Wisdom* (*Speculum sophicum rhodo-stauroticum*, 1618). Wings demonstrate the purely spiritual nature of the fraternity's dwelling, while the inscription *moveamur* shows they are 'impelled [by the Holy Spirit]'. To the right a pious enquirer after the fraternity acknowledges his ignorance as he looks to God and clutches the anchor of faith and hope, while to the left the 'well of errors and opinions' is the destination for those seekers after the brethren who cannot overcome accursed *philautia* (love of self) to uncover the spark of divine goodness within (Mögling, 1618: 11–12, 23). With permission of the Sächsische Landesbibliothek – Staats-und Universitätsbibliothek Dresden.

hierarchy corresponding to the angelic hierarchy represented at its ceiling. The names of these 'lower rulers' are said to be a secret of the brethren, who fear their misuse by those not possessing the heavenly 'antidote' to their malevolent power – a sentiment consonant with Trithemian and Agrippan demonology (Agrippa, 1533: 310; *Fama fraternitatis*, 1615: 38–39). However the 'brethren' might have utilized these demonic names, the *Fama fraternitatis* also appears to refer to communication with Paracelsian elementary spirits. Thus it is said that Christian Rosenkreuz learnt his arts from the elementary inhabitants (*Elementarische Inwohner*) of Fez, which in the earliest known manuscript copy of the *Fama fraternitatis* are specifically contrasted with human beings (*Fama fraternitatis*, 1998: 11, 76, 104).

Perplexingly, the inspirationist and addressative magical elements of the manifestos are at odds with their explicit description of the brethren's faith. Thus the *Fama fraternitatis* employs the language of Luther when it distinguishes the fraternity from 'all enthusiasts (*Schwärmer*), heretics and false prophets' (*Fama fraternitatis*, 1615: 45) – words specifically designed to deflect suspicions the brethren promoted an inspirationist religiosity unmediated by the clergy or the formal principle of *sola Scriptura*. The *Fama fraternitatis* goes on to state the brethren partake of 'two sacraments' as the 'first reformed Church' employs them. This statement suggests they are followers of Luther (*Concordia*, 1580: 216 *verso*, 221 *verso*). Nevertheless, the Calvinists also professed two sacraments, and for contemporary Calvinist readers the theological orientation implied by the fraternity's confession of faith remained ambiguous (Budova, 1616: 249), while hostile authors felt free to refer to the 'Calvinist-Rosicrucian brethren' (Germanus, 1626: 92). License for such a characterization had been given by the catalogues of the Leipzig and Frankfurt book fairs, which had advertised the manifestos as 'German theological books of the Calvinists' because they were published at Kassel with the specific authorization of the Calvinist Landgrave Moritz of Hessen-Kassel (1572–1632).

Further ambiguity is evident in the manifestos' attitude towards secular authority. Once again certain passages indicate a desire to distance the fraternity from an anti-institutional position: thus in the *Confessio fraternitatis* the brethren declare they are not heretics intending to overthrow worldly governments, and they offer the emperor their prayers, secrets and great treasures of gold (*Confessio fraternitatis*, 1615a: 55–56). It is unlikely this is a reference to Emperor Rudolf II (r. 1576–1612) or his usurping brother Matthias (r. 1612–19), who both followed an aggressive policy of re-Catholicization within the empire. It is a future successor who will be the recipient of the brethren's gold: as the *Fama fraternitatis* states, 'Europe is pregnant and will bear a strong child who must have a great christening gift' (*Fama fraternitatis*, 1615: 32). The millennialist tendencies apparent in both manifestos are more pronounced in the *Confessio fraternitatis*, which speaks of the coming of a 'lion' who will use the brethren's treasures to 'fortify his empire' (*Confessio fraternitatis*, 1615a: 69). In another place the prophecy continues with the foretelling of the 'final downfall' of a papacy already weakened by the onslaught of the Reformers (*Confessio fraternitatis*, 1615a: 66).

THE AUTHORSHIP OF THE MANIFESTOS

According to one widely disseminated narrative, the lion of the manifestos represents the 'Palatinate lion': the Calvinist Elector Palatine, Friedrich V (1596–1632), whom the Protestant Union of Calvinist princes and their Lutheran allies sought to install on the Bohemian throne, thus lending the Protestants a majority at the college of electors (*Kurfürstencollegium*) responsible for the election of the emperor (Yates, 1978: 54, 56). Nevertheless, the lion motif in the *Confessio fraternitatis* is derived from a vision of the Tübingen Paracelsian Tobias Hess (1568–1614), which has been recorded for posterity in a letter written by Hess in 1605 to his patron Friedrich I, the Lutheran Duke of Württemberg (1557–1608). Here the roar of the apocalyptic lion shakes the world to its foundations, and his wrath is directed towards an eagle and the whore of Babylon (Gilly, 1994a: 88). As the two-headed eagle was the emblem of the Holy Roman Emperor, it seems Hess' vision referred on at least one level to that office, while the whore of Babylon – the Pope – represented the power behind the imperial throne.

For the prophet Hess, the lion of his vision was the herald of the third age of the Holy Spirit foretold by the medieval theologian Joachim of Fiore (c. 1132–1202). Joachimite millennialism was an integral element of the thought of Paracelsus and his followers. According to this view of history, the Old Testament corresponded to the age of the Father and the rule of the law, while the New Testament announced the age of the Son and the rule of grace – and in the pages of the Book of Revelation, the Joachimites discerned a coming golden age of the Holy Spirit ushered in by an angelic pope and ruled by unmediated divine inspiration. For his part, Tobias Hess predicted this age would arrive in 1620. This belief did not please the authorities at the University of Tübingen, who launched proceedings against him as a 'disciple of that impious Paracelsus' (Gilly, 1995: 47).

Millennialistically inclined Protestants identified the lion of the *Confessio fraternitatis* with a worldly defender of the Protestant faith against the Catholic League, which had been formed in 1609 in response to the emergence of the Protestant Union. For Hess this defending lion had been his own patron, Duke Friedrich I of Württemberg (Gilly, 1994b: 470), who strove to bring the Lutheran states into closer alliance with the Calvinists. Subsequently the lion was identified with a number of Protestant leaders, most prominently the Elector Palatine Friedrich V, and later King Gustav II Adolf of Sweden, whose intervention in the Thirty Years' War briefly turned the tide in favour of the Protestant forces.

Tobias Hess formed the focal point of an 'intimate league of friends' in Tübingen that included the young Lutheran theologian Johann Valentin Andreae (1586–1654), the grandson of the editor of the Lutheran *Book of Concord* (1580). Although Andreae's authorship of the manifestos has been refuted on the grounds of his supposedly unwavering Lutheran orthodoxy (Montgomery, 1973: 210), today his involvement in what he came to describe as a youthful folly is well established (Brecht, 1977: 286–90). Indeed, the conflicting religious tendencies evident within their message give the impression the manifestos were written by a Paracelsian inspirationist and a Lutheran more inclined to orthodoxy. It is not entirely clear whether this disjuncture can be explained in terms of the respective worldviews of Hess and Andreae, particularly given the fact a third party is also implicated in the authorship of the manifestos (Gilly, 2001: 28–32). Nonetheless, the addressative, supernatural magical practices alluded to in the manifestos stand in stark contrast to Andreae's later conception of a purely natural magic (Andreae, 1618: 201–3), which he understood merely as a synonym for the experimentally based mathematical and mechanical arts also practiced by the brethren depicted in the manifestos.

This doctrinal tension within the manifestos is also reflected in the mixed response they elicited from Lutheran theologians. In his *Theological Judgment* (*Iudicium theologicum*, 1616), David Meder (1545–1616) points to the manifestos' explicit confession of faith as proof the brethren are orthodox Lutherans who accept the terms of the Peace of Augsburg (1555). He also defends the brethren's magic and alchemy, as he states he has himself been a lifelong practitioner of these arts. Their magic – like his own – is purely natural, having nothing to do with diabolical pacts, the help of evil spirits and other forbidden practices, while their alchemy – like his own – is that same chemical medicine the apostles used to cure the poor in body just as they cured souls with the word of Christ (Meder, 1616: Aiii *recto*-Aiv *verso*, Bi *recto*).

Yet Christopher Nigrinus (c. 1580–after 1637), a Lutheran pastor at Großkniegnitz in Silesia, put forward a very different interpretation of the brethren's religion in his *Rosy Sphinx* (*Sphynx rosacea*, 1619), which indicates political considerations were often paramount in the conflicting Lutheran judgements upon the fraternity. Treating the manifestos as texts with coded crypto-Calvinist messages, Nigrinus argues that the brethren with their admonitions to the unworthy are in fact the Calvinist elect, predestined to be saved since the beginning of the world. Likewise, the fraternity's statements concerning alchemical transmutation are a coded attempt to confuse the true Lutheran doctrine concerning the Eucharist. The Machiavellian purpose of the 'brethren' in publishing their manifestos is to bring the Lutherans into closer alliance with the Calvinists in the empire (Nigrinus, 1619: 82–84, 99, 108–9). Thus Nigrinus associates the manifestos and their message with the political ambitions of the Elector Palatine Friedrich V; his views reflect the precarious position of Lutheran Silesia under its feudal overlord, Archduke Ferdinand of Styria, who personally tore up the Letter of Majesty guaranteeing Protestant religious freedom following his assumption of the imperial throne in 1619.

THE SECRET TEACHINGS OF CHRIST

Among the many competing visions of the 'true' Rosicrucian fraternity that emerged in response to the ambiguous manifestos, the Paracelsian interpretation is exemplified by Adam Haslmayr's *Answer to the Praiseworthy Brotherhood of the Theosophers of Rosenkreuz* (*Antwort an die lobwürdige Brüderschafft der Theosophen von Rosencreutz*, 1612). In the course of his tract Haslmayr associates the lion of the *Confessio fraternitatis* with the pseudo-Paracelsian prophecy of the Lion of Midnight, which described the discovery of three treasures and the apocalyptic lion's defeat of 'the eagle' (i.e. the emperor) following the demise of 'the last Austrian emperor, Rudolf' (Paracelsus, 1933: 545–46; Haslmayr, 1615: 93). Although Paracelsians such as Haslmayr believed this to be a true prophecy of Paracelsus, the apparent reference to Rudolf II suggests it was created after that emperor assumed the imperial throne in 1576. In his *Answer to the Praiseworthy Brotherhood* Haslmayr portrays the Rosicrucian brethren as harbingers of the millennium; their role is to illuminate the way for the Lion of Midnight with 'the light of Christ and nature's sanctuary', a reference to the Paracelsian lights of grace and nature (Haslmayr, 1615: 98). With inspired language – 'so come, O you pious and pure priests, anointed with eternal wisdom and abounding with miracles' – Haslmayr implores the brethren to bring the darkening world their *Theophrastia* (Haslmayr, 1615: 97). He goes on to enumerate the elements of this wisdom: the Kabbalah, the 'angels of good counsel', the 'necrolic' (life-preserving) medicine, the 'sacred magic of Bethlehem', the prophetic interpretation of heavenly signs through the *evestrum* or astral spirit, and the 'blessed *nectromantia*', defined by Paracelsus as the revelation of things hidden in nature and the human heart through crystal-gazing, divining, dreams, etc. (Paracelsus, 1929: 148–57; Haslmayr, 1615: 97–98).

As the title page of the first published edition of the *Fama fraternitatis* announced, Haslmayr was sentenced by the Jesuits to many years' imprisonment on a Mediterranean galley due to his authorship of the *Answer to the Praiseworthy Brotherhood*. Just as Hess had seen Duke Friedrich I of Württemberg as the lion of his vision, so Haslmayr imagined his own patron in the same role. Prince August of Anhalt-Plötzkau (1575–1653) was a nominal Calvinist whose sympathies were firmly with the anti-institutional inspirationists; he created a secret printing press for the purpose of disseminating the theological works of Paracelsus and Weigel, which contributed in no small degree to the contours of the inspirationist reception of the manifestos (Gilly, 1988: 76).

In an intriguing passage, Haslmayr also refers in his apology to 'Paul and the Cabalists or *Aniadi*' who remained after the Ascension to propagate Christ's teachings among the Jews and heathens (Haslmayr, 1615: 88). The Paracelsian term *Aniadum* refers to the 'celestial body' received from the Holy Spirit via the sacraments, or alternatively to '*homo spiritualis* regenerated within us' (Dorn, 1612: 42). Thus Haslmayr envisages the Rosicrucians as transfigured men who have received the 'seed' of Christ (Gantenbein, 2008: 26) – a vision that draws not only from Paracelsus but also from Origen's explicit reference to 'esoteric' teachings of Jesus disseminated by Paul among a select 'assembly of the perfected' (Origen, 1605: 7–8; Origen, 2005: 79; cf. 1 Corinthians 2.6).

Through the work of the Christian Cabalist Julius Sperber (15?-1616?) – an advisor to Prince August's brother, Johann Georg I of Anhalt-Dessau – the Rosicrucian brotherhood was again portrayed as the inheritor of an esoteric magical tradition transmitted orally by Jesus to those few disciples capable of comprehending it. A tract of Sperber's dating to 1597 was printed as the *Echo of the Divinely Enlightened Fraternity of the Praiseworthy Order R. C.* (*Echo der von Gott hocherleuchteten Fraternitet des löblichen Ordens R. C.*, 1615), together with an anonymous introduction dedicating it to the Rosicrucian fraternity on account of its corroboration of the manifestos' assertions (Sperber, 1615: Diii *verso*-Div *recto*). In his tract Sperber depicted Jesus as a consummate exponent of the 'Merkabah', i.e. the Jewish Kabbalistic tradition of heavenly ascent to attain the vision of God's throne. For Sperber, this art entails intoning the names of God in order to speak with angels, receive revelations and ascend to the heavens to 'befriend' and even become one with God. However, Jesus did not receive this high wisdom in the synagogue, as the Jewish Kabbalah had become corrupted by his time; rather, he brought it directly from heaven and instituted a new 'magical college' for his disciples, to whom he taught the secret meaning of his parables (Sperber, 1615: 14, 20–26).

Sperber's conception of the Merkabah as the esoteric teaching of Christ is derived directly from Agrippa's *On the Uncertainty and Vanity of Sciences and Arts* (*De incertitudine et vanitate scientiarum et artium*, 1531; chapter five). Recognizing the manifest similarity of Kabbalistic doctrine with Marcosian Gnostic heresy, Agrippa had portrayed the latter as a corrupted derivative of the Kabbalistic *prisca sapientia* (rather than as the source it truly was); nevertheless, he also associated this heresy with Origen's notion of the esoteric teachings of Jesus and Paul to the 'perfected' (Agrippa, 1531: Hvii *recto*-Hvii *verso*, Ii *recto*). For Sperber only the members of this 'magical college' have the ability to prophesy during the age of the Son. Clearly Sperber counts himself among their number, as he describes his use of an 'archetypal mirror' in which he has attained the vision of the Merkabah, and from which he has gained knowledge of the imminent age of the Holy Spirit and its new third Testament, covenant and religion (Sperber, 1615: 159–60, 172–75).

In his Rosicrucian apologies the English Christian Cabalist Robert Fludd (1574–1637) also portrays the Kabbalah as the secret teaching of Christ, and like Sperber he derives the notion from Agrippa (Fludd, 1633: 44; Fludd, 1617: 28–29; cf. Agrippa, 1531: Hvii *verso*). Fludd's *Apologetic Treatise defending the Integrity of the Society of the Rosy Cross* (*Tractatus apologeticus integritatem Societatis de Rosea Cruce defendens*, 1617) was directed against the anti-Paracelsian alchemist Andreas Libavius, an orthodox Lutheran who had written at length against the fraternity depicted in the manifestos. Libavius had accepted that the parables of Christ possessed an esoteric significance, but he argued that the misuse of such symbolic language leads to just the sort of diabolical (addressative) magic advocated by the brethren (Libavius, 1615: 283). He also castigated the fraternity for spreading its apocalyptic prophecies concerning the Lion of Midnight – such ideas were a dangerous spark that might ignite another Peasants' War or Münster Rebellion (Libavius, 1616: 13–14). In his reply to Libavius, Fludd defends the practice of conversing with angels, and argues that the Rosicrucian brethren may well have foreseen the Second Coming in the new star of 1604, just as the Magi once read the seal of Christ imprinted in the star they followed to Bethlehem (Fludd, 1617: 25–26, 65). Moreover, the fraternity has knowledge of the dominion of the planetary angels or 'world rulers' over historical epochs, a doctrine of Trithemius that Fludd also attributes to Christ (Fludd, 1617: 130–38; cf. *Confessio fraternitatis*, 1615a: 62).

THE CHEMICAL WEDDING AND THE ALCHEMY OF THE BRETHREN

The alchemy of the brethren depicted in the manifestos is not of a 'spiritual' or allegorical nature; rather, it involves the laboratory pursuits of *chymiatria* (chemical medicine, hence the first law of the brethren to cure the sick *gratis*) and *chrysopoeia* (gold-making, hence the vast hoard of gold possessed by the brethren). These arts were patronized by many contemporary Protestant rulers in the empire, most notably Moritz of Hessen-Kassel. Chemical medicine promised monarchs a means of maintaining the health of the populace and hence the strength of the state, while the art of manipulating metals was a tried and true means of waging economic warfare on territorial rivals (Nummedal, 2007: 151–53). While it is true that the *Fama fraternitatis* impugns 'the godless and accursed art of gold-making', its polemic is directed towards alchemical frauds (*Betrüger*), as it goes on to state that gold-making is possible for the 'true philosopher', albeit as a mere by-work (*parergon*) rather than their main work (*ergon*) (*Fama fraternitatis*, 1615: 48). In a slightly different vein, the *Confessio fraternitatis* condemns those alchemists who swindle simpletons with 'obscure language' and misuse the Holy Trinity – a reference to the work of the Christian Cabalist Heinrich Khunrath (1560–1605), whose association of the Paracelsian *tria prima* with the Holy Trinity offended orthodox Lutheran sensibilities by blurring the boundaries between the natural and supernatural realms (*Confessio fraternitatis*, 1615a: 78).

It is likely those orthodox sensibilities belonged to Johann Valentin Andreae himself, as a very similar critique appears in the 'third Rosicrucian manifesto' published under his name: the *Chemical Wedding of Christian Rosenkreuz, 1459* (*Chymische Hochzeit: Christiani Rosencreütz, Anno 1459*, 1616) (Andreae, 1616: 46–47). This is without doubt the most famous work of Protestant alchemical allegory, a literary genre which had been sanctioned by Luther's own allegorical employment of alchemical symbolism (Luther, 1568: 361), and which flourished in the early Rosicrucian milieu through an early Baroque love of ornament. The *Chemical Wedding* concerns the seven-day journey of Christian Rosenkreuz, who has been invited by an angelic female figure to a royal wedding, and who is accepted into an order known as the Knights of the Golden Stone governed by a mysterious 'virgin'. This is manifestly Sophia of the Wisdom literature, in the same guise as we find her with her 'invisible fortress' in the allegorical writings of the Paracelsian Gerhard Dorn, which served as an important inspiration for the *Chemical Wedding* (Dorn, 1659: 238–39).

With its traditional alchemical motifs of death, resurrection and the *coniunctio oppositorum*, the *Chemical Wedding* may be read as a depiction of the soul's union with Christ in the tradition of Origen's allegorizing interpretation of the Song of Songs. Nevertheless, as Andreae's allegory is a portrayal of universal correspondences and archetypal laws, the reader will search in vain for a final referent. This did not prevent the appearance of Christoffer Rotbard's *Elucidarius maior* (1617) and the anonymous *Practica leonis viridis* (1619), which both claimed Christian Rosenkreuz's surreal journey was a veiled reference to laboratory alchemy. Rotbard argues the Rosicrucian brethren do not mean to bring strife to the empire, for that universal Reformation will be brought about soon enough with the return of Christ; rather, like all good alchemists they have hidden the 'high secret of the blessed Philosophers' Stone' within the opaque words of the manifestos and the *Chemical Wedding* (Rotbard, 1617: 65–67).

Although alchemy was only one element of the *prisca sapientia* possessed by the brethren of the manifestos, in his influential Rosicrucian apologies the alchemist Michael Maier (1568–1622) portrayed it as their primary pursuit. In *Silence after the Clamour* (*Silentium post clamores*, 1617), Maier argued that the fraternity's failure to answer the many published queries and requests for admittance should not be taken as proof of its non-existence; rather, the brethren are merely observing the oath of silence kept by earlier 'philosophical societies' such as the Pythagoreans, Brahmans and Egyptian priests (Maier, 1617: 26–46). According to Maier's monomythic perspective, the chief arcanum of the fraternity and their forebears is the Philosophers' Stone: hence in *Golden Themis* (*Themis aurea*, 1618) he argues the initials 'R. C.' are in fact alchemical 'hieroglyphs' and do not refer to a 'rosy cross' (Maier, 1624: 210–13). By proclaiming the 'true' meaning of the fraternity's laws, Maier wrote as if from the inside of an organized secret society; although he had no personal acquaintance with the Tübingen circle of Andreae, his aim thereby was to distinguish true Rosicrucianism from false and establish himself as the chief spokesman of the former. His success in this regard is evident from the words of the Jesuit polemicist François Garasse, who in his *The Strange Doctrine of the Allegedly Great Minds of this Time* (*La doctrine curieuse des beaux esprits de ce temps, ou pretendus tels*, 1623) described Maier as the 'secretary' of a 'pernicious company of sorcerers' threatening the church, the state and good morals (Garasse, 1623: 82–93).

THE ROSICRUCIAN TRIALS

With the outbreak of the Thirty Years' War the tide turned against those assuming the Rosicrucian mantle within the Protestant territories of the empire. The Defenestration of Prague on 23 May 1618 marked the beginning of a full-scale insurrection by the Bohemian Protestants, who elected the Elector Palatine Friedrich V as King of Bohemia on 26 August 1619. But many Lutheran German states wavered in their support for his venture, and the aspirations of the 'Winter King' were to end on 8 November 1620 at the Battle of the White Mountain; there a Catholic League army sent by Emperor Ferdinand II took less than an hour to defeat the combined Protestant forces.

It is in the context of these events that we should understand the Rosicrucian trials that took place in Lutheran and Calvinist Germany from 1619 onwards. With the heightening of sectarian hostilities and the outbreak of war, external territorial pressure prompted draconian measures to maintain the internal stability and cohesion of Protestant states that had once tolerated or even tacitly supported the Rosicrucian phenomenon, leading to the marginalization and persecution of those advocating an anti-institutional, inspirationist reception of the manifestos. Indeed, the manifestos' depiction of the brotherhood as an invisible cabal of transfigured beings and the fear it engendered assisted in this process of social disciplining, as the mere word *Rosenkreuzer* could be used to conjure up images of conspiratorial intrigue and thus marginalize political targets (be they truly 'Rosicrucian' or not) within the popular consciousness.

In 1619 proceedings were initiated by the Lutheran Church in Württemberg against the Rosicrucian apologist Johann Faulhaber (1580–1635), who was condemned as an 'enthusiast' and accused of being one of at least seventy 'Rosicrucian brethren' communicating by letter and meeting in the region (Schneider, 2005: 323). Soon thereafter Moritz of Hessen-Kassel himself oversaw proceedings against two men accused of being Rosicrucians: Philipp Heinrich Homagius and Georg Zimmermann. Homagius appeared at his hearing in the red woolly shirt of a jester, brandishing a bauble and declaring in an inspired manner that he had been called upon by God through special revelations and visions to appear as His fool (Hochhuth, 1862: 91, 98). Among other heresies, the Calvinist inquisitors assembled by Moritz condemned Homagius and Zimmermann for their Paracelsian pantheism ('God is material and corporeal') and their Joachimite belief in an imminent age of the Holy Spirit in which the invisible church would be made visible (Hochhuth, 1862: 113–20). They were also accused of disseminating magical texts such as the *Arbatel* alongside the works of Agrippa, Paracelsus and Weigel (Hochhuth, 1862: 87–88). As Homagius and his hundreds of 'Rosicrucian' co-conspirators were allegedly planning a Reformation which would begin on Christmas Day, 1621, Landgrave Moritz declared this to be a matter of utmost importance to the security of the state, and urged the inquisitors to pass the severest of sentences. Thus Homagius was sentenced to 'perpetual imprisonment', a ruling that drove him insane (Hochhuth, 1862: 128–29, 131).

Despite his harsh sentence, apparently Homagius was released after serving only a few years, as he became embroiled in another 'Rosicrucian' trial in 1623, this time in neighbouring Hessen-Darmstadt under the auspices of Landgrave Ludwig V (1577–1626). Although Ludwig was a cousin of Moritz of Hessen-Kassel, Hessen-Darmstadt was a staunchly Lutheran landgraviate allied to the imperial forces. In December 1622 Homagius met with the Rosicrucian apologist Heinrich Nolle (158?-1626) in Gießen, and when Ludwig heard of their presence in his capital he formed a commission to investigate this 'new sect of enthusiasts' and its leaders (Hochhuth, 1863: 216). While Nolle and Homagius fled its clutches, Ludwig's inquisition pitted the strictly Lutheran faculty of theology at the University of Gießen – whose duty was to prevent any further 'reform' of the teachings of Luther – against a number of professors in the faculties of medicine and law who had associated with the two 'sect leaders' (Klenk, 1965: 42). During the trial it was alleged the accused had gathered at secret meetings in which participants addressed one another as 'brother' and 'sister'; furthermore, a letter to Nolle from one of these 'brethren', professor of medicine Samuel Stephani, was signed 'Stephani, Rosen✠er' (Klenk, 1965: 54).

Ludwig's wrath was also provoked by the publication of Nolle's *Mirror of the Philosophical Parergon* (*Parergi philosophici speculum*, 1623) by the Gießen university press. This elegant allegory describes a young man's quest for the Brethren of Wisdom in their Castle of Fortune; during his journey Galen, the Aristotelian apologist Julius Caesar Scaliger and the Calvinist theologian Thomas Erastus attempt to lead him astray, but he is guided along the right path by Paracelsus, Hermes and the archangel Gabriel. As in his previous work, Nolle argues that divine inspiration may be received not only through the Bible but also via the macrocosm of nature and the microcosm of the human being, as meditative 'introversion' reveals the human soul to be the quintessence of the world. Although 'petty theologians' have branded him an enthusiast, Weigelian and Rosicrucian, Nolle states one need not be a brother of the Rose Cross to find wisdom: for he is a Christian and a theodidact (one taught by God), not a 'sectarian' bent on forcing his beliefs on the entire world (Nolle, 1623: 139–40).

The Gießen inquisitors pointed specifically to these sentiments in the *Mirror of the Philosophical Parergon*, as well as Nolle's portrayal of communication with angels, when they found him guilty of enthusiastic inspiration in contravention of article five of the *Confessio Augustana* (Hochhuth, 1863: 230–31). This article deals with the ministry of teaching the Gospel, and emphasizes the Church as the mediator between God and the faithful, stating that the Holy Spirit may only be received through partaking of the sacraments and hearing the Gospel. It goes on to state: 'Damned are the Anabaptists and others who teach that we may receive the Holy Spirit without the corporeal word of the Gospel, through our own preparation, thoughts and works' (Melanchthon, 1530: Bi *recto*). Stephani and one of his co-accused were eventually imprisoned, the victims of a witch-hunt in which the term 'Rosicrucian' emerged as a potent polemical weapon ensuring greater conformity of the citizenry with the political and religious goals of the state.

THE FATE OF THE ROSICRUCIANS

Members of the Hessen-Kassel and Hessen-Darmstadt 'Rosicrucian' circles were not only acquainted with one another, but also with other participants in the early Rosicrucian affair such as the apologist Georg Molther and the first publisher of the manifestos, Wilhelm Wessel (the father-in-law of Homagius). At the very least, these relationships suggest an informal network had emerged among readers of the Rosicrucian manifestos who found themselves united by their inspirationist sympathies. However, inquisitorial trial records are unreliable evidence for the existence of an organized secret society – and Rosicrucian history is just as much concerned with the powerful myth of such a society. Hence the appearance of placards proclaiming the entrance of the 'invisible' Brethren into staunchly Catholic Paris in 1623 created panic among the city's population; yet the report was a mere fantasy that incited polemicists to associate demonized caricatures of the brethren with various ideological targets, among them libertines, Lutherans and magicians (Kahn, 2001).

In England the fraternity lived on as a literary conceit in the satirical works of Ben Jonson (e.g. Jonson, 1625: 5) and in William Vaughan's *The Golden Fleece* (1626), in which the brethren appear as the four patron saints of the British monarchy (Vaughan, 1626: 86). Although there was a revival of interest in Rosicrucianism around the time of Thomas Vaughan's publication of the Rosicrucian manifestos in English translation in 1652, depictions of 'Rosicrucian' influence upon the Royal Society (Yates, 1978: 181–92) or even a 'Rosicrucian Interregnum' (Bamford, 1999: *passim*) commit the *pars pro toto* fallacy of designating as 'Rosicrucian' quite distinct manifestations of the Baroque vogue for reform societies.

Firmer evidence for the emergence of Rosicrucianism as an organized secret society is to be found in an Italian manuscript entitled *The Inviolable Laws observed by the Fraternity of the Golden Cross, or rather the Golden Rose* (*Osservazioni inviolabili da osservarsi dalli fratelli dell'Aurea Croce o vero dell'Aurea Rosa*, 1678), and in a series of later versions of the fraternity's laws that give the cumulative impression of an organization growing in numbers and geographical reach (Richter, 1710: 100–101; *Testamentum*, n.d.: 10 *recto*, 11 *verso*). The last of these, the Bohemian *Testament of the Fraternity of the Rosy and Gold Cross* (before 1735) forms the basis for the *Treasure of Treasures* (*Thesaurus thesaurorum*, c. 1765), the chief manuscript compendium of the quasi-Masonic Gold and Rosy Cross (*Gold-und Rosenkreuz*). Organized into an opaque pyramidal hierarchy, the Gold and Rosy Cross was an absolutist reaction to the erosion of aristocratic and ecclesiastical authority by democratic, republican and materialist ideologies during the Enlightenment. The order's chief concern was the production of an alchemical agent by which the Rosicrucian's 'earthly body is transformed into a spiritual body'

(Albrecht, 1792: 228); the summoning of planetary angels was also practiced (*Thesaurus*, n.d.: 144–51), and in the highest grade prophecies were received via the Urim, a ritual magical object manufactured from *electrum magicum* and inlaid with five different types of Philosophers' Stone (*Kabbalistische Geheimnisse*, 1767: 2; cf. Edwards, 1692: 46). High-grade initiates of the Gold and Rosy Cross (among them the kings of Prussia and Sweden) also employed the Abramelin operation for the summoning of guardian angels (Wöllner, 1804: xix, 299; c.f. *Magia divina*, n.d.), which would become a central practice within the Golden Dawn's *Ordo rosae rubeae et aureae crucis*.

Although Yates contentiously portrayed the early Rosicrucian phenomenon as a kind of proto-Enlightenment, by the close of the eighteenth century Rosicrucian doctrines had become an anachronism amidst the advance of mechanistic science and Enlightenment philosophy, which rejected divine inspiration as a legitimate path to scientific knowledge and discarded the ambiguous esoteric discourse of alchemy. Ideas and practices that were once condemned as heresy became the object of mere ridicule: in Voltaire's words, 'The philosopher is not an enthusiast and does not claim to be inspired by the gods; therefore I would not count the ancient Zoroaster, nor Hermes, nor the ancient Orpheus amongst the philosophers. Those who called themselves children of the gods were the fathers of deception; and when they used lies to teach truth, they were not philosophers, but rather very clever liars at best' (Voltaire, 1994: 427). Thus the entire notion of a *prisca sapientia* was – in Mulsow's words – 'dead', having been refuted philologically and defeated historico-critically by the elimination of mythic pseudo-histories (Mulsow, 2004: 12–13). However, eliminating a potent myth is no easy task, and Rosicrucian pseudo-histories continue to legitimize the authority of groups such as AMORC, the Lectorium Rosicrucianum and a plethora of Rosicrucian and Golden Dawn splinter groups. Indeed, artefacts of the imagination may convey truths of a different order to those of modernity's dominant intellectual paradigms – and they may also exercise their own considerable influence on the course of history, as the events precipitated by the Rosicrucian manifestos testify.

REFERENCES AND FURTHER READING

Agrippa von Nettesheim, Heinrich Cornelius (1531) *De incertitudine et vanitate scientiarum declamatio invectiva*, Cologne: Eucharius Cervicornus.

——(1533) *De occulta philosophia libri tres*, Cologne: Johann Soter.

Albrecht, Heinrich (1792) *Geheime Geschichte eines Rosenkreuzers*, Hamburg: n.p.

Andreae, Johann Valentin (1616) *Chymische Hochzeit: Christiani Rosencreütz Anno 1459*, Strasbourg: Lazarus Zetzner.

——(1618) *Menippus sive dialogorum satyricorum centuria inanitatum nostratium speculum*, Strasbourg: n.p.

Augustine (2002) *The City of God Against the Pagans*, Cambridge: Cambridge University Press.

Bamford, Christopher (ed.) (1999) *The Rosicrucian Enlightenment Revisited*, London: Steiner Books.

Brecht, Martin (1977) 'Johann Valentin Andreae. Weg und Programm eines Reformers zwischen Reformation und Moderne', in Brecht, Martin (ed.) *Theologen und Theologie an der Universität Tübingen*, Tübingen: J. C. B. Mohr, pp. 270–343.

Budovec z Budova, Václav (1616) *Circulus horologii Lunaris et Solaris*, Hanover: Johannes Aubrius.

Concordia: Christliche, widerholete/einmütige Bekentnüs nachbenanter Churfürsten/ Fürsten und Stende Augspurgischer Confession (1580) Dresden: Stöckel.

Confessio fraternitatis oder Bekanntnuß der löblichen Bruderschafft deß hochgeehrten Rosen-Creutzes/ an die Gelehrten Europae geschrieben (1615a) in *Fama fraternitatis, oder Entdeckung der Bruderschafft deß löblichen Ordens deß RosenCreutzes*, Frankfurt am Main: Johann Bringer, pp. 54–82.

Confessio fraternitatis R. C. ad eruditos Europae (1615b) in Philippus a Gabella, *Secretioris philosophiae consideratio brevis*, Kassel: Wilhelm Wessel, ff. G4 *recto*-I2 *verso*.

Dorn, Gerhard (1612) *Lexicon alchemiae sive dictionarium alchemisticum*, Frankfurt am Main: Zacharias Palthenius.

Dorn, Gerhard (1659) *Speculativa philosophia*, in *Theatrum chemicum*, vol. 1, Strasbourg: Eberhard Zetzner, pp. 228–76.

Edwards, John (1692) *A Farther Enquiry into Several Remarkable Texts of the Old and New Testament*, London: Robinson.

Fama fraternitatis, oder Entdeckung der Bruderschafft deß löblichen Ordens deß RosenCreutzes (1615) Frankfurt am Main: Johann Bringer.

Fama fraternitatis: Das Urmanifest der Rosenkreuzer Bruderschaft (1998) Haarlem: Rozekruis Pers.

Fludd, Robert (1617) *Tractatus apologeticus integritatem Societatis de Rosea Cruce defendens*, Leiden: Godefridus Basson.

Fludd, Robert (1633) *Clavis philosophiae et alchymiae Fluddanae*, Frankfurt am Main: Wilhelm Fitzer.

Gantenbein, Urs Leo (2008) 'Einleitung', in Paracelsus, *Vita Beata – Vom seligen Leben*, Neue Paracelsus-Edition: Theologische Werke I, Berlin: Walter de Gruyter, pp. 3–122.

Garasse, François (1623) *La doctrine curieuse des beaux esprits de ce temps, ou pretendus tels*, Paris: Sébastien Chappelet.

Germanus, Johannes (1626) *Der siebenden apocalyptischen Posaunen/ von Offenbarung verborgener Geheimnussen Heroldt*, Newenstatt: Knuber.

Gilly, Carlos (1988) 'Iter Rosicrucianum. Auf der Suche nach unbekannten Quellen der frühen Rosenkreuzer', in *Das Erbe des Christian Rosenkreuz. Vorträge gehalten anlässlich des Amsterdamer Symposiums 18.-20. November 1986*, Amsterdam: In de Pelikaan, pp. 63–89.

Gilly, Carlos (1994a) *Adam Haslmayr (1562–1631). Der erste Verkünder der Rosenkreuzer*, Amsterdam: In de Pelikaan.

Gilly, Carlos (1994b) '"Theophrastia Sancta". Der Paracelsismus als Religion im Streit mit den offiziellen Kirchen', in Joachim Telle (ed.), *Analecta Paracelsica. Studien zum Nachleben Theophrast von Hohenheims im deutschen Kulturgebiet der frühen Neuzeit*, Stuttgart: Franz Steiner Verlag, pp. 425–88.

Gilly, Carlos (1995) *Cimelia Rhodostaurotica. Die Rosenkreuzer im Spiegel der zwischen 1610 und 1660 entstandenen Handschriften und Drucke. Ausstellung der Bibliotheca Philosophica Hermetica Amsterdam und der Herzog August Bibliothek Wolfenbüttel*, Amsterdam: In de Pelikaan.

Gilly, Carlos (2001) 'Die Rosenkreuzer als europäisches Phänomen im 17. Jahrhundert und die verschlungenen Pfade der Forschung', in Gilly, Carlos and Friedrich Niewöhner (eds) *Das Rosenkreuz als europäisches Phänomen des 17. Jahrhunderts. Akten zum 35. Wolfenbütteler Symposium*, Amsterdam: In de Pelikaan, pp. 19–56.

Goldammer, Kurt (1952) 'Einleitung', in *Paracelsus. Sozialethische und sozialpolitische Schriften*, Tübingen: J. C. B. Mohr, 1952.

Haslmayr, Adam (1615) *Antwort an die lobwürdige Brüderschafft der Theosophen von Rosencreutz*, in *Fama fraternitatis, oder Entdeckung der Bruderschafft deß löblichen Ordens deß RosenCreutzes* (1615) Frankfurt am Main: Johann Bringer, pp. 83–101.

Hochhuth, Karl (1862) 'Mitteilungen aus der protestantischen Secten-Geschichte in der hessischen Kirche', *Zeitschrift für die historische Theologie*, 32 (1), pp. 86–159.

Hochhuth, Karl (1863) 'Mitteilungen aus der protestantischen Secten-Geschichte in der hessischen Kirche', *Zeitschrift für die historische Theologie*, 33 (2), pp. 169–262.

Hunnius, Nicolaus (1619) *Principia theologiae fanaticae*, Wittenberg: Johannes Richter.

Jonson, Ben (1625) *The fortunate isles and their union Celebrated in a masque design'd for the court, on the Twelfth night. 1624*, London: n.p.

Kabbalistische Geheimnisse de Magia Divina worinnen allerhand rare unerhoerte Dinge enthalten (1767) Munich: Bayerische Staatsbibliothek, Kiesewetteriana 18.

Kahn, Didier (2001) 'The Rosicrucian Hoax in France (1623–24)', in Newman, William and Anthony Grafton (eds) *Secrets of Nature: Astrology and Alchemy in Early Modern Europe*, Cambridge, MA: The MIT Press, pp. 235–344.

Klenk, Heinrich (1965) 'Ein sogenannter Inquisitionsprozeß in Gießen anno 1623', *Mitteilungen des Oberhessischen Geschichtsvereins*, 39, pp. 39–60.

Libavius, Andreas (1615) *Analysis confessionis Fraternitatis de Rosea Cruce*, Frankfurt am Main: Peter Kopff.

Libavius, Andreas (1616) *Wolmeinendes Bedencken/ von der Fama, und Confession der Brüderschafft deß Rosen Creutzes*, Frankfurt am Main: Peter Kopff.

Luther, Martin (1520a) *An den Christlichen Adel deütscher Nation/ von des Christenlichen standes besserung*, Basel: Petri.

Luther, Martin (1520b) *Ein sermon von dem hochwirdigen sacrament des heyligen waren leichnamß Christi*, Nürnberg: n.p.

Luther, Martin (1547) *Kirchen Postilla/ das ist: Auslegung der Episteln und Euangelien/ an Sontagen vnd furnemesten Festen*, Wittenberg: Hans Lufft.

Luther, Martin (1568) *Colloquia oder Tischreden Doctor Martini Lutheri*, Frankfurt am Main: Schmid.

Magia divina (n.d., late 18th century) Stockholm: private collection of the Sodalitas Rosae+Crucis et Solis Alati.

Maier, Michael (1617) *Silentium post clamores*, Frankfurt am Main: Lucas Jennis.

Maier, Michael (1624) *Themis aurea*, Frankfurt am Main: Lucas Jennis.

Meder, David (1616) *Iudicium theologicum/ oder Christlichs und kurtzes Bedencken von der Fama et Confessione der Brüderschafft des löblichen Ordens deß Rosencreutzes*, Danzig: Andrea Hünefeld.

Melanchthon, Philipp (1530) *Anzeigung und Bekantnus des Glaubens unnd der Lere, so die adpellierenden Stende Key. Maiestet auff yetzigen Tag zuo Augspurg öberantwurt habend: M.D.XXX*, Zürich: Froschauer.

Mögling, Daniel (1618) *Speculum sophicum rhodo-stauroticum*, n.p.: n.p.

Montgomery, John Warwick (1973) *Cross and Crucible: Johann Valentin Andreae (1586–1654), Phoenix of the Theologians*, The Hague: Martinus Nijhoff.

Mulsow, Martin (2004) 'Ambiguities of the *Prisca Sapientia* in Late Renaissance Humanism', *Journal of the History of Ideas*, 65 (1), pp. 1–13.

Nigrinus, Christopher (1619) *Sphynx rosacea/ das ist, der Entdeckung der Bruderschafft deß löblichen Ordens deß Rosen Creutzes*, Frankfurt am Main: Simon Schaumberger.

Nolle, Heinrich (1623) *Parergi philosophici speculum*, Gießen: Chemlin.

Nummedal, Tara (2007) *Alchemy and Authority in the Holy Roman Empire*, Chicago: University of Chicago Press.

Origen (1605) *Contra Celsum libri VIII*, Augsburg: Franck.

Origen (1980) *Contra Celsum*, Cambridge: Cambridge University Press.

Origen (2005) *Homilies on Leviticus, 1–16*, Washington, DC: Catholic University of America Press.

Osservazioni inviolabili da osservarsi dalli fratelli dell'Aurea Croce o vero dell'Aurea Rosa (1678) Naples: Biblioteca Nazionale di Napoli, MS. XII-E-30.

Paracelsus [Theophrastus Bombastus von Hohenheim] (1929) *Astronomia magna: oder die ganze Philosophia Sagax der grossen vnd kleinen Welt*, in Sudhoff, Carl (ed.), *Paracelsus: Sämtliche Werke*, vol. 12, Munich: Oldenbourg, pp. 1–507.

Paracelsus [Theophrastus Bombastus von Hohenheim] (1933) *Extract einer prophecei doctoris Theophrasti*, in Sudhoff, Carl (ed.), *Paracelsus: Sämtliche Werke*, vol. 14, Munich: Oldenbourg, pp. 545–46.

Paracelsus [Theophrastus Bombastus von Hohenheim] (2008) *Vita Beata – Vom seligen Leben*, Neue Paracelsus-Edition: Theologische Werke I, Berlin: Walter de Gruyter.

Practica leonis viridis/ das ist: Der Rechte und wahre Fussteig zu dem königlichen Chymischen HochzeitSaal F. C. R (1619) Frankfurt an der Oder: Thieme.

Richter, Samuel (1710) *Die Warhaffte und vollkommene Bereitung des Philosophischen Steins/ Der Brüderschafft aus dem Orden des Gülden-und Rosen-Creutzes*, Breslau: Fellgiebel.

Rotbard, Christoffer (1617) *Elucidarius maior/ oder Erleuchterunge über die Reformation der ganzen weiten Welt/ F. C. R. auß ihrer Chymischen Hochzeit*, Lüneburg: bey den Sternen.

Schneider, Ivo (2005) 'Between Rosicrucians and Cabbala – Johann Faulhaber's Mathematics of Biblical Numbers', in Koetsier, Teun and Luc Bergmans (eds) *Mathematics and the Divine: A Historical Study*, Amsterdam: Elsevier B. V., pp. 311–30.

Sperber, Julius (1615) *Echo der von Gott hocherleuchteten Fraternitet des löblichen Ordens R. C.*, Danzig: Andrea Hünefeld.

Sudhoff, Karl (1936) *Paracelsus, ein deutsches Lebensbild aus den Tagen der Renaissance*, Leipzig: Bibliographisches Institut.

Thesaurus thesaurorum à fraternitate roseae et aureae cruces testamento consignatus. 1580 (c.1765) Darmstadt: Hessische Universitäts-und Landesbibliothek, Technische Universität Darmstadt, Hs3262.

Testamentum der Fraternitet Roseae et Aureae Crucis…Anno 580 (n.d., before 1735) Vienna: Österreichische Nationalbibliothek, Cod SN 2897.

Vaughan, William (1626) *The Golden Fleece*, London: Francis Williams.

Voltaire (1994) 'Philosophe', in Pons, Alain (ed.) *Dictionnaire philosophique*, Paris: Gallimard, p. 427.

Weill-Parot, Nicolas (2002) 'Astral Magic and Intellectual Changes (Twelfth-Fifteenth Centuries): "Astrological Images" and the Concept of "Addressative" Magic', in Bremmer, Jan and Jan Veenstra (eds) *The Metamorphosis of Magic from Late Antiquity to the Early Modern Period*, Leuven: Peeters, pp. 167–88.

Wöllner, Johann Christoph von (1804) *Der Signatstern oder die enthüllten sämmtlichen sieben Grade der mystischen Freimaurerei*, Berlin: Schöne.

Yates, Frances (1978) *The Rosicrucian Enlightenment*, Boulder, CO: Shambhala.

CHAPTER TEN

EMANUEL SWEDENBORG

Jane Williams-Hogan

Emanuel Swedenborg (1688–1772) was a polymath and a visionary who provided a radical and rational interpretation of Christianity in his theological works, which departed in several respects from traditional interpretations concerning the Trinity, original sin, the atonement and justification. His writings also included rich and detailed descriptions of his 'experiences' in the world of spirits.

BACKGROUND

Emanuel Swedenborg was born on January 29th, 1688, in Stockholm, Sweden. He was the second son and third child of the Lutheran cleric, and later Bishop, Jesper Swedberg (1653–1735), and Sara Behm (1666–96). The family moved to Uppsala in 1692, when Swedberg was appointed a Professor of Theology, following which, he was soon appointed Dean of the Cathedral. Hence, Swedenborg's childhood and adolescence were spent in Uppsala. Swedenborg graduated from Uppsala University in 1709, having produced a thesis in philosophy. He confessed, however, that his real love was 'mathesis,' that is mathematically based universal science.

He went abroad in 1710 for five years to study with the principal astronomers and mathematicians of his day. He spent time in England, which he saw as the frontier in the development of natural science, the Netherlands, and France before traveling home via Hanover, Rostock and Greifswalde, Pomerania. In his notes he detailed the plans for several inventions, including an airplane, a submarine, and a machine gun.

Upon his return to Sweden in 1715, he began to work for the great Swedish inventor, Christopher Polhem (1651–1751). They engaged in various public works projects commissioned by the King, Karl XII (1682–1718). Swedenborg enjoyed conversations about mathematics with the King. In December of 1716, Karl XII appointed Swedenborg as an extraordinary Assessor to the Board of Mines. The death of the King in Norway, at the end of 1718, put Swedenborg's commission in doubt, and he labored over the next six years to have its legitimacy recognized. His family was ennobled in 1719, and took the name Swedenborg.

In 1724, when Emanuel Swedenborg's position as Assessor on the Board of Mines was at last salaried and secure, he turned his attention to exploring 'the secrets of nature.' Not only did he wish to reveal secrets for the sake of their usefulness, he wanted to discover the origins or 'first things' of existence.

Swedenborg's first project was to seek to understand the origins of the universe. In *Principia Rerum Naturalium* (1734), he, among other things, developed a nebular hypothesis to explain the origin of our solar system (arguably, a forerunner to the Kant–Laplace theory). His second project was to understand the soul. In fact, in this undertaking the aim was 'to demonstrate the immortality of the soul to the very senses' (Swedenborg, 1734b, 230). Here, too, he made important discoveries: the function of the ductless glands in the brain and the relationship between the motion of the brain and respiration. He published his findings, first, in the two volume *Oeconomia Regni Animalis* (1740–41), and, second, in the multi-volume *Regnum Animale* (1744–45) – the last of which he abandoned after producing three volumes.

Until 1744 it is clear that Swedenborg, an admirer of Newton, had a scientific and mechanistic worldview. He was convinced that everything in the natural world could be examined and demonstrated within an empirical framework. Although he could not, as Newton could not, be described an unbeliever, prior to his 1744 crisis (see below), he was first and foremost a scientist, rather than a theologian.

SWEDENBORG'S CALL

Swedenborg's 'call' did not occur in an instant, or even over the course of a few days or weeks. It was a relatively slow process which took place over several years. As he explored the nature of his call, he went through five different sorts of experiences, each generating a written response, only one of which he published. His call began late in 1743 in Amsterdam, when he experienced vivid dreams, which he recorded in a personal journal.

His dream experiences led him to reorder his priorities and seek closer communion with God (Swedenborg, 1977, 15). To achieve this Swedenborg had to purge himself of his arrogance and self-love. In the end, he wanted nothing more than 'to live with Christ in a state of innocence' (1977, 88).

He abandoned empirical science to become a scribe of heaven. In this second phase, his first effort was to write a mythic poem about creation and the birth and life of Adam and Eve. Woven into this poem was a summary of his philosophic works. He published this in London in 1745. It was titled, 'Worship and Love of God' and it symbolized his new perspective. Not long after this, he left England and returned to Sweden.

In the autumn he moved into a new home on Södermalm, Stockholm, and resumed his work on the Board of Mines. He also continued to explore his 'calling.' To do this, he re-immersed himself in the study of Hebrew, read the Bible, and wrote. During this period Swedenborg wrote numerous manuscripts (comprising 5000 folio pages), which he never published. The first of these constituted the third phase, and is known as 'The Messiah about To Come.' It is a collection of messianic prophecies found in the Bible, which Swedenborg collected and wrote down in Latin. It is possible that Swedenborg felt God's call as he read these passages, because he wrote in his native Swedish: 'November 17, 1745. I begin to write. Lord Jesus Christ, lead me to and on the way that thou willest that I shall walk....This will be the testimony of the Kingdom of God' (Swedenborg, 1949, 105).

What can be designated as a fourth phase, is a period of systematic biblical exegesis. In this phase, his first attempt, *The History of Creation According to Moses*, was only about forty numbered paragraphs in length. He soon started again with a work commonly referred to as *The Word Explained*. Written between 1745 and 1747, it comprised seven volumes in English translation and 1,951 pages. Both of these exegetical works attempt to interpret the spiritual meaning of the unfolding creation of the physical universe recorded in the Bible as he understood it.

At the same time and integral to his exegetical efforts, he began a 'Bible Index' in which he attempted to interpret the words and symbols in the Bible. This could be understood as his first dictionary of 'correspondences.' His published works are noted for their foundation in his famous 'doctrine of correspondences.' According to Swedenborg, divine correspondences are the means of communication between the natural and the spiritual worlds. In his published work *Divine Love and Wisdom* (1763), he wrote, 'To illustrate this by example: heat in the natural world corresponds to the good of charity in the spiritual world, and light in the natural world corresponds to the truth of faith in the spiritual world....Although distinct they make one by correspondence....when a person reads, in the Word, of heat and light, the spirits who are with the person perceive charity and faith instead' (§ 83).

One additional work was begun during his transition, and marks its fifth phase, *Spiritual Experiences*. These experiences are different than the dreams of the first phase of his call, and are, according to Swedenborg, visions that occur in a state of full wakefulness. Swedenborg recorded these experiences in separate unpublished journals (1746–65). They can be likened to an anthropologist's field notes. Some of them, when rewritten, are included in published works.

Entry into the spiritual world or state of consciousness required Swedenborg to read or meditate on the Bible or what he referred to as 'God's Word.' He experienced God's Word as the gateway to the spiritual realm. In June of 1747, he resigned from the Board of Mines. Just before his resignation, he was invited to assume the position of President of the Board. This invitation, in fact, may have spurred his resignation, because of the increased responsibilities it would entail. In July of 1747, after taking leave of his colleagues on the Board, he sailed to Europe, in order to focus on what was to be the first volume of the *Arcana Coelestia* [*Secrets of Heaven*] published anonymously in London in 1749. With the publication of this work, Swedenborg fully entered into his role as the servant of the Lord. As he described it, his task, until his death in 1772, was to witness, reveal, and record the far-ranging meaning of the Apocalypse, which was spiritual in nature, for the sake of a New Christian Church.

KEY TEACHINGS OF PUBLISHED THEOLOGICAL WORKS

Content

Swedenborg published eighteen different titles, some of them in multiple volumes, during his career as a visionary. *Secrets of Heaven* (eight volumes) was his first work and *Vera Christiana Religio* [*True Christianity*] (1771) was his last. In it he exclaimed that 'Now it is permitted to enter with understanding into the mysteries of faith' (§ 508). *Secrets of Heaven* is a line-by-line, and at times word-by-word exegesis of the biblical books, Genesis and Exodus. As noted, Swedenborg's exegesis was made possible through his concept of spiritual correspondences. They are the foundation of what he calls the spiritual or internal meaning of the Word. According to Swedenborg, the earth's first people used this language to communicate. As Jonathan S. Rose explains, '...people saw heavenly qualities reflected in the trees, plants, and animals around them, as well as in each other and the events of their lives' (2005, 66). These individuals belonged to what Swedenborg calls the 'Adamic' church or first spiritual age on Earth. They could receive direct guidance from God through the lens of nature, dreams, or visions. (According to Swedenborg, there have been five churches or spiritual ages on Earth.)

After the fall, however, the ability to understand correspondences faded and eventually disappeared. Swedenborg believed that one of his tasks in his role of Revelator was to re-introduce knowledge of correspondences to the world by revealing the spiritual sense of the Bible, long hidden within the historical and literal meaning of the Word. Although there is much more that could be said concerning Swedenborg's concept of correspondences, suffice it to say that his use of the word is compatible with and fits well within Antoine Faivre's definition of correspondences (1995).

God

With the tools provided by the doctrine of correspondences, he outlined a new Christian religion. While it has much in common with traditional Christianity, it also signals a radical departure from several key Christian teachings. For example, Swedenborg states that God is one in essence and person, and that essence is love and wisdom. Furthermore, there is a divine Trinity [and] these three, the Father, the Son, and the Holy Spirit are three essential components of one God. They are one 'the way our soul, body, and the things we do are one' (2006, §163). Swedenborg employs this concept of the Trinity to explain the birth and mission of Jesus Christ: the Soul of the Father through the Holy Spirit was the infinite love animating Jesus, whose task was to combat the hells he had assumed within himself by taking on the body through Mary. His temptations throughout his life on earth, even to the temptation of the cross, permitted him to subjugate the hells and to glorify his human. In this process he restored human freedom in spiritual things, and he ascended into the heavens as a divinely human visible God. God, according to Swedenborg, must be visible, so that we may know him, and therefore love him. Swedenborg understood that the nature of human beings is such, that they cannot love what they do not know or understand.

Last Judgment

Swedenborg also claimed that he was called because the time for the long awaited 'Last Judgment' finally had come. It occurred in 1757 and was a spiritual event. The Judgment took place in the spiritual world because it was predicted in the Word, which is essentially a spiritual document that speaks to and about spiritual matters. The judgment on Christianity was necessary because over the centuries a fatal separation developed between the qualities of faith and charity within all the Christian churches, leaving them spiritually dead at the time of Swedenborg's call. This was a result of misunderstanding the nature of the Trinity, the act of redemption, and the means of salvation.

Salvation

According to Swedenborg the merit of Christ cannot be borrowed at the time of death, but it is a powerful gift that is freely available to everyone in times of spiritual temptation during his or her lifetime. People can find it, when they seek the Lord in his Word. The Lord, who is love itself, created humanity to be eternal recipients of his love. For love to exist, both reception and affirmative response are required; thus heaven is the eternal home provided for the human race. He grants eternal life to all people. Salvation is possible for everyone, regardless of their religion, if they choose to do good to the neighbor, and subordinate their self-love and their love of the goods and pleasures of the world, because these loves which separate and divide are barriers to loving God and humanity.

Swedenborg teaches that the Lord never withdraws his love from anyone. However, each of us may withdraw from him by freely choosing a life of evil. As an extension of this idea, Swedenborg claims that after death we create our own heaven or hell, based on our free choices over a lifetime. For those who subdue their love of self and worldly pleasures, for the sake of serving the Lord and the neighbor, a full, useful, and beautiful heavenly life awaits them. On the other hand, for those who have chosen to indulge their love of self and the world, and who inwardly despise the Lord, the neighbor, and a life of useful service, they make their home in hell. While the spirits there may love it, hell is hell primarily because it is filled with spirits, each of whom wants to be the center or focus of everything, and since that is not possible, frustration, conflict, mutual torment and ugliness reign.

Marriage

One additional concept that figures prominently in his religious writings is that of marriage. Marriage for Swedenborg is the basis of the world of life, and is the fundamental metaphor of creation. According to him, marriage defines reality – whether divine or human, spiritual or natural. It describes the relationship between the divine qualities of love and wisdom; it is the operating principle of nature, the foundation of regeneration, and the highest human calling. An elaboration of these ideas can be found in Swedenborg's work...*Amore Conjugiali* [*Marriage Love*] published in Amsterdam 1768. It is the first of his religious writings that he signed.

Form and Style

Swedenborg's writings contain, as Jonathan S. Rose writes, a 'garden of theology' (2005, 53). In that garden one can find textual exegesis and doctrinal discussion, as well as lively presentations of his spiritual experiences. Rose suggests that this content utilizes two different styles, one explanatory and the other poetic (2005, 92). In his first theological work, the explanatory style is more prominent; in his last, there is a balance between the two. His explanatory style is abstract and logical. Again, according to Rose, Swedenborg, in his religious works, consciously chose to use a very simple explanatory style. In fact, it was the simplest Latin he ever wrote (2005, 93). He also employed a poetic style in order to engage the imagination. His poetic vocabulary was vast, and in that style he used concrete nouns and verbs, often in the active voice. This is the style of his spiritual experiences, often called memorabilia (2005, 93–94). They are used sparingly until the publication of *Apocalypsis Revelata* [*Apocalypse Unveiled*] in 1766. After that, they are found at the end of every discursive chapter (2005, 94).

SWEDENBORG AS REVELATOR

When he sent copies of this work to friends and dignitaries, which was his usual practice, he pointed out the addition of these descriptions of his spiritual experiences. He wrote: 'as they contain several remarkable particulars, they may excite the reader to their first perusal' (Acton, 1955, 612). However, they appeared to have the opposite of the intended effect on his friend Baron Anders Von Höpken (1712–89). It was Von Höpken's opinion that the addition of the experiences detracted from the doctrinal presentation. He stated that their inclusion 'throw[s] so much ridicule on his doctrine, otherwise so rational' (Sigstedt, 1981, 320). Some other readers, however, such as, Friedrich Christoph Oetinger (1702–82) were only interested in the 'things seen and heard' in the spiritual world, and had no interest in Swedenborg's doctrinal exegesis. In fact Oetinger explicitly condemned it (Acton, 1955, 619).

According to Von Höpken, Swedenborg told him that he was instructed by the Lord to include his experiences in the spiritual world in his works and that any ridicule they received was unjust. This indicates that Swedenborg believed that he could not fulfill his revelatory mission without including both the rational and the 'occult.' That said, Swedenborg himself would not have used the word 'occult', preferring rather to use the word 'spiritual.'

He also had several clairvoyant experiences during his visionary period that were widely circulated in Europe during his lifetime. One experience occurred in 1759, when on July 19th, he witnessed a fire raging in Stockholm, 300 miles distant, while attending a dinner at the home of William Castel in Gothenburg with fifteen other guests. He excused himself several times during the party. Each time that he returned he commented on the progress on the fire on Södermalm, the area of Stockholm where he lived. He saw the home of a friend in ashes, and saw the fire approaching his property. At eight o'clock he returned to the company and said, 'Thank God.' The fire finally had been extinguished three doors from his property. His dinner companions were amazed and, later that evening the provincial Governor was informed. The Governor interviewed Swedenborg the next day about the fire. He asked questions about when it began, how it had started, and how long it had lasted, and how it was finally put out. When reports came from Stockholm, they confirmed Swedenborg's description in every detail. Needless to say, people were amazed (Sigstedt, 1981, 269–70).

There were two other stories that were widely circulated, one concerned a lost receipt, and the other a long held secret of the Queen of Sweden. In both cases, Swedenborg revealed something that was only known by persons who had died and passed into the spiritual world. In 1771, close to the end of his life, Swedenborg discussed the matter of the Queen's secret in letters to Pastor Venator and to His Serene Highness Duke Landgrave (1726–1810). In the letters he addressed the Duke's question, as to whether revealing the conversation he had with the Queen's brother was a miracle. This is what he wrote to the Pastor:

> These must by no means be classed as miracles, being merely testimonies that I have been introduced by the Lord into the spiritual world, and there into communication and speech with angels and spirits: and this to the end that the Church, which has hitherto been in ignorance of that world, may know that heaven and hell are actual, and that man lives as a man after death; that so, doubts may no longer flow into the human mind concerning immortality. Deign I pray you, to persuade the Duke your Prince, so that he will think, not that such things are miracles, but that they are merely testifications that I speak with angels and spirits. That miracles do not take place at this day, and for what reasons, see in the above mentioned work. [*True Christianity*, § 501]
>
> (Acton, 1955, 749–50)

The importance of this section is to indicate the significance to Swedenborg of the relationship between these two different aspects of revelation. They are essential not just to revelation but to each other – like the heart and the lungs, they cannot survive, the one without the other. The religious writings of Swedenborg cannot be classified as merely 'occult' or merely rational. They are not simply an expression of the process of rationalization, because integral to them is an eternal living vision of the world beyond.

Science provides the tools whereby we discover the order and the rules governing the natural realm of time and space. According to Swedenborg, the spiritual world also has an order, and the rules governing that world must take into account the idea of state and affinity. Swedenborg states that the rules which govern the spiritual world are much like those that govern the human mind. For example, in states of happiness, a sense of time often disappears, yet when we are unhappy and doing something we do not enjoy, time seems to slow down or drag. While the natural world is governed by the passing of time, such as morning, noon, evening, and night; in the spiritual world there are morning states, high noon states, and then states of evening (it is never night in heaven, because the sun there never sets) which represent a need for rest and for revivification from the Lord. Location in the spiritual world is based on the proximity of mutual loves. Those whose loves are similar, dwell near one another. In addition, in the spiritual world thought brings presence. In the natural world, thought often leads to reaching out to the person, object, or activity that comes to mind; in the spiritual world all that is necessary is the thought. Thought brings presence, it connects us with our loves, whether they are good or evil. That is why, according to Swedenborg, the Lord is with us when we read his Word with affection.

Thus, while some see the realm of the spirit as incomprehensible or inscrutable, Swedenborg wrote about and revealed the orderliness of the supernatural world. He portrays a world that we can know and understand, as well as provides the tools that show us the relationship between the choices we make, here and now, and the place and nature of the eternal home we are constructing for ourselves there.

Swedenborg traveled frequently during his revelatory period, in order to publish his works which he could not publish in Sweden due to the censorship of the Lutheran Church. A group of readers of his works first emerged in Gothenburg, in the late 1760s. The two Lutheran priests who were part of the group were accused of heresy in 1769, and put on trial before the Consistory. The results were inconclusive, and the case was forwarded to Stockholm for review. Some in the Lutheran hierarchy also wanted to charge Swedenborg, but Swedenborg had both friends and connections in the highest places in Sweden, and he was never charged. Swedenborg left Sweden in July of 1770 for the last time. He traveled to Amsterdam where in 1771 he published *True Christianity*, which he inscribed, 'Emanuel Swedenborg, Servant of the Lord Jesus Christ.'

ASSESSMENT OF SWEDENBORG'S CALL AND TEACHINGS

Having set forth the stages of Swedenborg's call, it would be useful to see how they might be interpreted within the framework of occultism. First and, perhaps foremost, we see a man of scientific and empirical temperament and vision become drawn into the world of dreams, intense emotions, and extraordinary experiences. He was drawn quite literally into an alternative reality, separate and apart from the taken-for-granted world of every day life – separate from his scientific endeavors, his disciplined publishing activities, and the simple routines that keep body and soul together.

Significantly, he does not reject this alternative world that came to him unbidden (which as a scientist, he easily could have); rather, it appears that he took up residence there, not as a scientist, but initially as a sinner. During his dreams, his heart and soul were laid bare, and he suffered. In his torment he discovered humility and from time-to-time he caught glimpses of joy. Reading his journal, we descend with Swedenborg, into the depths and rise to see the light, not once, but over and over again. In the process, his heart is rent, and we feel his profound pain. But in the end, he experienced, and we witness, re-birth.

Reading the journal, we are not in the company of a scientist, but a religious seeker, even though like a disciplined scientist, Swedenborg recorded his dreams. In this journal we are exposed to the mysterious labyrinth of the human heart and enter into the secrets of a life, and life itself. The terror and sense of grace described are not just intellectual abstractions, but they are often portrayed as affecting Swedenborg physically. In his dreams journal, he described actually shuddering, weeping, kneeling, becoming prostrate or being cast down. Toward the end of October 1744, the images of terror subside, and more and more Swedenborg expressed feelings of love, and a growing tender, innocent companionship with his Lord. In the Spring 1745, he wrote, 'It seemed as if a rocket burst over me spreading a number of lovely sparkles of fire. Love for what is high, perhaps' (Swedenborg, 1977, 90).

It is important to realize that while all this was going on nightly over the length of a year, every day, upon waking, Swedenborg would continue to engage in the work of publication. While the activity remained the same, who he was and what he published dramatically changed. The Emanuel Swedenborg who departed from London in 1745, was not the same person who arrived in London the previous May. He was transformed.

What Swedenborg experienced was that angels and demons do not come from without, but dwell within. Nature, which is dead, is not the playground of spirits, but humanity is. The world of spirit and the world of nature do intersect and interact, but not everywhere, only within the human being. The spiritual calls and entreats in the mind and heart, leaving the world of everyday life untouched. The spiritual drama plays out within us and we choose which path to follow, accepting the Lord's help or not. Swedenborg, as he stated, chose not to do anything without the help of Christ.

In humility he set about a new mission, but he did not so much plot (or calculate) his way forward, as he found it unfold with guidance through prayer. The key for Swedenborg was to be found in the living Word of the Lord. Revealing the secrets of the world through science was no longer Swedenborg's goal. Rather, he believed he was led to reveal the secrets of life itself, the arcana of heaven. As a servant, he hoped to reveal the answer for modern humanity to 'our question, the only question important for us: "What shall we do, and how shall we live?"' (Weber, 1958, 143).

Weber restated Tolstoi's question in his essay, 'Science as a Vocation,' the essay in which he spells out the role of science, in an attempt to answer the question of salvation in what he called the disenchanted world. Swedenborg does not answer as a scientist but as a prophet or visionary. Unable to reconcile faith and reason within the framework of natural philosophy, Swedenborg was inspired to construct a reasonable faith. A faith that makes sense in the modern rational world.

Swedenborg claims that his rational religious vision was given to him by way of extra-ordinary spiritual experiences. Experiences that were part of his life for twenty-seven years. These extra-ordinary experiences eventually became part of his normal life, and thus, routine. They were made possible because of his call, but also because, according to Swedenborg every human being born on earth, actually lives in two worlds simultaneously. This is an essential part of what it means to be human. Most people are not conscious of this reality and, as Swedenborg wrote: 'He who knows not the arcana of heaven, may believe that angels subsist without men and men without angels. But...There is a mutual and reciprocal conjunction...The human race and the angelic heaven make one...' (Swedenborg, 1996, § 9).

The religious teachings that were the result of these ongoing extra-ordinary experiences, or to use Weber's terminology, charismatic experiences, were radical and rational. Although they were deeply Christian, they departed from the received tradition of Christianity, and, in fact, declared the death of the 'old' Christian church and the coming of the 'new.'

These new spiritual teachings were made possible, according to Swedenborg because he was taught or initiated into the ancient language of correspondences. A spiritual language that, over the course of time, became corrupted and associated with nature and natural things. Without a knowledge of correspondences the Bible appears to be just like any other book. In Swedenborg's day, many sophisticated and educated people had come precisely to that conclusion. And today, that belief is certainly widely held.

Swedenborg wrote that at the end of the first age or 'Adamic' church, a Word was begun, recorded in correspondences, that would safeguard spiritual truths until the end of times, when they would not only be required, but they could be rationally understood. Swedenborg referred to that time as the Last Judgment. The people of that ancient church experienced correspondences, they lived in what could be called a correspondential world. When it disappeared, their experience was codified for the use of posterity and the long process of rationalization was begun. The scientific age is the final legacy of that process. But perhaps, as with all the redemptive myths woven by humanity over the years, we are not left empty handed.

According to Swedenborg, we have not been left empty handed. Rather, we have been given the 'holy grail': the internal or spiritual sense of the Lord's Word suited to who and what we are are (rational beings with a passionate love of freedom). This 'third testament,' as it is sometimes called, was, according to Swedenborg, given by a loving God and filled with his wisdom for our use, should we first, find it and then, choose to respond to it.

SWEDENBORG'S LEGACY

When Swedenborg died in London in 1772, there were perhaps a handful of men who had accepted what he had written as a new revelation or the 'Second Coming of Christ.' Swedenborg had not organized a church anywhere, but his books were fairly widely distributed throughout Europe and England. By 1787, and the founding of the first organized church based on Swedenborg's religious writings, in England, his works also were being read in Denmark, France, Germany, Russia, Sweden, and North and South America. The next year, in 1788, a box of his religious writings was on its way to Botany Bay, Australia. Today they can be found on every habitable continent, and world-wide via the internet. Many of them have also been translated into the major languages of the world. Churches have sprung up wherever the books are found. Today, there are several branches of the New Church (Swedenborgian) found in the Americas, Europe, Africa, Asia, Australia. The cultural impact of his vision has been enormous, affecting social movements, such as antislavery, the abolition of serfdom, infant schools, women's rights, and civil rights. Swedenborg's writings were also a source of inspiration for Spiritualism, and for many artists, from William Blake (1757–1827) to Ralph Albert Blakelock (1847–1919); and for writers from Honore de Balzac (1799–1850) to Jorge Luis Borges (1899–1986). More and more these connections are being explored by scholars. Perhaps it will not be too long before it will be necessary for scholars to engage Swedenborg's religious and cultural contributions in order to gain a greater understanding of the nature of our times.

REFERENCES AND FURTHER READING

Acton, A., ed. & trans. (1955) *The Letters and Memorials of Emanuel Swedenborg*. Bryn Athyn, PA: The Swedenborg Scientific Association

Block, M. B. (1968) *The New Church in the New World*. New York: Octagon Books

Cox, R. S. (2006) 'Spiritualism', in E.V. Gallagher & W. M. Ashcraft, eds., *Introduction of New and Alternative Religions in America*, vol. 3. Westport, CT: Greenwood Press, 26–47

Faivre, A. (1994) *Access to Western Esotericism*. Albany: State University of New York Press.

——(1995) 'Introduction 1', in A. Faivre & J. Needleman, eds., *Modern Esoteric Spirituality*. New York: Crossroad, xi–xxii

Faivre, A. & Needleman, J., eds. (1995) *Modern Esoteric Spirituality*. New York: Crossroad.

Hanegraaff, W. J. (1996) *New Age Religion and Western Culture: Esotericism in the Mirror of Secular Thought*. Leiden: E. J. Brill

——(2005) 'Occultism', in W. Hanegraaff, ed., *Dictionary of Gnosis & Western Esotericism*. Leiden: Brill, 884–89

Häll, J. (1995) *I Swedenborgs Labyrint: Studier i de gustavianska swedenborgarnas liv och tänkande*. Stockholm: Atlantis

Lenhammar, H. (1966) *Tolerans och Bekännelsetvång: Studier i den svenska swedenborgianismen 1765–1795*. Uppsala: Acta Universitatis Upsaliensis

Jonsson, I. (1988) 'Swedenborg and His Influence', in E. J. Brock et al., eds., *Swedenborg and His Influence*. Bryn Athyn, PA: The Academy of the New Church

Rose, J. S. (2005) 'Swedenborg's Garden of Theology', in J. S. Rose et al., eds., *Emanuel Swedenborg: Essays for the New Century Edition on His Life, Work, and Impact*. West Chester, PA: Swedenborg Foundation, 53–97

Rose, J. S., Shotwell, S., & Bertucci, M.L., eds. (2005) *Emanuel Swedenborg: Essays for the New Century Edition on His Life, Work, and Impact*. West Chester, PA: Swedenborg Foundation

Sigstedt, C. O. (1981) *The Swedenborg Epic: The Life and Work of Emanuel Swedenborg*. London: The Swedenborg Society

Swedenborg, E. (1734a) *Principia Rerum Naturalium sive Novorum Tentaminum Phaenomena Mundi Elementaris Philsophice Explicandi*. Dresden: Fredrick Hekel [Basic Principles of Nature]

——(1734b) *Prodromus Philosophiae Rationcinantis de Infinito, et Causa Finali Creationis: Deque Mechanismo Operationis Animae et Corporis*. Dresden: Frederick Hekel [Swedenborg, E. 1908. The Infinite and the Final Cause of Creation. trans. James J. G. Wilkinson. London: The Swedenborg Society]

——(1740–41) *Oeconomia Regni Animalis in Transactiones Divisa: Quatrum Haec Prima, de Sanguine, Ejus Arteriis, Venis, et Corde Agit: Anatomice, Physice, et Philosophice Perlustrata. Cui Accedit Introductio ad Psychologiam Rationalem*. Amsterdam: François Changuion [Dynamics of the Soul's Domain]

——(1744a) *Regnum Animale, Anatomice, Physice, et Philosophice Perlustratum. Cujus Pars Prima, de Viseribus Abdominis seu de Organis Regionis Inferioris Agit*. The Hague: Adrian Blyvenburg [The Soul's Domain Part I]

——(1744b) *Regnum Animale, Anatomice, Physice, et Philosophice Perlustratum. Cujus Pars Secunda, de Visceribus Thoracis seu de Organis Regionis Superioris Agit*. The Hague: Adrian Blyvenburg [The Soul's Domain Part II]

——(1745) Regnum Animale, *Anatomice, Physice, et Philosophice Perlustratum. Cujus Pars Tertia, de Cute, Sensu Tactus, et Gustus; et de Formis Organis in Genere Agit*. London [The Soul's Domain Part III]

——(1917) *The Schmidius Marginalia together with The Expository Material of The Index Biblicus*, E.E. Iungerich, ed. Bryn Athyn, PA: Academy of the New Church

——(1928) 'The History of Creation According to Moses', in Vol. I *The Word of the Old Testament Explained*. Posthumous work. Trans. A. Acton. Bryn Athyn, PA: Academy of the New Church

——(1928) *The Word of the Old Testament Explained*. Vol. I – VIII. Posthumous work. Trans. A. Acton. Bryn Athyn, PA: Academy of the New Church

——(1949. *Concerning The Messiah About to Come and Concerning The Kingdom of God and The Last Judgment*. Posthumous work. Trans. A. Acton. Bryn Athyn, PA: Academy of the New Church

——(1977) *Swedenborg's Journal of Dreams*. Trans. J. J. G. Wilkinson. W. R. Woofenden, ed. New York: Swedenborg Foundation

——(1996) 'The Last Judgment and Babylon Destroyed', in *Miscellaneous Theological Works*. Trans. John Whitehead. West Chester, PA: Swedenborg Foundation

——(1997) 'Doctrine of Life', in *Four Doctrines*. Trans. J. F. Potts. West Chester, PA: Swedenborg Foundation

——(1998) *Conjugial Love* (Marriage Love). Trans. S. M. Warren. West Chester, PA: Swedenborg Foundation

——(2002) *Heaven and Hell*. Trans. G. F. Dole. West Chester, PA: Swedenborg Foundation

——(2002) *Spiritual Experiences, Records and Notes made by Emanuel Swedenborg between 1746 and 1765 from his experiences in the spiritual world*. Published Posthumously. London: The Swedenborg Society

——(2003) *Divine Providence*. Trans. G. F. Dole. West Chester, PA: Swedenborg Foundation

——(2006) *True Christianity*. Vol. I. Trans. J. S. Rose. West Chester, PA: Swedenborg Foundation

——(2008) *Secrets of Heaven*. Trans. L. Cooper. West Chester, PA: Swedenborg Foundation

——(2012) *True Christianity*. Vol. II. Trans. J. S. Rose. West Chester, PA: Swedenborg Foundation

Weber, M. (1958) 'Science as a Vocation', in H. Gerth & C. W. Mills, eds., *From Max Weber: Essays in Sociology*. New York: Oxford University Press, 129–57

Williams-Hogan, J. (1998) 'The Place of Emanuel Swedenborg in Modern Western Esotericism', in A. Faivre & W. J. Hanegraaff, eds., *Modern Western Esotericism and The Science of Religion*. Leuven: Peeters, 201–52

——(2001) 'Emanuel Swedenborg and the Kabbalistic Tradition', in R. Caron & J. Godwin, eds., *Ésotérisme, Gnoses, & Imaginaire Symbolique: Mélanges Offerts À Antoine Faivre*. Leuven: Peeters, 343–60

——(2005) 'Emanuel Swedenborg', in W. Hanegraaff, ed., *Dictionary of Gnosis & Western Esotericism*. Leiden: Brill, 1096–1105

Wilson, C. (2004) *The Occult*. London: Watkins Publishing

CHAPTER ELEVEN

FREEMASONRY

Jan A. M. Snoek and Henrik Bogdan

INTRODUCTION

With roots going back to the medieval guilds of stonemasons, Freemasonry is the oldest initiatory society in the West not dependant on a religious institution.[1] Having lodges in virtually every major city in most parts of the world, it has changed from an originally British institution to a worldwide phenomenon with a wide range of local idiosyncratic features and characteristics. Numbering millions of active members it is also the largest fraternal organisation in the world, still managing to attract new members in the postmodern society of the twenty-first century. The continued presence and development of Freemasonry with its rich diversity in practices and interpretations, raises the question of what it is that makes such an old phenomenon seem relevant to so many diverse people for over three hundred years? There is no single answer to the question, but part of it surely rests on the fact that despite its emphasis on tradition, transmission and authority, Freemasonry has always been a non-dogmatic organisation in the sense that its rituals, symbols and practices have not had official and final interpretations. On the contrary, Freemasonry is characterised by a striking diversity of interpretation—it is thus possible to find purely moral interpretations of its central symbols, but also scientific, psychological, esoteric, political, philosophical, religious, etc. interpretations of the same symbols. It should furthermore be stressed for readers unfamiliar with the study of Freemasonry, that Freemasonry is not *one* organisation, but in fact represents a plethora of organisations (independent Grand Lodges, Rites and Systems), each one of which might recognise some organisations as Freemasonry, while dismissing others.

However, despite its diversity, ever since its reformation in the early eighteenth century there are certain recurrent phenomena, that can be regarded as basic features of Freemasonry. Some masonic authors speak in this context about the 'ancient landmarks', although they do not seem to agree on what these landmarks actually consist of. For the present purposes, it suffices to mention the following features: (1) the practice of rituals of initiation (i.e. those for the three Craft or Symbolic degrees, Entered Apprentice, Fellow Craft and Master Mason, and those for the 'high' or 'additional' degrees which differ from system to system); (2) the use of a particular set of symbols (as often encountered in the rites of initiation), such as symbols taken from the Bible or the Christian tradition (for example the Temple of Solomon with its two pillars Jachin and Boas and the chequered floor, or the Eye in the Triangle as symbol for the Great Architect of the Universe [= God]), tools and other objects adopted from medieval stonemasonry (for example the square and the compass, the rough and perfected ashlars or stones, the white apron and gloves, tracing boards for each degree), and so on; (3) an organisational structure with hierarchical degrees, officers of the lodge, local lodges, Provincial and Grand Lodges; (4) emphasis on tradition and legitimacy where the members often see themselves as transmitters of an unbroken chain of initiation; (5) the individual's quest for improvement through the initiatory system, where each degree is interpreted as a step in a process leading to perfection (interpreted, of course, in different ways); (6) often an emphasis on charitable works; (7) an emphasis on a universal brotherhood, fraternity and conviviality (the latter often expressed through more or less formal dinners and banquets held in connection with the performance of the rituals of initiation); (8) the advocacy of privacy and the praxis of secrecy; and (8) opposition, or what is often referred to as 'anti-masonry', as an historically accompanying phenomenon.

Freemasonry has no founder or founding date. It developed slowly towards the point where we, now, recognize it as such, and developed onwards ever since. Therefore, it has no canonical form. Indeed, around 1600, the time when it can be identified with certainty, there seem to have existed at least two distinct forms, one in Scotland and one in England. A century and a half later, there exists also an Irish form, while in England at least three forms are found side by side, that of the so-called 'Premier' Grand Lodge, or 'Moderns', that of the 'Athol' Grand Lodge, or 'Antients', and a third tradition including among others the 'Harodim' and the 'Grand Lodge of All England, held at York'. Even if we assume that the tradition of the 'Antients' in fact developed out of a combination of the Irish and the 'Moderns' ones, there were still at this time at least four different forms in existence, of which we know nothing about what relationships existed between them. Right from the time that they can be historically grasped, then, there never was one Freemasonry, but rather a diversity of Freemasonries.

ORIGINS AND EARLY HISTORY IN SCOTLAND AND ENGLAND

The number of theories about the origins of Freemasonry runs in the dozens. Most famous, probably, is the Gould Thesis, first formulated by Robert Freke Gould and his friends around the time when they founded the first research lodge in the 1880s, the Quatuor Coronati Lodge No. 2076. According to this theory, at first there were simple, so called 'operative', stonemasons, who had their Craft and their lodges, but who did not 'speculate' about their Craft or their working tools, that is, they did not interpret them symbolically. Then, at the beginning of the eighteenth century, more and more 'gentlemen masons' became members of the lodges, who introduced, during a period of transition, the speculative element, out of which arose modern 'speculative' Freemasonry. This theory would be regarded as fact for about a century, but we know now that it is wrong (Hamill 1986). First, Freemasonry is significantly older than 1717. Second, the early Freemasons were anything but simple folk. 'Freemason' being short for 'Freestone mason', the term refers to the highest trained members of the Craft, the sculptors and architects, those who were allowed to work with the most expensive material: freestone. It is, third, also clear now that these freestone masons *did* 'speculate' about their craft, its tools, etc. Freemasonry, then, was speculative right from its start. And precisely this explains why 'gentlemen masons' were interested in it in the first place. It was not them who introduced the speculative element, but rather the other way round: they learned it from the stonemasons. Consequently, we should no longer oppose speculative to operative masons, but rather gentlemen masons to stone masons, all of whom were speculative masons, while the last ones were also operative (see Snoek 2010).

The oldest documents, which are usually associated with Freemasonry, are the so-called 'Old Manuscript Constitutions' or 'Old Charges'. Among the oldest ones are the Constitutions of the Masons of York (1352, 1370, 1409), the *Ordonnances des masons de Londres* (1356), the Constitutions of the Carpenters Guild of Norwich (1375), the Regius MS and the Cooke MS (both from between 1425 and 1450), and the *Constituciones artis geometricae secundum Euclidem* (fifteenth century). From 1583 onwards there are more than a hundred. Most of them are English and date from between 1675 and 1725. Especially these later ones often state that they should be read during the 'acception' of a candidate. This shows that these ones were related to the English 'acception' (see later), but we do not really know much of the context of the older ones. Most of them have the same structure: they start with a prayer, after which follows a legendary history of the craft. Then follow the actual 'Articles and Points' or 'Charges', as well as rules for the Grand Meetings, and instructions for the administration of justice. Finally follow instructions for the adoption of new members, such as the text of the oath to be administered, and a closing prayer. Especially interesting in the light of later developments are these old forms of the oath, such as:

> These Charges that you haue Received you shall well and truly keepe not discloseing the secresy of our Lodge to man woman nor Child : sticke nor stone : thing moueable nor vnmoveable soe god you helpe and his holy Doome Amen.
>
> (*Buchanan MS. 1*, ca. 1670)

The contents of these documents are explicitly Christian. You should serve God, the (Roman Catholic) Church, your Master, and the members of your lodge. You should behave properly, that is, bury the dead, support widows, go to church regularly, and so on. The Craft and its tools are interpreted symbolically (Prescott 2005).

In 1598 and 1599, William Schaw, the King's Master of Works and General Warden of the Craft, signed new 'statutes' for the lodges of the masons in Scotland. Three then existing lodges are named explicitly: those of Edinburgh St Mary's Chapel, Kilwinning, and Sterling. From the information these texts give there can be no doubt that these are masonic lodges, more or less in the modern sense. Their members are called Masons, and there is at least one ritual reception, namely when, after one has passed his examination as a Master Mason in the Incorporation, one is brought into the lodge and 'made' a 'Brother and Fellow in the Craft'. Such a lodge was presided over by a Warden and his two Deacons. The candidate paid an entrance fee, with which the dinner at the occasion was financed, and presented gloves to the members.

In the statutes of 1599—which are a complement to, rather than a replacement of, those of 1598—Schaw confirmed that the lodge of Edinburgh was the oldest one. The lodge of Kilwinning did not agree. It took some years before a successor to Schaw decided that both would get the status 'time immemorial', meaning that there was no longer anyone alive who could remember when one of them did not yet exist. Thus we must assume that at least these two lodges existed around the middle of the sixteenth century, but possibly already much earlier (Stevenson 1988; Snoek 2002).

The archives of the Mason's Company of London go back a long time. After a gap, probably resulting from the Great Fire of London in 1666, they continue from 1619 onwards. Almost at once there now occur terms, which were not there before the gap: 'the making of Masons' (1621), masons are 'accepted' (1630), or the 'acception' (1645–47, 1649–50). There is no reason to assume that the phenomenon to which these terms refer, the 'acception', was an invention of 1621 only, rather it was in existence at that moment for some time already. In 1646 Elias Ashmole wrote in his so-called diary: 'I was made a Free Mason at Warrington in Lancashire, with Coll: Henry Mainwaring of Karincham in Cheshire. The names of those that were then at the Lodge, Mr. Rich. Penket Warden, Mr. James Collier, Mr. Rich: Sankey, Henry Littler, John Ellam, Rich: Ellam & Hugh Brewer.' And in 1682 he noted: 'I rec[eive]d a Sumons to appe[ar] at a Lodge to be held the next day, at Masons Hall London....I was the Senior Fellow among them (it being 35 years since I was admitted)....' All the members mentioned in Ashmole's first entry were senior members of the Mason's Company of London, as well as members of the 'acception', and from the lodge mentioned in the second entry, we now know that there is a continuous link to the four lodges which James Anderson in his second edition of his *Constitutions*, of 1738, claims to have united in 1716, forming the start of the development which led to the 'Premier Grand Lodge' (Hamill 1986; Snoek 2002; Snoek 2010).

THE DEVELOPMENT OF FREEMASONRY IN ENGLAND

In 1666 London was devastated by the Great Fire. As a result, workmen from the building trade came to the English capital in order to rebuild it. Some of them joined the London lodges, which thus flourished. Once George of Hanover had become King of England at the end of 1714, the building activity in London came to an end. London had been largely rebuilt and there was no money left. So, the workmen went to other places, leaving the lodges of London with only a few members. According to Anderson's *Constitutions* of 1738, Sir Christopher Wren had been elected Grand Master in 1685, an office he supposedly held until 1695, and was 'again chosen Grand Master, [in] A.D. 1698'. However, he 'neglected the Office of Grand Master', 'some few years after' 1708. Further, still according to Anderson, in 1716 the lodges in London found 'themselves neglected by Sir Christopher Wren'. Anderson's complaint that Wren neglected the lodges is not at all surprising, if we remember that in 1716 he was eighty-four years old. Consequently, one can easily imagine that he was just too aged to continue his work of organising the Quarterly Communications, i.e. the four main annual meetings of the Grand Lodge. Still, the lodges felt the need to assemble in order to discuss their problems. Set against this background, Anderson's story of what happened in 1716 and 1717 makes eminent sense.

> [Four London lodges] and some old Brothers met at the Apple-Tree [Tavern], and having put into the Chair the oldest Master Mason [present] ([making him for that evening what we would] now [call] the Master of a Lodge) they constituted themselves a Grand Lodge pro Tempore in Due Form, and forthwith revived the Quarterly Communication of the Officers of Lodges ([which Quarterly Communications are also sometimes] call'd the Grand Lodge) [and] resolv'd to hold the Annual Assembly and Feast, and then [i.e. at that next Annual Assembly] to chuse a [new] Grand Master from among themselves.
>
> (Anderson 1738: 109)

What happened on St John's Day in 1717—according to Anderson's report, which is the only account of that event we have—was definitely *not* the foundation of a new organisation, but no more than the continuation of an old one. Surely, there can be little doubt that in the decade *following* this event, the Grand Lodge was reorganised into a form which had not existed in London before, mainly by developing itself into an organisation completely independent from the London Company of Masons and by considerably modifying and simplifying its ceremonial practice in order to adapt it to its new, less educated target group, the gentlemen masons (Snoek 2004a; Snoek 2004b). But there was no significant discontinuity between the Quarterly Communications before and after 1716, apart from the gap caused by Wren's inactivity (Snoek 2010).

According to Anderson, it was on St John's Day (24 June) 1717 that the already-mentioned four lodges from London met again and chose Anthony Sayer as their new 'Grand Master' for 1717–18. Soon, the most important and influential members would become John Theophilus Desaguliers, James Anderson and George Payne. Anderson was a minister of the Church of Scotland. Desaguliers was a minister of the Church of England, assistant to Isaac Newton, and a member of the Royal Society. After Sayer, Payne and Desaguliers occupied the post of Grand Master for three successive years during the formative period: 1718–19 (Payne), 1719–20 (Desaguliers), and 1720–21 (Payne). Then, in 1721, the Duke of Montague became the first aristocratic Grand Master. From then on, all further Grand Masters have been aristocrats. In 1720, Payne signed new regulations, which were included in Anderson's *Constitutions* of 1723.

At the end of the seventeenth and the start of the eighteenth century, the Scottish and English forms of Freemasonry seem to have discovered and influenced each other. As a result, whereas previously they seem to have had only one initiation degree each, there now developed a two-degree system, which we find referred to in Anderson's *Constitutions* of 1723: the 'acception', of London origin, had now become the first degree, which the Scotsman Anderson called 'Entered Apprentice', while the Scottish 'Master Mason or Fellow in the Craft' became the second degree, now called 'Fellow Craft or Master Mason'. Around 1725 the contents of these two degrees were in London redistributed over three degrees, now called 'Entered Apprentice' (containing part of the old first degree), 'Fellow of the Craft' (containing the rest of the old first degree), and 'Master Mason' (containing the old second degree) (Vibert 1967; Snoek 2002). There was, of course, only one possibility to persuade the lodges to work with the new trigradal system: in 1730 its rituals were published as Samuel Prichard's *Masonry Dissected* (Snoek 2003a). This pamphlet, first published in October 1730, is perhaps the most influential of all masonic exposures published in the eighteenth century, and it ran into no fewer than thirty editions in the eighteenth century. With the publication of this book the development of the Craft degree system had reached its completion in the sense that there were now three degrees: Entered Apprentice, Fellow Craft and Master Mason. It was to a very large extent because of *Masonry Dissected* that these three degrees and their particular rituals of initiation were implemented in the masonic initiatory system.

In 1723–24 the Grand Lodge of Ireland was formed, and in 1736 the Grand Lodge of Scotland followed. After 1725, Freemasonry started spreading over continental Europe and the British colonies: lodges were founded in Paris (1726), Mannheim (1727?), Madrid (1728), Gibraltar and Bengal (1729), Lisbon (1730), Florence (1733), The Hague (1734), Hamburg (1737), and so on. Next, other colonial powers such as France and the Netherlands started founding lodges in their colonies as well, while from 1732 onwards, lodges were attached to military regiments.

In 1725, the old lodge in the City of York formed itself into the 'Grand Lodge of All England'. It was related to a particular tradition in English Freemasonry, the practitioners of which called themselves the Harodim. When a conflict arose within William Preston's 'Lodge of Antiquity', the Grand Lodge ('Moderns') expelled it, whereupon it founded in 1779, on a warrant by the York-based Grand Lodge, the 'Grand Lodge of England, South of the River Trent', which disappeared again after ten years. Within this Grand Lodge, Preston created in 1787 the 'Ancient and Venerable Order of Harodim' (Hills 1967). It is becoming more and more clear at the moment, that this Harodim/York tradition of English Freemasonry is the source of most English 'high degrees', as well as the Royal Order of Scotland and the Adoption Rite (Snoek 2012).

There were in the eighteenth century large numbers of Irish day labourers in London. If they tried to visit lodges of the 'Premier' Grand Lodge, they would either not be let in because of their low social status, or if they were, they would be rather surprised by the rituals they saw there. From the 1730s onwards, they thus formed lodges of their own, which in 1750–52 united in a separate English Grand Lodge, which referred to itself as that of the 'Antients'. In 1756, their Grand Secretary, Laurence Dermott, published the Constitutions of this new Grand Lodge under the title *Ahiman Rezon*. Of course, their lodges too needed printed rituals, and thus 'exposures' of those were published in the 1760s. The two most important ones were *Three Distinct Knocks* of 1760 and *Jachin and Boas* of 1762 (Snoek 2003a).

After more than half a century of rivalry between the Moderns and the Antients, an attempt was made to merge these two English Grand Lodges. During the years 1809 to 1811 the Lodge of Promulgation, created especially for that purpose, prepared the merger and formulated the Articles of Union. In 1813 the Duke of Sussex was Grand Master of the Moderns, and his brother, the Duke of Kent, his Deputy Grand Master. At the same time, the Duke of Kent was also the Grand Master of the Antients. And so it came that on 27 December 1813 the two Grand Lodges merged into the United Grand Lodge of England and Wales with the Duke of Sussex as Grand Master. At once the Lodge of Reconciliation was formed to effectuate the merger. It functioned from 1813 to 1816. One of the things it did was to create new rituals for the new Grand Lodge, which were approved and confirmed by the Grand Lodge, based on their performance, in 1816. Then it was dissolved, while in the next few years several Lodges of Instruction or of Improvement were formed to instruct the lodges in the country how to perform the new rituals. It was pretended that there existed no written text of these rituals, but we know today that texts in cipher existed perfectly well. They were first published by Richard Carlile in 1825 (Carlile 1831; Hasselmann and Snoek 2010).

FREEMASONRY GOES INTERNATIONAL

In 1720–21 there had been an unofficial lodge in Rotterdam, composed of British Freemasons (Snoek 2000), but, as stated earlier, the spread of Freemasonry to the Continent and the rest of the world really started after 1725. The first country where it appeared was France. In 1688, William III had forced James II Stuart to abdicate the British throne, and to flee to France, where he lived until his death in 1701 at his court in exile in Saint-Germain-en-Laye, west of Paris. His son, James (III), was called 'the Old Pretender', and his son, Charles Edward, 'the Young Pretender'. They too stayed at Saint-Germain-en-Laye, where they were surrounded by large numbers of men from Scotland. Given the popularity of Freemasonry in Scotland between 1688 and 1725, it seems more likely than unlikely that there were enough Freemasons at this court to form a lodge, but no documentary evidence is known which could prove this. In 1704 the Stuarts were by law excluded from the English throne and in 1713, England and France concluded the Peace of Utrecht, as a result of which the Stuarts lost the support of France. The next year, George of Hanover became King of England and in September 1715 Louis XIV died and was succeeded by Louis XV. From September to November that year James (III) invaded England, but without success. Still, the Jacobite court in exile in France was maintained until the Young Pretender tried for the last time to gain the his throne in 1745. In 1717 the French concluded an alliance with England. Soon, everything English became en vogue in France. It is, no doubt, against this background also that Freemasonry was introduced in France. The first lodges in Paris, founded from 1726 onwards, were Jacobite ones, probably working within the Harodim tradition, but from 1729 onwards also Hanoverian lodges, working in the tradition of the 'Moderns', were founded. The first Grand Masters of the French Grand Lodge were British Jacobites. Only in 1738 the first French one was elected (Lefebvre-Filleau 2000).

The first interdict against Freemasonry came from the states of Holland and West Friesland in 1735. The first lodges had been founded here in 1734 (The Hague) and 1735 (Amsterdam and The Hague again), and they had elected their own Grand Master. Then the states demanded certain documents from the lodges, including Anderson's *Constitutions* (1723), and Prichard's *Masonry Dissected* (1730). The interdiction of 30 November 1735 formulated three reproaches: the Freemasons would support a certain political party (the supporters of the Prince of Orange), they would be responsible for certain riots, and they would practice sodomy. Bouman and Van den Brand have shown that all three of these accusations were unfounded and in fact no more than what at that time were the usual arguments to make an interdiction acceptable in the face of the general public (Bouman 1993; Van den Brand 1993). However, it is perfectly possible to read between the lines of the several documents pertaining to the interdict in the archives in order to conclude that authorities were concerned (1) that the Order demanded an oath with imprecations, that a sword of sovereignty was carried before the Grand Master of the Order and before the Master of a lodge, and that the Order had its own Book of Constitutions, all indications that the Order claimed *sovereignty*, and thus formed a 'state within a state', and (2) that the Master of a lodge, as well as the Grand Master of the Order, were elected *democratically* (Snoek 1994).

The French King had ordered the police officer Hérault to find out what the Freemasons were doing. In 1737 Hérault succeeded in obtaining a copy of a ritual, used by one of the Paris lodges, which he published on 5 December (Snoek 2001). The next year it was reprinted, together with a French translation, of the Dutch translation of ca. 1735 (Bernheim 1993), of Prichard's *Masonry Dissected* (1730), as part of *La Réception Mystérieuse*, purportedly published in London. However, as Freemasonry became popular in France, better printed rituals were required. As a result, in 1744 no fewer than four 'exposures' were published: *Le Secret des Francs-Maçons* by the Abbé Gabriel Louis Calabre Perau gave the rituals for the first two degrees of the tradition of the 'Moderns' (for the date of this publication see Bernheim 1993), while *Le Catéchisme des Francs-Maçons* by Louis Travenol, writing under the name Leonard Gabanon, added the third degree. Both established a new style of presentation, narrative rather than catechetic, and added much more information about the actions to be performed than the older publications had done. The rituals presented in *La Franc-Maçonne* seem not to relate to any known masonic tradition, but it tells a story about the beginnings of the initiation of women in Adoption lodges. *Le Parfait Maçon* seems to present rituals of the first four degrees of the tradition of the Harodim (Snoek 2012). In 1745 *Le Sceau Rompu* gave a number of corrections on *Le Secret* and *Le Catéchisme*, after which *L'Ordre des Francs-Maçons Trahi*, published in Amsterdam, merged all three into one. Therewith the French version of the rituals of the tradition of the Moderns was established, and it was this form that now spread rapidly over all of the European continent, almost completely replacing whatever traditions might have been worked in lodges founded there earlier (on the early French 'exposures', see Carr 1971).

'HIGH DEGREES' AND RITES

In or shortly after 1730, it seems, the first masonic knightly Order, the *Ordre Sublime des Chevaliers Élus*, was founded in France (Kervella and Lestienne 1997; Bernheim 1998). Around the same time, there were in England the first 'Scots Masons Lodges'. In one of them, the (French) Union lodge in London, the Italian painter Jacopo Fabris was initiated. In 1742, Fabris in his turn founded the Scots Masters lodge 'L'Union' in Berlin (Mollier 2002). From there this degree of Scots Master (probably of Harodim origin) spread over the continent. Soon new degrees were created, especially in France, England (Harodim tradition) and Germany. These degrees were at first mainly practiced in normal lodges, but soon separate bodies (Scots lodges, Chapters, and so on) were formed which accumulated a number of these, now called 'high degrees', and usually ordered them into a system, a Rite. Examples of these are the 'Strict Observance' (1751/1763–82, Germany), the Swedish Rite (1756/1759, Sweden), the Bavarian 'Illuminati' (1776–85, Germany), the 'Rectified Scottish Rite' (1778, France), the 'French' or 'Modern Rite' (1786, France), the York Rite (1797, United States of America), and the 'Ancient and Accepted Scottish Rite' (1801, United States of America).

Once the tradition of the 'Moderns' became the more successful one on the continent, the lodges there working in the Harodim tradition seem to have found other ways to survive: some of them, such as the lodge 'Zur Eintracht' or 'Zur Einigkeit' (= Union!) in Mannheim (Germany), turned into Scots Master lodges, while others started, from approximately 1744 onwards, to initiate women. The rituals of the first two degrees, practiced by these lodges, were transformed in a new trigradal system: the Adoption Rite (Snoek 2012). It took until the last quarter of the nineteenth century before women were initiated in the lodges, working in the continental tradition of the 'Moderns', forming the mixed Order 'Le Droit Humain' in France. Early in the twentieth century, the British branch of this Order adopted rituals, which were based on rituals from the Grand Lodge of Scotland. Later this branch started to work also with the rituals of the United Grand Lodge of England. Mainly after the Second World War, purely female Orders began to be founded. As a result, there are today male, mixed and female masonic Orders.

During the latter part of the eighteenth century a new form of masonry appeared which, to a certain extent, was a reaction against the 'Écossais' and the Templar Rites. This form of masonry did not place the origins of the Order of Freemasons with the medieval Crusades, but in ancient Egypt. That the origins of Freemasonry might be found in ancient Egypt was hinted at before Egyptian masonry as such appeared on the scene; for instance, in the 1745 publication *Le Sceau Rompu* (Carr 1971: 208). While Egyptian masonry never became a real threat to the predominance of the other forms of high degree masonry, it has remained on the fringes of conservative masonry to this day. One of the earliest propagators of Egyptian masonry was Karl Friedrich von Köppen (1734–97) who founded the Order of the *Afrikanische Bauherren* (African Building Masters) in 1767 (Caillet 1994: 17). This order was based on a short text by Köppen and Bernhard Hymmen (1731–87), entitled *Crata Repoa* (published only in 1770). Another influential system was Cagliostro's *Egyptian Rite*, which was founded in Naples in 1777, with a Supreme Council established in Paris in 1785 (Introvigne 2005: 225). Allesandro di Cagliostro (the pseudonym of Guiseppe Balsamo, 1743–95), was one of the most famous and charismatic adventurers of the eighteenth century. Among other things, he claimed to have been initiated at the pyramids in Egypt, and that he possessed the knowledge to transmute base metals into silver and gold. Other claims included the ability to evoke spirits, and that he had lived for no less than two thousand years. In 1785 he announced that both men and women should be entitled to the mysteries of the pyramids, and thus he opened his Rite to women (McIntosh 1975: 30–31). Cagliostro's preoccupation with esoteric matters apparently found its way into the initiatory system of his Egyptian Rite, and the Rite included alchemical aspects, the search for a spiritual immortality, and angelic theurgy (Caillet 1994: 19; Introvigne 2005: 225–27). Other influential Egyptian Rites worth mentioning are the Rites of Memphis and Misraim, which were founded during the first half of the nineteenth century.

Masonic Rites of a more outspoken esoteric bent included Rites and orders such as *L'Orde des Élus Coëns* and the *Rite Ecossais philosophique*, but Rosicrucian Rites and degrees can also be counted into this category. The first of these, *L'Orde des Élus Coëns*, or the *The Order of the Masonic Knights Élus Coëns of the Universe*, was founded by the theosophist and kabbalist Martines de Pasqually (1708/1709–74) in the 1760s, and it included a peculiar form of theurgy mixed with the philosophy and theosophy of its founder (see Le Forestier 1987 [1923]; Nahon 2005: 332–34). Although this order possessed all the outward characteristics of a masonic organisation such as a hierarchical degree system, rituals of initiation and lodges, and employed a typical masonic terminology, it is perhaps more fitting to label the *Orde des Élus Coëns* a religious movement. The reason for this is not only the peculiar religious teachings derived from Pasqually, but also the marked religious life that the members were expected to live, which is referred to in the name of the order: 'chosen priests', from the Hebrew *kohen* (meaning priest). Pasqually's teachings centre round the Gnostic idea of the Fall of Man through which humankind became separated from God. Through the initiatory system of the order the members were expected to reverse the Fall, and make an upward journey in which the seven degrees of the order (not counting the three Craft degrees) corresponded to the seven gifts of the Spirit. The final goal of the initiatory process was 'reintegration', a return to the primitive and primordial state of man characterised by union with God. The theurgy employed in the order was a means to this goal, through which divine energies were invoked and the communion with good spirits was sought. According to Jean-François Var this theurgy was not aimed at acquiring natural or supernatural powers, but it was part of a religious 'cult' which included a liturgy (Var 2005: 935). As mentioned, the initiatory system of the order consisted of a total of ten degrees, of which the preliminary Craft degrees were not seen as part of the Order as such. The degrees were divided into four different classes (again, not counting the Craft degrees), with the degree of Réau-Croix as the highest degree, which constituted a class of its own. After the death of Pasqually in 1774 Caignet de Lester (1725–78) succeeded him as the leader of the order (Grand Souverain de l'Ordre), followed by Sebastian de Las Casas in 1778. Although *L'Orde des Élus Coëns* was formally dissolved in 1781 it continued to have active lodges, most notably the one in Lyon under the leadership of Willermoz (Nahon 2005: 332–34; Var 2005: 931–35). The *Rite Ecossais philosophique* was the successor of an esoteric Rite called *Rite Hermétique d'Avignon*, which was founded in 1774. It is often stated that Dom Antoine Joseph Pernety (1716–96) was the founder of not only the *Rite Hermétique d'Avignon*, but also of the *Rite Ecossais philosophique*. Modern scholarship, however, contests this assumption (Snoek 2003b: 28–32). In 1776 the *Rite Hermétique* was exported from Avignon to Paris, where it changed its name to *Rite Ecossais philosophique*. It is uncertain when the Rite was dissolved, but it probably occurred sometime between 1844 and 1849 (Snoek 2003b: 70).

THE NINETEENTH CENTURY

The second half of the eighteenth century was a time in which Freemasonry flourished all over the world. However, it was also a time when major changes in the Western worldview were incubating. These changes then became manifest between 1780 and 1820. In 1789 the French Revolution shocked the Western world. In France, masonic activity came to a halt for ten years. Then Napoleon created a new world order, but was defeated himself in 1815. It is striking to see that in a large number of Western countries the masonic rituals were, for the second time,[2] dramatically changed during this period, reflecting a new Western culture, which was middle class, rather than aristocratic. In Germany, the rituals 'Schröder' of 1801 were among the first to reflect this new bourgeois worldview. They were followed by those for the 'Craft' degrees of the Ancient and Accepted Scottish Rite, written in 1804 in Paris (Noël 2006). The new rituals for the United Grand Lodge of England, approved in 1816, were Victorian in their moralistic outlook, even though Queen Victoria was not yet born. Although superficial comparison of the new rituals with the older ones may suggest that little had changed, what actually had changed was the heart of the matter. Instead of aiming at inducing a mystic experience in the Candidate, the new rituals reflected the conviction that proper moral behaviour can be learned by repetitive performance of proper model behaviour (Hasselmann 2009). For example, in the third degree the candidate is identified with Hiram Abiff, the architect of the Temple of Solomon, who, according to the masonic tradition, was murdered shortly before the completion of the work. The eighteenth-century rituals made clear that Hiram was in fact God, so that the candidate experienced a ritual *Unio Mystica*. In the ritual of the Ancient and Accepted Scottish Rite (AASR), however, Hiram reincarnates in the human candidate, and in the ritual of the United Grand Lodge of England, Hiram steadfastly refuses to give his murderers the Master's Word, thus showing the model behaviour of a man. The Swedish and American rituals escaped this process, at least for the time being (Snoek 2004a; Snoek 2004b).

The nineteenth century was the era of colonialism *par excellence*. Jews had been initiated from the 1730s onwards, and the first Muslim initiated into masonry was probably the Persian diplomat Askar Khan Afshar, in Paris in 1808. Both Jews and Muslims, however, knew the most central symbol of Freemasonry, the Temple of king Solomon, from their own Holy Scriptures, wherefore the masonic ritual could make at least some sense to them. That, of course, was not the case with people who identified strongly with another religious background. To them, Freemasonry could only mean something if they had assimilated thoroughly into Western culture. It thus took until the 1840s before the first one of them, a Parsee from India, was initiated. And since Freemasonry traditionally works 'to the Honour of the Grand Architect of the Universe', in singular, it took until the 1870s before Hindus—regarded by the English as polytheists *par excellence*—were admitted. Colonial politics, using Freemasonry to assimilate the 'locals' to the Western culture, were no doubt a major driving force behind this process. The other way round, however, the majority of the non-Christian members—Jews and Muslims included—seem to have used Freemasonry intentionally as an emancipation tool, in order to get recognition from members of the dominant culture with whom they were confronted in daily life. Another feature of nineteenth-century masonic history was the culmination of anti-masonry. In the first place, the so-called 'Morgan affair' triggered a strong anti-masonic movement in the United States of America, resulting even in an explicitly anti-masonic political party. Second, the Pope, confronted with the nationalist movement in Italy, realised that he would lose (as indeed happened in 1870) most of the Church–State (the largest part of Northern Italy, with the exception of mainly Tuscany and the Republic of Venice), and fought against it with the weapons he had: Papal Bulls. Because the two leaders of the Nationalist movement, Count Cavour and Guiseppe Garibaldi, were both Freemasons, the Pope seems to have hoped that Bulls condemning Freemasonry would hurt these two men. The predominantly Roman Catholic French Freemasons did not understand that these Bulls were not aimed against them. So, they tried to convince the Pope that there was nothing incompatible between Freemasonry and the Church. But whatever they did, it could not stop the stream of anti-masonic Bulls. Once Rome was invaded by the Nationalists and the Church–State integrated into Italy in 1870, the Papal Bulls against Freemasonry became even harsher, indicating frustration on the part of the Vatican. And thus, in 1877, the provoked *Grand Orient de France* took an explicitly anti-clerical stand. In 1896 Pope Leo XIII finally organised an anti-masonic conference and two years later the Anti-Masonic Liga was founded in Rome. The last anti-masonic Bull was Leo XIII's *Annum Ingressi* from 1902.

In the eighteenth century, an important accusation had been that, by demanding that the candidates would take an oath with imprecations, Freemasonry not only infringed on Biblical interdictions against swearing such an oath generally (Matthew 5:34, 37; Exodus 20:7), but also against the tradition in Western Church and State law, that only sovereign powers were allowed to do so. But this argument did not recur in the nineteenth century. The arguments against Freemasonry, forwarded in the Papal Bulls, were partly directly related to the real reason of their existence: Freemasons were supposed to plot against Church and State. Other recurrent arguments were (1) the fact that Freemasons accepted that their members were of any (Christian) religion they wanted, instead of demanding their conversion to the Roman Catholic Church ('indifferentism'), and (2) Freemasons wanted the separation of State and Church—which would cost the Pope his worldly power, and the Church its monopoly over education. These last two points were correct.

THE TWENTIETH CENTURY

After 1870, the feminist movement became ever more powerful in a number of countries. Once on 11 November 1875 Countess Ilona (i.e. Helena) Hadik-Barkóczy had been initiated in the male lodge 'Egyenlöség' ('Equality') at Ungvár, working under the *Grand Orient of Hungary*, Spain followed with the initiation of Countess Julia Apraxin-Batthyany in the lodge 'Fraternidad Ibérica' in Madrid in 1880. As opposed to the Hungarian male lodges, those in Spain did not stop after the initiation of one woman, but continued initiating more of them with the 'male' rituals of the AASR. Indeed, the phenomenon became rather popular. The struggle to initiate women into French masonic lodges at the end of the nineteenth century must be seen in the context of the struggle for women's political rights. Central to this process, on the masonic side, was the relatively short-lived *Grande Loge Symbolique Écossaise* (GLSE), which brought together the most progressive masons of its time. The lodge 'Les Libres Penseurs' belonged to this Grand Lodge. During a short interval as an independent lodge, it initiated the feminist leader Maria Deraismes in 1882, resulting in 1893 in the creation of what is now the mixed masonic order *Le Droit Humain* (LDH). This new Grand Lodge adopted the rituals of the GLSE for the initiation of all its members, male and female. This rise of mixed Freemasonry in France, Allen argues, has in fact its origins in the remarkable synergy of men and women feminists (Allen 2008), who worked together in the name of women's interests everywhere, not just in the Craft.

In the early twentieth century it was the British branch of *Le Droit Humain* where the third significant change of the masonic rituals took place. In 1902, Annie Besant was initiated in this mixed Order. She was not only an important feminist, but also one of the leading figures in the Theosophical Society. For her, *Le Droit Humain* and the Theosophical Society were both tools, which she could use in her feminist enterprise. The rituals she created from 1904 onwards for that part of *Le Droit Humain*, which she held under her control, were imbued with Theosophical symbolism. Given the enormous influence, which the Theosophical Society had on Western culture in the first third of the twentieth century, the form of Freemasonry she created was extremely well adapted to what was wanted by Freemasons, not only in her own masonic Order, and as a result, *Le Droit Humain* grew explosively. But with the Second World War, the Theosophically influenced Western culture came largely to an end (Prescott 2008).

Anti-masonry experienced a second culmination in the twentieth century. Ever since Augustin de Barruel had in 1797 published the ideas he had stolen from his friend John Robison about a World Conspiracy, in which the Jews, the Freemasons and the Illuminati (regarded by Barruel as distinguished from the Freemasons) cooperated in order to overthrow all monarchies as well as the Vatican, and to found a World Republic instead, conspiracy theories have lived a life of their own. From now on, anti-Semitism (which was much older) became almost inseparable from anti-masonry. The culmination of this development formed the *Protocols of the Elders of Zion*, written in 1897 or 1898 in Paris on the initiative of the Okharana, the secret police abroad of the Russian Tsar, led by Pyotr Ivanovitch Rachkovsky. The author was maybe Matvei Golovinsky, a member of Rachkovsky's group. It was based on Maurice Joly's *Dialogue aux Enfers entre Montesquieu et Machiavel* from 1864, an attack on the despotism of Napoleon III, but the Protocols reversed the argument, attacking exactly modernism. They were intended as propaganda against the progressive Count Sergey Witte, who was since 1892 minister of finances of Russia. As such they were published in Russia in the period 1903 to 1907. But with an intelligent preface, one could use the *Protocols* as propaganda for virtually any cause, as long as one could present the Jews and the Freemasons as the enemies. From 1919 onwards, translations were published in most European languages, and they played a central role in Nazi propaganda during the period 1929–45. Consequently, masonic activity came to a halt in Germany in 1935 and in all occupied countries during the Second World War. After it a significant number of Nazis fled to the Middle East and spread there their anti-Semitic ideas, using the *Protocols* again. Anti-Zionist Muslims from then on adopted them and use especially Arabic translations in their propaganda against Israel, in passing producing strong anti-masonic sentiments as well (Cohn 1967; Taguieff 1992).

The twentieth century saw, however, also an attempt at rapprochement. After Vaticanum II (1962–65), the Roman Catholic Church took the initiative to start conversations with representatives of Freemasonry. No doubt under the influence of those, the formulation of Canon 2335 in the first edition of the *Codex*, of 1917, that a Freemason is excommunicated automatically, was dropped in the second edition of 1983. It only contained now in Canon 1375 the statement that someone who becomes a member of an organisation, which plots against the Church, should be punished with a just punishment. The word 'Freemasonry' does not occur in it anymore. Ever since, Bishops-Conferences in many countries have declared that the Grand Lodge in their country is not an organisation, which plots against the Church. Regrettably, Bishop Ratzinger takes a different position, which is, however, understandable if one realises that the German Bishops-Conference had declared membership of the Church and of Freemasonry incompatible in 1980—three years before the second edition of the *Codex*—and that he is the last one still living of those who signed this declaration.

In 1985, British Freemasonry was for the first time confronted with serious opposition, and that by a Protestant Church: the 'Faith and Works Committee' of the 'Methodist Conference' published its *Report*, in which the position was taken that one cannot be a Freemason and a Christian at the same time. As a reaction, the 'Association of Methodist Freemasons' was founded, which demonstrated that the report was based on incorrect information. Thereupon the *Report* was referred back to the Committee for revision, but no new version ever appeared, so that it counts as withdrawn now. In 1986, the General Assembly of the United Reformed Church discussed the same theme, but did not come to any negative conclusions about Freemasonry. A Working Group of the Church of England, appointed in 1985 to study the Methodist *Report*, published in 1987 its *Freemasonry and Christianity. Are they compatible? A Contribution to discussion*. It did not answer the question posed in the title, but formulated certain critical remarks. One of them concerned the imprecations of the masonic oath. These had been declared no longer obligatory already in 1964, but now, in 1986, they were definitely abolished by the United Grand Lodge of England. No doubt anti-masonry in England reached its lowest ebb with the parliamentary inquiries of the Labour party, broadcasted by the BBC in the 1990s.

Once the *Grand Orient de France* had taken an explicitly anti-clerical stand in 1877, the United Grand Lodge of England (UGLE) at once declared that Grand Lodge—the largest one in France—irregular. It could do so easily, having itself hardly any Roman Catholic members. Yet, it took still more than a half century before the Grand Lodges of England, Ireland and Scotland together formulated what exactly, from then on, would be the rules which they would use to decide if a Grand Lodge was 'regular' or not. These rules were published in 1929 as the 'Basic Principles for Grand Lodge Recognition'. At first these and additional rules served to expel more and more Grand Lodges from the pool of 'recognised' Grand Lodges, thus at the same time creating a second group, usually referring to themselves as the 'liberal' (as opposed to the 'conservative') ones. In the last two decades, however, attempts can be observed to reconcile the two groups. For example, at least some of the so-called 'Prince-Hall' Grand Lodges in the United States of America, composed of Blacks, are now recognised by the UGLE, and it has also abandoned the position that an organisation which has female members can, by definition, not practice Freemasonry: friendly relations are now maintained with the 'Order of Women Freemasons' in England.

That Order was founded in 1908 as a mixed one, split-off from *Le Droit Humain*. In the 1920s it was decided to initiate no male candidates anymore, and in 1935 the Order became female only, after which it took its current name in 1958. It thus was the first female-only Grand Lodge. After the Second World War, purely female Grand Lodges were founded in many countries. The Adoption lodges of the *Grande Loge de France* were formed into one in 1945, which since 1952 is called the *Grande Loge Féminine de France*. It has founded daughter Grand Lodges in many countries, including Belgium, Switzerland, Italy, Portugal, Spain and Venezuela. In others, such as Germany and The Netherlands, female Grand Lodges were created on the initiative of male masons and/or their female relatives. One of the fastest growing ones seems to be the Female Grand Lodge of Turkey! Since the fall of the Soviet Union in 1991, moreover, male, mixed and female masonic lodges and Grand Lodges have been founded in most of the countries which once belonged to it.

NOTES

1 This chapter is based on the introduction and Chapter 2 in *The Handbook on Freemasonry* (Leiden: Brill Academic Publishers, 2014), edited by Henrik Bogdan and Jan A. M. Snoek.
2 The first time was the period 1715–25, see earlier.

REFERENCES AND FURTHER READING

Allen, J. S. 2008. 'Freemason Feminists: Masonic Reform and the Women's Movement in France, 1840–1914.' In A. Heidle and J. A. M. Snoek, ed., *Women's Agency and Rituals in Mixed and Female Masonic Orders*. Leiden and Boston: Brill, 219–34.

Anderson, J. 1723. *The Constitutions of the Free-Masons*. London.

——. 1738. *The New Book of Constitutions of the Antient and Honourable Fraternity of Free and Accepted Masons*. London: Ward and Chandler.

Bernheim, A. [pseud. Henri Amblaine]. 1993. 'Masonic Catechisms and Exposures.' *Ars Quatuor Coronatorum*. 106, 141–53.

——. 1998. 'La Stricte Observance.' *Acta Macionica*. 8, 67–97.

Bouman, M. 1993. *De Uitvaert van het Vryje Metzelaersgilde; Een anti-maçonnieke klucht uit 1735*. Amsterdam: Rodopi.

Caillet, S. 1994. *Arcanes & Rituels de la Maçonnerie Égyptienne*. Paris: Trédaniel.

Carlile, R. 1825. 'An Exposure of Freemasonry.' *The Republican*. XII.

——. 1831. *Manual of Freemasonry*. London: author.

Carr, H., ed. 1971. *The Early French Exposures*. London: Quatuor Coronati Lodge No. 2076.

Cohn, N. 1967. *Warrant for Genocide. The Myth of the Jewish World-Conspiracy and the Protocols of the Elders of Zion*. London: Eyre & Spottiswoode.

Hamill, J. 1986. *The Craft. A History of English Freemasonry*. Wellingborough: Crucible. Second edition: *The History of English Freemasonry*, 1994.

Hasselmann, K. 2009. *Die Rituale der Freimaurer. Zur Konstitution eines bürgerlichen Habitus im England des 18. Jahrhunderts*. Bielefeld: Transcript.

Hasselmann, K. and J. A. M. Snoek. 2010. 'Entwürfe eines neuen Rituals für die Vereinigte Großloge von England im Jahr 1816. Einige Bausteine deutsch-englischer Ritualgeschichte' (Teil-I: Einführung; Teil-II: Text). *Zeitschrift für Internationale Freimaurer-Forschung*. 23 (2010), 96–141 and 24 (2010), 76–109.

Hills, G. P. G. 1967. 'Brother William Preston: An Illustration of the Man, his Methods and his Work' (The Prestonian Lecture for 1927). In H. Carr ed., *The Collected 'Prestonian Lectures' 1925–1960*. London: Quatuor Coronati Lodge No. 2076, 1–30.

Introvigne, M. 2005. 'Cagliostro, Allesandro di (ps. of Giuseppe Balsamo).' In W. J. Hanegraaff ed., *Dictionary of Gnosis and Western Esotericism*. Leiden & Boston: Brill, 225–27.

Kervella, A. and P. Lestienne. 1997. 'Un haut-grade templier dans des milieux jacobites en 1750: l'Ordre Sublime des Chevaliers Elus; aux sources de la Stricte Observance.' *Renaissance Traditionnelle*. 28/112, 229–66.

Köppen, K. F. von and B. Hymmen. 1770. *Crata Repoa. Oder Einweyhungen in der alten geheimen Gesellschaft der Egyptischen Preister*. [Berlin].

Lefebvre-Filleau, J.-P. 2000. *La franc-maçonnerie française: Une naissance tumultueuse (1720–1750)*. Caen: Maître Jacques.

Le Forestier, R. 1987 [1923]. *La Franc-Maçonnerie Occultiste au XVIIe Siècle & L'Ordre des Élus Coens*. Paris: La Table d'Émeraude.

McIntosh, C. 1975. *Eliphas Lévi and the French Occult Revival*. London: Rider and Company.

Mollier, P. 2002. 'L "Ordre Écossais" à Berlin, de 1742 à 1751.' *Renaissance Traditionnelle*. 33/131–32, 217–27.

Nahon, M. 2005. 'Élus Coëns.' In W. J. Hanegraaff ed., *Dictionary of Gnosis and Western Esotericism*. Leiden & Boston: Brill, 332–34.

Noël, P. 2006. *Guide des maçons Écossais. Les grades bleus du REAA: genèse et développement*. Paris: A l'Orient.

Prescott, A. 2005. 'Some Literary Contexts of the Regius and Cooke MSS.' In T. Stewart ed., *Freemasonry in Music and Literature* (The Canonbury Papers 2). London: CMRC.

——. 2008. '"Builders of the Temple of the New Civilisation": Annie Besant and Freemasonry.' In A. Heidle and J. A. M. Snoek (eds.), *Women's Agency and Rituals in Mixed and Female Masonic Orders*. Leiden & Boston: Brill.

Snoek, J. A. M. 1994. Review of *De Uitvaert van het Vryje Metzelaersgilde; Een anti-maçonnieke klucht uit 1735* door Machteld Bouman. *Mededelingen van de Stichting Jacob Campo Weyerman*. 17.1, 28–31.

——. 2000. 'Rotterdam (La Première Loge sur le continent).' In E. Saunier ed., *Encyclopédie de la Franc-Maçonnerie*. [Paris]: La Pochothèque/Librairie Générale Française, 762–63.

——. 2001. 'A Manuscript Version of Hérault's Ritual.' In R. Caron, J. Godwin, W. J. Hanegraaff and J.-L. Vieillard-Baron (eds.), *Ésotérisme, Gnoses & Imaginaire Symbolique: Mélanges offerts à Antoine Faivre*. Leuven: Peeters, 507–21.

——. 2002. 'The Earliest Development of Masonic Degrees and Rituals: Hamill versus Stevenson.' In M. D. J. Scanlan ed., *The Social Impact of Freemasonry on the Modern Western World* (The Canonbury Papers 1). London: CMRC, 1–19.

——. 2003a. 'Printing Masonic Secrets – Oral and Written Transmission of the Masonic Tradition.' In H. Bogdan ed., *Alströmersymposiet 2003. Föredragsdokumentation*. Göteborg: Frimureriska Forskningsgruppen i Göteborg, 39–56.

——. 2003b. 'Swedenborg, Freemasonry, and Swedenborgian Freemasonry: An Overview.' In M. Rothstein and R. Kranenborg (eds.), *New Religions in a Postmodern World*. Aarhus: Aarhus University Press, 23–75.

——. 2004a. 'Drei Entwicklungsstufen des Meistergrads.' *Quatuor Coronati Jahrbuch für Freimaurerforschung*. 41, 21–46.

——. 2004b. 'Trois phases de développement du grade de Maître.' *Acta Macionica*. 14, 9–24.

——. 2010. 'Researching Freemasonry; Where are we?' *Journal for Research into Freemasonry and Fraternalism*. 1.2, 227–48.

——. 2012. *Initiating Women in Freemasonry. The Adoption Rite*. Leiden & Boston: Brill: = *Le Rite d'Adoption et l'initiation des femmes en Franc-Maçonnerie, des Lumières à nos jours*, Dervy: Paris, 2012.

Stevenson, D. 1988. *The Origins of Freemasonry. Scotland's century, 1590–1710*. Cambridge: Cambridge University Press.

Taguieff, P.-A. 1992. *Les Protocoles des Sages de Sion*. 2 Vols, Paris: Berg international.

Van den Brand, A.M.M. 1993. *De vrijmetselarij in de Republiek der Verenigde Nederlanden tot 1737, Vestiging en verbod*. Master thesis, university of Utrecht, The Netherlands.

Var, J.-F. 2005. 'Pasqually, Martines de.' In W. J. Hanegraaff ed., *Dictionary of Gnosis and Western Esotericism*. Leiden & Boston: Brill, 931–36.

Vibert, L. 1967. 'The Development of the Trigradal System' (The Prestonian Lecture for 1925). In H. Carr ed., *The Collected 'Prestonian Lectures' 1925–1960*. London: Quatuor Coronati Lodge No. 2076, 31–45.

CHAPTER TWELVE

ILLUMINISM

Andreas Önnerfors

INTRODUCTION

'Illuminism' is an expression that since the last decade of the eighteenth century has been used to denote a proto-romantic, esoteric and largely subversive undercurrent of Enlightenment reason. The origin of the concept lies within post-revolutionary conspiracy theories (primarily expressed by Augustin Barruel and John Robison) where 'illuminism' was used as a derogative term describing various esoteric practices such as somnambulism, Swedenborgianism or Martinist theosophy. But at the same time, illuminism was conflated with the ideology and teachings of the Bavarian Order of Illuminati (1776–85) and thus, current discussions often associate it with the assumed Illuminati agenda of radical political change. Hence it is sometimes difficult to make a clear-cut distinction between these two ambiguous usages of illuminism that can be found in the literature. Illuminism might refer to the principles and doctrines of the Illuminati themselves or to beliefs in and claims to extraordinary spiritual or intellectual enlightenment and its societal application. As it will emerge in the subsequent discussion, the academic treatment of illuminism has not always contributed to the clarification of the matter, but rather has preserved some ungrounded preconceptions concerning its meaning. This article treats the development of the concept in its original context, misconceptions as to its use, scholarly definitions and, finally, presents an epistemological revaluation identifying illuminism as a form of psychology *avant la lettre*.

REVOLUTIONARY ILLUMINISM: BETWEEN ATHEISM AND THEOSOPHY

In 1799 the British parliament passed the 'Unlawful Societies Act', a piece of legislature which was only repealed in 1967. It regulated the terms of existence of societies, such as reading and debate clubs or the much more radical 'United Englishmen' that were perceived to conspire against political order (Prescott 2002). At the time of passing the act, public opinion had been stirred up by the violent events of the French revolution and fear of an imminent invasion by the victorious Republican armies. In particular the Irish rebellion of 1798 illustrated painfully that Britain not was immune to popular uprising. In what sense is this dramatic governmental infringement of the free right of association related to a discussion of 'illuminism'? The search for scapegoats who could be held responsible for the overthrow of *l'Ancien regime* (the 'Old Regime') accelerated in the immediate aftermath of the French revolution and played into public opinion during the subsequent decade. The period witnessed the birth of a virulent culture of 'conspiracism' (Berlet 2009), which has occupied the Western imagination ever since. Indeed, there is a sense in which conspiracy can be considered a constitutive component of Western political discourse. Most prominent in this regard are the writings of a French émigré to Britain, abbé Augustin Barruel (1741–1820) and Edinburgh professor John Robison (1739–1805), blaming secret societies for orchestrating radical political change (Roberts 2008 and Oberhauser 2013). In part three of his *Memoirs illustrating the history of Jacobinism* (1798), outlining the 'antisocial conspiracy', Barruel established a chronology of the rise of various forms of illuminism. Whereas he devotes the lion's share of his writings to the historical Bavarian Order of Illuminati, Barruel identified 'the worst of the whole clan [as] a sort of Illuminees, calling themselves Theosophs' (Barruel 1798: 119), in direct relationship to Swedenborg and Martinism. Hence it is in this context the term 'illuminism' was originally coined and for the first time applied to an analysis of certain ideas and practices that had developed and flourished within Western secret societies.

That the term was understood in the sense Barruel used it emerges for example from the correspondence of Swedish envoy to Britain, George Ulrik Silfverhielm (1762–1819, a relative to Swedenborg). In early 1799, in a letter to duke Charles of Sudermania, prominent Grand Master of the Swedish Order of Freemasons 1774–1818, Silfverhielm discussed the political impact of Barruel's and Robison's anti-masonic writings on public opinion in Great Britain. He outlined that there existed two kinds of 'Illuminatism', one 'atheistic' (Adam Weishaupt and the Illuminati) and one 'mystical' (represented by John Joseph Gassner, Alessandro Cagliostro and 'other charlatans'). These two types of Illuminatism had made use of the three craft degrees of freemasonry, but a particular shadow had been thrown on its 'supreme secrets' (Silfverhielm's letter quoted extensively and translated in Önnerfors 2012: 171).

In the opinion of contemporaries, there was no doubt that illuminism in both guises had contributed to the undermining of the foundations of *l'Ancien regime*. These ideas were transported across the Atlantic: In 1802 Charlestown congregational preacher Seth Payson (1758–1820) published his *Proofs of the real existence and dangerous tendency of illuminism*, drawing on the writings of Barruel and Robison 'with collateral proofs and general observation'. For Payson illuminism was a 'system of deception' in which 'it is intimated, that there exist doctrines solely transmitted by secret traditions' (Payson 1802: 155–56). According to the author this was the first step in a recruitment process luring adepts into anti-Christian, anti-monarchical and anti-social ideology and action. Illuminism was cultivated in 'occult masonry' (Payson 1802: 64–80). As we can see, at the time of its first usage the term was loaded with considerable ambiguity that has blurred and inspired its general and scholarly understanding ever since.

Illuminism, therefore, does not identify a consistent phenomenon, and nor was it chosen as a term for self-referencing and identification. Movements with considerably diverging agendas could claim illumination, whether it be from radically different sources, such as the Christian esoteric sect, 'La Societé des Illuminés de Avignon', or the historical Bavarian Illuminati. This confusing situation had already begun to emerge at the time of both organisations. For instance, in Jean-Pierre-Louis de Luchet's *Essai sur la secte des Illuminés* (1789), freemasonry, martinism and theosophy are treated together with the Bavarian Illuminati, a continuity Barruel and Robison later repeated. Consequently, those working within exoteric, secular Enlightenment (*Aufklärung*) circles were placed, by their contemporaries, on a single common scale with those searching for an inner, esoteric and sacred light—no matter what their agenda was. Many thinkers and visionaries during early modernity claimed to have been 'enlightened' through different practices, whether through the processes of pure reason or ecstatic imagination. And it is precisely this ambiguity that has to be taken as a starting point for a deeper understanding of the powerful stream of 'illuminism' that has since informed esoteric occulture.

ILLUMINISM DOES NOT DENOTE A COHERENT PHENOMENON

Earlier definitions are not particularly helpful to capture the dualist nature of illuminism. In a seminal article Christine Bergé (2006) treats 'illuminism' and 'illuminists' as a more or less coherent movement with shared traits and characteristics, but admits at the same time that this movement is 'complex' and not easily opposed to intellectual Enlightenment. She states that it would be a simplification to see 'one as the partisan of reason, and the other as defending the irrational'. Rather illuminism has to be understood as a 'process of cross-fertilization that ended up engendering a modern kind of spirituality' matching 'the problem that the new society had to resolve: the collapse of Christianity and the emergence of secularism' (Bergé 2006: 601). However the image is consistently reinforced that 'illuminism' should be perceived as a significant Other to intellectual enlightenment, operating within spiritual realms demarcated by sentimentalism and mystical exaltation, impregnated with apocalyptic and milleniarist rhetoric, searching for 'secrets of creation and of the other world… sealed in the mysteries of ancient tradition' (Bergé 2006: 601). Illuminism is portrayed as a combination of pietist and masonic practices, ignoring the fact that these two movements from the outset appeared in clear opposition to each other. Bergé also points out, without quoting substantiating evidence, that Illuminists formed a vast network 'over the whole of Europe…attested by their voluminous correspondence in which they sought to exchange their "secrets"' (Bergé 2006), working in an operative and oracular path 'communicating with the beyond' towards 'a universal science' (Bergé 2006). Thus, from reading Bergé, the overall impression remains that 'illuminism' is a phenomenon that can easily be objectified and generalised, with clear beliefs, aims and objectives, and an identifiable community of practitioners.

ILLUMINISM AS A FORERUNNER OF CONTEMPORARY ESOTERICISM

In examining the underlying dynamics of rejected knowledge in Western culture, Hanegraaff (2012) points out that the occult occupied a significant place within the marketplace of Enlightenment print culture. Esotericism became an extremely fashionable commodity, 'culminating in a very large wave dominated by illuminism and mesmerism during its final decades' (2012: 220). For example, by publishing voluminous source material, Lekeby (2010) has demonstrated the rich variety of such practices in Swedish court circles during the decades around 1800. Illuminism is here best understood as a form of (introspective) imagination, establishing a correspondence between invisible and visible and the real possibility for observation of a '*mundus imaginalis*' in the sense of Corbin (Hanegraaff 2012: 300). Platon and in his tradition German idealism (with Immanuel Kant) made a clear cut distinction between the material world and the world of 'pure' ideas, existing in separate and mutually exclusive spheres. But in illuminist imagination, this split between idea and object is overcome in favour of an all-embracing worldview in which concept and matter coexist. They are placed on a shared scale of (potential) perception, the object just representing the most obvious and visible physical representation of the idea and the idea only invisible to the biological senses, not to imagination. There is a striking resemblance of this 'illuminist' outlook to the renaissance ideas of a 'visio intellectualis' (Cusa) and the Swedish-German early Romanticist Thorild's philosophy of an all-encompassing 'vision of all': the 'All-Blick' (Önnerfors 2008). Subsequent research, however, led to a rejection of this significant stream of the Enlightenment knowledge as inconsistent with the more powerful secular discourses and their more straightforward rational theories of knowledge. As a consequence, major overlaps with Romanticism, such as the philosophy of Schelling, were overlooked.

A more accurate understanding of Illuminism began to emerge when Auguste Viatte published his seminal two-volume work, *Les sources occultes du romantisme: Illuminisme-Théosophie* (1928). In it, neglected dimensions of the Enlightenment were investigated, including the religious concern of a great section of European intelligentsia, which had been considered, until that time, 'antireligious or religiously indifferent' (Eliade, quoted in Hanegraaff 2012: 338). Viatte's work sparked off an explosion of research into French illuminism, which began to challenge Francis Yates's concept that the hermetic tradition had been all but completely subdued by the progress of modern science and modernity. This, as we now know, was not the case. On the contrary, as the French scholar Antoine Faivre emphasised, illuminism and Christian theosophy, grounded in Renaissance 'hermeticism', had not only survived, but had flourished during the Enlightenment and had been developed within Romantic circles, peaking with German *Naturphilosophie* (Hanegraaff 2012). From here, it had been transported into the nineteenth century and beyond. Faivre's view of Illuminism was heavily influenced by a distinctive Christian theological reading and by his close association with a Christian neo-Templar system of masonry, which had a direct relationship with the so-called Swedish rite of freemasonry (Hanegraaff 2012: 340f.). This led Faivre to define constitutive features of illuminism, comprising of 'an Inner Church, initiation, the myth of fall and reintegration, and the centrality of nature as a web of correspondences' (Hanegraaff 2012:341). Hanegraaff, in his discussion of Faivre's contribution, describes 'illuminism' as a term, which had been used in scholarly circles, prior to the emergence of the concept of (Western) esotericism.

None of these eminent scholars, however, appear to have considered the ambiguous nature of the term illuminism in the context of its formation and its reception history. Why is it that a generation of French scholars (and many after them) returned to a term that was coined in a culture of counter-revolutionary conspiracism?

CROSSING THE BOUNDARIES OF HUMAN UNDERSTANDING

Faivre located the emergence of illuminism in a particular Christian esoteric context culminating during the final decades of the eighteenth century. This approach has clear methodological merits. But since the term was hardly used consistently within the 'illuminist movement' and, indeed, any such movement was, in reality, extremely disparate, it can be questioned what the term actually refers to.

Dan Edelstein in his volume, *The Super-Enlightenment: Daring to Know Too Much* (2010), which, of course, paraphrases the classical quote '*sapere aude*' ('dare to know'), investigates how far it holds true that the Enlightenment was not interested in crossing John Locke's 'limits of human understanding'. Interestingly, the first thinker discussed in Edelstein's work is Dom Antoine Joseph Pernety (sometimes spelled Pernetti, 1716–96), one of the foremost figures in 'les Illuminés d'Avignon' (noted earlier). According to Edelstein 'les Illuminés d'Avignon' was a para-Masonic cult that flourished in the late eighteenth century and attracted Parisian and foreign dignitaries (Edelstein 2010: 2). Pernety, who was a Swedenborgian,is chosen as an example because he, in 1758, published a treatise on ancient myths, *Les Fables égyptiennes et grecques, dévoilées et réduites au meme principe*, in which he compares his methodology to those in use in natural sciences. Surprisingly his science of deciphering ancient myths is rooted in alchemy and hermetic philosophy, which, he argued, simply represented sciences of nature, which were just as valid and rigorous as any other science. This odd case, 'a *philosophe* in search of the philosophers stone', is according to Edelstein (2010: 2) an example of the confluence of the worlds of mysticism and the Enlightenment, as also mirrored by Pernety's personal career, which included scientific voyages, a period at the court of Frederick the Great, and his establishment of a masonic sect in Avignon. According to Edelstein, he belongs to a host of writers, philosophers and agitators venturing beyond the boundaries of Lockean thought, who waded deep into metaphysics, metaphysical speculation and even otherwordly visions. This crowd of thinkers also includes, interestingly, Weishaupt, founder of the Illuminati (for whom Pernety invented mysterious Masonic rituals), as well as those interested in solar mythology, animal magnetism and the search for Atlantis. Edelstein, however, challenges the traditional (and still prevailing) view among historians, that these developments represent the dark, occult and irrational side of the Enlightenment. For such historians, 'illuminism' is shorthand for intellectual currents that were in opposition to the '*esprit philosophique* of the age'. Viatte, however, had already hinted at possible connections between Enlightenment thought and illuminist enquiries. The American cultural historian, Robert Darnton, had also pointed out that the natural philosophy of the age relied upon 'imaginative fictions for explaining the universe' and Faivre, as we have seen, referred to the 'contrary yet conflicting faces of Enlightenment and the light of the illuminists' (Edelstein 2010: 4).

Complementarity and confusion between Enlightenment thought and illuminism challenges the view that these two currents were indeed opposed. How is it possible, asks Edelstein, that illuminists conceived of themselves as members of the Enlightenment? A reductionist definition of the Enlightenment in line with the secularisation narrative is not helpful. Hence, the term 'Super-Enlightenment' is suggested by Edelstein as a non-historical attempt to create an umbrella concept under which it is possible to unite dramatically diverging theories of knowledge: 'an epistemological no-man's-land between *Lumières* and *illuminisme*' (Edelstein 2010: 33). Also, it should be noted that, because 'illuminé' and 'théosophe' were mainly pejorative terms in the eighteenth century, 'illuminists' would refer to themselves as 'philosophes'. This was certainly the case for Pernety—and also for other thinkers, such as Saint-Martin, who referred to himself as the 'Philosophe inconnu'. In defining the 'super-enlightened' approach, Edelstein states that 'hermetic' and 'ordinary' philosophers often shared an identical epistemological framework. This viewpoint is convincingly underpinned by David Bates, who argues that the 'modern, empirical sphere of thought requires a forbidden realm of esoteric knowledge against which to define itself, and thus in one respect incorporates this exteriority' (Bates 2010: 55). Illuminism is thus to be considered an occult space, within which a variety of practices and ideas were conceived and developed—practices and ideas that could not, at that point in time, be explained by the empirical sciences. Following his discussion of the not-so public sphere of the Enlightenment and 'enlightened mythologies', Edelstein argues that the period witnessed the emergence of important counter-mythologies 'designed to sap the foundations of Church authority, or to lay the foundations for a new conception of political power' (2010: 15).

In conclusion, the overall point is that the Enlightenment is characterised by a significant 'epistemological fuzziness' in which 'illuminst' ideas competed with and supported those of Enlightenment rationalism and vice versa. Hence, it was 'a movement continuously oscillating between opposing poles' (Edelstein 2010: 31). This raises a further question as to how we might understand illuminism.

ILLUMINISM AS A VISION OF POLITICS AND A POLITICS OF VISIONS

Europe of the late-1780s was in desperate need to reconfigure the basis for its politics. American independence, growing pressure for reforms, the success of the Enlightenment project and, finally, the collapse of the 'Old regime' in connection with the French revolution led to a situation in which any vision for societal change attracted the interest of European elites. 'Illuminist' practices such as hypnosis, the consultation of oracles, necromancy and alchemy provided answers to pressing questions of the time and presented ready visions of the future. As Hans-Georg Soeffner has stated, the desire for formal rituals tends to reflect a state of crisis, a need to come to terms with the world ('*Weltbewältigung*') and the breakdown of traditional, everyday order (2010: 40, 69). Another explanation for the attractiveness of illuminist practices is the position of secrecy within its performative culture. Georg Simmel (1906) pointed out that secrecy secures the possibility of a second world alongside mundane existence. Associational culture of secrecy (the form of the 'secret society') fills a significant sociological function in that it offers freedom and independence from the outside world. Clandestine forms of sociability present differentiation of interpersonal relations as a consequence of the modernisation process. In opposition to existing powers, these forms of sociability are predestined to develop and convey counter-hegemonic 'new life content' (Simmel 1906: 471). Kristiane Hasselmann (2009) has also studied the complex relationship between 'transparency and opacity' in secret societies and notes a constant playing with ideas of openness and closedness, which relate to the arcane secrets communicated within the societies, as well as to their way of coping with different socio-political contexts.

This fits into a larger picture of political escapism among the European elites of the period, expressing itself through an increased interest in mysticism, non-conformist religiosity, freemasonry and other esoteric initiatory traditions. Indeed, it is clear that the line between political visions and visionary politics was very thin. It is interesting to examine, for example, the role played by esoteric utopianism in the formation of political ideas within European elites during the revolutionary period. This, of course, relates directly to their keen interest in illuminist practices. Was esoteric utopianism simply an expression of political and philosophical escapism or even of politically reactionary dispositions anticipating Romanticism? Without retreating into conspiracy discourses, it is important not to overlook the political interests of those within masonic, or masonic-like fraternities. They were, first, able to provide networks of non-conformists and political dissidents and, second, to serve as a screen on which could be projected a variety of religious, ethical and political concepts relating to utopia. While the ideological foundations and the authority of the *Ancien Régime* were eroding rapidly, groups like les Illuminés d'Avignon could offer a substitute ideology that was both visionary and political, but not necessarily democratic nor secular. In the case of les Illuminés d'Avignon, a social environment was provided in which ideas were cultivated which, even in the revolutionary context of the Enlightenment, promoted occult interpretations of Christianity.

ILLUMINISM: PSYCHOLOGY *AVANT LA LETTRE*?

Regardless of its stigmatisation in post-revolutionary conspiracist narratives, and the perpetuation of generalising terminology in some twentieth-century scholarship on Western esotericism, and the recent attempts to unite disparate Enlightenment theories of knowledge, and the intricate relationship between esoteric utopianism and political theory, it is worth reflecting on the nature of the practices that have been associated with Illuminism. It continues to be a disorienting experience to work through the wealth of eighteenth century sources which reveal men and women of the Enlightenment age interpreting dreams, engaging in magical practice, searching for the philosopher's stone, speaking to angels, wandering in churchyards on moonlit nights, or decoding the 'Great Cipher of Nature'. Although a great deal of time and energy has been spent on these activities, a proper understanding of Illuminist practices within the lives of privileged and educated elites still remains somewhat elusive. The more we study the phenomenon (e.g. Lekeby's comprehensive 2010 collection of Swedish late-eighteenth-century sources) the less convincing it appears that Enlightenment thought was simply naïve, tragically misled by advanced superstition and plain credulity. Even if it disrupts the popular explanation of militant apologists of the secular narrative, key players within that very same narrative were attracted by illuminist practices. During the day, so to speak, they were engaged in the master-projects of the Enlightenment, as critical journalists, unprejudiced medical doctors and rational state reformers; during the evening, they might dress up as spiritual Knights Templar and initiate candidates into alchemical teachings. It would be deeply unfair and unhistorical to dismiss the collective biography of an entire generation, simply because it oscillated between these two poles of knowledge. And it would make no sense, following Hanegraaff, to reject and subdue one source of knowledge, which they were equally committed to and influenced by.

A common denominator of what we perceive as illuminist practices is their character of persistently opening up hitherto unknown, invisible or hidden (occult) dimensions of conscience, the soul or the mysteries of creation. A further important element is their focus upon the individual human, as medium, channel or subject/object of these processes of enhanced and enlarged perception and understanding. And another striking characteristic is the almost stubborn repetitiveness that one can read into complex alchemical formulas, elaborate rituals of initiation or symbolic cipher systems. Soeffner has noted that ritual performance represents a proto-rational structure, anticipating the scientific experiment as the master method of modernisation (2010). Ritual and experiment have many similarities, such as, most notably, a high degree of formalism and strict regularity of sequence and repeatability. Again, rituals and experiments are carried out by experts using special equipment and occupying specially designated places/spaces. They are both withdrawn from everyday life, which is underlined by special outfits, the rigorous spatiotemporal structure of performance and their position in more or less clandestine seclusion. Soeffner concludes that magic and ritual—we could add the entire spectrum of what might be called illuminist practices—aim at a quasi-rational mastery of nature, of the transcendent, and of social environment. If we summarise (from an imagined illuminist point of view): 'knowledge' is not only elicited through the application of reason, but it is possible for every individual to access advanced knowledge about oneself, nature and the transcendent through the application of specially designed methods and practices. Indeed, through such occult methods, it is possible to access more refined levels of consciousness and perception. The manipulation of thought processes might eventually lead to the transformation of physical matter and, hence, social reality. Such an epistemology does not run contrary to Enlightenment reason (if perceived as a reductionist rationalisation of the world), but outlines the possibility of knowledge and social action beyond Locke's narrow 'limits of human understanding'. Seen from this perspective, the phenomena we associate with illuminism can be understood as a psychology *avant la lettre* aimed at—to recall Kant's comment—humanity's emergence from self-imposed immaturity.

REFERENCES AND FURTHER READING

Barruel, A. (1798) *Memoirs illustrating the history of Jacobinism*, London: Burton.

Bates, D. (2010), 'Super-epistemology', in Edelstein, D. ed. *The Super-Enlightenment: daring to know too much*, Oxford: Voltaire Foundation.

Bergé, C. (2006) 'Illuminism', *Dictionary of Gnosis and Western Esotericism*, Leiden: Brill, 600–606.

Berlet, C. (2009) *Toxic to Democracy. Conspiracy Theories, Demonization and Scapegoating*, Boston: Political Research Associates.

Edelstein, D. (ed) (2010) *The Super-Enlightenment: daring to know too much*, Oxford: Voltaire Foundation.

Hanegraaff, W. (2012) *Esotericism and the Academy. Rejected Knowledge in Western Culture*, Cambridge: CUP.

Hasselmann, K. (2009) *Die Rituale der Freimaurer. Zur Konstitution eines bürgerlichen Habitus im England des 18. Jahrhunderts*, Bielefeld: transcript.

Lekeby, K (2010) *Gustaviansk mystik*, Stockholm: Vertigo.

Luchet, J.P.L. de (1789) *Essai sur la secte des Illuminés*, Paris: n a.

Oberhauser, C. (2013) *Die verschwörungstheoretische Trias: Barruel – Robison – Starck*, Innsbruck: Studienverlag.

Önnerfors, A. (2012) 'Envoyés des Glaces du Nord jusque dans ces Climats' Swedish Encounters with *Les Illuminés de Avignon* at the End of the Eighteenth Century' in Beaurepaire, P.Y.; Loiselle, K.; Mercier, J.-M.; Zarcone. T. eds., *Diffusions et circulations des pratiques maçonniques, XVIIIe-XXe siècle* Paris: Classiques Garnier, 167–96.

——(2008) 'Dichter der Meßkunst? – Zeit und Denken Thomas Thorilds im "Exil" 1795–1808' in Häntsch, C.; Krüger, J.; Olesen, J.E. eds., *Thomas Thorild: ein schwedischer Philosoph in Greifswald* Greifswald: Publikationen des Lehrstuhls für Nordische Geschichte, 53–92.

Payson, S. (1802) *Proofs of the real existence and dangerous tendency of illuminism*, Charlestown: Etheridge.

Prescott, A. (2002) 'The Unlawful Societies Act of 1799', in Scanlan, M.J.D. ed., *The Social Impact of Freemasonry on the Modern Western World*, London: Lewis Masonic, 116–34.

Roberts, J.M. (2008) *The mythology of the secret societies*, London: Watkins.

Simmel, G. (1906) 'The Sociology of Secrecy and of Secret Societies', *American Journal of Sociology*, 11(4): 441–98.

Soeffner, H.-G. (2010) *Symbolische Formung. Eine Soziologie des Symbols und des Rituals*, Weilerswist: Velbrück Wissenschaft.

Viatte, A. (1928) *Les sources occultes du romantisme: Illuminisme-Théosophie*, Paris: Champion.

CHAPTER THIRTEEN

MARTINISM IN EIGHTEENTH-CENTURY FRANCE

Christian Giudice

INTRODUCTION

Arthur Edward Waite, a *fin de siècle* author who wrote extensively on occult matters, argued that, during the second half of the eighteenth century, the intellectual and political centre of all things was the kingdom of France (Waite 1922: 7). As will be seen, while Waite's assessment is not incorrect, it does tend to ignore the mystical inspiration engendered by the distinctive thinkers of the *siècle des Lumières*. The Age of Reason in France saw the rise, during the second half of the eighteenth century, of a cultural revolution which would bring radical social and intellectual changes in the country (Porter 2001; Brewer 2008). Representative of the essence of French Enlightenment was the publication of the *Encyclopaedia* (1751–72), edited by Denis Diderot (1713–84) and Jean-Baptiste le Rond d'Alembert (1717–83), which, according to the aims of its editors and contributors, proposed to incorporate all world-knowledge in one oeuvre, under the rigorous scrutiny of scientific thought and reason. According to nineteenth-century occultist Papus (1895: 146) – the pseudonym of Gérard Encausse (1865–1916) – the intellectual revolution was not the only upheaval to be witnessed during this period. There was also an occult revolution that took place inside Masonic lodges. If most felt this to be a time to create a new society with a rational set of commandments to guide it, some felt lost in an age devoid of spirituality. Indeed, the power of religious sentiment has been widely overlooked in assessments of the period, in that, at the margins of the mainstream intellectual turmoil, lay the remnants of a rooted appeal to a more magical approach to life and nature (Roberts 2008: 106). Thus, far from being simply a reassuring and positivist era, disillusionment and a retreat into the realms of what would have then been considered irrationalism were a hallmark of the times too. As argued by Waite, 'it was a time of wonder-seeking, of portents, and prophets, and marvels: it was the time of Cagliostro and Mesmer, of mystic Masonry and wild Trancendentalism' (1922: 9). Illuminism and its champions stood against Enlightenment values, with the aim of finding a connection to a superior, moral order, and most of the *Illuminée* were likely to belong to the new Masonic lodges which spread in numbers throughout France from 1750 onwards. Here, those unsatisfied with the materialistic outlook on life could discover occult ways of seeking reconciliation and reintegration with the moral, religious dimension. Here, the tenets of Freemasonry blended with theosophical ideas in order to create a new, esoteric approach to Christianity. Martinism, comprising the doctrines set forth by Martinès de Pasqually (1726/7–1774) and his two most eminent followers Jean Baptiste Willermoz (1730–1824) and Louis Claude de Saint-Martin (1743–1803), is an excellent example of a new current born as an attempt to provide a path for mankind to return to a more spiritual quality of existence. When Papus published his volume *Martinésisme, Willermosisme, Martinism et Franc-Maçonnerie* in 1899, the French occultist clearly described the wider concept of Martinism as the combination of the influences of the three aforementioned eighteenth-century characters.

MARTINÈS DE PASQUALLY AND THE ORDER OF THE ÉLUS COENS

As Jean-François Var has pointed out, 'In the beginning was Martinès de Pasqually and above all his doctrine' (2006a: 770). Pasqually represents one of the greatest advocates of mystical doctrines within a masonic framework in eighteenth-century France (Le Forestier 1987). His origins are shrouded in mystery, although recent research conducted by Michelle Nahon (2011: 37) seems to establish that he was born in Grenoble. In 1762, he managed to open a chapter of his Masonic order in Foix after the name of *Temple des* Élus *Ecossais*, then changed to Élus *Coen,* or *elect priests* (Von Baader 1900: xx). As was common in Freemasonry at the time, Martinès's order contained degrees that went beyond the traditional symbolic ones (Mazet 1992: 265), and culminated in the *Réaux-Croix* grade, in which Pasqually's most occult doctrines were made manifest. His doctrine posits the fall of humanity into a state of unhappiness, which engenders a desire to amend previous sins and to be reconciled with the divine through a process of purification and the reestablishment of human integrity. Pasqually's theosophy is expounded in his *Traité sur la Réintégration des* Êtres, which circulated among the highest ranking members of the order in manuscript form, before being published in 1899. Pasqually's influences, on which he wrote very sparingly, are certain to include aspects of Hebrew Kabbalah, and Franz Joseph Molitor, in his *Philosophie der Geschichte* (1824: 487), did not hesitate to define him a great kabbalist. The *Traité* bears all three common traits that the scholar of Western esotericism, Antoine Faivre (2000: 7–8), postulated for theosophical works: it deals with the triangle formed by God, Man and Nature; it privileges the most mythic elements of biblical tradition; finally, it theorises a direct access to a superior dimension, the reintegration of beings with God. In his treatise, Pasqually formulates the main concepts of his worldview which also can be summed up in three broad tenets (Papus 1895: 115): First, the fall was universal for all material beings and the reintegration will similarly be universal; man is the only divine agent capable of causing the reintegration; lastly, man himself will be reintegrated by love. To convey a sense of urgency and closeness to the biblical stories narrated, Pasqually resorts to the use of what he calls 'types': an archetypal biblical event is documented in such a way that what is said to have happened in the past retains its validity in the present day. Thus typology employs events and people in the Old Testament, reflecting some aspect of future Christian dispensation.

According to Pasqually, reconciliation and reintegration could only happen through theurgical practices, which were at the core of his system. As Gilles le Pape has rightly emphasised, Martinès firmly believed in the idea that every man is a prophet and, via theurgic practices, could cause the apparition of intermediary beings, which would help in the process of reintegration with God (2006: 10). Embedded within a Christian framework, theurgy was the only means of contacting intermediary beings, although the nature of these beings has always been unclear and a persuasive comprehension of the phenomenon is even harder, given the name Pasqually attributed to the apparition conjured: *la Chose*. Whatever *la Chose* was, we know that there were essentially two ways of obtaining contact with it, first, by prayer and, second, by a strict adherence to the requirements of this special brand of ceremonial magic. Clothes of a particular colour and fabric were to be employed; circles and semi-circles were to be diligently traced on the floor; special incenses and exact times at which the rituals were preferably executed were to be provided to the initiate. At the conclusion of the theurgic operations there appeared fleeting apparitions, called '*Passes*' by Pasqually, which the *Coen* was supposed to quickly register. When asked by his pupils on the difficulty of manifesting such visual and auditory apparitions, Martinès replied that the phenomena would occur on the day they were worthy to see them. Pasqually died in 1774 in Haiti, having left Europe to receive an inheritance. The subsequent history of Martinèsism saw it develop in new directions as a result of the work of Willermoz and Saint-Martin.

JEAN-BAPTISTE WILLERMOZ AND THE RECTIFIED SCOTTISH RITE

Jean-Baptiste Willermoz, a wealthy silk merchant, had been initiated into Freemasonry in 1750 at the age of 20, and two years later was elected Venerable Master of his lodge in Lyon (Var 2006: 1170). Accepted among the Élus *Coen* in 1776, he quickly realised that Pasqually's doctrine, to which he would devote the rest of his life, was too esoteric, when compared to the theories circulating in more conventional lodges; at the same time, he recognised the *Coen* teachings of reintegration to be the only ones worth pursuing, although they were not systemised in a coherent structure that other Masonic guilds could guarantee. It was with the discovery of the Rite of Strict Templar Observance, which was very popular in Germany thanks to the efforts of Karl Gotthelf, Baron von Hund (1722–76), but less so in France, that Willermoz realised he had found the perfect infrastructure to which he could adapt Pasqually's teachings. According to Jean-Marc Vivenza (2012: 131), Willermoz's was an '*idée de génie*', and during the Masonic *Convent de Gaules* in 1778 and that in Wilhelmsbad in 1782, the seeds were sown for the birth of a new order, which would encapsulate Pasqually's theosophical teachings in a more strict Masonic structure.

At the convent of Wilhelmsbad, the Rite of Strict Templar Observance was dissolved, and Willermoz was able to create what is commonly known as Rite Écossais Rectifié, or R.E.R. The R.E.R. was divided into three different Classes, the first concerning the classic three fundamental Grades of Apprentice, Companion and Master, with an added fourth Grade which would hint at the mysteries experienced in the first three; a second Class constituted the Inner Order, Templar in spirit, which was comprised of the Grades of Noviciate and Knighthood; the third Class was represented by acceptance in the 'Profession', which instructed the advanced mason in the theories and practices of Pasqually's Élus *Coen*. This Class was to be shrouded in the utmost mystery and Willermoz himself seldom wrote about the subject (Var 2007: 25). The reticence of the German delegates at the convent of Wilhelmsbad, and especially the climate of social unrest generated by the French revolution did not allow for a substantial development of Willermoz's idea of R.E.R. It was the execution of theurgic rites with his friend Saint-Martin in the 1770s that had convinced Willermoz to place Pasqually's doctrine at the pinnacle of his masonic structure (Ambelain 1946: 102), and it is to the *Philosophe Inconnu*, whom Joseph de Maistre described as 'the most knowledgeable, the wisest and most elegant of modern theosophers' (de Maistre 1837: 208), that we must now turn.

LOUIS-CLAUDE DE SAINT-MARTIN: *LE PHILOSOPHE INCONNU*

Louis-Claude de Saint-Martin is probably the most famous of the three characters discussed here, and he too was initiated in the Order of the Élus *Coen* in 1768. Thanks to his copious correspondence with Nicholas Antoine Kirchberger, Baron of Liebistorf (1739–99), we know that, for twenty years after the death of his master, Saint-Martin still cherished the memories of his days as a *Coen*. Even after he had abandoned the Order, he still thought that Pasqually's method was a valid one – if he found a fault in somebody, it was in himself: 'I have had some physical communications also…but less abundantly than when I followed my school; and even in those proceedings I had less of the physical than my comrades' (de Saint-Martin 1982: 75). His first publication under the *nom de plume Philosophe Inconnu*, 'the Unknown Philosopher,' still demonstrated Pasqually's considerable influence. In his *Des Erreurs et de la Vérité* (1775) the recurrent theme of the work is clearly affected by the *Traité*: by an act of the will, humanity has lapsed from unity with God, but the Repairer, or Restorer, is always ready to help humans return to their primordial state (de Saint-Martin 1775: 34). In his following opus, *Tableau Naturel des Rapports qui Existent Entre Dieu, l'Homme et l'Univers* (1782), several sections are actually marked by parentheses, appearing less attached to the text. These sections correspond to Pasqually's doctrines, employed to corroborate the author's theories. The *Tableau*, for example, likens nature to a temple, with the stars as its lights, the earth representing the altar, and all corporeal beings are sacrificial victims that Man offers to God (de Saint-Martin 1782: 25). Faivre helps us draw a parallel, arguing that for Pasqually the Universal Temple was divided in a similar fashion, and proceeds with descriptions in which Nature is likened to a Temple, where the Élus are the priests who carry out the sacrifices (Faivre 1994: 157–59).

In his account of Martinism, Franz Von Baader argues that Saint-Martin's admiration for German mystic Jakob Böhme (1575–1624) became more and more noticeable as the years went by and that Böhme represented more than a kindred spirit for the Unknown Philosopher, becoming almost a cult figure. It is difficult to determine the date on which Saint-Martin was introduced to the works of the German mystic, but most scholars seem to agree with the *Nouvelle Notice Historique* attached to Von Baader's *Les Inseignments Secrets de Martinès de Pasqually*, in which the French philosopher is said to have encountered Böhme's works during his residency in Strasbourg between 1788 and 1791. It must be noted, though, that this is not the only theory. Trevor Stuart suggests that Pasqually held Böhme in great esteem and recommended the reading of his books to a then young Saint-Martin (de Pasqually 2009: xiv). Whatever the truth may have been, it is only with his *Ecce Homo* (1792: 36), that Saint-Martin actively advocated the attainment of the goal of reintegration through the imitation of Christ, as laid out in Böhme's *The Way of the Christ* (1624). But why did the works of Böhme impact so profoundly on Saint-Martin? I tend to agree with Waite's thesis that the French author believed Böhme to have penetrated more deeply into similar ideas and that adding Böhme's theories did not diminish the importance of Pasqually's grand oeuvre, since his early days as a *Coen* had also prepared him for a more spiritual, less materialistic approach (Waite 1922: 39). Saint-Martin simply saw in Böhme's work a more direct and less artificial way to God, declaring that the spiritual approach 'is more substantial, and leads more directly to the essential' (de Saint-Martin 1982: 27). Saint-Martin, in the end, was persuaded by the fact that the inner way represented the principle of all things and that, if the centre was not open, then the wonders of the external world were only to have a negative effect on the individual.

If one of Pasqually's main principles was that every human could become a prophet, Saint-Martin brought this theory one step forward, claiming that each and every individual could be called a Christ, and not merely a Christian (Von Baader 1900: 11). To him, every individual was capable of achieving communion with God through an inner way that did not include theurgy and ceremony. The Unknown Philosopher called this approach *la voie centrale*, or central, direct way. God was to be found within, and not without, Man. Individuals, in Saint-Martin's view, should become so engulfed by the Divine that they should start nurturing within them a bright shining sun; they should turn their gaze inwards and appreciate the presence of God within, rather than being distracted by physical phenomena. Perhaps Von Baader (1900: xcix) was right, when he wrote that, if his ancient master was a true theurgist, Saint-Martin truly was a contemplative mystic.

REFERENCES AND FURTHER READING

Ambelain, R. (1946) *Le Martinisme: Histoire et Doctrine*, Paris: Editions Niclaus.

Brewer, D. (2008) *The Enlightenment Past: Reconstructing Eighteenth-Century French Thought*, Cambridge: Cambridge University Press.

de Maistre, Joseph (1837) *Les Soirées de Saint Pétersbourg, ou Entetiens sur le Gouvernement Temporel de la Providence: suivies d'un Traité sur les Sacrifices*, Vol. II, Bruxelles: Meline, Cans et Compagnie.

de Pasqually, M. (2009) *Traité sur la Réintégration des Êtres dans leur Première Propriété, Vertu et Puissance Spirituelle Divine*, trans. by T. Stewart, Sunderland: Septentrione Books.

——(2010) *Traité sur la Réintégration des Êtres dans leur Première Propriété, Vertu et Puissance Spirituelle Divine*, VII ed., Le Tremblay: Diffusion Rosicrucienne.

de Saint-Martin, L. (1775) *Des Erreurs et de la Vérité, ou Les Hommes Rappellés au Principe Universel de la Science*, Edinburgh: n.p.

——(1782) *Tableau Naturel des Rapports qui Existent Entre Dieu, l'Homme et l'Univers*, Edinburgh. Reprinted: Hildesheim: Georg Olms Verlag, 1980.

——(1792) *Ecce Homo*, Paris: l'Imprimerie du Cercle Social.

——(1982) *Theosophic Correspondences 1792–1797*, trans. by E. Burton Penny, Pasadena, CA: Theosophical University Press.

Encausse, G. [Papus] (1895) *Martinès de Pasqually: sa vie, ses practiques magiques, son oeuvre, ses disciples*, Paris: Bibliothèque Chacornac.

——(1899) *Martinésisme, Willermosisme, Martinism et Franc-Maçonnerie*, Paris: Bibliothèque Chacornac.

Faivre, A. (1994) 'The Temple of Solomon in Eighteenth-century Masonic Theosophy' in *Access to Western Esotericism*, ed. by D. Appelbaum, Albany, NY: State University of New York Press.

——(2000) *Theosophy, Imagination, Tradition*, trans. by C. Rhone, Albany, NY: State University of New York Press.

Le Forestier, R. (1987) *La Franc-Maçonnerie Occultiste au XVIII° Siècle & l'Ordre des Elus Coens*, Paris: La Table d'Émeraude.

Le Pape, G. (2006) Les Écritures Magiques: Aux Sources du Registre des 2400 Noms d'Anges et d'Archanges de Martines de Pasqually, Milan: Archè.

Mazet, E. (1992) 'Freemasonry and Esotericism', in A. Faivre and J. Needleman, eds., *Modern Esoteric Spirituality*, London: SCM Press.

Molitor, J.F. (1824) *Philosophie der Geschicte Oder Über die Tradition*, Vol. II, Frankfurt am Main: Verlag der Hermannchen Buchbandlung.

Nahon, M. (2011) *Martinès de Pasqually: Un Énigmatique Franc-Maçon Théurge du XVIII° Siècle Fondateur de l'Ordre des* Élus *Cöens*, Saint-Malo: Pascal Galodé Éditeurs.

Porter, R. (2001) *The Enlightenment*, London: Palgrave Macmillan.

Roberts, J.M. (2008) *The Mythology of Secret Societies*, London: Watkins.

Var, J-F. (2006a) 'Martinism: First Period', in W. Hanegraaff, ed., *Dictionary of Gnosis and Western Esotericism*, Leiden: Brill, 770–79.

——(2006b) 'Jean-Baptiste Willermoz', in W. Hanegraaff, ed., *Dictionary of Gnosis and Western Esotericism*, Leiden: Brill, 1170–74.

——(2007) *The Life and Work of Jean-Bapriste Willermoz* (1730–1824), trans. by T. Stewart, Sunderland: Septentrione Books.

Vivenza, J. (2012), *Le Martinisme: l'Enseignement Secret des Maîtres Martinès de Pasqually, Louis-Claude de Saint Martin et Jean Baptiste Willermoz, Fondateur du Régime Écossais Rectifié,* Grenoble: Le Mercure Dauphinois.

Von Baader, F. (1900) *Les Enseignements Secrets de Martinès de Pasqually, Prècèdes d'une Notice sur le Martinezisme et le Martinism*, Paris: Bibliothèque Chacornac.

Waite, A.E. (1901) *The Life of Louis-Claude de Saint-Martin, the Unknown Philosopher, and the Substance of His Doctrine*, London: Philip Welby.

——(1922) *Saint-Martin, the French Mystic, and the Story of Modern Martinism*, London: W. Rider.

CHAPTER FOURTEEN

ANIMAL MAGNETISM AND MESMERISM

Adam Crabtree

Animal magnetism (also called 'mesmerism') is the name given to a system of physical healing developed in the latter half of the eighteenth century by the German physician Franz Anton Mesmer (1734–1815). Mesmer named his system 'animal magnetism' (Mesmer 1779) because it was based on the premise that there exists all through the universe something that he called 'magnetic fluid' which permeates every living thing ('animal' here meaning anything that is animate, especially human beings). His theory was that when a person became ill it was because the body had developed blocks to the natural flow of magnetic fluid throughout the organism, and if the person was to be healed, the physician must find a way to remove or break down those blocks. At the beginning of his practice of the system, he relied on iron magnets (only recently coming into general use) to accomplish that task, but he soon came to the conclusion that the most powerful 'magnet' was the physician's own body and that he could heal his patients by directing magnetic fluid in a concentrated form (through what he called 'magnetic passes' or sweeping movements of the hands over the body) into the patient. Once the blocks had been removed, the body was capable of healing itself through its natural processes (see Ellenberger 1970; Crabtree 1988; 1993; Gauld 1992).

Mesmer was a true son of the Enlightenment and he insisted that his system could be tested through scientific experimentation. He believed that all is matter and motion and that his system was simply a specific application of that state of affairs. Mesmer was not an occultist, and he firmly opposed any interpretation of this method that involved occult principles. Nevertheless, there were those mesmerists or practitioners of animal magnetism who developed their own explanations that involved occult forces or disembodied spirits.

For approximately seventy-five years after the publication of Mesmer's foundation paper in 1779, animal magnetism flourished as a medical and psychological specialty, and for another fifty years it continued to be a system of some influence. When one examines the history of animal magnetism and its offshoots, it seems incredible that this once powerful system fell into such obscurity. The fact that animal magnetism as such is no longer practiced is hardly surprising, for the theory of animal magnetism in its original form would be difficult to for most moderns to accept. What is puzzling is that the story of animal magnetism became so neglected. Animal magnetism is not comparable to certain medical fads which flourished for a time and then died out. Such crazes did not significantly shape medical or psychological theory and practice, nor did they, as a rule, significantly affect the evolution of those disciplines. Animal magnetism, on the other hand, had a profound impact on medicine, psychology, and psychical research (today called parapsychology), as a brief examination of its history shows.

Although Mesmer's personal fortunes and fame waned after about 1790, animal magnetism flourished. This was due in no small part to the work of the Marquis de Puységur (1751–1825), one of Mesmer's most loyal and enthusiastic pupils. Puységur discovered that some individuals fell into states of trance when animal magnetism was applied to them.

Although appearing to be asleep, magnetized subjects were still conscious and could reply to questions and convey information. In this state of 'magnetic sleep,' as Puységur called it (Puységur 1784), the patient was very suggestible. Upon awakening from magnetic sleep, the patient would remember nothing that had taken place while asleep. Although magnetized subjects had no memory in the waking state of occurrences in the state of magnetic sleep, they did retain a continuous memory from sleep state to sleep state. Noting these two separate chains of memory that accompanied the two distinct states of consciousness, he came to view magnetic sleep and the waking states as 'two different existences.' From this beginning, the notion that we all possess a mind seemingly separate from ordinary awareness operating covertly within the human psyche began to take root.

Puységur also noted the similarity between magnetic sleep and the natural phenomenon of 'sleepwalking' or 'somnambulism,' the only difference between the two states being that in magnetic sleep the subject is in a special connection or 'rapport' with the magnetizer, whereas in sleepwalking the sleeper is in rapport with no one. For that reason magnetic sleep also came to be referred to as 'magnetic somnambulism' and 'artificial somnambulism.'

Another thing that Puységur frequently noticed was a remarkable change in the personality of the magnetic subject, with the entranced individual exhibiting a greater alertness and engagement than normal. In addition the subject would sometimes exhibit certain metanormal abilities, such as the capacity to read the magnetizer's thoughts and a certain degree of clairvoyance, taking the forms of diagnosing the subject's own illness and those of others, along with the ability to prescribe effective remedies. These and other characteristics of magnetic sleep were assiduously studied during Puységur's lifetime and in the following decades after his death.

The implications of this discovery for the development of our modern culture are momentous. Up to this point in the history of the West, there were few ways to explain the human experience of being divided against oneself. The question was: Why do people think, feel, and do things that they do not want to think, feel, and do? Why do we seem to have such limited control of our psychical life? Before Puységur there were two basic kinds of answers given. One was to say that we think, feel, and do things that we do not like because we are taken over or influenced by some outside being or occult force, something intruding from the outside. This explanation could fittingly be called the *intrusion paradigm* for explaining these experiences. A second way was to declare that such unwanted thoughts, feelings, and actions were due to imbalances in the physical body—e.g., disorders of the bodily 'humors.' These physiologically based explanations can be called the *organic paradigm* for explaining such aberrations. With Puységur's discoveries a brand new way of explaining things came into being. We find ourselves thinking, feeling, and doing things we do not want to do because we are essentially *divided beings*. We all have a hidden region of mental activity that can affect our thoughts, our feelings, and our actions in ways that can go contrary to our conscious intentions. Because this region is hidden, we are not aware that this alternate mental reality is at work in us. Thus we have a new explanation and a new paradigm, one that can fittingly be called the *alternate consciousness* paradigm for explaining our distressing experiences (Crabtree 1993).

THREE STREAMS OF CULTURAL INFLUENCE

The influence of this new paradigm has established itself in the popular cultural attitudes of our era, as an examination of the history of animal magnetism and its offshoots brings home. The history points to three important streams of cultural influence arising from this new way of looking at ourselves. The most important of the three streams from a cultural point of view is the psychological stream. It can justly be said that Mesmer's discovery of animal magnetism was a pivotal moment in the evolution of modern psychology and psychotherapy. It led to Puységur's investigation of the consciousness manifested in magnetic sleep and the eventual discovery of a subconscious realm of mental activity. It also led to Braid's teaching about hypnotism as a psychological phenomenon and the resulting exploration of the psychotherapeutic power of suggestion.

Already in Puységur's lifetime the first cases of dual personality began to be reported, providing a naturally occurring confirmation of the notion that we have a second world of mental activity that manifests attitudes and intentions significantly different from those of the normal self. From the growing fund of experience with magnetic sleep over the course of the nineteenth century, two powerful beliefs were evolved: (1) that we have a dynamic inner mental world that is operating in us all the time, one that constantly influences us and is at the center of our being, and (2) that in exploring that world we discover undreamed of inner resources which can be effectively mobilized through the induction of trance states.

As magnetic sleep came to be more and more widely used, puzzling phenomena were noted that required explanation. It would often happen that a person in the somnambulistic state would do things of which he or she had no memory afterwards and which were effectively disowned by the magnetic subject. Are these things being done by a different person? If so, where does this new personality come from, and how can one explain the fact that it seems so alien? Around the middle of the nineteenth century physiologists began to develop an explanation based on the notion of 'automatism' or automatic reflex action. Their idea was that it is the physical brain, deprived of 'mind,' that carries out these actions. So although appearing to do intelligent things, magnetic subjects were really merely recreating actions encrypted in the brain from earlier experiences (Crabtree 2003).

However, this explanation came to be seen as inadequate, especially considering the complexity and often remarkable creative originality of the mental activity that occurred in the altered state. Searching for a better solution, Frederic Myers pioneered the notion of a 'psychological automatism' (Myers 1903). He pointed out that the mistake had been to consider the human mind a single unified thing. In fact it is a complex reality. The human psyche has an ordinary self which Myers called the 'supraliminal self' that exists 'above' the 'threshold' (limen) of consciousness. Below that threshold is the 'subliminal self' that houses any number of separate and relatively independent centers of consciousness. These intelligent subliminal personalities have their own thoughts, their own values, and their own intentions, and they can influence the individual's conscious or supraliminal self in striking ways. Thus there is a dynamic inner world that carries on a life of its own and which harbors both hidden problematic elements of the person, but also, and more importantly, a great storehouse of creativity, paranormal capacity, and spiritual awareness. This schema of Myers was capable of providing a place for and a profound understanding of the whole spectrum of human experience from the lowest to the highest (Kelly et al. 2007: chapter 5).

Myers's groundbreaking work cleared the way for the important psychological and psychotherapeutic work of Pierre Janet, and eventually the discoveries of Joseph Breuer and Sigmund Freud. The new view of the inner dynamics of the human psyche gave rise to 'dynamic psychiatry,' 'dynamic psychology,' and 'dynamic psychotherapy' as described by the great historian of the unconscious, Henri Ellenberger (Ellenberger 1970). The effects of this vision of the nature of human mental and emotional experience on the Western world have been vast. Without the findings of Puységur and those who built upon his work, we would not have the notion of a subconscious mind, obsessions, compulsions, psychological defenses, multiple personality, hypnosis, trance states, altered states of consciousness, and many other concepts that are now part of our popular culture.

THE HEALING STREAM

In its origins, animal magnetism was a healing system. It was based on a view of the human organism as a self-healing entity requiring the proper balance of a universal 'magnetic fluid' that affects the ebb and flow of the life force. Although Puységur's work diverted the attention of many magnetizers to psychological pursuits, there remained a powerful current of interest in the healing work Mesmer originally envisioned. Puységur himself had pointed out that many individuals when put into a state of magnetic sleep, would spontaneously diagnose their own illnesses and those of others, as well as prescribe effective remedies. He also acknowledged and made use of magnetic passes directly for healing. In the early decades of magnetic practice, it was discovered that the energetic and lengthy application of magnetic passes could act as an analgesic. Because of this, they were used as an aid to surgery and dental work. In our time, we have become familiar with what might generically be called 'energy healing' systems or 'healing touch' systems. The method of application and healing results are very similar to those described in the literature of animal magnetism. While some of these contemporary approaches (such as Reiki and Qi Gong) have clearly been imported from other cultures, the Western world has had a continuous tradition of healing methods of its own all the way back to Mesmer.

OCCULT AND PARAPSYCHOLOGICAL STREAM

Psychical research, the scientific study of the paranormal, had its official beginning in 1882 with the establishment of the Society for Psychical Research in Britain. Psychical research was the direct result of certain developments arising from animal magnetism. These were: (1) the occult medico-philosophical tradition in Germany that adopted animal magnetic theory, (2) the development of 'magnetic magic' in France, and (3) the rise of spiritism in France and Spiritualism in the United States.

In Germany animal magnetism developed a strong early following among those influenced by romantic philosophy, which was prominent at the end of the eighteenth century. These thinkers found the notion of a universal magnetic agent that connects all beings and is the source of life and health a most congenial concept. The philosophy of Emanuel Swedenborg had its part to play in these developments and many magnetic somnambulists began to have Swedenborgian-style visions, communicating with the spirit world in magnetic ecstasy. Paranormal phenomena, such as clairvoyance and precognition were common in these circles.

The French developed their own particular melding of animal magnetism and occult tradition. The most influential magnetizer of this kind was the Baron Du Potet de Sennevoy (1796–1881). He devised a system called 'magnetic magic' that revised animal magnetism's traditional doctrine of a universal magnetic fluid by incorporating it into the older notion of a universal spiritual power, which serves as the basis for 'natural magic.' This concept, so different from the mechanical view of Mesmer, considered magnetism to be the bond between spirit and matter, or body and soul. In Du Potet's view, mesmerizers who recognized the true nature of magnetism could work 'magic,' producing marvelous cures and a variety of paranormal phenomena (Du Potet 1852).

From very early, there were those who believed, contrary to Mesmer and Puységur, that spirits were the true source of animal magnetic action. In 1787, the Stockholm Exegetic and Philanthropic Society declared that the wisdom exhibited in diagnosis and healing requires an intellectual, spiritual agency beyond the somnambulist. Johann Jung-Stilling claimed that magnetic somnambulists have direct access to the spiritual world and in that way came into possession of information not available through ordinary means. Jung-Stilling (1808), Justinus Kerner (1824), Guillaume Billot (1838), and Louis Cahagnet (1848–54) investigated the apparent ability of magnetic somnambulists to communicate with spirits in the state of magnetic sleep.

However, the most influential magnetically inspired movement involving communication with departed spirits was American Spiritualism. Animal magnetism began making significant inroads in the United States from the mid-1830s on. Lectures by Charles Poyen St. Sauveur (d. 1844) on animal magnetism excited the imagination of the country and led to the emergence of magnetic practitioners of a peculiarly American type. Itinerant magnetizers wandered the countryside with professional somnambulists at their sides, stopping in local towns to give medical clairvoyant readings. At each stop, for a fee the magnetized somnambulist would diagnose illnesses and prescribe remedies. One of these itinerant magnetizers was Andrew Jackson Davis (1826–1910) who became an author of great popularity, whose books prepared the way for the rise of Spiritualism. Spiritualism had its birth in the 'spirit rappings' that occurred in the home of John Fox in 1848. This spirit activity centered around the daughters of the household, and news of the purportedly paranormal activity of the Fox sisters spread rapidly throughout the United States, reaching England, France, and Germany within a few years. Spiritualist mediums appeared who claimed to be able to communicate with the departed on the 'other side.' Typically, the medium would go into a self-induced trance and produce paranormal phenomena of the mental type (clairvoyance, telepathy, precognition, etc.) or the physical type (levitation of objects, materializations of forms, production of mysterious lights, etc.).

The successful spread of Spiritualism was to a large extent due to the popularity of a fad that grew out of spiritualistic circles and emigrated to Great Britain and Europe in 1853. This was the practice of 'table tipping,' 'table turning,' or 'table tapping,' as it was commonly called. A group of people would gather around the parlour table, rest their hands in a circle on its surface, and wait for spontaneous movements to occur. Sometimes the table would produce knocking sounds in the surface; at other times it would rise and fall on one side, tapping a leg on the floor. The tapping would be read as an alphabetical code, and a message would be deciphered. Many explained the phenomenon in terms of the actions of spirits of the dead communicating with the living; others attributed the movements and messages to the action of animal magnetic fluid emanating from the participants; still others believed the participants were simply deluding themselves, the movement being produced by their own unconscious physical exertions (Crabtree 1993). When the Society for Psychical Research was formed in England in 1882, it undertook to investigate not only the validity of spiritualistic phenomena, but also the nature of animal magnetism and hypnotism.

In the thirty years preceding the Society's foundation there had been a number of attempts to carry out a systematic investigation of the phenomena of Spiritualism. Some were carried out by scientists, others by individuals untrained in the procedures of empirical research. The results were uneven and inconclusive. So when a group of academics, most of them associated with Cambridge University, decided to set up a society that would undertake a study of the phenomena employing stringent scientific criteria, there was enthusiasm for the idea both from academics and the Spiritualists themselves. The British Society for Psychical Research was fortunate to have the nearly full-time involvement of a number of highly gifted investigators and within a few years began publishing its *Proceedings* and a journal. This activity generated a great many similar studies of the paranormal by some of the brightest minds of the day. The result was the publication of a mass of material on psychical research that continued well into the twentieth century.

CONCLUDING COMMENT

The histories of animal magnetism, hypnotism, and psychical research are inextricably intertwined. The three streams flowing from the discovery of animal magnetism often merged over the two hundred years following Mesmer's first exposition. The crossover is evident, for example, in the fact that both those interested in the psychological stream and those drawn to psychical research often investigated the healing and medical aspects of animal magnetism. In the process of developing these streams, the ideas of animal magnetism exercised a profound influence on the institutions of Western culture. Although the process of identifying these multifaceted influences over modern thought has begun, there remains much to be done to adequately appreciate the full impact of animal magnetism on our way of looking at the world.

REFERENCES AND FURTHER READING

Billot, G. P. (1838) *Psychological Investigations of the Cause of Extraordinary Phenomena (Recherches psychologiques sur la cause des phénomènes extraordinaires)*, 2 vols., Paris: Albanel et Martin.

Braid, J. (1843) *Neurypnology or the Rationale of Nervous Sleep Considered in Relation with Animal Magnetism*, London: John Churchill.

Cahagnet, L. A. (1848–54) *Magnétisme. Arcanes de la vie future devoilés*, 3 vols, Paris: Bailliére.

Crabtree, A. (1988) *Animal Magnetism, Early Hypnotism, and Psychical Research 1766–1925: An Annotated Bibliography*, White Plains, New York: Kraus International Publications, 1988. Online: www.esalenctr.org (accessed 2010).

——(1993) *From Mesmer to Freud: Magnetic Sleep and the Roots of Psychological Healing*, New Haven: Yale University Press.

——(2003) '"Automatism" and the Emergence of Dynamic Psychiatry', *Journal of the History of the Behavioral Sciences* 39: 51–70.

Du Potet de Sennevoy, J. D. (1852) *La magie dévoilée, ou principes de science occulte*, Paris: Pommeret et Moreau.

Ellenberger, Henri (1970) *Discovery of the Unconscious*, New York: Basic Books.

Gauld, A. (1992) *A History of Hypnotism*, Cambridge: Cambridge University Press.

Jung-Stilling, J. (1808) *Theorie der Geister-Kunde*, Nuremberg: Raw.

Kelly, E., Kelly, E., Crabtree, A., Gauld, A., Grosso, M., Greyson, B. (2007) *Irreducible Mind: Toward a Psychology for the 21st Century*, Lanham, Maryland: Rowman & Littlefield.

Kerner, J. (1824) *Geschichte zweyer Somnambulen*, Karlsruhe: G. Braun.

Mesmer, F. A. (1779) *Mémoire sur la découverte du magnétisme animal*, Geneva and Paris: Didot le jeune.

Myers, F. (1903) *Human Personality and Its Survival of Bodily Death*, 2 vols., London: Longmans, Green.

Puységur, Marquis de (1784) *Mémoire pour servir à l'histoire et à l'établissement du magnétisme animal*, Paris: Dentu.

PART IV

NINETEENTH CENTURY

CHAPTER FIFTEEN

SPIRITUALISM

Cathy Gutierrez

Spiritualism refers to the loosely affiliated religious movement begun in America in 1848 by the three Fox sisters, Leah (1814–90), Margaret (1833–93), and Kate (1837–92). Marked primarily by domestic séances in which a small group would attempt to contact the dead through the use of a medium, Spiritualism also had a more public face where the famous dead could be contacted for advice on contemporary matters like politics and philosophy via trance speakers in tent revivals or lecture halls. While trance speech and states of possession are by no means restricted to Spiritualist phenomena, 1848 is generally agreed upon by scholars because it is the turning point at which people could self-identify as Spiritualists, which carried, at least in the United States, associations with progressive politics as well as religious pluralism.

While the Spiritualist movement lacked a formal governing structure and had no process for training or regulating mediumship—the primary religious role of Spiritualism—there were a number of points of agreement among nearly all who seriously practiced it: the complete abolishment of hell; the continuity of the individual upon death; the advancing of the soul through several (most frequently seven) tiers of heaven; and the use of heaven as a model for what an ideal earth might become. These were all core theological mainstays. One of the problems of collecting demographic data on nineteenth-century Spiritualism is that one can encounter it in a number of spheres, ranging from dabbling for entertainment to experimentation after the loss of a loved one to complete commitment to its theology of progress and its concomitant implications for this-worldly politics. Scholars have estimated that half of Americans experienced Spiritualism in some manner and certainly hundreds of thousands adhered to it rigorously enough to belong to organizations or to subscribe to Spiritualist newspapers.

Within the months following Catherine and Margaret Fox's communication with a ghost in their Hydesville, New York home via a laborious version of Morse code, mediums sprung up all over America and the phenomenon appeared in England within the year. In France, it was heavily influenced by Hippolyte Léon Denizard Rivail, better known by his pen name, Allen Kardec. Kardec crafted a more Christian-influenced Spiritualism that also embraced reincarnation and this combination proved to be fruitful among the populations of Latin American Catholics: Spiritism, as the Kardecian version is frequently called, stood vehemently against the rising materialism of the nineteenth century and it continues to influence Afro-Caribbean religions from New Orleans to Brazil.

While many countries and cultures espoused some form of Spiritualism it was primarily the American Civil War that catalyzed a national fascination with talking to the dead, one that would not be echoed as strongly in Europe or Canada until after the First World War and the ravages of Spanish influenza. Understood as empirical evidence of the continuation of a soul in the afterlife and providing access to dead loved ones, Spiritualism intrigued those who wished to mine history for all of its great minds and served as an effective balm to the grieving.

HEAVENS AND HELLS

The primary influence that Spiritualism had was the complete disbanding of hell. As a consequence, it developed a universalist theology in which members of all races and religions went to heaven, opening the afterlife to all of humanity and dispensing with exclusive claims to knowledge and truth that pervaded most mainstream religions of its day. Other progressive traditions such as the Universalist General Convention had also dispensed with hell (see Buescher 2006). Other new religions of the same era, such as Mormonism, shrunk hell to contain only apostates, so members of all other religions enjoyed an afterlife on one of the three tiers of heaven. While tremendously progressive and multicultural for its day, Spiritualist heaven did not evade racist narratives and colonialist rhetoric, as dead Others proved interesting—and significantly safer—to think about at a remove (see Tromp 2007; Lowry, forthcoming). However, the triumph of religious pluralism should not be underestimated.

The hallmark of heaven was progress, and this ideal both provided the greatest focusing lens for thinking about time and meaning. It also insulated Spiritualists from a host of logical pitfalls such as inconsistencies between messages received from the afterlife. Since the dead were not perfected at the moment of ascent to heaven, they journeyed through it replete with their human foibles and ignorance. An inconsistent, incorrect, or even cruel communication from the dead merely meant that the medium had contacted spirits on the lower realms who were simply 'unprogressed.' Constant learning and spiritual refinement also meant that the dead could change their minds posthumously, and many did—Michael Faraday, prominent British scientist who refuted Spiritualism, became an ardent believer after death, and even William Shakespeare re-wrote his sonnets to more accurately reflect what he posthumously understood as truth.

This fluidity of the afterlife can be directly traced to the works of Emanuel Swedenborg (1688–1772), an eighteenth-century scientist and mystic whose journeys to the afterlife generated much influence over Protestant thinking and gave birth, not only to an eponymous church, but also served as the backbone to several new religious trajectories. While still a Christian who espoused a dualistic cosmos with heaven and hell, Swedenborg breathed new life into the vision of heaven, describing an afterlife teeming with societies, learning, and the continuation of human institutions such as marriage. In Swedenborg's work, three tiers of heaven are counterbalanced by three tiers of hell, echoing a Protestant version of Dante's *Inferno* and *Paradisio*.

In writing a fully evocative vision of heaven and hell as a first-hand experience, Swedenborg simultaneously competes with a Catholic imagination of the afterlife while at the same time critiquing it. As John Casey argues, 'Swedenborg brings out implications of the Renaissance and Protestant conviction that a life of activity is superior to one of contemplation. Perhaps this is the sort of heaven that a Protestant ought logically to countenance—one in which the active virtues are paramount and which represents a purified version of a cheerful active society as it ought ideally to be in this life' (2009: 355). Swedenborg also maintained a dualistic notion of the afterlife, while shielding God from ever directly causing suffering: upon death, the soul reviews her entire life in the company of angels and then either ascends directly to the appropriate place in heaven or quite literally dives into hell in recognition of shame. No devil figure administers hell. The inhabitants are evil creatures that cause other souls to suffer because that is their nature.

Spiritualism expands Swedenborg's cosmos to the more classically Neo-Platonic seven spheres and relegates the vicious dead to the bottom rungs where they, too, wander around inflicting pain on each other. Descriptions of the lowest spheres of heaven show little difference from typical depictions of hell, except that they lack any central administration. However, the primary point of departure from Swedenborg's hells to Spiritualism's lower heavens is mobility: in disbanding hell, Spiritualists also dismantled the concept of sin, such that wrongdoings were understood to be the product of ignorance and poverty rather than spiritual inclination toward evil. The most vile soul was expected to learn and advance, with the odd consequence that the living could occasionally aid the dead (see Gutierrez, forthcoming). Progress was eternal and individual and each soul had to fervently desire to improve before being able to ascend the ranks of heaven.

TRANCE STATES

While Swedenborg provided an intellectual structure for Spiritualism, its main rituals were dependent on the legacy of Franz Anton Mesmer (1734–1815). An eighteenth-century medical doctor from Austria, Mesmer, as well as many colleagues of his day, was in search of a single cause that could explain all illness. Just as the discovery of gravity had seemingly unlocked the secrets of physics, scientists sought parallel explanations in their related fields. Mesmer argued that he had indeed found a medical panacea in what he called 'animal magnetism.' He theorized that the universe was interconnected by invisible strains of magnetic fluid that caused the motion of the planets and the tides through laws of attraction and repulsion. The human body, too, was filled with this fluid, which could get blocked or otherwise disrupted thus creating illness. Using magnets, magnetized items, or even his own magnetic field, the doctor could cure the patient by felicitously adjusting the flow of the fluid through the body.

Mesmer spent years attempting to receive the imprimatur of the Parisian medical academy to no avail. However, the public found his methods beneficial, if a bit unconventional, and Mesmer had hundreds of cures attributed to his clinics. And while he tried to contain the use of his methods to a small band of students, the use of animal magnetism became widespread and slipped out of his control rather quickly. However, animal magnetism was a physical cure for a physical illness—the eponymous (and erroneous) discovery of Mesmerism, as an induced trance state, was the bailiwick of Mesmer's former student and rival, Armand-Marie-Jacques de Chastenet, Marquis de Puységur (1751–1825). In the course of conducting a magnetic healing, he noticed that his patients would fall into an alternate state of consciousness. Moreover, the second state was recognized by him as a preferable one: his patients (many of whom were in his employ or their families) became noticeably more articulate, intelligent, and moral than in their 'waking' state.

This second self would advise Marquis de Puységur on the patient's own treatment and even on occasion exhibit paranormal abilities, although he did not have much interest in that aspect of his discovery. So-called Mesmerism was promptly compared to sleep walking. As Adam Crabtree has shown, the Mesmeric second self, has a continuous memory of the waking self and the alternate state (see Crabtree 1993), which is not usual for sleepwalking. The ability to induce a trance state at will proved to have its own therapeutic uses but, much to Mesmer's dismay, was also quickly absorbed into mystical rhetoric and speculation about the occult.

While the terminology for, and value of a created trance state would be bandied about for a century, reclaimed by hard science under James Braid's term 'hypnotism,' and ultimately abandoned by Freud in favor of the talking cure, an at-will trance state was essential to Spiritualist mediumship. Mediums, most often young women, were understood to act as conduits between this world and the next by entering a trance state and allowing the spirits of the dead to use their voices and bodies to manifest once again in the material world. As Ann Braude has so rightly pointed out, this is an ultimate paradox of passivity: women were allowed to expound on matters of political and intellectual importance to the precise measure that they were understood not to be the agents of those ideas. In fact, the veracity of the exercise was often gauged by the perceived inability of women to answer such lofty questions—if a young woman could adequately discuss science and theology, then surely the dead spoke through her.

Thinkers as widely divergent as Nicholas Spanos and Homi Baba have noted that possession and trance states allow those outside of dominant power structures, a space in which to speak. Possession has legitimated women's religious authority from the Pythia of Delphi to contemporary Latin American shamans and seems to be one of the truly cross-cultural and trans-historical phenomena of religious experience. However, the cultural valence to be given to trance speech is debated, particularly among feminist scholars. Braude, for example, argues that Spiritualist trance speech functioned as an intermediary state that eventually ushered in women's public speaking. Others like Marlene Tromp have articulated how much cultural leeway mediums were given in otherwise constrained Victorian England—hosting the spirits of pirates and criminals allowed women to drink, curse, and threaten bodily violence, while eroticized Others flirted and kissed outside the boundaries of that which was considered culturally proper. It is important to understand, however, that while, on the one hand, this created intellectual and transgressive opportunities, on the other hand, it reinforced social roles of passivity and the instrumentalizing of the female body.

Nevertheless, it is clear that trance speech did allow women, poorer whites, and the occasional persons of color a public reputation, an independent means of income, and travel opportunities. It also provided a degree of self-definition that was not always possible in the nineteenth century. Having dispensed with the need for a Mesmerizer, mediums were not patients in an unequal power relation, but rather lay clergy and frequently authors and circuit speakers. The trance state that allowed for the dead to use the body as a vessel, was understood as an aperture onto higher modes of consciousness as residents of heaven and the accumulated wisdom of the ages spoke through them. The more-than-second self was multiple and pointed firmly up toward theology rather than toward the pathology of illness or insanity.

TECHNOLOGY

In 1844 a revolution in communication took place with the first telegram sent from Washington, D.C. to Baltimore, Maryland. 'What hath God wrought,' a biblical quotation chosen by a daughter of one of Samuel Morse's colleagues, proved to be quite prescient as the first message, both in terms of the rapid expansion of technology and the religious implications of telegraphy. The first practical use of electricity, telegraphy made instant and invisible communication available for the first time. By 1866, international telegraphy became possible. While limited railroads for steam engines had been laid as early as 1827, the first transcontinental railway would not be completed until 1869. Both the rail and the telegraph entirely outpaced the distance a human or a horse could cover. The telegraph, however, was not only immediate, it also eradicated the experience of space.

The telegraph would become the primary metaphor for Spiritualist communication since the wondrous ability to send messages to the territories from New York suggested to many that the ability to create similar technology pointing toward heaven was a logical next step. As discussed above, women were the favored vehicles for the alleged objectivity their inexperience lent them as well as for fuzzy notions of electricity, which posited that women were negatively charged thus making the positively charged heaven more attracted to them. Just as the machine did for electrical impulses, the body-as-telegraph demonstrated the existence of invisible forces without making the forces themselves visible:

> Hudson Tuttle explained that when 'a sympathetic cord is established' between two spirits 'in such a manner that thoughts flow on it, from mind to mind, as electric fluid on the telegraphic wire,' minds become united and their thoughts become 'in unison.' The extent of this fusion should not be underestimated: as one of the earliest spirit mediums declared, the fusion was so thoroughgoing that 'space was nearly annihilated' and time had little meaning.
>
> (Cox, 2003: 88)

Mediumship that began with the Fox sisters' 'alphabet raps' (one for *a*, two for *b* and so forth) quickly metamorphosed into more immediate—and more entertaining—methods, such as trance speech, automatic writing, and materialization séances, in which gifts of gloves or flowers were produced from the spirit world, and soon created a demand for full-blown ghosts and other theatrics that came to be associated with 'table tipping.'

Recent scholarship by Jill Galvan has persuasively argued that Spiritualist mediumship created a social code in which women became the perfect vehicles for a host of new communication technologies at the *fin de siècle*. The 'automatism,' as she calls it, of Mesmeric trance states and Spiritualist messages set the stage for a new sphere of female white-collar workers, who could deal with sensitive information without inflecting it with their own voices. Court stenographers, touch typists, shorthand takers, and telephone operators who were expected to listen in without processing information all benefited from and contributed to the mixed blessing that was trance speech. The idea that information could be filtered through the woman's body without being altered by it created some of the first 'respectable' jobs for women who had financial obligations, but expected one day to marry and drop out of the work force.

For many, however, the seeming automatism of trance states was insufficient for Spiritualist claims of absolute objectivity and many believers went to extraordinary lengths to create machines that would obviate any charges of cheating. In 1855 Spiritualists achieved a major *coup* with the conversion of Dr. Robert Hare (1781–1858), a professor at the University of Pennsylvania and the country's most prestigious chemist. Hare, who had begun experimenting specifically to disprove the claims of Spiritualism, was convinced by his own inability to do so and began making public test trials for mediums in earnest. In the course of this, he created multiple machines designed to ensure objectivity. The Spiritoscope was a prime example of his efforts. A medium would power something akin to a sewing treadle and this in turn spun a wheel with numbers and letters on it, much like a circular Ouija board. The medium had no control over where the wheel landed and at first was not even allowed to see the previous letters. Hare was also rigorous in the difficulty of the questions he put to his test mediums often requiring knowledge of specific quotations in Latin and details of American battles.

Perhaps the most ambitious machine associated with the Spiritualists was John Murray Spear's New Motive Power. Spear (1804–87), a Universalist Church of America minister-turned-medium, had a long track record of laboring for progressive causes. He worked with William Lloyd Garrison on the Underground Railroad (a secret network of routes and safe houses in the United States that enabled slaves to escape to the free states and Canada), freed an enslaved woman in New Bedford, Massachusetts (for which he received a near-fatal beating), and earned the nickname 'The Prisoner's Friend' for his attempts at jail reform (Buescher 2006). In 1853, Spear announced in the Boston weekly paper, *The Banner of Light*, that the spirits were planning to give humanity the ultimate gift from heaven, a 'mechanical messiah,' designed to usher in an unspecified but clearly utopian future for the living.

Spear's mechanical messiah is illustrative of one of the fondest hopes of Spiritualists and other progressive religious groups, namely that spirituality and science would be shown to be utterly compatible. The machine was designed to come alive, in that the fusion of the human and the technological would be assisted by an unnamed woman who would give birth to its spirit. Spear wrote of colorfully named associations forming in heaven, each bringing a particular gift to humanity. One of these heavenly associations was the Association of Electricizers, a gathering of spirits including Benjamin Franklin and Thomas Jefferson. Under the instruction of Franklin, Spear built the New Motive Power on a hill outside Lynn, Massachusetts. Perching 170 feet over the city, the machine was made of zinc and copper and cost an astonishing 2000 dollars. Despite claims that onlookers had seen signs of motion after the machine's gestation by the anonymous 'Mary of the New Dispensation,' it failed to actually do anything and was dismantled by angered Spiritualists.

The most perspicacious observer of Spiritualism at the time remains Emma Hardinge Britten (1823–99), who in 1870 stepped back from her own twenty-year career as a medium to become an 'impartial historian' of the movement in her exhaustive and detailed *Modern American Spiritualism*. Hardinge notes the superlatives used in the Boston Spiritualist press about the event and captures the core excitement: '[T]he "great discovery"...left little room to doubt that a modern Frankenstein had arisen, who, like Mrs. Shelley's famous student, was prepared to show a living organism, created at the hand of its fellow-man, only that the new "monster" was a being of metal and wood, instead of flesh and blood like its German prototype' (Britten 1870: 221). The fusion of human and machine began, in both Victorian literature and Spiritualist experience, as a scientific frontier that ultimately failed by overstepping the bounds of creation.

The search for unassailable empirical proof of Spiritualism's claims seemed, for a moment, finally to have found its perfect technology, photography. In 1861 William Mumler (1832–84) was learning the art of wet-plate processing when he accidentally developed a self portrait that included another image. Mumler attributed this to his own inexperience but showed the image to a Spiritualist friend as a joke. A week later, Mumler discovered himself being hailed in Spiritualist newspapers up and down the north coast. Mumler began specializing in spirit photography, charging five times what a regular photo sitting would for a picture with a ghost. Many such photographs, such as the famous ones Mary Todd Lincoln procured of her dead husband, reinforced domestic relations beyond death and suggested that one's loved ones hovered close to home. More curiously, many sitters would get a ghost whom they did not know, a phenomenon that some adherents argued was further proof of the existence of spirits, since the dead must want to be recognized if they appeared randomly in photographs.

At a time when photography was little understood by the vast majority of people, this did seem irrevocable and empirical justification for Spiritualist claims. If a photograph could uncannily, faithfully, and seemingly objectively reproduce a known image, then the appearance of an additional, unseen image meant that the human, and not the machine, was flawed. That is to say, some theorized that human sight was limited to a certain range on the light spectrum. Spirits existed invisibly on the human plane, but were captured by the superior sight of the camera. Spirit photography was enormously popular but delivered different and perhaps less satisfying results to believers—the dead were transported to the masculine and commercial world of professional photography where they were present but silent and often unrecognized.

In 1869, Mumler was brought up on charges of fraud. The prosecution put P. T. Barnum on the stand where he showed the viewers no fewer than ten different ways to manipulate images in wet-plate photography. Nevertheless, Mumler was acquitted on all counts and was compared by his lawyer in his closing argument to Galileo who persevered for science in the face of danger and ridicule. Spiritualists faced criminal charges for ghost photographs and séances in several countries, mostly for fraud, but in Great Britain and Canada for their transgression of sorcery laws as well. For the majority of believers, these incidents reinforced Spiritualist claims in the face of a common enemy, the small-mindedness of run-of-the-mill Christians.

The long nineteenth century saw enormous strides in technology and science that significantly improved the quality of human life in the West. The transition, however, was not always easy. The main tenets of Christianity took a bit of a thrashing: biblical criticism proved the Pentateuch to not be written by Moses, but rather by the hands of many men over many generations; biblical archaeology came up nearly empty handed for signs of Jesus in the Holy Land; and Charles Darwin struck the final blow to humankind's descent from Adam and Eve. Within some Protestant communities, this led to the creation of the anti-scientific rhetoric of faith-based knowledge that remains with us today.

However, for Spiritualists, as well as left-leaning Protestant groups and religious utopias like the Oneida Community, science was embraced as increasingly proving religious claims. Lord Alfred Russell Wallace, Darwin's own competitor to publish a theory of natural selection, became a Spiritualist convert and projected evolution past the threshold of death (Kontou 2009). Darwin's evolution became quickly conscripted (and inaccurately understood) as progress that could be extended through the entirety of heaven, such that the single largest threat to mainstream religiosity became an asset and an ally of Spiritualism. Ready to experiment with new machines, medical theories, and avant-garde forms of knowledge, Spiritualism remained convinced that science would further rather than erode religion.

DECLINE AND LEGACY

Spiritualism began at the juncture of grief and nascent pluralism, where the category of sin itself was coming under fire and where progressive thinkers were ready to abandon exclusive truth claims. It served as an effective aid to those in mourning and a hope for technologies that would expand beyond the bounds of earth. Spiritualism's denouement was mostly due to internal fractures in the structure of the movement itself. Its fierce individualism and refusal to create governing hierarchies with any power, its reliance on the young and inexperienced for its priestcraft, and its sheer democratic impulse of who might become a medium all caused the foundations to shake.

In addition to structural weaknesses, Spiritualists also increasingly demanded more showiness from their séances and lectures, a trend that resulted in inviting trickery and even charlatans into their realm. What began as the occasional glove or flower presented to a sitter from the spirit world spiraled into full-blown materializations of ghosts, shimmering instruments being played by invisible hands, and tables that rocked and spun for the sitters. Increased theatricality brought with it increased criticism, as tell-all books explaining how to reproduce these effects were published and Harry Houdini began what we currently know as stage magic in a specific refutation of Spiritualist other-worldly phenomena. Spiritualism began as a method of bringing the invisible to life with words, photographs, and then gifts from the dead, and was challenged by critics who could mimic their methods while refuting that any of the process belonged to the supernatural realm (see Nadis 2005).

Tatiana Kontou has recently argued that the decline of Spiritualism set the cultural stage for women's increased roles and importance in theatre. The turn of the twentieth century witnessed an astonishing jump in the quantity and caliber of good roles for women, with Henrik Ibsen's plays leading the way. The profession of acting concomitantly gained in reputation and desirability. As mentioned above, new white-collar jobs for women opened up in the field of communications that furthered the main impulses of Spiritualism but remained fully material in their roles and gains.

Many Spiritualists became Theosophists or other more hard line occultists, with some like Emma Hardinge Britten remaining in both camps without conflict. Theosophy had its roots in Spiritualism: both Helena Petrovna Blavatsky and her life-long follower and patron, Colonel Henry Olcott, were Spiritualists prior to the founding of the Theosophical Society in 1875. From the outset Theosophy had a more conspiratorial tone and sought to pry secrets purposefully hidden in history rather than merely asking the usually genial dead for advice and information. As its theology progressed, Theosophy became increasingly exclusive and initiatory with the goal of becoming an adept.

Others with a more scientific mindset explored Spiritualist communications as a form of thought transference. The Society for Psychical Research and later paranormal studies housed in psychology departments endeavored to explore and explain uncanny moments of human experience in systematic and rigorous settings. Long after having lost their association with Mesmer, magnets continue to be used in folk medicine as a cure for sore muscles in shoe inserts, back braces, and even disguised as jewelry. The ghosts of popular culture continue to experiment with new technologies and internet sites replace the mediums of old with electronic forms of communicating with the dead and even God.

One of the clearest examples of Spiritualism's ethos is the phenomenon of channeling, in which a person, usually female, abdicates her body for it to be governed by a spirit of immense age and wisdom who then dispenses advice to large audiences. As the telegraph shaped and bolstered Spiritualism, so too is channeling aided by television, which brought its messages directly into hundreds of thousands of homes. The communications from these sages are less personal and more aimed at the self-help generation which embraces goals of positive thinking and self-knowledge. Channeling is an arm of and functions in tandem with New Age religions that, like Spiritualism, deny an anthropomorphized deity who judges individuals and insists instead on eternal progress and education. With the additional knowledge of a century of exposure to Asian religions, New Age posits multiple reincarnations for each soul thus extending the range of progress through many lifetimes as well as time spent between them.

Television shows and movies abound in representations of contemporary forms of talking to the dead, some for the purpose of crime fighting and others for more traditional uses like grief counseling and righting wrongs posthumously. Religious dogma is almost always left unstated in these venues but the dead are generally portrayed as completely inclusive—that is, all dispositions, races, and presumably religions are in the same heaven and all will eventually be reunited with their loved ones. Like the ghosts they interact with, other Victorian monsters have been resurrected, updated, and cast into a multiverse where the ethics of exclusion are explored with ideas of death; gay and lesbian rights, race relations, and postmodernity itself are all thought through with ghosts, vampires, and zombies in prime time.

Spiritualism undoubtedly had its moments of lapses of decorum, outright quackery, and untrammeled racism. However, in the final analysis, Spiritualism's greatest legacy was the dismantling of hell. By opening heaven to all and repeatedly finding an inclusive and superior culture in the afterlife, Spiritualists carried a new moral code across a century and several continents to inaugurate what would become multiculturalism in the current world. The dead, while no longer perfect, were also no longer damned.

REFERENCES AND FURTHER READING

Braude, Ann (1989) *Radical Spirits: Spiritualism and Women's Rights in Nineteenth-Century America*, Boston: Beacon Press.

Britten, Emma Hardinge (1870) *Modern American Spiritualism: Twenty Years' Record of the Communion between Earth and the World of Spirits*, New York: self-published. Online: http://archive.org/stream/modernamericans01britgoog#page/n11/mode/2up.

Buescher, John (2006) *The Remarkable Life of John Murray Spear: Agitator for the Spirit Land*, Indiana: University of Notre Dame Press.

Casey, John (2009) *After Lives: A Guide to Heaven, Hell, and Purgatory*, New York: Oxford University Press.

Cloutier, Crista (2004) 'Mumler's Ghosts', in Clément Chéroux et al., eds., *The Perfect Medium: Photography and the Occult*, New Haven: Yale University Press, 20–28.

Cox, Robert S. (2003) *Body and Soul: A Sympathetic History of American Spiritualism*. Charlottesville: University of Virginia Press.

Crabtree, Adam (1993) *From Mesmer to Freud: Magnetic Sleep and the Roots of Psychological Healing*, New Haven: Yale University Press.

Galvan, Jill (2010) *The Sympathetic Medium: Feminine Channeling, the Occult, and Communication Technologies*, Ithaca, New York: Cornell University Press.

Gutierrez, Cathy (forthcoming) 'Crimes of the Soul: Spiritualism and the Dismantling of Hell', in Christopher Moreman, ed., *The Spiritualist Movement: Speaking with the Dead in America and Around the World*, Santa Barbara: Praeger/ABC-CLIO.

——(2010) *Plato's Ghost: Spiritualism in the American Renaissance*, New York: Oxford University Press.

Kontou, Tatiana (2009) *Spiritualism and Women's Writing: From the Fin de Siècle to the Neo-Victorian*, Houndmills: Palgrave Macmillan.

Kripal, Jeffrey J. (2010) *Authors of the Impossible: The Paranormal and the Sacred*, Chicago: University of Chicago Press.

Lowry, Elizabeth (forthcoming) 'Pinkie at Play: Postcolonialism, Politics, and Performance in Nettie Colburn Maynard's *Was Abraham Lincoln a Spiritualist?*' in Cathy Gutierrez, ed., *Handbook of Spiritualism and Channeling*, Leiden: Brill.

Nadis, Fred (2005) *Wonder Shows: Performing Science, Magic, and Religion in America*, New Jersey: Rutgers University Press.

Tromp, Marlene (2007) *Altered States: Sex, Nation, Drugs, and Self-Fashioning in Victorian Spiritualism*, Albany: SUNY Press.

Versluis, Arthur (2001) *The Esoteric Origins of the American Renaissance*, New York: Oxford University Press.

CHAPTER SIXTEEN

NEW THOUGHT TRADITIONS

Jeremy Rapport

INTRODUCTION

New Thought is a term that refers to a variety of religious expressions and movements with common roots in the mid-nineteenth-century United States. New Thought tenets and practices are premised on the idea that humans have within themselves all they need to connect with a larger, more perfect reality, and that creating and using this connection is a matter of using the powers of mind that all humans possess. This connection will allow individuals to heal themselves of physical and mental infirmities, deal with poor economic and social situations, and realize salvation through creating a happy, healthy, fulfilled life. Often couched in Protestant Christian language and practice, New Thought movements introduced teachings and rituals with esoteric elements to mainstream cultures.

This chapter surveys major New Thought philosophies, tenets, and practices, as well as overviews some major New Thought groups. The most important of the remaining New Thought movements, the Unity School of Christianity, is considered in greater detail. I conclude with an overview of contemporary New Thought trends. (For a more detailed examination of the history and historiography of New Thought, see Rapport 2010.)

MAJOR TENETS AND PRACTICES

Although metaphysical religion in the United States has historical links with traditions going back at least 600 years, it most clearly developed out of a variety of thought coming to prominence in the early nineteenth century in America, particularly three rising influences at that time: the writings of Swedish mystic Emanuel Swedenborg (1688–1772); the work of a group of romantic, idealist New England dissidents who came to be known as the Transcendentalists; and the mind cure phenomenon begun by Phineas Parkhurst Quimby (1802–66). These people and groups expressed ideas about the nature of divinity, the nature of the physical world, and the human's relation to divinity and the universe that were radically different from the Protestant Congregationalism that dominated early nineteenth-century New England (Ahlstrom 1972).

The first comprehensive, academic history of New Thought was Charles Braden's *Spirits in Rebellion: The Rise and Development of New Thought* (1963). While he acknowledged a wide variety of philosophical and religious sources, Braden argued the primary philosophical precedents of New Thought lay in the Transcendentalist movement. That influence can be directly established since, as Braden points out, many New Thought writers quote and cite the seminal Transcendentalist Ralph Waldo Emerson extensively as well as adopting many of Emerson's philosophical and religious hermeneutics. Emerson's conceptions of God as the all-encompassing source of the universe and of the natural and intimate connection of humans with God, particularly as those are expressed in his essay 'The Over Soul,' were especially influential on the New Thought conceptions of God, humanity, and the relation between the two. Braden also presented evidence that suggests that early New Thought practitioners believed that Emerson practiced a type of mental healing that foreshadowed New Thought healing techniques. Emerson, according to many early New Thought leaders, understood intuition to be a basic source of the knowledge of ultimate reality, advocated the idea that humans are essentially divine, and taught that the mind controls all matter, all of which are basic premises for New Thought (Braden 1963).

Braden based his general description of New Thought on statements published by the Metaphysical Club of Boston and the various incarnations of the group eventually known as the International New Thought Alliance. Braden was the first scholar to codify a list of basic New Thought characteristics: ideas are real things that have actual effects in the world; mind is primary, while matter is secondary; the way to cure all individual and societal problems is by understanding and using metaphysical principles; God is immanent, indwelling, Spirit, wisdom, goodness; because of those divine characteristics, and because humans are intimately connected with God, evil cannot have a permanent place in the world, or in individual human lives; and all religions have some truth and value (Braden 1963).

Subsequent academic work demonstrated the depth and width of New Thought sources and practices. J. Stillson Judah, in *The History and Philosophy of the Metaphysical Movements in America* (1967), one of the first comprehensive examinations of such traditions, argued the New Thought movement and its various religious groups along with several other groups that have similar philosophies, sources, and characteristics constitute a unique strain of religiosity called metaphysical movements. Judah describes fifteen characteristics that define metaphysical movements, stressing in particular the idea of God as an impersonal, yet all good and all-powerful force, human beings as essentially divine, an emphasis on self-realization and knowledge, and healing through the power of the mind. Metaphysical movements, for Judah, reflect an American concern with and aspiration for self-reliance. Thus a major mark of difference in these traditions is a transformed understanding of the human relation with the divine from one of utter dependence and submission to one of partnership and relationship. One way metaphysical movements are different is because they mark a departure from traditional Protestant teachings about God and humanity. God is no longer a sovereign with total control and power to grant grace and salvation to the individual, but a fount of life and the forces that shape it. For metaphysical religions the conclusion is obvious, the individual both can and must play a role in his or her salvation (Judah 1967).

Catherine Albanese, and many other scholars, now advocate the term 'metaphysical religion' to describe the New Thought movements and other, similar religious groups. Thus New Thought is a type of metaphysical religion. However, metaphysical religion itself refers to a wide variety of religious groups and philosophical stances and practices in America. The diversity of religious groups ranges from nineteenth-century expressions of this tendency such as Spiritualism and Theosophy, to early twentieth-century developments such as New Thought, to such contemporary expressions of the tendency as UFO religious groups, self-avowed Gnostic revival groups, and the various practices that are often termed 'New Age.' Albanese's *A Republic of Mind and Spirit* (2007) i s the first major examination of metaphysical religion in America since Judah's 1967 book. It both updates Judah's and adds a significant amount of historical detail to the development of metaphysical movements, both in America and the Western world. Albanese's reconfiguration of the major contours of American religious history places metaphysical religion in relationship to the other major trends in American religious history, allowing scholars not only to contextualize metaphysical religion better, but also to understand the basis of Albanese's claims about metaphysical religion's unique characteristics.

That contextualization frames Albanese's argument about the central place of metaphysical religion and New Thought in Western religions. She argues that three major forms of American religion can be identified. The first is the evangelical form, which cultivates emotional experience and sudden, life changing events. In the United States that is the religion of revivals and the Great Awakenings. The second form is the liturgical, which dominates the mainstream denominational traditions and focuses on communally organized ceremonial action. The third form is the metaphysical. Metaphysical religion encompasses four major themes: a focus on 'mind,' broadly conceived to include psychic abilities as well as cognitive abilities; an emphasis on the 'theory of correspondence,' the idea of a macrocosmic–microcosmic equivalence in which the larger, more perfect world can be accessed and made use of by humans in the smaller, less perfect realm; movement and energy as key themes in the practical presentation of ideas in metaphysical religion; and a central concern with salvation that is focused on therapy for and healing from both physical and psychological ills (Albanese 2007).

Taking as a characterization of New Thought Albanese's claim about the four elements of the metaphysical religion, describing and analyzing metaphysical religions, and thus New Thought, requires understanding how they create logical religious systems out of those four basic elements. One key element of that logical system, according to Albanese, is best understood as metaphysical magic, the ritual practices in metaphysical religions. Ritual in metaphysical religion is that system of thought and practice that allows the individual to connect with and make use of the macrocosm, which, as the source of the microcosm, is the realm where the failings and shortcomings of the microcosm disappear. Practitioners of metaphysical religions use ritual as a type of enacted metaphor that involves the use of artifacts and 'stylized accoutrements' as well as meditation in order to produce a transformation of physical conditions, usually the repair of flaws or problems. That notion of transformation using ritual techniques is so fundamental to metaphysical religion that Albanese calls it the 'heart of American metaphysics' (Albanese, 2007). Primarily in the form of various types of healing rituals, it is also the heart of New Thought practice.

The premise behind metaphysical magic is the theory of correspondence. According to Albanese, the basic notion of all forms of metaphysical religion is the idea of correspondence. Correspondence, in the religious sense of the word, posits that the universe has many levels that all reflect one another. The human world reflects the larger, cosmic world. A metaphysical religion says that sympathy exists among all things, meaning that actions in the human realm have consequences beyond just the human world. Humans have the power to bring themselves into harmony with the larger realms of the universe and so to heal themselves, among other abilities. For Albanese, a key point about correspondence is that it implies a world of fluid boundaries and creative syntheses of human religious expression: 'A universe in which microcosm and macrocosm shared the same reality and in which any action had truly cosmic repercussions could not be neatly divided into separate compartments...Metaphysical believers floated, seemingly, in universal space. They were cosmic migrants for whom everything was religious and every place was home. And they were, preeminently, combinationists' (Albanese 1999: 253). Metaphysical religion is different not only because of its ideas about divinity, humanity, and the nature of the universe, but also because of its general lack of attention to boundaries. Because it posits a world in which all things are connected and related, it also claims a world in which lines are meant to be crossed. Indeed, in the fullest understanding of metaphysical religion, boundaries and lines do not, ultimately, even exist.

For Albanese, the ideas of correspondence and metaphysical magic in American religion are central in the American religious world. In *Corresponding Motion: Transcendental Religion and the New America* (1977), she argues that correspondence first clearly manifested itself in the American setting among the Transcendentalists. These themes of correspondence that form a clear part of Emerson's *Nature* became a part of Transcendentalist tradition and from there worked their way into numerous other American religious modes. Albanese also has argued, in *Nature Religion in America: From the Algonkian Indians to the New Ages* (1990), that mind cure and nature religion, two American religious styles that she contends have strong links to Emerson and the Transcendentalists, can be read as attempts by human beings to wrest control of their lives and the world around them from an all-powerful, yet also mysterious, God (Albanese 1990). It is largely through ideas about the divine expressed in Emerson's *Nature* that the material world can become spiritualized, and so become an object worthy of veneration. Furthermore, it is possible to read the healing work central to New Thought's early development as largely a material version of metaphysical principles. These ideas and themes are at the foundation of what will become the New Thought movement.

NINETEENTH-CENTURY DEVELOPMENTS

New Thought's documented history begins with the work of Phineas Parkhurst Quimby (1802–66). Quimby was a clock maker in Maine when he attended a lecture and demonstration on hypnotism sometime in 1838. Quimby was fascinated by what he saw and soon began to study and practice hypnotism. Shortly thereafter he met Lucius Burkmar, on whom he practiced hypnotism for several months. Quimby came to believe that while under hypnosis Burkmar possessed clairvoyant abilities, and that Burkmar could diagnose and prescribe treatment for disease while hypnotized.

The two began to work together healing patients, traveling the northeastern United States conducting mesmerist demonstrations and healings (Braden 1963).

Burkmar's prescriptions frequently consisted of simple remedies such as a single herb or some tea, which Quimby believed could have no real healing efficacy. Quimby suspected that this might mean that the treatment's success was based, at least in part, on the effect it had on the patient's mind. Quimby confirmed this when Burkmar treated him for a back ailment. Doctors had told Quimby that he had a diseased kidney. Under hypnosis Burkmar confirmed the diagnosis and treated Quimby by laying his hands on Quimby's back and assuring him that the kidney would be healed within a couple of days. Two days later, again under hypnosis, Burkmar told Quimby that he was healed, and Quimby confirmed the proclamation. For Quimby, that experience meant that the cures he and Burkmar had been performing had more to do with manipulating the patient's state of mind than hypnotic discovery and treatment of illness.

Quimby began to experiment again and discovered that the same results could be achieved without hypnosis. Disease, Quimby decided, is the result of misinformation:

> Disease is what follows the disturbance of the mind or spiritual matter...This disturbance contains no knowledge or thought...It embraces mind without truth or error, like weight set in motion without direction...So is mind set in motion by spiritual power. Both are governed by laws of truth or error, the fruit shows which of the powers governs...Disease is what follows an opinion, it is made up of mind directed by error.
>
> (Quimby 1921: 180–81)

In other words, disease is not caused by outside organic forces but by an incorrect perception planted in the mind. Because the mind is open to suggestion, if the suggestion is received, perhaps from a doctor, that one is ill, then one will develop the illness.

Quimby's cure is therefore a logical result of his premise about disease. If disease is caused by an incorrect perception in the mind, then the perception must be corrected. Quimby treated his patients 'partly mentally and partly by talking till I correct the wrong impression and establish the Truth, and the Truth is the cure' (Quimby 1921: 194). By getting his patients to see that the errors in their minds caused their diseases and injuries, Quimby was able to cure them by convincing them of the inherent healthy condition of the matter that made up their bodies.

Quimby's method of healing is the basis for all subsequent New Thought healing, but it came primarily through the work of his students, not his own writings or personal reputation (Satter 1999). Quimby's manuscripts were not published until 1921, fifty-five years after his death. He did write a few articles and circulate some pamphlets to his students, but the majority of his writings were not widely known until Horatio Dresser published them. Quimby influenced some of the people he cured by inspiring them to follow in his footsteps. Two of those people who followed Quimby into healing did write and publish during their lifetimes and did become well known: Warren Felt Evans and Mary Baker Eddy.

Warren Felt Evans (1814/1817?–1889) was the first person to write systematically about New Thought ideas. Evans's life prior to meeting Quimby was not well documented. He was a New England Methodist minister who had been suffering from an unidentified ailment when he consulted the prominent healer P. P. Quimby. After a second visit to Quimby, Evans believed he was completely healed and was so taken with Quimby's method that he became a disciple. Evans set up a healing practice based on Quimby's teachings in Claremont, New Hampshire. Meanwhile, he had begun to read the works of Emanuel Swedenborg, and in 1863 he joined the Swedenborgian Church of the New Jerusalem. Evans continued to successfully practice Quimby's healing method, first in Boston, where he opened an office in 1867, and then in Salisbury, Massachusetts, where he opened an office in 1869 and continued to practice until his death in 1889.

Evans blended the more idealistic strains he inherited from Swedenborg and the Transcendentalists with the practical healing approach of Quimby. Although he published six books, Evans's basic content is similar across the books. It is this, more than the number of his publications, that is most relevant to understanding Evans's contribution to New Thought. Evans was the first person to write down many of the ideas that later become important to New Thought, in particular New Thought ideas related to central Christian ideas. He emphasized a separation between the historic Jesus and the Christ. The man Jesus was not born as a Christ; rather through intense personal effort he became a Christ. Evans taught the preexistence of the soul and that the body was a projection of the soul. He also taught that sin was an error of ignorance, not a condition into which all humans are born. Like Quimby, Evans believed disease resulted from wrong belief and that if the belief changed, the disease would be cured. He believed he was rediscovering the methods of Jesus. Evans supported affirmations as a method to change one's condition. Finally, Evans employed 'absent treatment'; he treated patients who were not even in his office. All of these ideas became basic tenets for most New Thought groups (Braden 1963: 89–128; Satter 1999: 70–73; Teahan 1979).

Mary Baker Eddy (1821–1910), the founder of Christian Science, is another vital person in the development of New Thought. Quimby healed Eddy in 1862, after she had serious health problems for much of her adult life. Inspired by Quimby, Eddy went on to write *Science and Health with Key to the Scriptures* (1875). Eddy argued that God is all and God is good; therefore evil cannot be real. Evil, sin, and disease are the result of the lesser human mind creating an illusory world. Humanity is not made up of matter, but of spirit. Matter is an illusion of the lesser human mind. The only true reality is the spiritual reality of God. The problem, therefore, is that the human mind is separated from the divine mind. Healing in Christian Science involves stopping the force of the mortal mind with the divine mind. Eddy's technique for accomplishing this was remarkably similar to Quimby's healing method. The patient had to be convinced that the disease was a result of a false belief and so it had no reality.

Eddy worked diligently for many years spreading her Christian Science. The work progressed slowly at first, but in 1879 Eddy and a small group of followers founded the Church of Christ, Scientist in Boston. Christian Science quickly became a widespread movement that included an educational institution, the Massachusetts Metaphysical College, and a magazine, the *Christian Science Journal*.

One of Eddy's early students and workers was Emma Curtis Hopkins (1851–1925). Hopkins is now known as the teachers' teacher in New Thought circles because so many important New Thought leaders took her classes and were ordained by her, including Malinda E. Cramer (1844–1906), Annie Rix Militz (1856–1924), and Charles and Myrtle Fillmore (1854–1948 and 1845–1931 respectively). But Hopkins was first affiliated with Mary Baker Eddy's Christian Science. Hopkins 'was a sickly thirty-two-year-old housewife and mother married to a debt-ridden and violent husband' when she met Eddy at a mutual friend's house in Manchester, New Hampshire, in 1883. The women discussed Christian Science, and Hopkins became enthralled with it. The neighbor, Mary F. Berry, used Christian Science techniques to cure Hopkins, and Hopkins next decided to take a class from Eddy. A woman who was apparently 'articulate, well-read, and beautiful,' Hopkins quickly rose through the ranks of the new Christian Science organization and within a year of her initial introduction to Eddy and Christian Science, Hopkins was editor of the *Christian Science Journal* (Satter 1999: 81).

Barely over a year later, however, Hopkins left Christian Science due to a dispute with Eddy. Eddy was apparently upset about an article Hopkins wrote in which she suggested that she (Hopkins) might have also had a divine revelation. Shortly afterwards, Hopkins moved to Chicago and began to teach her own versions of Christian Science classes. In Chicago, she also founded the Hopkins Metaphysical Association. That group began to affect the New Thought movement, such that, as Satter puts it, 'By December 1887 there were at least seventeen branches of the Hopkins Metaphysical Association in cities across the nation' (Satter 1999: 82).

Hopkins worked tirelessly to promote her teachings, traveling to centers around the country and writing in journals, in addition to continuing her work in Chicago. Hopkins was not only becoming immersed in New Thought, the major rival to Eddy's Christian Science, but she was helping to shape the growing movement. Her writings appeared alongside those of Warren Felt Evans; she was the star of the 1887 Mental Science convention in Boston; and most importantly, she was teaching people her ideas. By the end of the first half of the twentieth century, New Thought had become an established religious alternative throughout the United States. With numerous publications, groups across the country, recognized leaders and teachers, an umbrella organization, and training schools, the movement functioned as de facto denomination with at least five major subgroups. It will be instructive to look briefly at the most successful New Thought group, the Unity School of Christianity.

The contribution of Emma Curtis Hopkins to the early development of New Thought is critical, especially for the founders of the most important New Thought movement, the Unity School of Christianity. Charles and Myrtle Fillmore were both ordained by Hopkins. Most of the influential New Thought proponents that the Fillmores interacted with were students of Hopkins. More than just a teacher, however, Hopkins became a close friend of Charles and Myrtle Fillmore who worked to promote the Fillmores' growing movement. The relationship was mutual, and Hopkins apparently called on the Fillmores to aid her on occasion. Hopkins also taught in Kansas City several times, while the Fillmores stayed with Hopkins when they took classes in Chicago. The relationship continued with Hopkins exchanging letters with Myrtle Fillmore until two years before Hopkins's death. Gail Harley characterizes the relationship between Hopkins and the Fillmores as more than cordial, citing the personal insights that Hopkins confided to Myrtle Fillmore, Hopkins's apparent joy at the Fillmores' success, and arguing that Hopkins considered the Fillmores as people with whom she had developed spiritual bonds (Harley 2002).

THE UNITY SCHOOL OF CHRISTIANITY

The story of the Unity School of Christianity begins, as did many creative religious impulses of the late nineteenth century, with a search for healing. Sometime during the spring of 1886, Myrtle Fillmore attended a lecture by the Christian Science practitioner Eugene B. Weeks. Fillmore, convinced that she suffered from numerous serious physical ailments including incessant hemorrhoids and tuberculosis, came away from the lecture with the affirmation, 'I am a child of God and so do not inherit sickness' in her mind. She used this affirmation in conjunction with prayer to heal herself of her physical afflictions. She began to practice her healing technique with friends and eventually convinced her somewhat skeptical husband, Kansas City, Missouri, real estate man Charles Fillmore, that her beliefs and practices warranted further investigation. A formal healing practice was begun, and in 1890 Charles and Myrtle Fillmore founded their first magazine, *Modern Thought*. Thus was born the organization that would become the Unity School of Christianity, widely known today as Unity (Freeman 2000; Vahle 2002).

The Unity School of Christianity (henceforth Unity) is one of the largest and most stable of the New Thought Movements in America. The movement is more than 120 years old, and Unity materials reach millions of people worldwide not officially affiliated with the movement via outreach publications such as the *Daily Word* and its prayer service, Silent Unity. Unity is a significant, albeit largely unrecognized, player in the American religious world.

Contemporary Unity frequently describes itself as 'practical Christianity,' although like most New Thought groups, Unity espouses a general monotheistic worldview combined with teachings about the power of human beings to access and make use of the divine. It has a modified congregational polity, with movement headquarters located at Unity Village, a small town adjacent to Lee's Summit, Missouri, 17 miles southeast of Kansas City, Missouri. Unity has individual congregations in forty-nine states, many with a great deal of autonomy. As of January 3, 2006, the Association of Unity Churches, the ministerial support arm of the movement, reported 905 ministries worldwide, 659 of which are in the United States. Individual Unity congregations do not report membership levels, so it is difficult to make an accurate estimate of the total number of Unity adherents. Unity certainly is, however, the largest New Thought group in the United States, and it is arguably the most important New Thought-inspired religion in the United States (Rapport, 2010).

Unity became a worldwide movement over the course of the twentieth century. It boasts one of the largest religious printing houses in the Midwest. Unity Village operates with a full-time staff of over 600 employees. It also houses a formal ministerial training program and a prayer request service, called Silent Unity, which operates twenty-four hours a day, 365 days a year, handling over two million prayer requests annually. The Unity publication *Daily Word* has a circulation of over one million and is printed in nine different languages. A sister organization, the Association of Unity Churches, has developed to oversee and provide services to the individual congregations worldwide. These support organizations and production facilities have made Unity the de facto leader of the otherwise fairly amorphous American New Thought world (Rapport, 2010).

While Unity was originally intended to be an extra-ecclesiastical organization without a formal creed, the Fillmores gradually developed the elements of a formal religious organization, culminating in a 'Statement of Faith' for Unity in 1921 in response to demands from practitioners who had begun to look to Unity for their whole religious lives. The 'Statement of Faith' went through some variations, was solidified by 1939, and remained in that form for the next fifty years. In 1989, after approximately ten years had passed in which no formal copies of the 'Statement of Faith' were issued, a new doctrinal statement, known as the 'Five Principles,' appeared. A radical departure from the detailed, thirty-point 'Statement of Faith,' the 'Five Principles' distilled Unity's doctrine into a brief, thematic form in which the basic tenets of the organization were briefly summarized (Rapport, 2010).

The movement also has a well-established hermeneutic system embodied in its periodical literature and ministerial training system. Unity has thus developed a formal doctrinal system, even if they do not call it such, as well as an interpretive tradition that allows for creative reflection upon and revision of doctrines and practices. These developments are the result of complex evolution and growth processes. Over the course of its nearly 130 years, Unity grew from a healing and publishing movement endemic to the Kansas City area to an American religious denomination with both a clear affinity for the mainstream Protestant world and a method for espousing its alternative take on Protestant Christian belief and practice.

Unity's religious life depends on combining New Thought principles and practices with the 'Protestant grammar' of the American religious world. Unity takes as legitimate and makes use of basic Protestant assumptions, such as the principles of sola scriptura and the priesthood of all believers, and practices, such as the focus on prayer and scriptural exegesis, in its religious life. Unity employs the unspoken assumptions of the Protestant grammar, such as the legitimacy of writing and of texts, the authority of the individual, and the primacy of belief, to build the principles and practices of its religious life. By structuring the discourse of their religious movement on this Protestant grammar, the Fillmores appropriated the primacy of belief, the authority of the Bible, and the centrality of the individual experience to their own ends while also adopting the recognized forms of the majority of the American religious culture (Rapport, 2010).

These notions of mainstream religion and Protestant grammar are central to understanding Unity, and by extension New Thought, because they reveal important facets of the history and development of one important American religious alternative, while also serving as a primary way in which Unity sought legitimacy for its unconventional claims. By intertwining their movement with what they considered to be legitimate Christian expression in early twentieth-century America, the Fillmores negotiated a stable place for Unity, which had New Thought–inspired claims and practices that could have easily been interpreted as highly unconventional and destabilizing. Unity shows us one important way that New Thought movements, despite unorthodox religious claims that directly contradicted the most prominent religious tradition in the United States, managed to establish themselves during the first half of the twentieth century.

CONTEMPORARY NEW THOUGHT

A good number of New Thought movements remain active in the early twenty-first century, including Religious Science, Divine Science, and most prominently, the Unity School of Christianity. However, New Thought's real influence moved outside of its specific groups beginning in the mid-twentieth century. New Thought teachings and practices were also infiltrating the Protestant mainstream and non-religious areas of American culture. Figures such as Norman Vincent Peale brought New Thought into the American mainstream, albeit largely without the sectarian elements of the New Thought movement proper. New Thought leaders, with their basic teaching that thought creates reality, brought a form of esoteric practice to the American mainstream.

However, New Thought's real influence is with the prominent cultural icons who have adopted and espoused New Thought principles and with the widespread cultural discourse about the power of mind. Understanding New Thought as a cultural phenomenon requires opening the field upon which religious and esoteric forms of thought and practice usually operate to include such areas as self-help literature, popular psychology, and television talk shows. New Thought in this format is enmeshed with the capitalist, free-market exchange system of the modern, Western world. Indeed, much of New Thought's success, such as it is, has depended upon the ability of its proponents to present it as commodity in the marketplace of ideas and practices. The fact that New Thought tenets and rituals lend themselves to such commodification has played a vital part in the process. In other words, by using New Thought as the basis for the creation of marketable goods and services, the people who transformed the movement from a sectarian religious alternative to a commodified, cultural phenomenon were taking advantage both of marketing techniques to sell religious ideas and of the way in which New Thought's inwardly focused, esoteric elements lent themselves to books, videos, and other goods intended to be consumed by private individuals.

The first major transitional figure in this vein is clearly Norman Vincent Peale (1898–1993). An ordained Methodist minister who eventually converted to the Dutch Reformed tradition when he took over as the pastor of Marble Collegiate Church in 1932, Peale wrote numerous books with New Thought teachings central to the book's message, including most famously, *The Power of Positive Thinking* (1952). Peale's form of New Thought–laced Christianity developed relatively early in his career, possibly as result of his work with Ernest Holmes, an early twentieth-century New Thought leader and founder of the Religious Science branch of the New Thought movement. Peale's sermons were filled with accolades to positive thinking, but his real influence was in his prolific media output. His radio show, television appearances, work with Smiley Blanton on religion and psychology, his *Guideposts* magazine, and his political connections and activities all supplemented a literary output of forty books (George 1993).

More recently, New Thought has been repackaged and rebranded in the work of the Australian writer Rhonda Byrne and her movie and book, *The Secret*. *The Secret* purports to teach a method for cultivating the power of one's mind that has been used by famous philosophers, scientists, rulers, and religious leaders throughout human history (http://thesecret.tv). Based on the law of attraction teachings, a sub-category of New Thought concerned with using the techniques of affirmation for personal gain, Byrne is continuing on the path first marked by New Thought writers such as Wallace Wattles, whose *The Science of Getting Rich* (1910) teaches prayer techniques intended to enable practitioners to become financially successful (Wattles 2008). The media success of *The Secret* was due in no small measure to it being picked by Oprah Winfrey (1954–present). With the force of Winfrey's talk show and media empire behind it, *The Secret* brought New Thought back into the American consciousness in 2006.

Winfrey's role in the popularization of New Thought tenets and practices is more than just as a conduit for exposure to wider audiences. She is the most important contemporary adopter and adapter of New Thought. Winfrey's work as an author, businesswoman, and television talk show host is influenced by New Thought principles, in particular New Thought's focus on the power of the individual mind. Winfrey's work as a talk show host is premised upon her ability to convince her guests and viewers that their problems and issues are all subject to their control. As Kathryn Lofton has argued, Winfrey functions as priest whose sermons are the interviews she conducts, the books and products she recommends, and the special events she orchestrates (Lofton 2011). Winfrey's message relies upon several tenets of New Thought, which have been absorbed by mainstream American culture. Aimed primarily at women, Winfrey presents New Thought in the form of practices of counseling, consumption, and reading that, when done correctly, i.e. the way Oprah recommends, help women overcome what they lack and become the best people they can be. Winfrey's technique here is important. She facilitates the creation of narratives for her guests that are usually variations on personal transformation resulting from a difficult inner struggle (Lofton 2011). Winfrey's emphasis on the individual and the individual's responsibility for her own situation reinforces the New Thought tenet that it is one's personal relationship with a greater reality that affects one's well being in this world. The pinnacle of New Thought's modernization is reached in the techniques Winfrey uses to sell products to her viewers and readers. Her endorsements are not based only on her own celebrity, though no doubt that plays a central role in the product's success. Rather, Winfrey explains her product endorsements in terms of how the products make her feel, or help her cope with certain situations. In essence, it is possible for women to buy their way into Oprah's transformative mindset.

Thus Oprah Winfrey has recreated New Thought for an explicitly consumer age by representing its tenets and practices as simple beliefs, private rituals, and consumer goods the purchase of which can help individual women cope and overcome any challenges they might face. Oprah demonstrates how New Thought, and by extension esotericism, is adapted to new cultural settings. Moreover, Oprah shows how New Thought has become integrated into the American mainstream, therefore revealing how its influence and power continues to expand even though the number of actual religious movements espousing New Thought has continued to shrink.

CONCLUSION

The modern transformations of New Thought suggest at least two important points about esotericism as a religious practice. First, its appeal for many people is in its inward focus, which allows for its practitioners to paint the details of its practice in their own ways. Second, because esotericism's focus is the individual and the individual's mind, it lends itself to being described and taught through easily marketable and sellable goods such as books, magazines, and videos. Thus esotericism, in its New Thought forms, is an example par excellence of the contemporary notion of 'spiritual, but not religious,' in which people with religious problem-solving mindsets eschew institutional religions for ideas, philosophies, and practices available in a literal spiritual marketplace.

REFERENCES AND FURTHER READING

Ahlstrom, S.E. (1972) *A Religious History of the American People*. New Haven: Yale University Press.

Albanese, C.L. (1977) *Corresponding Motion: Transcendental Religion and the New America*. Philadelphia: Temple University Press.

——(1990) *Nature Religion in America: From the Algonkian Indians to the New Age*. Chicago: University of Chicago Press.

——(1999) *America: Religions and Religion*. Belmont: Wadsworth.

——(2007) *A Republic of Mind and Spirit: A Cultural History of American Metaphysical Religion*. New Haven: Yale University Press.

Braden, C.S. (1963) *Spirits in Rebellion: The Rise and Development of New Thought*. Dallas: Southern Methodist University Press.

Byrne, R. (2006) *The Secret*. New York: Atria Books.

Capps, D. (2009) 'Norman Vincent Peale, Smiley Blanton and the Hidden Energies of the Mind.' *Journal of Religion and Health* 48: 507–27.

Eddy, M.B. (1994) *Science and Health: With Key to the Scriptures*. Boston: First Church of Christ, Scientist.

Emerson, R.W. (1883) *Essays*. Boston: Houghton Mifflin.

Freeman, J.D. (2000) *The Story of Unity*. Unity Village, Mo.: Unity Books.

George, C.V.R. (1993) *God's Salesman: Norman Vincent Peale & the Power of Positive Thinking*, Religion in America series. New York: Oxford University Press.

Haller, J.S. (2012) *The History of New Thought: From Mind Cure to Positive Thinking and the Prosperity Gospel*. West Chester, Pa.: Swedenborg Foundation Press.

Harley, G.M. (2002) *Emma Curtis Hopkins: Forgotten Founder of New Thought*. Syracuse, N.Y.: Syracuse University Press.

Judah, J.S. (1967) *The History and Philosophy of the Metaphysical Movements in America*. Philadelphia: Westminster Press.

Lofton, K. (2011) *Oprah: the Gospel of an Icon*. Berkeley: University of California Press.

Meyer, D.B. (1965) *The Positive Thinkers, a Study of the American Quest for Health, Wealth and Personal Power from Mary Baker Eddy to Norman Vincent Peale*. Garden City, N.Y.: Doubleday.

Peale, N.V. (1952) *The Power of Positive Thinking*. New York: Prentice Hall.

Quimby, P.P. (1921) *The Quimby Manuscripts, Showing the Discovery of Spiritual Healing and the Origin of Christian Science*. Edited by H.W. Dresser. New York: T. Y. Crowell Company.

Rapport, J. (2010) 'Becoming Unity: The Making of an American Religion.' Ph.D. dissertation. Indiana University.

Satter, B. (1999) *Each Mind a Kingdom: American Women, Sexual Purity, and the New Thought Movement, 1875–1920*. Berkeley: University of California Press.

Teahan, J.F. (1979) 'Warren Felt Evans and Mental Healing: Romantic Idealism and Practical Mysticism in Nineteenth-Century America.' *Church History* 48: 63–80.

Vahle, N. (2002) *The Unity Movement: Its Evolution and Spiritual Teachings*. Philadelphia: Templeton Foundation Press.
Wattles, W.D. (2008) *The Science of Getting Rich*. Waiheke Island: Floating Press.
Witherspoon, T.E. (1977) *Myrtle Fillmore, Mother of Unity*. Unity Village, Mo.: Unity Books.

CHAPTER SEVENTEEN

ELIPHAS LÉVI

Christopher McIntosh

Eliphas Lévi (1810–75), whose real name was Alphonse-Louis Constant, lived a remarkably many-faceted life. At various stages he was a would-be priest, a revolutionary socialist, a utopian visionary, an artist, an actor, a poet and, above all, the author of a number of books on magic and occultism which helped to make these subjects accessible to a much wider public than ever before and played a seminal role in the upsurge of interest in occultism in the modern world. Lévi was part of a remarkable constellation of occultists in nineteenth-century France, but his influence went far beyond his native country. Many of his ideas were admired by Madame Blavatsky and passed into Theosophy, the magicians of the Hermetic Order of the Golden Dawn were strongly influenced by him, and the English magus Aleister Crowley believed himself to be Lévi's reincarnation. Lévi also influenced a number of writers and poets, including Joris-Karl Huysmans, Charles Baudelaire and W.B. Yeats.

LIFE AND WORK

Lévi's life divides into three fairly distinct phases, only in the final phase of which he adopted the name Eliphas Lévi. So, we shall begin by calling him by his real name, Alphonse-Louis Constant. He was born in 1810, the son of a poor shoemaker, in the Saint-Germain district of Paris. He received his first education at a free school for the poor run by priests on the Ile Saint Louis. There he developed an early vocation for the priesthood and was sent to the seminary of Saint-Nicolas du Chardonnet, run by a man who was to have a big influence on him, the Abbé Frère-Colonna. The Abbé was an expert on Mesmerism, although entirely from a hostile, orthodox Catholic standpoint. Nevertheless the young Constant became fascinated by what he heard about Franz Anton Mesmer (1734–1815) and his system of animal magnetism. What probably fascinated Constant particularly was Mesmer's theory of an all-pervading invisible fluid or force field, which was the medium he operated on when he was doing his cures.

Another important idea that the Abbé introduced him to, was the idea of millennialism, particularly the notion that history unfolds in a series of ages and that a new and better one is approaching. This runs through the whole history of western esotericism right up to the present day and includes Crowley's idea of the Age of Horus and Alice Bailey's concept of the Age of Aquarius. In the history of millenarian thinking, the key thinker is the twelfth-century Italian mystic Joachim of Fiore, who conceived of history as unfolding in three successive ages, corresponding to the three persons of the Trinity. First came the Age of the Father, which was the age of the Old Testament and the Law. Then came the Age of the Son, that of Christian faith and the Gospel. And finally there would come the Age of the Holy Spirit or the Paraclete, which would be an age of love, joy and freedom, when knowledge of God would be revealed directly in the hearts of all humanity. The young Constant was very taken by this notion and later it played a central role in his thinking.

In due course, Constant went on to the Seminary of Saint-Sulpice to train for the priesthood. After about three years at Saint-Sulpice he was ordained deacon and was given the task of preparing the young girls of the district for their first communion. He was on the point of taking his final vows as a priest when he fell platonically in love with one of his pupils, a girl of Swiss origin called Adèle Allenbach. This made him realize that he could never remain celibate, so he decided to abandon the priesthood and leave the seminary. Allenbach remained friendly with him throughout his life and was one of the mourners at his funeral.

After his departure from the seminary he made a brief attempt at monastic life in a Benedictine monastery, but soon quarreled with the superior and left. This marked the end of the first phase of his life. The second phase might be called the revolutionary phase. While scraping together a living in various ways – teaching in a school, acting and illustrating books – he began to move in politically radical circles. One of the people who had a great influence on him at this time was Flora Tristan, who became the grandmother of the painter Gauguin but is important in her own right as a socialist, a feminist and an early advocate of trade unions and author of a number of books on these causes. It was partly under her influence that he wrote his first important book, a radical socialist tract called *La Bible de la Liberté* (*The Bible of Liberty*), published in 1841, which interpreted the scriptures in a revolutionary sense.

It was only just over fifty years since the French Revolution, and the country was very polarized between left and right. The latter was intent on preserving the traditional order that had been restored after the Revolution, so a book like *The Bible of Liberty* was seen as profoundly threatening. On the day it was published virtually the entire edition was seized by the authorities and Constant was sentenced to eight months in prison. While he was in prison he started to read the works of the Swedish visionary Emanuel Swedenborg. At first found them rather turgid and impenetrable, but later on he came to appreciate Swedenborg's ideas and particularly the idea of correspondences – the notion that things in the world are symbols for things in the divine realm – and also the idea that one can only understand the deeper meaning of the scriptures if one treats them as a coded message based on correspondences, analogies and number symbolism. If one reads them in this way, Swedenborg believed, one could extract the true, universal religion, which lies concealed behind all the exoteric religions of the world.

The Bible of Liberty was followed by a very different sort of book, *L'Assomption de la Femme* (*The Assumption of Woman*). This reveals another characteristic of Constant/Lévi, namely his idealization of women. He sympathized with women in the oppression that they had suffered so often – in this, he was conspicuously ahead of his time.

Already at this point, Constant was beginning to develop an esoteric view of the world. But he still had some way to go before he became transformed into Eliphas Lévi. He was now in his mid-30s and already fairly well known as a radical thinker and writer. And at this time two significant events happened in his private life. He had a love affair with a schoolmistress, Eugénie C. (her full name is not recorded), which resulted in an illegitimate son. However, instead of marrying the schoolmistress, he married one of her pupils, a girl called Noémi Cadiot, who was only 18 when they married. She later became famous in her own right as a novelist and sculptress under the pseudonym of Claude Vignon. Soon after the marriage, in 1847, Constant found himself in prison again for six months for writing another inflammatory book called *La Voix de la famine* (*The Voice of Famine*). The following year, 1848, was the Year of Revolutions, and France had its own revolution – yet another one – which ended with the deposition of King Louis-Philippe and the proclamation of a Republic. In Paris there were violent riots in the streets and some 10,000 people were killed. While this was going on, Constant and his wife were both campaigning actively in the socialist cause, during which he unsuccessfully sought election as a deputy to the National Assembly. In the same year he wrote yet another radical treatise, *Le Testament de la liberté* (*The Testament of Liberty*). The following passage from the book reveals how closely religion and politics were tied together in his mind. He writes:

> Now the fourth stage of the revolution is in preparation: namely that of love... And it is thus that the reign of the Holy Spirit, proclaimed by Christ, will be realised on earth. Already the workers of God have cleared the ground for new constructions. The great heretics have burned the dead woods; the revolutionaries, axe in hand, have cut down and uprooted the old stumps; everywhere the socialists are sowing the new word, the word of universal association and communal property.
>
> (Constant 1848)

Interestingly, this was published in the same year as Karl Marx's *Communist Manifesto*. Like Marx, Constant presents a socialist teleology of history, but, instead of Marx's entirely secular teleology, Constant bases his scheme essentially on Joachim of Fiore's idea of the coming reign of the Holy Spirit.

When Constant was in his early 40s a number important things happened to him. One was that his wife, Noémi, left him. Another was his meeting with a curious Polish philosopher, mathematician and visionary called Josef Hoëné-Wronski who, like Constant, believed in the coming reign of the Holy Spirit. Wronski believed that there was no conflict between science and religion. On the contrary, he argued that through science one could discover the true religion. Moreover, once the true religion was revealed, a new and better age for humanity would be ushered in. Wronski had also invented a remarkable machine called a prognometer, which was a sort of compendium of all knowledge and supposedly could answer any question, including predicting the future. After Wronski's death, Constant – or Lévi, as he had become by then – found the machine in a junk shop and bought it. This is his description of it:

> The form is that of the [Hebrew] letter Shin. The double branch which stems from the base of the machine ends in two copper balls surmounted by two triangular pyramids; one represents divine knowledge, the other human knowledge, coming from the same base and functioning together...The main globe, which is composed of two spheres, one inside the other, has two alternative movements of rotation...This philosophical machine is an entire encyclopedia, and the inner globe is covered with long equations...On the wheel, which bears the signs of the zodiac, doors are constructed which open and close. On these doors are written the fundamental axioms of each science. There are thirty-two doors, and on each door are the names of three sciences.
>
> (McIntosh 2011: 99)

Wronksi was intent on creating an all-embracing system of knowledge, a key to the universe. Lévi was inspired by Wronksi to attempt something similar. But Lévi took it a step further with his concept of magic, because magic was, for Lévi, not simply a system for understanding reality, but a system for operating actively on reality and on oneself. And this is where Lévi was really innovative. Although he was drawing on earlier antecedents, the way he presented magic was something new, namely as a complete system of knowledge and a path that any individual could follow, given sufficient study and dedication.

He presented his theory of magic in his magnum opus *Dogme et rituel de la haute magie* (published in English as *Transcendental Magic, its Doctrine and Ritual*), first published in complete form in 1856 (by Germer Baillière, Paris), which appeared under the name of Eliphas Lévi, intended as a Hebrew version of his Christian names, Alphonse-Louis. The first part of the book, the *Dogma*, has 22 chapters, each corresponding to a letter of the Hebrew alphabet. It is arranged numerologically, so, for example, Chapter 4 deals with fourfold schemes like the four elements, 5 deals with the pentagram, 7 deals with the planets, 10 deals with the 10 Sephiroth in the Kabbalah, and so on.

The second part, the *Ritual*, deals with the practical side of magic. Lévi insists that, while theory is all very well, the point is to act. In this part of the book he provides a range of practical advice, such as how to consecrate a sacred space, how to work with elemental spirits, how to make and consecrate talismans, and so on. In a particularly interesting chapter, he deals with what he calls 'magnetic chains', meaning invisible links between groups of people. Here he deals with a number of questions addressed in modern social psychology. What is it that enables a skilled orator to move a crowd of thousands of people? Why do people in a group act in ways that they would not if they were on their own? Lévi conceived of these magnetic chains as thought forms imprinted on 'the astral light' (see below).

The publication of the *Dogme et rituel de la haute magie* marked the beginning of the third phase of his life, when he called himself Eliphas Lévi, the Professor of High Magic, and devoted himself to propagating his own particular form of occultism.

One of the first things he did in his new incarnation was to visit England, where he became friendly with the novelist Sir Edward Bulwer-Lytton, later Lord Lytton, whose books are full of occult themes, especially his novel *Zanoni*, which is the story of a Rosicrucian adept. It is obvious, when one reads Bulwer-Lytton's books, that he had a deep personal interest in occult matters. Evidently, he and Lévi found each other to be kindred spirits, and a few years later Lévi made a second visit to England in the company of a Polish friend, Count Alexander Braszynsky, who was a practicing alchemist, and the two of them went to stay at Bulwer-Lytton's house, Knebworth in Hertfordshire.

While he was in London he performed an evocation of the ancient Greek magus, Apollonius of Tyana, in a full-scale ritual, complete with altar, incense, robes and magical weapons, using the same procedure as he describes in Chapter 13, the chapter on necromancy, in the *Ritual of Transcendental Magic*. He describes how Apollonius appeared as 'a lean, melancholy and beardless' man, dressed in a grey shroud, who correctly answered certain questions that Lévi put to him (McIntosh 2011, 101–4). However, he ends the account by cautioning his readers against attempting similar operations of necromancy.

Another person who helped to spread Lévi's reputation in England was Kenneth Mackenzie, a Freemason and Rosicrucian, who later became one of the key figures behind the creation of the Hermetic Order of the Golden Dawn. Mackenzie visited Lévi in Paris and has left a detailed account of the meeting.

This was now the 1860s, and Lévi was in the full flower of his career. He was not only well known for his books on magic, but he had also become a charismatic figure who taught his system of occult knowledge to a select group of pupils. These included the Pole Count Braszynsky, an Italian nobleman named Baron Spedalieri, and a woman of Irish parentage called Mary L'Estrange, who was a particularly devoted pupil. She later married Gustav Gebhard, a wealthy German businessman, and moved to Germany, where Lévi stayed with her and her husband in 1871 when he had fallen on hard times. Later on she and her husband became keen Theosophists and friends of Madame Blavatsky, who also stayed with the Gebhards in the 1880s. Another pupil was an Englishwoman, Louise Hutchinson, who went to Paris to study with Lévi and took two lessons a week for a year. In an account of her experience, she wrote that, 'Alphonse Constant was the only man I have known who had attained true inner peace. His good humour was unalterable; his gaiety and liveliness knew no end...He initiated me into the Holy Science by revealing to me what was within my reach, saving me from all excessive mental fatigue. As soon as he saw me become enthusiastic for one idea, he led me to consider its opposite, thus producing equilibrium' (Williams 1975: 155–56). These pupils were typically deeply devoted to Lévi. He appears to have had a strong personal charisma, and clearly they felt they had benefited from his teaching. In person, he was evidently a very warm and convivial person with a lively sense of humour. During the last years of his life up to his death in 1875, he lived a rather poor existence, supported largely by his disciples.

KEY IDEAS

It is not easy to extract a coherent message from his works, because they are rather incoherent. Not only did he rarely re-read or correct what he had written, but his writings tend to be rather rambling and verbose. Also he was not a great scholar. He was careless and often got things wrong. But if one perseveres with his works, one finds that they contain some fascinating ideas, many of which must have seemed very new and exciting to his contemporaries.

I have already mentioned his millenarian view of history and the idea that the world was on the threshold of a new age, the Age of the Paraclete. Later on Lévi became attracted to a different millenarian theory, namely that of the fifteenth-century Abbot Trithemius, who believed that the world was ruled successively by seven archangels and that the rule of the Archangel Michael would begin in 1879. Writing in 1855 Lévi said: 'We see, therefore, that in 1879...in twenty-four years' time – a universal empire will be founded and will secure peace to the world' (McIntosh 2011: 151). Lévi believed that France was going to have this role. Later the idea of the Age of Michael was taken up by Rudolf Steiner.

Another of Lévi's key ideas already touched upon is what one might call perennialism, namely the idea that there is an essential truth informing all the religions of the world and that religious truth and scientific truth are the same. By the same token, what we call the supernatural does not really exist, nor do miracles. The magician is merely performing a superior type of science and working with higher planes of nature.

Nature, for Lévi, is organized according to a system of analogies. Everything is linked by a sort of web of correspondences. The occultist knows how to perceive this web and how to act accordingly. For Lévi, there were two supreme keys to this whole system of correspondences. One was the Tarot, which he referred to as a kind of Rosetta Stone. If you could understand the Tarot, you could interpret all of nature's hieroglyphs and all systems of symbolism. Much of his writing is concerned with the Tarot and he himself designed a pack of cards. In the *Doctrine and Ritual of Transcendental Magic*, he writes of the Tarot: 'It is, in truth, a monumental and extraordinary work, strong and simple as the architecture of the pyramids, and consequently enduring like those – a book which is the summary of all sciences, which can resolve all problems by its infinite combinations, which speaks by evoking thought, is the inspirer and moderator of all possible conceptions, and the masterpiece perhaps of the human mind' (Lévi 1896: 'Introduction').

The second major idea for Lévi was the significance of the Kabbalah. 'All true dogmatic religions,' he wrote 'stem from the Kabbalah and return to her; all that is scientific and grandiose in the religious dreams of all illuminated ones, such as Jakob Boehme, Swedenborg, Saint Martin and so on, is taken from the Kabbalah. The Kabbalah alone...links reason with faith, power with freedom, knowledge with mystery; she has the key to the past, present and future' (Lévi 1896: 'Introduction'). Lévi linked the Kabbalah and the Tarot by assigning the 22 Tarot trumps to the 22 letters of the Hebrew alphabet. Possibly he was the first person to do this. Certainly he was the first to popularize the Tarot as a magical and occult system, and so he is certainly at least partly responsible for the hundreds, maybe thousands of different Tarot packs that are available today.

Language, the word, was very important to Lévi. He attached great importance to the Hebrew alphabet and the idea that the letters with their corresponding numbers represented certain primal forces in the universe: 'In order to pronounce duly the great words of the Qabalah, one must pronounce them with a complete intelligence, with a will that nothing checks, an activity that nothing daunts. In magic, to have said is to have done; the word begins with letters, it ends with acts' (Lévi 1969: 174).

Another very important concept in Lévi's work is what he called the 'astral light', a term that later became familiar to Theosophists through the works of Madame Blavatsky. She also used the term *akasha*. In the *Dogma and Ritual of High Magic*, Lévi argues that

> There exists in nature a force infinitely exceeding that of steam, a force that would enable the man capable of seizing and directing it to change the face of the world. The ancients knew this force: it consists of a universal agent whose supreme law is equilibrium and whose direction is directly related to the great arcanum of transcendental magic. Through the use of this agent one can change the very order of the seasons, produce the phenomenon of day in the middle of the night, enter instantly into contacts with the farthest ends of the earth, see events on the other side of the world, as Apollonius did, heal or attack at a distance, and confer on one's speech universal success and influence.
>
> (Williams 1975: 101)

Here again Lévi is very much ahead of his time anticipating some of the ideas of modern psychology. For example, Wilhelm Reich in the 1930s, with his concept of 'orgone energy', was postulating something very similar to Lévi's concept of the astral light. Orgone energy, as Reich saw it, was a vital, omnipresent substance which pervaded all of life and could be directed to cure diseases and even manipulate the weather. The astral light, according to Lévi, has another important function, as a sort of universal archive, where everything that happens is recorded. This reappears as 'the akashic records' in Blavatsky's thought.

Lévi has some other interesting things to say about the astral light. He sees it as an explanation for spiritualistic phenomena. At that time, spiritualism was a new phenomenon, and one of its most famous mediums was the Anglo-American Daniel Dunglas Home (1833–86), who had caused quite a sensation in Paris with his séances, during which ghostly ectoplasmic figures and other strange phenomena would appear. Lévi's explanation was that these were simply traces of the living left in the astral light before they had died. He also talks about how the astral light operates in the formation of a child in the womb. He writes: 'At the moment of conception the astral light changes into human light and becomes the first sheath of the soul, combining with the finest of fluids and forming the etheric body or sidereal phantom, of which Paracelsus writes in his Philosophy of Intuition' (Lévi 1896: 'Introduction').

For Lévi the astral light enables all magical operations to take place. The instrument that the magician uses to operate on the astral light is the faculty of imagination, used in combination with intelligence and will. As he puts it in *Transcendental Magic, its Doctrine and Ritual*,

> Intelligence and will are tools of incalculable power and capacity. But intelligence and will possess as their help-mate and instrument a faculty which is too imperfectly known, the omnipotence of which belongs exclusively to the domain of magic. I speak of the imagination…The imagination, in effect, is like the soul's eye; therein forms are outlined and preserved; thereby we behold the reflections of the invisible world; it is the glass of visions and the apparatus of magical life. By its intervention we heal diseases, modify the seasons, warn off death from the living and raise the dead to life, because it is the imagination which exalts the will and gives it power over the Universal Agent.
>
> (Lévi 1896: 'Introduction')

The aim of the magician, Lévi says, is to gain mastery over the astral light through the use of the imagination and the will. In order to do this the magician has to develop equilibrium – balance between the polarities that exist in the astral light and between which powerful currents are always flowing back and forth. So the magician is constantly striving for this equilibrium, striving to strike a balance between masculine and feminine, positive and negative, dark and light, heaven and earth, freedom and authority, and so on. This is symbolized by the figure of the Juggler or Magician in Lévi's Tarot pack, showing the adept, poised between the polarities and in perfect command of himself and the invisible forces around him.

In this work the magician has a whole variety of instruments at his disposal – signs, symbols, words of power, magical weapons. Pentacles or talismans also played a role in his magic – objects inscribed with symbols of power and then charged by the magician. Thus every magician, according to Lévi, is engaged in a great work of self-transformation, and the ideal that he or she is aiming at is symbolized by the pentagram, signifying the dominion of intelligence and will over the forces of our lower nature. This is a condition that can only be won through long, patient study and discipline.

One of Lévi's remarkable drawings, included in *Dogme et rituel de la haute magie*, is called *The Sacerdotal Hand*. It shows a priestly hand, raised in benediction and casting a devilish shadow on to a wall. The text accompanying it reads '*Per benedictionem maledictus adumbratur*' ('by benediction the maledicted one [the Devil] is shadowed forth'). (Lévi has spelt '*benedictionem*' wrongly, with an 'n' instead of an 'm' – an example of how careless he could be.) The message appears to be: where there is light there is shadow. In other words, if one concentrates only on what is light and agreeable one will create a shadow within oneself. Here again, Lévi is ahead of his time. This anticipates the Jungian concept of the shadow, as does his concept of the imagination as the key tool in magic, where the active imagination plays an important role in the psychotherapeutic process.

Even more famous is Lévi's drawing, also from *Dogme et rituel de la haute magie*, entitled *Baphomet* or the *Goat of Mendès*, which has been reproduced innumerable times in books and magazines dealing with magic and the occult. It has often been mistaken for a satanic image, which it is most definitely not. In fact the image symbolizes the balance that is necessary for working with the 'astral light'. The goat represents dense, earth-bound nature, but has angel's wings representing heavenly aspiration. It has female breasts, but a male phallus. The four elements are shown by the hooves resting on the globe (earth), the fish scales on the belly (water), the wings (air) and the torch rising from the head (fire). Darkness and light are present in the black and white crescent moons and in the black and white serpents curled around the caduceus-like phallus. The right arm points up, the left down, and the words written on the arms, 'SOLVE' and 'COAGULA', taken from alchemy, refer to the two key operations necessary to working successfully with the astral light. First, the light must be fixed and concentrated (*coagula*) and then projected as a flow of energy (*solve*). In the centre of the goat's forehead is a pentagram, which, for Lévi, represents the dominion of will over the astral light. In the iconography of esotericism this figure has become one of those instantly recognized images like – in a wider context – Leonardo's *Vitruvian Man*, or Munch's *The Scream* or Andy Warhol's portrait of Marilyn Monroe. It has been widely commercialized and appears on everything from t-shirts to carrier bags.

THE RECEPTION OF LÉVI

Lévi's influence quickly spread outside France. Important for his reputation in England were the translations of his works by A.E. Waite. Lévi's writings had already been available in French in England, but the first translation by Waite was *The Mysteries of Magic. A Digest of the Writings of Éliphas Lévi with Biographical and Critical Essay*, published in 1886. Waite's translation of *Transcendental Magic, its Doctrine and Ritual* appeared in 1896 and of *The History of Magic* in 1913 – published by Rider, one of the major esoteric publishing houses in Britain. When *The History of Magic* appeared, the *Daily Citizen* newspaper gave it an almost full-page review, written very sympathetically by a reviewer called A.E. Manning Foster, who ended the review by saying that 'on the whole, Eliphas Lévi fulfils his message clearly and triumphantly after the manner of all great teachers and prophets'.

Waite, in his autobiography, *Shadows of Life and Thought*, writes: 'I have mentioned a general debt which I owed to *Isis Unveiled*, and there is another to be recorded now. H.P.B. [i.e. Helena Petrovna Blavatsky] brought me to Eliphas Lévi, Alphonse Louis Constant, "the French occultist" – so he was termed then, as if *par excellence*' (Waite 1938: 73). At the same time, Waite was sometimes derogatory about Lévi's knowledge: 'Over occult literature he had troubled next to nothing but had a gift of suggesting to readers that he knew everything' (Waite 1938: 98).

Another of Lévi's works, *The Key of the Mysteries*, was translated by Aleister Crowley (1959), who had an extraordinarily high regard for Lévi, and in his Introduction wrote that 'this is the masterpiece of Lévi. He reaches an exaltation of both thought and language which is equal to that of any other writer known to us' (Crowley 1959: 8).

The Theosophists repeatedly expressed admiration for Lévi. For example, in 1881, Lévi's former pupil Baron Spedalieri wrote a letter to *The Theosophist* at a time when the Theosophical Society was being attacked in the journal *The Spiritualist*. An editorial comment printed with Spedalieri's letter reads: 'It is with feelings of sincere gratitude that we thank Baron Spédalieri for his most valuable contribution. The late Éliphas Lévi was the most learned Kabalist and Occultist of our age in Europe, and everything from his pen is precious to us, in so far as it helps us to compare notes with the Eastern Occult doctrines and, by the light thrown upon both' (*The Theosophist*, Vol. III, No. 1, October 1881).

Mention should also be made of Lévi's influence on the Hermetic Order of the Golden Dawn, which incorporated parts of Lévi's work directly into its rituals – for example, Lévi's prayers of the elementals. Lévi's concept of the elementals is described very interestingly in *Transcendental Magic*, where he writes:

> Elementary spirits are like children; they torment chiefly those who trouble about them, unless they are controlled by high reason and great severity. We designate such spirits under the name of occult elements, and it is these who frequently occasion our bizarre or disturbing dreams, who produce the movements of the divining rod and rappings upon walls or furniture, but they can manifest no thought other than our own, and when we are not thinking, they speak to us with all the incoherence of dreams.
>
> (Waite 1896)

Translated into modern psychological terms, what he appears to be saying is that these elemental beings are fragments of our own unconscious, which can haunt us unless we bring them under our conscious control. This is in effect part of what the Golden Dawn was trying to teach its initiates. So, for example, the Theoricus grade of the Golden Dawn was attributed to the element air, and at the closing of the ceremony the participants recited the *Prayer of the Sylphs*, which was taken directly from Lévi:

> Spirit of Life! Spirit of Wisdom. Whose breath giveth forth and withdraweth the form of all things:
>
> Thou, before Whom the life of beings is but a shadow which changeth, and a vapour which passeth:
>
> Thou, who mountest upon the clouds, and Who walkest upon the Wings of the Wind.
>
> Thou, Who breathest forth Thy Breath, and endless space is peopled:
>
> Thou, Who drawest in Thy Breath, and all that cometh forth from Thee returneth unto Thee!
>
> Ceaseless Motion, in Eternal Stability, be Thou eternally blessed!
>
> We praise Thee and we bless Thee in the changeless empire of Created Light, of shades, of Reflections, and of Images –
>
> And we aspire without cessation unto Thy Immutable and Imperishable Brilliance.
>
> (Regardie 1978: 89–90)

Here it is not the sylphs themselves who are being addressed but rather God in his aspect as lord of the element air. Similarly, the ritual for the Zelator grade, which corresponds to the element earth, includes Lévi's *Prayer of the Gnomes*.

In the United States Lévi's ideas were taken up by the masonic writer Albert Pike – almost an exact contemporary of Lévi – who became prominent in the Southern Jurisdiction of the Scottish Rite, re-wrote its rituals and wrote an immense book called *Morals and Dogmas of the Ancient and Accepted Scottish Rite of Freemasonry*, a vast compendium of esoteric lore, published in 1871, which for many years was considered a sort of Bible of the Scottish Rite. Many passages in it are taken directly from Lévi.

We also find Lévi's influence in a group called the Hermetic Brotherhood of Luxor, active on both sides of the Atlantic from 1884, with certain similarities to the Golden Dawn, but where the members operated on their own, receiving the lessons by mail. Some of these lessons included elements taken directly from Lévi (Godwin et al. 1995).

As Wouter Hanegraaff has said of Lévi, 'the brilliance of his literary style, and arguably his synthesis as a whole has not always received the appreciation it deserves...It makes...sense to see him as what he was: an intelligent and creative amateur of considerable although unsystematic erudition, driven by sincere idealism and an enthusiastic joy of discovery, who had to work with scattered and chaotic fragments of learning but somehow managed to create something new and quite original out of it' (Hanegraaff 2010: 107–28).

REFERENCES AND FURTHER READING

Chacornac, P. (1926) *Eliphas Lévi, rénovateur de l'occultisme en France*, Paris: Chacornac.

Constant, Alphonse-Louis (1841) *La Bible de la Liberté*, Paris: Le Gallois.

——(1841) *L'Assomption de la femme*, Paris: Le Gallois.

——(1848) *Le Testament de la liberté*, Paris: J. Frey.

Godwin, J., Chanel, C. and Deveney, J.P. eds. (1995) *The Hermetic Brotherhood of Luxor: Initiatic and Historical Documents of an Order of Practical Occultism*, York Beach, Maine: Samuel Weiser.

Hanegraaff, W. (2010) 'The Beginnings of Occultist Kabbalah: Adolph Franck and Eliphas Lévi' in Boaz Huss, Marco Pasi and Kocku von Stuckrad, eds., *Kabbalah and Modernity*. Leiden: Brill.

Laurant, J-P. (2005) 'Eliphas Lévi', in Wouter J. Hanegraaff, ed., *Dictionary of Gnosis and Western Esotericism*, Vol. II, Leiden: Brill, 2005, 689–92.

Lévi, E. (1896) *Dogme et Rituel de la Haute Magie*, trans. by A.E. Waite as *Transcendental Magic, its Doctrine and Ritual*, London: George Redway; Rider, 1968.

——(1969) *La Clé des grandes mystères*, trans. by Aleister Crowley as *The Key of the Mysteries*, London: Rider, 1969.

McIntosh, C. (2011) *Eliphas Lévi and the French Occult Revival*, Albany: State University of New York Press.

Regardie, I. (1978) *The Golden Dawn*, St. Paul, Minnesota: Llewellyn Publications.

Williams, T. (1975) *Eliphas Lévi: Master of Occultism*, Tuscaloosa: University of Alabama Press.

CHAPTER EIGHTEEN

PASCHAL BEVERLY RANDOLPH

Hugh Urban

Paschal Beverly Randolph (1825–75) was an American spiritualist, Rosicrucian, and sex magician. Although not well known today, Randolph was one of the most important figures in the development of nineteenth-century esotericism, an eloquent advocate of social reform, and arguably the founding father of modern sexual magic.

Born in the slums of New York City, Randolph was a poor, 'free black' – an African American who was not a slave, prior to abolition. Orphaned at an early age, he was largely self-educated, but quickly emerged as one of the most important and prolific figures in the blossoming American Spiritualist movement during the 1850s and 1860s. In 1855 and 1857, Randolph left the U.S. to travel widely abroad, exploring not only Europe, but also Asia Minor and the Middle East. According to his own account, it was while traveling in the areas of Jerusalem and Bethlehem that he met a dark Arab maiden who first revealed to him the spiritual mysteries of love; afterward, he claimed to have encountered a group of fakirs or Sufis (possibly members of the Shi'ite group the Nusai'iri or Ansairi) who initiated him into a variety of occult and alchemical arts (1874, 48, 218; Deveney 1997, 211; Urban 2005, 66).

In the United States, Randolph earned a widespread reputation as an eloquent trance speaker and medium, particularly for his channeling of the more 'reform-minded spirits.' Like other Spiritualists of the mid-nineteenth century, Randolph spoke in his trance states not only about otherworldly matters but also about very immediate social, political, and gender issues, such as abolition, race, gender roles, marriage, and women's rights. Speaking at the Harmonial Convention of 1854, Randolph urged his audience to 'look forward to an age of gold in which peace on earth would prevail, and all men could meet...without distinction of color, sex or money' (Godwin 1994, 250). Although by no means a feminist in any modern sense of the term, he did engage enthusiastically in the most intense sexual debates of his era. Like other Spiritualists he decried the practice of marriage in his day as a form of institutionalized slavery in which women were mere property for male enjoyment; and he was a rare advocate of women's sexuality, believing that mutual pleasure in conjugal love was essential for both a healthy marriage and a healthy society (Urban 2005, 70–76).

Indeed, Randolph's writings on love and marriage would eventually become a tremendous source of scandal (and entertainment) when he was put on trial for the charge of disseminating dangerous 'free love' literature and all manner of sexual indecency to the public. In response Randolph published his own fictionalized account of the 'The Great Free Love Trial' in 1872. In the end, he took a certain delight in poking fun at his prosecuting attorney, who was unable to prove anything more against him than that he 'encouraged women to think of themselves as equal to men' (Godwin 1994, 256).

Perhaps Randolph's most lasting contribution to modern esotericism, however, was his practice of sexual magic or 'affectional alchemy.' While there is a long association between magic and sexuality in the Western esoteric tradition, Randolph was arguably the first to really develop the technique of using physical intercourse and the moment of orgasm as a source of magical power (Urban 2005, 21–80). In Randolph's view, male and female are complementary physical and spiritual forces, polarized in their heads and genitals like two magnets. The moment of sexual union is in turn the most 'solemn, energetic and powerful moment he can ever know on earth,' as the instant in which the physical realm is suddenly opened up to the energies of the cosmos and new life is infused from the spiritual realm into the material. Indeed, 'true sex power is God power'; by harnessing this tremendous creative power, the magus can achieve whatever he prays for at the moment 'when Love is in the ascendant' (Deveney 1997, 339–40).

Randolph listed a wide array of uses for sexual magic, ranging from the mundane to the sublime: it may be used to win the affections of a straying lover or secure financial gain; but it may also be the means to achieve 'the loftiest insight possible to the earthly soul' (Deveney 1997, 337). Ultimately, however, Randolph saw in sexual magic not simply a form of personal fulfillment but also the key to proper relations between male and female and thus the means to creating a harmonious social order and even a kind of 'social millennium.' In sexual love, 'he saw the greatest hope for the regeneration of the world...as well as social transformation and the basis of a non-repressive civilization' (Rosemont 1997, xv).

Randolph suffered a series of personal misfortunes in his later years. After falling from a train in 1873, he was left a paralyzed invalid. Intoxicated and suspicious that his wife had betrayed him, he committed suicide in 1875. However, his influence would extend long beyond his death. His writings on sexual magic would have an impact – either directly or indirectly – on virtually all later forms of sexual occultism, including important esoteric groups such as the Hermetic brotherhood of Luxor and the Ordo Templi Orientis, the Russian occultist Maria de Naglowska (who translated his work into French in the hugely influential text *Magia Sexualis* in 1931), and the greatest sexual magician of modern times, Aleister Crowley (Urban 2005, 81–161; Godwin et al. 1995). In sum, 'through Randolph's influence the genie had been released from the bottle,' and a wide array of sexual practices flourished throughout the modern esoteric tradition (Deveney 1997, 252).

REFERENCES AND FURTHER READING

Deveney, John Patrick (1997) *Paschal Beverly Randolph: A Nineteenth-Century American Spiritualist, Rosicrucian and Sex Magician*, Albany, NY: SUNY Press.

——(2008) 'Paschal Beverly Randolph and Sexual Magic', in Wouter H. Hanegraaff and Jeffrey J. Kripal (eds.), *Hidden Intercourse: Eros and Sexuality in the History of Western Esotericism*, Leiden: Brill, 355–68.

Godwin, Joscelyn (1994) *The Theosophical Enlightenment*. Albany, NY: SUNY Press.

Godwin, Joscelyn, Christian Chanel and John Deveney (1995) *The Hermetic Brotherhood of Luxor*, York Beach, ME: Samuel Weiser.

Naglowska, Maria de, trans. (1931) *Magia Sexualis*, Paris: Robert Telin.

Randolph, Paschal Beverly(1861–62) *The Great Secret: or Physical Love in Health and Disease*, San Francisco: Pilkington & Randolph.

——(1872) *P.B. Randolph: The 'Learned Pundit' and 'Man with Two Souls,' His Curious Life, Works and Career: The Great Free Love Trial*, Boston: Randolph.

——(1874) *Eulis! The Mystery of Love*, Toledo, OH: Randolph.

——(1978) *The Immortality of Love: Unveiling the Secret Arcanum of Affectional Alchemy*, Quakertown, PA: Beverly Hall.

Rosemont, Franklin (1997) 'Foreword' to John Patrick Deveney, *Paschal Beverly Randolph: A Nineteenth-Century American Spiritualist, Rosicrucian and Sex Magician*, Albany, NY: SUNY Press.

Urban, Hugh B. (2005) *Magia Sexualis: Sex, Magic and Liberation in Modern Western Esotericism*, Berkeley: University of California Press.

CHAPTER NINETEEN

WILLIAM WYNN WESTCOTT

Francisco Santos Silva

William Wynn Westcott (1848–1925) was a medical doctor, writer, editor and occultist, most famous for being one of the co-founders of the Hermetic Order of the Golden Dawn, together with Samuel Mathers and William Robert Woodman. Born in Leamington, England, the youngest of six siblings, his parents died early in his life and he was adopted by his uncle, Richard Westcott Martyn, who, like his father, was a surgeon. Westcott attended Queen Elizabeth Grammar School at Kingston-upon-Thames, following which he studied medicine at University College in London. In 1871, he became a partner at his uncle's practice in Martock, Somerset. It was during this period that he met and married Elizabeth Burnett, with whom he had five children. (Unfortunately for Westcott, she did not share his interest in occultism.)

Other than his interests in esoteric and occult topics, which took up much of his time, Westcott worked on medical texts, such as (with W.H. Martindale) *The Extra Pharmacopeia of Unofficial Drugs* and, in 1885, *Suicide: Its History, Literature, Jurisprudence, Causation and Prevention.* In 1918, Wescott moved to Durban in South Africa with his wife, in order to live with one of their daughters. He eventually died there in 1925, surviving his wife and all of his four children.

If the contours of Westcott's non-occultist life can be easily traced, his involvement with esoteric and occult movements is a more complex task. As with his co-founder of the Golden Dawn, Samuel Liddell Mathers, Westcott began his career with Freemasonry, joining the Parrett and Axe Lodge, in Crewkerne, in 1871 and becoming its Worshipful Master in 1874. He also joined other lodges, such as the Lodge of Brotherly Love in Yeovil, and William de Irwin Mark Lodge, also in Yeovil. In 1875, he applied to the 'Societas Rosicruciana in Anglia' (SRIA), although he did not become a member until 1880, shortly before he moved to London, in 1881. Indeed, it's worth noting that following his uncle's death in 1879, he took time away from work and retired to Hendon in order to study Kabbalah, hermeticism, alchemy and Rosicrucianism. The point is that, it was this period of study that seems to have sharpened his interests and led him to join the SRIA. Eventually he became the General Secretary of the SRIA in 1882 and, in 1892, was elected Supreme Magus, a position he held for 33 years.

Two years after joining SRIA, he met Mathers and, with Woodman, the Supreme Magus of the SRIA, he developed ideas that would lead to the foundation of the Hermetic Order of the Golden Dawn. Influenced by Anna Kingsford and Edward Maitland's Hermetic Society, as well as the Theosophical Society, Westcott and Mathers set out to create a practical order focused on Western esotericism. As such, they moved away from the broadly Oriental interests of the Theosophical Society and provided a practical interpretation of the more theoretical teachings of the Hermetic Society. In 1887, Westcott claimed to have acquired a manuscript from Reverend A. F. A. Woodford, an elderly Masonic scholar who died soon after passing the papers on. Written in a cipher that Westcott claimed to be able to interpret, the cipher manuscripts contained a rough draft of a series of ritual initiations. These became central to the construction of the rituals of the Golden Dawn. In actual fact, the manuscript was almost certainly produced within the SRIA and was probably the creation of Kenneth R. H. Mackenzie, the author of *The Royal Masonic Encyclopedia.* The cipher manuscripts also contained the name and address of a German adept, Fraulein Sprengel, who Westcott claimed to have given him the charter for the foundation of the British chapter of the Goldene Dämmerung, which would become the Hermetic Order of the Golden Dawn. Indeed, he appears to have forged, or to have commissioned forgeries of correspondence from this person. Although this would indicate that the idea for the creation of the Hermetic Order of the Golden Dawn was Westcott's, it is clear that from the outset he and Mathers considered themselves equal partners, with Woodman, busy with the affairs of SRIA, in their shadow. Westcott and Mathers collaborated in creating the rituals of the outer order and planning out its structure and body of teachings. Woodman's part in the process seemed to be one of simply lending the authority of the Supreme Magus of the SRIA. Indeed, he died soon after the foundation of the Golden Dawn. The official inauguration of the Order was in 1888 and, despite Westcott's initial dominant role in the early years of the Golden Dawn, it gradually became clear that the principal figure was Mathers, not least because he began developing the ideas and rituals for a second or inner order of the Golden Dawn. Moreover, following Woodman's death, Westcott's election as Grand Magus of the SRIA in 1892 made it difficult for him to continue a high level of involvement. However, perhaps the most important break with the organization came as a result of his professional life as Coroner for North East London and Central Middlesex, a post he took up 1881 and held until his retirement in 1918. In March, 1897, his occult interests became known to the authorities, when some of his papers, on which were printed his name and address, were left in a cab. The authorities advised him that the consequences would be serious if it were to become known that a Coroner of the Crown was also an occultist. Westcott resigned from the Golden Dawn, although remaining as an *ex officio* advisor. He was replaced as Chief Adept in Anglia by Florence Farr.

In 1900, Mathers admitted to Farr that Westcott had fabricated the Fraulein Sprengel narrative and that there was no German Order which had supposedly chartered the English temples of the Golden Dawn. Hence, Westcott was again drawn into the politics of the Golden Dawn, as members insisted on knowing the truth. Although maintaining his version of events, he could offer no proof.

In 1910, Aleister Crowley published Golden Dawn material in his periodical *The Equinox*, which led Mathers to institute legal proceedings. In the same publication,

Crowley also printed part of the letter from Mathers to Farr in which Westcott is accused of forgery. However, Westcott, in a letter to Golden Dawn member, John William Brodie-Innes, makes it clear that, as far as he is concerned, the best thing to be done about it is to simply to 'grin and bear it', as Crowley is a 'very bad man', who seems to relish the fact that Mathers would need him (Westcott) to prove the copyright of the Golden Dawn's rituals. Feeling mistreated by Mathers and hurt by his accusations, Westcott is clearly pleased with the situation. Indeed, because of this, he was able to compel Mathers to retract his accusations of forgery in exchange for help in the case.

Westcott's significance for modern esotericism can be found, not only in his involvement with the establishment of the Golden Dawn, but also in numerous influential publications exploring subjects as diverse as numerology, alchemy, astrology, freemasonry, kabbalah, Rosicrucianism, Theosophy and magic. He also edited the *Collectanea Hermetica*, an important nine-volume collection of esoteric texts from ancient and modern sources. Finally, of particular note are his translations of classical texts, such as the Jewish *Sepher Yetzirah*, the Neo-Platonist *Chaldaean Oracles*, and Eliphas Lévi's *Magical Ritual of the Sanctum Regnum*.

REFERENCE AND FURTHER READING

Gilbert, R.A. (1997). *Revelations of the Golden Dawn*, Slough: Foulsham.

——(1997) 'Afterword – From Cipher to Enigma: The Role of William Wynn Westcott in the Creation of the Hermetic Order of the Golden Dawn', in C. P. Runyon, *Secrets of the Golden Dawn Cypher Manuscript*, Pasadena: C.H.S.

Pasi, M. (2006) 'Westcott, William Wynn', in W. Hanegraaf, ed., *Dictionary of Gnosis and Western Esotericism*, Leiden: Brill, 1168–70.

Howe, E. (1978) *Magicians of the Golden Dawn*, Boston: Red Wheel/Weiser.

Kuntz, D. (1996) *The Golden Dawn Source Book*, Edmonds: Holmes.

Westcott, W.W. (1887) *Sepher Yetzirah or The Book of Creation*. Online: http://www.sacred-texts.com/jud/yetzirah.htm (accessed: 3 March 2013).

——(1895) *The Chaldean Oracles of Zoroaster*. Online: http://www.esotericarchives.com/oracle/oraclez.htm (accessed: 3 March 2013).

CHAPTER TWENTY

THE HERMETIC ORDER OF THE GOLDEN DAWN

Robert A. Gilbert

THE ORIGINS OF THE GOLDEN DAWN

The Hermetic Order of the Golden Dawn was created in response to a demand among occultists for a society in which the occult arts and sciences could be practised rather than simply studied. It was a child of the late Victorian era that survived fitfully into the first decades of the twentieth century and received a new lease of life in 1969 when its rituals were re-published. It is now far more widely known – and publicly accessible – than it ever was in its early years.

But what exactly *was* the Golden Dawn, who created it and what is its history? 'The Esoteric Order of the Golden Dawn in the Outer', as it was first styled, conformed to Dion Fortune's definition of such a body as a fraternity: 'Wherein a secret wisdom unknown to the generality of mankind might be learnt, and to which admission was obtained by means of an initiation in which tests and ritual played their part' (1928: ix). This 'secret wisdom' comprised the whole spectrum of divinatory and magical practices that constitute the occult arts and sciences, and the theoretical 'occult philosophy' that was believed to underpin them.

The basic model for all such societies was the one described in 1614 in the *Fama Fraternitatis*, but that 'Rosicrucian fraternity' had no existence in the real world. It was simply a ground plan for an ideal Christian community designed to bring about a socio-religious reformation of society. Its spiritual philosophy was taught by way of symbolic imagery, and its members vowed to heal the sick – but it had no ceremonial structure and was not an initiatic Order. Despite all this there were many subsequent attempts to establish 'real' Rosicrucian Orders.

Such Orders arose across continental Europe in the eighteenth century in the wake of speculative Freemasonry. The most spectacular was the German quasi-masonic Order of the Golden and Rosy Cross, which flourished in various forms during the later eighteenth century. It developed its own rituals and produced a series of complex symbolic drawings, the *Geheime Figuren* (Secret Symbols), that formed a compendium of Rosicrucian, alchemical and apocalyptic imagery to illustrate its doctrines. Although these were known in Britain to a small number of masonic occultists, no specifically Rosicrucian society existed in England until the *Societas Rosicruciana in Anglia* (SRIA) was founded in 1867 (see, Greensill, 2003).

The SRIA was, however, a study society restricted to Christian freemasons, and although it was initiatic, with graduated rituals of admission and advancement based on the stages of the kabbalistic Tree of Life, it was not designed for practical occultists. But after twenty years of theory three of the society's most senior members – Dr. W.R. Woodman, Dr. William Wynn Westcott and S.L. Mathers – perceived a demand, both within and beyond the SRIA, for an order that would add practice to theory, and in 1887 one of them, Dr. Westcott, decided that the time was right for its creation.

This was not a capricious decision. There was a public demand for such esoteric movements as Spiritualism and Theosophy, both of which – unlike Freemasonry – were open to women. What they lacked, other than mediumship, was any practical esoteric pursuit, and the occultism of Theosophy was largely oriental and dismissive of Christianity. To counter this two Christian esotericists, Anna Kingsford and Edward Maitland, founded the Hermetic Society in 1884. Both Westcott and Mathers became active members, but when Kingsford fell seriously ill in 1886 the society came to an end.

Earlier in 1886 Westcott had obtained the papers of Kenneth Mackenzie, a masonic writer and occultist who had recently died, and found among them a manuscript containing a series of outline ritual texts for an unidentified, non-masonic, esoteric order. The rituals were composed in English but Mackenzie had written them out, on old paper, in a cipher taken from the sixteenth-century *Polygraphia* of Trithemius. Westcott, who was familiar with the cipher, soon translated the texts and began to create the Golden Dawn. The first steps were taken in tandem: the conversion of the outline texts into coherent and workable rituals, and the parallel creation of a legend – the mythical history of the new order.

This history was important. Almost all esoteric and masonic bodies claimed fanciful pre-histories and the shadowy presence of Masters or Secret Chiefs. None of them, however, could match the false claims and false documents that Westcott fabricated for the Golden Dawn. His first inventions concerned his discovery of the cipher manuscript.

Westcott claimed that he had obtained it from a masonic historian, the Rev. A.F.A. Woodford. But the claim, and copies in Westcott's hand of supporting letters, were not produced until after Woodford's death in December 1887. One letter advised Westcott to see 'old Soror "Sapiens Dominabitur Astris" in Germany', who was identified as 'Fr. A. Sprengel' of Stuttgart. He promptly wrote to her – his letters being put into German, and the replies translated for him by a business colleague – and she raised Westcott to the '7 = 4 [Grade] of the Second Order in England', authorising him to 'Begin a new Temple No. 3'. He was also authorised to sign documents on her behalf, while a final letter, of August 1890, advised Westcott of her death (for the texts of these letters and of other related letters, public and private, see Küntz, 1996b).

THE FOUNDATION OF THE ORDER

Although the paper is dated 1809, textual references in the manuscript indicate that it was composed by Mackenzie around 1880 (for a facsimile and English translation, see Küntz, 1996a). The associated letters are either forgeries or fantasies, written by or for Westcott. They formed only a part of the mythical history of the Golden Dawn, but they convinced his fellow Chiefs and the future membership that it had existed in the real world. The official history, given to members and potential members of the Order, went through at least four versions between 1888 and 1895 – altered so that additional past members could be inserted once they were conveniently dead.

This 'Historical Lecture' defines the Order as 'an Hermetic Society whose members are taught the principles of Occult Science and the Magic of Hermes', among which are alchemy, the Hebrew kabbalah and the 'the magic of the Egyptians'. What follows is a rambling history of the ancient Mysteries and of the Order's descent from the Rosicrucian Fraternity, down to its revival by Westcott and his fellows. The new initiate is also provided with an outline of the Order's grade structure and the mode of progress through the grades.

Initiates are also given the names of various former members – among them Eliphas Levi and Kenneth Mackenzie – and learn that an earlier English Temple, 'Hermanubis No. 2...had ceased to exist' by 1850. Westcott's discovery of the cipher manuscripts is then described in all its falsity, and the 'Historical Lecture' closes by reminding the Neophyte of the continuing importance of female occultists and of the non-masonic nature of the Golden Dawn.

From this point onwards the 'Hermetic Order of the Golden Dawn' (as it should now be called) begins its material existence, but is there any truth in Westcott's 'pre-history'? Alas, there is none. All of Westcott's accounts of the origins of the Golden Dawn are misleading and deceitful, for there is no evidence that any earlier Temples existed while the masonic lodges that Westcott claimed as forerunners were nothing of the sort and none of his named adepts were ever members of the Golden Dawn (see Gilbert, 1998: 122–23).

Of course, being dead none of them could give the lie to Westcott's fictions, while potential sceptics in the SRIA, who might have asked awkward questions, were not informed of the imminent rebirth of the ancient Order that supposedly lay behind their modern, and well-documented, society.

But why did Westcott create this fantasy of origin ? For an Order that claimed to be Rosicrucian, a German source was essential and for esoteric Orders 'Secret Chiefs' had become a *sine qua non* in the late nineteenth century. With his German adepts Westcott had provided both, but he probably did believe in the reality of Secret Chiefs in the abstract, even though he knew that his own variety were unreal. Westcott's forgeries and inventions should, perhaps, be seen as a prime instance of believing that the end justifies the means. It is also certain that he did believe that his Order – the whole system of rituals, ceremonies and instruction – was spiritually sound and would benefit aspirant practical occultists, to a far greater degree than would the available alternatives.

Westcott had also convinced his co-Chiefs, Woodman and Mathers, that the cipher manuscripts and the associated letters were genuine and their role in the Order's creation was, at least initially, that of innocent enthusiasts. However, inconvenient truths cannot be buried forever, as Westcott was to find out to his cost.

THE BEGINNINGS OF A NEW ORDER: THE GOLDEN DAWN IN PRACTICE

Set against the hyperbole of its mythical origins, the reality of Westcott's Order was more mundane. The three co-Chiefs had established their authority to found and govern the Order on 12 February, 1888, when they elevated each other to the Grade of Adeptus Exemptus (7 = 4);[1] chartered themselves 'to constitute and rule the Isis-Urania Temple, No. 3'; and pledged secrecy as to the work, membership and very existence of the Order. Documents were thus signed only with their mottos. Within weeks they began to initiate candidates into Isis-Urania Temple, but without any public fanfare.

From the beginning, 'any approved person *Male* or *Female*', who believed in One God could become a candidate for 'Initiation and Advancement' in the Order, provided also that they were willing to take an Obligation to keep secret everything relating to the Order. In addition, aspiring members were required to choose a motto – usually in Latin – which would become their recognised name within the Order.

And despite the heavy emphasis on secrecy, potential candidates seeking practical occultism soon came forward. Thus at the first meeting of Isis-Urania Temple, on 1 March 1888, nine candidates, of whom three were women – a proportion by gender that prevailed throughout its history – were initiated. This, like all subsequent meetings of Isis-Urania, was held in rooms at Mark Masons' Hall in Great Queen Street, London, but it was soon apparent that Temples elsewhere were necessary.

Before the end of the year the Golden Dawn had more than fifty members, mostly in London and the south-east, but with other Temples established in Weston-super-Mare (Osiris Temple, No. 4) and in Bradford (Horus Temple, No. 5). Horus at Bradford was successful (eleven members initially, rising to fifty-seven), but Osiris Temple soon declined (with only ten members) and by 1895 it was defunct. Other Temples followed – Amen Ra, No. 6 at Edinburgh in 1893 (fifty-four members) and Ahathoor, No. 7 at Paris (twenty-five members).

By 1900 some 350 candidates had been initiated into the Golden Dawn. The common factor that drew them to the Order was an enthusiasm for occultism in both theory and practice, but of the total number more than eighty – one member in four – resigned after taking only the Grade of Neophyte (details of members' names, addresses, mottos and progress were recorded in the Order's address book, for the contents of which see, Gilbert, 1986).

The majority of the membership remained content to accept the disciplined structure of the Golden Dawn and to dedicate themselves to its system of spiritual development by way of ceremony and study. As occultists they were familiar with, and believed in, the concepts of a hierarchical Order and graduated advancement under the guidance of spiritual teachers who could act as intermediaries between the seeker and the Secret Chiefs. Most members of the Golden Dawn were well-educated, cultured men and women, eminently respectable and drawn from the commercial, artistic and professional middle classes. Others were financially independent, and husbands and wives often joined the Order together.

There was also no obvious bias in terms of occupation. Fourteen members, including two of the Chiefs, were medical practitioners, but there were only three clerics – perhaps a reflection of the unorthodox spirituality of the Order.[2] A similarly small number of minor artists entered the Golden Dawn, as did few professional scientists, including the chemist and physicist William Crookes. Literary figures were more prominent in the Order, notably the poet W.B. Yeats. There were many other writers, among whom the best-known were Arthur Machen, Algernon Blackwood, A.E. Waite, the actress Florence Farr, and the infamous Aleister Crowley.

But what was it that drew this disparate community of occultists together into Westcott's esoteric Order? The principal lure seems to have been its unique combination of dramatic ceremonial initiation and advancement, with its complex symbolism and rich visual imagery, and a systematic course of study and instruction in occult theory and practice. And with the suggestion of something beyond all this: the attainment by the initiate of true Adeptship.

This was the expectation of candidates, and after following the path opened up by the Golden Dawn, some of them believed that they had truly become adepts: magicians, of a kind, rather than mere occultists. Others were less sure, unconvinced that this was a suitable spiritual path and unhappy with the way that the Order's governance changed, after the unexpected death of Dr. Woodman in 1891. As Imperator of the Order Woodman had balanced the conflicting attitudes and demands of his co-Chiefs, Westcott and Mathers, but from 1892 onwards Mathers ruled the Order autocratically as Imperator. Westcott became Praemonstrator, in charge of the instruction of members, but without an administrative role.

Previously Westcott had used his diplomatic skills to smooth over tensions with the Theosophical Society by persuading Mme. Blavatsky that the Hermetic Order of the Golden Dawn, despite its Western bias, posed no threat to her society – in which many members of the Golden Dawn, especially in London and Edinburgh, were active. However, in Bradford the differences between dedicated theosophists and masonic Rosicrucians were difficult to reconcile and led to the first major signs of open dissension within the Order.

Both institutions sought to promote occultism, but their emphases and *modus operandi* were very different. The Theosophical Society was a public body with an effective administration, reasonably democratic and open to all through its many branches (lodges) across the country. It sought to disseminate esoteric knowledge by way of public lectures, private study groups and openly published books and journals. In contrast to this the Golden Dawn was a rigidly hierarchical, tightly disciplined and completely private body of initiates, giving instruction to a very limited membership that was obligated to keep the teaching and practices of the Order absolutely secret.

This did not pose any moral or social problems for members from a masonic Rosicrucian background, who were familiar with the hierarchical nature of initiatic Orders and with injunctions to secrecy. But the average theosophist who entered the Golden Dawn was often unable to reconcile these very different approaches to occultism as a way of spiritual development, and was thus likely to resist attempts at enforcing discipline. In 1892 such resistance split the Horus Temple and although some degree of harmony was restored, the exodus of members subtly altered internal perceptions of the Golden Dawn and created the first cracks in its structure. At this point the nature of that structure and of its working practices must be described and explained in some detail.

THE ORGANISATION AND WORKING OF THE GOLDEN DAWN

The Hermetic Order of the Golden Dawn was strictly hierarchical and was governed, in its early years, by a self-appointed triumvirate of Chiefs. Individual Temples were similarly ruled by three Chiefs and all of the officers required for the ceremonial working of the Temples were appointed rather than elected. It was these Chiefs who decided whether or not candidates for admission should be accepted, although they did seek advice when the candidates were unknown to them. From 1892 to 1900, even under Mathers' autocratic rule, officers, while still appointed, were selected on the basis of ability and of acceptability to the members. Despite rigid control the Golden Dawn worked smoothly: its officers were conscientious administrators rather than mere bureaucrats.

Their function was to ensure that the rules and regulations of the Order were maintained and that its basic aims were attained. These were quite clear: the ceremonial initiation and advancement of candidates, and their instruction in the essential features of what is now known as the Western Hermetic Tradition. This instruction was given partly through set lectures and courses of private study, but mostly – and more dramatically – by means of a progressive series of initiatory ceremonies that presented the various aspects of that tradition in symbolic form.

The setting and the working structure of the ceremonies were modelled on those of English Freemasonry, but they were far more colourful and dramatic, and the graduated progress of candidates represented a symbolic ascent of the kabbalistic Tree of Life rather than the building of King Solomon's Temple (an outline account of the arrangement of Temples, the names, functions, robes and regalia of the officers, and the 'secrets', regalia and symbolic correspondences of the various grades is given in Gilbert, 1986. For the complete, illustrated texts of the rituals, see Regardie, 1969). The symbolism employed in Golden Dawn ceremonies was also eclectic: drawn from the Hebrew Kabbalah, Egyptian mythology, the Eleusinian Mysteries and – in the Adept Grades – from Rosicrucian texts.

Masonic parallels were also present in the layout of the Temple on an East–West axis, and in the placing of the officers. Also as in Freemasonry, there was a ceremonial opening and closing for the working of each grade and the ceremony of initiation or advancement followed, to a large extent, the masonic pattern. In the Neophyte grade the candidate, wearing a plain black robe, enters blindfolded, receives a new name (the chosen motto) and is conducted, clockwise, on a symbolic journey around the Temple, during which he is challenged, purified and consecrated by the appropriate officers.

After the first stage of this journey the candidate takes a long and intimidating 'Obligation', with an alarming penalty for any violation, to maintain absolute secrecy with respect to the Order, and 'to prosecute with zeal the study of the occult sciences'. A further procession around the Temple then takes place and the candidate is given the secrets – the signs, grips, words and password – belonging to the grade. After this the principal officer, the Hierophant, instructs the candidate in the symbolic meaning of the furnishings of the Temple, and of the implements and visual imagery employed in the ceremony. The meeting closes with a symbolic meal of bread, salt and wine.

If the initiate persevered in 'the study of the occult sciences' and passed the stiff examinations, then he (or she) might progress through the four further grades of the

Outer Order – those of Zelator, Theoricus, Practicus and Philosophus – that represented the four lower Sephiroth of the Tree of Life (i.e. Malkuth (1 = 10), Yesod (2 = 9), Hod (3 = 8) and Netzach (4 = 7)). There was also the prospect of further examinations that would lead them to becoming notional Adepti Minores (5 = 6), and thus qualified to hold the office of Hierophant. Beyond this was the notional Second Order.

Every member of the Golden Dawn was familiar with the concept of a Second Order, but it was assumed to be dormant. In reality it did not exist until 1891 when Mathers began to create the impressive rituals, based on the discovery of the tomb of Christian Rosencreutz, and the elaborate robes, regalia, fittings and furnishing that would be needed for ceremonial admission to the Adept grades. The ceremony itself was high drama indeed: the candidate took the Obligation in the course of a symbolic crucifixion, after which he was instructed in the legend of Christian Rosencreutz and taken to the door of the Vault. In the next stage the candidate entered the vault, with its dazzling array of painted symbols, and found the entombed Chief Adept. Finally the resurrected Adept received the candidate as a full Adeptus Minor of the R.R. et A.C. – properly the *Ordo Rosae Rubeae et Aureae Crucis* – and instructed him in the symbolism of the grade.

This was only the beginning, for the Adept of the R.R. et A.C. was required to engage in practical magic. The entire system involved making and consecrating magical implements; invoking and banishing elemental beings; practising divination by astrology, geomancy and tarot; Enochian magic; spirit vision and astral projection. In all of these instruction was provided by ritual texts known as 'Flying Rolls', there were constant examinations to be passed and Adepts were obliged to keep records of their magical work (a summary of the working and administration of the Second Order is given in Gilbert, 1986).

The first Vault was established in London in 1892, followed by a second Vault in Edinburgh. Although Adepts were sworn to secrecy about the very existence of the R.R. et A.C., the more perceptive and enthusiastic members of the Golden Dawn soon sought admission and the majority of suitable candidates were duly advanced. By 1900 there were 130 members of the Second Order, evenly divided between men and women, but opposition to Mathers' autocratic rule led to indiscipline, resentment and resignations, and differences over magical practices resulted in the rise of warring factions. Annie Horniman – better known as a theatre manager – was effectively driven from the Order in 1896, and in 1897 Westcott gave up all active involvement in the Golden Dawn, supposedly because of official displeasure over his membership.

Although the Golden Dawn and the R.R. et A.C. continued to gain new recruits, the antagonism between Mathers – who by the later 1890s was living permanently in France – and the bulk of the British membership grew to breaking point, coming to a head early in 1900. From this time onwards disillusionment within the Order grew rapidly until the disintegration of the Golden Dawn became inevitable, hastened by the conflicting agendas of senior members.

THE END OF THE OLD ORDER

The later history of the Golden Dawn thus becomes less the story of a quest for spiritual enlightenment than one of the pursuit of power by competing factions, driven by strong-minded individuals rather than by schools of thought. The process of destruction began with a letter from Mathers to Florence Farr, then a senior member of the R.R. et A.C.

Westcott, Mathers told her, 'has NEVER been at any time either in personal or in written communication with the Secret Chiefs of the Order, he having either himself forged or procured to be forged the professed correspondence between him and them'. He further stated that he had been aware of Westcott's deceit from the beginning, that the entire teaching of the Order was his, and that he alone had been in communication with the Secret Chiefs.

After considering this bombshell, Florence Farr discussed the letter with other senior members of the R.R. et A.C. in early March. They promptly wrote to Mathers for proof of his allegations, and to Westcott for his admission or rebuttal of the truth of Mathers' claims. Westcott denied the charge but provided no evidence in support, while Mathers wrote further intemperate letters asserting his own supremacy in the Order and dismissing from office all those involved in 'rebellion' against him.

A subsequent attempt by Aleister Crowley to seize the Vault of the Adepts on Mathers' behalf failed, but the uproar in the Order led to an immediate schism between those for Mathers and those against him. Some Adepts simply continued with their work, but although the Order became more democratic, further divisions occurred. Then, in October 1901, came a sensational criminal trial that exposed the Order to public ridicule.

Early in 1900 Mathers had been duped, in Paris, by an American couple, Theo and Laura Horos – who pretended to be the real Anna Sprengel. At first Mathers believed them and wrote his sensational letter to Florence Farr, but they soon decamped to London and established a spurious Order modelled on the Golden Dawn. This was simply a criminal enterprise and they were eventually tried for fraud and rape, found guilty and gaoled – but not before the Neophyte ritual had been exposed in court and the original Golden Dawn derided in the press.

As a consequence many members, either disillusioned or fearing public exposure, resigned from the Order during 1902 and its governance became increasingly chaotic. It stabilised to some degree under a triad of new Chiefs during the second half of the year, but they and their proposed Constitution were rejected at the next annual general meeting of the Second Order.

What followed in 1903 was a virtual *coup d'état* by A.E. Waite, who took over both Isis-Urania Temple and the Vault of the Adepts, and renamed the Order 'The Independent and Rectified Rite of the Golden Dawn'. The ethos of the new Order was decidedly 'mystical' rather than magical and it was overtly Christian in nature, but it consisted of no more than a few dozen members.

The 'magical' Adepts under Felkin and Brodie-Innes carried on independently but eventually established a concordat with Waite's Order, and by 1907 their branch of the old Golden Dawn had become the Stella Matutina, with the Outer Order grades worked in a new temple, named Amoun. Both Felkin and Brodie-Innes believed themselves to be in touch with Secret Chiefs and they received, by psychic means, new ritual and instructional material that enabled them to develop even higher grades.

There was also a small group of members who remained loyal to Mathers and set up the Alpha et Omega Temple in London. By 1912 Brodie-Innes had become sceptical of Felkin's supposed German sources and transferred his allegiance to

Mathers, who continued to work in the Ahathoor Temple in Paris until his death in 1918. In 1928, when Mrs. Mathers died, Ahathoor ceased to function.

While all this was taking place Waite had created a new set of rituals and had drawn in some sixty members, but his Independent and Rectified Rite came to an end in 1914 when he closed it down because of internal dissension and founded The Fellowship of the Rosy Cross, which had no connection whatsoever with the old Order. Some of his former members preferred the Golden Dawn and entered the Stella Matutina, which enjoyed steady growth and established new Temples in England and in New Zealand (a detailed history of the Golden Dawn up to 1923 is provided by Howe, 1972).

REBIRTH IN THE NEW WORLD

The Stella Matutina did survive in the inter-war period, but although its Temples continued to operate well into the 1950s, they had suffered from internal dissent and from the oath-breaking of one American member: Israel Regardie.

An American Golden Dawn Temple, Thoth-Hermes No. 8, had been chartered by Mathers in 1897, established in New York in 1904 but had failed to achieve a significant following. The rituals of the Order were also worked, however, by the non-masonic Societas Rosicruciana in America, which was open to both sexes. In March 1926 Regardie was initiated into this society and began his career in the Golden Dawn. He came to England, entered the Hermes Temple of the Stella Matutina and in 1937, after a quarrel with other members, proceeded to publish the entire system of Golden Dawn working and instruction. After this act Regardie lost interest in the Order, only regaining his enthusiasm when persuaded to reissue his book in 1969.

Since then there has been a significant revival of the Golden Dawn, notably in the U.S.A., and variants of 'The Hermetic Order of the Golden Dawn' have proliferated, aided to a great degree by the spread of the Internet and the potential for 'virtual initiation'. What drives this revival is unclear, but there is no sign that enthusiasm for these new versions of the Golden Dawn is declining.

Perhaps it is a case of empty vessels making the most noise, for the Golden Dawn cannot be said to have ever had any cultural significance. Apart from W.B. Yeats, no great literary figures were members of the Order and its only marks on popular culture were the Tarot pack designed by Waite and Pamela Colman Smith, and the literary genre of the 'psychic detective' story.

NOTES

1. The grade system of the Golden Dawn was based on the ten sephiroth of the kabbalistic Tree of Life and a dual numbering was used to show the number of grades through which the candidate had advanced and the number attributed to the sephirah that corresponded to the grade attained.
2. A greater number of clerics, most of them 'High Church' Anglican priests, joined the various branches of the divided Order after 1900. The occupations of many of the more prominent members are given in Howe 1972.

REFERENCES AND FURTHER READING

Armstrong, A. & R.A. Gilbert, eds. (1998), *Golden Dawn: The Proceedings of The Golden Dawn Conference London 1997*. Bristol: privately printed.

Colquhoun, I. (1975), *Sword of Wisdom: Macgregor Mathers and The Golden Dawn*. London: Spearman.

Fortune, D. (1928), *The Esoteric Orders and their Work*. London: Rider.

Gilbert, R.A. (1986), *The Golden Dawn Companion: A Guide to the History, Structure, and Workings of the Hermetic Order of the Golden Dawn*. Wellingborough: Aquarian Press.

——(1987), *The Golden Dawn and The Esoteric Section*. London: Theosophical History Centre.

——(1997), *Revelations of The Golden Dawn. The Rise And Fall of a Magical Order*. London: Quantum.

——(1998), 'Trail of the Chameleon: The Genesis of the Hermetic Order of the Golden Dawn'. In A. Armstrong & R.A. Gilbert (eds.), *Golden Dawn: The Proceedings of The Golden Dawn Conference London 1997*. Bristol: privately printed, 117–35.

Greensill, T.M. (2003), *A History of Rosicrucian Thought and of the Societas Rosicruciana in Anglia*, second edition. London: privately printed.

Hanegraaff, W.J., ed. (2005), *Dictionary of Gnosis and Western Esotericism*, 2 vols. Leiden: Brill.

Howe, E. (1972), *The Magicians of The Golden Dawn: A Documentary History of a Magical Order 1887–1923*. London: Routledge & Kegan Paul.

Küntz, D., ed. (1996a), *The Complete Golden Dawn Cipher Manuscript: Deciphered, Translated, and Edited*. Edmonds, WA: Holmes Publishing Group.

——(1996b), *The Golden Dawn Source Book*. Edmonds, WA: Holmes Publishing Group.

Macgregor Mathers, S.L. (1987), *Astral Projection, Ritual Magic And Alchemy*, edited by King, Francis. Wellingborough: Aquarian Press.

Regardie, I. (1969), *The Golden Dawn. An Account of the Teachings, Rites and Ceremonies of the Order of the Golden Dawn*. Wellingborough: Aquarian Press. Originally 4 vols. Chicago: Aries Press, 1937–40.

Torrens, R.G. (1973), *The Secret Rituals of the Golden Dawn*. Wellingborough: Aquarian Press.

Waite, A.E. (1938), *Shadows of Life and Thought: A Retrospective Review in the Form of Memoirs*. London: Selwyn & Blount.

Westcott, W.W. (2012), *A Magus Among the Adepts: Essays & Addresses*, edited by R.A. Gilbert. York Beach: Teitan Press.

CHAPTER TWENTY-ONE

SAMUEL LIDDELL MATHERS

Francisco Santos Silva

Samuel Liddell 'MacGregor' Mathers (1854–1918) was one of the founders of the Hermetic Order of the Golden Dawn, the creator of its inner order rituals, and a translator and popularizer of both magical grimoires and kabbalistic texts. As such, he can be seen as a key figure in the development of modern esotericism with a broad influence, which can now be found in a wide spectrum of magic-oriented new religious movements and alternative spiritualities.

Very little is known of Mathers' personal life. We can, however, derive some information about his early life from a brief biographical note provided by William Wynn Westcott – his co-founder of the Hermetic Order of the Golden Dawn – which tells us that he was born on 8 January 1854, in Hackney, London and mentions that his father, William M. Mathers, died early in his life and that he lived with his mother in Bournemouth until 1885. He attended Bedford Grammar School, and worked in Bournemouth as a clerk. Moreover, while still young, prior to the death of his mother, Mathers had already started down the path that would lead him to the foundation of the Golden Dawn, being initiated in the Freemason Lodge of Hengist in Bournemouth in 1877. However, he never became a lodge master. After his mother's death, Mathers moved to London 'enjoying the hospitality of Dr. Westcott for many years'.

Mathers adopted the surname 'MacGregor' early in life, claiming to be a descendent of Ian MacGregor of Glenstrae, an ardent Jacobite. There is, however, no evidence for this, the adoption of the surname being an example of his frequent fabrication. Another example of this is related by his wife Moina Mathers. In a note written after his death, she reports that, while living with his mother in Bournemouth and before his joining a Masonic Lodge, Madame Blavatsky invited him to collaborate in the formation of the Theosophical Society (1875), which he promptly refused to do. Again, there is no evidence for this. Likewise, later in his life he claimed expertise, such as that of an Egyptologist – when he attempted to 'revive' a cult of Isis.

His earliest writings, in fact, were not on occult subjects, but rather on military history. Mathers' first publication in 1884 was entitled *Practical Instruction in Infantry Campaigning Exercise*. He thought of himself as a warrior, perhaps as a way to honour his 'MacGregor ancestry'. However, he never rose above the rank of private in the First Hampshire Infantry Volunteers, although one of the most famous pictures of Mathers has him dressed up as a Lieutenant of the Volunteer or Militia Artillery.

In 1888, he co-founded the Hermetic Order of the Golden Dawn and in 1890 married Mina Bergson – sister of the philosopher Henri Bergson – who changed her name to Moina Mathers to fit in with Mathers' obsession with Celtic culture and traditions. In 1892, the couple moved to Paris where he would keep his main residence for the rest of his life. Throughout their lives together, they experienced financial difficulties, the move to Paris itself being a result of these problems. Annie Horniman, a rich heiress and member of the Golden Dawn, lent Moina money to pursue a career as a painter in Paris and Samuel Mathers simply followed his wife there. Mathers continued controlling the Golden Dawn while in Paris until the dissolution of the Order in 1901. He died in Paris, on 20 November 1918, of unknown causes, although there are claims by Dion Fortune that he died of Spanish influenza.

As noted above, Mathers' path into the occult world began in Bournemouth on 4 October 1877, when he was initiated into Freemasonry. Following this initiation, his interest in Christian mysticism led him to join the 'Societas Rosicruciana in Anglia' (SRIA) in 1882. While Freemasonry was then, as now, an organization comprising a diverse cross-section of society, some of the members having no particular interest in occultism, esotericism or mysticism, the same was not true of the SRIA. According to Westcott, Robert Wentworth Little, the founder of SRIA, was 'a student of the works of Eliphas Lévi'. Lévi wrote almost exclusively about magic and by that time, the French occultist's name was already well known in London. Mathers adopted a Gaelic motto for his entrance into the SRIA, *'S rìoghail mo dhream'* ('royal is my tribe'). This was also the motto that he would use as a member of the 'Second Order' – the inner circle – of the Hermetic Order of the Golden Dawn.

Following his initiation into the SRIA and prior to 1887, he came into contact, either personally or through their works, with Blavatsky and Anna Kingsford of the Theosophical Society. Kingsford and her associate Edward Maitland founded the Hermetic Society in 1884 in order to study the western Hermetic tradition and Kabbalah. In 1887, Mathers dedicated his *The Kabbalah Unveiled* to Kingsford and Maitland. It was a natural match for Mathers, for while the Theosophical Society was becoming more oriented towards the East, the Hermetic Society and the SRIA were far more concerned with western traditions. The Golden Dawn would eventually develop many of the core elements of these two orders.

Mathers' first significant contribution to western esotericism was his translation of *The Kabbalah Unveiled* (1990) in 1887, a translation of Knorr Von Rosenroth's Latin work *Kabbalah Denudata* – which is essentially a translation of excerpts of the *Zohar*: *The Book of Concealed Mystery*, *The Greater Holy Assembly* and *The Lesser Holy Assembly*. The wide ranging importance of this translation goes beyond the field of esotericism, as this was the first time that excerpts of the *Zohar*, a core Kabbalistic text, were translated into the English language. Westcott helped him with his translation and, indeed, in the same year, Westcott himself published the first translation of the *Sepher Yetzirah* into the English language. In 1888, Mathers not only co-founded the Golden Dawn, but published *Fortune Telling Cards: The Tarot, its Occult Significance and Methods of Play*, and, a year later, published *The Key of Solomon the King: Clavicula Salomonis*. After moving to Paris in 1896, he began the translation of one of his most influential publications, the *Sacred Magic of Abramelin the Mage*, which was finally published in 1899. Finally, another important text edited by Mathers, *Goetia: The Lesser Key of Solomon*, was never actually published by him, but was rather stolen and published by Crowley. This was the first book of a longer work, *Lemegeton,* from the Isis-Urania Temple of the Golden Dawn. Mathers was not even credited as an editor of the book.

Mathers, however, made his most original contribution to western esotericism when he merged the ritualistic elements of Freemasonry and the SRIA with the study of the *Hermetica*, which Kingsford was developing. That said, as noted above, the Hermetic Order of the Golden Dawn was not founded solely by Mathers. Rather, it was a joint effort with Mathers, Westcott and William Robert Woodman as equal partners. Indeed, the idea for the creation of the Order seems to have been principally Westcott's. The Order derived its charter from a fictitious German order led by Fräulein Sprengel, who was supposedly in written contact with Westcott, although it is widely accepted that their letters were forged, possibly by Westcott. Other forgeries involved in the foundation of the Golden Dawn – possibly by the linguist and orientalist scholar, Kenneth R. H. Mackenzie – were the 'cipher manuscripts', a collection of sixty folios outlining a series of initiation rituals, around which much of the Order was based. However, the final form of the rituals and practices was constructed by Mathers and Westcott, while the inner order rituals were mainly the work of Mathers.

Eventually Westcott left the Order due to incompatibilities with his work as a Coroner – his superiors made him choose between being an adept or a doctor. Following Westcott's departure, Mathers – who had already moved to Paris – revealed that no one but him had ever been in contact with the 'Secret Chiefs', a version of Blavatsky's Mahatmas or Ascended Masters, and became more dictatorial in his attitude to other members. This led to tensions with the organisation and, eventually, the Golden Dawn fractured into Mathers loyalists, including Moina Mathers, Aleister Crowley and Edmund William Berridge, and separatists, who comprised most of the other members, particularly those of the Second Order in London. Mathers was expelled from the London temple in 1901, the head of the Order was deposed and what might be considered the classical period of the Golden Dawn came to an end. The loyalists resumed the Hermetic Order of the Golden Dawn under Mathers' rule, renaming it 'Alpha and Omega'. Finally, after his death, Moina Mathers took over leadership of the Order.

REFERENCES AND FURTHER READING

Gilbert, R. A. (1997) *Revelations of the Golden Dawn*, Slough: Foulsham.

Howe, Ellic (1978) *Magicians of the Golden Dawn*, Boston: Red Wheel/Weiser.

Kuntz, Darcy (1996) *The Golden Dawn Source Book*, Edmonds: Holmes.

Mathers, S., ed. (1912 [1887]) *The Kabbalah Unveiled.* Online: http://www.sacred-texts.com/jud/tku/index.htm (accessed: 3 March 2013).

Mathers, S. & Crowley, A. (eds.) (1997 [1904]) *The Goetia: The Lesser Key of Solomon the King*, Boston: Red Wheel/Weiser.

Mathers, S. (2002 [1889]) *The Key of Solomon the King*, Boston: Red Wheel/Weiser.

Pasi, Marco (2006) 'Mathers, Samuel Lidell "Macgregor"', in W. Hanegraaf, ed., *Dictionary of Gnosis and Western Esotericism*, Leiden: Brill, 783–85.

CHAPTER TWENTY-TWO

THEOSOPHY

Olav Hammer

INTRODUCTION

The Theosophical Society was founded in 1875 in New York City. It functioned as the vehicle for the dissemination of a religio-philosophical message that drew on a vast fund of Western esoteric sources, and was presented as a third option besides dogmatic religion and materialistic science, able to transcend the differences between the two. The primary spokesperson for this message was Helena Petrovna Blavatsky (1831–91), who synthesized and interpreted a host of esoteric teachings in numerous articles and several books. After her death, schisms followed, and several organizations claimed to carry on Blavatsky's legacy. For very different reasons, both of the two main Theosophical bodies – one based in Adyar, India, the other with headquarters in Point Loma, on the outskirts of San Diego – experienced setbacks toward the end of the 1930s. Theosophy has nevertheless continued to play an important role in the religious landscape, not only through Theosophical organizations in the strict sense (the topic of this chapter), but also through various movements with a looser doctrinal affiliation to the mother society (see the chapter 'The Theosophical Current in the Twentieth Century,' in the present volume), and via the kind of non-affiliated folk religiosity often referred to as 'New Age' (see the chapter of that name, also in the present volume). The cultural influence of Theosophy is pervasive, and readers can pursue the topics presented in those three chapters in considerably more detail in Hammer and Rothstein (2013).

BLAVATSKY AND THE FIRST GENERATION OF THE THEOSOPHICAL MOVEMENT

Helena Blavatsky, *née* Fadeevna von Hahn, led a life that was turbulent, at times impossible to trace, and often controversial. For these reasons, the definitive scholarly biography may perhaps never be written. The following brief account of Blavatsky's life, and of the history of the Theosophical Society, is compiled from a number of sources, in particular Cranston (1993—a very detailed account of her life, but to be used with caution due to its hagiographic tenor), Campbell (1980: 1–29), de Zirkoff (n.d.), Goodrick-Clarke (2008: 211–28), and Godwin (2013).

Helena was born in 1831 in the Russian city of Ekaterinoslav (now in the Ukraine). Due to her father's profession as army officer, the family relocated repeatedly, and as an adult Helena would continue to travel and resettle. At the age of 18, she married Nikifor Vassilyevich Blavatsky, a vice-governor in the province of Armenia. She left him after only a few weeks, but kept her husband's last name. She departed for Istanbul, and then set out on a series of voyages that have still not been retraced to the satisfaction of historical-critical scholarship.

Among the more securely documented journeys is an extended stay in Cairo, where she met a 'Coptic magician,' Paulos Metamon. Presumably closer to the domain of legend are her forays into Tibet, a daunting feat for a single woman of Russian extraction given that the Tibetan borders were closely guarded and would-be visitors were immediately expelled. Somewhere between fact and legend is her account of having met a spiritual Master in London's Hyde Park in 1851. In Theosophical parlance, Masters are beings that have evolved beyond the stage of ordinary humans, and are able to tap into and relay an ancient wisdom tradition. The encounter with her Hyde Park Master may, perhaps, have been a more mundane meeting with a person of flesh and blood, and only reinterpreted as a Theosophical Master in view of a much later terminological and ideological shift. Whatever the facts may be behind her accounts of these voyages and meetings, they established her – rhetorically if nothing else – as an extraordinarily successful seeker after hidden spiritual wisdom.

Blavatsky's life becomes much easier to trace after her departure for America in 1873. She settled in New York, and had within a very short time established contacts with the spiritualist and occultist milieus of the surrounding area. Here she also met Henry Steel Olcott (1832–1907), who would become a life-long friend and supporter.

Nineteenth-century Spiritualism was a very loosely organized movement, and individual Spiritualists had quite divergent interests. In the Anglo-American world, Spiritualist séances had until the 1870s been mainly devoted to mediums relaying brief messages from the departed and manifesting various putatively paranormal phenomena. In Germany and France, mediums were also liable to formulate wide-ranging cosmological doctrines: well-known examples include Justinus Kerner's book *Die Seherin von Prevorst*, published in 1829, relating the visions of the medium Friederike Haufe, and Allan Kardec's series of books on Spiritism beginning with *Le livre des esprits*, published in 1857. Anglo-American Spiritualism was beginning to manifest a similar expansion of its ambitions. Andrew Jackson Davis (1826–1910) had already in 1845 published a series of trance-induced messages under the title *The Principles of Nature*. William Stainton Moses (1839–92) began in 1872 to write a series of texts under dictation from an entity he identified as Imperator+. Emma Hardinge Britten (1823–99) in 1876 published *Art Magic*, a book supposedly transmitted in an altered state of consciousness. The formation of the Theosophical Society, and the promulgation of a highly complex Theosophical cosmology, can be seen as part of this historical shift.

A small group of about twenty people gathered in Blavatsky's apartment on 7 September 1875 in order to hear a lecture on 'the Kabbalah of the Egyptians and the Canon of Proportions of the Greeks.' Henry S. Olcott and William Q. Judge (1851–96) suggested forming a society that could investigate a variety of similar occult topics. Olcott was elected President of the Theosophical Society, and formally inaugurated the new organization on November 17, 1875. In the same year, Blavatsky had begun composing the first articles in what was to become a massive occultist oeuvre (her *Collected Writings* edited by Boris de Zirkoff comprise 15 volumes).

In 1877 she published her first book, *Isis Unveiled*. This massive work of over 1300 pages consists of a volume on Science and one on what she styled Theology. Blavatsky drew mainly on esotericists of the past in order to convey the message that the ancient wisdom tradition which she ostensibly transmitted was a viable alternative beside organized 'exoteric' religions (especially most Church-based forms of Christianity, which she reviled) and nineteenth-century materialistic science. The ancient wisdom tradition is in perennialist fashion traced back variously to Egypt, India, various Platonists, Kabbalists, and Hermeticists. Considerable space is devoted to magic and paranormal phenomena, explained here as practical manifestations of a true form of science that bigoted materialists have yet to understand and accept.

Isis Unveiled became the focus of considerable controversy, most famously after William Emmette Coleman shortly after the publication of Blavatsky's book accused her of extensive plagiarism. Olcott, on the contrary, maintained that Blavatsky wrote her book in an altered state of consciousness, in which the text appeared to be transmitted to her from a personality or personalities that were not her own.

Despite the apparent initial success of the Theosophical Society, some difficult years lay ahead. Membership dwindled, and Blavatsky decided to leave together with Olcott for a hopefully more receptive environment. In December 1878 they embarked for India, arriving in Bombay in February 1879. There, the founding duo not only established contact with Indian intellectuals, but also made influential friends and converts. The most important for the further development of the Theosophical Society and its world view were Alfred Percy Sinnett (1841–1921), editor of *The Allahabad Pioneer*, and Allan Octavian Hume (1829–1912), civil servant in the Indian administration.

Sinnett and Hume (and particularly the former) became the recipients of a series of letters, ostensibly sent by paranormal means by two Masters by the names of Koot Hoomi and Morya. Sinnet used these letters as background material for his books *Occult World* (1881) and *Esoteric Buddhism* (1883), that presented the Theosophical message for a broader readership.

Several years before, in Cairo, Blavatsky had struck up an acquaintance with a couple, Alex and Emma Coulomb, and had provided them with employment at the Theosophical headquarters. In early 1884 a conflict with the Coulombs erupted. In May 1884 they were fired, and took revenge by contacting a local newspaper, the Madras Christian College, with stories of how Blavatsky had faked 'supernatural' phenomena. In England, the Society for Psychic Research commissioned Richard Hodgson to travel to Adyar in order to look into the affair. After three months of investigation, Hodgson's verdict was devastating: Blavatsky, he asserted, had merely faked the mysterious phenomena. On March 31, 1885 Blavatsky left India for Europe, and spent the remaining years of her life in various European cities, writing and receiving visitors.

The most important work from this period is *The Secret Doctrine* (1888), consisting of over 1500 pages in two volumes: 'Cosmogenesis' and 'Anthropogenesis.' It is structured as a commentary on the 'Stanzas of Dzyan,' an otherwise unknown text in an equally unknown language, Senzar. *The Secret Doctrine*, like her preceding book, devotes considerable space to the errors of conventional science and to the folly of Christianity and other exoteric traditions, but also presents a vast cosmological vision that is barely hinted at in *Isis Unveiled*, and to which I will return later in this chapter. As a side effect of the publication of *The Secret Doctrine*, one of the most influential Theosophists of the next generation joined the society. Annie Besant (1847–1933), freethinker and social reformer, agreed to review Blavatsky's book for the *Pall Mall Gazette*, and was almost instantly converted to Theosophy (for a detailed biography of Besant, see Nethercot 1960, 1963).

The year 1888 also saw the founding of an inner, secret circle within the Theosophical Society: the Esoteric Section. Formally, the Section was ruled by the Masters, but Blavatsky was 'outer head' and thus in charge of the Section on a more mundane level.

Further written works followed in 1889. A popular introduction to Theosophy, in question-and-answer format, was published under the title *The Key to Theosophy*. *The Voice of the Silence*, published in the same year, is a more poetically formulated devotional work. Helena Petrovna Blavatsky was in her last years in increasingly ill health, and died in London on May 8, 1891.

Theosophical Cosmology

Blavatsky's world view underwent some changes over the years, sometimes in substance and sometimes in terms of a shift in focus. *The Secret Doctrine* is, for instance, more concerned with Oriental religions and less attentive to magical or paranormal abilities than *Isis Unveiled*, and accepts the reality of the mechanism of reincarnation that is explicitly denied in the earlier work. A brief section on the Theosophical world view risks glossing over some of these changes, and it should be emphasized that the following thumbnail sketch corresponds best to the views expressed in late works, notably *The Secret Doctrine*. This work presents considerable interpretive challenges, given that it tends to treat any given subject rather unsystematically, typically in passages dispersed throughout the text. In the interest of brevity, references to each individual item of information will not be given here. For that level of detail, readers are encouraged to consult Blavatsky's text, a task somewhat simplified by the detailed index (cf. also Elwood 1986, a sympathetic insider's account).

If, as Alfred North Whitehead famously claimed, philosophy consists of a series of footnotes to Plato, it is equally fair to say that esoteric cosmologies largely consist of a series of footnotes to Neo-Platonism. One recognizes the emanationist perspective of the Neo-Platonic philosophers in Blavatsky's view that an ineffable ultimate reality underlies everything. All that manifests itself in the cosmos is the result of a procession from this ultimate reality, and all the major events that occur over the vast eons of time described in *The Secret Doctrine* are predicated on the basic idea that consciousness as well as matter proceed from this ultimate reality, and will again return to it. We humans are sparks of consciousness, in principle identical in essence with the ultimate reality. At the present point in time we are – or have just passed – the lowest point of this process, and are now poised to return (on this grand historical scheme see in particular Trompf 1998, 2005, 2013).

In order to unpack this ultra-brief description, I will attempt to give an impression of Blavatsky's cosmology and its vast panorama over a cosmos in cyclical change, and her anthropology, a description of how individual sparks of consciousness incarnate innumerable times, passing through various manifestations identified in characteristic nineteenth-century terminology as 'races.'

Theosophical cosmology suggests that the monads or individual sparks of consciousness that constitute the core of each sentient being begin a long evolutionary journey on the first and most subtle or spiritual of a series of seven 'globes.' After having completed their span of time on that globe, they proceed to the next, and so on in succession until they reach the fourth and most materially dense globe. This represents the *nadir* of what might be called a cosmological U-curve, since from there evolution again propels each monad upward through subtler globes until the seventh globe has been completed. The totality of such globes constitutes a round; at the end of such a round the entire manifest cosmos is dissolved, after which a new round begins. The time spans involved are enormous, and the magnitude of the scale is apparent from the fact that a series of seven rounds constitute an even more extensive unit, one *manvantara*, each of which is an evolutionary unit in a seemingly endless row.

Just as *The Secret Doctrine* is based on an evolutionary cosmology, Blavatsky's anthropology focuses on the evolution of the sparks of consciousness that ultimately constitute human beings. These entities have incarnated, and will continue to incarnate, again and again over millions of years in what Blavatsky describes as a number of discrete stages or Root-Races. In the first of these stages, humans (or perhaps more accurately, pre-humans) are described as 'ethereal,' implying that they still had no distinct physical shape. Blavatsky's descriptions of this first stage add few details as to the mode of life of these beings. More specifics are given on the second Root-Race, the hyperborean. As the name indicates, they lived in the far north of our planet. Their bodies were fluid, and they were able to take on various shapes. They reproduced by dividing their bodies in half, in amoeba-like fashion.

Sexual reproduction enters human history in the third Root-Race, as (proto-) humans came to inhabit the continent of Lemuria. Originally hypothesized by biologist Philip Sclater (1829–1913) as a sunken land bridge that might explain why lemurs were found in Madagascar and in India, it was via Blavatsky that Lemuria entered occult lore on fabled continents. *The Secret Doctrine* describes Lemurians as tall beings, governed by kings, some of whose 'elect' fled the destruction of their continent and settled in the legendary city of Shamballah.

The fourth Root-Race is identified with the denizens of Atlantis (Godwin 2011: 82–87). Blavatsky describes these as the first truly human-shaped beings. When their continent became submerged, Atlanteans migrated to other continents. From these survivors emerged the present, fifth Root-Race. This so-called Aryan Root-Race is subdivided into seven epochs, or sub-races, that have their names after civilizations that in Blavatsky's perspective were important at various historical stages. After the Hindu sub-race come the Arabian, Persian, Celtic, and Teutonic sub-races. Blavatsky saw her own time as near the end of the fifth and just before the beginning of the sixth sub-race, an epoch that was to be characterized by the emergence of a new level of consciousness in parts of the United States. In a distant future, sixth and seventh sub-races will inhabit our planet, until the fifth Root-Race has lived out its course and a sixth Root-Race is born. An even more distant future will see the rise and development of a seventh Root-Race.

From Blavatsky's numerous but often vague and cryptic mentions of the civilization and way of life in such past continents as Lemuria and Atlantis it is all but impossible to piece together a coherent view of 'occult historiography.' This became a major topic with other Theosophical writers. The most influential writer in this genre is William Scott-Elliot (d. 1930), who fleshed out the details in books such as *The Story of Atlantis* (1896).

Reincarnation and Karma

Seen from one perspective, the various root-races and sub-races are hierarchically ordered in a way that recalls the racist and evolutionist discourse current in the late nineteenth century (Lubelsky 2013). Seen from another point of view, 'races' are just the temporary abodes of reincarnating spiritual entities (Santucci 2008). Precisely how reincarnation operates is – as with so many other topics mentioned in her *magnum opus* – not easy to deduce from *The Secret Doctrine* (for Theosophical reincarnation doctrines more generally, see Zander 1999: 477–99).

One of the few extended discussions of the topic (such as in *The Secret Doctrine*, vol. II: 302–6) affirms that the each monad retains its individuality over the countless incarnations. Up to a point in the Atlantean period, new monads were created, but since then the same individuals have been reborn in new bodies. The law of karma is the mechanism that decides into which body a given monad is reborn, but a waiting period of several centuries elapses before it incarnates again. The body into which we are born is a mere shell or even illusion: the true, inner person sheds one body and takes on another in an almost endless succession.

The related subjects of reincarnation, karma, and the post-mortem state are discussed with much more detail and precision in *The Key to Theosophy*. Here (esp. in section 7) the constitution of the human being is elucidated. The picture that emerges is complex: the human being is divided into two parts, a lower physical part with four elements and a higher spiritual part with three, together making up a septenary constitution of the human being. All seven elements are identified by Sanskrit terms. Of the upper, spiritual triad, the lowest element, called *manas*, is individual. The two upper, *buddhi* and *atma*, are universal spirit and its vehicle in the individual human being, respectively. In Platonic fashion, the *manas* can be inclined toward the lower, physical body or toward its higher counterpart, *buddhi*, and one's post-mortem destiny and next incarnation depend on this inclination. For those who aspire toward a spiritual life, the combined *manas* and *buddhi* will after death pass into a state referred to as devachanic bliss, and will after a delay of centuries reincarnate at a higher evolutionary stage.

Masters and Other Higher Beings

Although Blavatsky's theory of races suggests that we reincarnate in cohorts at roughly similar stages of development, there are according to Theosophical lore individuals who have taken such immense evolutionary strides that they vastly surpass the rest of us in spiritual development. These Mahatmas, Masters or Adepts reside in some of the world's spiritual foci – Egypt, the Himalayas – and guide humanity. The ancient wisdom tradition that Blavatsky claimed to transmit was in part derived from her contact with these august personalities. *The Secret Doctrine* has little to say of precisely who they are, or where and how they live.

Besides Masters, there are other beings at stages of spiritual evolution above the merely human. Blavatsky's texts speak of Manus, Dhyan-Chohans, Maha-Chohans, and several classes of Planetary Spirits. The unsystematic nature of the sources complicates efforts to determine more precisely the role of and relations between these members of the cosmic hierarchy.

THE SECOND THEOSOPHICAL GENERATION

Schism and Continuity in the Theosophical Society

After the death of Helena Blavatsky the Theosophical Society was marked by schisms, due to power struggles between several of the top echelon Theosophists (for details, see e.g. Campbell 1980: 103–11, Wessinger 2013: 44–47). Leaders claimed to be in contact with the Masters, and the acceptance of the authenticity of these new messages – or accusations of the lack thereof – triggered controversies. A dispute arose between Judge, who claimed to have received a message from a Master, and Besant who believed that Judge had written it himself. In 1894 matters came to a head. Besant pressed charges against Judge. The American Section sided with Judge and seceded from the mother organization, forming 'The Theosophical Society in America,' with Judge as President. Besant remained head of the Adyar-based Theosophical Society, and associated with Charles W. Leadbeater (1854–1934), a former clergyman of the Church of England who had converted to Theosophy (Tillett 1982). Leadbeater claimed clairvoyant abilities, and these were the source of numerous books that were published either by Besant and Leadbeater, or by the latter as sole author. As will become apparent in the following section, a number of doctrinal innovations were formulated during their leadership of the Theosophical Society.

Judge died on March 21, 1896, and was for a short period of time succeeded by his secretary, Ernest Temple Hargrove (d. 1939). Hargrove, however, was soon ousted from power by Katherine Tingley (1847–1929), who in 1900 moved the American society to Point Loma, near San Diego. Tingley conceived of and brought to life a full-scale Theosophical utopian commune, to which we shall briefly return below.

Although these were the most important schisms in view of the long-term developments within the Theosophical current, several other organizations were also formed in these turbulent years. Some, with names such as the Temple of the People, The Theosophical Society of New York, the Blavatsky Association, and The United Lodge of Theosophists (or ULT), remain doctrinally within the Theosophical fold. Others, such as the Anthroposophical Society, are more distantly related to the mother organization. Yet others are the result of independent entrepreneurs setting up movements that borrow freely from Theosophical sources, but are not the result of organizational schisms: the I AM Religious Activity, the Summit Lighthouse, and numerous others. Information on these and other groups can be found in Campbell (1980: 131–65 *et passim*), and in the contributions in Hammer and Rothstein (2013).

Doctrinal Innovations in the Besant–Leadbeater Writings

Besant and Leadbeater published prolifically during their years as Theosophical leaders. Whereas much of Blavatsky's oeuvre is poorly organized and difficult to read, the literature composed by this second generation of Theosophical ideologues is detailed, clearly structured, and lucidly written. Their works have, presumably not least for precisely that reason, been singularly influential. Some of the views they propose represent quite fundamental alterations compared to Blavatsky's Theosophy – either changes in emphasis, or more profound changes of substance. The following represents a partial list of such doctrinal innovations.

Blavatsky's Masters were hierarchically organized, but it was in second generation Theosophy (also known as neo-Theosophy, a term that at first was derogatory but is now also used as a descriptive label) that the ranks and positions within the hierarchy proliferated and increasingly came to resemble a great cosmic bureaucracy. Leadbeater's book *The Masters and the Path* (1925) mentions Arhats, Adepts, Masters, Manus, Bodhisattvas, Chohans, Maha-Chohans, Planetary Spirits, great Angels, karmic Deities, Buddhas, Christs (in the plural), and so forth. These are titles, occupied by beings who can graduate from one level to another by means of a series of initiations. For instance, Kuthumi, the ostensible writer of numerous Mahatma letters, will progress up the evolutionary ladder and will become the bodhisattva of the coming sixth race (*The Masters and the Path*, §94).

Blavatsky's hostility toward many manifestations of Christianity did not prevent her from writing about Jesus in positive terms. In her writings, Jesus is humanized: 'If we do not accept Jesus as God, we revere him as a man' (*Isis Unveiled*, vol II, p. 530). Leadbeater and Besant, on the contrary, assigned him a place in the spiritual hierarchy: Jesus had given up his body as a vehicle for the Christ, one of the Masters of Wisdom.

As with Blavatsky, one of the main roads to spiritual ascent is successive reincarnation. Whereas Blavatsky's description of reincarnation remains quite abstract, Leadbeater's professed clairvoyance allowed him to trace the destinies of specific individuals thousands of years back in time.

Clairvoyance was also involved in attempts to describe hitherto unknown aspects of the constitution of matter, and of human physiology. The former is represented by occult chemistry, the topic of a book by Leadbeater with the same title (cf. Morrisson 2007). While clairvoyant attempts at describing the structure of atoms have remained a topic of interest to more limited circles of readers, the latter discussion of occult physiology has influenced new religions and popular culture up to our own time. The *chakras* and the human aura, popularized in works such as *Man Visible and Invisible* (1902) and *The Chakras* (1927), are today widely known concepts.

The new doctrine that seems to have caused the most stir was that of the World Teacher. Blavatsky's view of history implied a gradual ascent over vast periods of time. The second generation Theosophical leaders added a millenarian twist to this historical scheme: spiritual change was imminent, and was to be ushered in by a process that involved a young Indian Boy, Jiddu Krishnamurti (1896–1986) becoming the bodily vessel of Maitreya, a high-ranking member of the spiritual hierarchy.

Point Loma and the Quest for Theosophical Utopia

Adyar Theosophy under Leadbeater and Besant took a distinctly occult direction. American Theosophy under Tingley was conceived of as a much more practical pursuit. Tingley transformed the American Theosophical Society from its lodge-based form into a community with global aims, with headquarters at Point Loma, California (see Greenwalt 1978).

The Point Loma site was rebuilt at great expense, with a large domed Temple of Peace, buildings for the headquarters of the Society, residential quarters, and a Greek theater as a setting for Tingley's dramatic productions. In order to educate future generations in accordance with Theosophical ideals, The Raja Yoga School was inaugurated in 1900. By combining intellectual achievement with a strict control over one's 'lower nature,' a morally and spiritually balanced character would be achieved. Over the years, the school was gradually expanded, until the educational program covered the entire span from kindergarten to University.

Despite financial backing by wealthy sponsors, Tingley's ambitions exceeded her resources. After her death in 1929, Tingley's successor Geoffrey de Purucker was unable to maintain the Point Loma community. In 1941 the school was closed and just prior to de Purucker's death on September 27, 1942 he sold the Lomaland site and moved the International Headquarters to Covina, California. The American branch, now named Theosophical Society (Pasadena), has since then mainly been active in carrying out more traditionally Theosophical tasks such as publishing.

THE THIRD GENERATION AND BEYOND

Within the space of a few years around 1930, Krishnamurti had renounced his role as vehicle for the World Teacher, and the leaders of both of the largest Theosophical organizations had passed away. Membership dwindled, and although all the main bodies of Theosophists exist today, they lead a rather subdued existence. Research on the history of Theosophy since the 1930s is still in its infancy, but a pioneering study by Michael Ashcraft (2013) suggests that the three main trends have been a gradual decline in membership; a series of unsuccessful attempts to heal the rifts after Adyar Theosophy and American Theosophy parted ways; and an opening up to a broader range of occult and popular topics in Theosophical publications and lectures, in order to cater to the interests of the 'baby boom' generation. There is at present nothing to suggest that Theosophy, as a distinct current with discrete organizational structures, will regain the importance that it had in its golden age from 1875 to the mid-1930s. The main conduits of Theosophical concepts have over the last many decades been a host of Theosophically based new religious movements, and the New Age. These are covered in separate chapters in the present volume.

REFERENCES AND FURTHER READING

Ashcraft, W. M. (2013) 'The Third Generation of Theosophy and Beyond,' in O. Hammer & M. Rothstein, eds., *Handbook of the Theosophical Current*, Leiden: Brill, 73–89.

Campbell, B. F. (1980) *Ancient Wisdom Revived: A History of the Theosophical Movement*, Berkeley: University of California Press.

Cranston, S. (1993) *HPB: The Extraordinary Life and Influence of Helena Blavatsky, Founder of the Modern Theosophical Movement*, New York: G.P. Putnam's Sons.

Elwood, R. (1986) *Theosophy: A Modern Expression of the Wisdom of the Ages*, London: Quest Books.

Godwin, J. (2011) *Atlantis of the Occultists and the Cycles of Time*, Rochester Vt.: Inner Traditions.

——(2013) 'Blavatsky and the First Generation of Theosophy,' in O. Hammer & M. Rothstein, eds., *Handbook of the Theosophical Current*, Leiden: Brill, 15–31.

Goodrick-Clarke, N. (2008) *The Western Esoteric Traditions: A Historical Introduction*, Oxford: Oxford University Press.

Greenwalt, E. (1978) *California Utopia: Point Loma, 1897–1942*, Point Loma: Point Loma Publications.

Hammer, O. & M. Rothstein, eds. (2013) *Handbook of the Theosophical Current*, Leiden: Brill.

Lubelsky, I. (2013) 'Mythological and Real Race Issues in Theosophy,' in O. Hammer & M. Rothstein, eds., *Handbook of the Theosophical Current*, Leiden: Brill, 335–55.

Morrison, M. S. (2007) *Modern Alchemy: Occultism and the Emergence of Atomic Theory*, Oxford: Oxford University Press.

Nethercot, A. H. (1960) *The First Five Lives of Annie Besant*, Chicago: University of Chicago Press.

——(1963) *The Last Four Lives of Annie Besant*, Chicago: University of Chicago Press.

Santucci, J. (2008) 'The Notion of Race in Theosophy,' *Nova Religio* 11:3, 33–63.

Tillett, G. (1982) *The Elder Brother: A Biography of Charles Webster Leadbeater*, London: Routledge & Kegan Paul.

Trompf, G. (1998) 'Macrohistory in Blavatsky, Steiner and Guénon,' in A. Faivre & W. J. Hanegraaff (eds.), *Western Esotericism and the Science of Religion. Selected Papers presented at the 17th Congress of the International Association for the History of Religions, Mexico City 1995*, Gnostica 2, Louvain: Peeters, 269–96.

——(2005) 'Macrohistory,' in W. J. Hanegraaff et al., eds., *Dictionary of Gnosis and Western Esotericism*, Leiden: Brill, 701–16.

——(2013) 'Theosophical Macrohistory,' in O. Hammer & M. Rothstein, eds., *Handbook of the Theosophical Current*, Leiden: Brill, 375–403.

Zander, H. (1999) *Geschichte der Seelenwanderung in Europa*, Darmstadt: Wissenschaftliche Buchgesellschaft.

de Zirkoff, B. (n.d.) 'Helena Petrovna Blavatsky. General Outline of her Life prior to her Public Work,' *Blavatsky Collected Writings* I: xxv–lii. Online: www.katinkahesselink.net/blavatsky/articles/v1.

CHAPTER TWENTY-THREE

FREDERIC W. H. MYERS

Jeffrey J. Kripal

INTRODUCTION

Frederic W. H. Myers (1843–1901) was a Cambridge-trained classicist who was one of the leaders of the Victorian psychical research tradition that crystallized around the London Society of Psychical Research (or S.P.R.), which he helped found in February of 1882. Myers is best known for his massive, two-volume tome that was posthumously published as *Human Personality and Its Survival of Bodily Death* (Myers, 1903), which was in turn largely based on a series of papers that he published between 1880 and his death in 1901, mostly in the journal of the S.P.R. Many of his other earlier published writings were expressions of what we would today call literary criticism. For example, he published two separate collections of essays on various authors, both ancient and modern (Myers, 1883, 1897). He also published a separate monograph on William Wordsworth, who was a friend of his mother's family, and a collection of metaphysical essays entitled *Science and a Future Life with Other Essays* (Myers 1881, 1901). He was also an award-winning poet (Myers 1904).

LIFE

Frederic W. H. Myers was the son of Frederic Myers, who was a pastor, and Susan Myers (born Susan Harriet), who loved poetry and nature. He was born on February 6, 1843, in Keswick, Cumberland, and spent his childhood in a parsonage, where his father taught him Latin from his sixth birthday on. At sixteen, he was sent to a classical tutor, then to a mathematical tutor, and then, at seventeen now, on to Trinity College at Cambridge University. At the age of twenty-two, in 1865, Myers was elected Fellow and Classical Lecturer at Trinity. He resigned four years later, to work for educational reform and the higher education of women. In 1871, he accepted a temporary post as an inspector of schools and, in 1872, took a similar but now permanent position. He was appointed to the Cambridge district in 1875, a job which he held until his health collapsed shortly before his death in 1901 (Gauld 1968).

In 1880, at the age of thirty-seven, Myers stepped into Westminster Abbey in order to marry a twenty-two-year-old woman named Eveleen Tennant. Evie, as she was called, came from a wealthy family and had her own social circles and intellectual interests, which never quite melded with those of her husband. The new couple took up residence in 1881 in Leckhampton House, on the Western edge of Cambridge. There they had three children over the next few years. Most of the historians agree that theirs was a stable marriage, but not an entirely happy one. This situation was not helped much by the fact that Myers would fall in love with the wife of a cousin who had killed herself and with whom Myers believed he was in communication via a medium. This material, which Myers believed was some of the strongest of *Human Personality*, was removed from the published volume by Evie (Blum 2006, 118).

Myers's spiritual and intellectual lives went through four separate stages, which he himself framed as Hellenism, Christianity, Agnosticism, and 'the Final Faith.' His early life was dominated by the Greek and Latin classics, particularly Virgil and Plato. This period ended in 1864 when Myers visited Greece and realized that this was a vanished world. He traveled to America in 1865, where on the night of August 28 he swam the dangerous currents of the Niagara River from the Canadian shore to the American one, an act which he himself saw as symbolic, that is, as a marker of a new stage in his life. After his return to England, he converted to a particularly emotional form of Christianity through the ministrations of a young and beautiful woman named Josephine Butler in whose particular form of sanctity (and Myer's excessive response to it) many of Myers's friends suspected more than piety.

But such a faith eventually faded too. It was a simple lack of evidence and the rigorous methods of science that did in his worldview this time. Agnosticism and materialism set in, and with them a dull pain and a certain horror before a completely indifferent universe. It was at this time that he became deeply impressed with the methods and findings of early professional science, particularly early Darwinian evolutionary biology.

What he calls his Final Faith developed slowly and gradually, partly out of his rejection of traditional religion (read: Victorian Christianity), partly out of his admiration for Darwinian biology, mostly out of his extensive field encounters with mediums and his textual research with the reports of ordinary people on both sides of the Atlantic. It was finally evolutionary biology, put into deep dialogue with classical mystical theorists like Plato and Plotinus, that gave him the grid on which he could then locate and make sense of the psychical data. As Myers himself explained it, there were three creedal points: (1) 'the fact of man's survival of death'; (2) 'the registration in the Universe of every past scene and thought'; and (3) a 'progressive immortality' or 'progressive moral evolution' moving always 'towards an infinitely distant goal' (Myers 1904, 40, 46–47). We might reframe these as a conviction in the survival of the human personality after death, a kind of cosmic mind or storehouse of knowledge based on the Platonic epistemological doctrine of true philosophical knowledge as a kind of 'remembrance' of things previously known before one's present incarnation, and an early evolutionary spirituality that fused spiritualist revelations and a non-Darwinian notion of progress. As Trevor Hamilton, Myers's most recent and extensive biographer puts it, Myers 'was trying to use Darwinian classification methods to show that normal, abnormal and paranormal phenomena were related manifestations of the same core processes' (Hamilton 2009, 4). The category of the paranormal would not arrive on the scene until around the turn of the century. Myers, however, had already created his own: the supernormal.

HISTORICAL CONTEXT AND THE THIRD WAY

In order to understand such convictions and methods, it is necessary to understand the cultural and historical context in which they arose and the dialectical epistemology out of which they spun. The category of the 'psychical' or the 'psychic' (first coined around 1881 by the British chemist Sir William Crookes) arose into prominence at a particular moment in Western intellectual history, a moment when Darwinism, materialism, and agnosticism (a word newly coined by 'Darwin's bulldog,' Thomas Huxley, to capture and advance the spirit of the new era and free the scientists from religious authority) were becoming increasingly dominant.

There were, of course, different responses to these developments. Some individuals embraced reason's science and rejected completely the now defunct and unbelievable claims of faith. Others embraced the claims of faith and chose to reject the science, or at least those parts of it that could not be reconciled with their particular belief system. There was a third option, however, a *tertium quid*, as its proponents often referred to it in the Latin they all could still effortlessly read. Myers had been schooled in the mid-nineteenth-century liberalism of John Stuart Mill, who had argued that new knowledge is created by avoiding the extremes and taking truths from both sides of an honest argument. In this liberal spirit, he sought to reconcile and move beyond position A and position B to what he sometimes referred to as simply 'X.' This was the X-option, as it were, that, as Myers once put it in less Latin and more humor, has 'fallen between two stools' (Myers 1901, 4).

Myers, in other words, belonged to a group of elite intellectuals who refused to be dogmatic about *either* their religion *or* their science. Put less metaphorically, they embraced science as a method that could throw new light on old religious questions. They attempted to work through the polarities of reason and faith toward what they thought of as a new and hopeful 'science of religion.' By such a shocking combination of words (and it *was* shocking), these Cambridge friends did not mean what their much more famous contemporary Max Müller meant by the same phrase over at Oxford, that is, they did not understand religious systems as comparable languages whose family organizations, grammatical structures, and devolving histories of literalization could be speculatively traced through time (whereby, for example, the ancient awe before the sun became the worship of a literal, personalized sun-god). What they meant by a science of religion was a fully rational and fundamentally comparative exercise of collecting, organizing, and analyzing experiential data that could not be fully explained by either the theological categories of the churches or the reductive methods of the sciences.

In other words, they did not discipline the reported spiritual experiences with the theological categories of institutional religion, nor did they equate rationalism with materialism. And here the reported experiences were the key: collected and compared in astonishing numbers, these frustrated and offended both the religious and the scientific registers and functioned as the base of what William James would call their 'radical empiricism' (today such historical events are brushed aside as 'anecdotal' within a dogmatic physicalism and a weak or faux empiricism).

By a science of religion, then, they did not intend a method that would necessarily reduce the religion to the science (although it just might). But neither did they intend a way of doing things that would somehow 'respect' religion or protect it from the powerful gaze and hard questions of the new scientific method. Rather, what they intended was a still future method that would move beyond both materialistic science and dogmatic religion into real answers to ancient metaphysical questions that had never really been convincingly answered. In other words, belief was irrelevant. What mattered now was evidence – empirical, experiential evidence.

BRAVE NEW WORDS

Always the poet, classicist, and philologist, that is, always the lover of words, Frederic Myers dwelt on all of these extraordinary events through long personal meditations on various Latinized and Hellenized coinages, brave new words that he fashioned out of his own ethnographic research, personal experiences with mediums, and intuitions. Basically, he took the altered states of consciousness and anomalous historical events that he encountered in the field and the correspondence and transformed them into the altered words that he expressed in his writing practice. There were at least four major new categories here, which were either original with Myers or whose specific uses he helped fashion. These were: (1) the telepathic; (2) the subliminal; (3) the supernormal; and (4) the imaginal. For the sake of space and time, I can only treat the first two here, but I have described and analyzed each elsewhere (Kripal 2011).

Myers's most well-known (if also misunderstood) neologism is the term 'telepathy,' which he coined around 1882. As Myers intended it, the word had little, if anything, to do with predicting the stock market or the next horse race (hence the misunderstandings). It was much more serious than that. The word rather had everything to do with suffering, trauma, and, above all, the horrors and agonies of physical death.

Here is how it came to be. The work of the SPR involved numerous channels, one of which was the Census of Hallucinations. This involved 410 collectors interviewing 17,000 individuals with a standard set of questions and demographic markers. This census, along with other recorded stories solicited in newspaper ads, resulted in an immense pool of data. Individuals like Myers sifted through these collections, selected out what they considered to be the most reliable, and then back-checked the facts through interviews, coroner reports, obituaries, and so on. They discovered a number of stable comparative patterns through this process.

They noted, for example, that the subject would often receive extremely accurate information about the death of the loved one in a dream or waking vision, regardless of how distant he or she was from the event. To use their language, they referred to these as 'veridical hallucinations' or 'crisis apparitions.' Even more bizarrely, often this information would come *before* the event actually occurred. It looked very much like a form of communication was occurring outside the normal parameters of space and time. Myers coined the term *tele-pathy* to describe these communications.

The word means, literally, '*pathos* at a distance.' This was the key. What Myers intended to communicate here is that such communications outside the reaches of the normal sense channels appeared to depend upon two fundamental processes: (1) an extreme emotional state, often connected to serious danger, physical trauma, or actual death; and (2) a level of the human psyche that is not bound by the normal parameters of space and time.

Myers called the latter dimension of the psyche the 'subliminal Self,' which he usually, but not always, capitalized, and which is not to be confused with the social ego. The word *subliminal* was Latin for 'under the threshold.' It was Myers's central organizing idea and, as such, did a great deal of work for him. He suggested, for example, that the subliminal Self is the source of intellectual genius and literary creativity through moments he called 'subliminal uprushes.' He also became convinced that individuals commonly receive telepathic communications from their loved ones below the same threshold of awareness. Such regions, however, cannot speak to the conscious self or ego directly, and so they generally emerge into consciousness indirectly through a dream image, a waking hallucination, or an overwhelming intuition. In short, the subliminal Self speaks to the ego through signs.

This, of course, sounds a lot like the unconscious of psychoanalysis and depth psychology. Myers certainly saw as much. He would in fact be the first person to introduce the writings of Freud to the English public, and Freud himself would write not one, not two, but *six* papers on telepathy, which he called 'thought transference' and knew from various profound therapeutic experiences. Still, there are major differences between the psychology of Myers and that of Freud, and the two should not be confused. In the end, Myers arrived not at a rational materialistic model of the human being, as Freud did, but at a kind of mind–body dualism. He was fully convinced that a mind uses a brain, and that the 'human brain is in its last analysis an arrangement of matter expressly adapted to being acted upon by a spirit' (Myers 1904, vol. 2, 254).

RECEPTION HISTORY AND FILTER THESIS

The ethnographic and epistolary methods of Myers and his colleagues focused on robust psychical events around trauma and death as these were encoded in texts of various sorts. At the end of the day, theirs was a literary method of the extreme. As the British psychical research tradition gave way to American parapsychology in the 1930s, 1940s, and 1950s, largely under the dominating presence of J. B. Rhine of Duke University, controlled laboratory studies and statistical methods came to the fore. The result was mixed, as such laboratory studies provided a much desired replicability and mathematical models but could not, in principle, study psychical phenomena in their natural habitat, that is, in and around human suffering and death. The result was that what once were dramatic, often life-changing phenomena 'shrunk' to statistical anomalies that needed countless boring trials and statistical analyses to be recognized at all.

Perhaps Myers's greatest influence on subsequent generations has been through his close friend and colleague William James, whose famous *The Varieties of Religious Experience* draws heavily, if silently, on Myers in key places, particularly in its theorization of a 'door' in the subconscious through which religious truths might enter and transform the human psyche. This idea was what eventually came to be known as the 'filter thesis,' whereby consciousness is theorized to be filtered through, transmitted, reduced, and translated by the brain, but not finally produced by it (see Kelly 2007 and Kripal 2012). As contemporary neuroscience continues to fail at solving the 'hard problem' of consciousness by looking for consciousness in and as the material brain, this filter or transmission thesis of Myers and James remains a promising, if seldom pursued possibility.

NOTE

This entry is based on chapter 1 of Kripal (2011), used with permission.

REFERENCES AND FURTHER READING

Blum, Deborah (2006) *Ghost Hunters: William James and the Search for Scientific Proof of Life After Death*, New York: Penguin.

Gauld, Alan (1968) *The Founders of Psychical Research*, New York: Schocken Books.

Hamilton, Trevor (2009) *Immortal Longings: FWH Myers and the Victorian Search for Life after Death*, Exeter: Imprint Academic.

Kelly, Edward F., Emily Williams Kelly, Adam Crabtree, Alan Gauld, Michael Grosso, and Bruce Greyson (2007) *Irreducible Mind: Toward a Psychology for the 21st Century*, Lanham: Rowman & Littlefield.

Kripal, Jeffrey J. (2011) *Authors of the Impossible: The Paranormal and the Sacred*, Chicago: University of Chicago Press.

——(2012) 'Mind Matters: Esalen's Sursem Group and the Ethnography of Consciousness,' in Ann Taves and Courtney Bender, eds., *What Matters? Ethnographies of Value in a (Not So) Secular Age*, New York: Columbia University Press.

Myers, F. W. H. (1881) *Wordsworth*, London: Macmillan and Co.

——(1883) *Essays: Classical*, London: Macmillan and Co.

——(1897) *Essays: Modern*, London: Macmillan and Co.

——(1901/1893) *Science and a Future Life with Other Essays*, London: Macmillan & Co.

——(1904/1903) *Human Personality and Its Survival of Bodily Death*, 2 vols., London: Longmans, Green, & Co.

Myers, Frederic W. H. (1904) *Fragments of Prose & Poetry*, edited by Eveleen Myers, London: Longmans, Green, & Co.

CHAPTER TWENTY-FOUR

THE SOCIETY FOR PSYCHICAL RESEARCH

Egil Asprem

INTRODUCTION

The British Society for Psychical Research (SPR) is the historically most influential organization dedicated to the study of 'psychic' and supernormal events. Founded in 1882 by a group of Cambridge-based scholars, the SPR set out to bring the torch of science to the dim region of the occult: the phenomena of spiritualism, apparitions, haunted houses, and psychic abilities were to be the focus of their careful investigations. From the very start the Society consisted of esteemed scientists, philosophers, and scholars, and was organized as an academic learned society that strove for serious recognition by the broader scientific community (cf. Gauld, 1968). The SPR was very much an *elite* phenomenon, fully networked not only with the upper echelons of higher education, but with the ruling classes of late-Victorian Britain. The SPR could sport the names of some of Britain's top intellectuals, cultural personalities, and politicians on its membership lists and board of officers. The considerable amount of work and resources that these people invested in the elusive endeavor of 'psychical research' resulted in a large number of articles and lengthy reports published in the Society's *Journal* and *Proceedings*, and numerous books written for broader audiences. In doing all this, the SPR established some intellectual credibility for belief in paranormal events; it popularized concepts such as 'telepathy' (coined by one of the SPR's founders, Frederic Myers), and laid the foundations of experimental parapsychology that would emerge in the twentieth century. Ironically, perhaps, by opening up for empirical and experimental study of occult phenomena, the SPR also contributed to the emergence of the modern skeptics movement. Thus, the legacy of the SPR is equally felt in contemporary spiritualism and psychic mediumship, in the methodologically rigorous parapsychological laboratory, and in the contemporary skeptics movement's debunking of psychics.

BACKGROUND AND CONTEXT: VICTORIAN PSYCHICAL RESEARCH

While unrivalled in terms of cultural influence and longevity, the SPR was not the only, and not the first society of its kind. It took part in a discourse of 'psychical research' that had emerged from the encounter between spiritualism and Victorian scientific naturalism in the 1860s, and addressed vital questions concerning the possibilities of scientific knowledge, and the relation between religious beliefs and rational knowledge about the world (see Asprem, 2013, 289–316). Scientists and other intellectuals who got interested in the phenomena of mediumism in this period – including such men as Alfred Russel Wallace, the co-designer of the theory of natural selection – did not thereby abandon reason and scientific method, but sought instead to approach ostensible contact with the dead through novel applications of science (cf. Noakes, 2004). For these men (the psychical researchers were, unlike the mediums they studied, mostly men), the activities of spirits and magical powers could be made proper objects of naturalistic science: the possible reality of spiritualism and other occult phenomena would not constitute a break with a naturalistic worldview, but rather indicate that our picture of the natural world had to be radically expanded. Psychical research was, in this way, predicated on an *open-ended* naturalism (cf. Asprem, 2014, 299–306).

Victorian psychical research thus arose from a genuine scientific and philosophical interest in the phenomena associated with spiritualism and related currents. In Britain, serious intellectual interest in this body of beliefs, practices, and behaviors began when the London Dialectical Society established a special commission to investigate spiritualism and psychic phenomena in 1869. The commission's report, written by thirty-three learned gentlemen, concluded that the bulk of evidence concerning spiritualistic phenomena could not at present be discounted as fraudulent, and it advised that more research be conducted on the topic (London Dialectical Society, 1871, 5–6). In 1875, only a few years after the publication of the report, the lawyer Edward Cox established a scientific organization for this type of research entitled the Psychological Society of Great Britain (Richards, 2001; Luckhurst, 2002, 47–51). It is notable that the words 'psychological' and 'psychic' were both associated with spiritualism at this point, with the establishment of psychology as a wholly 'secular' academic discipline still decades away (see Sommer, 2012). Cox's Psychological Society was an important forerunner for the SPR, as it aimed to translate the 'spiritual' and 'occult' into the language of science, and locate it within the strictures of a new scientific society (cf. Richards, 2001). Cox's pamphlet from 1871, *Spiritualism Answered by Science*, is characteristic of this scientizing approach: here he launched the influential concept of 'psychic force' (often falsely attributed to the physicist William Crookes, who was another important pioneer of psychical research prior to the establishment of the SPR), which was conceptualized as a scientifically acceptable alternative to the spiritualist hypothesis that mediumistic phenomena were caused by the activity of the disembodied spirits of the dead. By contrast, psychic force was a completely 'natural' force, connected to the biological organism and fit for naturalistic rather than 'supernatural' explanation.

Cox's Psychological Society was, however, largely a one-man show, and when its founder passed away in 1879 the society was buried with him. Three years later the SPR emerged, taking up the mandate established by the London Dialectical Society, mobilizing those who were already active in the field of psychical research and recruiting new allies. Indeed, the success of the SPR, which is enormous when compared to the preceding Psychological Society, is not due to a radically new approach to psychic events – the essential discursive and theoretical tools were already at hand, provided by the pioneering efforts of men like Cox, Crooks, and Wallace. The SPR added a strong *social* base, built on the investment of a group of independently wealthy, well-established scholars, with ties to the upper echelons of Victorian social, cultural, and political life. This secured the institutional stability and social respectability of the new society, providing a stable platform for the study of psychic phenomena, as well as significant cultural capital bestowed by the class distinction of its key players.

NOTABLE MEMBERS AND THEIR CONTRIBUTIONS

The Sidgwick Circle

Who were these distinguished advocates of a science of the supernatural? The core group of the SPR in the 1880s centered on the influential Cambridge philosopher Henry Sidgwick (1838–1900) and his wife, Eleanor (1845–1936), and is informally known as the 'Sidgwick circle' (Gauld, 1968). Henry was a leading utilitarian moral philosopher, but also an influential advocate of educational reform: he actively supported the entry of women into higher education, and played a role in the campaign against the religious tests that were required for teaching in most British universities until 1885 (cf. James, 1970). He oversaw the establishment of Newnham College, which was the second Cambridge college to accept women. Henry's wife, Eleanor, would later serve as principal of Newnham. Eleanor, whose maiden name was Balfour, belonged to one of the most powerful political families of Victorian Britain. Her brother, Arthur Balfour (1848–1930), would later become Prime Minister of Great Britain. He was an influential ally of the Sidgwick circle, and even served as the SPR's President between 1892 and 1895. Another powerful member of the extended Sidgwick–Balfour family, Lord Gerald Balfour (1853–1945; Member of Parliament, Chief Secretary for Ireland, President of the Board of Trade, member of the Queen's Privy Council, etc.), was in charge of some of the SPR's most extraordinary experiments in the early twentieth century, known as the 'cross-correspondences' (more on which below).

The Balfour family connection was no doubt useful for establishing a status of high distinction for the SPR, but other members of the Sidgwick circle were more important for actual scientific work during the first decades of the Society's existence. In addition to Henry and Eleanor, the most prolific and intellectually influential scholars were the Cambridge classicists Edmund Gurney (1847–88) and Frederic Myers (1843–1901), and the Australian émigré Richard Hodgson (1855–1905), who had enrolled at Cambridge in 1878. Collectively, this small group of people had their names attached to half of the approximately 14,000 pages of research reports, theorizing, and experimental notes that were published by the SPR's journal and proceedings between 1882 and 1900 (Gauld, 1968, 313). These publications were, moreover, made possible by avail of the group's independent financial means, particularly those of Edmund Gurney. In other words, the level of activity that the SPR was able to uphold in this period would have been completely unimaginable without the enormous financial, intellectual, and social investment of this most elite group of people.

Notable Contributions, 1882–1902: Phantoms of the Living, Skeptical Exposés, and Subliminal Selves

The first really significant work produced by the SPR was a massive two-volume book edited by Edmund Gurney (with Myers and Frank Podmore), entitled *Phantoms of the Living* (1886). The book collected thousands of case stories of paranormal events, mostly apparitions of the dead, impossible communications between minds over large distances, strange meaningful coincidences, and eerie premonitions of impending crises. The sheer magnitude of this survey suggested that the kind of experiences the SPR was interested in were indeed very common. The editors also made an attempt to apply probability analyses of the likelihood that these cases were due to chance. These analyses were, however, deeply flawed even for the period, amounting to rather absurd figures. In one case Gurney et al. wrote that 'the odds against the occurrence, by accident, of as many coincidences of the type in question… are about *a thousand billion trillion trillion trillions to 1*.' Sometimes the authors did not even bother spelling the figures out: '[t]he argument for thought-transference… cannot be expressed here in figures, as it requires 167 nines – that is, the probability is far more than the ninth power of a trillion to 1' (Gurney et al., 1886, vol. 2, 17; vol. 1, 34). These amateur uses of probability sparked a sharp debate in the first volume of the *Proceedings* of the American branch of the SPR, where the philosopher, logician, and mathematician Charles Sanders Peirce (1839–1914) lashed out at the SPR researchers: 'I shall not cite these numbers, which captivate the ignorant, but which repel thinking men, who know that *no* human certitude reaches such figures of trillions, or even billions, to one' (cf. Hacking, 1988, 444–45).

The most significant contribution of *Phantoms of the Living* was, however, to launch the hypothesis that crisis-induced experiences of seeing the newly departed loved ones or learning of an accident far away just before, or just as, it happens, were a result of spontaneous 'thought-transference.' Apparitions were, in other words, phantoms of the *living* (or in the process of dying), rather than phantoms of the dead. The theory of mental action across vast distances became a major heuristic for the early work of the SPR (cf. Luckhurst, 2002). It got its most sophisticated expression in the work of Frederic Myers, who coined the new term 'telepathy' (literally 'distant touch,' or 'distant feeling'). The concept inspired much of the early quantitative work of the Society, through card-guessing trials and other attempts to experiment with the transfer of mental content (images, words, numbers, scenes) from one mind to another. This work became the object of much theoretical and methodological controversy in the SPR and beyond.

SPR researchers were, however, not only looking to create evidence for obscure mental faculties. They were also skilled and critical observers who set out to find ways to debunk any fraudulent means that could possibly be involved with the production of various 'occult' phenomena. The so-called *physical* phenomena of spiritualism were a particularly common target for SPR investigators, who took pride in finding the techniques of stage magic employed to fake phenomena such as levitation, materialization of objects, and the playing of instruments from a distance. It was Richard Hodgson, an energetic and forthright Australian who had little patience for Victorian courtesy (a trait which almost cost him his Cambridge diploma), who was the chief debunker of the early SPR. Hodgson's first and perhaps most significant contribution to this critical side of the SPR's work, at least from the perspective of the history of modern occultism, was the famous exposé of the methods of Theosophy's founder, H. P. Blavatsky, in 1884–85. After relocating to Adyar, India, Blavatsky had started receiving mysterious letters containing esoteric knowledge, which purportedly came from secret chiefs known as the Mahatmas. Hodgson went to India to investigate; he found hidden doors installed in the shrine where the letters materialized, and internal evidence suggesting that it was Blavatsky herself who was writing the letters (Hodgson, 1885; cf. Coleman, 1895). Another noteworthy and influential work of skepticism came ten years later, when Hodgson accused his fellow researchers Richet, Myers, and the physicist Oliver Lodge of having been fooled by the Italian medium Eusapia Palladino (1854–1918) during séances in France in 1894. In follow-up trials run at Myers' house in Cambridge the year after, Hodgson proceeded to thoroughly expose Palladino's fraud with the help of the professional stage magician Nevil Maskelyne (1863–1924; cf. Carrington, 1909, 51–57). Together, these two episodes had serious repercussions for the credibility of two of the most influential occult movements of the late nineteenth century: Spiritualism and Theosophy.

The crowning achievement of the SPR's first two decades was nevertheless Frederic Myers' posthumously published *Human Personality and Its Survival of Bodily Death* (1902). This book represents Myers' remarkable attempt to systematize all the knowledge that had been gathered and all the theories and hypotheses that had been tried and tested in the work of the SPR, and embed them in an overarching theoretical and philosophical framework. It is the *locus classicus* of a number of neologisms on the border of parapsychology and mainstream psychiatry, including 'telepathy,' 'cryptesthesia,' 'hypnopompic,' 'retrocognition,' 'cosmopathic,' and many others (see Myers, 1902, vol. 1, xiii-xxii). Myers' book also launched the notion of the 'subliminal self,' which was essentially a psychological theory of personality and selfhood related to Romantic notions of the unconscious. According to Myers' theory, our everyday conscious selves are only a small fraction of a vast entity that lies mostly submerged under the threshold (*sub – limen*) of consciousness. This monumental subliminal self may from time to time erupt – in dreams, automatisms, during hypnosis, and in creative ruptures. Some people had easier access to their subliminal selves, and could make it manifest more or less at will. This is what the psychic mediums, clairvoyants, and telepaths did, according to Myers, and it was also the mechanism of religious prophesies, and the visionary abilities of great artists and writers. In short, the subliminal self was the source of what Myers called 'genius.'

Although a curious work of romantic, 'gothic psychology,' *Human Personality* and Myers' theories in general had a significant influence on several noteworthy thinkers of the early twentieth century. Myers' concept of telepathy was an important influence on Sigmund Freud and the broader psychoanalytic movement. Freud, Ferenczi, and Jung all wrote on the topic of telepathy, and incorporated it in one way or another into their psychological theories. But the most significant influence of Myers' work in psychical research was on William James – well-known today as a towering figure in American psychology and pragmatic philosophy, but also a deeply committed psychical researcher and the main representative of the SPR in the United States (cf. Blum, 2006). James' famous *Varieties of Religious Experience* (1902) draws considerably on Myers' theory of genius, and rests, as James himself pointed out at the end of the book, on Myers' notion of the subliminal self (for more information on this topic, see the article on Myers elsewhere in this volume).

SCHISMS AND DECLINE: THE SOCIETY FOR PSYCHICAL RESEARCH IN THE TWENTIETH CENTURY

The Demise of the First Generation and the Return of Spiritualism

The Sidgwick circle was the 'hard core' of the SPR, guaranteeing stability and a minimum of progress in the Society's scientific work. With the exception of Eleanor Sidgwick, who lived to 1936, all its members were dead by 1905. The dawn of the twentieth century thus marked a generational shift for the Society, and it was not an easy transition. The Society had no problems keeping an active membership: new branches were opening up in new countries, and sister and daughter organizations supporting similar work were taking shape in countries such as France and Germany (for these contexts, see Lachapelle, 2011; Wolffram, 2009). But the consistency of the Society's research focus was suffering from a lack of continuity, and the new generation tended to open up old avenues that their forebears had already closed, with good reason and after due consideration, as being unproductive and riddled with methodological dangers (cf. Asprem, 2014, 317–73). Thus the spiritualist hypothesis made its return, and verified fraudsters such as Palladino found new support among an enthusiastic younger generation.

We may list three reasons for the increased popularity of spiritualism in the SPR after 1900. The first reason is theoretical, and concerns the failure of the generally mechanistic theories of telepathy. When Gurney et al. had suggested that thought-transference explained apparitions of the (newly) dead, it was generally assumed that this was a mental faculty that worked through the transmittance of 'brain-waves' in electromagnetic fields in the ether. The main theorist here was the physicist Oliver Lodge, who was also one of the leading developers of the Maxwellian field theory (see Hunt 1992). Taking the physics seriously, Lodge and other physicists in the SPR grew concerned when noticing that the *positive* studies of telepathy did not seem to respect the inverse square law: telepathic effects did not diminish with distance. This meant that whatever was going on, it could have nothing to do with the fields and waves of physics. In a presidential address to the SPR in 1902, Lodge instead opened the door to non-physical theories, whether in the style of Myers' 'subliminal self' or the disembodied souls of the spiritualists (cf. Asprem, 2014, 214–16).

The second reason for the return of the spiritualist hypothesis was experimental (and perhaps a little sentimental), and had to do with the ghostly return of Frederic Myers and other first-generation SPR researchers through the mediation of spiritualists. In what became known as the cross-correspondence experiments, the spirit of Myers spoke through a number of mediums working as far away from each other as Boston, Bombay, and Cambridge. The statements were collected at the central offices of the SPR and analyzed through an increasingly esoteric set of hermeneutical strategies. When the data were massaged in this way, SPR researchers convinced themselves that dead Myers had invented a clever way of proving the survival of *his* personality by planting different hints to different mediums, requiring the researchers to collect all the pieces to make out the whole. While leaving strict experimental and quantitative methodologies behind, the hermeneutic evidence of the cross-correspondences was persuasive for many in the Society, including some of the most scientifically minded researchers, and the experiments would continue well into the 1920s (see e.g. Saltmarsh, 1938).

The third reason for the return of spiritualism is of an altogether different order: the horrors of the First World War. The killing of a generation of young boys in the trenches boosted the enterprise of crossing the veil of death. Many who had been mildly sympathetic to spiritualism before the war emerged as zealous advocates in its wake. Among these were Oliver Lodge, who lost his son Raymond in the trenches in 1915. Lodge believed he had made contact with his son through a number of different mediums, and wrote the bestseller *Raymond, or Life and Death* (1916) to bring the evidence to the world. The now retired physicist would spend the 1920s giving incredibly popular lectures on spiritualism, and writing countless articles, pamphlets and books on the survival of death and related topics (cf. Asprem, 2014, 208–25).

Science vs. Spiritualism: A Parting of Ways

The SPR continued to maintain a high public profile throughout this period, and attracted a number of internationally known intellectuals to serve as presidents of the society. The list of SPR presidents between 1900 and 1939 include Nobel laureates such as the philosopher Henri Bergson (1913) and the physicist Lord Rayleigh (1919), famous politicians such as Gerald Balfour (1906–7), and well-known public intellectuals such as the German biologist and philosopher Hans Driesch (1926–27), the British pioneer of academic psychology William McDougall (1920–21), and the analytic philosopher Charlie Dunbar Broad (1935–36).

Nevertheless, the rising influence of spiritualism within the Society's membership following the First World War had lasting effects on its future development. A chasm was growing between a 'scientific' wing and a 'spiritualist' wing of the SPR. The scientific wing held that the most important thing for the SPR was to develop proper scientific methods, acceptable to colleagues in disciplines such as biology, medicine, and psychology (which were getting increasingly more sophisticated), and to withhold judgment until these had been properly tested. By contrast, the spiritualist wing held that the matter had already been resolved, spiritualism had been vindicated, and the job now consisted in spreading the message to the people. In 1925 this ideological divergence materialized in the form of a series of institutional schisms. In England, the stage magician Harry Price convinced the University of London to support him in establishing the National Laboratory for Psychical Research, which was to act as a more scientific counterpart to the SPR. Price's 'Laboratory' would, however, turn out to be more of a stage for high profile debunking than a research laboratory. The 1932 'Brocken experiment' was a highlight: a full 'black magic' operation was performed on a midsummer's eve on the mountain Brocken in Germany, traditionally associated with the witches' Sabbath. With the world press attending, the magical experiment attempted to transform a goat into a young man. Sensationally, nothing happened.

A more serious institutional schism took place in the United States in the same year, as a response to a controversy that had erupted over tests run with the famous Boston physical medium Mina Crandon, better known as 'Margery.' An investigation committee had been set down, consisting among others of William McDougall (1871–1938), perhaps the most outspoken advocate of the pro-science line in psychical research, and Harry Houdini (1874–1926), the famous escape artist and skeptic. When the committee's report concluded that Margery was fraudulent, the American SPR took a curious course of action: it disregarded the verdict of the report, fired critics from positions of power in the Society, and started circulating apologetic articles, books, and pamphlets defending Margery against her critics (Prince, 1926; cf. Asprem, 2014, 337). Delicately, one of the orchestrators of this development was the influential Boston surgeon Le Roy Crandon, who happened to be Margery's own husband. One of the people who had been disowned by the board of trustees of the American SPR following the Margery case was Walter Franklin Prince (1863–1934), who had been the editor of the *ASPR* journal, a member of the Margery committee, and a clear supporter of the scientific wing of the Society. Prince, who was not an enemy of spiritualism *per se*, but insisted that scientific methods had to be respected, now became an outspoken critic of the new leadership line. In 1925, he established the Boston Society for Psychical Research (BSPR) to act as a scientific counterpart to the American SPR, which, to his mind, had been hijacked by spiritualists and turned into a propaganda machine.

The BSPR remained the standard bearer of scientific psychical research in America until it ceased operations due to its founder's premature death in 1934. Significantly, the very last thing the BSPR did was to publish a book that would become immensely influential: Joseph Banks Rhine's *Extra-Sensory Perception* (1934). This book, based on Rhine's experimental work under the supervision of McDougall at Duke University, represented a fully experimental, methodologically rigid program of psychical research, and is now generally regarded as the paradigmatic text of experimental parapsychology (e.g. Mauskopf & McVaugh, 1980; cf. Asprem, 2014, 398–407). The publication of *Extra-Sensory Perception* by BSPR thus initiated a new phase in the history of psychical research, where new institutions, often connected to mainstream research universities, pursued the scientific track through what became professional parapsychology. Although the SPR's publications would continue to host some important scientific and philosophical discussions in this field, the emergence of professional parapsychology marked the end of the SPR as an institution of any serious scientific promise.

THE SOCIETY FOR PSYCHICAL RESEARCH TODAY

The SPR is still active today, and is thus by far the most successful institution for psychical research in terms of longevity. In the shadow of professional parapsychology, which depends on highly specialized methodological training in experimental psychology and statistical methods, the SPR is not directly involved with research anymore, taking an educational role instead. It hosts public lectures at its offices in Kensington, London, organizes annual conferences on paranormal research and historical issues related to the field of psychical research, and offers some minor grants for researchers. In tune with its Victorian legacy, the SPR also continues to collect anecdotes of paranormal experiences, including premonitions, haunted houses, and poltergeist phenomena.

Most importantly, however, the SPR is in charge of managing its own vast heritage, holding extensive libraries of the entire psychical research literature. In recent years, much of this has been digitized and made available to SPR members online. Thus the Society's bibliographic and archival services are indispensable to parapsychological researchers, but also increasingly important to historians working in the fields of history of science (and 'pseudoscience'), and historians of modern esotericism. The SPR is today a somewhat museal institution of primarily historical interest – but a significant one at that.

REFERENCES AND FURTHER READING

Asprem, Egil (2014), *The Problem of Disenchantment: Scientific Naturalism and Esoteric Discourse, 1900–1939*, Leiden and Boston, Brill.

Blum, Deborah (2006), *Ghost Hunters: William James and the Search for Scientific Proof of Life after Death*, New York, Penguin Press.

Brown, Nicola, Carolyn Burdett and Pamela Turschwell, eds. (2004), *The Victorian Supernatural*, Cambridge, Cambridge University Press.

Carrington, Hereward (1909), *Eusapia Palladino and Her Phenomena*, New York, B.W. Dodge & Company.

Coleman, William Emmette (1895), 'The Sources of Madame Blavatsky's Writings', Appendix C in Vsevolod Sergyeevich Solovyoff, *A Modern Priestess of Isis*, 353–66, London, Longmans, Green, and Co.

Gauld, Alan (1968), *The Founders of Psychical Research*, London, Routledge & K. Paul.

Gurney, Edmund, F. W. H. Myers, and Frank Podmore, eds. (1886), *Phantasms of the Living*, two volumes, London, Society for Psychical Research/Trübner and Co., Ludgate Hill, E.C.

Hacking, Ian (1988), 'Telepathy: Origins of Randomization in Experimental Design', *Isis* 79, 427–51.

Hodgson, Richard (1885), 'Account of Personal Investigations in India, and Discussion of the Authorship of the "Koot Hoomi" Letters', *Proceedings of the Society for Psychical Research* 3, 207–380.

Hunt, Bruce J. (1992), *The Maxwellians*, Ithaca, NY, Cornell University Press.

Huxley, T. H., Henry Wace, et al. (1889), *Christianity and Agnosticism: A Controversy*, New York, The Humboldt Publishing Company.

James, David Gwilym (1970), *Henry Sidgwick: Science and Faith in Victorian England*, Oxford, Oxford University Press.

Lightman, Bernard (1987), *The Origins of Agnosticism: Victorian Unbelief and the Limits of Knowledge*, Baltimore & London, Johns Hopkins University Press.

Lodge, Oliver (1916), *Raymond: or Life and Death: With Examples of the Evidence for the Survival of Memory and Affection After Death*, London, Methuen.

London Dialectical Society (1871), 'Report on spiritualism of the committee of the London Dialectical Society: Together with the evidence, oral and written, and a selection from the correspondence', London, Longmans, Green, Reader and Dyer.

Luckhurst, Roger (2002), *The Invention of Telepathy 1870–1901*, Oxford, Oxford University Press.

Mauskopf, Seymour H. and Michael R. McVaugh (1980), *The Elusive Science: Origins of Experimental Psychical Research*, Baltimore, Johns Hopkins University Press.

Myers, F. W. H. (1902), *Human Personality and Its Survival of Bodily Death*, two volumes, New York, London & Bombay, Longmans, Green, and Co.

Noakes, Richard (2004), 'Spiritualism, Science and the Supernatural in mid-Victorian Britain', In Nicola Brown et al. (eds.), *The Victorian Supernatural*, 23–43, Cambridge, Cambridge University Press.

Rhine, J. B. (1934), *Extra-Sensory Perception*, Boston, Boston Society for Psychic Research.

Saltmarsh, Herbert Francis (1938), *Evidence of Personal Survival from Cross Correspondences*, London, G. Bell & Sons.

Sommer, Andreas (2012), 'Psychical research and the origins of American psychology: Hugo Münsterberg, William James and Eusapia Palladino', *History of the Human Sciences* 25, 23–44.

Turner, Frank Miller (1974), *Between Science and Religion: the Reaction to Scientific Naturalism in Late Victorian England*, New Haven, Yale University Press.

PART V

TWENTIETH CENTURY AND THE CONTEMPORARY WORLD

CHAPTER TWENTY-FIVE

ORDO TEMPLI ORIENTIS

Christian Giudice

EARLY STIRRINGS AND ORIGINS OF THE ORDER

The Ordo Templi Orientis is an occult order founded at the beginning of the twentieth century. As with most orders currently in existence, it has been very difficult to put forth a clear analysis of the structure, succession rights and main ideas of the order, but recent scholarship has allowed a much more informed and impartial point of view than previously possible. The initiatic organization arose in the backdrop of fin de siècle occultism, and its links to major personalities, such as anthroposophist Rudolf Steiner (1861–1925), Freemason and occultist John Yarker (1833–1913) and Papus (1865–1916), are proof that the prime movers and founders of the order were well connected in the English, German and French occult milieux. The first steps leading to the foundation of the order may be found in four major figures: the first, Henry Klein (1866–1913), has only recently been reassessed as a major contributor to the future founding of the O.T.O. (Kaczynski 2012: 1–32): through contacts in the music industry, Klein, in London, March 1886, met singer, socialist and Freemason Theodor Reuss (1855–1923), a figure 'reminiscent of Cagliostro' (Howe & Möller 1978: 28). The third member of the triumvirate, defined by Kaczynski as 'world-class occult authority' (2012: 49) was Dr Franz Hartmann (1838–1912), a doctor and illustrious member of the German section of the Theosophical Society. While bonds of friendship were tighter between Klein and Reuss, Hartmann was closer to the fourth figure, without whose financial aid, the O.T.O. would have never come into existence (Pasi 2005: 898): Carl Kellner (1850–1905), a wealthy Austrian businessman, with interests as varied as alchemy, yoga and Freemasonry. His interest in yoga was manifested by an account of his many years of experience, in the 1896 booklet *Yoga: Eine Skizze*. The myth surrounding the early O.T.O. history also depicts pictures of Kellner studying under the guidance of three Eastern masters, who according to Crowley-biographer John Symonds, were the Arab Soliman Ben Aïssa (b. 1865), Bheema Sena Pratapa (b. 1872) and Sri Agamya Guru Pramahamsa (b. ca. 1841), and Hartmann himself, in his 'Dr. Karl Kellner' (1924) confirmed the yogic teachings imparted upon Kellner by these individuals. Whether or not Kellner ever travelled to the East, where he has been credited with learning techniques of sex-magic, studies have yet to find out, although it must be pointed out that reference to sexual magic appears in Reuss's writings only after Kellner's death (Pasi 2005: 899). Around the year 1901, Reuss obtained charters from the chief of the *Societas Rosacruciana in Anglia*, William Wynn Westcott (1848–1925) and from Freemason John Yarker to found various high-grade masonic rites on German soil. Reuss, Hartmann and Kellner all seem to have been involved in this masonic milieu, and a journal, *Oriflamme*, was launched by Reuss, in order to better coordinate the growing number of groups. An *Inneres Dreieck*, or Inner Triangle (König 2001: 62) seems to have existed behind the façade of the high-grade orders, presumably teaching sex-magic techniques and more advanced occult practices, in most likelihood formed by Reuss, Hartmann and Kellner themselves. In 1905 Kellner died, and Reuss lost the financial backing he had enjoyed up until then. Scandals concerning homosexual rites within his organization forced him to seek refuge in England once again. Nevertheless Reuss was undeterred, and in 1906 wrote four distinct works: The first *Lingam-Yoni*, followed almost verbatim the theories found in Hargrave Jennings's (1817–90) *Phallism: a Description of the Worship of Lingam Yoni* (1889), according to which all religions could be elucidated by sexual symbolism. This seems to be the one of the sources of the sex-magic techniques of the O.T.O., as convincingly argued by Kaczynski (2012: 246–48). The other three were the two English and one German versions of the first constitution of the Ordo Templi Orientis: it must be noted that, because of the scandal that had surrounded Reuss, the year of publication was delayed considerably (König 2001: 63).

For years, Reuss abandoned his project, until, for the first time in 1910, and successively in 1912, he met the British rising star of occultism Aleister Crowley (1875–1947), who helped Reuss to definitely give the O.T.O. a proper identity. As Ellic Howe and Helmut Möller wrote, 'it seems unlikely that the O.T.O. was in any sense active as early as 1905–6 and we believe that it was not effectively launched until 1912 when Aleister Crowley got involved' (1978: 38). Appointed head of the order for the British Isles, Crowley set out to revise the initiation rituals and appoint delegates in English-speaking countries. As Hartmann had already noticed in his 'Light for Italy' (1888: 19), the order needed to break away from the masonic habit of not initiating women within its ranks. If sexual-magical techniques were to be the core of the order, female initiates would have had to be a desideratum. From the very beginning of his rule as British head, Crowley openly advocated female initiation, and added one new element to the already peculiar blend too. A text, which he had received in Cairo, in 1904, dictated to him by an allegedly praeternatural being, *Liber L*, or *The Book of the Law*, was to be embraced as a holy book in each of the lodges he supervised, and the tenets of the new religion of *Thelema*, which the book advocated, were to be accepted by it members. Meanwhile Reuss felt it was time to fully publicize the O.T.O.'s strongpoint, and, in the 1912 'jubilee issue' of *Oriflamme*, for the first time it was clearly stated: 'Our Order possesses the KEY which opens up all Masonic and Hermetic secrets, namely, the teaching of sexual magic, and this teaching explains, without exception, all the secrets of Nature, all the symbolism of Freemasonry and all systems of religion' (1912: 21).

THE O.T.O. DURING THE CROWLEY AND GERMER YEARS

Under Reuss's supervision, the O.T.O. initiatic path was divided in ten degrees, the tenth being purely administrative and representing the *Rex Summus Sanctissimus*, governing each country, while the eighth and ninth concerned the study and practice of sex-magic, with the former concerning masturbatory practices and the latter involving sexual intercourse. Crowley's addition of a subsequent eleventh degree was based on anal intercourse, be it hetero- or homosexual, while the twelfth degree represented the *Frater Superior*, or Outer Head of the Order, O.H.O. During WWI Crowley relocated to the US, where he made a living writing German propaganda, while Reuss sought asylum in neutral Switzerland, and more specifically in the artistic community of *Monte Verita'*, near Ascona. There, popular Austrian dancer Rudolf von Laban (1879–1958) represented a focus around which an O.T.O. lodge was created, and, through many changes and vicissitudes, still exists to this day as the only surviving O.T.O. body from the Reuss era. Crowley's pro-German propaganda articles, which he published in the US, culminated to a raid of the London lodge, where documents and paraphernalia were seized by the authorities (Pasi 2014: 16; Crowley 1978: 856–58). On Crowley's return to Europe, the relationship between Reuss and Crowley had become strained. A letter dated 9 November 1921 sent by Reuss to Crowley clearly demonstrates that the German occultist had intercepted a letter destined to one of Crowley's followers: 'your brotherly suggestions that I am demented and your other suggestion to have your nominee, so to say "depose" me as O.H.O. – makes all arrangements impossible' (König 2001: 76–77). Undeterred, Crowley wrote back: 'It is my will to be the O.H.O. *Frater Superior* of the Order, and avail myself of your abdication [sic] – to proclaim myself as such' (König 2001: 77). Upon Reuss's death in 1923, there seemed to be no other suitable candidate, and two of the remaining tenth degrees, Charles Stansfeld Jones (1886–1950) and Heinrich Tränker (1880–1956), respectively representatives for the US and Germany, gave their vote of confidence to Crowley. The *Pansophia* movement in Germany, a neo-Rosicrucian umbrella organization, which comprised several occult orders and was headed by Tränker, split into different factions. Among those who refused to accept Crowley's religio-philosophical tenets of Thelema fully was Eugen Grosche (1888–1964), who proceeded to found the *Fraternitas Saturni*, an order in many doctrinal and ritual aspects similar to the O.T.O., but independent from it. The Fraternitas Saturni is still active to this day, with members mostly in Germany and Canada.

Although German initiates did follow Crowley after Grosche's departure, most notably Karl Germer (1886–1962) and Martha Küntzel (1857–1941), the rapid rise of totalitarian regimes, and the consequent anti-masonic sentiment, which derived from these political movements, convinced Crowley to concentrate his efforts on expanding the O.T.O. in the US. Crowley agreed that Wilfred Talbot Smith (1885–1957), who had formerly been a charter member of O.T.O. Agapé lodge in Vancouver in 1915, would liaise with his former student, Jane Wolfe (1875–1958), in order to create a fully functioning body of the order on North-American soil (Seckler 2003: 146–47). Agapé lodge #2 was thus born in Los Angeles in 1933. By the end of WWII, close to Crowley's death in 1947, Agapé #2 was the only functioning O.T.O. body remaining, its headquarters having moved to Pasadena, and its new head being John Whiteside

Parsons (1914–52), a charismatic figure and well-respected aerospace engineer. In the meantime, Karl Germer, who had suffered internment in a Nazi camp for 'seeking students for the foreign resident, high grade Freemason, Crowley' (Starr 1995: 150) had been able to leave Germany and move to the US. When Crowley died, in 1947, he had already made provisions that Germer, 'the most valued member of the Order, with no exception' (Starr 2003: 263) succeed him at the head of the order. Despite vetoing new initiations within the order and *de facto* creating a stall in the expansion of the O.T.O., Germer's years as O.H.O. proved vital for the perpetuation of the O.T.O. and Crowley's legacy: The Beast's letters and documents between Germer and long-time Crowley friend Gerald Yorke (1901–83) were copied, exchanged and preserved for posterity (Richmond (ed.) 2011: xlvi–xlvii) and Germer himself supervised the publication of several texts penned by his predecessor, such as *The Vision and the Voice* (1952) and *Magick without Tears* (1954). At the time of Germer's death, in 1962, the Agapé #2 lodge had disbanded, and interest in keeping the order alive was at an all-time low.

A THELEMIC RENAISSANCE

From 1962 onwards, out of the many groups belonging to the Thelemic milieu, four in particular seemed to have stronger claims to successorship than others. In March 1951, Crowley's last secretary, the London-based Kenneth Grant (1923–2011) had successfully received a charter from Germer to found an English body of the O.T.O. The London camp soon developed into something different, and after alleged extra-terrestrial communications from a planet which was identified as being called Nu, Grant issued a manifesto of his new creation: the New Isis Lodge. Germer was swift to expel Grant from the order, and Grant in turn disavowed Germer's authority as O.H.O. and continued to promote his particular blend of Thelemic magic, which included Eastern tantra, the mentioned communications with extra-terrestrials and an emphasis on the works of artist Austin Osman Spare (1886–1956) and pulp-horror author H.P. Lovecraft (1890–1936). That Grant would consider himself to be the rightful head of the O.T.O. is backed by documentation. Crowley himself had written, shortly before his death: 'value of Grant: if I die or go to the USA, there must be a trained man to take care of the [...] O.T.O.' (Evans 2007: 287). In 1972 Grant embarked in a writing *tour de force* which would only end in 2002: the results are nine books, better known as the *Typhonian Trilogies*, which elucidate Grant's magical system, and Crowley's role within it, in all of its aspects. The order survives to this date as the Typhonian Order, and is primarily based in the United Kingdom. It no longer claims links to the O.T.O. and has changed substantially in structure since the days of the New Isis Lodge.

While Grant was organizing his lodge in England, Herman Metzger (1919–90) was busy rebuilding the Swiss O.T.O., which Reuss had founded in the pre-Crowley days. Germer had accepted this lineage as valid and kept in touch with Metzger, monitoring his attempt at rebuilding Reuss's legacy. After Germer's death, Metzger claimed the grade of O.H.O. for himself, since his claim to leadership, in his eyes, was stronger than Grant's, who had only entered the scene during the last years of Crowley's life. After Metzger's death, his friend and follower Annemarie Aeschbach (1926–2008) succeeded in leading the order up until her death, in April 2008. The Swiss branch is today no longer operative.

The biggest and only active group today, to have been recognized as O.T.O. by courts of law, is the so-called 'Caliphate' O.T.O. The O.T.O. was revived by Grady Louis McMurtry (1918–85), who had received direct instructions from Crowley to succeed after Germer's death. The two had met in the 1940s, when McMurtry had been stationed in Britain during WWII. Crowley had then written in clear terms that Germer was to be his successor, but that, at any moment, he could 'take charge of the whole work of the Order in California to reform the Organization' (Cornelius 2005, vol13: 46). Helped by notable thelemic representatives of the Agapé #2 lodge days, McMurtry slowly started rebuilding the order from its ashes. Far from being a model of efficiency, McMurtry's focus on his occult workings was at times unclear and he was often found to be intoxicated during initiation rituals, and there are many accounts, which corroborate this statement (Wasserman 2012): but the carefree attitude of the late 1960s and McMurtry's undeniable charisma enabled the O.T.O. to grow and prosper. In 1979, the order was incorporated under the laws of the State of California and the corporation attained federal tax exemption as a religious entity under IRS Code 501(c)3 in 1982. The last contender for the position of O.H.O. of the order was Brazilian occultist Marcelo Ramos Motta (1931–87): during the 1950s, Motta had been a student under Germer, and, at the time of the latter's, had proclaimed himself O.H.O. and, in this claim, he had been backed by Germer's widow, Sascha. Motta and his followers set up an enterprise named Society O.T.O., or S.O.T.O., and had begun publishing new editions, often followed by his commentaries, of Crowley's writings. McMurtry sued Motta over copyright issues, and the trial dragged on for years, until 1985, when, shortly before McMurtry's death, the court ruled in favour of McMurtry's group, and assigned them sole custody of Crowley copyrights. After the death of McMurtry, according to his wishes, all of the ninth degrees were summoned to elect the next O.H.O. William Breeze was chosen and is currently still head of the Caliphate O.T.O., expanding the order from the relatively few active in 1985 to the thousands affiliated to the order today.

REFERENCES AND FURTHER READING

Breeze, William [Hymaeneus Beta] (ed.), (1986) *The Equinox – The Review of Scientific Illuminism – The Official Organ of the O.T.O.*, vol. III-10, York Beach, ME: Samuel Weiser.

Cornelius, Jerry, (2005) *In the Name of the Beast: A Biography of Grady Louis McMurtry, a Disciple of Edward Alexander Crowley, Red Flame 12–3*, Berkeley, CA: Red Flame Productions.

Crowley, Aleister, (1952) *The Vision and the Voice, with Commentary by the Master Therion*, Barstow, CA: Thelema Publishing.

——, (1954) *Magick without Tears*, Hampton, N.J.: Thelema Publishing.

——, (1978) *The Confessions of Aleister Crowley: An Autohagiography Edited by John Symonds and Kenneth Grant*, London: Penguin Arcana.

Crowley, Aleister and Reuss, Theodor, (1999) *O.T.O. Rituals and Sex Magick*, Thame, I-H-O.

Evans, Dave, (2007) *The History of British Magick after Crowley: Kenneth Grant, Amado Crowley, Chaos Magic, Satanism, Lovecraft, the Left Hand Path, Blasphemy and Magical Morality*, Milton Keynes, Hidden Publishing.

Goodrick-Clarke, Nicholas, (2005) 'Hartmann, Franz', in W. Hanegraaff, A. Faivre, R. van den Broek, Jean-Pierre Brach (eds.), *Dictionary of Gnosis and Western Esotericism*, Leiden: Brill.

Hakl, H. Thomas, (2013) 'The Magical Order of the Fraternitas Saturni', in *Occultism in a Global Perspective*, Gordan Djurdjevic and Henrik Bogdan (eds.), Durham: Acumen, pp.37–56.

Hartmann, Franz, (1888) 'Light For Italy', *Lucifer* III:13, pp.18–20.

——, (1924) 'Dr. Karl Kellner, ein Opfer des Okkultismus', *Teosophische Rundschau* XII:6, pp. 306–9

Howe, Ellic and Möller, Helmut, (1976) 'Theodor Reuss: Irregular Freemasonry in Germany: 1900–923', *Ars Quatuor Coronati*, 91, pp. 28–46.

——, (1986) *Merlin Peregrinus: Vom Untergrund des Abendlandes*, Königshausen-Würzburg: Neumann.

Jennings, Hargrave, (1889) *Phallism: a Description of the Worship of Lingam Yoni in Various Parts of the World*, n.p., privately published.

Kaczynski, Richard, (2010) *Perdurabo: The Life of Aleister Crowley: Revised and Expanded Edition*, Berkeley, CA: North Atlantic Books.

——, (2012) *Forgotten Templars: The Untold Origins of Ordo Templi Orientis*, n.p., privately published.

Kellner, Carl, (1896) *Yoga: Eine Skizze* über *den psycho-physiologischen Teil der Alten Indischen Yogalehre*, München: Kastner & Lossen.

King, Francis (ed.), (1973) *The Secret Rituals of the* O.T.O., New York, Samuel Weiser.

König, Peter R., (1994) *Materialen zum OTO*, München: Arbeitgemeinschaft für Religions- und Weltanschauungsfragen.

——,(2014) The O.T.O. Phenomenon < parareligion.ch > (Last accessed 2 May 2014).

——, (2001) *Der O.T.O Phänomen Remix*, München: Arbeitgemeinschaft für Religions-und Weltanschauungsfragen.

Pasi, Marco, (2005a) 'Ordo Templi Orientis', in W. Hanegraaff, A. Faivre, R. van den Broek, Jean-Pierre Brach (eds.), *Dictionary of Gnosis and Western Esotericism*, Leiden: Brill.

——, (2005b) 'Crowley, Aleister', in W. Hanegraaff, A. Faivre, R. van den Broek, Jean-Pierre Brach (eds.), *Dictionary of Gnosis and Western Esotericism*, Leiden: Brill.

——, (2014) *Aleister Crowley and the Temptation of Politics*, Durham: Acumen.

Seckler, Phyllis, (2003) *Jane Wolfe: Her Life With Aleister Crowley, Red Flame 10–11*, Berkeley, CA: Red Flame Productions.

Starr, Martin P., (2003) *The Unknown God: W.T. Smith and the Thelemites*, Bolingbrook, IL: Teitan Press.

Reuss, Theodor, (1906) *Lingam-Yoni oder die Mysterien des Geschlechts-Kultus als die Basis der Religionen aller Kulturvölker des Altertums und des Marienkultus in der christlichen Kirche sowie Ursprung des Kreuzes und des Crux Ansata*, Berlin: Wilsson.

——, (1912) 'Unser Orden', in *Jubilæums-Ausgabe Der Oriflamme*, No. VII (1912), p. 21.

Richmond, Keith (ed.), (2011) *Aleister Crowley, the Golden Dawn, Buddhism: Reminiscences and Writings of Gerald Yorke*, York Beach, ME: Teitan Press.

Wasserman, James, (2012) *In the Center of the Fire: A Memoir of the Occult, 1966–1989*, Lake Worth, FL: Ibis Press.

CHAPTER TWENTY-SIX

ARTHUR EDWARD WAITE

Alison Butler

Arthur Edward Waite (1857–1942) mapped his own path through the terrain of the British occult revival. While his fellow occultists focussed more on magical experimentation and its intersections with contemporary scientific theories, he embraced the mystical and religious aspects of the traditions that made up nineteenth and twentieth-century occultism. As an author and critical historian of modern occultism, he also stood in stark contrast to the seemingly indiscriminate and all-accepting perspective of many of his occult colleagues.

Waite's legacy is largely characterized by this mystical bent and the numerous volumes he has left behind examining and analyzing esoteric traditions throughout the ages. Waite authored, translated or edited more than eighty works on various branches of occultism including, Freemasonry, Rosicrucianism, tarot, kabbalah and alchemy. As such, his influence on late nineteenth- and early-twentieth-century occultism and indeed contemporary magic is profound. He translated Eliphas Lévi's major works and co-produced one of the most renowned and used tarot decks. He was a member of many of the esoteric societies of his day and founded two himself, 'The Independent and Rectified Rite' and 'The Fellowship of the Rosy Cross'. Despite this, he shunned the magical and spent much effort debunking the fantastical claims of his contemporaries in favour of the mystical and his personal quest for divine union.

Born in Brooklyn, New York on October 2, 1857, Waite apparently entered the world as the illegitimate child of an American ship's captain, Captain Charles F. Waite, and an upper middle-class English woman, Emma Lovell (Gilbert 1987: 16). After his father's death, he moved to England in 1859 at the age of two with his mother and infant sister. There, his mother's family promptly disowned Emma and her children (Gilbert 1983: 12). His mother converted to Catholicism and turned to the Church for the support and community denied her by her blood. The Roman Catholic church was a strong influence on Waite as a child. His education was sporadic. There are records of him having attended St. Charles' College in Bayswater for two terms (Gilbert 1983: 12–13). It is this general lack of education that some have identified as the source of his rather ponderous and lengthy writing style (Gilbert 1983: 11). The Catholic influence of his childhood was tempered somewhat by the rather Protestant themes in the literature he consumed. He voraciously read the penny dreadfuls and epic poems of the day and by the age of 17 began to write his own poetry, a passion he would indulge in for the rest of his life (Gilbert 1983: 12).

Waite experienced a crisis of his Catholic faith when his sister died in 1874 from complications following a bout with scarlet fever (Gilbert 1987: 23). Waite turned to Spiritualism, which was at its height in Britain at the time, immersing himself in its literature and attending séances. Waite's initial enthusiasm for Spiritualism waned early although he continued to write on the subject for many years oftentimes critically and occasionally cynically, remarking how in the past our only desire of the dead was peace for the soul – nowadays we want to chat with them continuously (Waite 1908: 41). Mysticism proved more alluring and he placed more value on the mystical experience than the psychical. Eventually, he became interested in Theosophy, but was no happier with its ideas. It wasn't until he discovered Eliphas Lévi that he began to settle. Like many burgeoning occultists of his day, Waite set up camp in the British Museum, reading Lévi, and running into future Golden Dawn members such as William Butler Yeats and Samuel Liddell MacGregor Mathers. Waite was enamoured with Lévi calling him the 'most brilliant, the most original, the most fascinating interpreter of occult philosophy in the West' (Waite 2010: xiii). He translated his major works, beginning in 1886 with *Dogme et Haut Rituel*, which was published in 1891 as *The Mysteries of Magic*. This was followed in 1913 with *Transcendental Magic*, a translation of Lévi's *Histoire de la Magie*.

Despite Waite's many other accomplishments he is probably best known for his membership in the most notorious occult society of the day, the Hermetic Order of the Golden Dawn. Waite was admitted to the Golden Dawn in January of 1891, but resigned after six months. He had apparently begun to hear things indicating that he should not be involved, not due to issues of morality as the Order had yet to draw public scrutiny on such matters, but rather 'a question of things which had an equivocal legal aspect' (Gilbert 1987: 111). Moreover, Waite was not overly impressed with the teachings of the Golden Dawn, nor with the capabilities of its founders. He criticized Mathers for accepting 'too freely what texts and traditions tell him on these subjects' (Waite 1908: 4). Of both Westcott and Mathers he commented that he was 'certainly not an occultist after their manner; that I knew them sufficiently well to loathe their false pretences, their buskined strutting and their abysmal ignorance of the supposititious arcane which they claimed to guard' (Waite 1938: 99).

This initial break was not the end of Waite's association with the Golden Dawn. He applied to join again and was readmitted in 1896. Waite ascended through the ranks of initiates reaching the second order, the 'Rosae Rubae et Aureae Crucis', in 1899 (Gilbert 1987: 112). Following the general insurrection that took place as the order self-destructed in the early 1900s, Waite took over the Golden Dawn's London temple, the Isis-Urania Temple, and established his Independent and Rectified Rite. Waite's order replaced the magical focus of the Golden Dawn with a Christian mystical emphasis that stood in direct opposition to the other offshoot of the Golden Dawn that had survived its destruction, Robert William Felkin's 'Stella Matutina', which pursued a magical agenda.

Waite's faction attracted many of the original Golden Dawn members and new initiates including the poet and mystic Evelyn Underhill. The Rite lasted until 1914 when Waite was forced to dissolve it amidst further disputes and disagreements. The following year, he persevered with the creation of the Fellowship of the Rosy Cross and created rituals for his new Order that relied purely upon Rosicrucian and Christian imagery. Despite including some members of the dissolved Independent and Rectified Rite (and also the novelist Charles Williams), the Fellowship was very much a new creature and not a further evolution of the Golden Dawn magical system. In this new society, it is apparent that Waite had no further use for the Egyptian or Pagan aspects upon which the Golden Dawn had relied so heavily. In the Fellowship, he finally had full rein to pursue his mystical interest in the theory of a 'Secret Tradition' underlying all western esoteric traditions (Gilbert 2006: 1165).

Waite's desire for initiatic experience in search of mystical union with the divine had naturally led him to Freemasonry and he became a mason in 1901, joining many rites and degrees including the 'Societas Rosicruciana in Anglia' in 1902. Also, his interest in the idea of an underlying 'Secret Tradition' led him to kabbalism, about which he published several works, including *Doctrine and Literature of the Kabbalah* (1902) and *The Secret Doctrine in Israel* (1913).

Throughout the late nineteenth and early twentieth centuries he also joined various short-lived esoteric groups and served as the vice-president of the rather unique Quest Society (1908/9) established by the author and fellow occultist G. R. S. Mead. The goals of this society were to 'promote the study of religion, philosophy and science on the basis of experience' and to 'encourage the expression of the ideal in beautiful forms' (Gilbert 1987: 103).

Waite established himself as a competent and diligent scholar of esotericism through his translations, his edited work and his own writings. In 1888 he edited *Lives of Alchemystical Philosophers* and *The Magical Writings of Thomas Vaughan*. He also published his own occult scholarship as *The Real History of the Rosicrucians* in 1887 and *The Occult Sciences* in 1891. Indeed, he gradually shifted his research focus to alchemy in the 1890s, which led to the publication of a series of edited works of translations of alchemical texts as well as his vice-presidency of the Alchemical Society, founded in London in 1912 (Caron 2006: 53).

During this time he also edited one of the first esoteric journals of the time that was not purely spiritualist or Masonic in focus, *The Unknown World*. His publications did not always pay the bills however, and often he would turn to more practical forms of editing and writing to make a living, including a stint as the commercial manager of Horlicks, the malted milk manufacturer.

The publications which most clearly portray Waite's Christian mystical bent and western focus are those written during the period of the Independent and Fortified Rite. These include *The Hidden Church of the Holy Graal* (1909), *The Secret Tradition in Freemasonry* (1911), and *The Way of Divine Union* (1915). This emphasis upon Christian mysticism is further exemplified in *The Brotherhood of the Rosy Cross* (1924) and *The Secret Tradition in Alchemy* (1926). Waite also contributed many articles and letters to the occult journals of the day including *The Occult Review*. Some of his own works were reviewed in the pages of this very publication. Isabel de Steiger, a fellow occultist and mystical seeker, in her review of Waite's *Strange Houses of Sleep*, writes that '...rarely, it seems to me, has any poet sung so beautifully and mystically as has Mr. A. E. Waite in this most singular volume...' (1907: 49). While clearly some of his contemporaries praised his poetic writing, others took issue with his style. Perhaps his most hostile critic was Aleister

Crowley, who was vitriolic in his condemnation of Waite's writing style and, indeed, his very character (see Gilbert 2012).

Despite Waite's mystical turn and seeming hostility in his later years to the occultism in which he was so much involved, it would be incorrect to imagine that he had little time for occultism. Rather he had an immense amount of time and interest in the esoteric traditions that informed the occultism of his day and he wrote volumes on such topics. As Gilbert comments, 'No other writer sympathetic to the saner beliefs of occultists has succeeded so thoroughly as Waite in demolishing, both historically and critically, their lunatic claims upon history and metaphysics' (1983, 11).

Waite was never terribly healthy or rich and this combination led to a move from London to the coast of Kent in 1919. Having always suspected his heart was weak, he succumbed to heart problems in 1942, leaving behind one daughter, Sybil, from his first marriage. He had published 46 monographs, more than 40 translated, edited or introduced works, and 40 rituals created for the two orders he had established.

Waite's influence on twentieth-century mysticism and occultism is undeniable. However his work and ideas were also influential on the often overlapping literary world. This included his good friend and author Arthur Machen (a fellow member of the Fellowship of the Rosy Cross), Charles Williams, and Evelyn Underhill (his colleague in the Independent and Rectified Rite). Waite's interest in Christian mysticism freed, to some degree, from its orthodox religious underpinnings, was an interest shared by many artists and writers of the time. This common desire for mystical union with the divine brought many from the artistic world together with the occultists and the mystics in the numerous esoteric circles in operation at the time.

Waite's quest for mystical union led him to Spiritualism, Theosophy, ritual magic, kabbalah, alchemy and Freemasonry. He sought ultimate union with the divine through the variety of experiential processes offered by each movement or tradition. Content with none, he ended his days pursuing mystical union on his own terms. On this quest, the contribution he made through his translations, edited works and original writing was and is, crucial and enduring to his fellow seekers.

REFERENCES AND FURTHER READING

Butler, A. (2011) *Victorian Occultism and the Making of Modern Magic: Invoking Tradition*, New York: Palgrave Macmillan.

Caron, R. (2006) 'Alchemy V: 19th and 20th Centuries', in W. Hanegraaff, ed., *Dictionary of Gnosis and Western Esotericism*, Leiden: Brill, 53–58.

Gilbert, R. (1983) *A. E. Waite. A Bibliography*, Wellingborough, Northamptonshire: Aquarian Press.

——(1987) *A. E. Waite. Magician of Many Parts*, Wellingborough, Northamptonshire: Crucible.

——(2006) 'Arthur Edward Waite', in W. Hanegraaff, ed., *Dictionary of Gnosis and Western Esotericism*, Leiden: Brill, 1164–65.

——(2012) '"The One Thought That Was Not Untrue": Aleister Crowley and A.E. Waite', in H. Bogdan & M. P. Starr, eds., *Aleister Crowley and Western Esotericism*, Oxford: Oxford University Press, 243–54.

Steiger, I. de (1907) 'Review: A. E. Waite, *Strange Houses of Sleep*', *The Occult Review* 5:2, 49–50.

Waite, A.E. (1902) *Doctrine and Literature of the Kabbalah*, London: Theosophical Publishing Society.
——(1908) 'Notes of the Month', *The Occult Review* 7:1, 1–6.
——(1909) *The Hidden Church of the Holy Graal*, London: Rebman Limited.
—— (1911) *The Secret Tradition in Freemasonry*, New York: Rebman Company.
——(1913) *The Secret Doctrine in Israel*, London: William Rider and Son.
——(1915) *The Way of Divine Union*, London: W. Rider.
——(1924) *The Brotherhood of the Rosy Cross*, London: W. Rider & Son.
——(1926) *The Secret Tradition in Alchemy*, London: K. Paul, Trench, Trubner & Co.
——(1938) *Shadows of Life and Thought*, London: Selwyn and Blount.
——(2010) *The Mysteries of Magic: A Digest of the Writings of Eliphas Levi*, Whitefish, Montana: Kessinger Publishing.
——(2012 [1886]) *Mysteries of Magic: A Digest of the Writings of Eliphas Lévi*, Whitefish, Montana: Kessinger.

CHAPTER TWENTY-SEVEN

CHARLES FORT

Jeffrey J. Kripal

LIFE AND BOOKS

Charles Fort (1874–1932) was the son of a middle-class grocer of Dutch descent who grew up in Albany, New York, and became a journalist, a humorist, and a novelist before he turned to the personal study of what he called 'the damned' in the second and third decades of the twentieth century. Through his self-mocking writing on the latter, Fort effectively laid the intellectual and literary foundations for what would later crystallize—through the pulp magazines and science fiction of the 1930s, 1940s, and 1950s, the counterculture of the 1960s and 1970s, the New Age movement of the 1980s and 1990s, and the contemporary entertainment industry—'the paranormal' (Steinmeyer 2008, Kripal 2011a).

Fort composed and published four volumes dedicated to these anomalous phenomena: *The Book of the Damned* (1919), *New Lands* (1923), *Lo!* (1931), and *Wild Talents* (1932). The first and last books border on a genius prophetic of things to come later in the century (including and especially the UFO phenomenon). The third book is at once an extension of the first and a preparation for the fourth (on the paranormal powers of human beings as evolutionary potentials actualized and suppressed in different historical and cultural moments). The second book, though filled with insight, is more forgettable and at times embarrassing because of its crank rejection of modern astronomy.

THE DAMNED

By 'the damned' Fort referred to all those bizarre and seemingly inexplicable events commonly reported in the newspapers that could find no explanation either in the dominant religious or scientific registers of the time and so were almost immediately forgotten, ignored, or, in some cases, actively ridiculed and shamed. His primary sources were journals and newspapers. From about 1906 until his death in 1932, the man sat at a table in the New York Public Library (or the British Museum in London), spending much of every working day for a quarter century reading the entire runs of every scientific journal and newspaper that he could find, in English or French, all the way back to 1800.

He had to stop somewhere, he joked. True enough, but this unusual historical method had a number of profound implications for his theorizing, and this for at least two related reasons. First, this 1800-rule forced Fort to deal with what had traditionally been framed as the miraculous, the magical, and the demonic not in traditional religious sources of the distant past, much less in the canonized biblical world, but on the common streets and in the homes of otherwise perfectly ordinary people. Second, the same rule removed this bizarre material from the disciplining of traditional religious authority and so opened it up to other forms of modeling.

What we might call the Fortean mysteries, then, do not involve the spiritual flights of canonized saints, unions with beloved deities, historically distant prophetic revelations, or some singular Asian enlightenment. Fort would have none of that. What he would have are tablecloths and lace curtains bursting into flames around abused or emotionally conflicted teenage boys and girls (mostly girls, it turns out), or rains of fish, periwinkles, frogs, crabs, or unidentified biological matter falling from the sky and piling up in the ditches for anyone to see. He was particularly fond of stories of falling fishes. The latter image became a kind of signature or icon for his writing and was featured on the Dover edition of his collected works.

There is no way to capture Fort's humorous genius without reading him. He is at turns hilarious, philosophically profound, eerie, ridiculous, and oh so quotable. Indeed, he was such a definitive writer that his name has become an adjective—'Fortean'—to describe and capture both the trickster spirit of these phenomena and a particular no-holds-barred method of collecting them. He was a kind of paranormal Mark Twain, who was also fascinated by psychical phenomena, or what he himself framed as 'mental telegraphy,' his expression for telepathy, which he in turn linked to the sources of his literary inspiration (Kripal 2014, 249–50).

FORT THE COMPARATIVIST

There are numerous ways into Fort's thought. One of the simplest is to observe that what Fort is most interested in is how much of the world a system, *any* system, must exclude to form an opinion or a philosophical position. Put anachronistically, there is something oddly postmodern about his work, *way* before any French author would develop his or her critique of Enlightenment reason and the certainties of modernism (Bennett 2002). In his own terms, Fort was deeply bothered by how easy it is to disregard or damn a datum, a phenomenon which is linked to another insight of Fort's: how every system is, in principle, incomplete and so incapable of explaining everything.

Fort has a specific means for locating the damned or the anomalous, that stuff that does not fit in. He knows exactly what it feels like to bump up against something strange and inexplicable, something uncanny. That feeling he called a 'coincidence.' And his method for organizing these coincidences into some greater speculative context or meaningful whole? Comparativism. Here is a typical comparative moment in Fort's books, this one involving the slow falling of stones from the sky or from a specific point in the ceiling of a house:

> Somebody in France, in the year 1842, told of slow-moving stones, and somebody in Sumatra, in the year 1903, told of slow-moving stones. It would be strange, if two liars should invent this circumstance—And that is where I get, when I reason. (LO 566)

It is easy to disregard one such report. Merely an 'anecdote,' as the materialist scientists like to say in their pseudo-explanation these days. But two now? Then three? Then, with enough time in the library, three dozen from different parts of the world and in different decades? Just how long can we go on like this until we admit that this is real data, and that we haven't the slightest idea where to put it, that our present system does not, and cannot, explain it? Fort was a weird comparativist who believed that the patterns of his damned data gave witness to a different kind of world, just beyond the reach of our senses and simplistic reasons. Comparison done right could thus become what he called an 'awakening.'

The Fortean comparative practice works through the dialectical progression of three Dominants or Eras: (1) the Old Dominant of religion, which he associates with the epistemology of *belief* and the professionalism of priests; (2) the present Dominant of materialistic science, which he associates with the epistemology of *explanation* and the professionalism of scientists; and (3) the New Dominant of what he calls Intermediatism, which he associates with the epistemology of *expression* or *acceptance* and the professionalism of a new brand of individuating wizards and witches. Whereas the first two Dominants work from the systemic principle of Exclusionism, that is, they must exclude data to survive as stable systems, the New Dominant works from the systemic principle of Inclusionism, that is, it builds an open-ended system and preserves it through the confusing inclusion of data, theoretically *all* data, however bizarre and offending, toward some future awakening. Obviously, the New Dominant was what Fort was advancing and proposing.

Fort gives a date when the Old Dominant or former Era of religion finally gave way to the present one of science: 'around 1860.' This is when he noticed that the learned journals he was reading begin to lose their 'glimmers of quasi-individuality,' that is, this is when the data of the damned start to fade away before the higher organizations of aggressively and defensively intolerant scientific explanations (NL 239). This is also, of course, the precise period of Darwin's ascendance. *The Origin of Species* had just appeared the previous year, in 1859.

The Old Dominant of religion holds a special place in Fort's rhetoric. It is *the* model of intolerance, delusion, and Exclusionism. Deeply immersed in psychical research and its metaphors, Fort often preferred to see the power of religion as a psychological one akin to hypnosis. The present Dominant of science has taken over and copied the Old Dominant of religion. The priests have changed their vestments for lab coats and exchanged religious dogmas for scientific ones.

As his language of 'old' and 'new' Dominants makes crystal clear, the new Dominant of science is an unmistakable advance over the old Dominant of religion for Fort. This hardly makes science omniscient or absolute, however. Where science errs for Fort is in its pride, in its arrogance, in its failure to recognize its own limitations. Its absolute materialism and mechanism are particularly odious as well: they are powerful half-truths that imagine themselves to be the whole Truth.

He does not imagine, of course, that his particular expressions of the new Era are absolute, only that they include more and exclude less and so better approximate the Truth of things. This is why he also calls his New Dominant a species of Intermediatism. This is hardly a grand or arrogant term. It is a humble term. It implies, after all, its own demise. It is an open-ended system 'intermediate,' in between, on its way to the Truth. But it is *not* the Truth, and it too must some day be displaced by another quasi-delusion. It is this sense of being intermediate, of thinking in-between, that constitutes Fort's central insight.

In order to hasten this eventual awakening, Fort shifts his epistemology within the New Dominant. Both *belief* and *explanation*, or faith and reason, are now replaced by a more humble *acceptance* and a more daring *expression*. The latter two ways of knowing are derived from a historical consciousness that recognizes how bound people's beliefs and explanations are to their time period and, as we say now, its social construction of reality. 'All phenomena are "explained" in the terms of the Dominant of their era,' Fort points out in his own terms. 'This is why we give up trying really to explain, and content ourselves with expressing' (NL 306). The epistemology of expression, in other words, is a self-conscious knowing that recognizes its own construction and its own relativity and so opens itself up to further evolution. Hence Fort's hostility to naïve religious beliefs, which lock us into a previous era's revelations, which prevent us from progressing into the future.

SCI-FI RECEPTION HISTORY

Almost none of this, it must be said, is what made Fort so beloved among his later metaphysical, countercultural, and occult readers. Again, Fort has not generally been read as a systematic thinker, much less as a paranormal postmodern philosopher. He has been read rather, in the words of his first biographer, the science fiction writer Damon Knight, as a 'prophet of the unexplained.'

And there was a lot left unexplained. This is where things cease to be abstract and philosophical and become downright eerie and numinous. This is the same fantastic narrative that would later take on visionary, even physical, forms within the UFO phenomenon (what Fort called 'super-constructions in the sky'), a stranger story still that Fort saw in almost every detail over thirty years before it finally appeared on the public stage in the late 1940s. Prophet indeed. Here Fort argued in so many words that the earth was being visited by space ships, that these visitors were of various kinds (some beneficent, some cheats, some just curious), and that we were essentially a colony or 'farm' of these beings (a suggestion that finds a precedent in the observation of William James that we might well be like 'pets' in relationship to higher intelligences in the universe). In one of his most eerie and influential lines, Fort wrote this:

> Would we, if we could, educate and sophisticate pigs, geese, cattle? Would it be wise to establish diplomatic relation with the hen that now functions, satisfied with mere sense of achievement by way of compensation? I think we're property.
> (BD 163)

In a kind of postcolonial frame in *New Lands* (again, *way* before its time), he often compared our reactions to these encounters with the early reactions of the Native

Americans to the European colonists. Such ideas about a dark galactic colonialism and Earth as an alien farm or experimental zoo would come to form the backbone of hundreds of later science fiction stories and Hollywood movies.

NOTE

This entry is based on Chapter 2 of Kripal (2011b), used with permission.

REFERENCES AND FURTHER READING

The standard source for Fort's writings is the Omnibus volume, Introduction by Thayer, Tiffany (1941) *The Books of Charles Fort*, New York: Henry Holt and Company and later re-issued as *The Complete Books of Charles Fort* (1974), with a new Introduction by Damon Knight, New York: Dover. Most recently, the Omnibus volume has been re-issued again as *The Books of the Damned* (2008), with a new Introduction by Jim Steinmeyer, New York: Jeremy P. Tarcher. References above are to the Dover edition, with BD as *The Book of the Damned*, NL as *New Lands*, and LO as *Lo!*

Bennett, Colin (2002) *The Politics of the Imagination: The Life, Work and Ideas of Charles Fort*, with a Foreword by John Keel, Manchester: Headpress.

Knight, Damon (1970) *Charles Fort: Prophet of the Unexplained*, New York: Doubleday.

Kripal, Jeffrey J. (2011a) *Mutants and Mystics: Science Fiction, Superhero Comics, and the Paranormal*, Chicago: University of Chicago Press.

——(2011b) *Authors of the Impossible: The Paranormal and the Sacred*, Chicago: University of Chicago Press.

——(2014) *Comparing Religions: Coming to Terms*, Oxford: Wiley-Blackwell.

Steinmeyer, Jim (2008) *Charles Fort: The Man Who Invented the Supernatural*, New York: Jeremy P. Tarcher.

CHAPTER TWENTY-EIGHT

ALEISTER CROWLEY
A Prophet for the Modern Age

Henrik Bogdan

The figure of Aleister Crowley (1875–1947), so far as one exists in the dominant culture, defines him as a stock figure of transgression and evil, the godfather of contemporary Satanism and the advocate of every kind of excess, from sex to drugs, and with some posthumous assistance from pop musicians, rock and roll. What claim does a countercultural life more fit for tabloid coverage possess for contemporary academic attention?

The study of Crowley reveals a developing notion of his legacy and influence. Crowley was an influential twentieth-century religious synthesist. His esotericism was not a reversion to a medieval world view but instead in its questing for a vision of the self it was a harbinger of modernity. Crowley acknowledged that his negative reputation served as a useful filter for the credulous and a near-complete bar to acceptance of his philosophy from his peers. He stood apart and claimed for his intellectual isolation a cosmic purpose. His mission was a charismatic prophet of a new dispensation for mankind that proclaimed the absolute liberty of the individual to self-actualize without regard for the moral codes and religious strictures of prior ages. The individual means to this end was through the practices of his occult bricolage which he termed 'Magick,' a thoroughly eclectic and highly personal combination of spiritual exercises drawn from Western European magical traditions and primarily Indic sources for meditation and yoga disciplines. To this journey of self-liberation Crowley added the power of sexuality as a magical discipline. Crowley saw sexual magic as a simple and direct method of achieving the talismanic ends of the operator without the material trappings of ceremonial magic; the power was in the mind of the practitioner.

Yet Crowley as a proponent of a new religious movement does not fit neatly into a generalized construct of a charismatic revelator. Rather, it was a position into which he grew without seemingly abandoning his prior worldview. Before he assumed the role of prophet of a new age and the promulgator of a scripture, *The Book of the Law* (1904), that could not be changed 'so much as the style of a letter,' as a university student he sought to be a student of philosophy and empirical science. His reaction against the fundamentalist faith of his childhood predicated on biblical inerrancy led him to seek for religious truths that could be justified in terms of the science and philosophy he was first exposed to while at Cambridge. Crowley's signal contribution to western esotericism was his attempt to legitimate his essentially religious approach to reality by appeals to elements of philosophical and empirical skepticism. His first critical interpreter, J. F. C. Fuller, described Crowley's philosophical position as 'Crowleyanity: or in other words, according to the mind of the reader—Pyrrhonic-Zoroastrianism, Pyrrhonic-Mysticism, Sceptical Transcendentalism, Sceptical-Theurgy, Sceptical-Energy, Scientific-Illuminism, or what you will; for in short it is the conscious communion with God on the part of an Atheist, a transcending of reason by scepticism of the instrument, and the limitation of scepticism by direct consciousness of the Absolute' (Fuller 1907: 212). In Crowley's view, contemporary science and revealed religion had failed to answer their own questions due to their inherent methodological limitations; the ultimate truths were only to be found in a union of their epistemological strengths. Crowley chose as the motto of his occult journal, *The Equinox*, 'The Method of Science; the Aim of Religion.' Magick was the third way.

Crowley was a multifaceted character, and his activities spanned everything from mountaineering, poetry, comparative religion, politics, fiction, chess, mysticism, and art to Thelema and magic—this chapter will focus on the two latter facets of Crowley's work.

THE LIFE OF THE WANDER OF THE WASTE

Crowley's individualist personality is tightly bound with the development of his theory and praxis. Although he has received several full-length biographies, the abundant details of his chronicled life tend to obscure the dominant trends in the development of his intellectual and spiritual topoi.[1] Crowley was born in 1875 into a normative British upper-middle-class Victorian family. What set them apart from the mainstream of society was their commitment to the totalizing religious culture of the Exclusive Brethren sect of the Plymouth Brethren, an Evangelical Christian restorationist movement. The high demand religious practices combined with the rigid moralism (and apparent hypocrisy) of the Plymouth Brethren nurtured in the adolescent Crowley a sense of anomie. He rebelled, and in the process of the separation from his family he defined himself oppositionally to their God, taking as his model the 'Great Beast' of Revelation, a primary text in the Plymouth Brethren's historical–grammatical method of scriptural interpretation. John Nelson Darby, a central figure in the movement, developed a premillennial dispensational theology whose constructs shaped Crowley's world-view. Dispensationalism understood biblical history as a series of ages marked by covenants between God and his people. Premillenialism points to a blissful future in which God's rule will be established on earth by the return of Jesus. For Crowley there was little doubt that the comfortable world into which he was born was destined to be overthrown by a messiah (Bogdan 2012).

Crowley attended Cambridge but did not receive a degree, having had a revelation to devote his life to religion. The form which his devotion took was twofold from the start: sex and esotericism. He needed no schooling in the former, but by 1898 he found the Hermetic Order of the Golden Dawn (GD), which appeared to offer authentic instruction in western esotericism and an initiatic gateway to the true invisible Rosicrucian order. His involvement with the GD was short-lived, as the London body broke apart over disputes on the legitimacy of its historical claims and the derived authority of one of its founders, S. L. Mathers. The lasting influences were the GD's hierarchical structure of initiation based on the structure of the kabbalistic Tree of Life and its synthesis of western esotericism.

With the seeming failure to find the 'Hidden Church of the Holy Grail' incarnate in the GD, Crowley turned to the east and explored yoga and Buddhism in India and Burma. Mysticism as such had not been a part of the curriculum of the GD. Crowley found that the training of concentration through yogic exercises formed a useful adjutant to the ceremonial methods of western esotericism.

What Crowley described as a break from his past took place in Cairo in April of 1904. He was practicing ceremonial magical invocations with his wife, who (as Crowley relates the story), suddenly began to state that the Egyptian god Horus was waiting for him. Following her ritual instructions, Crowley claims to have received a text via direct voice, *The Book of the Law*, a revelation of a new age of which Crowley in his persona of the 'great beast' was the prophet. The past age or aeon of Osiris, manifested as patriarchal religion and society, was to be replaced by the coming age of Horus, the divine child, an eidolon of individual freedom. The Greek word 'thelema' (will) was the 'word' of the 'law' of the eon of Horus, encapsulated in its seemingly antinomian dictum of 'Do what thou wilt.'

Crowley was not quick to accept in its totality the charismatic authority granted him by *The Book of the Law*. His sense that its revelation put him at the head of the spiritual hierarchy vacated by S. L. Mathers first led him to form the A.·.A.·. in 1909, which combined the ceremonial magic of the GD with the eastern practices he had learned, structured as a teacher–student chain of authority. He published the teachings of the order in a semi-annual journal, *The Equinox* (1909–13). Mathers sued Crowley over his publication in *The Equinox* of the 'Rosicrucian' inner order ritual of the GD; the publicity led Crowley to a leadership role in another neo-Rosicrucian group, the Ordo Templi Orientis (OTO), a liberal masonic group that had at its center a closely guarded secret: the theory and practice of sexual magic. By the close of 1913 and Crowley's departure for America, he had two interconnected esoteric movements under his direction that he turned gradually to vehicles for the promotion of his revelation of Thelema and the Aeon of Horus. Like the GD, both groups had small memberships.

The First World War kept Crowley in the USA, from which he led the small groups of his followers in Canada, Britain, South Africa, and Australia. The movements did not flourish and Crowley, unable to find a market for his books, wandered Europe and North Africa in obscurity only briefly broken by the furor over the publication of his roman-a-clef, *The Diary of a Drug Fiend* (1922). In 1920 Crowley founded an utopian community at Cefalù, Sicily, called the Abbey of Thelema. To Crowley and his followers this community was a 'Collegium ad Spiritum Sanctum', A College towards the Holy Spirit, where the members practiced A.·.A.·. teachings, such as yogic practices and ritual magic. The community faded out after Crowley had been expelled from Italy by Mussolini in 1923. His textbook, *Magick in Theory and Practice* (1930), had little distribution; other occult texts were published privately in small editions principally for his disciples. His last major work, *The Book of Thoth* (1944), was his exposition of the Tarot, with the cards designed under his direction. Crowley died in Hastings, England, in 1947, with his life framed by accounts in American news magazines such as *Time* and *Newsweek* as a fringe religious eccentric, which view was to dominate for several decades.

THE GREAT BEAST 666, FOUNDER OF A NEW RELIGION

Crowley saw himself as the prophet of a new religion, Thelema, which had been revealed to mankind in 1904 when *The Book of the Law* was dictated to Crowley by a 'discarnate being' called Aiwass, the 'Minister of Hoor-Paar-Kraat.' The central doctrine of this new religion is that every man and every woman has a unique purpose or essence which to most people is unknown, hidden, or repressed. This essence is not only our true or higher self (a common notion in the history of western esotericism from late antiquity to modern times), but it also implies a praxis, something which needs to be performed. *The Book of the Law* identified this as the Will—or *True* Will as Crowley later would describe it: 'Do what thou wilt shall be the whole of the Law,' and 'Thou hast no right but to do thy will. Do that, and no other shall say nay.' Crowley identified the True Will with a higher self, or to use Crowley's preferred terminology, the Holy Guardian Angel (see below). The nature of the Law of Thelema was, furthermore, understood as a form of love: 'love is the law, love under will'. To Crowley the Law of Thelema was the answer to all the political, religious, social, ethical, and psychological problems facing mankind: since each one of us is a unique being ('every man and every woman is a star'), there can be no identical wills, we cannot want the same things and therefore all forms of conflicts are rooted in the fact that at least one of the parties involved in the conflict is not aware of his or her True Will.

Based on the revelations of *The Book of the Law*, Crowley saw human history as divided into three ages or aeons, each of which lasts for approximately two thousand years. These aeons mark evolutionary leaps in the development of humankind, and each is ruled by certain magical formulas. The new Aeon of Horus was preceded by the Aeons of Isis and Osiris, and it will in the future be superseded by a fourth aeon, that of Maat (Ma/Hrumachis), also termed the 'Aeon of Justice.' Crowley's understanding of history as a succession of aeons, or dispensations, can be seen as a reflection of the teachings of John Nelson Darby and the Plymouth Brethren that he encountered during his childhood. Darby's description of human history as divisible into a series of chronologically successive dispensations is paralleled by Crowley's succession of aeons. The Christian end-times theology of premillennialism, with its belief in the tribulation preceding the millennium, is reinterpreted as the birth pangs of the New Aeon of Horus. To Crowley, human evolution had passed through a stage of matriarchy (the aeon of Isis) and a stage of patriarchy (the aeon of Osiris), and in 1904 mankind entered a new, spiritually more advanced age (the aeon of Horus). This new age is characterized by individuality and freedom from oppressive systems (Bogdan 2012).

The Book of the Law is a relatively short text, consisting of three chapters and a total of 220 verses. The three chapters are attributed to three Egyptian gods: Nuit, Hadit, and Ra-Hoor-Khuit, respectively. Although aspects of these gods might be traced back to the rituals of the Golden Dawn (the rituals of the Golden Dawn were heavily colored by the fin-de-siècle egyptosophy), they represent a radical reinterpretation of ancient Egyptian religion: Nuit, the sky goddess of ancient Egypt (Nu), represents in the thelemic tradition the vastness of the space and the female principle; Hadit (in ancient Egypt this went by the name of Heru-Behdeti or Horus of Behdet, and Hadith in Greek) is the male principle, the infinitesimally small, the point within the circle which is Nuit; Ra-Hoor-Khuit (from the ancient Egyptian Ra-Hoor-Khu-It, Ra-Har-Khuti or possibly Ra-Har-Akht, more commonly referred to by the Greek transliteration Ra-Herakhty, meaning 'Ra [who is] Horus on the Horizon'), is in the thelemic tradition referred to as a god of war and vengeance (AL III:3), the lord of the new aeon, and as the symbolic union of Nuit and Hadit. According to Crowley, a period of war and conflict would mark the onset of the new age.

The trinity of Nuit, Hadit, and Ro-Hoor-Khuit is complemented by other gods and deities in the thelemic pantheon, of which The Great Beast and Babalon are the two most important. The Great Beast 666 from the Book of Revelation is in the thelemic tradition interpreted as a solar–phallic principle and an office which Crowley himself assumed. Babalon (not mentioned in *The Book of the Law*), is an allusion to a variant spelling of the Whore of Babylon, which in the thelemic tradition is usually interpreted as the earthly, sexual manifestation of Nuit. To Crowley Babalon also represented a magical office or title, which several of his lovers assumed over time.

Crowley claims that he was reluctant to agree with the message of *The Book of the Law*, and that it took three years before he finally accepted the role as the prophet of a new aeon. The year 1907, in which Crowley came to accept the role trust upon him, marked a high-point in the thelemic movement: not only did Crowley take the oath as a Magister Templi (one of the highest degrees in the Golden Dawn initiatory system), but he also founded the first thelemic organization, the Order of the Silver Star or A∴A∴, which in effect was a new version of the Golden Dawn. More important, however, for the development of the thelemic tradition, was a series of short automatic writings which Crowley wrote between October 29 and December 14. These poetic works were later published as *The Holy Books of Thelema*, and together with *The Book of the Law* and *The Vision and the Voice* (Liber 418) they make up the central canon of Thelema to this day. The latter text, *The Vision and the Voice*, is the record of Crowley's exploration of the 30 Æthyrs of the Enochian system, which Crowley had encountered during his time in the Golden Dawn—the system was originally developed by the Elizabethan magician John Dee and Edward Kelley. Through these visions, which Crowley obtained in Mexico in 1900 and in Algeria in 1909, many key doctrines of Thelema can be found, especially those related to Babalon mentioned above (Crowley et al. 1998).

Although Thelema developed into a complex theological system, particularly through Crowley's exegesis of *The Holy Books* and *The Vision and Voice*, the basic doctrine remains simple: discover the True Will, and act according to it. But how does one go about to discover this will? To Crowley, the answer was simple: through the practice of Magick.

MAGICK

Central to Crowley's religious system lies the practice of magic, or Magick as he preferred to spell it in order to distinguish it from earlier, superstitious forms of magic. To Crowley, Magick was to be based on 'scientific' premises: objective and verifiable observations and facts. In its simplest form, Crowley regarded every intentional act as an act of Magick, as famously described in his magnum opus, *Magick in Theory and Practice*:

> *Magick is the Science and Art of causing Change to occur in conformity with Will.* (Illustration: It is my Will to inform the World of certain facts within my knowledge. I therefore take 'magical weapons', pen, ink, and paper; I write 'incantations' – these sentences – in the 'magical language' i.e. that which is understood by the people I wish to instruct; I call forth 'spirits', such as printers, publishers, booksellers, and so forth, and constrain them to convey my message to those people. The composition and distribution of this book is thus an act of *Magick* by which I cause change to take place in conformity with my Will).
>
> (Crowley 1930: XVII)

The central point in Crowley's definition is the importance attributed to the will, Thelema, and it is only the acts based on the will of the practitioner that can be considered as acts of Magick. Furthermore, in a more restrictive sense, Crowley argued that it is only the acts that are carried out in accordance with the True Will that can be seen as lawful forms of Magick, and the first task of the apprentice would thus be to train the mind through mystical techniques (Crowley in particular recommended Indic yogic practices), and to perfom magical ceremonies aimed at reaching knowledge of one's True Will, symbolized by a mystical experience called the 'Knowledge and Conversation of the Holy Guardian Angel.'

Although the notion of a Holy Guardian Angel (HGA) has a long history in western esotericism, it was a concept which Crowley had encountered in particular within the Golden Dawn, where a conscious identification with the HGA or Divine Genius was believed to take place in the Adeptus Minor degree (the first degree of Golden Dawn's inner order, the R.R. et A.C.). In the Adeptus Minor initiation ritual, the candidate is obliged to take the following obligation:

> I further promise and swear that with the Divine Permission I will, from this day forward, apply myself to the Great Work – which is, to purify and exalt my Spiritual Nature so that with the Divine Aid I may at length attain to be more than human, and thus gradually raise and unite myself to my higher and Divine Genius, and that in this event I will not abuse the great power entrusted to me.
>
> (Regardie 1938: 214)

The Divine Genius that the members of the Golden Dawn sought to unite with was referred to by different names, such as the Higher Self, the Daemon, but perhaps most commonly as the Holy Guardian Angel. Although occultists differ in how the Divine Genius is interpreted the basic idea is that it constitutes a divine aspect in man that the profane or unenlightened person is not aware of. This idea can, for instance, be found in Gnosticism of Late Antiquity and the belief that man's soul is nothing but a spark of the divine Godhead, that through a primordial fall has been entrapped in the material world. The goal of the Gnostic was to free the divine aspect in man and to re-unite it with its divine source. In a similar manner the occultist sees the Divine Genius as the microcosmic counterpart of the macrocosmic Godhead, and the goal is to reach a conscious awareness of, or union with, the Divine Genius. This union is often referred to as the Knowledge and Conversation of the Holy Guardian Angel. With the secularization and psychologization of the occult the Divine Genius or Holy Guardian Angel was increasingly seen as an aspect of man's psyche. To Crowley, the

Holy Guardian Angel was nothing but the unconscious aspect of the mind, and consequently the object of his magical system was to become conscious of the unconscious.[2] Furthermore, Crowley believed that the unconsciousness contained the very essence of each human being (the True Will), and by discovering this essence one would find the answers to man's basic existential questions: Who am I, and what is the purpose of my life? Or to put it in the words of Crowley himself:

> It should now be perfectly simple for everybody to understand the Message of the Master Therion [i.e. Crowley]. Thou must (1) Find out what is thy Will, (2) Do that Will with (a) one-pointedness, (b) detachment, (c) peace. Then, and then only, art thou in harmony with the Movement of Things, thy will part of, and therefore equal to, the Will of God. And since the will is but the dynamic aspect of the self, and since two different selves could not possess identical wills; then, if thy will be God's will, *Thou art That.*
>
> (Crowley 1919: 42)

The identification of the True Will with God's Will, shows that to Crowley the goal of Magick is to become aware of the divine aspect in man. In fact, to Crowley 'there is no God but Man' as he blatantly stated in *Liber Oz* published in 1944. This does not mean that Crowley was an atheist, but rather that he believed that God is Man, or *Deus est Homo* which is one of the mottos of Ordo Templi Orientis, a German initiatic order that Crowley joined in 1912 and later became the head of, and which remains to this day one of the largest occultist orders in the west (for a discussion of the early history of the O.T.O., see Kaczynski 2012). It was through this order he discovered a powerful aid in the practice of Magick: sex.

SEXUAL MAGIC

In 1914 Crowley made the following statement concerning sexual magic in his diary *Rex De Arte Regia*:

> This Art was communicated to me in June [1912] by the O.H.O. [Outer Head of the Order, i.e. Theodor Reuss, the leader of the O.T.O.]. It was practised by me in a desultory way until [1 January 1914] when I made the Experiments recorded elsewhere of the Art derived from and parallel to this. The Knowledge thus gained enabled me to make further research with more acumen and directness, so that I was able definitely to assert that I had produced certain results at will. For example, my bronchitis, which had been most intractable was cured in a single day. I obtained money when needed. I obtained 'sex-force and sex-attraction' so strongly that for months after I was never at loss. Better than all, I was able to excite my art-creative power and my magical intuition so that much of the very great work done by me all this summer may be considered due entirely to this Art.
>
> (Crowley 1972: 3)

From that year on, Crowley experimented with the sexual magic that he had learned from the O.T.O., and he would continue to practice this form of magic for the rest of his life. Crowley's diaries, both published and un-published, show that he kept a careful scientific record of all 'operations,' stating the object; partner(s); quality of the 'elixir'; and the apparent results. The use of sex in magical and religious rituals fitted well with the principles of Thelema, and it is clear that Crowley and his students considered sexual liberation to be directly linked to spiritual development.

What, then, did the sexual magic that Crowley use actually consist of? The sexual magic of the O.T.O. was initially confined to the Eighth and Ninth degrees (the Tenth degree was the highest, administrative degree of the Order). In the Eighth degree, Perfect Pontiff of the Illuminati, the initiate was instructed in the practice of auto-sexual magic, or masturbation. In the Ninth degree, Initiate of the Sanctuary of the Gnosis, the initiate was taught a particular form of magic which involved heterosexual intercourse. In addition to this, Crowley quickly developed a new form of sexual magic which involved anal sex in a newly created Eleventh degree. A number of authors have stated that this degree was a homosexual degree, but a close reading of Crowley's diaries reveal that he performed this particular form of sexual magic with both men and women. In Crowley's sexual magic the mere use of sex was not enough in itself. The sexual energy was used to charge, as it were, mental images created by the magician. To a certain extent, this form of magic is similar to the so-called talismanic magic taught by the Golden Dawn which aimed at charging or empowering magical talismans.

During the operation, as Crowley called his acts of sexual magic, the performer had to concentrate his will on a particular object, such as inspiration to write poetry, and to create mental images that would stimulate the ecstatic nature of the ritual. Crowley would, for instance, imagine showers of gold pouring over him at the moment of orgasm in rituals whose aim was to raise money. Moreover, the mental state of the practitioner had to be 'energised' or charged with an ecstatic feeling or energy which Crowley apparently connected to sexual energy.[3] It seems as if Crowley sought to transcend the limits of normal rational consciousness in these forms of rituals and to reach into layers of the consciousness which are normally inaccessible. In discussing sexual magic in his 1920 diary, Crowley noted:

> Union of the conscious mind, made stable moreover, with the subconscious, is evidently necessary to any Operation in which the Result is to be formulated beforehand.
>
> (Crowley 1972: 150)

The union of the conscious mind with the subconscious appears to have been a central aspect of Crowley's spiritual system as he evidently identified the subconscious with the Holy Guardian Angel, as previously discussed. One significant characteristic of the O.T.O. version of sexual magic is the sacramental consumption of the so-called Elixir (in the Ninth degree the elixir consists of a mixture of male and female sexual fluids, gathered from the vagina). The Elixir could also be used to anoint objects such as talismans, thereby empowering them with the force that was released at the moment of orgasm. Crowley's systematic experimentation with sexual magic resulted in a few short secret documents entitled *De Arte Magica* (1914), *Agape vel Liber C vel Azoth* (1914), and *Emblems and Mode of Use* (1944). It is interesting to note that after Crowley had been initiated into the secrets of sexual magic two significant changes took place: first, Crowley practically stopped performing complex forms of ceremonial magic in favor of the much simpler sexual magic, and, second, practically all his subsequent recorded acts of sex are limited to the performance of sexual magic. Crowley's sexual liberation can thus be seen as a new form of regulation, which prevented him from performing sex for mere pleasure.

CROWLEY TODAY

The late 1960s and early 1970s witnessed a revival of the interest in Crowley, and many works by Crowley that had been out of print for decades were now re-issued. Instrumental in these publishing ventures were two former secretaries of Crowley, Israel Regardie in the United States, and Kenneth Grant in England. Regardie, who had been Crowley's secretary in 1928–32, was a prolific author and central to the re-emergence of the Golden Dawn. Apart from his biography of Crowley's *The Eye in the Triangle* (1970), Regardie edited and introduced Crowley's *AHA* (1969), *The Vision and the Voice* (1972), *The Holy Books of Thelema* (1972), Book Four (1972), *Magick without Tears* (1973), *The Qabalah of Aleister Crowley* (1973), *The Law is for All* (1975), and *Gems from the Equinox* (1974), a massive volume which included the bulk of the magical and mystical writings from first volume of the Equinox. Kenneth Grant, who had acted as Crowley's secretary for a period in 1944, collaborated with Crowley's literary executor John Symonds in introducing and editing a number of Crowley's books, including *The Confessions of Aleister Crowley* (1969), *The Magical Record of the Beast 666* (1972), *The Diary of a Drug Fiend* (1972), *Moonchild* (1972), *Magick* (1973), *Magical and Philosophical Commentaries on the Book of the Law* (1974), *The Complete Astrological Writings* (1974), and by writing an introduction to *The Heart of the Master* (1973). It was also during this period that Grant began to publish his three so-called Typhonian Trilogies commencing with *The Magical Revival* in 1972, which were completed twenty years later with *The Ninth Arch* (2002).

The parallels of key-discourses between Crowley's magical system of Thelema and the early New Age movement of the late 1960s and early 1970s and so-called Self Spiritualities are striking: the dawning of a new age (the Age of Aquarius) characterized by a higher spiritual evolution which will lead to a utopian society free from conflicts, and the belief in a higher, sacred self (Self Spirituality). Crowley's writings on magick, mysticism, sexuality, and drugs appealed to tastes of the time, and Crowley quickly became something of an antinomian icon in the counter-culture movement and the flower-power generation. In fact, Beatles included him on the cover of the album 'Sgt. Pepper's Lonely Hearts Club Band' (1967) as the second person from the left in the back row, and Led Zeppelin inscribed the vinyl of their album 'Led Zeppelin III' (1970), with Crowley's central motto 'Do what thou wilt,' while David Bowie sang 'I'm closer to the Golden Dawn/Immersed in Crowley's uniform/Of imagery' in the song 'Quicksand' included in the album *Hunky Dory* (1971). The increasing number of books in print by Crowley, coincided with a resurgence of activity within thelemic organizations. Some of these groups were quite small and were only active for a few years, such as the Solar Lodge which was active in the United States during the late 1960s, while others have established themselves quite firmly on the esoteric scene. The largest of these latter groups is Ordo Templi Orientis which was re-activated around 1969 in California by a number of old-time members of the O.T.O. under the leadership of Grady Louis McMurtry, who assumed the title of Caliph. McMurtry's authority was challenged, however, by the Brazilian thelemite Marcelo Motta and his Society Ordo Templi Orientis. In 1985 a court in California ruled in favor of McMurtry, and the O.T.O has since then established itself as an international organization with a few thousand members worldwide.

The continued importance of Crowley in western culture was made evident in the BBC's 2002 '100 Greatest Britons' poll, in which, with more than 300,000 votes, Crowley ranked at number seventy-three, before authors such as Geoffrey Chaucer (eighty-one) and J. R. R. Tolkien (ninety-two). Crowley is firmly imbedded in what Christopher Partridge has called the occulture (Partridge 2005), and is probably more known today than ever before (a quick search on google.com will come up with almost 900,000 hits). The Beast is very much alive.

NOTES

This chapter is based, in part, on the introduction to Bogdan and Starr 2012.

1 Several biographies have been published on Aleister Crowley. The most recent ones are Richard Kaczynski, *Perdurabo: The Life of Aleister Crowley* (2010) and *Tobias Churton, Aleister Crowley: The Biography* (2011).

2 Crowley's view on the nature of the HGA changed over time, and he would also interpret the HGA as a distinct being, separate from his mind.

3 See Aleister Crowley 'Energized Enthusiasm' (1913) for more information on this particular state of mind.

REFERENCES AND FURTHER READING

Bogdan, H., 'Envisioning the Birth of a New Aeon: Dispensationalism and Millenarianism in the Thelemic Tradition,' in Bogdan and Starr, Eds., *Aleister Crowley and Western Esotericism* (2012), 89–106.

Bogdan, H. and M.P. Starr, *Aleister Crowley and Western Esotericism*. New York: Oxford University Press, 2012.

Churton, T., *Aleister Crowley: The Biography*. London: Watkins 2011.

Crowley, A., 'Energized Enthusiasm: A Note on Theurgy,' *The Equinox* I(9), 1913, 17–46.

——'The Message of the Master Therion,' *The Equinox* III(1), 1919, 39–43.

——*The Magical Record of the Beast 666*. Montreal: Next Step Publications, 1972.

——*Magick in Theory and Practice*. Paris: Lecram Press, 1930.

Crowley, A., V. Neuburg, and M. Desti, *Vision & the Voice with Commentary and other papers*. York Beach, Maine: Samuel Weiser, 1998.

Fuller, J.F.C., *The Star in the West: A Critical Essay upon the Works of Aleister Crowley*. London: Walter Scott Publishing, 1907.

Kaczynski, K., *Perdurabo: The Life of Aleister Crowley*. Berkeley, Calif.: North Atlantic Books, 2010.

——*Forgotten Templars: The Untold Origins of Ordo Templi Orientis*. Private publication, 2012.

Partridge, C., *The Re-Enchantment of the West*. London: T&T Clark, 2005.

Regardie, I., *The Golden Dawn. An Account of the Teachings, Rites and Ceremonies of the Order of the Golden Dawn*. Chicago: Aries. Volume 2, 1938.

CHAPTER TWENTY-NINE

AUSTIN OSMAN SPARE

Phil Baker

Artist and occultist Austin Osman Spare (1886–1956) was, after Aleister Crowley, perhaps the most influential magical thinker of the twentieth century, basing his magical practice on the manipulation of the unconscious mind. He was a seminal influence on the late twentieth-century 'chaos magic' movement, and became a legendary figure to occult readers after the mythologized account of his life promulgated by his younger friend and associate Kenneth Grant.

Spare was born into a 'respectable' working-class family, son of a policeman, in the Smithfield area of London, making him an authentic Cockney. He spent his early years near the Smithfield meat market, before the family moved south of the river to Kennington. Spare showed a precocious talent for drawing, which was encouraged by his family and at evening classes. After elementary schooling he was apprenticed to a printing firm and then a glass factory, where he made drawings for stained glass, before being recommended for a scholarship to the Royal College of Art: he attended the RCA from 1902 to 1905, but left without completing the course. He was meanwhile feted in 1904 as a remarkably young exhibitor at the Royal Academy, aged seventeen, leading to a number of 'boy genius'-style newspaper stories.

Spare published his first book, *Earth: Inferno*, in 1905, and followed it with *A Book of Satyrs* in 1907, the year that saw his first West End show at the Bruton Gallery, Bruton Street, London. This was controversial, with some critics seeing his work as unhealthy: George Bernard Shaw is alleged to have said 'Spare's medicine is too strong for the average man' (cited Grant 1975a: 16; variants compared in Baker 2011: 48), and Spare wrote of himself 'Strange Desires and Morbid Fancies, / Such do I give' (Spare 1905: 10). Spare had absorbed the ambient ideas of the decadent 1890s, the Beardsley era, which included a strong sense of the world's hypocrisy and evil; a widespread Paganism, leading to the Edwardian popularity of Pan; and a sense of diabolism as sophisticated, with critic Roger Fry labelling Beardsley 'the Fra Angelico of Satanism' (Fry 1904: 628). These ideas were combined with the various supernatural tendencies of the late Victorian period, which gave birth to the occult revival and the Order of the Golden Dawn, the more Eastern-inspired ideas of Theosophy, and an interest in spiritualism and psychic research.

Spare was briefly an associate of Aleister Crowley and in 1909 he became a Probationer in Crowley's post-Golden Dawn magical order the A∴A∴, or Argenteum Astrum, but the two men fell out and Spare left the A∴A∴, having failed to progess from Probationer to the first proper grade of Neophyte. Crowley's comment, written on Spare's probationer card, was 'An artist; can't understand organisation, or would have passed' (cited Richmond 1999: unpaginated).

Spare rejected Crowley-style ceremonial magic in favour of a more free-form, psychologically oriented style of magic that pivoted on the unconscious; he believed the unconscious was all-powerful, and that it was necessary to bypass the conscious mind. Spare did this by deliberately forgetting wishes, believing that this would repress them into the unconscious and give them the power more often associated with complexes, neuroses, and the Freudian return of the repressed. Spare claimed that Freud had used some of his ideas, and that he had received a letter from Freud deferring to his greater genius (see Letchford 1996: 55, Grant 1975b: unpaginated introduction, Baker 2011: 106).

Spare's central method of communicating with the unconscious was the use of sigils. Relatively conventionalized or traditional sigils – graphic occult signs, akin to seals, which can represent demons, angels, planets or other entitities – go back a long way in Western magic (see Gettings 1981), but Spare's sigils simply consisted of writing a wish in a simplified form, removing the duplicate letters, and combining those that were left into a design which was to be imprinted on the mind and then forgotten. Spare's inspiration for sigils was the artist's monogram, a stylized design of an artist's initials; he meant it literally when he wrote 'Sigils are monograms of thought, for the government of energy' (Spare 1913: 50). This manipulation of the mind was the key to magic for Spare, as he wrote in his major work *The Book of Pleasure (Self-Love): The Psychology of Ecstasy*, which he self-published in 1913: 'This being the only system, any result other than by it is accidental. Also, you do not have to dress up as a traditional magician, wizard, or priest, build expensive temples, obtain virgin parchment, black goat's blood, etc., etc., in fact no theatricals or humbug' (Spare 1913: 50).

This aspect of Spare's practice is an instance of the 'psychologizing' tendency of twentieth-century magic, also to be seen in Crowley's 1904 edition of *The Goetia of Solomon the King*, where he suggests less compellingly that spirits are really portions of the brain, so a spirit said to bring treasure is supposedly the part of the brain that governs business abilities (Crowley 1904: 3–4). Spare's idea of spirits and familiars extended to 'obsessions' and 'automata', obsessions being derived from the spiritualist idea of obsession (when the obsessing entity or force is still separate, as opposed to possession when it has taken over) and automata from the work of French psychologist Pierre Janet (1859–1947). According to Janet's theories, seeing visions or hearing voices could be described as 'sensory automatisms' and glossolalia, mediumistic possession or automatic drawing as 'motor automatisms'. Spare's exposure to spiritualism also led him to claim more straightforwardly that he was sometimes possessed by the spirits of dead artists (Swaffer 1950: 72).

Spare was fascinated by evolutionary as well as unconscious strata, and Darwinism was another inspiration. He believed in the kinship of all life, and that we can draw on animal 'atavisms' – ancient throwbacks and reversions – latent within us, to obtain animal strengths and tap into ancestral talents. In some respects Spare represents a self-educated man idiosyncratically inspired by the intellectual currents of his time: Darwin and Freud, for example, come together when he explains, in *The Book of Pleasure*, that a bat evolved wings because it unconsciously (or 'organically') desired to fly – whereas, because man's desire to fly is merely conscious, we have to rely on machines (Spare 1913: 48).

The Book of Pleasure also outlined Spare's idea of the Kia, a slippery concept akin to the Tao and the Jungian pleroma. The Kia is both a fertile void behind or above all being, and something which can be tuned into as a higher state of consciousness, offering the non-duality of what Spare called 'the free or atmospheric "I"' (Spare 1913: 43). Spare's ontology paired the Kia with the Zos (the bodily animal self, with which he identified) and one way of uniting the Zos and the Kia in practice was the 'death posture' (e.g. Spare 1913: 17–19), a quasi-yogic relaxation almost certainly deriving its name from the yoga term *shavasana* or 'corpse pose'. The 'self' of Spare's self-love also had a yogic aspect, partly deriving from the 'atman' or higher self of Hindu philosophy.

As the title of his book suggests, Spare's thinking has a strong narcissistic component; so strong that his narcissistic pleasure flips over into what Freud termed the 'oceanic' (Freud 1930: 72–73), moving from the oneness of the self to a sense of oneness with everything. In this sense Spare was something of a mystic, a calling he defined in 'The Logomachy of Zos' as 'someone who experiences more of himself than he can articulate' (Spare 1998: 186). The title of his early show '*Pleasure and Obsession*' (Ryder Gallery 1912) already suggests his dual mystical–magical aspect, with his 'pleasure' inclining towards mysticism and his 'obsession', and the manipulation of obsessions, to magic.

There is a further eroticized manifestation of deep narcissism in Spare's 'New Sexuality' (Spare 1913: 6–7, 18–19, 29, Spare 1921: 6–10, Baker 2011: 129–31). This was an ecstatic means of becoming erotically self-sufficient, identifying with both male and female: an empathetic way of having all the sex in the world, without necessarily having any in the ordinary sense. In contrast to Crowley's emphasis on intercourse, Spare's sexuality was auto-erotic and largely solitary, and he experimented with masturbation as a magical technique within various modes such as focusing intent, charging sigils, attaining vacuity of mind, and auto-erotic abstinence. He hints at such practices with his dictum 'He has found wisdom who knows how to spend', spend being an old euphemism for ejaculation (Spare 1972: penultimate page; see also 'urning', Spare 1998: 223, and Baker 2011: 283–84). Spare married Eily Shaw in September 1911 but they parted during the war, without children.

The New Sexuality is further manifest in Spare's androgynous self-portraits as a woman; these are already present in his early work, and there is a particularly notable suite of pictures – unpublished and unpublishable in their day – in an album related to Spare's 1921 book *The Focus of Life*: once owned by the novelist E. M. Forster, they were long unseen until the album resurfaced in 2009 (see Baker 2011: 171–72, Spare 2012). These pictures of the artist-as-other, in some respects anticipating the practice of artists such as Cindy Sherman, now seem quite radical in art-historical terms.

Spare's artistic career stalled after the First World War, and the 1924 collapse of *The Golden Hind*, the magazine he co-edited with Clifford Bax, was a watershed of failure. Around this time Spare fell back to a council tenement south of the river, living – as he put it – as 'a swine with swine' (Rogers 1991: 21) and re-embracing his Cockney identity.

Spare's art did not keep pace with modernism, and it was unfashionably concerned with spirits and the occult. He nevertheless produced a remarkable range of work between the wars, from pastel portraits of local people to exquisite stylisations and perspective distortions of film stars, in a manner he came to call 'siderealism'. Spare's output seemed to take on a new aspect when surrealism came to Britain with the 1936 International Surrealist Exhibition. His long-held interest in automatism and the unconscious led to his friends and champions, such as Oswell Blakeston, dubbing him an original British surrealist, and even to a newspaper headline 'Father of Surrealism – He's a Cockney!' (*Daily Sketch*, 25th February 1938), although Spare's closest artistic affiliation is probably with the Symbolist movement. In fact Spare's automatism had roots in the late nineteenth-century spiritualistic unconscious, and was part of what had already made him dated by the 1920s, along with his belated allegiance to spirits and Edwardian-style satyrs: the ridiculous Mr Barbecue Smith, in Aldous Huxley's satirical 1921 novel *Crome Yellow*, shows how unfashionable claims of trances and automatic inspiration had become by this time.

Often said to be reclusive, Spare needed publicity, and he was prepared to play along with the surrealist angle, producing his *Surrealist Racing Forecast Cards* in 1936. Around the same time he also gained press coverage by allegedly refusing a request from Hitler for a portrait, but he tried to relaunch the story a couple of years later by claiming he had been to Germany and completed the picture.

Spare's South London studio at the Elephant and Castle was destroyed during the Blitz. He found refuge in the Brixton basement of a friend, Ada Pain, and survived a low period to attempt a post-war comeback, holding exhibitions in South London pubs. It was at this time that he was befriended by occultist Kenneth Grant and his wife Steffi, a young couple who cultivated Spare as a character, encouraged him to write about magic, and provided a collusive audience for his stories.

Spare had a strong tendency to confabulation, claiming that he had studied hieroglyphics in Egypt and been the only survivor of a torpedoed troopship, and this reached new heights in the subsequent writings of Kenneth Grant. The Grants also knew the witchcraft revivalist Gerald Gardner at the time they knew Spare, stimulating thoughts about witches, and Grant and Spare evolved a shared fantasy of an old South London witch who had initiated Spare, 'Mrs Paterson' – a name Spare may have encountered in a 1942 local newspaper story of a woman who lived to be 102 years old, but who was not a witch (*South London Press*, 27th January 1942, Baker 2011: 239–40). Grant coined a magical name for Spare, 'Zos vel Thanatos', and presents a highly confabulated version of him within his own para-fictional oeuvre, influenced by the work of Sax Rohmer, Arthur Machen and HP Lovecraft. Grant's mythologized Spare is a maverick magus of wide sexual experience and dark magical expertise, although Grant's contemporary diary entries show that Grant also found him to be a somewhat comic figure (see Spare 1998).

Spare died in 1956 from complications following appendicitis. His legend has grown through the writings of Kenneth Grant, notably *Images and Oracles of Austin Osman Spare* (1975a), but there is also a valuable account in Frank Letchford's memoir (Letchford 1996), and a vivid novelistic glimpse of Spare as 'Old Nick' in Blakeston 1969 (156–69, 194, 204). Spare has not only been adopted as the precursor of 'chaos magic', and taken up by avant-garde musicians including the bands Throbbing Gristle and Coil, but there has more recently been a wider appreciation of his art outside the occult community.

REFERENCES AND FURTHER READING

Ansell, R. (2005) *Borough Satyr*, London: Fulgur.

Baker, P. (2011) *Austin Osman Spare: The Life and Legend of London's Lost Artist*, London: Strange Attractor.

Blakeston, O. (1969) *For Crying Out Shroud*, London: Hutchinson.

Crowley, A. (1904) *The Book of the Goetia of Solomon the King*, Foyers: Society for the Propagation of Religious Truth.

Freud, S. (1930), 'Civilization and its Discontents', *The Standard Edition of the Complete Psychological Works of Sigmund Freud, Volume XXI*, London: The Hogarth Press.

Fry, R. (1904) 'Aubrey Beardsley's Drawings', in *The Athenaeum* 4019, 5th November, 1904, 627–28.

Gettings, F. (1981) *Dictionary of Occult, Hermetic and Alchemical Sigils*, London: Routledge and Kegan Paul.

Grant, K. (1975a) *Images and Oracles of Austin Osman Spare*, London: Frederick Muller.

——(1975b) 'Introduction', in Spare, *The Book of Pleasure*, Montreal: 93 Publishing: available at: http://fulgur.co.uk/artists/austin-osman-spare/introduction-to-the-book-of-pleasure (accessed 16 July 2013).

Letchford, F. (1996), *Michelangelo in a Teacup*, Thame: First Impressions.

Richmond, K. (1999), 'Discord in the Garden of Janus', in *Artist Occultist Sensualist* (exhibition catalogue), ed. Geraldine Beskin, Bury St. Edmunds: Beskin Press.

Rogers, G. (1991) 'Austin Osman Spare', *The Goth*, Vol. 6 [*sic* i.e. issue 6], 20–22.

Spare, A. O. (1905) *Earth: Inferno*, London: the author.

——(1913) *The Book of Pleasure (Self-Love): The Psychology of Ecstasy*, London: the author.

——(1921) *The Focus of Life*, London: The Morland Press.

——(1972) *A Book of Automatic Drawings*, London: The Catalpa Press.

——(1998) *Zos Speaks!* ed. Kenneth and Steffi Grant, London: Fulgur.

——(2012) *The Focus of Life (Redux)*, with essays by R. Ansell and P. Baker, London: Fulgur.

Swaffer, H. (1950) 'The Mystery of an Artist', *London Mystery Magazine*, vol. 1, no. 5, 69–76.

CHAPTER THIRTY

RENÉ GUÉNON AND TRADITIONALISM

Peter King

INTRODUCTION

The idea that the world's major religions are linked to some form of overarching perennial doctrine is not a new one. It was a view notably propounded in the English-speaking world by Aldous Huxley in his book, *The Perennial Philosophy*, first published in 1944 (Huxley, 2009). But the idea can be traced back to the fifteenth century and the ideas of Italian thinkers such as Bruno and Ficino (Sedgwick, 2004). However, the most important recent exponent of this idea can be found in the work of René Guénon and his followers in what has become known as Traditionalism (Sedgwick, 2004).

Guénon was born in 1886 in Blois, France. After failing to progress in his academic career he began dabbling in occult and masonic organisations in early twentieth-century Paris. However, within a decade he had became a fervent critic of modern esoterism and spiritualism (Guénon, 2001b, 2001c) and turned instead to a form of perennialist metaphysics heavily influenced by Hindu philosophy. Despite this, Guénon converted to Islam in around 1911, and following the death of his first wife, moved to Cairo in 1930 and spent the rest of his life living as a traditional Muslim until his death in 1951 (Chacornac, 2001). In total, he was the author of 23 books (some of these produced posthumously), all now published in a uniform English edition by the American publisher, Sophia Perennis.

What makes Guénon so fascinating, but also so disconcerting for those educated to think along the lines of modern rationality, is that he completely reverses our presumptions about intellectual progress. Instead of believing that we know more than the ancients, in reality we have only a shallow and very much degraded understanding of the world. We have become separated from what is truly important in our lives, having placed material progress before any spiritual and traditional modes of living. Accordingly, his work is concerned with informing us of what we once were and could be again if we could find the traditional ways that we have lost.

Sedgwick (2004) has argued that Guénon's thought can be seen as a unique synthesis of several longstanding elements, all of which had some currency in the late nineteenth and early twentieth centuries. None of these elements was original to

Guénon, but their synthesis into a coherent whole is distinctive. We shall accordingly look at each of these in turn.

INVERSION

Instead of progressing to a better future, Guénon would have it that Western civilisation is in decline (Guénon, 2001d, 2001e). This idea of inversion can be found in the Hindu tradition but also in Greek and Roman thinking. Instead of a linear progression, history should be seen as an ever-quickening decline from a once golden age to a period of ignorance and perversion. According to Guénon, we are now in this last period – the Hindu Kali Yuga – as exhibited by the forgetting of traditional ways of life and the placing of materialistic and profane values at the centre of our lives. We are inevitably heading towards some sort of apocalypse, after which a new golden age will be established and the cycle will begin again.

The main cause of this decline has been the placing of the profane above the sacred, with the Renaissance and the Reformation – usually seen as leaps forward in Western culture – here portrayed as the destroyers of the ancient tradition in Europe. Guénon (2001f) argues that the Renaissance 'was in reality not a rebirth but the death of many things' (p. 15). Much of the traditional sciences of the Middle Ages were lost, and in its place was left only profane science and philosophy. The decline of the West reached its nadir with the French Revolution, which completely rejected all tradition. What became the predominant concern for modern science and philosophy was the material and the quantifiable, and Guénon deals with this development in what is perhaps his most significant work, entitled *The Reign of Quantity and the Sign of the Times* (2001g). This is his most concerted and metaphysically informed consideration of the problems of modernity. He seeks to explain the roots of the malaise that is modernity and alights on the overriding concern for 'quantity' in the modern world. It is this need to quantify, the emphasis on the material, that runs through modern life and serves to denigrate the spiritual.

EAST AND WEST

If the West is in decline then for Guénon any remaining traditional wisdom may be found in the East (Guénon, 2001d, 2001e). Guénon opposes the profane and decadent West with a generalised – and perhaps also idealised – view of the East. Indeed, as Sedgwick (2004) has argued, Guénon uses the terms 'East' and 'West' as cyphers and he might just as easily have used the terms 'traditional' and 'modern'. However, using this distinction, he builds up a detailed critique of the profane West in thrall to material progress, and contrasts this with what he sees as the persistence of ancient values remaining in the East. His vision of the East – a view he developed before he had travelled outside Europe – was therefore essentially a means to critique the modern world and its placing of the material above the sacred or symbolic. His concern was to show that modernity was an aberration or an anomaly, and that most civilisations can be characterised by the placing of traditional sacred values at their centre. Guénon sees traditional societies, which emphasise stability and a lack of change, as superior to Western societies that seem to treasure innovation and follow what is currently fashionable (Guénon, 2001a). For Guénon, originality is something to be avoided as it presumes that we moderns are superior to those that preceded us, a view that he claims would be summarily dismissed in more traditional societies.

THE PERENNIAL TRADITION

Perhaps the key to understanding Guénon's thought is the belief in perennialism. Guénon, consistent with perennialist thinkers since Marsilio Ficino in the fifteenth century, suggests that there was a primal truth that underpinned, and so was able to unite, all the major belief systems of the world. This truth necessarily predates all these systems of belief and was presented to humanity by some transcendent means, fully formed in the first age of the world. Since then civilisation has been in an ever-quickening decline. Human history can therefore be seen as the forgetting and ultimate rejection of the perennial philosophy in the mistaken belief that humanity can be self-contained and determined by its own development, free from any metaphysical or supra-human manifestation.

It is pertinent to look here at what is meant by tradition. For Guénon and his followers there is not a multiplicity of traditions, neither does tradition merely refer to cultural practices. Instead tradition is a set of universal principles that underpin all modern religions and systems of thought. Tradition is the primordial basis of all ancient thought. Tradition is what is elemental – or 'principial' as he often denotes it – and necessary for any society: it is not merely wisdom but *the* wisdom, and so we can speak of Tradition rather than a series of traditions.

Several of Guénon's followers have sought to clarify precisely what he means by tradition. For example, Robin Waterfield (2002, p. 80) states that:

> Tradition was essentially the body of knowledge and self-understanding which is common to all men in all ages and nationalities. Its expression and clarification forms the basis of all traditional wisdom and its application the basis of all traditional societies.

It is through Tradition that we can come to understand the world that we are in and find our place in it. As Luc Benoist (2003, p. 14) states:

> It is concerned with origins: tradition is the handing on of a complex of established means for facilitating our understanding of the immanent principles of universal order, since it has not been granted mankind to understand unaided the meaning of his existence.

Tradition is nothing less than a metaphysical system that allows us to understand the true nature of the world. It can be seen perhaps as the manual for our life in the world: it is how we understand our place and our purpose.

As we move away from this wisdom, the more obscure it becomes, and so we become incapable of seeing the essential unity of Tradition. So Tradition is a particular type of wisdom, which forms the basis of all human understanding. The modern need for individual expression and aspiration is part of this falling away from Tradition as we become ever more ignorant of the underpinning principles that give meaning to our place in the world.

As Tradition is spiritual in nature its main threat is from materialism, and it is this that Guénon takes as defining modernity. He argues that 'materialism has insinuated itself into the general mentality' (2001g, p. 194) to become a form of common sense that needs no 'theoretical formulation' (p. 194) but which is now a sort of instinct. This is only reinforced by the 'industrial applications of mechanised science' (p. 194): 'Man "mechanised" everything and ended at last by mechanising himself, falling little by little into the condition of numerical units, parodying unity, yet lost in the uniformity and indistinction of the masses' (p. 194). A fellow Traditionalist and collaborator of Guénon, Ananda Coomaraswamy (1989), has argued that industrialisation and civilisation are incompatible. If civilisation depends on Tradition, and therefore religion, it must be opposed to those forces that seek to perpetuate industrialisation and globalisation. Civilisations, for Traditionalists like Guénon and Coomaraswamy, are local and particular, even as they are based on the idea of a single primordial Tradition.

This latter point is important because Guénon is not seeking to create some world civilisation in which all peoples follow the same direction. Rather he argues that all traditional societies have a shared root, and therefore all longstanding systems of thought, such as the great religions and the Chinese, Greek and Egyptian philosophical systems, have this in common. However, they have developed separately in a legitimate manner representative of how these civilisations have adapted the traditional wisdom to their own situations. Guénon's sense of Tradition is primordial, not universal. Therefore it is most definitely not legitimate to impose one particular system, be it Islam or Christianity, on all the others, neither is the aim of Guénon to advocate a synthesis of all these religions. Traditionalists see all the great religions as possible paths to the same end. Some of these religions may be older than others, and some, like Christianity, might have drifted further away from the shared root, but the task is to restore the essential elements within these religions rather than promote one over the others or to synthesise them.

INITIATION

The final element within Guénon's thought is the notion of initiation into esoteric knowledge through the following of spiritual discipline. What has been lost in Christianity and in other religions is the esoteric element. Modern religions – and Guénon sees the Protestant churches as the worst example – have almost entirely lost their esoteric core with its emphasis on initiation into a secret wisdom gained by following a required path and by accepting the disciplines of the esoteric order. Guénon argues that all religions have an exoteric or public side, which is what the majority see and can share. Yet underpinning this exoteric part is the hidden esoteric element whereby the secret wisdom is maintained and passed on. This element is only available to an elite minority and can only be understood through an appreciation of the symbols that are hidden within exoteric religion. For Guénon, modern Christianity is now merely public display, with the esoteric elements almost completely lost, having been subverted by the Renaissance and the Reformation with their opening up of Christian doctrine and the democratisation of faith. The role of the traditionalist is therefore to demonstrate the importance of the esoteric and, in doing so, to show the connected nature of all the various ancient systems of thought.

Guénon sees that the key aim of Traditionalists is to build up a new elite capable of properly interpreting and maintaining that Tradition. They are to do this by locating and joining orthodox forms of esoteric spirituality. It is for this reason that Guénon and many of his followers turned to the Sufi branch of Islam, which Guénon took to be an authentic path to initiation. Guénon argued that there might still be some hidden vestiges of esoterism in the West, perhaps within Catholicism but more probably with Freemasonry. However, for him the Protestant Churches were all corrupt examples of modernity and he was equally scathing in his criticism of what he saw as the modern inventions of theosophy (Guénon, 2001b) and spiritualism (Guénon, 2001c).

GUÉNON'S INFLUENCE

Sedgwick (2004), in his historical overview of the development of Traditionalism, argues that its reach is now worldwide and even includes parts of the Islamic world. However, he gives two caveats to this: first, there has been only a limited impact in the academic community, and second, the influence has tended to be more effective where traditionalism has been diluted or modified to what Sedgwick calls 'soft Traditionalism'.

One area that needs to be mentioned, but is beyond the scope of this work to develop more fully, is the political influence of Guénon's work (see King, 2012, 2014). One of his most prominent contemporaries was the Italian writer and artist Julius Evola (2002, 2003). Evola declared Guénon to be a major influence, but he was also clearly influenced by Nietzsche and German conservatives such as Spengler. Evola is controversial because of his links with both fascism and National Socialism, and his continued influence on the European radical right (Dahl, 1999). However, Evola might also be said to have perverted a crucial aspect of Guénonian thought by his transposition of action above knowledge and hence, in Guénon's terms, placed the secular above the sacred. We should note here that Guénon was scathing in his comments on National Socialism and its attempted appropriation of traditional symbols such as the swastika. To him Nazism and fascism were modernist aberrations with no links to genuine tradition. In arguing that knowledge should precede and dominate action, Guénon sees political action as suspect and his priority is always the exposition of tradition, with the ambition of enlightening those capable of understanding. Clearly, the achievement of Guénon's aims would have political implications, but he leaves these largely unstated, as merely a by-product of spiritual renewal.

During Guénon's lifetime there were a number of early followers of which the most notable was Frithjof Schuon (1907–98). Indeed, in some quarters, Schuon is taken to have superseded Guénon in his influence over Traditionalist thought. Schuon has certainly popularised the perennialist notion, stressing what he termed the transcendent unity of religion (Schuon, 1984). But Schuon is also a more controversial figure, particularly in the manner in which he moved away from Guénon's orthodox route to initiation. Over time Schuon's thinking developed to incorporate a number of practices from Islam and Native American Indian rituals, as well as the cult of the Virgin Mary. Schuon has also often been accused of setting up a cult, particularly after his move to the United States late in his life, and this has affected his reputation.

However, he certainly writes with greater clarity than Guénon and can be said to have extended the reach of Traditionalist ideas far beyond what Guénon achieved.

Perhaps the leading contemporary scholar influenced by Guenon is the Islamic philosopher, Seyyed Hossein Nasr. Nasr is an American-educated Iranian who has written widely on humanity's engagement with the natural world, as well as seeking to widen Western understanding of Islam (Nasr, 1997, 2011).

Most interesting for the development of Traditionalist thought is a developing literature in France that seeks to integrate Guénon's work into Catholicism in the hope of awakening what is seen as the latent Western esoteric Tradition. The two most notable examples of this work are Jean Borella (2004) and Jean Hani (2007a, 2007b, 2008, 2011). Hani's work is concerned with drawing out the Traditional elements in Catholic symbolism, as manifested in its architecture and liturgy. What is significant about the work of Hani in particular is that it seems to find it possible to firmly locate Guénonian Traditionalism within mainstream Western Catholicism and so connect the esoteric with the exoteric.

Perhaps the most surprising influence of Traditionalism is on the future British monarch. The Prince of Wales has on several occasions made his affinity with Traditionalism quite plain, using it to justify his concerns for conservation, organic farming, traditional architecture and crafts (Prince of Wales, 2010). The Prince has gone so far as to make explicit reference to Guénon and his critique of modernity (Prince of Wales, 2006). In this regard the Prince's links with the Temenos Academy, a body that seeks to promote perennialist ideas in the UK, is significant. As the future King of England it will be interesting to see whether there will be any major transformation in the perception of Guénon's ideas.

REFERENCES AND FURTHER READING

Benoist, L (2003): *The Esoteric Path: An Introduction to the Hermetic Tradition*, Hillsdale, NY, Sophia Perennis.

Borella, J (2004): *Guénonian Esoterism and Christian Mystery*, Hillsdale, NY, Sophia Perennis.

Chacornac, P (2001): *The Simple Life of René Guénon*, Hillsdale, NY, Sophia Perennis.

Coomaraswamy, A K (1989): *What is Civilisation?: And Other Essays*, Ipswich, Golgonooza Press.

Dahl, G (1999): *Radical Conservatism and the Future of Politics*, London, Sage.

Evola, J (2002): *Men Amongst the Ruins: Post-War Reflections of a Radical Traditionalist*, Rochester, Vermont, Inner Traditions.

——(2003): *Ride the Tiger: A Survival Manual for the Aristocrats of the Soul*, Rochester, Vermont, Inner Traditions.

Guénon, R (2001a): *Introduction to the Study of the Hindu Doctrines*, Hillsdale, NY, Sophia Perennis.

——(2001b): *Theosophy: History of a Pseudo-Religion*, Hillsdale, NY, Sophia Perennis.

——(2001c): *The Spiritist Fallacy*, Hillsdale, NY, Sophia Perennis.

——(2001d): *East and West*, Hillsdale, NY, Sophia Perennis.

——(2001e): *The Crisis of the Modern World*, Hillsdale, NY, Sophia Perennis.

——(2001f): *Spiritual Authority and Temporal Power*, Hillsdale, NY, Sophia Perennis.

——(2001g): *The Reign of Quantity and the Signs of the Times*, Hillsdale, NY, Sophia Perennis.

Hani, J (2007a): *Divine Craftsmanship: Preliminaries to a Spirituality of Work*, San Raphael, Sophia Perennis.

——(2007b): *The Symbolism of the Christian Temple*, San Raphael, Sophia Perennis.
——(2008): *The Divine Liturgy: Insights into its Mystery*, San Raphael, Sophia Perennis.
——(2011): *Sacred Royalty: From the Pharaoh to the Most Christian King*, London, The Matheson Trust.
Huxley, A (2009): *The Perennial Philosophy*, New York, Harper Perennial.
King, P (2012): *Reaction: Against the Modern World*, Exeter, Imprint Academic.
——(2014): *The Antimodern Condition: An Argument Against Progress*, Farnham, Ashgate.
Nasr, S H (1997): *Man and Nature: The Spiritual Crisis of Modern Man*, Chicago, ABC International.
——(2011): *Islam in the Modern World: Challenged by the West, Threatened by Fundamentalism, Keeping Faith with Tradition*, New York, HarperOne.
Prince of Wales (2006): 'An Introduction from His Royal Highness The Prince of Wales', *Sacred Web* Conference, University of Alberta, Edmonton, Canada, 23 September 2006. (http://www.sacredweb.com/conference06/conference_introduction.html, accessed 16 April, 2014).
——(2010): *Harmony: A New Way of Looking at Our World*, London, Blue Door.
Schuon, F (1984): *The Transcendent Unity of Religions*, 2nd revised edition, Wheaton, Quest Books.
Sedgwick, M (2004): *Against the Modern World: Traditionalism and the Secret Intellectual History of the Twentieth Century*, New York, Oxford University Press.
Waterfield, R (2002): *René Guénon and the Future of the West: The Life and Writings of a 20th Century Metaphysician*, Hillsdale, NY, Sophia Perennis.

CHAPTER THIRTY-ONE

DION FORTUNE AND THE SOCIETY OF THE INNER LIGHT

Alison Butler

Dion Fortune (1890–1946) has played a significant role in shaping modern magical ritual and has been particularly influential through her synthesis of the occult with the psychological. Indeed, she has become one of the most influential occult authors and figures in the development of the contemporary Western Esoteric Tradition. As a prominent occultist and lay psychoanalyst her exploration of perceived hidden powers of the mind resulted in the development of a magical–psychological system that is still practised within many esoteric and occult societies worldwide. At the heart of her system is the idea that humans are evolving spiritual beings. This evolutionary process has led to the emergence of adepts who function on higher levels of existence or 'inner planes' (Fielding and Collins 1985: 9, 10). It is from these inner planes that Fortune received the rituals and knowledge she used to establish her Society of the Inner Light. The purpose of this society was to enable initiates to fulfill their full potential as near gods, immortal and indestructible, and to bring about God's plan for humanity.

Fortune was born Violet Mary Firth in Llandudno, North Wales, on December 6, 1890, to Arthur Firth, a solicitor, and Sarah Jane Firth (née Smith). Her mother was a member of the Christian Science Church and this influence further encouraged Fortune's spiritual interests (Chapman 1993: 3). As a child, she was made to feel different and special (Fielding and Collins 1985: 11). According to Fortune, her mother told her a story that very much marked her as different. On enquiring as to, she says, 'the cause of my strangeness' (Knight 2000: 13), she was told that she had died in her mother's lap as a baby, lying for hours there until she came back to life. However, having returned to life, she now looked at her mother with different eyes, eyes that were not those of a child. Her mother suspected she was actually a different person come back to her. Moreover, by the age of four she was experiencing visions (Knight 2000: 14). Her literary career began almost as early as her mediumship. She began writing at a young age and produced her first book of poetry which was published by her family when she was 13 (Knight 2000: 16).

Fortune both attended and then later worked in a residential commercial school for women with emotional problems in Weston-super-Mare. According to Fortune, the school warden was fond of mental cruelty and endlessly harassed and ridiculed her employees and students. Fortune fell out of favor with this woman after a particular incident in which she was attempting to help another girl. Fortune was berated and interrogated for hours by her employer until she finally fell into a semi-conscious state for 30 hours (Fielding & Collins 1985: 14–17; Knight 2000: 24–27). It was this episode that supposedly helped to steer Fortune in the direction of psychology in order to further explore the power of suggestion and its effects on the mind (Knight 2000: 27).

Her first exposure to ideas and experiences that straddle the occult and psychological realms was through psychology. Although one biographer of Fortune claims that she studied psychology and psychoanalysis at the University of London (Chapman 1993: 5), Fortune herself simply claims to have been one of the first 'to take up the study of psychoanalysis [in] a clinic [that] opened in London just before the war' (Fortune 1932: 22). The Medico-Psychological Clinic, located in Brunswick Square, opened in 1913 under the direction of Jessie Murray and Julia Turner and was the first clinic to offer psychoanalytic training in Britain. Prominent students and staff included Hugh Crichton Miller, Francis Aveling, and William McDougall (Raith 2004: 63–64). The clinic was immensely influential on the development of British psychoanalysis and Fortune studied and worked there for about three years, beginning in 1913. She claims that she was the highest paid lay analyst in London at that time (Fortune 1932: 22). Fortune's experiences and education at the clinic greatly affected and influenced her future occult interests. When she began to investigate occultism she claims she did so 'from the psychological standpoint: for I believe that it is in psychology we find the key to the mysteries of magic, and its motives and modus operandi' (Fortune 1993: 102). And so, for Fortune, psychological explorations naturally led to occult experimentation.

It was at this time that Fortune met the Irish physician, Freemason, and occultist, Theodore Moriarty (1873–1923). Moriarty played a profound role in developing Fortune's interest in and knowledge of the occult. He had a special interest in psychology and healing and was particularly fascinated with alternative therapies for mental afflictions. Under his tutelage, Fortune explored the use of such therapies, including understanding past incarnations as the source for a current emotional disorder. Fortune's interest in alternative mental therapies led her further into the occult and she became convinced that occultism might hold the key to understanding the powers of the mind.

She joined one of the offshoots of the leading occult society of the day, The Hermetic Order of the Golden Dawn. In 1919, she was initiated into the London temple of the 'Alpha et Omega,' later transferring into Mina Mathers' section, the 'Stella Matutina.' Finally, Fortune and Mathers fell out in a now infamous and supposedly astral confrontation. This wasn't the only falling out Fortune had with prominent occult organizations. After having been involved in and even holding the presidency of the Christian Mystic Lodge of the Theosophical Society, a further rift ensued, this time with the Theosophists, following a squabble over the more Western focus of Fortune's lodge. This gave Fortune added incentive to establish her own group, or rather to facilitate the transition of the lodge into a new form, the Community of the Inner Light. Fortune's society initially was set up as an outer court of the Golden Dawn system and prior to Fortune's rift with Mathers, it had full approval from the 'Stella Matutina.' After their falling out, Fortune's society became independent of any contemporary Golden Dawn organization yet continued to make use of its magical system.

It was during this time that Fortune met the Welsh physician, Dr. Thomas Penry Evans (1892–1959). He too was a member of the Christian Mystic Lodge and the two married in April of 1927 as Community of the Inner Light was being established. As well as being an occultist, Evans held a diploma in Psychiatric Medicine. Evans was very much involved in the Inner Light and played a crucial role in Fortune's occult experimentations. The marriage ended somewhat amicably in 1945 (Fielding and Collins 1985: 93; Knight 2000: 240).

Meanwhile, Fortune's Fraternity of the Inner Light, as it later came to be called, had acquired land at the foot of the Tor in Glastonbury and there established Chalice Orchard. Fortune believed that Glastonbury held great mystical power because of its associations with Arthurian legend. It was also associated with Christian mysticism and had occult status as a power source for elemental contacts. Glastonbury remained central to Fortune's magical–psychological system. However, for practical reasons, the Inner Light's headquarters were based in London. The purpose of the fraternity was to train initiates in Fortune's theory and practice of spiritual evolution so that in becoming a superior life form, one might have an effect on the world for good. A second goal of the society was to disseminate such methods and goals to the general public in the form of literature and lectures (Fielding and Collins 1985: 54). Due to increasing demand from remote parts of the UK and abroad, the fraternity soon developed a correspondence course for neophytes unable to meet regularly in person (Fielding and Collins 1985: 56). Recommended reading for the study course included Mallory's *Morte d'Arthur*, the works of C. G. Jung, and of course Fortune's own publications and lectures (Fielding and Collins 1985: 58).

During the Second World War, the organization took on a rather more social and political role in engaging in a magical battle against the forces of evil at work within the ranks of the enemy. This 'magical battle of Britain' is described in great detail in Gareth Knight's book on the subject (1993). Fortune's occult system involved the belief that magic could be used as a social or political tool. Hence, The Society of Inner Light, as it eventually became known, attempted to influence political and social life through monthly and then weekly group meditations with the purpose of bolstering the war effort, protecting the realm, and defeating the enemy.

Fortune was a prolific writer on occult topics, both in fiction and non-fiction. She used her pseudonym for most of her occult publications, using her birth name for those works that dealt purely with psychology. The pseudonym comes from the magical motto she took in the Golden Dawn, *Deo non Fortuna* ('through God, not luck'). Most of her non-fiction expounds the principles and theories behind her psycho-spiritual system and she claims that much of the material was acquired from inner plane adepts through the process of trance mediumship. Such works include *Sane Occultism* (1929), *Psychic Self Defense* (1930), and her occult masterpiece, *The Mystical Qabalah* (1935). Her occult fiction often featured heroes and heroines based on her real life colleagues or associates. These include *The Secrets of Dr. Taverner* (1926), *The Demon Lover* (1927), *The Winged Bull* (1935), *The Goat Foot God* (1936), *The Sea Priestess* (1938) and the influential *Moon Magic* (1956), which, unfinished at her death, was, it is claimed, written posthumously by dictation to one of the Society's mediums (Fielding & Collins 1985: 166).

Fortune's mediumship places her in an interesting position at the intersection of occultism and Spiritualism. Many occultists, particularly those within the Golden Dawn, were hostile to Spiritualism and what were perceived to be its fraudulent and dangerous methods. Fortune, however, attempted to 'break down the distrust and antagonism that has so long prevailed between the two movements', encouraging fellow occultists to 'familiarise themselves with the methods of the Spiritualist séance' (Fortune 1942: 102). Having said that, The Society of the Inner Light was not always very receptive to Spiritualism. Members were originally banned from participating in Spiritualist activities resulting in many resignations (Knight 1993: 101). Fortune eventually removed the ban, but clearly distinguished between safe and dangerous forms of mediumship.

In much of her writing, Fortune clearly demonstrates the psychologisation of esotericism, increasingly typical of much twentieth-century occultism. As a lay analyst she was greatly influenced by the work of Sigmund Freud and Carl Jung, and in her occult non-fiction she appropriates both contemporary psychological terminology and theory. This appropriation stems from her recognition of parallel concepts within the developing field of psychology and recognition of easier public accessibility to occult concepts through the use of psychological terminology and theory. Fortune quite openly referred to Aleister Crowley, Israel Regardie and herself as the 'unholy trinity of revealers of the Mysteries' (Fortune 1933: 16).

Fortune accomplished her goal of making the secrets of the Western Mystery Tradition more accessible and, at the time of her death in 1946, her Society numbered around 50–60 men and women. Fortune died at the age of 55 from late-detected leukemia and it is suspected that her efforts during the magical battle of Britain exhausted her and made her more susceptible to the disease (Richardson 1991: 227–45). Her legacy continues in the many occult organisations practicing her system such as the 'London Group', the 'Star and Cross', 'Servants of the Light' and, of course, the modern day manifestation of the original 'Society of the Inner Light', which continued on after her death. Her influence upon other occult and neo-pagan groups is also part of her legacy. While it is debatable whether Fortune actually had any direct influence on the formation of neo-pagan traditions of the twentieth century, her fictional work with its Arthurian, Atlantean and goddess themes, has certainly been significant within such groups and her writing has been incorporated into neo-pagan rituals (Hutton 2009).

The significance of the magical tradition Fortune founded lies in its synthesis of some of the more appealing and enduring legends of the West with the already clearly established magical system of the Golden Dawn. In contributing to the further psychologisation of occultism, Fortune further enhanced the accessibility and relevance of this system, better suiting it to the needs of subsequent practitioners.

REFERENCES AND FURTHER READING

Butler, A. (2011) *Victorian Occultism and the Making of Modern Magic: Invoking Tradition*, New York: Palgrave Macmillan.

Chapman, J. (1993) *Quest for Dion Fortune*, York Beach: Samuel Weiser.

Fielding, C. & C. Collins (1985) *The Story of Dion Fortune*, York Beach, Maine: Samuel Weiser.

Fortune, D. (1926) *The Secrets of Dr. Taverner*, London: Noel Douglas.
——(1927) *The Demon Lover*, London: Noel Douglas.
——(1929) *Sane Occultism*, London: Rider.
——(1930) *Psychic Self Defense*, London: Rider.
——(1932) 'The Broken Tryst,' *The Occult Review*, 56:1, 21–25.
——(1933) 'Ceremonial Magic Unveiled,' *The Occult Review*, 57:1, 13–24.
——(1935a) *The Mystical Qabalah*, London: Williams and Norgate.
——(1935b) *The Winged Bull*, London: Williams and Norgate.
——(1936) *The Goat Foot God*, London: Williams and Norgate.
——(1938) *The Sea Priestess*, London: V. Firth.
——(1993 [1942a]) 'The Fraternity of the Inner Light and Spiritualism,' in G. Knight, ed., *The Magical Battle of Britain*, Bradford-on-Avon: Golden Gates Press, 100–104.
——(1993 [1942b]) 'Modus Operandi of Trance Communication,' in G. Knight, ed., *The Magical Battle of Britain*, Bradford-on-Avon: Golden Gates Press, 98–99.
——(1956) *Moon Magic*, London: Aquarian Press.
Hutton, R. (2009) 'Dion Fortune and Wicca.' Online: http://www.companyofavalon.net/documents/RonaldHuttonaddress.DF.doc (accessed December 10, 2012).
Knight, G. (1993) *The Magical Battle of Britain*, Bradford-on-Avon: Golden Gates Press.
——(2000) *Dion Fortune and the Inner Light*, Longborough, Leicestershire: Thoth Publications.
Raith, S. (2004) 'Early British Psychoanalysis and the Medico-Psychological Clinic,' *History Workshop Journal*, 58:1, 63–85.
Richardson, A. (1991) *The Magical Life of Dion Fortune*, Wellingborough, Northamptonshire: Aquarian Press.

CHAPTER THIRTY-TWO

JOHN WHITESIDE PARSONS

Nicholas Campion

John Whiteside Parsons (1914–52), better known simply as Jack Parsons, is one of the most interesting characters in the history of the occult in the early to mid-twentieth century, by virtue of his vital role in the American space programme. Parsons was born in Pasadena in October 1914 and became a noted chemical engineer and explosives expert. His scientific activities have been well-documented, as has his involvement in magick and the occult (Carter 2004; Pendle 2005). Inspired partly by science-fiction, he became part of a group of rocket enthusiasts who were determined to make space travel a reality and named themselves the 'suicide squad', in view of the danger of their work, and who were attached to the California Institute of Technology. Their work laid the foundation for the Jet Propulsion Laboratory, founded in 1944 (Conway n.d.), and so for the NASA space programme. Parsons eventually blew himself up in Pasadena in 1952, a martyr to his dream of travelling to the Moon.

Parsons joined Aleister Crowley's Ordo Templi Orientis (OTO) in 1941, together with his wife, the artist Marjorie Cameron (Kansa 2011) and became master of the Agapé Lodge, based in a mansion in Pasadena, which acted as a commune for Parsons and his close associates. He fell out with Crowley in 1946 and also had a brief friendship – and falling out – with L. Ron Hubbard (Miller 1988, 146–68), the founder of Scientology.

Although Carter and Pendle have documented the facts of Parsons' life as both an occultist and magician, and as a pioneer of the American space programme, neither deals with the details of his ideas concerning the role and nature of the occult. These can be inferred from Crowley's teachings, which served as Parsons' primary source in magick, as well as from Parsons' own writings, chiefly a collection of essays written in the 1940s, and published posthumously in 1989. In Grant's words, Parsons' mission as an occultist can be summed up as 'the discovery of his True Will' (2010, 169). His definitions and discussion of magic are clearly rooted in the European tradition, referring explicitly to the doctrine of sympathies (Parsons 1989, 46) and correspondences which, appropriately for Parsons' dreams of space travel, were described by Crowley as essential for a proper understanding of the planets (1979, 53). 'Magick,' Parsons wrote, 'is a system of philosophy and a way of life which, as a common denominator of all cultures, is universal to mankind' (1989, 45). As a scientist, Parsons was clear that the scientific and magickal worldviews are compatible. 'It is therefore essential,' he wrote, 'that the magician have a comprehensive knowledge of the various planes whose interaction results in comprehensive reality' (1989, 47). In Parsons' worldview, knowledge of rocket fuel was therefore as important to the practice of magick as were the rules and rites set out by the OTO. He continues, 'In its absolute basis, magick is a passion and a discipline which relates the mystery of love, and through which man is capable of attaining to any ultimate knowledge and love of himself, his fellow man and the universe in all its aspects' (1989, 46). Grant commented on Parsons' revolutionary tendencies, and radical and counter-cultural statements concerning the need for love as the basis of human life, as well as the necessity for new forms of social organisation, pervade his work (2010, 170). For example, he wrote that an education in magick should be a training in 'total consciousness', the object being 'the unfoldment of society in all the ways of love', the consequence of which, he hoped, would be 'a more conscious, better integrated, and more interesting and significant social order' (Parsons 1989, 47).

The legacy of such rhetoric in the counter-cultural thinking of the 1960s, two decades later, is clear. Parsons' vision of a new society was encompassed by his Crowleyesque millenarianism (Crowley 2011, 15–18), and what he believed to be the current historic transition from the 'Age of Osiris'. This, Parsons thought, had begun around 4000 BCE and had resulted in what he saw as the debased, patriarchal, oppressive, violent, self-loathing, militaristic, dogmatic and sexually warped culture of Judeo-Christianity. Parsons described the condition of humanity at the end of the Age of Osiris in despairing terms: 'Feeling himself unloved and unknowing of the way to live, Western man moves in a sterile wasteland of the mind, lacking the knowledge, understanding and will to save himself by an act of love' (1989, 49). All this, he hoped, was to change with the arrival of the imminent 'Age of Horus'. A new and better world was to come about through psychological revolution, that is, through the self-aware recognition and full expression by each individual of their dual male/female nature. However, he was not optimistic. Like Crowley, this prophetic historiography places Parsons within the wider context of Theosophical and New Age millenarianism (Campion 2012), as espoused particularly by H.P. Blavatsky, Rudolf Steiner and Alice Bailey, accompanied by a denunciation of modern materialism, and a belief in a spiritual equivalent of a Bolshevik revolutionary vanguard, whose task was to promote the arrival of the new world order. In Parsons' occult politics, the revolutionary vanguard was the OTO, its activism being magickal ritual and psychological self-awareness, rather than violent revolution.

The evidence from Parsons' own writings suggests that Crowley's cosmology was central to this own, including his desire to travel into space. Crowley's writings open many questions in relation to Parsons' own ideology. For example, Parsons was born on 2 October 1914: did he note Crowley's statement that those born with Uranus in Aries, as he was, possess 'a character intrepid, dauntless, fiery and indomitable'? (Crowley 1979, 124) In his rituals, did he note that emerald is the colour of Libra (Crowley 1986, 104), the zodiac sign containing the sun at his birth? Was he inspired by Crowley's statement that 'every man and woman is a star' (2011, 25)? Did Crowley's injunction, 'Plunge from the height, O God, and interlock with Man!' (1981, 69), encourage his determination to travel to the stars? Crowley had claimed that a star, in its metaphysical sense, is an aggregate of experience, in effect a 'God' (2011, 15). In what sense did such statements alter what Parsons' saw when he looked at the night sky? Such questions are yet to be explored, as is the significance of other aspects of life in the OTO. It is known, for example, that the OTO rituals, which Parsons both participated in and presided over, were explicitly astrological. One, the 'Ritual of the Lesser Hexagram', required the participant to face the East (the rising sun) and utter words such as 'Virgo, Isis, Mighty Mother, Scorpio, Apophis, Destroyer' (DuQuette 2003, 110), words that Parsons interpreted as code for the coming of the 'New Aeon' of Horus (1989, 60). When Crowley complained that 'men take the Son of Science, and burn him for a Heretic' (1991, 117), Parsons, for whom magick and science were part of the same, single cosmos, would have understood that the 'Scientist' in Crowley's terms, was the visionary who understood the true laws, of life, death and love, which, he believed, underpinned the world within which ordinary scientists – including rocket scientists – operated.

Parsons was not a leading occultist, but assumes prominence in the history of twentieth-century occultism as a consequence of his wider historical importance. He both confounds simple arguments that scientific education is the antithesis of superstition, occult practice or religious affiliation, and contributes to the study of the wide spread of ideas concerning the importance of human exploration of space (Bell and Parker 2009) which was later to drive the Apollo Moon programme.

REFERENCES AND FURTHER READING

Bell, D. & M. Parker, eds. (2009) *Space Travel and Culture: From Apollo to Space Tourism*, Oxford: Blackwell.

Campion, N. (2012) *Astrology and Popular Religion in the Modern West: Prophecy, Cosmology and the New Prophecy Age Movement*, Abingdon: Ashgate.

Carter, J. (2004) *Sex and Rockets: the Occult World of Jack Parsons*, Port Townsend WA: Feral House.

Conway, E. (n.d.) 'JPL History: 1936–58'. Online: http://www.jpl.nasa.gov/jplhistory/early/index.php (accessed 30 December 2012).

Crowley, A. (1979) *The Complete Astrological Writings*, ed. John Symonds and Kenneth Grant, London: Duckworth.

——(1981) *The Book of Lies*, San Francisco: Weiser Books.

——(1986) *777 and Other Qabalistic Writings of Aleister Crowley*, San Francisco: Weiser Books.

——(1991) *Liber Aleph vel CXI: The Book of Wisdom or Folly*, York Beach, Maine.

——(2011) *The Book of the Law*, San Francisco: Red Wheel/Weiser.

DuQuette, L. M. (2003) *The Magick of Aleister Crowley: A Handbook of Rituals of Thelema*, San Francisco: Weiser Books.

Grant, K. (2010) *The Magical Revival*, Vol. 1, London: Starfire Publishing.

Kansa, S. (2011) *Wormwood Star: the Magickal Life of Marjorie Cameron*, Oxford: Mandrake.

Miller, R. (1988) *Bare Faced Messiah: the true story of L. Ron Hubbard*, London: Sphere Books.

Parsons, J.W. (1989) *Freedom is a Two-Edged Sword*, Tempe, AZ: New Falcon Publications.

Pendle, G. (2005) *Strange Angel: the Otherworldly life of Rocket Scientist John Whiteside Parsons*, London: Weidenfeld and Nicholson.

CHAPTER THIRTY-THREE

KENNETH GRANT AND THE TYPHONIAN TRADITION

Henrik Bogdan

INTRODUCTION

The presence of the British author Kenneth Grant (1924–2011) looms large over the history of modern occultism. Apart from having collaborated with, and later promoted the works of influential occultists such as Aleister Crowley (1875–1947) and Austin Osman Spare (1886–1956), Grant is known as the expounder of a particular current in contemporary occultism usually referred to as the 'Typhonian Tradition.' This current can best be described as both a synthesis and re-reading of history through the lenses of an occultist worldview composed of such diverse traditions as Thelema, Neo-Vedanta, Hindu Tantra, Western Sexual Magic, Surrealism, ufology, and Lovecraftian gnosis; but the Typhonian Tradition as described by Grant in his 'Typhonian Trilogies' can also seen as a practical epistemological system aimed at spiritual enlightenment and the transcending of the illusion of duality.

Part of the appeal to the works of Grant is probably due to the fact that little is known about him as a person apart from the bits and pieces of his autobiography which are revealed in his writings. Grant led a private and quiet life in Northern London and for the last two or three decades he became increasingly reclusive, which helped to foster the image of Grant as a mysterious and enigmatic person. In contrast to many other occultists, Grant never gave any lectures or participated in public events. To Grant, the prime and most efficient mode of communication was through the written word, as expressed in the only interview that he ever gave: 'The silent or printed word is more potent than its spoken counterpart...and it reaches those for whom it is intended...Books...have been known to change lives. My own life was changed by Crowley's *Magick*' (Grant 1990: 5–7).

The book referred to above is Aleister Crowley's magnum opus *Magick in Theory and Practice* (1930), which Grant came across at the age of 15 at Zwemmers in Charing Cross Road. Grant, who had already read occultist authors such as Blavatsky, was deeply impressed by the book and eventually he managed to get in contact with the author personally. After a brief exchange of letters, Grant was invited on 10 December 1944 to visit Crowley at the Bell Inn, in Buckinghamshire. As noted by

Crowley in his diary, he took a liking to Grant and shortly thereafter hired the then 20-year-old Grant as his secretary for a brief period when he had relocated to Netherwood, a lodging house outside Hastings. Although Grant's stay with Crowley at Netherwood was short, it had a profound impact upon him and he would for the rest of his life continue to study the works of 'the Beast 666' (i.e. Crowley) and identify himself as a thelemite, an adherent of the new religion Thelema of which Crowley was the prophet.

In 1948, the year after Crowley had died, Grant was formally acknowledged as a ninth degree member of the Ordo Templi Orientis (OTO) by Karl J. Germer (1885–1962) who had succeeded Crowley as the head of the order. The OTO was a mixed masonic organisation of German origin which Crowley had seized control of in 1922, and which taught sexual magic in its highest degrees, i.e. the ninth and eleventh degrees (the tenth degree was an administrative degree reserved for national heads of the organisation). Later, on 5 March 1951, Germer issued a charter to Grant to open a camp of the order in London and Grant devoted himself to organising OTO work in London and publishing a manifesto of the British Branch of the OTO (1952) with the help of Cecil Williamson (1909–99), the founder of the Museum of witchcraft at Castletown on the Isle of Man.

The 1950s proved to be a turbulent and formative period for Grant. It was mainly during this period that Grant encountered and experimented with many of the diverse traditions that subsequently were synthesised into the Typhonian Tradition. Chief among these influences were—apart from the works of Crowley which Grant at this period was in a unique position to study since he was being employed by the Crowley collector Gerald Yorke (1901–83) to copy all of Crowley's unpublished writings, including letters and diaries—Hindu traditions such as Tantra and Advaita (see below) and the eldritch work and art of Austin Osman Spare. Grant was introduced to Spare through his wife Steffi in 1949 and a deep and lasting friendship developed between Spare and the young couple. The interest that they took in his art helped to rekindle not only Spare's artistic output, but also the development of his magical system, which was codified with the help of Grant into the Zos Kia Cultus (Baker 2011). Upon Spare's death in 1956, Grant acted as his literary executor and he would later be instrumental in the renewed interest in Spare through his Typhonian Trilogies and his books *Images and Oracles of Austin Osman Spare* (1975), and *Zos Speaks! Encounters With Austin Osman Spare* (1998), the latter co-written with Steffi Grant.

The first part of the 1950s was characterised by experiment and innovation in terms of the magical work carried out by Grant within loosely formed groups connected to the OTO and other obscure orders such as the I.B.A., of which very little is known. Much of this work culminated in the formation of the New Isis Lodge, founded in 1955. The lodge, which was founded as an OTO body, was announced in an eight-page pamphlet entitled *Manifesto of New Isis Lodge O.T.O.* (1955). The most conspicuous aspect of this manifesto is the claim that 'a new and compelling influence is enveloping the earth' and that 'its rays proceed from a source as yet unexplored by those who are not at one with it in essence and in spirit and it finds its present focus in the outer universe in the transplutonic planet Isis' (Grant 1955: 1). This alleged planet is, according to the manifesto, to be linked to the goddess Nuit, and thereby to the first chapter of Crowley's *The Book of the Law,* and it was the special task of the New Isis Lodge to channel the power and energy that emanates from the planet (Grant 1992). Germer, however, strongly objected to the manifesto and on July 20, 1955, he formally revoked the charter and expelled Grant from the OTO. Grant ignored Germer's letter of expulsion and continued to operate the New Isis Lodge until 1962 on the basis of 'inner Plane' powers. The group had, according to Grant, around 30 active members, who met every seventh Friday at the lodge premises in London, which at least for a while were located in the basement of a furrier's shop on 7a Melcombe Street, just off Baker Street (Bogdan 2010). The experiences drawn from the ritual workings of the New Isis Lodge seem to have had a profound effect upon Kenneth Grant, and he frequently returns to this lodge in his later published works, especially in *Hecate's Fountain* (1992) which is one of Grant's most popular books.

The break with Germer and the expulsion from the OTO are important for the understanding of Grant's subsequent activities in the New Isis Lodge, as this made it possible for Grant to develop his own, idiosyncratic understanding of Thelema and the OTO. While Grant does not explain the nature of the inner plane powers on which he based his legitimacy as a leader of the OTO subsequent to the falling out with Germer, it seems probable that they are connected to the transmissions related to the New Isis planet, and in particular the two texts *Wisdom of S'lba* and *OKBISh*, or *The Book of the Spider.* These texts were channelled by the members of the New Isis Lodge in the 1950s and later published by Grant in *Outer Gateways* (1994) and *The Ninth Arch* (2002).

After the closure of the New Isis Lodge in 1962, there followed a seven-year hiatus of which time little is known, but by 1969 and the publication of Crowley's autobiography, *The Confessions* (which Grant co-edited with John Symonds), Grant would start to refer to himself as the Rex Supremus or international leader of the OTO. During 1970s *The Confessions* was followed by several other works by Crowley that were co-edited by Grant and Symonds, and in 1972 the first book in a series of three trilogies (nine books in total) was published, entitled *The Magical Revival.*[1] As mentioned, these trilogies are referred to as the Typhonian Trilogies, and the ninth and final volume, *The Ninth Arch*, was published thirty years later, in 2002. It was also around the time that the first volume of the trilogies appeared that the so-called Typhonian OTO emerged, with its first official announcement published *ca.* 1973. The Typhonian OTO preserved the degree structure of the OTO under Crowley, but dispensed of virtually all masonic-style rituals, revised the teachings of sexual magic and became tightly connected to the Typhonian Tradition as laid out in the trilogies. The Typhonian OTO would later (in 2011) change its name to the Typhonian Order, and after Kenneth Grant's passing in 2011, the leadership of the order was passed to his friend and collaborator Michael Staley.

THE TYPHONIAN TRADITION AND THE NIGHTSIDE OF EXISTENCE

The Typhonian Tradition as described by Grant in his books, can be seen as both a particular interpretation of history and as a specific form of epistemology. In many ways the notion of a Typhonian Tradition lies at the core of Grant's work and he claimed that Crowley's religio-magical system—and by extension his own work—was a revival of this 'ancient' tradition. Grant's understanding of the Typhonian

Tradition evolved over the course of the thirty-year period that it took to complete the Typhonian Trilogies, from 1972 to 2002. Although the basic concept of this tradition is present already in the first book of the series, *The Magical Revival* (1972), it is from the third book, *Cults of the Shadow* (1975) and onwards that the reader encounters the actual term, and Grant devoted increasing attention to exploring and explaining the Typhonian Tradition in the subsequent books. Drawing heavily on the works of the self-taught Egyptologist Gerald Massey (1828–1907) and his comparative approach to ancient mythologies, Grant described the Typhonian Tradition as 'the primal African Cult in its ancient Egyptian or Draconian form. Typhon, or Taurt, represented the first light in darkness as the circumpolar complex of seven stars that gave her the name of the Dragon of the Deep. Her seven stars, or souls, were manifested by Set, her son in the South, who, as the eighth was the culmination or height of her light and the first male deity ever to be worshipped'(Grant 1975: 231). In other words, the arch-monster Typhon, opponent to Zeus according to the Greek mythology, is identified with the Egyptian goddess Taurt (Taweret, 'the great [female] one'), described by Grant as either the mother or a feminine aspect of Set. To Grant, the worship of Taurt or Typhon represented the oldest form of religion known to mankind, a religion that centered on the worship of the stars and the sacred powers of procreation and sexuality. The Egyptian god Set plays a particularly important role in the Typhonian Tradition; not only is he believed to have been the first male god ever worshiped, but he is also considered to have evolved into Satan, the adversary to the Christian God. Due to the antinomian nature of this deity, he has throughout history been identified with evil and sinister forces by its adversaries. Through an etymological analysis, inspired by Crowley and others, Grant argues that Set was transformed into Shaitan (according to Grant the prime God worshipped by the Yezidis), and later into Satan. Probably inspired by nineteenth-century theories on the possibility of understanding the essence of religion through the study of its origins, Grant maintained that the Typhonain Tradition, and in particular the god Set, represents the 'hidden', 'concealed' or repressed aspect of our psyche which it is vital to explore in order to reach gnosis or spiritual enlightenment.

In his trilogies Grant discusses various techniques whereby initiates can explore the hidden aspects of the psyche. Chief among these, is the 'nightside' or reverse of the kabbalistic Tree of Life, the Qlipoth (Woudenberg 2010). The Tree of Life is the most common glyph or diagram used by occultists to describe the order of the universe as well as the human mind, as expressed for instance in the initiatory system of the Hermetic Order of the Golden Dawn and in Crowley's initiatic order the A∴A∴ (1907), of which Grant became a member after he had met Crowley in 1944. Just as Grant gradually came to emphasise the Typhonian Tradition in his trilogies, the emphasis on the practical means of exploring the Qlipoth increased after the publication of the fifth book in the series, *Nightside of Eden* (1977). In the introduction to this book, Grant stated:

> Full magical initiation is not possible without an understanding of the so-called qliphotic paths which are, in practice, as real as the shadow of any object illuminated by the sun. (...) It is only after mastering the world of the shadows within himself in the form of arch-demons, anger, lust, and pride, that man may

> truly claim to be the Lord of the Shining Wheels or Disks [i.e. the ten Sephiroth of the Tree of Life].
>
> (Grant 1977: 1–2)

Again, Grant's understanding of key-topics covered in his books evolved, and the nature of the Qlipoth changed drastically as they increasingly became identified with a means of establishing contact with extraterrestrial life-forms, or powers beyond terrestrial consciousness.

CONTACT WITH NON-HUMAN ENTITIES AND THE MAUVE ZONE

The Mauve Zone, a key-concept in Grant's system first mentioned in *Hecate's Fountain* (1992), is related to a practical formula of dream control evolved by Grant during the years 1955–62, when 'New Isis Lodge was founded for the purposes of traffic with the Outer Ones' (Grant 1994: 7). In his writings, Grant repeatedly stresses the importance of establishing contact with higher beings for the spiritual evolution of the practitioner, but also for the future of mankind. Grant goes a long way in trying to explain the nature of these higher beings, drawing not only on traditional esoteric concepts, but also on the notion of aliens in the post-1947 UFO-milieu, and the Lovecraftian mythos of the Great Old Ones—ancient beings from Outer Space who are waiting to re-enter the human world. It should be emphasised that Grant differs from Crowley in his understanding of these entities: whereas Crowley adopted an agnostic approach to the nature of the entities encountered in ritual magic, Grant argues that they are actual entities existing outside of man's consciousness although they are to be accessed through a mental state which Grant calls the Mauve Zone:

> Above and beyond this, the book endeavours to follow the workings of these phenomena in dimensions that scientists are only just beginning to explore. These dimensions, which may be considered as existing outside or between the two states of dreaming and waking, I have called the Mauve Zone. It includes and excludes both simultaneously. The designation comports occult overtones needing no explanation to those acquainted with the function of Daäth [i.e. the 'hidden' sphere on the Tree of Life which Grant sees as the entrance to its nightside] as the gate of Ingress and of Egress to the other side of the Tree of Life. To those not so acquainted, the Mauve Zone may be said to have mythical analogue in the symbol of the *Crimson Desert* of the Arabs, which, according to Lovecraft, was the ancient equivalent of the *Roba el Khaliyeh*, a zone reputedly haunted by evil spirits and monsters of death.
>
> (Grant 1992: Foreword)

Grant was, however, ambivalent towards extraterrestrial contacts. On the one hand he warned against the Outer Ones or extraterrestrial powers and that they would somehow be linked to an imminent catastrophe or worldwide destruction of civilisation, as we know it. On the other hand, he argued that it is only through contact with these alien forces that mankind can progress, and that his books 'indicate certain "gateways" through which alien forms of consciousness may manifest to Man, and through which Man may go to meet them' (Grant 1990).

NECRONOMICON GNOSIS AND THE DERANGEMENT OF THE SENSES

The reference to Lovecraft in the quote above regarding the Mauve Zone was not accidental. In fact, according to Grant, Lovecraft had through his dreams unconsciously tapped into the same magical current that Crowley was consciously in contact with (Levenda 2013). The fictional works of Lovecraft—particularly those connected to the Chtulhu mythos (or Necronomicon Gnosis as Grant calls it), did not only correspond to Crowley's Law of Thelema and *The Book of the Law,* but more importantly explain and give deeper understanding of them. But Grant went beyond a mere interpretation of Thelema through the works of Lovecraft and he claims to have performed (during the days of the New Isis Lodge) rituals to invoke entities from the Chtulhu mythos: he describes for instance a ritual carried out at the Summer Solstice aimed at invoking the Great Old One Yog-Sothoth, and on another occasion he refers to the lodge-members of New Isis as votaries of Chtulhu (Grant 1992). It is apparent that Grant's use of Lovecraft's fictional work—but also that of other authors such as Arthur Machen (1863–1947) and Sax Rohmer (Arthur Henry Sarsfield Ward, 1883–1959)—was not restricted to a comparative enterprise, but seems to have had a more practical function in the sense of challenging the way that the reader sees fiction and reality. In this Grant was influenced by Surrealists such as Salvador Dalí (1904–89) and their method of challenging the notion of the real, and in particular referred to Arthur Rimbaud's (1854–91) formula of total derangement of the senses, which to Grant meant an active overstimulation of the senses which would lead to the mind opening up for the experience of, and communication with, entities in the Mauve Zone. In fact, when asked what the purpose of his books is, Grant replied: 'To provide concepts that are essentially strange so that the faculty of intuitive insight may be awakened and aligned with such alien concepts [as UFO's and similar phenomena]' (Grant 1990).

NEO-VEDANTA, TANTRA, AND THE LEFT-HAND PATH

It could be argued that Grant's use of fiction is directly linked to the fact that he embraced teachings of non-duality and Hindu Advaita. In the 1950s Grant immersed himself in Hindu philosophy and religion, especially the teachings of 'the Sage of Arunachala,' Bhagavan Sri Ramana Maharshi (1879–1950), and wrote a number of articles on Advaita Vedanta for Indian journals such as *The Call Divine*, published in Bombay. According to Grant, the notion that reality is composed of an objective and a subjective world, or an inner and outer world, is an illusion that one has to be freed from. By mixing fiction with historical fact the border between these worlds is increasingly being questioned, and ultimately it can be transcended.

The encounter with advaita during the early 1950s, was probably prompted by a deep-seated fascination with the Orient, especially with the religious and mystical traditions of India. In fact, Grant had volunteered for the army at the age of eighteen, with the expectation of being sent to India, where he had hopes of finding a guru

(Grant 1991). Although ill health led to his discharge from the army and thus prevented him from reaching India, he did manage to find an Eastern guru of sorts, in the unlikely person of David Curwen (1893–1984), a furrier of Jewish origin living in London. Grant met Curwen through Aleister Crowley, who had admitted the former to the ninth degree of the OTO in 1945. Curwen was, however, no newcomer to the occult and he had been taught Tantrik theory in the 1930s by an Indian guru, Swami Pareswara Bikshu (Bogdan 2010). After Crowley's death Curwen initiated Grant into the mysteries of Tantra, and Grant would later incorporate this knowledge in his version of the OTO; as with Crowley, the eighth degree dealt with masturbation and the ninth degree with heterosexual sex while the eleventh degree in contrast to Crowley's system did not deal with anal sex, but with heterosexual sex during menstruation. According to Grant, Crowley was not aware of the Tantric theories on the importance of the female sexual fluids (that Grant had learnt from Curwen), which Grant calls *kalas*. Grant describes the *kalas* as psycho-sexual secretions of the Tantric *suvasini* or female tantric adept of the Left-Hand Path, and goes on to state that there are sixteen different *kalas* that practitioners of sexual magic deal with and that these form the bases, together with the male fluids, of the Elixir (Grant 1973: 211–12). Furthermore, Grant argued that the Left-Hand Path was, in fact, an Indian manifestation of the Egyptian pre-dynastic cult of the Great Goddess, and that tantra is thus essential for the understanding of the Typhonian Tradition.

NOTE

1 The Typhonian Trilogies consist of; First series: *The Magical Revival* (1972), *Aleister Crowley & the Hidden God* (1973), *Cults of the Shadow* (1975); Second series: *Nightside of Eden* (1977), *Outside the Circles of Time* (1980), *Hecate's Fountain* (1992); Third series: *Outer Gateways* (1994), *Beyond the Mauve Zone* (1999), *The Ninth Arch* (2002). For a complete bibliography of Grant, see Bogdan 2014.

REFERENCES AND FURTHER READING

Baker, P. (2011) *Austin Osman Spare: The Life and Legend of London's Lost Artist*, London: Strange Atractor Press.

Bogdan, H. (2010), 'Introduction.' In Crowley, A. & D. Curwen, *Brother Curwen, Brother Crowley: A Correspondence*. Edited with an introduction by Henrik Bogdan, York Beach, ME: Teitan Press.

——(2014) *Kenneth Grant: A Bibliography*, 2nd edition. London: Fulgur Limited.

Crowley, A. (1930) *Magick in Theory and Practice*. Paris: Lecram Press.

Evans, D. (2007) *The History of British Magick After Crowley*, No place: Hidden Publishing.

Giudice, Christian (2011) 'Typhon Rising: Kenneth Grant and the Typhonian Tradition in post-Crowleyan Magic.' Unpublished MA thesis. University of Exeter.

Grant, K. (1955) *Manifesto of New Isis Lodge O.T.O.*, London: privately printed.

——(1972) *The Magical Revival*, London: Frederick Muller.

——(1973) *Aleister Crowley & the Hidden God*, London: Frederick Muller.

——(1975) *Cults of the Shadow*, London: Frederick Muller.

——(1975) *Images and Oracles of Austin Osman Spare*, London: Frederick Muller.

——(1977) *Nightside of Eden*, London: Frederick Muller.

——(1980) *Outside the Circles of Time*, London: Frederick Muller.

——(1990) 'Kenneth Grant Talks to Skoob: Interview with Kenneth Grant'. In *Skoob Occult Review* 3 (Autumn): 5–7.
——(1991) *Remembering Aleister Crowley*, London: Skoob Books.
——(1992) *Hecate's Fountain*, London: Skoob Books.
——(1994) *Outer Gateways*, London: Skoob Books.
——(1999) *Beyond the Mauve Zone*, London: Starfire.
——(2002) *The Ninth Arch* London: Starfire.
——(2006) *At the Feet of the Guru*, London: Starfire.
Grant, K. and Grant, S. (eds.) (1998) *Zos Speaks!: Encounters with Austin Osman Spare*, London: Fulgur.
Levenda, P. (2013) *The Dark Lord: H.P. Lovecraft, Kenneth Grant and the Typhonian Tradition in Magic*, Lake Worth, FL: Ibis Press.
Staley, M. (2011) 'Scintillations in Mauve: An Introduction to the Work of Kenneth Grant.' In *Starfire* II(4), pp. 9–26.
Woudenberg, G. (2010) 'Kenneth Grant's Nightside: The Reinterpretation of Kabbalistic Kelipot in Modern Occultism.' Unpublished M.A. thesis. University of Exeter.

CHAPTER THIRTY-FOUR

ROBERT ANTON WILSON

Erik Davis

Robert Anton Wilson (1932–2007), born Robert Edward Wilson, was an American novelist, essayist, editor, playwright, and lecturer whose playful and prolific writings helped make him one of the most stimulating and influential popular thinkers in the 'head' or 'freak' currents of the American counterculture in the 1970s, 1980s, and 1990s. Wilson's large, often digressive novels, including the seminal 1975 *Illuminatus!* trilogy written with Robert Shea, exploited the lore of conspiracy theories and occult secret societies to explore philosophical, political, and mystical themes with a satiric and willfully 'pulp' sensibility influenced by drug culture, American vernacular humor, modernist fiction, and the bawdy slapstick of underground comics. Wilson was also an original thinker whose witty, accessible, and highly discursive nonfiction texts drew from a wide range of discourses, including existentialism, phenomenology, general semantics, occultism, mysticism, sociology, anarchism, and quantum physics, not to mention his own experiments in 'hedonic engineering.' Developing an expansive skepticism rooted in the phenomenology of the nervous system, Wilson argued that that 'the only "realities" (plural) that we actually experience and can talk meaningfully about are perceived realities – realities involving ourselves as editors – and they are all relative to the observer' (Wilson, 1977: iv). For Wilson, this neurological relativism demanded a 'guerilla ontology' that critiqued, rejected, and culture-jammed the 'reality tunnels' that dominate modern society and individual behavior. Beyond this critique, Wilson also trumpeted and embraced the creative, hedonistic, and libertarian 'meta-programming' possibilities of self-reflexive reality-creation. Though his writings have not received the academic or mainstream recognition they warrant, their infectious ethos strongly influenced a number of cultural discourses that emerged from or passed through the counterculture, including occultism, libertarianism, transhumanism, psychedelia, and 'New Edge' cyberculture.

Born to a working-class Brooklyn family, Wilson contracted polio as a child, and suffered the effects of post-polio syndrome off and on throughout his life. Though raised a Roman Catholic, Wilson became a committed philosophical materialist as a teenager, dabbling in Marxism and studying engineering and mathematics at New York University. In his 20s, he underwent various courses of psychotherapy, studied existentialism, phenomenology and anarchism, and developed the 'model agnosticism' he would refine throughout his life and work. In 1958, Wilson married Arlen Riley, with whom he had four children; despite Wilson's celebration of the 'Tantric' and hedonistic currents of the counterculture, they remained a devoted pair until Arlen's death in 1999. In 1962, after reading a positive article about psychedelics in the conservative *National Review*, Wilson embarked on an extensive exploration of peyote and eventually LSD. In 1964 he traveled as a journalist to Millbrook to meet Timothy Leary, who would become a life-long friend; Wilson's debt to both psychedelics and Leary's ideas was profound, and he remained until the end of his days a tireless evangelist for Leary's SMI²LE program (Space Migration, Intelligence Increase, Life Extension). In 1965, Wilson became an editor at *Playboy*, a job he kept until 1971. Though he later earned a degree in psychology from Hawthorne College, Wilson remained an independent author and freelance writer for the rest of his life. His blue-collar beginnings, his journalist's commitment to entertaining (and sometimes chatty) writing, and the wayward bouts of poverty he experienced raising a family as an underground intellectual helped inform the down-to-earth character of both his writing and his libertarian politics.

Wilson's work can be conveniently divided into fiction and nonfiction, though the division is perhaps ultimately an artificial one. Wilson larded his stories with historical data and philosophical argument, and laced his essays with synchronicities and unsystematic evocations of concepts and possibilities. His quantum physics trilogy, *Schrödinger's Cat*, represents an innovative and well-informed narrative exploration of quantum weirdness, but his most important fiction remains the *Illuminatus!* trilogy, co-written with Robert Shea (another *Playboy* editor) in the late 1960s and early 1970s, but not published until 1975. Inspired by the wilder conspiracy theories mailed in by readers of the 'Playboy Forum,' the two authors wove together a restless, baggy, satirical science fiction famously described by Greil Marcus as 'the longest shaggy dog joke in literary history.' An exemplary postmodern text, though without literary pretension, *Illumninatus!* anticipates the conspiracy fictions later penned by Umberto Eco and Dan Brown, as well as the ongoing Masonic conspiracies associated in the 2000s with some hip-hop stars.

The novel follows various characters as they discover, combat, and propagate the feverish plots of the Illuminati, a conspiratorial global organization secretly run by a German rock band called the American Medical Association. The Illuminati lie behind the assassinations of John F. Kennedy and other 1960s figures, and may or may not be responsible for myriad other plots and possibilities the novel teasingly and only partly unpacks. The ultimate aim of the organization is to 'immanentize the eschaton,' a phrase popularized by William F. Buckley and drawn from the conservative historian Eric Voegelin, who warned against a modern utopian drive to forcibly realize the millennial kingdom on earth. Arrayed against the Illuminati are the Discordians, an underground cabal who worship and foment chaos and are headed by the submarine captain Hagbard Celine (who may or may not be the Illuminatus Primus, or supreme potentate, in disguise). Wilson and Shea based the group on an actual Discordian Society, then one of the counterculture's more obscure, satirical, and innovative engagements with religious mysticism, and an important influence on Wilson. Largely the invention of two Americans, Gregory Hill and Kerry Thornley (aka Malaclypse the Younger and Omar Khayyam Ravenhurst, who both appear in *Illuminatus!*), Discordianism holds that chaos is as least as fundamental to reality as order, and that it should be honored with paradox, contradiction, principled anarchism, and an irony so profane (or so silly) that it suggests the sacred. The principal Discordian text, originally published in 1965 in five copies and revised a number of times and by numerous hands, is the *Principia Discordia*, a parodic (and possibly sincere) collage of cartoons, bad puns, Beatnik Zen, tongue-in-cheek religious language, and a deeply irreverent strain of American vernacular humor. Wilson became both an Episkopos and Pope of the Discordian Society, and was later considered 'Pope Bob' by the Church of the Subgenius, which appropriated a good deal of Discordian DNA.

Placing the Discordian current within modern magical history, Margot Adler credits Kerry Thornley with first using the word 'Pagan' to refer to emerging nature religions like Wicca. However, the Discordian materials themselves are not deeply marked by occult currents. In *Illuminatus!*, however, Wilson and Shea weave in dense historical threads about Freemasonry and ceremonial magic, make copious references to H.P. Lovecraft and other occult fiction writers, and stage scenes tinged with pop Satanism, like the obscene black mass led by Padre Pederastia in the third of the trilogy's ten chapters, which correspond to the ten sephirot of the Tree of Life. But it was the mysterious events (or perceptions) that occurred to Wilson following the completion of the bulk of *Illuminatus!* in 1971 that turned him into a philosopher of the modern occult. Wilson relates these experiences in his 1977 book *Cosmic Trigger: Final Secret of the Illuminati*, the first volume in what would eventually become Wilson's *Cosmic Trigger* trilogy of autobiographical essays. Inspired by his continuing *Illuminatus!* research into esoteric conspiracies and revisionist histories, Wilson embarked on a course of ceremonial magic and other psycho-spiritual practices that catalyzed a series of synchronicities, conceptual insights, and robust altered states of consciousness. The conspiratorial fictions he had co-written began to bleed into his personal reality, and from July 1973 until roughly October 1974, Wilson came to inhabit a 'reality tunnel' in which he was receiving telepathic messages from an extraterrestrial intelligence linked to the double star system Sirius.

One of the more important catalysts for this explosion of high weirdness was Wilson's close reading of Aleister Crowley, whose writings Wilson had begun to explore in 1970 at the recommendation of Alan Watts (Crowley also appears as a character in Wilson's 1981 novel *Masks of the Illuminati*). Drawn to the encryption and pun-filled misdirection of Crowley texts like *The Book of Lies*, Wilson began to decode and then experiment with ritual regimens involving drugs and sexual magic. Over time, these and other practices seemed to catalyze what Wilson called – using the language of Timothy Leary's psycho-cybernetic model of consciousness – a new evolutionary 'circuit' lying *in potentia* in his nervous system and DNA. Wilson came to suspect that the techniques for hedonically engineering this state were the secrets that lay at the core of Illuminism and other esoteric traditions. With apotropaic doses of irony, Wilson narrates a widening paranoid web of significance that involves telepathic agents from the Dog Star, the number 23, Leary's 1973 'Starseed' communications, Sufism, Horus, and other florid arcana.

Cosmic Trigger can be read as an extended engagement with the uncanny conceptual and psychological powers of synchronicity, as well as an insightful spore print of California's occult and psychedelic demimonde. But the occultist significance of this book and many of the nonfiction books that followed lies precisely in Wilson's ability to largely come through the other side of the disturbing synchronistic web he called 'Chapel Perilous.' He did so with his deployment of what Wilson calls 'neurological model agnosticism.' One important inspiration for this method was Wilson's take on the Copenhagen interpretation of quantum physics, which asserts, roughly speaking, that the manifest character of quantum objects is dependent on the instruments used to measure them. Applying this model to consciousness, Wilson held that the synchronistic or apparently supernatural effects associated with ceremonial magic do not reveal truths about reality but rather evidence for the autopoetic capacities of the human nervous system. At the same time, Wilson was not claiming simply that it is all 'just in the brain.' Inspired by parapsychology, Leary's 8-circuit model, and the possible entanglement of consciousness with quantum effects, Wilson hewed to an optimistic vision of the transformative potential of the brain that significantly exceeded the boundaries of conventional naturalism. In this, Wilson can be seen as an outlier of the New Age, whose platitudes he often mocked but whose concerns—quantum physics, directed evolution, the Aquarian conspiracy—he overlapped. Indeed, Wilson's philosophical effort may be understood as a neuro-sociological and skeptical corrective to the essential New Age gambit that we 'create our own reality.'

As an occultist thinker, Wilson needs to be seen in light of his reading of Crowley, and specifically of the pragmatist and even reductionist thread that runs, inconsistently, throughout Crowley's work. In the introduction to his 1903 edition of the Goetia, for example, the young Crowley argues that 'the spirits of the Goetia are portions of the human brain.' Crowley later voiced something closer to Wilson's own model agnosticism in 'Liber O vel Manus et Sagittae,' an instruction manual for the A.:A.: that Wilson often quoted. Alerting students that they will encounter the discussion of things – like gods and spirits – which may or may not exist, Crowley asserts that 'it is immaterial whether they exist or not. By doing certain things, certain results follow; students are most earnestly warned against attributing objective reality or philosophical validity to any of them.' Though offering a simplistic portrayal of the contradictory Crowley, Wilson helped propagate an influential 'countercultural' vision of the Beast.

With his allergy to gurus and grand narratives, Wilson helped articulate and define a distinctly 'postmodern' theory and method of occultism. Conceptually, Wilson affirms the rich phenomenology of occult and mystical experiences while emptying them of ontological, idealist, or supernatural claims. The negative or critical character of such doubt is balanced with the exuberant 'meta-programming' possibilities rooted in the hedonic body, in experimental practice, in human intelligence, and in the virtual possibilities of the imagination and the transformative fictions it breeds. In this sense, Wilson may be productively placed in the context of a self-reflexive American reformulation of Paganism. Fellow travelers here include Discordianism, the science-fictional and originally libertarian Church of All Worlds, and the New Reformed Orthodox Order of the Golden Dawn (with whom Wilson practiced ritual); all of these groups acknowledged and celebrated their own contingent religious invention.

Wilson should also be considered an important progenitor of chaos magic. Like Wilson, many chaos magicians adopt a skeptical instrumentalism or 'guerilla ontology,' a methodology that is sometimes coupled with a taste for social critique, absurdist humor, and the meta-fictional use of science-fiction and fantasy materials. Especially important here is the work of H.P. Lovecraft, whose Yog-Sothery saturates *Illuminatus!* Wilson also placed magical and mystical concerns into dialogue with a heterogenous and productive set of discourses whose influence on various counter- and subcultural fields of production remains under-appreciated. These include transhumanism, libertarianism, psychedelia, science fiction, rave culture, and the 'New Edge' of early cyberculture. Wilson's continued online influence, as well as the fellow feeling inspired by his generous disposition, was demonstrated in the months before his death in early 2007, when an Internet campaign started by Douglas Rushkoff and publicized through Slashdot and Boing Boing raised over sixty thousand dollars for Wilson's care in three days.

REFERENCES AND FURTHER READING

Adler, M. (1986) *Drawing Down the Moon: Witches, Druids, Goddess-Worshippers, and Other Pagans in America Today*, Boston: Beacon.

Cusack, C. (2010) *Invented Religions: Imagination, Fiction, and Faith*, London: Ashgate.

Gorightly, A. (2003) *The Prankster and the Conspiracy: The Story of Kerry Thornley and How He Met Oswald and Inspired the Counterculture*, New York: Paraview.

Malaclypse the Younger and Omar Khayyam Ravenhurst (1980) *Principia Discordia: or, How I Found Goddess And What I Did to Her When I Found Her*, Port Townsend, WA: Loompanics.

Robertson, D. (2012) 'Making the Donkey Visible: Discordianism in the Works of Robert Anton Wilson,' in C. Cusack and A. Norman, eds, *Handbook of New Religions and Cultural Movements*, Leiden: Brill.

Wilson, R.A. (1977) *Cosmic Trigger I: Final Secret of the Illuminati*, Phoenix, AZ: New Falcon.

——(1983) *Prometheus Rising*, Phoenix, AZ: New Falcon.

——(1991) *Cosmic Trigger II: Down to Earth*, Phoenix, AZ: New Falcon.

Wilson, R.A. and R. Shea (1975) *Illuminatus!*, New York: Dell.

CHAPTER THIRTY-FIVE

NAZISM AND THE OCCULT

Julian Strube

ASSOCIATION OF NAZISM AND 'THE OCCULT'

In the post-war period, especially since the 1960s, ideas of an 'esoteric National Socialism' were widely disseminated by best-selling books, movies, and other media (Goodrick-Clarke 2002, 107–27). The National Socialists were depicted as black magicians or occultists and associated with 'magic,' 'irrationalism,' 'occultism,' or 'superstition,' vaguely summarized by the term 'the occult.' In the vast majority of those publications, 'the occult' is used as a waste-basket category (Hanegraaff 2012, 221), which included a diffuse mass of negative 'otherness.' When it was not done for commercial reasons and sensation-seeking, this 'othering' resulted from an attempt to understand the often-incomprehensible atrocities of the National Socialists, in order to exclude them from 'normal' people by depicting them as 'irrational' or 'evil.'

An opposite 'esoteric' interpretation was developed by far-right and neo-Nazi authors since the 1950s (Sünner 1999, 141–70; Goodrick-Clarke 2002, 128–92). Those authors attempted to rationalize the crimes committed by the National Socialists by placing their actions in the revisionist context of a dualistic battle of good against evil. According to their writings, an 'esoteric SS' took up the ancient tradition of defending 'light and truth.' After the war had been lost, those esoteric troops retreated to secret bases and have continued their fight until today, giving hope and confidence to the admirers of the lost 'Third Reich.' Such ideas have been widely disseminated since the 1970s, gaining considerable importance since the 1990s.

Both of these 'discursive networks' (Bergunder 2010, 26–27), which can be discussed in terms of 'popular reception' and 'esoteric neo-Nazism,' are usually significantly detached from reliable historical sources. It will be shown that these networks were interdependent and created credibility through systematic cross-referencing. A comprehensive study of that process of sedimentation (Bergunder 2012, 38–39) remains a desideratum. The following discussion will only be able to point out several key topoi. It will become clear, however, that the most commonly discussed 'esoteric' influences on National Socialism were either marginal or entirely invented.

Before and During World War II

The process of associating National Socialism and signifiers like 'magic' and 'occult' already started after 1933 (Hakl 1997/2004). As early as 1934, the French author René Kopp published an article in the journal *Le Chariot*, stating that Bonaparte, Mussolini, and Hitler were 'masters' sent to earth by higher powers. In 1939, Kopp asserted that pictures of Hitler proved his possession by 'a ghost of unknown origin.' In his *Le tyran nazi et les forces occultes* (1939), Edouard Saby identified Hitler as a medium, a magician, and an initiate of a secret 'Rosicrucian society' with links to Tibet and the *Vehm*. In the most influential of such publications, *Hitler Speaks* (1939) by Hermann Rauschning, the reader is informed about Hitler's practice of black magic and his possession by evil forces. Rauschning's accounts, which were based on entirely fictitious conversations with Hitler, were produced in English, French, and German, establishing the 'occult' image of Hitler and serving as key sources for later authors. The year 1940 saw the publication of Lewis Spence's *Occult Causes of the Present War*, a book that was to establish a still flourishing genre devoted to the exploration of links between Nazism and Satanism. The common reason for the success of those various publications was their explanation for the incredible triumph of National Socialist Germany so shortly after its defeat in World War I. Indeed, the shocking fall of France in 1940 contributed significantly to the cogency of that new literary genre.

Popular Post-War Reception

In the 1960s, a wave of enormously successful publications continued the earlier 'occultization' of National Socialism and its leaders. The most influential was *The Morning of the Magicians* (1960) by Louis Pauwels and Jacques Bergier, translated into several languages and selling millions of copies. The French authors presented the National Socialist elite as an order of black magicians initiated and controlled by secret societies such as the Thule Society or the fictitious Vril Society (on the latter, see Strube 2013). Especially the *Schutzstaffel* (SS) and its 'research institution,' the *Ahnenerbe*, were described as 'a religious order' whose 'monks' received their occult initiation on SS castles, performing dark magical rituals. Pauwels and Bergier were the most influential authors to coin the idea of an 'esoteric National Socialism' or 'magical Socialism.' They included esoteric organizations such as the Hermetic Order of the Golden Dawn and the Theosophical Society in their narrative. Through their occult connections, the initiated German elites were supposedly maintaining links to Tibetan Lamas and the Eastern esoteric realms of Agartha and Shamballah (on the changed spellings, cf. Godwin 2007, 94–173). Pauwels and Bergier also emphasized the development of 'Nazi science,' a mix of irrational magic and futuristic technology that developed into a major topos in popular culture.

Such ideas were widely spread in popular texts, such as Robert Charroux's bestseller, *Le Livre des secrets trahis* (1965). Even more successful was *The Spear of Destiny* (1973) by Trevor Ravenscroft, which elaborated the alleged magical operations of Hitler and his apprentices, adding the hunt for the Holy Lance and its 'occult powers.' These bestsellers led to a wave of speculative occult literature, including J. H. Brennan's *Occult Reich* (1974) and Francis King's *Satan and Swastika: the Occult and the Nazi Party* (1976). The perception of National Socialism in popular culture was heavily influenced by such publications. The idea of 'occult Nazis' can be found in

Hollywood movies such as *Raiders of the Lost Ark* (1981), *Indiana Jones and the Last Crusade* (1989), *Hellboy* (2004), and *Captain America* (2011), or the independent movie *Iron Sky* (2012). Likewise, similar ideas are reproduced in countless comic books, music records, or successful video games like *Return to Castle Wolfenstein* (2001) and its successor *Wolfenstein* (2009). Despite its mix of half-truths and entirely fictitious accounts, the popular invention of 'esoteric National Socialism' remains highly influential. It is backed up by a great variety of pseudo-scientific books and documentaries that decisively outnumber serious approaches to the subject.

Esoteric Neo-Nazism

Notions of an 'esoteric National Socialism' were not only discussed in popular literature, but also in far-right and neo-Nazi circles. In the early 1950s, a group gathered in Vienna, consisting of the former Austrian SS members Wilhelm Landig (1909–97) and Rudolf Mund (1920–85), as well as the engineer Erich Halik. This 'Vienna Circle' laid down the foundations for the development of an 'esoteric neo-Nazism' (see Goodrick-Clarke 2002; cf. Sünner 1999). The first publications from the Vienna Circle sphere date from the 1950s when Halik published a series of articles in the Austrian journal *Mensch und Schicksal*. Halik maintained that the UFO sightings that had caused a sensation since 1947 were not extraterrestrial spaceships, but rather 'cultic devices' used by 'the highest hierarchy of Gnostic Christianity and accordingly of earlier Gnostic Paganism' to influence society. In order to support his theory, Halik referred to the 'research' of Otto Rahn (1904–39), who had identified the medieval Cathars as the inheritors of a suppressed Pagan tradition reaching back to the Gnostics and who were, he argued, the keepers of the Holy Grail. Later, Halik revealed that the supposed UFOs were nothing but secret German aircraft used by 'esoteric forces' in the SS. Those 'SS-Cathars' had retreated to subterranean bases under the poles after the defeat of Germany and were still operating under their emblem, the 'Black Sun.'

Wilhelm Landig extended those topoi to his influential *Thule* trilogy, published in 1971 (*Götzen gegen Thule*), 1980 (*Wolfszeit um Thule*), and 1991 (*Rebellen für Thule*), respectively. The novels transported a trivial but still complex narrative that reinterpreted the SS as successor of an ancient 'heretical' tradition fighting a perennial battle against the 'forces of evil,' the adherents of the 'false god Jahwe.' On the 'good side,' the reader would not only find Germans but also Arabs, Indians, Japanese, Chinese, South Americans, Mongolians, and, especially, Tibetan Lamas. The latter enabled extensive elaborations of the Shamballah/Agartha topos that was already familiar in the writings of authors like Pauwels and Bergier. It becomes evident that the Vienna Circle had been influenced by popular writings about 'esoteric National Socialism' and blended them with their positive reception of earlier authors like Rahn and the 'Aryan Atlantis' writer Herman Wirth (1885–1981).

A younger generation of authors continued the work of Landig and his companions in the late 1980s (Strube 2012, 239–53). At that time, the so-called *Tempelhofgesellschaft* (Temple Court Society) took up its publishing activities and organized various meetings. The *Tempelhofgesellschaft* was then led by the former policeman Hans-Günter Fröhlich and had close ties to the German-speaking far-right network. There was a vivid exchange between the older generation of the Vienna Circle and the *Tempelhofgesellschaft*, revolving around the 'Black Sun' symbol and the supposed

'Babylonian/Assyrian/Sumerian' origins of 'the Germans.' Like Landig, they referred to earlier discourses from the nineteenth and early twentieth century to back up those claims. In 1991, the *Tempelhofgesellschaft* authors Norbert Jürgen-Ratthofer and Ralf Ettl published *Das Vril-Projekt*, another brochure that wildly elaborated the popular narratives of the Thule and Vril Societies, putting a great emphasis on the UFO aspect and maintaining the extraterrestrial origin of 'the Germans' who descended from a civilization in the star system Aldebaran, where they reigned over inferior races in an empire of 'National Socialism on a theocratic basis.'

Besides the vast distribution of photos, drawings, and blueprints of 'Nazi UFOs' (*Flugscheiben*), the principal influence of the *Tempelhofgesellschaft* remains its reinterpretation of the 'Black Sun' symbol. While the 'Black Sun' had been a central motif of esoteric neo-Nazism since the 1950s, it has only been related to a motif in the floor of the Wewelsburg castle in the novel *The Black Sun of Tashi-Lhunpo* (1991) by the pseudonymous author Russell McCloud. The *Tempelhofgesellschaft* authors, however, who identify this motif with the 'Black Sun,' understand it to be an ancient Babylonian, Assyrian, and thus German or Aldebaranian symbol expressing the 'bright power of the true divinity.' This description also resurfaced in Landig's *Rebellen für Thule* (1991), making the exchange of the *Tempelhofgesellschaft* authors with their mentor evident. After the THG had split up, Ralf Ettl founded the *Freundeskreis Causa Nostra* in 2005. It remains active and maintains relations to far-right publishers and networks.

HISTORICAL SOURCES

It has been indicated that the discursive networks of popular and neo-Nazi ideas about 'esoteric National Socialism' are not independent. For example, on the one hand, popular stories about the Thule and Vril Societies have conspicuously influenced the construction of esoteric neo-Nazism. On the other hand, ideas about Nazi UFOs and the Black Sun were widely disseminated in popular culture. While most of the mentioned topoi are post-war inventions, the question remains if there is a diachronic dimension to the association of National Socialism and esotericism. For example, various pre-National Socialist groups and individuals in the heterogeneous *völkisch* milieu have evidently been influenced by esoteric ideas. This might lead to the assumption that esoteric ideas have also found their way to the core of National Socialist ideology. Indeed, the personal convictions of a few high-ranking individuals, as well as the symbolism developed by organizations such as the SS, seem to confirm that assumption. The following section will approach that complex question by shedding some light on key aspects that dominate post-war discourses surrounding the relationship between esotericism and National Socialism. Unfortunately, the recently published studies by Peter Staudenmaier, which contribute significantly to our understanding of the relationship between occultism and National Socialism, could not be taken into account in the present text, but should be consulted (Staudenmaier 2013, 2014; also cf. Kurlander 2012).

The SS, the Wewelsburg, and the Ahnenerbe

No historical organization is as central to discourses about esotericism and National Socialism as the *Schutzstaffel* (SS), particularly its depiction in popular publications. In academic literature, initially the idea of a monolithic 'SS state' (Kogon 1946) consisting of elite warriors was generally accepted. However, in the 1960s and 1970s, scholars began to revise this perspective. It was demonstrated that the SS was a disunited body of sub-organizations and individuals struggling for power, indicative of a National Socialist *polycracy* (Hüttenberger 1976; cf. Schulte 2009, XV). It became clear that the image of an 'elite force in black uniforms' was primarily indebted to SS propaganda. Moreover, the organizational chaos within the SS was one of the main reasons why its history was subject to speculation in the post-war period, which focused primarily on the obscure projects of the *Ahnenerbe* and the megalomaniac plans of Heinrich Himmler (1900–45), the head of the SS (*Reichsführer-SS*). Indeed, Himmler is the primary example cited of a leading National Socialist with esoteric affinities. It has been shown, however, that his interests in subjects such as astrology and Ariosophy were restricted to his private life (Longerich 2008, 289–96). Moreover, Himmler's private esoteric interests have been exaggerated in such a wide variety of publications that the few serious studies to examine this aspect of his life are easily overlooked. (A comprehensive, reliable study of Himmler's relationship with esotericism has yet to be written.)

Perhaps the most conspicuous connection to Ariosophy is Himmler's patronage of Karl Maria Wiligut (1866–1946) who was known in the SS by the pseudonym 'Weisthor.' Little is known about Wiligut's actual thought and it remains unclear as to what degree his ideas influenced SS symbolism (such as the SS ring) and plans for the extension of the Wewelsburg castle. The accounts of the astrologer Wilhelm Wulff and Karl Wolff, the head of Himmler's personal staff, are of questionable credibility (cf. Howe 1967; Wulff 1968; Hüser 1987; von Lang 1989; Schulte 2009, 8). It is certain that Wiligut exerted a direct influence on Himmler's personal thought and that Himmler continued his relationship with his advisor even after he was forced to officially dismiss him in 1939, when his stay in a mental asylum in the 1920s became public. In the *Rasse-und Siedlungshauptamt* (RuSHA), Wiligut was responsible for the archive and exerted significant influence on the department of *Vor-und Frühgeschichte*. There is no comprehensive, serious study of the life of Wiligut and his role in the SS – within which he was generally detested (see Lange 1998 for sources). The Vienna circle author Rudolf Mund has produced a thoroughly unreliable hagiography of him (Mund 1982 and 2002; cf. Mund and Wefenstein 2004; Goodrick-Clarke 1985/2004, 155–66 has adopted many of the ideas within Mund's book).

Another curious case is Otto Rahn, one of the idols of post-war esoteric neo-Nazism. Rahn's quest for the Holy Grail and its supposed guardians, the Cathars, greatly impressed Himmler. Becoming a co-worker of Wiligut, he officially joined the SS in 1936 and a special edition of his book *Luzifer's Hofgesind* (1937) was given to Hitler by Himmler. However, his background is little known and deserves further attention (cf. Lange 1995 and 1999). He wrote his main work, *Kreuzzug gegen den Gral* (1933), before his contact with the SS. Moreover, despite Himmler's interest in his studies of the Cathars, his theories remained private and exerted no influence on SS ideology. After leaving the SS in 1939, most likely because of his homosexual leanings, Rahn committed suicide.

The Wewelsburg castle has been identified, within both popular literature and scholarly studies, as the location for a number of occult rituals performed by the SS, or even as the repository of the Holy Grail and the Holy Lance (Hüser 1987; Höhne 1967; Siepe 2009). Indeed, popular narratives about SS 'rituals' even found their way into the studies of esteemed experts (Fest 1963, 159–60; cf. Hüser 1987 68). Recent scholarship, however, has shown that no 'cults' or 'rituals' of any kind have ever been performed at the Wewelsburg (Schulte 2009). Himmler's plans for turning the castle into a *weltanschauliches Zentrum* and an organizational base for the SS were never realized.

In popular literature, the supposed occult machinations of the SS were closely linked to the *Ahnenerbe*. This 'research society' was founded in July 1935 by Himmler, Walther Darré (1895–1953, the head of the RuSHA), and Herman Wirth (Kater 1974; Kroll 1998). The latter's attempt to prove the existence of an ancient Aryan empire that had disappeared with the destruction of Atlantis was one of the driving forces when the society was established (Kater 1974, 41–46; cf. Wiwjorra 1995; Halle 2002; Löw 2009). The 'research' of the *Ahnenerbe* was conducted for ideological and propaganda reasons in order to establish an SS influence on the German academic landscape (Kater 1974; cf. Kroll 1998, esp. 230–34; Halle 2002). The output of the *Ahnenerbe*, however, was never acknowledged within German academia. When Wirth cofounded the *Ahnenerbe*, his reputation as a scholar had already been seriously questioned. Additionally, one of the main critics of Wirth had been Alfred Rosenberg, who contributed to the frequent power struggles between the *Ahnenerbe* and Rosenberg's *Amt* (office). Eventually, Wirth was pushed out of the *Ahnenerbe* in 1937.

Early in its history, the *Ahnenerbe* spawned several sub-divisions and offices to conduct research within various fields. These included Hanns Hörbiger's (1860–1931) *Welteislehre* (World Ice Theory) that was widely discussed in popular science in the 1920s. The *Welteislehre*, which was also held in high esteem by Himmler, was another example of a failed attempt to establish an obviously pseudo-scientific theory amongst German scholars (Wessely 2006 and 2008; and although it should be read with caution, see Nagel 1991). Another famous project, Ernst Schäfer's expedition to Tibet, was not carried out for any 'occult' reasons, but rather in order to explore the Caucasian terrain, to explore alternative ways to produce vegetable and animal materials, and to confirm racial theories (Mierau 2006). When the war began in 1939, the 'research' of the *Ahnenerbe* focused increasingly on 'practical' projects, including human experiments. However, the *Ahnenerbe* largely failed to establish its ideologically informed science. This failure was primarily due to the organizational chaos within the SS and the *Ahnenerbe* itself. It was no 'occult bureau' as suggested by authors such as Trevor Ravenscroft who have greatly exaggerated the importance and influence of this fragmented organization.

There is no historical evidence to suggest that there has been anything like a powerful 'esoteric circle' within the SS. It is clear that Himmler consistently had to hide his private esoteric interests from the public and other party elites like Hitler and Goebbels. His future plans for the SS, including the Wewelsburg or the Externsteine, never left the planning stage (Halle 2002; Schulte 2009). Those individuals within the SS who were following an esoteric agenda – notably Wiligut and Rahn – were pushed out of the organization and met tragic ends. Certainly, there is no evidence to indicate that those individuals interested in esotericism in the SS had the power to develop secret weapons or to build subterranean bases and worldwide networks. (However, more research is needed to fully understand the complexity of the relationship between Himmler's interest in esotericism and his development of the SS.)

The Thule Society

The Thule Society was the successor of the *Germanenorden*, a secret branch of the *völkisch* society, *Reichshammerbund*, both of which were founded in 1912 and were radically anti-Semitic. They propagated a Germanic racism that was based on the *völkisch* biological re-interpretation of 'Aryanism,' which was influenced by the Ariosophy of Guido von List and Lanz von Liebenfels (Goodrick-Clarke 1985/2004, 112–20; cf. Bönisch 1999). When the Thule Society was founded in 1918, Rudolf von Sebottendorff (Adam Alfred Rudolf Glauer, 1875–1945) became its leading force. During extensive travels, Sebottendorff had developed a keen interest in esotericism that was increasingly influenced by Ariosophical ideas. Officially, the Thule Society was founded for 'the research of German history and the promotion of German nature (*Art*),' as well as the research of the *Edda*, the *Sagas*, and similar subjects. The choice of the name 'Thule' was probably inspired by writings that had combined the Thule myth as the origin of the 'Aryan' race with the topos of Atlantis. The society played an active role in the opposition to the Bavarian Soviet Republic in 1918/19, but quickly dissolved after its fall in May 1919. Certainly, Sebottendorff did not participate in the activities of the society after June 1919, although he did try to revive the Society within the Third Reich in 1933. However, he was discredited by Nazi authorities for claiming a pioneering role in the formation of early National Socialism. Following a brief period of internment, he travelled to Turkey, where he found employment in the German Intelligence Service in Istanbul. He committed suicide on 9 May, 1945 (Goodrick-Clarke 2004, 121–35).

The Thule Society was not an esoteric or 'occult' order (Rose 1994; Gilbhard 1994). Its importance for the *völkisch* struggle against the Bavarian Soviet Republic made it a focal point for a disparate group of individuals and ideas. That the society's emblem included a swastika is not particularly significant, in that, not only was it taken from the *Germanenorden* and Ariosophers such as Guido von List, but it was common in *völkisch* and nationalist currents at that time. That is to say, it does not indicate an esoteric orientation of the society. Sebottendorff sometimes propagated Ariosophical and other esoteric ideas, but those tended to be met with suspicion. Furthermore, the Thule Society cannot be seen as a direct predecessor of the Nazi Party. Indeed, as noted above, when, in 1933, Sebottendorff claimed in his book *Bevor Hitler kam* that the Society had been central to the development of National Socialism, he incurred the wrath of the Party and was briefly interned in 1934.

Hitler, who expressed contempt for the '*völkisch* wandering scholars' (cf. Schirrmacher 2007, vol. 1, 318–37; vol. 2, 585–600), was never a member of the Society. Neither was Himmler. That said, later Nazi Party functionaries such as Dietrich Eckart and Alfred Rosenberg were granted 'guest' status and Rudolf Hess and Hans Frank were, for political reasons, members for a brief period. However, again, this does not allow us to conclude that the Thule Society operated as an elite pre-National Socialist school. Indeed, in order to argue this point, later authors, such as Pauwels and Bergier, have distorted the facts about the Thule Society, reframing it as an occult order, which initiated and controlled key figures within the Nazi Party. Their imaginative accounts include, for example, Karl Haushofer (1869–1946), who was never a member of the Society, nor the 'initiator' of Hitler, not, indeed, did his ideas concerning geo-politics have anything to do with occult masters from the East (Jacobsen 1979).

Ariosophy

Ariosophy is primarily a combination of *völkisch* nationalism, eugenic racism, anti-Semitism, and esoteric currents, especially Blavatsky's Theosophy. The term was coined by Jörg Lanz von Liebenfels (Adolf Joseph Lanz, 1874–1954). Lanz was a Cistercian monk who had entered the novitiate in Vienna in 1893 and left the order in 1899 (Goodrick-Clarke 1985/2004; Hieronimus 1991). He developed the idea of an 'Aryan' Christianity that was rooted in *völkisch*-Christian discourses, propagating the biological superiority of the 'Aryans' over inferior races that were believed to be the result of sexual intercourse with beasts. Lanz dubbed his teachings *Theozoologie*, expressing the importance of both the theological and biological aspects. From 1905–18, he spread his ideas in his journal *Ostara*. In 1907, he founded the Ordo Novi Templi in Vienna. He was also becoming increasingly influenced by the Theosophical writings of Helena Petrovna Blavatsky (1831–91), as well as by a range of other esoteric ideas taken from, for example, Kabbalah and Rosicrucianism. From 1925 to 1933, he collaborated with the publisher Herbert Reichstein (1892–1944) and succeeded in spreading Ariosophy amongst German-speaking esotericists. Initially enthusiastic about the rise of National Socialism, Lanz soon distanced himself from what he considered to be a principally 'boorish' movement. Under the restrictions imposed by the Nazi Party from 1937 onwards, the Ordo Novi Templi was forbidden. However, Lanz revived the order in 1947 and remained its leader until his death in 1954.

The second most important influence on the development of Ariosophy was the popular writer Guido von List (Guido Karl Anton List, 1848–1919). List's thought was formed in the Austrian Pan-German, *völkisch* milieu of the late nineteenth century. After a modest success with *völkisch*-romantic novels in the 1880s and 1890s, List significantly developed his ideas in 1902 during a period of enforced rest following an eye operation to remove a cataract. At that time, he articulated the first synthesis of German nationalism and Blavatsky's Theosophy. Increasingly his ideas found followers and, in 1908, a List Society was founded. In 1911, he created the *Hoher Armanen-Orden*, the aim of which was to propagate his ideas about an ancient Germanic elite called the *Armanen*. In his books *Die Rita der Ario-Germanen* (1908) and *Die Bilderschrift der Ario-Germanen* (1910), List articulated an esoteric interpretation of runes that remains influential today, even in circles that are hostile to Ariosophy.

Members of the List Society disseminated his ideas in the *Reichshammerbund* and *Germanenorden*, thus exerting a significant influence on the milieu that later fed into National Socialism. However, as Nicholas Goodrick-Clarke (1985/2004) has shown, Ariosophy must not be seen as a direct predecessor to National Socialism. Post-war publications (e.g. Daim 1958) have exaggerated the influence of Lanz and Ariosophy on Hitler and early National Socialism. Those elements of Ariosophy that later resurfaced in National Socialist ideology (e.g. eugenics and 'Aryan' supremacy) were not limited to Ariosophy. It should also be noted that the Ariosophical interpretation of Theosophy is quite distinct from that of the Theosophical Society. Again, additional research is required to understand the precise relationship between the 'esoteric milieu' in German-speaking countries and the emergence of Ariosophy. Also, the apparent differences between the 'Christian' developments following Lanz and the 'Germanic' developments following List deserve further attention (see Goodrick-Clarke 2004; von Schnurbein 1992, 1993).

Official Attitude Towards Esoteric Groups

The official stance of the state towards esoteric individuals and organizations became increasingly hostile after 1933. While there is evidence of continuities between esoterically inclined currents, such as Ariosophy, and National Socialism, those affinities never resulted in 'occult' influences at a state level. Esoteric groups influenced by such movements as Theosophy, Anthroposophy, Rosicrucianism, Ariosophy, Mazdaznan, or New Thought were classified as 'sects hostile to the state.' In the view of state officials, their unwillingness to adapt to the National Socialist *Weltanschauung* encouraged disunity amongst the *Volksgemeinschaft*. As Corinna Treitel (2004) suggests in her study of German occultism, two specific transgressions led to the persecution of esoteric groups by the authorities: the first was the denial of rigid racial hierarchies that, for example, became evident in the Theosophical proclamation of a 'brotherhood of humanity'; the second was the accusation of 'superstition' that would poison the minds of the German people. Hence, in July 1937, all Freemasonic lodges, Theosophical circles, and related groups were dissolved and *okkultistische* as well as *spiritistische* publications and activities were forbidden.

The famous flight by Rudolph Hess, who, in an attempt to bring an end to the war, had parachuted over Scotland in 1941, led to an increased suspicion of occult influence. It was, for example, claimed that the influence of astrologers and other 'charlatans' surrounding Hess had led to his 'insanity.' Hitler and, especially, Goebbels had always protested against 'superstition' and 'mysticism,' which now had to be finally eradicated. The resulting crackdown in June 1941 led to a brutal suppression of esoteric activity in Germany, to the interning of occultists and the forcing of many underground. Ironically, this purging of the occult and the sectarian took place under the aegis of the police chief, Himmler, who, while privately expressing an interest in esotericism, officially supported the crackdown on superstition, which he perceived to be a threat to the unity of the German people (cf. Dierker, Staudenmaier, and Meyer in Puschner 2012).

CONCLUDING COMMENTS

An examination of the most discussed 'occult' or 'esoteric' elements of National Socialism demonstrates that they were either marginal or fictional. Historical evidence confirms that the private occult interests of certain individuals such as Himmler and Hess did not, after all, translate into official Nazi policy. Additionally, it is arguably problematic to classify several of those interests as 'occult.' For instance, Himmler's enthusiasm for natural healing was also common in the *Lebensreform* movement, whose adherents did not necessarily have any occult interests (Buchholz et al. 2001). The Romantic fascination for everything 'Germanic' was shared by many Germans, including those adhering to *völkisch* currents that were declared enemies of *Okkultismus* (Treitel 2004, 218–20). To some extent, this highlights a number of general theoretical and methodological problems. What is exactly included under the umbrella terms 'occult' and 'esotericism'? Can it be equated with *Lebensphilosophie*, Idealism, anti-modernism, anti-materialism, or even a tradition of irrationalism that ultimately led to National Socialism (Lukács 1954)? To what degree is there a confluence with the *völkisch* milieu?

It should be noted that the discursive networks discussed above were typically heterogeneous. Consequently, it is sometimes difficult to identify the various esoteric currents, which is further complicated by the fact that their self-designations varied constantly. After all, 'esotericism' could not be exclusively linked to right- or left-wing politics. An identification of 'irrationalism' with esotericism is certainly an oversimplification, yet still common even in academic discourse where 'irrationalism' is often suggested as a common basis for National Socialism and esotericism (since Adorno 1951). That problematic assumption is further complicated by the fact that esotericists were persecuted by the National Socialist authorities as a result of their perceived 'irrationality' and 'superstition.' Again, National Socialism's relationship to 'the occult' is far more complex and tenuous in many cases than previously imagined and still requires significant analysis, particularly the esoteric aspects of the heterogeneous *völkisch* discourses that partly prepared the ground for National Socialism (Puschner 2001 and 2012; Breuer 2008; cf. Mohler 1972, esp. 214–15). Ariosophy, for example, was a product of *völkisch* and occult ideas, but how exactly it was perceived in the various milieus in which it was developed and circulated and in what ways it shaped ideology is still not entirely clear. Again, what was the nature of its relationship to other 'occultural' elements?

The relationship between esotericism, or 'the occult,' and National Socialism is not only relevant for the comprehension of the past, in that, as we have seen, the subject has become an essential feature of post-war culture. Since the conclusion of the Second World War, a neo-Nazi esotericism has adopted the teachings of Wiligut and Rahn, developing them into motifs such as the 'Black Sun' and the Aryan 'Thule' topos. This becomes most evident in the writings of the Vienna circle author Rudolf Mund, who rose to the highest rank in the post-war Ordo Novi Templi. Such thinkers developed a number of scattered occult and *völkisch* ideas into a monolithic system that had not existed before and that had certainly not exerted an influence on National Socialism. Hence, it is necessary to differentiate between post-war esoteric neo-Nazism and historical National Socialism. Additional research is needed to understand the complex relationship between the *völkisch*, esoteric, and National Socialist networks, as well as their reception in the post-war period. That research should, of course, focus on a careful historical contextualization and avoid popular oversimplification that still exerts a considerable influence.

REFERENCES AND FURTHER READING

Adorno, T. (1951) 'Thesen gegen den Okkultismus,' in T. Adorno, ed., *Minima Moralia. Reflexionen aus dem beschädigten Leben*, Berlin/Frankfurt am Main: Suhrkamp.

Bergunder, M. (2010) 'What is Esotericism? Cultural Studies Approaches and the Problems of Definition in Religious Studies,' *Method and Theory in the Study of Religion* 22, 9–36.

——(2012) 'Was ist Religion? Kulturwissenschaftliche Überlegungen zum Gegenstand der Religionswissenschaft,' *Zeitschrift für Religionswissenschaft* 19, 3–55.

Bönisch, M. (1999) 'Die "Hammer"-Bewegung,' in U. Puschner, W. Schmitz, J.H. Ulbricht, eds., *Handbuch zur 'Völkischen Bewegung' 1871–1918*, München: Saur.

Breuer, S. (2008) *Die Völkischen in Deutschland. Kaiserreich und Weimarer Republik*, Darmstadt: Wissenschaftliche Buchgesellschaft.

Buchholz, K., Latocha, R., Peckmann, H. and Wolbert, K., eds. (2001) *Die Lebensreform. Entwürfe zur Neugestaltung von Leben und Kunst um 1900*, Darmstadt: Häusser.

Daim, W. (1958) *Der Mann, der Hitler die Ideen gab. Von den religiösen Verirrungen eines Sektierers zum Rassenwahn des Diktators*, München: Isar Verlag.

Fest, J. (1963) *Das Gesicht des Dritten Reiches. Profile einer totalitären Herrschaft*, München: Piper.

Gilbhard, H. (1994) *Die Thule-Gesellschaft. Vom okkulten Mummenschanz zum Hakenkreuz*, München: Kiessling.

Godwin, J. (2007) *Arktos. Der polare Mythos zwischen NS-Okkultismus und moderner Esoterik*, Graz: Ares Verlag.

Goodrick-Clarke, N. (2002) *Black Sun. Aryan Cults, Esoteric Nazism and the Politics of Identity*, New York: New York University Press.

——(2004) *Die okkulten Wurzeln des Nationalsozialismus*, Wiesbaden: Marix Verlag; (1985) *The Occult Roots of Nazism: Secret Aryan Cults and Their Influence on Nazi Ideology, 1890–1935*, New York: New York University Press.

Hakl, H. T. (1997/2004) 'Nationalsozialismus und Esoterik,' in N. Goodrick-Clarke ed., *Die okkulten Wurzeln des Nationalsozialismus*, Wiesbaden: Marix Verlag.

Halle, U. (2002) *'Die Externsteine sind bis auf weiteres germanisch!'. Prähistorische Archäologie im Dritten Reich*, Bielefeld/Gütersloh: Verlag für Regionalgeschichte.

Hanegraaff, W. J. (2012) *Esotericism and the Academy. Rejected Knowledge in Western Culture,* Cambridge: Cambridge University Press.

Hieronimus, E. (1991) *Lanz von Liebenfels. Eine Biographie,* Berg: Toppenstedt.

Höhne, H. (1967) *Der Orden unter dem Totenkopf. Die Geschichte der SS,* Gütersloh: S. Mohn.

Howe, E. (1967) *Urania's Children. The Strange World of the Astrologers,* London: William Kimber.

Hüser, K. (1987) *Wewelsburg 1933 bis 1945. Kult-und Terrorstätte der SS,* Paderborn: Verlag Bonifatius-Druckerei.

Hüttenberger, P. (1976) 'Nationalsozialistische Polykratie,' *Geschichte und Gesellschaft* 2, 417–42.

Jacobsen, H.-A. (1979) *Karl Haushofer. Leben und Werk*, Boppard am Rhein: Boldt.

Kater, M. H. (1974) *Das 'Ahnenerbe' der SS 1935–1945. Ein Beitrag zur Kulturpolitik des Dritten Reiches*, München: Deutsche Verlags-Anstalt.

Kogon, E. (1946) *Der SS-Staat. Das System der deutschen Konzentrationslager*, München: Albert.

Kroll, F.-L. (1998) *Utopie als Ideologie. Geschichtsdenken und politisches Handeln im Dritten Reich*, Paderborn: Schöningh.

Kurlander, E. (2012) 'Hitler's Monsters: The Occult Roots of Nazism and the Emergence of the Nazi "Supernatural Imaginary",' *German History* 30(4), 528–49.

Lang, J. V. (1989) *Der Adjutant. Karl Wolff. Der Mann zwischen Hitler und Himmler*, Frankfurt am Main/Berlin: Ullstein.

Lange, H.-J. (1995) *Otto Rahn. Leben und Werk*, Engerda: Arun.

——(1998) *Weisthor. Karl-Maria Wiligut. Himmlers Rasputin und sein Erbe*, Engerda: Arun-Verlag.

——(1999) *Otto Rahn und die Suche nach dem Gral*, Engerda: Arun.

Longerich, P. (2008) *Heinrich Himmler*, München: Siedler.

Löw, L. (2009) 'Völkische Deutungen prähistorischer Sinnbilder. Herman Wirth und sein Umfeld,' in U. Puschner and G.U. Großmann, eds., *Völkisch und national. Zur Aktualität alter Denkmuster im 21. Jahrhundert*, Darmstadt: Wissenschaftliche Buchgesellschaft.

Lukács, G. (1954) *Die Zerstörung der Vernunft*, Berlin: Aufbau-Verlag.

Mierau, P. (2006) *Nationalsozialistische Expeditionspolitik. Deutsche Asien-Expeditionen 1933–1945*, München: Utz.

Mohler, A. (1972) *Die Konservative Revolution in Deutschland 1918–1932*, Darmstadt: Wissenschaftliche Buchgesellschaft.

Mund, R. (1982) *Der Rasputin Himmlers. Die Wiligut-Saga*, Wien: Volkstum-Verlag.

——(2002) *Wiliguts Geheimlehre. Fragmente einer verschollenen Religion*, Berlin: Deutschherrenverlag.

Mund, R. and Werfenstein, G. V. (2004) *Mythos Schwarze Sonne. Karl Maria Wiligut/Weisthor, der heilige Gral und das Geheimnis der Wewelsburg*, Berlin: Deutschherrenverlag.

Nagel, B. (1991) *Die Welteislehre. Ihre Geschichte und ihre Rolle im 'Dritten Reich'*, Stuttgart: Verlag für Geschichte der Naturwissenschaften und der Technik.

Puschner, U., Schmitz, W. and Ulbricht, J. H., ed., (1999) *Handbuch zur 'Völkischen Bewegung' 1871–1918*, München: Saur.

Puschner, U. (2001) *Die völkische Bewegung im wilhelminischen Kaiserreich. Sprache, Rasse, Religion*, Darmstadt: Wissenschaftliche Buchgesellschaft.

Puschner, U. ed. (2012) *Die völkisch-religiöse Bewegung im Nationalsozialismus. Eine Beziehungs-und Konfliktgeschichte*, Göttingen: Vandenhoeck and Ruprecht.

Rose, D. (1994) *Die Thule-Gesellschaft. Legende – Mythos – Wirklichkeit*, Tübingen: Grabert.

Schirrmacher, T. (2007) *Hitlers Kriegsreligion. Die Verankerung der Weltanschauung Hitlers in seiner religiösen Begrifflichkeit und seinem Gottesbild*, Bonn: Verlag für Kultur und Wissenschaft.

Schnurbein, S. V. (1992) *Religion als Kulturkritik. Neugermanisches Heidentum im 20. Jahrhundert*, Heidelberg: Carl Winter Universitätsverlag.

——(1993) *Göttertrost in Wendezeiten. Neugermanisches Heidentum zwischen New Age und Rechtsradikalismus*, München: Claudius-Verlag.

Schulte, J. E. ed. (2009) *Die SS, Himmler und die Wewelsburg*, Paderborn: Schöningh.

Siepe, D. (2009) 'Die Rolle der Wewelsburg in der phantastischen Literatur, in Esoterik und Rechtsextremismus nach 1945,' in J.E. Schulte ed. *Die SS, Himmler und die Wewelsburg*, Paderborn: Schöningh.

Staudenmaier, P. (2013) 'Nazi Perceptions of Esotericism: The Occult as Fascination and Menace,' in A. Manthripragada, ed., *The Threat and Allure of the Magical*, Newcastle: Cambridge Scholars Publishing.

——(2014) *Between Occultism and Nazism: Anthroposophy and the Politics of Race in the Fascist Era*, Leiden/Boston: Brill.

Strube, J. (2012) 'Die Erfindung des esoterischen Nationalsozialismus im Zeichen der Schwarzen Sonne,' *Zeitschrift für Religionswissenschaft* 20(2), 223–68.

——(2013) *Vril. Eine okkulte Naturkraft in Theosophie und esoterischem Neonazismus*, Paderborn: Wilhelm Fink.

Sünner, R. (1999) *Schwarze Sonne. Entfesselung und Missbrauch der Mythen in Nationalsozialismus und rechter Esoterik*, Freiburg: Herder spektrum.

Treitel, C. (2004) *A Science for the Soul. Occultism and the Genesis of the German Modern*, Baltimore: The Johns Hopkins University Press.

Wessely, C. (2006) 'Karriere einer Weltanschauung. Die Welteislehre 1894–1945,' *Zeitgeschichte* 33, 25–39.

——(2008) 'Welteis. Die "Astronomie des Unsichtbaren" um 1900,' in D. Rupnow, V. Lipphardt, J. Thiel, and C. Wessely, eds., *Pseudowissenschaft*, Frankfurt am Main: Suhrkamp.

Wiwjorra, I. (1995) 'Herman Wirth. Ein gescheiterter Ideologe zwischen "Ahnenerbe" und Atlantis,' in B. Danckwortt, ed., *Historische Rassismusforschung. Ideologen – Täter – Opfer*, Hamburg: Argument-Verlag.

Wulff, W. (1968) *Tierkreis und Hakenkreuz. Als Astrologe an Himmlers Hof*, Gütersloh: Bertelsmann.

CHAPTER THIRTY-SIX

THE THEOSOPHICAL CURRENT IN THE TWENTIETH CENTURY

Olav Hammer

INTRODUCTION

Theosophy is in many ways the first truly successful global, new religion. The Theosophical Society and the message it disseminated have attracted numerous entrepreneurial individuals, who have produced new twists on well-known themes familiar from the foundational texts of Theosophy. Some stayed close to the Theosophical worldview as expounded in books by Helena Blavatsky and her successors, while others added many innovative concepts and practices to those inherited from their ideological ancestor. New religious movements have been created as institutional frameworks around such innovative receptions of Theosophy. Theosophical concepts have also profoundly influenced the loose folk religiosity often referred to as 'New Age.'

This discussion examines a sample of post-Theosophical movements, as well as Theosophically inspired New Age elements, but is by no means an exhaustive catalog. For a much more detailed presentation of the Theosophical current in the twentieth century, see the contributions in the volume edited by Olav Hammer and Mikael Rothstein (2013). Much of the information summarized in the present chapter is indebted to the information presented in that volume.

ALICE BAILEY

Of the various post-Theosophical currents to be examined here, the one associated with Alice Bailey (1880–1949) is perhaps the most 'orthodox,' and therefore a good place to begin our exploration. Born Alice LaTrobe Bateman, Bailey was brought up in an affluent and thoroughly Anglican family. Her autobiography (Bailey 1951) describes her as an unhappy but deeply spiritual child. Several incidents recorded in that book served to sever her ties with mainstream Christianity and led her towards an affiliation with Theosophy. A meeting with a mysterious stranger in 1895 was later reinterpreted as a first encounter with a Theosophical Master. Her marriage to and subsequent divorce from an Episcopalian priest, Walter Evans, described by her as an abusive husband, led to further disaffection with organized Christianity. In the mid-1910s, she joined the Theosophical Society. In 1920 she and her future husband

Foster Bailey (from whom she received the family name by which she is generally known) were expelled from the Theosophical Society. For the nearly three remaining decades of her life, she pursued a career as an organizationally independent religious teacher in the Theosophical tradition.

Alice Bailey presented most of her work as the result of dictation from a spiritual teacher that she purportedly came into contact with in 1919, and whom she called 'The Tibetan,' Master Djwhal Khul (often simply referred to as DK). The first volume that resulted from this revelatory encounter, *Initiation, Human and Solar*, was published in 1922. Besides numerous titles produced as merely the 'amanuensis' of this Tibetan Master, Alice Bailey also produced works published under her own name. This voluminous corpus of teachings (below, for ease of reference, credited to Bailey) reveals many points of direct continuity with the teachings of Blavatsky. Topics such as the spiritual evolution of mankind, karma and reincarnation, the subtle 'bodies' of the human being, and the existence of a hierarchy of Masters, are found throughout Bailey's writings. In the interest of brevity, the main innovations into the Theosophical teachings introduced by Alice Bailey will be summarized in a few points. A caveat is in order at this point: much of this corpus is formulated in a style that poses significant interpretive challenges.

In the teachings imparted by the Tibetan, a complex and detailed cosmology emerges. Ultimate reality manifests itself in seven distinct forms or energies, that Bailey calls the seven rays. Each ray is associated with specific qualities, described in Bailey's writings by means of capitalized abstract nouns: the first ray is associated with Will and Power; the second with Love-Wisdom; the third with Active Intelligence; the fourth with Harmony, Beauty and Art; the fifth with Concrete Knowledge and Science; the sixth with Devotion and Abstract Idealism; and the seventh with Order and Ceremonial Magic. This cosmological structure is so fundamental to Bailey's cosmology, that a five-volume work is entitled *Treatise on the Seven Rays*.

One of the most fundamental ways in which these seven rays affect humans is through the seven planets of astrology. Bailey devoted a major volume (the third of the five-volume *Treatise on the Seven Rays*) to what she called esoteric astrology. In contradistinction to the generally event-oriented astrology current in the first half of the twentieth century, Bailey's esoteric astrology deals with personal spiritual evolution based on the qualities symbolized by the planets. Her writings on the topic assume complex systems of correspondence between planets, constellations, rays, and elements of the human constitution, and differ in many ways from other contemporary non-Theosophical versions of astrology, e.g., by assuming the existence of an occult planet, Vulcan.

Like Blavatsky's Masters or Mahatmas, the beings who have come furthest on this path of spiritual evolution serve as teachers who can guide us. This hierarchy of Masters is similar to, but not identical to the gallery of advanced beings found in Blavatsky's texts, and in its profuse array of levels and titles more closely resembles the second-generation Theosophy of Charles W. Leadbeater and Annie Besant. To some extent such differences can be seen as changes in emphasis. Blavatsky mentions a Master Djual Khool, but this is a being who plays a minor role in her writings. By contrast, Bailey's Tibetan, Djwhal Khul, has become the principal transmitter of esoteric teachings. Blavatsky's Theosophy focuses on Masters living in our own world (e.g. the Himalayas). Although Bailey's principal Master is associated with a physical location on our planet, her hierarchy is also associated with extraterrestrial locations (Venus, Sirius) and places that may not even be geographical locations at all, but denote other dimensions of existence (Shamballa).

Blavatsky's sense of evolutionary history presupposes that we are collectively progressing toward a new spiritual age. Blavatsky is rather vague about the particulars of the transition, but appears to see it as the distant end result of a long process. Bailey gives this teaching a millennialist turn, predicting that this transition would take place suddenly and in the near future. Bailey repeatedly referred to this epoch as the 'New Age' and used the term in her 1944 volume *Discipleship in the New Age*.

One of the most striking innovations in Bailey's Theosophy is the reintroduction of a strong strain of esoteric Christianity, which positions the Christ as a paramount member of the hierarchy of Masters. Whereas Blavatsky was decidedly critical of much of the Christian heritage, and anchored her teachings in a synthesis of Western esoteric elements and Oriental terminology, Bailey's writings are replete with references to the figure of Christ, albeit a figure that differs in crucial respects from that of mainstream denominations (O'Callaghan 2013).

ANTHROPOSOPHY

While it is hardly contentious that the teachings of Alice Bailey are firmly situated within a Theosophical context, considerable controversy surrounds the Theosophical connections of Rudolf Steiner (1861–1925), and in particular the Theosophical influence on his creation, Anthroposophy. That Steiner was in a historical sense affiliated with the Theosophical Society is accepted by Anthroposophists and academic outsiders alike: Steiner joined in 1902 and left again toward the end of 1912. The disagreement regards the question whether (as most scholars suggest) Steiner's teachings were decisively influenced by Theosophy, especially as formulated by its second generation leaders Annie Besant and Charles W. Leadbeater, or (as most Anthroposophists insist) the Theosophical Society was merely the institutional shell within which Steiner could work and formulate a spiritual vision that was entirely his own, and that he could access thanks to his immense powers of suprasensible cognition.

Clearly, Anthroposophy presents many different aspects, only some of which even from a scholar's point of view are manifestly Theosophical. There is an immense corpus of writings, by Steiner as well as his followers, outlining a vast and detailed esoteric conception of the world and of humanity. There are numerous practical applications, including Waldorf pedagogy, eurythmy (a distinctly Anthroposophical performance and therapeutic art), and biodynamic farming. There is an Anthroposophical-Christian institution, The Christian Community. There is also a substantial Anthroposophical visual and material culture, manifested in architecture, in mystery plays, even in commercial products such as Weleda cosmetics and natural medicines. For many people, the practical applications will be much more familiar than the occult doctrines, and these applications are at best indirectly connected to a Theosophical current of thought. For the present chapter the most relevant aspects of Anthroposophy are Steiner's cosmogony, anthropogony, and concepts regarding the occult physiology of the human being, all of which bear a strong resemblance to similar Theosophical doctrines (for a fuller presentation, with references to further literature, see Brandt and Hammer 2013).

Steiner had an eclectic intellectual background, and had published several works on subjects such as Goethe's philosophy of nature, Ernst Haeckel's monist philosophy, Max Stirner's radical and atheist individualism, and the works of Friedrich Nietzsche, before joining the Theosophical Society in 1902 together with his wife Marie von Sivers. Steiner rapidly rose in the organization. In 1904 Annie Besant appointed Steiner national manager of the Esoteric School for Germany and Austria. Conflicts soon arose and in 1907 Steiner positioned himself as a representative of a European, esoteric Christian tradition, as opposed to the more Indian-inspired tradition of the mother organization. The official foundation of a breakaway Anthroposophical Society took place on 28 December 1912. Steiner and von Sivers abandoned the Theosophical Society and increasingly distanced themselves from it.

Rudolf Steiner claimed visionary abilities, by means of which he could reconstruct any given detail in the development of the cosmos and of mankind. Events of world history, the occult constitution of the human body, and the mechanisms of reincarnation ranked prominently among the topics discovered in these spiritual forays. All of these were described in books and lectures, in terms reminiscent of Theosophical doctrines.

The history of our planet and of humanity is treated in great detail by Steiner, in terms reminiscent of the 'globes' and 'races' of Theosophy. He suggested that today's Earth was preceded by three planetary incarnations, 'old Saturn,' 'old Sun,' and 'old Moon.' In the distant future three more incarnations of the Earth will follow, stages of evolution that he called the future Jupiter, Venus, and Vulcan. The present Earth stage is further divided into seven root races or epochs, again according to a scheme with distinct echoes of Blavatsky's Theosophical terminology. These are the Polar, Hyperborean, Lemuric, Atlantic, and Aryan epochs, as well as two future epochs that have no specific names in Steiner's writings. Each root race or epoch is again divided into seven sub-races or stages. His classification places present-day humans in the fifth post-Atlantean stage of the Aryan epoch, a stage that roughly began with the advent of the early modern period in European history (for details of this historical scheme, see Zander 2007: 624ff).

Steiner introduced a model of the human being as constituted of four bodies, or *Wesensglieder*: the physical body, etheric body, astral body, and self. Steiner's conceptual proximity to Theosophical sources is apparent from the fact that he at first added the Indian terms used in Theosophical literature to the designations that he had chosen.

Finally, Rudolf Steiner's discussion of reincarnation is contemporaneous with that of the second generation of Theosophists, and resembles Leadbeater's and Besant's account. Steiner's claim to being able to access records of the past by suprasensible means resulted both in a very detailed exposition of the fate of the human being between successive incarnations, and a wide-ranging narrative of individual past lives.

OCCULT HISTORY, RACES, AND THE ARIOSOPHIC MOVEMENT

Blavatsky's *Secret Doctrine* devotes much space to the history of the human species. As a rule, Blavatsky was dismissive of mainstream scientific theories, and used then-current perspectives of the planetary and human past as raw materials to construct a distinct, occult history. Central to Blavatsky's historiography is an underlying super-diffusionism that claims that all of human (spiritual) culture has a single origin and has spread to various locations around the world via processes of migration. The carriers of this spiritual and civilizational impulse were identified as various Root Races and Races, some of which populated mythical continents such as Lemuria and Atlantis. Individual 'monads' or souls incarnated again and again throughout history, and all races are thus in a sense interconnected. At the same time, not all monads are equally advanced on the evolutionary path, and there are numerous suggestions in *The Secret Doctrine* that some races are primitive remnants left behind in the evolutionary grand scheme. Depending on whether one prefers to focus on the interconnectedness of all of humanity due to the same monads reincarnating in new shapes, or on the differential valuation of some races and peoples as more primitive than others, Theosophical historiography will come across as either benign or racist (Santucci 2008; Lubelsky 2013). Post-Theosophical writers such as Alice Bailey and Rudolf Steiner reproduce or subtly rearrange Blavatsky's historical scheme. Bailey's writings include passages on well-known elements from Theosophical history, such as root races, Atlantis, and Lemuria, and have been accused of introducing an added focus on the purportedly negative characteristics of Jews. In Steiner's case, racial discourse is complicated further by his inheritance from national Romanticism and the *völkisch* movements of the idea that individual ethnic groups or nations have essential characteristics rooted in biology. Thus, in a lecture held in 1906, entitled *Blut ist ein ganz besonderer Saft,* Steiner suggests that national and racial characteristics are due to different types of blood. Perhaps unsurprisingly, considerable controversy surrounds this aspect of Bailey's and Steiner's writings, with some authors (writing from an outsider's perspective) insisting that racist and anti-Semitic references can be found in both bodies of text, and others (those who are sympathetic to the post-Theosophical currents in question) claiming on the contrary that such accusations are due to misinformed critics quoting out of context, or distorting the wording of the sources.

While disagreement continues to surround this entire lineage of occultist historiographies, another group of post-Theosophical writers and currents is unambiguously racist and anti-Semitic. As documented in the work of the late Nicholas Goodrick-Clarke (1992), several German occultist writers active in the first decades of the twenteth century, and in particular Guido von List (1848–1919) and Jörg Lanz von Liebenfels (1874–1954), combined Theosophical race mythology with a highly idiosyncratic and radically racist understanding of the soteriological role of the 'Aryans.' These so-called Ariosophic writers and movements drew on many other sources than Blavatsky's historiography. Guido von List at first based his religious views on a reading of Old Norse texts, and on his conviction that the runes were the key to occult insight. In 1908, a List Society was formed, with the purpose of propagating List's *völkisch* occultism. His ideas, which he subsumed under the label Wotanism, increasingly came to consist of an original synthesis of his reading of Germanic mythology with Theosophy. Wotanism postulated that the ancient Germanic peoples had followed a system of mystical initiations, and that the secrets imparted by this Germanic path were identical to those of 'Hindu' (i.e. Theosophical) doctrine.

Lanz von Liebenfels was in many ways an ideological disciple of Guido von List. He came to understand world history as the struggle of Aryan and non-Aryan races, where the Aryans' superiority (as manifested by their possession in ancient times of electric sense organs that enabled extrasensory perception) was threatened by racial degeneration. Besides basing his theories on Guido von List's Wotanism, he embarked on an allegorical reading of biblical texts that concluded that the passion of Christ as depicted in the gospels was in fact a veiled allusion to the struggle of a representative of the superior Aryan race against ape-like creatures.

Such syntheses of extreme right-wing politics, racism, and Theosophy were most influential before World War II, but there have been quite a few attempts since then to revive Ariosophical thinking, or to produce new combinations of such themes (Godwin 2011: 124–56). For instance, the Armanen-Orden was founded in 1976 as a revival of Guido von List's Wotanist ideology. Perhaps more anti-modernist than strictly post-Theosophical, this organization sees its mission as a revitalization of ancient Germanic pagan religion (von Schnurbein 1992). Another, truly original perspective on Theosophical race theory is provided by the work of Pekka Siitoin (1944–2003), a Finnish occultist who combined Theosophical and Anthroposophical metaphysics with Satanist ideology. He founded several occultist societies and wrote books that combined Theosophically inspired ideas of racial evolution with Nazism, UFOs, Satanic symbolism, and black magic (Granholm, forthcoming).

NATIONALISTIC THEOSOPHY

One notable aspect of the Theosophical current is its ability to adapt to changing, local circumstances, such as by incorporating the racist obsessions of interwar Germany. More benign alignments with nationalist agendas can also be found in the Theosophical family of currents. The Theosophical message could with equally seamless integration become a nationalistically tinged message for an American or a Russian audience. Theosophical historiography is, as we have seen, super-diffusionist, its sacred geography predicated on the idea that certain places are spiritual hot spots for human evolution. One mode of Theosophical innovation is to assert that one's own country and particular sites in it are the *fons et origo* of cultural diffusion, or play key roles in the grand evolutionary scheme.

The first of the two Theosophically based movements to be covered in this section is the I AM Activity (Mayer 2005; Rudbøg 2013). This organization was founded by Guy W. Ballard (1878–1939) after his alleged meeting in 1930 with a spiritual being by the name of Saint Germain on Mount Shasta, a volcanic mountain in northern California. Ballard describes how he was hiking on the mountain when a young man suddenly appeared behind him. This was obviously no mundane encounter, since the young man began to tell Ballard about the Eternal Law of Life, or the idea that whatever a person thinks and feels will manifest in his life through hidden spiritual laws. Ballard's interlocutor then revealed his true identity as an Ascended Master – a title related to but not identical with the Masters or Mahatmas of 'classical' Theosophy.

Ballard returned to his home in Chicago, where he and his wife Edna established the I AM Activity in order to disseminate the insights obtained on Mount Shasta. In 1932 they founded the Saint Germain Foundation and a publishing house, the Saint Germain Press, and in 1934 Ballard's first book *Unveiled Mysteries* was published (under the pen name Godfré Ray King). Over the years a series of twenty I AM books were written.

Just as Ballard's original revelatory event was placed in an American setting, these books continued to affirm the centrality of the USA in the cosmic scheme of things. Ballard built on Blavatsky's idea of the spiritually evolved Mahatmas or Masters, but added new names to this pantheon, and asserted that a group of these Masters were particularly concerned with the unique occult mission of America. Paramount among these is Saint Germain, a figure known from earlier Theosophical literature, but now placed at the apex of the brotherhood of Masters and personally in charge of the destiny of the USA.

Another American member of the Theosophical family of currents, the Summit Lighthouse, has produced a similarly nationalistic version of Theosophical mythology (Whitsel 2003; Abravanel 2013). Founders Mark Prophet (1918–73) and Elizabeth Clare Prophet (1939–2009) saw themselves as messengers for the Ascended Masters. This vast pantheon comprises Masters who are central to Blavatsky's work, such as Morya and Kuthumi, but also, as in the I AM movement, specifically American Masters, including Saint Germain. After his death, Mark Prophet was considered one of these Masters, having adopted the name Lanello upon ascension. Numerous statements by the leaders asserted that America had a key historical and spiritual role. Most notably, the Summit Lighthouse in the late 1980s adopted an extreme form of cold war rhetoric. After Saint Germain in 1986 supposedly had warned Elizabeth Clare Prophet of a nuclear attack from the Soviet Union, bomb shelters were established at the headquarters of the organization.

Agni Yoga (also known as Living Ethics) is a Theosophical movement founded by the Russian couple Nicholas (1874–1947) and Helena Roerich (1879–1955) (Stasulane 2005, 2013). After resettling in the USA in 1920, the Roerichs claimed to receive messages from Master Morya, published a series of books based on these messages, and organized groups where these books could be read and discussed. The existence and involvement in earthly affairs of the Masters became a key tenet of their movement. Over the years, a dualistic worldview developed, according to which true revelations to the Masters were accorded to the Roerichs, whereas other post-Theosophical writers were severely criticized, and even denounced as agents of dark powers.

Like many other post-Theosophical writers, the Roerichs built on the foundation laid by Helena Blavatsky, but could shift focus and highlight elements that were not central to works such as *The Secret Doctrine*. Among the core doctrines of Agni Yoga is the suggestion that symbols from various religions can, when understood through an evolved consciousness, reveal underlying spiritual truths. The Masters themselves appear in symbolic form throughout the world. The symbol of fire, they contended, is also universal, as is the symbol of the Mother of the World. The two were combined in an apocalyptic prediction: an 'epoch of fire' is approaching, a dangerous period when someone is needed who can transform the higher cosmic energies so that humanity would be able to receive them. According to Nicholas Roerich, this was done by his wife – the Mother of Agni Yoga.

The nationalist element of Agni Yoga comes clearly to the fore in connection with Nicholas Roerich's expeditions in 1925 to 1928 to the Altai Mountains (on which, see McCannon 2002). Here he hoped to find a mythic land called Belovodye – a kind of Russian counterpart of such sites of the occult and Romantic imagination as Shamballa and Shangri-La. Roerich's grand utopian ambition was to create a Siberian kingdom where an earthly manifestation of Maitreya, the Buddha of the Future, could lead humanity into a golden, new age. Roerich's reason for choosing the Altai was his deeply held conviction that human culture came from there, and that this was the home of our spiritually awakened ancestors.

EDGAR CAYCE

From one perspective, the American psychic Edgar Cayce (1877–1945) can be seen as merely one among presumably hundreds of people who have claimed to transmit messages with a distinctly Theosophical flavor from Masters, the Akashic Records, their Higher Selves, or other alleged supramundane sources. From another perspective, Cayce, due to the fame he accrued and the fact that he was active in the culturally and linguistically dominant USA, became perhaps the most important link in the transmission of Theosophical doctrine from the golden age of the Theosophical Society (and its various branches), roughly spanning from the late 1880s to the early 1930s, to the modern countercultural and New Age milieus – i.e. from the 1970s to the present (Hanegraaff 1996: 34–36; Trosper Schorey 2013).

Cayce's work can be seen as an integration of at least three different currents: alternative medicine as practiced in Cayce's days, conservative Christianity, and Theosophical occultism. Biographies stress Cayce's Christian upbringing, and his life-long devotion to the Bible (which he is said to have read once a year throughout his life). A key biographic element concerns an illness that incapacitated Cayce, and that was resistant to treatment until he underwent hypnosis in 1910. The sources relate that Cayce discovered that he was able to diagnose the maladies of others while in a trance-like state and also to suggest successful treatments. From now on, Cayce would provide free advice on health issues. Cayce's fame rapidly spread and led to a crucial encounter when, in 1923, Arthur Lammers, a wealthy printer interested in 'metaphysics' (i.e. Theosophically tinged occultism) persuaded him to give trance readings on more broadly spiritual topics. Presumably as the result of prolonged contact with and instruction by Lammers in metaphysical matters, Cayce's health readings were now increasingly supplemented by readings on Theosophical themes such as reincarnation and karma. Elements of the Theosophical view of history were incorporated into these messages, and alternative views of Egypt and details of life on Atlantis became prominent topics. Many of Cayce's clients had, it seemed, previously lived in these places and, in particular, readings could disclose details of life in Atlantis. Cayce's Christian background was integrated into this overall Theosophical scheme: Jesus appears here as a spiritual master who has accumulated wisdom by reincarnating in successively higher forms.

After Cayce's death in 1945, his fame continued to spread. Several books with a hagiographic perspective have appeared since then; one of the most influential is Thomas Sugrue's 1945 volume *The Story of Edgar Cayce: There is a River*. Other works are collections of his readings on occult topics such as Atlantis or alternative views of Christ. When a subculture of 'spiritual seekers' emerged in the 1970s, such widely available biographies and anthologies provided easy access to occultist topics.

BENJAMIN CREME AND SHARE INTERNATIONAL

Most of the authors and currents reviewed above have integrated a millennialist perspective on human history in their message. Whether as a dramatic transformation of human collective consciousness in a dawning new age (as for Bailey), or as a cataclysmic event (nuclear war, for the Prophets; a pole shift, for Cayce), the historiographic vision predicted that an imminent change was to be expected. One Theosophical group is particular has become known for its millennialist promise: Share International, founded by Scottish esotericist Benjamin Creme (b. 1922).

The second-generation leaders of the Theosophical Society, Annie Besant and Charles W. Leadbeater, predicted that a coming World Teacher would usher in the new, utopian age. Theosophists identified this figure as Maitreya, a name perhaps more familiar from Buddhist tradition as the Buddha of a future age. Benjamin Creme is influenced by several post-Theosophical currents, including Theosophical UFO movements and the teachings of Alice Bailey. He became convinced that different religious traditions all shared the same core teaching of a messianic figure, who will soon make his presence known to humanity, and announced that he in 1975 had been telepathically contacted by this being. Creme has published extensively on the imminent arrival, in anticipation of the day when Maitreya will declare himself openly as 'World Teacher for the Age of Aquarius.' In order to spread his message and facilitate the messianic event, Creme founded an organization, Share International, which *inter alia* disseminates Creme's books, provides an insider's perspective on who Maitreya is, and publicizes apparently miraculous events said to document that Maitreya is already amongst us and has merely chosen to temporarily remain in anonymity.

In what is perhaps the most innovative element in Creme's teachings, the traces of these miraculous events effectively function as Theosophical icons. They are claimed to embody particular healing energies that can be tapped. A picture of Maitreya's hand is said to have 'extraordinary healing properties' that can be 'invoked from Maitreya when you place your hand over the image or simply look at it. You are, in effect, calling forth his healing or blessing or help – whatever is possible within the karmic law. The same effect can be produced even with a photocopy of the image' (www.share-international.org/maitreya/ Ma_approach.htm).

THEOSOPHICALLY INSPIRED UFO MOVEMENTS

Blavatsky's and Leadbeater's Masters were presented as spiritually highly evolved beings, but they were nonetheless distinctly human creatures. Most seemed to live in the Himalayan region, and according to Leadbeater's description of them in *The Masters and the Path* even lived in housing that resembled that of ordinary humans (see, e.g., www.anandgholap.net/Masters_And_Path-CWL.htm, section 64). The American post-Theosophical movements transformed the Masters into altogether more lofty and exotic entities, suggesting that they had 'ascended,' presumably into a radically different mode of existence. The distance, geographically as well as ontologically, between ordinary humans and the Masters grew even further when in the 1950s a number of so-called contactees claimed to have received messages from benevolent beings arriving to our planet in UFOs.

The message imparted by these gentle aliens in many ways resembled classical Theosophical topics. Mankind had mismanaged the planet, and in particular created the threat of nuclear holocaust. However, a new age was now about to dawn, ushered in by our brothers from space. This latest intervention was merely one in a long series, since humanity had throughout its history been guided in its evolutionary journey by these beings from space. Most post-Theosophical space age prophets, such as George Adamski (1891–1965) and George van Tassel (1910–78), spread their versions of this story through informal networks, lectures, books, and the media. Only a very few have founded lasting religious movements. One of the most significant of these is George King, creator of the Aetherius Society (Rothstein 2013). King presents yet another variation on the familiar themes of human spiritual evolution, reincarnation, and space brothers as cosmic guides. Besides a Master Aetherius, who appears to be a distinct innovation of this group, King's publications describe Master Jesus as a physical being from another world, who intervenes in earthly affairs in order to help humanity.

THEOSOPHICAL ELEMENTS IN NEW AGE RELIGIOSITY

As will be apparent from the chapter on New Age in the present volume, the label 'New Age' is contested, and when used in scholarly literature, denotes a very diverse, malleable, and loosely connected form of religiosity. The historical roots of the New Age are also very diverse, and the Theosophical current is only one of the many sources that have fed into it. The challenge for the historian is compounded by the fact that much New Age literature is singularly uninterested in documenting the source of its ideas, and even where the Theosophical influence can seem completely self-evident to an outsider, the connection can be explicitly denied.

The Theosophical link manifests itself in many ways, from an *air de famille* due to a general cultural climate expressed by Theosophists and New Agers alike, via themes that may not have been of crucial importance to the main figures of the Theosophical Society but were created or popularized by members of the Theosophical Society, to specific terms and concepts prevalent in the New Age milieu that can be directly traced back to specific works by Theosophical authors (Hammer 2013). Themes that are ubiquitous in Theosophical as well as New Age literature, but where the influence need not be direct, include the suggestion that we are embarked on a voyage of spiritual evolution; that this is a journey that via the mechanism of reincarnation takes place over many lives; and that the spiritual insights that we may arrive at as we rise in evolutionary level can be found among various ancient or exotic peoples, including India, Tibet, and ancient Egypt. These topics familiar from Theosophical and New Age discourses are ubiquitous in the general occultist milieu, and anybody with an interest in 'alternative spiritualities' will sooner or later come across them. Direct borrowing from, say, the works of Blavatsky or Leadbeater, is certainly possible, but not necessary.

The Theosophical Society attracted a segment of people that, employing Colin Campbell's term, could be characterized as the cultic milieu of the late nineteenth and early twentieth century (Campbell 1972). Besides a membership in the Theosophical Society, these individuals could have a wide range of interests that only partly overlapped with the core Theosophical message. Astrology, for instance, is mentioned at various places throughout Blavatsky's *oeuvre*, but was of limited interest to her. Organizationally, nevertheless, there are strong connections between the astrological and Theosophical milieus, and this link has played a pivotal role in the current revival of astrology after a long period of decline. A key figure in this astrological revitalization was Alan Leo (1860–1917, given name William Frederick Allan; see Spencer 2000: 82–86 and Campion 2009: 231–37 et passim). Leo, who in 1915 founded an Astrological Lodge of the Theosophical Society, was a prolific writer and a practicing astrologer, and numerous people became acquainted with astrology via him. Modern astrology has one of its many sources in Leo's Theosophical interests.

Finally, a number of quite specific claims presented in Theosophical literature appear also in modern New Age books, and here historical transmission would seem evident. A number of Theosophical works, and in particular titles by Charles Leadbeater such as *Man Invisible and Visible* (1903) and *The Chakras* (1927) describe an occult physiology discernible only to spiritually advanced individuals. The two main terms associated by Leadbeater with these occult human elements have become household terms in contemporary culture. The aura is described as a colored sheath surrounding the physical body. Leadbeater's 1927 title further states that the vital forces of the human being form seven nodes or *chakras*, that the clairvoyant observer will discern as rotating discs with a complex internal structure. In the late 1960s and early 1970s, parts of Theosophical lore on the chakras entered the emerging New Age. Leadbeater's book has gone through numerous reprints, and has been easily available ever since the first year of publication. Once the *chakras* became an integral and ubiquitous part of New Age discourse they have been described in ways that are not entirely consistent with the Theosophical sources. The majority of New Age texts present the *chakras* as a sequence of centers aligned roughly vertically along the spine. Each such center has a distinctive function and color.

THEOSOPHICAL INFLUENCES ON ART AND LITERATURE

All of the sections above deal with the post-Theosophical current understood as a family of (from a scholarly point of view) religious movements, writers, and texts. Theosophy has also exerted considerable influence on other cultural domains than the religious, and in particular on literature, art, and music. At the 'high' end of the cultural scale, Theosophy had a major impact on the emergence of abstract art at the cusp of the twentieth century.

It has for long been recognized that the Theosophical interests of such painters as Kandinsky and Mondrian influenced their move away from figurative art (an early study is Robsjohn-Gibbings 1947; for an up-to-date summary of the links between Theosophy and art, see Bauduin 2013). They and other artists participated in the utopian impulse shared by many Theosophists: a new spiritual epoch was about to dawn and abstract art was its herald. This art was meant to capture a spiritual or sacred geometry, for instance by depicting a dualistic principle of male versus female or heaven versus earth. Some artwork was intended as an even more concrete manifestation of the hidden realities that Theosophical visionaries could perceive, and that they called thought-forms.

Theosophy has also influenced a more popular art form, namely occult novels (see Gilhus and Mikaelson 2013). Talbot Mundy (1879–1940), Algernon Blackwood

(1869–1951), Kenneth Morris (1879–1937), Dion Fortune (1890–1946), and a host of other once highly popular writers reworked Theosophical topics in fictional form, and thus contributed to making themes such as reincarnation and hidden Masters familiar to a readership well beyond the borders of any Theosophical organization. Many of these authors may be largely unknown to present-day readers, but the bestselling charts of the last few years show that topics well-known from the Theosophical milieus remain staples of modern popular fiction – that the Christian churches present a false picture of the life and teachings of Jesus (cf. Dan Brown's *The Da Vinci Code*), or that mankind is embarked on a voyage of spiritual evolution and will soon experience a major shift in consciousness (cf. James Redfield's *The Celestine Prophecy*).

In this sense, although Theosophy as an organization may have been reduced to marginal importance since the golden days of the Theosophical Society, Theosophy as a broader current has entered the cultural mainstream.

REFERENCES AND FURTHER READING

Abravanel, M. (2013) 'The Summit Lighthouse: Its Worldview and Theosophical Legacy,' in Hammer and Rothstein, eds., *Handbook of the Theosophical Current*, Leiden: Brill, 173–92.

Bailey, A. (1951) *The Unfinished Autobiography*, London: Lucis Press.

Bauduin, T. (2013) 'Abstract Art as "By-Product of Astral Manifestation": The Influence of Theosophy on Modern Art in Europe,' in Hammer and Rothstein, eds., *Handbook of the Theosophical Current*, Leiden: Brill, 429–52.

Brandt, K. and O. Hammer (2013) 'Rudolf Steiner and Theosophy,' in Hammer and Rothstein, eds., *Handbook of the Theosophical Current*, Leiden: Brill, 113–34.

Campbell, C. (1972) 'The Cult, the Cultic Milieu and Secularization', *A Sociological Yearbook of Religion in Britain* 5, 119–36.

Campion, N. (2009) *History of Western Astrology*, 2 vols, London: Continuum.

Gilhus, I. S. and L. Mikaelson (2013) 'Theosophy and Popular Fiction,' in Hammer and Rothstein, eds., *Handbook of the Theosophical Current*, Leiden: Brill, 453–72.

Godwin, J. (2011) *Atlantis of the Occultists and the Cycles of Time*, Rochester Vt.: Inner Traditions.

Goodrick-Clarke, N. (1992) *The Occult Roots of Nazism: Secret Aryan Cults and Their Influence on Nazi Ideology; The Ariosophists of Austria and Germany, 1890–1935*, New York: New York University Press.

Granholm, K. (forthcoming) 'Theosophically Inspired Groups in Finland,' in Henrik Bogdan and Olav Hammer, eds., *Western Esotericism in Scandinavia*, Leiden: Brill.

Hammer, O. (2013) 'Theosophical Elements in New Age Religion,' in Hammer and Rothstein, eds., *Handbook of the Theosophical Current*, Leiden: Brill, 237–58.

Hammer, O. and M. Rothstein (2013) *Handbook of the Theosophical Current*, Leiden: Brill.

Hanegraaff, W. (1996) *New Age Religion and Western Culture: Esotericism in the Mirror of Secular Thought*, Leiden: Brill.

Lubelsky, I. (2013) 'Mythological and Real Race Issues in Theosophy,' in Hammer and Rothstein, eds., *Handbook of the Theosophical Current*, Leiden: Brill, 335–56.

Mayer, J-F. (2005) '"I AM" Activity,' In Wouter J. Hanegraaff et al., eds., *Dictionary of Gnosis and Western Esotericism*, Leiden: Brill, 587–88.

McCannon, J. (2002) 'By the Shores of White Waters: the Altai and its Place in the Spiritual Geopolitics of Nicholas Roerich,' *Sibirica*, Vol. 2, No. 2, 166–89.

O'Callaghan, S. (2013) 'The Theosophical Christology of Alice Bailey,' in Hammer and Rothstein (eds.), *Handbook of the Theosophical Current*, Leiden: Brill, 93–112.

Robsjohn-Gibbings, T.H. (1947) *Mona Lisa's Mustache: A Dissection of Modern Art*, New York: Alfred A. Knopf.

Rothstein, M. (2013) 'Mahatmas in Space: The Ufological Turn and Mythological Materiality of Post-World War II Theosophy,' in Hammer and Rothstein, eds., *Handbook of the Theosophical Current*, Leiden: Brill, 217–36.

Rudbøg, T. (2013) 'The I AM Activity,' in Hammer and Rothstein, eds., *Handbook of the Theosophical Current*, Leiden: Brill, 151–72.

Santucci, J. (2008) 'The Notion of Race in Theosophy,' *Nova Religio: The Journal of Alternative and Emergent Religions*, Vol. 11, No. 3, 37–63.

Spencer, N. (2000) *True as the Stars Above: Adventures in Modern Astrology*, London: Orion.

Stasulane, A. (2005) *Theosophy and Culture: Nicholas Roerich*, Rome: Pontificia università gregoriana.

——(2013) 'The Theosophy of the Roerichs: Agni Yoga or Living Ethics,' in Hammer and Rothstein, eds., *Handbook of the Theosophical Current*, Leiden: Brill, 193–216.

Trosper Schorey, S. (2013) 'Sleeping Prophet: The Life and Legacy of Edgar Cayce,' in Hammer and Rothstein, eds., *Handbook of the Theosophical Current*. Leiden: Brill, 135–50.

von Schnurbein, S. (1992) *Religion als Kulturkritik: neugermanisches Heidentum im 20. Jahrhundert*, Heidelberg: Winter.

Whitsel, B. (2003) *The Church Universal and Triumphant: Elizabeth Clare Prophet's Apocalyptic Movement*, Syracuse: Syracuse University Press.

Zander, H. (2007) *Anthroposophie in Deutschland. Theosophische Weltanschauung und gesellschaftliche Praxis 1884–1945*, 2 vols, Göttingen: Vandenhoeck and Ruprecht.

CHAPTER THIRTY-SEVEN

CONTEMPORARY PAGANISM AND THE OCCULT

Graham Harvey

Paganism has a number of sources, some more influential than others. Confluences and conflicts between such sources have shaped not only the evolution of the movement but also its diversification. Sometimes Pagans fuse previously or apparently discrete elements of other traditions, practices or ideologies. Sometimes they pay more or less attention to matters that others (Pagans or not) might deem central or peripheral to their interests. In this chapter, I survey the influence and inspiration of esotericism on the founders of significant Pagan movements in the early to mid-twentieth century and then consider the continuing performance of esotericism within some twenty-first-century Paganisms. In particular, I note that although esotericism has been of vital importance and major significance within Pagan movements and practice, it has always been tangled or braided with other sources of inspiration. These are not necessarily unique to Paganisms but the particular fusions that result are generative of specific groups or traditions. Naturism (of several kinds), for example, played a lively role in the creation of both Wicca and Pagan Druidry, while animism is now provoking considerable interest among diverse Pagans.

MAGIC AND WORSHIP

It has been a common habit of scholars and other people interested in such matters to distinguish magic from religion. A theme in such contrasts is that religion is defined by acts of worship offered to deities, recognising the power of such beings and seeking their aid. Magic, by contrast, is alleged to involve efforts to manipulate situations by various means under the control of the practitioner. Both religion and magic, so understood, can require training and involve techniques (and the validation of *appropriate* techniques) but magic may be thought to require more from the practitioner precisely because religion (focused on divinities) subjugates the practitioner to another being's greater ability. Such distinctions rarely operate so clearly in lived reality. Worshippers of deities might expect obvious and even dramatic changes in their conditions. Sometimes prayers or hymns are offered with the explicit and declared expectation that improved health, wealth or happiness will follow. Deities can be cajoled: they can be told not to expect more devotion if good (as the devotee defines it) does not follow. Similarly, the practice of magic can easily and regularly involve expressions of humility and limitation by the practitioner. Aid from more powerful beings or forces may be requested rather than engineered. It is, then, unlikely that esotericism should be treated simply as a technology or technique by which people seek to cause change (in themselves or their world) while religion should be treated as obeisance to greater beings. Indeed, the whole approach to defining 'religion' has been misdirected since the early modern European conflicts of nation state formation (mis-identified as 'the Wars of Religion') re-formed religion as a private and personal matter. (I have argued this more fully, and proposed a redefinition of religion as something like 'etiquettes of relationship between humans and the larger than human world', in Harvey, 2013. But see also Cavanaugh 1995 and King 2007.) Although misguided, such reforming and modernist approaches to religion and magic do form the context in which esotericism flourished and, more particularly, in which some Victorians and Edwardians, including some esotericists, valorised 'religious' Paganism.

Writers and poets (Rossetti, Swinburne, Wilde, Hardy, Lawrence and Forster, for example) met increasing urbanisation and industrialisation with evocative and romantic celebrations of the countryside, or 'nature',[1] and of bodies, or 'natural vigour'. They proposed that a nature-venerating Paganism (imagined as once having respected the countryside, rural life and wildlife) could worthily repair the damage being done by modernity. Even if this fondly held idea did not significantly diminish the further development of industry and the increasingly global trend towards urbanisation, it was immensely popular. Perhaps, indeed, it was popular because it was not fully or energetically realised in significant re-ruralisation or in alternative systems of production and consumption. It remained an urban myth just as 'wilderness' remains a utopian imaginary among present-day city dwellers. An element of this kind of 'naturism' (or 'religious naturalism') was the notion that deities of nature or elemental beings (of earth, air, fire and water) were – and could once more be – venerated in rural or wilderness retreats. Its attraction was perhaps rooted in romantic nostalgia but it has sometimes resulted in anarchic communalism or radical activism. Networks of nudist 'naturists' were foundational to the new Pagan movement while eco-activism has been generative (albeit contested) in its continuing evolution.

In a parallel development, a widespread fondness for classical (imagined) rural Paganism meshed with a growing fascination with female deities. At its most dramatic, this evoked a new deity: 'the Great Goddess' or 'the Mother Goddess'. The definite article is significant here. As the historian of ancient Paganisms and contemporary Paganisms Ronald Hutton has demonstrated (1998; 2011: 239),[2] the notion of a singular all-encompassing goddess is a modern novelty, albeit a powerful one that has proved resonant, popular and satisfying to many. While ancient pagans may have acknowledged the existence of such a being – for example, Isis as the one goddess who is all goddesses in Apuleius' *Metamorphosis* (Clifton and Harvey 2004: 15–18) – they only built shrines and venerated local or national deities for immediate rather than global or utterly transcendent purposes. In the nineteenth and early twentieth centuries, the cult and myth of 'the Goddess' were elaborated. This process has been so effective that it is now projected back into antiquity so that people imagine that a 'Great/Mother Goddess' associated with changing moon phases and with women's changing social roles (virgin, mother, crone) was a preeminent feature of ancient West Asian and European religions.

These emphases on putatively 'natural' or rural deities and/or female deities seem to have generated at least wistful hopes among some people for a revival of pagan religion. Hutton sums up much of this in saying:

> To the classical ancient world, as to the succeeding centuries until the nineteenth, the favourite deities had been those of civilisation. Now, however, the wild, horned, and goat-footed god came into his own, featuring as the patron of Kenneth Grahame's *The Wind in the Willows*, being hailed by Oscar Wilde, and appearing in the work of a host of lesser writers. Others preferred to adopt another ancient Greek image, that of Gaia, the presiding female spirit of the globe itself, so that references to Mother Earth and Mother Nature began to multiply, reverently, in the literature of the age. By 1900, the poetic vision of the English, when contemplating the rural world, was dominated as never before by the great goddess and the horned god.
>
> (Hutton 1996: 9)

Interest in 'fertility religion' and/or 'nature religion' increased significantly and became pervasive features of European and American popular cultures (Albanese 2002). This is the larger cultural context in which some esotericists contributed to the re-imagining and evocation of a new Paganism. In the idiom of the time their efforts were initially about 'magic' rather than 'religion'. Hutton, for example, comments that Aleister Crowley 'amalgamated pagan deities, Hebrew demons and redeveloped Christian ritual to produce a personal set of rites and beliefs linked by what may be termed therapeutic blasphemy'. He continues, 'as in all documented ceremonial magic of this period, the central impulse was not essentially religious; it was not to worship or honour supernatural beings so much as to gain personal power from them' (1996: 5). Whether or not the distinction works, esotericism was noticeably fusing with religiously inflected ideas about and engagements with 'nature'.

ESOTERICISM INTO PAGANISM

Wouter Hanegraaff has traced the historical trajectory by which esoteric ideas and practices have evolved into various twentieth- and twenty-first-century movements. He writes about the 'secularisation of esotericism' (e.g. Hanegraaff 2009: 349–51). Aspects of pagan (especially Egyptian, Greek and Roman), Jewish and Christian religions formed Renaissance Hermeticism and related esoteric currents. The European Enlightenment pressured this broadly religious esotericism into more technical and rationalist occultism. In one arena of that wide milieu of evolving religious/spiritual creativity, the worldview and especially the ritual structures of esotericism and occultism continue to have a significant role in shaping the activities and interests of contemporary Pagans.

From the 1930s to 1950s increasing numbers of people influenced by movements such as the Golden Dawn, the Theosophical Society and a number of Masonic or quasi-Masonic groups (e.g. esoteric and friendly society Druid Orders) identified themselves as Pagans. Gerald Gardner and Ross Nichols are the best known of these.

Short introductions to them will offer a flavour of the nascent Pagan movements that emerged from their efforts.

Gardner founded Wicca by bringing elements of esotericism together with other ideas and practices, especially those generated by Margaret Murray's spurious interpretation of the early modern 'witch' trials as a Christian persecution of a hidden pagan fertility cult. (Ronald Hutton details Murray's ideas, methods and influence in various works, including in his article on 'Revisionism and Counter-Revisionism in Pagan History', 2011.) Esoteric influence is evident, for instance, in the ways in which Gardner's new witches cast circular ritual working spaces using symbolic tools or daggers, purifying them with salt and water, and greeting forces, elements or beings associated with the cardinal directions. The robes and 'occult' symbols of Wicca are recognisably those of esotericists modelling themselves after Christian clergy or earlier pagan priesthoods. For example, five pointed stars are common Wiccan symbols but no longer refer to the five wounds of Christ (as they did in early medieval and mystical Christianity) but remain associated with protection. Similarly, the cords and blindfolds used in initiations, and Wicca's initiatory structures or 'degrees', are recognisably drawn from those of esoteric ritualism. In line with Hanegraaff's depiction of the secularising and popularising processes involved, these can also be depicted as 'democratising'. While there are hierarchies within Wicca there are only three degrees involved even for those who seek to run their own covens within a lineage of related groups. Even 'first degree' Wiccans are priestesses and priests. The language of esotericist magic predominates in Wiccan discourses so that a ritual is 'work' or 'working' in a 'temple' or 'circle'. This is not to say that Gardner and more recent Wiccans have not innovated. Not all Wiccans continued the ritual scourging that Gardner included in rituals, but nudity (when Wiccans are 'working' in closed, close-knit groups rather than in public ceremonies) remains significant.

Ross Nichols' formation of the Order of Bards, Ovates and Druids (OBOD) followed a popularising of previously more esotericist Druidry. While Welsh, Cornish and Breton Druidry were largely movements of resistance to the dominance of English and French cultures, English Druid Orders (prior to the 'paganisation' of the 1960s onwards) fused esotericism and the mutualism of Friendly Societies. Ceremonial practices and regalia paralleled those of Freemasonry or Co-Masonry but emphasised or added pointers to imagined Iron Age or 'Celtic' Druidry (e.g. golden sickles or pruning hooks for the cutting of mistletoe). In forming OBOD Nichols maintained interests in esoteric materials but increased the nature spirituality. Like Gardner, Nichols was a naturist, enjoying nudist retreats in woodlands in southern England and elsewhere. The movement he formed was not explicitly a Pagan one, and many OBOD members still identify with other religions or none, even while Pagan Druidry has proliferated with the creation of explicitly Pagan Orders. Nichols and his companions imagined an alternative historical lineage from Gardner's Wiccans. Rather than a fertility cult surviving Christian persecution, Druidry was identified as a nature-religion with significant precursors in antiquity and among antiquarians, such as John Aubrey and William Stukeley, and among inspired poets, such as William Blake. (Some of those claimed as ancestors or precursors did claim to be some sort of Druid, others however are likely to have objected to such an attribution.) OBOD used similar style clerical robes to Wiccans – and therefore to esotericists – but used colours to differentiate initiated bards, ovates and druids. Sometimes these sub-groups seem like parallels to the three 'degrees' of Wicca (i.e. as a progression from those who join to those who lead) but there is a common insistence that it is appropriate to want to improve as a bard or ovate without seeking the status of druid. There are other similarities and differences between the movements initiated by Gardner and Nichols but this brief outline is intended to highlight esoteric and naturist inspirations.

THE EIGHT FESTIVALS

In addition to discussing broader sweeps of the development of Paganisms within or out of earlier sources, Hutton's article on 'Modern Pagan Festivals' (2008) demonstrates precisely how Paganism materialised. The calendar or cycle of festivals celebrated by the majority of Pagans is noted by most commentators on Paganism (including Harvey 2006: 1–16). It provides an unrivalled lens through which to examine not only the performance and material cultures of the Pagan movement as a whole, or of particular traditions or subgroups, but also almost every conceivable feature of Paganism. Hutton demonstrates the analytical value of the festival cycle in a dialogue between the critical issues of the disciplines of History and Folklore.

The result is the possibility of stating a number of facts (all evidenced in Hutton 2008). Most Pagans now take it for granted that an annual cycle of eight seasonal festivals is central to their religion. Most Pagans (and many others) take it for granted that this calendar and its constituent festivals are of ancient origin. It is assumed that many of the celebratory practices associated with the 'eight festivals' are drawn from historical and folkloric evidence. A significant degree of adaptation is acknowledged as people today fit putatively ancient celebrations to contemporary needs or interests (such as ecology or feminism). However, there is no evidence of the existence of this cycle of festivals prior to its evolution in the 1950s. There is evidence of some of the constituent festival dates being significant in antiquity or more recent historical eras. For instance, Stonehenge's alignment to the midsummer solstice sunrise and midwinter solstice sunset strongly suggests the ancient celebration of those festivals. Precisely how these or other festivals were celebrated in the ancient past is either undocumented or poorly evidenced. (For example, Pliny's short evocation of a Druidic mistletoe ritual has been influential but only by a selective reading that ignores Pliny's dismissal of its frivolity and his insistence that it is a lunar festival; see Clifton and Harvey 2004: 19–20.) Two different cycles of festivals were brought together in the 1950s as Pagan Witchcraft and Druidry were creatively formed. The influence of the Welsh revivalist, Edward Williams (better known to Druids now as Iolo Morganwg) is evident in the identification from the late eighteenth century until now of the solstices and equinoxes as Druid festivals. The influence of Margaret Murray is evident in the celebration of 'the quarter days' (the first days of February, May, August and November) as the key festivals of witchcraft. Both Williams and Murray have been found to have taken a creative approach to evidence. Most Pagans are aware of this and have adjusted their origins narratives to deal with it. This adjustment can include the acknowledgement that Gerald Gardner and his colleagues were responsible for fusing the two festival cycles and relating them to celebrations of new and full moons. Doreen Valiente's liturgical and literary abilities, and the insistence of particular covens within Gardner's system, are important in the bedding down of these festivals as a taken-for-granted way of being or doing Paganism.

Particular features of this process demonstrate the originating and continuing relationship between esotericism and Paganism. Hutton notes, for example, that in Gardner's initial instructions, the influence of Murray is evident in the emphasis 'on dancing, feasting, games, songs or chants, and spell-casting, rather than on seasonal rites as such, in which the witches of the early modern imagination had shown no interest' (Hutton 2008: 256). Similarly, Hutton evokes a tension between witchcraft and priestcraft (not his word) in the performance of Gardner's Wicca: arguing that a priestess or priest 'can be simply a passive servant of the divine' while a witch 'is presumed to be a more active and productive agent' (Hutton 2008: 264). He shows that the festivals (initially at least) 'are essentially about the empowerment of the human participants, in making them (at least to themselves) more effective as inhabitants of the present world and assisting them to understand it and themselves to a greater extent' (2008: 265). The festivals are not about the veneration or propitiation of deities. There is no (non-symbolic) sacrifice and there is rarely a sense that deities might be dangerous or too powerful to be amenable to supporting the wishes of ritualists. What is evident here is an inheritance within the lineage from Hellenistic Egyptian magical papyri, through Renaissance Hermeticism to nineteenth-century esotericism. The festivals, although related to larger-than-human cosmic cycles, are opportunities for humans to achieve and utilise powers (variously conceived). They are 'magical rather than religious' in the way Hutton uses this distinction.

As an emphasis on 'nature' and 'nature-religion' increased among Pagans, the festivals did not entirely turn from magic to religion (understood in this way). They continued to place the practitioner or worker of magical rites at the centre. Hutton illustrates this with a series of examples. In *The Spiral Dance* (1979), Starhawk (perhaps the most famous feminist witch) and her Reclaiming colleagues created a 'series of seasonal rites that addressed human hopes and fears at each point of the Wiccan eight-festival cycle'; while the 'avowed aim' of Janet and Stewart Farrar's *Eight Sabbats for Witches* (1981) 'was to reintroduce urban people to the archetypal rhythms of the natural world' rather than to emphasise deity worship. In Vivianne Crowley's *Wicca* (1989) 'the seasonal rites featured as exemplifications of human maturation, as featured in Jungian psychology'; and more recent forms of ecologically orientated and/or non-denominationally organised Paganisms 'are essentially about the empowerment of the human participants, in making them (at least to themselves) more effective as inhabitants of the present world and assisting them to understand it and themselves to a greater extent' (Hutton 2008: 266–67). In these ways, Hutton admirably demonstrates that the new Pagan cycle ('wheel') of eight festivals served the purposes of people seeking a contemporary magical or esotericist spiritual practice.

LIVING NATURE

According to Antoine Faivre, 'living nature' is one of four 'fundamental characteristics' the simultaneous presence of which is required for something to be 'included in the field of esotericism' (Faivre and Needleman 1993: xv; Faivre 1994: 10–15). Within esotericism this *can* refer to notions of a cosmos replete with living beings or to a planet imbued with consciousness and/or agency. The Kabbalistic 'tree of life', with its ten spheres of concentrated powers, attributes or emanations from/to the ultimate divine, is sometimes utilised as a map of possible relationships by esotericists and Pagans. Versions of it are published in Pagan guides to magical practice and it structures the meditative visualisations association with recent elaborations of Tarot decks. Susan Greenwood makes excellent use of the tree glyph in describing the process by which she and others learn 'the language of another mode of reality' (2000: 49). She notes that there are tendencies to translate the whole process into an understanding of the training of consciousness or cognition but also demonstrates that magical training can be about learning to engage differently with a living world. Many beings not normally encountered in daily life are discovered and worked with. In her discussion, the continuing esoteric practice of many Pagans is brought into sharp focus.

I propose, however, to consider a contrast. As with all comparisons there is a danger that this will suggest stronger boundaries than actually exist. Indeed, the point of the following vignette is to demonstrate the fluid mingling of esotericism and animism (defined carefully below) in Pagan rituals. To be clear, esotericism continues to be an important source even when it mingles with more recent animistic notions of the 'living world'. So, the vignette is of a typical Pagan festival celebration and just happens to have taken place among Druids.

It is the feast of Lughnasad, 1 August. Saying what the festival is about is difficult without prejudicing expectations of what might happen. In several senses, it is about harvest. It is timed around the traditional beginning of the grain harvest in Britain. It could be a first fruits harvest festival. It is also (to suggest only one other possibility) considered a suitable time to meditate on 'inner harvests', i.e. on the results of a longer period of personal growth, or fulfilled or thwarted intentions and ambitions. Herein lies a tension between esoteric and animist ritualism.

In a pasture field somewhere near ancient sacred sites but relatively secluded, away from non-participating others, a Druid group is gathered. They have camped here for up to a week prior to this central Lughnasad ritual, and most will continuing camping here for a few more days. Episodes of conviviality and learning have structured the camp's days and nights so far. But this day has involved a quite serious mood almost entirely anticipating this ritual. Subgroups have prepared elements of the event. Some attending to the physical location, others to practicing appropriate songs or ritual gestures to be performed for or with the full community. One small group has gone to a nearby organic barley field and cut grain, offering greetings and gratitude in the process. Some have ground grain and baked flour in a replica Iron Age–style oven built for the purpose. Experimentation and enthusiasm have synthesised in these spiritual exercises. Finally, people have donned costumes and jewellery, floral wreaths or other signs of festivity. Led by senior Druids and musicians, a procession slowly forms a circle. Variations on standard purificatory demarcations of the circle and on the greeting of the four cardinal directions (and associated elements, guardians or powers) are conducted by pre-selected officers or volunteers. Esoteric heritage is most evident here. A ritual drama of the harvest is presented – mixing entertainment into the serious business of focusing attention on the key matter. Following a number of other offered contributions to the celebration, loaves of bread and cups or horns of barley wine or mead are shared around the circle. Community is celebrated and created. A speech is made about Lughnasad and its place in the ever-turning wheel of the year. All participants are invited to say something about the festival. Both the speech and the short statements evidence a considerable variety of understanding. Finally, ritualised farewells are offered to the quarters, the ceremony is closed and people depart from the circle.

The variety in the speech and statements demands more attention because they are expressive of a creative tension that has been growing within Paganism. The ritualist privileged to speak about the festival fairly concisely summed up an esotericist or at least highly symbolic understanding of the ritual. It was, he asserted as if it were uncontentious, the purpose of Lughnasad celebrations to provide this opportunity to reflect on who we have become since we set out our intentions for the year. The bread and drink symbolise the 'inner' harvest of better lives. They represent nourishment of the joy of fulfilled desires or hopes. For many people, this was almost certainly uncontentious. Lughnasad is one of eight festivals in which each person seeks personal growth towards being a more spiritual person. They do so in company and with pleasure, but it is as individuals, as a 'priesthood of all believers', that they engage in ritual. (The Protestant influence on British versions of esotericism is unmistakable.) For others, however, it was something of a surprise to find that in this particular celebration of Lughnasad, a whole other distinct but complementary emphasis went unremarked in this speech. Some of those who had cut the grain, ground the flour, baked the bread and shared the meal had thought that they were taking an opportunity to acknowledge and be grateful for the nourishment provided (self-sacrificially) by grain. A more animistic communion with specific other-than-human persons was forefront to them. Personal growth, for some, could remain a personal (relatively private) matter. Communion with others or the etiquette of relationship in a larger-than-human world was the reason for participating in communal seasonal rites.

ESOTERICISM AND ANIMISM

In this and similar events no voice was raised in objection. No protest or division occurred. Perhaps only the few people who explicitly told me about their experience in this ritual were aware of the tensions they expressed. In many Pagan events there is an easy flow between different notions of the 'living world' and different ways of acting that they express. Esotericism has much to do with the inner life of individuals who seek to transmute their ordinary existence and habits into more elevated, intentional, or spiritual awareness. It draws on long-established traditions and practices to represent, evoke and empower new consciousness. It generates rich ceremonies and profound changes in people's lives. The Eleusinian words 'know thyself' might sum up much of esotericism – and are revisioned at the heart of Wicca processes. However, because of the flow of other sources into the streams of Paganism, esotericism is braided with the somewhat different world of 'animism'.

This label requires care because it can still be associated with the kind of phenomena imagined by Edward Tylor for whom, in his *Primitive Culture* (1871), 'animism' meant 'belief in spirits'. Certainly there are Pagans (and others) who express beliefs about spirits. But there is a 'new animism', a new theory that uses the same word to speak of phenomena widespread in time and space. Elsewhere I have summed up much of the new approach to animism as research concerned with ways of treating the world as a community of persons, most of whom are other-than-human but all of whom deserve respect (Harvey 2005, alluding to the foundational work of Irving Hallowell 1960). It invites attention to relationships, performance and materiality of religion rather than to beliefs or intentions. It does not ignore the fact that some religious practitioners, including esotericists, emphasise intentionality and interiority. However, it places these more solidly in the context of performative and material relationality.

Alongside growing academic attention to such matters (e.g. in Vásquez 2011), animism has been gaining resonance among Pagans. Esotericism, naturism, feminism and environmentalism have played important roles in the post-1950s evolution of Paganisms. Increasingly, these and other currents have cast light on the co-dwelling of humans alongside other species in a material and relational world. For some Pagans, animism seems to sum up a current phase of seeking to relate more respectfully with the world than the larger late-modern culture encourages. It sums up an emphasis of many celebrants in the Lughnasad ritual for whom gratitude to grain and bread is more important than any symbolic or representational role such things might be given or afforded in more-esoteric rituals.

It is important, again, to emphasise the difficulties of writing about two trajectories within Paganism without strongly suggesting that they are absolute contrasts. In lived reality, the esoteric spring continues to flow into animist rituals, mingled with influences from many or all of the other sources that have been significant. These are, perhaps, only heuristically useful distinctions except when, on a few occasions out of many, a particular speech or act stresses one theme or ignores other possibilities. Generally, Pagans are adept at multivalent speaking and simultaneous translation. That is, they can say 'Goddess' when they mean (at the same time) 'the one deity', 'the community of all deities', 'the non-theistic complex of the cosmos', 'all of us in this together' and more. Just as one person can say 'Goddess' and mean these many things (or just one of them in some cases), Pagans hearing the word regularly take it to mean just 'whatever they want it to mean, neither more nor less' (to paraphrase Lewis Carroll's Humpty Dumpty, Carroll 1872). Only rarely does a specific emphasis weigh too heavily to allow other ideas to grow. Thus, when some ritualists insist (as some more esotericist Pagans do) that the intention of a ritual determines all then there might be less room for others to lay stress on acts performed towards others (as more animist Pagans might). Even in such cases, other conditions and sources of influence are involved. In short, my efforts to point out one of the current tensions with esotericism in Paganism is not intended to have any particular point of the vibrant tapestry of possibilities identified as 'more definitively Pagan' than any other. This is, rather, an effort to see Pagan esotericism and its fuzzy boundaries more clearly by attending to one relationship, that of esotericism with animism.

UNIVERSALISM TO PARTICULARISM

Ronald Hutton has identified four 'direct lines of connection' between ancient Paganism and the present. These are 'high ritual magic, "hedge" witchcraft, the general love affair of the Christian centuries with the art and literature of the ancient world, and folk rites' (1996). His disciplined exploration of the links between the Paganisms of the past and the present Paganisms contrasts with the early twentieth-century academic practices which provided a major impetus to the birth of Paganism.

What Gardner, Nichols, Valiente and many others created was not a revival of ancient religions (whether of peasants seeking fertility or elites seeking wisdom). It was a fusion of esotericism with other culturally vibrant forms in their time. Esotericism and naturism (of several kinds) assembled together to make various forms of Paganism relevant to their contemporaries. Magical training and ritualism allied with creatively imagined calendar customs played starring roles. Tensions with the Protestant denigration of ritual (or ritualism) were evident among esotericists but perhaps become more dramatic when the stuff being celebrated was as ordinary as sunrises, moonrises, fecundity and health. The democratisation of esotericism was spurred on by experiments with new authority structures consequent on the rise of feminism and its impact among Pagans. A dramatic shift away from fertility towards the celebration of vitality almost certainly made a better match with the desires of Victorian and Edwardian romantics but absolutely certainly made more sense from the 1960s onwards. When Pagans were confronted by increasing assaults on ecological diversity, their naturism became more about environmentalism than nudism (though the latter has not disappeared). Animism emphasised one characteristic of esotericism but braided it into the ecological engagement with a larger-than-human world in which relational etiquette is at least as significant as personal consciousness.

This sketch of the origins and evolution of contemporary Paganism has paid particular attention to Druidry and Wicca. Other important traditions such as Heathenry and Goddess Spirituality could provide material to enrich this picture. European esoteric traditions and practices underlie much of Paganism today – especially but not only the most common ritual patterns and protocols. As popularised forms of esotericism, Paganisms fuse and hybridise other available or appropriated cultural forms to advance the particular variation that Pagan individuals or groups deem most interesting or important. The influence of Protestant Christianity and Enlightenment rationalism are evident in a number of places, including when more universalist themes (such as consciousness or intentionality) are determinative. Recently, however, a more animistic trend has become evident, especially as or when Pagans devote increasing attention to their more immediate locality and larger than human community. If, as Ronald Hutton has said on a number of occasions, Pagan witchcraft is the only religion the English have given the world, the varied ways in which Pagans mix their sources means that Paganism (in its varied forms) does not remain 'English' for long. It interacts excitingly with local needs, perceptions, relations and protocols to become yet more diverse and, probably, continuously relevant to its time and place.

NOTES

1 My use of scare quotes around 'nature' indicates that while this term evokes emphases of importance to Pagans and their scholarly observers, I reject the false nature/culture dualism with which it is entangled. I tackle this more carefully in Harvey (2013).

2 I am grateful to Ronald Hutton for the excellent quality of his research which, as will be clear throughout this chapter, provides an unrivalled foundation for understanding the evolution of Paganisms.

REFERENCES AND FURTHER READING

Albanese, C.L. (2002) *Reconsidering Nature Religion*, Harrisburg: Trinity Press.

Carroll, L. (1872) *Through the Looking Glass*, Published in a combined volume in 1962 with *Alice's Adventures in Wonderland*, London: Puffin.

Cavanaugh, W.T. (1995) 'A Fire Strong Enough to Consume the House: "The Wars of Religion" and the Rise of the State', *Modern Theology* 11.4: 397–420.

Crowley, V. (1989) *Wicca*, London: Aquarian.

Clifton, C.S., and Harvey, G., eds. (2004) *The Paganism Reader*, London: Routledge.

Faivre, A., and J. Needleman, eds. (1993) *Modern Esoteric Spirituality*, London: SCM Press.

Faivre, A. (1994) *Access to Western Esotericism*, Albany: State University of New York Press.

Farrar, J., and S. Farrar (1981) *Eight Sabbats for Witches*, London: Hale.

Greenwood, S. (2000) *Magic, Witchcraft and the Otherworld: An Anthropology*, Oxford: Berg.

Hallowell, A. I. (1960) 'Ojibwa Ontology, Behavior, and World View', in Stanley Diamond, ed., *Culture in History: Essays in Honor of Paul Radin*, New York: Columbia University Press, 19–52. Reprinted in Harvey, G., ed. (2002) *Readings in Indigenous Religions*, London: Continuum, 18–49.

Hanegraaff, W. (2009) 'New Age religion,' in L. Woodhead, H. and C. Partridge, eds., *Religions in the Modern World: Traditions and Transformations* (second edition), London: Routledge, 339–56.

Harvey, G. (2005) *Animism: Respecting the Living World*, London: C. Hurst & Co.; New York: Columbia University Press.

——(2006) *Listening People, Speaking Earth: Contemporary Paganism* (second edition), London: Hurst.

——(2013) *Food, Sex and Strangers: Understanding Religion as Everyday Life*, London: Routledge.

Hutton, R. (1996) 'The Roots of Modern Paganism,' in Graham Harvey and Charlotte Hardman, eds., *Paganism Today*, London: Thorsons, 3–15.

——(1998) *The Triumph of the Moon: A History of Modern Witchcraft*, Oxford: Oxford University Press.

——(2008) 'Modern Pagan Festivals: A Study in the Nature of Tradition,' *Folklore*, 119.3: 251–73.

——(2011) 'Revisionism and Counter-Revisionism in Pagan History,' *The Pomegranate*, 13.2: 225–56.

King, R. (2007) 'The Association of "religion" with violence: Reflections on a modern trope,' in John R. Hinnells and Richard King, eds., *Religion and Violence in South Asian Theory and Practice*, 226–57.

Starhawk (1979) *The Spiral Dance*, San Francisco: Harper and Row.

Tylor, E. (1871) *Primitive Culture*, 2 vols, London: John Murray.

Vásquez, M.A. (2011) *More than Belief: A Materialist Theory of Religion*, Oxford: Oxford University Press.

CHAPTER THIRTY-EIGHT

NEW AGE

Olav Hammer

INTRODUCTION

In a West where the Christian churches no longer have any ideological hegemony, various forms of 'alternative' religion have become widespread indeed. Whereas organized new religious movements (NRMs) tend to attract few people, looser forms of religiosity have entered the cultural mainstream. These include such miscellaneous interests as astrology, Reiki healing, channeling, past life regression, aura photography, swimming with dolphins, and positive thinking. In much of the scholarly literature that has appeared on these topics, the term New Age is used to sum up these interests (e.g., Heelas 1996; Hanegraaff 1996). Other authors insist, on the contrary, that the epithet 'New Age' is meaningless, derogatory, or a term made up by the mass media (e.g., Wood 2007; Bochinger 1994; see Chryssides 2007 for a discussion of the issues involved).

The term New Age originally arose in Theosophical milieus in connection with the expectation that humanity stood poised to take a bold leap into a millenarian epoch, a time when the consciousness of our species would take a collective bound forward. Theosophist Alice Bailey (1880–1949) is credited with having coined the term.

In the 1960s, a cohort of young people in particular were inspired by astrological language, and by the belief that an astronomical phenomenon known as the precession of the equinoxes would take us into a new Aquarian Age, to expect the imminent dawning of a new era. Many of those who were sympathetic to these utopian strivings were interested in pursuits such as healing, channeling, and divination, but saw them as tools in this overall transformation, rather than as ends in themselves. As the years passed and global consciousness did not morph into a higher mode, the millenarian aspiration became less common. It does have its defenders even at the time of writing (e.g., among those who in 2012 awaited the end of the Mayan Calendar, or speculate that a new breed of Indigo Children are being born into the world, ready to finally make the grand dream of spiritual transmutation come true). More commonly, however, the label New Age has been retained in the media and in the terminology of outsiders in order to refer to the wide variety of practices listed above, with no hint of a collective aspiration. Today, most individuals interested in tarot cards or *chakra* healing have more modest expectations, and usually hope first of all to improve their own situation. In fact, one of the earliest attempts to find a common element uniting the many offers on the New Age market was the contention that the basic message is that there is something wrong with us, but also that there are almost magical methods and remedies at hand (Heelas 1996: 18–19, 24–26). The term New Age, it should be noted, is rarely used by those who experiment with these remedies and methods, but no generally accepted sobriquet has come to replace 'New Age.'

Even a short sample of New Age components, such as those listed above, illustrates that diversity characterizes the field. Not only is the list of common components quite diverse – New Age interests also have a tendency to emerge, peak, and subside again with bewildering rapidity. Books on New Age thinking that it was *de rigueur* to read at one point in time can be virtually obsolete five or ten years later. One might suspect that we are dealing with a field of spiritual anarchy where anything goes, and that 'New Age' is just convenient shorthand for whatever happens to be in fashion in religious popular culture at any particular time. The first part of this chapter is an attempt to counteract this first impression, and to uncover some commonly shared presuppositions that show that 'New Age' is more than an empty signifier.

The second section of this chapter will examine some of the main components of the New Age in somewhat closer detail. The third section will address the question why the New Age is so volatile and heterogeneous. The concluding fourth and fifth sections will examine the historical background and the processes of change that have made New Age into what it is at present. In particular, this account of the New Age will show that many of the conceptions and activities prevalent in New Age milieus can be understood as an adaptation of older beliefs and practices to the characteristics of contemporary society.

CORE CONCERNS OF NEW AGE RELIGIOSITY

We are prey to an uncertain destiny, the prospect of disease and, ultimately, death. Such existential concerns are in most forms of folk religiosity addressed in a practical and unsystematic fashion, often through a process of *bricolage* from already available narratives and rituals. Only rarely does the theological impulse arise to systematically formulate an overarching vision of the human condition in religious terms.

In this respect, much of the New Age is indeed a mode of folk religiosity. Illness is remedied by a variety of healing rituals. Astrologers, tarot readers, and other diviners attempt to ritualistically foretell the future. Narratives about our previous incarnations offer the hope that physical death is not the end, but merely a transition to something new and perhaps better. However, details of how the various healing systems are supposed to work can be left open, the specific views presented by different tarot readers and astrologers can be vague and mutually inconsistent, and the particular theories of reincarnation found in New Age texts can be nebulous. A minimal shared worldview, rarely spelled out explicitly, can nevertheless be reconstructed from the mass of conflicting details (Hammer 2005):

- The underlying 'stuff' of the cosmos is not matter but something intangible, perhaps identifiable as consciousness or energy.

- We humans contain a spark of this energy or consciousness within us, a resource that we can tap into in order to change reality and create our own worlds.
- The human being is thus not only a material body, but also comprises a mind and a spiritual element. When ill, one needs to address all of these elements, rather than merely treat individual physical symptoms.
- Each of us is embarked on a journey of spiritual development, a development that will not stop at the death of the physical body but will continue over many lives.
- There are better ways to get to understand the world we live in and our own place in it than via the intellect. Perhaps we can gain spiritual insight in flashes of intuition. Perhaps there are prophetic states in which we can access knowledge from various highly developed beings, or from a divine part of our selves. A variety of techniques such as astrology or the tarot can also have this function.
- Similar insights into the workings of the cosmos and into our own selves were granted to a number of ancient cultures, ranging from Egypt, India, and Tibet, to the native Americas.
- Such insights are confirmed by the most recent developments of Western science, especially quantum mechanics.
- Spirituality is not a matter of accepting doctrines formulated by others, but rather a highly individual quest, that should be based primarily on personal experience.
- We can either as individuals or collectively change the world into a better place by adopting such a spiritual vision.

Besides comprising a diffuse worldview, as summarized in the list above, the New Age is also an intensely ritualistic form of religion. The belief that body, mind, and spirit form a whole and should be treated as such has led to a profusion of systems of ritual healing that New Agers understand to be holistic. The idea that there are states of consciousness in which it is possible to access spiritual knowledge has led to the emergence of ritualized means of reaching such states, generally termed *channeling*. The belief in a plan of spiritual evolution has generated a variety of divinatory techniques that purportedly allow us to gain insight into this plan.

CONCEPTS AND PRACTICES OF NEW AGE RELIGIOSITY

Healing

Medical anthropology distinguishes disease (which is definable from a biomedical perspective) from illness (which is defined within a given local worldview). Although Western forms of complementary medicine certainly also attract clients with biomedically definable diseases, the spiritual aspect of healing within a New Age framework typically implies addressing culturally defined states of illness. Indeed, New Age conceptions of health can imply such an optimal level of physical, emotional, and spiritual functioning that much more vaguely perceived conditions – social and existential problems, a less than optimal level of vitality – can be seen as issues that need to be addressed.

The methods employed in healing vary from the laying on of hands to the use of a broad variety of ritual substances and objects. Reiki and Therapeutic Touch involve the use of the healer's hands. Crystal healing presupposes that gems and minerals possess healing properties. Color therapies and Aura-Soma therapy assume that colors influence physical and spiritual well-being. Bach Flower Remedies attempt to derive similar effects from plant extracts.

These ritual methods rely on a few basic – and often vaguely formulated – presuppositions about the cosmos and the constitution of the human body. Three such presuppositions are common to a diverse set of practices. First, it is generally held that there are normally invisible vital forces ('energies') that surround and/or pass through the human body, and that the therapist is able to manipulate. This hidden physiology is often understood to comprise seven or more centers of vital force, the *chakras*. Second, the body is a holistic system. The body as a whole is mirrored in the feet (reflexology), on the outer ears (as in one modern, Western development of acupuncture), or in the eyes (iridology). Theories of Chinese origin, according to which the vital forces flow through channels connecting the diverse parts of the body into an integrated whole, are frequently referred to by New Age healers. Third, body and spirit are also part of a whole. By treating the body, the spirit can be healed. Conversely, by treating the spirit the body is healed. In a kind of epistemological circle, healers can feel assured of the validity of these ideas because they can see that healing works, and explain why healing works in terms of those ideas.

Channeling

In traditional cultures throughout the world, religious specialists have functioned as links between human beings and what each culture understands to be a suprahuman reality. The New Age counterpart of this process of prophetic revelation is generally known as channeling.

There are, broadly speaking, two main types of channeled messages. The first presents an alternative view of cosmology and history. Information is given about legendary continents such as Atlantis, Lemuria, and Mu. We are told of mysterious events in the near future, predictions that we will experience a shift in dimension or consciousness, or even have our DNA restructured. Readers of such channeled texts are presented with communications from beings living in distant parts of the galaxy. Much of this material feeds into and feeds off popular culture, and is ultimately (albeit often implicitly) influenced by the works of Theosophical and other occultist authors.

The second type of channeled texts conveys a synthesis of psychology and religion, a genre of self-help spirituality that has constituted an important part of Western religious thought since the late nineteenth century. The underlying message is, once again, that we live suboptimal lives, and the channeled messages attempt to diagnose our condition and provide help. The root cause of our problem can be fear and guilt, excessive rationality, and materialism. Since we create our own reality and attract events and people that match our level of awareness (an axiomatic truth in much New Age literature), we need the necessary tools to reprogram our minds. If we bring out our true, high or divine selves, the world will be miraculously transformed. Health, happiness, creativity, even material affluence, will then be ours.

Divination

Although obviously an ancient system of divination, astrology has become part of the New Age milieu, and has adopted many of the traits that underlie New Age religiosity. Predictive astrology, as e.g., in sun-sign columns, still has many users, but many contemporary astrologers prefer seeing astrology as a method for achieving inner, spiritual change. The chart is perceived as a blueprint of a person's character, and consultations with psychologizing astrologers will often address the challenges perceived to be inherent in that blueprint. Tarot cards, perhaps the most popular method of divination within the New Age milieu, have been provided with similar psychologizing modes of interpretation.

SOCIAL CHARACTERISTICS OF THE NEW AGE MILIEU

Besides a number of underlying presuppositions and a set of common practices, the New Age is also characterized by the self-perception of its members, and by its social structures. People who are interested in New Age pursuits and accept most of the underlying presuppositions engage in what an outsider might characterize as a religious current: there are conceptions regarding a transcendent dimension, ritual means of getting in touch with that dimension, afterlife beliefs, prophetic writings – all of which are part of the basic setup of what most of us would be willing to characterize as 'religion.' Nevertheless, most New Agers would never accept the term 'religion' for their own beliefs and practices, they perform rituals without being aware of doing so, and frequently do not regard their own beliefs and practices as part of any wider New Age movement but rather as an expression of their individual quest.

An important reason for this self-perception is the culture critique intrinsic to much of the New Age (see also Hanegraaff 1996: 515–17). For many, the very word 'religion' is hopelessly tainted with what they see as authoritarian structures, where people at the top of the organizational hierarchy impose their views on others, while the term 'ritual' can seem to connote mere outward appearance and meaningless repetition. A widespread linguistic distinction sets apart more loosely organized beliefs and practices as 'spiritual,' and the more fixed as 'religious.'

The qualifier 'loosely organized' is of key importance in this context. New Age beliefs and practices are characterized by being created and disseminated by very different social channels than the churches of mainstream Christianity, or the institutional pillars of society that ensure that a science-based worldview is at least minimally familiar to most people. Astrology and channeling belong to a different kind of religiosity, the *cultic milieu* identified by Colin Campbell (1972). The cultic milieu consists of the vast numbers of individuals who have adopted a variety of beliefs and practices that from the majority point of view may seem more or less unorthodox, but are unwilling to join a tightly organized new religious movement. Campbell suggested that religious innovations tend to arise out of the cultic milieu, thrive for a while, and will typically pass into oblivion after a few years.

The cultic milieu can support unrelated and at times even mutually contradictory beliefs, simply because they share an inherent culture critique. Reiki healing, astrology, and spiritually uplifting messages channeled from space beings may seem to be very different phenomena, but they do share the characteristic of thriving without any support from churches, publicly funded schools, the health care system, corporations, or the legal system. People who want to defend the value of New Age religiosity often do so in defiance of the worldview espoused by the majority. Some believers may be tempted to explain their minority position as the effect of a spiritual awakening that sets them apart from the more skeptically inclined. Others can accuse a powerful materialistic establishment for ignoring or suppressing inconvenient truths.

Out of this sentiment of constituting an alternative to the cultural mainstream, a cultic milieu arises: People in a minority position find common interests, gradually form a social network, and become aware of each others' interests: tarot readers meet healers, UFO enthusiasts read texts produced by channelers. In this meeting ground of unorthodox pursuits, narratives are exchanged, experiences shared, and new syntheses between previously unrelated ideas and practices can arise. Some of these innovations become important new religious trends, while others remain the more or less idiosyncratic products of their originators.

Since the innovative spokespersons of the New Age are deeply immersed in the cultic milieu, they will rarely build their new doctrines and rituals from nothing. More commonly, already available methods of healing, divination, or channeling will be reformulated or recombined in new ways. In this manner, a historical chain of doctrines and their predecessors can be traced back in time, and the New Age emerges as a tradition with less diffuse contours than might be suspected at first. Out of all the possible modalities of, say, healing or divination that ethnographic studies have documented, very few have any following among New Agers in the West. Reiki-style laying on of hands, or Chinese-inspired methods of manipulating 'energies' are common ways of tackling illness; sacrificing a fowl to the ancestors is not.

ROOTS: THE ESOTERIC BACKGROUND

New Agers are by no means unaware that their practices have a historical background, and can insist that their own doctrines and rituals have roots in ancient or exotic cultures. Egypt, India, China, Tibet, the Native Americas, or even mythical continents of Atlantis and Lemuria, or locations in outer space such as Sirius or the Pleiades, can be seen as the ultimate origins of one's own methods and creeds. Academic studies are more inclined to see the New Age as an eclectic blend of numerous historic sources of inspiration, most prominently several varieties of Western esotericism (Hanegraaff 1996). To the extent that imported elements and more distant origins in India or China are involved, these are often quite radically reinterpreted to suit the preconceptions that Westerners hold.

Some mainstays of New Age thinking have very early predecessors in Western intellectual culture. The suggestion that human beings have a divine self within resonates with anthropologies of late Antiquity. Other historical links, as demonstrated by Wouter J. Hanegraaff (1996), can be traced back to esoteric movements in the Renaissance and early modern period. Arguably, the New Age has its most direct predecessors in the nineteenth century. New Age healing practices are prefigured by the mesmerist movement that was in vogue in the early nineteenth century. Mesmer's methods resemble the rituals of contemporary healing. His attempts to explain his success in scientific terms anticipate similar appeals to the scientific validity of New Age practices. The more mystical mesmerism of several of Mesmer's disciples is reminiscent of New Age interests in esoteric cosmologies, in paranormal phenomena, and in the purported latent powers of the mind. Out of these late-nineteenth-century circles came the first 'channeled' texts.

Although New Age religiosity is eclectic, three historical sources of inspiration are particularly important. A first major source is Theosophy, founded by Helena Petrovna Blavatsky, but significantly modified by her successors Annie Besant and Charles W. Leadbeater. Theosophy is the most obvious source for many of the occult and speculative elements that one finds in the New Age. Contemporary conceptions of reincarnation and karma are by New Agers often attributed to Indian roots, but have more do with Theosophical understandings of rebirth as a didactic, evolutionary process, than with Hindu or Buddhist understandings of transmigration. Theories about lost continents such as Atlantis, and alternative histories of ancient civilizations such as Egypt, also have Theosophical roots. Moreover, Theosophy is the source of widespread beliefs in an occult physiology of the human body, as described earlier.

A second major source is the 'harmonial' or New Thought movements of the late nineteenth century. These were currents based on a creed of personal well-being and prosperity, and on the conviction that our beliefs and attitudes shape the world in which we live. Whatever we experience is the result of the mind-set that we project onto our surroundings. If we have negative thoughts, we will come to live in a fearful and negative reality; if we manage to practice positive thinking, our world will reflect that positivity back on us.

A third, more recent source is constituted by various twentieth-century syntheses between psychology and religion. No single person or movement is responsible for this merging of psychology and religious belief. The harmonial religions sketched above, with their conflation of attitude and reality, have clearly contributed to this historical process. Other important factors have been the popularization of the theories of Carl Gustav Jung, and the emergence in the 1950s and 1960s of humanistic and transpersonal psychology.

In the second half of the twentieth century a small cultic milieu emerged in which Theosophy, the harmonial religions, and popular, 'spiritualized' psychology could combine in innovative syntheses. These religious innovations were at first of marginal significance, but with the explosion of the counterculture in the 1960s and early 1970s, this situation soon changed. Traditional Christianity was seen as ossified and uninteresting by many young people, and various alternatives were explored. Some gravitated toward Asian religions such as Zen Buddhism or Advaita Vedanta, others experimented with New Religious Movements, and yet others with the mixture of esoteric religiosities mentioned earlier. A high level of commitment to Oriental religions or NRMs remained an option for a small minority; the eclectic, experimental, and largely esoteric religiosity outlined above attracted much larger numbers of 'spiritual seekers.' In the 1960s, a loose network of vaguely like-minded people committed to a utopian vision built on such a variety of doctrinal foundations had formed, and, by the early 1970s, the term New Age had become an increasingly common label for this network.

Forty years have at the time of writing passed since the New Age label was first adopted, and significant changes have taken place. Some are perhaps superficial, and can be attributed to the volatile nature of any cultic milieu: new practices (innovative methods of healing, swimming with dolphins, speculations regarding the Mayan calendar) have been introduced, bestselling books (*The Celestine Prophecy*, *Conversations with God*) have been introduced on the market, and were on the bestseller lists for a while until interest largely faded out again.

Other changes are more profound or structural. Over time, New Age appears to have transformed from a network or social movement with a utopian focus, into a form of vague shared discourse and a fund of common practices. The belief in the imminent spiritual transmutation, which originally gave the New Age its name, has lost much of its strength. Some New Age beliefs and practices have entered mainstream society: positive thinking is found in many sectors of society, and complementary medicine based on New Age ideas of occult physiologies and invisible and intangible 'energies' attracts clients from all walks of life. The most radically countercultural elements of the first generation of New Age belief have tacitly been dropped. There has been a shift in the New Age constituency from younger people to a larger and perhaps more middle age group. And, as noted earlier in this chapter, whereas the first generation of New Age spokespersons used 'New Age' as a self-designation, the term has become increasingly understood as a pejorative, even meaningless epithet. No new self-designation for their collective identity seems to have formed, signaling that there is no longer the same awareness of forming part of a coherent milieu. The New Age *movement* may be on the wane, but the wider New Age *religiosity*, i.e., a historically related group of doctrines and rituals, linked by a tenuous and largely invisible set of common underlying presuppositions, shows no sign of fading away.

NEW AGE RELIGION AND MODERNITY

Whereas the preceding chapter has emphasized historical roots, the New Age can also be seen as a religious phenomenon that reflects characteristically modern, Western conditions and preoccupations. Four such symptoms of modernity will concern us here: globalization, commodification, individualism, and the appeal to scientific rationality.

The very fact that so many diverse cultures and traditions are mined for inspiration is the result of a contemporary phenomenon, namely massive globalization. Admittedly, earlier forms of esotericism were also the result of a *bricolage* of biblical, Platonic, kabbalistic, hermetic, and other elements of quite diverse origins, but modernity has vastly expanded the fund of available cultural elements from which one can pick and choose. A small sample of exotic ingredients that may interest New Agers, picked largely at random, can include Chinese medicine, Hawaiian huna, Egyptian mysteries, Celtic legends, the putatively healing effects of Mongolian chanting, and Siberian shamanism – all of which, in the process of incorporation into the New Age, are adapted and transformed, sometimes almost beyond recognition.

Commodification is the process by which New Age rituals, courses, books, and other products are marketed and sold in the same way as other goods and services in modern society are sold. Since there are no large top-down organizations that can impose a list of canonical writings, or prescribe the 'correct' mode of performing rituals, New Age pursuits are to a large extent formed by the forces of supply and demand. Best-selling books, for instance, will influence a large readership, but will on the other hand probably only become bestsellers if they resonate with the already existing interests of a potential readership.

Individualism, i.e., the assumption that our own sentiments are more important than the suggestions of external authorities, is a key element in the self-understanding of the New Age milieu, and New Age texts will characteristically suggest that their readers only retain from a given doctrine what is perceived as useful and subjectively true. The metaphor of the spiritual supermarket is commonly employed as a way of describing a vast market of New Age goods that one can pick or discard *ad libitum*. An apt but sometimes overlooked aspect of the supermarket metaphor is that the goods on offer are manufactured by others, and that consumer choice is powerfully influenced by external factors such as the media, markets forces and the predilections of other people in one's personal networks (Hammer 2010).

Finally, although New Age texts are concerned with affirming the ancient roots of the New Age, they are equally interested in demonstrating the scientific nature of their endeavors (Hammer 2001, esp. ch. 5). New Age texts may abound with terminology borrowed from science: energy, vibration, dimension, frequency, and quantum. New Age rituals can use simulacra of technological apparatuses as ritual objects, e.g., cameras purportedly able to capture the aura surrounding the body. Attempts to gain scientific legitimacy have resulted in the publication of several influential texts that attempt to show that physics and mysticism point at the same reality. The paradigmatic example of New Age science is Fritjof Capra's *The Tao of Physics*. Capra (b. 1939) claimed that there are suggestive parallels between the statements made by mystics of various Eastern traditions and those made by twentieth-century physicists. New Age exegetes of science after Capra have radicalized his claims, arguing that quantum mechanics can explain ESP or healing.

The modernity of the New Age is, however, limited. Thus, New Age understandings of personal experience are in a sense pre-critical. They usually eschew any discussion of the constructed nature of experience, and typically view spiritual experience as a faithful representation of underlying reality. Furthermore, in a characteristic paradox of New Age religiosity, the notion of an entirely individualistic spiritual quest can imply participating in rituals scripted by others and adopting explanatory frameworks expounded by authoritative spokespersons.

CONCLUDING REMARKS

As noted above, a number of concepts associated only a couple of decades ago with the New Age, such as the millennialist aspirations, have become marginal interests. Other beliefs, such as the existence of Atlantis, are also mainly found in small, occultist segments of the New Age, presumably due to the difficulties in reconciling such views with elementary scientific literacy. At the same time, other forms of New Age thinking have become vital parts of popular culture. Prominent New Age authors such as Deepak Chopra (b. 1947) and James Redfield (b. 1950) sell millions of copies of their books and become celebrities far beyond the confines of an underground cultic milieu. In some cases, esoteric rituals such as healing seem even to attempt to move toward full-scale incorporation into the societal and cultural mainstream. Stripped of their controversial New Age label, such practices and beliefs have effectively lost their links with a cultic milieu and are increasingly perceived as part of everyday life.

REFERENCES AND FURTHER READING

Bochinger, C. (1994) *'New Age' und moderne Religion: religionswissenschaftliche Analysen*, Gütersloh: Kaiser.

Campbell, C. (1972) 'The Cult, the Cultic Milieu and Secularization', *A Sociological Yearbook of Religion in Britain* 5, 119–36.

Chryssides, G. D. (2007) 'Defining the New Age,' in D. Kemp & J. R. Lewis, eds., *Handbook of New Age*, Leiden: Brill, 5–24.

Hammer, O. (2001) *Claiming Knowledge: Strategies of Epistemology from Theosophy to the New Age*, Leiden: Brill.

——(2005) 'New Age Movement,' in W. Hanegraaff et al., eds., *Dictionary of Gnosis and Western Esotericism*, Leiden: Brill, 855–61.

——(2010) 'I did it My Way? Individual Choice and Social Conformity in New Age Religion,' in S. Aupers & D. Houtman, eds., *Religions of Modernity: Relocating the Sacred to the Self and the Digital*, Leiden: Brill, 49–67.

Hanegraaff, W. J. (1996) *New Age Religion and Western Culture: Esotericism in the Mirror of Secular Thought*, Leiden: Brill.

Heelas, P. (1996) *The New Age Movement: The Celebration of the Self and the Sacralization of Modernity*, Oxford: Blackwell.

Kemp, D. (2004) *New Age, a Guide: Alternative Spiritualities from Aquarian Conspiracy to Next Age*, Edinburgh: Edinburgh University Press.

Kemp, D. & J. R. Lewis, eds. (2007) *Handbook of New Age*, Leiden: Brill.

Lewis, J. R. & J. G. Melton, eds. (1992) *Perspectives on the New Age*, Albany: State University of New York Press.

Rothstein, M., ed. (2001) *New Age Religion and Globalization*, Århus: Aarhus University Press.

Sutcliffe, S. & M. Bowman (eds.) (2000) *Beyond New Age: Exploring Alternative Spirituality*, Edinburgh: Edinburgh University Press.

Wood, M. (2007) *Possession, Power and the New Age: Ambiguities of Authority in Neoliberal Societies*, Aldershot: Ashgate.

York, M. (1995) *The Emerging Network: A Sociology of the New Age and Neo-Pagan Movements*, Lanham: Rowman & Littlefield.

CHAPTER THIRTY-NINE

CONTEMPORARY RITUAL MAGIC

Egil Asprem

INTRODUCTION

'Ritual' and 'magic' are elusive concepts with long and complicated histories in academic discourse (Styers 2004; Otto & Stausberg 2013). One could easily get lost in a thicket of semantic and theoretical problems when combining the two to talk about 'ritual magic'. It is, therefore, crucial to stipulate from the outset that 'ritual magic' here refers to a historically specific constellation of texts and practices, and their receptions, reinterpretations, and transformations. We are *not* here discussing 'magic' as a cross-cultural type, embedded in (or supporting) 'ritualized' behavior, which would require the scope to be truly global. Instead, we will focus on 'ritual magic' as a (largely) emic designation for certain forms of practice in the context of modern Western esotericism. (Hence, all figures, practices, and representations mentioned in this article recognize themselves as 'magicians' and their practices as ritual or ceremonial 'magic,' although, as we shall see, the understandings of what that implies may vary dramatically.) Thus *contemporary* ritual magic refers to a set of cultural phenomena that are historically related to this historiographical category. This chapter probes the variety of contemporary ritual magic, and explores how changing conditions in society, technology, media, and economy have influenced the practice of ritual magic in contemporary esotericism.

A BRIEF HISTORY OF MODERN MAGIC

The historiographic category of 'ritual magic' covers sources and discourses that stretch from Antiquity, through the Middle Ages and the Renaissance, to post-Enlightenment and contemporary times. To say anything meaningful about what is going on here and now it is necessary to look briefly at this history in order to know something about how we got here. First of all, it is important to note that all the periods mentioned above are marked by distinct developments and changes that make it impossible to talk of a stable and uniform 'magical tradition,' with contemporary custodians. Despite what some contemporary practitioners might say, there is no evidence of an unbroken tradition of ritual magic from ancient times until today. That, however, does not mean that there is no continuity whatsoever: certain sources and ritual liturgies have indeed inspired similar practice throughout the past two millennia. But we must be clear about what we are dealing with: namely, a number of different sets of ritual practices, codified in ritual texts and liturgies authored in different centuries and cultural contexts, that have been subject to loss, rediscovery, reinterpretation, innovations, and abridgements, and which have furthermore inspired and spawned new literature as centuries have passed. Ancient sources such as the Greek magical papyri and the 'technical' Hermetica are thus not only sources for ritual magical practice in antiquity, but have also been of great inspiration for *new* ritual practice in later centuries. The same can be said for the philosophical and theological discourse on the magical practices of 'theurgy' and 'goetia,' associated with neoplatonic thinkers such as Porphyry and Iamblichus; these writers not only kept a ritual-magical discourse alive in late antiquity, but also inspired later interpretations of magic. They provided elements for new intellectual frameworks of understanding magic in the Renaissance, through figures such as Marsilio Ficino, Pico della Mirandola, and Henry Cornelius Agrippa. For each new context, however, such sources are subject to entirely new interpretations. Thus the renaissance scholars mentioned above could draw not only on the *Hermetica* and Iamblichus, but a broad variety of folk magical practices as well as 'orthodox' Christian sources – a framework that was obviously missing in earlier 'pagan' sources. Meanwhile, another set of ritual texts took shape through the middle ages with the tradition of grimoires, or magical books (Davis, 2010). These books, including famous liturgies such as the *Key of Solomon*, the *Lemegeton* or 'Lesser Key of Solomon,' the *Ars Almadel*, and the *Heptameron*, continued to be copied and adapted throughout the early modern period, and constitute an influential set of sources for ritual magic.

These sources were, however, dispersed, and tended to differ widely in their practices, goals, and theological claims. The gradual reception and interpretation of older sources of ritual magic in the context of nineteenth-century occultism is of supreme importance for understanding the dynamic of contemporary ritual magic. In the wake of the Enlightenment we find a synthesis of 'modern ritual magic.' To a large extent, this synthesis bases itself on early-modern works such as Agrippa's *De occulta philosophia*, and the rediscovered grimoires, while also drawing significantly on the Christian cabala of Knorr von Rosenroth's *Kabbalah Denudata*, and the mythology of Rosicrucianism, Templars, and secret societies. All of this is, furthermore, supplied with new frameworks for *explaining* magic, increasingly in terms of 'sciency' discourses such as Mesmerism, electromagnetism, and ether physics, along with 'Romantic' theories of the unconscious mind and the 'night-side of nature'. In a sense, Doctor Faustus meets Doctor Frankenstein, and the result is a modern synthesis of magic understood as a practice in-between science and religion, equal parts 'technology' and 'ritual.'

The main figures and groups involved with the creation of modern ritual magic are all discussed elsewhere in the present volume. They include people such as Éliphas Lévi, Pascual Beverly Randolph, Samuel Liddell Mathers, William Wynn Westcott, and Arthur Edward Waite, and organizations such as the Hermetic Brotherhood of Luxor and the Hermetic Order of the Golden Dawn. It was with their contributions, roughly spanning the period 1850–1900, that the *groundwork* of modern ritual magic was created. The next fifty-year period saw further developments, in the form of schisms of old occult institutions, and the crystallization of new 'schools' or 'currents' of ritual magic. Aleister Crowley invented the new religion Thelema, and spent an enormous amount of his time developing a new approach to ritual magic. It amounted to a reform of the Golden Dawn system, the incorporation of sexual magic, and the development of an ostensibly 'scientific' or 'naturalistic' way of practicing magical ritual in what he called 'Scientific Illuminism' (Asprem 2008). The artist and sometime member of Crowley's magical order, the A.·.A.·., Austin Osman Spare, invented new techniques of magic and improvised ritualization in the 1910s. Dion Fortune split with the Golden Dawn in the 1920s and created her Fraternity of Inner Light, gradually revising the practices. Israel Regardie published the rituals of the Golden Dawn in the late 1930s, adding his own psychologized interpretations of magical practice filtered through his involvement with psychoanalysis and Reichian therapy. In continental Europe, the Czech occultist and writer Franz Bardon published his 'Hermetic' theories of ritual magic, while in Italy, the occultist and fascist Julius Evola established Gruppo di Ur, which published on ritual magic, pagan religion, and other esoteric subjects. After WWII the complexity increases, with new waves of schisms and the foundation of novel magical frameworks. Thelema splintered after Crowley's death in 1947; different lineages of Crowley's magical order, A.·.A.·., came to emphasize different aspects of his system, and occasionally expand upon it. Likewise, Kenneth Grant's 'Typhonian' current took Crowley's magic in novel directions from the 1950s onwards. Another acquaintance of Crowley's, Gerald Gardner, invented the modern Wiccan movement in Britain in the 1940s, paving the way for a self-described 'pagan' and 'witchcraft' oriented practice of ritual magic – soon enough to split into several fractions as per the usual procedure. In California, modern religious Satanism was born with the activities of Anton Szandor LaVey, presenting new and increasingly 'secularized' practices of ritual magic that became the subject of further reinterpretations and new syntheses when schisms hit the Church of Satan before a decade had passed. Thus, we also have the 'left-hand path' magical practice of Michael Aquino's Temple of Set emerging in the 1970s, adding new sources, new theories, and new ways of practicing ritual magic. Meanwhile, in Great Britain, 'chaos magic' started taking shape (if that is not an inappropriate metaphor) with the activities of a number of anarchically oriented occultists, notably Peter Carroll, Ray Sherwin, and Phil Hine, drawing inspiration from a number of sources including Crowley and Spare, but also writers and artists like Brion Gysin and William Burroughs (Duggan, 2013, 95–97).

There is much, much more – this is in no way an exhaustive list of all the different magical currents and spokespersons that were taking shape during the first eighty years or so of the twentieth century. It merely serves to make the point that we are dealing with a great number of consecutive transformations of magical ritual, leaving us with a vast variety of impulses informing contemporary magical practice.

THE VARIETIES OF CONTEMPORARY RITUAL MAGIC: THEMATIC DEVELOPMENTS

When we talk about 'contemporary' ritual magic we should focus our attention on the novel developments of the last few decades. Although it is tricky to periodize the contemporary, it makes sense to start in the early 1990s: the Soviet Union has collapsed, the cold war ended, Western capitalism and consumerism reign supreme, and the great ideologies of the twentieth century die as postmodernism goes mainstream. Meanwhile, a communications and media revolution is underway that rapidly changes the rules of the game: the emergence of the Internet and the development of the World Wide Web have had a remarkable effect on the production and dissemination of ritual magical texts, but also on the actual *practice* of magical ritual. In this section I shall outline how some of these broad structural changes in society and technology have impacted on the way magic is produced, disseminated, and practiced. When we have framed these important changes in the environment we can continue to look at some of the variety in the actual fauna of contemporary ritual magic. Taken together, these considerations will suffice as an overview of the 'biotope' of magic today.

Rise of the Occult Information Society

Probably the most significant characteristic of the contemporary occult world is the enormous wealth of free information now available. The rise of an 'occult information society,' or the adaptation of occultism to an emerging information society, started before the Internet became a public utility. Through the 1970s' 'occult explosion,' and continuing through the 1980s, there was a massive growth in the occult publishing industry. Publishing houses such as Weiser, New Falcon, Feral House, and Llewellyn, made a great number of previously rare materials available to a broad audience, while emerging currents such as Satanism and chaos magic generated new occult subgenres of their own. The previously hard-to-get literature on Golden Dawn rituals was made easily obtainable, as were the almost inaccessible works of Crowley.

Meanwhile, something else was happening: a number of 'scholar-magicians,' mostly based in the UK, took to the archives of the British Library and the Bodleian Library at Oxford, dug up rare early modern print works and old magical manuscripts, edited and published them – not to an audience of scholars, but to fellow occultists and magical practitioners. Smaller publishing houses such as Askin Publishers, Element, and Aquarian Press were releasing primary material on obscure topics such as Enochian magic. Daniel Driscoll's 1977 edition of the *Sworn Book of Honorius the Magician* did much to foster a scholar-like interest in grimoires among practitioners. Stephen Skinner published new editions of older print works, such as Meric Causaubon's famous account of Dee's angel conversations (*True & Faithful Relations*) and the *Fourth Book of Occult Philosophy,* spuriously attributed to Agrippa. In 1979, Adam McLean established the 'Magnum Opus Hermetic Sourceworks Series,' which set the standard for scholar-magicians of the following decade. Throughout the 1980s, McLean published works by Trithemius, Khunrath, Dee, Robert Fludd, and Michael Maier, as well as previously unpublished magical manuscripts, including an intriguing seventeenth/eighteenth-century grimoire attributed to 'Dr. Rudd,' combining angelic and demonic magic (see Asprem, 2012, 32–42). Also in the 1980s, Robert Turner and Geoffrey James published source-driven accounts of Elizabethan ritual magic, fostering an attempt to reconstruct 'original' renaissance magic.

Thus when the dissemination of magical texts went online around 1994, there was already a wealth of information available, far surpassing the state of affairs in earlier periods. The threshold of access to occult knowledge was lower than ever before, and the variety of sources and perspectives on the theory and practice of magic much vaster. This unprecedented freedom of occult information had significant implications. One of the most crucial effects of the occult information boom is that one could now easily get access to works pertaining to different 'schools' of magic without any direct institutional involvement or affiliation. One could pick up *The Satanic Bible* in any well-assorted bookstore, and compare its version of the Enochian keys with the material found in Regardie's *Golden Dawn*, Crowley's *Equinox*, or even the new editions of John Dee's original work. Indeed, with the publication of primary material, such as goetic manuscripts and facsimiles of early modern magical reference works, occultists now had access to magical texts that were more or less unmediated by the occult schools of the turn of the century. By contrast, it took two decades before a few members of the late-nineteenth-century Golden Dawn noticed there were discrepancies between the order's teachings of specific rituals and what the original sources said – simply because the sources were not known or available to anyone but one or two leaders. A century later, one could easily be an unaffiliated magician, aiming to reconstruct Elizabethan ritual magic, goetic demon conjurations, or rituals from the Greek magical papyri. Indeed, one effect of the explosive growth in magical information has been the emergence of a form of *magical 'purism'* – a return to older source material, and a revolt (at least on the surface) against the great magical syntheses of the nineteenth and early twentieth centuries.

The Internet greatly enhanced this already pre-existing trend. Through email lists, forums, and file sharing, and later (with Web 2.0) through blogging, YouTube, and social networking sites (especially Facebook), magicians could publish, share, and access material much more easily, and irrespective of geographical boundaries. More importantly, one could discuss the theory and practice of magic with other magicians, publish accounts of one's own experiences, compare notes, and develop new systems. All of this could happen *without* the social space of occult institutions with dogmatic commitments. Thus, the new occult information society means a *weakening of occult institutions*. No single school has a monopoly on the interpretation of magic; existing institutions such as Golden Dawn temples, O.T.O. lodges, Wiccan covens, and Satanic grottoes will all have to live with the fact that their members will read up broadly online, and experiment with different types of magic as they please. One illustrative example of the impact of this infrastructural revolution is found in the Open Source Order of the Golden Dawn, established by Sam Webster in 2002 (see website). Reasoning that the digital information revolution makes old institutional frameworks obsolete, this online magical order is based on the free dissemination of magical teachings, democratic leadership, and an open profile regarding which 'traditions' its members bring in and work with. Webster himself is hard to pin down in terms of affiliation, as he simultaneously identifies as a Thelemite, an initiate of Wicca, a Gnostic bishop, and a practitioner in the Golden Dawn current.

Finally, one interesting trend of the recent two decades should be framed as a counter-development to the wide online dissemination of magical texts. In the 1990s and continuing through the 2000s a significant number of micropublishers specializing in limited craft editions of rare magical material, of ancient as well as contemporary provenance, have emerged. David Rankine and Stephen Skinner's Golden Hoard Press, for example, has released a number of grimoires since 2004, many of which published for the first time, and with leather-bound special editions to complement the cheaper versions. Other craft book publishers specializing in ritual magical texts include Fulgur, Ouroboros Press, and Scarlet Imprint, all producing relatively expensive, handcrafted magical books. These works become collector's items, but also function as a sort of magical fetish in their own right: they constitute a new and sophisticated material culture of ritual magic, emerging as a response to the digital overflow of free magical information. Anyone can download the text of the *Heptameron*, but only the true aficionado would own the full imperial vellum edition, priced at $225, from Ouroboros Press. The value of this material culture can also be gauged from the occult second-hand book market: the catalogue of Weiser Antiquarian, for example, lists first, second, and even third editions of Crowley's magical works ranging up to $ 1,000.

Virtual Magic

The effect of the new forms of communication provided by the Internet cannot simply be seen as amplifying existing trends by providing an increase in the quantity of information. The new form of mediation has also inspired radical *qualitative* changes in the way magic is being *practiced* (cf. Cowan 2005). In the 1990s, chat protocols such as IRC were used by 'tecnopagans' for group rituals, where participants scattered around the world would get together and play their parts through instant messaging in plain text. There has even been an intriguing overlap of people involved with cutting-edge programming and occultist magic, who have embraced the emerging global Internet as a magical tool in its own right. The computer programmer Mark Pesce, for example, stated in a 1995 interview that the 'astral plane' would be reborn in cyberspace (Davis, 1995; cf. Crow, 2013).

The innovative effect of cyberspace on magical practice is clearly visible in the emergence of ritual practices in virtual reality. The development of simulated 3D environments through virtual reality platforms such as Second Life has provided the possibility to do much more than was possible with the text and static images of websites and chat forums. Virtual worlds provide a flexible, modifiable environment in which one can move about in the shape of an 'avatar,' interact with other avatars, chat with them through text or voice, purchase property, buy, build and sell items, and use scripts that animate avatars to perform specific gestures and movements in specific settings. The avatar itself can in principle be modified to any imaginable shape, and it may also fly or teleport to other locations. Unlike game platforms with similar features, e.g. massively multiplayer online games (MMOGs) such as World of Warcraft, there are no predetermined goals or objectives in Second Life: it is whatever its users make it. Occult and pagan users have increasingly made it a place of magic and ritual, a site of virtual enchantment (see especially Cowan 2005; Crow 2013). If, for example, one visits the virtual village of Covenstead, one finds temples and magic circles where avatars can be animated to do rituals and invocations, solitary or in groups. Such cyber-rituals pose about as many challenges as they open possibilities: while the virtual world of Second Life is flexible and full of opportunities, its possibilities for movement, and physical and mental experience are still incredibly limited when compared to the real world. Thus, some contemporary cyber magicians improvise by combining real life and virtual practice in a singular ritual act: laptop computer running the Second Life software can be put on a physical altar and take the function of a ritual object, on a par with a crystal ball or magical mirror (Crow, 2013, 178). This practice potentially opens a range of metaphysical questions for the magician: does the magic happen 'in-world,' or is the computer-mediated imagery merely a convenient tool for inducing 'magical consciousness' in a real-life ritual setting? Could the visions on the screen even be comparable, in terms of their ontological status, as those encountered in crystal visions – in other words, is it an actual, real magical world that now manifests in software? Some magicians apparently opt for this interpretation, arguing that the landscapes of virtual reality are not just *similar* to the experiences involved in the magical techniques of astral travel, but that the virtual *is* the astral plane (ibid., 179–80).

CONTEMPORARY CURRENTS OF RITUAL MAGIC

In an occult world where magical institutions are weakened, frameworks are fluid, and practices always improvised, it is problematic to describe what is going on by a rigid classification of 'schools' and 'currents.' The previous section should have made clear that some of the most interesting developments in contemporary ritual magic have less to do with 'currents' than with infrastructural changes in communication, technology, and social organization. The following section on 'currents' is thus clearly not intended to pick out stable and autonomous 'traditions'. If, however, we follow Kennet Granholm's (2013) proposal and define esoteric 'currents' as *discursive complexes* instead, the concept may indeed help us to grasp another dimension of the contemporary ritual magical landscape. In this sense, 'currents' are seen merely as 'collections of specific discourses in specific combinations' (ibid., 51). The advantage of this conception is that we will find certain discursive elements to be shared by a number of different currents – which by specific combinations give the element in question a specific flavor or meaning.

It is crucial to note that these currents or discursive complexes must *not* be confused with the *sources* of magical practice. An A∴A∴-affiliated Thelemite, an 'Alexandrian' Wiccan, and a rationalist 'Satanist' (see below for these labels) may in principle work with precisely the same ritual text (say, the Lesser Key of Solomon), but will typically attach different ontological and ethical commitments to this magical practice, expressed through discourses that are essentially at odds with each other. While their building blocks may be the same, they construct the totality of their ritual-magical practice differently. Thus, talking about currents in this sense makes it possible to home in on the fact that special ways of working with the same ritual sources have emerged, that are unique to a specific current, or cluster of currents. In the corpus of 'Enochian magic,' for example (a set of systems for angel magic, originating in the work of John Dee and subsequently the object of a series of reinterpretations and modifications), the Golden Dawn created a whole new way of conceptualizing and working with it that is not found in the original Elizabethan sources. Golden Dawn magicians today will typically continue to work with these innovations, while unaffiliated magicians, or magicians embedded in currents that do not have any particular view on Enochian, may decide on a more 'purist' approach, and work with what can be reconstructed from primary material (see Asprem, 2012). Thus 'Enochian magic' means different things in different currents.

This important point should be kept in mind as I continue to list some of the most prevalent currents of ritual magic that are around today. Some of these have deep roots, and may in some sense be seen as contemporary inheritors of older lineages. However, even in those cases it will be clear that contemporary spokespersons have to adapt to contemporary circumstances. Additionally, factors that are specific to each current have in most cases led to significant innovation. Some of these will be mentioned for each of the currents discussed. I will, however, be brief, and the following should only be seen as suggestive of certain trends, deemed by the present author to be particularly significant or interesting – a rough roadmap to navigate in this rather complex landscape.

Contemporary Golden Dawn Currents

The Golden Dawn was extremely influential on early twentieth-century developments of ritual magic, and in some sense the broad variety of currents that will be mentioned below are all inconceivable without the Golden Dawn impulse. As an institution, however, the Golden Dawn fell apart already in the first decade of the 1900s. Different splinter groups continued to operate temples and train new magicians in the following decades, most notably MacGregor Mathers' Alpha et Omega temple in Paris, and the Stella Matutina, which had lodges in the UK and New Zealand, and was the faction that Israel Regardie was acquainted with before publishing the order's rituals in the late 1930s. After the Second World War, however, most of these groups died out in their original form. Then in the 1970s, as a response to the new publications of primary sources, especially the Llewellyn edition of Regardie's version of the Golden Dawn rituals, a number of groups tried to resuscitate the tradition by forming new groups. Over the years this Golden Dawn revival has led to a confusing and controversial 'Golden Dawn current': at present there are at least four groups that claim to represent the 'real deal,' all of which have been involved with legal battles over the Golden Dawn 'trademark' in various countries, and frequently engage in rather hostile polemics with each other online.

The first of these groups appears to have been Charles 'Chic' Cicero's Hermetic Order of the Golden Dawn Inc., started in the late 1970s with the blessing of Israel Regardie – who in the United States was metonymic for the Golden Dawn current as a whole. Chic and his wife, Sandra 'Tabatha' Cicero, have since established themselves as leading 'authorities' in Golden Dawn-style initiation and ritual magic through numerous publications. They also have to take some dubious credit for the 'businessification' of occultism in this period, as they incorporated the Golden Dawn under state of Florida legislation in 1988 in order to get rid of competitors through legal action.

One of the competitors of Hermetic Order of the Golden Dawn Inc. is the Order of the Golden Dawn®, a registered trademark in Quebec, Canada, originating with the New Zealander Pat Zalewski. This group currently runs a temple in Montreal, besides being active in Australia and New Zealand. Its teachings appear to be relatively standard Golden Dawn material, derived from the Stella Matutina faction that survived in New Zealand.

Two other Golden Dawn orders are notable for their more extravagant claims and novelties of practice. Robert Zink's Esoteric Order of the Golden Dawn has attracted some notoriety in occult circles for its emphasis on 'astral initiation.' To become an initiate, all one needs to do is pay the fees to the higher chiefs, enter the astral plane, and receive initiation from a distance. It easily comes across as the ritual-magical equivalent of a post-order Ph.D. Zink's version of the Golden Dawn current is perhaps the clearest example of occult ritual magic incorporating discursive elements from the general 'alternative spirituality' landscape: for example, Zink not only claims the ceremonial titles of the traditional Golden Dawn hierarchy, but adopts contemporary trends by styling himself 'Miracle Mentor' and 'Alchemy Life Coach,' while inventing other hybrids such as 'neuro-linguistic alchemy' and playing with the 'law of attraction' (Zink, 2013).

Zink's fiercest critic has been Robert Griffin, himself an eccentric magical adept and the leader of another 'original' Golden Dawn current. Completely immersed in the legal side of the Golden Dawn franchise, Griffin sports a number of trademarks in Canada, the US, and Europe, and seems to spend a lot of time making this fact known to the world. A unique stamp of Griffin's current is a strong emphasis on the role of 'secret chiefs': these legendary figures are, according to Griffin, real people that have obtained a state of near immortality through the workings of Rosicrucian initiation and alchemical practice. Griffin in fact claims to have been in touch with the very same adepts that once gave Mathers the authority and means to run the 'inner order' of the Golden Dawn, and consequently has gone on to claim that his order teaches certain forms of magic, apparently of an alchemical and erotic character, that have successfully been kept a secret through all exposés and publications of Golden Dawn documents (Griffin, 2009).

The Thelemic current

Thelema, the new religious framework established by Crowley in the early decades of the twentieth century, and embodied in a number of institutions, has inspired another broad current of ritual magic. The main institutional carrier of Thelema today is the 'Caliphate' O.T.O. It should, however, be noted that the O.T.O. is not in itself a ritual magical organization, comparable to the Golden Dawn – it is an initiatory fraternal organization working for the development of the individual in compliance with Thelemic principles (thus especially the discovery of the 'True Will'), and the concerted effort of creating a Thelemic society by promoting the Law of Thelema ('Do what thou Wilt shall be the whole of the Law'). As for the development and practice of 'Thelemic magic' (or 'magick,' to follow the Crowleyan jargon) this has been done in particular through the lineages of Crowley's magical order, the A∴A∴. In modern and contemporary times, authors and magicians such as Marcelo Ramos Motta, James Wasserman, Christopher Hyatt, Lon Milo DuQuette, Rodney Orpheus, J. Daniel Gunther, and many others have continued to develop a distinctly Thelemic take on ritual magic, extending the heritage of Crowley's work.

It must also be noted that the Thelemic current, like most others, has been shaken by schisms and the formation of new sub-currents. Kenneth Grant's Typhonian current is beyond doubt the most significant of these. Through a corpus of six books known as the Typhonian trilogies (the first appearing in 1972, and the last in 2002) Grant crafted an original ritual magical current mixing 'classic' Thelemic elements with elements taken from sources such as Lovecraftian fiction, UFO-lore, Austin

Osman Spare, and the emerging chaos current (cf. Evans, 2007). A final sub-current emerging from the Thelemic mainstream may be discerned in the 'Franco-Haitian' O.T.O. current associated with Michael Bertiaux. Bertiaux's approach to magic, equally original, combines the Thelemic framework with elements of Haitian voodoo and what the author calls a 'Gnostic' impulse (e.g. Bertiaux, 2007).

Wiccan currents

Along with the emergence of Thelema, the invention of the Wiccan witchcraft religion by Gerald Gardner in post-war UK has meant a lot for the changing perceptions and practices of ritual magic in the West (see Hutton, 1999). For our present purposes, it will suffice to say that this current, in general, combines Golden Dawn practices with witchcraft folklore and the notion of a suppressed Pagan religion based on the worship of a horned god and a mother goddess. This current has, as the others discussed, broken up into a number of different currents and local practices. The most noteworthy sub-currents are the 'Gardnerian' and 'Alexandrian' (after Alex Sanders, known in the 1960s as the 'king of witches') schools, operating as initiation systems organized in 'covens,' carrying the religious practice of the god and goddess and the teaching of a variety of ritual magical practices. There is, however, a lot more going on. For example, the 'Dianic Wicca' that has grown out of the activities of Hunagrian-American activist Zsuzsanna Budapest rejects the gender-duality of the British groups, replacing it with an exclusive focus on the goddess and casting itself as 'feminist' spirituality. Yet other forms of Wicca may be classified as 'eclectic,' lacking any formal organization and blending in seamlessly with the Pagan segments of contemporary occulture.

Other Neopagan currents

The broader Neopagan current is thus another important factor to consider. It is, however, hard to describe this as a single current, even in the sense of a discursive complex – and the discernible currents that are collected under the heading of Neopaganism are far too many and diverse to be given justice here. We should nevertheless note that the attempt to reconstruct pre-Christian religious traditions, whether these be Norse, Germanic, Roman, Celtic, Greek, or 'Shamanic,' have provided additional discursive elements as well as 'raw materials' for contemporary magical practice. The use of runes for divination and spell-casting is one clear example of this, and the incorporation of techniques such as drumming, dancing, and the use of psychoactive agents to induce extravagant visionary experiences, indicate another area of innovation that can be roughly related to the Neopagan movement.

Satanic and Left-Hand Path currents

It is slightly easier to delineate a cluster of Satanic and (post-Satanic) Left-Hand Path currents, that build on and renew the magical discourses and practices of the Golden Dawn and Thelema (but cf. Petersen, 2012). In itself, the contemporary 'Satanic milieu' is, however, yet another fragmented and complex field. Anton LaVey created a discourse on magical ritual that is quite distinct in its thorough 'secularization' of magical efficacy. In this 'rationalistic' line of Satanic magic, the boundary between magic and ordinary social-psychological mechanism (i.e. dressing or speaking a certain way to manipulate one's social surroundings) is blurred. On the more 'esoteric' pole of the spectrum, however, we find something rather different: magicians affiliated with one of the pylons of the Temple of Set are, for example, more likely to conceive of ritual magic in supernatural, or at least 'esoteric' terms: one evokes powers and beings that are quite real, quite distinct from ordinary social or psychological mechanisms. What the 'rationalist' and the 'esoteric' Satanist have in common is that the magic is conceived of in antinomian and strongly individualistic terms, and that they place themselves in opposition to schools of 'white magic' – which to these practitioners would typically include Golden Dawn, Thelemic, and witchcraft groups.

More recently, other Left-Hand Path organizations have appeared, expanding this current of ritual magic in new directions by incorporating various 'pagan' elements from e.g. Norse sources. This is notably the case with Stephen Flowers (a.k.a. Edred Thorsson), who mixed scholarship on rune magic (the subject of his Ph.D. in Germanic languages) with influences from the Church of Satan, Temple of Set, and reconstructionist Ásatru when forming his new organization, the Rune-Gild. Similarly, the Swedish scholar and magician Thomas Karlsson (another Ph.D., this time in the history of religion) founded the Dragon Rouge in the early 1990s, today one of the most successful Left-Hand Path organizations in the world. It practices a form of ritual magic that draws heavily on grimoire traditions for liturgical inspiration, and on a mix of 'gothic' literary romanticism, psychology, and previous Left-Hand Path ideologies for its 'theological' outlook (cf. Granholm, 2014).

Chaos currents

Since, for pedagogical reasons, we have already been rather liberal with the use of the term 'current' we may as well continue to give the label to yet another dubious entity. Chaos magic was, as mentioned briefly, an anarchic magical phenomenon emerging in the late 1970s and early 1980s. Even though things have changed since then, and chaos magic never really became fixed in the first place, we may nevertheless speak of a chaos current running into the 1990s and continuing today. New generations of (primarily very young) occultists have picked up the published books of main 'chaos magic' authors, such as Peter Carroll's *Liber Null* and Phil Hine's *Prime Chaos*, taking inspiration from them in order to play and improvise with magic, focusing on what is simple, fun, and 'seems to work.' Since the mid-1990s, countless chaos-themed personal websites have emerged, collecting personalized spells and advice for using techniques such as 'banishing by laughter,' making magic sigils, or employing video games as a focus for channeling emotional energy in order to 'charge' such sigils (e.g. Ellwood, 2004).

As a whole, however, chaos magic is symptomatic of a number of intersecting trends and currents. Thelema, Satanism, and the Left-Hand Path coalesce, and form new expressions in the meeting with 'underground' artistic milieus and dissemination structures. Indeed, chaos magic has always been interwoven with intricate and innovative channels of dissemination, whether through the anarchist/artist 'zine scene,' online file sharing, or eclectic underground periodicals. One notable example of the latter is *The Fenris Wolf*, run by Swedish occultist and author Carl Abrahamson.

The first three volumes of this journal, published between 1989 and 1993 gathered notable spokespersons from the broader international 'chaotic' and Left-Hand Path milieu, including author William Burroughs, Satanic pope Anton LaVey, artist, musician, and magician Genesis P-Orridge, chaos magician Lionel Snell, Thelemite Rodney Orpheus, O.T.O. 'caliph' Hymenæus Beta, and Church of Satan high priest Peter Gilmore. *The Fenris Wolf* has recently been revived, with the fourth volume appearing in 2011.

CONCLUSION: NEW LOCATIONS OF RITUAL MAGIC

A major conclusion of this survey must be that ritual magic is migrating to new locations.

With the emergence of new media, through connections with new artistic scenes and forms of expression, and by way of new channels of dissemination and consumption, ritual magic is becoming embedded in intricate feedback loops with other aspects of contemporary culture. We have already dealt with the way that the Internet and especially virtual reality has functioned as a new location for magic, a new environment that also invited drastically new ways for magic to be practiced. In closing, we should focus on two other significant developments, both having to do with the migration of ritual magic, and its integration in other areas of culture.

The first of these is the interface of ritual magic and underground art and music scenes. The interest of 'underground' artists and musicians in magical practices is by no means new, but it appears to have taken a radical new spin around the 1980s (cf. Partridge, 2013). The chaos magic scene is important here, as already mentioned, being intricately connected with new expressions on the intersection of ritualized art, magical practice, and a punked up esoteric esthetic. Musical acts such as Throbbing Gristle and performance artists such as Genesis P-Orridge are key examples of this integration of magic and artistic expression, while the activist art collective known as Center for Tactical Magic (CTM) serves as an example of more recent developments. On its website, CTM defines its magical approach ('tactical magic') as a 'fusion force summoned from the ways of the artist, the magician, the ninja, and the private investigator,' leading to 'an amalgam of disparate arts invoked for the purpose of actively addressing Power on individual, communal, and transnational fronts' (CTM website). The magical theories and practices discussed on the website are clearly derived from the chaos current.

Another development concerns the integration of ritual magic in products of 'popular culture' with truly broad exposure, especially through films and television programs. While most such integration is purely *representational* (that is, reconstructions and representations of magical practice as plot devices), there are also intriguing examples of popular culture being used *as* magic – again, unsurprisingly, with reference to chaos magic. Thus, the Scottish comic book writer Grant Morrison has claimed that his graphic novel, *The Invisibles* (running from 1994 to 2000), was intended to function as a 'hypersigil,' one giant magical invocation to push culture and society in a certain direction by imprinting on readers' psyches (cf. Kripal, 2011, 21). While Morrison may remain a rather exotic example (always 'occultural,' but more 'cult' than 'pop'), we should not dismiss the representational expressions mentioned above either. This is because the descriptive, in fact, easily becomes *pre*scriptive, and thus we find that a new generation of occultist magicians, coming of age in the late 1990s and 2000s, are likely to have had their first encounter with witchcraft through shows such as *Charmed*, or to have learnt about the binding and exorcism of demons with the Key of Solomon through the episodes of *Supernatural*. Thus, the extensive popular dissemination of ritual magical representations must be considered an integral part of the ritual-magical landscape today. While fiction, folklore, and mythology have no doubt always been major sources for beliefs and practices of magic, present-day representations tend to borrow primarily from the occultist syntheses that have emerged since the nineteenth century, rather than from earlier mythological sources. Thus, the practices and beliefs of occult ritual magic are being passed on primarily through a massive popular occulture, rather than through secret lodges.

REFERENCES AND FURTHER READING

Websites

Center for Tactical Magic, http://www.tacticalmagic.org
Esoteric Order of the Golden Dawn, http://www.esotericgoldendawn.com
Hermetic Order of the Golden Dawn, Inc (Chic Cicero), http://www.hermeticgoldendawn.org
Open Source Order of the Golden Dawn, http://www.osogd.org
Order of the Golden Dawn (Zalewski), http://www.orderofthegoldendawn.com/theorder.html
Order of the Golden Dawn, Alpha et Omega (Griffin), http://www.golden-dawn.com

Literature

Asprem, Egil (2008) 'Magic Naturalized? Negotiating Science and Occult Experience in Crowley's "Scientific Illuminism"', *Aries*, 8(2), 139–65.

——(2012) *Arguing with Angels: Enochian Magic and Modern Occulture*, Albany, State University of New York Press.

Asprem, Egil and Kennet Granholm, eds. (2013) *Contemporary Esotericism*, Sheffield, Equinox.

Bertiaux, Michael (2007) *The Voudon Gnostic Workbook: Expanded Edition*, San Francisco, CA: Red Wheel/Weiser, LLC.

Cowan, Douglas E. (2005) *Cyberhenge: Modern Pagans on the Internet*, London, Routledge.

Crow, John L. (2013) 'Accessing the Astral with a Monitor and Mouse: Esoteric Religion and the Astral Located in Three-Dimensional Virtual Realms', in Egil Asprem and Kennet Granholm (eds), *Contemporary Esotericism*, Sheffield: Equinox, 159–180.

Davis, Erik (1995) 'Technopagans: May the Astral Plane be Reborn in Cyberspace', *Wired* 3.07, http://www.wired.com/wired/archive/3.07/technopagans.html (accessed 28 February 2013).

Davis, Owen (2010) *Grimoires: A History of Magic Books*, Oxford, Oxford University Press.

Duggan, Colin (2013) 'Perennialism and Iconoclasm: Chaos Magick and the Legitimacy of Innovation', in Egil Asprem and Kennet Granholm, eds, *Contemporary Esotericism*, Sheffield, Equinox, 91–112.

Ellwood, Taylor (2004) 'How to Charge & Fire a Sigil by Playing a Video Game', *Spiral Nature*. Online: http://www.spiralnature.com/magick/chaos/sigilvideogame.html (accessed 25 February 2013).

Evans, Dave (2007) *The History of British Magic after Crowley: Kenneth Grant, Amado Crowley, Chaos Magic, Satanism, Lovecraft, The Left Hand Path, Blasphemy and Magical Morality*, n.p., Hidden Publishing.

Granholm, Kennet(2013) 'Esoteric Currents as Discursive Complexes', 43(1), 46–69.

——(2014) *Dark Enlightenment: The Historical, Sociological, and Discursive Contexts of Contemporary Esoteric Magic*, Leiden and Boston: Brill.

Griffin, Robert (2009) 'The True Nature of Hermetic Alchemy, *Hermetic Order of the Golden Dawn* website, http://www.golden-dawn.com/eu/displaycontent.aspx?pageid=102-true-nature-of-hermetic-alchemy (accessed 25 February 2013).

Hutton, Ronald (1999) *The Triumph of the Moon: A History of Modern Pagan Witchcraft*, Oxford, Oxford University Press.

Kripal, Jeffery (2011) *Mutants and Mystics: Science Fiction, Superhero Comics, and the Paranormal*, Chicago, University of Chicago Press.

Partridge, Christopher (2013) 'Occulture Is Ordinary', in Egil Asprem and Kennet Granholm (eds.), *Contemporary Esotericism*, Sheffield: Equinox, 113–33.

Petersen, Jesper Aa. (2012) 'The Seeds of Satan: Conceptions of Magic in Contemporary Satanism', *Aries* 12.2, 91–129.

Otto, Bernd-Christian and Michael Stausberg, eds. (2013) *Defining Magic: A Reader*, Sheffield, Equinox Publishing.

Styers, Randall (2004) *Making Magic: Religion, Magic, and Science in the Modern World*, Oxford, Oxford University Press.

Zink, Robert (2013) *The Law of Attraction – Ancient Wisdom Applied to Modern Living*, website, http://www.personal-magic.com (accessed 25 February 2013).

CHAPTER FORTY

CONTEMPORARY SATANISM

Jesper Aagaard Petersen

The figure of Satan is part of a select group of pervasive cultural icons in popular culture of the late modern West. Alongside Jesus, Santa Claus and the alien Greys, to name a few, Satan regularly appears in various forms and genres as a recognizable, yet constantly reinterpreted figure. Thus we are primed through popular culture to recognize Satanists and the satanic as cultural tropes within certain registers of meaning (Petersen, 2013a; Petersen & Dyrendal, 2012).

Although religious and political extremists dominate the news today, the occasional reference to 'satanic' activities still pops up from time to time in national and international media. Usually, these instances are the result of professionals or commentators misinterpreting a hodge-podge of occult paraphernalia at a crime scene. In rare cases, single individuals and small bands self-identify as Satan worshippers (or at least in league with the devil) in court testimonies, academic research or media reports, fueling blanket statements by external observers about the moral state of society and the permissiveness of modern culture. Parallel to these frames dealing with confrontation and crime, we also find self-declared Satanists dealing less in inchoate 'rebellion' and more in adversarial modes of living transcending the cultural and normative framework of 'ordinary' society. These individuals form a diffuse satanic milieu with partially overlapping interests, tastes, aesthetics and references, sometimes cohering into groups of varying permanence. Nevertheless, both permeable and hard boundaries exist between this milieu and external parallels, boundaries which become invisible when examples are lumped together as 'occult' and 'satanic', i.e. dangerous devil worship, by outsiders.

Consequently, in order to recognize Satanism as a contemporary religious phenomenon, we must distinguish between broader interpretations of the satanic and satanic interpretations coming from within, and it is the latter which we will examine in some detail in the following.

DISCOURSE ON THE SATANIC AND SATANIC DISCOURSE: OTHER OR SELF?

Within modernity, Christianity itself is a complex phenomenon. On the one hand it is associated with humanitarianism and charity, on the other with state religion and social order (at least in the old world). By default, the negative other, Satanism, must be characterized by inhumanity and egoism, but also anarchy and rebellion. In the modern period the underlying value system seems to shift, mainly because of new impulses by Enlightenment philosophers, Romantic poets, Bohemian artists and countercultural currents affecting ever larger segments of society. Government and order becomes inhuman and elitist, while Satan's eternal rebellion and anarchistic ethos gradually assumes a human and almost charitable guise. Even egoism is transformed into self-actualization, autonomy and individuality. In effect, Satan becomes our ally or mentor.

Today, the words 'Satanism' and 'Satanist' connote a variety of unpleasant things fully in tune with their speckled history: Obscenity and perversion, blind transgression, violence and heresy, and so on. Yet these developments have also realigned Satanism to more positive values and attributes such as self-reliance and power, bohemian and esoteric pursuits, and carnal knowledge (Lewis, 2009). Thus the concepts mean different things to different groups across different contexts – they have no fixed meaning in themselves, but are actively filled with content by social actors in relation to their view of identity and tradition. This process is negotiated through conflict and compromise, both internally, in specific groups and milieus, and externally, in the market of identity located in the wider field of socio-cultural relations. Here, Satanism and Satanist play a role not unlike terms such as 'witchcraft/witch', 'islam/muslim', or a number of other identity terms based on religious, national, ethnic, political and sexual orientation (Petersen, 2011a).

To make sense of this pluralistic chaos, Satanism can be viewed from two vantage points: discourse on the satanic and satanic discourse. The first perspective understands Satanism as cultural phantasms or social imaginations connecting Satan, Devil worshippers, crime and obscenity with popular receptions of the occult. It can be found in horror movies, metal music, educational literature (whether Christian, secular or fellow occult), and contemporary folklore and urban myths. Whether religious or secular, discourse on the satanic promotes the virtues of society (and by extension, the speaker) by highlighting someone else as 'evil' or even 'the wholly Other.' As such, it is a socially enforced and culturally amplified 'Satan code' about dark forces, transcending individual media, subcultures and worldviews. This amorphous code is rooted in pre-Christian, pre-modern and modern conceptions of evil, integrating popular mythology, psychology and history in a diffuse blend (Partridge, 2005, ch. 6).

The second perspective, satanic discourse, denotes constructions and articulations of the satanic put forth by self-declared Satanists such as Anton S. LaVey's Church of Satan and its spin-offs and rivals, as well as the many independent Satanists found online. Although these Satanists relate to the 'Satan code' discussed above, it is actively redefined in satanic discourse into positive images of self. We are thus dealing with interpretations combining old and new discourses on the satanic with satanic meaning-making and identity. This is rather new; satanic discourse coheres into a viable alternative in California in 1966 with the establishment of the Church of Satan. This group combines a visible organization with a leadership and hierarchy, beliefs and practices defined by accessible literature, and a clear identification with Satan as a symbol of the Satanists' self-image.

Conflating discourse on the satanic and satanic discourse is a common mistake across popular literature on Satanism past and present. To assume from the outset that a stable relation exists between the Satanism of individuals and groups today and the historical scarecrow found in theological literature or various ill-documented performances of the past is simply wrong. Similarly, to equate modern Satanism with broader currents such as the occult sciences of western esotericism and comparable phenomena like neo-paganism or heavy metal culture erases the specific features of Satanism and makes it more widespread and dangerous than it actually is.

THE SATANIC MILIEU: LOCATING SATANIC DISCOURSE

A second mistake is to ignore the internal plurality within self-declared Satanism as a socio-cultural phenomenon. One way to realize this is to relate individual expressions and groups to a satanic milieu actively stimulating the dissemination of satanic ideas and practices and thus the formation of identities and communities. This milieu is not a literal entity, a specific group or even a 'movement' in the common sense of a loose group moving in the same direction. It is rather an analytical term describing a satanic ecosystem or habitat upheld by partly overlapping activities and networks, such as books, magazines, websites, spokespersons, media products and so on. These activities predate the individual or group and will exist after they are gone, yet they encourage an abstract communality through common references and tastes which bind them together (Campbell, 1972). The satanic milieu is both local and global, as it is anchored in specific activities and scenes on the one hand and international trends on the other. Similarly, the boundaries to analogous milieus, such as thelemic groups or neo-paganism, are not definite, but are constantly renegotiated.

Going back to the discussion on satanic discourse above, there is no doubt that Anton LaVey (1930–97) and the Church of Satan were instrumental in stimulating a coherent discourse and nascent milieu, partly by galvanizing already existing groups and networks by acting and writing in certain ways. But at the same time neither LaVey nor his Church was (or is) the entirety of satanic discourse or the satanic milieu. Apart from a broader cultural discourse on the satanic and witchcraft which was quite popular in the 1960s, individuals and groups relating to the figure of Satan did exist before LaVey; in the 1920s and 1930s, for example, the German Fraternitas Saturni and the French La Flèche d'Or, led by sexual magician Maria de Naglowska (1883–1936), were both using Satan and Lucifer in their literature and rituals. So did Helena Blavatsky (1931–1891), founder of modern Theosophy, Eliphas Levi (1810–75), influential writer on ceremonial magic, and Aleister Crowley (1875–1947), perhaps the most recognizable of western occultists. But in all cases Satan was not the center of attention, and the interpretation of Satan was usually quite skewed towards noble esoteric goals. None of these figures understood themselves or their organizations as satanic in any unequivocal sense.

In the same vein, LaVey certainly had competitors on the market for witchcraft and occultism in the 1960s, and Satan had a certain level of countercultural capital in that period. Yet no unified satanic identity or milieu existed before a 'dominant' group and a 'dominant' discourse suddenly ascended to national (and international) fame. This in turn prompted the evolution of an autonomous satanic milieu through networking and mutual references as well as a de facto satanic tradition by selectively appropriating and reinterpreting various existing discourses on the satanic. In essence, what LaVey did was to codify an extremely influential satanic discourse opening up a hitherto unused religious identity organized as a satanic religion. However, any stability was short-lived, and this space was quickly filled with alternative interpretations combining elements in different ways while retaining their identity as satanic. The most famous example is the schism within the Church itself, culminating in 1975 with the establishment of Michael Aquino's (1946–) Temple of Set, which still exists today.

This is the present situation: the satanic milieu is visibly pluralistic, especially online, where individual groups are often intensely competitive and dismissive of each other (Petersen, 2013b). By adopting one interpretation of Satanism as explanation for the whole milieu, as is done when the Church of Satan's distinction between 'Satanism' and 'pseudo-Satanism' is used, we misrepresent the plurality of 'Satanisms' all claiming to be 'true'.

SATANIC PERSPECTIVES: SHAPING SATANIC DISCOURSE

With that in mind it is possible to isolate distinct satanic perspectives by studying movement texts, images, activities and practices found within the milieu. I have focused on three types that can be used to understand actual groups or individuals: an oppositional anti-Christian orientation, an esoteric, transformatory outlook, and a rationalist and materialist position (Petersen, 2009a). All of these perspectives locate authority within the self (making them 'self-religious') and exhibit an antinomian character, in other words they prioritize self and transgression as ultimate values in a project of self-discovery or creation. This is not necessarily satanic, however. What makes them distinctly satanic is the narrative use of Satan and related beings alongside an orientation towards a specific subcultural ancestry to define and explain themselves. Conversely, what makes them internally different is the orientation to and use of cultural discourses of the satanic and the occult, something which affects their understanding of Satan, satanic practices and beliefs, and organization.

Anti-Christian Satanism

> I am your disciple/And therefore my own/Your weapon I will be/With the demons that possesses me [sic] (...) The sign of your horns/Is my dearest vision/They impale all holy and weak.
>
> (Darkthrone, 'To Walk the Infernal Fields', 1993)

The oppositional and anti-Christian perspective is an inversion of Christian narratives in order to confront and oppose society, making the Satanist an inverted image of societal norms. Whether they actually worship the Devil or simply identify with the enemy is less important. Basically, the self-image and understanding of Satanism is closely dependent on cultural images and values, making this perspective a (frequently aesthetic) living-out of a mythical framework. This is most apparent in the black metal scene and as youth culture, although some people keep the anti-Christian perspective active well into adulthood. That said, while it is no less authentic to the people involved, it is more determined by emotional and experiential factors than ideological choices, making it difficult to sustain over time as a coherent identity and lifestyle (Lowney, 1995; Petersen, 2011b).

To fully appreciate this perspective, we must make certain reservations. First, we cannot assume a stable connection between music or style and a satanic identity. People can be involved in black metal without identifying as Satanists or even sympathizing with Satanism; equally, Satanists of other convictions can enjoy a bit of musical rebellion or aesthetic frisson. Second, the use of anti-Christian rhetoric and aesthetic aligns on a scale of satanic commitment moving from purely aesthetic consumption to rather radical occult practices, with provocation and shock as well as nostalgia for pre-Christian modes of life in between. What is important here is that these practices seldom devolve into criminal acts; and those who do express deeper psychological issues rather than Satanism as such. Likewise, delving deeper into occult practices often blends with the esoteric outlook, transforming it from provocation to magic. In any case, Satanists of this persuasion seem somewhat marginalized by dominant groups in the satanic milieu exactly because of their literal interpretation of Christian stereotypes.

Post-Christian Satanism

> Here is Satanic thought from a truly Satanic point of view.
>
> (Anton LaVey, *The Satanic Bible*, 1969, 22)

The esoteric and rationalist perspectives, as exemplified by the Temple of Set and the Church of Satan, respectively, go beyond anti-Christian inversion in order to articulate a philosophical worldview or religious system transcending current norms and values in society. What they share is a definite post-Christian orientation. By establishing a range of modern interpretations of Satan and Satanism based on Enlightenment critique, countercultural expressions, and esoteric knowledge, Christianity no longer takes first place in supplying the context for contemporary Satanism. This has two main consequences. First, devil worship, violence and obscenity are replaced by autonomy, antinomianism and liberation, positive values opposed to the staleness and security of modern life. In contrast to classical theology and folklore is a modern programme for self-development, aptly summarized in the ideological move from Satan to the Satanist. Where the former is a figure borrowed from the Christian narrative, the latter is free to define what is satanic, hence transforming a derogatory term into a positive symbol of reclamation, like 'nigger' or 'gay'.

Related to this, by dis-embedding Satan from the Christian context, modern Satanists are selectively using elements of the Satan-figure to express their particular interests and ambitions while also ignoring or reinterpreting other aspects. This relationship to mythology and tradition is nothing new or even particular to Satan or Satanism, but is a widespread strategy in the history of religion. In my research, I conceptualize this as the 'sanitization' and 'satanization' of Satanism, strategies which have to be seen alongside processes of 'normalization' and 'exclusivity' (or universality and particularity) (Petersen, 2011a). To understand this it is necessary to go back to California and the Summer of Love.

From the outset, the Church of Satan and its High Priest confirms expectations, engaging in blasphemy, carnality and provocation (Barton, 1990). But it quickly becomes evident that this is more than anti-Christian theatre or an occult lodge. In three books published after the founding – *The Satanic Bible* (1969), *The Compleat Witch* (1971; later reissued as *The Satanic Witch*) and *The Satanic Rituals* (1972) – LaVey formulates a set of beliefs, practices and values central to the Church. By borrowing from various mythologies, sociology and psychology, occult philosophy and writers such as Ayn Rand, Friederich Nietzsche and Ragnar Redbeard, these volumes articulate satanic discourse on an esoteric, religious, philosophical and oppositional level. Nevertheless, they are held together by consciously defining Satanism against contemporary trends. Thus, LaVey chastises occult 'fraud', 'white light' spirituality, organized religion, countercultural currents and simple Christian inversion equally, positioning Satanism as the best of all worlds.

In particular, Satan is both emphasized as a symbol of modernity and individuality, as we saw earlier, and disassociated from crime, violence and perversion. This is particularly manifest in The Book of Lucifer, the most reflected and critical part of the bible, and the 'Nine Satanic Statements' establishing the core dogma of indulgence and vital existence (LaVey, 1969: 25, 37–107). This is a double move of 'sanitizing' Satanism and 'satanizing' the modern to obtain an optimal balance of satanic 'bite' and popular appeal. In the same vein, the balance between the universal or normal and the particular or exclusive is also established through the use of esoteric beliefs and practices. On the one hand, esoteric traditions, folklore and mythology are consistently incorporated in Lavey's understanding of satanic magic, thus 'satanizing' them and making them part of a postulated satanic tradition. On the other hand, magic is reinterpreted through a naturalistic and psychological lens, as theatre or 'psychodrama', sanitizing it to make it less antagonistic and marginal (Faxneld, 2013; Petersen, 2011c, 2012; see also Asprem, 2008). Finally, aside from the blatant anti-Christianity of The Book of Satan, the first part of *The Satanic Bible*, blasphemy mainly serves a purpose in rituals, as a specific practice and not the defining ideology. It is thus sanitized and made applicable in a modern context, as an adversarial stance rather than a specific religious statement. In that sense, The Church of Satan is more inspired by Coney Island and the carnival than theological imagination.

Of course, the interpretation of LaVey's texts and organization has changed repeatedly in the past forty-odd years, especially after LaVey's death in 1997 and the explosive development of the Internet from the mid-1990s. Today, the Church of Satan is led by Peter H. Gilmore, who is continuing the dual project by underscoring the atheistic and Epicurean nature of Satanism, yet increasingly promoting a satanic public presence through rituals and literature (Gilmore, 2007). Paradoxically, he has also chosen a rather exclusive take on what Satanism is, that is Church property, even though internal outlooks vary substantially. This reinforces the internal boundary between the Church and the wider milieu, even if many individuals and groups orient themselves by *The Satanic Bible* or consider their association in tune with LaVey's intentions.

Post-Satanic Satanism

> For the serious LHP [left-hand path] practitioner, Satan became powerless when he became cool.
>
> (Don Webb, *Uncle Setnakt's Essential Guide to the Left Hand Path*, 1999, 100)

Post-Christian Satanism as represented by the Church of Satan and modern variants is in many ways prototypical in the satanic milieu and seems both ideologically and numerically dominant. But it is not alone. Visible online and in publishing circuits are various 'theistic' and 'spiritual' Satanisms proposing a return to more explicitly religious interpretations. Here, the relation between Satan and the Satanist is the core of an esoteric project of transformation, based on a personal or mystical relationship. Examples of this position include Diane Vera's many groups and websites combining devil worship and personal growth, and the highly eclectic, fascist Joy of Satan, which offers a range of occult techniques alongside conspiracy theory and Sumerian mythology.

Other types of esoteric Satanism which seem to be increasingly popular are 'anticosmic' Satanism (also called 'Chaosophy' or 'the 218 current') and 'The Sinister Tradition'. Groups such as the anti-cosmic Temple of the Black Light and the sinister Order of the Nine Angles advocate a return to the invocation of medieval demons and radical occult practices (even intimating animal and human sacrifice) in order to unravel the fabric of the cosmos and evolve into truly godlike beings (Petersen, 2012; Senholt, 2013; Sieg, 2014). More broadly, the appeal to the Left Hand Path, tantric practices and occult aims are also prevalent in Luciferian Witchcraft and dark paganism, although the specific perspective and aims vary considerably (Gregorius, 2013).

What is common between these examples is first of all their ephemeral nature. All of these groups are primarily known through publications and websites, and if they have any real presence, it is extremely small in number and exclusive in nature. Second, they all seem to expand Satanism to include a wide range of religious, philosophical and artistic material centred on magic in order to obtain mystical experience. Nevertheless, it is unclear whether the described beliefs and practices are mainly literary, actual blueprints or real events. Third, and this is crucial here, they all seem to broaden the scope and reintegrate Satanism into the wider occult world. The appeal to the Left Hand Path in particular indicates an emerging field of correspondence between Satanism, Paganism and ceremonial magic, borrowing from all. As a consequence, Satan seems to have limited importance the further we move along the esoteric axis and into the 'Left Hand Path milieu'.

In fact, some scholars have proposed the term 'post-Satanism' to highlight the decreasing appeal of Satan in groups such as the Temple of Set, which broke away from the Church of Satan to establish an occult academy based on initiatory magic and self-divinity (Granholm, 2009, 2013). The central principle of the Temple, Xeper (pronounced Kheffer), 'to come into being', can be said to be satanic in the same way Set is misrepresented as Satan – that is, not the whole picture. Becoming or evolution is paramount, and in that is implied a challenge to the status quo and a longing for something more. Setian 'Satanism' is thus 'psychecentric', subsuming all beliefs and practices (which include magical work and esoteric study) under the goals of self-awareness and self-creation (Aquino, 1985 [1975], 2002 [1975]). In essence, the Temple of Set might be the most accessible example of post-Satanic Satanism, insofar as the move from Satan to Set and from Coney Island carnival to Egyptian mystery school marks a return to a pre-LaVeyan emphasis on magical study and initiatory practice in a framework determined explicitly by esoteric, that is idealistic, aims.

Even though I doubt the analytical value of the concept of post-Satanism, it makes good sense to describe many of the emerging currents in the satanic milieu as 'post-satanic', as Satan increasingly is subsumed in larger groups of mythological beings, such as Set, Lilith, Hecate, and Chaos, instead of being the centre of attention. Further, the emphasis on the Satanist is generally retained, while external factors are downplayed. As we saw earlier, most Satanists interpret Satan as their self, a symbol of their highest ideals or a model for living; what is evident here is that even with Satanists who are actually worshiping a real entity or are using magic and demonology without a shred of irony, it is ultimately directed towards themselves. The identification with or imitation of the demons are affecting change and transformation, not demonic intervention as such (or at least, self and demon cannot be divided). This indicates an added distance from the satanic in both a stereotypical and post-Christian sense, as we move away from any intimation of familiarity.

CONCLUDING REMARKS

When looking at any actual example, it is immediately apparent that no group, individual or text fits perfectly within one outlook. Actually, any satanic group will selectively utilize aspects of the three types. A good example is the oppositional and anti-Christian position, which can be found in activities and statements from any number of groups; as indicated above, the focus on grey areas, shadows, forgotten ideas, transgression and provocation is a core element in the satanic project of the self, namely antinomianism and autonomy. Similarly, religious transformation and initiation is not the purview of esoteric Satanism – again, personal expression and self-discovery is central to all Satanists, and indeed most affluent people of the late modern West. Finally, the focus on philosophical reinterpretation of myth and magic into science and psychology so prominent in LaVey's books and the modern Church is continued in a number of satanic perspectives, fitting Satanism into the larger trend of naturalizing religious content. As with any categorization, the types are fuzzy at the edges and speak of relative clarity, not absolute fit.

Furthermore, we should not overstate the differences between LaVey's more philosophically inclined, carnivalesque Satanism and the various post-Satanic developments. First of all, these differences are also a result of the strategies mentioned above, sanitizing and 'satanizing' in order to appeal to smaller or wider audiences. LaVey's ambiguity regarding magic and the occult (that is, if these forces and practices are to be understood literally or metaphorically) has to be seen alongside his extensive use of the same and his complete dismissal of previous and contemporary occultists and 'pseudo-Satanists'. Conversely, LaVey and The Church of Satan are viewed with both jealousy and indifference; the former because of the wide success and popular appeal, the latter because of the shallowness of beliefs and rituals and the lack of focus coming from widespread dissemination. Thus, by mapping the similarities and differences between submilieus and groups within the satanic milieu and the wider 'Left Hand Path' milieu, as well as their relations to popular culture and the occult in general, we see the plurality of contemporary satanic trends.

REFERENCES AND FURTHER READING

Aquino, M. (1985 [1975]) *The Book of Coming Forth By Night*, San Francisco: Temple of Set.

——(2002 [1975]) *Black Magic*, San Franscisco: Temple of Set.

Asprem, E. (2008) 'Magic Naturalized? Negotiating Science and Occult Experience in Aleister Crowley's Scientific Illuminism', *Aries* 8, 139–65.

Barton, B. (1990) *The Church of Satan*, New York: Hell's Kitchen Productions.

Campbell, C. (1972) 'The Cult, the Cultic Milieu and Secularization', in M. Hill, ed., *A Sociological Yearbook of Religion in Britain* 5, London: SCM Press, 119–36.

Dyrendal, A. (2008) 'Devilish Consumption: Popular Culture in Satanic Socialization', *Numen* 55(1), 68–98.

——(2009) 'Darkness Within: Satanism as a Self-Religion', in J. A. Petersen, ed., *Contemporary Religious Satanism: A Critical Anthology*, Farnham; Burlington, CT: Ashgate, 59–74.

Faxneld, P. (2013) 'Secret Lineages and de Facto Satanists: Anton LaVey's Use of Esoteric Tradition', in E. Asprem & K. Granholm, eds., *Contemporary Esotericism*, London: Equinox, 72–91.

Faxneld, P., & Petersen, J. A., eds. (2013) *The Devil's Party: Satanism in Modernity*, New York: Oxford University Press.

Frankfurter, D. (2006) *Evil Incarnate: Rumors of Demonic Conspiracy and Satanic Abuse in History*, Princeton: Princeton UP.

Gilmore, P. (2007) *The Satanic Scriptures*, Baltimore, MD: Scapegoat Publishing.

Granholm, K. (2009) 'Embracing Others than Satan: The Multiple Princes of Darkness in the Left-Hand Path Milieu', in J. A. Petersen, ed., *Contemporary Religious Satanism: A Critical Anthology*, Farnham; Burlington: Ashgate, 85–102.

——(2013) 'The Left-Hand Path and Post-Satanism: The Example of the Temple of Set', in P. Faxneld & J. A. Petersen, eds., *The Devil's Party: Satanism in Modernity*, New York: Oxford University Press, 209–29.

Gregorius, F. (2013) 'Luciferian Witchcraft: At the Crossroads between Paganism and Satanism', in P. Faxneld & J. A. Petersen, eds., *The Devil's Party: Satanism in Modernity*, New York: Oxford University Press, 229–50.

LaVey, A. S. (1969) *The Satanic Bible*, New York: Avon Books.

——(1972) *The Satanic Rituals*, New York: Avon Books.

——(2002 [1971]) *The Satanic Witch*, second edition, New York: Feral House.

Lewis, J. R. (2009) 'Infernal Legitimacy', in J. A. Petersen, ed., *Contemporary Religious Satanism: A Critical Anthology*, Farnham; Burlington, CT: Ashgate, 41–58.

Lowney, K. (1995) 'Teenage Satanism as Oppositional Youth Subculture', *Journal of Contemporary Ethnography* 23(4), 453–84.

Moynihan, M., & Søderlind, D. (1998) *Lords of Chaos: The Bloody Rise of the Satanic Metal Underground*, Venice, CA: Feral House.

Partridge, C. (2005), *The Re-Enchantment of the West: Alternative Spiritualities, Sacralization, Popular Culture and Occulture*, vol. 2, London: T&T Clark.

Petersen, J. A. (2009) 'Introduction: Embracing Satan', in J. A. Petersen, ed., *Contemporary Religious Satanism: A Critical Anthology*, Farnham; Burlington, CT: Ashgate, 1–24.

——(2011a) 'Between Darwin and the Devil: Modern Satanism as Discourse, Milieu, and Self' (doctoral thesis), NTNU, Trondheim, Norway.

——(2011b) '"Smite Him Hip and Thigh": Satanism, Violence, and Transgression', in J. R. Lewis, ed., *Violence and New Religous Movements*, Oxford; New York: Oxford University Press, 351–76.

——(2011c) '"We demand bedrock knowledge": Modern Satanism between Secularized Esotericism and "Esotericized" Secularism', in O. Hammer & J. R. Lewis, eds., *Handbook of Religion and the Authority of Science*, Leiden: Brill, 67–114.

——(2012) 'The Seeds of Satan: Conceptions of Magic in Contemporary Satanism', *Aries*, 12(1), 91–129.

——(2013a) 'The Carnival of Dr. LaVey: Articulations of Transgression in Modern Satanism', in P. Faxneld & J. A. Petersen, eds., *The Devil's Party: Satanism in Modernity*, New York: Oxford University Press, 167–89.

——(2013b) 'From Book to Bit: Enacting Satanism Online', in K. Granholm & E. Asprem, eds., *Contemporary Esotericism*, London: Equinox, 134–58.

Petersen, J. A., ed. (2009b), *Contemporary Religious Satanism: A Critical Anthology*, Farnham; Burlington, CT: Ashgate.

Petersen, J. A., & Dyrendal, A. (2012) 'Satanism', in O. Hammer & M. Rothstein, eds., *Cambridge Companion to New Religious Movements*, Cambridge: Cambridge University Press, 215–31.

Senholt, J. C. (2013) 'Secret Identities in the Sinister Tradition: Political Esotericism and the Convergence of Radical Islam, Satanism, and National Socialism in the Order of the Nine Angles', in P. Faxneld & J. A. Petersen, eds., *The Devil's Party: Satanism in Modernity*, New York: Oxford University Press, 250–74.

Sieg, G. (2014) 'Angular Momentum: From Traditional to Progressive Satanism in the Order of Nine Angles', *International Journal for the Study of New Religions* 4, 251–83.

Webb, D. (1999) *Uncle Setnakt's Essential Guide to the Left Hand Path*, Smithville, TX: Rûna-Raven Press.

CHAPTER FORTY-ONE

CHAOS MAGICK

Colin Duggan

Chaos Magick is a development in twentieth-century occultism, strongly influenced by individuals like Aleister Crowley, Austin Osman Spare, and Kenneth Grant. It comprises a radically individualized discourse on magic and is therefore difficult to accurately define and characterize. It proves more useful to consider Chaos Magick as a set of discourses deploying conceptions of chaos where issues concerning magic, science, art, politics, and individual identity were negotiated and debated, primarily in the 1980s and 1990s. Chaos Magick not only provided a foil against which many individuals involved in more conventional forms of occultism in this period could develop their own ideas, but a space in which new ideas, not only concerning magic, but also sexuality and politics, were allowed to flourish. Although there are numerous discursive transfers between those involved, two general, but overlapping strands of concern can be traced among the myriad opinions of individuals involved in Chaos Magick as to the discursive role played by ideas of chaos. The first strand concerns theories and mechanisms of magic where its efficacy is constructed in terms of scientific chaos theory. The second concerns ideas of chaos characterized by unpredictability, instability, or disorder that provide the ontological basis for individuals to embrace iconoclasm, creativity, potentiality, uncertainty, and above all, change itself.

The first strand includes those individuals who identify with Chaos Magick directly and are most likely to identify as 'Chaos magicians.' They see their practice as scientific, results-based, and experimental. This focus on a new theoretical model of magical efficacy derived from chaos theory distinguishes Chaos Magick from other forms of occultism. In mathematics, chaos theory accounts for dynamical systems that behave in apparently complex ways as if they are being affected by erratic external signals. Chaotic behavior is observed when minor fluctuations in the initial states of the system result in large-scale changes as the system evolves. Even simple systems that are insulated from external interference, which one would expect to be predictable and deterministic, can still display chaotic behavior and this has allowed chaos theory to be appropriated as a mechanism for magical efficacy. Individuals inclined towards this strand of the discourse emphasize the development and explanation of magical models linked to chaos theory such as the 'cybernetic model.'

One notable Chaos Magick author, Phil Hine, has explained that as part of a non-deterministic universe, the neurological activity created in the brain through magical techniques can be used to effect very small changes in the universe which can cause much greater changes.

The second strand describes the broader milieu of interest in ontological ideas of chaos. This strand overlaps with earlier ideas from Discordianism and includes other loose associations such as Thee Temple ov Psychick Youth. Discordianism uses ideas of order and disorder, humor, and the myth of the Greek goddess of chaos to interrogate power structures and individual perceptions of reality. Thee Temple ov Psychick Youth (TOPY), founded by Genesis P-Orridge in 1981, was a collective of artists, musicians, and magicians that emphasized 'sigilisation,' sex, performance, and culture criticism. This broader second strand includes the engaged, knowledgeable, and often polemic writings of many authors contributing to a vital discourse on occultism in this period.

Individuals who participated in the Chaos Magick discourse tended to be involved in practical activities like politics, music, art, and science, and it is in these areas where the greatest changes were taking place. The radical individualism of Chaos Magick drove engagement with new expressions of political, sexual, artistic, musical, and scientific identities, visible in the growth of interest in anarchist politics, the spectrum of sexualities, adoption of new technologies, individualized dissemination of knowledge, shocking and culture critical performance art, and experimental and drug-related musical cultures. The division of Chaos Magick discourse into two strands, an efficacy strand and an ontological strand, does not mean that individuals participated in one or the other, but illustrates sets of inclinations and trends in the overall discourse. Many individuals successfully navigated both of these broad conceptions of chaos and found ways to combine them.

ORIGIN AND DEVELOPMENT

Conventionally, the formal origins of Chaos Magick are traced to the writings of Peter Carroll and Ray Sherwin who published *Liber Null* and *The Book of Results* in 1978 through Sherwin's own publishing venture, The Morton Press. These were followed by Carroll's *Psychonaut* in 1981 and Sherwin's *Theatre of Magick* in 1982. It was during this early period that a number of inchoate concerns regarding the modernization of magic developed into the results-based, practical, and chaos theory–infused magic that distinguished Chaos Magick from other forms of occultism. Lionel Snell (who adopted the alias, Ramsey Dukes) was an important early contributor to the discussions of occultism in the mid- to late 1970s, and the 1980s and 1990s saw numerous publications on the subject that expanded the scope and variety of Chaos Magick discourse by authors like Phil Hine, Joel Biroco, Stephen Sennitt, and Genesis P-Orridge.

Chaos Magick sought to legitimize itself through sets of appeals to tradition and science. The appeal to science is present from the very beginning in the preoccupation with results-based magical practice. The encouragement to record all magical practice as experimentation in magical diaries recalls Aleister Crowley's approach and gives the first air of scientism to Chaos Magick discourse. This is compounded by the direct appeal to scientific chaos theory as an explanation for the efficacy of magic in their new development of occultism and taking the word chaos as an identifier.

In terms of results-based magic, individuals inclined towards efficacy also tended to be more concerned with recording data pertaining to both positive and negative results. Those more inclined towards ontological discourses were primarily concerned with creative acts. So, in this case, performances of music or art, and the production of material works such as 'zines' (abbrev. 'fanzine' or 'magazine': small circulation, often self-produced publications) were part of the desired results and the effects of these creations on an audience, viewer, or reader were also believed to be the results of magic. This can be understood in terms of an 'art as magic' discourse, which can be traced to Austin Osman Spare and can be best explained as the creative labor of the individual being equivalent to a magical practice or the act of creating works while performing other types of magical practice in order to influence the production. This type of result, the effects created, could not be as meticulously recorded, but sometimes reports in the local paper proved to be a record of public reaction to performances.

Generally, appeals to tradition occur in one or both of two ways. In the first case, Chaos Magick is traced back to a pre-modern shaman who is presented as the ancient and universal precursor of all magic. In placing itself in a constructed, perennialist tradition of magic, Chaos Magick attempts to claim legitimacy through heritage and the unbroken tradition of magical knowledge. Perennialism here refers to the general idea of unbroken chains of wisdom through history and the processes of selective construction employed by individuals in creating these 'traditions.' Late twentieth-century radical individualist discourses have seen these constructed perennialist traditions become more varied and subjective.

The second way in which Chaos Magick appeals to tradition is in the form of iconoclasm, which is understood figuratively as the strategy of disregarding the established ideas of one's predecessors in favor of one's own innovations. In this case, the appeal is made by claiming to be the next, newest, and most vital instance of a constructed, perennialist tradition while heavily criticising and polemicizing against existing conventions or dominant ideas. Due to the emphasis on individualism, Chaos Magick seeks legitimacy both for its rightful place in a tradition of magic and its iconoclastic impulse which calls for criticism, polemics, and symbolic destruction of all that precedes it. Therefore, Chaos Magick claims legitimacy for its innovations both at the level of the broader discourse and the individual. Iconoclasm is the active form of perennialism in Chaos Magick discourse as tearing down existing structures and hierarchies makes way for new systems, cultural spaces, and individualism that can be included in the tradition.

Chaos Magick has sometimes been characterized as nihilistic due to its strong relativism, iconoclasm, and negative representations of how ideas of chaos or self are employed in the discourse. This results primarily from a lack of engagement with the source materials, but also an underestimation of the extent of discussion and debate within Chaos Magick leading to a non-representative analysis of particular elements only. Contrary to some portrayals, Chaos Magick discourse is primarily concerned with criticism, creativity, and potential.

Chaos Magick differs from other forms of occultism, both in this period and the early twentieth century in its strong rejection of the hierarchical structures of other magical orders or groups. Although groups like the Illuminates of Thanateros (while founded by Carroll and Sherwin, as a loose network, it became an organized group) are often discussed, this is more the exception than the rule. Individuals choosing to involve themselves in the practice of Chaos Magick more often work alone or in loose networks. The anarchic elements of Chaos Magick and of the milieu with which it is associated, allow each individual to create or choose their own mode of participation in the discourse. This accounts for the scope and diversity of ideas and discussion in the literature. Thee Temple ov Psychick Youth is a primary example of a loose network of individuals in which Chaos Magick interacts with culture criticism, politics, and performance art.

IDEAS AND PRACTICE

Given the radical individualism and inherent fluidity of Chaos Magick, there are no defining features of theory or practice that must be present in order to warrant the categorization. Individuals involved in Chaos Magick can, and have, used the full range of magical practices and systems drawn from a long history. However, there are a number of key components that are often associated with Chaos Magick and are commonly discussed in the literature.

The first of these is the process of sigilization in which the practitioner creates a sigil by encoding a desire into a personalized glyph. For example, one simple way of encoding a sigil is to write down the desire, remove the vowels and any repeats of letters, and arrange the remaining letters into a glyph that should be entirely personal to its creator. The extent to which this process is personalized and varied is often linked to the potency of the sigil. The sigil is then cast into the sub-conscious mind by bringing it into focus at a moment of intense ecstatic trance reached through excitatory or inhibitory techniques including, but not limited to, sexual excitement, sexual exhaustion, drug use, music, dance, and meditation. These techniques can be employed singly or in combination as long as the result is a trance-like, ecstatic, short-circuiting of the conscious mind in order to allow the sigil and its coded desire direct access to the sub-conscious. The idea and process of sigilization is prevalent in Chaos Magick discourse and in this form is often traced back to the English occultist and artist, Austin Osman Spare who is noted by many writers as an important influence on Chaos Magick.

Together with this idea of sigils, Spare provides the idea of chaos as the aspect of the universe that is unformed potentiality, that which contains everything in a state prior to conception. This was the source of Spare's rejection of belief because for him, belief is responsible for all the limiting conditions placed on the subjective individual and therefore, in order to break free of the conditions, one must break free of belief and learn how to use it as a tool for the development of the self. Hence, in Chaos Magick, belief has often been presented as such, a tool to be used when required, switching from one belief system to another at the will of the practitioner. This is connected to another part of Chaos Magick discourse, ideas of conditioning and deconditioning where the practitioner strives to form and break habits in order to develop the will and free the self from the conditioning of society.This radical subjectivity and, in effect, the process of testing the boundaries of that subjectivity encapsulates the influence of Crowley's Thelema on Spare and Chaos Magick.

Ideas of the self in Chaos Magick are ambivalent and the singularity of self, the essentialism of the idea that there is one self, sometimes in two parts, and that that self corresponds to the physical individual, and to that one individual only, has been a source of contention. Chaos Magick has been called post-modern by many commentators but its status as such is irrelevant. The discourse has obviously been influenced by post-modern and post-structuralist thought and conceptions of the self in Chaos Magick are complex. The existence of the individual and sovereign self is one of the last bastions of modern thought and the implications of its fragmentation and fragility lead to a paradox when it comes to the idea of 'self development.' Many magical practices are supposed to act upon the individual self in order to improve or develop that self but the implication of post-modern thought would prompt questions as to whether that self exists. If it does, doubt would still remain as to the permanence of such a self that would enable it to be acted upon, to retain change, to experience improvement. This paradox can be resolved when Chaos Magick is considered in terms of the ontology of creativity, potential, and renewal. In many ways, the exercises provide the method of exposing the self as an entity unable to do the work thrust upon it by early twentieth-century occultists. Through this breaking down of self and undermining of the concept of the essential individual, there is space for creating new consciousness, ideas, societies, politics, sexualities, art, music, and a new way of combating the modern alienation of the essentialized individual.

DISSEMINATION AND INTERACTION

Like the occultists of the early twentieth century, one of the ways in which knowledge and information concerning Chaos Magick was disseminated in the 1980s and 1990s was through the pages of self-published texts known as zines. Zines are a representation of the democratization of knowledge production and access to information. The creation and dissemination of zines and their contents is a political act. They affirm the status of certain types of knowledge that have been neglected in other media. Zines are inherently a criticism of hierarchical structures, centralized authority, organized religion, and society in general. As well as the political and artistic act of producing zines, they were a vehicle for knowledge about political systems, anarchy, and social criticism. Due to the publishing history of influential individuals and groups involved in occultism in the late nineteenth and early twentieth century, Chaos zine producers have often referred to their productions as periodicals. While other zine producers have made every effort to distance themselves from more established forms of printing and producing, there is still a legacy issue with regard to occultism where authenticity is not lost if one is following in the footsteps of publications like Aleister Crowley's *Equinox*.

Zines provided the opportunity for candid debate and are a historical record of the Chaos Magick discourse throughout the 1980s and 1990s. Some operated a publish everything policy that fostered lively debate and discussion of occultism and their number and scope are expressions of this discourse. Zines contained a wide range of subject matter including Chaos Magick explanation, interpretation of magic as it had been (iconoclasm), gender, sexuality, sexual politics, establishment politics, art, music, science, and technology. Chaos Magick engendered polemical discussions as to the nature of these subjects and zines were an important vehicle for this type of knowledge. While providing a forum for discussion of Chaos Magick and other topics, zines also facilitated network building among interested participants regardless of location. Zines often contained a networking section and/or a review section of other zines along with contact details of their producers and information on how to obtain them. The democratic aspect of zine production means that zine consumers are zine producers, and the act of distributing zines becomes the act of gaining access to other zines.

The importance of individualism in Chaos Magick discourse cannot be overstated. The emphasis on personal experience, personal experimentation, personalized rituals, personal beliefs, self-development, self-conditioning, individual potential, individual creativity, and individual creation and dissemination of knowledge is evident in all aspects of Chaos Magick discourse. In addition, its fluidity and easy interactions with other forms of occultism and various cultural knowledge forms prevents easy characterization but encourages analysis of pluralized and individualized discourses.

REFERENCES AND FURTHER READING

Carroll, P. (1987 [1978, 1981]) *Liber Null and Psychonaut: An Introduction to Chaos Magic*, San Francisco: Red Wheel/Weiser. Originally published as two volumes, *Liber Null* (East Morton: The Morton Press, 1978) and *Psychonaut* (East Morton: The Morton Press, 1981).

Duggan, C. (2013) 'Perennialism and Iconoclasm: Chaos Magick and the Legitimacy of Innovation,' in E. Asprem & K. Granholm, eds., *Contemporary Esotericism*, Sheffield: Equinox, 91–112.

Hanegraaff, W. (2007) 'Fiction in the Desert of the Real: Lovecraft's Cthulhu Mythos,' *Aries* 7, 85–109.

Hine, P. (1992) *Condensed Chaos*, London: Chaos International Publications.

Sherwin, R. (2005 [1978]) *The Book of Results*, Morrisville: Lulu Press.

——(2006 [1982]) *Theatre of Magick*, Morrisville: Baphomat Publishing/Lulu Press.

Urban, H. B. (2006) *Magia Sexualis: Sex, Magic, and Liberation in Modern Western Esotericism*, Los Angeles, CA: University of California Press.

CHAPTER FORTY-TWO

VAMPIRISM, LYCANTHROPY, AND OTHERKIN

Jay Johnston

INTRODUCTION: ON BEING OTHER THAN 100 PERCENT HUMAN

This chapter explores subcultures and individuals found in the occult world that celebrate their difference from humans. Vampire, Lycanthrope, and Otherkin are the terms used to designate individuals who understand themselves to be either not human or only partially human, with the rest of their subjectivity comprised of some 'other' species: 'real' or metaphysical. The identity terminology is slippery, for example some accounts of Otherkin include vampires, others do not and not all who identify as non-or-partially human use such labels at all. Nonetheless, the terms have gained increasing currency in both the identity politics of numerous subcultures and the academic study of religion, therefore, despite the noted contestation they will be employed herein.

Vampires, Lycanthropes and Otherkin traverse – indeed inhabit – boundaries: boundaries between matter and spirit; between the human and the animal and the human and non-human species, with 'species' taken as it can be most broadly conceived. Each of these represent enormous fields of study in themselves and the focus of this chapter is not to give an exhaustive historical or literary account of vampire or werewolf figures for example; but, rather, to provide an overview of where these figures have intersected with, and featured in occult belief and practice. Emphasis will be placed on their presence in the contemporary occult world.

Although this discussion will identify and consider a series of different subcultures linked to the figures of vampire, werewolf, and Otherkin identities (and indeed, discuss each in turn) there are certain shared qualities, or more precisely, processes, encapsulated in their very concept of ontological 'being' which are features of all. To start with: their status as boundary dwellers and boundary breakers. That is, each of these figures cross, disrupt, and inhabit boundaries common to everyday forms of reason: animal/human; real/unreal (fantasy); actual/virtual; physical/metaphysical; culture/nature; fact/fiction. They are figures of potentially dangerous transgression (both ontologically and epistemologically): this is the heart of their appeal and abhorrence.

Further, each of the forms of subject discussed here are marked by processes of metamorphosis: the capacity to change from one state of being or species to another; and/or the process by which one comes to understand the self as not entirely human (and as having been born as such), that is a metamorphosis in perception leading to a revision of one's identity: whether this is an involuntary 'development,' for example the reported 'awakening' when an individual becomes aware of their vampire or Otherkin self; or a consciously cultivated skill (via techniques like guided visualization, contemporary shamanic journeying, and other forms of ritual performance) leading to an understanding that the individual can shape-shift into other forms. Enchantment inhabits the very transmogrifying flesh of these figures and in some cases – as discussed further below – they are themselves the custodians and agents of certain types of magic. Indeed, contemporary renderings of vampires and werewolves are marked by their status as practitioners of magic more than previous historical renderings – in literature and folktale – of such figures (Partridge 2005). Their occult agency has grown; and, in turn, so has their allure.

These figures may not only have the capacity to change from one state to another (whether cyclical or permanent); they are also hybrid subjects, composed of more than one species. In regard to Otherkin, what counts as an 'other' species is a perpetually expanding field that includes, for example, animals, angels, elves, mythical beasts, machines, and cartoon characters. Otherkin subjectivities confound such hybridity even further in cases where an individual is understood to be composed of three or more species (these are known as 'multiples'), or more than one subjectivity.

Hybridism and the capacity for metamorphosis have long been the traits not only of magicians but also gods and demons. Early Christian magical handbooks – that provide instructions and spell formulae – are replete with images of snake-legged and bird-beaked humans and spiritual beings, as well as forms of hybrid animals (for examples see Meyer and Smith 1999). Of course, the capacity for spiritual beings and 'special' humans to shape-shift is a feature of many belief systems, especially those marked by what are now designated as animistic or 'shamanic' beliefs and practices. These include those Nordic traditions which have influenced many Otherkin subcultures (Johnston 2014). A swift 'nod' to this conceptual heritage before commencing a more detailed account of vampires, lyncanthropes, and Otherkin is useful, as it signals the deep foundations of the contemporary versions of these figures. It is not just that they share the features and processes previously discussed; but, also, to varying degrees they partake of the same field of conceptual influences as are filtered through numerous forms of discourse including scholarly analysis and popular genres of film, TV, novel, and game.

As the discussion of several subcultures below will seek to illustrate, the contemporary renderings of vampire and Lycanthrope figures and the formations of subjectivity embraced by Otherkin can *both* challenge dominant concepts of the human and animal, the real and unreal for example, but also reproduce and re-affirm dominant concepts of normal/abnormal boundaries including gender ascription. As figures of deviance they hold enormous popular appeal. The degree to which such deviance challenges dominant discourse or merely forms an 'other' which reinforces its binary structure – including the bounds of normality – varies considerably.

VAMPIRE TEMPLE AND WEREWOLF CATHEDRAL: NOTES ON OCCULT VAMPIRE AND LYCANTHROPE GROUPS

Vampirism

> Show a vampire a clove of garlic and s/he is likely either to laugh or think about pasta possibilities.... Vampires can fly – but only in airplanes, gliders and helicopters.
>
> (Lupa 2007: 152)

For contemporary youth of western culture, nothing says vampire more than the *Twilight* series. Despicably handsome, powerful, romantic figures populate the books by Stephenie Meyer, and the subsequent films have garnered broad adolescent appeal; a decidedly more occult version of the iconic 1980s *The Breakfast Club* (1985). While this popularity can be considered as yet another development in the general fascination with vampire myth and legend – in the wake of other previous literary, filmic, and folktale precursors like Dracula and Nosferatu – *Twilight's* particular figure of the vampire builds most clearly upon the less horrific and more cult-iconic vampires that emerged in the 1980s out of Anne Rice's books, notably *Interview with the Vampire* (1976), and their filmic adaptations; as well as other movies like *The Lost Boys* (1987). These more recent cultural forms have certainly presented vampires as viable individuals with unique personalities and capacities. Accompanying these newer forms of the 'media' vampire has been the development of vampire subcultures which include vampire role-players, blood fetishists, vampire religions, and of course vampires – as a distinct subjectivity – and their 'donors' (those that voluntarily feed them whether with blood or energy) (Keyworth 2010: 355).

Vampire subcultures inhabit numerous socio-cultural spaces and produce an assortment of beliefs and practices. There are clearly different degrees of commitment and styles of engagement. Following Ramsland, Keyworth reads the popularity of the figure of the vampire in popular culture and the emergence of contemporary subcultures and religion as a response to the 'malaise and confusion, feelings of abandonment and loneliness, and the need to be "somebody"' that is given as the characteristic of Generation X (those who grew up in the 1970s and 1980s). What he terms 'the pretence of a vampire existence' – the term 'pretence' carrying unfortunate dismissive connotations of charade, or even deceit – is interpreted as offering 'a heightened sense of self–esteem, imparted the strength to overcome adversity... encouraged a sense of community...and led credence to the notion of being an outsider and social outcast' (2010: 356). This is a vampire subjectivity that celebrates its difference from the 'normal' human and is not overtly interested in challenging the concepts upon which the normal is predicated: it keeps such dominant logic in place. Although usually read as a form of deviance (often with attempts to pathologize adherents), as Williams argues 'upon closer examination, many self-identified vampires and their rituals and practices can be understood as artistic, expressive, and rather normal and healthy' (2008: 513). One suspects that most 'living' vampires would find the attribution to them of the label 'normal' to be anathema.

These are subjects that consider themselves inherently and 'naturally' to *be* vampires. It is core to how they understand themselves, including their physical body and their relations to others and the world in general. This identity can be linked to more formalized vampire religions or groups, for example Clan of Lilith, or like other forms of self-directed spirituality it can form the foundation of an eclectic set of practices chosen, developed, and adapted by the individual. On-line surveys also record vampires as members of a variety of other religions including Wicca, Satanism, and (very) low percentages of Christianity and Islam (Keyworth 2010: 365). Hence, for example one can understand oneself to be a vampire and a Christian simultaneously.

There have been a number of academic studies of vampire religion (including Keyworth 2010; Laycock 2010; Partridge 2005; Melton 1999) which highlight the occult heritage of organizations like Order of the Dragon, House Kheperu and The Temple of the Vampire, and their similarities and differences to Anton LeVay's Church of Satan. The Temple of the Vampire founded by Lucis Martel is usually dated to 1989, the year that *The Vampire Bible* was published and when it was registered with the United States Government (Partridge 2004b: 353). As previously identified by Christopher Partridge, many of the Temple's core beliefs are aligned with Satanists, especially the focus on the power and 'might' of the self; while in contra-distinction their worship of Undead Gods (set to return at a Final Harvest) is a distinguishing feature. Like all of the groups and communities discussed in this chapter the Temple is an on-line phenomenon, with vampires able to form local 'cabals' for off-line meetings and rituals as well. Membership is by application, and certain texts – for example *The Vampire Sorcery Bible*, freely available until 2003 – are now restricted to members as they move through the Temple's hierarchy of vampire development. According to Temple discourse, individuals are inherently born vampires ('born to blood') and the role of the Temple is to draw together and develop those of vampire heritage. Unlike many Elven groups (to be discussed below) this is no egalitarian setup. Not only is there a hierarchy within the Temple itself, but vampires perceive themselves to be more advanced, 'of a higher evolution' than humans. Their discourse is indeed quite dismissive of the human species (Partridge 2005: 237–38).

In addition to, and for some in association with, these occult organizations, are individuals of vampire subjectivity, both 'sanguine' and 'psychic' who understand themselves as Otherkin. Sanguine vampires are understood to literally feed on human and animal blood and are usually encouraged to find a willing donor; whilst psychic vampires feed on energy. In *A Field Guide to Otherkin* (2007) Lupa recounts three forms of energy snacking: 1. 'ambient': feeding on group energy absorbed in a crowd and considered a form of 'junk food' (Lupa 2007: 143); 2. 'contact': which requires closer 'auric' contact; 3. 'Deep feeding': directly drawing on an individual's psychic energy, usually done during times of heightened states of physical or sensory experience, for example during sex (2007: 142–43). In hir advice to both vampires and donors regarding understanding and working with energy, Lupa advises consulting Barbara Brennan's *Hands of Light* (1988), the 'classic' tome for alternative therapists working with energy medicine (see Chapter 65, The Body in Occult Thought, for further details on these theories).

Lycanthropes

Lycanthropy, like vampirism, can be found in numerous forms in contemporary occult practice. Some forms are strongly influenced by contemporary shamanism of the Michael Harner variety; in which it is presented as a technique that can be learnt by anyone, and a feature of which is working with totem animals either as guides to (and in) other worlds or in shape-shifting rituals (Harner 1980). Timberwolf's website and suggested practice is an example of this form of Lycanthropy (2009: np.). Individuals are trained – via meditation and visualization techniques – to release their wolf within: to tap into and connect with their innate Lyncanthropic spirit:

> I exist mentally and in spirit as both wolf and human (I am *one* person, *one* character, *one* being). When I shift, mentally, the outside world usually notices. The change produces a change in my demeanour [sic] that is recognizable. Even without shifting, there are facets in my mind that are pure wolf, and make me different to the people around me.
>
> (anon qtd Timberwolf 2009: np.)

According to Timberwolf, the inner wolf agency has the capacity to affect a 'shift,' and thereby override human will if it 'senses that you need guidance or protection' (Timberwolf 2009: np.). As will be illustrated in discussion of Otherkin below, the individualized, shamanic heritage advocated by Timberwolf is also a feature of many Therian practices and beliefs.

Occult groups of Lycanthropes – werewolves – have also been established. The Werewolf Cathedral is a noted example; indeed, its founder, High Priest Christopher Johnson, is a member of the Church of Satan and the Temple of the Vampire (images of membership cards are shown on the Cathedral website). Like both, the Cathedral has a creed 'The Oath of the Werewolf' and a guide text, in this case *Manifesto of the Wolf* written by Johnson. Both stress the individual as that which is to be revered – 'I shall have no other gods before mine own self' – and in particular the valorization of instinct (the beast) over intelligence (Johnson 2009).

While the Cathedral rejects any concept of good and evil it reifies another dualism of predator and prey: 'I am predator not prey and shall conduct myself as such' ('The Oath of the Werewolf'). Such conduct according to the website includes taking responsibility for one's own destiny via a 'lycanthropic transformation.' This unleashing of the beast is undertaken through occult training. Johnson's biography lists eleven years of participation and training in occult organizations including Italian Wicca and various pagan groups. He is, therefore, more precise than many about the practical and conceptual heritage of the werewolves' ritual and worship: 'These teachings are based off an amalgam of teachings from the works of Aleister Crowely, Boyd Rice, The Hermetic Order of the Golden Dawn, Classical Hermetics, Occultism, and the works of Dr. Anton Szandor LaVey, Ragnar Redbeard, and various Chaos Magick systems' (Johnson 2009: 12).

The Manifesto contains references to becoming an 'esoteric werewolf' via training in visualization techniques and energy manipulation; descriptions of rituals, ritual objects, and invocations are also provided (Johnson 2009: 12–13), with the final line of the Oath being: 'I shall have no pity for those, which I seduce with my magick' (ibid.: 3). Magick is one of the features that distinguishes werewolves from 'lower' species like humans. They are proudly misanthropic, although they do revert to other animal metaphors when castigating mass belief and consumer practices: 'We are werewolves not sheep. We do not watch TV or advertising that is designed to brainwash and conform us' (ibid.: 9). A heightened sense of individual authority and a celebration of the physical life are endorsed beastly features.

Like The Vampire Temple, the Cathedral proposes a group of 'higher' beings – the Werewolf Elders – that are evoked in rituals. Johnson's experience with other occult groups has led to very upfront responses in the website's FAQ section as to what distinguishes the group from The Temple of the Vampires or The Church of Satan. Working with the Werewolf Elders is a defining feature, and he considers the Cathedral as a form of paganism with the website advocating: 'Those that do believe in the spiritual realms are encouraged to find and work with a patron God and Goddess much like wiccans do' (anon. werewolfcathedral.com: np.). However, certain wiccan forms are definitely not encouraged, with new members directed to avoid associating with 'Feminist, Wiccan-orientated, consciousness-raising groups who practice more male-bashing than magick' (anon. werewolfcathedral.com: np.).

There is a hierarchical order to the Cathedral, with Johnson a member of The Order of Marchosias, an 'inner order' about which nothing much else is given publicly. The organization works to facilitate links between members, forming on- and off-line Packs to whom they are asked to hold allegiance (but not to the degree that it undermines their own authority). The 'animal' in the werewolf Cathedral is celebrated for its difference from humans and as representative of a visceral, physical type of 'gut'-knowledge. Predator dominance is an overarching theme, one that is not characteristic of wolf Therianthropes to the same degree.

OTHERKIN

> This is not a roleplaying game. When a person says s/he is a dragon, or a wolf, or an elf, s/he is not referring to a character that s/he only becomes during the gaming session. That which is Other is a constant part of the person; s/he is the Other at all times.
>
> (Lupa 2007: 27)

There is a vast – and ever increasing – range of 'types' of Otherkin (or 'kin), and any attempt at producing a comprehensive catalogue is destined for redundancy at the outset. Indeed, such multiplicity and elusiveness is core to understanding Otherkin. In the brief overview that follows information is drawn primarily from internet sites – Otherkin is a strongly net-mediated subculture (see Kirby 2009) – and from Therian Lupa's on-line survey research published in *A Field Guide to Otherkin* (2007).[1]

At the heart of Otherkin belief is the visceral, lived understanding that the individual is something other than 100 percent human. For many, but not all, accompanying this understanding are various spiritual beliefs that provide causal reasons for their unique ontological status. As will be taken up in more detail below, Otherkin subjectivities offer very useful critiques of normative concepts of the human, whilst simultaneously reinforcing concepts of species difference. In the creation of the numerous identities found in the subculture, Otherkin individuals draw on a vast and eclectic range of spiritual and religious beliefs, with occult knowledge, especially magic and energetic concepts of the body, an evident feature.

The most recognized groups of Otherkin are Therians, Elves and Fey, Angels and Demons, Kitsune, Otakuken, Mythological beasts (for example dragons and unicorns), Mediakin, and as previously noted vampires are often considered a class of 'kin as well. Therians are animal–human Otherkin, with their animal element drawn from a great range of the recognizable animals that inhabit this world. From squirrel to salamander, Therianthropic identity incorporates aspects of contemporary Shamanism, especially the tendency to see their animal self in totemic, abstract, or archetypal terms. That is, whether the reference is to 'wolf spirit' or 'fox spirit,' the animal identity is generic rather than particular (for which their concept of the animal can be critiqued). Crossovers with other subcultures, like werewolves and Furries (Furry Fandom), also exist; although there has been noted animosity between groups as well. Many Therians are critical of the Furries' part-time 'fursona.' Lupa states: 'Therians do not take off their animal selves at the end of a convention – they are human and animal at all times' (2007: 131).

However, like Furry Fandom, Therian subjectivity also holds the potential to confound dominant, dimorphic concepts of gender (male/female); hence Lupa's choice to use non-specific pronouns like 'hir' throughout the text (Lupa 2007: 26; Probyn-Rapsey 2011). Indeed, the capacity for animal and other non-human species' gender and sexuality (whether elf or vampire) to confound (to Queer) dominant male–female logics (often discussed as 'animal trans'), as well as the possibilities engendered by Other–human hybridity, has become a feature of gender and feminist scholarship (Giffney and Hird 2008; Ferreday 2011).

American counter-culture groups of the 1960s, nature-based spirituality, J. R. R. Tolkien's fantasy novels (and Peter Jackson's more recent film versions of *Lord of the Rings*), European mythology: These all strongly inform faery, elven and mythological beast 'kin (Lupa 2007: 153–71). As a contentious example, Tië eldaliéva are an Elven group (officially founded August 23, 2005) whose spiritual path is entirely founded upon Tolkien's works, with *The Silmarillion* described as the closest text the group has to a Bible. While they do not exclude other elven lineages, Tië eldaliéva elves (Quendi) consider Otherkin elves as not 'real' elves, but rather 'Elven friends' (www.lassiquendi.com: np.). For this group being Otherkin is about resonating with Elven energy but NOT being Elven (lacking in Elven DNA or Elven Soul). Obviously, many elvenkin would disagree with such an assessment. The Tië eldaliéva claims exemplify those debates about authenticity that are a feature of the Otherkin community.

Similarly, the Fey (or Faerie) 'kin are informed by modern and contemporary fantasy literature, and their forms can embrace everything from Doreen Virtue style angels (as depicted in her books and divination cards) of winged elemental beings to animal-fey. As Lupa notes of hir survey results:

> I received surveys from all sorts of fey, including phoukas, a satyr, a selkie, and 'just call me a faerie.' Bandora describes herself as 'a mix of a couple of faery species. My particular kind have accented face features including ears, almond shaped eyes, dragonfly type wings, bluish-glowy skin, very thick wiry yet fairly straight hair and joints that can bend to any angle…'. Needless to say, there's no one right way to describe faerie.
>
> (Lupa 2007: 165–66)

Otherkin physiology has both physical and energetic components. Like many forms of self-directed contemporary spirituality, esoteric energy bodies feature, characteristically, 'kin appendages. Wings, talons and tails are often described as parts of the individual's subtle body: energetic phantom limbs. Physical and medical evidence is also referenced to account for, or to demonstrate, one's 'kin affiliation; for example, a diagnostic for Fey is an allergy to iron (Lupa 2007: 183; 170).

Kitsune Otherkin claim a fox spirit 'other' – and are therefore a mix between Therianthrope and Mythological beast – found in Japanese, Chinese, and Korean mythological traditions. Iconographically, Kitsune usually take the form of a fox; but the spirit-being is traditionally renowned as a shape-shifter, and this quality is often considered an aspect of Kitsunekin. Japanese *manga* and *anime* culture has furnished Otakukin with a range of non-human elements. Characters from popular culture forms like film, cartoon, game, and fiction feature as much as figures from mythology or medieval beasteries. Mediakin denotes 'kin types whose 'other' is derived from culturally diverse media genres, including Disney cartoon characters (Lupa 2007: 197–206).

In addition to identifying as a particular type of Otherkin, individuals can understand themselves as being comprised of a number of different species ('multiples'); or, as their physical body housing an entirely other being (or two) known as 'walk-ins.' Very much the same terminology is found in UFO-based religions, equally the channelling culture of the 1980s. Some Otherkin, like vampire and Werewolf subcultures, demonstrate an antipathy towards their human 'part' and term 100 percent humans as 'mundanes.' Fey, Lysander, is clear in hir contempt: 'socializing with regular humans (mundanes) I find rather boring, and dealing with them too often or in too large of doses is frustrating to me because they're just so, ugh, dull' (qtd. in Lupa 2007: 168). Nevertheless, this statement is then qualified to not include *every* human (some are apparently fun). In contrast, information for prospective Tië eldaliéva elves advises: 'the danger zone with this category is that some think Elves are superior to Humans…The position that Tië eldaliéva takes on this topic is that there is already enough racism in the world and do not wish to add to it' (www.lassiquendi.com: 10). Misanthropy is therefore not necessarily a feature of the broader Otherkin community, as it is for members of The Werewolf Cathedral; but the 'human' certainly remains that which 'kin subjectivity is defined against.

These are debates that are central to the numerous, complex, and contradictory information that Otherkin subcultures produce; they are discourses focused on how to negotiate difference. 'Kin difference is not only from 'mundanes' (100 percent humans) but also from different types of 'kin or groups within a single 'kin. This difference is key to Otherkin identity politics, it is the grist that drives authenticity claims and/or claims from within the community that cast doubt on an individual's status ('pretendakin'). The valorization of 'alternative' epistemologies, for example imagination and intuition, as the source of realizing one's true Otherkin nature (a process called 'awakening'), like many New Age and Wellbeing self-directed spiritualities, places the authority of knowing the truth of ontological being on the individual. Claims and counter-claims about one's kin status are inherently unverifiable by any external agent; not that this has hindered the development of technologies to help identify one's Otherkin type (which many groups suggest are best avoided).

Many 'What Kind of Otherkin Are You' on-line surveys exist. Selectsmart.com (2,269 results since 2008) asks for example: 'Is your appearance somewhat feral?' and 'Do you have any magick abilities?' While the more involved 'The Kintype Indicator' (HelloQuizzy.com) results break down each individual to a percentage of different types of 'kin and human with accompanying graphics to demonstrate how the individual compared to other respondents. For example one may be: 15 percent human; 54 percent Therian; 53 percent Faerie; 57 percent Angel; 29 percent Demon; 56 percent Elf, 30 percent Kitsune; 16 percent Machine-kin; 31 percent Starseed; 13 percent Shadow; 46 percent Dragon, and 19 percent Polymorph. A final 'this is your type' answer is given (which unsurprisingly matches the highest percentage). Although its detail and pseudo-scientific presentation carries an aura of authority, it is only another reductive form of personality testing. The species difference seems to have been utterly erased in the process. That is, the sense that there is in Otherkin identity an 'other' that is never entirely knowable by the individual or in some way retains its foreign, incommensurate nature; a difference that cannot be accommodated in dominant epistemologies or concepts of human agency. This central but mysterious aspect of self for Otherkin can only be known by the employment of ritual practices, visualization, imagination, and energy work.

This unknown aspect to the 'other' is evidenced in the starting point for many Awakening narratives which recount profound feelings of body dimorphia: of not fitting in one's body; not being able to make the body do what one desires to do. That is, a profound disjuncture between the concept of self and the physical body. For Otherkin, both the Other and the Human are part of their lived, everyday, subjectivities and it is the use of occult theories and practices, especially of magical ritual and energetic concepts of the self that provides a foundation for understanding their sense of dimorphism or displacement.

Unsurprisingly, the communities have offered a varying array of beliefs about their origins, many of which use popular science, religious belief, and mythological discourses as foundation narratives. These include, reincarnation (Neoplatonic transmigration of the soul rather than Buddhist cyclic rebirth) where the individual soul, the locus of the 'other,' is understood to have had previous lives as the relevant animal or spirit being. There are also (loosely) Gnostic proposals of incarnation in the human body as being a punishment, as well as more general New Age (of the Shirley McLaine variety) notions that the incarnation is for learning a specific lesson (Lupa 2007: 57–58). Reincarnation ideas also include the belief that the self is comprised of a series of multiple fragments that have coalesced for this life-time only. These soul fragments could be drawn from any number of species, hence:

> one fragment may have been part of an elf in another life, while another was part of a tiger. The fragments may collect around a central primary energy to create a complete soul, or the soul may be entirely comprised of fragments. When a person dies the soul becomes fragments again and each piece goes on its separate journey.
>
> (Lupa 2007: 62–63)

Genetic inheritance is also used to explain the difference, some Otherkin claim to possess anomalies in the genome – to have Elven DNA for example – or to have been born into a family of kin. Solo, a vulpine canine multiple, explains:

> Our biological father, when he was young, would tell people that he wanted to be a fox when he grew up. He also had eyes that, under average circumstances

> are green, but've [sic] been known to randomly turn very yellow, and he has rather pronounced canines. He also has an amazing, almost hypnotic effect on dogs, and he considers them his favourite animals and feels he can strongly relate to them...
>
> (qtd in Lupa 2007: 69)

Such physical/genetic heritage is often traced back to an ancestor having had interspecies sexual relations. On the whole though, shared physical characteristics do not seem to feature as much in the discourse as does energetic or soul connections. The Other is strongly conceptualized as something of essence: of soul or spirit. It is more ephemeral than physical. This is evidenced in the Quendi's conceptualization of elven subjectivity, which is at its 'essence' a form of 'bridge' (in much the same way that subtle bodies are conceived to bridge the physical and metaphysical worlds). As explained on the Tië eldaliéva FAQs:

> Elves seemed to 'bridge' with many entities and life forms, including trees, plants, and animals, with virtually no effort at all – likely because they were 'between' many different energies and could likely 'blend' more easily with what was at hand.
>
> (n.d.: 2)

In summary, a vast array of reasons from conventional science and biomedicine to spiritual composition, soul essence, parallel universes, and reincarnation, are deployed to 'explain' being Otherkin; with the ubiquitous haunting understanding that one's lived, felt subjectivity is not 'normal.'

OCCULT SELVES: ON DIFFERENCE AND CRITIQUE

Vampires, Lycanthropes and Otherkin have had a presence as on-line occult groups and subcultures for several decades now (not counting the pre-dating 'real world' counter-culture communities) and they have from the outset been read as a critique of the contemporary world. Mamatas in 'Elven Like Me' for the *Village Voice* reported in 2001:

> Like so many other subcultures, the Otherkin have found a place on the Internet, where they make friends and build communities. The Otherkin are both a sign and a portent of a widespread dissatisfaction with the modern world.
>
> (Mamatas 2001: 35)

The critiques these discourses contain are numerous but not consistent: some rally against dominant faith traditions like Christianity, others against empirical reason and the suppression of imagination and creativity, yet others against the desecration of the 'natural' world. There is no cohesive point that can be identified; except, that they are – to some degree – not human. In an effort to understand and identify their subjectivity occult ideas and techniques from antiquity to popular culture are employed. The occult world is that which they inhabit; it is their everyday reality and as such vampires, Lycanthropes, and Otherkin live in the interstices; they understand themselves as enchanted and capable of enchanting. Magic is part of their being and like any other perceptual skill capable of being developed.

At its most mundane the ontological difference these boundary subjects champion simply maintains abnormal–normal binaries; at its most potent they offer serious and important challenges to the limits and knowledges that characteristically define the modern human. Like Donna Haraway's figure of the cyborg (1991), they are at the very least to be celebrated for the confounding of fact and fiction, real and unreal, that they embody. For those committed to ontological stability and precise categorization they are dangerous subjects; for those who delight in the unknown but clearly destructive and creative possibilities of their fluid, processural concepts of self, they undermine normalcy in enchantingly subversive ways.

Credulity closely accompanies their identity politics. Are they serious? Yes, they are. Should they be taken seriously? Yes, they should. More importantly, however, they should be considered with the same confounding of reason and the imagination, of naivety and sophistication, of humor and gravity, which vampires, Lycanthropes and Otherkin approach themselves and their communities. This confounding of categories is perhaps the crucial endowment that their occult subjectivities offer the more conservative members of the (equally heterodox) mundane community.

NOTE

1 In April 2013, a year or so after the drafting of this chapter, Lupa publicly renounced her Therian identity (thanks to Venetia Robertson, a scholar of Therianthropy, for swiftly drawing this to my attention) and the dwindling relevance of her previous research. In doing so, she cites the nature of her own development since the publication of the text, the need to 'take a break' from the community, and how it transpired that she never returned. In short, Otherkin as a 'framework' ceased to adequately explain how she/he understood her/his identity – a 'personal narrative' subject to revision like all narratives (http://therioshamanism.com/2013/04/02/letting-go-of-therianthropy-for-good, accessed 3 November 2013). Rather than a wholesale undermining of the salience of such subject positions, this declaration serves to emphasize the transitory nature of identity formation in such subcultures, and further, the concept of the self as fluid and multiple. This multiplicity is forever open to ambiguous futures and newer frameworks of understanding.

REFERENCES AND FURTHER READING

Brennan, B. A. (1988) *Hands of Light: A Guide to Healing Through the Human Energy Field*, Toronto; New York; London; Sydney; Auckland: Bantam.

Ferreday, D. (2011) 'Becoming Deer: Nonhuman Drag and Online Utopias,' *Feminist Theory* 12.2: 219–25.

Gerbasi, K. C. et al. (2008) 'Furries from A to Z (Anthropomorphism to Zoomorphism),' *Society and Animals* 16.3, 197–222.

Giffney, N. and Hird, M. (eds.) (2008) *Queering the Non/Human*, Aldershot: Ashgate.

Haraway, D. (1991) *Simians, Cyborgs and Women: The Reinvention of Nature*, London: Free Association Books.

Harner, M. (1980) *The Way of the Shaman*, New York: Harper and Row.

Johnson, C. (2009) *Manifesto of the Wolf*. Online: http://www.werewolfcathedral.com (accessed 30 December 2011).

Johnston, J. '(2014) 'Arctic Otherkin: The Influence of Northern Mythology and Fauna on a Contemporary Spiritual Subculture,' *Contributions to Circumpolar Studies*. Vol. 3.

Keyworth, D. (2010) 'The Socio-Religious Beliefs and Nature of the Contemporary Vampire Subculture,' *Journal of Contemporary Religion* 17.3, 355–70.

Kirby, D. (2009) 'From Pulp Fiction to Revealed Text: A Study of the Role of the Text in the Otherkin Community,' in *Exploring Religion and the Sacred in a Media Age*, C. Deacy and E. Arwick, eds, Farnham: Ashgate, 141–54.

Laycock, J. (2010) 'Real Vampires as an Identity Group: Analyzing Cause and Effects of an Introspective Survey by the Vampire Community,' *Nova Religio: The Journal of Alternative and Emergent Religions* 14.1, 4–23.

Lupa (2007) *A Field Guide to Otherkin*, Stafford: Megalithica Books.

Mamatas, N. (2001) 'Elven Like Me,' *Village Voice* 20 (February), 35.

Melton, G. (1999), *The Vampire Book: An Encyclopedia of the Undead*, Detroit: Visible Ink Press.

Meyer, M and Smith, R., eds. (1999) *Ancient Christian Magic: Coptic Texts of Ritual Power*, Princeton: Princeton University Press.

Partridge, C. (2004a) *The Re-Enchantment of the West*, Vol. 1., London: T & T Clark.

Partridge, C., ed. (2004b) *New Religions: A Guide: New Religious Movements, Sects and Alternative Spiritualities*, Oxford: Oxford University Press.

Partridge, C. (2005) *The Re-Enchantment of the West*, Vol. 2, London: T & T Clark.

Probyn-Rapsey, F. (2011) 'Furries and the Limits of Species Identity Disorder: A Response to Gerbasi *et al*,' *Society and Animals* 19.3, 294–301.

Tië eldaliéva (n.d.) *Tië eldaliéva: The Elven Path*. Online: http://www.lassiquendi.com (accessed 30 December 2011). This website is now defunct, but other sites have replaced it. See particularly, http://elvenspirituality.wordpress.com/ (accessed 16 April 2013).

Timberwolf (2009) *Lycanthropy – Shape-Shifters – Werewolves*. Online: http://timberwolfhq.com (accessed 30 December 2011).

Williams, D. J. (2008) 'Contemporary Vampires and (Blood Red) Leisure: Should We Be Afraid of the Dark?' *Leisure/Loisir* 32.2, 513–39.

CHAPTER FORTY-THREE

HAKIM BEY

Christian Greer

Peter Lamborn Wilson (1945–) dropped out of Columbia University to pursue an autodidactic, and largely peripatetic course of education that would be as wide-ranging as it was unorthodox. This began with an initiation into the Moorish Orthodox Church, which was fashioned after Noble Drew Ali's Moorish Science, Tantra, Hazrat Inayat Khan's 'Universal Sufism' and the sacramental use of hallucinogenic substances ('entheogens'). As a member of the church, his interest in psychedelics was accented when the Moorish Orthodox Church installed itself alongside the Neo-American Church and the League for Spiritual Discovery at the Millbrook 'ashram,' then under the direction of Dr. Timothy Leary. As a conscientious objector to the Vietnam War and with the foreboding sense that the spirit of the counterculture was lost, Wilson expatriated in 1968 and embarked upon what would become a decade of spiritual sojourning throughout North Africa, the Indian subcontinent, and the Middle East. After his tutelage under Ganeesh Baba (Shri Mahant Ganesh Giriji Maharaj – a teacher in the tradition of Kriya Yoga) and an initiation in Tara Tantra in India, Wilson spent the following years trekking what became known as the 'hash trail' through Nepal, Afghanistan, and Pakistan where he followed itinerant Qalandariyyah Sufis, sought initiations from Hindu gurus and Sufi masters, and availed himself of the abundant supplies of opium and *bhang*. Following the recommendation of Vilayat Inayat Khan, upon reaching Iran, Wilson sought out the Nimatullahi Sufi order. However, after an introduction to Seyyed Hossein Nasr, it has been plausibly suggested that he joined Frithjof Schuon's Maryamiyya order instead. His affiliation with Nasr and connection with the Maryamiyya led him to an editorship of *Sophia Perennis*, which was published under his guidance from 1975 to 1978 and functioned both as the Imperial Iranian Academy of Philosophy's journal and a mouth piece for Schuon's Traditionalist Sufi order. Also working as the director of English language publications for the academy, Wilson worked alongside Traditionalist luminaries Henry Corbin, Toshihiko Izutsu, and William C. Chittick. At this time, Wilson's own scholarship reflected a traditionalist bias. However, in the following years, his literary output would be transformed through a closer engagement with anarchism, hermetic philosophy, and post-structuralism.

After the fall of the Shah of Iran in 1979, Wilson returned to the US. Once there, he escalated his involvement in the underground press by publishing prodigiously under the name 'Hakim Bey,' named after the eccentric sixth Fatimid caliph, Hakim bi Amr al-Lāh. It was not long until the work of this mysterious figure became a staple in numerous anarchist, queer, and esoteric zines (abbrev. 'fanzine': small circulation, often self-produced publications) and underground newspapers. As distinct from his previous traditionalist scholarship, Bey's writings amalgamated Nietzschean philosophy and Individualist Anarchism with Hermeticism and esoteric themes to form a powerful brand of mystical anti-authoritarianism. Unique within the anarchist circles in which his work appeared, Bey's spiritual anarchism was summarized in the name of his own esoteric order, the Association for Ontological Anarchism (AOA) founded in the early 1980s. His voluminous output termed, 'communiqués of ontological anarchism,' as well as the mystery surrounding Bey's identity, garnered the author (and more specifically his alter ego) a great deal of attention within underground Pagan, anarchist, and queer milieus. Bey's underground notoriety continued to grow as a result of his radio show, The Moorish Orthodox Crusade, his editorial work for Semiotext(e) publishing, and his controversial contributions to the newsletter of NAMBLA (North American Man-Boy Love Association), not to mention the vitriolic attacks made against his brand of anarchism by notable anarchists such as Murray Bookchin. His most famous work to date, *The Temporary Autonomous Zone: Ontological Anarchy, Poetic Terrorism* (commonly abbreviated to *TAZ*) is an expansion on an earlier collection of Bey's writings culled from notable zines like *Factsheet Five*, *Popular Reality*, and *Kaos*. Apart from his science fiction, man-boy love novel *Crowstone* published in 1983 under the name 'Hakim,' *TAZ*, published in 1991, was Bey's first full length book and the one with which both identities are routinely associated. This is due in large part to the profound influence the text has had on, for example, Chaos Magick, rave culture, Post-Anarchism, and the Cacophony Society, who later founded the massive temporary autonomous zone event known as Burning Man. Alongside the vast array of Bey's anarcho-mystical publications, Wilson continued to write numerous learned books on esoteric and heretical sects of Islam, psychedelic spirituality, and angels.

In the late 1990s, Bey's identity became a public secret largely due to the internet, but little changed in terms of the use his *nom de plume* served. Essentially, he articulates the same premises concerning esoteric non-authoritarianism in two different voices, for Wilson they functioned as historiographic tools, and for Bey they were fodder for ontological anarchist agitation and utopian engineering. The basis of these premises lay in his anarchist refashioning of traditionalism, whereby the non-authoritarianism and 'shamanic spirituality' of paleolithic society is identified as a more traditional form of traditionalism. Much of Wilson's historical work traces the contours of this proclivity for nonauthoritarianism as it expressed itself in dissenting and esoteric doctrines, beliefs, and groups. In his reading, this loose lineage originates with the 'shamanic spirituality' of the hunter-gatherers and continues in medieval 'free spirit' movements, 'heretical' traditions, and renaissance hermeticism. In his works, Wilson attempts to show how the Anarchist tradition has a lost prehistory in the utopian aspirations of a number of heretical, antinomian, and esoteric discourses, and enumerates the ways in which these discourses can revitalize what he considers to be the obsolete logic of leftist anarchism. Writing under the name Bey, he claims that a paradigm shift must occur within Anarchism if it is to remain relevant and, more importantly, effective against the 'technopathocracy' of global capitalism. To do this, he argues, it must base itself in an ontological framework defined by chaos. Anarchism scholars such as Lewis Call have traced the origin of the postmodern turn within anarchism, termed 'Post-Anarchism,' to Bey's theorization of ontological anarchism, although post-anarchists general ignore its thoroughly esoteric nature.

Arguably today's foremost anarchist writer, Wilson has spent the latter portion of his career participating in art exhibitions, once notably with fellow 'Beats' Brion Gysin and William Burroughs, publishing a number of poetry chapbooks, promoting his brand of environmental esotericism termed 'green hermeticism,' and teaching alongside Allen Ginsberg at Naropa University.

REFERENCES AND FURTHER READING

Bey, Hakim (2003 [1985]) *T.A.Z.: The Temporary Autonomous Zone, Ontological Anarchy, Poetic Terrorism*, second edition, Brooklyn: Autonomedia.

Wilson, Peter Lamborn (1993) *Sacred Drift: Essays on the Margin of Islam*, San Francisco: City Lights.

——(1999) *Ploughing the Clouds: The Search for Irish Soma*, San Francisco: City Lights.

——(2005) *Queer Rain*, Boulder: Farfalla Press.

PART VI

POPULAR CULTURE AND THE ARTS

CHAPTER FORTY-FOUR

THE OCCULT AND THE VISUAL ARTS

Tessel M. Bauduin

INTRODUCTION

In 1969 German artist Sigmar Polke (1941–2010) created a large canvas with one black corner and a typed message reading '*Höhere Wesen befahlen: rechte obere Ecke schwarz malen!*' ('Higher beings command: paint the upper right corner black!').

The painting has variously been interpreted as satirical, ironical, humorous, or a critical commentary of contemporary artistic styles and culture. Suggesting the involvement of 'higher beings', the painting also refers to mediumistic and spiritualist art, or artworks made by mediums under the guidance of, it was claimed, spirits or similar entities. This practice was widespread in Europe during the late nineteenth and early twentieth century. The painting can further be said to refer more generally to the relationship with metaphysical, spiritual and occult thought that is a very significant, possibly even integral, part of modern art.[1] Even as the art historians and critics of the 1960s attempted to write a history of modern art without any mention of anything spiritual or occult – or, indeed, of anything religious (Tuchman 1986b: 17–18) – in fact, artists such as Polke were not only deeply interested in occult sources and ideas themselves, but also very much aware of the occult interests of their direct predecessors.

This chapter presents a brief overview of selected artists who, since the late nineteenth century, have shown some interest in occultism. It will first explore the relationship between Symbolism, Spiritualism and Theosophy in the late nineteenth century, and subsequently the modern European avant-gardes between the 1910s and 1940s, finally touching briefly upon artists since the 1950s and their relation to occultism. The main focus of discussion is the visual arts, principally, fine art painting. This is not, of course, to say that the other arts – such as literature, music and dance – were less involved with occultism. They were not.

While the discussion here is limited to those artists who have shown an interest in occultism, this is not intended to convey the notion that *all* modern artists looked favourably upon occultism (or were even familiar with it). Occultism is but one current (besides stylistic developments and other cultural influences) informing the various movements and individuals categorised under headings such as 'modern art'

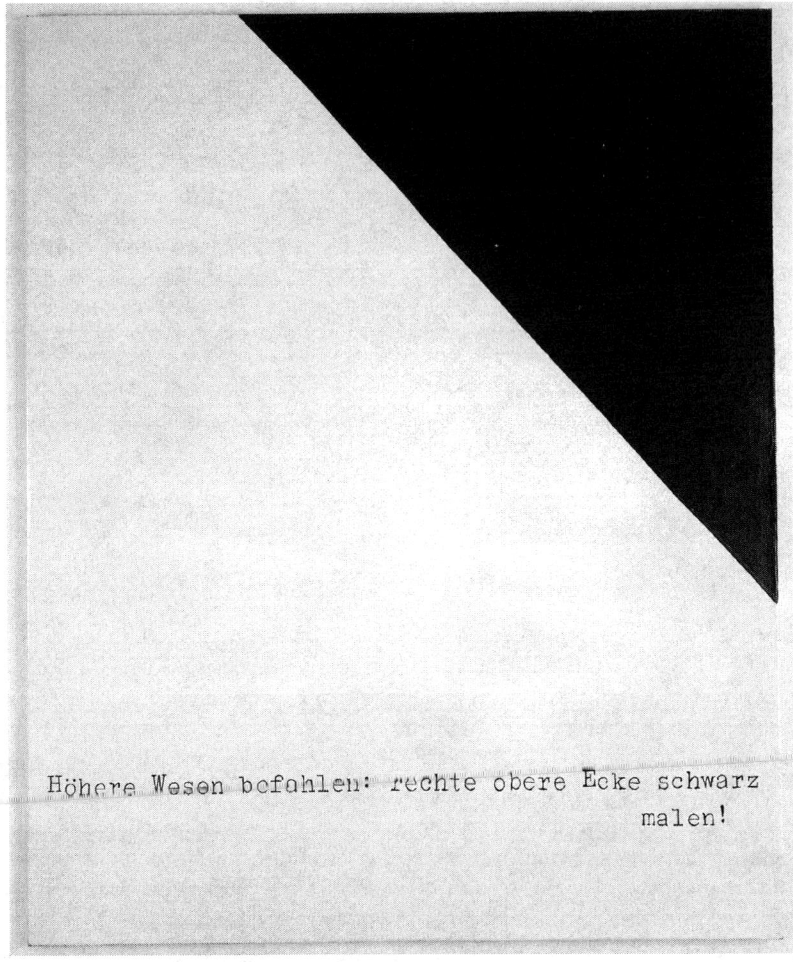

Figure 44.1 Sigmar Polke, *Höhere Wesen befahlen: rechte obere Ecke schwarz malen!, 1969*. Froehlich Collection, Stuttgart. © The Estate of Sigmar Polke, Cologne, DACS 2014.

(from the second half of the nineteenth century up to the 1970s) and 'the historical avant-gardes' (from the turn of the twentieth century to the Second World War). Still, as occultism is quite closely tied to the experience of modernism, as Treitel (2004) and Owen (2004), among others, have argued, it is only to be expected that the movement left a distinct trail in modern art.[2] Occult views, ideas, beliefs and practices permeated modernist artistic culture to a significant extent, and a great many artists in literature, music, dance, architecture and the visual arts (painting, sculpture, photography, and film) drew on occult ideas and experiences to fuel their creativity. We should note that the interest in occultism varied considerably between individuals, groups and movements. It ranged from the briefest and most incidental of references to a single source, on the one hand, to active membership of occult organisations and full commitment to occult beliefs on the other. Most artists occupied a position somewhere in-between these two poles. Some artists became practicing occultists;

others attended lectures or read occult material; others eschewed any personal involvement in or even knowledge of occultism but still made occult topics the subject of works of art. With regard to works of art, the spectrum stretches between an artwork that employs the occult as subject, plot device, topos or atmospheric scheme – e.g. many of the works of Spanish artist Francisco Goya, for instance – to an artwork that functions foremost as an object of devotion or tool in spiritual praxis, as a traditional icon does. Such 'occult art', as it were, will not be discussed here. Still, while the focus here lies upon art that is foremost art – even if the artists themselves participate in occult milieus – it will nonetheless become clear that besides offering content and/or providing an inspirational worldview and spiritual concepts, occultism's own visual culture (in particular that of Spiritualism and Theosophy) extended a considerable influence over modern art.

Finally, it should be noted that this chapter provides a brief overview, which barely penetrates the surface of modern art's deep and complex interaction with occultism. The groundwork for a revaluation of the spirituality (including occultism[3]) of modern art was laid with an important 1986 exhibition curated by Maurice Tuchman (1987). Other curators since then have followed in his footsteps and their catalogues are the starting point for any serious investigation of this topic (Lampe and de Loisy 2008; Loers 1995; Pijaudier-Cabot and Faucherau 2011).[4] As the (occult) spirituality of abstraction has been the initial driving force behind much research, the relationship between early abstract art and Theosophy and Anthroposophy has now become an accepted fact in art history. Only recently, however, has the considerable influence of Spiritualism, and its visual culture in particular, upon modern art been pointed out. Hence, this will be discussed more extensively below.

AROUND THE FIN-DE-SIÈCLE

Mediumistic Art and Automatism

Let us return to Polke's *Höhere Wesen befahlen...*(see Figure 44.1). Stylistically, it can be placed in one of modern art's most famous traditions, abstract art. Already there was a strong connection to occultism. Lauded abstract artists such as Russian artist Wassily Kandinsky (1866–1944), Dutchman Piet Mondrian (1872–1944), and František Kupka (1871–1957), originally Czech – to name the most famous[5] – were during their lifetime all interested in occult movements, particularly Theosophy (see below).

Regardless of whether the artist is being serious, playful or ironic, the painting's title and apparent message about 'higher beings' refer, as stated, to a modern Western tradition of mediumistic art, also known as spirit or Spiritualist art, automatic art, or trance art, which stretches from the early days of French Spiritism in the 1850s to, at least, the invention of the category of *art brut* or outsider art in the 1950s.[6] Relatively quickly after the dawning of Spiritualism, the means of spirit communication changed from raps and turning tables to mediumistic writing, aided by such inventions as the Ouija-board and planchette, and then to drawing as well. The actual techniques are frequently referred to as 'automatic' (e.g. 'automatic writing' and 'automatic drawing'). This designation more or less sidesteps the rather thorny issue *who* (or *what*, perhaps) is actually doing the drawing – a spirit, a person's subconscious, the unconscious, or some alternate part of their personality. At the same time, it makes clear that the person drawing is in some way dissociated, operating like an automaton or 'recording instrument' (Edelman 1995; Shamdasani 1993; Will-Levaillant 1980).[7]

Spiritualism attracted many artists and intellectuals, and several began experimenting with automatic techniques. A well-known example is the French poet and novelist Victor Hugo (1802–85). During a series of séances he, his son and others produced various phrases, sentences, poems and drawings, in several cases apparently dictated or even authored by a spirit (Godeau 2012). Eventually, automatic creative techniques moved beyond drawing to watercolours, etching and even oil painting. Automatic artist and medium Hélène Smith (Catherine-Elise Müller, 1861–1929) was celebrated during her lifetime, and much admired by artists such as the Symbolists and Surrealists. From writing and speaking in tongues, her talents developed within a couple of years to drawing, water colouring and painting (Deonna 1932). Her works mirror her Spiritualistic endeavours. *Martian Landscape* (1896–99), for instance, is the result of her astral journeys to Mars under spirit guidance (see Figure 4.2).

Psychiatrist Théodore Flournoy, who participated in Smith's séances and wrote several books about her (e.g., Flournoy 1994), considered all her creations to be automatic expressions of her (inventive and original) creative subconscious. This viewpoint was also current among the Surrealists and other artists (Morehead 2009: 77–80; Shamdasani 1994).[8] This brings us to an essential point: artists were attracted to automatism because it appeared to be a means to achieve artistic freedom – that is to say, creative expression in a manner outside the borders of academic training. André Breton (1896–1966), the founder of Surrealism, is a good example of this. In an essay discussing mediumistic artists such as Fernand Desmoulin (1853–1914),

Figure 44.2 Hélène Smith, *Paysage martien*, 1896.

Victorien Sardou (1831–1908) and Augustin Lesage (1876–1954)[9] – whose work is considered to be *art brut* or outsider art (Peiry 2008)[10] – he commented that they worked in a manner 'without any order', without preparatory sketches, without composition or 'final aim', without apparent plan or proper technique, from the top to the bottom corner (such as Lesage), 'everywhere at once', or, even, 'in the dark [blindfolded], upside down [and] obliquely' (Breton 2007: 45). The aim was to paint in a manner completely contrary to the norm and therefore, from the viewpoint of many modern artists, in a manner more *authentic* and *original*.

Visual Culture of Spiritualism: Spirit Photography

Spiritualism, of course, was not an art movement (although writer Jules Bois wrote of a 'spirit aesthetic', Bois 1897), but we can certainly speak of a visual culture of Spiritualism. Besides automatic drawings by mediums, its main constituent was spirit photography.

Photography, newly invented, was embraced by Spiritualists and psychical researchers as 'the ultimate documentary evidence' of Spiritualist events (Keshavjee 2013: 43), based upon the understanding of photography as objective. Treated with special substances and sensitive as it was, the photographic plate was thought to be able to capture things the ordinary eye could not, but which were nevertheless present – such as spirits and ghosts, but also fluids, auras, ethereal energies and the like (Fischer 2005; Chéroux 2005).[11] Science too confirmed that the human eye was a rather limited visual instrument, with the discovery of, for instance, X-rays, or infrared and ultraviolet (see also Natale 2011; Bauduin 2012). Photography was employed to capture ghostly phenomena materialising, a development startlingly paralleled by a new form of dance developed by French-American dancer Loïe Fuller (1862–1928). It incorporated dramatic and colourful lighting and the dancer appearing and disappearing amidst a continual swirl of veils, materialising in a sequence of fluid forms, as it were (Rousseau 2013: 169).[12] Besides dance, Spiritualism's visual culture similarly influenced Symbolist theatre, as Keshavjee (2009) has shown, including play writing, stage design and promotional material.

Towards the fin-de-siècle Spiritualism constituted a pervasive presence in artistic culture with a distinct visual impact. A typical example is American-British artist James McNeill Whistler (1834–1903). As Jonathan Shirland (2013) has argued in a study of Whistler's portraits from the 1860s to the 1890s, Spiritualism was not only a practice the artist participated in, but something that informed the technique, style and even subject of these paintings. Moreover, Spiritualism also functioned as the lense through which his audience received and perceived Whistler's art (Shirland 2013: 82–87).

Symbolism and Occultism

Spiritualism's visual culture left its mark upon Symbolism, the major artistic moment of the late nineteenth century, as Morehead (2009) and Keshavjee (2009) have shown. Other occult movements too are relevant, including Theosophy, and the particular blend of Rosicrucianism, other esoteric thought and fringe-Catholic mysticism evident in the work of Joséphin Péladan (1858–1918), the founder of the French Mystical Order of the Rose+Croix and its Salons.

Péladan espoused a form of esoteric Catholicism mediated through a mystical art, in which the artist, as initiate, played a key role (Chaitow 2013; Pincus-Witten 1976; idem 1968). He promoted his ideas and movement through his prolific writings (e.g. Péladan 1888; idem 1894). Six Salons were organised in Paris between 1892 and 1897, and works by over 230 artists were included. The majority were Symbolists, such as Belgians Fernand Khnopff (1858–1921) and Jean Delville (1867–1953), Dutch Jan Toorop (1858–1928), Swiss Arnold Böcklin (1827–1901) and German Carlos Schwabe (1866–1926), who designed the promotional poster for the first Salon in typically Symbolist fashion (Da Silva 1991).[13]

Connecting the works exhibited at these Salons was their (Symbolist) subject matter: myths, legends, mysticism and esotericism. Realism and naturalism were not permitted, nor were subjects to do with modern life. The Salons encompassed literature and music as well. For example, the composer Erik Satie (1866–1925) composed several pieces on the occasion of the opening of the first Salon.[14]

While some artists became members of Péladan's Rose+Croix order, others participated only once in the Salons and can hardly be associated with his ideas. It seems that Péladan's direct influence upon art is mainly limited to the introduction of the motif of the androgyne, as Clerbois has shown (2002a). This is typical of the problem of defining 'influence'. Although it can be shown that many artists moved in occult circles and were familiar with occult sources or individuals, it is questionable how much occultism can really be said to have played a defining role in their art – and even if some influence can be discerned, it is difficult to determine whether it constitutes intellectual inspiration, whether it features as content, or whether it leads directly to particular stylistic elements. Further complicating matters is the pronounced occult eclecticism of many artists, as Clerbois (2002b) and others have shown. For example, Jean Delville's Salon d'Art Idéaliste, founded in 1886 in Belgium – successor of the Salon de la Rose+Croix in Brussels – combined Péladan's ideas with Theosophy.

Les grands initiés (1889) by the French writer Édouard Schuré (1841–1929) became a key work in transmitting Theosophical concepts to the Symbolists. It expounds upon the notion of a lineage of world teachers 'initiated' into the ancient secret mysteries, including Plato, Orpheus, Buddha and Jesus (Schuré 2010). Delville's painting, *L'Ecole de Platon* (1898), depicts an 'initiated' teacher who appears as a combination of Plato and Christ, but who also has, like Péladan, rather androgynous features. The triangular composition may reflect Theosophical ideas concerning sacred geometrical forms (Clerbois 2002a; idem 2002b; Welsh 1987).[15]

The occult eclecticism and synthesis of artists reflects that of Theosophy and, indeed, of occultism *per se*. *Esoteric Buddhism* (1883) by Alfred Percy Sinnet formed the basis for Paul Ranson's enigmatic painting *Christ and Buddha* (1880), which also builds upon the artist's knowledge of Schuré's *Great Initiates: A Study of the Secret History of Religions* (1989).[16] It shows a crucified Christ, based upon an original by Paul Gauguin, a seated Buddha, and a partial Buddha face (Welsh 1987: 73). Ranson was a member of a group known as the *Nabis* (the 'prophets' or 'inspired'), whose frontman was Paul Sérusier (1864–1927). The latter's deep and lifelong commitment to (French) Theosophical thought has been outlined by Davenport (2007) and certainly influenced other Nabis. However, Spiritualism as well as contemporary Christian mysticism interested the Nabis too; the last leaving a distinct trace in the semi-ecclesiastical 'Nabi costume' they wore during their regular meetings, depicted in the portrait Sérusier painted of Ranson (1890).[17]

Visual Culture of Theosophy

Many of the Symbolists moved in occult and in particular Theosophical circles, but it was the visual culture of Spiritualism we find reflected in some of their work, as argued above – even as subject matter might be inspired by Theosophy. This is an interesting development, as it shows that even though Theosophists and Spiritualists maintained a distinct distance from one another – indeed, construed their movements in opposition to one other – artists were susceptible to both and felt apparently no qualms about incorporating elements from either into their art.

Theosophy too developed its own visual culture, although it only took shape after the turn of the twentieth century, with the publications by Theosophists Annie Besant (1847–1933) and Charles Webster Leadbeater (1854–1934), such as *Thought-Forms* (1901), *Occult Chemistry* (1908) and *Man Visible and Invisible* (1902; by Leadbeater alone). The need to make the invisible visible, of which spirit photography was one result, was also prevalent in Theosophy and other occult currents. Besant and Leadbeater undertook a series of occult experiments in which they discovered through clairvoyance the astral, ethereal or otherwise occult form, shape and outlook – i.e., the *appearance* – of thought-forms and auras, but also chemical elements. In line with the well-established tradition of esoteric illustration,[18] they illustrated their books with schemata illustrating occult concepts. More importantly, the books also include depictions that, although they may appear abstract, should be considered more or less *mimetic*, that is, forms representing something seen (albeit clairvoyantly in this instance), such as auras with thought forms.[19] In all these forms elements such as form, line, colour and density were of particular importance as they convey intention and intensity of emotion on the supra-normal plane (Besant e.a. 2005: 16).

THE TWENTIETH CENTURY

Abstraction

Even as the dominant styles of the time were figurative, already during the nineteenth century mediumistic automatic drawing led in a few cases, such as that of Georgiana Houghton (1814–84), to artistic results that might be qualified as 'abstract' (Oberter 2006: 221–23).[20] Several decades later, Swedish artist Hilma af Klint (1862–1944) also experimented with automatic drawing in a Spiritualist setting. Trained as a conventional artist of landscapes and flowers, she moved beyond that training by means of automatism. Indeed, I would argue that af Klint eventually employed the technique specifically to that end; thereby showing that automatism could indeed function as a means to achieve artistic change and innovation. She created several series of impressive paintings exploring spiritual or sacred concepts (Müller-Westerman 2013: 38, 41), developing a unique style that combined geometric and biomorphic form with a free line very reminiscent of (her and others') automatic drawing. An example is *Old Age*, from a series exploring the ages of mankind (see Figure 4.3).

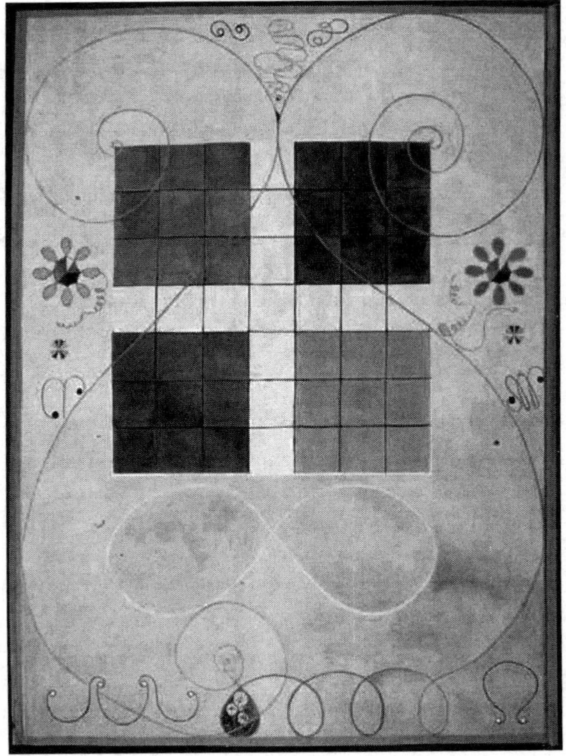

Figure 44.3 Hilma af Klint, *The Ten Largest, no 10: Old Age* (Group IV), 1907. © Stiftelsen Hilma af Klints Verk

As we know that af Klint was deeply interested in Theosophy, and later Anthroposophy, we can assume that Theosophical and Anthroposophical concepts formed the inspiration for many of her works. While among the more renowned abstract artists of the first decades of the twentieth century af Klint may stand out for being a woman,[21] her interest in Theosophy and involvement in contemporary occult movements are by no means exceptional. Today the interests of many abstract artists in Theosophy and Anthroposophy are well charted and generally accepted. Groundbreaking studies by Sixten Ringbom of Kandinsky have paved the way (Ringbom 1966; 1970; 1986).

Theosophy found an audience among the intelligentsia from all over Europe, artists prominently included among them. The Theosophical alliances of, for example, Mondrian and Kandinsky, illustrate well that an artist's interest in Theosophical sources, integration of Theosophy into one's life and worldview, and possible incorporation of Theosophical ideas into one's art diverges considerably between individuals – the very complexity of 'Theosophy' as a movement, extending and changing over time as well, is mirrored in the complexity and idiosyncrasy of artists' engagement of Theosophy in their own life and art. For instance, Mondrian was a lifelong member of the Dutch Theosophical Society and follower of Steiner, and hardly interested in other forms of occultism. He professed to be inspired primarily by the works of Theosophy's founder, Helena Blavatsky (1831–91), such as *Isis*

Unveiled (1877) and *The Secret Doctrine* (1888), and claimed his own art style *Nieuwe Beelding*, neoplasticism, to 'exemplify theosophical art (in the true sense of the word)' (Evelein 1996: 122). Kandinsky, for his part, was foremost inspired by the ideas of second-generation Theosophists Besant and Leadbeater, *Thought-Forms* (1901) in particular, but also deeply interested in other forms of occultism, besides, as well, Steiner. As he proclaimed in *Concerning the Spiritual in Art* (2004), art expressed a spiritual experience or need, it was a manifestation of *inner necessity* (see further Bauduin 2013).

Theosophy's visual culture (i.e. the illustrations from Besant and Leadbeater's books), with its aim to capture the invisible (emotions, spiritual concepts), in particular combinations of lines, forms and colours, resonated with many artists, not least Kandinsky (Alderton 2011; Ringbom 1970) and af Klint.

Continental artists in particular drew upon Theosophical ideas, such as, in Germany, Heinrich Nüßlein (1897–1947) and Bô Yin Râ (Joseph Anton Schneiderfranken, 1876–1943), and Blue Rider artists such as Franz Marc (1880–1916), Hans (Jean) Arp (1886–1966), Marianne von Werefkin (1860–1938), János Mattis Teutsch (1884–1960), and in particular Wilhelm Morgner (1891–1917); in France, Marcel Duchamp (1887–1968), Constantin Brâncusi (1876–1956), and Kupka; and in the Netherlands, Mondrian's fellow De Stijl-members, such as Theo van Doesburg (1883–1931), the architects Karel C.P. de Bazel (1869–1923) and Mathieu Lauweriks (1864–1932), Jacoba van Heemskerck (1876–1923), and several others. This list is by no means exhaustive but rather reflects the artists whose occult alliances have come under scrutiny recently (Bax 2006; Bax 1995; Huussen et al 2005; Faucherau 2011: 228ff.; Loers 1995: 240; Treitel 2004: 126–31; for more Lampe and de Loisy 2008; Loers 1995; Pijaudier-Cabot and Faucherau 2011).

Suprematism and Futurism

Theosophy had less of a following among the Russian avant-garde, Kandinsky excepted. Other forms of occultism, as well as (Christian) mystical thought, did find an artistic following; Suprematist artists such as Kasimir Malevich (1879–1935), Maria Ender (1897–1942) and Mikhaïl Matiouchine (1861–1934), for instance, were inspired by occult theories of time and space. Of particular relevance are the theories concerning the occult fourth dimension of Pjotr Ouspensky, set forth in *The Fourth Dimension* (1909) and *Tertium Organum* (1912), and further expanded upon and introduced to a non-Russian reading audience by Claude (Bragdon 1929; Ouspensky 1922; Wagner 2011: 259–61). *Primer* and *Tertium Organum*, together with a few earlier and other works discussing the occult fourth dimension, found a wide following in Europe among artists and intellectuals (Henderson 2010), including the Russian and Italian Futurists.[22] Typical of the occult eclecticism we have also encountered with many Symbolists, the Futurists further showed an avid interest in Theosophical ideas concerning clairvoyance and the astral plane, as well as contemporary experiments of psychical research (Bauduin 2012: 36–40; Celant 1981; Henderson 1981).

Bauhaus, Klee

Kandinsky took his occult background and interests with him to the Bauhaus, where occult thought formed a large part of the collective Bauhaus-worldview. Many were familiar with Theosophy, Anthroposophy, and with nineteenth-century Freemasonry and esoteric-reformist thought besides (Wagner 2011: 261–63; see also Wagner 2005). Artists such as Walter Gropius (1883–1969), Johannes Itten (1888–1976), Paul Klee (1879–1940), Gunta Stölzl (1897–1983) and others can be counted among them. Mazdaznism, a modern form of Zoroastrianism, flourished at the Bauhaus, although mainly in the group around Itten – a figure whose occult interests and knowledge may have been instrumental for many, as Wagner (2009) has shown.

Although it sometimes appears as if occultism of the Theosophical kind is the main occult inspiration for twentieth-century artists, I would emphasise that Spiritualism and its visual culture (incorporating also the visual testimonies of psychical research) continued to be a source of inspiration for many. Take for instance Swiss artist Klee, whose idiosyncratic artistic trajectory took him from the Blue Rider to the Bauhaus and finally to French Surrealism. He was very much interested in Spiritualism and mediumistic phenomena, such as automatic writing, materialisations (of spirits, ectoplasm, etc.) and levitation, throughout his career. Partly or entirely materialised forms were the apparent subject of several drawings made in the 1910s and 1920s, entitled, for instance, *Incomplete Materialisation* (1915) or *Materialised Ghost* (1923) (Okuda 2011: 278–80).[23] Towards the end of the 1930s he undertook several works incorporating 'secret' hieroglyphs and signs, which were clearly inspired by the Martian script of Hélène Smith. As this example illustrates, various aspects of Spiritualism – belief in the existence and manifestation of spirits, mediums and their practices, the techniques of automatism, the visual culture of spectral forms and thin, uncertain lines – continued to inspire art well into the twentieth century. Klee, for his part, found kindred spirits in French Surrealism, where, as I have detailed (Bauduin 2014), mediumism and automatism served as inspirational examples of artistic practice, while towards and during the 1940s, a deeper investment in occultism took place.

Postmodern and Contemporary Art

Occultism continued to inspire many artists after the Second World War. Only a very few can be mentioned here,[24] but this does not mean that occultism was mainly a concern of modern artists; indeed, many postmodern and contemporary artists have shown not only a distinct interest in the occult – for instance in spirit photography[25] – as well as a more general susceptibility to occulture, but their works often reflect upon modern art's relation with occultism. Polke's painting has already been mentioned. Joseph Beuys (1921–86) stands out because his spiritual search was hardly limited to occultism; shamanism, for instance, played a considerable role in his work (Taylor 2012). Americans Mark Rothko (1903–70), Barnet Newman (1905–70), Alfred Jensen (1903–81) and Frenchman Yves Klein (1928–62) also found subjects as well as inspiration in occultism (Kuspit 1986). Several postmodern artists have engaged occult currents or individuals that were significantly less prominent in the artistic culture of their own time, but went through a revival in the counterculture of the 1960s. Experimental filmmaker Kenneth Anger (1927), for instance, has shown a consistent fascination for Crowley and his religion of Thelema in many of his works (Déjean 2008). Mention should also be made of British occultist Austin Osman Spare, for whom automatic drawing formed the core of his artistic practice.[26]

Contemporary art has occult, but also spectral and paranormal qualities, as Bang Larsen (2007) has pointed out. Again, therefore, we see a combination of (the legacy of) the visual culture of Spiritualism and psychical research, with occult currents such as Theosophy, as well as with occulture generally. Matthew Barney (b.1967), for example, has engaged the ritualistic and symbolic elements of occultism in the *Cremaster Cycle* (Taylor 2012). Goshka Macuga's (b.1967) sculpture *Mme Blavatsky*, finally, reflects upon Theosophical heritage even as it playfully references the occulture of stage magic as well.

CONCLUSION: ART IN OCCULTISM

The interest of modern artists in occultism was not always reciprocated. For all that Theosophical ideas found fertile ground with continental artists already from the 1870s onwards, the Theosophical Society itself was rather late to catch on. The first exhibition organised under its auspices occurred only in 1905, on the occasion of the annual meeting of European branches of the TS in London, and included works by Theosophical artists as well as by 'sympathetic non-member artists' (Clerbois 2002a). Exhibitions were organised regularly after that. But while art, or better, *the arts*, were an important concern in Theosophical thought and for many Theosophists personally, and while a significant number of avant-garde artists were deeply interested in Theosophy and other forms of occult thought, the two parties never really collaborated.[27]

A handful of studies have investigated the artistic works of Steiner and his direct Anthroposophical circle (Howard 1998; Kries 2011; see also Kugler 1995). Art was of considerable importance to Steiner as a possibly universal language of spiritual truths. Art's role as the vehicle of Anthroposophical ideas was embodied in the (first) Goetheanum, constructed in Dornach (Switzerland) and described by one researcher as 'built, sculpted and painted Anthroposophy' (Oberhuber 1995: 713). Steiner was closely involved in the construction of the Goetheanum and made many designs, such as a sketch for a design in the small cupola. It illustrates the position of humanity, here represented by a humanoid figure, between Lucifer above and Ahriman below.

Colourful and accomplished, the design is iconographically fairly conventional, which mirrors other Anthroposophical designs by Steiner and others for the Goetheanum and other Anthroposophical locations. Indeed, stylistically speaking many of the drawings and designs can be related to Symbolism, to Art Nouveau and styles favoured in the Vienna Secession, and the same can be said of Anthroposophical sculpture, architecture and furniture design (various essays in Kries 2011).[28] Many of the blackboard drawings by Steiner that have been exhibited recently[29] show similarities with the Theosophical illustrations made on the direction of Besant and Leadbeater. They confirm a Theosophical visual culture consisting in part of abstracted forms that should be considered representative.[30] In other words, for all that Steiner could count important and innovative abstract artists among his followers, his preferred style was figurative. The new language of abstract forms invented by the many artists inspired by Theosophy and Anthroposophy, abstract specifically so as to be better vehicles for spiritual truths and occult thought, was not employed *within* Anthroposophy – and neither was this case for Theosophy or other occult movements, for that matter.

Finally, of course this overview has only lightly scratched upon the surface of the deep interactions between occultism on the one hand, and modern art, movements and individual artists on the other. Even though the occult alliances of the canonical artists and movements such as Symbolism and abstraction are now largely charted, much more research into less famous artists and marginalised individuals such as af Klint and other women artists, as well as artists working in less valued media such as the applied arts and textiles, is still necessary. Moreover, Spiritualism and its attended visual culture is now coming to the forefront as much more influential than previously thought, a topic also deserving of more research.

NOTES

1 'Höhere Wesen befehlen' is a series (1968) (Hentschel 1996: 59–62).
2 The modern artist's turn towards the occult should therefore *not* lead to the conclusion that artists and/or their art are *anti-modern* but should be viewed as an essential part of being modern and engaging modernism.
3 Categories such as 'occultism', 'spiritualism' and 'esotericism' are rather problematic with regards to modern, and especially avant-garde, art. See Kokkinen 2013 and the sources mentioned therein.
4 Furthermore, Cardinal and Lusardy 1999; Dichter et al. 2007; *Entrée des médiums* 2012; Martinez and Schroeder 2008.
5 The origins of abstract art lie in the nineteenth century, Rosenberg and Hollein 2007.
6 Arguably mediumistic art continues today, cf. Danchin 1999; Dichter et al. 2007: 120–22.
7 Despite frequent comments to the contrary, automatic writing originated as a spiritualist technique and was subsequently co-opted by dynamic psychiatry, the forerunner of modern psychiatry and psychology. In the latter context, it is some part of the medium's personality that authors the writing or drawing, while in the former case the author may be an angel, higher elemental being, spirit, etc. 'Dissociation' is not quite a neutral term in this context either (because pathological), but it serves to illustrate that the medium is not (considered to be) in a 'normal' state of consciousness. Crabtree 2003; on the question of authorship see Enns 2012.
8 More on Smith and automatism in Surrealism in Bauduin 2014.
9 For examples of works (and biographies) of these and other artists, see Cardinal et al. 1999; *Entrée des médiums* 2012; and the abcd (Art Brut Collection).
10 Strictly speaking the categories 'outsider art' and 'art brut' are not the same, but for our discussion here both terms are more or less interchangeable. Both include creators of art variously qualified as mediumistic, trance, automatic or spiritist. See Cardinal 1972; Cardinal & Lusardy 1999; Maclagan 2009; Peiry 2001; Thévoz 1999.
11 Find abundant examples in *The Perfect Medium* (Metropolitan Museum of Art 2005).
12 http://www.youtube.com/watch?v=fIrnFrDXjlk (accessed 20 February 2013).
13 Image in the public domain and online available via https://en.wikipedia.org/wiki/File:Salon_de_la_Rose%2BCroix.jpg (accessed 22 April 2014).
14 Claude Debussy, also associated with occultists (Godwin 1995: 170–73).
15 Image: http://www.musee-orsay.fr/en/collections/index-of-works/notice.html?no_cache = 1&nnumid = 158 (accessed 08 February 2013).

16 Image: http://en.wikipedia.org/wiki/File:Christ_et_Buddha_by_Paul_Ranson_1880.JPG (accessed 13 February 2013).
17 Image: http://www.musee-orsay.fr/en/collections/works-in-focus/search.html?no_cache = 1&zoom = 1&tx_damzoom_pi1[showUid] = 109519 (accessed 27 February 2013).
18 See Taschen's *The Hermetic Museum: Alchemy & Mysticism*, by Alexander Roob (1997, 2003, 2011).
19 *Thought-Forms*, including the many colour illustrations of particular thought forms and the colour interpretation scheme, is available online via Project Gutenberg: http://www.gutenberg.org/files/16269/16269-h/16269-h.htm (accessed 22 September 2014).
20 Houghton participated as a medium in the photographs of spirit photographer Frederick Hudson, Fischer 2005: 30, 32.
21 She may have begun painting under the direction of spirits as a way to negotiate traditional gender roles (i.e. the understanding that artistic genius is beholden to the male); compare for instance another case detailed by Treitel 2004: 121–24.
22 Occultism is less relevant to Cubism as a whole (in spite of suggestions otherwise, but see Henderson 2010), but several individuals—not least Cubist leader Apollinaire—were familiar with occult thought (Henderson 2004: 450).
23 Images: http://www.emuseum.zpk.org/eMuseumPlus (accessed 22 September 2014).
24 For an extensive overview, see the many essays in Lampe e.a. 2008: 261–418; Martinez e.a. 2008; Kuspit 1986.
25 See *Art Journal* 62 (3), fall 2003, on contemporary art and spirit photography.
26 Spare's *Book of Automatic Drawing* (2005): http://www.scribd.com/doc/51425351/Austin-Osman-Spare-Book-of-Automatic-Drawings (accessed 22 September 2014).
27 Studies focusing on the artistic works created within the Theosophical Society and/or upon the role of art and aesthetics specifically within the Theosophical worldview are still lacking, with the exception of Kroon et al. 2005.
28 Several authors in Kries 2011 refer to an 'anthroposophic style', which seems generally to be Jugendstil and Secession in outlook.
29 See examples in Faucherau 2011: 250–51; Kries 2011: passim.
30 In line with the illustrative tradition of Western esotericism as mentioned earlier; compare for instance the images in Kries 2011: 64–69.

REFERENCES AND FURTHER READING

Alderton, Zoe (2011) 'Colour, Shape, and Music: The Presence of Thought Forms in Abstract Art', *Literature & Aesthetics* 21 (1), 236–58.

Audinet, Gérard (2012) 'L'Art de la table', *Entrée des médiums: Spiritisme et Art de Hugo à Breton*, Paris: Maison de Victor Hugo, 11–25.

Bauduin, Tessel M. (2014) *Surrealism and the Occult. Occultism and Esotericism in the Work and Movement of André Breton*, Amsterdam: Amsterdam University Press.

——(2013) 'Abstract Art as "By-Product of Astral Manifestation": The Influence of Theosophy on Modern Art in Europe', in O. Hammer and M. Rothstein, eds., *Handbook of the Theosophical Current*, Leiden: Brill, 429–52.

——(2012) 'Science, Occultism, and the Art of the Avant-Garde in the Early Twentieth Century', *Journal of Religion in Europe* 5 (1), 23–55.

Bax, Marty (2006) *Het web der schepping: theosofie en kunst in Nederland van Lauweriks tot Mondriaan*, Amsterdam: SUN.

——(1995) 'Theosophie und Kunst in den Niederlanden 1880–1915', in V. Loers, ed., *Okkultismus und Avantgarde: Von Munch bis Mondrian, 1900–1915*, Frankfurt: Schirn Kunsthalle, 282–319.

Bang Larsen, Lars (2007) 'The Other Side'. *Frieze* 106. Online: http://www.frieze.com/issue/category/ issue_106/ (accessed 25 February 2013).

Besant, Annie, and Leadbeater, Charles Webster (2005 [1901, 1925]) *Thought forms*, London: The Theosophical Publishing House. Online: http://www.gutenberg.org/files/ 16269/16269-h/16269-h.htm (accessed 20 February 2013).

Bois, Jules (1897) 'L'Esthétique des esprits et celle des symbolistes', *Revue des Revues* XX (January–March), 405–20.

Bragdon, Claude (1929 [1913]) *A Primer of Higher Space: The Fourth Dimension, to Which is Added Man the Square, a Higher Space Parable*, New York: Knopf.

Breton, André (2007 [1933]) 'The Automatic Message', in Claudia Dichter et al., eds., *The Message. Kunst und Okkultismus/Art and Occultism*, Bochum: Kunstmuseum, 33–55.

Cardinal, Roger (1972) *Outsider Art*, London: Praeger.

Cardinal, Roger and Lusardy, Martine, eds. (1999) *Art Spirite, Médiumnique, Visionnaire: messages d'outre-monde*, Paris: La Halle Saint-Pierre.

Celant, Germano (1981) 'Futurism and the Occult', *Artforum* XIX (5), 36–42.

Chaitow, Sasha (2013) 'How to Become a Mage (or Fairy): Joséphin Péladan's Initiation for the Masses', *The Pomegranate* 14, 185–211.

Chéroux, Clément (2005) 'Photographs of fluids. An alphabet of invisible rays', in Metropolitan Museum of Art, *The Perfect Medium: Photography and the Occult*. New York: The Metropolitan Museum of Art, 114–25.

Clerbois, Sebastien (2002a) 'In Search of the *Forme-Pensée*: the Influence of Theosophy on Belgian Artists, between Symbolism and the Avant-Garde (1890–1910)'. Online: http://www.19thc-artworldwide.org/index.php/autumn02/259-in-search-of-the-forme-pensee-the-influence-of-theosophy-on-belgian-artists-between-symbolism-and-the-avant-garde-1890-1910 (accessed 08 February 2013).

——(2002b) 'L'Influence de la pensée occultiste sur le symbolisme Belge: bilan critique d'une «affinité spirituelle» à la fin du 19e siècle', *Aries* 2 (2), 173–92.

Cole, Brendan (2006) 'L'École de Platon de Jean Delville: Amour, beauté et androgynie dans la peinture fin-de-siècle', *Revue du Louvre et des Musées de France* 56 (4), 57–63.

Crabtree, Adam (2003) '"Automatism" and the emergence of dynamic psychiatry', *Journal of the History of the Behavioral Sciences* 39, 1: 51–70.

Danchin, Laurent (1999) 'Création médiumnique aujourd'hui: leçons d'une rencontre', in Roger Cardinal, and Martine Lusardy, eds., *Art Spirite, Médiumnique, Visionnaire: messages d'outre-monde*, Paris: La Halle Saint-Pierre, 29–37.

Da Silva, Jean (1991) *Le Salon de la Rose + Croix (1892–1897)*, Paris: Syros-Alternatives.

Davenport, Nancy (2007) 'Paul Sérusier: Art and Theosophy', *Religion and the Arts* 11, 172–213.

Déjean, Gallien (2008) 'Kenneth Anger', in Angela Lampe and Jean de Loisy,eds., *Traces du Sacré*, Paris, Munich: Centre Pompidou, Haus der Kunst, 364–65.

Deonna, Waldemar (1932) *De la Planète Mars en Terre Sainte: art et subconscient: un medium peintre: Hélène Smith*, Paris: De Boccard.

Dichter, Claudia; Golinski, Hans Günter; Krajewski, Michael; and Zander, Susanne, eds. (2007) *The Message. Kunst und Okkultismus/Art and Occultism*, Bochum: Kunstmuseum.

Edelman, Nicole (1995) *Voyantes, guérissseuses et visionnaires en France, 1785–1914*, Paris: Albin Michel.

Enns, Anthony (2012) 'The Undead Author: Spiritualism, Technology and Authorship', in Tatiana Kontau and Sarah Willburn, eds., *The Ashgate Research Companion to Nineteenth-Century Spiritualism and the Occult*, Burlington: Ashgate, 55–78.

Entrée des médiums: Spiritisme et Art de Hugo à Breton (2012) Paris: Maison de Victor Hugo.

Evelein, F. (1996) '"Pure Theosophical Art": verslag van een werkreis', *Theosofia* 97(3), 121–23.

Faucherau, Serge (2011) 'La magie moderne', in Joëlle Pijaudier-Cabot, and Serge Faucherau, eds., *L'Europe des esprits ou la fascination de l'occulte, 1750–1950*, Strasbourg: Éditions de Musées de Strasbourg, 227–51.

Fischer, Andreas (2005) '"A Photograph of Marvels": Frederick Hudson and the beginnings of spirit photography in Europe', in Metropolitan Museum of Art, *The Perfect Medium: Photography and the Occult*, New York: The Metropolitan Museum of Art, 29–36.

Flournoy, Théodore (1994 [1899]) *From India to the Planet Mars: A Case of Multiple Personality with Imaginary Languages*, ed. by S. Shamdasani, Princeton: Princeton University Press.

Godeau, Jérome (2012) 'Esprit de famille', in *Entrée des médiums: Spiritisme et Art de Hugo à Breton*, Paris: Maison de Victor Hugo, 38–59.

Godwin, Joscelyn (1995) *Music and the Occult: French Musical Philosophies 1750–1950*, Rochester: Rochester University Press.

Henderson, Linda Dalrymple (2010) *The Fourth Dimension and Non-Euclidean Geometry in Modern Art*, Cambridge: MIT Press.

——(2004) 'Editor's Introduction: I. Writing Modern Art and Science – An Overview; II. Cubism, Futurism, and Ether Physics in the Early Twentieth Century', *Science in Context* 17 (4), 423–66.

——(1981) 'Italian Futurism and "the Fourth Dimension"', *Art Journal* 41 (4), 317–20.

Hentschel, Martin (1996) 'Plotting Pole's *Showcase Piece*: Irony and Parody as Vehicles of Criticism and Artistic Freedom', in D. Thistlewood, ed., *Sigmar Polke: Back to Postmodernity*, Liverpool: Tate Gallery/Liverpool University Press, 57–70.

Howard, Michael, ed. (1998) *Art as Spiritual Activity: Rudolf Steiner's Contribution to the Visual Arts*, Hudson, NY: Anthroposophic Press.

Huussen, A.H. jr., van Paasschen-Louwerse, J.F.A., de Ruiter, Peter, and Blokhuis, Marleen (2005) *Jacoba van Heemskerck van Beest, 1876–1923: schilderes uit roeping*, Zwolle: Waanders/Prins Bernhard Cultuurfonds.

Kandinsky, Wasily (2004 [1912, 1914]) *Concerning the Spiritual in Art*, trans. T.H. Michael. Online: http://www.gutenberg.org/ebooks/5321 (accessed 01 March 2013).

Keshavjee, Serena (2013) 'Science and the Visual Culture of Spiritualism: Camille Flammarion and the Symbolists in fin-de-siècle France', *Aries* 13 (1), 37–69.

——(2009) '*L'Art Inconscient*: Imaging the Unconscious in Symbolist Art for the Théâtre d'art', *RACAR–Canadian Art Review* 1, 62–76.

Kries, Mateo (2011) *Rudolf Steiner: Alchemy of the Everyday*, Weil-am-Rhein: Vitra Design Museum.

Kokkinen, Nina (2013) 'Occulture as an Analytical Tool in the Study of Art', *Aries* 13 (1), 7–36.

Kroon, Andrea, Bax, Marty, and Snoek, Jan, eds. (2005) *Masonic and Esoteric Heritage. New Perspectives for Art and Heritage Politics*, The Hague: OVN.

Kugler, Walter (1995) 'Wenn der Labortisch zum Altar wird – Die Erweiterung des Kunstbegriffs durch Rudolf Steiner', in V. Loers, ed., *Okkultismus Und Avantgarde: Von Munch Bis Mondrian, 1900–1915*, Frankfurt: Schirn Kunsthalle, 47–60.

Kuspit, Donald (1986) 'Concerning the Spiritual in Contemporary Art'. In: Tuchman, Maurice (ed.). *The Spiritual in Art: Abstract Painting 1890–1986*, Los Angeles, The Hague: Los Angeles County Museum, Haags Gemeentemuseum, 313–25.

Lampe, Angela, and de Loisy, Jean, eds. (2008) *Traces du Sacré*, Paris, Munich: Centre Pompidou, Haus der Kunst.

Leadbeater, Charles Webster (1902) *Man Visible and Invisible. Examples of Different Types of Men as Seen by Means of Trained Clairvoyance*, Adyar: The Theosophical Publishing House. Online: http://www.scribd.com/doc/31411/C-W-Leadbeater-Man-Visible-And-Invisible-1902 (accessed 01 March 2013).

Loers, Veit, ed. (1995) *Okkultismus und Avantgarde: Von Munch bis Mondrian, 1900–1915*, Frankfurt: Schirn Kunsthalle.
Maclagan, David (2009) *Outsider Art: From the Margins to the Marketplace*, London: Reaktion Books.
Martinez, Chus, and Schroeder, Katja, eds. (2008) *The Great Transformation: Art and Tactical Magic*, Frankfurt: Frankfurter Kunstverein.
Metropolitan Museum of Art (2005) *The Perfect Medium: Photography and the Occult*, New York: The Metropolitan Museum of Art.
Miles, Christopher J. (2006) 'Journey into the Neither-Neither: Austin Osman Spare and the Construction of a Shamanic Identity', *The Pomegranate* 8 (1), 54–83.
Morehead, Allison (2009) 'Symbolism, Mediumship, and the "Study of the Soul that has Constituted Itself as a Positivist Science"', *RACAR–Canadian Art Review* 1, 77–85.
Müller-Westerman, Iris (2013) 'Paintings for the Future: Hilma af Klint – A Pioneer of Abstraction in Seclusion', in I. Müller-Westerman and J. Widoff, eds., *Hilma af Klint – A Pioneer of Abstraction*, Stockholm: Moderna Museet, 33–51.
Natale, Simone (2011) 'The invisible made visible. X-rays as attraction and visual medium at the end of the nineteenth century', *Media History* 17 (4), 345–58.
Oberhuber, Konrad (1995) 'Rudolf Steiner – Das Erste Goetheanum', in V. Loers, ed., *Okkultismus und Avantgarde: Von Munch bis Mondrian, 1900–1915*, Frankfurt: Schirn Kunsthalle, 713–57.
Oberter, Rachel (2006) 'Esoteric Art Confronting the Public Eye: The Abstract Spirit Drawings of Georgiana Houghton', *Victorian Studies* 48 (2), 221–32.
Okuda, Osamu (2011) 'Le métamorphose médiumnique chez Paul Klee', in Joëlle Pijaudier-Cabot and Serge Faucherau, eds., *L'Europe des esprits ou la fascination de l'occulte, 1750–1950*, Strasbourg: Éditions de Musées de Strasbourg, 278–87.
Otto, Elizabeth (2012) 'Image as investigation: sciences of the otherworldly at the Bauhaus', *Environmentalist* 32, 318–25.
Ouspensky, Piotr D. (1922 [1912]) *Tertium Organum* (second revised edition), New York: Knopf. Online: http://www.sacred-texts.com/eso/to/index.htm (accessed 15 February 2013).
Owen, Alex (2004) *The Place of Enchantment: British Occultism and the Culture of the Modern*, Chicago: University of Chicago Press.
Peiry, Lucienne (2008) 'Le spiritisme et l'Art Brut', in Angela Lampe and Jean de Loisy, eds., *Traces du Sacré*, Paris, Munich: Centre Pompidou, Haus der Kunst, 132.
——(2001) *Art Brut: The Origins of Outsider Art*, trans. by James Frank, Paris: Flammarion.
Péladan, Joséphin (1888) *La Décadence Esthétique. Vol. I: L'Art Ochloratique, Salons de 1882 et 1883*, Paris: Dalou.
——(1894) *L'art idéaliste et mystique, doctrine de l'Ordre et du salon annuel des Rose+Croix*, Paris: Chamuel.
Pincus-Witten, Robert (1976) *Occult Symbolism in France*, New York: Garland.
——(1968) *Les salons de la Rose Croix, 1892 – 1897*, London: Piccadilly Gallery.
Pijaudier-Cabot, Joëlle, and Faucherau, Serge, eds. (2011) *L'Europe des esprits ou la fascination de l'occulte, 1750–1950*, Strasbourg: Éditions de Musées de Strasbourg.
Ringbom, Sixten (1987) 'Transcending the Visible: The Generation of the Abstract Pioneers', in M. Tuchman, ed., *The Spiritual in Art, Abstract Art 1890–1985*, Los Angeles, The Hague: Los Angeles County Museum, Haags Gemeentemuseum, 131–54.
——(1970) *The Sounding Cosmos: A Study in the Spiritualism of Kandinsky and the Genesis of Abstract Painting*, Åbo: Åbo Akademi.
——(1966) 'Art in "The Epoch of the Great Spiritual": Occult Elements in the Early Theory of Abstract Painting', *Journal of the Warburg and Courtauld Institutes* 29, 386–418.

Rousseau, Pascal (2013) 'Premonitory Abstraction – Mediumism, Automatic Writing, and Anticipation in the Work of Hilma af Klint', in Iris Müller-Westerman and Jo Widoff, eds., *Hilma af Klint – A Pioneer of Abstraction*, Stockholm: Moderna Museet, 161–75.

Rosenberg, Raphael, and Hollein, Max, eds. (2007) *Turner, Hugo, Moreau. Entdeckung der Abstraktion*, Frankfurt: Schirn Kunsthalle.

Schuré, Édouard (2010 [1889]) *The Great Initiates*, 2 vols, Whitefish: Kessinger.

Shamdasani, Sonu (1994) 'Encountering Hélène: Theodore Flournoy and the Genesis of Subliminal Psychology', in Théodore Flournoy, *From India to the Planet Mars: A Case of Multiple Personality with Imaginary Languages*, ed. by S. Shamdasani, Princeton: Princeton University Press, xi–li.

——(1993) 'Automatic Writing and the Discovery of the Unconscious', *Spring* 54, 100–131.

Shirland, Jonathan (2013) '"Enigmas So Occult That Oedipus Might Be Puzzled To Solve Them": Whistler, Spiritualism & Occulture in Late Victorian England', *Aries* 13 (1), 71–102.

Taylor, Mark C. (2012) *Refiguring the Spiritual: Beuys, Barney, Turrell, Goldsworthy*, Chichester, New York: Columbia University Press.

Thévoz, Michel (1999) *Art Brut, psychose et mediumnité*, Paris: Éditions de la Difference.

Treitel, Corinna (2004) *A Science for the Soul: Occultism and the Genesis of the German Modern*, Baltimore: Johns Hopkins University Press.

Tuchman, Maurice, ed. (1986a) *The Spiritual in Art, Abstract Art 1890–1985*, Los Angeles, The Hague: Los Angeles County Museum, Haags Gemeentemuseum.

——(1986b) 'Hidden Meanings in Abstract Art', in M. Tuchman, ed., *The Spiritual in Art, Abstract Art 1890–1985*, Los Angeles, The Hague: Los Angeles County Museum, Haags Gemeentemuseum, 17–61.

Wagner, Christopher (2011) 'Les avant-gardes et les dispositifs de l'ésotérisme', in Joëlle Pijaudier-Cabot and Serge Faucherau, eds., *L'Europe des esprits ou la fascination de l'occulte, 1750–1950*, Strasbourg: Éditions de Musées de Strasbourg, 253–71.

——(2009) 'Johannes Itten und die Esoterik: Ein Schlüssel zum frühen Bauhaus ?', in C. Wagner, ed., *Esoterik am Bauhaus. Eine Revision der Moderne* ? Regensburg: Schnell & Steiner, 109–49.

—— ed., (2005) *Das Bauhaus und die Esoterik. Johannes Itten, Paul Klee, Wassily Kandinsky*, Bielefeld: Dumont.

Welsh, Robert P. (1987) 'Sacred Geometry: French Symbolism and Early Abstraction', in Maurice Tuchman, ed., *The Spiritual in Art: Abstract Painting 1890–1986*, Los Angeles, The Hague: Los Angeles County Museum, Haags Gemeentemuseum, 63–88.

Will-Levaillant, Françoise (1980) 'L'analyse des dessins d'aliénés et de médiums en France avant le Surréalisme', *Revue de l'Art* 50, 24–39.

CHAPTER FORTY-FIVE

THE OCCULT AND FILM

Brian Baker

In many ways, the birth of cinema may be said to occur in the same period of rapid technological invention in the late nineteenth century that produced other machines of mass communication – the telephone, gramophone, and ultimately radio – that have been the focus of theorists and historians of media from Marshall McLuhan (*Understanding Media*, 1964) to Friedrich Kittler (*Gramophone, Typewriter, Film*, 1999). Cinema occurs at the point at which imaging technologies developed through the daguerreotype and photography proper were matched with the flexible and transparent medium celluloid, producing the possibility of cinematic reproduction of the world and, importantly, projection to a multi-member audience. Previous attempts, such as those by Eadweard Muybridge, to provide the effect of visual animation through spinning glass discs were hampered by the fragility of the technology: the cinematic apparatus, devised by the Lumière brothers and Thomas Edison, to produce the *illusion* of movement by the rapid succession of (24) frames per second, is reliant both on the invention of celluloid and on the mechanical flange that tricks the human eye.

We can, of course, trace cinema's roots back further, to proto-cinematic optical toys like the zoetrope that were something of a craze in the Victorian period, or further still, to the insistent visuality that has characterised studies of the popular culture of the nineteenth century and which can be found not only in the rise of photography, but in the popularity of panoramas, exhibitions and other forms of spectacular entertainment that are common to European and American culture in the period. Cinema can be seen, then, not as an invention of something entirely new (the affective implication of the legend surrounding the Lumière Brothers' first showing of 'The Train Arriving at Le Ciotat', where the audience tried to get out of the way of the approaching train), but as a spectacular technology that is the product of a popular culture of visuality and a concomitant penetration of technologies of spectacle into that culture.

If one of the vectors producing cinema is technological innovation, and another the culture of visual spectacle, a third is the kind of immersive entertainment known as the 'phantasmagoria'. These 'spectral entertainments', which proposed a manifestation of spectres and noumenal phenomena through 'mysterious projected images' and 'applications of the laws of optics and perspective', have been identified by Tom Gunning, Maria Warner and others as a proto-cinematic visual entertainment 'invoking the supernatural by projecting images of spirits of the dead in highly stage-managed eerie surroundings while simultaneously obeying Kircher's dictum on de-mystification' (Gunning 2004, p. 103). By this, Gunning means that the phantasmagoria offered *both* the frisson of seeing ghosts, the 'spirits of the dead', *and* the knowledge that these effects were produced by technological means. The phantasmagoria was, in a sense, the predecessor of special effects cinema (or the audio-visually enhanced contemporary theme park ride), offering illusionistic (and safe) terrors while also producing a 'how-did-they-do-that' or 'wow' factor. The phantasmagoria, and the magic lantern show, Gunning argues, transmits to cinema the 'intersection between a Renaissance preoccupation with the magical power of image (typified by Guilio Camillo's and Giordano Bruno's theories of memory) and a secular discovery of the processes of light and vision' (p. 102).

Gunning goes on to suggest that the phantasmagoria could only have been produced in a post-Enlightenment age, where 'the formerly sacred objects, stripped of official sanction, could now serve as entertainment'; but at the same time, this faith must be incompletely expelled, in order for the affective apparatus (producing the 'uncanny shudder') to work (p. 104). We can connect this to Foucault's (1980) suggestion in the interview/essay 'The Eye Of Power' that first-wave Gothic fiction, like the phantasmagoria a cultural product of the late eighteenth century, was directly related to the Enlightenment's banishing of unreason to the 'dark' spaces, of the cultural margins, in which transgressive desire, violence and the abject found representation. Cinema's inheritance from the phantasmagoria is, then, a metaphysical or even a theological one: its 'magical' illusionistic power rests, in part, on the unexpelled elements of belief in the 'other' world, the spiritual or numinous, which compounds the affect of technological spectacle.

The affective *power* of images is particularly apparent in the conception of one form of early cinema as the 'cinema of attractions'. This early cinematic form, before the advent of editing, demonstrated and exploited the spectacular capacities of cinema by offering not the *actualités* of the Lumière Brothers – a 'window on the world' representational power – but the staging of *cinema itself* as a spectacle. The films of Georges Méliès, who had also been a stage illusionist, embody the 'cinema of attractions', films which revel in the possibilities of representing the *un*real, the fantastic, the seemingly impossible. The 'cinema of attractions' foregrounds cinema *as* a special effect. Méliès' most famous film is *La voyage de la lune* (1902), a science fiction narrative which displays cinema's ability to create worlds of the imagination through model work, matte photography, double exposure/superimposition, and the kind of cinematic 'tricks' that Christian Metz enumerated as types of *trucage*, 'invisible' but 'perceptible' (that is to say, the spectator is aware of the technological artifice of the affect at the same time as being immersed in the illusion).

This simple binary, however, that separates out illusionistic power of cinema from its technical ability to *record* and represent the world is a false dichotomy, even though earlier histories of cinema proposed the 'cinema of attractions' as a 'primitive' form that was succeeded by a narrative cinema, in particular Hollywood continuity style. We should rather see that the power of *illusion* is embedded in narrative styles (such as continuity, which works hard to suppress spectatorial consciousness of the illusion), and that world-representing (or building) techniques are central to the generic inheritors of the spectacular emphases of the 'cinema of attractions', particularly science fiction film. Just as with Enlightenment and Gothic, illusion and representation (mimesis) remain interconnected, and expelled elements of each are found in the other.

The inheritance of the phantasmagoria, of access to or representation of *other* worlds or beings or forms, indicates that the *chemical* basis of cinema (silver nitrate emulsion on celluloid) is accompanied by an *alchemical* or magical one, in which the 'real' world is re-presented and *transformed* in the mirror of the cinematic image. The potentialities of cinematic transformation of the image – directly consequent from Méliès' 'discovery' of trick editing, where a passing autobus seemingly turned into a hearse as his camera jammed in the middle of the shot – leads to the symbolic substitutions and transformations that are characteristic of Surrealism, and particularly the dream-logic dissolves of Buñuel's *Un Chien Andalou* (1926) and *L'Age d'Or* (1929). In *Un Chien Andalou*, co-created with Salvador Dali, a series of cinematic transformations and trick effects are staged: a clothed woman becomes a naked one, a suit and tie laid out on a bed manifests the man, ants crawl from a hole in a hand. The uncanny, unsettling effects are, in part, the staging of cinema's power to penetrate beyond the logic of mimesis, of direct representation of the world, to reveal the *latent* world of desire, symbolism and art that lies beneath. Cinema's seeming ability to present access to the irrational, to *call up* the images of the unconscious, becomes a kind of magical act (and is not dissimilar to the eerie protoplasmic manifestations of the phantasmagoria, but these are spectres of the unconscious). Surrealism itself, and in particular André Breton's experiments with automatic writing, made manifest or called forth an alterity that may be explained through an occult *other* power, or a radical alterity *within*. The connection between Surrealism and the occult is well attested. Alan Ramòn Clinton (2004) argues:

> In noting the temporal coincidences between Yeats' and Breton's encounters with automatism, one would do well to remember that Breton's first public explanation of automatic writing was the article 'The Mediums Enter' published in *Littérature*. Describing his experiences of writing *The Magnetic Fields* with Soupault, Breton affirms, in almost cultic fashion, 'I have never lost my conviction that nothing said or done is worthwhile outside obedience to that magic *dictation*'. Just as for Yeats and his wife, for Breton automatic writing was always a spiritual event.
>
> (p. 25)

Clinton states that the Surrealists' 'experiments [with automatism] occurred under the aegis of spiritualist practices' (p. 26). Into Surrealist creative practice, then, was transmitted the gestures and practices of occultism. The influence of Surrealist cinema upon the twentieth-century history of avant-garde cinema and the cultural 'underground' is profound; and in what follows, this article traces elements of occultism in both the *practice* of avant-garde cinema (through ritual, symbolism and affect) and the stories of mainstream horror film (representation of the occult, the devil and witch craft).

MIRRORS

A vitally important conduit for what follows is the cinema of Jean Cocteau. Cocteau – whose work profoundly influenced both Maya Deren and Kenneth Anger, whose work will be considered shortly – worked across several fields, as a filmmaker, artist and writer. His films, and indeed his writings on cinema, propose an intimate connection between poetry and film. In his short essay 'Poetry and films', Cocteau (1994) suggests that even in the work of a 'cinema-poet' (like himself) 'understanding comes [...] in flashes and glimmers [...] that instantaneously reveal the unexpected arrangement of things' (p. 38). This literal enlightenment – the illumination provided by inspiration or the muse (a recurrent motif in Cocteau's work) – is the revelation of poetry 'as a product of the unconscious', whereas the 'poetic is conscious'. *Poetry* (elevated above a conscious striving for the 'poetic') enters almost by indirection or accident; using a 'tale or a legend as an everyday device and [believing] in acts of magic as he does in the most routine actions' will lead the cinema-poet towards poetry. Cocteau's intention, in cinema, is to 'create a world that is superimposed upon the visible and to make visible a world that is ordinarily invisible' (p. 38), through 'acts of magic', manifesting the 'invisible world'. While, in the same paragraph, Cocteau explicitly disavows the supernatural, the language used to describe his artistic practice is a form of magical ritual. While this could be explained as an instance of mystification of an otherwise workaday procedure ('everyday device [...] routine actions'), the transmission of the language of inspiration, ritual and 'magic' indicates the extent to which the conception of *interior* (other) inspiration drifts into an *exterior* (occult) one.

In Cocteau's *Orphée* (1950), a version of the Orpheus myth, the poet's source of inspiration is explicitly represented as deriving from exterior powers. Death, having fallen in love with Orphée, arranges a fatal accident for Orphée's young poet-rival, Cegeste, and then uses him to transmit poetry (in a code that echoes the wartime BBC broadcasts to agents operating in Nazi-occupied Europe) to Orphée, who sits, transcribing, listening to the radio in Death's own limousine. *Orphée* presents a poetics of *transmission* rather than interior *inspiration*; after Eurydice is taken by Death to the Underworld, Orphée follows to try to win her back. This scene is staged using the full resources of cinema *as* an illusionistic medium: film runs backwards, there are tricks with regard to cinematic space, and in particular the illusionistic use of a mirror. The passage into the Underworld is effected by means of shooting gloved hands entering a mercury bath. Rotated 90 degrees, this becomes a 'soft mirror' which allows the passage of Orphée *beyond*. The cinematic mirror (the screen) is diegetically repeated as a magic mirror, Orphée's entry into the space *behind*/beyond the mirror replicating the spectator's illusionistic entry into Cocteau's imagined world. The importance of *trucage* in the *mise-en-scéne* of *Orphée*, the self-reflexive use of cinematic and stage illusions (film director *as* illusionist/'magician') places Cocteau in direct lineage to the cinema of Méliès; this mode is passed down further to the avant-garde cinema of Maya Deren.

Deren was an experimental film maker, working entirely outside of mainstream production and distribution systems in the USA, and who claimed particular artistic and filmic inspiration from Cocteau, although P. Adams Sitney, in *Visionary Film*, suggests that Deren did not see any Cocteau films until after she began making her own. Lucy Fischer (2001), in an article called 'The Eye for Magic', draws a lineage directly between Deren and Méliès, and the title of the essay is taken from a phrase of Deren's, speaking of cinema as a mode of seeing or *vision* (a recurrent idea in avant-garde cinema) 'that perceives and reveals *the marvellous* in whatever it looks upon', an almost direct restatement of Cocteau's ideas in 'Poetry and film'. 'That Deren's films and writings would be informed by magic should come as no surprise to us,' suggests Fischer (p. 186), and she makes an interesting case for a *double* inheritance from Méliès: in terms of a cinematic prestidigitation (*trucage*), and in terms of a 'spiritualist' fascination 'by metamorphoses of identity facilitated by the intervention of cinema' (p. 195). That cinema provides access to what Deren characterised as 'the laws of the unknown forces which compulse the universe' (quoted Fischer, 2001, p. 191) and signifies a magical, or in Fischer's terms, 'a mythic/ritualistic perspective on the universe' (p. 194). Deren would later become an actual initiate of vodoun ceremonies in Haiti, 'mounted' by the *loa* Erzulie (as described in *The Divine Horsemen*, 1953, pp. 247–62), but Fischer (1994) uses this concept to propose a reading of Deren's own cinematic and artistic practice. The artist becomes 'one of the initiated who can make spirits known to those who remain in the dark', and cinema a form of 'magic [that] could link people to ritual and myth' (p. 197).

Deren's cinema draws from myth and ritual – one of her films is titled *Ritual in Transfigured Time* (1948–49) – and from the filmic resources of Surrealism. In Deren's most well-known work, *Meshes of the Afternoon* (1943–59), use of shadows and architecture recalls not only the paintings of di Chirico, but also Murnau's film of *Nosferatu* (1922). Deren herself plays the central character in *Meshes*, a dreamer whose multiple avatars populate the film; at one point, Deren encounters two other versions of herself seated at a table, while a third, the dreamer herself, sleeps in a nearby armchair. The dream-logic of the narrative rests upon repetition – Deren re-enters the same room several times, ascends the same staircase multiple times, pursues the same hooded figure along the same paved walkway – and upon the conjunction of uncanny objects – a bread knife, a telephone, a key. Dressed in black, Deren resembles a female version of Cesare, the somnambulist in *The Cabinet of Dr Caligari* (1919), tracing repeated and choreographed movements across a dislocated architecture. Dislocation is emphasised by ruptures in space and time. In several shots in the first half of the film, an arm reaches *into* the shot from off screen space (seeming to imply a point-of-view or first-person shot), but these dis-articulated limbs – and close-ups of Deren's legs and feet – disperse the dreaming subject *between* shots, and refuse a direct identification between viewer and dreamer-Deren, or viewer and actant-Deren. Time circulates in *Meshes*, becomes a form of space: an uncanny one, resembling a drawing by MC Escher. In a celebrated sequence, an avatar of Deren grasps the knife and seems to menace the dreamer. In the final sequence of shots of Deren's stepping feet, the actant steps on sand, soil, grass, paving and a rug in her passage between the table and the nearby armchair. Such radical dislocations reveal the logic of images which challenges the time of continuity cinema *and* everyday experience. Space becomes not a neutral container or physical architecture, but *meaningful*: psychologised, certainly, but also charged with the significant correspondences of the occult.

The blurring of interior and exterior spaces, ruptures in spatial continuity, and a use of the cinema to effect alterations in *time* (washed up on the beach at the start of the film, the waves roll backwards *away* from Deren's prone body), is also central to *At Land* (1944). When Deren levers herself up from the beach using a large piece of driftwood, the next shot shows her peering over a white tablecloth at the end of a long dining table in a large room. Both this film and *Ritual in Transfigured Time* bespeak a visionary isolation from the social – Deren is ignored as she crawls up the table – but here, ritual is invoked as a means by which a more profound connection to the world can be forged. When she stumbles along the beach, picking up and dropping stones, Deren appears to enact a Sisyphusian labour, in search of a kind of totem – the chess piece that plays a symbolic visual role throughout the film. Encountering two women on the beach, playing chess, Deren forms a triangulation, stroking their hair, before stealing a piece and running away. This triangulation of three women is also found in *Ritual*, which P. Adams Sitney reads as an articulation of the three Graces (1979) – Deren herself, the dancer Rita Christiani, and the writer Anais Nin – though the winding of a skein of wool also suggests, as Lucy Fischer (2001) notes, the three Fates (p. 197). We can perhaps read Deren's use of classical archetypes in a continuum with her interest in vodoun – both expressed a means by which to circumvent the alienating materialism of modernity, and return to a magical/occult understanding of the relation between human beings and the 'unknown forces which compulse the universe'. Deren's Modernism is clear; the magical *and* the mythic are forms of re-enchantment, a *return* to occulted knowledge to express *new* conditions of subjectivity and being.

P. Adams Sitney (1979) characterises Deren's cinema as 'trance film', and sees its motifs of interior quests for 'the erotic mystery of the self' in contradistinction to Surrealist predecessors, which instead encode 'a mad voyeurism and [the purpose] to imitate the very discontinuity, the horror, and the irrationality of the unconscious' (p. 11). This quest for the 'erotic mystery of the self', effected through a means of ritual and avant-garde cinematic practice, is also crucial to the work of Kenneth Anger. While Anger's work is considered in detail elsewhere in this volume, here it is necessary to concisely situate his work as a means by which occult motifs and practices are transmitted not only into more mainstream films of psychological horror, but into the counter-culture of the 1960s more widely and to the visibility of diabolism by the end of that decade.

DEVILS

The influence of Cocteau on Anger is more direct still than that of the films of Maya Deren. Anger's first film (the one still extant: he burned the negatives of his very early work) is *Fireworks*, in which a young man awakes in bed, rises and passes through a door marked 'Gents' and emerges on to a (literal and symbolic) stage upon which a psycho-drama of sado-masochistic homo-erotic 'awakening' takes place. Where, in the much more widely known *Scorpio Rising* (1964), Anger takes the pop-cultural figure of the outlaw biker as a queered masculine icon of desire and violence, *Fireworks* presents the lover/antagonist as an idealised American sailor. The film cuts between chain-wielding sailors and an increasingly brutalised protagonist, and an emphasis on the passage of fluids (blood/milk) becomes an analogy for ejaculation. The film enacts a sexual ritual, one of initiation, which leads directly to transformation or transfiguration: the final shots show the protagonist with a firework protruding through his fly as a spectacular and fiery penis, which then becomes a burning Christmas tree: both a parodic and hyperbolic phallus. In Anger's films, the inheritance of Surrealism – sexualised or eroticised dream imagery – becomes overt and transgressive. Where Deren's sexual dream-logic results in the smashed mirror of the self, in Anger's work the 'erotic quest' is queered, resolving itself in sado-masochistic subsection to the desired but terrifying Other. This becomes more striking still in *Scorpio Rising*, the first half of which soundtracks bubblegum pop of the early 1960s (including Bobby Vinton's 'Blue Velvet') over shots of an 'outlaw biker' re-building a motorcycle, in order to critique American popular culture's investment in fetishised icons of chrome and steel, violence and speed (velocity and amphetamine), leather and rubber. The building of the motorcycle is replicated in the fetishised clothing of the outlaw males themselves: studded jackets, buckled leather wristbands, *Wild One*-style caps. What kind of subjectivity is being constructed (and desired/feared) is the core of the film's second half, in which jagged editing lends an unpleasant and threatening overtone to the scenes of rough homosocial horseplay (and a disquieting note to the bubblegum pop soundtrack). When a biker totes a machine gun and seems to declaim in tyrannical fashion, Nazi flags visible in the background, a troubling matrix of eroticism, fascism, sado-masochism and a pop-cultural 'death trip' come together in a kind of occulted meditation on the 'dark side' of the 1960s.

Anger's influence on mainstream cinema can be felt in several ways. The first is through the use of pop music, which has a clear impact upon Martin Scorsese's first film *Mean Streets* (1973), where the use of the Rolling Stones' 'Jumpin' Jack Flash' over a lurid red-lit bar, as Harvey Keitel watches the entrance of Robert De Niro, recalls Anger's provocative and disjunctive counterposing of image and sound track. Still more powerfully, the underground imagery and practice of *Fireworks* and *Scorpio Rising* was transmitted to the work of David Lynch, whose first film, *Eraserhead* (1977) was shot on a tiny budget over several years, outside the mainstream systems of distribution and exhibition. (It made its reputation as a cult film on the 'midnight movie' circuit, where Anger's films were also shown.) In later films such as *Blue Velvet* (1986) – where the intrusion of an uncanny, diabolic world into white-picket-fence suburbia is organised around the same Bobby Vinton song used in *Scorpio Rising* – or *Fire Walk With Me* (1992) and *Lost Highway* (1997), dislocations of time and space, the play of unexplainable or occult forces, the destabilisation of unitary subjectivity, and the unleashing of repressed sexuality and violence are recurrent motifs.

The second influence is more direct, and concerns the increasing visibility of diabolic or occulted imagery in rock and roll and the counter-culture of the 1960s. As outlined by Gary Lachman in *Turn Off Your Mind* (2001/2010), Anger's *Invocation of My Demon Brother* (1969) is a key text that stitches together several elements of the occult and prominent members of the counter-culture. *Invocation of My Demon Brother*, a short film which intercuts speeded-up footage of Anger conducting an occult ceremony, a musical troupe playing then descending a stair well, and shots of the eye of Horus and swastikas, also features a soundtrack by Mick Jagger – repeated electronic signals pierced by a blast of white noise – and footage taken from the Stones' concert in Hyde Park and news images of U.S. Marines jumping from helicopters in Vietnam. Like *Scorpio Rising*, *Invocation* is an indictment of an American death trip, but elements of occult revelation only find final (and 'straight') expression in Anger's later film *Lucifer Rising* (1972/1980); in *Invocation*, the speeded-up ceremony represents both a hyperbolic circulation of images *and* a fall into parody: the magus becomes a whirling marionette. The tonal incongruities of *Invocation* – begging the question as to whether the film sends itself up as it progresses – leaves an ambiguous relation between the film and an end-of-the-60s narrative, where the Stones' disastrous performance at Altamont Speedway – and the murder of Meredith Hunter while the band played 'Sympathy for the Devil' – marks the end of the counter-cultural dream. In Anger's films, this imaginary is already bound up with violence and darkness. Affirming the connection between Anger, the Rolling Stones and their entourage is the director Donald Cammell, who co-directed *Performance* (starring Jagger and Anita Pallenberg), and who himself played Osiris in Anger's *Lucifer Rising*.

Cammell and Roeg's *Performance*, while not ostensibly a diabolic or occult film, does stage a form of ritual transfiguration which places it in a continuum with other films discussed in this chapter. The film falls into two halves: in the first, the London gangster Chas (James Fox) exceeds the (violent) bounds of his employment and kills an old rival, after being beaten up himself; in the second, on the run, he finds a strange sanctuary in the Notting Hill flat of a retired rock star, Turner (Mick Jagger). Having been dosed with psychotropic drugs, Chas undergoes a kind of breakdown, but upon 'recovery' it appears that Turner and Chas have become enmeshed. In a crucial scene in the film, where Chas is in bed with Pherber (Anita Pallenberg, Turner's and Keith Richards' real-life girlfriend), she holds a hand-mirror to his face and chest, whereupon her face and breast are superimposed on his body in the mirror. As we have seen in the work of Cocteau and Deren, the mirror has a peculiarly magical property in the occult cinema; here, it presages a kind of melding or interconnection between the male subjects, a disruption of individual subjectivity. After Chas shoots Turner in the brain (the bullet tunnelling towards a picture of Jorge Luis Borges), his old boss comes to apprehend him. As the white Rolls Royce drives away (we had seen a black Rolls earlier in the film, a clear nod to *Orphée*), 'Chas' is seen at the window, driven to his own death, but it is Turner's (Jagger's) face that looks out.

Performance was shot in 1968 but released in 1970. This delay indicates the difficulty that even the troubled Hollywood studio system at the end of the 1960s would have had in placing *Performance* in a mainstream market place, even with Jagger as a star presence and following *Easy Rider*'s success in 1969. That is not to say the occult ideas and themes were absent from mainstream cinema in this period; far from it. But it is clear that the presence of the occult, diabolism, the satanic, was more acceptable or marketable if it took the form of horror or the Gothic.

The rise of Hollywood horror, as a big budget rather than B-picture phenomenon, marks the period 1968–76. The year 1968 saw the release of George A. Romero's *Night of the Living Dead* (an 'underground' horror film achieving great success) and, equally influentially, Roman Polanski's *Rosemary's Baby*. Produced by William Castle, the director of gimmick-laden shockers as in the 1950s and 1960s, *Rosemary's Baby* is the story of a coven of witches who manage the coupling of Mia Farrow with the Devil, and then act as the satanic neighbourhood support system to help the baby to term. Paul Wells (2000), connecting this film to Polanski's *Repulsion* (1965), which narrated the psychological fragmentation of its female protagonist (leading to a 'murderous psychosis'), argues that '[b]y prioritising the fears of women Polanski further radicalises the genre[....] We are offered Rosemary's perspective and necessarily must believe that our life is being determined by a Satanist conspiracy' (p. 83). Wells suggests that *Rosemary's Baby* stages social anxieties, and inaugurates a generic motif whereby 'the body [becomes] the key site of ideological and creative struggle' (p. 83). The centrality of the *female* body to what Kim Newman calls the 'Devil Movies' of the period, and anxieties about design and reproduction, can be seen in many films that follow *Rosemary's Baby*. Newman (1988) diagnoses a 'paranoid world view' in the film, where 'the central characters are trapped in a vast nightmare parallel where intellects vast, cool and unsympathetic are out to get them' (p. 58) – a world view still more visible in the paranoid conspiracy thrillers of the early 1970s, such as *Klute* (1971) or *The Parallax View* (1974), but also present in the big budget revision of the satanic pregnancy theme in *The Omen* (1976).

In *The Exorcist* (1973), the highest profile of all the Satanic horror films of this period, anxieties about the nuclear family, as analysed by Paul Wells and others, predominate. Regan (Linda Blair), the subject of demonic possession, is being brought up by her mother; 'the problem may be', argues Mark Jancovich (1983), 'that the possessed child, Regan, is being raised by a one-parent family which lacks a male authority figure' (p. 94). As Jancovich suggests, the film restores patriarchal order in the shape of Fathers Merrin (Max Von Sydow) and Karras (Jason Miller), the latter assuming Merrin's values and, faith restored, sacrificing himself to save the family. Whether we see *The Exorcist* as a metaphor for disrupted familial organisation, conservative in its 'desire for security' (Jancovich, 1983, p. 95), or more challenging in its depiction of the monstrous and transgressive female body, it is still the source of much critical discussion and analysis. What is clear is that by the early 1970s, the occult in film, particularly organised around women or female bodies, had become a vehicle for expressing particular social anxieties and ideological formations. In several films about witchcraft in the 1970s, this becomes explicit.

WITCHES

Witchfinder General was directed by Michael Reeves, a young director who had one film on his CV, called *The Sorcerers*. Vincent Price, who had been the star of Roger Corman's Poe cycle earlier in the decade, was cast as the East Anglian Hopkins, bringing some American star power to the production in a strategy common to British pictures in the 1950s and 1960s. The film begins with lens flare, sun shining through leaves, almost a pastoral scene, the greenness of the East Anglian landscape. Along with films such as *Blood on Satan's Claw* (1970) and *The Wicker Man* (1973), *Witchfinder General* has been called 'folk horror', where the uncanny or horror elements of the narrative are set against pastoral landscapes. At the beginning of the film, shots of the countryside give way to sounds of hammering and the screams of a middle-aged woman being dragged to a gibbet on a hill by a mob. The scene is presided over initially by a priest, who sermonises as the woman faints, is revived by having a bucket of water thrown over her, and is then hauled up on to a stool with a noose around her neck. Sun, wind, hammering, 'Gather yourselves together': all the while, she screams.

Screaming is a crucial audio motif in *Witchfinder General*. It is present here at the beginning of the film, and it is present in the very last moments. The screams of victims overlay the pastoral and direct our attention to the horror of the scene: this is the judicial murder of a middle-aged woman. The film begins *in media res*: we see no trial, no accusation, no proof of witchcraft. This is every-woman, a victim, a sacrifice or scapegoat that stands in for the victims of communal violence, between parliamentarian and royalist, between Protestant and Catholic. *Witchfinder General* begins with this scene because it signals the corrosion of the communal in times of conflict. These communities cannot withstand the disorder and violence that surrounds them, but try to earth that violence through the ritual sacrifice of one of their members. As the woman swings from the gibbet, the film cuts to a man on a horse, a pale rider: Matthew Hopkins (Vincent Price), watching. His distance and gaze both authorise this killing within the diegesis and indicate to the viewer the real puppet master at work. Hopkins not only authorises the killing of witches, but he authors them: the malignancy of Hopkins and his assistant Stearne is everywhere visible in the film.

The opening voice-over of *Witchfinder General* suggest that Hopkins takes advantage of the lawlessness and disorder in the Civil War, but it is clear that Hopkins' activities are really an extension both of mid-seventeenth-century Puritanism and of Parliamentarian rule: Hopkins and his helpers would have required passes of parliamentarian forces to travel around East Anglia. This diagnosis is hinted at by the repetition of the word 'godliness' in speeches by Hopkins and Oliver Cromwell. Hopkins denounces female witches, and upon witnessing a burning, suggests that it was 'a fitting end for the foul ungodliness of women kind'; Cromwell, sitting with his men after victory at Naseby, sees his triumph as a 'victory for true godliness'. Though the film does not undermine Cromwell's righteousness directly, Hopkins' cynicism in deploying the language of religion at this point, and its expression of misogyny that is also apparent in his sexual exploitation of young women, tends to undermine the authority of such statements. The role of law is then a highly problematic and dubious one in *Witchfinder General*. Hopkins is himself a lawyer, not a man of the cloth; his activities are seemingly given space by 'lawlessness'; Marshall must disobey the letter of the law in seeking to destroy Hopkins, and while his commanding officer threatens to throw 'the whole weight of military law' at him if he abandons his post, once Marshall leaves he wishes him every success on his quest for revenge, validating his extra-legal violence; and Hopkins clearly perverts the law: there is no witchcraft here. There is no evidence, only fakery, abuse of power, and spectacle.

In Ken Russell's *The Devils*, released (after much trouble with the British censor) in 1971, the protagonist (and ultimate victim) Urbaine Grandier (Oliver Reed), a worldly but spiritually lost Catholic priest, marries a young woman in spite of his vows of chastity, in order 'to come closer to god'. Unlike Marshall, who turned away from the possibility of redemption to pursue revenge, Grandier does indeed achieve a kind of 'spiritual carnality', and the simple ceremonies he conducts later in the film attest to the change in him and his return to faith. Grandier, upon the death of the city's governor, chooses to exert his own authority to attempt to defend the walls of Loudun against Cardinal Richelieu's attempts to pull them down. Grandier's sin, besides that of sexual licence, is *pride*. He is physically vain (with twirled moustaches), but is educated, sophisticated as opposed to his simple or corrupt parishioners, witty and cynical – and his intellectual power, his superiority, makes him believe that he is protected from downfall, even when he makes the daughter of the presiding magistrate pregnant. He is not accused of his true sins of sexual incontinence, but of being the centre of the sexual possession and debauch of Sister Jeanne (Vanessa Redgrave) and other nuns. He is, of course, innocent of these crimes.

The second half of *The Devils* concentrates on the trial and martyrdom of Grandier, and is, in fact, his Passion. Reed is given several powerful speeches denouncing the proceedings and their contradictions. His audience, however, is *us*: he is condemned by the court from the very beginning. No matter how much law and logic he uses, the case is already lost. His refusal to repent, to confess, results in scenes of torture, which are very powerfully staged. These are explicitly meant to extract a confession from him, and where violence and pain does not work, his torturers attempt to apply a kind of moral blackmail: they offer him a chance of redemption if he accepts that confession will help the Catholic church. When asked whether he loves the church, he replies 'Not today'. The simple dignity of this refusal, and Reed's powerful performance, goes beyond even the violent extremity of Marshall's response to Hopkins. When Grandier is burnt at the stake, his suffering *and* his unrepentant refusal to partake of the game of witchfinding spectacle is powerfully represented. He ascends to Christ-like status: Marshall remains an earth-bound revenger.

While the moment of maximal visibility for occult images, narratives and themes in mainstream cinema is the end of the 1960s and the 1970s, particularly associated with horror and Gothic (and production houses such as Hammer), this chapter has suggested that the occult is foundationally implicated in cinema's creation, and so never goes away entirely. More recent expressions of the manifestation of occult forces has been, self-reflexively, through the recurrent return to media itself as the transmission-point for 'dark' energies. From Tobe Hooper's *Poltergeist* (1982) to *The Blair Witch Project* (1999), from the J-horror *Ringu* cycle to *White Noise* (2004) and *Paranormal Activity* (2007), film and television (the latter in particular) have themselves entered the stage as the means by which an 'other' world may access our own, or be accessed by ourselves. This penetration of worlds, a global variation on the body-possession narratives of the 1970s, extends the terrifying *frisson* of the depiction of occult phenomena beyond the safe stage of the phantasmagoria and its filmic inheritors, and out into the 'real'. In contemporary visual culture, it is the screen itself, the 'magic mirror' of the film or television screen (or the computer display) which is the locus of occult representation, a mirror in which we see ourselves *and* our shadows.

REFERENCES AND FURTHER READING

Bibliography

Clinton, Alan Ramòn, *Mechanical Occult: Automatism, Modernism, and the Specter of Politics* (New York: Peter Lang, 2004).

Cocteau, Jean, 'Poetry and films', *The Art of Cinema*, trans. Robin Buss, ed. André Bernard and Claude Gauteur (London and New York: Marion Boyars, 1994), pp. 37–39.

Deren, Maya, *Divine Horsemen: the Living Gods of Haiti* (1953) (New York: Macpherson, 2004).

Fischer, Lucy, 'The Eye for Magic: Maya and Méliès', in *Maya Deren and the American Avant-Garde*, ed. Bill Nichols (Berkeley and Los Angeles: University of California Press, 2001), pp. 185–206.

Foucault, Michel, 'The Eye of Power', in *Power/Knowledge: Selected Interviews and Other Writings, 1972 – 1977*, ed. Colin Gordon, trans. Colin Gordon et al. (Brighton: Harvester, 1980), pp. 146–65.

Gunning, Tom, '"Animated Pictures": Tales of the Cinema's Forgotten Future, After 100 Years of Film', *The Nineteenth-century Visual Reader*, ed. Vanessa R. Schwartz and Jeannene M. Przyblyski (New York and London: Routledge, 2004).

Jancovich, Mark, *Horror* (London: Batsford, 1983).

Kittler, Friedrich, *Gramophone, Typewriter, Film* (Stanford, CA: Stanford University Press, 1999).

Lachman, Gary, *Turn Off Your Mind: The Dedalus Book of the 1960s* (Sawtry, Cambs: Dedalus, 2010).

McLuhan, Marshall, *Understanding Media* (1964) (London: Ark, 1987).

Metz, Christian, 'Trucage and the Film', *Critical Inquiry*, v. 3, no. 4 (1977), 657–76.

Newman, Kim, *Nightmare Movies: A Critical Guide to Contemporary Horror Films* (New York: Harmony Books, 1988).

Sitney, P. Adams, *Visionary Film: The American Avant-Garde 1943–78*, 2nd edn. (Oxford: Oxford University Press, 1979).

Warner, Marina, *Phantasmagoria: Spirit Visions, Metaphors and Media into the Twenty-First Century* (Oxford: Oxford University Press, 2006).

Wells, Paul, *The Horror Genre: from Beelezebub to Blair Witch* (London: Wallflower, 2000).

Filmography

Anger, Kenneth (dir.), *Fireworks* (1947)
Anger, Kenneth (dir.), *Invocation of My Demon Brother* (1969)
Anger, Kenneth (dir.), *Lucifer Rising* (1970–80)
Anger, Kenneth (dir.), *Scorpio Rising* (1963)
Buñuel, Luis (dir.), *L'Age d'Or* (1929)
Buñuel, Luis, and Salvador Dali (dirs.) *Un Chien Andalou* (1922)
Camell, Donald and Nic Roeg (dirs.), *Performance* (1971)
Cocteau, Jean (dir.), *Orphée* (1950)
Deren, Maya (dir.), *At Land* (1944)
Deren, Maya (dir.), *Meshes of the Afternoon* (1943)
Deren, Maya (dir.), *Ritual in Transfigured Time* (1946)
Donner, Richard (dir.), *The Omen* (1976)
Friedkin, William (dir.), *The Exorcist* (1973)
Haggard, Piers (dir.), *Blood on Satan's Claw* (1970)
Hardy, Robin (dir.), *The Wicker Man* (1973)
Hooper, Tobe (dir.), *Poltergeist* (1982)
Hopper, Dennis (dir.), *Easy Rider* (1969)
Lynch, David (dir.), *Blue Velvet* (1986)
Lynch, David (dir.), *Eraserhead* (1977)
Lynch, David (dir.), *Fire Walk With Me* (1992)
Méliès, Georges (dir.), *Le voyage de la lune* (1902)
Murnau, F.W. (dir), *Nosferatu* (1922)
Pakula, Alan J. (dir.), *Klute* (1971)
Pakula, Alan J. (dir.), *The Parallax View* (1974)
Peli, Oren (dir.), *Paranormal Activity* (2007)
Polanski, Roman (dir.), *Rosemary's Baby* (1968)
Reeves, Michael (dir.), *Witchfinder General* (1968)
Romero, George A. (dir.), *Night of the Living Dead* (1968)

Russell, Ken (dir.), *The Devils* (1971)
Sanchez, Eduardo and Daniel Myrick (dirs.), *The Blair Witch Project* (1999)
Sax, Geoffrey (dir.), *White Noise* (2005)
Scorsese, Martin (dir.), *Mean Streets* (1973)
Wiene, Robert (dir.), *The Cabinet of Dr Caligari* (1919)

CHAPTER FORTY-SIX

KENNETH ANGER

Deborah Allison

Born Kenneth Wilbur Anglemyer, February 3, 1927, Santa Monica, California, he is best known as an American avant-garde filmmaker and the author of two volumes of *Hollywood Babylon*, which describe, in salacious detail, the scandals of movietown. As such, Anger has been a central countercultural figure for more than sixty years. His most acclaimed film works are nine short pieces, collectively titled *The Magick Lantern Cycle* (1947–80), of which *Fireworks* (1947) and *Scorpio Rising* (1963) have left the deepest cultural footprint. Between the 1940s and 1970s, Anger variously completed and began around a dozen other shorts, which are now lost. After a lengthy career hiatus, he resumed filmmaking in the 1990s and has since completed several further short films, including *Ich Will!* (2000), *Don't Smoke That Cigarette!* (2000), *The Man We Want to Hang* (2002), *Mouse Heaven* (2004), *My Surfing Lucifer* (2007), and *Missoni* (2010).

Alongside his ongoing commitment to creating entirely new works, Anger remains actively engaged in restoring and reworking his earlier films, which he continues to regard as works in progress. (Hence, filmographic details here and elsewhere cannot be considered definitive.) He has toured extensively in recent years, presenting and discussing selections of his film work and co-curating gallery exhibitions of its imagery. A renewal in interview activity spawned the feature-length documentary *Anger Me* (Elio Gelmini, Canada, 2006), in which he provided a first-hand overview of his life and career.

A longstanding fascination with myth, magic, and the occult suffuses Anger's work. An intricate and intoxicating brew of ceremony and occult signification, his filmmaking depicts and enacts rituals of invocation and transformation. In describing the origins and development of his distinctive brand of cinematic alchemy, he often cites four key influences. First, he credits his grandmother Bertha Coler with fostering an early fascination with the films and stars of Hollywood, on the fringes of which he was raised. Second, he notes the influence of the artist Jean Cocteau, whom he met in Paris in 1950, and who helped develop his self-identity as a 'film poet,' while nourishing the mythological elements of his work. Third, he mentions Henri Langlois, the co-founder and director of the Cinémathèque Française, who further enhanced his appreciation of cinema in its many forms. Finally – but by no means least – he notes the influence of the English occultist Aleister Crowley, who left behind a substantial body of teachings and writings, the central tenets of which became foundational to Anger's own life and oeuvre.

Anger has made two films centered on Crowley's visual art. The long-lost *Thelema Abbey* (1955) is a ten-minute documentary of the several months spent in Cefalu, Sicily, during which he stripped the whitewash that covered the erotic frescos with which Crowley had adorned his small temple. In *The Man We Want to Hang* (2002), his camera roams across a 1998 London exhibition of Crowley's paintings. More significant, however, is the extraordinary potency with which Anger's fusion of Crowley's 'Thelemic' philosophy with his own preoccupations shapes the subjects, styles, and purpose of *The Magick Lantern Cycle* from the mid-1950s onwards.

In his program notes for a 1966 presentation of *The Magick Lantern Cycle*, Anger described 'Thelema' as his religion and Magick as his lifework. Adopting a Crowlean notion of 'magick,' he characterized himself as a magician casting a spell on his audience, and his camera as the 'magickal weapon' with which he composed his filmic 'incantations.' Although Anger belongs to the Ordo Templi Orientis (of which Crowley had been a prominent member), he usually designates himself as 'Pagan.' His incantations pull from a broad mythological span, encompassing an abundance of ancient and modern world religions, which he often weds to the cult of Hollywood cinephilia and fandom, alongside other totems of popular culture.

The consummate artisan, Anger prefers to work alone on his 'film poems' as far as possible, yet his list of collaborators reads like a directory of the artificers of twentieth-century culture. His films and research have taken him to many countries where he has mingled and shared inspiration with a dazzling array of celebrated figures whose films, music, poetry, visual art, and scholarly studies have broadened our social, spiritual, and aesthetic landscape in countless ways. Among the notable countercultural icons appearing in or otherwise contributing to his films are Bobby Beausoleil, Michael Cooper, Donald Cammell, Samson de Brier, Marianne Faithful, Curtis Harrington, Mick Jagger, Alfred C. Kinsey, Anton LaVey, Anaïs Nin, and Jimmy Page.

Throughout his long career, Anger has documented movements in contemporary culture, drawing out their parallels with more ancient civilizations, ideas, and beliefs. Although the esotericism of his symbolism sometimes renders their full intent abstruse, he invariably succeeds in communicating their major tenets even to non-initiates. Part of their popularity derives from the fact that, typically, he presents his theses with an appealingly dry humor and an acute appreciation of the profundity of the absurd. Despite spawning countless imitators, Anger remains peerless in his marriage of the popular with the arcane: a powerful synergy he renders with intelligence and panache.

THE MAGICK LANTERN CYCLE

Fireworks (US, 1947, 15 minutes, black-and-white)

Anger's first extant film pays homage to key works of the European and American cinematic avant-gardes, in whose culture he was already steeped. Drawing inspiration from the surrealists, it also follows the tradition of American 'trance films' of the

1940s. Structured as a dream, this modest psychodrama works as an interior autobiography wherein the dreamer (played by Anger) ventures out in search of a light and is drawn into a homoerotic reverie in which his sadomasochistic encounter with a group of sailors suggests the ritualistic restitution of an initial psychological lack. Filled with symbolism, including an African fetish and a cheirognomist's hand, *Fireworks* introduces motifs that recur in Anger's later films. In particular, a focus on the potency of light heralds what would become the dominant metaphor of *The Magick Lantern Cycle* – the affiliation between the mechanics of cinema and the principal figure of Anger's personal pantheon, the rebel angel, Lucifer.

Puce Moment (US, 1949, 6 minutes, color)

Assembled from material shot for an aborted project, *Puce Moment* depicts a Hollywood starlet slipping into a series of sumptuously sequined and beaded 1920s evening gowns, which shimmer under the filmmaker's lamps until the reflected light assumes a mesmeric quality of its own. This dressing ritual, where external trappings assist the wearer's assumption of a desired identity, prefigures the self-invention of Anger's later protagonists. Pointing up this parallel, he would incorporate footage from *Puce Moment* into *Inauguration of the Pleasure Dome*, superimposing it over new footage of a magickal masquerade party.

Rabbit's Moon (France/UK, 1950–71/1979, 16/7 minutes, tinted black-and-white)

Combining characters drawn from the Italian *commedia dell'arte* with Japanese myth and the Tarot, *Rabbit's Moon* plays out the stripped-down tale of Pierrot, Harlequin, and Columbine. Pierrot (the Fool) yearns to possess the moon, the Apollonian symbol of unrequited love and the quest for the ideal. He also covets Columbine, a beautiful illusion emanating from the magic lantern of the devilish jester Harlequin, against whose Dionysian sexual mischief Pierrot proves no match. Indeed, Harlequin has been widely interpreted as Anger's first full-fledged Lucifer figure. Once again, the transformative effects of light are embedded in the visual style. The moonlit woodland set also pays homage to *A Midsummer Night's Dream* (1935), in which Anger has claimed a childhood role as the Changeling Prince. After archiving his unedited footage for twenty years, Anger produced a sixteen-minute cut in 1971, which he later replaced with a shorter version featuring a different score.

Eaux d'Artifice (Italy, 1952, 13 minutes, tinted black-and-white)

The last film of *The Magick Lantern Cycle* to be shot in black-and-white, the aesthetic of *Eaux d'Artifice* echoes *Rabbit's Moon*, with the stunning sixteenth-century water gardens of the Villa d'Este in Italy providing an equally otherworldly setting. Its title (which puns on the French translation of 'Fireworks' – *feu d'artifice*) highlights their similarities, as its protagonist draws out the spirits of a glistening nocturnal dreamscape. Although representing the only completed portion of a more ambitious project, Anger describes it as 'a perfect film,' not least for its exquisite fusion of image and music (the Winter Concerto of Vivaldi's 'Four Seasons'). None of Anger's films contain speech (he compares them to visions in a crystal ball) and his soundtrack selections became increasingly expressive as his career progressed.

Inauguration of the Pleasure Dome (US, 1954, 38 minutes, color)

Anger's longest and most technically ambitious film is a psychedelic re-enactment of a masquerade party hosted by Samson de Brier, in which ancient gods and goddesses rub shoulders with cinematic icons, and where luminaries of the contemporary art and occult worlds are recognizable beneath their glittering costumes. This dream, drug, and magick-inspired masterpiece extends Anger's established themes while also representing a pivotal moment in his career. His first overtly occult-inspired work, choreographed to Janáček's 'Glagolitic Mass,' is replete with hallucinatory colors, the symbolism of which draws directly from Crowley's system of correspondences, which would also provide the visual scheme of Anger's subsequent films. The most impressive of *Invocation*'s several versions was created for the 1958 Brussels World Fair, where, inspired by Abel Gance's *Napoleon* (1927), the last twenty minutes opened out onto on a triptych of screens.

Scorpio Rising (US, 1963, 29 minutes, color)

Anger's best-known film centers on motorcycle fetishism and the eroticism of the death wish. It shows a group of American bikers preening themselves and their lustrous chariots in preparation for a Walpurgisnacht party, which culminates in a fatal race. Employing a color palette symbolically dominated by the blacks and reds of Mars, Anger also steps up his use of montage to imply connections between a dizzying array of textual elements. The influence of the silent-era Soviet filmmaker Sergei Eisenstein is unmistakable, while incorporation of found footage partakes of a trend emerging with the 1960s American avant-garde. *Scorpio Rising* is most celebrated for its influential pop soundtrack, in which thirteen contemporary songs provide an ironic commentary on characters and events. This novel technique spawned a host of imitators and helped establish a now-common cinematic convention. Its brush within American law and the consequent ruling of the Supreme Court as to its 'redeeming social merit' proved a landmark case influencing later censorship decisions.

Kustom Kar Kommandos (US, 1965, 3 minutes, color)

Conceived as a companion piece to *Scorpio Rising* and representing a segment of yet another uncompleted project, *KKK* (as Anger would controversially dub the film) features a young man fetishistically polishing his gleaming customized car to the accompaniment of The Paris Sisters' song 'Dream Lover.' Although arguably the least complex and ambitious film of *The Magick Lantern Cycle*, its high production values (which ape the Hollywood mainstream) typify the technical refinement that sets Anger's work aside from that of his peers.

Invocation of My Demon Brother (US/UK, 1969, 11 minutes, color)

In the late 1960s Anger began shooting a version of *Lucifer Rising*, but the loss of his footage (allegedly stolen by the lead actor, the San Francisco musician Bobby Beausoleil) brought production to a halt. The incident prompted a depressed Anger to place an advertisement in the *Village Voice*, where he announced the death of his filmmaking career. He subsequently assembled *Invocation of My Demon Brother* from cutting-room scraps, which he combined with other oddments of material, including documentary clips of occult rituals in which he appears as the Magus, scenes featuring Church of Satan founder Anton LaVey, and stock footage of the Vietnam War. Composed almost entirely in black and red, and featuring an abrasive Moog synthesizer soundtrack from Mick Jagger, this work of rage and passion is the explicit product of coincident personal and cultural upheavals.

Lucifer Rising (UK/Germany/Egypt, 1970–80, 30 minutes, color)

Inspired by Crowley's 'Hymn to Lucifer,' Anger's second *Lucifer Rising* project was the result of more than ten years' labor, and he viewed it as a summation of everything he had hitherto worked toward. Filmed in England, Germany, and Egypt, it enacts rituals founded in intersecting ancient and modern theologies and, like *Inauguration* and *Invocation*, features a cast of prominent countercultural figures. Far more sedate than its immediate predecessor, it embodies a reconciliation between opposing ideologies – a sensibility underscored by its being the only film of *The Magick Lantern Cycle* credited as 'A Film by Kenneth Anger,' instead of opening with the aggressively hand-scrawled inscription, 'A Film by Anger.' Here at last, new hope is expressed as the Aeon of Horus dawns.

REFERENCES AND FURTHER READING

Henderson, Richard, 'Anger is an Energy,' The Wire 247 (September, 2004), 32–33.

Hunter, Jack, ed. (2002) *Moonchild: The Films of Kenneth Anger*, London: Creation Books.

Landis, Bill (1995) *Anger: The Unauthorised Biography of Kenneth Anger*, San Francisco: HarperCollins.

Pilling, Jayne and Michael O'Pray (1989) *Into The Pleasure Dome: The Films Of Kenneth Anger*, London: BFI.

Pouncey, Edwin, 'Industrial Light and Magick,' The Wire 247 (September, 2004), 34–35.

Sitney, P. Adams, (1979) *Visionary Film: The American Avant-Garde 1943–1978*, second edition, New York: Oxford University Press, 93–135.

Wees, William C. (1992) *Light Moving in Time: Studies in the Visual Aesthetics of Avant-Garde Film*, Berkeley: University of California Press.

CHAPTER FORTY-SEVEN

DENNIS WHEATLEY

Phil Baker

Dennis Wheatley (1897–1977), the author of a number of immensely popular 'black magic' novels, such as *The Devil Rides Out* (1934), did a great deal to shape the popular image of occultism and Satanism in twentieth-century Britain, from the 1930s through to the occult revival of the late 1960s and early 1970s. Although he portrayed Satanism as evil, the ambience of his books made it seem strangely seductive and luxurious.

Wheatley was the son of a Mayfair wine merchant, wealthy but unequivocally considered 'in trade' by the Victorian class system. He became an officer in the First World War, where he came under the influence of Eric Gordon Tombe, a fellow officer who encouraged him to read widely and inclined him towards Paganism. Tombe and Wheatley led a raffish life after the war, when Tombe was active as a gentleman criminal and fraudster before being murdered in 1922. Wheatley commemorated Tombe on his bookplate, which features Tombe as the god Pan – he originally designed him more explicitly as the Devil, pouring a bottle of Veuve Clicquot champagne with his tail.

Wheatley had meanwhile married, but he came to look back on his first wife as suburban after their divorce, and in 1931 he married the more aristocratic Joan Pelham Burn. He worked in the family wine business and in due course took it over, but ran into financial difficulties after the 1929 Wall Street Crash. Wheatley was bought out by a larger firm and relegated to being a junior director, before running into trouble with the new owners, largely because he had included his personal debts in the firm's liabilities. This led to allegations of fraud. Suspended from work pending investigation, he used his enforced idleness to write, publishing *The Forbidden Territory* in 1933, which was a thriller set in Communist Russia. He never looked back, receiving accolade such as 'Public Thriller Writer No.1' in the 1930s and 'Prince of Thriller Writers' in the 1940s. The largest figure usually estimated for his lifetime sales is fifty million and he ranked in popularity with Edgar Wallace and Agatha Christie. He published around seventy novels, of which only eight are centrally concerned with the occult, as well as innovative 'Crime Dossiers' and even board games.

Early in the Second World War, Wheatley began writing amateur essays on tactics and strategy, and he was able to use personal contacts to have them read by King George VI and the Joint Planning Staff (JPS) of the War Cabinet. He was then given a job with the JPS itself, working in strategic deception. This was a very successful part of the war effort, misdirecting the German forces about such things as the D-Day landings.

At the end of war, Wheatley bought Grove Place, a Georgian country house in Lymington, Hampshire, where he continued to write industriously, while settling into a more gentlemanly, smoking-jacketed life with an extensive library and wine cellar. He later acquired a large flat in London's Cadogan Square. Profiling him in 1970 and noting that he lived in 'some splendor,' journalist David Blundy commented: 'Wheatley's been grappling with the Devil for over thirty years now, and frankly, the Devil's been pretty decent about it.'

The Devil Rides Out is perhaps the greatest popular occult novel of the twentieth century, as Dracula was of the nineteenth. Like *The Forbidden Territory*, it features the Duke de Richleau and his friends Simon Aron, Rex Van Ryn, and Richard Eaton, a loyal band of friends who recur in Wheatley's books and are inspired by Dumas' Three Musketeers. Young financier Simon Aron begins to dabble with Satanism and his friends must rescue him, together with another new recruit, a beautiful girl named Tanith.

Imbued with the mystique of connoisseurship and the glamour of social class, the Duke de Richleau books embody what a contemporary reviewer referred to as 'the luxury traditions of the cheap novel.' The Duke is fond of Imperial Tokay wine and Hoyo de Monterrey cigars, and in his Mayfair flat he has a 'Tibetan Buddha seated upon the Lotus; bronze figurines from Ancient Greece. Beautifully chased rapiers of Toledo steel and Moorish pistols inlaid with turquoise and gold, Ikons from Holy Russia set with semi-precious stones, and curiously carved ivories from the East' (Wheatley 1934, 33).

Previous writers had often depicted Satanism as a downmarket affair (as in W.B. Yeats's characterization of a Dublin black magical group as 'mainly small clerks,' in his story 'The Sorcerers') but Wheatley assured readers that 'practitioners of the Black Art in modern times were almost exclusively people of great wealth' (1934, 117). Having followed the Satanists to a bleak spot on Salisbury Plain, the Duke and his friends see Rolls-Royces, Daimlers, Bentleys, and a golden Bugatti parked for a Satanic orgy.

The appeal of black magic in popular culture was bound up with eroticism and Wheatley's books contributed significantly to this perception. They were, consequently, very popular with adolescents. Wheatley-style Satanism tends to involve a promise of impending group sex: after 'the baptism of the neophytes' in *The Devil Rides Out* will come 'the foulest orgy, with every perversion which the human mind is capable of conceiving' (1934, 130). As a character in a later novel explains, 'They get hold of pederasts, lesbians and over-sexed people of all ages, and provide them with the chance to indulge their secret vices' (1953a, 102). As Timothy d'Arch Smith has commented, tongue-in-cheek, 'Wheatley actually did the occult a great disservice in that he reduced hermetic science to the rogering of virgins on altar tops' (correspondence from the author, cited in Baker 2009, 496). Wheatley's occult books often feature the impending sexual degradation of a woman, sometimes a new recruit (an idea dimly related to ancient practices of temple prostitution) such as Tanith in

The Devil Rides Out, Molly in *The Satanist* (1960), and Sally in *The Haunting of Toby Jugg* (1948). The climactic double-bind of Wheatley's plots is that this fate-worse-than-death cannot be allowed to happen, although the possibility is dwelt on as fulsomely as possible; the girl must be saved at the last moment.

Wheatley's books tended to be research-heavy, whether the subject was Napoleonic history or South American landscape, and this plays a special role in the occult books, particularly *The Devil Rides Out*, where the encyclopaedic packing of occult lore is so insistent that readers not only learn of the astral plane, elemental spirits, grimoires, and scrying, but it encourages a suspension of disbelief. The specialised vocabulary is also richly atmospheric, with 'the dispersion of Choronzon,' 'St.Walburga's Eve,' 'The Clavicule of Solomon,' 'Our Lady of Babalon,' and Golden Dawn–style grades such as Magister Templi and Ipsissimus.

Disbelief is further suspended by the Duke de Richleau's disquisition on magic, repeated in several books, which begins with the reality of hypnosis and moves down a slippery slope to telepathy, the powers of the human will – whether to good or evil – and finally the Manichaean conflict between the forces of 'Eternal Light' and 'Eternal Darkness.' While Umberto Eco has described the James Bond books as Manichaean – a tendency of thrillers in general – the universe of Wheatley is literally and theologically Manichaean.

Although the occult lore in Wheatley's work is notoriously superficial and confused, the main planks of an occult worldview are clear: mind rules matter; spirit is transcendent; the human soul is eternal; we move through successive incarnations 'towards the light'; and there are 'Hidden Masters' and 'Lords of Light.' This has affinities with Theosophy (although Wheatley had little interest in Madame Blavatsky or Theosophy as such) and Gnosticism. Such Gnostic and theosophical-style elements are drawn largely from Maurice Magré's 1931 book *The Return of the Magi*. Grillot de Givry's 1931 book *Witchcraft, Magic and Alchemy* was also a major source, particularly for more archaic and picturesque details, along with Camille Flammarion's *Death and its Mystery* (1923), and the works of Montague Summers. Borrowings from occult fiction also play a part in Wheatley's occult writing, particularly from William Hope Hodgson.

Wheatley made the acquaintance of several occult authorities for research, notably Summers, Harry Price, Rollo Ahmed, and Aleister Crowley. In later years Wheatley liked to suggest that he had Crowley to dinner several times, but there is little evidence for more than a single lunch at the Hungaria restaurant on Regent Street, after which Crowley gave him a specially inscribed and customised copy of his *Magick in Theory and Practice* (1929). Wheatley incorporated elements of Crowley's appearance into the figure of Mocata, the villain in *The Devil Rides Out*, as he used the figure of Montague Summers for Canon Copely-Syle in *To The Devil – A Daughter*. Summers is perhaps the greatest influence on Wheatley's work, with his sense of Satanism and witchcraft – which are barely distinguished – as a gigantic conspiracy threatening civilisation. A commentator in the 1970s partwork encyclopaedia *Man, Myth and Magic* noted that with his condemnations of occultism – despite the fact that his own work contributed considerably to its popularity – 'Wheatley...can almost be said to have taken on the cloak of the late Montague Summers' (Anon. 1970, 885).

Wheatley enjoyed a great resurgence of popularity with the occult revival of the late 1960s. *The Devil Rides Out* became a much-loved Hammer film in 1968, and in

1971 Wheatley published a non-fiction compendium of spiritual beliefs, *The Devil and All His Works*. The works of Montague Summers and even the *Malleus Malleficarum* were re-issued as mass-market paperbacks in the early 1970s with introductions by Wheatley. By this time he had become something of an occult uncle to the nation, and newspapers would seek his advice on crimes that might have an occult angle. He also lectured to clergymen, suggested that industrial strikes and anti-apartheid demonstrations were manifestations of Satanism, and warned that half of Britain's drug-pushing was in the hands of witch covens.

Privately, Wheatley was less absorbed in the occult than his public image would suggest, although he was a strong believer in reincarnation and had a general belief in the possibility of occult phenomena. He professed to pray to the 'Lords of Light' and did not believe in God (although God is mentioned approvingly in his fiction and journalism, largely with the aim of keeping the masses on a righteous path). Wheatley would like to have been taken more seriously as a historical novelist and a writer of general thrillers, but the occult was obviously what the public wanted from him and he bowed to this with two late novels – in series which had not focused on the occult – *The White Witch of the South Seas*, closing the Gregory Sallust series, and *The Irish Witch*, penultimate novel in the Roger Brook series. Neither is commonly included among his main occult novels.

Wheatley was more interested in history and politics than he was in the occult, and his books are remarkable for their calculated propaganda content. Propaganda was a key concept in his mind. For example, he suggested during World War II that propaganda was more important than armed force and, in a 1953 lecture, he suggested that a key role of novels was as a 'vehicle for propaganda' (1953b, 761; see also Baker 2009, 490). Of Wheatley's eight main occult novels, six or seven have a distinct propaganda message. *The Devil Rides Out* (1934), in which the Satanists are trying to unleash a new world war, has a message of peace with Hitler's Germany. *Strange Conflict* (1941) has an emphasis on astral projection and life after death intended to prepare a wartime readership for mortal danger and bereavement. *The Haunting of Toby Jugg* (1948) presented Communism as the new face of Satanism, and a Cold War subtext then goes through *To The Devil – A Daughter* (1953a), *The Ka of Gifford Hillary* (1956), which argues for Britain to have a strong nuclear deterrent, and *The Satanist* (1960) which features the menace of Satanic Trade Unionism, while in *Gateway to Hell* (1970) Wheatley turns his attention to Black Power. A lesser known high point in Wheatley's propaganda career occurred when, paid by a secret department within the Foreign Office, the Information and Research Department (IRD), he wrote a novel for a British scheme to promote Islam in the Middle East (in the hope that it would be useful against communism). This was published in Arabic in 1953 as *Ayesha*.

Despite his broader output, Wheatley now seems destined to be remembered for his occult books and their construction of occult practice, whether this is recalled for comic effect or, more seriously, in unpicking allegations of Satanic abuse. He seems unlikely to be as popular again at face value, but, in addition to their skillful narrative tension, the unintentional humor and richly enjoyable ambience of his books offer the pleasures of kitsch and nostalgia. Like Sax Rohmer and John Buchan, Wheatley's books have made the transition from merely dated to positively 'period,' and considered as period pieces they offer considerable insight into popular taste, social history, and popular conceptions of the occult.

REFERENCES AND FURTHER READING

Anon. (1970) 'Frontiers of Belief: Dangerous Ritual,' *Man, Myth and Magic* No. 31 (20 August), 885.

Baker, Phil (2009) *The Devil is a Gentleman: The Life and Times of Dennis Wheatley*, Sawtry: Dedalus.

Crowley, Aleister (1991 [1929]) *Magick in Theory and Practice*, Edison, NJ: Castle Books.

Flammarion, Camille (1923 [1921]) *Death and its Mystery*, 3 vols., trans. Latrobe Carroll, London: Fisher Unwin.

Givry, Grillot de (1931) *Witchcraft, Magic and Alchemy*, New York: Dover Publications.

Hutton, Ronald (1999) *The Triumph of the Moon*, Oxford University Press.

Magre, Maurice (1931) *The Return of the Magi*, London: Philip Allan & Co.

Wheatley, Dennis (1934) *The Devil Rides Out*, London: Hutchinson.

——(1941) *Strange Conflict*, London: Hutchinson.

——(1948) *The Haunting of Toby Jugg*, London: Hutchinson.

——(1953) *Ayesha*, Beirut: [British Foreign Office].

——(1953a) *To the Devil – A Daughter*, London: Hutchinson.

——(1953b) 'The Novelist's Task,' *The Journal of The Royal Society of Arts* 4908, 18 September, 761–70.

——(1956) *The Ka of Gifford Hillary*, London: Hutchinson.

——(1960) *The Satanist*, London: Hutchinson.

——(1970) *Gateway to Hell*, London: Hutchinson.

——(1971) *The Devil and All His Works*, London: Hutchinson.

CHAPTER FORTY-EIGHT

THE OCCULT AND MODERN HORROR FICTION

Douglas E. Cowan

> In moments they would be here—the one Kircher had called the Cenobites, theologians of the Order of the Gash. Summoned from their experiments in the higher reaches of pleasure, to bring their ageless heads into a world of rain and failure.
>
> (Clive Barker, *The Hellbound Heart*)

'A WORLD OF RAIN AND FAILURE...'

Though less well known than some of his longer, more intricate literary works—*Weaveworld* (1987), *The Great and Secret Show* (1989), or *Imajica* (1991)—in his 1986 novella, *The Hellbound Heart*, British writer, artist, and director Clive Barker (b. 1952) creates some of the most enduring images in modern horror and offers an encomium of occult riches for the perceptive reader. In the toymaker's puzzle box, for example, what Barker calls 'the Lemarchand configuration,' we have the occult technology that forces open a crack between the worlds, less a key, perhaps, than a bell-pull summoning those who walk in the outer darkness. In the 'world of rain and failure' that marks the relationships between the novella's human characters, we find the search for meaning in something more than we have, in anything beyond the mundane. In the Cenobites, the dark theologians, we see the good, moral, and decent fallacy, the soothing fiction by which so many religious believers live their lives, exposed like bone through riven flesh. And in all their dreadful interactions, we realize the consistent beat that lays at the heart of horror.

Consider the Cenobite. In prose worthy of the best of H.P. Lovecraft, Barker introduces them as 'theologians of the Order of the Gash. Summoned from their experiments in the higher reaches of pleasure, to bring their ageless heads into a world of rain and failure' (1986, 4). Playing a relatively minor role in Barker's novella and only slightly more in his 1987 film adaptation, *Hellraiser*, the unworldly creature now known to legions of fans around the world as 'Pinhead' has become a twentieth-century horror icon. 'Every inch of its head,' Barker writes, 'had been tattooed with an intricate grid, and at every intersection of horizontal and vertical axes a jewelled pin driven through to the bone' (1986, 8). Subpoenaed from the regions beyond, beside, and in-between time and space, in Barker's film the lead Cenobite explains its presence simply: 'We are explorers in the further regions of experience. Demons to some, angels to others.'

As I have pointed out elsewhere, though dealing with the enormously popular *Hellraiser* films which continue to appear despite Barker's long absence from the franchise (Cowan, 2008, 84–90), the Cenobites invert popular notions of religiosity, offering an occult variant of 'normal' patterns of belief. An early draft of Barker's screenplay includes a scene in which the Cenobites occupy what appear to be mediaeval monastic cells, while their dress resembles nothing so much as monkish cassocks—marred and torn, though, by the cruel instruments of their investigations. Indeed, of all those who have commented on the films, only a few recognize that 'cenobite' is an explicitly religious term, referring to those who dwell in monastic community, rather than live alone as hermits. Although it does not appear in Barker's novella, one line in *Hellraiser: Bloodline* captures the essence of the Cenobite, the occult inversion of the monk seeking communion with the divine. When confronted by a human character, who gasps in terror, 'Oh, my God!' the Cenobite responds imperiously, 'Do I look like someone who cares what *God* thinks?' What could possibly inspire deeper fear than something so utterly alien that it is beyond such concern? Rather than God, here is the horrific version of Karl Barth's *totaliter aliter*, that which is completely other.

'The oldest and strongest emotion of mankind is fear,' wrote H.P. Lovecraft (1890–1937) at the beginning of his 1927 essay, 'Supernatural Horror in Literature,' 'and the oldest and strongest kind of fear is fear of the unknown' ([1927] 2000, 21). Three principal aspects mark what Lovecraft called 'weird tales,' the 'literature of cosmic fear' ([1927] 2000, 22). First, rather than simply relying on 'secret murder, bloody bones, or a sheeted form clanking chains,' the true horror story requires 'a certain atmosphere of breathless and unexplainable dread of outer, unknown forces.' That is, however terrifying, the encounter cannot be explained—or explained away—as some mundane, albeit grotesque anomaly, a serial killer, a rogue comet, a deadly pandemic. For Lovecraft, more is needed. Second, the true horror story relies on 'atmosphere,' 'for the final criterion of authenticity is not the dovetailing of a plot but the creation of a given sensation.' This sensation, this *frisson*, raises the creeping flesh and crawling skin that marks the thrill of fear sought by fans around the world. It prompts the inadvertent shivers that make the reader wonder whether to put the book down and kindles the tricks of light by which shadows take on lives of their own. Finally, for Lovecraft and so many modern horror writers who have followed him, 'the one test of the really weird is simply this—whether or not there be excited in the reader a profound sense of dread, and of contact with unknown spheres and powers' ([1927] 2000, 23). In the midst of their failed relationships, with the help of the toymaker's box, through the cruel agency of the Cenobites, Barker brings his readers in touch with all these elements.

Whether we destroy or banish the monster, as so often happens in stories ranging from Mary Shelley's *Frankenstein* ([1818] 1996) to Stephen King's *It* (1980) and Dean Koontz's *Phantoms* (1983), or we make some kind of uneasy and tenuous peace with it, which is far more Barker's style, horror consistently challenges the boundaries not of what we think is real, but of everything we hope we can count on as real. If, as the Cenobite says, he does not care what God thinks, then what power has the divine in our 'world of rain and failure'? As it evolves from Gothic and

Victorian horror fiction, the best of which is canonized in writers such as Edgar Allan Poe, the worst mercilessly lampooned by Jane Austen in *Northanger Abbey* ([1817] 2000)—modern horror moves the reader into and out of ordinary time and space.

Rather than catalogue the scores of writers working in the various subgenres of modern horror, consider as brief examples two ends of the continuum between the ordinary and the extraordinary. M.R. James marks the transition from Gothic and Victorian melodrama to the more restrained, implied horror of the early modern period. Edward Lee, on the other hand, following in wake of writers such as Clive Barker, returns in late modernity to a much more visceral style. In the former, occult horror is, for the most part, held off-stage, while the latter places it squarely in the middle of the audience and dares them to keep reading.

OUT OF ORDINARY TIME AND SPACE: M.R. JAMES

Born almost a generation before Lovecraft, though dying within a year of the younger man, Montague Rhodes James (1862–1936) is one of the earliest writers to bring horror into the modern age. Indeed, Lovecraft considered James one of the few modern masters and a profound influence on his own work, extolling his 'almost diabolical power of calling horror by gentle steps from the midst of prosaic daily life' ([1927] 2000, 69). That is, rather than the deeply shadowed abbeys, tolling bells, and ominous portents of the early Gothic, or the work of late Victorian writers who steeped their Grand Guignol stories in gore sufficient 'to make a reader physically sick' ([1929] 2006, 259), James insisted that the modern ghost story arise naturally, as it were, from ordinary experience and everyday life. Rather than a setting in which the reader can be nothing more than a spectator, 'the charm of the best ghost stories,' wrote James in the introduction to the 1924 collection, *Ghosts and Marvels*, is one that will 'allow the reader to identify himself with the patient' ([1924] 2006, 248). That is, James wanted to avoid the kind of horror that would 'never put the reader into the position of saying to himself, "If I'm not very careful, something of this kind may happen to me!"' ([1911b] 2005, 255). Instead of characters with whom few readers could identify, virtually a hallmark of overwrought horror fiction to that point, 'let us see them going about their ordinary business, undisturbed by forebodings, pleased with their surroundings; and into this calm environment let the ominous thing put out its head, unobtrusively at first, and then more insistently, until it holds the stage' ([1924] 2006, 248).

In his classic essay, *The Uncanny*, James' contemporary Sigmund Freud (1895–1939) identified precisely the same aspects of experience that invoke the power of horror. 'The "uncanny",' Freud writes, 'belongs to the realm of the frightening, of what evokes fear and dread' ([1919] 2003, 123), an evocation, however, that is rooted in 'what was once well known and had long been familiar' ([1919] 2003, 125). Unfortunately, in English 'uncanny' does not reveal the full power of the concept. As Freud put it, 'the uncanny (*das Unheimliche*, "the unhomely") is in some way a species of the familiar (*das Heimliche*, "the homely")' ([1919] 2003, 134). The extraordinary that, bidden or unbidden, emerges from the ordinary; the unknown that presses in on the fragile edges of the known. In modern horror, ordinary people are confronted by extraordinary experiences, and it is in this intersection, in these dark crossings of the unimaginative and the unimaginable that modern horror reveals itself.

Although we lack period demographics for belief in the occult, the supernatural, and the paranormal, the popularity of spiritualism, scientific interest in paranormal investigation, and the simple fact that many of James' stories include ritual magic ('Lost Hearts'), vengeful divination and spell-casting ('Casting the Runes'), demonic invocation ('Canon Alberic's Scrap-book'), and other aspects of what I have called elsewhere 'the inversion of the sacred order' (Cowan, 2008, 61–92) indicates that these were never far from his readers' minds. Unlike Lovecraft, who, despite the efforts of modern devotees to paint him as a secret occultist (e.g., Tyson, 2010), was a thoroughgoing and unapologetic realist, James' relationship with the occult is more ambiguous. At least some of his interlocutors believe James far more interested in the occult than he himself was wont to admit, at least one of them intimating that no one *that* skilled at writing occult horror fiction could do so *without* believing (Pfaff, 1980; Weighell, [1984] 2007). For S.T. Joshi, however, his most erudite editor, James' belief in the existence of the occult did not translate into a willing acceptance of it. Indeed, writes Joshi, 'in his ghost stories, James uses such devices as occultism (the perversion of religion into impious magic and sorcery) and the misuse or misconstrual of biblical passages as a warning on the dangers of straying from the orthodox' (2005, xiv). That is, though he recognizes what American psychologist William James identified as 'the unseen order,' the principal constituent of his most useful definition of religion ([1902] 1999, 61), M.R. James is also firmly mired in what I have called elsewhere, 'the good, moral, and decent fallacy'—that is, 'the popular misconception that religion is always (or should always be) a force for good in society, and that negative social effects somehow indicate false or inauthentic religious practice' (Cowan, 2008, 15–16). Although his characters regularly encounter aspects of the occult, there remains a strict division between religion as a force for good, at least in an abstract sense, and the occult power of supernatural phenomena that haunt his stories. Wedged in-between these is the ambivalence that horror fiction reveals about the modern encounter with religion and horror: the belief that God still exists tinctured with the fear that he is either unwilling or unable to intervene on our behalf.

In 'Casting the Runes,' for example, Karswell, a malevolent author outraged that his paper has been rejected by 'the Association,' torments Dunning, the man who reviewed his work, by planting on him a note ensorcelled with 'Runic letters.' It does not occur to Dunning to turn to the church, to pray and light candles, to fight dark magic with the power of socially sanctioned religion. Somehow, for so many readers, that kind of *deus ex machina* simply doesn't ring true. Rather, Dunning works an elaborate plot to return the cursed paper to Karswell, whom some commentators interpret as a reference to the occultist Aleister Crowley, thus 'casting the Runes' back upon him. The occult is used to fight the occult. Dunning feels a bit guilty about this and wonders whether he should warn Karswell. Before that can happen, though, he learns that 'an English traveller, examining the front of St. Wulfram's Church in Abbeville, then under extensive repair, was struck on the head and instantly killed by a stone falling from the scaffolding erected round the northwestern tower, there being, as was clearly proved, no workman on the scaffold at that moment' (James, [1911a], 179). Here, an utterly ordinary event in the life of most scholars—peer-reviewing a manuscript and rejecting it; submitting an essay and having it rejected—becomes a tale of occult intervention and supernatural revenge.

Similarly, in 'Canon Alberic's Scrap-book,' an antiquarian, Dennistoun, whom Joshi identifies as an unusual moment of autobiography in James' ghost stories, finds a rare book—or, more accurately, pages from several rare books—while poking about an ancient church in southern France. Put together by the mysterious, but 'unprincipled Canon Alberic' (James, [1895] 2005, 6), the scrapbook contains leaves taken from a variety of illuminated mediaeval manuscripts. Recognizing its value, Dennistoun is surprised to learn how easily the sacristan at St. Bertrand's is willing to part with the book—and more surprised by the gift of a crucifix from the sacristan's daughter, something clearly meant to keep him safe. Though he 'hadn't much use for these things,' the antiquarian 'submitted to have the chain put round his neck' (James, [1895] 2005, 9). It does not banish the evil the reader knows is lurking somewhere in the pages of the book, but barely keeps at bay what Lovecraft called 'the assaults of chaos and the daemons of unplumbed space' ([1927] 2000, 23). Indeed, as soon as Dennistoun removes the crucifix, the demon spell-bound in the pages of the scrap-book manifests behind him, and is driven away—but not defeated—only when Dennistoun 'grasped blindly at the crucifix,' screaming 'with the voice of an animal in hideous pain' (James, [1895] 2005, 11). Once again, we are confronted with an ordinary moment transfigured by the extraordinary. What bibliophile has not hoped to find some rare prize while rooting through the shelves and boxes of an old house or out-of-the-way bookshop? Yet, like the deceitful book dealer, Lucas Corso, in Arturo Pérez-Reverte's *The Club Dumas* (1993), another tale in which a cursed book brings nothing but trouble, how certain can we ever be of our new treasure's provenance?

(SUB)URBAN DECAY: EDWARD LEE

Beyond the borders of devoted horror fandom, Edward Lee (b. 1957) is not nearly so well known as his contemporaries who crowd the stacks at generic box bookstores—Peter Straub, Stephen King, John Saul, or Dean Koontz. He is, however, easily as prolific and arguably more versatile. Lee works mainly in what has been called 'splatter-horror' or 'splatterpunk,' a subgenre of horror populated by writers such as Poppy Z. Brite, Robert Devereaux, and Wrath James White, and whose books are often published in limited editions through small houses such as Deadite Press, Bloodletting Press, and Necro Publications. Unless reissued by larger trade houses, few of these volumes ever see the inside of major bookstores, although most are regularly featured and reviewed in horror magazines such as *Cemetery Dance* and *Rue Morgue*, and command a devoted following among horror fans.

Early modern writers such as M.R. James, Algernon Blackwood (1869–1951; 2002), Arthur Machen (1863–1947; 2001, 2003, 2005), and Shirley Jackson (1916–65; 1959) eschewed what James called 'the merely nauseating' ([1929] 2005, 259), often keeping their occult actors offstage, where they beckon from the wings and are indicated only by the terrified aspect of the actors. Lee and his splatterpunk colleagues, on the other hand, place the horrific squarely, starkly, and viscerally before their readers. Often mingling the sexual and the savage—another major gaffe for M.R. James—Lee is regarded as a master of 'splatter horror.' Where he and his progenitor agree, though, is in the nature of the occult danger. Reticence aside, James had no patience with 'nice ghosts.' 'Don't let us be mild and drab,' he wrote. 'Malevolence and terror, the glare of evil faces,' together with 'a modicum of blood, shed with deliberation and carefully husbanded' were all part of the modern horror tale (James, [1929] 2006, 259).

So, too, for Edward Lee. Consider, for example, this passage from *Incubi*, his horror-cum-police procedural in which legendary sex-demons take on the personae of urban serial killers. In this scene, Veronica Polk wakes to find herself embraced not by her lover, Jack, but by a horrific vision of his animated corpse. 'It feebled to hands and knees,' Lee writes ([1991] 2011, 85). 'Steam rose off its dilapidated flesh as maggots squirmed their way through hot gray skin. Eventually the thing rose to its feet in wet crunching movements and turned its head to her. Veronica crawled back onto the bed. The cadaver beseeched her in its loss, holding out worm-riddled hands as if to divulge a crucial wisdom...' "This is what," Jack's corpse grated, "all love comes to. It falls to pieces in our hands." His scalp and the rest of his face slip off his skull, but only after the peeling lips uttered the final testament: "I...still...love you, Veronica."' Once again, the ordinary—a lover's tryst—is engulfed in the horrific extraordinary.

In *Succubi* ([1994] 2004), on the other hand, Lee locates his horror in the rediscovery of an ancient religion based on cannibalistic sacrifice and worship of female sex-demons. A female-dominated society, the Ur-locs are presented as precursors of Margaret Murray's long-discredited 'witch-cult hypothesis' (Murray, 1921). 'Witches, before the existence of witchcraft,' says one of the characters (Lee, [1994] 2004, 10). More than that, he builds his story on the kind of deeply rooted cultural fears of witchcraft that have animated tales of terror ranging from *Hansel and Gretel* to *The Blair Witch Project*, and in doing so creates one of his most fully realized religious visions. 'They plundered whole settlements,' explains Ms. Eberle, the archaeologist who functions as a prefatory chorus, 'not for spoils or territorial expansion, but for *infydels* to serve either as sacrificial victims, slaves, or food... Babies provided the ultimate sacrifice to the object of the Ur-locs' belief'—the Ardat-lil (Lee, [1994] 2004, 9). In-between her descriptions of the Ur-locs' culinary interests—'human brains, slow-cooked in the skull'; 'bone marrow potpourri'; 'womb-bread,' and 'gut-roll'—we learn that 'countless religious systems have worshipped a similar or even identical deity. Consider the derivations from Middle and Old English: the *loc* in Ur-loc, and the *lil* in Ardat-lil. Hence, *liloc*, which roughly translates as *sex-spirit*...The Ardat-lil was a succubus.'

Here is the good, moral, and decent fallacy in full. As I have written elsewhere in terms of horror cinema, though it applies equally to the literature of horror, many critics dismiss horror films, novels, or stories 'that have at their core some depiction of religiously motivated torture or human sacrifice, arguing that that this does not accurately represent "religion," that its depiction denigrates authentic (and, by implication, decent) religious impulses. As historian Jonathan Z. Smith reminds us, though, "Religion is not nice; it has been responsible for more death and suffering than any other human activity"' (Cowan, 2008, 16). As gruesome and vile as we may find the rites and beliefs of Lee's Ur-locs, they are no less religious activity—that is, world-constructing activity—than the modern sacrifice of the Mass or the burnt offering of a lamb on an ancient Israelite altar. It is difficult to overstate the importance of this when considering cultural products such as horror stories and films, especially when it is so tempting to dismiss the use of religious symbols and practices as mere trappings (see Cowan, 2008, 43–46).

From *Incubi* and *Succubi*, to a delightful series of novels paying homage to his principal influence, H.P. Lovecraft (Lee, 2009a, 2009b, 2010, 2011), to scatological meditations on his fascination with the mirror nature of good and evil (e.g., Lee and White, 2003), Lee constantly presses the boundaries of the ordinary and the extraordinary. Among the most intriguing is his reimagining of Hell in the *Infernal City* trilogy (Lee, 2001, 2004, 2007). Hell may have begun as a blasted plain or lake of fire, but just as humankind gathered together and built cities, so too Satan's domain evolved as a vast, seething metropolis. Class-ridden and fraught with bureaucracy, Mephistopolis has grown into the largest city in existence—no small comment on Lee's vision of humankind. If Clive Barker's Lemarchand configuration pries open the portal that allows the other side to enter our world, in the *Infernal* novels Lee uses the device of a 'deadpass' to permit humans to visit Hell. There, they walk the blood-brick boulevards of Rot-Port, avoid the diarrhea-spewing hydrants of Sewageton, or gaze at the monstrous fortress towering over the Boniface District—ruled over by the Antipope, Boniface VII (d. 985)—or wander the different demonic districts: Tepesville (named for Vlad Tepes, the Impaler), White Chapel (the infamous hunting ground of Jack the Ripper), or Osiris Heights (named after the Egyptian god of the underworld). Indeed, when I read *House Infernal* (Lee, 2007) for the first time, its monstrous mundanity struck me a bit like 'Harry Potter goes to Hell.' In much the same way J.K. Rowling completely reimagined the English public school experience as the wizard academy, Hogwarts, Lee has relocated all the problems of a late modern urban metropolis to the abode of the damned. As Father Alexander, a priest who has chosen to go to Hell as a kind of *agent provocateur* explains to Ruth, a newly arrived victim, because 'Fallen Angels themselves are pretty stupid':

> Everything here, since Lucifer's fall, every twisted science, every warped equation, all the architecture—every single thing that can be thought of as the product of innovation and creativity comes from the minds of the Human Damned. The Green River District, the De Rais Institutes of Occult Science, the Richard Speck Immemorial Medical Center. Hexegenic research, the Teratology Labs, where they use Human anatomical science to manufacture monsters, the Voudun Zombie Clinic—everything. It's all here because *Humans* are here.
>
> (Lee, 2007, 79)

I leave the reader to follow up on Lee's innumerable intertextualities.

DARK CONTINUANCE

Modern horror fiction exists as part of a continuum stretching back through the horror comic books of the 1950s and the pulps leading back to the 1920s, through Victorian tales of terror and gothic horror in the late eighteenth century—and it repays its debt with each retelling. A very brief essay such as this can do little more than offer a sign-post, a bell-pull into the world of modern horror and its ambivalent relationship with the occult. Besides those considered here, scores of other authors—some well-known, others toiling in obscurity—cry out for recognition and exploration. To hundreds of millions of readers, for example, Ray Bradbury (1920–2012) is best known as a science fiction writer, most conspicuously for his 1953 dystopia,

Fahrenheit 451. Far fewer know that he supported himself in his early years writing pulp erotica under the pseudonym Don Elliott, or that he is regularly included in fan lists of the top horror writers of the twentieth century for his 1962 novel, *Something Wicked This Way Comes*. In *Needful Things* (1991) and *Storm of the Century* (1999), Stephen King examines the notion of the Faustian bargain, in the former from the human perspective, in the latter from the demonic.

In *The Idea of the Holy*, German theologian Rudolf Otto (1869–1937), another contemporary of M.R. James, traced the etymology of primordial fear that he believed lay at the heart of human religious development. Calling it variously 'religious dread' and 'daemonic dread,' he continues: 'It is this feeling which, emerging in the mind of primeval man, forms the starting point for the entire religious development in history. "Daemons" and "gods" alike spring from this root, and all the product of "mythological apperception" or "fantasy" are nothing but different modes in which it has been objectified' (Otto, [1923] 1950, 14–15). 'That this is so,' he concluded, 'is shown by the potent attraction again and again exercised by the element of horror and "shudder" in ghost stories, even among persons of high, all-around education' (Otto, [1923] 1950, 16).

Whether Otto is correct or not, that a gnawing, enervating primal fear grounds the development of human religious consciousness, modern horror fiction continues to explore the dark spaces where the wonder of occult technology, the vagaries of human relationship, and the ambivalence we feel toward our varied gods meet. Whatever form they take, artwork from Fuseli's *The Nightmare* (1781) to Wayne Barlowe's *The Examination* (1998), novels from *The Castle of Otranto* to *City Infernal*, and simple campfire stories to extravagant Hollywood blockbusters, the tales we tell to frighten us most, tell us the most about who we are.

REFERENCES AND FURTHER READING

Austen, Jane (2000 [1817]) *Northanger Abbey*. New York: Dover.

Barker, Clive (1986) *The Hellbound Heart*. New York: HarperCollins.

——(1987) *Weaveworld*. New York: Pocket Books.

——(1989) *The Great and Secret Show*. New York: Harper & Row.

——(1991) *Imajica*. New York: HarperCollins.

Blackwood, Algernon (2002) *Ancient Sorceries and Other Weird Stories*, ed. S.T. Joshi. New York: Penguin Classics.

Bradbury, Raymond (1953) *Fahrenheit 451*. Ballantine.

——(1962) *Something Wicked This Way Comes*. Simon & Schuster.

Cowan, Douglas E. (2008) *Sacred Terror: Religion and Horror on the Silver Screen*. Waco, TX: Baylor University Press.

Freud, Sigmund (2003 [1919]) *The Uncanny*, trans. David McLintock. New York: Penguin Books.

Ingebretsen, Edward J. (1996) *Maps of Heaven, Maps of Hell: Religious Terror as Memory from the Puritans to Stephen King*. Armonk, NY: M.E. Sharpe.

Jackson, Shirley (1959) *The Haunting of Hill House*. New York: Penguin Classics.

James, M.R. (2005 [1895]) 'Canon Alberic's Scrap-book.' In *Count Magnus and Other Ghost Stories*, ed. S.T. Joshi, 1–13. New York: Penguin Classics.

——([1911a] 2005) 'Casting the Runes.' In *Count Magnus and Other Ghost Stories*, ed. S.T. Joshi, 158–79. New York: Penguin Classics.

—— ([1911b] 2005) 'Preface to *More Ghost Stories of an Antiquary*.' In *Count Magnus and Other Ghost Stories*, ed. S.T. Joshi, 255–56. New York: Penguin Classics.
——([1924] 2006) 'Introduction to *Ghosts and Marvels*.' In *The Haunted Dolls' House and Other Ghost Stories*, ed. S.T. Joshi, 247–53. New York: Penguin Classics.
——([1929] 2006) 'Some Remarks on Ghost Stories.' In *The Haunted Dolls' House and Other Ghost Stories*, ed. S.T. Joshi, 253–60. New York: Penguin Classics.
James, William ([1902] 1999) *The Varieties of Religious Experience*. New York: Modern Library.
Joshi, S.T. (2005) 'Introduction.' In *Count Magnus and Other Ghost Stories*, ed. S.T. Joshi, vii-xvii. New York: Penguin Classics.
Kendrick, Walter (1991) *The Thrill of Fear: 250 Years of Scary Entertainment*. New York: Grove Press.
King, Stephen (1980) *It*. New York: Signet.
——(1981) *Danse Macabre*. New York: Berkley.
——(1991) *Needful Things*. New York: Signet.
——(1999) *Storm of the Century*. New York: Pocket Books.
Koontz, Dean (1983) *Phantoms*. New York: Berkley.
Kristeva, Julia (1982) *Powers of Horror: An Essay on Abjection*, trans. Leon S. Roudiez. New York: Columbia University Press.
Lee, Edward ([1991] 2011) *Incubi*. Sanford, FL: Necro Publications.
——([1994] 2004) *Succubi*. Sanford, FL: Necro Publications.
——(2001) *City Infernal*. New York: Leisure Books.
——(2004) *Infernal Angel*. New York: Leisure Books.
——(2007) *House Infernal*. New York: Leisure Books.
——(2009a) *The Haunter of the Threshold*. Portland, OR: Deadite Press.
——(2009b) *Trolley No. 1852*. Portland, OR: Deadite Press.
——(2010) *The Innswich Horror*. Portland, OR: Deadite Press.
——(2011) *The Dunwich Romance*. Welches, OR: Bloodletting Press.
Lee, Edward, and Wrath James White (2003) *Teratologist*. Hiram, GA: Overlook Connection Press.
Lovecraft, H.P. ([1927] 2000) *The Annotated Supernatural Horror in Literature*, ed. S.T. Joshi. New York: Hippocampus Press.
Machen, Arhur (2001) *The Three Imposters and Other Stories: Vol. 1 of the Best Weird Tales of Arthur Machen*, ed. S.T. Joshi. Hayward, CA: Chaosium.
——(2003) *The White People and Other Stories: Vol. 2 of the Best Weird Tales of Arthur Machen*, ed. S.T. Joshi. Hayward, CA: Chaosium.
——(2005) *The Terror and Other Stories: Vol. 3 of the Best Weird Tales of Arthur Machen*, ed. S.T. Joshi. Hayward, CA: Chaosium.
Murray, Margaret Alice (1921) *The Witch-cult in Western Europe: A Study in Anthropology*. Oxford: Clarendon Press.
Otto, Rudolf ([1923] 1950) *The Idea of the Holy*, trans. John W. Harvey. Oxford and London: Oxford University Press.
Pérez-Reverte, Arturo (1993) *The Club Dumas*, trans. Sonia Soto. New York: Random House.
Pfaff, Richard William (1980) *Montague Rhodes James*. London: Scolar Press.
Shelley, Mary ([1818] 1996) *Frankenstein*, ed. J. Paul Hunter. New York: W.W. Norton.
Twitchell, James B. (1985) *Dreadful Pleasures: An Anatomy of Modern Horror*. New York and Oxford: Oxford University Press.
Tyson, Donald (2010) *The Dream World of H.P. Lovecraft: His Life, His Demons, His Dreams*. Woodbury, MN: Llewellyn Publications.
Weighell, Ron ([1984] 2007) 'Dark Devotions: M.R. James and the Magical Tradition.' In *Warnings to the Curious: A Sheaf of Criticism on M.R. James*, ed. S.T. Joshi and Rosemary Pardoe, 125–37. New York: Hippocampus Press.

CHAPTER FORTY-NINE

THE OCCULT AND SCIENCE FICTION/FANTASY

Brian Baker

On initial consideration, it would seem that the occult and science fiction make problematic bedfellows. Not so fantasy, where magic, the operation of mysterious or demonic powers, or quests for arcane knowledge are commonplace. This 'split' between fundamentally opposing world-views – one that banishes the occult, and one that places it centre-stage – that are constitutive of the two genres is the starting point for Adam Roberts' text *The History of Science Fiction* (2005), an extension and development of his earlier *Science Fiction* (2000), but one with very different emphases.

FANTASY AND SCIENCE FICTION: THE CASE OF *FRANKENSTEIN*

In *Science Fiction*, part of the Routledge New Critical Idiom series, Roberts argues that science fiction (SF) is a genre fundamentally implicated in the Age of Empires. He diagnoses a generic tradition that can be traced back to Milton's *Paradise Lost* in its depiction of a radical alterity; Satan, a being so Other that he is cast out of Creation, becomes a figure through which an exploration of literal 'alien' worlds (Pandaemonium/Hell) may be imagined and explored. Roberts argues that the figure of Satan, re-imagined in particular by Romantic poets such as William Blake (who famously declared, in *The Marriage of Heaven and Hell*, that Milton was 'of the Devil's party without knowing it') or Mary Shelley (whose *Frankenstein* [1818] channels Satan as a Faustian, transgressive scientist) is a means by which radical alterity may at the same time be represented as transgressive, malignant, Other, *and* as vital, vigorous and grandly attractive. This conflicted, problematic representation of the Other reflects and re-presents the troubled relation between colonial Europe and the colonised other, and bequeaths to Gothic fiction especially a subjectivity in which the ideological work of separation of self from other must remain incomplete. The Gothic is considered elsewhere in this volume, but the connection between the Gothic and science fiction, between the mysterious/irrational and the scientific/rational, has been a recurrent touchstone for critics and theorists of SF, not least Roberts himself.

The revision Roberts makes from *Science Fiction* to *The History of Science Fiction* is radical in terms of conceptualisation, if not in terms of historical duration (long) or of the texts analysed. Where *Science Fiction* uses alterity and empire as critical foci, in the later text Roberts proposes a far more radical and foundational rupture which, ultimately, brings SF into being. This split is between Protestantism, which leads to humanism, materialism and science; and Catholicism, which preserves mystery, magic and the numinous. Roberts supplants a formal or descriptive critical difference between SF and fantasy with a *theological* one. He states:

> the re-emergence of science fiction is correlative to the Protestant Reformation. During the late sixteenth and early seventeenth centuries the balance of scientific enquiry shifted to Protestant countries, where the sort of speculation that could be perceived as contrary to Biblical revelation could be undertaken with more (although not total) freedom.
>
> (2005, p. ix)

Roberts suggests that the death of Giordano Bruno, burned at Rome by the Inquisition in 1600, is predicated on his insistence on the possibility that 'the universe was infinite and contained innumerable worlds – an example of speculative rather than empirical science, and accordingly science-fictional' (p. ix). To orthodox Catholicism, Roberts argues, 'a plurality of inhabitable worlds becomes an intolerable supposition', whereas the Protestant imagination embraces 'the imaginative-speculative exploration of that universe' (p. x). Science fiction inhabits the Protestant world-view; fantasy the Catholic. '"Catholic" imaginations countenance magic and produce traditional romance, magical-Gothic, horror, Tolkienian fantasy, Marquezian magic realism', he adds, and suggests that the key to twentieth-century fantasy as a genre is, unsurprisingly, Tolkien; 'Protestant imaginations increasingly replace the instrumental function of magic with technological devices, and produce science fiction' (p. xi). Roberts' working definition of SF in this book is of 'that form of fantastic romance in which magic has been replaced by the materialistic discourses of science' (p. xi).

Roberts' generic boundary/binary, then, traces an epistemological or epistemic rupture that precedes the one diagnosed by Michel Foucault in his interview-essay 'The Eye of Power', where he proposes that the Gothic emerges as a textual repository of the elements of darkness, the irrational and the demonic expelled by Enlightenment discourses of order and rationality. The very disjunction between 'reason' and 'unreason' in post-Enlightenment thought is constituted, in Roberts' conception, by the divergence between Protestant and Catholic theologies. However, the text highlighted by another author-critic, Brian Aldiss, as the source text for science fiction is Mary Shelley's *Frankenstein* (1818) which, he argues, functions *both* as Gothic and as science fiction. While the novel's Faust-theme and elements of secrecy, transgression and the monstrous indicate its Gothic-ness, Aldiss argues that *Frankenstein* is 'the first real novel of science fiction: Frankenstein's is *the* modern theme, touching not only science but man's dual nature' (1973, p. 29).

It is not going too far, I would suggest, to propose that SF *itself* has a dual nature, and that elements of the mysterious, magical and occult remain unexpelled, tropes that still exist within its generic DNA. Roberts concedes that 'Catholic' writers, such as James Blish (who we will consider later in this chapter) or Gene Wolfe have used science fiction as a means by which to articulate the interconnection between 'science' and 'magic'; however, I would go further, and suggest that if we see both Gothic and SF histories passing through a single channel, the textual work of *Frankenstein*, then this suggests not a fundamental prior rupture but a mutual *implication* between the rational and the irrational, between science and the occult.

We should pause here to analyse *Frankenstein* (1993) in a little more detail, to indicate how Mary Shelley herself articulated a critique of science by indicating its implication in the transgressive, in occulted discourses of knowledge and power that scientific method and reason sought to dispel. Victor Frankenstein self-defines as a Natural Philosopher rather than a 'scientist', according to the terms of the day, though he notes his 'predilection for science' (p. 22); but soon he catalogues his research into the 'wild fancies' of Paracelsus and Albertus Magnus, the former particularly connected with alchemy as well as 'science'; and he attests that 'his family was scientifical, and had not attended any of the lectures given at the schools of Geneva. My dreams were therefore undisturbed by reality; and I entered with the greatest diligence into the search for the philosopher's stone and the elixir of life' (p. 23). Mary Shelley is careful to blur any distinction between 'scientific' experimentation and practices more properly aligned with the occult. The Faustian qualities of the narrative noted by Aldiss, and the Satanic influence analysed by Roberts and Mario Praz among many others, indicate that Frankenstein's particular quest for knowledge, for power over nature (or 'Creation') is transgressive from its very inception. Frankenstein reveals his determination to pursue the 'mystery' of the principles of life, soon to be discovered, he believes, 'if cowardice or carelessness did not restrain our enquiries' (p. 33). The sense of going *beyond* restraints – not only those of attention or want of courage, but ethical or philosophical considerations – is crucial to Frankenstein's implicit self-characterization. The quest to understand the 'principle of life' – Galvani's spark or spirit or life force – leads to scenes indistinguishable from conjuration. In vaults and charnel houses, revelation comes (literally, enlightenment: from 'the midst of this darkness a sudden light broke in upon me' [p. 34]). This 'discovery' is 'like a magic scene [...] opened upon me at once' (p. 34). This is a deliberate mixing of discourses on Mary Shelley's part: insistently, she indicates that Frankenstein's researches are at once scientific *and* occult.

The results, causally, are both extraordinary and monstrous. Frankenstein understands the morally transgressive nature of his own actions:

> I do not think that the pursuit of knowledge is an exception to this rule [that tranquillity should not be disturbed by passion]. If the study to which you apply yourself has a tendency to weaken your affections, and to destroy your taste for those simple pleasures in which no alloy can possibly mix, then that study is certainly unlawful.
>
> (p. 37)

Note the infection/destabilisation of tranquillity by passion, of reason by unreason; and Shelley herself uses the metaphor of the alloy and the proper (or improper) admixture. In pursuing knowledge through occulted (and secret) means, Frankenstein damns himself, and also his creature. The work is 'unlawful'; the creature itself is a 'demoniacal corpse' given life (p. 40). Later in the novel, in the Creature's own narration, he compares himself to Satan, 'solitary and detested' (p. 105), but this compounds his relation to his own deficient Maker, the equally isolated and scorned (self-loathing) Victor Frankenstein. As many readers have noted, the confusion between Frankenstein and the Creature is diagnostic, but it is also the *manner* of Frankenstein's actions – a conjuration of life from death, blurring of 'science' and magic – which produces the monstrous.

THE LOVECRAFTIAN WEIRD

The Faustian and Satanic implications of *Frankenstein* – and its rehearsal of what Aldiss diagnoses as '*the* modern theme' – are echoed in the depiction of 'mad scientists' in horror and pulp science fiction. The access of the *monstrous* into SF at this foundational juncture, as well as attesting to a fundamental generic hybridity also signifies the extent to which the Other in SF wears the clothes of monstrosity, from Frankenstein through to *Alien* (1979) and beyond. Monstrosity, or what may be characterised through Julia Kristeva's notion of the 'abject' outlined in her influential work *Powers of Horror* (1982) – waste, fluids, the expelled remnant of patriarchal culture, typed as 'the feminine' – is crucial to a mode of fantastic fiction which is a hybrid of Gothic and SF, the 'Weird', which is most identified with the work of H.P. Lovecraft. Characterised by Brian Aldiss in *Billion Year Spree* as 'that kind, lonely and influential man' (1973, p. 176) – increasingly influential in the 21st century – Lovecraft was the author of a series of stories that have been approached by fans and critics under the rubric of the 'Cthulu Mythos', named after one of and Lovecraft's more famous short stories, 'The Call of Cthulu'. Somewhat jokingly, Aldiss describes Lovecraft's work thus: 'The macabre, the eldritch, is Lovecraft's province. He developed a demoniac cult of hideous entities, the spawn of evil, which were seeking to take over Earth' (p. 176). This sounds like an occulted version of the invasion narrative that was influential in the late nineteenth century, and bore upon H.G. Wells's imagination to produce *The War of the Worlds* (1898) – for Martians, read 'the Old Ones' or 'Elder Race'. Aldiss places Lovecraft in the genre's margins: 'one or two [...] stories rank as science fiction', he argues, but he diagnoses a 'hatred of science and progress [and] in part a hatred of life' (p. 177), which would seem antithetical to the genre's core values and imperatives. Yet even the 'Cthulu' narratives often have the framework of science fiction. In 'At the Mountains of Madness', published in *Astounding Stories* in 1936, the scientific mission of Antarctic Exploration discovers a seemingly abandoned subterranean city evidently constructed by a non-human inhabitants, clearly much more ancient in origin than human beings. Horrible consequences ensue:

> From these foothills the black, ruin-crusted slopes reared up starkly and hideously against the east, again reminding us of those strange Asian paintings by Nicholas Roerich; and when we thought of the damnable honeycombs inside them, and of the frightful amorphous entities that might have pushed their foetidly squirming way even to the topmost pinnacles, we could not face without panic the prospect of again sailing by those suggestive skyward cave-mouths where the wind made sounds like an evil musical piping over a wide range.
>
> (Kindle loc 1727)

What connects Lovecraft's method to SF is his use of a radical (and malign) alterity to displace human beings from the centre of the cosmological narrative: the Old Ones are *much* more ancient, more powerful, and more 'advanced' than human beings, and were in possession of Earth far earlier. Human beings became rather puny usurpers, awaiting the return of the *real* owners. These ancient beings are at once all-too-present, their tentacular and alien shapes imprinting themselves indelibly on the imagination of the beholder; and at the same time the beings escape language, are literally 'un-nameable', their amorphousness a challenge to the descriptive properties of literature itself. In one of Lovecraft's short fictions, 'The Unnamable', published in *Weird Tales* in 1925, the failure of language is staged within the textual apparatus itself. Two friends, sitting in a graveyard, are overcome by the malignant influence of some nearby presence. Upon waking one says to the other: '"My God, Carter, it was the unnamable!"' This is where the story ends: with a word that signifies the incapacity of language to signify the true nature of the horror. Everything else is the white space of the page. In his essay 'M.R. James and the Quantum Vampire', China Miéville suggests that the 'spread of the tentacle – a limb-type with no Gothic or traditional precedents – signals the epochal shift to a weird culture' (2009a, p. 105), the influence of Lovecraft felt across genres and popular cultures. This rise of a 'New Weird' is a return to the kind of fiction inaugurated by Lovecraft, but also found in the works of William Hope Hodgson, where cosmological horror runs up against a kind of cosmic SF found in the works of Olaf Stapledon. Miéville, in another article, conceives of the Weird as the 'bad conscience of the Gernsback/Campbell SF paradigm', proposing a generic hybridity that encompasses 'a dark fantastic ("horror" plus "fantasy") often featuring non traditional alien monsters (thus plus "science fiction")' ('Weird fiction', 2009b, p. 510).

Miéville's conception of the Weird is of a fiction that asserts that the mode 'allows swillage of [sublime] awe and horror from "beyond" back into the everyday' (2009b, p. 511). This undermining of the quotidian through a focus on tentacular horrors behind the walls, a collision of ontologies or worlds (everyday/numinous) is, of course, not only confined to the Weird. It is constitutive of a particular mode of contemporary fantasy, particularly associated with children's fiction, where the protagonist stumbles upon, or is introduced to a world of magic that underlies, and is hidden from the everyday real. This mode is found in Alan Garner's *The Weirdstone of Brisingamen* (1960), for instance, where two children discover the world of magical conflict physically *beneath* the hills of Alderley Edge in Cheshire; and, most famously, J.K. Rowling's Harry Potter novels, where the eponymous young hero discovers a world of magic that coexists, secretly, with contemporary Britain. We shall return to this mode in relation to the access of the *demonic* into the real shortly.

The Weird, in Miéville's reading, is opposed to the Gothic in its insistence upon both the *materiality* and *historicity* of the tentacular Others: these are no revenants, ghosts called up from secret transgressions, but monsters that are always-already present, an alterity that coexists with the 'real'. This materiality and historicity is often figured through language itself. The *Necronomicon*, a Lovecraftian grimoire of secret knowledge, has entered popular culture more widely as a means by which transmission of occult knowledge and the operation of magical powers may be effected. Literally, knowledge is power, not only in 'magic words' and invocations, but in the ontological proof that the tentacular others are indeed *real*. Miéville suggests that the Weird is produced out of a dual crisis, in modernity and in fantastic fiction itself, in attempting to deal with a post-WWI world in which the 'cruder nostrums of progressive bourgeois rationality [were] shattered' on the killing fields of Flanders, 'the global and absolute catastrophe implying poisonous totality' ('Weird fiction', p. 510). The *horror* of Cthulu is the horror of modernity recognising that the irrational remains unexpelled from the core of reason.

Lovecraft's insistence upon Cthulu as an effect of language (for all its failures of signification), while at the same time in 'The Call of Cthulu' using the formal apparatus of a textual archive as the means of revelation of the other world, indicates the extent to which the *book* itself, the repository of knowledge, is the means of transmission of the occult. Leon Surette's book on the relationship of Modernist literature more generally and the occult, *The Birth of Modernism: Ezra Pound, T.S. Eliot, W.B. Yeats, and the Occult* (1993), takes the preservation and transmission of knowledge to be crucial to occultism: 'the revelation is preserved and handed down in written texts and in the oral traditions of communities of initiates and adepts', he argues (p. 13). Surette connects occultism both to mysticism and to a belief in the divine, but it is in this particular transmission of 'special knowledge (wisdom, gnosis)' that has been preserved in forms only understandable to adepts, that occultism finds its characteristic form. Secrets become 'secret history', encoded in the passage of these books in and through history. It is in this connection in particular that Surette binds literary Modernism to the occult, in ways that exceed the actual participation of a figure like William Butler Yeats in 'séances, spirit manipulations, evocations and the like' (p. 23).

Occultism, for Surette, is not a belief in a numinous realm, nor in magical powers, nor in transactions with the dead or other beings, but is a practice of *reading*. 'The occult hermeneutic is based upon a relatively simple binary set of an exoteric or manifest meaning apparent to the uninitiated, and an esoteric or latent meaning encrypted "beneath" the "surface" meaning' (p. 27). This depth-hermeneutics is, in a sense, literary study; it is little wonder, then, that occultism in fantastic fiction *tout court* often turns to motifs of self-reflexivity, and the presence of books of 'secret knowledge' within these stories. Still less surprising is the presence of occult elements in generically hybrid texts that attempt to deal with paranoia or conspiracy-inflected notions of a 'secret history' of the twentieth century, from Robert Anton Wilson's *Illuminatus!* trilogy (1975) to Dan Brown's *The Da Vinci Code* (2003). Both texts weave a narrative fabric that combines elements of 'real' history and the arcana of conspiracy theory, the occult, and the promise of revelation of the 'true' or 'hidden' powers underlying everyday life, patterned more-or-less explicitly on a game of encryption and decoding. The reader herself is implicated in a rite of initiation: to 'solve' the mystery of the book we, like the protagonists, must become adepts of 'symbology'.

This thread in post-war speculative fiction has been taken up by contemporary writers, often using generic hybridity, to import elements of the occult and 'magic' directly into science fiction itself. This is most visible in the SF/Gothic/fantasy hybrid known as 'steampunk', alternate Victorian-era worlds in which machine technologies have achieved a revolutionary and socially transformative power that corresponds to the penetration of digital technologies into contemporary life. Tim Powers, whose *The Anubis Gates* (1983) and *Declare* (2001) combine SF elements with the imagination of occult powers, has been a major influence on the development of steampunk; and the latter novel's intersection with the espionage form presages the 'Laundry' novel series of Charles Stross, which combine the imaginative realms of spy fiction (in particular Len Deighton), H.P. Lovecraft and cyberpunk SF. The 'Laundry' novels feature the adventures of Bob Howard, an operative in a shadow-secret service (more secret than MI5, which is itself represented as an inter-agency rival or 'enemy') that uses and combats occult techniques. Howard embodies the laconic, anti-authoritarian manner of Deighton's protagonist in *The Ipcress File* (1962) and other 1960s spy novels, and who was named Harry Palmer in the screen adaptations of Deighton's books. Where Deighton's narrator is a Grammar-school educated 'Other Ranker', a version of the bright, upwardly mobile male subject who recurs in British fiction and film in the 1950s and 1960s and represents a shift in constructions of post-war masculinity, Bob Howard is a 'computer nerd', whose ostensible function is to root around in the computer networks of his employers, and research using these methods to collate information of security interest. The first novel in the series, *The Atrocity Archives* (2001) narrates Howard's path from backroom boy to field agent. He is sent to contact a British scientist working in a Californian university, whose research on 'probability manipulation' has brought her to the attention not only of the US occult security services, but a terrorist organisation bent on using occult means to open a 'portal' in time-space and wreak devastation.

Although *The Atrocity Archives* was written before 9/11, Stross has stated that he altered some details of the narrative to explicitly differentiate the storyline from 'Islamist' terrorism on the US mainland. That said, its espionage narrative, deployment of discourses of security and terrorist violence and focus upon the *secret*, conspiratorial workings of the occult secret service and their antagonists aligns it both with a post–Cold War, 'War on Terror' imaginary *and* representations of the occult in fiction. The debt to Lovecraft in particular is demonstrated in a scene where the endangered scientist (become love-interest), Mo, is escorted back to her London flat by Howard, where they encounter a Lovecraftian assassin:

> Mo is on the floor up against an inner doorway, screaming her head off. What looks like a nest of pythons has wriggled under the woodwork and is trying to drag her in by the neck. [...] Behind her, the door is bulging; the light from the bulb overhead is attenuated to a dull, candlelike flicker.
>
> (2001, ch. 4)

This is not the only door to act as a portal in the narrative; although Bob saves Mo from the tentacles here, later she is snatched though a bathroom door in an Amsterdam hotel room, and taken to an alternate Earth, once populated by escaped Nazi occultists from Earth but now the habitat of an ancient entity that is sucking the life out of the entire universe and which wants to use the portal to force its way into *our* universe and consume that in turn. Stross splices a Lovecraftian Weird with alternate-world SF tropes, but *both* suggest that there is some other material existence *behind the door*, indicating the common estranging device between Weird/occult fiction and some modes of SF: there is more to *material* reality than is dreamt of in your philosophy.

THE DEMONIC

The Lovecraftian occult is then a material one; however, there is another strand in SF and fantasy that is more explicitly mythological or theological (or perhaps demonological). We noted above that Milton's *Paradise Lost* has been cited by Adam Roberts as an ur-text for SF, and that the Satanic figure was transmitted (through Faust) into Romanticism, and thereby appeared in the crucial SF/Gothic narrative *Frankenstein*. The Frankenstein/Faust figure of the transgressive experimenter becomes overtly connected to the occult in Arthur Machen's 'The Great God Pan' (1996/1892). The story opens with a man named Clarke visiting the house of Dr. Raymond, a clinician whose researches led him to be called a 'quack and charlatan' (p. 361). Raymond intends to perform brain surgery on a young woman named Mary, 'a trifling rearrangement of certain cells' (p. 362). In a moment of enlightenment recognisable from other texts in this vein – 'a great truth burst upon me, and I saw, mapped out in lines of light, the whole world, a sphere unknown' (p. 363). Raymond's ecstatic moment of vision is the revelation, once again, of the other world:

> it was a summer evening, and the valley looked much as it does now; I stood here, and saw before me the unutterable, the unthinkable gulf that yawns profound between two worlds, the world of matter and the world of spirit; I saw the great empty deep stretch deep before me, and in that instant bridge of light leapt from the earth to the unknown shore, and the abyss was spanned.
>
> (p. 363)

What the operation will effect is a *material* vision or encounter, rather than Dr. Raymond's intellectual ravishment: 'Clarke, Mary will see the god Pan!' (p. 363). The moment of Mary's annunciation is also described in terms of vision: 'her eyes opened [and] shone with an awful light, looking far away, and a great wonder fell upon her face'; but this enlightenment is so total, the revelation so overwhelming, that sublimity turns from awe to terror, and annunciation to an idiot vacancy. Raymond's response – 'it could not be helped; and after all, she has seen the Great God Pan' (p. 367) – is an index of his amorality, his focus on the experiment itself rather than upon its catastrophic effects. For those effects continue: Mary gives birth, and her daughter, once grown, taking on innumerable disguises, sets out on a path that delivers men to their ruin. Using the name Helen Vaughan, this woman becomes not just a *femme fatale*, but a *femme maudit*, allowing these men to see and to hear such horrors that they are driven into depression and suicide.

Helen Vaughan is herself 'the most beautiful woman and the most repulsive' (p. 377), an embodiment of the two worlds: beautiful/disgusting, fantastic/hideous, Angelic/demonic, light/dark. She is the progeny of human and Pan, 'our' world and the terrifying numinous, and embodies both qualities. At the point of her death, Helen Vaughan dissolves, melts into a 'horrible and unspeakable shape, neither man nor beast [and as it] was changed into human form, a cane finally death' (p. 400). This form itself is 'too foul to be spoken of', just as in the Lovecraftian *mythos*, but the shape is recognised as an ancient darkness given material form. What this actually *is*, is revealed, somewhat by indirection, a few pages before Helen Vaughan's death is described:

> We know what happened to those who chanced to meet the Great God Pan, and those who were wise enough to know that all symbols are symbols of something, not nothing. It was, indeed, an exquisite symbol beneath which men long ago veiled their knowledge of the most awful, most secret forces which lie at the heart of all things; forces before which the souls of men must wither and die and blacken, as their bodies blacken under the electric current. Such forces cannot be named, cannot be spoken, cannot be imagined, except under a veil and a symbol, a symbol to most of us appearing a quaint, poetic fancy – to some, a foolish tale. (p. 396)

Here, language itself is a disguise, a form for the formless, indeed the *negation* of form. Language provides no true access to the other world, as it does in Lovecraft, in 'The Great God Pan', for exposure to that secret power is to risk insanity and total vacancy. At the same time, Machen asserts the power of the symbol: it stands for *something*, something which otherwise cannot be named, something that exists beyond language, reason, humanity.

That this secret power is named 'Pan' rather than 'Cthulu' suggests a pre-Christian, 'magical' apprehension of a world of intention and of power; it also suggests, as does the use of the name 'Mary', that Helen Vaughan is a literal anti-Christ, a demonic being produced from the forced violation of a human woman by a terrifying (here demonic) Other. The implicit blasphemy pushes the transgressive elements of the Frankenstein myth deeper into a kind of dark theology or demonology, where the discourse of revelation results not in enlightenment, transfiguration or rapture, but in terrifying death or dissolution.

I will return to representations of the Satanic shortly, but first would like to turn to the connection between fantasy and a particular conception of the 'demonic' that is present in the work of Rosemary Jackson and Ewan Fernie. Jackson's *Fantasy: The Literature of Subversion* (1981) remains a classic critical text, and largely applies a Freudian depth-hermeneutic to the study of 'realism' and fantasy. 'Fantastic narratives,' wrote Jackson,

> confound elements of both the marvellous [Todorov's category of supernatural explanation of phenomena] and the mimetic. They assert that what they are telling is real – relying upon all the conventions or realistic fiction to do so – and then they proceed to break that assumption of realism by introducing what – within those terms – is manifestly unreal. (p. 34)

This is the collision *between* worlds, and between fictional modes, alluded to earlier. Lovecraft's insistence on the materiality of the Cthulu realm/the 'Old Ones' through gestures of textual documentation (books within the narrative) can be understood through the application of the techniques of realism: redundancy of detail producing the illusion of concrete materiality, what Roland Barthes calls 'the reality effect'. The intrusion of one world into another, however, produces an ontological destabilisation, which Jackson argues is 'fantasy's central *thematic* issue: an uncertainty as to the nature of the "real"' (p. 48). Jackson conceptualises fantasy as shifting 'from one "explanation" of otherness to another in the course of its history. It moves from supernaturalism and magic to theology and science to categorise or define otherness' (p. 158). What these explanations fail to reveal is an absence at the core of modernity, an absence which is the 'absolute', the divine: the revelation of total meaning. Modernist texts, Jackson suggests, turn to silence or absence to denote this empty space, the impossibility of reaching the 'absolute'.

A *theological* reading of fantasy, rather than a Freudian one (where fantasy is the subconscious of realism, wherein the expelled latent material is made manifest in monsters and ghosts and others) then connects language, subjectivity and desire; once again, we find, in Jackson, a tracing of the genre's history through the Faust myth:

> The demonic pact which Faust makes signifies a desire for absolute knowledge, for a realisation of the impossibility, transgressing temporal, spatial and personal limitations, becoming as God. This desire is represented as increasingly tragic, futile and parodic. In a general shift from a supernatural to a natural economy of images, the demonic pact comes to be synonymous in an impossible desire to break human limits, it becomes a *negative version* of desire for the infinite.
>
> (p. 57)

The demonic, then, comes to stand for the radical absence of the ability to approach the absolute or divine; this by the result in a kind of splitting of the subject and ejection/projection of the other in the form of the monstrous or demonic, or in a form of otherness that 'threatens this world, this "real" world, with dissolution' (p. 57). The demonic is at once *internalised* and secularised, transformed from a supernatural agency into one of effects human desire (and the consequences of the transgressive nature of that desire).

This reading of the Faust myth is confirmed in Ewan Fernie's *The Demonic* (2013). 'Faustus hankers after the infinite,' Fernie writes of Marlowe's transgressive Mage, but 'what he gets is nothing' (p. 47). Faustus should have expected this, Fernie adds: 'the shapeless limitlessness of infinity is necessarily *no thing*, beyond all specificity' (pp. 47–48). At the heart of their desire for the infinite is the possibility of annihilation, and throughout his book Fernie proposes an insistent interrelation of the demonic (Faust, Satan, in Nietzsche) with a kind of radical negativity: Milton's Satan, he suggests, 'steps away from the banquet of creation into all the nullity and possibility of the uncreated' (p. 7). The paradoxical inter-relation of the divine and the demonic, the indissociable connection of destruction and death with 'demonic creativity' (p. 23) are what separates Fernie's conceptions of the demonic (and its relation to annihilation) from the death drive of late Freud. 'The goal of all life is death', asserts Freud in *Beyond The Pleasure Principle*; 'the inanimate was there before the animate' (p. 20). The death drive is then the 'hypothesis that all instincts have as their aim the reinstatement of an earlier condition', a condition of absence of pain, and suffering, and the striving of life (p. 20). Fernie, in writing about Aldous Huxley's *The Devils of Loudon* (1952), suggests that the manipulative Jesuit exorcist, Father Surin, achieves a kind of oceanic 'bliss' in the months before his own death, which 'could be seen in Freudian terms, of the death drive, but to see it *only* thus would be to mislay Surin's experience of its spiritual fullness' (p. 243). Again, the 'proximity of the demonic to the sacred' (p. 242) emphasises the difference between the kind of ecstatic annihilation, the achievement of non-being, that is figured in demonic fantastic fictions and a biological drive to quiescence at the heart of Freud's conception. The roots of the death drive are organic, biological; the roots of the demonic are ecstatic, theological.

We can find these ecstasies of annihilation in forms of SF which take on theological (often explicitly Christian) discourses and iconography in attempting to narrate the encounter between human and the radically other, usually unknowable and powerful alien beings. In some texts such as the Arthur C. Clarke novel and Stanley Kubrick film *2001: A Space Odyssey* (1968), Stanislaw Lem's *Solaris* (1963) and its screen adaptations by Andrei Tarkovskii (1972) and Steven Soderbergh (2002), the representation of alien others takes on the figuration of the divine. There are repeated visual motifs in these films which indicate the connection between the willed dissolution of the subject and an explicitly Christian iconography. The crucial gesture appears in Soderbergh's *Solaris* when the space station Prometheus is about to enter the ionosphere of the planet Solaris. Kelvin, the wounded psychiatrist (George Clooney) has opted not to return to Earth, but to stay to uncover the mystery of the 'visitors' to the space-station's crew, Solaris-engendered manifestations of human loss or desire: in Kelvin's case, his wife. As Kelvin lies prostrated on the corridor floor, the light and noise of the station's disintegration overwhelming him, a young boy appears. It is another visitor, the 'son' of Kelvin's friend Gibarian who had committed suicide while on the station. The boy, standing above the prone man, reaches out his hand: Kelvin reaches up. The pose is held for a moment, whereupon the boy grasps Kelvin's hand, and the man 'enters' Solaris. In *2001: A Space Odyssey* (1968), the gesture appears in the strange seeming-coda of the film, when Bowman (Keir Dullea) is translated to a room with an illuminated floor and Regency furnishings, having passed through the Stargate. He encounters rapidly ageing versions of himself, then is reduced (as a very ancient man) to laying in the double bed, a version of the monolith present at his feet. As 'Also Sprach Zarathustra' plays upon the soundtrack, he reaches out with his arm towards the monolith, one finger extended. The iconography at work here is obvious: it is Michaelangelo's fresco on the ceiling of the Sistine chapel, God's finger approaching that of the prostrated Adam in a moment of Creation. Here, the moment of transcendence is typed in cosmic SF terms (the alien planet Solaris or the monolith) but the insistence of the Christian tradition is clear. Why do we find these images at this point? It is, perhaps, that the most powerful visual register available for SF filmmakers wanting to invoke a radically transcendent alterity is, in fact, Christian iconography.

SATAN AND SCIENCE FICTION

In moving towards a conclusion, let us return to Adam Roberts's conception of the Protestant and Catholic world-views encoded in SF and fantasy respectively. Roberts cites examples of SF which inhabit a 'Catholic' imaginary, including Gene Wolfe's *Book of the New Sun* tetralogy (1980–87) and *Long Sun* tetralogy (1993–96), that feature not only far-future scenarios and a high technology indistinguishable from magic, but also figurations of the divine in many guises. Two other writers to consider in more detail here, also cited by Roberts, are James Blish and C.S. Lewis, the latter particularly well known, of course, for the Christian symbolism of his children's fantasy novels, the Narnia books. Lewis memorialised in a dedication to Blish's novel

Black Easter (1968), which stages the apocalyptic end of the Earth at the hands of Satan, and it is here that I will begin. Blish demonstrated a continuing interest in Catholicism which appears in several of his SF novels; in *A Case of Conscience* (1958), which begins the 'After Such Knowledge' trilogy (and won the 1959 Hugo award), a Jesuit priest encounters an alien species and proceeds to exorcise them, believing them to be the product of a Satanic imperative. In *Black Easter*, a wealthy industrialist approaches the magician Theron Ware with an unusual request: he wishes to release all the demons of Hell for a night to witness what will happen. The book – and its sequel, *The Day After Judgement* (1971) – are predicated on the world in which magic and the invocation of diabolical entities exist as material facts, and mages such as Ware are for hire by corporations or individuals who seek some kind of intervention or outcome. Ware is shadowed by a Catholic conclave of white magicians, and one, Father Domenico, is present in the apocalyptic rite that brings *Black Easter* to a conclusion. Much of the book is concerned with the preparations for, and enactment of the ritual, once the bargain is agreed upon between Ware and the industrialist Baines. The bargain is indeed Faustian, for neither Baines nor Ware has an understanding of the consequences of their actions; their act precipitates a war in heaven, and the rules and law by which Ware presumed all transactions with demonic others might be regulated have been broken. The 'Sabbath Goat' appears to the men contained in a magical circle, while outside the world is consumed, and says (in upper case):

> TOO LATE, MAGICIAN. EVEN THE BEST EFFORTS OF YOUR WHITE COLLEGE ALSO HAVE FAILED – AND AS THE HEAVENLY HOSTS WILL ALSO FAIL. WE ARE ABROAD AND LOOSE, AND WILL NOT BE PUT BACK.
>
> (ch. 17)

Father Domenico, whose crucifix and attempt to invoke Christ to send the demon back to Hell both literally explode, asks:

> 'If you would be so kind…I see that we have failed…would you tell us, *where* did we fail?'
>
> The Goat laughed, spoke three words, and vanished.
>
> (ch. 17)

These three words end the novel: 'God is Dead'. The final image of the novel, with the 'last magicians wait[ing] for the now Greatest Powers to come back for them' in 'circles of desolation' (Earth *as* Hell), the final three words foreclosing any possibility of hope or salvation, is as bleak as science fiction or fantasy endings get. This is somewhat undone in the sequel, where it is revealed that God may not be dead after all, but some power restrains the demons (what John Clute called, in a review of the books, a '*real* shaggy God story' [1983, p. 338]), but this does not vitiate the power of *Black Easter* and its reading of both Faust and catastrophe narratives through occultism.

Blish's nod to C.S. Lewis points us towards a previous text that connects SF, the apocalyptic and demonology: Lewis's *That Hideous Strength* (1945). This novel is the third of a trilogy of books that are clearly informed by theological concerns, and which combines the traditions of planetary romance (from Verne and Wells through Edgar Rice Burroughs and, particularly and explicitly, Olaf Stapledon) with theology and demonology. In *That Hideous Strength*, which begins almost as a pre–*Lucky Jim* satire of university life, the dystopian narrative unfolds in which Mark Studdock, a sociologist at Bracton college, is drawn into the settlement of a research institute on the grounds of the college (in fact a wood, in the midst of which is a well, apparently the resting place of Merlin). The scientists of N.I.C.E., the National Institute for Combined Experiments, seemed to represent a vigorous technocratic masculinism, which quickly shades into more disturbing territory. Lord Feverstone, an amoral member of the college who promotes the interests of N.I.C.E. and thereby himself, outlines to Studdock the proposed programme:

> Quite simple and obvious things at first – sterilisation of the unfit, liquidation of backward races (but we don't want any dead weights), selective breeding. Then real education, including prenatal education [....] Of course, it'll have to be mainly psychological at first. But we'll get on to biochemical conditioning in the end and direct manipulation of the brain.
>
> (ch. 2)

Here, a Huxleyan dystopia of genetic and psychological programming wears the clothes of Nazism, inescapable connotations for a book published in 1945. This revelation of the Fascist ideology of N.I.C.E., a secret imperative of domination, is restated on the theological level when it is revealed that the organisation is a front for Satanic forces that, in fact, govern the Earth. Earth has been quarantined, but as the narrative reaches a resolution, a revived Merlin is inhabited by Angelic forces of good, and his own invocation of the curse of Babel precipitates the destruction of N.I.C.E. and the reign of evil.

The main agent of the forces of light is Elwin Ransom, a former Cambridge don who, in his travels in the previous books of the trilogy to Mars and Venus, has come into contact with the Elohim. He assumes the status of inheritor of the kingdom of Arthur, 'Pendragon', and the community he organises at the village of St Anne's – in the spatial and moral opposition to the forces of evil arrayed at Bracton – becomes the heir to an Arthurian Albion ('Logres'). Lewis, in splicing cosmological SF and the planetary romance, Arthurian legend and a Christian cosmology (a battle between forces of good and evil) comes to the opposite resolution to Blish: in *That Hideous Strength*, deliverance from evil is indeed through the intervention of God and his angels. Where Blish's text, at the end of the 1960s, depicts a ruined world without hope or grace, Lewis, towards the end of World War Two, offers the possibility of salvation, even if it is not through human agency.

CONCLUSION

The occult is present in both SF and fantasy, and attempts to draw strict generic markers between the two in terms of their handling of science and the occult, even in such a thorough and rigorous text as Adam Roberts, *The History of Science Fiction*, end up admitting their mutual implication. The centrality of the Faust mythos to SF, and the transmission of Satanic elements through foundational texts such as *Frankenstein*, indicates that knowledge is deeply embedded in both transgression *and* encounters with a radical otherness, an alterity that is often represented through the iconography of the divine or transcendent. In fantasy, magic and the occult are everywhere; in SF, the occult is at times itself occulted or effaced, but it remains part of the genre's DNA.

REFERENCES AND FURTHER READING

Aldiss, B.W. (1973) *Billion Year Spree*. London: Weidenfeld and Nicolson.

Barthes, R. (1989), *The Rustle of Language*, trans. R. Howard. Berkeley CA: University of California Press, 141–48.

Blish, J. (2000/1958) *A Case of Conscience*. London: Gollancz.

——(2011/1968) *Black Easter*. London: Gateway.

Clute, J. (1983/1972) 'Scholia, Seasoned With Crabs, Blish Is', *New Worlds: An Anthology*. London: Flamingo, 331–40.

Fernie, E. (2013), *The Demonic: Literature and Experience*. London: Routledge.

Foucault, M. (1980) 'The Eye of Power', *Power/Knowledge: Selected Interviews and Other Writings, 1972 – 1977*, ed. Colin Gordon, trans. Colin Gordon et al. Brighton: Harvester, 146–65.

Freud, S. (2010/1922) *Beyond the Pleasure Principle*. Memphis TN: General Books.

Garner, A. (1992/1960) *The Weirdstone of Brisingamen*. London: HarperCollins.

Jackson, R. (2003/1981) *Fantasy: The Literature of Subversion*. London: Routledge.

Kristeva, J. (1982) *Powers of Horror: An Essay on Abjection*, trans. Leon S. Roudiez. New York: Columbia University Press.

Lewis, C.S. (2005/1945) *That Hideous Strength*. London: HarperCollins.

Lovecraft, H.P. (2011) *The Complete Collection*. Signature Kindle edition [n.p.].

Machen, A. (1996/1892) 'The Great God Pan', in *Tales of Terror and the Supernatural*. London: Random House.

Miéville, C. (2009a) 'M.R. James and the Quantum Vampire: Weird; Hauntological: versus and/or and/or or?', *Collapse: Philosophical Research and Development* IV: 105–28.

——(2009b) 'Weird fiction', in M. Bould, A.M. Butler, A. Roberts and S. Vin, eds., *The Routledge Companion to Science Fiction*. London: Routledge, 510–16.

Praz, M. (1970) *The Romantic Agony*, trans. Angus Davidson, second edition. Oxford: Oxford University Press.

Roberts, A. (2000) *Science Fiction*. London: Routledge.

——(2005) *The History of Science Fiction*. London: Palgrave.

Shelley, M. (1993/1818) *Frankenstein; or, The Modern Prometheus*. Oxford: Oxford University Press.

Stross, C. (2001) *The Atrocity Archives*. London: Orbit.

Surette, L. (1993) *The Birth of Modernism: Ezra Pound, T.S. Eliot and the Occult*. Montreal and Kingston: McGill-Queen's University Press.

CHAPTER FIFTY

H.P. LOVECRAFT

Erik Davis

Howard Phillips Lovecraft (1890–1937) was an American writer principally known for his weird fiction, a largely British and American sub-genre of speculative narrative that he helped both characterize and, as a critic, define. In his tales, Lovecraft blended elements of fantasy, horror, and science fiction into a strikingly original, infectious, and highly influential narrative universe. Lovecraft's weird fiction is characterized by a fascination with occult grimoires and forbidden knowledge; a pantheon of bizarre extraterrestrial pseudo-gods who are essentially inimical to human life; a nostalgic attachment to the history and landscape of New England; and a heavily racialized concern with human degeneration and atavistic cults. In contrast to the implicit supernaturalism of ghost stories or the gothic tale, the metaphysical background of Lovecraft's stories is a 'cosmic indifferentism' rooted in the nihilistic and atheist materialism that Lovecraft professed at great length in his fascinating letters. This lifelong philosophical stance led Lovecraft to embrace the disillusioning powers of science, but also to pessimistically anticipate science's ultimate evisceration of human cultural norms and comforts. His weird tales were imaginative diversions from this nihilism, but their horror reflected it as well. Lovecraft's literary vision was also amplified by the vivid, often nightmarish, and intensely detailed dreams he experienced throughout his life. A crucial influence on his fiction, Lovecraft's dreaming can be seen as a phantasmic supplement to the reductive naturalism of his intellectual outlook, lending his work an uncanny dynamism that helps explain its continued power to stimulate thought, imagination, and cultural creation.

Lovecraft was born in Providence, Rhode Island to a privileged and pedigreed New England family. For the rest of his life, he would remain under the spell of the manners, aesthetics, and class attitudes he associated with that heritage. Lovecraft's father was committed to an insane asylum when the boy was less than three years old, most likely due to tertiary syphilis. Lovecraft grew up an only child in a household dominated by doting and indulgent women; alongside the pampering, he began to experience recurrent nightmares peopled by terrifying 'night-gaunts.' When his beloved maternal grandfather died in 1904, the family fell on hard times; for the rest of Lovecraft's life, with some exceptions, and partly due to his own hyper-sensitivity, he lived on the margins of poverty. Through a precocious intellect, Lovecraft dropped out of high school, falling into a period of intense social isolation that was relieved when he discovered the world of amateur journalism. In 1919, his psychologically unstable mother was also committed to an asylum. Shortly after her death two years later, Lovecraft met and eventually married Sonia Greene, an older Jewish woman and the only obvious love interest in Lovecraft's rather asexual life. His relationship with Greene brought him to New York City for a few years but the marriage did not last long and Lovecraft returned to his beloved Providence, where he lived with his aunts. A teetotaler with a simple diet, he generally hewed to an ascetic existence, but he traveled some and maintained an extraordinarily voluminous and thoughtful correspondence with many friends and peers, including amateur journalists and weird fiction writers like Robert E. Howard, Clark Ashton Smith, and other members of the 'Lovecraft circle.' He died of intestinal cancer in 1937 at the age of 46.

Publishing his fiction chiefly in *Weird Tales*, Lovecraft was not widely read during his life, and his archaisms and other stylistic mannerisms turned off some pulp fans just as they continue to challenge readers today. Drawing inspiration from earlier masters of the weird tale like Poe, Arthur Machen, Lord Dunsany, and William Hope Hodgson, Lovecraft wrote scores of striking short stories and novellas that, for all their inconsistency and even contradiction, are held together by an enigmatic intertextual web that includes the invented New England geography of 'Arkham country'; grimoire titles like the *Pnakotic Manuscripts* and the dread *Necronomicon*; a cosmology of multiple dimensions and recurrent Dreamlands; and a pantheon of barbarously named beings like Cthulhu and Azathoth, who are generally known as the 'Great Old Ones' or the 'Outer Gods.' During his lifetime, Lovecraft encouraged members of his literary circle to contribute stories to what Lovecraft informally called, after one of his principal beings, his Yog-Sothery. Following Lovecraft's death, August Derleth, who founded Arkham Horror largely to publish the work of his friend and mentor, coined the term 'Cthulhu Mythos' to describe this shared fictional universe, which Derleth and others in the Circle continued to elaborate and extend. Over time, thousands of amateur and professional writers across the globe would come to do the same, as well as numerous filmmakers, illustrators, sculptors, game and toy designers, and comic-book artists. Lovecraft's work has also spawned a thriving and appropriately arcane domain of Lovecraft scholarship, and has even been addressed by philosophers like Graham Harman and Gilles Deleuze. Arguably the most unusual response to Lovecraft's work, however, has come from occultists, who have made his work perhaps the single most significant fictional inspiration for contemporary magical theory and practice, particularly within chaos magic and various left-hand and Thelemic currents.

LOVECRAFT'S REPRESENTATION OF THE OCCULT

To illuminate Lovecraft's fictional transformation of the occult, it is helpful to conceptually distinguish two streams of lore and practice of the Western magical arts. On the one hand, there is an elite stream of learned magic associated with literacy, arcane knowledge, and to some degree fraternal orders—an 'esoteric' cultural orientation that includes medieval monks as well as, for example, Victorian Freemasons enthralled with Egyptian mysteries. On the other hand, there is the vast, amorphous, and often highly localized body of folklore, seasonal ritual, herbcraft, hexing, and healing techniques associated with rural life or communities with low degrees of social status and formal education. This 'popular' magical culture has in many ways left scant traces in the historical record, which in turn has allowed scholars and occultists alike to invent sometimes highly speculative accounts of its characteristics—accounts that themselves sometimes become part of the occultist milieu.

Lovecraft's most extended engagement with the Western esoteric stream occurs in his short novel *The Case of Charles Dexter Ward*, written in 1927 but not published until after his death. Relatively free of Yog-Sothery, the work also stands as Lovecraft's most thorough treatment of his recurrent theme of ancestral possession, as well as a monument to the man's love for the architecture and history of Providence. In the story, we learn of the young Charles Ward's obsession with and eventual resurrection of his forefather Joseph Curwen, an eighteeth-century necromancer, alchemist, and psychopathic murderer who discovered the art of using 'essential Saltes' to re-animate dead shades. Though not as scholarly as many of Lovecraft's heroes and villains, Curwen is a man of education and high status. At one point we are given a brief catalog of Curwen's library, which includes books of occult and natural philosophy by Paracelsus, Van Helmont, Trithemius, and Robert Boyle, as well as classic esoteric texts like the Zohar and the Hermetica. Lovecraft's regular inclusion of rare books, as well as the narrative device of a young researcher studying his or his locality's past, helps set up his central concern with the ironic dialectics of forbidden knowledge. Charles Dexter Ward, for example, is killed by the object of his genealogical research. But perhaps the most succinct expression of this dialectic lies in the game play of Chaosium's highly successful Call of Cthulhu RPG franchise: the more a character learns about the Mythos, the closer they come to going insane.

In his catalogs of grimoires, Lovecraft usually includes a copy of one of his most famous fictional inventions: the dreaded *Necronomicon*, a book by 'the mad Arab Abdul Alhazred' concerning the lore and invocation of the Old Ones. By including the *Necronomicon* alongside esoteric books, Lovecraft helped heed his own admonition that, for a weird story to be effective, it must be devised 'with all the care and verisimilitude of an actual hoax.' Some readers, then and now, believed that *The Necronomicon* was an actual text, and Lovecraft himself wrote a brief pseudo-history of the book, which we learn was translated into Greek by Theodorus Philetas, into Latin by Olaus Wurmius, and later into an unpublished, fragmentary English edition by the Renaissance mage John Dee. Despite his playful references to esoteric literature, however, Lovecraft did not have enough respect for the occult to become a scholar of it; in the mid-1920s, with his Yog Sothery already underway, Lovecraft admitted that his knowledge of the history of magic was largely restricted to the *Encyclopedia Britannica*. That said, Lovecraft did recognize that learned magic is in part characterized by the intertextual web of referentiality that grows between largely inaccessible and cryptically entitled books, a web that itself can be imaginatively extended. Alongside the *Necronomicon*, whose name came to Lovecraft in a dream, Lovecraft's Mythos stories include references to many other invented grimoires, like the *Book of Eibon* and *De Veris Mysteriis*, both of which, in a second-order instantiation of the intertextual web, were concocted by other writers in Lovecraft's circle.

Alongside Lovecraft's inventive engagement with esoteric occultism, he also wrote obsessively about primitive or atavistic magical cults, often composed of rural, marginal or impoverished communities, in the West or abroad. One important scholarly source for this vision was Margaret Murray's 1921 book *The Witch-Cult in Europe*, which also went on to play an important role in the establishment of modern Wicca. Controversially, Murray argued that beneath the violent ecclesiastical machinery of the European witch trials lay the remnants of an actual pre-Christian fertility religion. For Lovecraft, who grew up 65 miles from the home of the Salem witch trials, Murray's vision of the ancient witch-cult—which included accusations of child sacrifice—gave him license to develop the theme of an archaic and savage magical religion that continues to persist in modern times. Inspired as well by the fiction of Arthur Machen, who linked witchcraft with the fairy lore of the 'little people,' Lovecraft also associated the witch-cult with pre-Aryan or 'Mongoloid' peoples, which he readily combined with his racist concerns with degeneracy and immigrant populations. Examples of such cults in his fiction include the mixed-blood voodoo sect in 'Call of Cthulhu' and the Yezidi devil-worshippers in 'The Horror at Red Hook,' a New York-inspired tale not usually classed with the Mythos.

Though Lovecraft separately re-imagined these two streams of elite and popular magic, he achieved his unique vision of the occult in part by promiscuously commingling them. In 'The Dunwich Horror,' for example, Wilber Whateley and his isolated rural family are declared to be of degenerate stock, and practice strange rituals on the sinister Sentinel Hill, topped by an altar-like stone and featuring caches of ancient, possibly Indian bones. At the same time, Whateley needs to get the words of one his invocations exactly right, so he travels to Miskatonic University in order to compare their Latin edition of the *Necronomicon* to the fragmented Dee version he possesses. In Lovecraft's world, learned magic unleashes atavistic and prehistoric powers rather than hierarchies of angels or devils; as such, he is able to depict an ancient but vital left hand path that is free of Satanism or Christian demonology. On the other side of the coin, Lovecraft's primitive cults, including the sort of exotic tribes that haunt the anthropological imaginary, are characterized by their ongoing relationship with the ultimate forces of the cosmos. Lovecraft first makes this ground-breaking move in his famous 1928 story 'The Call of Cthulhu,' wherein Lovecraft reframes the primitive gods worshipped by voodou initiates and remote 'Eskimo wizards' as extraterrestrial or inter-dimensional beings.

Later entering popular culture as Erich von Däniken's 'ancient astronaut' theory, Lovecraft's atavistic science-fictional cosmology allowed his fictions to undermine the progressive Enlightenment view of religious history popularized by Tylor and Frazer while still upholding the scientific course of civilization. The savage mysteries that animate the most primitive human cults are no longer the result of ignorance and neurosis but instead encode actual truths about the cosmos, including powerful extraterrestrial entities and dimensions of reality—like Einsteinean space-time and the non-Euclidean geometry used to describe it—that early twentieth-century astrophysics is only beginning to understand. Lovecraft's most explicit intertwining of the witch-cult and weird science occurs in the 1932 story 'The Dreams of the Witch-House.' At first, the demonic characters that the folklorist Walter Gilman glimpses in his nightmares and in the oddly shaped corners of his room seem unusually traditional for Lovecraft: the evil witch crone Keziah Mason, her evident familiar spirit, and a 'Black Man' who is possibly Lovecraft's most unambiguously Satanic figure. But Gilman is also a student of quantum physics and non-Euclidian geometry, and his nightmares also seem to take place within an 'indescribably angled' hyperspace. Within these seething abysses, Gilman regularly encounters a small polyhedron and a mass of 'prolately spheroidal bubbles' that turn out in the end to be none other than Keziah and her familiar. Lovecraft is thus able to 'save the appearances' of supernatural folklore by superimposing them onto an expansively naturalistic if no less disturbing cosmos.

THE OCCULTIST RECEPTION OF LOVECRAFT

From the time of Lovecraft's death, his name and work was kept alive by August Derleth and other members of the Lovecraft circle. But a mass Lovecraft revival would have to wait until the 1960s, when his stories, along with work by his friends Robert E. Howard, Clark Ashton Smith, and other weird fiction writers, starting appearing in affordable paperbacks designed to exploit the market for adult fantasy opened up by Tolkien's *The Lord of the Rings*—as well as, arguably, the growing use of cannabis and LSD. Inevitably, the exotic aura of dark magic that suffuses Lovecraft and the best writers in his circle fed into the 'occultic milieu' that characterized much countercultural spirituality. The first explicitly occult appropriation of Lovecraft's fiction can be traced to the British magician Kenneth Grant, one of the most vivid and controversial figures to emerge from the Thelemic current begun by Aleister Crowley, and the renegade head of the New Isis Lodge and the Typhonian Ordo Templi Orientis. Writing for *Man, Myth and Magic* in 1970, and two years later in his book *The Magical Revival*, Grant argued that, through his remarkable dream life, Lovecraft was linked to actual traditions of ancient and contemporary magic; in this view, *The Necronomicon* is a 'real' book tucked away in the akashic records that Lovecraft's waking mind was too hidebound and timid to accept. Grant was particularly keen on lining up curious similarities between names and other elements of Thelemic and Lovecraftian lore, like Yog-Sothoth and Crowley's Sut-Thoth. In all this, Grant's own degree of irony or diabolic playfulness is, as ever, hard to assess. Given his florid imagination and parsimonious use of scholarship, Grant's texts—which include ruminations on Bela Lugosi—already scramble the borderlines between occult originality and fiction.

The year 1972 also saw the publication of Anton LaVey's *The Satanic Rituals*, a companion text to the Church of Satan leader's popular *The Satanic Bible*. The book includes two Lovecraftian rites written by LaVey's deputy Michael Aquino, the 'Ceremony of the Angles' and 'The Call to Cthulhu.' In his introduction, Aquino legitimizes the occult appropriation of Lovecraft along much less supernaturalist lines than Grant, emphasizing instead Lovecraft's own amoral philosophy and the subjective, archetypal, and possibly prophetic power of fantasy. This argument accorded with the language of 'psychodrama' that LaVey himself offered as non-supernatural explanations for the transformative power of blasphemous ritual. As a pragmatic corollary to this constructionist view, Aquino developed a meaningless ritual language for his rituals, a 'Yuggothic tongue' based on the alien speech Lovecraft provides in 'The Dunwich Horror' and 'The Whisperer in the Dark.' The efficacy of such guttural and semantically empty speech is also described by Grant in his discussion of the Cult of Barbarous Names.

Within the Church of Satan, LaVey founded an informal 'Order of the Trapezoid' whose name was inspired in part by Lovecraft's story 'The Haunter of the Dark,' which features a 'shining trapezohedron' used by an extinct cult called the Church of Starry Wisdom. The Order of the Trapezoid would later become the supreme executive body of Aquino's Church of Set, where the Lovecraftian current was interpreted in part as a force of apocalyptic subjectivity. Other notable Lovecraftian orders over the decades have included the Lovecraftian Coven, founded by Michael Bertiaux, a practitioner of 'Gnostic Voudon'; Cincinatti's Bate Cabal; and The Esoteric Order of Dagon, a Thelema- and Typhonian-inspired sect founded by Steven Greenwood, who in the 1960s became magically identified with Lovecraft's fictional hero Randolph Carter. Lovecraftian magic has also became an important, almost signal leitmotif for chaos magicians, whose 'postmodern' (and largely left-hand) approach to the contingency of traditional occult systems is resonantly affirmed by the adaptation of a fictional and profoundly anti-humanist cosmology that has the additional feature of being concocted by a philosophical nihilist.

Having achieved an intertextual virtual reality, the *Necronomicon* eventually manifested in the physical world of publications as well. In 1977, Avon Books—who also published LaVey—released a version of Alhazred's book by the pseudonymous 'Simon.' Emerging from Herman Slater's New York occult bookstore Magickal Childe, Simon's text, which has never gone out of print, is a practical grimoire featuring a fictional frame and rituals that mash up Sumerian lore and European Goetic magic. Less popular was the *Necronomicon* published by George Hay, a hodge-podge that includes literary essays, fabricated translations of John Dee, and an introduction by Colin Wilson. The most faithfully Lovecraftian version of the *Necronomicon* was arguably written by Donald Tyson and published by Llewellyn in 2004. Tyson has since become a one-man font of Lovecraftiana, including spell books, a Tarot deck, and an intelligent literary biography that combines sober critical analysis with a Jungian and paranormal twist on Grant's strategies of legitimization.

Regardless of such strategies, the occult appropriation of Lovecraft can be traced in part to the intertextual and metafictional dynamics of the texts themselves. The central theme that Lovecraft critic Donald Burleson identifies as 'oneiric objectivism' is itself the central vehicle for occultist legitimization; from this perspective, occultists impose a second-order level of objective dreaming onto the textual circuit that Lovecraft himself established between his actual dreams and his fictional worlds. Occultists could certainly be accused of turning Lovecraft the writer into something he's not and would moreover abhor. The irony, however, is that this supernaturalist overwriting of the author's materialism is itself inscribed in Lovecraft's fiction, which—unlike the detective fiction it occasionally resembles—usually encourages the reader to piece together the horrifying cosmic scenario long before the bookish and blinkered protagonists put the pieces together. In a larger sense, occultists might simply be seen as culture makers who have, like thousands of writers, accepted Lovecraft's invitation to play the game of imaginatively co-creating the Mythos. In the occultist version of the game, however, players risk the element of verisimilitude that Lovecraft himself saw was a key element of the 'hoax.' And like the empty networks of referentiality that undergird the substance of occult literature, such games may have a life of their own.

REFERENCES AND FURTHER READING

Burleson, D. R. (1991), 'On Lovecraft's Themes: Touching the Glass,' in S.T. Joshi, ed., *An Epicure in the Terrible: A Centennial Anthology of Essays in Honor of H. P. Lovecraft*, Fairleigh Dickinson University Press: Rutherford, New Jersey, 135–47.

Davies, O. (2010), *Grimoires: A History of Magic Books*, Oxford University Press: Oxford.

Davis, E. (1995), 'Calling Cthulhu: H.P. Lovecraft's Magickal Realism,' *Gnosis* 37, 56–64.

Joshi, S.T. (1982), *A Subtler Magick: the Writings and Philosophy of H.P. Lovecraft*, Wildside Press: Gillette, New Jersey.

——(2001), *A Dreamer & A Visionary: H. P. Lovecraft in His Time*, Liverpool University Press: Liverpool.

Lachman, G. (2001), *Turn Off Your Mind: The Mystic Sixties and the Dark Side of the Age of Aquarius*, Sidgwick & Jackson: London.

Price, R. (1985), 'H. P. Lovecraft and the Cthulhu Mythos,' *Crypt of Cthulhu* 35, 9.

Tyson, D. (2010), *The Dream World of H.P. Lovecraft*, Llewellyn: Woodbury, MN.

Waugh, R. H. (1994), 'Dr. Margaret Murray and H.P. Lovecraft: The Witch-Cult in New England,' *Lovecraft Studies* 31, 2–10.

——(2006), *The Monster in the Mirror: Looking at H.P. Lovecraft*, Hippocampus Press: New York.

CHAPTER FIFTY-ONE

THE OCCULT AND COMICS

Kennet Granholm

Studies of religion and popular culture are increasing in number, but it is still fairly uncommon to find treatments of comic books in general introductions and collected volumes. This is a shame, as comic books are perhaps *the* popular cultural products where the occult is most prominent, as well as one of the few remaining popular cultural arenas where creators are still relatively free to experiment with unorthodox subject matter. Both of the above mentioned are likely due to comic books being viewed as an 'unworthy pursuit', mirroring the sentiments directed towards the occult itself for centuries, even when compared to areas such as heavy metal to Science Fiction TV-shows starting to be recognized as valid subjects of study.

Comic books form a broad and diverse field, including a great number of different genres and massive variations in intended readership, approach, and thematic content. In this essay I will primarily focus on material from the major superhero comic book companies, DC Comics and Marvel Comics. This means that I will mostly, though not exclusively, deal with the superhero genre and secondary genres derived from and/or connected to this primary one. There are two main reasons for this: First, superhero comics are by far most well known, not least due to having been adapted into numerous Hollywood blockbuster films in the last decade, and which thus have the greatest cultural impact. Second, the genre of superhero comics can in and by itself be interpreted as a genre of occult literature, which makes a treatment of it doubly significant in a discussion of comics and the occult (Kripal 2011).

When the page numbering of comic books and albums is unclear I have chosen to refer only to issue or volume number. As for comic book authors, I have chosen only to name writers, except in cases where an artist has worked on a series throughout its publication run and when referring to particular issues of a comic rather than whole series.

'AGES' AND OCCULT PHASES IN SUPERHERO COMICS

The history of superhero comics is commonly divided into different phases or 'ages', which, although being somewhat simplifying (Kripal 2011, 26), give a rough sketch of major developments. The most common division is into the golden, silver, bronze and modern ages. The golden age commences in 1938 with the first appearance of Superman in Detective Comics' (renamed DC Comics in 1977) *Action Comics* #1 (Siegel and Shuster 1938; see Coville 2011a). This era was characterized by a great optimism with superheroes commonly portrayed as perfected human beings, representing the next evolutionary step of humanity (Kripal 2011, 75). This, combined with the superheroes often gaining their powers from advanced scientific experimentation, introduces an important occult dimension, and is why the superhero comic can in itself be regarded a form of occult fiction, preceded by the occult novels of the late 1800s and the UFO magazines of the 1950s (Kripal 2011, 85). The loss of popularity of superhero comics after the Second World War combined with a growing critique of them due to their perceived detrimental effect on youth motivated the comic book industry to create a self-censoring organ in the Comics Code Authority (CCA) in 1955 (Coville 2011b).

From 1956, there was renewed interest in superhero comics, giving rise to the silver age (Coville 2011c). Where DC Comics had dominated the golden age, Marvel Comics in many ways came to dominate the silver age with its new breed of heroes who besides battling villains also struggled with everyday human problems and concerns. The 'Marvel age' started with the publication of *Fantastic Four* #1 in 1961 (Lee and Kirby 1961), and in the next two years several popular superheroes and superhero teams were created, such as Spider-Man (1962), the Hulk (1962), Thor (1962), X-Men (1963), the Avengers (1963) and Iron Man (1963). Like their golden age counterparts, silver age superheroes were often imagined as the next steps of human evolution.

In the bronze age, from 1970, '[c]omics got more complex, rules changed, and different characters and stories were told', increasingly revolving around real-life social and political problems (Coville 2011d). The CCA relaxed its rules which made it possible to again publish horror comics, and titles such as *Vampire Tales* (Gerber and Moench 1973–75), *The Tomb of Dracula* (Conway et al. 1972–79), *Werewolf by Night* (Conway et al. 1972–75), *Ghost Rider* (Friedrich, Wolfman and Moench 1973–83), *Swamp Thing* (Wein and Wrightson 1971; 1972) which often dealt with explicitly occult themes were launched.

The modern age, variously seen as starting in 1980 with Frank Miller's dark realistic envisioning of Marvel's Daredevil (1980–83; see Coville 2011d) or the mid-1980s with Alan Moore and Dave Gibbons' deconstruction of the superhero genre in *Watchmen* (1986–87) and Miller's in the dystopian future-vision of Batman in *The Dark Knight Returns* (1986), represents a 'loss of innocence' for superhero comics and is sometimes called 'The Dark Age' due to its overall darker tone in themes and stories. The occult characters introduced during the bronze age had mostly disappeared from mainstream comics by the early 1980s, but this was in turn compensated by an increasing number of more adult-oriented comic books which dealt with occult subject matter, particularly evident in the launching of DC Comics' Vertigo imprint in 1993. Vertigo collected existing series such as *Saga of the Swamp Thing/Swamp Thing* (1982–96, 2000–1, 2004–6; see particularly Moore 1984–87), *Doom Patrol* (1987–95; see particularly Morrison 1989–93), *Hellblazer* (Delano et al. 1988–2013), *Sandman* (Gaiman 1989–96), *Shade, the Changing Man* (Milligan 1990–96), and *The Books of Magic* (Gaiman 1990–91; Rieber and Gross 1994–2000), and launched many new ones such as *Death: The High Cost of Living* (Gaiman and Bachalo 1993), *Enigma* (Milligan and Fegredo 1993), *Preacher* (Ennis and Dillon 1995–2000), *The Invisibles* (Morrison 1994–2000) and *Lucifer* (Carey 2000–2006).

CLASSIC OCCULT THEMES AND COMIC BOOKS

Magic has more or less always played a role in comic books. In the pre-superhero age we find the character Mandrake, who in full stage magician attire, top hat and all, relied on illusionist tricks in his fight against evil. In the golden age of comics we find characters such as Captain Marvel (Parker and Beck 1939), a young boy who through the intervention of an ancient Egyptian wizard can transform into a Superman-like super being by shouting the magic formula SHAZAM! (for the wisdom of Solomon, the strength of Hercules, the stamina of Atlas, the power of Zeus, the courage of Achilles, and the speed of Mercury). Even for Superman magic played a role, as it was one of the few weapons, aside from kryptonite, that he was vulnerable to. In the silver age we have characters such as Doctor Strange (Lee and Ditko 1963) and Zatanna (Fox and Anderson 1964) who are first and foremost magicians. However, even though these characters wield magical powers and classic occult notions such as the astral plane are included, magic appeared simply as any other superpower. In the bronze age, we find explicitly occult characters and the use of occult symbolism, as detailed above, but it is really in the modern age that occult magic properly becomes a theme in comic books.

Much of the changes in mainstream comics in the 1980s, including more complex and mature engagements with the occult, came with the so-called British Invasion in American superhero comics and writers such as Moore with *Saga of the Swamp Thing* from 1984, Neil Gaiman with *Sandman* from 1989, and Grant Morrison with *Animal Man* (1988–90). The most obvious example is the character John Constantine, who was introduced in *The Saga of the Swamp Thing* #37 (Moore, Veitch and Toutleben 1985), and got his own ongoing series *Hellblazer* in 1988 (Delano et al. 1988–2013). In stark contrast to most earlier magical characters, John Constantine is not a superhuman being wielding vast supernatural powers in a fight against super villains. Instead, Constantine possesses vast knowledge of the occult arts and engages with non-human realms and beings by ritual magic or other conventional occult means. For example, in the famous storyline 'Dangerous Habits' (Ennis and Simpson 1991), which was the main influence of the movie *Constantine* (2005), John Constantine is diagnosed with terminal lung cancer. As no medical intervention can save his life Constantine relies on occult means. In a magical ceremony he calls on Azazel, one of the most powerful demon rulers of Hell, and sells his soul, then carefully cleans and prepares his magical circle before evoking Beelzebub and selling his soul again. When he then slits his wrists and both demons, along with the 'First of the Fallen' – who has avowed to personally drag Constantine's soul to Hell, come to collect his soul they have no other recourse than to heal his wounds and cure his cancer or engage in a disastrous civil war. Constantine's trademark is that he relies on his knowledge of the occult arts and his wit, outsmarting supernatural beings who are far more powerful than he is.

Ceremonial magic also plays a role in Gaiman's *Sandman*-series, which starts in the second decade of the twentieth century with a group of magicians summoning (by use of the 'Magdalene Grimoire') and trapping the personification of dream (in their attempt to trap Death), the titular Sandman. The leader of this group, Roderick Burgess, is clearly modeled on Aleister Crowley, although he is envisioned as a rival of Crowley as he right before performing the evocation says: 'After tonight I'd like to see Aleister and his friends try to make fun of me!' (Gaiman and Kieth 1989, 4). Though not explicitly named, Crowley's influence is evident in the sex magic–loaded series *The Witching* as well (Vankin and Gallagher 2004–5). Elsa Grimston, one of the three witches in the series, is a 'Moonchild' conceived magically by her magician father. The father, Henry Grimston, is most likely modeled on John Whiteside Parsons (1914–52), who was one of the first followers of Crowley in the US, and who with his magical partner Marjorie Cameron attempted to create a Moonchild in the sex magical 'Babalon working'.

Another interesting example is Pat Mills and Kevin O'Neill's *Nemesis the Warlock* (1980–2000). The titular warlock of the series is a demon-looking alien fighting a fanatically religious church-like Termight led by Tomas de Torquemada, who seek to rid the galaxy of all non-human life forms. Nemesis, as a warlock, uses magic and sorcery in his battle against the Termight.

A final example I will give is Kieron Gillen and Jamie McKelvie's *Phonogram* (2006–7). Drawing inspiration from chaos magick, the series does not contain much in the way of conventional occult symbolism or ritual magic, but instead operates with the notion of pop culture as a magical realm. The lead character is a phonomancer, a magician who works with pop music, and in a segment of the series he evokes the goddess of Britpop, who has since the early 1990s slowly withered away. In a magical working in the third issue of the series the phonomancer puts on a record with The Manic Street Preachers, dresses in the clothes and puts on the makeup he wore when being involved in Britpop, does drugs and drinks alcohol in the same way as he used to, puts a book of Sylvia Plath's collected poems in his back pocket, goes to the club he went to in the early 1990s (which is no longer a Britpop club), puts a cassette tape with the band Pulp in his Walkman and dances to the music. The inner dialogue goes: 'Ten years ago this was my church. If I can hold this self together maybe I've enough belief left for one last mass' (Gillen and McKelvie 2006, 20–24).

PAGAN SENSIBILITIES

A feature that became popular in comics since the 1980s is a catering to pagan sensibilities, both in a nature- and non-human orientedness and the use of preexisting and newly created non-Christian mythologies. Moore's *Saga of the Swamp Thing* is a pioneer in this respect. When introduced in 1972 the character was conceived of as a scientist turned into a monster due to science gone awry (Wein and Wrightson 1972), a standard origin story in comics. When Moore started writing the series in 1984 he made a dramatic revelation: 'We thought that the Swamp Thing was Alec Holland, somehow transformed into a plant. It wasn't. It was a plant that *thought* it was Alec Holland!' (Moore 1984, 12). The revelation was made in a equally dramatic fashion. The Swamp Thing is shot and the doctor dissecting it finds to his astonishment that its 'organs' are nothing more than crude non-functional approximations of human ones (Moore 1984, 7). As '...you can't kill a vegetable by shooting it through the head' (Moore 1984, 15), the Swamp Thing revives, exacts revenge, and escapes, going on to assume a role as protector of all plant life on earth, being in contact with all plant life through the astral plane-like 'the Green', and gaining new powers such as being able to travel vast distances near instantaneously simply by dissolving its body and re-growing it somewhere else (Moore, Veitch and Turtleben 1985, 15;

Moore, Bissette and Turtleben 1985, 12–13, 17–22; Moore, Woch and Randall 1986). The notion of a living nature is a classic and widespread feature of occult philosophy, as is the monistic worldview presented in Moore's *Saga of the Swamp Thing*.

Morrison's *Animal Man* continues in the same vein. When created in 1965 Animal Man was a superhero who in contact with crash-landed aliens gained the power to mimic the abilities of different animals, but when Morrison started writing the character in 1988 he made drastic changes. In a entheogen-assisted Native American vision quest Animal Man comes to realize that his powers are the result of him being in contact with all animal life on earth through the astral plane-like 'the Red', and it is through this contact that he can 'borrow' the powers of different animals (Morrison, Truog and Hazlewood 1989). In Animal Man's newfound affinity with non-human animals he becomes a strict vegetarian, starts increasingly working for animal liberation and ecological welfare, and eventually even starts to take on physical non-human characteristics when borrowing animal powers. The same theme of animal liberation continues in Morrison and Frank Quitely's *WE3* (2005), which revolves around a trio of animals, a dog, a cat, and a rabbit, who have been modified by the military to be super soldiers. The animals escape, are hunted by the military – with humans thus being the evil antagonists, and eventually two of them reach freedom (the rabbit having sacrificed itself in order to save the other two). The series is also of occult interest as it portrays the transfiguration, and indeed transmutation, of beings to a higher evolutionary state through technological means.

Gaiman's *Sandman* creates its own non-Christian mythology, in presenting the Endless, a 'family' of eternal principles manifested in personified form; Destiny, Death, Dream, Destruction, Despair, Desire, and Delirium (who first manifested as Delight). The series engages heavily with existing mythologies, including that of Christianity, but the Endless embody principles that are more ancient and fundamental in the fabric of the cosmos than gods and other supernatural beings. A story that always struck me as particularly interesting in portraying the power of *imaginatio* (as in the power of dreams) is the self-contained 'A Dream of a Thousand Cats' (Gaiman and Jones 1990). In the story a cat meets Sandman in the form of a black cat (as *Dream* will appear in the form expected by the dreamer), who tells the cat the story of how humans in times past were the pets of cats, and miniscule compared to them, but how they collectively dreamed themselves as the rulers of earth, and thus changed reality to always having been so. The cats meet in groups, discuss, and the story ends with one cat sleeping and in his sleep hunting something – to the adornment of the cat's unwitting owner – implying that the cats are now dreaming a new reality into existence.

COMIC BOOKS AND OCCULT PRACTICE: GRANT MORRISON

In terms of the occult, Scottish comic book writer Grant Morrison is of particular interest. Morrison identifies as a magician, and his work not only reflects and expresses his occult interests, but sometimes even becomes a tool for magical practice.

Born in Glasgow in 1960, Morrison began doing comics at a young age, publishing his first work in the Scottish alternative comics magazine *Near Myths* in 1978. At around the same time, at age 19, he did his first magical working, purportedly because he wanted to prove that Aleister Crowley's magic was nothing but fantasy. When a demon showed up, however, he was hooked for life (Babcock 2004; cf Cowe-Spigai and Neighly 2003, 237). Morrison's comic book career really took off when he started writing *Zenith* for the comics anthology *2000AD* (Morrison and Yeowell 1987–1992). The success of *Zenith* got the attention of DC Comics, and he was commissioned to re-imagine the company's B-list character Animal Man. After this Morrison was given increasingly prestigious comic book work, eventually even writing flagship titles such as *New X-Men* for Marvel (2001–4) and *Batman* (2006–8, 2010) for DC. In 1992 Morrison had started experimenting with drugs in magical workings, and in 1994, while in Kathmandu, Nepal, he 'was taken out of Four-D reality, shown the entire universe as a single object, shown the world as it is from the outside' (Babcock 2004) – an experience which greatly affected him and flowed into his comic book work. Morrison has also written on his take to magic, an approach greatly influenced by chaos magick that he calls Pop Magic (Morrison 2003).

The occult figures prominently already in *Zenith*. For example, the Nazi super being Masterman is a genetically engineered human body possessed by 'Iok Sotot, Eater of Souls' – which is a name strongly reminiscent of beings in H.P. Lovecraft's Cthulhu mythos, which is popular in modern occultism – through the 'Ritual of Nine Angles' – named after a ritual described in Anton LaVey's Satanic Bible (1969) – in which in 'The Order of the Black Sun' – with the Black Sun being a symbol which figures prominently in discussions of (primarily imagined) Nazi occultism – communes with a formless 'Dark God' – again showing an influence from H.P Lovecraft (Morrison and Yeowell 1987). Other examples are: a story titled 'A Separate Reality' (Morrison and Yeowell 1989) – clearly referencing Carlos Castaneda's famous neoshamanic book, a character called 93 Mantra – clearly referencing Crowley's religiomagical philosophy of Thelema (Morrison and Yeowell 1989), and the chaos magickal group Thee Temple ov Psychick Youth (see Partridge 2013) mentioned in passing (Morrison and Yeowell 1990).

Kid Eternity (Morrison and Fegredo 1991) has even clearer occult symbolism and more elaborated occult themes, and also demonstrates some of Morrison's chaos magickal leanings such as the mind creating its reality – e.g. Hell adapting to the mindsets of individual souls trapped there (79) and duality ultimately being an illusion (105), popular cultural icons representing archetypical occult forces (123), and the inclusion of a 'chaosphere engine' devised to speed up human evolution (101).

Occult themes are explored most clearly and deeply in Morrison's *The Invisibles* (1994–2000), which is directly influenced by his experiences in Kathmandu. The series portrays a terrorist cell of chaos magickians fighting a conspiracy of the political and economic establishment governed by outer-dimensional beings seeking to control and passivize humanity. To give just a few examples of the occult ideas and practices contained in *The Invisibles*: A heavy-handed push by a magical mentor shifts the initiate's perception (Morrison and Yeowell 1994b, 7) – as described in Castaneda's books – and extreme experiences being able to do the same (Morrison and Yeowell 1994c, 10; cf Cowe-Spigai and Neighly 2003, 235); the idea of sigil-magic being used in mainstream corporate culture – the McDonald's golden arc described as 'the sigil of the dark emperor Mammon' (Morrison and Yeowell 1994b, 16; cf Morrison

2003, 20); the alphabet described as the name of a demon, 'a spell word, an "abracadabra," implanted in the brain of every English-speaking child, the root mantra of restriction' (Morrison and Jimenez 1996c, 7); and, again, popular cultural icons, John Lennon this time, being invoked as archetypical occult forces (Morrison and Yeowell 1994a, 18–19). Morrison writes, '[Ragged Robin]: The Beetle's supposed to stand for death and resurrection, isn't it. Is that why you invoked John Lennon? [King Mob]: Yeah. I figured he's got all the attributes of a god now, so I used traditional ceremonial magic methods and summoned him for advice' (Morrison and Yeowell 1994a, 26).

Morrison has described *The Invisibles* as a hypersigil, 'a sigil extended through the fourth dimension...an immensely powerful and sometimes dangerous method for actually altering reality in accordance with intent' (Morrison 2003, 21). According to Morrison, the series 'consumed and recreated my life during the period of its composition and execution' (Morrison 2003). He wrote himself into the stories, as the musician and author 'Kirk Morrison' and the superspy Gideon Stargrave, whom Morrison had used as a character in his stories in *Near Myths*, as imaginary 'shield-personas' used by the character King Mob when being tortured and interrogated (Morrison and Jimenez 1996a; 1996b; 1996c). King Mob became both a reflection of Morrison and a character that influenced his circumstances, with things written for the character manifesting in various, often unpredictable, ways in Morrison's own life (Morrison 1996b, 26; Cowe-Spigai and Neighly 2003, 233–34, 246–47). As a magical working the series was intended to both change the world and Morrison himself, and at a point when sales of the series where down to the degree of cancelled Morrison implored his fans to engage in a 'wankathon' as 'a magically charged global mastubation session initiated in order to increase the sales of The Invisibles' (Morrison 1996a, 25; Brother Yawn 2002), instead of simply asking the fans to buy more copies or to encourage their friends to do so.

FINAL WORDS: THE OCCULT AND COMICS IN NON-ENGLISH-LANGUAGE CONTEXTS

The occult is naturally not only a factor in English-language superhero comics, but for a proper treatment I am limited by the scope of this essay, my language skills, and the plain fact that the world of comics is simply too vast for a single person to be fully familiar with. I will, however, end this essay with one short example from a non-English-language context.

An interesting example of the occult in comics in a French context is Alejandro Jodorowsky and Moebius' (Jean Giraud) *L'Incal* (translated into English as *The Incal*). Jodorowsky is more famous for being a film director, and particularly his *The Holy Mountain* (1973) is ripe with occult themes inspired by the 'Fourth Way' philosophy of George Ivanovich Gurdjieff. *Incal* is set in a massive futuristic city, where the protagonist John DiFool receives the crystal-like 'light incal', which is in turn sought by, among others, a cult that worships the 'dark incal'. As an alien/higher intellect the incal educates and temporarily transforms the protagonist, quite literally by butchering his body, into four beings representing the classic elements air, water, fire, and earth, while asking '...who is John DiFool? And just how many of you are there?' (Jodorowsky and Moebius 1988, #1). Further on in his adventures DiFool encounters a nude woman called Animah, to whom he promptly gives the black incal he just obtained and also instantly develops a deep longing for (Jodorowsky and Moebius 1988, #1). This theme of the union on gendered opposites is expressed elsewhere in the series as well, such as in the being Foetus – composed of a male and a female joined at the head (Jodorowsky and Moebius 1988, #1), the union of the light and dark incals – in a ritual-like performance by DiFool and Animah – which grants them greater power than each of them holds separately (Jodorowsky and Moebius 1988, #2), and the child character Sunmoon – whose 'heart is that of a perfect androgyne' (Jodorowsky and Moebius 1988, #2). Animah is a being of great spiritual wisdom and power, who teaches Difool's company to gain control of gigantic 'psycho-rats' through meditation: 'Control your minds! Rid yourselves of fear and violence', she says (Jodorowsky and Moebius 1988, #2). Later, she identifies herself and the rest of DiFool's company as 'the seven keys' who can open the 'portal of transfiguration'. She says to the group: '...we cannot open the portal unless we strip ourselves...of our self-images! Bare our souls for the transfiguring process!', and to Sunmoon who will form the centre of the portal: 'you must now leave your childhood behind! Become your essential self. Reconstruct your own axis!' after which the child reaches its full potential as an androgynous being (Jodorowsky and Moebius 1988, #2). Further, books three and four of the series are named 'That Which is Above' and 'That Which is Below', which in combination form a phrase which has been widely used in occultism. It can be added that the series should seem familiar to anyone familiar with science fiction movies of the last two decades, as it is clearly a direct inspiration for Baz Luhrman's movie *The Fifth Element* (1997). Very little in Luhrman's movie is not derived from *Incal*, including the title of the movie itself. The fifth and sixth books of *L'Incal* are named 'La Cinquième essence', or 'The Fifth Essence' in English (Jodorowsky and Moebius 1988, #3).

REFERENCES AND FURTHER READING

Babcock, J. (2004) 'One Nervous System's Passage Through Time', *Arthur* 12. Online: http://www.arthurmag.com/magpie/?p=1644 (accessed 31 January 2013).

Brother Yawn (2002) 'Interview with an Umpire'. Online: http://www.barbelith.com/old/interviews/interview_9.shtml (accessed 31 January 2013).

Coville, J. (2011a) 'Creating the Superhero', *TheComicsBooks.com – The History of Comic Books*. Online: http://www.thecomicbooks.com/old/Hist1.html (accessed 16 January 2013).

——(2011b) 'The Comic Book Villain, Dr. Fredric Wertham, MD', *TheComicsBooks.com – The History of Comic Books*. Online: http://www.thecomicbooks.com/old/Hist2.html (accessed 16 January 2013).

——(2011c) 'The Silver Age', *TheComicsBooks.com – The History of Comic Books*. Online: http://www.thecomicbooks.com/old/Hist3.html (accessed 16 January 2013).

——(2011d) 'The Bronze Age', *TheComicsBooks.com – The History of Comic Books*. Online: http://www.thecomicbooks.com/old/Hist4.html (accessed 16 January 2013).

Cowe-Spigai, K. and P. Neighly (2003) *Anarchy for the Masses: The Disinformation Guide to The Invisibles*, New York, NY: The Disinformation Company Ltd.

Kripal, J. J. (2011) *Mutants and Mystics: Science Fiction, Superhero Comics, and the Paranormal*, Chicago, IL: University of Chicago Press.

LaVey, A. S. (1969) *The Satanic Bible*, New York, NY: Avon Books.

Morrison, G. (2003) 'Pop Magic!' in R. Metzger, ed., *Book of Lies: The Disinformation Guide to Magick and the Occult*, New York, NY: The Disinformation Company Ltd., 16–25.

Partridge, C. (2013) 'Occulture is Ordinary', in E. Asprem and K. Granholm, eds., *Contemporary Esotericism*, London: Equinox Publishing, 113–33.

Comics

Carey, M. 2000–2006. *Lucifer*. DC Comics/Vertigo.

Conway, G., Goodwin, A., Fox, G. and Wolfman, M., 1972–79. *The Tomb of Dracula*, vol. 1, #1–70. Marvel Comics.

Conway, G., Wein, L., Wolfman, M., Friedrich, M. and Moench, D., 1972–75. *Werewolf by Night* #1–43. Marvel Comics.

Delano, J., Ennis, G., Campbell, E., Jenkins, P., Ellis, W., Macan, D., Azzarello, B., Carey, M., Mina, D., Diggle, A., Milligan, P., 1988–2013. *Hellblazer*. DC Comics/Vertigo (from 1993).

Ennis, G. and Dillon, S., 1995–2000. *Preacher*. DC Comics/Vertigo.

Ennis, G. and Simpson, W., 1991. 'Dangerous Habits', *Hellblazer* #41–46. DC Comics.

Fox, G. and Anderson, M., 1964. *Hawkman*, Vol. 1, #4. Detective Comics. (Character: Zatanna.)

Friedrich, G., Wolfman, M. and Moench, D., 1973–83. *Ghost Rider*, Vol. 2. Marvel Comics.

Gaiman, N., 1989–96. *Sandman*, Vol. 2. DC Comics/Vertigo (from 1993).

——, 1990–91. *Books of Magic*, Vol. 1, #1–4. DC Comics.

Gaiman, N. and Bachalo, C., 1993. *Death: The High Cost of Living*. DC Comics/Vertigo.

Gaiman, N. and Jones, K., 1990. 'A Dream of a Thousand Cats', *Sandman*, Vol. 2, #18. DC Comics.

Gaiman, N. and Kieth, S., 1989. 'Sleep of the Just', *Sandman*, Vol. 2, #1. DC Comics.

Gerber, S., McGregor, D. and Moench, D., 1973–75. *Vampire Tales* #1–7, 10–11. Curtis Magazines. Continued in: Friedrich, M., Gerber, S., Moench, D. and Mantlo, B., 1974–75. *Adventure into Fear* #20–31. Marvel Comics. (Character: Morbius the Living Vampire.)

Gillen, K. and McKelvie, J., 2006. *Phonogram* #3. Image Comics.

Jodorowsky, A. and Moebius (Giraud, J.), 1988. *Incal* #1–3. Epic Comics. Originally published in six French-language albums by Les Humanoïdes Associés, 1981–88.

Lee, S. and Ditko, S., 1963. *Strange Tales* #110. Marvel Comics (Character: Doctor Strange.)

Lee, S. and Kirby, J., 1961. *Fantastic Four* #1. Marvel Comics.

Miller, F., 1980–83. *Daredevil* #166–91. Marvel Comics.

——, 1986. *Batman: The Dark Knight Returns*. DC Comics.

Milligan, P., 1990–96. *Shade, the Changing Man*, Vol. 2. DC Comics/Vertigo (from 1993).

Milligan, P. and Fegredo, D., 1993. *Enigma*. DC Comics/Vertigo.

Mills, P. and (primarily) O'Neill, K. 1980–2000. *Nemesis the Warlock*. In (mainly): *2000AD* #167, 178–79, 222–44, 246–57, 335–49, 387–88, 430, 435–45, 482–87, 500–504, 520–24, 534, 546–57, 586–93, 605–8, 824, 901–3. Fleetway.

Moore, A., 1984–87. *(The Saga of the) Swamp Thing*, Vol. 2, #20–64. DC Comics.

Moore, A., Bissette, S. and Totleben, J., 1984. 'The Anatomy Lesson', *The Saga of the Swamp Thing*, Vol. 2, #21. DC Comics.

——, 1985. 'Fish Story', *Swamp Thing*, Vol. 2, #39. DC Comics.

Moore, A. and Gibbons, D., 1986–87. *Watchmen*. DC Comics.

Moore, A., Veitch, R. and Totleben, J., 1985. 'Growth Patterns', *Swamp Thing*, Vol. 2, #37. DC Comics.

Moore, A., Woch, S. and Randall, R., 1986. 'The Parliament of Trees', *Swamp Thing*, Vol. 2, #47. DC Comics.

Morrison, G., 1988–90. *Animal Man* #1–26. DC Comics.

——, 1989–93. *Doom Patrol*, Vol. 2, #19–63. DC Comics/Vertigo (from 1993).
——, 1994–2000. *The Invisibles*. DC Comics/Vertigo.
——, 1996a. Invisible Ink, In: *The Invisibles* #16. DC Comics, 25–26.
——, 1996b. Invisible Ink, In: *The Invisibles* #24. DC Comics, 25–26.
——, 2001–4. *(New) X-Men* #114–54. Marvel Comics.
——, 2006–8, 2010. *Batman* #656–58, 663–83, 700–702. DC Comics.
Morrison, G. and Fegredo, D., 1991. *Kid Eternity*. DC Comics.
Morrison, G. and Jimenez, P., 1996a. Entropy in the U.K. Part 1, *The Invisibles*, Vol. 1, #17. DC Comics/Vertigo.
——, 1996b. Entropy in the U.K. Part 2, *The Invisibles*, Vol. 1, #18. DC Comics/Vertigo.
——, 1996c. Entropy in the U.K. Part 3, *The Invisibles*, Vol. 1, #19. DC Comics/Vertigo.
Morrison, G. and Quitely, F., 2004–5. *WE3*. DC Comics.
Morrison, G., Truog, C. and Hazlewood, D., 1989. 'At Play in the Field of the Lord', *Animal Man* #18. DC Comics.
Morrison, G. and (Primarily) Yeowell, S., 1987–92. Zenith. In: *2000AD* #535–50, 558–59, 589–606, 626–34, 650–62, 667–70, 791–806. Fleetway.
Morrison, G. and Yeowell, S., 1987. Zenith, Phase I, 2: Blow Up. In: *2000AD* #537. Fleetway.
——, 1989. Zenith, Phase III, 3: A Separate Reality. In: *2000AD* #629. Fleetway.
——, 1990. Zenith, Phase III, 22: Stairway to Heaven. In: *2000AD* #667. Fleetway.
——, 1994a. 'Dead Beetles', *The Invisibles*, Vol. I, #1. DC Comics/Vertigo.
——, 1994b. 'Down and Out in Heaven and Hell, Part 2', *The Invisibles*, Vol. 1, #3. DC Comics/Vertigo.
——, 1994c. 'Down and Out in Heaven and Hell, Part 3', *The Invisibles*, Vol. 1, #4. DC Comics/Vertigo.
Parker, B. and Beck, C. C., 1939. *Whiz Comics* #2. Fawcett Publications. (Character: Captain Marvel.)
Rieber, J. N. and Gross, P., 1994–2000. *Books of Magic*, Vol. 2, #1–75. DC Comics/Vertigo (from 1993).
Siegel, J. and Shuster, J., 1938. *Action Comics* #1. Detective Comics. (Character: Superman.)
Vankin, J. and Gallagher, L. 2004–5. *The Witching*. DC Comics/Vertigo.
Wein, L. and Wrightson, B., 1971. 'Swamp Thing'. In: *House of Secrets* #92. Detective Comics. (Character: Swamp Thing [Alex Olsen].)
Wein, L. and Wrightson, B., 1972. *Swamp Thing*, Vol. 2, #1. Detective Comics. (Character: Swamp Thing [Alec Holland].)

CHAPTER FIFTY-TWO

THE OCCULT AND POPULAR MUSIC

Christopher Partridge

There is something about music's ability to manipulate emotion that has, throughout history, made it peculiarly conducive to metaphysical interpretation. In particular, popular music's important relationship with emotion—its ability to create affective spaces within which identity construction and meaning-making occur—has been explored to great effect since the early 1960s. This confluence of popular music and spirituality has been conspicuous within a number of influential subcultures. There has been a particularly keen focus on occult practice and rejected knowledge, which have often been a source of fascination within transgressive youth cultures—which, nowadays, extend well beyond adolescence. Indeed, popular music, which has been so central to subcultural identity construction, has been particularly significant within the 'occulture' of the late-modern world (see Partridge, 2013a).

OCCULTURE

Some years ago, I began reflecting on the 'spiritual' environment in the West, within which there seemed to be a socially significant confluence of competing discourses, many of which appeared to be related to everyday life through popular culture and the media (see Partridge, 2004, 2005). On the one hand, it was difficult to ignore the force of the arguments and the evidence marshalled in support of widespread secularization driven by the currents of modernization. It is, for example, irrefutably the case that traditional forms of institutional Christianity in Western liberal democracies (particularly Europe) are experiencing a significant decline in power, popularity and prestige. Institutional religion may be flourishing beyond the West and it may still occupy a place of significance in the public life of the United States, but, generally speaking, the evidence seemed to support secularization. On the other hand, within this progressively secular environment, where modernization appeared to be highly corrosive of religion, there was clear evidence of a widespread and vibrant interest in the paranormal, the pursuit of experiences of transcendence, a fascination with the acquisition of occult knowledge, and the development of some form of inner-life spirituality. Consequently, the ostensibly secular Western mind seemed to be haunted by the possibility of an enchanted world.

While such enchantment often emanates from the rarefied worlds of the bizarre and the exotic, it gradually becomes quotidian and ordinary. This process of mainstreaming is principally indebted to the media and popular culture. From the advertising of everyday products that claim to promote wellbeing to the ubiquity of sonic and visual cultures fascinated with experiences of the paranormal, discourses antagonistic to secularization are circulated within everyday life. In short, there appears to be an influential culture of enchantment, which encompasses the marginal and the mainstream, the deviant and the conventional, and which circulates ideas, creates religio-cultural synergies, and forms new trajectories, all of which are driven by wider cultural forces. Indeed, although hegemonic, broadly secular cultures in the West considered many of these ideas trivial and peripheral, in actual fact they are socially significant. Although 'officially' rejected as profane, ridiculed and marginalized by society's religious and intellectual gatekeepers, such discourses are actually deceptively significant in the construction of 'lifeworlds'—those latent, taken-for-granted core values, beliefs, and understandings about who we are, how we relate to others, what the world is like, and how we fit into it (see Habermas, 1987). This is occulture.

Not only are the processes of occulture important in everyday life, but popular music has been central to them. Indeed, since the 1960s there has been a pronounced preoccupation with the occult and the folkloric embedded within popular music 'occulture': the much-mythologized Crowleyesque/Thelemic preoccupations of Jimmy Page and the speculation surrounding the occult signification within the music and cover art of *Led Zeppelin IV* (see Davis, 2005); the bewitching influence of Crowley's *Diary of a Drug Fiend* on Peter Perrett of The Only Ones (see Antonia, 1996, 93–94); the hippie, neo-Romantic mysticism of Gong's *Magick Brother* (1970); the occultural interests articulated on Blue Öyster Cult's *Agents of Fortune* (1976); the 'esoterrorist' agendas of bands such as Psychic TV, Coil, and Burial Hex (see Partridge, 2013b); the understated traces of M.R. James, Arthur Machen, and H.P. Lovecraft in the work of Mark E. Smith of The Fall (see Fisher, 2010; Goodall, 2010); the far more explicit influence of occult popular literature and film evident in the music of some doom and stoner albums, such as Electric Wizard's *Witchcult Today* (2007) and *Black Masses* (2010); the kitsch vampiric eroticism that led to the composition of Bauhaus's genre-defining classic, 'Bela Lugosi's Dead' (1979—see Carpenter, 2012, 37–39); the cosmic fantasies and channeled ramblings articulated on Ramases' *Space Hymns* (1971), Sun Ra's *Space is the Place* (1973) and the various projects of Funkadelic, Parliament, Hawkwind, and Acid Mothers Temple and the Melting Paraiso U.F.O. (see Hollings, 2002; Valcic, 2012); the idiosyncratic and often quaint musings on the bucolic and the Pagan in the songs of The Watersons, The Incredible String Band, Andy Partridge, The Waterboys, Julian Cope, Björk, Natasha Khan/Bat for Lashes, and Blood Ceremony (see, Weston & Bennett, 2013; Harley, 2006); the penchant for the occult in Goth culture from Siouxsie and the Banshees onwards (see, Pitzl-Waters, 2013); the enigmatic references, such as 'Western Esotericism' by The Flaming Lips (featuring Erykah Badu), which is the title given to the controversial video of their haunting version of Roberta Flack's 'The First Time Ever (I Saw Your Face)' (available on: *The Flaming Lips and Heady Fwends*, 2012); Scandinavian Black Metal's litanies to the Southern Lord and the affective spaces shaped by its broadly Heathen meditations on the dark solitude of

Northern wildernesses (see Howells, 2012; Dyrendal, 2009a; Granholm, 2011, 2013); the disturbing contorted esotericism of Wold's *Freermasonry* (2011); the eclectic fascination with global esoteric currents evident on albums such as Bill Laswell's *Hashisheen: The End of Law* (1999) and his various 'Sacred System' dub projects; the interest in occultural celebrities, such as the Swedish artist Ouijabeard's (Andreas Sandberg) fascination with Rasputin (*Die and Let Live*, 2012) and Damon Albarn's operatic celebration of John Dee (*Dr. Dee*, 2012); and the focus on local occult folklore, such as the atmospheres inspired by Lancashire witch mythology in the darkly atmospheric electronica of Pendle Coven and Demdike Stare. Interestingly, on 13 December 2013, Sean Canty and Miles Whittaker (Demdike Stare) performed a live score for Benjamin Christensen's classic silent film, *Häxan: Witchcraft Through the Ages* (1922), at the British Film Institute's festival in London, 'Gothic: The Dark Heart of Film.'

PSYCHEDELIC FOLK OCCULTURE

While many popular musicians have articulated a sense of the sacred in nature, which they are happy to refer to as 'Pagan,' since the mid-1960s there has been a gradual increase of interest in Pagan faith and practice within popular music culture—an interest which has been cultivated at music festivals. The Green Man festival in Wales, for example, which has won several awards, is annually blessed by Druids and described on their website as follows: 'In the beating heart of the breathtaking Black Mountains, where mystical leylines converge amid ancient oak trees, something truly magical is stirring' (Green Man, 2013).

This interest emerged quite naturally out of a fascination with traditional folk culture and a quest for authenticity. Rooted in a burgeoning folk scene, several of the more experimental bands were particularly significant in this respect. For example, drawing on folkloric myth and magic, Comus (e.g. 'Song to Comus', *First Utterance*) and The Watersons (e.g. *Frost and Fire: A Calendar of Ritual and Magical Songs*) both sought to introduce their listeners to an often dark and visceral enchanted world: 'the cycles of nature are those with which humanity should commune, even to the point of human sacrifice as a means of ensuring fertility. Encompassing every type of activity and emotion in a celebration of rural life, the song-cycle is also about work as a means of engaging with the land' (Hegarty & Halliwell, 2011: 56). Musically, bands such as the Incredible String Band and Comus began to plough what was to become a distinctive furrow within folk culture, a furrow that would lead them to progressive acid folk and folk-rock that had, to some extent, sloughed off traditional folk. As Hegarty and Halliwell say of Comus, 'the band twisted traditional instrumentation into an ecstatic, mounting discordance where a lost, sexual and often deadly nature could be summoned. The pastoral is about an unleashing of energy that taps into a host of Pagan gods and stories…' (2011: 56; see Leech, 2013). Even some artists who were, musically, more traditional, were attracted to folk occulture, explicitly articulating a Romantic embrace of Pagan traditions. For example, in the mid-1960s, the folk duo Dave and Toni Arthur began exploring Wicca, following a meeting with Britain's occult celebrity, Alex Sanders (who rejoiced in the title 'King of the Witches').

> We'd talk about magic, as we'd got into witchcraft and studying it, to find out how witchcraft was reflected in the traditional song—if magical ballads were anything to do with what was perceived then as Wicca, the witch covens that were going round in England, and whether they were actually related or whether it was a separate thing. And so we started going to meetings of witches and going through their ritual books and things, and we were invited as guests to all sorts of coven meetings, and then we were stuck in 'Tam Lin' and all these magical ballads and somehow trying to relate them to what was going on in the occult world and find out what the connections were.
>
> (Dave Arthur, quoted in Young, 2010: 440)

As the guitarist Richard Thompson put it, 'you find a lot of magic in traditional music...A lot of songs about Faery Queens and people cavorting with the elemental beasties' (quoted in Heylin, 1989: 7). This made traditional music peculiarly attractive to those seeking to establish continuities with premodern Paganism. For example, the title of Dave and Toni Arthurs' album, *Hearken to the Witch's Rune* (1970), is taken from Alex Sanders' 'Witch's Chant,' based on a chant composed by the famous British Wiccan, Doreen Valiente: 'Darksome night and shining moon/ East, South, West, the North/ Hearken to the witch's rune/ Here I come to call thee forth...By all the power of land and sea/ By all the might of Moon and Sun/ As I do will, so might it be/ Oh chant the spell and be it done.' The fact that it's not actually sung on the album, but only printed on the back cover and used in the title indicates its significance for the couple and its perceived appropriateness for a folk album. More than this, the text effectively transformed the record into a sacred artifact, the implication being that the album's true significance lay beyond mere entertainment. This was 'musick'—a sonic grimoire.

Such discourses, whilst largely restricted to a vibrant and burgeoning occult underground, surfaced spectacularly into the mainstream in Robin Hardy's 1973 film, *The Wicker Man*. Based on David Pinner's 1967 novel, *Ritual*, which related the occult murder of a child in a remote Cornish village, *The Wicker Man* depicted the survival of an isolated Pagan community on a small island off the Scottish coast. Leaning heavily on the ideas developed by the late-Victorian anthropologists Edward Burnett Tylor and James Frazer (whose magnum opus, *The Golden Bough*, is particularly significant in this respect), the film, through its gentle evocation of sacred awe, communicates a sense of the emotional power of Pagan occultural discourse at the time. Watching it nowadays is like stumbling through a hidden door into the secret garden of late-1960s occulture. In a society in which Christian hegemony is still conspicuous, it depicts a level of commitment to natural forces that is both fascinating and frightening, both attractive and repelling. The viewer is drawn, not just into the narrative arc, but also into a Romantic Pagan space. Certainly, as a reflection of the changes taking place in 1960s' and early 1970s' religion and society, the film is particularly interesting. As in the affective spaces evoked by much early psychedelic folk music, it is imagined that there is a place, Summerisle, where there survives a pre-Christian religion, in tune with nature, unfettered by the mean morality of conservative Christianity, but savage at its core. The screenwriter, Anthony Shaffer, was drawn to the swelling tide of popular occultural interest in folklore and magic, as well as to the rural Romanticism of, for example, the Incredible String

Band's album *The Hangman's Beautiful Daughter* (1968). Central to the occultural impact of the film is the soundtrack composed by Paul Giovanni and played by his band, Magnet, which was formed specifically for the purpose (see, Fitzgerald & Hayward, 2009; Rossi, 2013). Throughout the film, folk music is explicitly identified with the survival of pre-Christian indigenous religion. Indeed, it is used to create a boundary between the Christianity of the staunchly Presbyterian policeman, Sergeant Howie (Edward Woodward), and the Pagan space inhabited by the islanders and overseen by Lord Summerisle (Christopher Lee). The use of music and dance evokes the vibrancy of nature religion and the occult over against the dry formalism of mainland Calvinist theology. However, it does so in a way that problematizes the boundary, in the sense that it is not always clear whether the music identifies the profane—'the demonic', as Sergeant Howie understood it—or the sacred—the pure, the innocent, and natural, occult lores as the Summerisle community understood it.

This ambiguity and the core themes within the film, which reflect the religious and cultural shifts that had begun to gain ground during the 1960s, have ensured its continuing presence within popular music culture. Numerous musicians still directly reference the film: Iron Maiden, 'The Wicker Man' (*Brave New World*, 2000); Momus and Anne Laplantine, *Summerisle* (2004); Plague Lounge, *The Wicker Image* (1996); Us and Them, *Summerisle* (2011); Agalloch, 'Summerisle: Reprise' (*Whitedivisiongrey*, 2012). More directly, many have registered their interest in the occultural content of the film by covering songs from the soundtrack. For example, the Italian neo-folk band, The Green Man, produced a version of 'The Maypole Song' ('Summerisle', *From Irem to Summerisle*, 2009). Again, 'Willow's Song,' the most popular from the soundtrack, has been covered by artists as disparate as Doves (*Lost Sides*, 2003), The Sneaker Pimps ('How Do', *Becoming X*, 1996), The Go! Team (as a bonus track on the Japanese release of *Proof of Youth*, 2007), Nature and Organization ('The Wicker Man Song', *Beauty Reaps The Blood Of Solitude*, 1994), Faith and the Muse (*The Burning Season*, 2003), and Us and Them (*Summerisle*, 2011). As the Pagan writer Jason Pitzl-Waters comments, 'It is hard to overstate the influence *The Wicker Man* soundtrack has had on Pagan and occult-themed music. It not only became a reference point for Pagan artists, but a touchstone for a wide variety of musicians from seemingly disparate genres, entranced by the atmospherics and authenticity of the music' (2012; see Letcher, 2013). However, it is within the neo-folk and post-industrial scenes that the film has had its most conspicuous impact, largely because of its cementing of the relationship between folk music and imagined pre-modern occult discourse. For example, not only does the online magazine *Compulsion*—dedicated to post-industrial culture—seem to be committed to documenting the continuing significance of *The Wicker Man*, but the influential compilation *Looking for Europe: A Neofolk Compendium* (2005) includes Magnet's version of 'Willow's Song' taken directly from the film. Again, 'The Unbroken Circle' website, which discusses contemporary 'Wyrd Folk,' insists that the film is 'the point where...the perceived realization of folk music as important in the social and magical context was made. It does not matter whether this realization was factual or just a perception, what matters is the transformation it created in the minds of many' (quoted in Jason Pitzl-Waters, 2012).

The Romantic confluence of folk and the occult at the heart of *The Wicker Man* is particularly evident in the music of the neo-folk pioneer, David Tibet. Emerging out of the transgressive culture that gave shape to industrial music, his work in the early 1980s is essentially an occultural reading of Christian apocalyptic thought through a Crowleyan lens (see Fava, 2012). Indeed, he named his band Current 93, which is itself an important Thelemic reference. Using the system of isopsephy, which, like gematria, allocates numerical value to letters, Crowley identified the number 93 as a distillation of the central ideas of Thelema: 'Do what thou wilt shall be the whole of the Law' and 'Love is the law, love under will.' The point is that the numerical value of 'thelema'/'will' is 9 and that of 'agape'/'love' is 3 (see, Churton, 2012: 182). Thelemic thought is never far from the surface in the work of Current 93. Crowley, says Tibet, 'was someone I grew up with. He was incredibly important to me. He gave me a great deal of confidence in a world I thought was very insecure and frightening. Crowley gave me a sense that I could control my environment to some degree, and I had a power, just as we all have' (Moliné, 2006: 93). Hence, as well as explicitly referencing his ideas, as on the EP *Crowleymass* (1987), which Tibet recorded with the Icelandic musician and Pagan thinker Hilmar Örn Hilmarsson, many early Current 93 albums betray a Thelemic influence. *Nature Unveiled* (1984), for example, the first Current 93 album, comprises two tracks, 'Ach Golgotha (Maldoror is Dead)' and 'The Mystical Body of Christ in Chorazaim (the Great in the Small),' both of which are intertextually complex, darkly liturgical compositions. Although the album is clearly seeking to engage with apocalyptic Christian esotericism, nevertheless Thelemic and Pagan discourses are dominant: chanting, bells, gongs, prayers, weeping, and screaming contribute to a disturbing cacophonic and primal energy, which, on 'Ach Golgotha (Maldoror Is Dead),' is haunted by a loop of Crowley chanting 'Om.' 'I was trying to make a truly majestic and apocalyptic album,' recalls Tibet, the aim being to construct a genuinely disturbing affective space. 'To me it's like a long song that builds up in power…It's not a Black Mass, but it is literally a diabolical record in some ways.' Crowley, once said, 'I fought all night with God and the Devil. Finally God won, but I'm not sure which God it was.' The album *Nature Unveiled*, he suggests, 'has that tension' (quoted in Moliné, 2006: 32; see also, Keenan, 1997: 34–37).

The influence of Current 93's work has, in recent years, extended to US free folk or what has become known as the 'New Weird America,' Having said that, the popular music of the United States has, of course, never been short of its own occult influences. A particularly important person in this respect was the proto-psychedelic occultist, folklorist, filmmaker, and music collector, Harry Smith. His three-volume *Anthology of American Folk Music* released in 1952, became the primary document of the American folk revival. However, not only did it introduce a host of musicians, including Pete Seeger, Bob Dylan, Joan Baez, John Fahey, and Jerry Garcia, to the music of the 1920s and 1930s, but the liner notes also introduced them to Crowley, to the seventeenth-century English Paracelsian philosopher and physician Robert Fludd, to the founder of Anthroposophy, Rudolf Steiner, and, rather bizarrely, to the anthropologist who succeeded Tylor at Oxford University, R.R. Marrett. In the conclusion of his lengthy and fascinating liner notes, he claimed (in rather obscure terms) that the following quotations had been useful in compiling his *Anthology of American Folk Music*: 'In elementary music the relation of Earth to the sphere of water is 4 to 3, as there are in the Earth four quarters of frigidity to three of water' (Fludd); 'Civilized man thinks out his difficulties, at least he thinks he does, primitive man dances out his difficulties' (Marrett); 'Do as thy wilt shall be the whole of the law' (Crowley); 'The in-breathing becomes thought, and the out-breathing becomes the will manifestation of thought' (Steiner) (Smith, 1952: 18). While even the most imaginative esoteric mind would have difficulty applying this collection of eclectic gobbets to the process of compiling an anthology of folk music, nevertheless the confluence itself is an interesting one, in that it shows a commitment to the significance of the relationship between popular music and the occult that has continued to flow underground, occasionally bubbling to the surface in springs of fresh countercultural creativity. Even Smith's surreal occult film, *Heaven and Earth Magic* (originally released in 1957 and then again in 1962), has attracted the attention of musicians such as John Zorn, who has performed live during screenings of it, as have Deerhoof ('Look Away', *Friend Opportunity*, 2007) and the producer Flying Lotus. Indeed, the liner notes for the album *Heretic: Jeux Des Dames Cruelles* (1992) by Zorn's improvisational project Naked City declare that 'this record is dedicated to Harry Smith. Mystical Animator, Pioneer Ethnomusicologist, Hermetic Scholar, Creator of "Heaven + Earth Magic", one of the greatest films of all time.' And the Brattleboro Free Folk Festival, the principal gathering of the New Weird America movement, constitutes 'an attempt to muster the same recurrent and archetypal forms that archivist and mystic Harry Smith saw manifest in the American folk music of the early twentieth century' (Keenan, 2003b: 34). Here, at Brattleboro, gather 'lone visionaries, hermetic isolationists, young marginalized artists, hippy revolutionaries, country punks, ex-cons, project kids, avant experimentalists, luddite refuseniks, psychedelic rockers and assorted misfits in an attempt to make space for an alternative American narrative, irreconcilable with the prevailing neoconservative vision of the "New American Century"' (Keenan, 2003b: 34). The point is that, like Smith before them, some of the key figures in American neo-folk think of their music as possessing a certain occult energy which has the potential to effect significant social change. Indeed, rooted in albums such as, again, The Incredible String Band's *The Hangman's Beautiful Daughter* (1968), 'one of the scene's founding documents' (Keenan, 2003b: 37), there is a clear sense that the New Weird America is creating, as Chasney puts it, alternative affective spaces within which one might 'summon up ancient forces that once only took shape in drawings in hermetic books' (quoted in Keenan, 2003b: 40). In going back to traditional folk instruments, there is an attempt to unearth an authenticity that connects the sound with the beyond. It's 'not that music that uses electricity cannot be transcendental. It's just a matter of studying the forms of sounds that are closer to human existence in order to understand the correspondence with higher forms, with the heavens' (Ben Chasney quoted in Keenan, 2003b: 40).

SYMPATHY FOR THE DEVIL

If *The Wicker Man* contributed to contemporary discourses about premodern Pagan occultism and its close relationship with the natural world, the films of Kenneth Anger can be read as reflecting the contours of contemporary Romantic individualism, particularly evident within Satanist discourses.

Popular music culture's relationship with Anger is a close one, not least because he used musicians in his films, notably Bobby Beausoleil and The Rolling Stones entourage, who he viewed as the provocative heralds of the new aeon (see Baddeley,

1999: 47; Landis, 1995). Moreover, both Beausoleil and Jimmy Page produced soundtracks for his film *Lucifer Rising* and albums reflecting the occult chic of the late 1960s, such as particularly *Their Satanic Majesties Request* (1967) by The Rolling Stones, betray Anger's influence. More significantly, however, there are two interrelated themes in Anger's work that are worth tracing through into popular music, both of which were conspicuous within the occulture of the period. The first and most obvious is that of Lucifer as an icon of individualism, whose name Anger had tattooed across his chest, and the second is that of art as a conduit for occult energy. We will deal with the former in this section and the latter in the following section.

In accordance with the Romantic conception of Satan (see Russell, 2005), Anger's Lucifer is not the biblical Devil, a personification of evil, but rather a more nuanced figure. Indeed, *Lucifer Rising*, he explained, was 'a film about the love generation—the birthday party of the Aquarian Age. Showing actual ceremonies to make Lucifer rise. Lucifer is the Light God, not the Devil—the Rebel Angel behind what's happening in the world today. His message is that the key of joy is disobedience' (quoted in Baddeley, 1999: 48). This disobedience, moreover, is interpreted Romantically in terms of a sacred individualistic act, arrogant in its transgressive assertion of personal rights and self-determination, and single-minded in its intention to subvert oppressive laws and attitudes informed by Western morality and religion. Popular music, in its subversion of political and religious hegemonies, and in its Dionysian excess, constituted a manifestation of this Luciferian energy. For Anger, Lucifer is quite literally 'the bringer of light,' 'the morning star,' 'the son of dawn' (Isaiah 14:12), who is related to the dawning of a new aeon of enlightenment and liberty. Anger's Lucifer is an exemplar of key features of the Romantic hero. As Jeffrey Burton Russell discusses of the nineteenth-century Romantics, their 'distaste for the Church was reciprocated, and clerical attacks on the Romantics only intensified their view that Christianity was evil and its opponents good. It followed that if the greatest enemy of traditional Christianity was Satan, then Satan must be good.' Of course, this was, 'a philosophically incoherent statement contradicting the core meaning of the Devil, and indeed the Romantics intended such a statement, not as a theological proposition, but rather as an imaginative challenge and as a political program' (Russell, 2005: 160). Their point was that, as symbolic of the challenge to unjust and repressive authority, Satan is the archetypal Romantic idea of the hero, which, 'derived from the concept of the sublime, stands in contradiction to the classic epic notion of the hero as one devoted to the welfare of his family and people. The Romantic hero is individual, alone in the world, self-assertive, ambitious, powerful, and liberator in rebellion against the society that blocks the way to progress toward liberty, beauty, and love; the Romantics read these qualities in Milton's Satan' (Russell, 2005: 160). Hence, just as the figure of Satan merged with that of 'the rock star' in the minds of those fearful of a threat to core Christian values in society, particularly within right-wing religion, so within some youth cultures, for very different reasons, Satan and rock stars were elided in the figure of the Romantic hero—both are champions of truth and liberty.

A good example of this interpretation of Lucifer is The Rolling Stones' song 'Sympathy for the Devil' (*Beggars Banquet*, 1968). Satan is the demonic Other necessary for the identification of the good. That is to say, Mick Jagger, who was closely involved with Anger for a short period, constructs an essentially Romantic Devil. Rather than being a transgressive exaltation of evil personified, as in the *ad hoc* satanic discourse of much black metal, his 'man of wealth and taste' is a far more ambiguous figure. Indeed, it is unsurprising that in an interview with Jann Wenner for the *Rolling Stone* magazine, he recalls that it was probably 'taken from an old idea of Baudelaire's' (quoted in Wenner, 1995). Certainly, the protagonist in 'Sympathy for the Devil' can be compared to the 'Prince of the exile' who has been 'wronged' in Charles Baudelaire's 'Les Litanies de Satan.' That said, there are also significant parallels with Mikhail Bulgakov's *The Master and Margarita*, which Jagger has also claimed as an inspiration, having received the book as a gift from Marianne Faithfull. Bearing in mind that Bulgakov's Satan is essentially 'a man of wealth and taste' who visits earth and attempts to argue the case for his existence, the core themes of the song suggest that this was indeed Jagger's primary source of inspiration. However, whether it was or not, the point is that the Devil is used to interrogate constructions of good and evil in society.

Finally, thinking more generally of the Romantic tendency to 'transpose the Christian God into a symbol of evil, the Christian idea of humanity into God (in the sense that humanity became the ultimate concern), and the Christian Satan into a hero' (Russell, 2005: 160), this is explicitly evident in Satanist discourse, which understands 'socialization as repression' and Satan as a 'force, model, symbol or expression of the self' (Petersen, 2009: 2; see also, Faxneld & Petersen, 2012). Satanism, in other words, was developed as a form of 'self-religion,' a project devoted to the excavation and empowerment of the authentic inner self, which has been corrupted by the profane forces of socialization (see Dyrendal, 2009b; Lap, 2012). As Anton LaVey—founder of the Church of Satan in San Francisco, in 1966—describes his philosophy, it is 'the ultimate conscious alternative to herd mentality and institutionalised thought.' Its aim is 'to liberate individuals from a contagion of mindlessness that destroys innovation.' Consequently, he says, 'Satanism means "the opposition" and epitomizes all symbols of nonconformity' (LaVey, 1992: 9–10). Satan, the Romantic hero, is 'the spirit of progress, the inspirer of all great movements that contribute to the development of civilization and the advancement of mankind. He is the spirit of revolt that leads to freedom, the embodiment of all heresies that liberate' (LaVey, quoted in Wolfe, 1969, 13). Again, it is hardly surprising that there are conspicuous lines of continuity linking popular music, the Romantic Satan, Satanism, and transgression. Having said that, they do need to be untangled a little, not least because there is a question as to whether, in the final analysis, the very idea of a Satanist Romantic hero is a contradiction in terms. While there are a few popular musicians, such as Boyd Rice, Marilyn Manson, and King Diamond of Merciful Fate, who have found LaVeyan Satanism appealing as a philosophy, others have clearly interpreted it in terms of a hindrance to individualism, unfettered excess, and self-determination. Indeed, LaVey was, as Jean LaFontaine notes, 'a firm believer in order and observing the rule of law' and opposed to the use of drugs (LaFontaine, 1999: 97). This is because, for all its discourse around individualism, Satanism is a system, a régime, a set of principles and techniques for the realization of 'self-godhood.' As Dyrendal notes (quoting Don Webb of the Temple of Set),

> Rulership of the inner world involves controlling the body, mind, emotions and will, and means that the initiate achieves 'a sense of reality and purpose in what one does.' To reach this goal, one should find factors that hinder development at all levels, and remove them. Forces opposing the *body* are 'those things which shorten life, remove energy, or dull the senses' and range from drugs to the wrong kind of food to cultural and environmental factors. Forces opposing the *mind* are all 'habits of non-thinking' involved in herd conformity.
>
> (Dyrendal, 2009b: 66)

This type of thinking, as LaFontaine puts it, 'appears somewhat inconsistent with rebellion against authority' (1999: 97). There is, in other words, an Apollonian–Dionysian tension. Organizational Satanism has routinized and reified Dionysian individualism. As such, it has subverted that which the Romantic hero holds sacred—an embrace of excess in the pursuit of liberty and enlightenment. This goes some way to explaining the negative attitude toward Satanic organizations evident within extreme metal. For example, the black metal label Deathlike Silence Productions, as Dyrendal comments, 'sometimes featured a picture of LaVey in a circle with a line drawn through it—similar to conventional "no smoking" signs.' Understood in terms of the above discussion, this rejection is directly related to the fact that, 'whereas LaVey's Church of Satan espouses "nine parts respectability to one part outrageousness", the discourse and ethos of transgression in the early black metal scene inverts the proportions.' That is to say, 'while the Church of Satan...values transgression as well as control, only a few individual Satanists, many of which are marginal, would value transgression to the extent implied in black metal discourse' (Dyrendal, 2009a: 29–30). The individualistic creed of the Romantic Satan resists control, order, and regulation, embracing excess in the pursuit of liberty.

There was also a concern within early black metal culture that, not only had the individualistic creed been eroded within organizational Satanism, but the idea of Satan had been detraditionalized, becoming little more than a principle of self-development, rather than the literal infernal being of traditional Western demonology. This humanist intellectualization and, in effect, sanitization, reduced Satan's potency as an occultural symbol of transgression and rebellion.

MUSICK

Turning to the Romantic idea that art might be a conduit for occult energy, at the center of Kenneth Anger's work is an almost devout commitment to occult ritual, which draws heavily on the work of Crowley. For Anger, films are, as Carel Rowe commented in an early analysis of his work, 'a search for light and enlightenment' (1974: 26). 'Making a movie is casting a spell,' claims Anger, and 'the cinematograph' is a 'magick weapon' (Anger, quoted in Rowe, 1974: 26). Hence, his films, which are densely symbolic, are understood in terms of 'evocations or invocations, attempting to conjure primal forces which, once visually released, are designed to have the effect of "casting a spell" on the audience. The magick in the film is related to the magickal effect of the film on the audience' (Rowe, 1974: 26). It is this conviction that most clearly reflects a particular fascination with the occult in popular music. While some have observed that Anger's 'concise body of films stretching over five decades has provided a mother lode of ideas mined to this day by rock video directors' (Henderson, 2004: 32), and while musicians have produced homages to his life and work as representative of late 1960s' psychedelic occultism, such as Death in Vegas's *Scorpio Rising* (2002), there are yet others—who do not necessarily look back to Anger—for whom the notion that music might be able to summon primal forces and manipulate energies is an attractive one. For these musicians, their work can be understood very literally in terms of alchemy and occult energy. Music becomes 'musick,' 'a conjuration of pagan forces,' 'a surge of spiritual and mystical power' (Anger, quoted in Pouncey, 2004: 35).

Such understandings are, of course, not new. The history of music is not short of shadowy magi obsessed with notions of the esoteric potential of sound. For example, Alexander Scriabin's Piano Sonata No. 9, Op. 68 (1913), was dubbed by his friend, Alexi Podgaetsky, 'The Black Mass'—a title the composer approved of, in that, through it, he was seeking to express an inexpressible darkness. Hovering around the interval of the diminished fifth, which is popularly understood as 'the Devil's interval,' Scriabin's notation reads as follows: 'a sweetness gradually becoming more and more caressing and poisonous' (quoted in Bowers, 1996: 244–45). As Faubian Bowers comments, 'its ritual is perverse. The rite is spitting at all that is holy or sacred... Corruption, perversity, diabolism recurs' (Bowers, 1996: 245). Scriabin was reaching into a particularly dark corner of contemporary Russian occulture. However, the point is that, like the music of Psychic TV, Coil, and Current 93, the performance of the 'Black Mass' wasn't simply understood as entertainment, but rather as a more dynamically metaphysical happening. Indeed, the Russian concert pianist Yevgeny Sudbin notes that Scriabin believed that 'he was "practising sorcery" whenever playing this sonata' (Sudbin, 2012).

Fifty-six years later, a similar, but cruder fascination with the occult potential of music surfaced in the United States in the work of Coven, who performed what they considered to be an authentic black mass, a recording of which was released on their debut album, *Witchcraft Destroys Minds and Reaps Souls* (1969). 'To the best of our knowledge, this is the first Black Mass to be recorded in written words or in audio. It is as authentic,' they claimed, 'as hundreds of hours of research in every known source can make it...' In actual fact, it was composed by their producer, Bill Traut, an ardent fan of H.P. Lovecraft, and much of it seems to have been lifted from the accounts of rituals in Dennis Wheatley novels. Nevertheless, whatever the source material, they provided a Wheatley-esque warning in their sleeve notes (and with this warning, deepened the record's occult gravitas): 'we do not recommend its use by anyone who has not thoroughly studied Black Magic and is aware of the risks and dangers involved.' This was immediately appealing to many young people, the implication being, of course, that the record was able to infuse the affective space created by the music with occult energy. Again, as with Dave and Toni Arthur's *Hearken to the Witch's Rune* (1970), it was believed to be far more meaningful than merely entertainment. Thus fetishized, it was an occult artifact with an energy waiting to be released by a stylus.

Likewise, in the UK, Black Widow's progressive rock single 'Come to the Sabbat' (from the album *Sacrifice*, 1970) sought to evoke a similar affective space: 'Help me in my search for knowledge/ I must learn the secret art,' sings Kip Trevor. The sense of occult energy was enhanced during their early performances by the inclusion of a mock sacrifice of a nude woman, choreographed by members of Leicester's Phoenix Theatre Company. Moreover, again, like Dave and Toni Arthur, they made it known that they had been tutored in ritual magic by the 'King of the Witches,' Alex Sanders. However, unlike the Arthurs, they produced a performance with his wife, Maxine, as the naked Lady Astaroth. 'Discard your clothes and come on foot...Join me in my search for power...Come to the Sabbat, Satan's there!' Indeed, this song is included on Nat Freedland's occulturally interesting double LP, *The Occult Explosion* (1973), which comprises a series of interviews with a number of occult figures, including a discussion by the founder of the Church of Satan, Anton LaVey.

Another musician fascinated with the confluence of music and the occult was Graham Bond, a gifted, but troubled man, who believed himself to be Crowley's son. A central figure in the British blues movement, he had, by the close of the 1960s, formed Magick, a group intended to channel his interests in the occult in much the same way that Anger had sought to do through film—although far more chaotically. The band released two albums, *Holy Magick* (1970) and *We Put Our Magick on You* (1971), both of which were occulturally eclectic, infused with obscure esoteric meaning and folklore, as indicated by the track titles: 'Meditation Aumgu'; 'The Word of Aeon'; 'The Qabalistic Cross'; 'Invocation to the Light'; 'The Pentagram'; 'The Holy Words'; 'Aquarius Mantra'; 'Enochian (Atlantean) Call'; 'Return of Arthur'; 'The Magician'; 'My Archangel Mikael'; 'Druid'; 'I Put My Magick on You'; 'Hail Ra Harokhite'; 'Time to Die.' Sadly, the last of these titles was rather prescient in that, in April, 1974, following a nervous breakdown, significant personal problems, and the failure of his next band, Magus, he died under the wheels of a train at Finsbury Park station, London. While myths circulated within popular music occulture about the relationship of his death to his esoteric interests, it is more than likely that he committed suicide as a result of severe depression.

Since this period, the notion that music might be used as a conduit for occult energy has been developed across an increasingly broad spectrum, both by the musicians themselves and by their fans, from Steve Hillage's *Rainbow Dome Musick* (1979), composed to be played at the 1979 Mind, Body, Spirit Festival in London, to contemporary 'ritual black metal,' which is 'characterized by explicit, systematic, and sustained engagements with the occult' (Granholm, 2013: 5). The latter is particularly interesting, in that musicians and fans within the black metal scene, 'not only demonstrate an interest in occult subject matter that surpasses most of what came before, but explicitly claim their artistry to be an expression of the occult in itself—as divine worship or communion, an expression of and tool for initiatory processes, and/or and explication of seriously held beliefs' (Granholm, 2013: 5). This is, in other words, explicitly 'musick' in the sense discussed above, being very similar to Graham Bond's and Kenneth Anger's theory of art as an occult tool. Indeed, a number of music and arts festivals have emerged in recent years, for which such an understanding is central. One of the most recent is Arosian Black Mass, established in 2011 and held 100 km west of Stockholm. Although black metal bands play at the event, the organizers are keen to promote it, not as a black metal music festival, but rather as being 'centered around occult esoterism in art, music and dark spiritual practice. The whole event will have it's focus upon an esoteric process within which all participating artists will play key roles' (Arosian Black Mass, 2013). Such events are constructed as serious occult happenings during which ritual is central. Hence, perhaps inevitably, from within these music subcultures there have emerged a number of occult fraternities, as well as alliances with established occult orders, such as Dragon Rouge and, particularly in the case of the band Dissection, the Misanthropic Lucifer Order (see, Granholm, 2013: 21–27). For example, concerning the formation of occult fraternities, the Luciferian Flame Brotherhood/ Serpent Flame Brotherhood consists of members of a number of black metal bands who are interested in occult belief and practice. The aim of this fraternity is 'not to become an initiatory order in itself, but to direct the musical expressions of the occult to align them with ritual magical practice' (Granholm, 2013, 20).

ESOTERRORISM

While black metal's relationship with the occult has been particularly prominent—which, in many cases, is more to do with marketing hype and media construction than with genuine conviction—some of the most distinctive and carefully theorized occult trajectories within popular music have their roots in industrial culture. Of particular note in this respect is Genesis P-Orridge, who developed several projects around ideas of 'esoterrorism' and Paganism as 'a form of anti-establishment activity' (P-Orridge, 2001: 122).

A founder of the experimental ritual magick network, Thee Temple ov Psychick Youth (TOPY), which drew on material developed by the Process Church of the Final Judgment, P-Orridge began his musical career as a naïve occultist. Although his friend Carl Abrahamsson notes that he 'read and studied…occultism all through his youth' (Abrahamsson, 2002: 29), in actual fact, at least initially, this was an area in which he tended to follow rather than to lead. While he may have had an early fascination with the occult and the supernatural, as many young people do, as the work of COUM Transmissions evolved into Throbbing Gristle and eventually into Psychic TV, several friends began to shape his thinking more formatively, notably his fellow musicians, the late John Balance (of the band Coil) and particularly David Tibet. For example, concerning the important influence of the occultist and artist Austin Osman Spare on P-Orridge's thought, especially the use of sigils, 'it was Balance, alongside Hilmer Örn Hilmarsson, who together thoroughly infused…Spare into the Psychic TV melting pot' (Gavin Semple, quoted in Keenan, 2003a, 41). Balance had become obsessed with the ideas of Spare: 'I'd go to the Atlantic bookshop…looking for books and paintings by him…But the thing is, I genuinely felt this instant connection…It wasn't joking around. Our thing was that we were going to try and follow in this guy's footsteps' (quoted in Keenan, 2003a, 104). He even claimed to have developed a form of what he has referred to as 'ancestor worship,' during which he communicated with the deceased artist through a Sparean method of meditating on his drawings. Again, acknowledging the significant influence of Tibet, P-Orridge notes that, not only was Tibet 'obsessed with Aleister Crowley,' but he 'wrongly assumed I was well read and researched in the museum of magick. *I am not*' (quoted in Keenan, 2003a, 40). Nevertheless, Paganism and the occult became important sites of exploration, which alongside a fascination with notorious cult leaders, such as Charles Manson and Jim Jones, as well as the ideas and rituals of the Process Church of the Final Judgment, provided a transgressive lens through which to analyze society.

As with Anger, P-Orridge came to believe that occult ideas and methods, communicated through music, could be used to change minds, subvert accepted social mores, and *convert* people to new ways of thinking and being. As Abrahamsson notes, his interest was always less in the 'the lure and romance of mediaeval magicians, cloaked in robes and waving wands,' and more in 'the apparent changing ability the human mind and activities actually have' (Abrahamsson, 2002: 29). Hence, during the late 1970s, P-Orridge became interested in 'how a small number of fanatical individuals could have a disproportionate impact on culture' (Ford, 1999: 10.29). He reasoned that occult ideas articulated and developed by film directors, authors, artists, and musicians are, through synergies and networks, able to have a disproportionate influence on large numbers of people and, consequently, on institutions and societies. This is 'esoterrorism.' However, to understand where this type of thinking is being drawn from, we need to return to the ideas of Spare.

Working from within a tradition of Romantic occultism, Spare demonstrated an aversion to moralism and taboos, as well as a fascination with the sexual and the bodily (particularly the significance of combining orgasm with the will and the sigil-focused imagination), and a keen interest in the potential of occult power to manifest desire. A talented artist and draughtsman, at an early age Spare became fascinated with the occult, a fascination that quickly found an outlet in his drawings. Following an early exhibition at London's Bruton Gallery in October 1907, at which the public were introduced to his highly sexualized drawings, which included much occult symbolism, he was contacted by Crowley. By 1910, after contributing four small drawings to Crowley's publication *The Equinox*, Spare had become a probationer of his Argenteum Astrum order, which he had formed following his estrangement from the Hermetic Order of the Golden Dawn. Although the two parted company, with Crowley referring to Spare as his 'black brother,' the latter's esoteric explorations continued. Developing a system of magical sigils, he became 'probably the first modern occultist to evolve a self-contained working hypothesis about the nature of psychic energy which could be applied without all the paraphernalia of traditional rituals, grimoires, and magical incantations' (Drury, 1994: 86). Without unpacking Spare's rather convoluted esoteric thought in detail (see Spare, 2001; Baker, 2010), the terms 'Kia' and 'Zos' do need to be introduced, the former being a primal and universal source of being, and the latter being the human body, a channel through which to communicate the occult energies of the psyche. The technique used to summon these primal energies he referred to as 'atavistic resurgence,' a method which involved 'focusing the will on magical sigils, or individualised symbols, which, in effect, represented instructions to the subconscious' (Drury, 1994: 86). It was these ideas that stimulated imaginations within industrial culture. P-Orridge even encouraged John Gosling to name his music project Zos Kia. The advice was accepted and several recordings were released under that name in the mid-1980s (e.g. *Transparent*, 1984). Since then, although still relatively obscure, Sparean esotericism and the terms 'Zos' and 'Kia' have entered popular music occulture (e.g. Behemoth, *Zos Kia Cultus*, 2002; Zero Kama, 'Prayer of Zos', *The Goatherd And The Beast*, 2001; Limbo, *Zos Kia Kaos*, 1994). And, as Davis notes, back in 1971, Jimmy Page, who had become interested in Spare, designed a personal symbol for the fourth Led Zeppelin album, 'Zoso,' which was probably intended to be a sigil for Zos. As Page himself commented enigmatically, 'it wasn't supposed to be a word at all, but something entirely different' (Davis, 2005: 42–43).

P-Orridge has been far less secretive about Spare's influence. Inspired by Kenneth Grant's *Images and Oracles of Austin Osman Spare* (to which he was almost certainly introduced by Tibet, who was a member Grant's Typhonian Ordo Templi Orientis), he developed a Sparean understanding of his own visual and musical creations as sigils. Spare's work also encouraged him to theorize and intellectualize the sexual, so that his fascination with the body (which is conspicuous throughout much of his work) was channeled into the formulation of an esoteric philosophy. Just as Spare had employed a technique of ecstasy, central to which was the orgasm, so P-Orridge states (using deliberately idiosyncratic spelling), 'thee moment ov orgasm is central to thee process. It is special and all should be done to make it so...Sex is thee medium for thee magickal act, enacted physically and with direct control ov thee Individual. It generates thee greatest power which, when released, is diverted from its ordinary object and thrust with thee intense force ov will towards thee fulfillment of desire' (2002: 133). This is pure Spare. The key here is deeply felt desire, the Romantic emphasis on powerfully felt emotion (which, of course, can be evoked by music), on feeling that moves and inspires, on the construction of a highly charged sonic environment for the purpose of meaning making. This, of course, is central to modern occult thought. Congruent with contemporary consumerism and the turn to the self in the modern world, there is a commitment to the belief that any desire deeply felt at the core of the human consciousness is capable of fulfillment. A carefully planned orgasm adds depth to the feeling, thereby increasing the chances of success in manifesting the desire. However, as we have noted, Spare's system also included an added extra—the use of sigils.

Spare's sigilization involved, for example, the writing down of a sentence as concisely as possible, which expresses one's desire; letters are then crossed out so that no letter is repeated; the remaining letters are then combined to produce a sigil. The sigil is then focused on and mentally absorbed, before being destroyed and, as far as possible, completely forgotten. The theory claims that, at the depths of the subconscious, occulted from the conscious mind, it begins to work. Innate psychic energies manifest the sigilized desire. It is not too difficult to understand how P-Orridge believed this occult practice of sigilization might be developed in relation to popular music. Indeed, the statements that music is 'a platform for propaganda' (Vale, 2007: 87), while probably taken from the title of George Orwell's collection of essays *All Art is Propaganda* (2008), needs to be understood in this Sparean sense, as the manifestation of sigilized desire. Of course, at a relatively mundane level, a musician is able to have a significant emotional impact on fans and, through that influence, to acquire the potential to subvert mainstream thinking and challenge established authorities. However, if one imagines that such activities can be coupled with the energies made available by sigilization, then the potential for esoterrorism is significantly increased. Music becomes a 'magick weapon' and performances become the 'casting of spells' (Kenneth Anger, quoted in Rowe, 1974: 26).

Returning to P-Orridge's spelling and grammar, it's worth noting here that this is understood to be a subversive technique, rather than simply a quaint idiosyncrasy. The spelling of 'magick' is, of course, simply taken from Crowley's usage. Hence, the addition of a 'k' to other words signifies esoteric meaning—e.g. Steve Hillage's *Rainbow Dome Musick* (1979) and Coil's *Musick to Play in the Dark* (1999). However, the other idiosyncratic spellings and grammatical constructions are intended to constitute a challenge to thought and ways of reading; a challenge to the ways in which we have learned to think; our angle of vision is bent during the process of reading; we are drawn into closer examination; words are given 'added levels of meaning' (P-Orridge, 2010: 313). In short, sigils, neologisms, idiosyncratic spelling, and dissonant sound subverts learned behaviors and challenges received worldviews. Again, as Davis says of Led Zeppelin's fourth album, the official title of which is spelled out with four well-known symbols/sigils, it seems 'to communicate something without saying anything at all.' He continues, 'when confronted with such inscrutable signs, our natural impulse is to *decode* them, to "know what they mean."' However, when it comes Led Zeppelin's four sigils, 'strict meanings are neither their nature nor their function. These sigils, and the musical sounds they announce, don't *mean* stuff so much as *make stuff happen*. And they make stuff happen by frustrating the conventional process of meaning' (Davis, 2005: 26). In the case of P-Orridge, he has an explicitly Promethean agenda in mind:

> We live in limbo and thirst for freedom...Vested interests of every kind want us lazy and atrophied...Man's fall from grace is his fall from inner security. His defeat is his surrender to conditioned boundaries imposed by the strict regime of acceptability instead of the natural honesty of his individual instinct that recognises all things to be in a state of flux...We are trained to not even *want* to think. Decondition the condition. Conditioning is control. Control is stability. Stability is safety for those with a vested interest in control. Let's go out of control. What breaks this cycle is a psychic jolt. *Music is magick*, a religious phenomena that short circuits control through human response. The moment we forget ourselves and end the limbo-dance we enter a world of struggle, joy and clarity. A tragic, but magickal world where it is possible to accept mortality and thereby deny death. Experience without dogma, anguish without shame or sham. A morality of anti-cult. Occult culture. Its rituals are collective, yet private, performed in public, but invisible...The rites of youth.
>
> (P-Orridge, 2007: 87)

William S. Burroughs, who has been an important influence on P-Orridge's thinking, had been articulating similar ideas for some years. Indeed, in an interview with Jimmy Page in 1975, not only did Burroughs argue that 'Western man has been stifled in a nonmagical universe known as "the way things are",' but he insisted that 'rock music can be seen as one attempt to break out of this dead soulless universe and reassert the universe of magic' (Burroughs, 2008: 168).

Again, it's important to understand here that such ideas are quite distinct from ritualized systems of magick, which introduce elements of control and reflect the conventions of hierarchical society. Unlike Page, P-Orridge was not interested in 'the magick of the Golden Dawn, designed for the stately Victorian manor.' Rather, his was a magick intended 'for the blank-eyed, TV-flattened, prematurely abyss-dwelling youth of the late twentieth century—like the punk kids in Derek Jarman's *Jubilee*, who have never ventured out of the council flats they were born in' (Louv, 1994: 18). Hence, 'rather than high ceremony, drawing-room intrigue and exalted initiatory ritual, the focus more often than not, became simple survival and defense of individual vision from a malevolently dehumanizing culture that the Victorians and Modernists...

could never have foreseen' (Louv, 1994: 18). Similarly, in *Thee Grey Book*—a compendium of techniques written for TOPY and significantly influenced by Tibet and Balance—he states that, 'recognizing thee implicit powers ov thee human brain (neuromancy) linked with guiltless sexuality focused through Will Structure (sigils)... magick empowers thee individual to embrace and realise their dreams and maximise their natural potential' (TOPY, 1982).

As well as P-Orridge's work, Balance's own music, particularly with Peter Christopherson as Coil, was an explicit attempt to experiment with occult power. Drawing on, he claimed, the divinatory theories of John Dee, Crowley, and Spare, he believed he was able to create 'a lunar consciousness musick for the foreseeable future' (quoted in Young, 2010: 605). As John Everall comments, Coil 'warped, twisted and transmitted sound in a manner pertinent to their immersion in the world of esoteric ideas' (Everall, 1995: 18). For example, the album *Scatology* (1985) was conspicuously focused on alchemy. 'I'm obsessed,' admitted Balance, 'with the idea of turning base matter into gold, transmuting base materials, i.e. raw sound, into something else—the gold in the process. We recorded some rather peculiar practices which we then transformed and manipulated in accordance with our specific aims' (quoted in Everall, 1995: 18). Indeed, rather enigmatically, Christopherson insisted that Coil was 'a code. A hidden universal. A key...a spell, a spiral...A whirlwind in a double helix. Electricity and elementals, atonal noise and brutal poetry. A vehicle for obsessions. Kabbalah and Khaus. Thanatos and Thelema. Archangels and Antichrists. Truth and deliberation. Traps and disorientation' (Coil, quoted in Neal, 1987: 117). 'Certain tracks on certain Coil records are designed to trigger altered states,' insists Balance. 'Without wishing to sound pompous, we want to make sacred music' (Balance, quoted in Everall, 1995: 18). Indeed, following Sparean thought, through the manipulation of sound they claimed to have developed 'sidereal sound': 'obviously the term sidereal relates to stars,' says Balance, 'but also through wordplay to looking at reality sideways, from a new angle or perspective. So as Spare twisted images in space, we adopt a similar process with sound. We've always been into sonic deviation and experimentation' (Balance, quoted in Everall, 1995: 18).

CONCLUDING COMMENTS

It is hardly surprising that music, which is so closely wedded to the imagination, to the manipulation of emotion, and to religious ritual (see Partridge, 2013a: 37–59) should be used to articulate esoteric ideas. Moreover, that popular music in particular has consistently been attacked by society's moral gatekeepers (see Partridge, 2013a: 13–36) and is often linked to Dionysian excess and transgression has made its marriage to occult discourse an easy and obvious one. Young (and, nowadays, not so young) people who are often keen to distance themselves from the previous generation's religion and morality, who seek to shape their own liminal identities, have found the cordial relationship between the occult and popular music an engaging and empowering one. Indeed, along with film, popular music has become one of the principal disseminators of occult thought in the modern world. There is little chance that this close and well-matched relationship will not continue to grow in the years that lie ahead.

REFERENCES AND FURTHER READING

Bibliography

Abrahamsson, Carl (2002) 'Changing Compositions,' in Genesis P-Orridge, *Painful but Fabulous: The Lives and Art of Genesis P-Orridge*, New York: Soft Skull Shortwave, 29–39.

Antonia, Nina (1996) *The One and Only: Peter Perrett—Homme Fatale*, Wembley: SAF Publishing.

Arosian Black Mass (2013) 'Information,' http://www.arosian-black-mass.se/info.html (accessed 9 July 2013).

Baddeley, Gavin (1999) *Lucifer Rising*, London: Plexus.

Baker, Phil (2010) *Austin Osman Spare: The Life and Legend of London's Lost Artist*, London: Strange Attractor.

Bowers, Faubian (1996) *Scriabin: A Biography*, vol. 2, second edition, New York: Dover Publications.

Bulgakov, Mikhail (1997) *The Master And Margarita*, trans. by Richard Pevear and Larissa Volokhonsky, London: Penguin.

Burroughs, William S. (2008) 'Uranium Willie and the Heavy Metal Kid: A Near-Forgotten 1975 Talk with Jimmy Page,' in Jon Bream, *Whole Lotta Led Zeppelin: The Illustrated History of the Heaviest Band of All Time*, Minneapolis: Voyageur Press, 166–69.

Carpenter, Alexander (2012) 'The "Ground Zero" of Goth: Bauhaus, "Bela Lugosi's Dead" and the origins of Gothic Rock,' *Popular Music and Society* 35, 25–52.

Churton, Tobias (2012) 'Aleister Crowley and the Yezidis,' in Henrik Bogdan and Martin Starr, eds., *Aleister Crowley and Western Esotericism*, New York: Oxford University Press, 181–208.

Culler, Jonathan (2001) *The Pursuit of Signs: Semiotics, Literature, Deconstruction*, London: Routledge.

Davis, Erik (2005) *Led Zeppelin IV*, New York: Continuum.

Drury, Neville (1994) *Echoes From the Void: Writings on Magic, Visionary Art and the New Consciousness*, Bridport: Prism Press.

Dyrendal, Asbjørn (2009a) 'Satanism and Popular Music,' in Christopher Partridge and Eric Christianson, eds., *The Lure of the Dark Side: Satan and Western Demonology in Popular Culture*, London: Equinox, 25–38.

——(2009b) 'Darkness Within: Satanism as a Self-Religion,' in Jesper Aagaard Petersen, ed., *Contemporary Religious Satanism: A Critical Anthology*, Farnham: Ashgate, 59–74.

Everall, John (1995) 'Obscure Mechanics,' *The Wire* 134, 18.

Fava, Sérgio (2012) '"When Rome Falls, Falls the World": Current 93 and Apocalyptic Folk,' in Christopher Partridge, ed., *Anthems of Apocalypse: Popular Music and Apocalyptic Thought*, Sheffield: Phoenix Press, 72–89.

Faxneld, Per, and Jesper Aagaard Petersen, eds (2012) *The Devil's Party: Satanism in Modernity*, New York: Oxford University Press.

Fisher, Mark (2010) '"Memorex for the Krakens": The Fall's Pulp Modernism,' in Michael Goddard and Benjamin Halligan, eds, *Mark E. Smith and The Fall: Art, Music and Politics*, Farnham: Ashgate, 95–110.

Fitzgerald, Jon, and Philip Hayward (2009), 'Inflamed: Synthetic Folk Music and Paganism in the Island World of *The Wicker Man*,' in Philip Hayward, ed., *Terror Tracks: Music, Sound and Horror Cinema*, London: Equinox, 101–11.

Ford, Simon (1999) *Wreckers of Civilization: The Story of Coum Transmissions and Throbbing Gristle*, London: Black Dog Publishing.

Frazer, James G. (1922) *The Golden Bough: A Study in Magic and Religion*, abridged edition, London: Macmillan.

Goodall, Mark (2010) 'Salford Drift: The Psychogeography of The Fall,' in Michael Goddard and Benjamin Halligan, eds, *Mark E. Smith and The Fall: Art, Music and Politics*, Farnham: Ashgate, 41–53.

Granholm, Kennet (2011) '"Sons of Northern Darkness": Heathen Influences in Black Metal and Neofolk Music,' *Numen* 58, 514–44.

——(2013) 'Ritual Black Metal: Popular Music as Occult Mediation and Practice', *Correspondences* 1.1, 5–33. Available at: http://correspondencesjournal.files.wordpress.com/2013/06/11302_2_granholm.pdf (accessed 9 July 2013).

Green Man (2013), 'About Green Man.' Available at: http://www.greenman.net/info/about-green-man (accessed 5 August 2013).

Habermas, Jürgen (1987) *The Theory of Communicative Action: A Critique of Functionalist Reason*, Vol. 2, trans. by T. McCarthy, London: Polity Press, 113–98.

Harley, Kevin (2006), 'Natasha Khan: Mystery and Magic,' *The Independent* (1 December): Available at: http://www.independent.co.uk/arts-entertainment/music/features/natasha-khan-mystery-and-magic-426447.html (accessed 5 August 2013).

Hegarty, Paul, and Martin Halliwell (2011) *Beyond and Before: Progressive Rock Since the 1960s*, New York: Continuum.

Henderson, Richard (2004) 'Anger is an Energy,' *The Wire* 247, 32–33.

Heylin, Clinton (1989) *Gypsy Love Songs and Sad Refrains: The Recordings of Richard Thompson and Sandy Denny*, Sale: Labour of Love Publications.

Hollings, Ken (2002) 'The Solar Myth Approach,' in Rob Young, ed., *Undercurrents: The Hidden Wiring of Modern Music*, London: Continuum, 99–113.

Howells, Tom, ed. (2012) *Black Metal: Beyond the Darkness*, London: Black Dog Publishing.

Keenan, David (1997) 'Childhood's End,' *The Wire* 163: 34–37.

——(2003a) *England's Hidden Reverse: A Secret History of the Esoteric Underground*, London: SAF Publishing.

——(2003b) 'The Fire Down Below: Welcome to the New Weird America,' *The Wire* 234: 32–41.

LaFontaine, Jean (1999) 'Satanism and Satanic Mythology,' in Bengt Ankarloo and Stuart Clark, eds, *Witchcraft and Magic in Europe: the Twentieth Century*, Philadelphia: University of Pennsylvania Press, 81–140.

Landis, Bill (1995) *Anger: The Unauthorised Biography of Kenneth Anger*, San Francisco: HarperCollins.

Lap, Amina Olander (2012) 'Categorizing Modern Satanism: An Analysis of LaVey's Early Writings,' in Per Faxneld and Jesper Aagaard Petersen, eds, *The Devil's Party: Satanism in Modernity*, New York: Oxford University Press, 83–102.

LaVey, Anton S. (1992) *The Devil's Notebook*, Portland: Feral House.

Lawson, Dom (2011) 'Occult Rock: Do You Believe in Black Magic?' *The Guardian* (24 November), http://www.guardian.co.uk/music/2011/nov/24/occult-rock-black-widow-ghost (accessed 19 April 2013).

Leech, Jeanette (2013) 'Comus Wakes, He Starts to Play…,' in Jon Mills and Andy Morton, eds, *Witches Hats and Painted Chariots: The Incredible String Band and the 5,000 Layers of Psychedelic Folk*, special issue of *Shindig!* (Cambridge: Volcano Publishing), 64–70.

Letcher, Andy (2013) 'Paganism and the British Folk Revival,' in Donna Weston and Andy Bennett, eds, *Pop Pagans: Paganism and Popular Music*, Sheffield: Equinox, 91–109.

Louv, Jason (1994) 'Introduction: On the Way to Thee Garden,' in Genesis P-Orridge, *Thee Psychick Bible: Thee Apocryphal Scriptures of Genesis P-Orridge and Thee Third MIND ov Psychic TV*, Port Townsend: Feral House, 17–28.

Moliné, Keith (2006) 'The Road to Salvation: Current 93,' *The Wire* 269, 28–33.

Neal, Charles (1987) *Tape Delay*, Wembley: SAF Publishing.

Orwell, G. (2008) *All Art is Propaganda: Critical Essays*. New York: Houghton Mifflin Harcourt.

Partridge, Christopher (2004) *The Re-Enchantment of the West: Alternative Spiritualities, Sacralization, Popular Culture and Occulture*, Vol. 1, London: T&T Clark International.

——(2005) *The Re-Enchantment of the West: Alternative Spiritualities, Sacralization, Popular Culture and Occulture*, Vol. 2, London: T&T Clark International.

——(2013a) *The Lyre of Orpheus: Popular Music, the Sacred and the Profane*, New York: Oxford University Press.

——(2013b) 'Esoterrorism and the Wrecking of Civilization: Genesis P-Orridge and the Rise of Industrial Paganism,' in Donna Weston and Andy Bennett, eds, *Pop Pagans: Paganism and Popular Music*, Sheffield: Equinox, 189–212.

Petersen, Jesper Aagaard (2009) 'Introduction: Embracing Satan,' in Jesper Aagaard Petersen, ed., *Contemporary Religious Satanism: A Critical Anthology*, Farnham: Ashgate, 2009, 1–24.

Pinner, David (2011 [1967]) *Ritual*, London: Finders Keepers Records.

Pitzl-Waters, Jason (2013) 'The Darker Shade of Pagan: the Emergence of Goth,' in Donna Weston and Andy Bennett, eds, *Pop Pagans: Paganism and Popular Music*, Sheffield: Equinox, 76–90.

——(2012) 'Musical Influence of The Wicker Man Soundtrack': http://www.adarkershadeofpagan.com/labels/The%20Wicker%20Man.html (accessed 1 May 2012).

P-Orridge, Genesis (2001) 'Genesis P-Orridge,' in V. Vale, ed., *Modern Pagans: An Investigation of Contemporary Paganism*, San Francisco: RE/Search, 122–27.

——(2002) *Painful But Fabulous: The Lives and Art of Genesis P-Orridge*, New York: Soft Skull Shortwave.

——(2007) 'The Lion in a Cage,' in V. Vale, ed., *RE/Search 4/5: William S. Burroughs, Brion Gysin and Throbbing Gristle*, San Francisco: RE/Search Publications, 87.

——(2010) 'The Splinter Test,' in John Zorn, ed., *Arcana V: Music, Magic and Mysticism*, New York: Hips Road, 297–313.

Pouncey, Edwin (2004) 'Industrial Light and Magick,' *The Wire* 247, 34–35.

Rossi, Marco (2013) 'The Incredible World of Wicker, with a Momentary Digression Into String Theory,' in Jon Mills and Andy Morton, eds, *Witches Hats and Painted Chariots: The Incredible String Band and the 5,000 Layers of Psychedelic Folk*, special issue of *Shindig!* (Cambridge: Volcano Publishing), 86–90.

Rowe, Carel (1974) 'Illuminating Lucifer,' *Film Quarterly* 27: 4, 24–33.

Russell, Jeffrey Burton (2005) 'The Romantic Devil,' in Harold Bloom, ed., *Satan*, New York: Chelsea House Publishers, 155–92.

Smith, Harry, 'Liner Notes,' *Anthology of American Folk Music* (Folkways, 1952). The Smithsonian Institution has made Harry Smith's liner notes, along with the notes from the 1997 release of the anthology, available at: http://www.folkways.si.edu/albumdetails.aspx?itemid=2426 (accessed 4 July 2012).

Spare, Austin Osman (2001) *Ethos: The Magical Writings of Austin Osman Spare*, Thame: I-H-O Books.

Sudbin, Yevgeny (2012), 'Scriabin Liner Notes': http://www.yevgenysudbin.com/artist.php?view=essays&rid=456 (accessed on 13 May 2012).

TOPY (1982) *Thee Grey Book*: http://www.kondole.com/theegreybook/greycover.htm (accessed 5 October 2010).

Valcic, Vuc (2012) 'Acid Mothers Temple,' *Rock-A-Rolla* 35 (December 2011–January 2012), 24–28.

Vale, V., ed. (2007) *RE/Search 4/5: William S. Burroughs, Brion Gysin and Throbbing Gristle*, San Francisco: RE/Search Publications.

Wenner, Jann S. (1995) 'The *Rolling Stone* Interview: Jagger Remembers,' http://www.jannswenner.com/Archives/Jagger_Remembers.aspx (accessed 5 February 2012).
Weston, Donna, and Andy Bennett, eds (2013) *Pop Pagans: Paganism and Popular Music*, Sheffield: Equinox.
Wolfe, Burton H. (1969) 'Introduction,' in Anton S. LaVey, *The Satanic Bible*, New York: Avon Books, 9–18.
Young, Rob (2010) *Electric Eden: Unearthing Britain's Visionary Music*, London: Faber & Faber.

Discography

Agalloch, *Whitedivisiongrey* (Licht von Dämmerung Arthouse, 2012).
Damon Albarn, *Dr. Dee* (Parlophone, 2012).
Dave and Toni Arthur, *Hearken to the Witch's Rune* (Trailer, 1970).
Bauhaus, 'Bela Lugosi's Dead' (Small Wonder Records, 1979).
Behemoth, *Zos Kia Cultus (Here And Beyond)* (Olympic Recordings, 2002).
Black Widow, *Sacrifice* (CBS, 1970).
Blue Öyster Cult, *Agents of Fortune* (Columbia, 1976).
Bobby Beausoleil and the Freedom Orchestra, *Lucifer Rising* (Disgust Records, 1981).
Flaming Lips, *The Flaming Lips and Heady Fwends* (Bella Union, 2012).
Graham Bond, *Holy Magick* (Vertigo, 1970).
Graham Bond, *We Put Our Magick on You* (Vertigo, 1971).
Coil, *Scatology* (Force and Form, 1985).
Coil, *Musick to Play in the Dark* (Chalice, 1999).
Comus, *First Utterance* (Dawn, 1971).
Coven, *Witchcraft Destroys Minds and Reaps Souls* (Mercury, 1969).
Current 93, *Nature Unveiled* (L.A.Y.L.A.H Antirecords, 1984).
Current 93, *Crowleymass* (Maldoror, 1987).
Death in Vegas, *Scorpio Rising* (Concrete, 2002)
Deerhoof, *Friend Opportunity* (Kill Rock Stars, 2007).
Doves, *Lost Sides* (Heavenly Records, 2003).
Electric Wizard, *Witchcult Today* (Rise Above Records, 2007).
Electric Wizard, *Black Masses* (Rise Above Records, 2010).
Faith and the Muse, *The Burning Season* (Metropolis Records, 2003).
Nat Freedland, *The Occult Explosion* (United Artists, 1973).
The Go! Team, *Proof of Youth* (Tearbridge International (Japan), 2007).
Gong, *Magick Brother* (Charly Records, 1970).
The Green Man, *From Irem to Summerisle* (Hau Ruck! SPQR, 2009).
Steve Hillage, *Rainbow Dome Musick* (Virgin, 1979).
The Incredible String Band, *The Hangman's Beautiful Daughter* (Elektra, 1968).
Iron Maiden, *Brave New World* (EMI, 2000).
Killing Joke, *The Courtauld Talks* (Invisible Records, 1989).
Bill Laswell, *Hashisheen: The End of Law* (Sub Rosa, 1999)
Led Zeppelin, *IV* (Atlantic, 1971).
Limbo, *Zos Kia Kaos* (Discordia, 1994)
Momus and Anne Laplantine, *Summerisle* (Analog Baroque, 2004).
Naked City, *Heretic: Jeux Des Dames Cruelles* (Avant, 1992).
Nature and Organization, *Beauty Reaps The Blood of Solitude* (Durtro, 1994).
Ouijabeard, *Die and Let Live* (High Roller Records, 2012).
Jimmy Page, *Lucifer Rising and Other Soundtracks* (Jimmypage.com, 2012).
Plague Lounge, *The Wicker Image* (New World Of Sound/Holy Mountain, 1996).

Ramases, *Space Hymns* (Vertigo, 1971).
The Rolling Stones, *Their Satanic Majesties Request* (Decca, 1967).
The Rolling Stones, *Beggars Banquet* (Decca, 1968).
Sneaker Pimps, *Becoming X* (Clean Up Records, 1996).
Sun Ra, *Space is the Place* (Blue Thumb Records, 1973).
Us and Them, *Summerisle* (Fruits De Mer, 2011).
Various artists, *Anthology of American Folk Music* (Folkways, 1952).
Various Artists, *Looking for Europe: A Neofolk Compendium* (Auerbach Tonträger, 2005).
The Watersons, *Frost and Fire: A Calendar of Ritual and Magical Songs* (Topic Records, 1965).
Wold, *Freermasonry* (Profound Lore Records, 2011).
Zero Kama, *The Goatherd And The Beast* (Athanor, 2001).
Zos Kia/Coil, *Transparent* (Nekrophile Records, 1984).

Filmography

The Devil Rides Out (1968). Directed by Terence Fisher.
Heaven and Earth Magic (1957). Directed by Harry Smith.
Lucifer Rising (1970–80). Directed by Kenneth Anger.
The Wicker Man (1973). Directed by Robert Hardy.

CHAPTER FIFTY-THREE

THE OCCULT ON THE INTERNET

Douglas E. Cowan

SCREENSHOTS FROM THE ONLINE OCCULT

In the summer of 2010, Salem, Missouri resident Anaka Hunter went to her local public library to research her Wiccan beliefs, as well as the religious traditions of various indigenous peoples in the region. Searching the Internet, however, she was astonished to find access to a number of Web sites blocked by the library's Internet filter software, much of which was designed originally to filter sexually explicit content from publicly accessible computers. When she complained to the librarian, Hunter was told that these sites would only be unblocked if the librarian 'felt patrons had a legitimate reason to view the content' (ACLU, 2012). In Hunter's case not only would most of the sites *not* be unblocked, but the librarian also said that she 'had an "obligation" to call the "proper authorities" to report those who were attempting to access blocked sites if she thought they would misuse the information they were attempting to access' (Patrick, 2013). The librarian would not comment on what she meant by 'misuse' nor who constituted 'the proper authorities.'

According to the brief filed by the American Civil Liberties Union, the librarian's response caused Hunter 'to be reasonably concerned that she would be reported to the police if she continued to attempt to access websites about Native American cultural and religious history and the Wiccan Church' (Hunter v. Salem et al.). Notwithstanding the implicit though not insignificant threat here, and the anxiety this can easily cause among members of 'minority religions in a majoritarian America' (Barner-Barry, 2005), the library's filter software categorized the sites Hunter wanted as 'occult' and 'criminal skills.' According to the ACLU, among other sites similarly categorized and blocked were: All About Spirituality; Astrology.com; the official site of the Wiccan Church; the Wikipedia entry on Wicca; and Witchvox.com, arguably the largest repository of modern Pagan material on the Internet (see Cowan, 2005). *Not* blocked, however, were a number of sites that considered the same subject matter, but from a Christian countercult perspective, including the online *Catholic Encyclopedia* entry on Wicca, 'Christian Paranormal Answers,' and 'What Does the Bible Say about Voodoo?' (Complaint, 2012).

Nearly three years later, in early March 2013, a federal judge E. Richard Webber prohibited the Salem library from 'reactivating' the filter software. Although this may seem like something of a victory for those who hold to principles of the freedom of religion and freedom of information, it raises a number of important questions, both in terms of ongoing social construction of the occult in late modern society and the ways in which such processes as Internet filtering invoke a surveillance culture on those prejudices. Put differently, how many people have searched for similar topics at public libraries, found nothing or were blocked, but did *not* take the issue up with library staff? How many did complain to staff, but were too frightened by the response to proceed any further?

Nearly 2000 kilometres southwest of Salem, in the posh community of Scottsdale, Arizona, Bob Larson sits in a basement office, staring intently into his computer screen. A young man stares back, his image blurred a bit by the screen, the camera that is recording the scene, and the fact that they are connecting over Skype. The young man, David, is in Norway and, according to Larson, is possessed by multiple demons. Larson is attempting to exorcise those demons over the Internet. Looking these days more like a Roman Catholic priest than the fundamentalist Protestant that he is, Larson raises his finger and traces the sign of the cross in front of the screen. 'I'm going to reach out, across the miles, and anoint you in the name of the Father, the Son, and the Holy Spirit' (Tuchman, 2014)—behavior evocative of early televangelists who encouraged viewers to place their hands on the television to feel the same Holy Spirit touch them across the miles. This is the same Bob Larson discussed in Chapter 73 who has been training his teenage daughter and her four friends as teen exorcists.

David, though, who looks as though he would be comfortable in a mosh pit at a black metal concert (see Moynihan and Søderlind, 2003), taunts Larson. 'Are you Bob the Builder?' he screeches, laughing in a parody of mania. He looks off-screen, 'I guess he's Bob the Builder.' Larson responds calmly, the same ornate pewter cross used by his daughter held up in front of the screen. 'You have mocked the servant of God,' he intones. Drawing back his arm, he flings the cross forward toward the young man's image. 'You will be struck with *judgment* for mocking the servant of God!' Alternating between the cross and a heavy, leather-bound Bible, which he moves in a circle in front of his computer, Larson engages the 'demon.' Toward the end of this session, and reminiscent of the famous *Exorcist* scene in which Fathers Karras and Merrin chant, 'The power of Christ compels you!' Larson shakes his cross at the screen, shouting at the image, 'Judgment strikes you! Judgment strikes you!'

According to Gary Tuchman, the *CNN* reporter who filed the story, it took more than an hour to rid David of his demons, 'for now,' he says. As they sign off, a young blonde woman appears in the background on David's screen. 'God bless, bye, bye,' says Larson cheerfully. 'OK, bye, bye,' David replies, the young woman waving from the background. 'With all due respect,' says Tuchman, 'some of what we just watched seemed like a very disturbing nightclub act' (2014). 'It isn't,' Larson replies simply. 'It's real. There would be no need to theatrically stage this for any reason. Why would anybody do that? I have no idea' (Tuchman, 2014). As we discuss below, though, it may be the nearly US$300 per hour Larson charges for his online exorcisms.

Although not all of them occur over the Internet, Larson claims to conduct between five hundred and one thousand exorcisms every year.

These two vignettes illustrate a number of aspects related to the occult on the Internet: the search for information about the occult, whether by practitioners or simply interested parties; the social opprobrium (and social control) that still attaches to popular interest in the topic and the fear this can generate; use of the Internet for what may be considered occult purposes, in this case, Larson's putative exorcism of David; and the Internet as a site for contested points of view, a venue for the range of conversation that Berger and Luckmann (1966) contend is crucial to worldview-maintenance and reinforcement. That is, as it is for so many things, the Internet is an environment for information, exploration, performance, and communication, though not so very different onscreen as off-.

THE OCCULT ON THE INTERNET

Although *Cyberhenge*, my book about modern Pagans on the Internet, appeared just prior to the invention of what we now know as 'social media' (Cowan, 2005), relatively little has changed in terms of how people use the online environment to pursue activities related to their occult interests. Even with the advent of social media and the increasing social penetration of smartphones, iPads, easily transportable notebooks, and widely available wi-fi networks—that is, technology that liberates the user from a fixed computing position—the majority of online activity remains (and, I would argue, will remain for the foreseeable future) a function of offline interests and pursuits. Only a small percentage of users will conduct their religious business, as it were, entirely in the online environment. And, for many of those, it will eventually translate into offline activity, or wither to insignificance. Thus, in very broad terms, the Internet and the occult come together in four principal modes.

First and foremost, like Anaka Hunter and tens of thousands of others like her, the Internet is a venue for *information about the occult*, most of which will be used in offline pursuits. Second, though, and intimately related, the Internet is a *contested information space*, a realm of shifting social controls and ideological conflicts the contours of which occasionally depend on nothing more than one's offline location. Put differently, would Hunter have encountered the same resistance from her local librarian if she were accessing the Internet at a branch of the public library in New York, Los Angeles, Toronto, or London? On the other hand, consider the Web sites to which the library's filter software *did not* limit access, specifically Christian sites claiming to 'expose' the dangers of the occult. However popular it may be, fear of the occult remains deeply embedded in the late modern West.

Third, and I would suggest this is the most significant in terms of identity-construction, maintenance, and experimentation, the Internet is a *communication tool*, a multimodal platform through which like encounters like, through which young women in Salem, Missouri find out they are not alone in their religious interests, and through which they can seek support in the emergence and development of their religious identities. Although this does not seem to be the case with Anaka Hunter, a considerable amount of modern Pagan online interaction involves identity experimentation. Young women (and some young men) try on, as it were, pagan or occult identities, identities that would never be sanctioned in their offline worlds. On the other hand, when one considers YouTube comments on Bob Larson's 'virtual exorcism,' especially comments skeptical of him, we experience the Internet as a vast kind of 'speaker's corner,' an interactive discussion that both challenges and reinforces one's beliefs about the world, both online and off-.

Finally, we have the ways in which the online environment is used *for occult practice*—a fundamentalist Christian exorcism over Skype or, as I saw in the boarding lounge at an Arizona airport, a woman clearly involved in New Age spirituality staring intently at her iPad while circling her hands over the image on the screen. Although this type of behavior is arguably the least common in terms of overall Internet usage, it is perhaps the most interesting in terms of the different ways technology shapes and informs religious belief and practice. That is, while there are modern Pagans who consider computer technology quite literally a kind of magic. In these cases 'magic' is almost a synonym for 'we don't understand how it works,' a theoretical position that wilfully ignores the fact that millions of people around the world understand precisely how computer technology works. Complex algorithms determine computer function based on user input, software design, firmware limitations, and hardware configuration. What happens, though, when users see all this as a function of their magical or occult worldview, when they map their understanding of the 'unseen order' onto the machine language and application code of computer programming? I think it's axiomatic that very few people will be conducting exorcisms over Skype or sending healing energies through their tablet computers, but this does not mean that the Internet is not used for occult practice. Let us consider the online manifestation of one of the most common occult practices: divination.

ORACLES AND ALGORITHMS

Apart from those whose religious identities are formed around different occult spiritualities—whether positive, negative, or skeptical—the most common occult involvement is arguably divination, specifically astrology (see Stark and Bainbridge, 1985) and Tarot (see, for example, Jorgenson, 1992). Unfortunately, the explosion of popular interest in all manner of divination practices, technologies, and textual resources has not been matched by significant academic interest. In the area of Tarot alone, for example, hundreds of different decks are now available, with dozens more in the design and production stages, all of which reflect a wide variety of spiritual interests, paths, and motivations.

And, not surprisingly, Tarot has moved online. Scores of Web sites offer Tarot readings over the Internet. Some of these provide the divination right on the screen, while others connect the visitor to a Tarot reader elsewhere. Some require the user to join a 'community,' the information from which is shared with other online service providers. Hundreds of discussion groups on a wide variety of portals have been created to discuss all aspects of Tarot history, imagery, and usage. Although, like the modern Pagan discussion groups I consider in *Cyberhenge* (Cowan 2005), relatively few of these groups have more than a handful of members who contribute regularly to discussions, that so many have emerged at all indicates something of the popular interest these practices hold.

Paul O'Brien is the founder, CEO, and 'chief visionary' of a Portland, Oregon, company called Visionary Networks, which operates Tarot.com, one of the most elaborate online divination services I have been able to find. Founded in 1988, O'Brien's company originally produced divination programs on CD-ROM, intending them for online purchase, but offline use. With the emergence of the Internet in 1995, his company's business plan shifted to the online environment. Tarot.com's 'mission is to provide universal access to time-honored divination systems that support deeper self-knowledge and genuinely mystical experiences, using the Internet and other interactive media' (2014)—practices O'Brien distinguishes from psychic hotlines and fortune tellers.

Currently, Tarot.com offers readings in Tarot, astrology, numerology, and the *I Ching*, and company press releases assert that the Tarot portion of these sites alone is providing between one and two million free readings per month. O'Brien's particular claim to fame in the growing field of online divination is the alleged complexity of the algorithms that control the readings, and what he calls the 'energetically authentic' manner in which the divination itself proceeds.

Free Tarot readings on Tarot.com are offered as a basic three-card spread—one card each is 'drawn' to represent the 'self' (i.e., how the inquirer views him- or herself), the 'situation' about which the question is being asked, and the 'challenges or opportunities' that inhere in the relationship between them; alternatively, this 'simple spread,' as it's also known, can be interpreted as indicating the present, past, and future of a particular situation. Visitors can either type in a few words about their specific question or select from more general situational descriptors: love, relationship, or one's personal situation. Once selected, the image of a deck of cards fanned face down appears on the screen and visitors are invited to choose from over fifty different Tarot decks for the specific images in their readings. Operationally, clicking anywhere on the fanned deck turns over a card and locates it in a particular place in the reading. Once all three cards are revealed, the program requires visitors to sign up for a 'free account,' before generating an interpretation based, according to the site operators, on both the general meaning of the card, and the more specific meaning relative to that particular card's position in the spread. To secure a more detailed reading, visitors can click to draw the other seven cards in a classic 'Celtic Cross' spread, but are required to pay for the more extensive online interpretation. Tarot.com remains, after all, a business.

Llewellyn Publications, the St. Paul-based publisher of hundreds of New Age, occult, and modern Pagan titles, also operates an online Tarot service on its commercial Web site (www.llewellyn.com/free/tarot.php). Here the service is entirely free and visitors have the choice of seven different spreads. There are, however, noticeable differences and arguable drawbacks to the algorithmic process on the Llewellyn site. Visitors, for example, have no option to input anything about their question or concern. They are simply instructed to 'select a deck and spread' for their readings, then 'think of a question or an object of concern.' That is, the program has no way of 'reading' the querent's question or concern; it cannot search for trigger words or phrases, nor tailor its response to input from the querent. The onscreen instructions, however, assure users that 'Your Web Tarot reading will help you find the answer.' Once 'your mind is focused,' 'click the button to proceed with your free tarot reading.' Rather than choose one card at a time, this program generates all the cards at once. Very general interpretative comments, 'canned readings,' as it were, accompany the Tarot images the program selects. Not nearly as detailed or positionally specific as the Tarot.com site, each reading is accompanied by various offers to purchase that particular deck of cards, other artwork by the artist, or books about the Tarot. Llewellyn Publications remains, after all, a business.

It is easy enough to dismiss such Web sites as the latest technological advance of the occult, or to explain them away as crass commercialism rather than trying to understand them as responses to cultural interest and investment. In the modern and late modern periods, numerous researchers have condemned divination practices as little more than the generic commentary of charlatans playing on the narcissistic specificity of the gullible. More than fifty years ago, for example, in what has become known as the 'Forer Effect,' or the principle of subjective validation, psychologist Bertram Forer (1949) found that subjects tend to interpret vague, general divinatory statements such as those produced by the Llewellyn and Tarot.com sites as though they were highly relevant and particular to themselves; repeating the experiment, others (e.g., Dickson and Kelly, 1985) found that the addition or highlighting of simple phrases such as 'for you' increases this effect significantly.

There are at least a couple of problems with approaches such as these. First, a scientistic tenor is reminiscent of Freud's rather uncharitable introduction to *Totem and Taboo* ([1918] 1950). Second, and more importantly, however, while they do proffer *an* explanation for the phenomena—its purveyors are charlatans, its participants either gullible, deluded, or regressively infantile—this kind of an explanation is overly simplistic sociologically, and does not even attempt to *account* for these phenomena in terms of (a) divination's cross-cultural (some would argue pan-cultural) existence; (b) its popular emergence and growth in North America over the past few decades; (c) the internal logics by which participants justify their participation; and (d) the myriad ways in which these participants negotiate meaning and establish hierarchies of authority within divination subcultures—especially now over the Internet.

In a brief article several years ago, Jürgen Sørenson (1999) suggested that comparative research into systems of divination—which we could extend to consideration of any occult systems, either online or offline—should be structured according to common constituents of the oracular process: the 'experiment,' that is, the actual mechanism of divination, the outcome of which is not available prior to the event; an 'exemplar text' to which this experimental outcome is applied (e.g., the *I Ching* or the Tarot images); and an '*ad hoc* interpretation' on the basis of which the divinatory reading itself is made. To these he added that researchers should consider the shared cosmology of diviner and inquirer, as well as 'the ways in which the verdicts of divination acquire authority' (Sørenson 1999, 186). To this model, I would propose two particular refinements, one fairly simple, the other more complex, both of which would be well served by more intentional cross-cultural investigation, analysis, and comparison, and both of particular interest to the exploration of the occult on the Internet.

First, there is 'the interaction factor.' That is, how much does the diviner know about the inquirer and his or her problem, and, between them, who makes the final divinatory interpretation? Though there are obviously nuances within the framework, two basic interactional positions emerge in the online examples above, positions we might call 'supply-side' interpretation and 'client-side' interpretation. In supply-side divination, the diviner both knows the inquirer's question and shapes the content of the interpretation according to that knowledge. In client-side interpretation, on the other hand, the diviner knows nothing about the inquirer and his or her question, but offers the divination for the inquirer to interpret entirely.

Online divination functions in both ways, at least in its freeware version. Freeware Tarot.com readings respond to specific questions, however rudimentary. While some might argue that simply typing in a short question stretches the concept of 'interaction,' the program does generate a portion of the 'exemplar text'—whether Tarot or *I Ching*—in response to online user input. In this, it is at least minimally supply-sided. The Llewellyn program offers no such option; it is 'client-sided' in that onscreen instructions simply encourage the visitor to 'hold your question in your mind' while 'choosing' the cards or pressing the button. Interpretation and application to one's own circumstance is entirely the responsibility of the client.

FURTHER DIRECTIONS

As I noted above, the majority of online activity is still related to offline pursuits, if for no other reason that that we are ineluctably embodied and, short of *uploading* (transferring our consciousness to a computer, à la Stephen King's *Lawnmower Man* or *The X-Files*' 'Kill Switch'), we live the majority of our lives offline. That said, how we understand the nature of our online involvement is changing significantly. For example, how do those who grew up with Facebook think about their online interactions? For me, such interactions are little more than a nuisance, a distraction from almost anything else I would rather be doing. For younger people, however, those for whom social interaction has been framed and shaped by social media—including their understanding of spiritual pursuits such as investigation of the occult or the practice of modern Paganism—this understanding is likely very different. Although I would not consider a Facebook discussion group on the occult *participation* in the same way I would a coven gathering together offline to celebrate one of their rituals, how do those who do participate online regard this behavior? This is an important question for future researchers to explore.

Elsewhere, I have written about the real-life emergence of new religious traditions based on the occult fiction of H.P. Lovecraft (Cowan, 2012). What about the use of online role-playing games as venues for occult performance? Some work has been done in this area, but very little of substance or theoretical weight. A number of the most popular MMORPGs are explicitly based on an occult worldview, a worldview in which the laws of nature can be bent, gnostic mysteries uncovered and used in the pursuit of one's goals, and powers gained as experience accrues and knowledge deepens in gameplay. How do players in these environments understand this behavior? Is it purely fantasy, a game-playing experience safely and completely left behind with log-off, or is it something more?

REFERENCES AND FURTHER READING

ACLU. 2012. 'Hunter v. Salem Public Library Board of Trustees.' Press release (January 3); retrieved from www.aclu.org/religion-belief/hunter-v-salem-public-library-board-trustees, December 12, 2012.

Barner-Barry, Carol. 2005. *Contemporary Paganism: Minority Religions in a Majoritarian America*. New York: Palgrave Macmillan.

Berger, Peter, and Thomas Luckmann. 1966. *The Social Construction of Reality: A Treatise on the Sociology of Knowledge*. Harmondsworth, UK: Penguin.

Complaint, *Hunter v. City of Salem, Missouri, et al.* (Eastern District of Missouri, 2012), Case No. 4:12CV00004 ERW.

Cowan, Douglas E. 2005. *Cyberhenge: Modern Pagans on the Internet*. London and New York: Routledge.

——. 2012. 'Dealing a New Religion: Material Culture, Divination, and Hyper-religious Innovation.' In *The Brill Handbook of Hyper-Real Religion*, ed. Adam Possamai, 247–65. Leiden: Brill.

Dickson, D. H., and I. W. Kelly. 1985. 'The "Barnum Effect" in Personality Assessment: A Review of the Literature.' *Psychological Reports* 57, no. 2: 367–82.

Forer, Bertram. 1949. 'The Fallacy of Personal Validation: A Classroom Demonstration of Gullibility.' *Journal of Abnormal and Social Psychology* 44, no. 1: 118–23.

Freud, Sigmund. [1918] 1950. *Totem and Taboo: Some Points of Agreement Between the Mental Lives of Savages and Neurotics*, trans. James Strachey. New York: W.W. Norton.

Jorgenson, Danny L. 1992. *The Esoteric Scene, Cultic Milieu, and Occult Tarot*. New York and London: Garland.

Moynihan, Michael, and Didrik Søderlind. 2003. *Lords of Chaos: The Bloody Rise of the Satanic Metal Underground*, rev. ed. Los Angeles: Feral House.

Patrick, Robert. 2013. 'Missouri library agrees not to block witch websites.' *St. Louis Post-Dispatch* (March 6); retrieved from http://www.stltoday.com/news/local/crime-and-courts/missouri-library-agrees-not-to-block-witch-websites, December 12, 2013.

Sørenson, Jürgen P. 1999. 'On Divination: An Exercise in Comparative Method.' In *Approaching Religion*, ed. Tore Ahlbäck. Åbo, Finland: Donner Institute for Research in Religion and Cultural History.

Stark, Rodney, and William Sims Bainbridge. 1985. *The Future of Religion: Secularization, Revival, and Cult Formation*. Berkeley and Los Angeles: University of California Press.

Tarot.com. 2014. Mission statement; retrieved from www.tarot.com/mission-statement, 10 January 2014.

Tuchman, Gary. 2014. 'Evangelical Christian reverend performs exorcisms by Skype.' *Anderson Cooper 360* (January 24); retrieved from www.cnn.com/video/data/2.0/ video/living/2014/01/25/ac-pkg-tuchman-reverend-exorcisms.cnn.html, 25 January 2014.

PART VII

BELIEFS, PRACTICES, ISSUES, AND APPROACHES

CHAPTER FIFTY-FOUR

KABBALAH

Peter J. Forshaw

MEDIEVAL JEWISH KABBALAH

Kabbalah has its origins in the Middle Ages, for it is in twelfth-century France that we find the first historical stages of this form of Jewish mysticism described as 'Kabbalah' and practitioners who call themselves 'Kabbalists' (Scholem 1978, p. 42ff). The Hebrew term Kabbalah is generally translated as 'reception', 'received lore', or 'doctrine received by oral tradition', referring to a series of revelations stretching back variously to Moses, Abraham and, for some, even Adam, that had been preserved in the form of a secret oral tradition, passed down over the generations from master to disciple. In Christian Cabala the most commonly reported tradition described a twin revelation on Mount Sinai when Moses, receiving both the Law and the knowledge of wondrous things, was told 'These words shalt thou declare, and these shalt thou hide' (2 Esdras 14:6). Consequently, while the Ten Commandments were revealed to all, a secret teaching was transmitted only to the elect few.

There are, of course, Jewish practices and texts that serve as precursors to the Kabbalah, for example, the Hekhalot or Heavenly Halls literature, dating back to late antiquity, and the influential *Sefer Yetzirah* or *Book of Formation*, variously dated as second to fourth century CE, which while classed as proto-Kabbalah is undeniably one of the most important sources of inspiration for Kabbalistic commentaries.

Strictly speaking, the first text generally recognized as a work of Kabbalah is the *Sefer ha-Bahir* (*Book of Illumination*), dated back to the second half of the twelfth century. The *Bahir* presents itself as a series of dialogues between master and disciples, providing commentaries on the first chapters of Genesis, on the hidden significance of the Hebrew letters, on statements from the *Sefer Yetzirah*, and so forth. It introduces for the first time the concept of the *ilan* or divine tree, with ten branches, a system of emanations, which constitute the divine *pleroma*. These emanations, the ten *sefirot* had already been introduced in the *Sefer Yetzirah* as corresponding to ten fundamental 'numerations', but it was in the *Bahir* that they first came to be regarded as divine attributes, powers emanating from the Godhead (Scholem 1978, p. 96ff).

The following century bore witness to the appearance of the *Sefer ha-Zohar* (*Book of Splendor*) by Moses ben Shem Tov de Leon in Spain, who claimed to be drawing from pre-existing manuscript material reaching back to the second-century rabbi Shimon bar Yochai. The *Zohar* is a vast collection of texts, including Sifra diTzni'uta (Book of the Hidden), Idra Rabba (Great Assembly), Idra Zuta (Smaller Assembly), Ra'aya Meheimna (Faithful Shepherd) and Midrash haNe'elam (Hidden Midrash), which present the reader with commentary on the Torah, ranging from the nature of God, the structure of the cosmos, the primordial man, Adam Kadmon, the emanation of the four worlds Atziluth, Beriah, Yetzirah, & Assiah, the nature of souls, the notion of redemption, the forces of evil (*kliphot*), and how the individual practitioner relates to God and the rest of creation. Two major points of focus involve *Ma'aseh Bereshit* (Work of Creation), based on the exegesis of Genesis 1 and 2, and *Ma'aseh Merkavah* (Work of the Chariot), visions and speculations involving the Throne on its Chariot in the first chapter of Ezekiel (Matt 1983; Liebes 1993; Giller 2001).

Following the expulsion of the Jews from Spain in 1492 and then from Portugal in 1497, these kabbalistic works and ideas enjoyed a wide dissemination throughout Europe in Sephardic and Hasidic communities, so much so that the *Zohar* became the authoritative text for most Jewish Kabbalists. By this time, as Moshe Idel has shown, there were three major models of Kabbalah: the ecstatic or prophetic Kabbalah of the school of Abraham Abulafia (1240–91) with its emphasis on the permutations of the *Shemot* (divine names) for possible union with the divine, the Theosophical-Theurgical Kabbalah, as exemplified by Menahem Recanati (1250–1310) with its focus on the *Sefirot*, and the astromagical Kabbalah articulated by Yohanan Alemanno (1435–c.1504) (Idel 2011, p. 328ff). Each of these represents different combinations and considerations of the balance between speculative and practical Kabbalah, between scriptural exegesis and action.

BEGINNINGS OF CHRISTIAN KABBALAH

Various candidates have been proposed for the origins of a specifically Christian Kabbalah. The oldest record of a conversion to Christianity due to kabbalistic exegesis of scripture is found in Abulafia's writing, where he reports a group of disciples who converted to Catholicism (Scholem 1997, p. 25). Early candidates are the conversos Raymund Martini (1220–85), whose *Pugio Fidei* (*Dagger of Faith*) contained Christological speculations that contributed to the notion of a Christian appropriation of Kabbalah and the philosopher and anti-Jewish polemicist Abner of Burgos (b. c.1270) (Scholem 1997, p. 18; Idel 2011, pp. 227–35). Also proposed is their contemporary, the Majorcan mystic Ramon Lull (1225–1315), under whose name appeared the pseudepigraphic *De auditu Kabbalistico* (*On Kabbalistic audition*), which, despite its title, displays little evidence of any knowledge of the Jewish tradition (Blau 1944, p. 117; Hames 2000, p. 27). Paulo de Heredia's (d. 1486) *Iggeret ha-Sodot* (*Epistle of Secrets*) is sometimes considered to be the first recognizable work of Christian Kabbalah, one cited by influential Christian exponents, including Petrus Galatinus (1460–1540) and Athanasius Kircher (1601/2–1680), though of a somewhat dubious reputation, given Heredia's tendency to cite from unidentified, possibly non-existent Kabbalistic works and to distort quotes from genuine sources like the Zohar (Scholem 1997, p. 30ff).

GIOVANNI PICO DELLA MIRANDOLA: FATHER OF CHRISTIAN KABBALAH

A watershed in the history of Hebrew studies in Europe, however, most convincingly occurs with the syncretic Italian philosopher Count Giovanni Pico della Mirandola (1463–94), the first Christian by birth known to have studied Hebrew and Aramaic in order to learn about Kabbalah and generally credited as being the first to introduce Kabbalah into Christian circles, thereby earning the title of Father of Christian Cabala (Idel 1993, p. 16). So great was Pico's enthusiasm for this Jewish mystical tradition that in 1486 at the age of 23 the 'Phoenix of his Age' published 900 *Philosophical, Kabbalistical and Theological Conclusions*, with plans for a debate in Rome before the Pope and leading theologians and scholars of his day. The debate never took place but the Pope ended up condemning a number of Pico's theses as heretical, including the declaration that 'There is no science that assures us more of the divinity of Christ than magic and Cabala' (Farmer 1998, p. 497). The forty-seven 'Cabalistic Conclusions according to the secret doctrine of the Hebrew Cabalist Wisemen' (taken directly from Jewish sources, such as Menahem Recanati's *Commentary on the Pentateuch*, Joseph Gikatilla's *Gates of Justice*, and the *Bahir*) and seventy-two 'Cabalistic conclusions according to my own opinion, strongly confirming the Christian religion using the Hebrew Wisemen's own principles' (drawing from works by Abulafia, Azriel of Gerona, and Recanati, whose writings contain numerous quotes from the *Zohar*), supplemented by further references to Kabbalah in other groups of Conclusions, and the claims that Pico made concerning the Kabbalah were to leave an enduring impression on early modern esoteric thought (Secret 1964 Cap. III; Reichert 1995, pp. 195–207).

Two of Pico's favoured authors were Recanati and Abulafia, who represent the bipartite division Pico proposes in his Cabalistic Conclusions Confirming the Christian Religion, where he asserts 'Whatever other Cabalists say, in a first division I distinguish the science of Cabala into the science of *sefirot* and *shemot*, as it were into practical and speculative science' (Farmer 1998, p. 519). This division implies two different conceptions of kabbalah: the speculative kabbalah of the *sefirot* and the practical or ecstatic, prophetic kabbalah of the divine names. Pico's first set of kabbalistic conclusions is almost exclusively concerned with the *sefirot*, while the second set, which begins with the above distinction, considers both approaches. Although Pico does not enter into a detailed or systematic discussion of the important Kabbalistic doctrines of the *sefirot*, the paths of wisdom, and the gates of intelligence, he does show that he is aware of these teachings and understands their relation to kabbalistic theories of creation and revelation. We find many of the themes to be adopted by later Christian Cabalists, such as the vital significance of the Hebrew letters and their connection to the *sefirot*, as well as the privileged status of the Hebrew language with relation to magic.

Pico expressly declares that his primary motivation for adopting certain exegetical techniques found in Kabbalah is their use for evangelical purposes against Jews and heretics. His interpretation of kabbalah attempts to fuse a specifically Christian concept of the Divine act of redemption through Jesus with notions of creation and revelation common to both Judaism and Christianity, in order to provide a Christian interpretation to existing texts and adopt recognizable doctrines, symbols and methods for apologetic and polemical purposes. The kabbalistic method of reading Hebrew texts without diacritic marks, that is, without any vowel indicators, increases interpretative possibilities, giving rise to multiple readings of a single text, including the possibility of proving the supremacy of the name of Jesus and the mystery of the Trinity.

The significance of Pico's Kabbalah should not, however, be restricted simply to Christian apologetics, for he goes beyond the confirmation of Christianity. In his desire to establish the unity of truth, he is keen to point out correspondences between not just Judaism and Christianity, but also show the relation between them and Platonism, between mysticism and magic. Chaim Wirszubski emphasizes that Pico viewed Kabbalah from an entirely new standpoint, arguing 'he is the first Christian who considered cabala to be simultaneously a witness for Christianity and an ally of natural magic' (Wirszubski 1989, p. 151). Indeed, the extreme nature of the claims Pico makes regarding the role of Kabbalah was instrumental in ensuring a widespread interest in this mystical Jewish tradition, among both sympathetic and antagonistic audiences.

A German contemporary of Pico, the humanist scholar Johannes Reuchlin (1455–1522) represents a more systematic and in-depth engagement with Kabbalah. Reuchlin was the first German scholar to promote the study of Hebrew, indeed the leading Christian Hebraist of his time. Amongst his publications are two of the most influential books of Christian Cabala, the *De Verbo Mirifico* (*On the Wonder-Working Word*, 1494) and the *De Arte Cabalistica* (*On the Cabalistic Art*, 1517). In these works Reuchlin introduced the Latin West to the names and theories of some of the important Jewish and Kabbalist thinkers, including Azriel of Gerona, Eleazar of Worms, Menahem Recanati, and most of all Joseph Gikatilla.

At the same time as being a propagator of Christian Cabala, Reuchlin also claimed to be a restorer of the doctrines of Pythagoras, one of the *prisci sapienti* or ancient wise men. Reuchlin propounds the fundamental similarity between Pythagorean and Kabbalistic teachings, the intention of both being 'to bring men's minds to the gods, that is, to lead them to perfect blessedness.' He defines Kabbalah in Pythagorean terms as 'symbolic theology' (Reuchlin 1993, pp. 233, 241). Both traditions communicate their mysteries by means of symbols, signs, adages and proverbs, numbers and figures, letters, syllables and words. Hence the symbolic similarities between the Hebrew *Tetragrammaton*, the powerful divine name of four letters YHVH, and the Pythagorean *Tetraktys* (Zika 1976).

One of the main reasons why Christians like Pico and Reuchlin were interested in the Kabbalah, was the novel use it made of hermeneutical techniques, an approach that introduced Christian exegetes to a radically new concept of language. The Jewish method of exegesis, employed in midrashic and kabbalistic texts, was fundamentally different to Christian methods of interpretation: while the latter concentrated on the semiotic level of meaning of text, the Jewish approach reshaped and transformed the text itself, seeing significance in the shapes and parts of the individual letters, the vocalization points, their numerical values, and so forth, discovering an almost infinite variety of new meanings in scriptural material (see Copenhaver 1999). These textual elements were combined and permuted following three main techniques, described in Joseph Gikatilla's (1248–c.1305) *Ginnat Egoz* (*Nut-Garden*), in which the three letters of the Hebrew word for 'Garden' (GNTh – Ginnat) denote the techniques of *Gematria* (arithmetical computations), *Notarikon/Notariacon* (manipulation of letters into acronyms and acrostics, e.g. Ginnat) and *Temura* or *Tseruf* (permutation, commutation, or transposition of letters) (Morlok 2011, pp. 72, 225).

Because every Hebrew letter possesses an inherent numerical value, every letter, word and phrase in the Torah has a mathematical significance by which correspondences can be found with other words, revealing internal resonances within seemingly disparate sources (Dan & Kiener 1986, p. 11). The 32 'wondrous paths of wisdom' with which the *Sefer Yetzirah* opens, for example, can be represented by the Hebrew letters *Lamed* (with the value 30) and *Beth* (with the value 2), which combine to form the Hebrew word '*Leb*,' meaning 'heart' (Kaplan 1979, pp. 23, 36). These two letters are also the first and last letters of the Torah – the *Beth* of *Bereshit*, the first word of Genesis 1:1 and the *Lamed* of *Israel*, the last word of Deuteronomy 34:12. Thus the five books of Moses constitute the 'heart' of the Kabbalah, together with the ten *sefirot* and the 22 letters of the alphabet that form all the *shemot* or divine names (Idel 1990, p. 67). One of the most influential examples of *Gematria* provided by both Pico and Reuchlin relates to the most powerful Jewish name for God, the ineffable *Tetragrammaton*, YHVH. By cumulatively adding up the values of these letters when they are aligned according to the points of the Pythagorean *Tetraktys*, that is by adding *Yod* (10) to *Yod-He* (15) to *Yod-He-Vau* (21) to *Yod-He-Vau-He* (26), we reach the significant total 72, associated, for example, with 72 psalmodic verses and related angelic powers (Farmer 1998, p. 543; Reuchlin 1983, p. 267). Reuchlin is fascinated with Kabbalistic ideas concerning the multiple names of God. The main thrust of *De Verbo Mirifico* reveals his interest in proving the supremacy of the Christian Kabbalist *Pentagrammaton* or five-letter name of Jesus, YHSVH, the 'true Messiah', that supersedes the Jewish four-letter YHVH.

Pico and Reuchlin stand at the head of a series of Christian thinkers who engaged with Kabbalah, including the Jewish converts, Paulus Ricius (1470–1541), who published an influential translation of Joseph Gikatilla's *Gates of Light* (1516), containing the first depiction of the Tree of Life outside a Jewish text and his own four-part religio-philosophical synthesis of kabbalistic and Christian sources, *De Cœlesti Agricultura* (*On Celestial Agriculture*, 1541) (Blau 1944, pp. 67–74; Black 2007) and Petrus Galatinus (1460–1540), who, at the request of Pope Leo X and Emperor Maximilian I, wrote *De arcanis catholicae veritatis* (*On the Mysteries of Catholic Truth*), published in 12 books in 1518, which quickly became an important text of Christian Kabbalah. Another significant figure is undoubtedly the Venetian scholar Francesco Giorgio (c.1460–1540), author of two large volumes that were widely read: *De Harmonia mundi totius cantica tria* (*Three Canticles on the Harmony of the Whole World*, 1525) and the *Problemata* (1536). In both books the Kabbalah is central to the themes developed, and the *Zohar*, for the first time, was used extensively in a work of Christian origin (Busi 1997). One of Giorgio's disciples, Arcangelo da Borgonuovo (d. 1571) published a *Dechiaratione sopra il nome di Giesu* (*Declaration on the Name of Jesus*, 1557), essentially an expansion of the final chapters in Reuchlin's *De Verbo Mirifico*, later followed by a commentary on Pico's kabbalistic theses, *Cabalistarum selectiora, obscurioraque dogmata* (*Very Select and Obscure Doctrines of the Cabalists*, 1569) (Wirszubski 1974). The famous preacher and humanist poet Egidio da Viterbo (1465–1532), who was to become the General of the Augustinian Order in 1503 and be elected cardinal in 1517, translated many of the texts fundamental to Christian Kabbalah. Aside from minor works on the Hebrew language, the majority are kabbalistic in nature, including passages from the *Zohar* and the *Bahir*, Gikatilla's *Ginnat Egoz* (*Nut-Garden*) and *Sha'areh Orah* (*Gates of Light*), *Sefer Raziel* (*Book of Raziel*), Recanati's *Commentary on the Pentateuch*, and the *Sefer Yetzirah*. In his *Historia viginti saeculorum* (*History of Twenty Centuries*) Giles writes a mystical history of the Church, stating that it cannot be understood without Kabbalah. One of Giles's most important treatises is the *Libellus de litteris hebraicis* (1517), which discusses the spiritual signification of the letters of the Hebrew alphabet. Drawing not only from kabbalistic literature, but also from the Greek and Latin poets and Neoplatonic philosophers, the longer *Scechina* (1530) treats of numbers, letters and divine names, with a focus on the importance and meaning of the tenth *sefira*, *Malkuth*, personified in kabbalistic literature as the *Shekinah*, the feminine manifestation of God in creation, who in Giles's work reveals the Kabbalah to Pope Clement VII and Emperor Charles V (Stein Kokin 2011; Secret 1964, pp. 106–26).

An important French representative of Christian Kabbalah is Guillaume Postel (1510–81), expelled from the Jesuits by Ignatius Loyola in 1545 due to unorthodox mystical tendencies, including prophetic visions and the unusual relationship he had with Mother Jeanne, his spiritual mother and guide, identified by Postel after her death as the Venetian Virgin, the *Shekinah*, the feminine manifestation God on earth. Postel's illuminism, in which the themes of the soul of the Messiah and the doctrine of *Gilgul* or metempsychosis, the 'revolution of souls' dominate, provoked censure in both Italy and France. For Postel, Hebrew was the key to true knowledge; once everyone spoke it the universe would be understandable and men would once more be able to communicate directly with God. Like Pico, Postel employs Kabbalah to show how a single current of truth runs through all philosophies, attaining its most profound expression in Christian revelation. In *De orbis terrae concordia* (*On the Concord of the Earth*, 1544), he advocated a universalist world religion, calling for the unification of all Christian churches, arguing that all Jews, Muslims and heathens could be converted once they recognized that the common foundations of all religions, i.e. love and praise of God, love and succor of Mankind, was best represented in the Christian religion. By 1548 Postel had made a translation with commentary of the *Zohar* and in 1552 he published Latin translations of the *Zohar*, the *Sefer Yetzirah*, and the *Sefer ha-Bahir*, predating the first Hebrew printing of these works by ten years; although his *Zohar* commentary was unpublished during his lifetime, it circulated in manuscript and was known to many Christian Kabbalists of his time (Bouwsma 1954; Kuntz 1981).

The figure arguably most responsible for shaping the Western image of early modern Christian Kabbalah is the German humanist theologian Heinrich Cornelius Agrippa (1486–1535), whose encyclopedia of esoteric thought, *De Occulta Philosophia libri tres* (*Three Books of Occult Philosophy*, 1533) was to become one of the most consulted sources for information about kabbalistic theories and practices, albeit a presentation of Kabbalah derived almost exclusively from the works of his co-religionists Pico, Reuchlin, Ricius and Giorgio. Agrippa presents a similar intermingling of Pythagorean, Neoplatonic and Kabbalistic ideas, emphasizing similar claims to the natural signification of Hebrew as the original language and the significance of its 22 letters as the foundation of the cosmos. Book Two of *De Occulta Philosophia* displays an interest in practical Kabbalah and arithmology, in the occult significance of numbers; Book Three indicates Kabbalah's importance for Agrippa's notion of a sacralized magic (Scholem 1978, p. 198; Lehrich 2003, pp. 149–59)

Strictly speaking, the first known author to write of a 'Christian' Kabbalah, is the Franciscan Jean Thenaud (d. 1542) whose unpublished manuscript *Traité de la Cabale* or *Traité de la Cabala chrétienne* (c.1521), summarizes some of the earlier Latin studies (Blau 1944, p. 89ff; Secret 1964, p. 153ff). The first published work to explicitly describe itself as 'Christian Kabbalist' is the *Amphitheatrum Sapientiae Aeternae* (*Amphitheatre of Eternal Wisdom*, 1595/1609) of the German theosopher Heinrich Khunrath (1560–1605), who openly acknowledges the influence of Reuchlin and Agrippa on his work, but goes further than either of them in arguing that 'Kabbalah, magic, and alchemy shall and must be combined and used together' (Scholem 2006, p. 91; Khunrath 1608, p. 87). Khunrath promotes an analogous harmony between alchemy and Christian Kabbalah, the former having as its goal the Philosophers' Stone as 'Son of the Macrocosm', the latter the union of man with YHSVH Christ, 'Son of the Microcosm' (Khunrath 1609, p. 203; Forshaw 2007, p. 263). The first circular figure of Khunrath's *Amphitheatre*, his Sigillum Dei (Seal of God), includes the Hebrew Decalogue, angelic orders, Hebrew alphabet, *sefirot*, *shemot*, and and Cruciform Christ at the centre, surrounded by the *pentagrammaton* in a fiery pentagram.

SEVENTEENTH-CENTURY DEVELOPMENTS

The mid seventeenth century was witness to two major esoteric publications that engaged with Jewish Kabbalah. The first of these is a work of the Jesuit polymath Athanasius Kircher (1601/2–1680), *Oedipus Aegyptiacus* (*Egyptian Oedipus*, 1652–54), which as well as discussing hieroglyphs also devotes hundreds of pages to the presentation of not only *Cabala Hebraeorum* (*Kabbalah of the Jews*), but also to *Cabala Saracenica* (*Kabbalah of the Arabs and Turks*), including information on divine and angelic names in kabbalistic amulets. Kircher approaches the subject with an antiquarian fascination for unraveling the significance of many of the magical amulets and talismans, but constantly maintains a highly condemnatory attitude to most of the beliefs and practices of the non-Christian subjects under study. He does, however, provide a great deal of information of value for understanding occult philosophy, with material drawn from Pico, Reuchlin, Agrippa, Galatinus, and many other primary and secondary sources. *Oedipus Aegyptiacus* contains two of the best-known images of early modern material on Kabbalah: Kircher's elaborate version of the Tree of Life, representing all four kabbalistic worlds (Archetypal, Angelic, Celestial and Elemental) and his 'Speculum Cabalae mysticae' (Mirror of Mystical Kabbalah), which serves as a visual distillation of major kabbalistic themes, revealing how Kircher adapts them to further the universalist ideology of the early modern Catholic Church (Stolzenberg 2004). Here too we find Reuchlin's YHSVH at the heart of the diagram, as 'Jesus Christ, the centre of all nature, in whose name all the other divine names are concentrated'. The intent viewer can find the Hebrew Kabbalist 12-letter divine name, from which emanates the 42-letter name, then a 72-letter name, or rather Kircher's variant of the Jewish tradition, with 72 four-letter names of God, representing the 72 nations that comprise all humanity. As Daniel Stolzenberg has argued, by this stratagem, Kircher transformed the notion of the divine names as instruments for theurgical invocation into the representation of the totality of humanity under the influence of the Christian-Kabbalist divine *Pentagrammaton*, as a universal revelation and promise of salvation to all peoples (Stolzenberg 2013, pp. 162–74).

The other major seventeenth-century publication was the great anthology of kabbalistic texts, *Kabbala denudata, seu doctrina Hebraeorum transcendentalis et metaphysica atque Theologica* (*The Kabbalah Unveiled, or the Transcendental, Metaphysical and Theological Doctrine of the Hebrews*), the first volume of which was published in Sulzbach between 1677 and 1678 by Christian Knorr von Rosenroth (1636–89), in collaboration with Francis Mercurius Van Helmont (1614–98), and dedicated to 'the lover of Hebrew, Chemistry, and Wisdom'. This compilation was superior to anything that had previously been published on Kabbalah in a language other than Hebrew, providing a non-Jewish readership with translations of authentic texts that were to be the principal source for Western literature on Kabbalah until the end of the nineteenth century.

The first volume includes a Key to the Divine Names of the Kabbalah, i.e., the explanation and division of all divine names according to the sefirotic degrees, derived from the *Zohar*, Moses Cordovero's *Pardes Rimmonim – Garden of Pomegranates* and Joseph Gikatilla's *Gates of Light*. It also included some of the works by, or inspired by, the originator of the modern school of kabbalistic thought, Isaac Luria (1533–72), *Emek ha-Melekkh* (*Valley of the King*) by the Lurianic Kabbalist Napthali ben Jacob Bacharach, an abridged version of the Portuguese Rabbi Abraham Cohen de Herrera's *Sha'ar ha-Shamayim* (*Gate of the Heavens*), along with a detailed Lurianic explanation of the Tree of Life, and a summary of a Jewish alchemical treatise, the *Esch Mezareph – The Refiner's Fire*, suggesting correspondences between the *sefirot*, planets and metals.

A second volume, *Kabbalae denudatae tomus secundus, id est Liber Sohar restitutus* (*The Second Volume of the Kabbala Unveiled, i.e., the Book of Zohar Restored*), published in Frankfurt in 1684, emphasizes Knorr's missionary intent. It begins with a systematic resumé of the *Zohar*'s doctrines, to which is added a Christian interpretation, in which Knorr juxtaposes various doctrinal points of the kabbalistic system with passages drawn from the New Testament, so as to show the intimate correlation between Jewish and Christian traditions. The same technique is used in the *Adumbratio Kabbalae Christianae [...] ad conversionem Judaeorum*, the last, anonymously authored, treatise in the *Kabbala denudata*, which was in fact written by Van Helmont and published separately because of its alleged importance in the task of converting Jews to Christianity. The *Adumbratio* is set as a dialogue between a 'Kabbalist' and a 'Philosophus Christianus', in which they explain their respective religious doctrines, enabling Van Helmont to show the concordance between the two traditions. This volume also contains *Pneumatica cabbalistica*, introducing kabbalistic ideas about spirits, angels and demons, the soul and various states and transformations included in the kabbalistic theory of metempsychosis; plus Latin translations of Lurianic works, including chapters on angelology and demonology from Abraham Cohen de Herrera's *Beth Elohim* (*House of the Lord*) and Hayyim Vital's *Sefer ha-Gilgulim*, translated as *De revolutionibus animarum* (*On the Revolutions of Souls*).

Several of the treatises in the two volumes of the *Kabbalah Unveiled* promote the magical creative power of language. Bacharach's *Valley of the King* describes the Hebrew letters as building blocks of the universe and Vital's *On the Revolutions of Souls* describes how just and pious men can create angels and spirits through prayers. Cohen de Herrera's *Gate of the Heavens* makes a similar claim that everything was created through combinations of Hebrew letters, connecting the letters with the creation and characteristics of the first man, *Adam Kadmon* and with the ten *sefirot*. All three of these works are by followers of Isaac Luria and it is worth noting that although the *Kabbala denudata* contains material by kabbalists from other traditions, there is a distinct bias in favour of Lurianic material, including the doctrine of *tzimutzum*, the withdrawal or contraction of God into Himself in order to provide room for Creation, elaborations on earlier kabbalistic doctrines of the shattering of the sefirotic vessels in their original emanation and their subsequent reformation into the stable structure of the Tree of Life, plus an emphasis on man's role in the process of *tikkun* or restoration, and the human actions by which souls, trapped among the shards of the shattered vessels, can be reunited with the divine light.

For Rosenroth and Van Helmont, the Kabbalah offered a permeable barrier between Christians and Jews. Inspired by the Lurianic Kabbalah with its optimistic philosophy of perfectionism and universal salvation, they rejected many of the orthodox Christian views of the Fall, Salvation and the Trinity, tending towards Arianism, with the Son regarded as a creation of the Father rather than his co-equal: in the *Adumbratio Kabbalae Christianae* one reads, 'Precisely what you call *Adam Kadmon*, we call Christ' (Coudert, *Impact of Kabbalah*, 1999, p. 127). Rather than an emphasis on the doctrine of original sin and on man's fallen nature, instead there was the implication that every individual was innately capable of salvation through their own efforts; all were potentially if not actually divine.

CONCLUSION

The early modern occult philosopher interested in Kabbalah had a wide variety of material at hand, both from genuine Jewish sources and in material adopted, adapted, distilled or despoiled, mutilated or transmuted by its Christian adherents. Much Christian Kabbalah is undoubtedly alien to Jewish practitioners, it is questionable whether some of the material ever was Kabbalah *strictu sensu* and orthodox Christians could be forgiven for wondering whether the ideas espoused by Rosenroth and Van Helmont belonged within the Christian fold. Be that as it may, the material contained in the publications mentioned exerted a profound influence on modern practitioners like A. E. Waite, Aleister Crowley, and Dion Fortune and Kabbalah represents an important current in Western esotericism.

REFERENCES AND FURTHER READING

Black, C 2007, 'From Kabbalah to Psychology: The Allegorizing Isagoge of Paulus Ricius, 1509–41,' *Magic, Ritual, and Witchcraft*, vol. 2, no. 2, pp. 136–73.

Blau, JL 1944, *The Christian Interpretation of the Cabala in the Renaissance*, Columbia University Press, New York.

Bouwsma, W 1954, 'Postel and the Significance of Renaissance Cabalism,' *Journal of the History of Ideas*, vol. 15, no. 2, pp. 218–32.

Busi, G 1997, 'Francesco Zorzi: A Methodical Dreamer,' in J Dan (ed.), *The Christian Kabbalah: Jewish Mystical Books and Their Christian Interpreters*, Harvard College Library, Cambridge, Mass.

Copenhaver, BP 1999, 'Number, Shape, and Meaning in Pico's Christian Cabala: The Upright *Tsade*, the Closed *Mem*, and the Gaping Jaws of Azazel,' in A Grafton and N Siraisi (eds), *Natural Particulars: Nature and the Disciplines in Renaissance Europe*, The MIT Press, Cambridge, Mass.

Coudert, A 1993, 'The *Kabbala denudata*: Converting Jews or Seducing Christians?' in RH Popkin & GM Weiner (eds), *Jewish Christians and Christian Jews*, Kluwer Academic Publishers, Dordrecht.

——1999, *The Impact of the Kabbalah in the Seventeenth Century: The Life and Thought of Francis Mercury van Helmont (1614–1698)*, Brill, Leiden.

Dan, J & Kiener, RC 1986, *The Early Kabbalah*, Paulist Press, New Jersey.

Dan, J 1997, 'The Kabbalah of Johannes Reuchlin and Its Historical Significance,' in J Dan (ed.), *The Christian Kabbalah: Jewish Mystical Books and Their Christian Interpreters*, Harvard College Library, Cambridge, Mass.

Farmer, SA 1998, *Syncretism In The West: Pico's 900 Theses (1486) – The Evolution Of Traditional Religious And Philosophical Systems*, Medieval & Renaissance Texts & Studies, Arizona.

Hames, HJ 2000, *The Art of Conversion: Christianity and Kabbalah in the Thirteenth Century*, Brill, Leiden.

Idel, M1990, *Golem: Jewish Magical and Mystical Traditions on the Artificial Anthropoid*, State University of New York Press, Albany, NY.

——1993, 'Introduction,' in Johann Reuchlin, *On the Art of the Kabbalah*, translated by Martin and Sarah Goodman, University of Nebraska Press, Lincoln.

——2011, *Kabbalah in Italy, 1280–1510: A Survey*, Yale University Press, New Haven.

Kaplan, A 1979, *The Bahir Illumination: Translation, Introduction, and Commentary*, Samuel Weiser, York Beach, Maine.

Khunrath, H 1608, *De Igne Magorum Philosophorumque secreto externo & visibili*, Lazarus Zetzner, Strassburg.

——1609, *Amphitheatrum sapientiae aeternae*, Guilielmus Antonius, Hanau.

Kilcher, A 2010, 'Philology as Kabbalah,' in B Huss, M Pasi, K Von Stuckrad (eds), *Kabbalah and Modernity: Interpretations, Transformations, Adaptations*, Brill, Leiden.

Kuntz, ML 1981, *Guillaume Postel: Prophet of the Restitution of All Things – His Life and Works*, Kluwer Academic Publishers, The Hague.

Lehrich, CI 2003, *The Language of Demons and Angels: Cornelius Agrippa's Occult Philosophy*, Brill, Leiden.

Liebes, Y 1993, *Studies in the Zohar*, translated by A Schwarz, S Nakache & P Peli, State University of New York Press, Albany, NY.

Matt, DC 1983, *Zohar, The Book of Enlightenment*, Paulist Press, New Jersey.

Morlok, E 2011, *Rabbi Joseph Gikatilla's Hermeneutics*, Mohr Siebeck, Tübingen.

Reichert, K 1995, 'Pico della Mirandola and the Beginnings of Christian Kabbala,' in KE Grözinger & J Dan (eds), *Mysticism, Magic and Kabbalah in Ashkenazi Judaism*, Walter de Gruyter, Berlin.

Scholem, G 1978, *Kabbalah*, Meridian Books, New York.

——1990, *Origins of the Kabbalah*, edited by R. J. Zwi Werblowsky, translated by Allan Arkush, Princeton University Press, Princeton NJ.

——1997, 'The Beginnings of the Christian Kabbalah,' in J Dan (ed.), *The Christian Kabbalah: Jewish Mystical Books and Their Christian Interpreters*, Harvard College Library, Cambridge, Mass.

——2006, *Alchemy and Kabbalah*, Spring Publications, Putnam, CT.

Secret, F 1964, *Les Kabbalistes Chrétiens de la Renaissance*, Dunod, Paris.

Stein Kokin, D 2011, 'Entering the Labyrinth: On the Hebrew and Kabbalistic Universe of Egidio da Viterbo,' in I Zinguer, A Melamed & Z Shalev (eds), *Hebraic Aspects of the Renaissance: Sources and Encounters*, Brill, Leiden.

Stolzenberg, D 2004, 'Four Trees, Some Amulets, and the Seventy-two Names of God: Kircher Reveals the Kabbalah,' in P Findlen (ed.), *Athanasius Kircher: The Last Man who Knew Everything*, Routledge, New York & London.

——2013, *Egyptian Oedipus: Athanasius Kircher and the Secrets of Antiquity*, University of Chicago Press, Chicago.

Wirszubski, C 1974, 'Francesco Giorgio's Commentary on Giovanni Pico's Kabbalistic Theses,' *Journal of the Warburg and Courtauld Institutes*, vol. 37, pp. 145–56.

——1989, *Pico Della Mirandola's Encounter with Jewish Mysticism*, Harvard University Press, Cambridge, Mass.

Zika, C 1976, 'Reuchlin's *De Verbo Mirifico* and the Magic Debate of the Late Fifteenth Century,' *The Journal of the Warburg and Courtauld Institutes*, vol. 39, pp. 104–38.

CHAPTER FIFTY-FIVE

ALCHEMY

Georgiana D. Hedesan

INTRODUCTION

Until relatively recently, scholars defined alchemy as the theory and practice of transmutation, particularly of baser metals into gold and silver. This description was often accompanied by the belief that alchemy was a pseudo-science that vanished around the time of the so-called Scientific Revolution. However, recent scholarship has shown that the separation of metallic-transmutation alchemy from other movements, such as Paracelsian 'iatrochemistry', spagyrics or distillation theory and practice is artificial. Today, alchemy is increasingly seen as a complex and wide discipline that had a variety of purposes distinct from simply the making of gold. For instance, Harry J. Sheppard (1996, 313) defined alchemy as the pursuit of three possible goals: (a) the search for the *lapis philosophorum* (the philosophers' stone) that could transform metals, (b) the preparation of an elixir of life for health and longevity, and (c) a spiritual-symbolic goal. This approach to alchemy may still be too restrictive to describe the domain, as it still does not take account of other medical goals of alchemy, or of the application of alchemical principles in other areas, such as agriculture or physics.

The following discussion views alchemy as a diffuse realm of theories and practices that involved the belief in the ability of human beings to transmute matter, spirit, or both from a qualitatively 'lower' state to a 'higher' state. The goal of alchemy in general was one of 'improvement', whether from a fundamental or simply pragmatic standpoint. This tentative definition implies that alchemy could be seen as a wider and fuzzier domain than chemistry, even as alchemy generally involved chemical techniques.

This description suggests that in some cases it may be necessary and fruitful to differentiate between different types of alchemy: 'metallic-transmutation alchemy' is referred to by the term 'chrysopoeia'—literally, the making of gold, even if transformation into other metals may have been involved; alchemy undertaken for medical purposes is referred to as 'medical alchemy'; 'spiritual alchemy' is used in reference to modern (post-Enlightenment) practices that did not involve the transformation of matter, but of the human spirit.

The following overview is primarily historical, concentrating on alchemy in the Mediterranean world. For a review of Chinese and Indian alchemy, the reader is invited to consult such works as Needham (1974–83), Sivin (1968), Cooper (1990) and White (1996).

ORIGINS OF ALCHEMY

The etymology of the word 'alchemy' is shrouded in mystery. While the '*al-*' part of the term has long been recognised as referring to the definite article in Arabic, the '*chem-*' root has been the subject of intensive debate. Some have attributed it to the Egyptian word '*keme*' (black), suggesting the Egyptian origin of alchemy, while others have preferred the Greek term '*cheo*', to pour. More fanciful explanations, deriving the word from the biblical Apocrypha or the name of a mythical hero, have long been rejected.

Like the obscure etymology, the origins of alchemy are disputed. Alchemists and some early scholars believed that the origin of alchemy was to be found in Egypt. By the mid-twentieth century, many scholars changed their mind in favour of China (after briefly considering Mesopotamia). Chinese alchemy may have started slightly earlier than the Greek–Egyptian counterpart, but that does not necessarily support the argument for transmission. As Sheppard (1970) and Halleux (1979) have shown, Chinese and Western alchemy may have formed parallel traditions without a common point of origin. Indeed, Chinese alchemy concentrated on long life from its earliest recorded beginnings, while the Greek–Egyptian variant apparently did not. Moreover, no Chinese etymological roots have been uncovered in Western alchemical terminology.

GREEK ALCHEMY

Our knowledge of Greek alchemy is mainly based on collections of texts compiled by Byzantine scholars. The earliest alchemical treatise is *Physika kai mystika*, which originates from around the third century BCE. *Physika* shares recipes with the Leiden-Stockholm papyri found in an Egyptian tomb. Despite this correspondence, the intentions behind *Physika* and the papyri appear different. The author of *Physika* seems committed to a belief in metallic transmutation, while the Leiden-Stockholm papyri are concerned with metallurgical techniques that transform base metals only into resemblances of gold or silver.

Physika kai mystika is traditionally attributed to the Greek pre-Socratic philosopher Democritus. However, scholarly agreement attributes this to Bolos of Mendes living in the third century BCE (Halleux 1979, 63). The treatise concerns the making of gold, silver, gems and purple, and evinces a belief in the homogeneity of matter, a theory which permits transmutation.

Also from around this period are many other treatises attributed to individuals such as 'Cleopatra', 'Mary the Jewess', 'Osthanes', 'Isis', 'Hermes' and others. While these alchemists generally used pseudonyms, the fourth century CE alchemist, Zosimus of Panopolis (known in Latin treatises as Rosinus) did not. Zosimus's ideas were strongly coloured by a Hermetic-Gnostic religious outlook. He described technical processes in allegorical terms, which encouraged a dual reading of his texts, one mystical and one literal. In particular, his 'visions' focussed on the symbolism of sacrifice, death and resurrection.

Following Zosimus, important Greek alchemists included Synesius and Olympiodorus. Their tradition was continued during the Middle Ages by Stephanos of Alexandria (eighth century), Michael Psellus (1018–78), Cosmas (eleventh century) and Nicephorus Blemmydes (1197–1272). The late medieval period was characterised by the increasing influence of Arab and Latin alchemy.

ARABIC ALCHEMY

Following the Islamic conquest of the Middle East and North Africa, knowledge of alchemy passed to the Arabs. The first important Arabic alchemist was said to be the Umayyad prince Khalid ibn Yazid (d. 704) who was instructed in alchemical secrets by the Christian monk Marianus or Morienus, a student of Stephanos of Alexandria (Holmyard 1957).

The most famous Arabic alchemists are Jabir ibn Hayyan (eighth century) and Rhazes (tenth century). The huge Jabirian corpus was not entirely authored by Jabir, as Peter Kraus (1942–43) has shown. Some parts of it can be attributed to the tenth century, when the corpus was compiled by members of the Islamic Ismaili sect. The Jabirian corpus was informed by Aristotelian thought and the short text of the *Emerald Tablet* was attributed to the mythical Hermes Trismegistus. Jabir proposed the formation of metals from sulphur and mercury, and also developed the concept of mass balance, or equilibrium of 'natures'.

An important anonymous alchemical piece, which has been dated to around the tenth century, is the *Turba philosophorum*, 'The Convention of Philosophers'. The treatise is written as a debate between nine Greek pre-Socratic philosophers, including Pythagoras and Empedocles. The purpose of this work, according to Martin Plessner (1954), is to demonstrate the superior truth of Islamic religion over Greek philosophy.

The Arab alchemical tradition flourished in the eleventh and twelfth centuries, when the important work *De aluminibus et salibus* and the pseudo-Avicennian texts were produced. Despite the famous denial of metallic transmutation by the Persian philosopher and physician Avicenna (980–1037) in his *Kitab al-Shifa'* (*The Book of Remedy*), his discussion of the generation of metals in terms of the sulphur-mercury theory proved highly influential. Translated into Latin as *De congelatione et conglutinatione lapidarum* and appended to Aristotle's *Meteorology*, the treatise was long considered to belong to Aristotle himself. At the same time, Aristotle's supposed denial of transmutation was complicated by the similarly incorrect attribution of the treatise *Secreta secretorum* to him. This work, also translated from Arabic into Latin, supported transmutation. The inconsistency helped to promulgate the idea that alchemy was an esoteric art, which had to be practiced in secret.

The twelfth century was the period of the 'great translation' of alchemical treatises into Latin, which marked the birth of Latin alchemy. The Arabic alchemical tradition continued unabated into the thirteenth and fourteenth centuries. Although no great works have been produced since, alchemy is practiced in Islamic lands even to the present day.

LATIN ALCHEMY IN THE HIGH MIDDLE AGES (1100–1300)

The first known translation of an Arab treatise into Latin is *The Testament of Morienus* (1144) by the English scholar Robert of Chester. He was followed by many others, the most famous of whom was Gerard of Cremona (1114–87), who founded a school of translators.

Many scholars in the High Middle Ages focussed on the subject of metallic transmutation (*chrysopoeia*). In his *Book of Minerals*, the great scholar Albertus Magnus (c. 1193–1280) followed Avicenna's lead in *De congelatione et conglutinatione lapidarum* to deny the possibility of transmutation. However, in the *Little Book of Alchemy* (*Libellus de alchimia*), which may be inauthentic, Albertus upheld the idea that alchemical gold can be made, albeit not to the perfection of natural gold. Albertus's pupil, Thomas Aquinas (1225–74), agreed that making gold and silver is possible, but extremely difficult to accomplish. He too was considered a 'closet' alchemist and several books were attributed to him, including the important but spurious *Aurora consurgens*, famous as an illuminated manuscript (Obrist 1982). The authority of Albertus and Thomas helped establish alchemy as a component of medieval knowledge. Nevertheless, alchemy was never able to become a subject of study in medieval universities.

Another famous chrysopoeian alchemist of the High Middle Ages was 'Geber', who used the pseudonym of the Arabic philosopher Jabir for his works. That is to say, modern scholarship has established that several works attributed to Jabir were actually written by Geber, who lived in the latter half of 1200 (Kraus 1942–43, Newman 1991). In fact, William Newman has persuasively argued that behind the name of Geber lay the Italian Franciscan monk Paul of Taranto.

Geber's masterpiece is *Summa perfectionis magisterii*, which was inspired by Jabir's theory of sulphur and mercury. Having said that, Geber was also an original philosopher who brought a unique corpuscularian interpretation to Jabirian theory, and believed that the true 'medicine of the metals' was mercury (Newman 1993). This led to the so-called 'mercury only' theory of transmutation, which was highly popular in the fourteenth and fifteenth centuries (Thorndike 1934, 58).

Besides Albertus and Geber, another key alchemical figure of the High Middle Ages was Roger Bacon (1214–92). Bacon was engaged in a vast project of reforming knowledge, and believed alchemy to be an important component of natural philosophy. He divided alchemy into two parts: speculative and practical. The speculative side was a philosophy concerned with the generation of new things, while practical alchemy taught not only the making of noble metals, but the creation of medicine as well. It was in this latter respect that Bacon was particularly original. He drew on the pseudo-Aristotelian *Secreta secretorum* to argue that it was possible to manufacture a universal medicine obtained from human blood which could radically extend life.

LATIN ALCHEMY IN THE LATER MIDDLE AGES (1300–1500)

The fourteenth century was a transformational period for alchemical thought. During this period, the pseudo-Arnaldian and pseudo-Lullian alchemical corpora were formed. Although both were attributed to two great medieval Catalan scholars, Arnau of Villanova (c. 1230–1311) and Ramon Llull (c. 1232-c. 1316), it is unlikely that they actually authored them.

At the root of the rich Pseudo-Lullian corpus stands the *Testamentum*, authored sometime before 1332 (Pereira 1989). The *Testamentum* is a highly original natural philosophical work. Inspired by Aristotelian and Lullian speculation, the treatise elaborates a theory of 'the elixir' as a chrysopoeian and medical instrument. The Pseudo-Lullian corpus became highly influential in the fifteenth century. One of its strengths lay in its assimilation of the work of the Franciscan John of Rupescissa (c. 1310–c. 1366), who will be discussed below.

The pseudo-Arnaldian corpus has received less scholarly scrutiny. Its best-known work is the *Rosarium philosophorum* (Telle 1992). The pseudo-Arnaldian corpus is characterised by a strong religious inclination and is particularly associated with the analogy between Christ and the work of alchemy, often referred to as the lapis-Christ analogy or parallel (Calvet 1993, 98). It also evinced a spiritual understanding of the 'water of life' (*aqua vitae*) obtained by distillation. Such speculations in turn influenced another important alchemist of the period, John of Rupescissa (Halleux 1981, 266–67), who is famous for his theory of 'the quintessence', a distilled medicine based on *aqua ardens* (alcohol) that had profound effects on the human body. Rupescissa drew on Aristotelian speculation on the fifth element of the heavens to argue that this could also be extracted by alchemical distillation from different earthly substances. Ingesting this quintessence would result in a profound reformation of the body that had religious and apocalyptic connotations (DeVun 2009).

As recent studies have shown, late medieval alchemy favoured medical alchemy in the detriment of chrysopoeia (Crisciani and Pereira 1996, 72). There were several reasons for this development. The medical applications of Rupescissa's quintessence theory led to an increasing interest in medical alchemy on the part of trained physicians, such as Guglielmo Fabri (fl. 1449), Michele Savonarola (1385–1468) and Marsilio Ficino (1433–99).

In the meantime, the position of chrysopoeian alchemy was seriously weakened by the condemnation of Pope John XXII in the 1317 Bull *Spondent quas non exhibent*. The situation was aggravated in 1396, when the Aragonese Inquisitor Nicholas Eymerich (c. 1316–99) further condemned alchemy in his *Tractatus contra alchimistas* (Newman 2004, 91–97). Outside of the church, prohibitions were also given by rulers such as, in France, Charles V (1380), in England, Henry IV (1403/4) and VI (1452), and by legislators in the cities of Venice (1488) and Nuremberg (1493). Such bans and criticism did not, of course, lead to the demise of chrysopoeia, which was still supported by such famous alchemists as George Ripley (c. 1415–90), Thomas Norton (c. 1433–1513), Giovanni Augurelli (c. 1441–1524) and Giovanni Bracesco (c. 1482–c. 1555). If anything, interest in metallic transmutation increased particularly at princely courts, which were always searching for ways to increase their finances (e.g. Moran 1991). Particularly significant, however, was that this period saw the propagation of a rhetoric that differentiated evil, greedy alchemists, from genuine and honest ones.

Late medieval alchemy also emphasised the association between the Christian religion and alchemy. The fourteenth and fifteenth century saw the proliferation of alchemical treatises containing Christian themes, including the *New Pearl of Great Price* (*Pretiosa margarita novella*) by Petrus Bonus of Ferrara, the anonymous *Book of the Holy Trinity* (*Buch der heiligen Dreifaltigkeit*), and the *Alchemical Mass* of Melchior Cibinensis. In the 1400s and early 1500s alchemical religious themes could also be found in the work of George Ripley, Ludovico Lazzarelli (1447–1500), and Giovanni Mercurio da Correggio (fl. 1451).

RENAISSANCE ALCHEMY AND PARACELSUS (SIXTEENTH CENTURY)

The sixteenth century saw a starker differentiation between the chrysopoeian and medical alchemy, with the latter often rejecting the pursuit of metallic transmutation on religious or ethical grounds. This period was also marked by the resurgence of esoteric philosophy, dominated by a renewed interest in Late Antique philosophy, particularly Neoplatonism and Hermeticism. The re-discovery of texts supposedly authored by the mythical founder of alchemy, Hermes Trismegistus, brought alchemy into a closer relationship with other esoteric forms of knowledge, such as magic, Kabbalah and prophecy. Consequently, Renaissance philosophers saw alchemy as being a component of a greater system usually dominated by ceremonial or learned magic. This is easily seen in Heinrich Cornelius Agrippa's famous *De occulta philosophia* (1531), but also in Paracelsus's *Astronomia magna* (c. 1537). Magi like John Dee (1527–1608/9) and Guillaume Postel (1510–81) also saw alchemy as part of a wider worldview that focussed on the manipulation of occult forces.

Theophrastus Paracelsus (1493–1541) can be seen as a transitional figure between Renaissance and early modern alchemy. On one hand, his interest in an eclectic philosophy dominated by high magic made him similar to other Renaissance figures like Agrippa or Dee; on the other hand, he departed from the traditional framework by rejecting learned authority, emphasising direct illumination and paying particular attention to medical alchemy. Paracelsus described medical alchemy as being one of the four pillars of medicine and was singularly outspoken in his rejection of Galenic-Aristotelian medicine. Instead, he argued that the new medicine had to strongly rely on alchemical preparations obtained from inorganic sources. Distinguishing between medical and chrysopoeian alchemy, he rejected the latter as being an unethical pursuit. Yet this rejection became muddled after his death, when several pseudo-Paracelsian treatises emerged: these works praised metallic transmutation and described the process of creating the philosophers' stone.

Paracelsus was such a towering figure in the alchemical tradition that most early modern alchemy was somehow indebted to his ideas. His theories transformed the way alchemists thought about themselves and their ideas. He single-handedly generated a new alchemical philosophy, which was no longer reliant on Aristotelian and Galenic thought, and put a renewed emphasis on Christian ideas. Indeed, he formulated the ideal of the unification of natural philosophy and Christian thought.

EARLY MODERN ALCHEMY (SIXTEENTH AND SEVENTEENTH CENTURIES)

Early modern alchemy can be defined as a reckoning with the thought of Paracelsus: whether adopting or rejecting his ideas, most if not all alchemists were somehow indebted to Paracelsian thought. Early modern alchemy is sometimes referred to as 'chymistry' to emphasise its transitional state between alchemy and modern chemistry (cf. Newman and Principe 1998).

The most prominent supporters of Paracelsus were chiefly learned physicians, notably Petrus Severinus (1540/2–1602), Oswald Croll (c. 1563–1609) and Joseph du Chesne (1544–1609). As several scholars have pointed out, Severinus was responsible for rescuing the thought of Paracelsus from relative disrepute and setting it in a clear medical framework (e.g. Shackelford 2004). In his 1571 work, Severinus sought to 'systematise' Paracelsian ideas in a more Renaissance-friendly context. Hence, he placed Paracelsus within a lineage of enlightened philosophers that included Hippocrates, Hermes Trismegistus and medieval alchemists.

Severinus's view strongly influenced the next generation of Paracelsian supporters, chief of whom were Croll and du Chesne. Croll's *Basilica chymica* (1609) advocated a Paracelsianism with strong Christian overtones, advancing the idea that alchemy was a sacred philosophy. Du Chesne emphasised the Severinian concept of a *prisca philosophia* of alchemical persuasion and connected it with Mosaic and Christian thought.

This emphasis on the religious nature of alchemical speculation was an increasingly popular trope at the beginning of the seventeenth century. Many alchemists expressed their belief in the compatibility between alchemy and Christianity. Some, like Robert Fludd (1573–1637) and Jan Baptist Van Helmont (1579–1644), went further in their attempts to construct new philosophical systems based on alchemical and religious principles.

This period also marked the birth of a long-surviving offshoot of alchemy, theosophical thought (which should not be confused with the ideas of the Theosophical Society in the nineteenth century). Central to this tradition was Jacob Boehme (c. 1575–1624), a mystical thinker who emphasised the religious side of alchemy over its practice. His followers would become increasingly perceived as a religious dissenting group with little connection to practical alchemy, even though some continued to be involved in alchemical work well into the eighteenth century—such as the theosopher Friedrich Christoph Oetinger (1702–82).

The early seventeenth century was also a period marked by an increasing concern with theological orthodoxy. Many intellectuals began to worry about the religious claims of alchemy and its tendency to emphasise personal illumination over orthodox canon. Consequently, alchemical philosophers came under the close scrutiny of theologians and intellectuals, most famously Marin Mersenne (1588–1648). In the eyes of some philosophers of the period, religion and natural philosophy had to be treated separately to ensure that theological doctrine remained intact. This was a belief propagated by such alchemical sympathisers as Andreas Libavius (1555–1614) or Pierre Gassendi (1592–1655). Libavius in particular is credited with defining chemistry (which he called 'alchemy') as an independent, but non-speculative branch of knowledge. The increasing institutionalisation of alchemy within older, conservative institutions, like the universities, would help to transform it into a purely natural-philosophical or 'scientific' endeavour.

Yet in mid-seventeenth century, it was not yet obvious that alchemy would become 'chemistry', as we know it today. The 1650s saw the dissemination of the writings of J.B. Van Helmont, a 'reformed' Paracelsian who firmly believed in the possibility of unifying alchemy and religion in a Christian philosophy. His view was embraced by a new wave of alchemical enthusiasts, including the reformists of the Hartlib Circle, George Starkey (1628–65) and young Robert Boyle (1627–91) (Newman and Principe 2002). Van Helmont propagated the ideas of a universal solvent (the Alkahest) which could reduce matter into its initial components, as well as a universal medicine that would remarkably extend life. Van Helmont was chiefly a medical alchemist, but he did not reject chrysopoeia as Paracelsus had done. Indeed, this period saw a flourishing of interest in metallic transmutation, promoted by the re-discovery of medieval tracts. An astounding amount of alchemical tracts and compendia were published in the seventeenth century, including the six-volume *Theatrum chemicum* (1604–62), the *Musaeum Hermeticum* (1625), the *Theatrum chemicum Britannicum* (1652), the *Bibliotheca chemica curiosa* (1702) and others. The result was a blurring of the lines between medical and chrysopoeian alchemy, as well as an increasing fascination with the latter. Some philosophers now saw chrysopoeia as a supreme and sacred art, or even as the culmination of all knowledge. Such thinkers included Boyle and Isaac Newton (1642–1727) whose incursions into chrysopoeia have been subject to much analysis in the twentieth century (e.g. Dobbs 1991).

Moreover, the exaltation of chrysopoeia contributed to an increased division between 'exoteric' and 'esoteric' knowledge at the end of the seventeenth century. This view distinguished levels of accessibility of alchemical knowledge, with the highest secrets being reserved for the 'adepts', alchemists who had reached a superior level of knowledge that set them apart from everyone else. Legends of alchemical adepts who performed metallic transmutation became increasingly popular during this period, particularly due to the testimonies of Michael Sendivogius (1566–1636), Van Helmont, Starkey, and Helvetius (1625–1709). In turn, they fuelled the literary trope of the lonesome or immortal alchemist that often appeared in Romantic and Victorian writings.

ALCHEMY IN THE ENLIGHTENMENT

In the eighteenth century, alchemy and chemistry began to part ways. Significantly, they were entered as two separate categories in Diderot's *Encyclopédie* (1751). That said, the author of the entry on 'alchemy', Paul Jacques Malouin (1701–78), could still relate the two by describing alchemy as 'the most subtle chemistry'.

The differentiation between alchemy and chemistry can be described in at least four ways. First, the goal of 'alchemy' came to be defined as predominantly chrysopoeian and centred on the philosophers' stone. That the philosophers' stone could both be an agent of metallic transmutation and human healing was, of course, a medieval trope that returned to prominence with the demise of Paracelsianism. Van Helmont still differentiated between the goals of making gold and those of prolonging life, but had accepted the idea that the stone also healed diseases. By the late seventeenth century many alchemists saw the philosophers' stone as the single goal of alchemy and medicine.

Second, 'alchemy' became associated with 'secrecy'. Malouin argued that once alchemical knowledge was diffused it lost its 'miraculous' character and became debased into chemistry. Increasingly, alchemy was associated with occult societies, arcane knowledge and theosophical circles. This was particularly so in the *Gold-und Rosenkreutz* current in Germany, which thrived under the leadership of Prussian King Frederick Wilhelm II (1786–97). The *Gold-und Rosenkreutz* still included practical alchemy in its curriculum, as did the members of the *Hermetische Gesellschaft* (c. 1796–1810), but many others may not have. In the freemasonic current established by Martinez de Pasqually (1727–74) and Louis-Claude de Saint-Martin (1743–68), alchemy was perceived in theosophical and religious-millenarian terms.

Third, the reality of the theory of transmutation came under increasing attack within the chemistry community. Yet chrysopoeian alchemy did not completely fall into disrepute. Chrysopoeian goals were pursued by respected Royal Society Fellow James Price (1752–83), German theologian J.S. Semler (1725–91), or the French author Dom A. J. Pernety (1716–96). Charismatic figures like the Count of Saint Germain (1701–84) and Giuseppe Cagliostro (1743–95) also perpetuated and further coloured the 'adept alchemist' legend.

Finally, seventeenth-century medical alchemy became subsumed within the iatrochemical school associated with Georg Stahl (1659–1734). Stahl was influential not only in promoting ideas from the previous century, such as the phlogiston theory, but also in supporting promoting a new current, vitalism, in opposition to mechanicism. His ideas were later developed by vitalist physicians at the Medical School of Montpellier.

During this period, medical alchemy lost some of its philosophical and religious force. Few dared to maintain that alchemy or chemistry had a privileged understanding of the nature of matter. An illustrious chemist like Hermann Boerhaave (1668–1738) accepted the primacy of Newtonianism and mechanical philosophy over chemical philosophy. Even so, chemistry remained a relatively autonomous science until the advent of the so-called 'Chemical Revolution' of Antoine Lavoisier (1743–94).

Besides the iatrochemical school and the vitalists, the Paracelsian-Helmontian alchemical tradition also indirectly influenced the Romantic current of *Naturphilosophie* in the German lands. The physician and scientist Samuel Hahnemann (1755–1843) clearly drew on the medical alchemical tradition and distillation techniques to 'invent' medical homeopathy (Goodrick-Clarke 2004). Other Naturphilosophs drew on alchemical ideas for inspiration in their theories of magnetism, electricity, psychology and mesmerism. However, these 'sciences' were only remotely connected to chemical laboratory work. Moreover, alchemical ideas, themes and symbolism, often passed via theosophical currents, also influenced Romantic philosophers such as J. G. Herder (1773–1803), Franz von Baader (1765–1841) and G. W. F. Hegel (1770–1831).

ALCHEMY IN THE NINETEENTH CENTURY

In the nineteenth century, both traditions of chrysopoeian and medical alchemy came under threat from the forces of modernity. Post-Lavoisierian chemistry rejected the theory of transmutation and uprooted the iatrochemical school. Homeopathy was similarly ostracised by the medical community. Aspects of the Paracelsian-Helmontian legacy remained, but became increasingly subsumed within the wider domain of the 'occult sciences'. Alchemical work in secret societies became less and less of a practical nature and increasingly linked with spiritual techniques.

Alchemical ideas, symbols and images gradually passed via theosophical and Pietistic circles as a form of inner, spiritual or sacred teaching. Indeed, it is only during this period that we can properly talk of a 'spiritual alchemy' removed from laboratory work. This interpretation was rooted in theosophy's appropriation of alchemical symbolism for religious purposes, as in the works of Angelus Silesius (1624–77), Georg Gichtel (1638–1710), and French Martinists (Coudert 2004). Alchemical symbolism was also increasingly absorbed in Masonic and Rosicrucian rituals as a path of self-development.

In mid-1850, Mary Ann Atwood (1817–1910) and Ethan Allen Hitchcock (1798–1870) developed the idea that alchemy was in fact a spiritual discipline rather than a practical one, arguing that its true subject was the perfection of humanity. These theses were consonant with the views current in the occult societies emerging at the end of the nineteenth century, and they found support in several quarters.

During the nineteenth century, practical alchemists remained active, but were few in number and usually reluctant to publish their ideas. Amongst those who did, the most famous was the mysterious French alchemist Cyliani, who published the influential *Hermes dévoilé* in 1832. Others included Karl von Eckartshausen (1752–1802) and Louis Cambriel (1764–c. 1850). Johann Gottfried Rademacher (1772–1850) and Carl Friedrich Zimpel (1801–79) also continued the Paracelsian-Helmontian tradition of medical alchemy through their research into plant spagyrics.

ALCHEMY IN THE TWENTIETH CENTURY

During the early twentieth century, alchemy became a popular subject that was treated in remarkably different ways. An important aspect was the rise of interest in the history of alchemy. An early devotee of alchemical studies was Arthur E. Waite (1857–1942), who translated and edited a large number of old alchemical texts. Other early historians of alchemy included E. J. Holmyard, F. Sherwood Taylor and J. R. Partington.

The revival of interest in alchemy can also be linked with the discovery of radioactivity by Ernest Rutherford (1871–1937) and Frederick Soddy (1877–1958). The transformation of nitrogen and radioactive materials into other elements was often interpreted as a confirmation of the truth of transmutation alchemy (Morrison 2007). Sir William Ramsay (1852–1916) even believed that the philosophers' stone and elixir of life would soon come within the reach of scientists.

The first half of the century was also marked by a flourishing of systems of spiritual alchemy. Traditionalists like Rene Guénon (1886–1951) and Julius Evola (1898–1974) or the anthroposophist Rudolf Steiner (1861–1925) explored this understanding of alchemy. Most famously, it bred the still-influential interpretation of Carl Gustav Jung (1875–1961), who used alchemy as a path of self-discovery.

The early twentieth century was also marked by the appearance of a number of societies that took an interest in alchemy. In France, Francois Jollivet-Castelot (1874–1937) founded the 'Societé alchimique française' at the turn of the century, followed by the 'Società alchemica italiana' (1909) and the English Alchemical Society (1912). These societies were eventually disbanded, but the Society for the History of Alchemy and Chemistry (set up in 1935) is still active today.

The twentieth century also saw a revival of practical alchemy. In the early twentieth century, famous alchemists included Archibald Cockren (c. 1880–1960) and Fulcanelli. After World War II, practical alchemy continued to find adepts. A famous modern alchemist was Eugene Canseliet (1899–1982), Fulcanelli's disciple. Other alchemists, some of whom are still alive today, include Baron Alexander von Bernus (1880–1965), Manfred Junius (1929–2004), René Alleau (b. 1917), Armand Barbault (b. 1906), Albert Richard Riedel alias Frater Albertus (1911–84).

REFERENCES AND FURTHER READING

Calvet, A. (1993) 'Alchimie et Joachimisme dans les "Alchimica" Pseudo-Arnaldiens', in Margolin and Matton, eds., *Alchimie et philosophie à la Renaissance*, 93–107.

Caron, R. (2005) 'Alchemy V: 19th and 20th Century', in Hanegraaff, ed., *Dictionary of Gnosticism and Western Esotericism*, 50–58.

Cooper, J.C. (1990) *Chinese Alchemy: The Daoist Quest for Immortality*, New York: Sterling Publishing.

Coudert, A. (2005) 'Alchemy IV: 16th–18th Century', in Hanegraaff, ed., *Dictionary of Gnosticism and Western Esotericism*, 42–50.

Crisciani, C. and M. Pereira (1996) *L'arte del sole e della luna: Alchimia e filosofia nel medioevo*, Spoleto: SISMEL.

Debus, A. (1977) *The Chemical Philosophy: Paracelsian Science and Medicine in the Sixteenth and Seventeenth Centuries*, London: Dover.

DeVun, L. (2009) *Prophecy, Alchemy and The End of Time: John of Rupescissa in the Late Middle Ages*, New York: Columbia University Press.

Dobbs, B.J.T. (1991) *The Janus Face of Genius: The Role of Alchemy in Newton's Thought*, Cambridge: Cambridge University Press.

Goodrick-Clarke, C. (2004) 'Rationalist, Empiricist, or Naturphilosoph? Samuel Hahnemann and his Legacy', *Politica Hermetica* 18, 26–45.

Halleux, R. (1981) 'Les ouvrages alchimiques de Jean de Rupescissa', in *Histoire Littéraire de la France*, 41, 241–56.

——(1979) *Les textes alchimiques*, Turnhout: Brepols.

Hanegraaff, W.J., ed. (2004) *Dictionary of Gnosticism and Western Esotericism*, Leiden: Brill.

Holmyard, E.J. (1957) *Alchemy*, London: Harmondsworth.

Kraus, P. (1942–43) *Jabir ibn Hayyan: Contribution à l'histoire des idées scientifiques dans l'Islam*, Cairo: Institute of Egypt.

Margolin, J.C. and S. Matton, eds (1993). *Alchimie et philosophie à la Renaissance*, Paris: Vrin.

McIntosh, C. (1992) *The Rose Cross and the Age of Reason: Eighteenth-Century Rosicrucianism in Central Europe and its Relationship to the Enlightenment*, Leiden: Brill.

Moran, B. (2005) *Distilling Knowledge: Alchemy, Chemistry and the Scientific Revolution*, Cambridge, MA: Harvard University Press.

——(1991) *The Alchemical World of the German Court*, Stuttgart: Franz Steiner.

Morrison, M. (2007) *Modern Alchemy: Occultism, Science, and the Ownership of Atomic Theory, 1895–1939*, Oxford: Oxford University Press.

Needham, J. (1974–83) *Science and Civilisation in China*, vol. V, Cambridge: Cambridge University Press.

Newman, W.R. and L.M. Principe (2002) *Alchemy Tried in the Fire: The Fate of Helmontian Chymistry*, Chicago: University of Chicago Press.

——(1998) 'Alchemy vs Chemistry: The Etymological Origins of a Historiographic Mistake,' *Early Science and Medicine*, 3:1 (1998), 32–65.

Newman, W.R. (2004) *Promethean Ambitions: Alchemy and the Quest to Perfect Nature*, Chicago: University of Chicago Press.

——(1993) 'L'influence de la "Summa perfectionis" du Pseudo-Geber', in Margolin and Matton, eds., *Alchimie et philosophie à la Renaissance*, 65–77.

——(1991) *The 'Summa perfectionis' of Pseudo-Geber: Edition with Commentary and English Translation*, Leiden: Brill.

Obrist, B. (1982) *Les débuts de l'imagerie alchimique (XIVe-XVe siècles)*, Paris: Le Sycomore.

Pagel, W. (1958) *Paracelsus: An Introduction to Philosophical Medicine in the Era of the Renaissance*, Basel: Karger.

Pereira, M. (1989) *The Alchemical Corpus Attributed to Raimond Lull*, London: Warburg Institute.

Plessner, M. (1954) 'The Place of the "Turba philosophorum" in the Development of Alchemy', *Isis*, 45, 31–38.

Shackelford, J. (2004) *A Philosophical Path for Parcelsian Medicine: The Ideas, Intellectual Context, and Influence of Petrus Severinus (1540/2–1602)*, Copenhagen: Museum Tusculanum Press.

Sheppard, H.J. (1996) 'La perfezione della materia', in Crisciani and Pereira, *L'arte del sole e della luna*, 313–18.

——(1970) 'Alchemy: Origin or Origins?' *Ambix* 17: 69–84.

Sivin, Nathan (1968) *Chinese Alchemy: Preliminary Studies*, Cambridge, MA: Harvard University Press.

Telle, J. (1992) *Rosarium Philosophorum: Ein alchemisches Florilegium des Spatmittelalters*, Weinheim: VCH Verlag.

Thorndike, L. (1923–58) *A History of Magic and Experimental Science*, 8 vols, New York: Columbia University Press.

White, D.G. (1996) *The Alchemical Body: Siddha Traditions in Medieval India*, Chicago: Chicago University Press.

CHAPTER FIFTY-SIX

SEX MAGIC

Hugh Urban

Magic and sexuality have a long and complex relationship in the history of Western esotericism. Sexual magic as a sophisticated ritual technique is largely a development of the modern era, beginning in roughly the mid-nineteenth century. However, sexual magic has roots that run much deeper in Western occult and esoteric traditions, some of them historical and some of them imaginary or fantastic (Urban 2005, 21–54; Versluis 2008; Hanegraaff and Kripal 2008).

The historical roots of modern sex magic lie in the Hermetic, Christian Gnostic and Jewish traditions from at least the first centuries of the common era. Throughout early Hermetic and Gnostic literature, the sexual union of male and female is used to describe the ineffable mystery of spiritual union (Urban 2005, 41; Hanegraaff and Kripal 2008). In some Gnostic traditions, such as the *Gospel of Philip*, the return of the soul to heaven is described as a kind of spiritual wedding, the 'mystery of the bridal chamber'; and it appears that the followers of *Philip* may have also practiced a form of mystical sexual union between male and female that mirrored the union of the soul and its heavenly counterpart (DeConick 2008). Another important source for modern sexual magic is Jewish mysticism and the esoteric tradition of Kabbalah. Throughout Kabbalistic literature, erotic symbolism is used to describe the relation between the Torah and her lover, the Kabbalist, and to portray the relationship between different aspects of the divine realm itself. However, because the human being is also a mirror of the divine, the physical union of man and wife can also serve as a spiritual technique to reunite the male and female aspects of the Godhead. According to the classic thirteenth-century text, the *Zohar*, this union of man and wife also symbolizes the union of God with his bride, the community of Israel (Wolfson 1995, 81, 96; Idel 1989).

During the Renaissance, many of these Hermetic, Christian and Kabbalistic sources converged in the magical revival in Italy. Indeed, perhaps the most famous formulation of the relationship between magic and sexuality was the classic work, *De Amore*, by the Italian philosopher and Hermeticist Marsilio Ficino (1433–99). In Ficino's words, magic and eros are intimately related arts, for both work by the power of attraction, the understanding of how like draws like: 'The whole power of Magic is founded on Eros. The way Magic works is to bring thing together through their inherent similarity' (Coulianu 1987, 87).

At the same time, in addition to these historical sources, there is also an equally long tradition of imaginary, fantastic and paranoid associations between magic and sexuality in Western history. Since at least the time of the Dionysian and Bacchic mystery religions in ancient Greece and Rome, and continuing with the Christian Gnostics and medieval heresies, there is a long and consistent narrative that links sexual transgression and orgiastic behavior with black magic and occult rituals (Urban 2005, 21–54). One of the most common charges leveled against the Gnostics by the early church fathers was that of hedonism and sexual abandon in the course of their obscene rites, and this accusation of sexual license and perverse ritual would recur throughout the later Middle Ages in the church's war against various heresies, from the Cathars in the thirteenth century to the Knights Templar in the fourteenth century to the witch trials in the fifteenth, sixteenth, and seventeenth centuries (Stephens 2002; Frankfurter 2008).

However, it is really not until the nineteenth century that we see the development of a sophisticated technique of sexual magic – that is, not simply the use of eroticism as a general metaphor for mystical experience but rather the explicit manipulation of physical orgasm and sexual emission as a source of magical power (Urban 2005). Arguably the most important figure in the development of modern sex magic was the American Spiritualist, Rosicrucian and medium, Paschal Beverly Randolph (1825–75). Born a poor, free black in the slums of New York city, Randolph was largely self-educated and traveled the world as a young man. During his journeys in the Middle East, he claims to have encountered a group of fakirs or Sufis (possibly members of the Shi'ite Nusai'ri sect) who instructed him in the arts of magic and alchemy, including the 'affectional alchemy' of sexual magic (Deveney 1997, 216–17). In Randolph's view, the moment of sexual union is the most 'solemn, energetic and powerful moment he can ever know on earth,' as the instant in which the physical realm is suddenly opened up to the energies of the cosmos and new life is infused from the spiritual realm into the material. By harnessing this tremendous creative power, the magus can achieve whatever he prays for at the moment 'when Love is an in the ascendant' (Deveney 1997, 339–40). Randolph listed a wide array of uses for sexual magic, ranging from the mundane to the sublime: it may be used to win the affections of a straying lover or secure financial gain; but it may also be the means to achieve 'the loftiest insight possible to the earthly soul' (ibid.). Ultimately, however, Randolph saw in sexual magic not simply a form of personal fulfillment but also the key to proper relations between male and female and thus the means of creating a harmonious social order and a kind of 'social millennium.' In sexual love, 'he saw the greatest hope for the regeneration of the world...as well as social transformation and the basis of a non-repressive civilization' (Rosemont 1997, xv).

Following Randolph, a wide array of sexual magical traditions began to proliferate throughout the US, England, and Europe. Among the most important of these were the Hermetic Brotherhood of Luxor, established by Max Theon in London in the 1870s, and the Ordo Templi Orientis (OTO), founded by Carl Kellner (1851–1905) and Theodor Reuss (1855–1923) in the late 1890s. The OTO is particularly noteworthy for its synthesis of Western traditions of sexual magic with newly important forms of yoga and Tantra drawn from India (Reuss 1906; Pasi 2005; Urban 2003, 2005, 2008). Following the European Orientalist scholars of the nineteenth century, Reuss (mistakenly) identified Tantra as primarily a form of spiritual sex and assimilated it into a largely Western tradition of sexual magic – where it has remained lodged in the popular imagination ever since (Urban 2003). Tantra, in Reuss' view, is the most ancient religious system in the world, as the worship of the male and female principles, Shiva and Shakti embodied in the male and female sexual organs (lingam and yoni), which is in turn the basis of all later religious traditions (Reuss 1906; Urban 2005, 100). Like Randolph, Reuss linked his sexual magical practices to a much larger vision of social transformation – indeed to the creation of a new morality and a 'new civilization.' In contrast to the morality of modern Christian society, this new civilization would be a 'Neo-Gnostic' society of 'Templar Christians' who would reject the false idea of original sin and accept the inherent divinity of the sexual act as a 'mystic marriage with God' (Urban 2005, 102–3).

The most influential leader of the OTO – and arguably the most important figure in the development of sexual magic in the twentieth century – was the controversial occultist, poet, and novelist Aleister Crowley (1875–1947). Not only was Crowley among the most prolific occultists of the modern era, but even more so than Reuss, he was also one of the first Western authors to incorporate elements of Buddhism, yoga, Tantra, and other Asian traditions into his magical practice. Long before meeting Reuss and the OTO, Crowley had already proclaimed his own new revelation and a new era in human history, based on the law of Thelema, from the Greek for 'will': 'do what thou wilt shall be the whole of the law' (1996). Indeed, when Crowley met Reuss in 1910, the latter recognized that he had already grasped and revealed in his work the innermost secret of the OTO, the secret of sexual magic. As Crowley later wrote in his autobiography, this secret of sexual magic is the most profound, powerful and creative force in human existence: 'if this secret, which is a scientific secret, were perfectly understood, as it is not by me after more than twelve years' almost constant study and experiment, there would be nothing which the human imagination can conceive that could not be realized in practice' (1989, 702; Crowley 1986). In contrast to both Randolph and Reuss – who were on the whole fairly conservative with regard to sexual matters – Crowley was far more explicitly transgressive and antinomian in his approach to sexual magic. Indeed, while previous authors had insisted that such magic be performed only between heterosexual married couples, Crowley opened the door to all manner of sexual experimentation, including homosexuality, masturbation, and occasional bestiality. Likewise, Crowley had a far more radical social and political vision – the birth not simply of a more harmonious society but rather of a whole new era in human history based on the sole principle of Thelema and the law of do what thou wilt (Urban 2005, 109–39; Crowley 1989, 850–51).

Crowley's work also inspired one of the most remarkable episodes in the history of modern occultism, a sexual ritual undertaken by an American named John (Jack) Whiteside Parsons in California during the late 1940s (Carter 2005, 86–99). A member of the American branch of the OTO, Parsons hoped to put some of Crowley's most radical rituals into practice – including the birth of a 'magical child' or 'moonchild.' As he described it in his diary of the 'Babalon Working,' Parsons' aim was first to identify a woman who would serve as his partner in sexual magical rites; this partner would then become impregnated with a magical child, a supernatural offspring that would be the embodiment of ultimate power, 'mightier than all the kings of the earth' (Parsons 1982). Parsons' accomplice and ritual partner in all of this was none other than L. Ron Hubbard – one of America's most prolific authors of science fiction and fantasy tales who would soon go on to found the hugely successful self-help movement of Dianetics and the new religion of Scientology. Indeed, Hubbard served as Parsons' 'scribe' during the rites and even as the voice of the Whore of Babylon, whom he channeled in March of 1946. Parsons' magical operation was never fully realized, however. Hubbard ended up running off with both Parsons' girlfriend and most of his money, and Parsons later accidentally blew himself up in his garage (Urban 2012; Carter 2005, 86–99).

While Randolph had seen sexual magic as the key to a more egalitarian 'social millennium,' and Crowley had seen it as the key to his new law of 'do what thou wilt,' others imagined that sexual magic might have very different sorts of social and political effects. One of the twentieth century's most important theorists of occultism, magic, and sexuality was Julius Evola (1898–1974) – an author also known for his far-right, radical Traditionalist views and his involvement with the Fascists and Nazis in the years before and during World War II (Urban 2005, 140–65; Hansen 2002). Like Reuss and Crowley, Evola was interested not only in Western sexual magical practice but also in the more transgressive left-hand (*vamachara*) forms of Hindu Tantra as the 'heroic' and 'virile' (*virya*) path most needed in this decadent modern era. Like previous authors, Evola too saw sexual magic as having larger social and political implications; in striking contrast to Randolph, however, Evola had a profoundly elitist hierarchical political ideal, one based on Imperial Rome and deeply opposed to modern democratic society. For Evola the radical techniques of sexual magic and left-hand Tantra are the extreme measures most needed in these extreme times, amidst the decadence and decline of modern Western society – a means of 'riding the tiger,' as it were, and harnessing the dangerous power of sexual magic as part of a larger 'revolt against the modern world' (Urban 2005, 140–65; Evola 1992, 188; Evola 1983, 109; Hakl 2008, 462).

During the 1920s, Evola was involved with another key figure in the development of modern sexual magic, the enigmatic Russian mystic, Maria de Naglowska (1883–1936). According to rumor, this involvement was not merely intellectual but also romantic. Although Naglowska is often mistakenly labeled a Satanist because of her controversial use of occult symbolism, her magical system centers on the third person of the Christian Trinity, the Holy Spirit, whom she identified as the divine feminine principle; and her magical practices centered on the reconciliation of the light and dark forces through the union of the male and female in sexual rites (Naglowska 2011; Hakl 2008). In 1931 Naglowska also published an important French translation of Randolph's work (supplemented with her own material) under the title *Magia Sexualis*, which introduced his hitherto little-known writings to a much wider international audience.

By the middle of the twentieth century, a modified form of sexual magic had also become part of the neo-pagan revival of witchcraft led by Gerald Gardner (1884–1964) and the early Wicca movement. A member of the OTO himself, Gardner borrowed heavily from Crowley's writings in his early Wiccan rituals. Although much of this influence was later removed or downplayed in the Wiccan tradition, the early drafts of Gardner's ritual manual, the *Book of Shadows* reveal a strong Crowleyian element (Hutton 1999, 217–23). One of the central rituals of Gardner's

Wicca is the 'Great Rite,' which centers on either the literal or symbolic union of (married) male and female partners as a source of magical power (Farrar and Farrar 1996; Urban 2005, 162–90) For many in the early neo-pagan movement, and particularly for feminist witches such as Starhawk, Z Budapest, and others, sexual magic again promised an element of social and political liberation – in this case the liberation from a patriarchal culture that had for millennia limited the spiritual and biological power of women. As Starhawk puts it, 'a true transformation of our culture would require reclaiming the erotic as power-from-within, as empowerment... The Goddess who is the mother is the love Goddess, the Goddess of the erotic' (Starhawk 1988, 138).

At roughly the same time that the neo-pagan revival was spreading rapidly across Europe and the United States, sexual magic began to take a very different form in the modern Satanist movement. The most well-known form of Satanism, the Church of Satan, was founded by Anton Szandor LaVey (1930–97), who might be said to represent the dark side of the sexual revolution – that is, affirming sexual liberation while fiercely rejecting feminism and women's rights (Urban 2005, 191–220). Like Crowley, LaVey was also particularly interested in power of sexual transgression, the explicit violation of social taboos and what he called 'the law of the forbidden.' Whereas Christianity (as LaVey understood it) seeks to confine sexuality within the limits of reproduction, Satanic sex explores and exploits every fetish, every deviant desire, every non-productive form of sexuality as a source of individual freedom and power (LaVey 1969, 147–48, 1989, 73, 235). Again, LaVey's view of sexuality is closely tied to an ideal of social and political liberation – only in this case, the liberation of the individual ego from the limitations of social conformity, conventional morality, and mainstream religion (Urban 2005, 191–221).

Although sexual magic as such was a fairly minor part of LaVey's early Satanic rituals, it became far more central to the more extreme and explicitly transgressive forms of Satanism that came in their wake. One of the most radical of these post-LaVey-ian Satanic currents is the 'Left Hand Path' espoused by LaVey's daughter Zeena and her partner Nikolas Schreck. As we see in their work, *Demons of the Flesh*, the Schrecks embraced a far more extreme ideal of sexual and social liberation that incorporated not only elements of Hindu and Buddhist Tantra but also sadomasochism, orgies, fetishism, sexual vampirism, and ritual intercourse with divine and demonic entities (Schreck and Schreck 2002).

By the late twentieth and early twenty-first centuries, a wide array of new forms of sexual magic had begun to proliferate, most of them combining Crowleyian style magic with a somewhat garbled version of South Asian Tantra. Thus we see a variety of groups such as NAMASTE (the 'New Association of Magical, Sexual and Tantrik Explorers') and the 'New Tantrik order in America' (Kraig 2002; Douglas 1997). Sexual magic in both its Tantric and Western esoteric forms has also been absorbed as one of many techniques into more radically eclectic movements such as Chaos Magic. For Chaos magicians such as Peter J Carroll, however, sexual magic is not simply a means of liberating the individual self or transgressing the limits of conventional society, as it has been for Randolph or Crowley; rather, it is part of a more radical attempt to shatter the limits of ordinary consciousness and reality itself: 'Eat all loathsome things until they no longer revolt, Seek union with all that you normally reject. Scheme against your most sacred principles in thought, word and deed. You will eventually have to witness the loss and putrefaction of every loved thing...The only clear view is from atop the mountain of your dead selves' (Carroll 1987, 48).

This article has provided just a brief overview and has necessarily had to omit many other figures, movements, and ideas in the development of modern sexual magic (see Versluis 2008; Hanegraaff and Kripal 2008; Hakl 2008). Yet virtually all these many forms of sexual magic have roots that stretch deeply into the Christian, Jewish, and Pagan origins of Western esotericism and flowered into a bewildering diversity of new forms in the modern era. One of the most consistent themes that we see throughout these many different forms of modern sexual magic, however, is the link between sexual and social liberation – the belief that the creative power of sexuality is in one way or another tied to the larger transformation of society as a whole. This hope for social liberation has assumed a great many different forms – ranging from the sexual and racial egalitarianism of P. B. Randolph to the radical Traditionalism and elitism of Julius Evola, from the feminism of Starhawk to the self-proclaimed misogyny of LaVey. But one recurring theme in all of these is the belief that sexuality carries with it a power that far exceeds mere physical orgasm, promising the hope of transcending the limits of the individual ego, the social world, and perhaps even conventional reality itself.

REFERENCES AND FURTHER READING

Carroll, Peter J. (1987) *Liber Null & Psychonaut: An Introduction to Chaos Magic*, York Beach, ME: Weiser Books.

Carter, John (2005) *Sex and Rockets: The Occult World of Jack Parsons*, Port Townsend, WA: Feral House.

Coulianu, Ioan P. (1987) *Eros and Magic in the Renaissance*, Chicago: University of Chicago Press.

Crowley, Aleister (1986) *Liber Agape: De Arte Magica*, Toronto: Kadath Press.

——(1989) *The Confessions of Aleister Crowley: An Autohagiography*, New York: Penguin.

——(1996) *The Law is for All: The Authorized Popular Commentary on Liber AL sub figura CCXX, The Book of the Law*, Tempe, AZ: New Falcon.

DeConick, April (2008) 'Conceiving Spirits: The Mystery of Valentinian Sex,' in Wouter J. Hanegraaff and Jeffrey J. Kripal (eds), *Hidden Intercourse: Eros and Sexuality in the History of Western Esotericism*, Leiden: Brill, 23–48.

Deveney, John Patrick (1997) *Paschal Beverly Randolph: A Nineteenth-Century American Spiritualist, Rosicrucian and Sex Magician*, Albany, NY: SUNY Press.

Douglas, Nik (1997) *Spiritual Sex: Secrets of Tantra from the Ice Age to the New Millennium*, New York: Pocket Books.

Evola, Julius (1983) *The Metaphysics of Sex*, New York: Inner Traditions.

——(1992) *The Yoga of Power: Tantra, Shakti and the Secret Way*, Rochester, VT: Inner Traditions.

Faraone, Christopher (1999) *Ancient Greek Love Magic*, Cambridge: Harvard University Press.

Farrar, Janet and Stewart Farrar (1996) *A Witches' Bible: The Complete Witch's Handbook*, Custer, WA: Phoenix.

Frankfurter, David (2008) *Evil Incarnate: Rumors of Demonic Conspiracy and Satanic Abuse in History*, Princeton: Princeton University Press.

Godwin, Joscelyn, Christian Chanel and John Patrick Deveney (1995) *The Hermetic Brotherhood of Luxor*, York Beach, ME: Samuel Weiser.

Hakl, Hans Thomas (2008) 'The Theory and Practice of Sexual Magic, Exemplified by Four Magical Groups in the Early Twentieth Century,' in Wouter J. Hanegraaff and Jeffrey J. Kripal (eds.), *Hidden Intercourse: Eros and Sexuality in the History of Western Esotericism*, Leiden: Brill, 445–79.

Hanegraaff, Wouter and Jeffrey J. Kripal, eds. (2008) *Hidden Intercourse: Eros and Sexuality in the History of Western Esotericism*, Leiden: Brill.

Hansen, H.T. (2002) 'Julius Evola's Political Endeavors,' in Julius Evola, *Men Among the Ruins: Post-War Reflections of a Radical Traditionalist*, Rochester, VT: Inner Traditions.

Hutton, Ronald (1999) *Triumph of the Moon: A History of Modern Pagan Witchcraft*, New York: Oxford University Press.

Idel, Moshe (1989) 'Sexual Metaphors and Praxis in the Kabbalah,' in David Kraemer (ed.), *The Jewish Family: Metaphor and Memory*, New York: Oxford University Press, 179–224.

Kraig, Donald M. (2002) *Modern Sex Magick: Secrets of Erotic Spirituality*, Llewellyn Publications.

LaVey, Anton Szandor (1969) *The Satanic Bible*, New York: Avon.

——(1989) *The Satanic Witch*, Los Angeles: Feral House.

Naglowska, Maria de, trans. (1931) *Magia Sexualis*, Paris: Robert Telin.

Naglowska, Maria de (2011) *The Light of Sex: Initiation, Magic and Sacrament*, Rochester, VT: Inner Traditions.

Parsons, John Whiteside (1982) *The Book of BABALON*, Berkeley, CA: Ordo Templi Orientis.

Pasi, Marco (2005). 'Ordo Templi Orientis,' in Wouter J. Hanegraaff et al (eds.), *Dictionary of Gnosis and Western Esotericism*, Leiden: Brill, II: 898–906.

Randolph, Paschal Beverly (1874) *Eulis! The Mystery of Love*, Toledo, OH: Randolph.

Reuss, Theodor (1906) *Lingam-Yoni*, Berlin: Verlag Willson.

Rosemont, Franklin (1997) Foreword to John Patrick Deveney, *Paschal Beverly Randolph: A Nineteenth-Century American Spiritualist, Rosicrucian and Sex Magician*, Albany, NY: SUNY Press.

Schreck, Nikolas and Zeena Schreck (2002) *Demons of the Flesh: The Complete Guide to Left Hand Sex Magic*, New York: Creation Books.

Starhawk (1988) *Dreaming the Dark: Magic, Sex and Politics*, Boston: Beacon Press.

Stephens, Walter (2002) *Demon Lovers: Witchcraft, Sex, and the Crisis of Belief*, Chicago: University of Chicago Press.

Wolfson, Elliot R. (1995) *Circle in the Square: Studies in the Use of Gender in Kabbalistic Symbolism*, Albany, NY: SUNY Press.

Urban, Hugh B. (2003) *Tantra: Sex, Secrecy, Politics and Power in the Study of Religion*, Berkeley: University of California Press.

——(2005) *Magia Sexualis: Sex, Magic and Liberation in Modern Western Esotericism*, Berkeley: University of California Press.

——(2008) 'The Yoga of Sex: Tantra, Orientalism and Sex Magic in the Ordo Templi Orientis,' in Wouter J. Hanegraaff and Jeffrey J. Kripal (eds.), *Hidden Intercourse: Eros and Sexuality in the History of Western Esotericism*, Leiden: Brill, 401–45.

——(2012) 'The Occult Roots of Scientology? L. Ron Hubbard, Aleister Crowley and the Origins of a Controversial New Religion,' *Nova Religio* 15, no. 3: 91–116.

——(forthcoming) 'Sexuality,' in Glenn Magee (ed.), *The Cambridge Handbook of Western Mysticism and Esotericism*, Cambridge: Cambridge University Press.

Versluis, Arthur (2008) *The Secret History of Western Sexual Mysticism: Sexual Practices and Spiritual Marriage*, Rochester, VT: Destiny Books.

CHAPTER FIFTY-SEVEN

TAROT

Helen Farley

INTRODUCTION

In a society increasingly intolerant of religious enquiry, where empirical scientific investigation and strict rationalism are afforded primary importance, tarot has been discredited, linked in the media and popular culture with dodgy soothsayers with a malignant intent to deceive and with weak-minded seekers clad in rainbow colours. The relatively small number of scholarly works relating to tarot is in marked contrast to the large numbers of popular tarot books, which crowd the shelves of New Age bookstores and 'Self-Help' corners of department stores.

In considering tarot in an academic context, it is first necessary to distinguish historical facts from the esoteric fictions which are endlessly recycled. For example, many authors still promulgate the falsehood that tarot is encoded with the lost Hermetic knowledge of an endangered Egyptian priesthood confronted with annihilation by powerful enemies. These fanciful tales cannot be substantiated and originate in a perceived need for legitimacy for tarot through an artificial association with a noble, wise and ancient people.

This discussion will provide an overview of tarot history, symbolism and divination. It begins by investigating the origins of tarot, gleaning evidence from the time of its first appearance in the courts of Northern Italy in the first quarter of the fifteenth century. At this time, the deck was used exclusively for game playing. Tarot was first viewed as an esoteric device in the last part of the eighteenth century in pre-Revolutionary France. This is where tarot's first significant links with esotericism were forged and tarot symbolism became associated with a perceived ancient Egyptian provenance, as well as esoteric Freemasonry and astrology in the milieu of the French occult revival. Occurring slightly later, England also underwent an occult revival, the most noteworthy group during which was the Hermetic Order of the Golden Dawn. Under their considerable influence, tarot underwent a substantial evolution, which laid the foundations for modern tarot interpretation.

WHAT IS TAROT?

Tarot decks exist in infinite variety, resplendent with symbolism from every religious, esoteric and cultural tradition. The creators of these different decks assert that each has a particular purpose and is suited to particular people. But, what constitutes the tarot deck?

Commonly, though not exclusively, the tarot deck consists of seventy-eight cards. Most of the deck has a comparable structure to the ordinary playing card deck. Fifty-six of the cards are distributed through four suits and this structure shows tarot's original purpose for use in games very similar to contemporary Bridge. Those who use the tarot for more esoteric purposes have a special name for this grouping, calling it the 'Minor Arcana'. As with the ordinary playing card deck, each suit consists of numbered cards from 1 (Ace) to 10, with the usual three court cards of Jack (Knight), Queen and King. Tarot suits however have an additional court card, the Page. When tarot first appeared, it featured the Italian suit signs of the regular card deck, namely Cups (*Coppe*), Batons (*Bastoni*), Coins (*Denari*) and Swords (*Spade*). These suits signs relate to the modern English and French marks of Hearts (*Coeur*), Clubs (*Trèfle*), Diamonds (*Carreau*) and Spades (*Pique*) respectively. As those card games played with both the regular deck and the tarot deck extended from Italy across Europe, the suit signs evolved into distinctive, region-specific patterns.

The remaining twenty-two cards of the tarot deck consist of twenty-one ordered trump cards and an unnumbered 'wild' or *Fou* (Fool) card. These cards are generally distinguished by the elaborate symbolism they display. Those who use the tarot deck for divination often use the term 'Major Arcana' to describe the grouping of the trump cards and Fool card. It is certainly the novel addition of these cards to the cards of the four suits that makes the tarot deck so intriguing. In this way, the structure of the tarot deck diverged markedly from that of the ordinary playing card deck. Originally unlabelled, the trumps bear the names of the Magician, the Popess, the Empress, the Emperor, the Pope, the Lovers, the Chariot, Strength, the Hermit, the Wheel of Fortune, Justice, the Hanged Man, Death, Temperance, the Devil, the Tower, the Star, the Moon, the Sun, Judgement and the World. The names of the individual trump cards, the form of the symbolism on them and their rank order, differed between decks, depending on where each was designed, the purpose for which they were created and the intent of the artist who crafted them.

THE BIRTH OF TAROT

No new invention first appears in a form that is final and complete. Instead, there are a number of false starts, incremental changes, revisions and redesigns and so it was with the invention of tarot. It seems most likely that the tarot deck evolved from the fifty-two-card playing deck common in many countries in the west. There are significant correspondences in structure and symbolism between the two kinds of deck which indicate a close developmental relationship. Indeed, circumstantial evidence supports this hypothesis. The ordinary playing card deck was first mentioned in sermons and prohibitions against gambling around fifty years before the first documented appearance of tarot (Depaulis 1984, 33). In 1371, Peter IV, King of Aragorn, commissioned a deck of cards from the Catalan Jaume March (Ortalli

1996, 175) and just six years later in 1377, Johannes of Rheinfelden in Switzerland, referred to a deck as consisting of thirteen cards in four suits, each made up of ten numeral cards and three court cards consisting of a King, an upper Marshal and a lower Marshal (Steele 1900, 189, 202). The 'game of cards' or *ludus cartarum* had arrived in Switzerland that same year but was swiftly prohibited (O'Donoghue 1901, 2–3). Almost concurrently, playing cards were alluded to in a range of bureaucratic documents including catalogues of possessions, edicts, city chronicles and account books in the cities of Florence, Siena, Paris and Basle (Dummett with Mann 1980, 10–32). The deck was most likely introduced into Europe through the prosperous seaport of Venice which conducted a busy trade with the countries of the East and the Near East (Hargrave 1966, 223). By this time, it is evident the deck consisted of fifty-two cards distributed through four suits. It is also evident that in the absence of transitional decks or obvious progenitors, the playing card deck was not of European invention (Dummett with Mann 1980, 33–34).

A likely progenitor was found in 1939 in an Istanbul museum by archaeologist L. A. Mayer. The deck was from the Egyptian Mamlūk Empire and was obviously the antecedent of the Latin playing card deck (Goggin 2003, 49–50). Through comparison with Egyptian illustrated manuscripts of known provenance, it was dated to the fifteenth century (Hoffmann 1973, 18–19). Forty-eight cards of the entire pack had survived with cards divided into four suits of Swords, Polo-Sticks, Cups and Coins, with each comprised of ten numeral cards and three court cards headed by the King (Dummett with Mann, 1980, 39). Having been imported into Italy via Venice, the cards were adapted to reflect the subtleties of the local culture by card-makers (Olsen 1974, 42–43). The most evident modification was the renovation of the suit of polo sticks into batons as polo was not well-known in Europe at that time (Chehabi & Guttmann 2002, 390).

As indicated at the outset, the oldest tarot decks so far unearthed are from northern Italy and have been dated to the first half of the fifteenth century. The first intriguing intimation as to the identity of tarot's creator came in a letter written by a Venetian military captain, Jacopo Antonio Marcello. The letter was dated 1449 and accompanied a deck of tarot cards (*carte de trionfi*), sent as a gift for Queen Isabella of Anjou, the consort of King René I, Duke of Lorraine (Olsen 1994, 1). In the letter, Marcello asserted that the famous artist Michelino da Besozzo painted the deck which had been invented by Duke Filippo Maria Visconti of Milan (Olsen 1994, 1). Although the deck of cards Marcello described did not survive, his letter and an instructive treatise in Latin penned by the eccentric Duke's secretary, Marziano da Tortono, still do (Dummett with Mann 1980, 82). The treatise, entitled *Tractatus de Deificatione Sexdecim Heroum*, maintained that the idea for the deck came from Duke Filippo Maria Visconti and that it was crafted by the acclaimed artist, Michelino da Besozzo (Olsen 1994, 106–7). Duke Visconti's biographer, Decembrio, writing in 1440, also described a deck of similar cards and it seems credible that this deck was the one described in Marcello's letter and Marziano's treatise (Moakley 1966, 52).

Decembrio described the deck as comprising 'sixteen celestial princes and barons' with four kings. Though the sixteen cards were sequential, as with the tarot deck, they were also distributed into four orders or suits, namely Virtues, Riches, Virginities and Pleasures (Pratesi 1989, 34). There is no doubt that this deck was very different to the deck that later became characterised as tarot, but it does seem to have represented an intermediate stage between regular playing cards and tarot. Though the sixteen deities were not present as trumps in later tarot decks, there is some similarity between the suits of Virtues, Riches, Virginities and Pleasures and those of both the regular tarot deck and regular playing cards. Pratesi suggested that the *denari* (coins) corresponded with the order of Riches; *spade* (swords) evolved into Virtues; *coppes* (cups) inspired Pleasures; and *bastoni* (batons) became known as Virginities (1989, 143–44).

An abundance of administrative documents from the various courts of northern Italy suggest that there was a surfeit of handcrafted decks produced between the time of Marcello's letter and the end of the fifteenth century. Even so, just twenty partial packs survive (Olsen 1994, 2). The earliest of these originated from the court of Milan presided over by Duke Filippo Maria Visconti. Though there is a broad correspondence between their structures, they do not resemble very closely the pack described in Marziano's treatise or Marcello's letter. Of the extant packs, there are three that are of particular interest because they are both the oldest and the most complete. The three decks share pip cards allocated to the traditional Italian suits of Coins, Swords, Cups and Batons (Dummett with Mann 1980, 68). One of these decks, known as the Visconti-Sforza deck, appeared to be the immediate progenitor of standardised decks with most of the familiar trumps.

It seems most likely that the tarot was invented by Duke Filippo Maria Visconti. The symbolism depicted on that first deck described by Marziano was replaced by something altogether more symbolic of the forces affecting the Duke's difficult passage through life. For example, the cards of the Emperor, Empress, Pope and Popess represented spiritual and temporal power in northern Italy in late Medieval and Early Modern times (Dummett 1986, 104). Milan was caught in a power struggle between the Pope, exerting influence from Rome, and the Holy Roman Empire to the north. These four cards are indicative of that struggle (Farley 2009, 52–58). Interestingly, the Popess has been linked to the figure of Sister Maifreda da Pirovano who was a relative of the Viscontis. She was a member of the heretical sect of the Guglielmites (Newman 2005, 28). Significantly, none of the extant decks possessed either the Devil trump or the Tower trump, standard in modern tarot decks. It has been theorised that the Devil was not a significant figure in the Renaissance so probably was omitted from the deck (Farley 2009, 88–92). The Tower or 'Torre' in Italian, however, was also the name of the main political rivals of the Visconti in Milan. It is not inconceivable that the Tower card, with its destructive and violent imagery, was present in the original decks, symbolising the eventual triumph of the Viscontis over the Della Torres (Farley 2009, 84–88).

The game of tarot was complex, requiring much skill and an excellent memory. The symbolism on the cards could be seen as an allegory for life, itself complicated and unpredictable. The particular character of the games played using those early cards remains mysterious as there were no recorded rules of play prior to the sixteenth century (Dummett & McLeod 2004, 13). However, there are a few clues as to how play proceeded. It can be deduced from Marziano's treatise that the order of cards of two of the pip suits was reversed in common with games described at a later date (Pratesi 1989, 24). It is feasible that the ordering of these cards would also have been reversed in games played with those first decks and shrewd players would have factored this complication into their game strategy. Initially, trump cards were not numbered and their order had to be memorised, serving to further complicate the game (Dummett 1986, 7–8). The game of tarot required cleverness and strategy, yet each player was still susceptible to the vagaries of chance introduced by the other players. In many ways a game is a reflection of life as inferred by the phrase 'the game of life' (von Franz 1980, 49), and the game of tarot with its evocative symbolism and complex rules of play, made this relationship overt.

In our society, tarot is primarily used as a divinatory device and it is worth considering why it did not serve such a function from the time of its creation. An explanation can be found in Renaissance attitudes to both divination and magic. At this time, it was widely believed that God embedded clues in nature that could be deciphered by anyone with sufficient knowledge. In this way, humans were able to discern the mind and will of God (Kieckhefer 1989, 90). It was thought that the causes of tempests, illness, misfortune or famine could be determined by a careful examination of omens, the movements of stars or even a reading of the physical attributes of the human body (Lessa 1958, 314–26). Any form of divination or fortune-telling which made use of invocations, written petitions or the use of sigils was considered to be devilish and could draw the unwelcome attentions of the Inquisition (Russell 1972, 143). Using tarot for fortune-telling or other forms of divination would have been akin to working with the Devil.

TAROT AND ESOTERICISM

We know tarot primarily as an esoteric or divinatory device. There are numerous books about how to use tarot to enhance various aspects of life. Yet, for many continental Europeans, tarot is a popular game requiring skill and patience. In many countries, tarot decks can be purchased solely for the purpose of game playing (see Dummett & McLeod 2004). The change was brought about by a shift in European culture, which saw a decline in the popularity and legitimacy of organised Christianity and allowed the emersion of more heterodox forms of spirituality which often combined Christian ideas with astrology, esoteric Freemasonry, Rosicrucianism, Kabbalah and other esoteric systems (Farley 2009, 95–101).

Just before the French Revolution that would so shake Europe, between the years 1773 and 1782, a Swiss-born Freemason and esotericist, Antoine Court de Gébelin, published his magnificent nine-volume opus entitled *The Primeval World, Analyzed and Compared to the Modern World*. This considerable work elaborated Court de Gébelin's dream to reconstruct primeval civilisation which he perceived to be in every way superior to contemporary culture. Part of the eighth volume was devoted to the origins of tarot (Depaulis 1984, 131). It was here that Court de Gébelin recounted how at some time in the last quarter of the century, he happened across some women playing the game of tarot. At that time, tarot cards were not known in Paris. As Court de Gébelin was interested in the Hermetic mysteries of ancient Egypt, it seemed obvious to him that he was regarding a sacred Egyptian book, the remnants of the lost *Book of Thoth* (Decker and Dummett 2002, 25). Court de Gébelin imagined that this *Book of Thoth* had been smuggled to Europe by the gypsies, at that time thought to have been from Egypt, who had been hiding it since it had been entrusted to them by Egyptian priests faced with annihilation by their enemies. He further inferred that the most secure way to preserve the Hermetic wisdom was to encode it as a game and to trust that one day a suitable adept would decipher it. This honour he claimed for himself (Court de Gébelin 1774).

Because tarot was purportedly of Egyptian origin, Court de Gébelin removed all traces of Christian symbolism from the deck. For example, the Pope holding the papal triple cross became the 'High Priest' or 'Hierophant and his cross was declared to be Egyptian. Likewise, the Popess emerged as the "High Priestess" apparently correcting the gaffe of the German card-makers' (Decker, Depaulis & Dummett 1996, 60). Remarkably, Court de Gébelin linked the twenty-two tarot trumps with the twenty-two letters of the Egyptian alphabet which he maintained was also common to the Hebrews and the Orientals (Decker, Depaulis & Dummett 1996, 62). Alas, there were not twenty-two letters in the Egyptian alphabet but notably, this was the first time the trumps had been linked to the Hebrew alphabet and subsequently Kabbalah, an association which was a central tenet of later esoteric theories of tarot (Auger 2004, 5).

The theory that posited an Egyptian origin for tarot was reinforced by other French esotericists such as Éliphas Lévi, Paul Christian and Gérard Encausse (popularly known as 'Papus') (Farley 2011). Each had their own particular slant on tarot's place in esoteric theory. Egypt was believed to be the source of all esoteric wisdom and the Egyptian hieroglyphics were considered an ancient magical language. This theory was able to gain currency because of France's infatuation with all things Egyptian, prior to the deciphering of hieroglyphics by François Champollion enabled by the discovery of the Rosetta Stone.

Just a few short years later, across the Channel from France, England was also in the grip of the occult revival. By this time hieroglyphs had been translated. Even so, Victorian society remained enraptured by Egyptian culture. One possible reason is the revelation of the grandeur and sophistication of Egyptian civilisation unearthed by extensive archaeological excavations (Luhrmann 1989, 40). Initially, the role of tarot in this esoteric climate was slight. However, guided by the influence of a small esoteric society, the Hermetic Order of the Golden Dawn, the tarot became significant. The Golden Dawn never possessed more than 300 members, yet it quickly became enormously influential on the practice of magic and tarot interpretation. The Order was the crowning glory of the British occult revival, fusing into a coherent whole, an immense body of material embracing Egyptian mythology, Kabbalah, tarot, Enochian magic, alchemy, Rosicrucianism and astrology (Farley 2002, 3). The trump sequence of the tarot deck was rearranged to better align with other esoteric systems and each Major Arcana card was linked to one of the twenty-two pathways between the *sephiroth* on the Kabbalistic Tree of Life. A divinatory meaning could be ascribed to each of the cards, borrowed from the meaning of the pathways. The modified trump order and divinatory interpretations underpin modern tarot divination. Two members of the Golden Dawn would also play a substantial role in the evolution of tarot, namely Aleister Crowley and Arthur Edward Waite.

Crowley extended the lists of correspondences between the tarot trumps and other esoteric systems. But it was Waite who was to be the major innovator. He designed a pack in which each Minor Arcana card was illustrated to expedite divinatory interpretation. Waite was also responsible for popularising the link between tarot and the Grail legends, which, at that time, erroneously claimed a Celtic origin. This invention of Britain's Celtic heritage came to be known as the 'Celtic revival'. In addition to Ireland and Scotland, this movement embraced the language, mythology and lore of Brittany, Cornwall, Wales and the Isle of Man (Webb 1974, 318–19). Further mining this inclination, Waite was the initiator of the Celtic Cross spread, a very commonplace method used to 'read' the cards even today. The deck he conceived, commonly known as the Rider-Waite deck after its designer and publisher, was to become the most popular in the history of tarot. Many modern tarot scholars prefer to call it the 'Colman-Waite' deck in order to acknowledge the contribution of Pamela Colman Smith who was the artist who painted the deck.

TAROT TODAY

With the advent of the New Age when esoteric, philosophical and religious systems are eclectically plundered to create individual spiritual systems for seekers, the tarot has undergone yet another transformation. The tarot deck preserved its primary function as an aid to divination, but the character of that divination has altered. The object of New Age tarot reading has become healing and self-development, rather than straightforward fortune-telling. During the French and British occult revivals, practitioners looked for the one true tarot, 'rectifying' the deck in accordance with their beliefs (Pollack 1989, 124). With the advent of the New Age, tarot designers felt able to 're-imagine' the deck, no longer afraid to experiment, comfortable with creating links to other cultures or to create decks that fulfilled roles other than divination (Pollack 1989, 124). The appropriation of the principles of analytical psychologist Carl Jung justified this practice. Jung's theory of archetypes validated borrowings and substitutions from other cultures in the symbolism of tarot (Nichols 1980, 7–10). Consequently, the structure and symbolism of the tarot deck is constantly shifting. Large numbers of decks lack Minor Arcana cards or variable numbers of Major Arcana cards. Trump titles are frequently substituted so that they are better customised within whatever scheme was pulled into service.

There are modern tarot decks aligned to every conceivable tradition, philosophy or culture (for example, see Tarot Catalog #61 2004). For example, the *Voyager Tarot* of Knutson and Wanless was created as a psychological tool of personal transformation. In contrast to the well-defined rubric of symbols used by esotericists to effect change, Wanless advocated using a larger, less conventional pool of symbolism. The images on this deck range from animals, vegetables and elements to minerals, art and extra-terrestrial worlds (Pollack 1989, 126). In contrast, the *Feng Shui Tarot* created by the mother-and-son team of Eileen and Peter Paul Connolly has incorporated the ancient Chinese geomantic tradition of *feng shui* into the schema of tarot. It is not intended for *feng shui* analysis and the traditional meanings of the Major Arcana cards are retained though illustrated using symbols relevant to *feng shui*. The suits of the Minor Arcana suits are renamed White Tigers (Swords), Black Tortoises (Wands), Red Phoenix (Cups) and Green Dragons (Coins) (Kaplan & Huets 2005, 35–37). These two decks are just examples of the many thousands of decks available for New Age divination and spiritual development.

CONCLUSION

Tarot began its life nearly 600 years ago in the court of Milan, most likely invented by a reclusive and eccentric nobleman, Duke Filippo Maria Visconti. At first, the tarot reflected the concerns of the Duke's life: his battles with the Papacy and the Holy Roman Empire, the trials and tribulations of love and marriage, the ever present spectre of death in the form of the Black Death. But once the deck was taken away from this cultural milieu, it appeared enigmatic and mysterious. Little wonder that Antoine Court de Gébelin, when he saw the tarot in pre-Revolutionary France, did not recognise the symbolism on the deck, mistaking it for the outpouring of an Egyptian priestly class faced with annihilation. The fiction was promulgated by esotericists in France and later in England into the nineteenth century. Once in England, the tarot underwent its most significant transformation under the auspices of the Hermetic Order of the Golden Dawn, and in particular, with two of its members, Aleister Crowley and Arthur Edward Waite. It was here that tarot's modern divinatory meanings were established along with long lists of correspondences, tying tarot to myriad other esoteric schemas.

With the emergence of the New Age in the late 1970s, tarot underwent further transformation in tandem to the cultural changes taking place. With the rise of interest in Eastern and indigenous spiritual systems, ecofeminism and other spiritual and cultural currents, the symbolism of tarot adapted to and incorporated those symbols. In addition, its purpose shifted from fortune-telling to become a tool of spiritual and holistic development. As culture undergoes further change, as will inevitably happen, tarot no doubt will act as a willing receptacle for those new patterns, symbols and systems that will arise.

REFERENCES AND FURTHER READING

Auger, E.E. (2004) *Tarot and Other Meditation Decks: History, Theory, Aesthetics, Typology*, Jefferson: McFarland & Company Inc.

Chehabi, H.E. & Guttmann, A. (2002) 'From Iran to All of Asia: The Origin and Diffusion of Polo', *The International Journal for the History of Polo* 19:2–3, 384–200.

Court de Gébelin, A. (1774) *Le Monde Primitif: Analysé Et Comparé Avec Le Monde Moderne, Considéré Dans L'histoire Naturelle De La Parole; Ou Grammaire Universelle Et Comparative*, 9 vols, Paris: Archives De La Linguistique Française.

Decker, R. & Dummett, M. (2002) *A History of the Occult Tarot: 1870–1970*, London: Gerald Duckworth & Co. Ltd.

Decker, R., Depaulis, T. & Dummett, M. (1996) *A Wicked Pack of Cards: The Origins of Occult Tarot*, London: Gerald Duckworth and Co. Ltd.

Depaulis, T. (1984) *Tarot, Jeu Et Magie*, Paris: Bibliothèque Nationale.

Dummett, M. (1986) *The Visconti-Sforza Tarot Cards*, New York: George Braziller, Inc.

Dummett, M. & McLeod, J. (2004) *A History of Games Played with the Tarot Pack: The Game of Triumphs*, vol. 1, Lewiston: Edwin Mellen Press.

Dummett, M. with Mann, S. (1980) *The Game of Tarot: From Ferrara to Salt Lake City*, London: Gerald Duckworth and Co.

Farley, H. (2011) 'Out of Africa: Tarot's Fascination with Africa', *Literature and Aesthetics* 21:1, 175–95.

——(2009) *A Cultural History of Tarot: From Entertainment to Esotericism*, London: I.B. Tauris.

——(2002) 'The History of the Hermetic Order of the Golden Dawn: 1887–1920', Masters thesis, Brisbane: University of Queensland.

Gilbert, C.E., ed. (1980) *Italian Art 1400–1500: Sources and Documents*, Englewood Cliffs: Prentice Hall, Inc.

Goggin, J. (2003) 'A History of Otherness: Tarot and Playing Cards from Early Modern Europe', *Journal for the Academic Study of Magic* 1:1, 45–74.

Hargrave, C.P. (1966) *A History of Playing Cards and a Bibliography of Cards and Gaming*, New York: Dover Publications.

Hoffmann, D. (1973) *The Playing Card: An Illustrated History*, Greenwich: New York Graphic Society.

Kaplan, S.R. & Huets, J. (2005) *The Encyclopedia of Tarot*, vol. 4, Stamford: U. S. Games Systems.

Kieckhefer, R. (1989) *Magic in the Middle Ages*, *Cambridge Medieval Textbooks*, Cambridge: Cambridge University Press.

Lessa, W.A. (1958) 'Somatomancy: Precursor of the Science of Human Constitution', in Lessa, W.A. & Vogt, E.Z., eds., *Reader in Comparative Religion: An Anthropological Approach*, Evanston: Row, Peterson and Co., 314–26.

Lessa, W.A. & Vogt, E.Z., eds. (1958) *Reader in Comparative Religion: An Anthropological Approach*, Evanston: Row, Peterson and Co.

Luhrmann, T.M. (1989) *Persuasions of the Witch's Craft: Ritual Magic in Contemporary England*, Cambridge: Harvard University Press.

Moakley, G. (1966) *The Tarot Cards Painted by Bonifacio Bembo for the Visconti-Sforza Family: An Iconographic and Historical Study*, New York: The New York Public Library.

Newman, B. (2005) 'The Heretic Saint: Gugliema of Bohemia, Milan, and Brunate', *Church History* 74:1, 1–38.

Nichols, S. (1980) *Jung and Tarot: An Archetypal Journey*, New York: Samuel Weiser.

O'Donoghue, F.M. (1901) *Catalogue of the Collection of Playing Cards Bequeathed to the Trustees of the British Museum by the Late Lady Charlotte Schreiber*, London: Longmans and Co.

Olsen, C. (1994) 'Carte Da Trionfi: The Development of Tarot in Fifteenth Century Italy', doctoral thesis, Philadelphia: University of Pennsylvania.

Ortalli, G. (1996) 'The Prince and the Playing Cards: The Este Family and the Role of Courts at the Time of the Kartenspiel-Invasion', *Ludica: annali di storia e civilta del gioco* 2, 175–205.

Pollack, R. (1989) *The New Tarot*, Wellingborough: The Aquarian Press.

Pratesi, F. (1989) 'Italian Cards – New Discoveries: 10. The Earliest Tarot Pack Known', *The Playing Card* 18:2, 33–38.

Russell, J.B. (1972) *Witchcraft in the Middle Ages*, Ithaca: Cornell University Press.

Steele, R. (1900) 'A Notice of the Ludus Triumphorum and Some Early Italian Card Games; with Some Remarks on the Origin of the Game of Cards', *Archaeologia, or, Miscellaneous Tracts Relating to Antiquity* 57, 185–200.

U.S. Games Systems, Inc. (2004) *Tarot Catalog #61*, Stamford: U. S. Games Systems.

von Franz, M. (1980) *On Divination and Synchronicity: The Psychology of Meaningful Chance*, Toronto: Inner City Books.

Webb, J. (1974) *The Occult Underground*, La Salle: Open Court Publishing Company.

CHAPTER FIFTY-EIGHT

SCRYING

Angela Voss

Imagination is nearer to the substance of the soul than the sense is.

(Agrippa 1997, 202)

Scrying, taken from the English word 'descry' (to catch sight of something that is difficult to discern), has been variously defined as 'the faculty of seeing visions in a smooth surface or clear deep, or both' (Besterman 1924, 2); 'an occult method for obtaining oracular visions in water, glass or crystal' (Tyson 1997, xvi); and 'the deliberate act of perceiving events that lie beyond the range of the physical senses by using the agents of the unconscious mind' (Tyson 1997, 3). As such, scrying is a form of clairvoyance or cryptesthesia, and as it would usually also involve the interpretation of the meaning of such visions, it can be considered to be a form of divination. That said, Donald Tyson defines scrying as divination only if it involves the 'unconscious mind', such as some form of subliminal intuition, rather than merely deduction according to a set of rules (Tyson 1997, 4–5). The idea of a mirror or shining surface revealing an occult dimension—an alternative world which cannot be seen via sense-perception alone but which requires an intuitive 'second sight' to reveal it—leads us to question what is being revealed, how it is revealed, and why humans have the capacity to see beyond the veil of consensual reality. The silvery, shiny and translucent surfaces of crystals, mirrors or water remind us of the moon, poetically associated with the role of mediator between the elemental life on earth and the immaterial life of the spirit. In a receptive state, it seems possible for the scryer to gain access to this other realm, which reveals itself in shapes, images and symbols to be deciphered by the conscious mind.

It is not my intention in this chapter to give a history of scrying or a description of its various techniques, as these topics are covered in other sources (see Besterman 1924; Tyson 1997; Thomas & Lang 2010). Suffice it to say that its many variants have been practised at all times and in all cultures. Theodore Besterman lists catoptromancy (mirror), crystallomancy (crystal), cyclicomancy (cup of water or wine), gastromancy (marks on belly), hydromancy (water, river, lake), lecanomancy (water in basin or open receptacle), lithomancy (stone), onychomancy (fingernails), pegomancy (spring water) plus any other method using reflective objects or precious stones or metals (1924, 2–8). Tyson adds telepathy, dowsing and psychometry (1997, 4–5). Two of its most famous exponents were Nostradamus (1503–66) and Dr John Dee (1527–1608/9) with his medium Edward Kelley. The latter believed they were summoning autonomous spirits via the famous 'shewstone', in whose black obsidian surface Kelley saw visions of angels who communicated to him in a complex language (see Harkness 1999; Suster 2003; Szönyi 2006a). However, in this chapter we will focus more closely on the metaphysics of scrying, locating the practice within an epistemological context, and to this end highlight some of the avenues by which we might approach the subject of clairvoyant and divinatory 'knowing' in ways which honour its verity and integrity.

We will begin by addressing the nature of divination itself, before considering theories of subliminal mind and cognitive imagination in relation to scrying. In my view, it is not sufficient to approach such an activity from a purely psycho-physiological perspective—a legacy of post-Enlightenment material science—but rather we should situate it in within a discourse of liminality, poetics and supra-rational paradigms of perception if we wish to gain insight into its *modus operandi*.

DIVINATION

It is all too easy to marginalise divinatory knowledge as superstitious, irrational or illusory from a standpoint of an 'objective' rationalist who fears usurpation by 'the dark tide of mud of occultism' as Freud put it (see Jung 1961, 150); and for such a rationalist, even the spiritual science of visionaries such as Rudolf Steiner or Henry Corbin, for whom research into transpersonal reality involved rigorous inquiry into interior experience, is likely to be critiqued as 'religionist'. Contemporary scholarship on divination, however, has certainly progressed from the 'self-congratulatory rationalism' of various historians of science and anthropologists of the past (see Szönyi 2006b, 74), with authors such as Patrick Curry, Geoffrey Cornelius and Barbara Tedlock (all practitioners as well as academics) addressing head-on issues of divinatory phenomenology, ontology and epistemology in a wide inter-disciplinary inquiry (see, Cornelius 2003, 2007, 2010; Curry & Willis 2004, Curry & Voss 2007; Curry 2010; Tedlock 2006). They all expose divination as an essentially ubiquitous and creative—or co-creative—process, whose rationale is *affective* and metaphorical rather than causal. Divining involves the derivation of meaning from signs, and this metaphorical seeing is a fundamental principle of esotericism in the West. As Plotinus (204–70 CE) reminds the reader of his second *Ennead*, 'All teems with symbol; the wise man is the man who in any one thing sees another', adding that this is a common, everyday experience (Plotinus, II.3.7. See also III.1.6.). In our positivist society, it tends to be overlooked that this kind of seeing may produce valuable knowledge for the participant, the bottom line of truth always being the natural, physical causation in the underlying medium. Signification is regarded as an arbitrary and unverifiable leap of an over-active imagination, and the 'seeing of one thing as another' (*pareidolia*) as either a useful tool for psychological diagnosis or nothing more than an amusing coincidence. However, it is not problematic for diviners to hold both rational and symbolic levels of perception as equally valid in their respective cognitive domains; in fact in esoteric epistemology, intuitive cognition (or 'the intuitive intellect' as Plato would call it) is logically prior to discursive reasoning, as it is an innate faculty of knowing in the soul which is intimately connected to its own ground of being. It is this faculty which transcends subject–object duality as it exists beyond time and space as we know them.

What then is divination? Cornelius has defined it as 'a work where human being submits intimate concern to a primordial intelligence or reality that goes under various names, such as "spirit-like" or "divine", or a named god' (Cornelius 2007, 247), and Tedlock defines diviners as 'experts who embrace the notion of moving from a boundless to a bounded realm of existence in their practice' (Tedlock 2006, 62). A divination is both 'functional and performative', always constituting a 'unique case' whose truth is realised in lived experience and is never mere speculation or correctness of propositions (Cornelius 2007, 234–38). In its authentic form, divination involves taking moral responsibility for actions and decisions. It is not primarily about predicting the future (although it may involve prophetic utterance) but about asking for guidance about 'right action', about how to follow the path of good fortune in one's life, for 'destiny is negotiable' on the level of human affairs. In neoplatonic and theosophical contexts, as well as many 'new age' ones, divination has the teleological aim to cultivate self-awareness and raise consciousness, in the understanding that the human soul has an innate duality—a human and a divine aspect—which need to be brought into single focus. The higher part, according to the Platonists, is aligned with the all-seeing divine mind, and therefore has the power to alter what may appear to be 'fated' to the more materially bound level of cognition. This power (whether it is conceived as 'internal' or 'external' to the diviner) is sought and possibly embodied through a ritual action such as scrying, as the image arising is interpreted as a message from the spirits, gods or 'higher self'. The divinatory act allows the present moment to reveal itself, as it were, and within this moment the future is implicit and will flow according to the choices made.

In the act of gazing into a crystal ball or shiny surface, an *abaissement du niveau mental* may take place in which shapes or forms appear and assume significance as omens. The visions may be either unbidden or bidden (*Omina oblativa* and *omina impetrativa*—see Cornelius 2010, 396); that is, either actively sought through ritual intention, or spontaneously observed without any preparation or expectation of their appearance. As an example of the former, Crystal Addey draws our attention to the tradition of catoptromancy in ancient Greece, where shiny surfaces or mirrors were used for divination (Addey 2007, 1). According to Pausanias, at the sanctuary of Demeter at Patras rituals for the prognosis of illness involved lowering a mirror into a spring—after various ritual activities the images in the mirror would reveal whether the person enquired about was alive or dead (quoted in Addey 2007, 2–3). As an example of the latter, Pausanias again describes a mirror on the wall of a temple at Lykosaura; apparently when the visitor looked into it they did not see themselves, but only the distant statues of deities which were brought into sharp focus. Here we have a concrete metaphor for any scrying practice which aims to reveal aspects of an invisible world to normal sight.

The two modes of rational (human) and revelatory (divine) knowledge in turn relate to two distinct forms of divinatory practice: artificial and natural. In other words, some things could be ascertained through inductive rituals requiring speculation, inference or deduction, but others were directly 'revealed' through visions, dreams or direct symbolic insight. Tedlock has termed these forms 'representational' and 'presentational symbolism' and notes:

> In representational symbolism, specific intentional inference is paramount, the medium of expression is straightforward, and inductive reality is dominant. In presentational symbolism, meaning emerges directly from experiential immersion in the expressive or emotional patterns of the symbolic medium that is grasped intuitively.
>
> (Tedlock 2006, 70)

In practice, it is not so easy to differentiate between the two modes as perception and interpretation are often instantaneously intertwined; but, as Cornelius has pointed out, post-Enlightenment thought 'has removed the ontological necessity [of the relation between reason and revelation] and with it, the ground of divination' (Cornelius 2010, 5). In other words, the notion that all rational analysis is ultimately grounded in a 'supra-rational', noetic or deeply intuitive insight is no longer considered valid. In an 'ontological inversion' of cognitive value, the material world has assumed the status of ultimate reality, whilst metaphysically speaking it is contained and governed by far more 'real' spiritual law. It is illuminating to view this duality in terms of the functions of the brain hemispheres, as researched by Iain McGilchrist. In his pioneering book *The Master and his Emissary* he posits that the left brain of rationality and abstraction has become severed from the right brain's intuitive, visionary and holistic capacity and is no longer its 'emissary' but strives to become the master, if not the tyrant. McGilchrist concludes that it is in fact the imagination which provides a bridge between the two modes, which can be equated with (but *not* reduced to) the connective function of the *corpus callosum* in the brain (McGilchrist 2009, 198–208). Jeffrey Kripal follows this line of enquiry in his suggestion that scholars and researchers of religious or paranormal experience should develop their capacity for engagement with trans-rational, transpersonal or 'sacred' reality as well as their critical minds, an argument which I have also pursued elsewhere (Kripal 2001: 5; Voss 2009, 2011, 2013a).

So how can we characterise the kind of revelatory knowledge gleaned via the image in a crystal bowl or pool of water? It would appear to embody a sympathetic resonance, a 'consubstantiality' or 'momentary identity of substance' between observer and observed: the omen, the vision, IS at the same time the numinous 'other', which is also implicated in the event it points to in the world (see Cornelius 2007, 235). The omen is unique in that it is *only an omen for the one who sees it*, to whose life it has direct relevance, and this sense of being 'meant' is often attributed to a daimonic agency, as it resists all our usual categories of understanding (Cornelius 2007, 235). However, it may also be attributed to an 'unconscious' dimension of the human mind, and to this theory I will now turn.

SUBLIMINAL MIND

The suggestion of the nineteenth-century psychic researchers and psychoanalysts that the human mind contained 'unconscious' powers which could produce all manner of precognitive and telepathic information, and that these powers were open to rational investigation, was a radical one and it continues to inform parapsychological approaches today. But such a view strains to accommodate either a magical cosmology of autonomous spirit-agency (on its own terms) or the validity of gnostic insight, as it remains firmly bound to a spirit of scientific inquiry.

William James (1842–1910) triumphantly reported on the rigour of the investigative activities of the Society for Psychical Research, founded in 1882, praising F.W.H. Myers' (1843–1901) theories of the 'subliminal self'—an 'ultra-marginal' or unmanifested part of human consciousness responsible for pre-cognitive or telepathic events. In his essay 'What Psychical Research has Accomplished', published in 1912 in *The Will to Believe*, James gives the example of a 'Miss X', who, on consulting her crystal ball, saw printed characters telling of the death of an acquaintance. On perusing *The Times* from the previous day, she saw the identical announcement in the newspaper, although she was not aware of having read it before her scrying session. With the theory of the subliminal mind, events such as this could now be explained coherently with no need to resort to supernatural explanations, for such information could have been 'unconsciously' remembered. But other phenomena were more difficult to explain. For instance, James, Myers and their colleagues struggled to incorporate into this paradigm their experience of mediumship, which often demonstrated a tangible and inexplicable presence in the séance room which was difficult to attribute to 'subliminal mind'. As James famously remarked on witnessing the skills of the medium Mrs. Piper: 'If you wish to upset the law that all crows are black, you must not seek to show that no crows are; it is enough if you prove one single crow to be white. My own white crow is Mrs. Piper' (1912, 319). James attempts to construct a paradigm of 'hallucination' which embraces everything from the powers of suggestion to hearing the warning voice of a deceased relative in a time of danger, but cannot avoid the suspicion that in the latter case there must be 'something else going on'. In fact, he cannot resist the speculation that the theosophists may be more correct in their theories of autonomous astral bodies.

For the psychical researchers, it was enough that scryers or mediums could peer into a super-sensory realm not bound by laws of time and space, into an unconscious mind which could access information from a mysterious source, yet which needed a vehicle of words or images. Myers observed that scryers were not in a hypnotised state, but scrutinised their visions in complete conscious detachment. He concluded that crystal gazing is 'an empirical method of developing internal vision; of externalising pictures which are associated with changes in the sensorial tracts of the brain, due partly to internal stimuli, and partly to stimuli which may come from minds external to the scryer's own' (Myers 1919, 150). It thus may involve telepathic activity, and Myers appears to leave it open as to whether these 'external' minds are embodied or not. Besterman follows a harder line and sees no 'evidence' for spirit activity, concluding that

> scrying is a method of bringing into the consciousness of the scryer by means of a speculum through one or more of his senses the content of his subconsciousness, of rendering him more susceptible to the reception of telepathically transmitted concepts, and of bringing into operation a latent and unknown faculty of perception.
>
> (Besterman 1924, 160)

The contemporary scryer and scholar Donald Tyson takes a more radical view. He uses the metaphor of the unconscious mind as a computer which can pick up information and convey it through an image on a screen—such images might be clear and concise such as the words seen by Miss X, or shady and symbolic therefore requiring interpretation (Tyson 1997, 144). He calls them sensory metaphors, which like dream images, may point to an important message for the recipient. The 'computer' tunes in as it were to autonomous presences from other frequencies which might be experienced on an inner level as form, voice or touch (Tyson 1997, 145). The scrying mirror here, he claims, acts as a reflector of images communicated by discarnate spirits to the scryer's 'inner mind' which projects them onto its surface, in the same way as automatic writing or drawing. We note with interest that in Myers' supposed post-mortem communication via the medium Geraldine Cummins, he confirms that indeed the 'minds external to the scryer's own' are not incarnate. From his position 'on the other side', he explains that the inner mind of the medium is like soft wax which receives the thoughts of the discarnate being, but it must then find the appropriate words or images in which to 'clothe' it:

> It is true that we communicate by pictures or images, by signs which the deeper mind of the sensitive apprehends, and sometimes we may convey by a sign or symbol, a name or word unknown to the medium. It would be well for you to note that what you call 'normal consciousness' means the raising up of the barriers between your mind and another human mind. But behind all that there is among human beings a deeper self, a subjective mentality that can trespass into the domain of other subliminal selves, that meets with few barriers.
>
> (Cummins 1967, 126)

Whatever the reader may make of that, we are certainly left with an unresolvable ambiguity around the potential of the subliminal mind to embrace the intelligent 'other', however it is conceived.

THE IMAGINAL WORLD

Myers draws our attention to the importance of the symbolic image as an interface between two dimensions or levels of consciousness, and this leads us now to consider traditions in which the imagination itself is regarded as *cognitive*. The psychical researchers were aiming for scientific respectability through adopting a rational, methodically thorough examination of non-ordinary consciousness. On the other hand, we find the esoteric stream of wisdom in the West concerned with a mode of cognition which transcends rationality *per se* and engages with an epistemology of transcendent intuition derived from the Platonic notion of 'intellect' as the path to *gnosis* or wisdom.

The neoplatonic theory which illuminates our theme of scrying hinges on the understanding I mentioned earlier, that the sensible world is a natural image or reflection of the divine or intelligible world which interpenetrates it (see Armstrong 1990). Here we find again the crucial distinction between artificial and natural images. According to Plotinus, artistic or sculptural images would be artificial, representing a 'perfected' nature, and therefore could act as *eikons* or symbols, pointing back to an essential, archetypal form (Plotinus V.8.1). Natural images on the other hand are reflections in surfaces, such as water or a mirror. The appearance of an image in a scrying mirror for instance could be seen as a natural, immediate imprint of an eternal dimension of reality, because the eternal world contains the temporal and nothing impedes their interpenetration. As Plotinus explains: 'because of their closeness to something else in the world of real being [i.e. the spiritual world], something like an imprint and image of that other suddenly appears, either by its direct action or through the assistance of soul…or of a particular soul' (Plotinus V.8 7). The shadow or image of the archetype is produced directly and spontaneously through the mirroring process, unlike the artist's creation which involves planning and construction; but most interestingly, Plotinus emphasises the co-creative aspect of these spontaneous visions, for as he says of dreaming nature, 'my act of contemplation makes what it contemplates' (Plotinus III.8.4). The amphibian soul has a dimension which continuously inhabits the archetypal, unchanging world, whilst its 'human' part is able to translate intimations of this world through visions into the world of the senses 'by casting the reflections and shadows which make it up…or by dreaming the dream which it is' (Armstrong 1990, 162–63). Thus our attention is drawn to the fact that the dreams and visions hold an essential truth, whilst our normal waking consciousness is a mere reflection of an eternal reality.

In relation to the art of scrying then, the more polished or transparent the mirror of the psyche, the more powerful the vision, but the accuracy of its interpretation must depend on the quality of intuition of the individual. Reflections and shadows on water for instance can be true signs for some, but bewitch and mislead those who do not understand them and take them to be ultimate realities, or try to grab and literalise them, fixing them in immutable meanings (Armstrong 1990, 173, 178). The idea that meaning and truth arise from a 'symbolic attitude' is central to esotericism, as it is to poetry, and it is necessary to side-step our habitual rationalist assumptions if we are to get to the heart of image-magic. We also need to suspend our notions of causality, for to ask if images in a shiny surface are produced *either* by the psyche of the operator *or* an autonomous, non-material being creates an unhelpful dichotomy which can never be resolved one way or the other.

The neoplatonist Iamblichus (245–325 CE) refers to theurgic rituals which involve different kinds of light shining on reflective surfaces, and he too is careful to emphasise the difference between the two orders of 'divine' and 'human' action. True divinatory acts, he says, are instigated by the gods, not by men, for it is their transcendent power which illuminates the human imaginative faculty and allows it to glimpse images of another order. As Addey explains: 'divine illumination emanates from the god's ethereal vehicle to the human's ethereal vehicle, which is wholly taken over by the gods and the oracular message is pictured on the soul's imagination: these "pictures" or images come from the gods, thus divine illumination irradiates the vehicle, causing divinely inspired images in it' (Addey 2012, 8; Finamore 1985, 89–93). The divine appearances within the soul vehicle then, set in motion by the gods' will, take possession of the imaginative power, the mirror or glass acting as a medium for the practitioner's imaginative faculty (see Synesius 1888; Addey 2012; Finamore 1985). This power of the imagination to access an eternal, omniscient realm leads philosophers in this tradition to consider it as the means of prophecy—and, interestingly, as a daimonic intelligence in its own right (Synesius 1888, 137; Voss 2013b).

Cornelius Agrippa in 1533 confirmed that prophecy occurs 'by the true revelation of some divine power in a quiet and purified mind; for by this our soul receives true oracles, and abundantly yieldeth prophecies to us' (Agrippa 1997, 633). He echoes Plotinus in his insistence that the 'imaginative spirit' must be pure and undisturbed, 'so that it may be made worthy of the knowledge and government by the mind and understanding: for such a spirit is fit for prophesying and...is a most clear glass of all the images which flow everywhere from all things' (Agrippa 1997, 633). For Agrippa as a Christian magus, it is religion which will lead the mind to the necessary state of purity (Agrippa 1997, 638). Likewise, Paracelsus (1493–1541) speaks of the twofold human soul, part of which can rise above the illusions of the senses and perceive the 'astral light' or hidden occult properties in all elements of creation. This 'inner man' is 'the natural man, and knows more than the one which is formed of flesh'. Paracelsus brings our attention back to the importance of intention and commitment, for 'imagination springs from desire' and is required for successful clairvoyance; when the active will ceases to dominate, the imagination is freed to 'act on the invisible substance of the soul' (Hartmann 2010, 106–7). Paracelsus reiterates the crucial neoplatonic distinction between 'fancy' and imagination, the former being 'the corner stone of superstition and foolishness', the latter the faculty which 'becomes pregnant through desire' and may enter into contact with spirits (Hartmann 2010, 112). This metaphor connects us directly with C. G. Jung's theory of active imagination, to which I will now turn.

> *Looking*, psychologically, brings about the activation of the object; it is as if something were emanating from one's spiritual eye that evokes or activates the object of one's vision.
>
> The English verb, 'to look at', does not convey this meaning, but the German *betrachten*, which is an equivalent, means also to make pregnant...And if it is pregnant, then something is due to come out of it; it is alive, it produces, it multiplies. That is the case with any fantasy image; one concentrates upon it, and then finds that one has great difficulty in keeping the thing quiet, it gets restless, it shifts, something is added, or it multiplies itself; one fills it with living power and it becomes pregnant.
>
> (Jung 1997, 7)

Jung notes that an attitude of active expectation is required for the images brought forth to be examined by the conscious mind, whereas a passive attitude may result in an indiscriminating identification with the mood of the image (such as in a dream). When the mind is active, it is able to start penetrating to the meaning of the symbol revealed through concentrating on it and bringing it alive (see Voss 2006). In this way the divination becomes 'co-creative' (Jung 1997, 6). For Jung then, the act of scrying would facilitate the arousal of unconscious contents prior to their shaping, interpretation, and subsequent conversion into moral obligation. Furthermore, when a union of conscious and unconscious contents occurs, the transcendent function arises, which 'makes the transition from one attitude to another organically possible, without loss of the unconscious' (see Jung 1958). In an interesting parallel Tedlock notes that 'whenever a theory of divination has been proposed by diviners, we find not only inductive or propositional thought and intuitive or compositional thought, but also integrative consciousness or ways of knowing' (Tedlock 2006, 68). Following McGilchrist, she reports that this integrative consciousness can be neurologically related to the inter-hemispheric connective passageways, thus providing a physical correlate for the function of the active imagination as go-between.

What Jung expresses in psychological terms is a process we can see as intimately related to the neoplatonic aspiration to access the wisdom of the higher soul. Of course not all visions in the scrying mirror will necessarily aid this therapeutic endeavour, for often they will appear to be random, obscure or inconsequential. But the devotee of higher wisdom will be seeking a form of communication which will not only lead to psychic integration, but to spiritual *initiation*. This brings us to Jung's contemporary Henry Corbin, the French historian of religion, on the function of the symbolic or visionary image. Cheetham shows how Corbin's theory of symbol owes much to Jung: it is 'the only means of saying something that cannot be apprehended in any other way' (Cheetham 2012, 134; Corbin 1998, 14; see also Wasserstrom 1999). Our scryer is here placed in a teleological context, where his or her second sight, or *imaginatio vera*, tunes in to a 'supersensible' reality which is not the shadowy unconscious mind but a highly delineated supra-rational realm of angelic beings. Steeped in the Islamic mysticism of Suhrawardi and Ibn'Arabi, Corbin's active imagination is a way of gnosis, of eventual participation of the soul in the angelic consciousness (Cheetham 2012).

> The whole task consists in purifying and liberating one's inner being so that the intelligible realities perceived on the *imaginal* level may be reflected in the mirror of the *sensorium* and be translated into visionary perception…We have already gone a considerable distance beyond the limits imposed by psychology…The vision of the angel does not emerge from the negativity of an *unconscious*, but descends from the a level of a positively *differentiated* super conscious.
>
> (Corbin 1986, 265–56)

James Hillman suggests that 'The difference between Jung and Corbin can be resolved by practising Jung's technique [of active imagination] with Corbin's vision; that is, active imagination is not for the sake of the doer and *our* actions in the sensible world of literal realities, but for the sake of the images and where they can take us, *their* realisation' (Hillman 1980, 33, n.5; see also Cheetham 2007, 104–9). For Corbin, 'spiritual hermeneutics' involves a 'simultaneous turning towards the Angel and the sensible' (Corbin 1998, 13) through engaging with the *mundus imaginalis*, a world 'as ontologically real as the world of the senses and the world of the intellect' (Corbin 1964), a world in which spiritual reality is reflected as living image and perceived through the power of the imagination. To go beyond the symbolic representation, to open the eye to the dynamic, eternal reality of spiritual being that constantly informs the material world, is for Corbin the way for modern man to overcome the 'divorce between thinking and being' that so plagues him (see Corbin 1978).

I have attempted, in this brief overview, to locate the practice of scrying within a wider framework of divinatory hermeneutics, to show how it may facilitate a process of reflecting an 'occult world' back to our senses. In my view, 'how' this may happen is—in a technical sense—of less importance than 'why' it may happen. It is surely not sufficient to resort to neurological explanations of hallucination, and yet it is deeply problematic in our current intellectual (and academic) climate to claim 'truth value' for a non-material dimension of purposive intelligence which may interact with our mind in some way (see Cornelius 2007). I would suggest that we need to reclaim a philosophical and metaphysical position which acknowledges that there is a middle ground, a mode of cognition in which the mysterious truth of clairvoyant phenomena such as scrying is most fully revealed by honouring and engaging the daimonic and unifying powers of the imagination. As for 'why', such a question must surely impinge on the nature and destiny of the human soul, themes which lie beyond the scope of this essay.

REFERENCES AND FURTHER READING

Addey, C. (2007) 'Mirrors and Divination: Catoptromancy, Oracles and Earth Goddesses in Antiquity', in Miranda Anderson, ed., *The Book of the Mirror: An Interdisciplinary Collection exploring the Cultural Story of the Mirror*, Newcastle: Cambridge Scholars Publishing, 42–46.

——(2012) 'In the Light of the Sphere: The Vehicle of the Soul and Subtle Body Practices in Neoplatonism', in G. Samuel & J. Johnston, eds., *Religion and the Subtle Body in Asia and the West: Between Mind and Body*, London: Routledge, 149–67.

Agrippa, C. (1997 [1531–33]) *Three Books on Occult Philosophy*, trans. J. Freake, St Paul: Llewellyn.

Armstrong, A. H. (1990) *Hellenic and Christian Studies*, Vol. 6, Aldershot: Variorum, 147–81.

Asprem, E. (2012) *Arguing with Angels: Enochian Magic and Modern Occulture*, Albany, New York: State University of New York Press.

Besterman, T. (1995 [1924]) *Crystal Gazing: A Study in the History, Distribution, Theory and Practice of Scrying*, Whitefish, Montana: Kessinger Publishing.

Blom, J. D. (2010) *Dictionary of Hallucinations*, Dordrecht: Springer.

Cardoso, A. (2010) *Electronic Voices: Contact with another Dimension?* Ropley: O-Books.

Cheetham, T. (2007) *After Prophecy: Imagination, Incarnation, and the Unity of the Prophetic Tradition*, Dallas: Spring Publications.

——(2012) *All the World an Icon: Henry Corbin and the Angelic Function of Beings*, Berkeley, California: North Atlantic Books.

Cooper, C. (2012) *Telephone Calls from the Dead*, Old Portsmouth: Tricorn Books.

Corbin, H. (1964) *Mundus imaginalis*. Online: http://hermetic.com/moorish/mundus-imaginalis.html (accessed 12 February 2013).

——(1998 [1969]) *Alone with the Alone: Creative Imagination in the Sufism of Ibn'Arabi*, Princeton: Princeton University Press.

——(1978) 'Letter to David Miller', in D. L. Miller, ed., *The New Polytheism*, Dallas: Spring Publications 1981.

——(1986) *Temple and Contemplation*, London: Wiley & Sons.

Cornelius, G. (2003) *The Moment of Astrology: Origins in Divination*, Bournemouth: The Wessex Astrologer.

——(2007) 'From Primitive Mentality to Haecceity: The Unique Case in Astrology and Divination', in P. Curry & A. Voss, eds., *Seeing with Different Eyes: Essays in Astrology and Divination*, Newcastle: Cambridge Scholars Publishing, 227–54.

——(2010) 'Field of Omens: a Study of Inductive Divination', University of Kent: unpublished doctoral thesis.

Cummins, G. (1967) *The Road to Immortality*, London: Psychic Press Ltd.
Curry, P., ed. (2010) *Divination: Perspectives for the New Millenium*, Farnham: Ashgate.
Curry, P. & R. Willis (2004) *Astrology, Science and Culture: Pulling down the Moon*, Oxford: Berg.
Curry, P. & A. Voss, eds (2007) *Seeing with Different Eyes: Essays in Astrology and Divination*, Newcastle: Cambridge Scholars Publishing.
Eason, C. (2007) *Scrying the Secrets of the Future: How to use Crystal Balls, Fire, Wax, Shadows, Spirit Guides to Reveal your Destiny*, Franklin Lakes, NJ: The Career Press.
Finamore, J. F. (1985) *Iamblichus and the Theory of the Vehicle of the Soul*, Chico, California: Scholars Press.
George, L. (1995) *Alternative Realities: the Paranormal, the Mystic and the Transcendent in Human Experience*, Bel Air, California: Checkmark Books.
Harkness, D. (1999) *John Dee's Conversations with Angels*, Cambridge: Cambridge University Press.
Hartmann, F. (2010) *Paracelsus: Life and Prophecies*, Whitefish, Montana: Kessinger Publishing.
Hillman, J. (1980) *Facing the Gods*, Dallas: Spring Publications.
Iamblichus (2003) *On the Mysteries*, trans. E. Clarke, J. Dillon & J. Herschbell, Atlanta: Society of Biblical Literature.
James, W. (1912) *The Will to Believe*, New York: Longmans, Green & Co.
Jung, C.G. (1958) *Collected Works*, vol. 8, Princeton: Princeton University Press.
——(1960) *Synchronicity, an Acausal Connecting Principle*, ed. S. Shamdasani, Princeton: Princeton University Press.
——(1961) *Memories, Dreams, Reflections* ed. A. Jaffe, trans. R. & C. Winston, New York: Pantheon.
——(1997) *Jung on Active Imagination*, ed. J. Chodorow, London: Routledge.
Kripal, J. J. (2001) *Roads of Excess, Palaces of Wisdom*, Chicago: University of Chicago Press.
——(2010) *Authors of the Impossible: The Paranormal and the Sacred*, Chicago: University of Chicago Press.
McGilchrist, I. (2009) *The Master and his Emissary: the Divided Brain and the Making of the Western World*, Yale: Yale University Press.
Milne, J. (2002) 'Providence, Time and Destiny'. Online: http://www.users.globalnet.co.uk/~alfar2/cosmos/provid.pdf (accessed 12 February 2013).
Myers, F.W.H. (1919) *Human Personality and its Survival of Bodily Death*, London: Longmans.
Paracelsus (1999) *Essential Readings*, ed. N. Goodrick-Clarke, Berkeley: North Atlantic Books.
Plotinus (1966–88) *Enneads*, 7 vols, trans. A. H. Armstrong, Cambridge: Harvard University Press.
Synesius (1888) *On Dreams*, trans. I. Myer, Cambridge: Harvard University Press.
Suster, G., ed. (2003) *John Dee*, Berkeley: North Atlantic Books.
Szönyi, G. (2006a) 'Paracelsus, Scrying and the *Lingua Adamica*', in S. Clucas ed., *John Dee: Interdisciplinary Studies in English Renaissance Thought*, Dordrecht: Springer, 207–30.
——(2006b) 'Talking with Demons. Early Modern Theories and Practice', in G. Klaniczay & E. Pocs, eds., *Demons, Spirits, Witches: Christian Demonology and Popular Mythology*, Budapest: Central European University Press, 72–88.
Tedlock, B. (2006) 'Toward a Theory of Divinatory Practice', *Anthropology of Consciousness* 17:2, 62–77.
Thomas, N.W. & A. Lang (2010 [1905]) *Crystal Gazing*, Whitefish, Montana: Kessinger Publishing.

Tyson, D. (1997) *Scrying for Beginners: Tapping into the Supersensory Powers of Your Subconscious*, St Paul: Llewellyn.

Voss, A. (2006) 'The Secret Life of Statues' in N. Campion & P. Curry, eds., *Sky and Psyche*, Edinburgh: Floris Books, 201–27.

——(2009) 'A Methodology of the Imagination', *Eye of the Heart Journal* 3: 3, 37–53.

——(2011) 'A Matter of Spirit: An Imaginative Perspective on the Paranormal', *Paranthropology* 2:3, 37–43.

Voss A. (2013a) 'Making Sense of the Paranormal: A Platonic Context for Research Methods', in O. Jenzen & S. Munt, eds., *The Ashgate Research Companion to Paranormal Cultures*, Farnham: Ashgate, 139–48.

——(2013b) 'Fireflies and Shooting Stars: Visual Narratives of Daimonic Intelligence', in A. Voss & W. Rowlandson, eds., *Daimonic Imagination: Uncanny Intelligence*, Newcastle: Cambridge Scholars Publishing, 244–65.

Warde Fowler, W. (1911) *The Religious Experience of the Roman People*, London: Macmillan & Co.

Wasserstrom, S. (1999) *Religion after Religion: Gershom Sholem, Mircea Eliade and Henry Corbin at Eranos*, Princeton: Princeton University Press.

CHAPTER FIFTY-NINE

ASTROLOGY

Nicholas Campion

Astrology is the name given to a raft of ideas and practices, which assume that the stars and planets possess significance for terrestrial affairs. In the modern west it is a familiar part of popular culture, as well as of 'occulture', to use Christopher Partridge's (2004) term, and anywhere from as low as 14 percent to as high as 73 percent of the adult population 'believes' in it, depending on how the question is asked (Campion 2012b, 153). In view of its popularity, descriptions such as 'fringe' tend to misrepresent astrology's cultural status.

Given that all forms of astrology share a reference to the sky, stars and planets, it is distinguished by its diversity (Campion & Greene 2011), and terms used to describe it have included art, psychology, magic, divination, spiritual tool, religion or quasi-religion, and science, divine science or pseudo-science. One label, occult, lingers amongst dictionary definitions of astrology, and is popular among Christian evangelical critics of astrology, but seems to be almost entirely rejected by astrologers. The *Concise Oxford Dictionary* (1952) defines astrology as the 'art of judging of reputed occult influence of stars upon human affairs (*judicial* ~)', while the *Encyclopaedia Americana* (1972, 557), describes it as 'the belief in the occult influence of heavenly bodies on human affairs'. Almost alone amongst those commentators sympathetic to astrology, Fred Gettings commented that 'Astrology appears to be one of the most ancient of the surviving occult sciences' (1985, 52–53). The problems with defining astrology as occult arise from the word's literal meaning as 'hidden,' and its associations with practices that are somehow dark and sinister. The self-defined community of modern astrologers is keen to present a rational, accessible, and democratic image to the world through its societies, schools and literature: anyone can learn astrology and all are welcome to attend its conferences. The word 'esoteric' is generally favored by astrologers and, even though its meaning as 'inner' can suggest that esoteric matters are hidden from the world and hence, strictly, occult, esotericism is perceived as light and welcoming, the direct antithesis of occultism.

The difficulties in defining astrology therefore result from three problems: first, its diversity; second, disputes over its definition between its practitioners and external critics; and, third, differences of opinion between its supporters concerning its nature. To adapt Hildred Geertz's comment on magic, the discussion concerns not just the content and practice of astrology but the label (1975, 76). And to borrow Stephen Sutcliffe's similar examination of difficulties relating to the term 'New Age', the word astrology is an 'emblem' which may mean different things to different people (2003, 9–11). The word astrology then becomes a symbol of human frailty and gullibility to its various critics, but of a path to the truth and the construction of meaning and identity to its competing groups of supporters. The history of astrology in relation to magic and the occult has been well-covered, particularly in the Renaissance (for example Walker, Couliano). However, most academic and secondary sources avoid anything later than the early twentieth century, a phenomenon discussed in relation to esotericism by Hanegraaff (2012). Instead, what academic studies that do have some relevance to astrology tend to focus on is Paganism and Witchcraft (Greenwood 2000).

The word astrology itself is Greek, from *astro-logos*, which may be translated variously as 'the word-,' 'logic-,' or 'reason-of-the-stars.' The inference is clearly that astrology is a means of communication, has an internal logic and is rational, three qualities which place it firmly within a Platonic context. The classical Greeks appear to be responsible for the particularly sophisticated form of astrology based on the use of horoscopes. These are mathematically precise, schematic diagrams of the sky which contain complex series of meanings based on the exact location of the planets and stars in the zodiac, and divisions of the sky known to modern astrology as houses; when we refer to 'horoscopic' astrology, it is to this complex form (Campion 2008, 203–23). Although the broader concept of a general relationship between terrestrial matters and celestial bodies appears to be a universal feature of human culture (Campion 2012a), this chapter will examine modern western astrology. Hence, from now on the word 'astrology' will refer to the modern western form and its predecessors in the ancient world.

The various rationales for astrology regularly provided by astrologers are located primarily in three schools of classical philosophy: the Platonic, Aristotelian, and Stoic. Astrology is itself an explanatory model, but there are also explanatory models that seek to justify it; these may not be entirely consistent, but neither are they necessarily mutually exclusive (Campion 2012b, 2013). In the syncretic model to which most astrologers subscribe, astrology is generally perceived as a symbolic language which allows the astrologer to interpret and engage with the Essence of the cosmos, whether this is perceived as Platonic Ideas or in modern terms, Jungian archetypes. As all things in the cosmos, whether emotional, spiritual or physical, are interdependent, astrology may deal simultaneously with physical influences and divine causes, as well as with acausal, synchronous (Jung 1963) connections between celestial and terrestrial events.

Central to an understanding of astrology's diversity in the western tradition is the distinction between 'Natural' and 'Judicial' Astrology, which originates in classical discourse in the first century BCE (Campion 2012a, 16). Natural astrology requires no more than the observation of seasonal phenomena and natural influences deriving from the planets, and was universally accepted in the medieval and Renaissance worlds. Judicial astrology, requiring the astrologer's interpretative judgment, depended on complex deductions made from horoscopes.

The literary roots of western astrology can be traced to third-millennium BCE Mesopotamia, and from there to the Hellenistic world of the last three centuries BCE, where the technical structure which survives to the present day was developed. To this should be added possible influences from the Egyptian temple tradition: Ronald Hutton (2004) has demonstrated continuity in astral magic from at least Hellenistic Egypt to the present day. The question of whether astrology is classed as magic or occult is, as I have argued, largely one of semantics. However, there are definite distinctions in practice which can lead to the identification of some astrology as more overtly magical or occult, in the simple understanding of those terms. If magic, loosely defined, is the attempt to engage with the world through the imagination or psyche, in order to obtain some form of knowledge, benefit or advantage, then astral, celestial or astrological magic engages with the cosmos using stellar, planetary or celestial symbolism, influences or intelligences as a medium. Similarly, if the rules and regulations for the practice of astral magic are secret rather than publically available, it can be defined as occult.

Some skeptics (Dean, Kelly and Mather 1996), borrowing from nineteenth-century anthropology (Tylor 1958, Vol. I, 133), regard all astrology as magical on the grounds that it makes links, which do not really exist, between different phenomena, such as the connection between, say, the Sun and kings (Lilly 1647, 71) or the Moon and women (Hone 1973, 25–26). This argument, as employed by skeptics, concludes that, because all astrology is magical it is therefore necessarily false. However, the astrological features of ritual magic as practiced, for example, by the Hermetic Order of the Golden Dawn, can be distinguished from the art of interpreting and analyzing horoscopes. The distinction between action on the one hand, and interpretation on the other, is implicit in both the narratives and the institutions which surround western astrology. For example, major modern astrological text books deal only with the interpretation of horoscopes, and not with any action which may be required as a result (see for example Hone 1973, and Parker and Parker 1971). Where action is discussed, it is in terms of the kind of behavior to which an individual inclines, rather than any kind of action, ritual or otherwise, which the astrologer may prescribe. There is a slight move amongst practitioners within this astrological milieu towards prescribed action as a result of counselling, but the emphasis remains very much on understanding the act, rather than performing the act, whether ritual or otherwise (Bogart 2012, 70–73).

If astrology is diverse, then astrologers must be similarly varied. Joscelyn Godwin identified three types of astrologer in the nineteenth century: ‘Firstly those yearning to be accepted as scientists, secondly those with a more religious approach and thirdly those attracted to the occult, magic and spiritualism’ (1994, 142–43). The third group, though, the occultists and magicians, have become invisible in modern astrology’s ‘own universe of discourse,’ to adopt Ann Geneva’s words (1995, xiv). Astrological magic in its ritual forms therefore makes almost no appearance in public astrology, and exists institutionally in an entirely separate network: individuals may move between the two communities, but the Ordo Templi Orientis, for example, occupies a cultural milieu which is entirely separate to the leading astrological societies in the USA, the names of two of which make their modernizing, secularizing aspirations clear; the International Society for Astrological Research, and the National Council for Geocosmic Research. Both groups embody an overt anti-occult tendency in modern astrology.

Much academic commentary assumes that astrology is a form of the occult (Webb 1980, 1981, 1988; Butler 2011, xii; Jorgensen and Jorgensen 1982). However, the slippage between the terms magic, occult, and esoteric, has been observed in the most recent academic studies, from Galbreath (1986, 1–27) to Butler (2011). Tiryakian distinguished esotericism from occultism on the grounds that the former is theory, while the latter is practice (1972, 265–66). Butler, though, illustrated the difficulties of distinguishing them: an esotericist need not be a magician or occultist, but magicians and occultists must study esoteric wisdom (2011, xii). Faivre pointed out that the distinction then breaks down further if esotericism has a practical application (1994, 34). In the context of what Galbreath identified as 'terminological confusion' (1986, 16), it is clear that magic and occultism are often considered coincident, in that to practice magic is to be an occultist. In this case, astrology's identity as an occult practice can be explored partly through the activities of those who apply astrology to magic, what we may call astral magic, as a particular application of astrology.

Recently, though, an additional strand has been introduced into the discourse, amid suggestions that the astrological consultation (the interpretation of the horoscope by an astrologer for a client) itself is, in a sense, a magical encounter, a view which can evoke Dean's opinion that all astrology is magic, but without assuming that it is therefore necessarily false. Liz Greene, who does not agree that all astrology is magic, nevertheless illustrates the argument for its magical nature (2011, 32). Writing of astrological symbols, she observes that, in a Platonic context, the essential identity of the astrological symbol with the thing symbolized is the basis of the use of astrology in medieval magic grimoires: by manipulating the symbol the thing itself is also affected. Greene thereby contested the assumption of much astrological historiography that the texts of astrological horoscope interpretation represent an entirely different genre to the texts of astral magic, and can be studied separately.

In a traditional context, as a practice, astrology is best understood through its functions. It has been called both a system of anthropology and sociology in the sense that its purposes include the understanding of human nature and the organization of society. Prediction of the future, one of astrology's primary functions, makes sense only in a context in which action in the present can be changed in order to alter the outcome of such predictions. This is then the prime function of astral magic. In this sense, sociologically, astrology's purpose is management of the present in order to preserve harmony between sky and earth, and maintain peace and stability. It may achieve this through a variety of means from the casting of spells to gain personal advantage, to the magician's ascent through the planetary spheres in order to gain enlightenment.

OCCULT ASTROLOGY 1: RITUAL MAGIC

The most obvious application of astral magic is for personal advantage, and personal advantage was often best served by medicine, and the use of amulets, talismans, and sigils. The following example from a Greek text illustrates the point.

> Another amulet for the foot of the gouty man: You should write these names on a strip / of silver or tin. You should put it on a deerskin and bind it to the foot of the man named, on his two feet: 'THEMBARATHEM OUREMBRENOUTIPE / AIOXTHOU SEMMARATHEMMOU NAIOOU, let NN, whom NN bore, recover from every pain which is in his knees and two feet'. You do it when the moon is [in the constellation] Leo.
>
> (Betz 1992, PDM xiv.1003–14, 244)

The first point to notice is the importance of timing. The Moon is in Leo for around two and a half days every month: all other aspects of the healing ritual are enclosed within a framework in which time is qualitative as much as quantitative and magical actions can only be effective at certain times. No matter how powerful the magician, a ritual will be ineffective if performed at an inauspicious moment. The second feature of astral magic is the notion that planets, stars, and zodiac signs have personalities: every identifiable entity in the cosmos is anthropomorphized. In Greek, Islamic, and Medieval astrology, the precise personality of the universe at any moment, down to the nearest minute and exact location, could be determined by the positions of the stars and planets (Lilly 1647). The practical, magical actions designed to exploit the benefits of moments in time have been handed down to the modern world through two major texts, the thirteenth-century *Picatrix* (Attalah 2002) and Cornelius Agrippa's *De Occulta Philosophia* (1651), via Eliphas Lévi (1896) and Aleister Crowley (1979). The basic principles of modern (considerably simplified from classical and medieval practice) astrological interpretation as set out by Crowley (1979) are as follows:

1 Every planet (a designation which includes the Sun and Moon), and some of the brightest stars, possess personalities, usually described as a range of symbolic principles or archetypal associations.
2 The twelve zodiac signs (divisions of the sun's apparent annual path through the sky) also have personality characteristics.
3 The twelve divisions of the sky known in modern astrology as houses indicate different areas of activity or circumstances, such as wealth, friends, and family.
4 The planets have relationships to each other based mainly on the angular differences between them, which define the way in which the principles they represent interact.

This much all astrologers agree on (see for example Parker and Parker 1971). Beyond this, the technical complications multiply, and, even though astrology is based in the cyclical repetition of planetary positions, such are the number of permutations possible in a single horoscope that the exact same combination of configurations never recurs.

The most important institutional disseminator of astral magic in the modern world is the Golden Dawn and, from the beginning, astrology was a part of its curriculum (Howe 1985, xvi). The Order's curriculum displayed its respect for the subject by referring to 'the true system of Astrological Divination' (Howe 1985, 289). Other evidence suggests that, while basic astrological computation and analysis was taught at lower grades, higher astrological wisdom was preserved for the Order's elite

(Fleming 2005, 5). In addition to the techniques of horoscope interpretation as set out by Crowley, and which are recognized by all modern astrologers, the Golden Dawn has been instrumental in preserving such features of medieval and Renaissance astral magic as planetary angels (Regardie 1993, 222–33) and magic squares (Greene 2012, 250–73). Astrology occupied a central, synthesizing role in other parts of the Order's magical training, as such topics as tarot, numerology, geomancy, and astral travel possess planetary and stellar correspondences. One ritual designed to facilitate astral travel held in 1900 illustrates the point. It began as follows: 'We sat in a semi-circle at the north side of the Altar, facing the South, when Mars was in Virgo at the time. Deo Date then made the Invoking Hexagrams of Mars around the room, and the Pentagram of Virgo and the Mars symbol towards the South' (Gilbert 1983, 132; see also Owen 2004, 156–57). The resulting astral journey was judged to be shaped by the earthiness of Virgo and the fiery nature of Mars, resulting from the dominant planetary configuration of the moment

A number of the Order's early members established its astrological identity. The most famous was probably the poet W.B. Yeats, who appears to have cast horoscopes in order to analyze his dreams (Heine 1997). Annie Horniman, another of the most notable early members also had, in Howe's words, 'a continuing preoccupation with astrology' (1978, 66). Howe records one instance of another early member and officer, F.L. Gardner, discussing a horary chart, a horoscope designed to provide an answer for the time of the asking of a question – in this case about a legacy expected by one of the Order's members (1978, 155–56). Gardner was consulted because Samuel Liddell MacGregor Mathers, one of the Order's founders, had already provided advice on so many horoscopes that it was thought he could not be troubled again.

On the other hand many ritual magicians regard astrology as an inferior practice on account of what they see as its passivity, in contrast to magic's active intervention in the world. In 1892 one Golden Dawn member, Frater Firth, was charged with claiming that astrology was 'mere divination' and showing 'a rebellious wish to pick and choose his subjects of study,' thereby challenging the authority of the curriculum (Howe 1978, 111). A.E. Waite, one of the Golden Dawn's most important early members, dismissed astrology (by which he meant the standard astrology of the late nineteenth century, as described by Crowley) as a species of Natural Magic, and hence not 'of service to the psychic student,' who would, by contrast, benefit from the superior benefits of 'Spiritual or Transcendent Magic' (Gilbert 1987, 51). All astrology was magic, then, in Waite's view, but only some of it was worthwhile magic; the rest was worthless. In line with such thinking, on one occasion, after a lecture to the Blavatsky Lodge of the Theosophical Society in London in 1986, I was firmly told 'Magicians do not practice astrology.' This is patently true neither on an individual level, nor on the institutional, but reflects a discourse amongst some magicians that their engagement with celestial entities is not astrological, and that most astrologers, meanwhile, are not aware of the true nature of the forces they study. Such opinions were encouraged by Waite, who believed that a pure and primitive astrology, which he sought to recover, had been degraded by what he called dismissively, 'the erectors of horoscopes' (Levi 1896, 81). He set out to restore this supposed pristine astrology in works such as his *Complete Manual of Occult Divination* (1972). Such attitudes as Waite's are becoming increasingly rare in the wake of skepticism of what are now seen as arbitrary categories, of which Geertz's argument concerning magic was one of the first indications. The Hermetic Order of the Golden Dawn website (2012) is in tune with modern pluralistic notions of astrology as embracing a variety of practices:

> The Golden Dawn stands as an inheritor of the Hermetic tradition with its Trivium Hermeticum, the triune spiritual disciplines of theurgy (magic), alchemy, and astrology. The role of astrology in the Golden Dawn as is also the case with the entire Hermetic tradition, is surprisingly not primarily one of divination or fortune telling. Rather it is used as an adjunct to theurgy and alchemy, as for example, in astrological magic, or in the use of specific astrological cycles in both alchemy and theurgy.

The website continues: 'The most noticeable aspect of the occult revival of modern times has been the widespread popularity of astrology.' For the Golden Dawn, then, astrology is itself occult or, at least, exists within a cultural framework provided by the occult. Astrology's function as interpretation or prediction is distinguished from the activity inherent in its use in theurgy and magic, but dismissive attitudes to the former are no longer evident.

OCCULT ASTROLOGY 2: ESOTERICISM AND NATURAL MAGIC

Edward Tiryakian's view that esotericism is important in the development of modernism, and Butler's view on the need for occultists to study esotericism, present a way into understanding a different kind of astrological occultism, arising out of the modernizing impact of theosophy. Larsen adds a complementary view, arguing that astrology establishes an important 'ritual' field in Western esotericism, constituting a ritual for expressing certain 'Ultimate Sacred Postulates,' and in so doing, for generating new ideas (2008, 13–45). Modern astrology is, as the term suggests, at one with the modernizing trends of nineteenth and twenty-first century society (Campion 2011). Modernity is evident in the astrology of the nineteenth and twentieth centuries in a number of areas, including an increased emphasis on astrology's interiorization, based on the assumption that whatever descriptions astrology may have of external events are dependent on the condition of the psyche, whether conceived of as mind or soul. There is a direct parallel between this feature of astrology and the development of depth-psychology, which was well-known to the astrologers of the time. The interiorizing trend in western astrology had been evident in the mid-nineteenth century through magicians such as Eliphas Levi, but was made explicit in the early twentieth century by the theosophist Alan Leo (1875–1917), one of the most influential astrological theorists of the early twentieth century. Drawing heavily on Neoplatonism as filtered through H.P. Blavatsky, Leo devised a system in which the planets and zodiac signs related primarily to levels of spiritual existence and stages of spiritual evolution, rather than physical descriptions or predictors of events. Leo's modernizing spirituality was developed by the American theosophist, Dane Rudhyar (1895–1985), possibly the most influential American astrologer of the twentieth century. According to Ertan (2009, 71), Rudhyar, who lived most of his life in the USA but had been born in France, deliberately set out to 'inject' the literary and artistic legacy of French occultism into American modernity. From his own combination of theosophy with depth psychology, Rudhyar devised a two-track astrology which he described by a pair of terms, Transpersonal and Humanistic. In Transpersonal astrology, inspired by theosophy, the individual's task is to integrate with the higher, spiritual, cosmos and to become a vehicle for the coming of the Age of Aquarius and (Rudhyar was an esoteric Christian) the advent of Christ consciousness. Humanistic astrology, by contrast, grew out of Rudhyar's encounter with depth-psychology and was intended to facilitate self-understanding. The technical structure of the horoscope was adapted and simplified, and prediction eschewed, the emphasis being on the needs of the client, rather than the projection of an astrological truth on to the individual. Rudhyar devised the term 'person-centred' (1980) to describe his approach to astrology. The pursuit of self-understanding, though, is not an end in itself, but a means to get to that point of enlightenment at which one loses one's individuality and becomes a cipher for a higher good. Rudhyar's book, *Occult Preparations for a New Age* (1975), made his purpose clear. Rudhyar was a Christian and his astrology was religious in a conventional sense: it was designed to subordinate humanity to high spiritual powers. It was therefore in a strict sense, supernatural, dealing with matters over and above the world of material phenomena. Rudhyar himself sounded a cautionary note: 'of course the thing you have to be careful of when you are dealing with so-called occult, or esoteric ideas,' he wrote, 'is that you never know too much how much you are dealing with symbols and how much you are dealing with what you might call a higher reality' (Rayner 1997, 99, cited in Ertan 2009, 84).

Rudhyar's astrology can be described as religious, perhaps as an occult (to use his own term) religion, or 'occultic,' to borrow Gunn's reconciliation of 'occult' with 'esoteric' (2003, 7), but this does not mean that his legacy is necessarily religious. Rudhyar's cosmology is pervasive in modern astrology, especially in the USA, thriving in a context in which most astrologers accept the general truths of theosophical cosmology, chiefly that the cosmos is fundamentally spiritual rather than material, and that individual spiritual growth is structured through the laws of karma and reincarnation (Campion 2012b, 175). In that Rudhyar followed in the Neoplatonic Renaissance tradition advocated by Marsilio Ficino (1989), in which magic operates through changes in behavior rather than the ritual invocation of higher powers, his astrology might be described as a species of 'sympathetic magic' (Frazer 1971, 14–15) on the grounds that it depends on the essential similarity between things rather than on ritual acts by the magician.

CONCLUSION

To call all astrology occult is to be an outsider. If we are historians or anthropologists, we have to respect astrologers' universe of discourse, and the terms in which they describe themselves. To describe astrology as necessarily occult fails to account for the diversity of its practices and claims, as do terms such as divination, religion, art or science. However, the term remains a useful one both for some insiders, and for academic commentators. Margot Adler's solution is probably the best. To the question of whether 'occult' groups are indeed occult, she replies, 'the real answer is yes and no, depending on the definition of the occult. Yes, because many of these groups deal with hidden or obscure forms of knowledge that are not generally accepted, and no, because a number of groups regard themselves as celebratory rather than magical or occult' (Adler 1986, 12). The problem therefore depends partly on astrologers' ontology and epistemology; on their truth claims and theory of knowledge on the one hand, and their self-identity on the other. Therefore, the more astrology makes itself accessible and secular, rejecting any need for the supernatural, the more difficult it becomes to describe it as occult. But the more astrology either regards itself as the bearer of secret knowledge or relies on the supernatural, the easier it becomes to call it occult. Just as some astrology may be described as New Age and some not (Campion 2012b, 216–17), so some may be classified as occult, but some not. With such a fluid approach it then becomes possible to broaden the scope of what may be occult. To return to Godwin's three categories of astrologer, then, the second group, the religious and spiritual, of which Alan Leo and Dane Rudhyar were the leading exemplars in the twentieth century, could be defined as occult, in addition to their more familiar designation, esoteric. Perhaps it is best to say that astrology as a single category of belief or practice is not occult, but particular uses of it can be. In addition, through its application to the correct timing of ritual and provision of a direct connection between the individual and the celestial realms, it plays a central part in occult practice.

REFERENCES AND FURTHER READING

Adler, M. (1986) *Drawing Down the Moon: Witches, Druids, Goddess-Worshippers, and Other Pagans in America Today*, Boston: Beacon Press 1986.

Agrippa, Henry Cornelius (1896) *Three Books of Occult Philosophy*, facsimile of the 1651 translation, London: Chthonius Books.

Atallah, Hashem, trans. (2002) *Ghayat Al-Hakim. Picatrix: the Goal of the Wise*, Seattle: Ouroboros Press.

Betz, H.D. (1992) *The Greek magical papyri in translation, including the Demotic Spells*, Chicago: Chicago University Press.

Bogart, G. (2012) *Planets in Therapy: Predictive Technique and the Art of Counselling*, Lake Worth: Ibis Press.

Brodie-Innes, J.W. (2005) *The Astrology of the Golden Dawn*, second edition, Sequim, WA: Holmes Publishing Group.

Butler, A. (2011) *Victorian Occultism and the Making of Modern Magic: Invoking Tradition*, New York: Palgrave Macmillan.

Campion, N. (2008) *A History of Western Astrology*, Vol. 1. The Ancient World, London: Continuum.

——(2009) *A History of Western Astrology*, Vol. 2, The Medieval and Modern Worlds, London: Continuum, 2009.

——(2011) 'Astrology's Place in Historical Periodisation: Modern, Premodern or Postmodern?' in N. Campion and L. Greene, eds., *Astrologies: Plurality and Diversity*, Lampeter: Sophia Centre Press, 217–54.

——(2012a) *Astrology and Cosmology in the World's Religions*, New York: New York University Press.

——(2012b) *Astrology and Popular Religion in the Modern West: Prophecy, Cosmology and the New Age Movement*, Abingdon: Ashgate.

——(2013) 'Astrology as Cultural Astronomy,' in C. Ruggles, ed., *Handbook of Archaeoastronomy and Ethnoastronomy*, Berlin: Springer-Verlag, 106–13.

Campion, N. & L. Greene, eds. (2011) *Astrologies: Plurality and Diversity*, Lampeter: Sophia Centre Press.

Concise Oxford Dictionary (1952), Oxford: Clarendon Press.

Couliano, I. (1985) *Eros and Magic in the Renaissance*, Chicago: University of Chicago Press.

Crowley, A. (1979) *The Complete Astrological Writings*, ed. J. Symonds & K. Grant, London: Duckworth.

Dean, G., I. Kelly & A. Mather (1996) 'Astrology,' in G. Stein, ed., *The Encyclopaedia of the Paranormal*, Amherst, New York: Prometheus Books, 47–99.

Encyclopaedia Americana (1972), Danbury CT: Grolier Inc.

Ertan, D. (2009) *Dane Rudhyar: his Music, Thought and Art*, Rochester: University of Rochester Press.

Faivre, A. (1994) *Access to Western Esotericism*, Albany: State University of New York Press.

Ficino, M. (1989) *Three Books on Life*, ed. C. Kaske & J. Clark, Binghamton: State University of New York at Binghamton.

Fleming, A. (2005) 'Introductory Notes,' in J.W. Brodie-Innes, *The Astrology of the Golden Dawn*, second edition, Sequim, WA.: Holmes Publishing Group, 3–6.

Frazer, J.G. (1971) *The Golden Bough: A Study in Magic and Religion*, abridged edition, London: Macmillan.

Galbreath, R. (1986) 'Explaining Modern Occultism,' in H. Kerr & C. Crow, eds, *The Occult in America: New Historical Perspectives*, Urbana: University of Illinois Press, 11–37.

Geertz, H. (1975) 'An Anthropology of Religion and Magic, I,' *The Journal of Interdisciplinary History* 6:1, 71–89.

Geneva, A. (1995) *Astrology and the Seventeenth Century Mind: William Lilly and the Language of the Stars*, Manchester: Manchester University Press.

Gettings, F. (1985) *The Arkana Dictionary of Astrology*, London: Penguin-Arkana.

Gilbert, R.A. (1983) *The Golden Dawn, Twilight of the Magicians: The Rise and Fall of a Magical Order*, Wellingborough: Aquarian Press.

——(ed.)(1987) Hermetic Papers of A.E. Waite: the unknown writings of a modern mystic, Wellingborough: Aquarian Press.

Godwin, J. (1994) *The Theosophical Enlightenment*, New York: State University of New York Press.

Greene, L. (2011) 'Signs, Signatures, and Symbols: the Languages of Heaven,' in N. Campion & L. Greene, eds., *Astrologies: Plurality and Diversity*, Lampeter: Sophia Centre Press, 17–45.

——(2012) *Magi and Maggidim: The Kabbalah in British Occultism 1860–1940*, Lampeter: Sophia Centre Press.

Greenwood, S. (2000) *Magic, Witchcraft and the Otherworld: An Anthropology*, Oxford: Berg.

Gunn, J. (2003) *Modern Occult Rhetoric: Mass Media and the Drama of Secrecy in the Twentieth Century*, Tuscaloosa: University of Alabama Press.

Hanegraaff, W. (2012) *Esotericism and the Academy: Rejected Knowledge in Western Culture*, Cambridge: Cambridge University Press.

Heine, E. (1997) 'W.B. Yeats: Poet and Astrologer,' *Culture and Cosmos* 1:2, 60–75.

Hermetic Order of the Golden Dawn (n.d.). Online: http://www.golden-dawn.com/eu/displaycontent.aspx?pageid=118-astrological-tradition (accessed 31 December 2012).

Hone, M. (1973) *The Modern Textbook of Astrology*, fourth edition, London: L.N. Fowler.

Howe, E. (1985) *The Magicians of the Golden Dawn: A Documentary History of a Magical Order 1887–1923*, Wellingborough: Aquarian Press.

Hutton, R. (2004) 'Astral Magic: The Acceptable Face of Paganism,' in N. Campion, P. Curry & M. York, eds., *Astrology and the Academy*, Bristol: Cinnabar Books, 10–24.
Jorgensen, D. & L. Jorgensen (1982) 'Social Meanings of the Occult,' *The Sociological Quarterly*, 23:3, 373–89.
Jung, C.G. (1963) 'Synchronicity: An Acausal Connecting Principle,' in *The Structure and Dynamics of the Psyche*, Collected Works, Vol. 8, trans. R.F.C. Hull, London: Routledge & Kegan Paul, 417–531.
Larsen, L.S. (2008) 'Western Esotericism: Ultimate Sacred Postulates and Ritual Fields,' doctoral dissertation, University of Lund, Sweden. Online: http://www.lunduniversity.lu.se/o.o.i.s?id=24732&postid=1236319 (accessed 1 June 2013).
Leo, A. (1913) *Esoteric Astrology: A Study in Human Nature*, London: Modern Astrology.
Lévi, E. (1896) *Transcendental Magic, its Doctrine and Ritual by Eliphas Lévi, (Alphonse Louis Constant)*, trans. A.E. Waite, London: George Redway.
Lilly, W. (1985) *Christian Astrology*, facsimile of the 1647 edition, London: Regulus Publishing.
McIntosh, C. (1972) *Eliphas Lévi and the French Occult Revival*, New York: Samuel Weiser.
Owen, A. (2004) *The Place of Enchantment: British Occultism and the Culture of the Modern*, Chicago: University of Chicago Press.
Parker, D. & J. Parker (1971) *The Compleat Astrologer*, London: Mitchell-Beazley.
Partridge, C. (2004) *The Re-Enchantment of the West*, Vol. 1. London: T&T Clark.
Rayner, S., ed. (1977) *Dane Rudhyar: Interviewed by Sheila Finch Rayner, Clare G. Rayner and Rob Newell*, Long Beach: California State University Library.
Regardie, I. (1993) *What You Should Know About the Golden Dawn*, Phoenix: New Falcon Publications.
Rudhyar, D. (1975) *Occult Preparations for a New Age*, Madras and London: Theosophical Publishing House.
——(1980) *Person Centered Astrology*, New York: Aurora Press.
Sutcliffe, S. (2003) *Children of the New Age: A History of Spiritual Practices*, London: Routledge.
Tiryakian, E.A. (1972) 'Towards the Sociology of Esoteric Culture,' *American Journal of Sociology*, November, 78:3, 491–512.
Tylor, E.B. (1958) *Primitive Culture*, New York: Harper Torchbooks.
Waite, A.E. (1972) *Complete Manual of Occult Divination*, New Hyde Park, NY: University Books.
Walker, D. (1975) *Spiritual and Demonic Magic from Ficino to Campanella*, London: University of Notre Dame Press.
Webb, J. (1980) *The Harmonious Circle: The Lives and Work of G.I.Gurdjieff, D.Ouspensky, and Their Followers*, Boston: Shambhala Publications.
——(1981) *The Occult Establishment*, Glasgow: Richard Drew Publishing.
——(1988) *The Occult Underground*, La Salle, IL: Open Court.

CHAPTER SIXTY

GRIMOIRES

Owen Davies

The term grimoire has become well-embedded in the English language over the last few decades, and numerous works of fiction and guides to modern Pagan practice include the word in their titles and their content. It was adopted in the late nineteenth century primarily as a result of Anglophone occult interest in a range of manuscripts and cheap print books of magic and conjuration that were illicitly published in eighteenth-century France, most notably the *Grand grimoire* and the *Grimoire du Pape Honorius*. One of the early members of the Order of the Golden Dawn, Arthur Edward Waite (1857–1942), was instrumental in spreading knowledge of these French grimoires through publishing extracts in his compendium of Western literary magic, *The Book of Black Magic and of Pacts* (1898). Recognition of the term was furthered by the publication in 1936 of a collection of short stories entitled *The Grimoire, and Other Supernatural Stories*, by the popular historian of witchcraft Montague Summers (1880–1948), who denounced the evil influence of grimoires in his history of black magic. Today, popular recognition of the grimoire derives in part from the advent and growth of the modern Pagan witchcraft movement after the Second World War, and the portrayal of modern witches in hit television series such as *Charmed* and *Buffy the Vampire Slayer*. An awareness of this chronology is useful as it explains why scholars of ancient and medieval literary magic generally refrain from using the term 'grimoire' – the word was not used in those periods.

But what is a grimoire? It is a book of magic of course, but not all books of magic are grimoires. The old books bearing the title in print or manuscript contained guidance on how to create protective talismans and to conjure spirits – in the notorious *Grand grimoire* to call up the Devil himself. They also sometimes contained a medley of Christian prayers, exorcisms, astrological information, lists of lucky days, remedies and mundane household tips. But some magic books cannot be described as grimoires as they were strictly concerned with natural magic, in other words the discovery and understanding of the occult or secret properties of plants, animals and stones. This was a tradition of literary magic that dated back to antiquity, with Pliny the Elder's *Natural History*, written in the 70s CE, forming the basis of numerous other compilations of secrets in the medieval Islamic and Christian worlds.

So, in essence, grimoires provide instructions that allow humans to magically manipulate the world around them through ritual, rite and invocation.

The keys to the enduring cultural power of the grimoire over the centuries are the ability to write them and the ability to read them. These are two different processes, and each has shaped how the grimoire has developed and spread. Considering the first skill, why record magical knowledge at all? David Harper, in discussing ancient and medieval Chinese occult books, sees the creation of such occult literature as to enrich the lives of the wealthy elites and also to codify oral folk magical knowledge for general benefit (Harper, 2010: 43). It is clear from the European archive, though, that grimoires were created for a wide range of motives, from the purity of the quest for divine knowledge to the venal desire for satanic power, from the desire to harness natural and celestial resources for humanity to the desire to control them for personal gain.

The act of recording and writing magic is shaped by the nature of the writing implement and the writing surface. The earliest written magic from Egypt and Mesopotamia was engraved on clay tablets, stone, and metal, but the first grimoires or magic books were made possible by the development of papyrus as a writing surface during the mid-first millennium BCE, and with it came the use of inks that could be imbued with magical properties. In other words the act of writing became an inherent part of the magic of the grimoire. The first boom in papyri magic books in the western hemisphere took place in the Hellenic world, their contents drawn from the fusion of Greek, Egyptian, and then Roman religious and magical traditions in the region. Over in China the first books were produced by stitching together bamboo slips. Numerous Chinese manuscripts have been discovered containing conjurations and charms dating from between the fourth century BCE to the tenth century CE. They exhibit a particular preoccupation with using magic to deal with nightmare spirits and ghosts, such as this spell from a medieval Chinese text:

> When a person has foul dreams at night, rise at dawn, and in the northeast part of the house unbind the hair and chant this incantation: 'Boqi, Boqi. He does not drink ale or eat meat, and regularly eats the earth of High Elevation. May the foul dreams return home to Boqi. Crushing dreams cease, give rise to great blessings.' Chant the incantation like this seven times and there will not be spirit odium.
>
> (Harper, 2010: 54)

Despite the concerted attempt by the Christian churches to suppress magic books, which were denounced as symbols of pagan superstition during the early centuries of the Christian ascendancy, a new fertile phase of grimoire production and use occurred in medieval Europe. Through intellectual exchanges with Jewish and Arabic scholars in Moorish Spain, southern France and Byzantium, new vistas of mystical and occult knowledge opened up for Western scientists and theologians. They were introduced to ancient texts and knowledge that had long been lost in the West, but which had been preserved through Arab and Judaic scholarship. Out of this flourishing exchange of ideas during the twelfth and thirteenth centuries new compilations of magic circulated across cultures (though some drew upon earlier texts), including grimoires with spurious venerable authorship. This was the age of such enduring works as the

Clavicule and the *Ars Notoria of Solomon*, the *Sworn Book of Honorius* attributed to a legendary ancient scholar of Thebes, the Harba de-Moshe (*Sword of Moses*) and the *Ghayat al-Hakim* or *Picatrix*. As well as these iconic intellectual texts, numerous diverse manuals of practical magic exchanged hands clandestinely that provided rituals and invocations to discover treasure, provoke love and to have power over others – all highly prized goals in the world of medieval aristocratic courtly intrigue.

In Christian Europe the monasteries were the principal producers of these grimoires, just as in medieval China Buddhist and Daoist (Taoist) monks seem to have been the main compilers of occult works. The clergy were, after all, amongst the very few people who were literate at the time. Yet how could the monasteries be central to the grimoire trade if the Churches had for centuries condemned magic literature? The intellectual milieu of the twelfth and thirteenth centuries generated new debates about the definition and categorisation of magic. The pursuit of natural magic – the scientific exploration of the occult properties of God's natural world – could be justified as a worthy devout task. Some argued, furthermore, that to seek dialogue with the angels through ritual invocations for the same ends was likewise a godly exercise. Thus angelic communication became central to the medieval grimoire. The counter argument was that to call upon the celestial spirits was presumptuous and even heretical: it gave an opportunity for the Devil and his demons to intercede. There were, indeed, grimoires that instructed in how to conduct 'pagan' rites or conjure demons for venal and carnal purposes. Consider these instructions from a fifteenth-century grimoire, *The Book of Angels, Rings, Characters and Images of the Planets*:

> Sacrifice a cock, write the character and name of the angel on the skin, of course, in which you should fold a penny. And no matter how often you give it away, it will return to you.
>
> Sacrifice a live white dove, write the name and character of its angel on the skin of a hare; if you show it to a woman, she will quickly follow you.
>
> (Lidaka, 1998: 49)

By the fifteenth century, grimoires such as these reinforced the authoritarian concern that grimoires were a tool of an increasingly powerful Satan. The age of the witch trials was dawning.

The Renaissance of the fifteenth century saw two juxtaposed developments in the European intellectual world. On the one hand the fear of a satanic conspiracy conducted through the agency of witches and magicians began to generate localised persecutions in central Europe. On the other, the Humanist movement inspired a renewed interest in the mystical and occult literature of the ancient 'pagan' world. Following in the footsteps of open-minded medieval theologians, Italian and German occult philosophers drew inspiration from 'new' discoveries, most notably the *Corpus hermeticum,* attributed to the ancient man-god Hermes Trismegistus, which was translated into Latin by Marsilio Ficino (1433–99) and published in 1471. Kabbalah was also introduced to new audiences through the *Three Books of Occult Philosophy* by the German Humanist Cornelius Agrippa (1486–1535).

Agrippa's name would become one of the most cited in future grimoires, not only due to his own writings but because of magical works that were attributed to him posthumously, in particular the *Fourth Book of Occult Philosophy*, which became notorious across Europe. Agrippa was not alone in attracting posthumous notoriety for penning grimoires he would have abhorred. Real but long-dead people were now joining those legendary figures of the Bible and antiquity who graced the titles of the medieval genre. So, in the early modern period manuscripts circulated that were ascribed to the renowned medieval scientists Roger Bacon (*c.* 1214–94) and Michael Scot (1175-*c.* 1232), while various medieval popes accrued noxious magical reputations that were readily spread by Protestant propagandists. The early ninth-century Pope Leo III became the author of a late seventeenth-century French grimoire, and around the same time Pope Honorius III (1148–1227) usurped his ancient Theban namesake as the originator of the *Grimoire du Pape Honorius*.

By the seventeenth century, print was having a profound impact on the nature of grimoires, their use and dissemination. As a technology, print certainly reduced the magical potency of the grimoire. The printing press and the rag paper it was developed to work with depersonalised the production of literary magic, limiting the diversity of inks and writing surfaces – the use of vellum in particular which had become integral to the medieval grimoire tradition. Yet the printed grimoire merely became the source material for a continuing, vibrant and democratic manuscript grimoire tradition, as is evident from the prosecution records of the early modern period. The Italian Inquisition conducted numerous raids on those who owned, traded, translated and copied grimoires and the records reveal a vibrant scribal culture in places like Venice, demonstrating how the culture of magic books touched every stratum of society from nobles to the illiterate, and involved women and men. The numerous manuscript grimoires confiscated by the inquisitors were compiled from a mix of illicit printed texts, such as those written by or attributed to Agrippa, and the more diverse secret manuscript archives that dated back to the late medieval period. Some were produced on a commercial basis – sometimes to order, and others for personal use or for groups of treasure seekers. The process was not only one of mere copying but of re-invention, so that three manuscripts bearing the title *Clavicula Salomonis* could differ markedly in terms of content. Then again, a book whose contents were based on a version of the *Clavicula* might end up being attributed to someone else.

Many of the prosecutions involving the possession of grimoires across Europe concerned treasure hunting. The main knowledge desired was how to identify the location of treasure through communication with the spirit world or how to deal with the spirits that were often thought to guard buried treasure. But a more humble use of grimoires was as a source for creating everyday protective charms and talismans against witchcraft, evil spirits and misfortune. In this respect the possession of a grimoire was an essential tool for many cunning-folk who were the key disseminators of literary magic in popular cultures. The mere possession of a grimoire was not enough to unleash its power. Grimoires could only be unlocked by experts who were thought to have special powers due to their learnedness, possession of innate powers bestowed through birth right, their association with the spirit world, and/or the association with the mystique of foreignness. While the possession of literacy was essential to the reputations of many cunning-folk, their education was often not sufficient to understand fully the Latin words and sentences, occult symbols and references contained in the grimoires they possessed. Yet this did not matter, as they were used to create bricolage charms that consisted of various passages, signs and symbols which looked magical. The result was a new form of literary magic that made no intrinsic sense from a learned perspective but had a clear purpose for the clients who purchased them. Such written talismans were often folded, sealed or placed in receptacles by cunning-folk, so the client had no idea what they contained anyway: what was important was that they derived from books of magic that clients could not access.

From the advent of the printing press the print production of magic books was effectively suppressed in the Mediterranean inquisition countries, though it proved more difficult to halt the trickle of books smuggled across the Alps and Pyrenees. The earliest centres of occult book publication were in Protestant parts of Germany and Switzerland. In the fertile radical publishing environment of Cromwell's Commonwealth the first English editions were printed of the *Three Books* and *Fourth Book of Occult Philosophy*, the *Arbatel of Magick* (first printed in Basel in 1575), and the *Notory Art of Solomon*. Then in the eighteenth century the centre of grimoire publication shifted to France and the developing market in small cheap magic books. Toward the end of the century a new genre of grimoires and spell books also began to be printed in small numbers in Germany and Denmark.

The interaction of popular print and manuscript grimoires during the late eighteenth century generated new regional grimoire traditions based around false attributions. Some distinctive French titles have already been mentioned. In Germany and Scandinavia there was an emphasis on grimoires attributed to the notorious, semi-legendary sixteenth-century magician Dr Faustus. A title that would come to have global reach was the *Sixth and Seventh Books of Moses*. In Scandinavia the genre of *svarteboken* or 'black books' also included those bearing the pseudo-authorship of Cyprianus. While Saint Cyprian, a legendary third-century Bishop of Antioch was the original inspiration for the attribution, in nineteenth-century black book folklore Cyprianus was variously an evil Dane or a humble student – one more example of the mutability of the grimoire tradition.

The age of the American grimoire began with the arrival of a German immigrant named John George Hohman in 1802. He supplemented his living by publishing cheap religious, medical and occult tracts in German for the Pennsylvania Dutch population. His most influential and enduring was *Der lang Verborgene Freund*, which contained a series of charms, rituals and spells for protection against witches, ill health and the promotion of good fortune. The contents derived primarily from a popular text published in his homeland in the late eighteenth century. During the mid-nineteenth century the first English language editions appeared and over the ensuing decades *The Long Lost Friend*'s influence began to filter far beyond the Pennsylvania Dutch and into African-American popular magic. Then in the early twentieth century an Ohio huckster named William Lauron Delaurence became a legend in parts of the Caribbean and West Africa due to his canny use of advertising in foreign newspapers, marketing techniques and mail order distribution. His overseas reputation as a master of magic derived from his outrageous plagiarism of several books of ritual magic compiled by nineteenth-century British ritual magicians, and the repackaging of the *Sixth and Seventh Books of Moses*. Delaurence died in 1936 but 'his' grimoires are still banned by the Jamaican Customs Service as part of the attempt to suppress the practice of Obeah.

As the democratisation and spread of grimoires across social levels and cultures accelerated during the nineteenth and early twentieth century, there also began a renewed intellectual engagement with ritual magic and the literary sources that underpinned it. Throughout the so-called Enlightenment solitary and small fraternities of intellectual occult explorers continued to practise ritual magic, with Freemasonry providing a conducive environment, ritual structure and means of networking. In 1801 one such British occultist explorer, Francis Barrett, wrote a compendium of the aforementioned published seventeenth-century English works. Published in 1801, *The Magus: Or Celestial Intelligencer* was a flop in Barrett's own lifetime but had considerable influence on popular and intellectual magic in the following century. Delaurence printed a profitable version under his own name and bearing the title *The Great Book of Magical Art, Hindu Magic and East Indian Occultism*.

It was those involved in or inspired by the late nineteenth-century ritual magical organisation – the Hermetic Order of the Golden Dawn – who ushered in a new golden age for the grimoire in intellectual and artistic circles. One of its members was Arthur Edward Waite, author of the *Book of Black Magic and of Pacts*, which contained extensive conjurations culled from early modern printed texts, eighteenth-century manuscripts and French chapbook grimoires. Waite had no practical interest in their contents; indeed his aim was to diminish the worth of such literature. Fellow member Samuel Liddell Mathers (1854–1918), by contrast, drew inspiration from grimoires for his and the Golden Dawn's rituals. Mathers produced the first English edition of a *Clavicule of Solomon* in 1889, and went on to publish an English translation of a late seventeenth- or early eighteenth-century French grimoire called the *Book of the Sacred Magic of Abra-Melin*, which purported to be the distilled knowledge of a fifteenth-century Kaballist. Aleister Crowley (1875–1947) drew inspiration from these sources in constructing his own conception of magical practice.

So by the early twentieth century, printed grimoires could be found in the cottages of European folk magicians, the indigenous and colonial populations of the French and British empires, and the libraries of European esotericists. New centres of popular grimoire publishing opened up in Brazil, Mexico and Argentina. But the manuscript tradition was far from dead. With the advent of Wicca shortly after the Second World War, and the subsequent growth of the Pagan witchcraft movement, a new reformulation of familiar grimoire features was recast as the literary expression of an ancient Pagan fertility cult, and a new grimoire tradition was born – *The Book of Shadows*. The democratisation of magic was not on the agenda in early Wicca: the *Book of Shadows* was to be kept a secret known only to initiates, and transmitted through manuscript copying. But as with the Golden Dawn and its secret rituals, it only took a few decades for the 'original' contents of the *Book of Shadows* to appear in print.

Versions of the most famous print grimoires from antiquity to the twentieth century are now available for free on the internet, thanks in particular to the likes of Joseph Peterson and his website esotericarchives.com, and over the last few years a number of edited versions of rare manuscript texts have also been published. David Rankine, for example, has helped make available the seventeenth-century French manuscript *Le Livre d'Or* lodged in the British Library Lansdowne collection, and the private magic manual of a seventeenth-century London magician named Arthur Gauntlet, the original manuscript being in the Sloane collection of the British Library.

While such modern editions are valuable resources for scholars, the editors, like Rankine, are sometimes practitioners working primarily for the benefit of the practitioner community. This is a fascinating development in the history of the grimoire. Non-practitioner academics of ancient and medieval magic are providing texts and analyses primarily for an academic audience but which are also being used by practitioners, and, vice versa.

For those Pagan practitioners who shun such Judaeo-Christian magic traditions, every year brings new personalised 'grimoire guides' for this diverse occult community. Inspired by the *Book of Shadows* these provide systems of ritual magic-working drawn from an eclectic mix of global traditions and feed off other practitioner-inspired texts as well as recent work by anthropologists, sociologists and historians. Yet while the contemporary western grimoire tradition draws upon an eclectic mix of western esotericism, oriental mysticism and the problematic category of shamanism, the modern Islamic expression of literary magic is rarely identified as an inspiration or engaged with by modern non-Islamic practitioners. The information is out there and maybe in the future, in the grand tradition of grimoires, new cultural exchanges and understanding will occur through the medium of magic and the internet.

REFERENCES AND FURTHER READING

Barbierato, F. (2011) 'Writing, Reading, Writing: Scribal Culture and Magical Texts in Early Modern Venice', *Italian Studies*, 66, 2: 263–76.

Butler, A. (2011) *Victorian Occultism and the Making of Modern Magic: Invoking Tradition*, Basingstoke: Palgrave.

Davies, O. (2003) *Cunning-Folk: Popular Magic in English History*, London: Hambledon and London Press.

——(2009) *Grimoires: A History of Magic Books*, Oxford: Oxford University Press.

Dillinger, J. (2012) *Magical Treasure Hunting in Europe and North America*, Basingstoke: Palgrave.

Eamon, W. (1994) *Science and the Secrets of Nature: Books of Secrets in Medieval and Early Modern Culture*, Princeton: Princeton University Press.

Fanger, C. (ed.) (1998) *Conjuring Spirits: Texts and Traditions of Medieval Ritual Magic*, Philadelphia: University of Pennsylvania Press.

——(2012) *Invoking Angels: Theurgic Ideas and Practices, Thirteenth to Sixteenth Centuries*, Philadelphia: University of Pennsylvania Press.

Green, M. (2011) 'The publication of and interest in occult literature, 1640–80', M.Phil. thesis, University of Hertfordshire.

Harari, Y. (2012) 'The Sword of Moses (*Harba de-Moshe*): A New Translation and Introduction', *Magic, Ritual, and Witchcraft*, 7, 1: 58–99.

Harms, D. (ed.) (2012) *The Long-Lost Friend: A 19th Century American Grimoire*, Woodbury: Llewellyn Publications.

Harper, D. (2010) 'The Textual Form of Knowledge: Occult Miscellanies in Ancient and Medieval Chinese Manuscripts, Fourth Century B.C. to Tenth Century A.D.', in F. Bretelle-Establet (ed.) *Looking at It from Asia: The Processes that Shaped the Sources of History of Science*, Dordrecht: Springer, 37–80.

Johnson, T.K. (2010) 'Tidebast och Vändelrot: Magical Representations in the Swedish Black Art Book Tradition', unpublished Ph.D. thesis, University of Washington.

Kieckhefer, R. (1989) *Forbidden Rites: A Necromancer's Manual of the Fifteenth Century*, Philadelphia: University of Pennsylvania Press.

Klaassen, F. (2013) *The Transformations of Magic: Illicit Learned Magic in the Later Middle Ages and Renaissance*, Philadelphia: University of Pennsylvania Press.

Lang, B. (2008) *Unlocked Books: Manuscripts of Learned Magic in the Medieval Libraries of Central Europe*, Philadelphia: University of Pennsylvania Press.

Lidaka, J. (1998) 'The Book of Angels, Rings, Characters and Images of the Planets: Attributed to Osbern Bokenham', in C. Fanger (ed.), *Conjuring Spirits: Texts and Traditions of Medieval Ritual Magic*, Philadelphia: University of Pennsylvania Press, 32–75.

Ohrvik, A. (2011) 'Conceptualizing Knowledge in Early Modern Norway: A Study of Paratexts in Norwegian Black Books', unpublished Ph.D. thesis, University of Oslo.

Rankine, D. and P. H. Barron (eds) (2010) *The Book of Gold (Le Livre d'Or)*, London: Avalonia.

Rankine, D. (ed.) (2011) *The Grimoire of Arthur Gauntlet: A 17th-Century London Cunning-man's Book of Charms*, London: Avalonia.

Saif, L. (2011) 'The Arabic Theory of Astral Influences in Early Modern Medicine', *Renaissance Studies* 25, 5: 609–26.

CHAPTER SIXTY-ONE

ORIENTALISM AND THE OCCULT

Christopher Partridge

The premise of 'Orientalism' is that there is an essential polarity between East and West. The taken-for-granted, often naïve acceptance of this opposition within particularly the arts, the media, and popular culture has not only shaped Western understandings of the 'Other', but has fostered an attitude of difference and the exotic. This, in turn, has often led to and is supported by the construction of caricatures and unsophisticated understandings of Oriental religions, cultures and societies. Images of meditating Buddhist monks in saffron robes filtered through a gentle mist of incense, advertisements for 'Turkish Delight' confectionary depicting images of tented Bedouin royalty, a majestic camel train making its way across rolling dunes, the eroticism of the East described in the writings of the British Orientalist Richard Burton (1821–90) and depicted in paintings such as John Fredrick Lewis's *The Hhareen* (c. 1850), John Auguste Domonique Ingres's *Le Bain Turc* (1862) and Sir Frank Dicksee's *Leila* (1892), and the mysticism of gravity-defying martial artists in recent films such as *House of Flying Daggers* (2004), *Hero* (2002) and *Crouching Tiger, Hidden Dragon* (2000). All these narratives and images are common in the modern West and, again, all trade in stereotypes, fostering a perception of the exotic and the essential otherness of the Orient. Perhaps the starkest statement of this relationship is Rudyard Kipling's 'Ballad of East and West': 'Oh, East is East, and West is West, and never the twain shall meet, Till Earth and Sky stand presently at God's great Judgment Seat...' Orientalism refers to this ideological division of East and West, underlying which are constructions of the sacred and the profane; it refers to discourses shaped by the Western curiosity with the Eastern 'Other'; and it refers to the concomitant Western hubris generated by those discourses, which are usually accompanied by misunderstanding and a sense of duty to convert, to civilize and to modernize.

Not all Orientalism, however, articulated explicit Western hubris. Western constructions of the Orient also proved to be fascinating to some Westerners. Those seeking access to occult truth, who had become convinced that the mainstream religious traditions of the West had little to offer, turned to the Orient for enlightenment. Helena Petrovna Blavatsky (1931–1891), the co-founder of the Theosophical Society and its most important thinker, provides a paradigmatic example of both this

Occidental 'othering' and the construction of the Oriental 'other', in that she was fascinated by the possibility of excavating a hidden knowledge protected from modernity in a timeless, Oriental realm of wisdom and spirituality. She understood Theosophy to be the 'Secret Doctrine *of the East*' (Blavatsky, 1893, vol. 1: xvii), the teaching of the Oriental Masters of Wisdom (Blavatsky, 1968: 289; Pert, 2006: 109). She became convinced that, if a timeless Wisdom existed, it would have to have been concealed in the East, away from the corrosive rationalism of Western modernity and Christian hegemony. This, for example, is the rationale for the *The Book of Dzyan*, knowledge of which, Blavatsky claimed, formed the basis of her *Secret Doctrine* (1888; Maroney, 2000). It is, she argued, one of several sacred and ancient manuscripts, written in the esoteric language of 'Senzar', and protected from the profane world by initiates of a 'Great White Brotherhood' based in Tibet. This 'chief work…is not in the possession of European Libraries. *The Book of Dzyan* (or "*Dzan*") is utterly unknown to our Philologists…' (Blavatsky, 1893, vol. 1: xxii), who were, it appears, rather too sceptical regarding its existence. For example, Max Müller is reported to have said, concerning the *The Book of Dzyan*, that 'she was either a remarkable forger or that she has made the most valuable gift to archeological research in the Orient' (Kuhn, 1930: 194). However, the point is that, the nineteenth-century confluence of Orientalism and occultism meant that it was almost inevitable that 'the trans-Himalayan esoteric knowledge which has been from time immemorial the fountain-head of all genuine occultism on this earth' (de Zirkoff, 1975; 130) would be recorded in an unknown Eastern language and hidden in the imagined landscapes of the Orient.

A good recent example of this type of occult Orientalism is the teaching of Benjamin Creme concerning the Theosophical doctrine of the Lord Maitreya (see Blavatsky, 2010, vol. 6: 266–68), 'the Cosmic Christ', the highest office in the Spiritual Hierarchy. Two thousand years ago, he claims, Maitreya manifested himself on earth through his disciple Jesus, but has, ever since, been living in a remote mountain retreat in the Himalayas (Creme, 1980). The hidden Orient, the remote mountain retreat, the Tibetan outback, becomes sacred space in the occult Orientalist's imagination.

Edward Said makes the important point that in the system of knowledge about the Orient, it is 'less a place than a *topos*, a set of references, a congeries of characteristics, that seems to have its origin in a quotation, or a fragment of text, or a citation from someone's work on the Orient, or some bit of previous imagining, or an amalgam of all of these' (2003: 177). This, we will see, is certainly true of occult thought.

ROMANTICISM AND ORIENTALISM

While the term 'Orientalism' has, particularly since the publication of Said's polemically charged *Orientalism* in 1978, become pejorative and contested, it was originally used simply to refer to the disinterested, objective study of the Orient. For example, when referencing such work, Blavatsky simply refers to its authors as 'the Orientalists' (e.g. 1893, vol. 1: xxviii, 32; 2010, vol. 2: 104). Of course, the idea that such study is disinterested or neutral is now fundamentally problematic, as Said's impressive reception history indicates. Whether one agrees with all the points of his analysis or with what some consider to be his sweeping generalizations – making him guilty of the essentialism he himself criticizes in European culture (e.g. al-'Azm, 1981) – it is difficult to deny his thesis that, by and large, the history of Western attitudes towards 'the East' is a history of the formation of a powerful European ideology constructed to deal with the 'otherness' of Oriental cultures.

As to 'Orientalism' *per se*, arguably with origins in 1784, with the work of William Jones (1746–94) and the establishment of the Asiatic Society of Bengal in Calcutta, the study of the Orient can be viewed as the academic and administrative catalyst for the Bengali Renaissance, a resurgence of intellectual interest in Hindu culture and Indian history. A founding father of comparative linguistics, Jones's work on Sanskrit, along with that of Thomas Colebrooke (1765–1837), sought to establish Sanskrit's links with European languages. Such work not only led to a flowering of interest in Indian history and culture, but also to Romantic speculation about the Orient as the cradle of Occidental civilization. It is this speculation which eventually informed Theosophy's construction of Oriental *topoi*.

This scholarly turn to the Orient, intersected closely with an increasing Romantic tendency, from the late eighteenth century, to emphasize 'the mystic East' by reference to the 'esoteric' nature of India's ancient texts. For example, in 1808, Friedrich Schlegel (1772–1829), whose brother translated the *Bhagavadgita* and *Ramayana*, published his *Über die Sprache und Weisheit der Indier* (*On the Language and Wisdom of the Indians*), which expressed what became characteristic of Romanticism, namely a yearning for spiritual guidance from the East. Also typical of this Romantic gaze was Johann Gottfried von Herder's (1744–1803) conviction that 'the archaic nature of the Hindu Vedas represented the origins of human civilization, the source of Indo-European mythology and language, and provided a window into the mysterious history of humankind' (King, 1999: 118). Without unpacking this Romantic fascination with the Orient, the point here is simply that, in a Romantic Orientalist milieu, it is hardly surprising that contemporary occult thinkers and philosophers were beguiled by it. Perhaps most famously, in his radical critique of fundamental themes in Judeo-Christian theologies, Arthur Schopenhauer (1788–1860) demonstrated a conspicuous readiness to integrate Indian philosophical ideas into his own thought and self-understanding. As Nicol MacNicol comments of Schopenhauer, 'these utterances of the Indian spirit seem to have so affected him as to determine from thenceforward the direction and tone of his teaching. He has himself described how profoundly he was affected when this new planet swam into his ken, even though those voices of the Indian sages reached him as a dim echo in a version that was twice translated, first from the original Sanskrit into Persian and then from Persian into Latin' (1936: 77–78; see also Halbfass, 1988: 106–20). Again, we have seen that there was, in Romantic Orientalism, a nostalgia for human origins, for 'authenticity'. Once India was identified as 'the cradle of civilization', there was, as is evident in Herder's work, an allied tendency to understand its religion and culture ahistorically, as frozen in time, a throwback to the infancy of the human race. Indeed, in seeking reasons for why this view was so readily accepted in early nineteenth-century Europe, it's important to understand that this apparently solid bedrock of Oriental civilization provided a welcome feeling of stability during a period when Western political and social sands were shifting. As Richard King comments, 'while Europe and the New World were undergoing enormous social and political changes, India seemed to have remained unchanged for thousands of years, representing a crucial example of static archaism with which the dynamic modernity of the West could be successfully contrasted' (1999: 118).

Put simply, nineteenth-century Western 'occulture' was Orientalist. That is to say, the imagined Orient appealed, not only to Romantic philosophy, but, as the nineteenth century progressed, also to occultism and to popular culture (each of which tended to inform the other). Geographically and intellectually diverse thinkers such as Edwin Arnold (1832–1904), Ralph Waldo Emerson (1803–82), Walt Whitman (1819–92), E.M. Forster (1879–1970), Edward Carpenter (1844–1929), and Blavatsky all developed a homogenized view of India as a culture which rejected materialism, reductive rationalism, and industrialization, in favour of the cultivation of a simple, spiritual life shaped by a philosophy of self-realization (e.g. Arnold, 2007; Carpenter, 1892; Emerson, 2000; Forster, 1924; Whitman, 1975). Put simply, it is difficult to ignore the fact that the Romantic fascination with Indian thought, which was typically Orientalist and essentialist, was an important moment in the West's reception of the East and, as such, the soil in which modern occultism took root. Indeed, it is significant that thinkers such as Blavatsky and René Guénon were clearly familiar, not only with the contemporary Orientalist scholarship, such as that of Müller, but also with Romantic and Transcendentalist speculation about the Orient in the writings of such as Emerson and Schopenhauer. In Blavatsky's essay on Schopenhauer, for example, she even claims that 'if ever he were studied, Theosophy would be better understood' (2010, vol. 1: 332).

A key tenet of Theosophy, as we will see, is the belief in the existence of a 'Divine Wisdom', 'Theosophia' (Blavatsky, 1968: 1), which constitutes an ageless, occult guide to the life of the universe and everything. However, this type of Orientalist perennialism, which sought archaic connections between disparate philosophies, religions and spiritualities, is likewise very typical of the period. For example, Abraham Hyacinthe Anquetil-Duperron (1731–1805), whose *Oupnek'hat* (the first European translation of the *Upanishads*) became an influential sourcebook of Indian wisdom,

> called upon the philosophers of many countries, and in particular the representatives of German Idealism – the 'followers and opponents of the profound Kant' – to study the teachings of the *Oupnek'hat* from a philosophical angle, not just seeing them as testimony about ancient India, but also to consider them as a serious philosophical challenge...He included many comparisons with Western philosophical teachings, e.g., with Plotinus and the Gnostics...Anyone who carefully examines the lines of Immanuel Kant's thought, its principles as well as its results, will recognise that it does not deviate very far from the teachings of the Brahmins, which lead man back to himself and comprise him and focus him within himself.
>
> (Halbfass, 1988: 66–67)

Moreover, as well as the Romantic penchant for Orientalist perennialism, it was also prevalent among nineteenth-century Hindu reformers. Dayananda Saraswati (1824–83) – referred to by Blavatsky as 'a most highly honoured Fellow of the Theosophical Society' (2010, vol. 1: 382) – and the Arya Samaj (Blavatsky, 2010, vol.1: 379–84) insisted on the primacy and superiority of Hinduism and the Vedas, even going so far as to argue that all knowledge, including contemporary Western scientific knowledge, has its origins in ancient India. Even the principal teachings of Christianity could be found in ancient Sanskrit texts. Another example of this type of thinking, representing a confluence of East and West, is that of Ram Mohan Roy (1772–1833), sometimes referred to as the 'the father of modern India', and certainly the first significant modern Hindu reformer. Not only did he seek to purify Hinduism and return it to the *Upanishads*, but he sought to do this in dialogue with Christian thought (see Klostermaier, 1994: 432–35). In so doing, drawing on Unitarian deism, he developed a universalist thesis that all the major religions had a common root (see Blavatsky, 2010, vol. 2: 130–35). It's worth noting that Roy's translations were read by American transcendentalists (see Christy, 1932) and subsequently by Blavatsky, who described him as 'one of the purest, most philanthropic, and enlightened men India ever produced' (2010, vol. 3: 56).

Finally, before looking at some of these ideas a little more closely, it's important to note that, while it's not difficult to be disparaging of occult Orientalism and its rather naïve romanticization of India, Tibet, and, indeed, Egypt, its social and cultural impact was, in several significant respects, positive. For example, as R.C. Zaehner comments of the Theosophist Annie Besant (1847–1933), 'from the moment she set foot on Indian soil she gave herself entirely to the Hindu people and far exceeded the indigenous reformers in her zeal to defend all things Hindu...Her energy was boundless, and it would be no exaggeration to say that no single person did so much to revive the Hindu's pride in his religious heritage as did she. She lifted Hindus out of the deep feeling of inferiority that had been induced in them by the subjugation of their land to an alien yoke and the attacks made on their religion by the self-confident zealots of another faith.' Indeed, Zaehner even goes so far as to claim that it is 'largely due to the Theosophical Society and its uncritical adulation of all things Hindu that Hinduism has been able not only to shake off its previous inferiority complex, but to face the other great religions of the world at least as an equal' (1966: 160–61). While there is exaggeration here and little account taken of the impact of colonialism and Orientalism, it is, nevertheless, a point worth noting when considering particularly the Theosophical Society's relationship to India.

THE OCCULT TRAVELLER

Orientalism *per se* began with travel. 'The idea of travel as a means of gathering and recording information is commonly found in societies that exercise a high degree of political power. The traveller begins his journey with the strength of a nation or an empire sustaining him (albeit from a distance) militarily, economically, intellectually and, as is often the case, spiritually' (Kabbani, 2008: 17). The traveller, as an imperial agent, becomes the interpreter of the exotic, selecting ethnographic data for Western curiosity, exaggerating difference, chronicling the alien, constructing cultural and racial stereotypes, seeking, in some cases, to convert, control and colonize. The general point, however, is that travelogues and the popular culture and the art they informed (see Mackenzie, 1995; Said, 2003), along with the intellectual reception of the Eastern thought, contributed to the construction of an Orientalist occulture which shaped the development of certain occult currents.

Alan Bennet, for example – a member of the Order of the Golden Dawn, a close friend of Aleister Crowley, and an affiliate of the Druidic organization, the British Circle of the Universal Bond – having read Arnold's *Light of Asia* in 1890, travelled

East to study Buddhism. He eventually became one of the first Westerners to enter the Theravadin sangha and was subsequently frequently referenced by Crowley as a great *yogi* (see Rawlinson, 1997: 159–62). Crowley himself, of course, had also travelled to Ceylon, where he studied yoga with Bennett, determined, he declared in typical Orientalist fashion, 'to work out the Eastern systems under an Eastern sky and by Eastern methods alone' (quoted in Pasi, 2012: 59).

However, again, arguably the most significant occult tourist was Blavatsky, who claims to have travelled widely in search of occult knowledge. Whether she travelled as extensively as she claimed is beside the point, for she was, at least to some extent, a tourist, a collector and interpreter of exotic ideas. Although it is difficult to construct a chronology or to verify much of what she recorded, she did describe numerous selected encounters and cultivate the image of the Victorian traveller. Of particular importance for Theosophy's hagiographical narrative, is her claimed solitary seven-year sojourn in Tibet (2010, vol. 7: 288), during which she was 'chosen' to study with a secret group of 'Himalayan Brothers' (2010, vol. 3: 262). This narrative of her as occult tourist-scholar imposed itself with some force on the Theosophical imagination. The tales of an occultist with considerable psychic powers travelling to Egypt and Tibet could hardly have been better contrived to fascinate. Not only was she an intriguing example of what nineteenth-century Westerners had come to expect of their intrepid travellers, but she was Russian and, therefore, in no small measure, exotic herself. She also, of course, travelled to lands that particularly piqued the imagination of her generation. Her persistence as an occult traveller, her intelligence, her pugnacity, and her claimed innate psychic abilities gave her, despite suffering shipwrecks and ill health, access to wisdom hidden in locations that had already begun to gain a considerable Romantic and occult symbolic significance: Egypt, India, Tibet. She travelled to what a Christian culture had learned to dismiss as the 'heart of darkness' and found light. Not greatly dissimilar to other travellers and writers of her generation, she produced selective Romantic accounts of the cultures and beliefs of others. Again, few narratives could be better designed to stimulate the interest of nineteenth-century Westerners drawn to occultism. She met with magicians, sat at the feet of spiritual Masters, and gained access to a foundational spiritual wisdom that 'relates to all the primeval truths delivered to the first Races, the "Mind-born," by the "Builders" of the Universe themselves' (Blavatsky, 2010, vol. 14: 46–47).

Of course, much of what she wrote about was probably gleaned from the published accounts of Orientalists and other travellers of the period. For example, concerning Tibet, despite Blavatsky's claims to have studied in the country under the mysterious Masters of Wisdom, her 'knowledge of Buddhism in *Isis Unveiled* could easily be found in western publications' and the 'geographical and ethnographical knowledge relating to Tibet was drawn from Abbé Évariste Régis Huc, *Travels in Tartary, Thibet China and India During the Years 1844–5–6* (1852), Emil Schlagintweit, *Buddhism in Tibet* (1863), and Clement R. Markham, *Narratives of the Mission of George Bogle to Tibet and of the Journey of Thomas Manning to Lhasa* (1876)' (Goodrick-Clarke, 2007: 21). Indeed, Buddhism and Tibet had become increasingly important features of contemporary occulture, particularly within Spiritualist circles. Spiritualists, like the Theosophists, 'responded to the Buddhist view that the soul was an immortal essence, independent of physical manifestation' (Goodrick-Clarke, 2007: 21). As to the attraction of Tibet, as with many other Westerners, the country appealed greatly to the Theosophist's Romantic imagination. Indeed, apart from the Western fascination with Egypt, it is difficult to think of another place so steeped in Orientalist myth and imagining. Whether we think of the convalescence and rebirth of Sherlock Holmes in Tibet following his attempted assassination at the hands of Moriarty at the Reichenbach Falls or James Hilton's book *Lost Horizon* (1933), or, indeed, David Lynch's FBI agent in *Twin Peaks* looking for inspiration from Tibet to assist him in solving the disturbing and bizarre murder of a young woman, Tibet has been a focus of Orientalist speculation about a wisdom and spiritual power unavailable in the West. As Peter Bishop comments, 'Tibet's location of the Western sphere of influence and at the fringe of its everyday concerns, has been directly responsible for the consistently rich fantasies evoked by that country. In a sense, Tibet's peripheral place has given permission for the West to use it as an imaginative escape: a sort of time out, a relaxation of rigid rational censorship. Time and again Tibet has been described with all the qualities of a dream, a collective hallucination' (1993: 16). This dream-like view of Tibet is typical of the occultism's love affair with the Orient.

THE EROTIC EAST

Another nineteenth-century occult tourist was Carl Kellner (1851–1905). A wealthy Austrian paper chemist with a keen interest in esotericism, he is said, by his disciples, to have travelled to 'the East' and to have 'studied with three Eastern masters' (Urban, 2006: 96). More importantly, with Theodor Reuss (1855–1923), he laid the foundations for the Ordo Templi Orientis (OTO), an organization which sought to bring together key elements of Freemasonry and Rosicrucianism, along with Oriental ideas, particularly those associated with Hindu Tantra. Indeed, Reuss, the principal architect of the OTO, came to understand 'sexual rituals and the cult of the Lingam (the Sanskrit word for the Phallus or male sexual organ) as the root of all religion, "the most ancient cult on earth", and the core of every spiritual tradition from prehistoric times...And the quintessential form of phallic worship is Tantra' (Urban, 2006: 98). In other words, typical of the Orientalist imagination, which understood the East to have developed attitudes towards sexuality unconstrained by Christian morality, there was a fascination with sex as an occult technology.

While the identification of Tantra with sex – which is central to much nineteenth-century Orientalist discourse – is misleading, the articulation of Tantra as 'sex magic' has remained prominent within some streams of modern occultism. Indeed, as Hugh Urban shows, the '(mis)equation of Tantra with sex has been a consistent theme in virtually every popular Western text on Tantra, from Omar Garrison's *The Yoga of Sex* to Judy Kuriansky's *Complete Idiot's Guide to Tantric Sex*' (2006, 105).

ORIENTAL MASTERS OF WISDOM

As indicated above, also important for the occult tourist, was not simply the geographical locations explored, but the exotic persons encountered. Whether we think of occultists and magicians in Egypt or gurus in India, occult works are peppered with references to 'meetings with remarkable men' as proof of some doctrine or practice. For example, Blavatsky 'pointed to the legends of the mysterious East and the renowned powers of Indian yogis as proof of the possibility of performing natural magic in accord with an occult science' (Bevir, 1994: 762). However, of the Oriental persons encountered by Blavatsky, none were as important as the Mahatmas of Tibet. Her particular interpretation of Buddhism within a larger narrative informed by Western esotericism, Spiritualism and contemporary evolutionary theory, along with the romance of Tibet's lost horizon – Shambhala/Shangri-La – provided the seedbed for a central doctrine of Theosophical Orientalism. 'If Tibet's remote location was a fitting source of esoteric doctrine, the cosmology of Tibetan Buddhism provided an elaborate world of esoteric intermediaries for the articulation of Theosophical cosmology…a descending hierarchy from the nameless Absolute to the human leaders of mankind in successive historical eras' (Goodrick-Clarke, 2007: 23). The guardians of occult knowledge, who were able to materialize and, through Blavatsky, speak to the world, became central to Theosophical thinking. Hence, there are numerous testimonies relating the mysterious appearance or disappearance of Masters, as well as much else that demonstrates their power and wise superiority. 'I am very glad to testify' declares Charles Leadbeater (1854–1934), 'that I have on many occasions seen the Masters appear in materialized form at the Headquarters in Adyar' (quoted in Besant, 1907: 13).

'We call them masters because they are our teachers; and because from them we have derived all the Theosophical truths' (Blavatsky, 1968: 289). Needless to say, such statements require a lot more discussion than is possible here. However, the principal point here is a simple one, namely Theosophical Masters/Mahatmas conform to nineteenth-century Orientalist stereotypes: the ethereal Brahmin, the world-denying, cross-legged guru, the spiritually penetrating 'swami', the psychically powerful 'fakir', detached from the material world and in touch with ancient wisdom and higher powers. In the Orient we find occultists *par excellence*, the 'Mahatmas', 'the men of great learning', those who 'remain apart from the turmoil and strife of your western world', those who are able to manifest themselves in their astral bodies (Blavatsky, 1968: 289; Besant, 1907). This view of the powerful, occult genius of the Orient was a conspicuous theme in contemporary popular occulture. Take the example of Sax Rohmer's (1883–1959) description of Fu Manchu in his 1913 novel, *The Insidious Dr. Fu-Manchu*. While a Theosophical master such as Koot Hoomi or Morya might appear very different from Fu-Manchu, in actual fact, interesting parallels could be drawn showing the latter as an inverse of the former:

> Imagine a person, tall, lean and feline, high-shouldered, with a brow like Shakespeare and a face like Satan, a close-shaven skull, and long, magnetic eyes of the true cat-green. Invest him with all the cruel cunning of an entire Eastern race, accumulated in one giant intellect, with all the resources of science past and present, with all the resources, if you will, of a wealthy government – which, however, already has denied all knowledge of his existence. Imagine that awful being, and you have a mental picture of Dr. Fu-Manchu, the yellow peril incarnate in one man.
>
> (Rohmer, 1997: 13)

Instead of using his mystical genius, his Oriental wisdom, to guide the human race, as Theosophical Masters do, Fu-Manchu seeks control, through the use of what

Blavatsky would describe as 'black magic'. However, the point is that Rohmer and Blavatsky were breathing the same Orientalist air as their imagined Masters.

It should be noted, however, that not all Theosophists were happy with the Eastern direction towards which Theosophy was facing or with the teaching regarding Masters. Anna Kingsford (1846–88), for example, encouraged the esoteric study of Christianity, believing Theosophy in England to be too concerned with Oriental ideas which were, she said, 'meaningless and unintelligible, save to a few' (quoted in Pert, 2006: 118–19). Similarly, she writes, 'Pray do not let yourself be drawn away from the original idea by giving your Society such a name as "Oriental". It will mean nothing, and will put you into communication with no one either in India or in England' (quoted in Pert, 2006: 108). More pointedly, she was highly critical of Theosophy's increasing focus on what the newspapers were referring to as Theosophy's 'Indian jugglers' (see Pert, 2006: 119). The following extract from one of her letters indicates both her distaste for the doctrine and also its growing importance in Theosophical circles:

> I look with sorrow and concern on the growing tendency of the Theosophical Society to introduce into its method...the exaggerated veneration for persons and for personal authority...There is far too much talk among us about the adepts, our 'MASTERS' and the like. Too much capital is made of their sayings and doings, doctrine is commended to us solely on the ground that they have affirmed it to be true, and reverence is expected for it to an excessive degree on that ground alone; insomuch that if one says 'I think Koot Hoomi is in error on such a point' or 'the Brothers appear to be insufficiently informed about so and so,' the statement is not unlikely to be regarded in the light of a sort of blasphemy, or at least as a disloyalty to Theosophy.
>
> (quoted in Pert, 2006: 117)

The fact that Koot Hoomi had been found to have plagiarized the American Spiritualist Henry Kiddle did nothing to allay her fears (see Pert, 2006: 116–17).

EGYPTOSOPHY

There are few countries that have attracted as much esoteric speculation as Egypt. A general fascination with Egypt grew during the nineteenth century, stimulated to some extent by numerous artefacts brought to the West as a result of military campaigns, such as Cleopatra's Needle, an obelisk, flanked by Victorian sphinxes, and erected on the Thames embankment in London. Initially, the obelisk was the gift of a Turkish governor in 1801 following the defeat of Napoleon by the British at the Battle of Alexandria, but it was only transported to London in 1877. Indeed, Napoleon's failed military campaign in Egypt at the end of the eighteenth century was, arguably, the midwife of modern Egyptology. Napoleon insisted that everything be recorded and mapped in an attempt to render Egypt, as Said puts it, 'completely open, to make it totally accessible to European scrutiny. From being a land of obscurity and a part of the Orient hitherto known only second hand through the exploits of earlier travellers, scholars and conquerors, Egypt was to become a department of French learning' (2003: 83). This learning, perhaps unsurprisingly, seeped into the occulture of the period. Gradually, the occult imagination began to make connections and seek answers. In France, for example, 'a highly speculative and widely influential interpretation of the Tarot cards...identified ancient Egypt as the source of the beguiling imagery' (Horowitz, 2009: 51). This type of speculation was, likewise, conspicuous in occult literature.

Having said that, while nineteenth-century occulture is particularly interesting in this respect, the idea of 'an ancient esoteric Egypt', what Erik Hornung refers to as 'Egyptosophy', 'an imaginary Egypt viewed as a profound source of all esoteric lore' (2001: 3), has a long history in the Western imagination. Notably, the Greeks attributed the highest degree of wisdom to the Egyptians. For example, Hermes was compared by Diodorus Siculus (c. 90–21 BCE) to both Moses and Zoroaster, the three forming an esoteric triad that would later influence both Renaissance and subsequent generations of European esotericists. Again, such as Herodotus and Pliny contributed to the construction of an imaginary Egypt, which has continued to influence a form of Western Orientalism. As is evident in Blavatsky's Theosophy, in some occult traditions ancient Egypt was understood to be the 'source of all wisdom'. Indeed, Egyptian hieroglyphs were understood by some Renaissance esotericists to be the primeval, secret language of Hermes. Again, Thoth becomes a central figure in Egyptosophy. The 'founder of religion', this winged messenger, scribe of the gods, and guardian of the Eye of Horus, whose priests were authors of the esoteric *Books of Thoth*, had, by the Ptolemaic period, become the primary Egyptian deity of occult magic, incantations and spells. Eventually, Thoth was transformed into Hermes Trismegistus and following 240 BCE, a historic religion of Hermes can be traced (see Goodrick-Clarke, 2008: 16ff.). The point is that 'Egyptosophy' emerges as a significant esoteric force during the Renaissance. For example, in the imaginations of key Renaissance thinkers, such as Marsilio Ficino (1433–99) and Giovanni Pico della Mirandola (1463–94), Greek wisdom originated with the Egyptian priests and the Chaldean (i.e. Zoroastrian) magi. Hence, rather unsurprisingly, European hermeticism, fundamentally indebted to Ficino's translation of the *Corpus Hermeticum* (see Copenhaver, 1992: xlvii–xlix), has a very clear Orientalist focus on an imaginary Egypt. This Orientalist gaze is later developed in the works of such as Ralph Cudworth (1617–88) and Athanasius Kircher (1602–80) and can be traced through into Rosicrucianism and Freemasonry, which included ideas from Renaissance Hermeticism and 'Egyptian mysteries', both of which find their way directly into Blavatsky's Theosophy (see Hornung, 2001: 141–54). As Godwin comments, 'everywhere she [Blavatsky] was involved with Freemasonry, Oriental secret societies, occult fraternities, and with the spiritualists who constituted, as it were, the exoteric "church" from which doors opened to the more esoteric circles' (1994: 281). Again, the point is that there emerged a general Orientalist fascination with esoteric Egyptian motifs during the eighteenth and nineteenth centuries. Whether we think of the founding of the short-lived Hermetic Brotherhood of Luxor (see Godwin, Chanel, & Devaney, 1995), or the establishment of the 'Rite de la Haute Maçonnerie Egyptienne' in 1784 by Count Alessandro di Cagliostro (1743–95), 'the great European impersonator of the Orient' (Said, 2003: 88) who claimed to have discovered a 'secret knowledge learned in the subterranean vaults of the Egyptian pyramids' (Hornung, 2001: 121), or the Egyptian influences evident in German Romanticism, occulture was soon peppered with references to what Blavatsky refers to as 'the Wisdom of the Egyptians' (2010, vol. 13: 76; see Sinnet, 1881: 2).

While there is room for considerable scepticism regarding Blavatsky's travels in Tibet (see Price, 2003: 173), this is not the case regarding her short time in Egypt. That said, regarding the witnesses, Albert Leighton Rawson (1829–1902) and Alfred Percy Sinnett (1840–1921), both of whom were admirers, their emic accounts do need to be treated with some caution. Nevertheless, Nicholas Goodrick-Clarke makes good use of their work to construct the following summary:

> In 1851...at Cairo she was introduced to Paolos Metamon, a Copt magician, with whom she studied occult and magical lore. While living in the backwoods of Mingrelia (Caucasus) in 1864, she sought out native sorcerers, Persian thaumaturgists and Armenian fortune-tellers, all the time increasing her own reputation as a magician. After a near-fatal accident, she fell into a coma for some months, but on recovery she found she had complete mastery of her psychic powers.
>
> Seven years later, in 1871, Blavatsky was again in Cairo, where she became interested in spiritualism, which had been widely publicized through Allen Kardec in France during the 1860s. She started *Société Spirite* for the investigation of mediums and phenomena according to Kardec's theories of spiritualism.
>
> (2007: 3; see also Godwin, 1994: 277–78)

This time spent in Cairo, during which she founded the *Société Spirite* – to which Max Théon (1848–1927) and the Hermetic Brotherhood of Luxor seem to have been tenuously linked (see Godwin, Chanel, & Devaney, 1995: 9) – can be understood as an initial Orientalist period, shaped by Western understandings of Egypt. While the Tibetan Other played a far more significant role in the formation of Theosophical Orientalism, it is nevertheless the case that, whether one considers occult organizations, such as the Hermetic Brotherhood of Luxor, or simply the popular culture of the period, Egypt held a particular fascination for the West. As Said comments in his discussion of the twenty-three-volume *Description de l'Égypte*, published between 1809 and 1828, Jean-Baptiste-Joseph Fourier, the author of its *préface historique*, argues that to study Egypt is to study 'a kind of unadulterated cultural, geographical, and historical significance'. Said continues, 'Egypt was the focal point of the relationships between Africa and Asia, between Europe and the East, between memory and actuality...Because Egypt was saturated with meaning for the arts, sciences and government, its role was to be the stage on which actions of world-historical importance would take place' (2003: 84–85). This type of thinking translated easily to the occult thinking of the period. As indicated by the gigantic monuments, the intriguing sacred texts, and what they knew of the exotic deities and mythologies, Egypt became a foundational reference in some theories of occult wisdom. Blavatsky was no exception (see 1893, vol.1: xxviii–xxx). It is significant, for example, that she entitled her first major work *Isis Unveiled* (1877). Again, drawing on current Hermeticism, she was convinced that an ancient science of occultism, traceable in 'the thousand riddles of the Egyptian hieroglyphic records' (Blavatsky, 1893, vol.1: xxxiv), could be traced back to the Gnosticism of the Egyptian Ophites.

Arguing that its origins lie deep in prehistory, over 400,000 years ago, Blavatsky understood Egypt to have emerged from a colony of Atlanto-Aryan migrants, from the northern Atlantean island-continent of Daitya. Theosophy itself is directly continuous with this ancient history through Egypt, in that, as she insists at the outset of *The Key to Theosophy*, the term 'Theosophy' was coined by 'the Alexandrian philosophers', notably, Ammonius Saccas (*c.*160–242), who started 'the Eclectic Theosophical system' (Blavatsky, 1968: 1–2). Seeking to establish the unity of all religions, she identified a 'Wisdom religion', of which Theosophy is a manifestation and turned initially to Egypt to locate its origins. 'The Neo-Platonists were a large body, and belonged to various religious philosophies; so do our Theosophists. In those days, the Jew Aristobulus affirmed that the ethics of Aristotle represented the *esoteric* teachings of the Law of Moses; Philo Judaeus endeavoured to reconcile the *Pentateuch* with the Pythagorean and Platonic philosophy; and Josephus proved that the Essenes of Carmel were simply the copyists and followers of the Egyptian Therepeutae (the healers)' (Blavatsky, 1968: 4–5). Likewise, she argues that 'occult alphabets and secret ciphers are the development of the old Egyptian *hieratic* writings, the secret of which was, in the days of old, in the possession only of the Hierogrammatists, or initiated Egyptian priests' (Blavatsky, 1968: 9).

CONCLUDING COMMENTS

'Simplistically speaking, we can speak of two forms of Orientalist discourse, the first, generally antagonistic and confident in European superiority, the second, generally affirmative, enthusiastic and suggestive of Indian superiority in certain areas. Both forms of Orientalism, however, make essentialist judgements that foster an overly simplistic and homogenous conception of [Oriental] culture' (King, 1999: 116). Much occult fascination, which certainly belongs to the latter form of Orientalism, was shaped within the context of Western political dominance and colonial expansionism. This is important, because all Orientalism is, to some extent, a 'Western style for dominating, restructuring, and having authority over the Orient' (Said, 2003: 3). Hence, for example, the Theosophical Society understands that a confluence of Blavatsky's sharp occult mind, the tuition of the Masters, and a significant breadth of experience as a traveller, led to a superior understanding of the individual beliefs of others. She was able to grasp the esoteric heart of Hinduism, Buddhism and Islam; she was able to sift out Theosophical orthodoxy from the heterodoxy of the wider tradition; she was actually a good example of Kabbani's argument that 'it is a commonplace of Orientalism that the West knows more about the East than the East knows about itself...' (2008: 31). As such, in a subtle, open-armed, enthusiastic, welcoming manner, she is an example of, to quote Said again, Orientalism as a 'Western style for dominating, restructuring, and having authority over the Orient'.

There is, we have seen, a particular narrative consciousness shaping occult Orientalism. While, like many Orientalists, many Western occultists believed they were studying and travelling in order to learn, in actual fact, they had already constructed occult narratives prior to their travels. Hence, drawing on other Romantic narratives of the Orient and adopting (to some extent, unwittingly) an Orientalist, Procrustean hermeneutic, Western occultists went in search of what they 'knew' was already there in order to meet their esoteric needs. Hence, for example, it was always important for Blavatsky and Theosophy that esoteric India remained frozen in religious history; its traditions, its spirituality, its Wisdom needed to remain pure and unaltered; there was, therefore, a need for protection from pollution by Western thought; this, to a large extent, was the reason for the secrecy of the Masters. Again, the point is that, this is typically Orientalist. 'In order for the Orient to continue to provide the Occident with such a wealth of personas to choose from, it must remain true to itself, in other words, truly Oriental. If it diverged at all from its given Orientalness, it became useless, a travesty of what it was *supposed* to be' (Kabbani, 2008: 32).

While, of course, no religions or cultures remain frozen in history, this being an Orientalist myth, Western occultism transformed what it took from India. Hence, for example, in the final analysis, the hidden Wisdom Theosophy received from its Masters in Tibet, was itself a product of Western Romantic and esoteric occulture, informed by earlier Orientalist interpretations of Indian and Egyptian texts. Indeed, Theosophy is a conspicuous example of the Orientalist appropriation and reinterpretation of Indian religion and culture. The Theosophical Society's understanding of karma and reincarnation is a good example, in that these doctrines are clearly viewed through a particular Western esoteric evolutionary lens. Wouter Hanegraaff puts it well: 'Progressive spiritual evolutionism was far more central than the belief in reincarnation *per se*. [Blavatsky] certainly did not adopt evolutionism in order to explain the reincarnation process for a modern Western audience; what she did was assimilate the theory of *karma* within an already-existing Western framework of spiritual progress...It is not the case that she moved from an Occidental to an Oriental perspective and abandoned Western beliefs in favour of Oriental ones. Her fundamental belief system was an occultist version of Romantic evolutionism from beginning to end' (1996: 471–72; see also Besant, 1912: 20–99).

REFERENCES AND FURTHER READING

al-'Azm, S.J. (1981) 'Orientalism and Orientalism in Reverse', *Khamsin* 8: 5–26.

Arnold, E. (2007 [1879]) *The Light of Asia: The Great Renunciation*. Charleston: BiblioBazaar. Available at: http://www.buddhanet.net/pdf_file/lightasia.pdf (accessed: 1 February 2010).

Besant, A. (1907) *H.P. Blavatsky and the Masters of Wisdom*. London: Theosophical Publishing House.

——(1909) *Revelation, Inspiration, Observation: An Approach to them for Theosophical Students*. Adyar, Theosophical Publishing House.

——(1912 [1910]) *Popular Lectures on Theosophy*, second edition. Adyar: The Theosophist Office.

Bevir, M. (1994) 'The West Turns Eastward: Madame Blavatsky and the Transformation of the Occult Tradition', *Journal of the American Academy of Religion* 62: 747–68.

Bishop, P. (1993) *Dreams of Power: Tibetan Buddhism and the Western Imagination*. London: Athlone Press.

Blavatsky, H.P. (1893) *The Secret Doctrine: The Synthesis of Science, Religion and Philosophy*, 2 vols. Pasadena: Theosophical University Press. Available at: http://www.theosociety.org/pasadena/sd/sd-hp.htm (accessed: 12 December 2009).

——(1968 [1889]) *The Key to Theosophy*. London: Theosophical Publishing House.

——(1972 [1877]) *Isis Unveiled: A Master Key to the Mysteries of Ancient and Modern Science and Theology*, 2 vols. New York: Bouton.

——(2010) *Collected Writings*, 12 vols. Wheaton: Quest Books. Available at: http://blavatskyarchives.com/collectedwritings.htm (accessed: 12 December 2009).

Carpenter, E. (1892) *From Adam's Peak to Elephanta* (London: Swan Sonnenschein). Available at: http://www.archive.org/details/fromadamspeaktoeoocarprich (accessed: 1 February 2010).

Christy, A.E. (1932) *The Orient in American Transcendentalism*. New York: Columbia University Press.

Copenhaver, B.P. (1992) *Hermetica: The Greek* Corpus Hermeticum *and the Latin* Asclepius *in a New English Translation, with Notes and Introduction*. Cambridge: Cambridge University Press.

Creme, B. (1980) *The Reappearance of the Christ and the Masters of Wisdom*. London: Tara Press.

de Zirkoff, B. (1975) 'A Messenger and A Message', in L.H. Leslie-Smith (ed.), *The Universal Flame: Commemorating the Centenary of the Theosophical Society*. Adyar: Theosophical Publishing House, 130–38.

Emerson, R.W. (2000) 'Brahma', in R.W. Emerson, *The Essential Writings of Ralph Waldo Emerson*. New York: Random House, 732.

Forster, E.M. (1924) *A Passage to India*. London: Edward Arnold.

Godwin, J. (1994) *The Theosophical Enlightenment*. Albany: State University of New York Press.

Godwin, J., C. Chanel, and J.P. Devaney (1995) *The Hermetic Brotherhood of Luxor: Initiatic and Historical Documents of an Order of Practical Occultism*. York Beach: Samuel Weiser.

Goodrick-Clarke, N. (2007) 'The Theosophical Society, Orientalism, and the "Mystic East": Western Esotericism and Eastern Religion in Theosophy', *Theosophical History* 13(3), 3–28.

——(2008) *The Western Esoteric Traditions: A Historical Introduction*. Oxford: Oxford University Press.

Guénon, R. (1941) *East and West*. Trans. by S. Perrenis. London: Luzac.

Halbfass, W. (1988) *India and Europe: An Essay in Understanding*. Albany: State University of New York Press.

Hanegraaff, W. (1996) *New Age Religion and Western Culture: Esotericism in the Mirror of Secular Thought*. Leiden: Brill.

Hilton, J. (1947 [1933]) *The Lost Horizon*. London: Pan Books/Macmillan.

Hornung, E. (2001) *The Secret Lore of Egypt: Its Impact on the West*. Trans. by D. Lorton. Ithaca: Cornell University Press.

Horowitz, M. (2009) *Occult America: The Secret History of How Mysticism Shaped Our Nation*. New York: Bantam Books.

Kabbani, R. (2008 [1986]) *Imperial Fictions: Europe's Myths of the Orient*. London: Saqi.

King, R. (1999) *Orientalism and Religion: Postcolonial Theory, India and 'the Mystic East'*. London: Routledge.

——(2005) 'Orientalism and the Study of Religions', in J.R. Hinnells (ed.), *The Routledge Companion to the Study of Religion*. London: Routledge, 275–90.

Klostermaier, K.K. (1994) *A Survey of Hinduism*. Albany: State University of New York.

Kuhn, A.B. (1930) *Theosophy: A Modern Revival of Ancient Wisdom*. New York: Henry Holt & Co.

LePage, V. (1996) *Shambhala: The Fascinating Truth Behind the Myth of Shangri-La*. Wheaton: Quest Books/Theosophical Publishing House.

Mackenzie, J.M. (1995) *Orientalism: History, Theory and the Arts*. Manchester: Manchester University Press.

MacNicol, N. (1936) *Is Christianity Unique? A Comparative Study of the Religions*. London: SCM.

Maroney, T. (2000) *The Book of Dzyan: The Known Text, The Secret Doctrine, Additional Sources, A Life of Mme Blavatsky*. Hayward, CA: Chaosium.

Oldmeadow, H. (2004) *Journeys East: 20th Century Western Encounters with Eastern Religious Traditions*. Bloomington: World Wisdom Inc.

Partridge, C.H. (2004) *The Re-Enchantment of the West: Alternative Spiritualities, Sacralization, Popular Culture and Occulture*, Vol. 1. London: T&T Clark.

——(2005) *The Re-Enchantment of the West: Alternative Spiritualities, Sacralization, Popular Culture and Occulture*, Vol. 2. London: T&T Clark.

——(2009) 'Religion and Popular Culture', in L. Woodhead, H. Kawanami, and C. Partridge (eds), *Religions in the Modern World*, second edition. London: Routledge, 489–522.

——(2013) 'Lost Horizon: H.P. Blavatsky's Theosophical Orientalism', in Mikael Rothstein and Olav Hammer (eds), *Handbook of the Theosophical Current*. Leiden: Brill, 309–33.

Pasi, M. (2012) 'Varieties of Magical Experience: Aleister Crowley's Views on Occult Practice', in H. Bogdan and M.P. Starr (eds), *Aleister Crowley and Western Esotericism*. New York: Oxford University Press, 53–88.

Pert, A. (2006) *Red Cactus: The Life of Anna Kingsford*. Watsons Bay: Books and Writers.

Price, L. (2003) 'Madame Blavatsky, Buddhism and Tibet': http://blavatskyarchives.com/price.pdf (accessed: 24 January 2010).

Radhakrishnan, S. (1940) *Eastern Religions and Western Thought*. Oxford: Oxford University Press.

Rawlinson, A. (1997) *The Book of Enlightened Masters: Western teachers in Eastern Traditions*. Chicago: Open Court.

Redfern, T.H. (1950) *The Work and Worth of Mme Blavatsky*. London: Theosophical Publishing House.

Rocher, L., ed. (1984) *Ezourvedam: A French Veda of the Eighteenth Century*. Amsterdam: John Benjamins B.V.

Rohmer, S. (1997 [1913]) *The Insidious Dr. Fu-Manchu*. Mineola, NY: Dover.

Said, E. (2003 [1978]) *Orientalism: Western Conceptions of the Orient*. Harmondsworth: Penguin.

Sinnet, A.P. (1881) *Occult World*. London: Trubner & Co.

Sugirtharajah, S. (2003) *Imagining Hinduism: A Postcolonial Perspective*. London: Routledge.

Urban, H.B. (2006) *Magia Sexualis: Sex, Magic, and Liberation in Modern Western Esotericism*. Berkeley: University of California Press.

Whitman, W. (1975) 'Passage to India', in W. Whitman, *Walt Whitman: The Complete Poems*. Harmondsworth: Penguin, 428–36.

Zaehner, R.C. (1966 [1962]) *Hinduism*, second edition. Oxford: Oxford University Press.

CHAPTER SIXTY-TWO

OCCULT WAR

George J. Sieg

As a thought-form emerging from the intersections of occultism and conspiracism in the twentieth century, 'occult war' has its genesis in the reception of dualism within the milieu of western esotericism. The first use of the term occurred in *La Guerre Occulte* (1936), translated from the work of Emanuel Malynsky (d.1936) into French by Vicomte Leon de Poncins (1897–1976). De Poncins was a French Catholic anti-Jewish, anti-Semitic conspiracist influenced by the work of the Abbé Barruel. Over the course of his life, de Poncins wrote twenty-six conspiracist works, beginning in 1921 with his own 'Introduction' to the *Protocols of the Learned Elders of Zion*. Emanuel Malynsky was a Russo-Polish Catholic émigré to France and advocate of integral monarchism, liberal neo-feudalism, and Pan-Europeanism. Despite the title, *La Guerre Occulte* does not introduce significant occult themes directly. Rather, it is a political and historical conspiracist text focusing on the transformation of Europe in the time of Bismarck, who is regarded as a mistaken reactionary subverted by malefic forces (De Poncins and Malynsky 1936: 71–82). He accuses a 'narrow-minded naturalist circle' of promoting a 'Platonic Germany' which was 'beyond the world, far from the currents which render its parts interdependent with much of universal history' (De Poncins and Malynsky 1936: 82). This is probably the most esoteric statement in the text, which seems to present the alleged ambitions of a given conspiracy in a philosophical context. Other than this, the text focuses on the historical development of Bolshevism in Germany, blaming the German government for promoting world subversion by sending Lenin back to Russia. In summary, Malynsky presents a world conspiracy directed by International Jewry, which temporarily promoted German interests in order to destroy the anti-Jewish Russian monarchy, and which then turned against Germany itself. Unlike many conservative conspiracists of his era, Malynsky did not predict a Boshevist victory, or foresee the downfall of western capitalism. Rather, he predicted the ultimate demise of socialism in Russia, along with its aspirations to world power. Instead, his account of the world-conspiracy culminated with the final victory of 'Judaeo-capitalism' by means of a democratic American world hegemony (De Poncins and Malynsky 1936: 207–17).

Malynsky's work passed into the milieu of esotericism when it was translated into Italian by Julius Evola (1898–1974) in 1939, with an extra chapter written by De Poncins especially for that edition. In 1961, Evola republished it with his own introduction and conclusion which summarized those aspects of de Poncins's extra chapter which remained relevant to the post-war world, and otherwise expanded it with Evola's own comments. These placed the conspiracist themes of the work in the context of 'Tradition,' an esoteric identification proximally originating with the work of René Guénon (1886–1951), who described 'anti-' and 'counter-traditional' forces as 'subversive' (Guénon 1945). Evola adopted the concept of 'subversion' from Guénon and applied it to the historical narrative of *La Guerre Occulte*. This indicates Evola as the direct progenitor of the 'occult war' concept within the domain of esotericism. While its dualist heritage demonstrates a lineage of antecedent ideas, and its autonomy from both esotericism and conspiracism as an independent thought-form can be established subsequent to Evola, his inclusion of occult war in the milieu of Tradition marks both its clearest definition and its most systematic manifestation.

THE STRATEGIES OF SUBVERSION

Guénon presents the cosmic cycle as culminating in a phase of materialism which gives way to destruction and dissolution, furthered by infra-human forces which seep into the world through 'fissures' analogically at the 'bottom' of a hardened shell in which humanity is sealed, cutting it off from superior spiritual forces from 'above.' These malign influences use the neo-spiritualist and psychic movements as their unwitting agents, since these movements are, according to Guénon, crypto-materialist and bereft of Traditional metaphysics which would protect them from this sort of subversion. He makes the analogy that black magicians can manipulate the psychic residue and detritus of vanquished civilizations in a manner analogous to the animation and manipulation of the otherwise witless shades of the deceased by mediums and necromancers. Although part of the cosmic order in the sense of fulfilling the necessary function of furthering dissolution, these 'anti-traditional' powers are necessarily destructive to traditional cultural order, given its spiritual orientation toward the preservation and maintenance of Tradition. In addition to wishing to pervert the psychic influences emanating from traditional centers of power, the forces of subversion also wish to appropriate these physical power centers due to their sacred geographical significance (Guénon 1945).

He contends that such subversive efforts are one of the reasons for the maintenance of secrecy by traditional esoteric and initiatory institutions. He affirms: 'since all effective action necessarily presupposes agents, anti-traditional action is like all other kinds of action, so that it cannot be a sort of spontaneous or "fortuitous" production, and, since it is exercised particularly in the human domain, it must of necessity involve the intervention of human agents.' He describes their action as the 'counter-initiation,' aiming to drag people into the 'sub-human' realms to counter-act the super-human influences which incarnate as the spirits of authentic traditions. He summarizes post-medieval counter-initiatory activity by describing the confining effects of Renaissance humanism which denied super-human, super-natural influences, contributing to the rise of rationalism and isolating individualism. Guénon ignores Florentine Neo-Platonism and Hermeticism, such as that of Ficino and Pico. It may be that he considered it too deviant from 'Tradition' to be worthy of consideration, given its assimilation into Renaissance humanism, or he may have considered its spiritual influence insufficient to prevail over the ultimately individualist and mechanist consequences of the whole movement.

According to Guénon (1945), these consequences ultimately made materialism possible because exclusive reliance on the senses and material science became standard, resulting not only in materialism but also in profane science, and finally producing 'mechanism.' He concludes his summary of subversion by reiterating that once mechanism reaches its most profane, solid extent, the subversive forces aim to go further toward absolute quantification by promoting outright dissolution. This allows the penetration of the corporeal world by subtle, infra-human forces which, when unleashed, will usher in the final destruction. This process of deviation from normal, traditional order culminates in outright 'subversion,' wherein no further deviation from tradition is possible and any remaining developments constitute the positive affirmation of a deliberately anti-traditional order, which Guénon describes as a 'satanic' counterfeit of spiritual reality. His detailed discussion of counter-initiatory symbolic subversion presents a description of techniques of deliberately confusing or switching beneficent or maleficent valences of a symbol, especially in the introduction of spurious dualistic concepts into symbolic interpretations. As one example of subversion considered at length, he castigates psycho-analysis as an inversion of traditional initiation and its symbolism, a descent into hell from which no re-ascent is possible, passed from analyst to subject in a perversion of esoteric spiritual transmission. Generally considering the proponents of counter-initiation to be unwitting pawns, he seems to reserve the designation of 'conscious satanism' for those who knowingly promote pantheism with the aim of encouraging beings to dissolve themselves in an undifferentiated cosmic consciousness.

Evola's most concise reference to the 'counter-initiation' was in a brief article 'Remarks on the Counter-Initiation' under the pseudonym Arvo, appearing in the publications of the UR-Group in the 1930s. The article credits Guénon for the term, and ascribes all subversive movements to negative occult influence. Evola supports Guénon by contending that the present tactic of counter-initiation is to mislead people out of materialism into sub-human and sub-personal realities, especially through the use of 'phenomena.' He specifically identifies the Theosophical doctrine of abolishing individual separateness in pantheistic, monistic unity as a counter-initiatory deception, along with humanitarianism and egalitarianism. After quoting from *The Reign of Quantity and the Signs of the Times*, he adds to Guénon's descriptions his own assertion that the counter-initiation involves blind forces from the infernal and demonic regions, as well as the intelligent, personal beings which Guénon would associate with degenerate, perverted chains of Satanic initiation.

In his introduction to *La Guerre Occulte*, Evola classifies the forces of subversion into two main groups: the international financial power of the Judaeo-Masonic democracies, and the revolutionary influence of Marxism, which would eventually produce Bolshevism. Various strategies of subversion are described, including the deliberate creation of massive inflation and a combination of cultural nihilism and pacifism, all designed to weaken 'any concept of authority, of tradition, of race, or of fatherland, and any form of idealism or heroism, while tending to highlight, at the same time, the lower and more material aspects of human nature.' Evola ascribes the initial success of Fascism and National Socialism to a moment of overconfident self-revelation on the part of the twin forces of Jew-influenced international subversion, hegemonic capitalism and communism. Summarizing the Second World War as a continuation of the First, he laments the defeat of the Axis, alleging that even genocide (while disputing the proportions claimed by the victors) would not have been too high a price to defeat the worse totalitarianism of the Soviet Union and prevent the communist takeover of China. He concludes that the current historical cycle will end with a 'sinister destiny' of 'cultural Bolshevism.'

More extensive comments on the occult war appear in *Gli uomini e le rovino*, Evola's 1953 exposition of his 'reactionary' post-war political conclusions. In a chapter specifically devoted to the concept, Evola defines *occult war*:

> The occult war is a battle that is waged imperceptibly by the forces of global subversion, with means and in circumstances ignored by current historiography. The notion of occult war belongs to a three-dimensional view of history: this view does not regard as essential the two superficial dimensions of time and space (which include causes, facts, and visible leaders) but rather emphasizes the dimension of *depth,* or the 'subterranean' dimension in which forces and influences often act in a decisive manner, and which, more often not than not, cannot be reduced to what is merely human, whether at an individual or a collective level.
>
> (Evola 1953: 235)

He explains that this third dimension of depth involves conscious, deliberate influence from various hidden intelligences, the true agents of history, often manifest through 'men of action and ideologies' who are in reality the objects rather than the subjects of historical forces.

Evola proposes that exclusively positivist explanations of history are probably promoted by antitraditional forces the better to conceal themselves. He asserts that when people begin to see through such obscurations, a *tactic of replacement* is used, in which some imagined, theoretical, or philosophically conceived agency or force is proposed as a cover, like the 'absolute Spirit' or the *elan vital*, or even the force of 'History' itself. A particular instance of this is the *tactic of counterfeits*, which is especially used to subvert possible traditional reawakening by presenting subtly distorted symbols which would originally have been traditionally appropriate. Often these distorted symbols can themselves then be attacked, criticized, and negated all the more convincingly. He uses as his example the concept of 'traditionalism' itself, which he suggests is deliberately misdefined and promoted as an adherence to outworn customs, allowing *Tradition* to be similarly derided as anachronism. Another tactic he describes is the *tactic of inversion*, in which the opposite of a given value is presented in its place. He makes neo-spiritualism his example, in its substitution of the sub-human for the super-human. He similarly criticizes occultism and Theosophy as promoting a mis-association to be made between themselves and authentic ancient or traditional Eastern doctrines, which slanders these doctrines by association when modern errors are pointed out, and also provokes misdirected defences, as when defenders of 'western' spirituality attack 'eastern' forms. He points out that this *tactic of inversion* promotes the direct influence of chaotic, infra-human forces. These instances relate to the *tactic of ricochet*, when traditional forces are manipulated in such a way as to end up attacking other traditional forces, leading to disunity which can then be exploited. As a historical example, he mentions the consequences of regimes attempting to benefit themselves by promoting revolution against rival regimes and ultimately undermining themselves thereby. He considers 'unconditioned loyalty to an idea' to be the only defence against such occult war tactics, another of which is the *tactic of dilution*, a particular aspect of the *tactic of surrogates*, in which traditional forces are weakened by being led into the promotion of a return to previously vanquished forms that were already flawed, such as the profane 'nationalism' opposed by revolutionaries but still in itself insufficiently Traditional. A more direct tactic is the *tactic of misidentification*, in which unworthy representatives of a principle, such as monarchy, are attacked as the principle itself. The final tactic he describes is *infiltration*, in which members of a traditional organization no longer recall its spiritual foundation and allow it to be taken over by the counter-initiation from within.

DUALIST HERITAGE

Dualism, an ideological preference for one of a pair of disconnected extremes, has been an influential mode of thought within western culture and civilization as a whole since its inception, and it has been accompanied by a wide variety of attendant antagonist projections. Forms of dualism can be categorized as either cosmological or ethical/moral. Cosmological dualism can include the 'absolute' opposition of two co-eternal principles or the 'monarchian' rule of one principle opposed by another derived from it. Cosmological dualism also includes preferences for or against the cosmic order (pro- or anti-cosmic), the material world (-hylic) or the body (-somatic). Another possible feature of cosmological dualism is a historical dialectic in which two principles are opposed but whose conflict moves in a particular direction. Perhaps the most extreme form of cosmological dualism is the *eschatological*, in which a final end is conceived as inevitable – and often as desirable.

Dualism was present in both Judaism and Christianity by the time of the fall of the Roman Empire. While the Roman world did not tend toward dualism, conspiracism flourished increasingly in its final centuries (Cohn 1975). Judaeophobia was increasingly common in both Classical and post-Classical periods (Schäfer 1997), and traditional Roman concerns about anti-social conspiracies converged with Roman mistrust of Jews, subversive Eastern cults, and magicians, to vilify the early Christian movement (Cohn 1975). Once Catholicism triumphed in Rome, its anti-Jewish tendencies became increasingly explicit (MacDonald 1998), and by the medieval period, full-blown demonic anti-Judaism was endemic throughout Western Christendom (Trachtenberg 1943). Catholic polemics against heresies and heterodox beliefs often included rhetoric against Manichaean absolute dualism and Gnostic monarchian dualism, as well as Gnostic anti-cosmism and anti-hylicism, despite the Catholic Church's own anti-somatic tendencies (Runciman 1947). Catholic moral dualism was not self-reflectively recognized as such, and 'dualism' came to be identified primarily with Gnostic cosmologies in the heresiology of the West. Conflicts with Gnosticism and Manichaean survivals persisted into the medieval period, most notably in the Albigensian crusade (Stoyanov 2000). While the Iranian Zoroastrian influence on the Manichaean dualists is perhaps the most obvious dualist transmission in the West, contributing to the association of dualism with gnosis and esotericism, the Iranian Zoroastrian influence on the formation of Judaism after Cyrus conquered Babylon is no less profound (Cohn 1993). It is clear that all the major players in the battle for ideological supremacy in Western civilization were dualist at least to some degree.

The most direct dualist influence on occult warfare beliefs is anti-Jewish and ultimately anti-occult *conspiracism*, drawing from the heritage of medieval Catholic anti-Judaism, but secularized through the course of the Enlightenment. Post-Enlightenment conspiracism has varied in its focus between 'Illuminati'-oriented conspiracy theories (referencing the brief but purportedly influential Bavarian Illuminati who infiltrated Freemasonry in the eighteenth century with the intention of promoting secularism), Jew-oriented conspiracy theories, and fully 'occult' conspiracy theories such as those exemplified in the work of Nesta Webster (1921–24) and Edith Star Miller, Lady Queensborough (1933). These influences united in the work of Leon des Poncins, but Julius Evola reoriented them within esoteric discourse in the context of Tradition. This distinguishes occult war itself from the milieu of dualism since Evola himself, and the Traditionalists in general, eschewed all dualism save the ethical.

OCCULT ALLIES

The anti-Jewish, anti-occult conspiracism suggested by Evola is opposed in the modern occult revival in the Allied world, although it also has its counterparts, such as 'Inquire Within,' Christina M. Stoddard, a member of the Hermetic Order of the Golden Dawn who ultimately rejected its purported Secret Chiefs as nefarious Jewish manipulators and wrote conspiracist exposés of the modern occult revival: *Light-bearers of Darkness* (1930) and *The Trail of the Serpent* (1936).

The heritage of Blavatskian Theosophy, the progenitor of the modern occult revival in the English-speaking world, is markedly pro-cosmic and morally dualist, and this trend continues through Neo-Theosophy in the work of Annie Besant and Charles Webster Leadbeater, Anthroposophy in the work of Rudolf Steiner, and also in the Neo-Hermetic philosophy of Anna Kingsford. These influences are all relevant to the Neo-Hermetic magical revival embodied in the Hermetic Order of the Golden Dawn (though less so in the Hermetic Brotherhood of Luxor), and the Golden Dawn's dualism interacted with Aleister Crowley's Plymouth Brethren heritage and interest in apocalyptic eschatology (Beskin 2007) to ensure that his Thelemic religion, a primary focus of the modern occult revival into contemporary western esotericism, is profoundly pro-cosmic and morally dualist. As Crowley himself was involved in intelligence work on behalf of the Crown throughout his life (Spence 2008) and also heavily involved in irregular Freemasonry, ultimately taking leadership of the Ordo Templi Orientis and using it as a vehicle to promote Thelema (in which the imagery of war, violence, and vengeance figure prominently), he represents the Allied world's epitome of what Evola deemed to be 'occult war' endeavors, as well as what the Traditionalists in general would regard as 'counter-initiation.' His contemporary Violet Mary Firth (Dion Fortune, from her magical motto *Deo non fortuna*, 'God not Fortune') was also a major influence on the modern magical revival in the English-speaking world, and she encouraged her disciples in practical magical attack against the Axis powers; by the end of her life, she had converted to Thelema (Sutin 2000). Condemnation of 'black magicians' and potential magical conflict with them has continued to be a feature of occult belief in contemporary traditions which derive from the modern occult revival.

CONTEMPORARY OCCULT WAR

Given its prevalence on both sides of the Second World War, it is unsurprising that occult warfare beliefs persist into contemporary esotericism as well as popular culture, such as in diverse occult conspiracist speculations concerning the involvement of secret societies (most prominently the Illuminati) in the promotion of terrorism and counter-terrorism, exemplified by 9/11 conspiracism in rap music, popular films widely available on the Internet such as *Zeitgeist* (2007), and so forth. In the specifically esoteric and/or occult milieu, Anthroposophy retains extensive conspiracist dualism; various interpretations of Tradition, including those influenced by the work of Evola, continue to attract adherents and have established themselves beyond the strictly 'far-right' and 'ultra-fascist' milieu, although those associations remain persistent within the 'Traditionalist' scene. The work of Neo-Eurasian Neo-Traditionalist Aleksandr Dughin (1992) features conspiracism and eschatology (Dughin 1992) and has acquired some influence in Russian political circles (Sedgwick 2004). 'Radical Traditionalism' in the West orients itself toward cultural conflict and occasionally aligns with the agendas of the New Right (Buckley, Cleary, and Moynihan 2002–8).

While most Satanic and Left-Hand Path groups ignore occult warfare beliefs even when they hold dualist beliefs, the 'sinister' family of traditions derived from the Order of Nine Angles are explicitly concerned with esoteric conflict against Jewish influences. The Order of Nine Angles first publicly appeared by that name in England in the 1970s and, like Evolian Traditionalism, evidenced no dualism (Long 2009) other than an ethical condemnation (Order of Nine Angles 2011) of 'Magian' Jewish influences, named for the Zoroastrian 'Magi' but proximately derived (via *Imperium* by Francis Parker Yockey, an American National Socialist writing in 1948 under the pseudonym Ulick Varange) from the 1918 work of philosopher of history Oswald Spengler, *Das Untergang das Abendlandes*. Some of the ONA's contemporary spin-offs are more dualistic, such as 'Progressive Satanism' which features the pro-cosmic and pro-hylic orientation of National Socialism with less of a focus on anti-Judaism, and Noctulian Vampirism, which presents an apocalyptic eschatology involving the return of the Elder Gods in the 'Final Harvest,' and violent anti-Judaism (Lord Karnac, Czar Azag-Kala and Drill Sgt. #333 2004).

In some cases, occult warfare beliefs manifest without any references to dualism at all, and this development indicates the development of 'occult war' into a thought-form ultimately separable and separate from its dualist heritage. The work of the founder of chaos magic, Peter J. Carroll, is marked since his 1987 *Liber Null and Psychonaut* by an interest in 'aeonics' (the magical manipulation of 'psycho-historical' forces, the same term used by the 'sinister' traditions) practiced particularly against the influences of transcendental religion and materialism. In his online article 'Wizards against Tyranny,' he presents a purely politicized occult war in the form of a conspiracist libertarian condemnation of the European Union as facilitating the occult 'synarchy' proposed in the work of St. Yves d'Alveydre, *Mission de l'Inde* (1882–87). Previously, in the course of Carroll's leadership of the premier chaos magical order, the Magical Pact of the Illuminates of Thanateros, he participated in a socio-magical conflict (which participants dubbed the 'Ice War') against a group of completely non-dualist magicians (the 'Ice' magicians) whom he believed were promoting totalitarian agendas within the Pact.

REFERENCES AND FURTHER READING

Beskin, G. (2007) 'The Moot With No Name,' unpublished lecture, 9 September 2007, Percy Community Centre, New King Street, Bath, Somerset, BA1 2BN

Boardman, T. M. (1998) *Mapping the Millennium: Behind the Plans of the New World Order*, London: Temple Lodge.

Buckley, J., Cleary, C., and Moynihan, M. eds. (2002–8) *Tyr: Myth-Culture-Tradition*, vols. 1–3. Atlanta: Ultra.

Cariou, B. (2004) 'Evola As He Is: Occult War (conclusion),' available at: http://thompkins_cariou.tripod.com/id48.html, accessed 26 September 2014.

Carroll, P.J. (1987) *Liber Null and Psychonaut*, York Beach, Maine: Weiser.

——(1992) *Liber Kaos*, York Beach, Maine: Weiser.

——(2009) 'Wizards Against Tyranny,' available at: http://specularium.org/index.php?option=com_content&task = view&id = 69&Itemid = 106, accessed 26 September 2014.

——(n.d.) 'The Ice War as Remembered by Stokastikos,' available at: http://philhine.org.uk/writings/ess_icewar.html

Cohn, N. (1975) *Europe's Inner Demons: An Enquiry Inspired by the Great Witch-Hunt*, London: Book Club Associates.

——(1993) *Cosmos, Chaos, and the World to Come*, New Haven: Yale University Press..

Coogan, K. (1999) *Dreamer of the Day: Francis Parker Yockey and the Postwar Fascist International*, New York: Autonomedia.

De Poncins, L. and Malynsky, E. (1936) *La Guerre Occulte* [*The Occult War*], trans. by Bruno Cariou (2009), Paris: G. Beauchesne et ses fils.

Dougouine, A. (2006a) *La grande guerre des continents* [*The Great War of Continents*], Paris: avatareditions.

——(2006b) *Le prophète de l'eurasisme* [*The Prophet of Eurasism*], Paris: avatareditions.

Dughin, A. (1992) 'The Great War of Continents,' in *Konspirologya*, Moscow: Arktogeya.

Evola, J. (1953) *Gli uomini e le rovine* [*Men Among the Ruins*], Rome: Edizione Mediterranee.

Fortune, D. (1993) *The Magical Battle of Britain*, Bradford-on-Avon, Wiltshire: Golden Gates.

Frater U.'.D.'. and David Rietti (2006) 'Ice Magic,' *Oracle Occult Magazine* 6, 8–18.

Goodrick-Clarke, N. (2002) *Black Sun: Aryan Cults, Esoteric Nazism, and the Politics of Identity*, London: New York University Press.

Guénon, R. (1945) *Le règne de la quantité et les signes des temps* [*The Reign of Quantity and the Signs of the Times*], Paris: Gallimard.

Julius Evola and the UR Group (2001) *Introduction to Magic*, Rochester: Inner Traditions.

Knight, G. (2000) *Dion Fortune and the Inner Light*, Loughborough, Leicestershire: Thoth Publications.

Long, A. (2009) 'The Wonder and Joy of Acausal Darkness,' available at: https://darknessconverges.wordpress.com/tag/chaos

Lord Karnac, Czar Azag-Kala and Drill Sergeant #333 (2004) *Liber 333: Tempel ov Blood – Discipline of the Gods – Altars of Hell – Apex of Eternity*, Tampere, Finland: Ixaxaar.

Mauri, C. (2006) 'Tre attentati al Duce: una pista esoteric,' in G. de Turris, ed., *Esoterismo e fascismo*, Rome: Edizioni Mediterranee, 245–58.

MacDonald, K. (1998) *Separation and Its Discontents: Toward an Evolutionary Theory of Anti-Semitism*, New York: Praeger.

Miller, E. S. (1933) *Occult Theocrasy*, Abbeville: F. Paillart.

Nesfield-Cookson, B. (1998) *Michael and the Two-Horned Beast: The Challenge of Evil Today*, London: Temple Lodge.

Ravenscroft, T. (1973) *The Spear of Destiny: The Occult Power Behind the Spear Which Pierced the Side of Christ*, New York: G. P. Putnam's Sons.

Reuveni, A. (1996) *In the Name of the 'New World Order': Manifestations of Decadent Powers in World Politics*, London: Temple Lodge.

Runciman, S. (1947) *The Medieval Manichee*, Cambridge: Cambridge University Press.

Saint-Yves d'Alveydre, Marquis J.A. (1882–87) *Mission de l'Inde*, self-published.

Schäfer, P. (1997) *Judaeophobia: Attitudes toward Jews in the Ancient World*, New Haven: Yale University Press.

Sedgwick, M. (2004) *Against the Modern World: Traditionalism and the Secret Intellectual History of the Twentieth Century*, Oxford: Oxford University Press.

Spence, R. (2008) *Secret Agent 666: Aleister Crowley, British Intelligence, and the Occult*, Port Townshend, Washington: Feral House.

Spengler, O. (1918) *Das Untergang das Abendlandes* [*The Decline of the West*], Vienna: Braumüller.

Stoddard, C. M. (1930) *Light-bearers of Darkness*, London: Boswell.

——(1936) *The Trail of the Serpent*, London: Boswell.

Stoyanov, Y. (2000) *The Other God: Dualist Religions from Antiquity to the Cathar Heresy*, London: Yale Nota Bene.

Sutin, L., (2000) *Do What Thou Wilt: A Life of Aleister Crowley*, New York: St. Martin's Press.

Trachtenberg, J. (1943) *The Devil and the Jews: The Medieval Conception of the Jew and Its Relation to Modern Antisemitism*, New York: Meridian.

Tradowsky, P. (1998) *Christ and Antichrist*, London: Temple Lodge.

Varange, Y. (1948) *Imperium: The Philosophy of History and Politics*, self-published.

Webster, N. (1921) *World Revolution: The Plot Against Civilization*, Boston: Small, Maynard, and Co.

——(1924) *Secret Societies and Subversive Movements*, London: Boswell.

Zeitgeist: The Movie (2007) Peter Joseph: www.zeitgeistmovie.com, accessed 26 September 2014.

CHAPTER SIXTY-THREE

THE COUNTERCULTURE AND THE OCCULT

Erik Davis

Perhaps the single most important vector for the popularization of occult spirituality in the twentieth century is the countercultural explosion associated with 'the Sixties'—an era whose political and culture dynamics hardly fit within the boundaries of that particular decade. A more useful term was coined by the Berkeley social critic Theodore Roszak, who used the word 'counterculture' to describe a mass youth culture whose utopianism and hedonic psycho-social experimentation were wedded to a generalized critique of rationalism, technocracy, and established religious and social institutions. As such, the counterculture significantly overlapped, though also sometimes resisted, the parallel rise of the New Left and its ideological and occasionally violent struggle against more-or-less the same 'System.' Within a few short years after its emergence in the middle of the 1960s, the counterculture had transformed social forms, creative production, personal lifestyles, and religious experience across the globe. Though the counterculture was a global phenomenon, its origins and many of its essential dynamics lie in America, which will be the focus of this chapter.

Many of the attitudes and practices associated with the counterculture were drawn from earlier and more marginal bohemian scenes. Arguably, the key catalyst for the emergence of a mass counterculture was the widespread availability and use of LSD and other charismatic psychoactive substances. For many, LSD's extraordinary noetic and emotional affects seemed direct evidence that the individual alteration or expansion of consciousness, coupled with corresponding shifts in the self and its values, could precipitate a new social and cultural order. These experiences were also characterized as early as Aldous Huxley's foundational 1954 mescaline text *The Doors of Perception* as having a pronounced mystical or religious dimension. Once people began 'turning on' *en masse*, an amorphous and visionary spiritual counterculture almost inevitably emerged.

In line with Catherine Albanese's argument that the American metaphysical tradition is essentially recombinant, the new seekers promiscuously and often superficially comingled Vedantic nondualism, tantric yoga, Zen meditation, Theosophy, Native American symbolism, and other religious discourses and practices. This visionary stew included many 'profane' elements as well: pulp fiction, parapsychology, ufology, cybernetic social science, and a Reichean hedonism that emphasized the erotic freedom from repression and restraint. Indeed, a primary source for the counterculture's thirst for spirituality was its only apparently paradoxical embrace of the intensified body. Permissive and experimental sexuality, coupled with the ecstatic and drug-fueled collective rituals of live rock shows, helped forge a Dionysian sensibility that readily looked to and absorbed the imaginal and energetic transports of occult phantasmagoria and the protocols of mysticism.

Over time, this explosion of esoteric novelty opened up the space for the crystallization of more defined religious structures and identities, and helps to explain the rise of new religious movements and 'cults' in the late 1960s and especially the early 1970s. At the same time, the counterculture also hosted a continuously informal cultic—or 'occultic'—milieu that included astrology, witchcraft, the *I Ching*, Tarot, chakras, reincarnation, Theosophical and ethnopharmacological lore. Though many of these ideas, symbols, and practices already circulated in the metaphysical fringes of twentieth-century America, and by no means exclusively among bohemians, the counterculture brought them more or less onto center stage, so that they helped define what we can authentically call a Zeitgeist. By the early 1970s, when the counterculture had transformed the engines of popular culture, the West found itself hosting a pervasive and commercialized 'pop occulture' whose long shadow we still live in today, from the New Age to black metal music to personal growth seminars to rave culture.

Needless to say, 'the counterculture,' 'spirituality,' and 'occultism' are all highly complex and multidimensional concepts that describe domains that also feature a high degree of informality and internal diversity—even contradiction. This makes compressed generalizations about their interaction particularly fraught. One particularly significant issue is the question of Easternization. The dominant language of countercultural mysticism in the 1960s was marked by translated Asian concepts and practices; is it right to think of these as part of 'occultism'? Without question, the turn East has been integral to Western occultism since Theosophy and early Crowley; moreover, Tibetan Buddhism, Taoism, yoga, and even Zen have their own forms of 'magic.' Still, while Christopher Partridge has helped to define a conception of 'occulture' broad enough to embrace Asian ingressions alongside Western esoterica, one must resist collapsing the popular emergence of Western Buddhism and non-ethnic Hinduism in the 1960s into the occult *per se*. For these reasons, it is perhaps better to consider a broader 'spiritual counterculture' within which we can identify Asian traditions as well as overlapping but also more specifically characterized occult currents.

THE BOHEMIAN ANTECEDENTS OF THE OCCULT COUNTERCULTURE

Depending on the angle and depth of approach, one could identify any number of crucial antecedents to the counterculture. One direct ancestor of the back-to-nature hippie is the West Coast 'Nature Boys' health-food scene, a subculture that was directly inspired by ideas and individuals associated with the German *Wandervogel* movement, and therefore with the organicist, neo-Romantic, and 'pagan' sensibility forged in the German-speaking esoteric underground of the nineteenth century. Similarly, the transformative aspirations, Atlantean lore, and Asian-inflected mysticism of the Age of Aquarius is inconceivable outside the context of Theosophy's spiritual evolutionism. But to track the specific antecedents for the occult counterculture, we are better off turning to painters, poets, and other bohemian artists of the postwar period. The informality (or incoherence) of later hippie mysticism is in part tied to the fact that, beyond popular literature, the influences closest to hand were not spiritual masters or organized sects, but rather artists whose cultivation of personal idiosyncrasy and singular expression lent their occult and religious explorations an unsystematic, visionary, and often hedonistic dimension.

One early and emblematic figure was Henry Miller, who was already in his 50s when he moved to Big Sur in 1944. Miller had already written the experimental erotic novels that would earn him both fame and infamy, but his influence on Big Sur was pivotal, as the place transformed into a minor mecca of artists, sexual adventurers, and political anarchists. Miller represents a genuine bridge between the generations and the continents. In 1930s Paris, he was already reading Blavatsky, Rudolph Steiner, and Gurdjieff. In California, he continued to study astrology and Eastern and Western spiritual teachers, wrote a book about the utopian mysticism of the Brethren of the Free Spirit, and transmuted his earlier pornographic obsessions into what Jeffrey Kripal calls a 'panerotic nature mysticism.' He also visited the baths that would later form the omphalos for the Esalen Institute, whose institutional devotion to mind–body practices would, by the 1970s, bring tai chi, tantra, and other esoteric practices of the enlightened body into the mainstream of American psychological culture.

Another singular figure of the postwar proto-counterculture was the polymath, ethnomusicologist, experimental filmmaker, and archivist Harry Smith. Raised by Theosophist parents in the Pacific Northwest, Smith lived in the Bay Area in the 1940s, smoking pot, hanging out in jazz clubs, and making hand-painted abstract animations inspired in part by esoteric color theory. Smith later moved to Manhattan, and in 1952, made his most lasting contribution to the counterculture: the Anthology of American Folk Music, a powerful and uncanny collection of early blues and old time music that became the Rosetta stone for folkies like Bob Dylan and The Fugs; among his obsessive notes Smith included quotations from Robert Fludd and Rudolf Steiner. Smith's films grew more iconographic, and featured animated montages of Tibetan godforms, interlocking Kabbalistic trees, and *Amanita muscaria* mushrooms. Smith was also a serious student of Aleister Crowley, a then-obscure predilection he shared with Kenneth Anger, a far more influential West Coast experimental filmmaker who started making films in 1947. Anger's shorts, often marked with occult and homo-erotic symbolism, later became mainstays of the midnight movie circuit; though no hippie, Anger saw the counterculture as the fulfillment of Crowley's prophesized Aeon of Horus.

The most direct ancestors of the spiritual counterculture remain the Beat Generation. Jack Kerouac, Allen Ginsberg, William S. Burroughs, and Gary Snyder were all seekers, and their earnest explorations of Buddhism, Scientology, magic, tantra, Zen, psychedelics, and Hinduism came to provide models for readers seeking a path out of America's crushing culture of conformity in the 1950s. That said, their spiritual journeys were divergent, and inflected the rising occult current in different ways. Kerouac, who often identified as a Catholic, started reading the Mahayana sutras in 1954; a year later he met the West Coast poet Snyder, whose deep embrace of Zen is immortalized in Kerouac's 1958 *The Dharma Bums*. Kerouac turned to the dharma out of his own painful self-struggle, and was inspired as well by Buddhism's rhetoric of immediacy, which resonated with his own formal practices of spontaneous prose. Wary of Zen, Kerouac found in the classic Mahayana sutras a language of paradox and visionary display that he later emulated in *Mexico City Blues* and *The Scripture of Golden Eternity*, with its 'fantastic magic imagination of the lightning, flash, / plays, dreams...'

Snyder's embrace of Buddhism was at once more formal and more grounded than Keruoac's. He studied for many years at a monastery in Kyoto, and his dharma, like his more hard-edged poetry, side-stepped Kerouac's romantic narcissism for a concrete and uninflected sanctification of the everyday that had little truck with hidden or anomalous powers of mind. In this sense, Snyder helps define the important difference between the spiritual counterculture, which he directly helped foment, and the occult revival, whose esoteric undertow he rejected. Nonetheless, even in its most minimalist forms, Zen did offer Snyder and other bohemian seekers a kind of illuminism, especially as it was articulated in Alan Watts' limpid and enormously influential texts on Zen.

Of all the Beats, Ginsberg performed the most instrumental role in the spiritual counterculture. Partly through his youthful visionary experiences, Ginsberg's work had an expansive, Blakean dimension from the beginning. Like Synder, his voice also insisted on a transformation of rather than an escape from materiality, and his later encounters with Hinduism and Buddhism took place within a solidly Whitman-inspired framework that helped define a more fleshy American dharma. In the early 1960s, after a visit to India with Synder and others, Ginsberg publicly adopted the trappings of a holy man; appearing at readings or protest gatherings in robes, he would often sing *kirtan*, chant 'Hare Krishna,' and play the harmonium. A mystical and hedonic bard of conscience, Ginsberg also joined Synder in refusing to honor the divide that many made between the spiritual counterculture and political activism.

The oldest and least humanist of the Beats, William S. Burroughs anticipated the darker and more paranoid dimensions of the occult counterculture. Burroughs distrusted language as a vehicle of self-expression and spontaneity, considering it more as an occult battleground where the forces of control waged war against subversive and even nihilistic attempts to break the spell of conventional signs. Sensitive to the rivalry and paranoia that court magical thinking, Burroughs was, in the early 1950s, already writing to Ginsberg about the use of curses and 'black magic'; he also traveled to South American in a prescient plunge into the serpentine depths of *yage* (*ayahuasca*). In Paris in the late 1950s, when he also studied Scientology, Burroughs developed the cut-up method of artistic composition invented by Brion Gysin, linking the sort of oracular juxtapositions already found in Dada and Surrealism to a postwar model of information processing and media manipulation. Gysin and Ian Sommerville, a crony of Burroughs', also constructed the dream machine in the early 1960s, an inexpensive device whose consciousness-altering flicker effect anticipated the countercultural quest to use drugs and media to, as Burroughs put it in 1964's *Nova Express*, 'storm the reality studio.'

LSD AS CHEMICAL MYSTERY RELIGION

Along with other psychoactive substances, LSD helped catalyze the transformation of marginal bohemian esotericism into the pop occulture of the late 1960s and 1970s. From the beginnings of its dissemination into youth culture, acid came already 'packaged' with associations linking it to mystical states of consciousness, thanks in part to *The Psychedelic Experience*, a popular 1964 trip guide by Timothy Leary, Richard Alpert, and Ralph Metzger that based its cartography of altered states on Evans-Wentz's Theosophical remix of the *Tibetan Book of the Dead.* More importantly, the acid experience itself gave immediate evidence of the transrational capacities of consciousness, states that might range from a sense of unitive vibratory fusion with the cosmos to a mythopoetic explosion of religious and supernatural symbolism to a perceptual merry-go-round of trickster synchronicities and paranormal possibilities. Acid undermined the instrumental schemes of individual agency, and it returned many users to baseline with a growing taste for loosely associational thinking, ecstatic states, and spontaneous collective happenings. Unsurprisingly, the use of LSD and other drugs encouraged a kaleidoscopic engagement with spiritual practices, metaphysical systems, and occult arcana, all of which came to supplement, refract, and to some degree substitute for acid's unsustainable noetic raptures.

The paradoxes of a chemical sacrament—whose sacred states were instrumentally catalyzed by a commodity molecule—are very much reflected in the career of Timothy Leary, who was as responsible as anyone for turning on the youth generation. (Ginsberg, to whom Leary first provided psilocybin, also played a vital role.) When Leary took psilocybin mushrooms in 1960, and LSD shortly thereafter, he was a successful professor of psychology who, although rejecting the reigning behaviorism of the day, was no humanist. Though firmly rooted in impersonal social science, his experiments with students and faculty led him toward more esoteric discourses and frameworks. His friend Huston Smith, a professor of religion at MIT, introduced him to the perennialist notion of a core 'mystical experience' lurking beneath the apparent variety of religious phenomenology, a controversial concept that fundamentally shaped subsequent psychedelic thinking. After a breakthrough experience at a local Vedanta temple, Leary's 60s persona was set: after leaving Harvard and becoming a countercultural leader, Leary adopted a snappy guru persona and wove Hindu mystical ideas and other hip esoterica into his rhetoric. But as his ongoing discourse of DNA and social 'games' suggests, he never really abandoned the frameworks of social science or philosophical materialism, and was spiritually most aligned with the sometimes manipulative 'trickster' approach of Gurdjieff, who Leary started reading in 1965.

Leary's elitist East Coast approach to psychedelia is conventionally contrasted with the more informal and carnivalesque West Coast style of Ken Kesey and the Merry Pranksters, one of whom memorably referred to Leary's fascination with the Tibetan bardos as a 'crypt trip.' In contrast, the 'spirituality' of the Pranksters can be seen as an anarchic, demotic, and sometimes goofy suspension of the difference between sacred and profane—more of a dodge of conventional rationality than a disciplined transcendence. One key focus for their non-stop happening was synchronicity, the uncanny phenomenon of strikingly meaningful coincidence first described as such by Jung. For the Pranksters and many other heads, synchronicity came to be seen as a kind of profane or psychedelic grace—in the fortuitously meaningful conjunction of ordinary events, synchronicity implies a paranormal order of correspondence while retaining a quotidian materiality. The multi-media Acid Tests that the Pranksters staged before California banned LSD in 1966 creatively deployed sound and light technologies along with jams from the young Grateful Dead, and thereby laid down a template for the mass psychedelic culture just around the corner. But the Acid Tests can also be understood as social synchronicity machines—an immersive, cybernetic, and McLuhanesque celebration of Burroughs' cut-up war on control.

Synchronicity does not demand explicitly occult interpretations, but it certainly lends itself to them. One traditional esoteric tool that was popular among the Pranksters, and that also saturates bohemian and psychedelic culture in general, is the *I Ching*. First published in the famed Wilhelm/Baynes edition in 1950, the *I Ching*, or the Classic of Change, is an ancient Chinese oracular system which uses the random throw of yarrow stalks (or, more simply, three coins) to generate figures that correspond to one of sixty-four hexagrams, each of which comes festooned with a variety of often enigmatic commentaries. Though presenting a cooler and more philosophical profile than the Tarot, the *I Ching* was still used by many as an occult tool, one that simultaneously rejected conventional notions of 'chance' while embracing an organic system of signs that promised to refigure agency along holistic cosmic powers rather than instrumentalist lines. Another significant divinatory system was astrology, which became a generally available typological framework and lingua franca for the counterculture as well as a tool to harmonize that emerging collective with the cosmic environment. Key astrologers for the counterculture included the Haight resident Gavin Arthur—who contributed to the Haight Street *Oracle*—and Dane Rudhyar, who decisively shaped modern astrology by introducing more humanistic and Jungian interpretative conventions. Though the popularity of astrology was by no means restricted to the youth generation—sun sign columns had been popular in American newspapers since the 1940s—the 'Age of Aquarius' became the most popular tag for that generation's widespread and gripping sense of an immanent and epochal shift.

One important popular vehicle for esoteric and occult symbolism was psychedelic art, particularly as it effloresced through the medium of concert posters, LP designs, and, to a lesser extent, underground comix. Indeed, if Leary's bardo manual and Kesey's Acid Tests can be understood as the development of psychedelic *form*, the semi-commercialized hippie culture they helped engender can be understood more in terms of developing psychedelic *content*. Album covers exploited explicitly occultist and mythopoetic imagery, with the Incredible String Band's *The 5000 Spirits or the Layers of the Onion* and the Jimi Hendrix Experience's *Axis: Bold as Love* being standout examples from 1967. On the other hand, underground comics were saturated with satiric and pornographic obsessions that made most publications considerably less mystical than, say, the Steve Ditko-illustrated exploits of Marvel Comics' *Dr. Strange*, which debuted in 1963 and was loved by many heads. One important exception was Rick Griffin, a comics creator as well as one of the key rock poster designers of the psychedelic era. Though he cut his teeth on surf art in the early 1960s, Griffin's mature style—often associated with the Grateful Dead—presented a heavy and idiosyncratic symbolism that drew from orange crate art, Manly Hall's

Secret Teachings of the Ages, blobular modernism, and his own intense imagination. Griffin remixed Kabbalistic and esoteric Christian imagery for Robert Crumb's *Zap* magazine, while the flying eyeball poster he designed for a Jimi Hendrix Fillmore gig remains perhaps the single most iconic image of the era, an unnerving mix of pop surrealism, eldritch nightmare, and divine invasion. Just as many psychedelic posters played with the tension between two-dimensional patterns and three-dimensional organic forms, so did Griffin's popular work superimpose the depths of esoteric imagery onto the pure surface of commercial design.

THE MAGICAL REVIVAL

Roszak ends his *The Making of a Counter-Culture* with the invocation of the shaman and the creative magic of the embodied visionary imagination. In religious terms, this spirit is manifested less in hippie interpretations of Zen or Vedantist mysticism than in the rise of explicitly magical religions: witchcraft, Satanism, and Paganism, the latter a self-description that itself emerged from the counterculture. Antecedents for these developments include British Wicca and Victor Anderson's American Feri tradition, but any broad view of magical currents in the 1960s must also consider the pulpier domains of popular culture, which circulated images and atmospheres that would later materialize as spiritual practice. Particularly important was the market in fantasy fiction established by the tremendous popularity of J.R.R. Tolkien's *The Lord of the Rings*, which became a campus hit after appearing in an unauthorized paperback edition in 1965. Imprints like Lancer and Ballantine were also repackaging (in often lurid covers) American weird fiction from the previous generation, making Lovecraft's alien necromancy and Robert E. Howard's sword-and-sorcery tales available. Though comics had long trafficked in supernatural powers, they developed a hipper resonance in the early 1960s; Marvel's *Dr. Strange*, whose Western wizard hero nonetheless draws his wisdom from Tibet, has already been mentioned. Supernatural horror films witnessed a sexy Hollywood revamp; examples include Roger Corman's feverish series of Poe adaptations starring Vincent Price.

Indeed, it is an interesting exercise to consider the exact difference between the Satanic rituals staged in, say, Corman's *Masque of the Red Death* and the Satanic 'psychodramas' staged by the most famous American occultist of the 1960s, Anton LaVey. Though too often dismissed as a simple huckster, LaVey mixed his libertarian philosophy of satisfied individualism with a strong sense of subversive showmanship and more than a touch of sleaze. He founded the Church of Satan in 1966, setting up sensationalist events at the 'black house' in San Francisco, and becoming, along with the popular British witch and astrologer Sybil Leek, one of the main sources for journalists writing about the rise of magic. Though LaVey himself was critical of the hippie drug scene, one of his dynamic co-conspirators was Kenneth Anger, whose tangled engagement with the Age of Aquarius is reflected in his dark and jagged 1969 short film *Invocation of My Demon Brother*, much of which was shot in the Haight. In one of the creepy synchronicities of the age, the film featured Bobby Beausoleil, a crony of Charles Manson who was later convicted for the Manson-inspired murder of Gary Hinman. Far more than the trendy devil-dabbling that led the Rolling Stones to call their 1967 record *Their Satanic Majesties Request*, Charles Manson crystallized, in the social imagination and to some extent in reality, the spiritual diabolism potentiated by the counterculture's wayward plunge into sex, drugs, and nondual metaphysics.

The infernal side of occult religion—real, imagined, or performed—was paralleled in the 1960s by more balanced and affirmative nature-based religions, which in part sacralized the countercultural ethos of the enchanted flesh. British Wicca made inroads across the country, but an arguably more important part of the magical revival was the counterculture's willingness to ground spiritual authority in imaginative invention rather than narratives of unbroken historical transmission. Emerging in 1961 from a prophetic stew of science fiction, libertarianism, and Maslow's psychology of human potential, the Church of All Worlds was already on its way to becoming a nature-focused magical group when it became the first earth religion to receive a formal charter in 1968. In California, the New Reformed Orthodox Order of the Golden Dawn formed when college students started mixing Gerald Gardner's *Witchcraft Today* with the radical ideas of Norman O. Brown and the creative possibilities of group performance and ritual play. Even the secular re-enactment scenes like the Society for Creative Anachronism and the Renaissance Pleasure Faire provided cultural context for the fabrication of explicitly Pagan identities. The lesson from the counterculture was that, magically speaking, the collective performance of the creative imagination was at least as important as initiation and the replication of 'tradition.'

Perhaps the most audacious public expression of this lesson, one that reached far beyond witchcraft or even the spiritual counterculture, was the 'exorcism of the Pentagon' that took place in October 1967. Following a massive rally held at the Lincoln Memorial to protest the Vietnam war, about 50,000 people marched on the Pentagon. Along with thousands of civil rights activists, peaceniks, and leftists, the crowd included many colorful and festive representatives of the counterculture. One protest group that explicitly sought to blend activism with such feral pageantry were the Yippies, whose co-founder Abbie Hoffman, in an act of knowing theater, attempted to use the gathered psychic energy to physically levitate the Pentagon, turn it orange, and end the war. Allan Ginsberg supported the effort with Buddhist chants, while Hare Krishnas danced and the crowd 'ommed.' At another point the New York underground folk group The Fugs led a (partly?) tongue-in-cheek exorcism of the Pentagon's demons, while Kenneth Anger performed Crowleyian magical spells on his own without the slightest bit of irony. The complex mixture of absurdism and sincerity that various actors brought to this galvanizing magical protest reflects the degree to which the occult had become a generalized cultural language of collective possibility and not merely a 'spiritual' orientation.

Progressive politics would also come to characterize the evolution of explicitly magical and pagan currents in the 1970s. The most notable of these was the development of feminist witchcraft, perhaps the most extreme example of the widespread feminization of religion and spirituality in the decade. In 1971, Z. Budapest established the women-only Susan B. Anthony Coven no. 1 along essentialist feminist lines. Budapest, who was arrested in 1975 for breaking a California law against 'fortune telling' that she later led the effort to overturn, fused the rhetoric of radical feminism with an exclusive focus on female deities rather than the sexual polarity of traditional Wicca; for her coven and many others, 'consciousness raising' had become the conscious raising of goddess energy. Budapest's most influential and important student was Starhawk, who widely popularized witchcraft with her 1979 book *The Spiral Dance*, and whose highly visible and politically active form of pagan practice channeled the older energies of the counterculture into the embattled political and environmental landscape of the 1980s and beyond.

POP OCCULTURE IN THE EARLY 1970S

Some peg the end of the counterculture to 1970, when Charles Manson went on trial for the Tate-LaBianca murders and national guards killed four protesting students at Kent State. A longer, more inertial view stretches the epoch into the mid-1970s, with the early 1970s characterized as a hazy twilight of the hippie idols. (Beyond this point, we may speak of countercultures—squatter punks, travelers, radical environmentalists, ravers—but the rhetoric of generational unity is over.) The 1960s had been marked by a pervasive sense of imminent collective transformation, but then the Age of Aquarius went into eclipse, just as Johnson's Great Society gave way to recession, Watergate, and the politics of paranoia. So even as 'liberated' or permissive mores began to transform mainstream social life, the ravages of drug abuse and the existential confusion introduced by the psycho-social dislocation endemic to the counterculture became impossible to ignore. Environmental consciousness grew in intensity—the first Earth Day was in 1970—but it was accompanied by the defeatist sense that the only way to keep the dream alive was to retreat into rural life or an idealized nonhuman nature.

These conditions all help explain the spiritual innovation that characterized the early 1970s, which from the perspective of the history of religions was an extraordinarily fertile if sometimes desperate era of discovery and reinvention. The most notable development was the unprecedented growth of new and transplanted religious movements, like the Unification Church, Siddha Yoga, and a wide variety of Jesus People sects. Accompanying these groups, and the parallel growth of earlier NRMs like the Hare Krishnas or Scientology, was a growing public discourse around 'cults.' Usually led by charismatic teachers or gurus and sometimes relying on the counterculture's already established occult sensibility—with the Los Angeles-based sect around Father Yod/YaHoWha/James Baker representing one group deeply in debt to Western esotericism—these movements internalized the era's utopian and collective expectations while providing crystallized social and metaphysical structures in the place of existential drift.

More important here, however, is the establishment in the early 1970s of a more informal but pervasive 'pop occulture.' This widespread cultural sensibility was produced in part by strong commercial forces that had already been building toward the end of the 1960s, when, for example, the number of newly published books on occult science and parapsychology increased by more than 100 percent annually. Similarly, while a number of popular television shows in the 1960s featured occult powers—examples include the gothic soap *Dark Shadows* and the comedy *I Dream of Jeannie*—the mediascape of the 1970s was saturated with supernaturalism, from the rise of heavy metal and progressive rock, to the increasingly cosmic iconography of comic books and poster art. Esoterica was big business—major publishers like Doubleday established occult imprints, while US Games issued their popular (and exclusively copyrighted) version of the famed Rider-Waite Tarot deck in 1971. The urge to publish also marked independent and underground outfits already identified with the spiritual counterculture: Llewellyn issued an American witch's version of Gerald Gardner's legendary Book of Shadows in 1971, while the Church of All Worlds and other nature religions developed Pagan discourse through a lively network of periodicals.

As with new religious movements and self-improvement regimens like est, the explosion of occulture—books, oracular tools, popular narratives, ephemerides, etc.—helped organize the deterritorialized flux of counterculture consciousness as it engaged a darker and more paranoid era with its yen for enchantment very much intact. One notable example of this fit is the bestselling series of books by Carlos Castaneda, in which the UCLA anthropologist described (or, more likely, invented) his long initiation by the Yaqui 'Man of Knowledge' Don Juan Matus, who gives Castaneda psychedelic drugs along with a variety of intriguing practices. Though the first volume appeared in 1968, it was the Don Juan books Castaneda published in the early 1970s that really resonated, presenting an accessible magical reality that was populated by somewhat ominous allies and required constant vigilance and self-discipline to navigate. This amoral and more indigenous 'shamanic' view stands in sharp contrast to earlier and more beatific Aquarian visions. Though Castaneda's books came to be seen by most (but not all) anthropologists as fabrications, this hardly made a difference to many readers; like Don Juan and many of the 'crazy wisdom' gurus of the era, Castaneda himself could be seen as a trickster capable of waking you up.

Timothy Leary too sensed the shift in the air. In his short 1973 'Starseed' pamphlet, written in Folsom prison, Leary advises readers to reject the 'Hindu trap' he had earlier embraced, with its 'soft, sweet, custard mush' of unity. Instead, Leary offered an expansive, futuristic, and increasingly transhuman 'Psi-Phy' perspective on the ongoing possibilities of re-programming the human nervous system. One of Leary's most important influences in this transition was Aleister Crowley, many of whose most important works (including the extraordinary Book of Thoth) were published or republished in the late 1960s and early 1970s, sparking a deep interest in Thelema that has yet to abate and that remains intertwined with certain streams of rock and other popular cultures. In many ways Crowley stands as the most important 'ancestor' of the occult counterculture: he loved drugs, tapped Eastern as well as Western esoteric sources, spear-headed a dysfunctional commune, and placed sexuality at the core of his controversial and counter-normative mysticism. His bald head appeared on the cover of the Beatles' 1967 *Sgt. Pepper's Hearts Club Band* (along with Jung, Aldous Huxley, Burroughs, and other counterculture heroes), but the Beast received his most important rock endorsement from Led Zeppelin guitarist and composer Jimmy Page, who sold Crowleyania through his occult bookstore and lived for a spell in the man's old mansion. The fact that myriad young fans across the globe were exposed to a scandalous Edwardian ceremonial magician through the medium of chart-topping rock and roll is as good a characterization as any for the dynamics of pop occulture in the 1970s, when the spiritual seeds of the counterculture spread far and wide, high and low.

REFERENCES AND FURTHER READING

Adler, Margot (1979) *Drawing Down the Moon*. Penguin: New York.

Clifton, Chas (2006) *Her Hidden Children*. AltaMira: Lanham, MD.

Ellwood, Robert S. (1994) *The Sixties Spiritual Awakening*. Rutgers University Press: Rutgers, NJ.

Greenfield, Robert (2006) *Timothy Leary: A Biography*. Harcourt: New York.

Kennedy, Gordon (1999) *Children of the Sun: A Pictorial Anthology from Germany to California 1883–1949*. Nivaria Press: Mecca, CA.

Kripal, Jeff (2007) *Esalen: America and the Religion of No Religion*. University of Chicago Press: IL.

Lachman, Gary (2001) *Turn Off Your Mind: The Mystic Sixties and the Dark Side of the Age of Aquarius*. Sidgwick & Jackson: London.

Lee, Martin and Bruce Shlain (1985) *Acid Dreams: The Complete Social History of LSD*. Grove: New York.

Lopez, Jr., Donald S. (2011) *The Tibetan Book of the Dead: A Biography*. Princeton University Press: Princeton, NJ.

McNally, Dennis (1987) 'Prophets on the Burning Shore: Jack Kerouac, Gary Snyder, and San Francisco,' *A Literary History of the American West*, J. Golden Taylor, ed., Texas Christian University Press: Fort Worth, TX, 482–95.

Partridge, Christopher (2004, 2005), *The Re-Enchantment of the West*, vols. 1 and 2. T&T Clark: London.

Roszak, Theodore (1968) *The Making of a Counter-Culture*. Doubleday: NY.

Tipton, Steven M. (1982) *Getting Saved from the Sixties: Moral Meaning in Conversion and Cultural Change*. University of California Press: Berkeley, CA.

Truzzi, Marcello (1972) 'The Occult Revival as Popular Culture: Some Random Observations on the Old and the Nouveau Witch,' *The Sociological Quarterly*, vol. 13, no. 1, 16–36.

Urban, Hugh B. (2006) *Magia Sexualis: Sex, Magic, and Liberation in Modern Western Esotericism*. University of California Press: Berkeley, CA.

Webb, James (1976) *The Occult Establishment*. Open Court Publishing: LaSalle, IL.

CHAPTER SIXTY-FOUR

INTERMEDIARY BEINGS

Egil Asprem

The theme of mediation plays a central role in much of Western esotericism (Faivre, 1994). Practices that are focused on achieving radical metaphysical insights, gaining higher knowledge, or transforming the self and the world, will always need to account for how the practitioner can get access to such rarefied goods. Interaction with mediating beings of various sorts often does the job; these postulated entities have access to powers and knowledge way beyond our own, but are still close enough to us to make contact and interaction possible. This overview chapter charts some of the main types of intermediary beings encountered in the world of Western esotericism, discusses some key functions these tend to perform, and considers some important trends in the historical development of intermediaries in this context.

TYPES OF INTERMEDIARY BEINGS

One encounters a broad variety of intermediary beings in the context of Western esotericism, from angels and demons, to aliens and the spirits of the dead. It may be helpful to attempt a crude classification of common intermediaries based on the natures ascribed to them as well as their cultural origin. While there is no claim of completeness to the following categories, they pick out some dominant trends that we will return to later in this chapter.

Beings Related to the Judeo-Christian Pantheon

The first and most dominant category contains intermediary beings related to the Judeo-Christian pantheon. This includes entities that are known from Christian liturgy and take on ritual functions there, such as the virgin Mary, the saints, Jesus Christ, and the major angels. Practices related to these intermediaries abounded in medieval magical ritual and heterodox visionary practice, as testified by the Ars Notoria, the *Liber visionum* and many other surviving magical books and grimoires (Davies, 2010; cf. Fanger, 2005). Contact with angels is especially pervasive in Western religious history. In occult and esoteric practices these beings often appear in visions or even as the object of ritual invocations.

But this class of 'Judeo-Christian' intermediaries does not limit itself to specific entities named by the liturgy, the biblical texts or commentaries, nor for that matter to intermediaries that are on the side of Heaven. The esoteric interaction with intermediaries is much too creative to be limited by canonical texts and established meanings; thus, we also include in this category the numerous angelic and demonic beings that theologians will never have heard of, and which, for that precise reason, have tended to be viewed with suspicion. In esoteric practice, all these subtypes may occur together, as excellently illustrated by John Dee's famous angel conversations of the late sixteenth century (Harkness, 1999). Here, known archangels such as Michael appear in the crystal ball alongside very idiosyncratic beings with names like Madimi, Ave, and Nalvage. At one point during the conversations, Jesus Christ himself appears to convince the magician in a particularly controversial issue. The angels, furthermore, instruct on ways to contact an enormous array of other spirit beings, some of them demons.

Besides the Christian liturgy and the innovation of individual practitioners, a major source of these mediators, as well as some of the practices surrounding them, is found in Jewish mysticism. With the spread of kabbalistic literature in Europe following the interest in it by Christian humanist scholars and the invention of printing, an enormous world of angelic and demonic mediators was opened up.

Cosmological Intermediaries

For lack of a better terminology, a second category of note can be referred to as cosmological intermediaries. This term is meant to designate a broad class of intermediary beings that have been postulated, theorized, and mapped in a number of philosophical and theological contexts since antiquity, most notably in neoplatonic philosophy (especially Iamblichus and Proclus), the *Chaldean Oracles* (second century), the *Hermetica* (second–third centuries), and in gnosticism. There is a degree of overlap with the previous category, especially through the influence that the neoplatonic cosmologies have had on hierarchical angelologies and demonologies through for example, Pseudo-Dionysius the Areopagite. The point about this category is however not only to identify a cultural pedigree separate from the Judeo-Christian one, but to pinpoint the centrality of intermediary spirits that are connected with cosmological functions. The seven Gnostic Archons were, for example, involved with the creation of the physical world, and connected to the seven classical planets. In the sixteenth century, Cornelius Agrippa gives the names, seals, and correspondences of both the (malevolent) spirits and (benevolent) intelligences that rule the planets. There are spirits that rule specific times, from hours and days to years and entire ages (see for example, Johannes Trithemius), and there are spirits connected to geographical regions of the earth. There are also spirits of the elements; the most influential arrangement of these come from Paracelsus, who talks of gnomes (earth), salamanders (fires), sylphs (air), and undines (water). All of these entities become available for evocation, conversation, and manipulation through ritual practices.

Initiated Humans

A third category of intermediary beings that has become very common in modern esotericism takes us somewhat closer to home: other human beings who have become initiated, transformed, or otherwise had their status elevated to such a degree that they can take the role of intermediaries for others. There is a key focus here on concepts such as initiation, personal transmutation, and apotheosis. From the perspective of comparative religion, this is not an uncommon category of intermediaries; we may, for example, think of the doctrines and practices associated with Bodhisattvas in Buddhism. In the West, something comparable only appears to have developed quite late, and primarily in the context of Western esotericism and the mythology of secret societies. In the seventeenth century, the Rosicrucian manifestos popularized the idea of a secret brotherhood of adepts working silently to perform benevolent acts to the transformation of the world and the salvation of humanity. In the developing mythology, these adepts would have acquired superhuman powers and possibly even immortality. The appeal to mysterious 'secret chiefs' became a central feature of the new institutional formations of the nineteenth century occult revival, often trading heavily on the Rosicrucian mythology (see e.g. Bogdan, 2007). The Hermetic Order of the Golden Dawn claimed to have been instigated by mysterious Rosicrucian adepts in Germany, while the Theosophical Society depended on contact with hidden masters in Tibet. In the twentieth century, the various splinters from Theosophy and the Golden Dawn have taken this mythology in new directions that radicalize the otherness of these adepts, chiefs, or masters. The masters are not only hidden in the sense of being in secret locations, but also disembodied or ascended to higher spheres of existence – from which they may still communicate with the chosen this-worldly adepts who know how to dial.

The Dead as Intermediaries

On a global scale, the spirits of the dead are among the most pervasive types of intermediary beings there are (Poo, ed., 2009). Ancestral spirits are at the center of religious praxis around the world, and non-institutionalized, improvised beliefs and practices concerning the dead (whether friendly or hostile) are abundant in mythology, literature, and folklore. When it comes to Western esotericism, the spirits of the dead have taken a special position as mediators of religious knowledge in the currents associated with Spiritualism. Emanuel Swedenborg opened the door to a more central theological role of dead spirits through his view that the angels and demons have themselves developed from human spirits, creating a continuity between ghosts and higher or lower mediators. Swedenborgian Christianity was an important influence on the development of spiritualist theology in the nineteenth century, as seen for example in the work of Andrew Jackson Davis. A different theological direction was taken by French 'spiritist' Allan Kardec, who combined spiritualist practice with (among other things) a doctrine of metempsychosis (cf. Monroe, 2008). Common for all the theologizing trends in spiritualism, however, is that the communication with the dead through mediums become something more than just an attempt to meet once again with lost loved ones: the spirits become full-blown mediators of higher knowledge about religious truths, and especially about the afterworld and the nature of the human soul.

Pagan Intermediaries

With the emergence of neopaganism in the twentieth century, the gods, heroes, and spirits of pre-Christian mythology have come alive again as viable intermediary beings. Not only are the gods of various pantheons (e.g. Greek, Roman, Norse) available for worship, but they can also be communicated with, and prayed to for help with specific problems. Moreover, with an increased valorization of 'pagan' belief systems, various nature spirits and magical beings such as gnomes, elves, and fairies become available and relevant once more as well.

Aliens

Extraterrestrial intelligences have become increasingly popular as intermediary beings. While UFO sightings, bedside visitations and alien abduction stories have had a broad cultural impact since Roswell, the aliens portrayed through the contactee movement in the late 1940s and 1950s have been particularly influential on their role as intermediary beings in esoteric contexts. The message from the 'Space Brothers' of global peace, nuclear disarmament, and universal brotherhood – coupled with warnings of impending doom, and a conspiracy to keep their wisdom hidden – have continued to funnel through the channellers of the New Age movement (cf. Hanegraaff 1996). But the cultural script of aliens is also available to other modes of experience and to different kinds of messages; thus, we find the alien as intermediary being in several other movements, from Kenneth Grant's Typhonian OTO to full-blown UFO religions such as Heaven's Gate or the Raelians.

Fiction-based Intermediaries

A final type of intermediaries that could be distinguished due to the specific cultural creativity that they signify are the beings that have been culled from explicit works of fiction, whether literature, film, comics or television (cf. Davidsen, 2013). While there is nothing new in works intended as fiction influencing religious thought and practice (think of Dante or John Milton), they have usually been successful in doing so by creatively elaborating on and visualizing the dominant established worldview. In more recent times we see works of fiction that portray a wholly alternative worldview getting adopted as prescriptive texts for practice. Thus, in terms of intermediaries, we find occultists incorporating Tolkien's mythology of Middle Earth, performing rituals to contact the Valar, or gods of Middle Earth (Davidsen, 2012). One of the most influential fictitious worldviews to have exerted influence on occult practice is H. P. Lovecraft's cthulhu mythos. The 'Great Old Ones' are invoked by real-life 'cultists,' mostly of a chaos magical and Left-Hand Path orientation. Rituals for working with Lovecraftian entities were published with *The Satanic Rituals* (1972), written by Michael Aquino, the founder of the Temple of Set. Several versions of the fictitious grimoire *Necronomicon* have since appeared in print (Harms and Gonce, 2003).

THE FUNCTIONS OF INTERMEDIARY BEINGS

What are all these intermediary beings good for? What do the mediators mediate? In this section I will discuss four distinguishable roles that contact with intermediary beings takes in esoteric practices: the mediation of knowledge, transformation, power/agency, and authority. The first three of these are goals that practitioners themselves would recognize and even consciously intend with their practice. The final function is a crucial effect that emerges on the social level, whether consciously intended or not.

Knowledge

Much esoteric practice is concerned with achieving higher forms of knowledge (von Stuckrad, 2005). Contact with intermediary beings is one of the primary routes that practitioners take to this end. Intermediary beings may appear in revelatory visions, such as the Poimandres figure in the *Corpus Hermeticum*. But there are also techniques for manipulating the intermediary beings to bestow knowledge on the practitioner. The medieval Ars Notoria tradition is focused on this practice, providing a magical shortcut to proficiency in the liberal arts by petitioning the angels. Grimoires dealing with the evocation of demons also frequently list the acquisition of knowledge and secrets as something the infernal servants could help with. A prototypical example of an esoteric quest for higher knowledge through intermediary beings is once again found in John Dee. Together with his scryers (notably Edward Kelly), Dee called on the angels to give knowledge of religious and cosmic mysteries, from metaphysical insights about the constitution of the cosmos, to eschatological insights on the end of the world and the salvation of humankind. It is notable that Dee, primarily a natural philosopher and a mathematician, turned to this course of action at a point when he felt all his intellectual efforts had been exhausted (Harkness, 1999). In the 'spiritual diaries,' where Dee meticulously kept track of the conversations with angels, the heavenly mediators take the form of schoolteachers, giving lessons on specific topics and answering questions from the student thirsting for knowledge.

Transformation

The quest for higher knowledge often bleeds into a more soteriological goal of personal transformation. This is in line with the notion of *gnosis* as a type of knowledge that is not merely 'higher' in terms of its superior content, but which possesses the power to transform the knower and set her free. Thus, the contact with intermediary beings in Western esotericism is often connected with a combined goal of achieving higher knowledge and achieving *salvation* through a personal transformation brought about by this knowledge. There is an emphasis on this in the theurgic traditions emanating from neoplatonists such as Iamblichus and Proclus, and resurfacing in the neoplatonic interests of the Renaissance humanists. In later periods, the focus has been retained and reinvented in light of changing intellectual contexts, including the turn to psychological understandings of the self.

In modern occultism, the goal of personal transformation is absolutely central to ritual practice. From the Golden Dawn onwards, magical ceremonies aimed at summoning and communicating with entities are typically understood within a broader theurgic framework where the ultimate goal is the transformation of the practitioner's self (cf. Asprem, forthcoming). In jargon stemming from the Golden Dawn and later developed in for example, the Thelemic context, this is expressed above all as achieving contact and communication with one's Higher Self, sometimes externalized into an entity known as the Holy Guardian Angel. This intermediary being is similar to the tutelary spirits of Greek antiquity, the personal *daimon* that, according to Plato, is assigned to each one of us before birth, and guides us through our earthly incarnation. Ritual practice in modern occult ritual magic is often bent on contacting this spirit directly and establishing a line of communication that will have a transformative effect on the practitioner's life.

Power/Agency

Intermediary beings may not only be the harbingers of knowledge and transformation, but may also bestow great power on the practitioner. In the class of ritual practices commonly classified as 'magic', the focus is often on having intermediary beings do things in the world for the practitioners, thus extending the magician's agency through that of the intermediary (cf. Sørensen, 2006). The evocation of demons through grimoires such as the Goetia exemplifies this: while the acquisition of knowledge may be a goal of such operations, the focus is often on having the demon perform tasks that are beneficent to the ritualist. They may also confer novel powers upon the magician, such as the power of invisibility, transportation to distant lands, or flying. In some of the occult lodges of the nineteenth and twentieth century, the power of intermediaries may also be exploited for the entire group itself, or for achieving goals that are much grander than those of an individual person. Thus, in the Ordo Templi Orientis – itself not primarily a magical group – the higher initiates are instructed to use magical techniques that involve intermediary spirits in order to strengthen the order itself and boost its mission to spread the Law of Thelema to society (cf. Asprem, forthcoming).

Authority

Intermediary beings have often played a role in the creation of new schools, currents or institutions within the occult world of modern times. This is, of course, not a new phenomenon in itself: messages from mysterious agents routinely show up in the hagiographic accounts of founders of religious movements, from Muhammed to Joseph Smith. Establishing the founder's message as authentic and special is easier if it originated with an angel of the lord or the emissary of an advanced alien civilization. Contact with intermediaries is thus often part of what Max Weber called charismatic authority.

This function of intermediaries takes a significant role in the relatively unorganized forms of esoteric practice where formalized authority structures are weak to non-existent. An example is the discourse on channelling (cf. Hanegraaff, 1996). The message of a channeler is deemed important not because it is uttered by the channel him/herself, but because it is attributed to an exotic source of higher knowledge. Access to the entity becomes crucial for claiming and retaining authority within this discourse. Thus, when a student of the American medium J. Z. Knight started channeling Knight's own favorite entity, the warrior Ramtha from Atlantis, this was a serious threat to her status as a unique link to higher knowledge. Consequently, Knight took appropriate legal action, resulting in Ramtha™ becoming a recognized trademark of J. Z. Knight. The ancient Atlantean spirit was now bound by copyright law, illustrating the close relationship between access to intermediary beings and the worldly authority of those who access them.

The access to intermediaries is also a recurring theme in schisms among institutionalized groups. Alice Bailey was notably ejected from the Theosophical Society after starting to receive messages directly from a hidden master, the 'Tibetan' Djwhal Khul. In the Hermetic Order of the Golden Dawn, a conflict over who the Secret Chiefs really were, whether they were real to begin with, and if so, who were still in contact with them, was at the centre of the break-up of the order and the reconstitution of new branches in the early twentieth century (cf. Howe, 1976). It was also out of these specific skirmishes that the first fully-fledged new religious movement would arise out of *fin de siècle* occultist ritual magic, namely Aleister Crowley's Thelema. The central holy text of Thelema was reportedly dictated to Crowley by a mysterious entity named Aiwass, and a host of intermediary beings, including angels, demons, pagan gods, and secret chiefs were involved at various stages in the development of its doctrines through Crowley's ongoing magical practice. Moreover, demonstrating that these communications were 'genuine' and that Aiwass was indeed more than just a hidden, higher portion of Crowley's psyche became central to establishing the authority of the Thelemic revelation (cf. Pasi, 2011). In a later generation, Thelemic and post-Thelemic positions, including Kenneth Grant's 'Typhonian' current and left-hand path positions such as Michael Aquino's Temple of Set have expanded the index of intermediary entities involved to include aliens, mythological beasts, and fiction-based entities (e.g. Evans, 2007).

TRENDS IN THE HISTORICAL DEVELOPMENT OF INTERMEDIARY BEINGS

Having charted some of the diversity of intermediary beings appearing in Western esotericism and the functions they perform, we should end this overview by looking at some trends in the historical development of these beings and their uses. Not surprisingly, the history of intermediaries is bound up with the history of Christianity, and the relative and changing power of the Churches and denominations to police orthodoxy and orthopraxy in society. One of the effects of the development and introduction of Christianity in late antiquity was that all sorts of intermediary beings that had previously flourished relatively freely were subjected to strict theological categorization and regimentation. Above all, the spirits were subsumed to a moral dualism and divided into 'good' angels of light, on the one hand, and 'evil' demons and wicked spirits, on the other. The Greek generic *daimon*, which could indeed be wicked, but equally well be neutral or even good (as the tutelary daimon, who comes closer to the notion of a 'guardian angel' as it would develop in the Christian sphere), underwent a drastic transvaluation, becoming a signifier for spirits in league with a deep ontological evil. Moreover, a theological hermeneutic of suspicion developed around this class of spirits, by which any *unknown* intermediary (encountered in foreign cultures, among 'pagans,' or in the personal experiences of individuals), whatever its claimed provenance, was a suspected demon in disguise. This suspicion extended ultimately to all claims of mediation, including those of angels and saints. As Paul had warned the Corinthians: 'Satan himself is transformed into an angel of light' (2 Cor. 11:14).

The Problem with Mediation

Thus, Christian theology introduced two aspects worthy of mention when it comes to the understanding of intermediary beings. First, a strict dichotomization of these beings into 'good' and 'evil' spirits; second, an unshakable doubt about the true nature of *all* intermediary spirits, even when claimed to be lawful. The first construction has been influential in informing distinctions between 'white' and 'black' magic, especially as appearing in the Renaissance. Cornelius Agrippa distinguished good 'theurgia' from bad 'goetia' on the grounds of the nature of the spirits involved – a distinction that was adopted by early modern demonologists such as Johann Weyer and Reginald Scot.

But the effect of the second construct is even more pervasive and historically influential. What it did was to throw all trafficking with intermediaries – except those that were sanctioned within the church (e.g. the veneration of Mary and the Saints) – into serious doubt. When someone starts receiving messages from the angels, the most economical interpretation from the orthodox perspective was to treat it not as divine favor, but demonic subterfuge. The theological problems posed by intermediaries within Christianity may in fact be considered a significant reason why contact with intermediary beings is so intimately connected with practices labeled 'occult' and 'esoteric' in the West: such actions were by definition heterodox, even when involving 'lawful' spirits. It is therefore not surprising that these practices have been relegated to the category of the rejected and marginal in Western culture (cf. Hanegraaff 2012).

Another important consequence of this theological problem with intermediaries is the development of specific techniques for the *discernment* of spirits (cf. Copeland and Machielsen, 2012). Experts within the Church needed to be able to distinguish genuine miracles and acts of God (whether direct interventions or through the mediation of angels or saints) from the trickery and illusions of demonic mediators. It is intriguing to note that this discourse on discernment went beyond the confines of the church and its authorities: esoteric spokespersons and practitioners of various non-liturgic techniques for interacting with intermediaries were frequently discerning as well. One excellent example from the early modern period is found in the reception history of Dee's angel conversations. The author of the mid-seventeenth-century 'Treatise on Angel Magic' (referred to in the text as one Dr. Rudd) went to great pains developing a technique for filtering out deceitful entities through a series of interrogative steps (cf. Asprem 2008b). This discerning magician also appears to have concluded that Dee's spirits were not angels at all, but rather demons in disguise: as a consequence, he altered the rituals for working with them in accordance with techniques for constraining and binding wicked spirits with holy names.

Post-Enlightenment Upheavals: Secularization, Pluralization and De-moralization

The decline in church institutions' power to police orthodoxy is one of the core meanings of 'secularization.' In this specific sense, secularization has had a revolutionizing effect on the use of intermediaries in Western religion. With the corrosion of centralized religious authority, we would expect to see a greater creativity and variety in practice and interpretation. Indeed, one of the most significant trends in discourses on intermediary beings since the Enlightenment is a tendency towards *pluralization*. Since about the middle of the nineteenth century we have seen a shift away from a dominance of Judeo-Christian intermediaries towards other forms of intermediaries that lack this grounding – such as pagan gods, mythological creatures, extraterrestrials, and entities described in fiction. The influx of 'eastern' material through the Theosophical Society has provided new resources for understanding intermediary entities as well; Theosophy proved to be a space for mixing ideas on initiates (hidden and ascended masters), aliens, and eastern concepts such as Bodhisattvas and avatars, feeding back into an emerging, post-Christian occulture. Moreover, when Judeo-Christian intermediaries *are* invoked, the range of functions to which they can be put is typically much wider than previously allowed, and the interpretations of the entities may diverge substantially from those sanctioned by established theology or canonized scripture. The understanding of 'angels' in the contemporary reconstruction of Dee's angelic magic (typically known as 'Enochian magic') is a good example of this. In modern Enochian magic, the angels are understood widely and idiosyncratically enough by practitioners to make it acceptable even for self-described Satanists to indulge in this form of 'angelic magic' (Asprem, 2012).

Related to the trend of pluralization is a trend towards the *de-moralization* of discourses on intermediary spirits. Beings are no longer understood simply in terms of 'good' versus 'evil,' but are typically viewed as parts of a continuous and complex ecology of spirits, with no intrinsic moral shades. Thus, we see in the context of Victorian occultism that the discourse on black and white magic that had been in place since the Renaissance started to crumble. New authors, starting with Samuel Liddell Mathers, Aleister Crowley, A. E. Waite, and Israel Regardie, and continuing with post-War inventors of Wicca and neopagan witchcraft, came to impose new ways of distinguishing between black and white that were not connected to the intrinsic nature of the intermediaries, but typically to the intentions of the practitioner instead.

The Problem of Disenchantment and Changes in the Explanation of Intermediaries

Max Weber argued that the thrust of monotheistic theologies is towards the disenchantment of the world, a project that has only been more or less completed with the transition from theological to natural-scientific and rationalistic interpretations of the world following the Enlightenment. Disenchantment may, however, be viewed as a change in Western plausibility structures, in which explanations of events in terms of 'mysterious, incalculable powers' become problematic, and events traditionally explained in such terms require new responses (Asprem, 2014). Understood this way, the postulation of and interaction with intermediary beings are affected by the impending problem of disenchantment. Those involved with such beings are prone to ask themselves: are these entities 'really real'? How can they be effective? Where do they come from? Are they perhaps part of our psyche? If so, how is our psyche to be understood? As a subjectively real realm of imagination and experience, ultimately reducible to neurochemistry, or as a shared, intersubjectively real 'collective unconscious'?

There are two things to say about these sorts of questions and their relation to a historical change towards disenchantment. First, they may take the form of a new sort of discernment. While in previous times it was important to discern a divine from a demonic entity, following the Enlightened age it has become important to discern between natural and supernatural causes, and thus between 'genuine' intermediaries and mere illusions (cf. Taves, 1999). This sort of discernment is dominant within the skeptical discourse that emerged in the wake of nineteenth-century scientific naturalism, among critics and debunkers of spiritualism, and among those dedicated to psychical research (Asprem, 2014). It was also important for at least some of the practitioners to use this naturalistic form of discernment to argue the validity of their experiences and the entities with which they communicated (Asprem, 2008a).

The second thing to say about these questions is that they concern processes of *attribution*; that is, of how individuals explain events and experiences. If we follow the lead of recent cognitive psychology of religion (e.g. Taves, 2009), we should expect attributions to vary not only from individual to individual, but across an individual's lifetime as well. When we look at the way modern and contemporary esoteric practitioners explain their interaction with intermediary beings – that is, what sort of reality they attribute to the entities, and how they understand them to be effective – we find a host of different answers. If we limit ourselves to discourses on 'demons' and 'angels' alone (e.g. Asprem, 2006; idem, 2012), we find that some understand these entities metaphorically, as names for subjective, psychological realities, while others express belief in their literal existence as supernatural beings. Some look to the Jungian collective unconscious, others to more naturalistic understandings of the mind/brain (cf. Asprem, 2008a). Moreover, some key spokespersons, including Aleister Crowley himself, are found to change attribution of such encounters several times over through their career (Pasi, 2011). These changing attributions are not arbitrary, but follow contexts such as the intended audience (existing followers, potential followers, outsiders, oneself) and the goal of the speech-act. In the case of Crowley and the reception of the Thelemic *Book of the Law* from the entity Aiwass, for example, we see a clear change from naturalistic, psychological, and reductionist attributions around the time of the event itself, to an increasingly supernaturalistic attribution as his investments in establishing Thelema as a valid religious alternative increase (Pasi, 2011).

What's Next? The Intermediary Beings' Population Boom in Popular Occulture

The processes of secularization, pluralisation, and de-moralization of intermediary beings have freed the discourse and practice of communicating with entities from theological policing. The effects of this have already been seen through the twentieth century, with a proliferation of new intermediaries entering the stage, and increasingly creative ways of handling them. In the twenty-first century, this creative process is increasingly powered by the interplay between individual religious experimentation and the mass-distribution of unusual religious representations through popular culture. As Christopher Partridge has argued (2004, 2005, 2013), we are currently witnessing the emergence of a dominant 'occulture,' which brings the creative efforts of previously marginal religious milieus to the attention of a vast audience. Through this process, occulture is becoming increasingly ordinary: representations belonging to the world of the occult become familiar as they are shared in a broad population (Partridge, 2013). Perhaps more than anything else, this goes for the intermediary beings that have populated the world of the occult but have tended to be marginalized from 'elite' culture. Angels, aliens, demons, monsters, ghosts, and spirits are making frequent appearances as characters and plot devices in a host of successful films and TV-series. The narrative grand structure of big shows like *Supernatural* and *True Blood* can even be seen to reflect this ongoing mainstreaming of occult intermediaries. At the start of *Supernatural*, we find the human protagonist 'hunters' chasing down a small number of supernatural entities, such as ghosts, vampires, and werewolves. As the show progresses, the protagonists find themselves in a warzone between angels and demons, with cameo appearances of increasingly bizarre entities, including pagan gods and Lovecraftian 'Old Ones.' Similarly, at the beginning of *True Blood*, the vampires are 'coming out of the coffins' and pursuing a policy of mainstreaming in human society; as the show progresses, it becomes clear that there are many more enchanted species hiding out among the humans, including shapeshifters, werewolves, maenads, witches, ghost seers – and fairies. While far from all of these beings take the function of 'intermediaries' in a strict sense, there can be little doubt that the scope of what sorts of non-human entities can be imagined, theorized, and become the subjects of creative appropriation by religious bricoleurs, is increasing through the mass-distribution of popular occulture. Moreover, the ordinaryness of occulture does not rely on viewers passively adopting content spread through these shows. Instead, we are expecting a creative interplay between the shared representations and meanings explored in the shows, and the creative input and uses on the receiving end. Popular occulture can thus become an arena for learning and socializing into more formal occultural practices (cf. Dyrendal, 2008). That *Supernatural* can do this in an effective way for ritual practices concerned with the summoning and interaction with demons and angels is not in doubt: The show draws heavily, and quite reliably, on esoteric lore and ritual techniques connected with the manipulation of different categories of intermediary entities; for example, Enochian language is used to command angels, while Latin does just fine for exorcising demons. Ghosts, on their part, retain the vernacular. Given the spread of this and similar shows, the twenty-first-century angel summoner is likely to start his or her occult learning process during Thursday night's TV entertainment rather than crouching over arcane books in a library.

REFERENCES AND FURTHER READING

Asprem, Egil, (2006), 'Thelema og ritualmagi: Med magi som livsholdning i moderne vestlig esoterisme,' *Chaos*, 46, 113–37.

——, (2008a), 'Magic Naturalized? Negotiating Science and Occult Experience in Aleister Crowley's "Scientific Illuminism",' *Aries* 8.2, 139–65.

——, (2008b), 'False, Lying Spirits and Angels of Light: Ambiguous Mediation in Dr Rudd's Seventeenth-Century Treatise on Angel Magic,' *Magic, Ritual, and Witchcraft*, 3.1, 54–80.

——, (2012), *Arguing with Angels: Enochian Magic and Modern Occulture*, Albany, State University of New York Press.

——, (2014), *The Problem of Disenchantment: Scientific Naturalism and Esoteric Discourse, 1900–1939*, Leiden and Boston, Brill.

——, (forthcoming), 'The Golden Dawn and the O.T.O.', in Glenn Magee (ed.) *The Cambridge Handbook of Western Mysticism and Esotericism*, Cambridge: Cambridge University Press.

Bogdan, Henrik, (2007), *Western Esotericism and Rituals of Initiation*. Albany, NY: State University of New York Press.

Brach, Jean-Pierre, (2005), 'Intermediary Beings III: Renaissance,' in Wouter J. Hanegraaff et al. (eds.) *Dictionary of Gnosis and Western Esotericism*, 898–906, Leiden: Brill.

Broek, Roelof van den, (2005), 'Intermediary Beings I: Antiquity,' in Wouter J. Hanegraaff et al. (eds.) *Dictionary of Gnosis and Western Esotericism*, 898–906, Leiden: Brill.

Copeland, Clare, and Jan Machielsen, eds. (2012), *Angels of Light? Sanctity and the Discernment of Spirits in the Early Modern Period*, Leiden: Brill.

Davidsen, Markus Altena, (2012), 'The Spiritual Milieu Based on J.R.R. Tolkien's Literary Mythology,' in Adam Possamai (ed.) *Handbook of Hyper-Real Religions*, 185–204, Leiden & Boston: Brill.

——, (2013), 'Fiction-Based Religion: Conceptualising a New Category against History-Based Religion and Fandom,' *Religion and Culture; An Interdisciplinary Journal* 14.4, 378–95.

Davies, Owen, (2010), *Grimoires: A History of Magic Books*, Oxford: Oxford University Press.

Dyrendal, Asbjørn, (2008), 'Devilish Consumption: Popular Culture in Satanic Socialization,' *Numen*, 55.1, 68–98.

Evans, Dave, (2007), *The History of British Magic After Crowley*. n.p.: Hidden Publishing Ltd.

Faivre, Antoine, (1994), *Access to Western Esotericism*, Albany: State University of New York Press.

Fanger, Claire, (2005), 'Intermediary Beings II: The Middle Ages,' in Wouter J. Hanegraaff et al. (eds.), *Dictionary of Gnosis and Western Esotericism*, 619–23, Leiden: Brill.

Hanegraaff, Wouter J., (1996), *New Age Religion and Western Culture: Western Esotericism in the Mirror of Secular Thought*, Leiden: Brill.

——, (2012), *Esotericism and the Academy: Rejected Knowledge in Western Culture*, Cambridge: Cambridge University Press.

——, (2013), *Western Esotericism: A Guide for the Perplexed*, London, etc.: Bloomsbury.

Harkness, Deborah, (1999), *John Dee's Conversations with Angels: Cabala, Alchemy, and the End of Nature*, Cambridge: Cambridge University Press.

Harms, Daniel, and John Wisdom Gonce III, eds., (2003), *Necronomicon Files: The Truth Behind Lovecraft's Legend*, York Beach: Red Wheel / Weiser.

Howe, Ellic, (1972), *The Magicians of the Golden Dawn*. London: Routledge and Kegan Paul Ltd.

——, (1978), *The Magicians of the Golden Dawn: A Documentary History of a Magical Order, 1887–1923*, York Beach: Samuel Weiser, 1978.

Monroe, John Warne, (2008), *Laboratories of Faith: Mesmerism, Spiritism and Occultism in Modern France*, Ithaca, NY: Cornell University Press.

Partridge, Christopher, (2004), *The Re-Enchantment of the West: Alternative Spiritualities, Sacralization, Popular Culture and Occulture*, vol. 1, London: T and T Clark International.

——, (2005), *The Re-Enchantment of the West: Alternative Spiritualities, Sacralization, Popular Culture and Occulture*, vol. 2, London: T and T Clark International.

——, (2013), 'Occulture is Ordinary,' in Egil Asprem and Kennet Granholm (eds.), *Contemporary Esotericism*, 113–33, London: Equinox Publishing.

Pasi, Marco, (2011), 'Varieties of Magical Experience: Aleister Crowley's Views on Occult Practice,' *Magic, Ritual, & Witchcraft*, 6.2, 123–62.
Poo, Mu-chou, ed., (2009), *Rethinking Ghosts in World Religions*, Leiden: Brill.
Stuckrad, Kocku von, (2005), 'Western Esotericism: Towards an Integrative Model of Interpretation,' *Religion*, 34, pp. 78–97.
Sørensen, Jesper, (2006), *A Cognitive Theory of Magic*, Walnut Creek, CA: Alta Mira Press.
Taves, Ann, (1999), *Fits, Trances, and Visions: Experiencing Religion and Explaining Experience from Wesley to James*, Princeton: Princeton University Press.
——, (2009), *Religious Experience Reconsidered: A Building-Block Approach to the Study of Religion and Other Special Things*, Princeton and Oxford: Princeton University Press.

CHAPTER SIXTY-FIVE

THE BODY IN OCCULT THOUGHT

Jay Johnston

Active, extensive and infused with meaning, the body in occult thought is anything but banal. It is utilised to create magic, understood as the locus of divine/demonic/alien agency, employed as an instrument in ritual, read symbolically to uncover secret wisdom, made extensive and expansive through energetic attributes; and, for some, it is positioned as an *axis mundi* linking the mundane 'physical' world to that of a larger metaphysical reality. For others its sheer visceral corporeality is worshipped and celebrated. In short, the body inhabits, generates and symbolises a significant place in many occult discourses and practices. This chapter will set out a typology of the main ways in which it has been conceptualised. It is not a historical survey, nor does it adequately represent the rich diversity of body concepts and body roles in occult discourse. Rather, it aims to identify the dominant tropes and functions attributed to the body across a number of occult traditions.

A feature of many examples discussed herein is the celebration of fleshly existence. Some groups, for example forms of Contemporary Paganism, consciously celebrate the body as a locus of the divine (diversely conceptualised) in contradistinction to its perceived negative positioning – or rejection – in dominant Judaeo-Christian traditions. In adopting dualist spirit–body constructions of the individual, such traditions seek to redress a perceived imbalance that is understood to have denigrated the body and its role in spiritual belief and practice. Such celebration of the corporeal extends to the way in which desire is understood to either enable (or disable) relations with the divine/occult force(s) and often invokes decadence and hedonism. Of course, the gender ascribed to an individual also impacts upon how the body is inscribed and read (treated in a separate chapter in this volume). Bodies and desires through such a lens are productive and central, indeed crucial, to spiritual practice. However, this is a far from straightforward relation as the following discussion seeks to unfurl. The occult body is magical in myriad ways.

STAR DUST, SPIRITUAL ENERGY AND GROSS MATTER: OF WHAT OCCULT BODIES ARE MADE

In many occult belief systems the conceptualisation of the body and its capacities is directly linked to the material of which it is understood to be comprised. From the astral substance of Renaissance Hermeticism to a form of quasi-matter infused with spiritual energy – subtle matter – popularised by the Theosophical Society, the occult body can challenge normative biological definitions regarding what actually constitutes a body. Before examining some of the different types of occult bodies in more detail, an overview of some of its proposed ontological constituents in general is given. This is requisite as it provides information about the foundation upon which the fulsome, fleshy, occult self is then established.

The modern 'western' individual, and the biomedical sciences that tend to the health of contemporary bodies, conceptualise an individual's body as a living, ideally self-regulating, organism that terminates at the skin boundary. Individuals are ontologically separate units and, except in rare cases of conjoined twins, are understood as physically separated from one another as well. Occult bodies can *both* incorporate this individualism and challenge the physical and ontological boundaries commonly attributed to the physical body. An occult body may have invisible agency that stretches well beyond the reach of the physical body, for example to work magic; it may have invisible anatomy, a subtle, energy body that extends beyond the flesh and out into the broader cosmos, or an esoteric anatomy that works as a microcosm of a larger macrocosm with established relations of sympathy between each; or it may be comprised of a form of matter understood as entirely different to gross, empirical matter. Some occult practices – especially contemporary ones – combine these various forms together. At the heart of many of them is a different concept of matter/materiality: a peculiarly animate substance.

Belief in the agency and efficacy of matter – especially that considered as lacking consciousness or agency by modern science – has long been a feature of magical traditions. From the use of semi-precious stone amulets to ward off illness in Antiquity, to the use of plant or mineral in contemporary pagan ritual, the very matter of empirical reality has been attributed special actions and qualities. Occult frameworks contend that these qualities can be activated or manipulated by a person with the requisite occult skill, often via a specific practice: for example, the work of the infamous and influential Marsilio Ficino (1433–99), translator of Plato and the *Corpus Hermeticum*. In his volumes on medicine – notably *The Book of Life* 1489 (1996) – he sought to effect healing of what were interpreted as constitutional disharmonies. These were associated with the medieval Galenic belief in four types of humour: phlegmatic, melancholic, sanguine, choleric (Yates, 2001: 59). One dominated the physiology of any individual through the use of tinctures, powders, salves, diets and certain types of physical activities (Ficino, 1996 [1489]). The selection and combination of ingredients was directed by the 'doctrine of signatures'; the belief that all material, physical, psychological and cosmic phenomena were governed by a dominant planetary correspondence. To heal a melancholic – attributed to an imbalance of Saturnian and Mercurial energies – remedies that bear Jupiter's signature were to be administered (1996 [1489]). Therefore material substance, considered inert and unconscious from the perspective of modern empirical science, was attributed agency and affectivity; derived from their ontological constituents which were implicitly interrelated with a particular celestial body. The physical body was intertwined – via these celestial correspondences – with the celestial and spiritual, as were all phenomena of the natural world (Johnston, 2008: 114–16).

Ficino's system has been built upon by contemporary astrologers. For example, the standard introductory text, Alan Oken's *Complete Astrology* [1980] provides lists of phenomena – colours, stones, plants, anatomy, occupations – ascribed to the 'rulership' of each planet. His proposition that the body is constituted by all the planets – to certain degrees – with one or two predominating, has also found further elaboration in relation to modern psychology. Thomas Moore, working within the area of Jungian depth psychology, published *The Planets Within: The Astrological Psychology of Marsilio Ficino* (1982). In this text Moore adapts Ficino's system with reference to Jungian archetypes and psychological techniques; including those of the inner male and inner female: the anima and the animus.

Another form of ontological energetic agency understood to comprise the 'stuff' of bodies is found in the esoteric healing advocated by Alice Bailey (amanuensis for the spiritual 'master' Djwal Khul), in the infamous 'blue books' (see especially *Esoteric Healing* 1953 and *A Treatise on White Magic* 1934). These present an individual as comprised of a series of bodies, with the physical (or 'gross') body the densest manifestation of the spirit–matter of which they are all comprised. Each of the other bodies interpenetrate this gross body and exceed it (and each other) in a hierarchical schema that stretches the individual's body from physical to metaphysical reality: it is an embodied bridge between self and divine (this conceptualisation is detailed further below in the discussion of the subtle bodies of Theosophical Society discourse). The healer's role is to perceive the action of the subtle energy bodies (invisible to 'everyday' sight) and to adjust their behaviour, action and agency accordingly. As with Ficino's system this may involve specific activities, especially meditation, and the use of various plants, stones and colours in ritual activity.

Core to both these examples of 'healing' the body is the belief that matter and consciousness are not ontologically distinct (the body is not a 'handbag' for the soul or spirit) rather that they are comprised to various degrees of the same animating substance. This is broadly the relation proposed in Process Philosophy (Rescher 1996) and one which is often exemplified by philosopher and parapsychologist Henri Bergson's proposition that it is not a difference in kind (kind of substance), but a difference in degree (1996[1896]). As I have noted elsewhere (2008: 57), Bergson is an intriguing figure regarding the philosophy and science of esoteric bodies. His sister Mina ('Moina' after initiation) was centrally involved in the nineteenth-century occult group the Hermetic Order of the Golden Dawn. Indeed, an 'esoteric' aspect of Bergson's work can be traced through its influence to more contemporary philosophers, especially Gilles Deleuze (and the concepts of the 'Body without Organs') (Johnston, 2008: 136–52). This ontological perspective allows both *matter* and *consciousness/spirit* to be comprised of the same 'stuff' and therefore placed in relations of effect and influence.

The occult practitioner is attributed the skill to perceive and/or manipulate this substance, including recognising its efficacy in various phenomena of the natural world. Therefore the capacity to *perceive* this subtle matter is an attribute of the occult practitioner and linked to various sensory capacities, especially intuition, extra-sensory perception and the 'second sight'. This includes the belief in a sixth sense that may take the form of clairvoyance, clairaudience, clairsentience and claircognisance (Howes 2009; Gee 1999; Virtue 1998).

In its most radical form subtle matter proposes a form of intersubjectivity: a proposition that views individuals as inherently interrelated with one another and always in the process of dynamic exchange that gives them 'being'. In this occult form of intersubjectivity the physical body is made expansive by invisible 'spiritual' material with which it interpenetrates (and vice versa) the broader world and cosmos. It gives an ontological foundation to the 'New Age' maxim, 'we are all one'; that is, inextricably bound together by a shared ontological substance (although, with Ruth Barcan, we have elsewhere discussed the distressing way this has been employed in neoliberal frameworks [2006]). This is a much-popularised concept of human subjectivity in contemporary wellbeing spirituality, underpinning many alternative health practices and is discussed further below.

A less radical form of permeability attributed to the physical body is that which underpins the phenomena of channelling. In contradistinction to the ontology outlined above in this model the 'self' (equated with consciousness) is considered distinct from the physical body and able to 'step aside' to enable another spiritual entity to inhabit the physical body and communicate through it (Brown 1997).

While spiritual concepts of matter, or belief in disembodied agencies able to direct physical matter, are a feature of many occult groups; not all forms of occultism hold such beliefs. For example, the pure fleshiness of the body divorced from any concept of the divine is celebrated in Satanism (La Vey 1969). However, in general, the occult body requires a particular way, a particular framework for viewing and interpreting anatomy and/or a specific approach of employing, using the physical body (often designated as ritual). The body is therefore implicit in the framework through which the occult practitioner understands their life and world.

CORPOREAL HIEROGLYPHS: BODY AS SYMBOL AND LANGUAGE

Reading the body as an occult text can be understood as an extension of the hermeneutic approaches to reading the 'book of nature' featured in numerous esoteric traditions. Here the body is seen as 'nature'. This is not a self-evident corollary but one fraught with conceptual and ethical issues that lie beyond the scope of this chapter; it is enough to signal that the equation body = nature is not necessarily 'natural'. This corporeal text is then 'read' by those with the requisite knowledge and special 'sight'. As Antoine Faivre defines it in his oft-cited (and now supplemented and challenged) tenets of western esotericism, Living Nature is:

> Multilayered, rich in potential revelations of every kind, it must be read like a book. The word *magia*, so important in the Renaissance imaginary, truly calls forth the idea of a Nature, seen, known and experienced as essentially alive in all its parts, often inhabited and traversed by a light…Thus understood, the 'magic' is simultaneously the knowledge of networks of sympathies and antipathies that link the things of Nature…
>
> (1994: 11)

Numerous versions of this approach are found in occult discourse: From specific anatomy being read as a symbolic manifestation of metaphysical 'truths' (the endocrine system being read as symbolically representing spiritual laws for example), to contemporary forms of holistic dentistry where each tooth is allocated a correspondent relationship with a specific organ or anatomical feature. In the endocrine example, the body presents sacred knowledge in its very physiology and attendant systems; one just needs to know how to read it to uncover the spiritual message. In the dentistry example, as with Iridology, one system of the body is considered a microcosm of its whole; and its marks, blemishes, decay, and shapes are read to interpret the state of the physical body in its entirety and by extension the state of body–mind–spirit harmony.

American Theosophist Manly P. Hall, synthesising ideas presented in H. P. Blavatsky's *The Secret Doctrine* (1888), produced *The Secret Teachings of All Ages* in 1928. This distillation provides the following on the body:

> All the gods and goddesses of antiquity consequently have their analogies in the human body, as have also the elements, planets, and constellations which were assigned as proper vehicles for the celestials. Four body centers are assigned to the elements, the seven vital organs to the planets, the twelve principal parts and members to the zodiac, the invisible parts of man's [sic] divine nature to various supermundane deities, while the hidden God was declared to manifest through the marrow of the bones.
>
> (Hall 1928: LXXV)

Here, then, the body is not only a microcosm for cosmic and worldly 'nature'; but also for the astrological zodiac, numerous gods, goddesses and intermediary spirits, as well as the locus of a overarching, singular divine source (God). Specific aspects of physiology are attributed particular relations/correspondences.

A more contemporary – and best selling – version of such logic has been popularised by Louise L. Hay (1984) and Annette Noontil (1994). Both texts read the body's ailments as communicating a body–mind–spirit disharmony. As Noontil puts it in *The Body is the Barometer of the Soul: So Be Your Own Doctor*, 'I see my body as a vehicle to learn from' (p. vi). Less concerned with viewing the body as a visceral compendium of all sacred knowledge, Hay and Noontil's schemas are heavily psychologised; for example, the health of bones is related to the concept of resentment for Noontil (p. 9), while Hay contends that pain is caused by guilt and that 'guilt always seeks punishment'. Both authors draw attention to what they perceive as the fundamental form of 'unhealthy' thinking they view as the cause; and Hay, now famously, provided a series of aphorisms as a tool for healing the imbalance.

ESOTERIC ANATOMY: BODY AS ENERGY

The logic that underpins many 'body as text' approaches – the logic of correspondences – is often built upon an understanding of the body as constructed from various types of energies. This is exactly the type of concept of the body that utilises the subtle matter ontology previously detailed. Popularised in the nineteenth century by the Theosophical Society, this version of the body incorporates and adapts Buddhist and

Hindu concepts of the Subtle Body (for further discussion and critique see Samuel and Johnston 2013) with occult concepts of the body; for example, Paracelsus' (c. 1493–1541) 'sidereal body' of celestial substance or Jacob Boehme's (c. 1575–1624) subtle forces of ontological desire (Deghaye 1995: 224). Indeed, from medieval to early modern accounts of subtle bodies, their constituent 'forces' were also understood to be comprised of spirits (including those of demons, see Göttler and Neuber 2008) and the distinction between the 'force' of subtle matter and spiritual entity was not always clear.

Theosophical subtle bodies are comprised of seven sheaths ('bodies') of subtle matter-consciousness, of which each body exhibits a different gradation; the physical body being the 'densest' form and the 'lowest' of the seven bodies on the spiritual evolutionary scale used by Theosophists. The other bodies interpenetrate and exceed one another on a hierarchical scale: the higher they are placed on the developmental scale the more refined their comprising subtle matter is perceived to be. Only four bodies are understood to manifest in physical reality: physical, etheric, astral and the 'manas' or 'mental' body. The other three link the individual to – and inhabit – other metaphysical/cosmological realms (Blavatsky 1971 [1887], Bailey 1953).

In addition to the interpenetrating sheaths, subtle bodies are attributed a network of energetic pathways and centres. These incorporate and adapt Hindu *nadi* and *chakra* schemas – utlised in systems of Yoga – along and through which spiritual energy is understood to flow (see de Michelis 2005 for an erudite account of Yoga's take-up in relation with western esoteric discourse). These pathways and centres have been aligned with specific organs and areas of the physical body (as well as sounds, colours, planets, elements, etc.). Quite detailed tables of correspondences have been produced, for example those found in Anodea Judith's *Eastern Body: Western Mind: Psychology and the Chakra System as a Pathway to the Self* (1996). For further discussion on the complexities of Theosophical and other traditions of the subtle body, including Jung's 'alchemical' version see Lockhardt (2010).

Although a nebulous and ephemeral concept of the body–self, subtle bodies have held a strong and enduring cultural presence. Contemporary versions, especially those found in the Wellbeing Spirituality (Heelas 2008) and the Alternative Health milieu, have been strongly psychologised. Such influence is clearly present in the title of Judith's aforementioned text. Barbara Brennan's *Hands of Light: A Guide to Healing Through the Human Energy Field* (first published in 1987) is now an iconic guide to 'working with' subtle bodies for health and healing. The type of subtle anatomy advocated by Brennan incorporates Annie Besant and C.W. Leadbeater's concept of 'thought-forms' as espoused in *Thought-Forms* (1901). These are shapes that form in an individual's subtle body (proposed to be comprised of energy drawn specifically from the Astral and Mental subtle bodies). They are often discussed as being present in a persons 'aura', another term for these energetic bodies (and that spawned the practice of Kirlian photography in an effort to capture these invisible energetic parts of the human as a visible, static image which is then interpreted). Like Besant and Leadbeater, Brennan espouses the thought-forms' relationship to particular emotions represented by colour and form, as in the *chakra* system in general.

These networks of energetic signs, to be read in diagnosis of health and psychological imbalance, are also found in Anodea Judith's *Wheels of Life: A User's*

Guide to the Chakra System (1987). She not only interprets them as directly informing the shape and mass of the physical body, and the state of an individual's psyche, but also as implicit in the working of magic (Johnston 2010); specifically, drawing a relationship to the sacred space of a circle cast in contemporary pagan magic ritual:

> The space created for a magical working is thought of as a circle, so that what occurs within the sacred space can then radiate outwards in all directions when the working is finished, and the 'circle' is taken down. One meaning for the work 'chakra' is a circle of worshippers, alternating men and women with a Priest and Priestess in the center.
>
> (Judith 1996: 438)

The use of subtle bodies in the practice of magic is detailed further in later sections of this chapter. In general, however, their contemporary occult manifestations are quite diverse. Numerous schemas exist. Indeed, volumes like Cyndi Dale's (2009) list together Theosophical versions and those found in various indigenous traditions without any consideration of cultural specificity, nor how the different schemas may be thought to exist in relation to one another. Can a white middle class man from Sydney, Australia, be comprised of an Incan subtle body system, 'shaped like a bagel' with its '*ojos de luz*, eyes of light' (correlated to the concept of *chakras*) (2009: 297–98)?

Aleister Crowley provides one final example of the mutability and range of energetic occult bodies. As recounted in Hugh Urban's *Magia Sexualis*, Crowley's concept of the human body incorporated a subtle body chakra schema to which he added an additional set of three sub-chakras below the base chakra. These were:

> The anal lotus is of eight petals, deep crimson, glowing to a rich poppy colour when excited...
>
> The prostatic lotus [prostrate gland in males/urethra-cervix in women] is like a peridot, extremely translucent and limpid....The petals are numerous, I think thirty-two....
>
> The third lotus is in the *glans penis* [clitoris in the female], close to the base.... It is of a startlingly rich purple....The centre is gold like the sun....
>
> (Crowley qtd. in Urban 2006: 126)

The colour and petal number associations of these three lower charkas are different for women. The occult body is always a gendered body (as discussed elsewhere in this volume). For Crowley the subtle body was distinct in the areas pertaining to the sexual organs. As with dominant, normative, western perspectives, the locus of sexuality and of sexual identity is 'fixed' onto the region of biological sex organs; even in subtle matter.

MAGICAL FLUIDS AND FORMS: BODY AS TOOL

The previous section has already gestured towards the way in which the body and its products are used as tools in occult practice. Specifically, the body is used as an agent in the practice of magic, of self-development on a spiritual path, or as a vessel through which the occult practitioner communes with the deity/divine.

Crowley's *chakras* (influenced by western versions of Tantra) were employed in the practice of sex magic; as was the ritual use/consumption of sexual fluids understood within an alchemical framework in which they were considered to be a spiritual elixir (Urban 2006; 123–28). The conceptual heritage adapted and assimilated here includes that of Medieval Siddhu traditions, in which the operations of the subtle body were combined with a belief in the sexual fluids as being internal power fluids that were – internally – combined and transformed to produce *amrta* (the divine nectar of immortality). This is a form of corporeal alchemy understood to be incorporated in tantric practices and hathayoga (White 1996); although, as Hugh Urban has artfully demonstrated, western forms of tantra have placed greater emphasis on sex and orgasm rather than body–mind cultivation practices and ritual ingestion of foods and sexual fluids (2003). A discussion of the 'meeting' of bodies of dimorphic gender ascription, the creation of spiritual hermaphrodites and the role of so-called 'deviant' gender positions in occult thought – although most certainly embodied – is taken up in the chapter on Gender and the Occult.

These perspectives present the body as both able to create and direct magical and/or spiritual energy. The drawing together of an individual's intention (or will), and celestial substance understood to inhabit matter, is also found in the work of Giordano Bruno [1548–1600], a central figure in the development of occult practices. For Bruno, magic involved the creation of 'chains' by the magician – through the use of imagination and images – with which they could bind another person. In *Cause, Principle and Unity: And Essays on Magic* [1584] he identified a specific type of magic that was orientated towards the binding and controlling of another's emotions (1998: 130). Magic here is constituted by the energetic manipulation of another. In short, it is about power, a power linked to ontological substance and spirit. Bruno considered *eros* as the strongest and most significant of these binding agents. Bruno's magical practitioner is one who is savvy in perceiving, creating and directing these binding agents. This may include focusing one's energy via the construction (visualization) – in spiritual matter – of a specific image or symbol. The legacy of this heritage is found in contemporary works like Caroline Myss' evocation of power as an affective and healing agent in *Anatomy of the Spirit* (1997): *Learning the symbolic language of energy means learning to evaluate the dynamics of power in yourself and others* (author's italics; 47).

Quite a different role for the body is developed in Channelling cultures, particularly those that flourished in the 1980–90s. The Spiritualist Church has long had members who provide information for individuals based upon what is communicated to them by a spiritual entity. Often these messages come in the form of physical sensations in the medium's body; for example, the deceased individual identifying themselves by previous ailments or cause of physical death. Here the medium interprets the messages via physical and metaphysical sense systems.

Other forms of channelling are less filtered, the 'medium' or 'channel' placing themselves in a trance-like state to enable the spirit to speak through them (understanding their own consciousness to have 'retreated'); or, indeed, the 'other' spiritual subjectivity – whether understood as alien, a deceased loved one, spiritual master or deity, animal (or even, as recorded by Michael F Brown, a Barbie doll) – entirely takes over the channel's body (1997). Such events are often signalled with a marked change in voice, especially pertaining to historical idiom or accent. These practices raise interesting questions about the conceptualisation of the self: Whether or not it is thought to have a transferrable essence, or to be implicitly related to a particular physical body.

DIVINE RESIDENCE: THE DEIFIED AND CELEBRATED BODY

Contemporary pagan traditions are often associated with the positive re-valuation of the physical body in spiritual practice. A feature of many forms of contemporary paganism is the understanding of the divine as immanent; manifest in the physical world and in the physical body. This includes movements like Wicca with its central focus on the physical body (and the 'body' of the earth) as the locus of the immanent God and Goddess. The Priest and Priestess are often understood to personify and manifest these divine agencies during ritual.

Such belief is also combined with the concept of subtle bodies. Contemporary Pagans Janet and Stewart Farrar and Gavin Bone outline in *The Healing Craft: Healing Practices for Witches and Pagans* a study of physical physiognomy and anatomy that incorporates the *chakra* system; e.g. 'The endocrine system is an important area of study for anyone interested in spiritual healing because of the correlations between the positions of the glands and the chakras' (1999: 55).

The centrality of the body to occult practice is also distinguished in Satanism; although here it is not valorised for its capacity to 'presence' any form of deity. Rather, the fleshy, corpulent self is revered for its *humanness*. The self – following a broadly Nietzschean 'superman' model – was one's own god, revered by physical indulgence and sense gratification without any recourse to a transcendent deity; certainly not one modelled on a transcendent Christian God or Devil (La Vey 1969). Celebration of one's physical form via sensual pleasure was viewed as a form of self-reverence.

AXIS MUNDI: BODY AS MAP AND SPIRITUAL HIGHWAY

The *axis mundi* is conceptualised as 'a pole situated at the centre of the world, holding up the canopy of heaven and connecting it with the earth' (Purce 1974: 17). It is envisaged as a connecting bridge or ladder between the terrestrial and the celestial; in esoteric traditions one that the human can ascend via the development of their spirit. In traditions that utilise a subtle body system, the body itself and the cultivation of its energetic anatomy forms such an *axis mundi*. It is an embodied bridge between the individual and the divine.

Another of the more common frameworks used in the conceptualization of body–cosmos and self–divine relations is that of the microcosm relating to the macrocosm: envisaging the self as a smaller version of the cosmos. As previously noted these schemas can be built upon a belief in correspondences and/or in subtle matter. Other models use the shape of the body to 'map' the relations between elements of diverse occult thought systems (and sometimes bring different systems, for example astrology and the tarot, into dialogue with one another). In medical astrology each sign of the zodiac is attributed with a specific part of anatomy; for example, Capricorn is associated with the knees, Scorpio with the genitals (Johnston 2011). Such associations are depicted in images of 'zodiacal man' found in manuscripts from the Middle Ages to contemporary times; for example, in *Les Très Riches Heures du Duc de Berry* (French ms, fifteenth century) or the works of Athanasius Kircher (1602–80) such as *Oedipus Aegyptiacus* (1653) (Kenton, 1974).

Yet another form is found in the Kabbalah, with the proposition of Adam Kadmon (the 'original' or 'primoridal' man) onto whom is mapped the *sefirot* or divine attributes that a devotee develops on that path of esoteric Judaism (a 'hermetic Kabbalah' was developed in Renaissance Italy) (Lurker 2004: 2–3). Similarly, when interpreted as stages in an individual's spiritual development the twenty-two major arcana cards of the tarot are placed in association with physical anatomy and/or can be read in card layouts that attribute placement correspondences to the human body. Nancy Garen provides interpretations for 'the physical body' for every card of the entire deck; e.g, the nine of swords is interpreted as 'You will have stomach problems, be subject to nausea, or have trouble with your prostate gland' (2011: 304). Therefore the tarot is interpreted as providing insights into the health of the inquirer's physical body and its associated emotional correspondences. Indeed, a whole market of 'healing cards' has developed: the selection of which is deemed to give intuitive advice – whether attributed to the internal 'self' or an extant deity – to the inquirer; for example Christine Northrup's *Women's Bodies, Women's Wisdom Healing Cards* (2003) or Doreen Virtue's *Archangel Raphael Healing Oracle Cards* (2010).

TRANSFORMING BODIES: BECOMING OTHER BODIES

> In ceremony, meditation and dreams they 'become' their chosen animal. This ritual experience clearly shades into the 'shamanistic' experience of animal companions, guides and totems.
>
> (Harvey 2007: 166)

Occult bodies may also be distinctly non-human, for example vampire or werewolf or trans-human. This can either be thought of as a permanent ontological state or a temporary embodiment bought about by magic; especially forms of shape-shifting embraced by contemporary shamanic practitioners. Akin to some forms of subtle body metaphysics, shape-shifting is commonly underpinned by an animistic belief that allows the suitably initiated or developed to manipulate matter–spirit to effect this change in subjectivity. Rich veins of folklore infuse contemporary paganisms with amorphous bodies that move across species boundaries.

Various mind–body cultivation techniques are often employed including creative visualisation, trance, psychotropic substances, forms of meditation, ritual movement, performance and dance. Terminology for explaining these experiences is slippery and tricky. The term 'imagination' is often employed. However, as exemplified in Susan Greenwood's description of becoming an owl, this is a particularly visceral form of imagination: 'I *smelt* my warm bird smell and it took me into the experience of flight; I could *feel* the pull of the air on my wing feathers' (2013: 211). Manuals like Ted Andrews' *Animal-Speak* (1998), Michael Harner's, *The Way of the Shaman* (1980), Sandra Ingerman's *Soul Retrieval* (1991) and Nicki Scully's *Power Animal Meditations* (2001) all describe various ritual, visualisation and mind–body cultivation practices to enable an individual to either experience the energetic aspects of their particular animal teacher or guide and/or to effect a shape-shift of their own body-image; either into an animal form, or into a magical form of self able to access and travel in otherworlds.

CONCLUSION: OCCULT BODIES AND THEIR POLITICS

The body in occult thought is no simple visceral appendage but deeply implicated, not only in spiritual worldviews and practices as detailed above, but also in its political and socio-cultural agency. Whether this is the extra-skilled body of the seer or the body attributed sexualised chakras in Crowley's system, many of these bodies emerged critiquing normativity. That is, through their very conceptualisation they challenge normative ideas of what a body is, what it is capable of doing and what it should be allowed to do.

While bodies with magical tails and invisible wings may remain the purview of counter-culture groups and self-directed spiritual practices, other forms of the occult body have become distinctly mainstream. The subtle body of alternative therapies interprets the body to speak personal, emotional and spiritual narratives that underpin an ever-expanding multi-million dollar industry (Barcan 2011); while the continuing technological developments engender disembodied occult bodies, including avatars and forms of Otherkin that inhabit virtual spaces and on-line worlds.

The body in occult thought, its anatomy and capacities, speak its subject's beliefs. Whether considered made of stars or pure indulgent flesh, whether expansive and ephemeral or non-human, this is a body that is and enacts *relation*, between the self, the divine and the cosmos...however those slippery terms are interpreted.

REFERENCES AND FURTHER READING

Andrews, T. (1998) *Animal-Speak: The Spiritual and Magical Powers of Creatures Great and Small*, St Paul: Llewellyn.

Barcan, R. (2011) *Complementary and Alternative Medicine: Bodies, Therapies, Senses*, London: Berg.

Barcan, R. and J. Johnston (2011) 'Fixing the Self: Alternative Therapies and Spiritual Logics,' in *Mediating Faiths: Religion and Socio-Cultural Change in the Twenty-First* Century, Eds. M. Bailey and G. Redden, Surrey: Ashgate, 75–87.

Bailey, A. A. (1974 [1934]) *A Treatise on White Magic*, New York: Lucis Publishing Company.

——(1989 [1953]) *Esoteric Healing*, New York: Lucis Publishing Company.

Bergson, H. (1996 [1896]) *Matter and Memory*, trans. N. M. Paul and W. S. Palmer, New York: Zone Books, Urzone.

Blavatsky, H. P. (1971 [1877]) *Isis Unveiled, Vol. 1 Science; Vol 2 Theology*, London: Adyar and Wheaton: Theosophical Publishing House.

Brown, M. F. (1997) *The Channeling Zone: American Spirituality in An Anxious Age*, Cambridge MA: Harvard University Press.

Bruno, G. (1998 [1584]) *Cause, Principle and Unity: And Essays on Magic*, Ed. and trans. R. J. Blackwell and R. de Lucca, Cambridge: Cambridge University Press.

Dale, C. (2009) *The Subtle Body: An Encyclopedia of Your Energetic Anatomy*, Boulder: Sounds True.

Deghaye, P. (1995) 'Jacob Boehme and His Followers,' in *Modern Esoteric Spirituality*. Vol 21 *World Spirituality*, Eds. A. Faivre and J. Needleman, New York: Crossroad, 210–47.

de Michelis, E. (2005) *A History of Modern Yoga: Patanjali and Western Esotericism*, London: Continuum.
Farrar, J., S. Farrer and G. Bone (1999) *The Healing Craft: Healing Practices for Witches and Pagans*, Blaine: Phoenix Publishing.
Faivre, A. (1994) *Access to Western Esotericism*, Albany: State University of New York Press.
Ficino, M. (1996 [1980; 1489]) *The Book of Life*, trans. C. Boer, Woodstock: Spring Publications.
Garen, N. (2011 [1989]) *Tarot Made Easy*, London: Piatkus.
Gee, J. (1999) *Intuition: Awakening Your Inner Guide*, York Beach, Maine: Samuel Weiser.
Göttler, C. and W. Neuber (2008) 'Preface: Vapours and Veils: the Edge of the Unseen,' in *The Representation of Subtle Bodies in Early Modern European Culture*, C. Göttler and W. Neuber, Leiden and Boston: Brill.
Greenwood, S. (2013) 'On Becoming An Owl: Magical Consciousness,' in *Religion and the Subtle Body in Asia and the West: Between Mind and Body*, Eds. G. Samuel and J. Johnston, London: Routledge, 211–23.
Hall, M. P. (1988 [1928]) *The Secret Teachings of All Ages: An Encyclopedic Outline of Masonic, Hermetic, Qabbalistic and Rosicrucian Symbolical Philosophy: Being an Interpretation of the Secret Teachings Concealed Within the Rituals, Allegories and Mysteries of All Ages*, Los Angeles: The Philosophical Research Society.
Harner, M (1990 [1980]) *The Way of the Shaman*, New York: Harper and Row.
Harvey, G. (2007) *Listening People Speaking Earth: Contemporary Paganism*, London: Hurst & Company.
Hay, L. L. (1988 [1984]) *You Can Heal Your Life*, Concord: Specialist Publications.
Heelas, P. (2008) *Spiritualities of Life: New Age Romanticism and Consumptive Capitalism*, Malden and Oxford: Blackwell.
Howes, D. Ed. (2009) *The Sixth Sense Reader*, Oxford and New York: Berg.
Ingerman, S. (1991) *Soul Retrieval: Mending the Fragmented Self*, New York: Harper Collins.
Johnston, J. (2008) *Angels of Desire: Esoteric Bodies, Aesthetics and Ethics*, Gnostica Series, London and Oakville: Equinox.
——(2010) 'Physiognomy of the Invisible: Ritual, Subtle Anatomy and Ethics' in *Ritual Dynamics and the Science of Ritual: Body, Performance, Agency, Experience*, vol. IV. Eds. J. Weinhold and G. Samuel, 351–59.
——(2011) 'Reading the Body Invisible: Subtle Bodies, Astrology and Energetic Healing,' in *Astrologies: Plurality and Diversity*, Eds. N. Champion and L. Greene, Ceredigion: Sophia Centre Press, 201–16.
——and R. Barcan (2006) 'Subtle Transformations: Imagining the Body in Alternative Health Practices' *International Journal of Cultural Studies* 9.1: 25–44.
Judith, A. (1987) *Wheels of Life: A User's Guide to the Chakra System*, St Paul: Llewellyn.
——(1996) *Eastern Body, Western Mind: Psychology and the Chakra System as a Path to the Self*, Berkeley: Celestial Arts.
Kenton, W. (1974) *Astrology: The Celestial Mirror*, London: Thames and Hudson.
La Vey, A. (1969) *The Satanic Bible*. New York: Avon Books.
Lockhardt, M. (2010) *The Subtle Energy Body: The Complete Guide*, Rochester: Inner Traditions.
Lurker, M. (2004 [1987]) *The Routledge Dictionary of Gods, Goddesses, Deities and Demons*, London: Routledge.
Moore, T. (1990) *The Planets Within: The Astrological Psychology of Marsilio Ficino*, Hudson NY: Lindisfarne Press, 2d Ed.
Myss, C. (1997) *Anatomy of the Spirit: The Seven Stages of Power and Healing*. New York: Bantam.

Noontil, A. (1994) *The Body is the Barometer of the Soul So Be Your Own Doctor II*, Nunawading: self-published.
Northrup, C. (2003) *Women's Bodies, Women's Wisdom: Healing Cards*, Carlsbad: Hay House.
Purce, J. (1997 [1974]) *The Mystic Spiral: Journey of the Soul*, London: Thames and Hudson.
Rescher, N (1996) *Process Metaphysics: An Introduction to Process Philosophy*, Albany: State University of New York Press.
Samuel, G. and J. Johnston (2013) *Religion and the Subtle Body in Asia and the West: Between Mind and Body*, London: Routledge.
Scully, N. (2001) *Power Animal Meditations*, Rochester: Inner Traditions.
Urban, H. (2003) *Tantra: Sex, Secrecy, Politics, and Power in the Study of Religion*, Berkeley: University of California Press,
——(2006) *Magia Sexualis: Sex, Magic and Liberation in Modern Western Esotericism*, Berkeley: University of California Press.
Virtue, D. (1998) *Divine Guidance: How to Have a Dialogue with God and Your Guardian Angels*, Los Angeles: Renaissance Books.
——(2010) *Archangel Raphael Healing Oracle Cards*, Carlsbad: Hay House.
White, D. G. (1996) *The Alchemical Body: Siddha Traditions in Medieval India*, Chicago: The University of Chicago Press.
Yates, F. (2001 [1979]) *The Occult Philosophy in the Elizabethan Age*, London and New York: Routledge.

CHAPTER SIXTY-SIX

DRUGS AND THE OCCULT

Dan Merkur

In 1829, Eusèbe Salverte published *Des Sciences Occultes*. An English translation appeared in 1846. A lawyer by profession, Salverte adduced the evidence of the classics, Eastern religions, and ethnography. He argued that alleged prodigies and miracles should not be dismissed as fictions when their improbability could be shown to be merely apparent. Salverte devoted a full chapter to the use of psychoactive drugs in occult initiations, including, for example, the Eleusinian Mysteries. He cited evidence of drugs that were unidentifiable, but he also specifically named opiates, belladonna, datura, and cannabis (1846: II, 3, 6, 10–12). The following chapter, dealing with perfumes in sorcery, again documented unidentifiable drugs, together with hemp, henbane, and belladona (pp. 37, 38). Salverte also proposed that the witches' sabbat occurred, not in the flesh, but as the content of dreams induced by opium, henbane, solanum and other drugs in witches' ointments (pp. 42–46). Interestingly, Salverte mentioned in passing, much earlier in his book, that 'bearded darnel,' mixed with wheat, produces a bread that 'occasions violent giddiness' (1846: I, 79); he referred presumably to darnel infested with ergot, which is psychedelic.

Salverte's candid discussion of the role of drugs in sorcery and magic was part of the European encounter with the East, which had brought hashish and opium to the attention of Western literati (Hayter 1968; Mickel 1969; Boon 2002). The use of marijuana, chiefly in the form of hashish, spread from India through Islam in the high Middle Ages (Rosenthal 1971) and presumably reached Europe in the thirteenth or fourteenth century. François Rabelais (1999: 401–12) famously devoted four chapters to 'the herb Pantagruelion,' which he likened to hemp (p. 402), described as though it were hemp (p. 402), but named for 'its virtues and special properties' (p. 407). Hemp seems otherwise to have been unimportant in European letters until 1809, when Silvestre de Sacy connected hashish with the legend of Hasan-i Sabbâh, the medieval founder of the Assassin sect. The linkage, which rests on an error in philology, was given wide currency by Alexandre Dumas, Gérard de Nerval, Baudelaire, Théophile Gautier, Moreau de Tours, and others (Mickel 1969: 57, 64). These writers are counted among the French Romantics. They were interested in Swedenborgianism or, more generally, in Neoplatonic philosophy (p. 70), and in their view, drugs provided access to spiritual realities.

A second trajectory of drugs in the occult began with the rehabilitation of witchcraft in the 1830s and 1840s, when secular historians first suggested that witches perpetuated pre-Christian paganism. Jules Michelet counted mandrake, datura, henbane, and belladonna as key ingredients of witches' ointments (Mickel 1969: 71). These atropine-bearing plants began to influence occultism in the decades that followed. The extent of witchcraft's earlier influence on European occultism remains unknown. Western esotericism was a learned practice, whereas witchcraft belonged to the lower classes. Drugs of choice overlapped; but to what extent did the two subcultures mix prior to the occult revival of the late nineteenth century? Niccolo Machiavelli's play *The Mandragola* bears witness to Renaissance theatregoers' ignorance of witches' knowledge about the plant. Machiavelli implicitly conformed to a conventional but mistaken reading of Genesis 20:14–23 in crediting it with promoting conception (Penman 1978: 27). Mandrake's magical use as an aphrodisiac was known to the biblical author (Rätsch 1997: 136–38), as also to European witches and, interestingly, Agrippa, but apparently not to Machiavelli and his Italian audiences.

In 'The Tale of the White Powder', Arthur Machen (2001), a late Victorian fantasy and horror writer who was also a member of the Hermetic Order of the Golden Dawn, imagined a mysterious pharmaceutical that transformed a man into 'a lover of pleasure, a careless and merry idler,' who hunted 'snug restaurants' and criticized 'fantastic dancing' (p. 198). In a matter of days, he grew incredibly fat and, still later, into 'two eyes of burning flame...in the midst of something as formless as my fear, the symbol and presence of all evil and all hideous corruption' (p. 204). He ended as 'a dark and putrid mass, seething with corruption and hideous rottenness, neither liquid nor solid, but melting and changing before our eyes, and bubbling with unctuous oily bubbles like boiling pitch' (p. 207). The transition from joy to formlessness was attributed, at the tale's end, to 'the powder from which the wine of the Sabbath, the *Vinum Sabbati*, was prepared' (p. 210).

Machen's allegorization of mystical oneness as a horrific physical formlessness made a horror story of occult ideas that Aleister Crowley developed differently in a short story titled 'The Drug.' The first person narrative speaks of a visit to a friend who shows him a secret alchemical laboratory and gives him an alchemical liquor to drink. 'I lifted the glass and drank. Its taste was subtle and sweet as a kiss is; an ecstasy woke in me for an instant. Then I sank down, out of things, into a rich red gloom that grew blacker and blacker. Meseems that much time passed; but who can measure the time of a consciousness that is but the negation of all things? Yet was I content in annihilation, and – as it seemed – at rest' (Crowley 2010: 79). The narrative continues with a considerable discussion of the visions and apperceptions that followed the phase of annihilation. Students of Islam will be aware, as Crowley was, that 'annihilation' translates the Arabic term *fana*, which designates the consummate mystical experience in Sufi tradition. Crowley was asserting that alchemists used a drug that precipitated mystical experiences.

Gustav Meyrink (1913), whose occult training included Masonic, Rosicrucian, and Theosophical influences, wrote a number of fantastic tales with drug motifs. In 'Petroleum, Petroleum,' he referred in passing to a man who 'made millions out of a lively trade in mescal, a new anaesthetic and social drug, whose preparation he had developed' (p. 46). In 'Bal Macabre,' he wrote of a club named 'Amanita,' whose patrons ate 'poison fungi, along with Veratrum album, the white Hellebore' (p. 168).

In 'Coagulum,' the protagonist blends together 'mandrake root, henbane, wax, spermaceti and – he shuddered in disgust – a child's corpse, rendered into a soup' (p. 178). In addition, 'gorse, nightshade, thorn-apple' are cast into the fire, providing smoke with a 'narcotic effect' (pp. 178–79). In his novel *The Angel of the West Window* (1927), Meyrink referred to two alchemical drugs. They are kept in 'two small ivory spheres, the one red and the other white' (p. 46). The color coding referenced the red king and white queen, or sun and moon, of the alchemical wedding. The white sphere and its powder do not play a role in the novel. The 'red ivory sphere' contains 'the royal powder, the "Red Lion",' which consists of 'flaky purple granules' (p. 180). It can be used to transform base metals into gold (p. 184), but when it is prepared as an incense (p. 233), it has a psychoactive effect. 'Inhaling the red smoke enables them to "step out" of their bodies and cross the threshold of death; there, through marriage with their female "other half", which in their earthly existence almost always remains hidden, they acquire unimaginable magical powers such as personal immortality as the wheel of birth comes to a standstill; in short, they achieve a kind of divine status which is denied other mortals as long as they are ignorant of the secret of the blue and red spheres' (p 231). Meyrink narrated two experiences of the red powder. After the first, the protagonist concluded from 'the mild headache and the slight feeling of nausea the noxious fumes had left' that he 'had taken opium or hashish' (pp. 233–36).

The wide variety of drugs in Meyrink's stories was consistent with the experimentation of several occultists of his period: Stanislas de Guaita and Edouard Dubus (Boon 2002: 51–52, 145), as well as Crowley (1922; Regardie 1968). Occultists continue to value drugs in visualization (Conway 1988: 81) but discourage their use in ceremonial magic.

> Drink, drugs, and sex can be used to produce a state of mingled exhaustion and exaltation in which the magician's powers are raised to their highest pitch, but it is essential that the magician does not indulge himself for pleasure, which would distract him from the necessary iron concentration on the business in hand, but with the clear and sole purpose of building up his magical energies. The force to be evoked may show itself by taking temporary possession of the magician or one of his assistants and [should] one of those present...be weakened to the point of exhaustion by drink, drugs, wounds and the ceremony itself...he can put up the least possible resistance to the invading force.
>
> (Cavendish 1967: 212)

In all, Salverte's *Sciences Occultes* seems to have inaugurated an era when occultists wrote candidly about several drugs, and references to alchemical elixirs and powders became increasingly transparent as drug references. Drug use in the occult prior to Salverte was generally more discrete.

AMBROSIA AND NECTAR IN THE RENAISSANCE

Several Renaissance esotericians referred to ambrosia and nectar, the food and drink of the Olympian gods in classical mythology. Marsilio Ficino, who inaugurated the Platonic-Hermetic revival of the Renaissance, discussed the consumption of ambrosia and nectar in language that implied a pagan communion.

> The perfect food of man is...God, with whose nectar and ambrosia human hunger and thirst are continuously aroused and increased till, at length, they are wonderfully and abundantly satisfied. Thus in Him alone does the highest pleasure coexist forever with the highest satisfaction.
>
> (Ficino 1978: 54–55; see also 1944: 79; 1994: 26, 107–8)

Ficino's disciple, Giovanni Pico della Mirandola wrote less guardedly about the psychoactive properties and significance of nectar. Like Plotinus (*Enneads* VI vii 35), Pico associated nectar with the Active Intellect, 'the fountain fullness of holy and inexpressible intelligence, whence the angels are drunken on their own nectar' (1965: 12). He made clear, however, that he referred to the practices of the pagan mysteries of antiquity.

> For what else is meant by the degrees of initiation that are customary in the secret rites of the Greeks?...Then lastly...came...a vision of divine things by means of the light of theology. Who does not seek to be initiated into such rites? Who does not set all human things at a lower value and, contemning the goods of fortune and neglecting the body, does not desire, while still continuing on earth, to become the drinking-companion of the gods; and, drunken with the nectar of eternity, to bestow the gift of immortality upon the mortal animal? Who does not wish to have breathed into him the Socratic frenzies sung by Plato in the *Phaedrus*, that by the oarlike movement of wings and feet he may quickly escape from here, that is, from this world where he is laid down as in an evil place, and be carried in speediest flight to the heavenly Jerusalem.
>
> (Pico 1965: 13)

Here, nectar was drunk by a person 'while still continuing on earth.' Its intoxication had the power 'to bestow the gift of immortality.' It produced 'the Socratic frenzies sung by Plato in the *Phaedrus*,' visions of the ascension to heaven.

Henricus Cornelius Agrippa von Nettesheim (1993: 652) referred only briefly and equivocally to nectar, but he asserted that it was available for human consumption: 'Now man is returned to God by prayers, by which coming he (saith *Plato* in Phaedrus) stops horses, and enters into the chambers of repose, where he feeds upon ambrosia, and drinks nectar.' Giordano Bruno, by contrast, candidly discussed the psychoactivity of nectar. 'Nectar...distorts and saddens our nature, and perturbs our imagination, making some gay and without purpose, others unrestrainedly happy, some superstitiously devout, others vainly heroic, others choleric, others builders of great castles in the air' (Bruno 1964a: 143–44). Bruno asserted that responsibility attended the privilege (pp. 145–46). 'He stops living according to the world of folly, of sensuality, of blindness and of illusion, and begins to live by the intellect; he lives the life of the gods, he feeds upon ambrosia and is drunk with nectar' (Bruno 1964b: 126).

The pagan context of ambrosia and nectar in Plotinus, Ficino, Pico, and Bruno suggests that they associated the psychoactive substances with classical paganism and not with Christianity. Something similar may be found in Francesco Colonna's *Hypnerotomachia Poliphili*, written in 1467 but not published until 1499. Using the literary convention of a dream, Colonna (1999: 12) presented fictionalized accounts of extraordinary visionary experiences. In the visionary world, nymphs have magic ointments that transform people into birds and asses (p. 86). The protagonist, Poliphilo, discovers to his surprise that the transformative ointment aroused him sexually (p. 86). Much later in the book, there is a sequence where a priestess plucks three fruits of a red rose bush that bears 'somewhat rounded fruits of marvellous fragrance that were white tinted with red' (p. 233). The fruits prove psychoactive.

> No sooner had I tasted the miraculous and sweet fruit than I felt my crude intellect renewed, my anxious heart revived in amorous joy...This caused even more amorous flames to burn incontinently within me, and I seemed to be transmuted with the sweeter torment of novel qualities of love. I began to know directly and actually to feel the graces of Venus...after the devout and sacred communion of the prophetic fruits, the divine plant disappeared.
>
> (p. 234)

Poliphilo is told that 'to pluck the roses was forbidden at the time, but the priests trafficked in them' (p. 237). The idea that forbidden fruits were clandestinely used by priests may be transferred, I suggest, from the visionary world to Renaissance Italy. Fruits with a related appearance are mentioned later in the book. The phrasing 'some with blood-red fruits and others still white' (p. 295) specifies plants that commence white and become blood-red as they mature. Several sentences later, reference is made to 'larches overgrown with fungi and agarics' (p. 295), possibly intimating a concern with *Amanita muscaria*, the fly agaric, which matures from white to increasingly red. Psychoactive mushrooms were occasionally portrayed in medieval church art (Irvin & Herer 2008; Rush 2011); *Amanita muscaria* sometimes appeared as the forbidden fruit of biblical Eden.

Like the *Hypnerotomachia Poliphili*, an erotic or pornographic work, *Comte de Gabalis* by N. de Montfaucon de Villars (1922) teaches the occult practice of human marriage to the sylphs, gnomes, nymphs, and salamanders of the visionary world. The text dates to 1670, and attributes access to the visionary world through 'the very Holy Medicine' (p. 29), 'the Holy Catholic Medicine (government of Solar Force)' (p. 30), or 'the Catholic Cabalistic Medicine' (p. 65). Like Colonna, Villars was addressing the aspect of spiritual alchemy that Meyrink associated with the red powder.

THE ANGELIC STONE IN ENGLISH ALCHEMY

An English alchemical manuscript, entitled 'The Epitome of the Treasure of all Welth,' was written in 1562 by 'Edwardus Generosus Anglicus Innominatus.' The text attributed an alchemical teaching to St Dunstan and maintained that he departed from the standard tripartite description of the philosophers' stone as animal, vegetable, and mineral, when he introduced the concept of a fourth and angelic stone that was 'preservative to the state of mans body.' The angelic stone was entheogenic: 'by this stone shall mans body be kept from corrupcion also he shal be endued with divine giftes & foreknowldge of things by dreams and revelations.' Although the angelic stone was invisible, it could be smelled and tasted. 'Therefore in St Dunstans worke itt is said that Solomon King David's sonne did call itt the foode of Angell, because a man may live a long time without any food having som taste of this stone' (Kassell, 2001, p. 364). The Bible called manna the bread or food of angels (Psalm 78:25), and a considerable series of Jewish and Christian commentators had secretly considered manna psychoactive (Merkur, 2000b). Here, in an early Elizabethan alchemical text, the angelic stone was psychoactive and identified with manna.

The motif of the angelical stone that was identical to manna may be traced in English alchemy for over two centuries. It occurs in the writings of Simon Forman, a London astrologer, magician, and alchemist of the late sixteenth and early seventeenth centuries (Kassell 2001: 354, 359, 364), and in the *Theatrum Chemicum Britannicum* (1652) of Elias Ashmole (see Merkur 1993, 2000a), where, for purposes of mystification, it is additionally called the red stone (Ashmole 1652: B2i). Robert Boyle adopted Ashmole's trope, stating that it was 'possible or lawfull...by the help of a red powder which is but corporeall and even an inanimate thing to acquire communion with incorporeal spirits' (Principe 1998: 312). Lastly, the essay on alchemy in Francis Barrett's *The Magus* (1801: 57) reverted to the motif of manna. Barrett asserted that 'the true *aqua vita*,' 'the celestial spiritual manna,' fills the alchemist with the grace of God and opens his spiritual and internal eye.

THE PAIRING OF PSYCHOACTIVES IN THE ALCHEMICAL WEDDING

In *Monas Hieroglyphica* (1564), the foundation text of spiritual alchemy, John Dee eliminated the role of the intellect and ideas (Paracelsian salt) and proposed that 'this whole magisterial work depends upon the Sun and the Moon' (Josten 1964: 165). If we interpolate the symbolism in Meyrink's *Angel of the West Window*, we arrive at the concept of a pairing of two types of psychoactives, the one color-coded red and the other white. The colors, which Dante's *Paradiso* had associated with positive and negative theologies, respectively, were also coded as solar and lunar. In an article on 'Spiritual Alchemy in *King Lear*,' I demonstrated that Lear's madness may be divided into two phases, the first associated with 'mildew' in 'white wheat' (*King Lear* II iv 112–15), and the second with a 'physic' (III iv 33), or Paracelsian preparation, that consisted of:

> ...rank fumiter and furrow-weeks,
> With hardocks, hemlock, nettles, cuckoo-flowers,
> Darnel, and all the idle weeds that grow
> In our sustaining corn.
>
> (IV iv 3–6)

Elizabethan writers discussed hemlock (*Conium maculatum*) as a poison (Byrd 1971: 15–16). It was also known as an ingredient in witches' flying ointments (Schleiffer 1979: 8, 15, 139, 142). In doses less than poisonous, hemlock produces delirium and excitement, and also works as a sedative (Rudgley 1993: 112). Thomas Cooper's *Thesaurus linguae Romanae & Britannicae* (1565) called *Lolium temulentum*: 'A vitious graine called ray or darnell, which commonly groweth among wheate. If it be eaten in hote breade it maketh the head giddie' (King 1968: 141). This Elizabethan entry was consistent with such European folknames as German *Taumellolch*, 'delirium grass,' French *ivraie*, 'inebriating,' and Spanish *borrachera*, 'drunkenness.' Witches' flying ointments sometimes contained darnel, as did occasional beers as late as the nineteenth century (Ott 1993: 155).

A simpler recipe for the alchemical marriage occurs as the final paragraph of Nicolas Flamel's *Exposition of the Hieroglyphicall Figures which he caused to bee painted upon an Arch in St. Innocents Church-yard*, which was first published in French in 1612; the English translation followed in 1624. Although Nicolas Flamel (d. 1417) was a historical person, the text is a pseudepigraphic fiction of the original Rosicrucian period. At my reading, the text is mostly concerned with metallic alchemy, but its final paragraph is notable in the present context for its mention of two plants: grain and poppy. Here is Flamel's highly coded statement.

> The *vermilion red* colour of this *flying Lyon*, like the pure & cleere *skarlet* in graine, which is of the true *Granadored*, demonstrates that it is now accomplished in all right and equality. And that shee is now like a Lyon, devouring every pure *mettallicke* nature, and changing it into her true substance, into true & pure *gold*; more fine then that of the *best mines*...Praised be *God* eternally, which hath given us grace to see this most fair & all-perfect *purple* colour; this pleasant colour of the *wilde poppy* of the *Rocke*, this *Tyrian*, sparkling and flaming colour, which is incapable of *Alteration* or *change*, over which the *heaven* it selfe, nor his *Zodiacke* can have no more domination nor power, whose bright shining rayes, that dazle the eyes, seeme as though they did communicate unto a man some supercoelestiall thing, making him (when he beholds and knowes it) to be astonisht, to tremble, and to be afraid at the same time.
>
> (Flamel 1994: 53)

Flamel conformed to the same symbol system that led Ashmole to identify the angelic stone with the red powder. Where, in metallic alchemy, pale green milky vapours, containing acids, attack metals, absorbing their colors, so that the Green Lion matures to become the Red Lion, so here where the motifs were appropriated for the purposes of spiritual alchemy, the alchemist who employs 'graine' or, more precisely, the ergot that infests grain, takes over the purple colouration of 'the wilde poppy,' resulting in a compromise that appears 'vermilion red' and is the 'true & pure gold' of the alchemical wedding. *King Lear* presented a different and more magical practice that substituted hemlock for opium. In both cases, psychedelics were paired with a deliriant or other non-psychedelic psychoactive, confronting the practitioner with a logical need to develop one or another philosophy of drug experience. The options ranged from mystical to magical.

Some of E. T. A. Hoffmann's fantasy fiction drew on related alchemical lore. His short story, 'The Golden Flower Pot' (1813), mentioned Gabalis (Hoffmann 1967: 66) and had a preparation of arrack (pp. 51, 67) induce otherworldly visions (pp. 52, 68–69) in which men marry salamanders. The novel *The Devil's Elixirs* (1816) concerns elixirs with which Satan had anciently tempted Saint Anthony. Among other reactions, a painter envisions 'all the pagan subjects he had ever painted...as living forms before his eyes' (p. 217). When he tries to paint Saint Rosalia Venus appears and he paints her 'looking at him with eyes full of voluptuous passion' that inflame him 'with wild, sensual lust' (p. 218). Opiates are mentioned in connection with a rape (p. 224), the physical equivalent of the vision. Two motifs imply an additional concern with ergot. Ergotism was called Saint Anthony's fire and there is a poisoned wine that causes death by eating or corroding flesh (Hoffmann 1963: pp. 69–70, 241–42, 250). The falling off of limbs is symptomatic of gangrenous ergotism.

REFERENCES AND FURTHER READING

Agrippa, H. C. (1993) *Three Books of Occult Philosophy*, trans. J. Freake, St. Paul, MN: Llewellyn.

Ashmole, E. ed. (1652) *Theatrum Chemicum Britannicum: Containing Severall Poeticall Pieces of our Famous English Philosophers, who have written the Hermetique Mysteries in their owne Ancient Language, Faithfully Collected into one Volume with Annotations thereon*, new intro. A. G. Debus, London, 1652; reprinted New York: Johnson Reprint, 1967.

Barrett, F. (1801) *The Magus, or Celestial Intelligencer; Being A Complete System of Occult Philosophy*, London: Lackington, Allen & Co.; reprinted York Beach, ME: Samuel Weiser, 2000.

Boon, M. (2002) *The Road of Excess: A History of Writers on Drugs*, Cambridge, MA & London: Harvard University Press.

Bruno, G. (1964a) *The Expulsion of the Triumphant Beast*, trans. A. D. Imerti, New Brunswick, NJ: Rutgers University Press.

——(1964b) *The Heroic Frenzies: A Translation, with Introduction and Notes*, trans. P. E. Memmo, Jr., Chapel Hill: University of North Carolina Press; reprinted Ann Arbor, MI: UMI Books on Demand, 2002.

Byrd, D. G. (1971) 'Weed Imagery in "King Lear",' *Antigonish Review*, 2(2): 14–26.

Cavendish, R. (1967) *The Black Arts*, London: Capricorn; reprinted New York: Penguin, 1983.

Colonna, F. (1999) *Hypnerotomachia Poliphili: The Strife of Love in a Dream*, trans. J. Godwin, New York: Thames & Hudson.

Conway, D. (1988) *Magic: An Occult Primer*, London: Aquarian.

Crowley, A. (1922) *The Diary of a Drug Fiend*, reprinted San Francisco, CA: Red Wheel/Weiser, 2010.

——(2010) *The Drug: and Other Stories*, ed. W. Breeze, London: Bibliophile.

Ficino, M. (1944) *Commentary on Plato's Symposium*, trans. S. R. Jayne, Columbia: University of Missouri.

——(1978) *The Letters of Marsilio Ficino, Vol. II*, London: Shepheard-Walwyn.

——(1994) *The Letters of Marsilio Ficino, Vol. 5: being a translation of* Liber VI, London: Shepheard-Walwyn.

Flamel, N. (1994) *His Exposition of the Hieroglypicall Figures* (1624), ed. L. Dixon, New York: Garland.

Hayter, A. (1968) *Opium and the Romantic Imagination*, Berkeley & Los Angeles: University of California Press.

Hoffmann, E. T. A (1963) *The Devil's Elixirs*, trans. R. Taylor, reprinted Richmond, UK: Oneworld, 2008.

——(1967) *The Best Tales of Hoffmann*, ed. E. F. Bleiler, New York: Dover.

Irvin, J. R., with Herer, J. (2008) *The Holy Mushroom: Evidence of Mushrooms in Judeo-Christianity*, Grand Terrace, CA: Gnostic Media.

Josten, C. H. (1964) 'A Translation of John Dee's "Monas Hieroglyphica" (Antwerp, 1564), with an Introduction and Annotations,' *Ambix*, 12:2–3, 83–221.

Kassell, L. (2001) '"The Food of Angels": Simon Forman's Alchemical Medicine.' In W. R. Newman and A. Grafton, eds., *Secrets of Nature: Astrology and Alchemy in Early Modern Europe*, Cambridge, MA & London: MIT Press.

King, T. J. (1968) '"Darnel" in "King Lear", IV.iv.5,' *Notes and Queries* NS, 15: 141.

Machen, A. (2001) *The Three Impostors: and other stories. Vol. 1 of the Best Weird Tales of Arthur Machen*, ed. S. T. Joshi, Hayward: Chaosium.

Merkur, D. (1993) *Gnosis: An Esoteric Tradition of Mystical Visions and Unions*, Albany: State University of New York Press.

——(2000a) 'Methodology and the Study of Western Spiritual Alchemy,' *Theosophical History*, 8:2, 53–70.

——(2000b) *The Mystery of Manna: The Psychedelic Sacrament of the Bible*, Rochester, VT: Park Street Press.

——(2002) 'Spiritual Alchemy in *King Lear*,' *Theosophical History* 8:10, 274–89.

Meyrink, G. (1913) *The Opal (and Other Stories)*, trans. M. Raraty, Sawtry, UK: Dedalus, 1994.

——(1927) *The Angel of the West Window*, trans. M. Mitchell, Sawtry, UK: Dedalus, 1991.

Mickel, Jr., E. J. (1969) *The Artificial Paradises in French Literature. I. The Influence of Opium and Hashish on the Literature of French Romanticism and* Les Fleurs du Mal, Chapel Hill: University of North Carolina Press.

Ott, J. (1993) *Pharmacotheon: Entheogenic Drugs, Their Plant Sources and History*, Kennewick, WA: Natural Products.

Penman, B. ed. (1978) *Five Italian Renaissance Comedies, Machiavelli: The Mandragola, Ariosto: Lena, Aretino: The Stablemaster, Gl'Intronati: The Deceived, Guarini: The Faithful Shepherd*, Harmondsworth: Penguin.

Pico della Mirandola, G. (1965) *On the Dignity of Man. On Being and the One. Heptalus*, trans. C. G. Wallis, P. J. W. Miller, and D. Carmichael, Indianapolis: Bobbs-Merrill.

Principe, L. M. (1998) *The Aspiring Adept: Robert Boyle and His Alchemical Quest, Including Boyle's 'Lost'* Dialogue on the Transmutation of Metals, Princeton, NJ: Princeton University Press.

Rabelais, F. (1991) *The Complete Works of François Rabelais*, trans. D. M. Frame, Berkeley: University of California Press.

Rätsch, C. (1997) *Plants of Love: The History of Aphrodisiacs and A Guide to Their Identification and Use*, Berkeley, CA: Ten Speed.

Regardie, I. (1968) *Roll Away the Stone: An Introduction to Aleister Crowley's Essays on the Psychology of Hashish, with the complete text of Aleister Crowley's The Herb Dangerous*, Saint Paul, MN: Llewellyn; reprinted North Hollywood, CA: Newcastle, 1994.

Rosenthal, F. (1971) *The Herb: Hashish Versus Medieval Muslim Society*, Leiden: E. J. Brill.

Rudgley, R. (1994) *Essential Substances: A Cultural History of Intoxicants in Society*, New York: Kodansha International.

Rush, J. A. (2011) *The Mushroom in Christian Art: The Identity of Jesus in the Development of Christianity*, Berkeley, CA: North Atlantic Books.

Salverte, E. (1846) *The Occult Sciences. The Philosophy of Magic, Prodigies and Apparent Miracles*, 2 vols., trans. & ed. Anthony Todd Thomson. London: Richard Bentley. (First French edition: *Des Sciences Occultes, ou, Essai sur la Magie, les Prodiges, et les Miracles.* Paris: Sëdillot, 1829).

Schleiffer, H. (1979) *Narcotic Plants of the Old World: An Anthology of Texts from Ancient Times to the Present.* Monticello, NY: Lubrecht & Cramer.

Villars, N. de Montfaucon de. (1922) *Comte de Gabalis* [Paris, 1670], trans. Lotus Dudley. New York: Macoy.

CHAPTER SIXTY-SEVEN

GENDER AND THE OCCULT

Jay Johnston

The consideration of gender as an aspect of occult discourse and practice is an essential, if complex, topic. Concepts of dimorphic gender (that is the existence of only two gender positions: male and female), ambiguous, hermaphroditic or 'deviant' gender positions are often a central feature of the discourse. For example Swedenborg's androgynous *homo* as representative and ideal of spiritual development, or Alastair Crowley's misogyny captured in expressions like: 'Man is the guardian of the Life of God; woman but a temporary expedient; a shrine indeed for the God, but not the God' (qtd in Urban 2006: 133). Yet, both the concept of gender and occult traditions themselves are not static entities and as scholarship on both develops – changing to reflect different socio-cultural bias, accommodate new historical 'finds,' theoretical frameworks and emergent groups – so too does both the history of occult belief and practice and the understanding of contemporary forms. Gender, like other critical concepts with which it is interwoven, including the body, subjectivity, race, and class, is an implicit element of this scholarship.

In this chapter gender is acknowledged as a contested term. As I have argued elsewhere (2013) the term has been used to denote various concepts: including women's subjectivity, identities that are understood as socially constructed and even reproductive biology. In general its current usage in contemporary critical discourses reflects an understanding of gender as designating a spectrum of possible identities and subject positions. In addition, the ontological foundation upon which such identities are built is considered the result of the mutual interrelation of both biological and socially constructed aspects of the self (2013: 411). Therefore, while acknowledging that at different times the term gender has been used to designate women, as a correlate of 'sex' or as a socio-cultural product differentiated from biological sex, it is not employed carrying those meanings or senses herein. Rather, it is understood as a critical concept, which designates numerous identities and ontologies, and further, that its conceptualisation is subject to specific socio-cultural and political contexts. Indeed, 'gender' intersects with conceptualizations of the body, power, spirit, soul, self, and identity in a myriad of ways.

This chapter identifies a series of approaches towards gender in occult thought via discussion of selected examples. It encapsulates discourses that explicitly tie sexual acts and/or different gendered identities to occult belief and practice. It also examines the way in which gender has (or has not) been a feature of scholarship on the occult, including how it also evidences a tendency to assume the 'I' of the scholar/researcher to be masculine, reflecting a long endured bias in western modes of reasoning that associated the male with consciousness and thinking and the female with body and nature (see Lloyd, 1993). The mind–body/spirit–matter dualism is a pervasive one in western epistemology, however, there is also much content amongst occult traditions that challenges and disrupts this binary logic.

As gender encompasses an embodied understanding of subjectivity, this chapter intersects with themes developed in the consideration of the occult body found elsewhere in this volume. Overall the emphasis in this chapter is on the perceived role of gender as a distinct part of the *practice* of occult traditions. Indeed, certain activities and types of knowledges are themselves gendered.

GENDER IDENTITY AS MAGICAL INGREDIENT

Occult discourse contains many examples in which a dimorphic concept of gender is employed in ritual practice. This includes traditions of alchemy, astrology, and sex magic. As illustrated in the examples below, gender can be understood in these traditions as reflecting set ontological positions that are inherently linked to broader metaphysical themes. That is, through the conceptual associations, a belief in only two gender positions existing – the male and the female – is 'naturalised,' collectively viewed as an implicit truth rather than a specific interpretation. Indeed, as these examples of alchemy and sex magic demonstrate, these two gender positions have been considered as polarities, the interaction of which is requisite for magical efficacy.

Gender within such frameworks is viewed as an implicit aspect of the universe and directly related to both the functions of lived individuals and their spiritual agency and development. Through the logic of correspondences (a typical esoteric form of reasoning) gender is thus attributable to, for example, plants, metals, planets; also activities as well as bodies and subjectivities. When interpreting the interaction of these aspects of the world, many occult traditions emphasize the gender attributes of the specific phenomena, and privilege heteronormative associations: this is the 'men are from Mars and women are from Venus' logic. Aside from the New Age relationship manual (Gray 1992) this phrase represents long-held gender ascriptions given to those particular celestial bodies and phenomena associated with them.

Rich and complex alchemical traditions have travelled across cultures from Antiquity to the present day. Contemporary manifestations include the psychologization of alchemy where the interactions or 'mixtures' of 'substances' are equated with psychological archetypes (Jungian) and interpretations of soul and spirit (see for example Myss 2004). Indeed, alchemy as an inner practice of spiritual refinement was strongly developed from the nineteenth century (Principe 2006: 13). Stressing the diversity of alchemy traditions, it can be noted that they usually incorporate a series of processes that 'destroys a base metal by eliminating its specific nature, and then infusing the remaining matter with a new, nobler essence' (Haage, 2006: 18). However, these metals are not considered as purely empirical substances, but rather have been associated with spiritual 'elements,' planets, and colors. Such associations carry with them the beliefs in ruling deities, magical efficacy, corresponding 'energetic' networks and indeed, gender ascriptions.

The production of a magical elixir, for example 'the philosopher's stone,' was often depicted during the seventeenth century as the outcome of a 'chemical wedding' between a King and Queen. Indeed, alchemical vessels were viewed as wombs in which the child of this encounter would gestate. This offspring was commonly conceptualized as a hermaphrodite (the 'resolution' of the meeting of the two polarized genders). Thus, prints from John Daniel Mylius's *Philosophia reformata* of 1622 depict this process of transmutation in a series of images which feature the King ('hot and dry') and Queen ('cold and wet') in the alchemical bed as the first part of the process. The resulting child of this union – philosopher's stone – is understood to reconcile these states (perceived as opposite) and is designated Mercury, which is considered like the 'Hermaphrodite' to possess both the nature of the alchemical male (King) and alchemical female (Queen).

Indeed, the process of their merging, a stage of alchemical transubstantiation in which they become the Hermaphrodite is depicted with them sharing one body with two heads. These heads are sometimes human (the King and Queen) and sometimes orbs of their associated celestial bodies, Sun (king) and Moon (queen). Thus the alchemical process was understood as the outcome of the meeting of gendered materialities (elements and celestial forces), their offspring attributed aspects associated with both and was thereby positioned as superior in a hierarchy of substance and sexuality. This illustrates a not uncommon positioning of the figure of the hermaphrodite as reconciling gender dimorphism as a sign of spiritual development (cf. Swedenborg). Such ideas have been carried into contemporary culture, for example the belief in 'sexless' spirit guides, their spiritual maturity signaled by their transcendence of the physical body. Or in channeling cultures the 'pairing' of a male spirit guide with a female channel; albeit this reproduces a male (spirit/consciousness) female (body/host) dualism (Brown 1997).

Sexual union as a magical practice has an equally diverse and cross-cultural heritage. Indeed. David Gordon White has published several volumes on *tantra* traditions including the consumption of sexual fluids associated with alchemical substances ('inner alchemy') in the Medieval Siddhu tradition (1998; 2006). The interpretation of such traditions in western contexts has provided a powerful fascination and influence for occult practitioners. The most notorious of these is Aleister Crowley (on tantric tradition in the west and occult sex magic traditions see Urban, 2003; 2006).

For Crowley, the sex act itself (between lovers of any gender, but he especially valorized male homosexual encounters) resulted in a mystical dissolution of self that generated and released magical force and power. As Urban summarizes, the erotic magician could: 'unleash the ultimate magical energy and subdue all of reality' (2006: 133). Indeed, the outcome of such practices for Crowley had the potential to generate a 'divine foetus,' not born of the 'defiled' flesh of woman, but purely out of spiritual power (Urban 2006: 133). The resulting being however was attributed a masculine gender. Such a child has clear parallels with the resulting 'child' (philosopher's stone) of alchemical traditions.

While a self-conscious, cultivated sensationalism accompanied Crowley's prescriptions for, especially debauched, ritual sex, they share an occult heritage in which a magical effect is realized via the meeting of polarized subjects, agencies, and actions; whether those polarities were dimorphic genders, spiritual (subtle) bodies, body fluids or two individual consciousnesses. For many (but not all) of these practices specifically gendered bodies were required to create the occult force, the 'magic' energy/manifestation. Crowley's promotion of sexual excess engendering magical efficacy was founded upon some very normative and conservative gender stereotypes, especially the degradation of women and the re-inscription of the deviant–normal binary.

Often, because of its association with the deviant, the occult itself has been sexualized: Viewed as something illicit, covert and pitched in a dyadic relation against the normal or orthodox. However, this simplistic binary relation should be questioned. Not least because as Partridge has so clearly demonstrated, much of the contemporary occult is far from covert (2004/5); but also, as developed in Foucauldian analysis, the belief which equates 'gender' with an individual's 'true' or 'inner' self is a modern development. The mapping of this idea onto the interpretation of occult and esoteric traditions, especially those utilizing sexual practices, metaphors or embodied ritual, needs to be closely scrutinized, especially for the way in which such positioning of discourse and interpretation reproduces the binary logic of normalized discourse (Johnston 2013).

GENDER AND OCCULT PRACTITIONERS: NORMATIVE ALLEGIANCE

That the male subject has historically been positioned as the scholar, the holder of knowledge, including what would now be designated occult knowledge, is reflected in dominant interpretations of the magician as male. This connotation also reflects broader class, gender, and socio-cultural restrictions placed on access to education in 'western' contexts. Hence Giordano Bruno writes on the opening page of his two essays on magic, in (the aptly titled) *On Magic*:

> First, the term 'magician' means a wise man; for example the trismegistes among the Egyptians, the druids among the Gauls, the gymnosophists among the Indians, the cabalists among the Hebrews, the magi among the Persians (who were followers of Zoroaster), the sophists among the Greeks and the wise men among the Latins.
>
> (1998: 105)

Bruno – for whom magic involved the manipulation of powers of attraction (and was thus intimately tied to the dynamics of eros) – refers here to a standard genealogy of esoteric knowledge that is perceived as a tradition of groups (including secret societies) and individuals who are bearers of initiatory and profound wisdom. This is a list from which any other gender subject, except the masculine, is commonly (although not always) excluded. As such, Bruno is emblematic of the scholar–occult–practitioner whose realm of knowledge includes those of 'natural magic' but necessarily excludes more dangerous forms of practice that would link them to heresy, demonic communion, and witchcraft. Infamously however, an association with heresy was not one that Bruno was able to avoid, being burned at the stake in 1600.

In considering the Renaissance tradition that Bruno inherited and was deemed to transgress, the operations of a gendering of epistemology and associated practices can be identified. Bruno inherited 'natural magic' traditions developed by Renaissance scholars such as Marsilio Ficino (1422–99) and Giovanni Pico Mirandola (1463–94), as have many modern and contemporary esoteric groups. As Zambelli (2007) argued, 'natural magic' developed in a socio-cultural context (in which religious belief was foundational and implicitly embedded) that required distinctions between different types of magic. This is what Zambelli demarcates as 'black' and 'white' magic, a binary that persists into contemporary times. The development of 'natural' magic needed to remain on the right side of the Church with regard to issues of the reaches of human agency and the capacity of human intelligence to understand divine creation. It was such a boundary that Bruno was charged with transgressing.

In order safely to continue their studies (which included various types of practice, for example Ficino's role as physician) they needed to clearly distinguish their thought and practice from that deemed demonic. Demonic magic was associated with invoking demons and transgressing sexual mores as well as species boundaries. Zambelli writes:

> Ficino and Giovanni Pico Mirandola were undoubtedly very different in culture and influence from the simple countrywomen accused of witchcraft. Nonetheless, these two scholars aimed at establishing a natural theory of magic urgently needed in a period when more and more witches were being burned at the stake. It is impossible to see all this as a mere coincidence. Only then could they return – without incurring too much danger – to their readings and hymns...
>
> (2007: 22)

Here, while noting the very significant factors that influenced the way that 'natural magic' was developed, especially its need to remain safe from charges of heresy and collusion with the demonic, Zambelli reproduces what have unfortunately become normalized gender attributions. Natural magic, the 'white magic' of the male scholar, is defined against the 'black magic' of the 'simple' (uneducated) country (uncultivated) woman. A very clear nature–culture binary. No doubt, as Zambelli notes, these were differing socio-cultural realms of life, and it is true that more women than men were killed as a result of the 'witchcraft craze' periods in Europe as a whole (Mitchell 2011: 175). However, the legacy of this cultural foundation for 'natural magic' is the continuing association of the masculine subject with a learned magical practice and women with a magical practice tied to romantic concepts of 'nature,' folk belief, and superstition. Not only this, but women's bodies were seen as more easily penetrated by demons; 'naturally' more susceptible to unruly and evil possession (as association also characteristic of Spiritualism discussed below). This division between folk belief and superstition and occult/esoteric practice is an unfortunately enduring one – overly ripe for critique and rethinking.

Another gendered dualism sits at the heart of such conceptual formations; the feminized and less-valued *practice* (body) contra the masculinized and more respected *theory* (mind). This division has been employed by scholars to characterize different types of theurgic texts. Indeed, Garth Fowden has critiqued the historical division of Hermetic texts into 'technical' and 'philosophical' with the latter being considered more important to scholarship. Fowden argues such genre divisions impose an inappropriate framework that affects the interpretation and understanding of the traditions (1986).

Even at Hogwarts, the magical school of fictional wizard-student Harry Potter (created by J. K. Rowling) divination and herbalism were taught by female professors while potions and protection against the dark arts were taught by masculine subjects including the effeminate Quirinus Quirrell who 'rebirths' Lord Voldemort (with the one exception being the subject's usurpation by evil Dolores Jane Umbridge). Even the senior figure of Professor Minerva McGonagall is more closely associated with concepts of 'witchery' via her skill in transfiguration and her resulting form as a cat.

This leap in discussion from Renaissance 'high' culture to contemporary popular culture while enormous in socio-cultural difference is alarmingly similar with regards to epistemological gendering. Both evidence an association of the masculine with hermeneutic, learned magical 'arts' and the feminine with practical knowledges, including Herbology (taught by Pomona Sprout), Divination, and Transfiguration that aligns them with the environment or animal world as well as practices, such as mediumship and crystal-gazing in which their individual agency is suppressed or seen as unstable. Such examples demonstrate the interweaving of a normative male–female gender binary with both a practitioner's gender identity and also the types of knowledge they are considered able to possess. Ficino could interpret the 'book of nature' and the invisible, celestial relations between all things via a form of logic and reason (the 'law of correspondences'); witches of the period gained their special knowledge via collusion with the devil and 'unnatural' relations. The flaky and unimpressive Sybill Patricia Trelawney (distinctly a flower child, counter cultural stereotype) in the Harry Potter novels taught a feminized intuitive knowledge in Divination classes: a knowledge which was subject to ridicule and scorn by the student, including the more bookish – i.e. intellectual – Hermione Granger. It would seem the Renaissance gendering of magic remains alive in contemporary popular culture.

As I have argued elsewhere (2013: 412), what I find most disturbing regarding the men are magicians/women are witches trope is that the historical traditions upon which the gendered stereotypes have been constructed have not in themselves been subject to widespread scrutiny. Consideration needs to be paid to the degree that individuals and groups who challenge this normative gender ascription remain unseen in the historical record due to the biases of normative reportage. A few scholars however are undertaking such investigations, for example Elizabeth Pollard's continuing work on women's magical activity and its representation in Late Antiquity (2008) and the edited collection *Women's Agency and Rituals in Mixed and Female Masonic Orders* (Heidle and Snoek 2008).

This conceptual stereotype also misrepresents the central role men played in the development of contemporary Wicca, for example Gerald Gardner and Alex Sanders. It has also allowed women-only groups to claim knowledge forms like intuition as a particularly feminine epistemology, which, while trying to redress the devaluing of such epistemologies also implicitly reproduces a form of gender essentialism (for example see Stein 1995). Despite numerous challenges to such stereotypes – and histories that refute their simplistic claims – the women lack intellect and men lack intuition tropes remain resoundingly familiar. Further, these particularly gendered capacities direct engagement in occult practices.

Henrik Bogdan notes in his analysis of *Western Esotericism and Rituals of Initiation* that 'a common characteristic of secret societies is that they often (but not always) are restricted to a single sex' (2007: 37). Indeed, Bogdan references Mircea Eliade's claim that the desire for an individual to live more 'intensely' with the sacred is key to an engagement with secret societies; and that, further, this engagement is gender specific: 'sacrality peculiar to each of the two sexes' (qtd. 2007: 37). Here again, only two gender positions (male–female) are considered viable. That the 'spiritual' be specific to gender identity is not an uncommon proposition. The gender of demon and deity are read and interpreted through the same conceptual frameworks as the gender of occult practitioners, including the gendering of their specific activities and knowledges. The conceptualization of Gods, Goddesses, and spirits of all kinds can also work to reinforce gender stereotypes, or undermine them. Indeed the crossing of normative boundaries by some deities marks out their supernatural status, for example Loki in the Norse traditions who assumed the form of a mare and gave birth (*Loksenna* 23; 33. Orchard 2011).

RESISTANCE AND DEVIANCE: OCCULT PRACTICES, NORMATIVE CRITIQUE, AND GENDER AMBIGUITY

Just as some occult groups and beliefs have reinforced gender stereotypes (even those most intent on disrupting social mores), others have embraced agendas that challenge normative categories and expectations. In this final section a number of these groups will be exemplified. In addition, continuing the article's focus on *practice*, one example of an association of magical practice with ambiguous gender identity will also be explored.

The prominent role of women in occult movements like Spiritualism and the Theosophical Society has been well noted and examined (e.g. Braude 2001; Owen 2004; Galvan 2010; Dixon 2011). Part of the broad popular appeal of these groups has been understood to be the opportunities they gave women to take up senior positions in spiritual groups and religious organizations. Yet, as with channeling culture of the 1980s, some epistemological gender stereotypes were also reproduced. Women predominating as the channels for spirits reinforced the general attitude that the female was more susceptible to such spirit possession, because of their emotional and potentially hysterical natures. Even the spiritual masters for whom Blavatsky and Alice A. Bailey (Arcane School) acted as the amanuensis were gendered masculine (and tied to racial stereotypes). Yet, readings of these phenomena have also worked to view the spirit–channel relationship as outside of a binary male–female framework. For example Molly McGarry's study of Spiritualism from a queer perspectiv e (2008) emphasizes the way the movement disrupted and challenged gender binaries and explores its embodiment of sexual deviance.

Queer references a concept of gender identity that is multiple and unstable. That is, that one's identity is not fixed; nor does it derive from any type of binary (e.g. hetero–homo or male–female). As a mode of analysis it developed out of Lesbian and Gay critiques of post-structuralism (Jagose 1996: 3). However, its application in many academic disciplines and its employment as a definitional noun for specific identities has led to critiques of the term's usefulness and its ability to enact a 'deviant' step now that it has been embraced by academic discourse (see Hall and Jagose 2012).

As McGarry's work illustrates, the act of 'queering' religious studies discourses and of developing queer readings of spiritual phenomena and groups is underway in the academic study of religion. Occult practices are the site of such analysis and the practice of magic itself has been presented as particularly suited to such, due to its deviant socio-cultural positioning. This is clearly exemplified in contemporary readings of Norse paganism.

Scholars of Old Norse religion have long debated the ambiguous nature of the divine pantheon (albeit the textual sources upon which they base their analysis have been filtered through the prism of Christianity). The Norse Gods are admixtures of good and bad; benevolence and malevolence. Many of the Gods and Goddesses were noted for their capacity to cross ontological boundaries and for their sexual prowess and exploits. As already mentioned, Loki was particularly adept at shape-shifting and changing gender ascription (see *Loksenna* in trans. Orchard 2011). Recently more substantial attention has been paid to the representation of magical practice in the Eddic and Saga literature and its interrelationship with gender (e.g. Mitchell 2011) and this is equally true of scholarship on its representation and practice in contemporary North European paganism (Blain 2002).

Seiðr is the crux of the issue in terms of magic. As a form of magical practice it was associated in the textual evidence with female practitioners. In fact, citing etymological precedents, Heide argues it was about 'spinning a mind emissary, or attracting things or doing other things with such an emissary' (2006: 164). Spinning designated a particularly female task. As a practice *seiðr* is understood as a form of sorcery, one which involves altered states of consciousness, elicits the capacity to prophesy, and the practitioner has the capacity to send out aspects of themselves in another form, including animal, to do their bidding (the influence of Sami traditions is also featured in contemporary scholarship, for example Dubois 1999; Hedeager 2011; Schnurbein 2003).

However, although the textual sources depict *seiðr* as a predominantly female undertaking, they also present Odin as particularly adept at it (Solli 2008: 194). This presents – at least to contemporary scholars' eyes – a paradox, detailed by Brit Solli as follows:

> Odin was also the master of *seid* (sorcery). The knowledge of *seid* came from gods called *vanir*, and *seid* was considered to be an activity carried out by women....Odin knew this art well. He could foresee the future and know the destiny of people and things yet to happen. He could also cast spells and cause people's death, and he could both take away and procure wisdom. He also could cure disease. However, the art of *seid* was associated with so much *unmanliness* (in Old Norse *ergi*) that men could not practice it without shame. As a god Odin thus constitutes a paradox: He is the *manliest* god of warriors, but he is also the *unmanly* master of *seid*.
>
> (2012: 194–95)

Thus a God associated with skill in battle was also associated with a designated effeminate practice. Considering this relation via a contemporary concept of masculinity this tension is indeed hard to resolve. Similarly Mitchell argues that such a gender association with the practice of *seiðr* was operative in Viking-Age culture:

'That this distinction was operative appears to be borne out by the fact that, among the many male practitioners of magic to be found in medieval Icelandic literature, male witches are overwhelmingly portrayed as villainous characters set in opposition to the hero, generally a Christianizing king or a dowdy native son, rather than as dabblers in love magic and so on' (2011: 190).

Jenny Blain (2002) examines the way in which these associations have been incorporated into contemporary shamanism and Northern European Paganism. In particular she emphasizes that the ritual practices undertaken have a fluid ontological basis, with practitioners slipping across identities and species, and as such 'conventional labels of "gay" and "straight" need not apply.' Therefore *seiðr* can be viewed as queer in a very productive way, rather than in any derisory association. In particular her examination of a range of possible interpretations for the term *ergi* alights upon the vulnerable state that the *seiðr* practitioner enters, understood as a form of deep trance (2002: 139–40). In such a state the practitioner would seemingly become passive (although it is entirely likely that they are in active relation with the spirits) and unable to defend themselves. Such a passive state would not be necessarily at odds with conceptualizations of the feminine, but it would sit uneasily with a (reductive) understanding of masculinity that was tied to activity and especially violent activity. Thus *seiðr* practitioners were deemed *ergi* due to the state of consciousness evoked by the practice and its contrast to other forms of gathering knowledge and effecting social change. From such a perspective Blain records the reclaiming of the term to posit non-binary and fluid subject positions (albeit her description starts from that framework):

> Men and women who engage with seiðr [sic] today are shaping their own understandings of *ergi* as they deal actively with discourses of gender and sexuality, positioning themselves as active agents of change as they seek to understand their own worlds. Some are actively attempting to reclaim the term to describe themselves, their practice, their philosophy. Seiðr therefore is political practice, and 'queer' practice, existing within gendered political dimensions today.
>
> (2002: 141)

The repetition of the term 'active' in this quotation highlights that this is not only a reclamation of a term laden with derisory gender connotations, but a practice that constructs occult practitioners' personal identities, and that this is *both* a personal and political undertaking.

CONCLUSION

As this reductive and short foray into the intertwining of gender and occult practice has sought to illustrate, it is easy to find examples in occult discourse and practice that reproduce the esoteric–exoteric, occult–orthodox binary. Yet, contemporary scholarship has resoundingly undermined such a straightforward binary via its close examination of practice. For example Partridge has drawn attention to the very public and popular aspect of contemporary occultism (2004/5). Similarly, it is also not difficult to find examples where the often assumed 'deviant' occult practices actually reproduce and reinforce dominant gender stereotypes.

Occult traditions utilize concepts of gender in the understanding of magical efficacy (for example the meeting of two gendered polarities which either result in a requisite 'balance' or produce a desired 'synthesis' as part of a magical process) and it utilizes gender to understand the capacities of specific occult practitioners and metaphysical agents. Whether highlighted or not, gender is implicit in occult practices from antiquity to the contemporary world.

Scholarship of this implicit association can continue to grow in myriad ways including increased scrutiny of the political nature of gendering in occult practices and their attendant epistemologies. Further, the taint of sexual deviance that often accompanies the occult in western discourse (as a discrete body of knowledge – although that could be usefully contested) is also well overdue critical analysis. This includes its positioning – including by scholars in the field – in a binary relationship with other fields of academic knowledge. The occult is so easily 'othered,' so often read as inherently deviant (with an accompanying sexualization of its discourses and practices). Considering developments in gender theory, particularly with regard to fluid identity positions, the potential to disrupt this implicit 'othering' of the occult is now front and center for contemporary scholarship in the field. Gender and the occult are not two elements joined together; but mutually constituting discourses and practices.

REFERENCES AND FURTHER READING

Anon (n.d. [2011]) *The Elder Edda: A Book of Viking Lore*. Trans. A. Orchard. London: Penguin.

Blain, J. (2002) *Nine Worlds of Seid-Magic: Ecstasy and Neo-Shamanism in North European Paganism*. London and New York: Routledge.

Bogdan, H. (2007) *Western Esotericism and Rituals of Initiation*. Albany: State University of New York Press.

Braude, A. (2001) *Radical Spirits: Spiritualism and Women's Rights in Nineteenth Century America*. Bloomington: Indiana University Press.

Brown, M. F. (1997) *The Channeling Zone: American Spirituality in an Anxious Age*. Cambridge: Cambridge University Press.

Bruno, G. (1998) *Essays on Magic* [c 1588], Trans. and Ed. R. J. Blackwell. Cambridge: Cambridge University Press.

Dixon, J. (2001) *Divine Feminine: Theosophy and Feminism in England*. Baltimore: Johns Hopkins University Press.

Dubois, T. A. (1999) *Nordic Religions in the Viking Age*. Philadelphia: Univeristy of Pennsylvania Press.

Fowden, G. (1986) *The Egyptian Hermes: A Historical Approach to the Late Pagan Mind*. Princeton: Princeton University Press.

Galvan, J. (2010) *The Sympathetic Medium: Feminine Channeling the Occult and Communication Technologies, 1859–1919*. Ithaca: Cornell University Press.

Gray, J. (1992) *Men Are From Mars, Women Are From Venus: The Classic Guide to Understanding the Opposite Sex*. New York: Harper Collins.

Haage, B. D. (2006) 'Alchemy II: Antiquity – 12th century,' in *Dictionary of Gnosis and Western Esotericism*, Ed. W. J. Hanegraaff, Leiden and Boston: Brill, 16–34.

Hall, D. E. and A. Jagose Eds. (2012) *The Routledge Queer Studies Reader*. London and New York: Routledge.

Hedeager, L. (2011) *Iron Age Myth and Materiality: An Archaeology of Scandinavia* AD *400–1000*. London: Routledge.

Heide, E. (2006) 'Spinning *Seiðr*,' in *Old Norse Religion in Long-Term Perspective*, Eds. A. Adren, K. Jennbert, and C. Raudvere. Lund: Nordic Academic Press, 164–70.

Heidle, A. and J. A. M. Snoek, Eds (2008) *Women's Agency and Rituals in Mixed and Female Masonic Orders*. Leiden: Brill.

Jagose, A. (1996) *Queer Theory: An Introduction*. New York: New York University Press.

Johnston, J. (2013) 'A Deliciously Troubling Duo: Gender and Esotericism,' in *Contemporary Esotericism*. Eds E. Asprem and K. Granholm, London: Equinox, 410–25.

Lloyd, G. (1993 [1984]) *The Man of Reason: 'Male' and 'Female' in Western Philosophy*. London: Routledge.

Mitchell, S. A. (2011) *Witchcraft and Magic in the Nordic Middle Ages*. Philadelphia: University of Pennsylvania Press.

McGarry, M. (2008) *Ghosts of Futures Past: Spiritualism and the Cultural Politics of Nineteenth-Century America*. Berkeley: University of California Press.

Myss, C. (2004) *Fundamentals of Spiritual Alchemy*. Carlsbad CA: Hay House.

Orchard, A. Trans. (2011) *The Elder Edda: A Book of Viking Lore*. London: Penguin.

Owen, A. (2004) *The Darkened Room: Women, Power, and Spiritualism in Late Victorian England*. Chicago: University of Chicago Press.

Partridge, C. (2004/5) *The Re-enchantment of the West: Alternative Spiritualities, Sacralization, Popular Culture and the Occult*, 2 vols. London: T. &T. Clark International.

Pollard, E. (2008) 'Witch-crafting in Greco-Roman Art,' *Classical World*, volume 102, no. 1, 49–64.

Principe, L. M. (2006) 'Alchemy: Introduction,' in *Dictionary of Gnosis and Western Esotericism*, Ed. W. J. Hanegraaff, Leiden and Boston: Brill, 12–16.

Schnurbein, S. v. (2003) 'Shamanism in the Old Norse Tradition: A Theory Between Ideological Camps.' *History of Religions*, volume 43, no. 2, 116–38.

Solli, Brit (2008) 'Queering the Cosmology of the Vikings: A Queer Analysis of the Cult of Odin and "Holy White Stones",' *Journal of Homosexuality*, volume 54, no. 1–2, 192–208.

Stein, D. (1995) *Women's Psychic Lives*. St Paul, MN: Llewellyn.

Urban, H. (2006) *Magia Sexualis: Sex, Magic and Liberation in Modern Western Esotericism*. Los Angeles: University of California Press.

——(2003) *Tantra: Sex, Secrecy and Politics, and Power in the Study of Religion*. Los Angeles: University of California Press.

White, D. G. (1996) *The Alchemical Body: Siddha Traditions in Medieval India*. Chicago: University of Chicago Press

——(2006) *Kiss of the Yogini: Tantric Sex in Its South Asian Contexts*. Chicago: University of Chicago Press.

Zambelli, P. (2007) *White Magic, Black Magic in the European Renaissance*. Leiden and Boston: Brill.

CHAPTER SIXTY-EIGHT

CRIME, MORAL PANIC, AND THE OCCULT

Jeffrey S. Victor

INTRODUCTION

This chapter offers readers a way of understanding how false accusations of crime may be attributed to people who hold socially unpopular religious beliefs, such as those associated with 'the occult.' (In the United States, examples include Spiritualists, Pagans, Satanists, and Santerians.) The chapter first presents an explanation of the unusual social phenomenon of a moral panic. Then, it offers research findings about the satanic cult moral panic, as an example of a recent worldwide moral panic. The chapter presents a summary of false clues, 'red herrings,' which can mislead criminal investigators during a moral panic, resulting in convictions of innocent people. It explains how innocent people can easily be convicted of horrendous crimes, such as incest, child abuse, and murder. Finally, the chapter offers an application to the famous case of the West Memphis Three.

CHARACTERISTICS OF A MORAL PANIC

The term 'moral panic' was coined by British sociologist Stanley Cohen (1972) in a study of British public reaction to the deviant behavior of the 'mods' and 'rockers' youth. Cohen used the term to identify a form of collective behavior characterized by widely circulating rumor stories disseminated by the mass media, which exaggerates the threat posed by a type of moral deviants. Goode and Ben-Yehuda (1994) refined the concept a bit further. They suggested that a moral panic is a form of collective behavior characterized by: (1) suddenly increased concern and hostility in a significant segment of a society; (2) in reaction to widespread beliefs about a newly perceived threat from moral deviants; (3) however, careful, empirical examination at a later time reveals that the perceived threat was greatly exaggerated or even nonexistent. Local rumor-panics may occur in reaction to belief in the threat. However, the motivational dimension of a moral panic is belief, not emotion. The main observable behavior during a moral panic is the communication of claims, accusations, and rumors.

The past offers numerous examples of moral panics during which widespread, fearful rumors and accusations about dangerous deviants resulted in false accusations of crime against many innocent people. In some cases, the widely feared deviants are products of ethnic, racial, or religious stereotypes. Members of unpopular religions may certainly become targets. Jews, for example, were targets of widespread panics and mass murders during the Middle Ages, and even later, in response to stereotypes spread by belief in the 'blood libel.' In some cases, the deviants are creations of pure imagination. The classic example is the European witch-hunt, during which perhaps over one hundred thousand people were executed, because they were believed to possess evil magical powers. In still other cases, the deviants are stereotypes of members of groups that are widely believed to be a political threat in a society. An example is the anti-Communist 'Red Scare' in the U.S. of the 1950s, during which many thousands of Americans were labeled as subversives and lost their jobs. The satanic cult rumor panics offer an example relevant to the practice of occult religions. These moral panics erupted in many countries beginning in the early 1980s, and then gradually diminished during the mid-1990s. However, the rumors and accusations of satanic cult crime have continued sporadically until the present time. (For a recent U.S. case, see Caron, 2011.) They will continue well into the future, as long as there are large numbers of people who believe that an evil supernatural entity has human co-conspirators.

THE MORAL PANIC ABOUT SATANIC CULTS CRIME

Focusing on the Claims-makers

Exaggerated claims-making about deviants is central to understanding moral panics. Therefore, the sociological study of moral panics and deviant behavior focuses upon an analysis of the claims-making process (Victor, 1998a). The content of claims about deviance may include matters such as stereotypes of deviants, typologies of deviants, and descriptions of the dangers caused by deviants. (It is important to keep in mind that a social 'deviant' is a socially constructed definition.) Sociological research and analysis focuses upon the claims-makers, rather than the targets of their claims. It focuses on the rhetoric and propaganda of the claims-makers, their vested interests, and their authority and power.

Content of the Claims

A wide variety of crimes have been claimed to have been committed by secret satanic cults, including ritual murder, and ritual child sexual abuse (hereafter abbreviated as SRA). Most claims made about satanic ritual abuse assert that there exist secret, criminal organizations, which commit horrible crimes against children, motivated by worship of Satan. Some claims assert the existence of an international conspiratorial network. Less extreme versions assert that the secret networks consist only of intergenerational family clans. Ritual torture and sexual abuse of children is done supposedly to 'program' children to reverse good and evil. The purported aim is to 'brainwash' children into the ideology of Satan worship. In their Satan-worshipping rituals, these criminals supposedly sometimes kill and sacrifice infants born to impregnated 'breeders' and commit cannibalism with the body parts. Some claims-makers even assert that satanic cults kidnap runaway youth for ritual sacrifice, commit random murders of indigent people, and engage in the criminal businesses of child pornography, forced prostitution, and drug dealing. According to the claims-makers, these criminals are able to maintain their secrecy and avoid detection, because satanists have infiltrated all the institutions of society.

There is no research on the precise number of people who have made accusations of SRA against their parents, or childcare workers and others in the United States. There is also no precise count of the number of criminal prosecutions. However, a random sample national survey of 2,272 clinical psychologists found almost 3,000 cases of SRA allegations. These psychologists reported seeing 1228 cases of adults who they defined as victims of SRA, and 1500 cases of children who they defined as victims of SRA (Bottoms, Shaver & Goodman, 1996). The actual numbers of SRA cases are much higher, because many thousands of psychotherapists are psychiatrists, clinical social workers, and diverse kinds of counselors.

Innocent People Convicted for Crimes

Hundreds of innocent people in the United States, and perhaps thousands worldwide, have been victimized by false accusations. Innocent people have been convicted for such crimes as incest, sexual child abuse, and even murder. Accusations of satanic cult crime have surfaced in many countries other than the United States, since the mid-1980s. The countries include: the United Kingdom, Canada, Australia, New Zealand, the Netherlands, Norway, and Sweden. Many SRA accusations have been taken to the criminal courts. One American national survey of district attorneys, social service workers and law enforcement agencies found that these agencies had dealt with 302 SRA cases of criminal accusations (Goodman et al., 1995).

A legal survey done by the American False Memory Syndrome Foundation involving criminal allegations of child sexual abuse based upon so-called 'recovered memories' offers useful information about accusations made by adults against their parents. A legal survey of 78 criminal cases done in September, 1996, found that in the United States from 1989 through early 1996, 47 cases (60 percent) involved adult allegations of ritual abuse (FMSF, personal communication, 9/96). By the early 1990s, many adult former psychotherapy patients had retracted their memories of SRA and filed malpractice lawsuits against their former therapists and hospitals. Another legal survey done by the False Memory Syndrome Foundation conducted on 59 civil lawsuits between 1991 and 1997 found 34 cases (57 percent) involved purported memories of SRA (FMSF Legal Survey, 1998).

No Evidence to Support Claims of Satanic Cult Crimes

The misleading clues to support these claims consist primarily of accusations made by hundreds of adult psychotherapy patients who report decades-old memories of ritual torture and sexual abuse by their parents, and similar accusations made by children against their parents or child care workers. The authorities making these claims include some psychotherapists, social workers, local law enforcement officials, fundamentalist clergy, and members of anti-cult organizations (Victor, 1994).

No law enforcement agency or research study has found any physical evidence to support claims about SRA. No one has turned up written or electronic communications, bank account records, meetings in process, members who can identify leaders, or any of the vast number of bodies of people supposedly murdered by satanic cults. Official government reports from several countries could find no evidence to support claims about SRA. These reports include those from the Department of Health of the United Kingdom (La Fontaine, 1994); from the Netherlands Ministry of Justice (1994); from the Behavioral Science Unit of the FBI (Lanning, 1992); and state agencies in Michigan (Michigan State Police, 1990), Virginia (Virginia State Crime Commission Task Force, 1991), and Washington (Parr, 1996). In addition, a national survey of psychotherapists could not find a single SRA accusation reported by the psychotherapists, where there was reliable evidence to corroborate SRA accusations from children or adults (Bottoms et al., 1996).

The Underlying Causes

Satanic cult rumor-panics illustrate sociologist I. W. Thomas' fundamental principle of social interaction: 'If people define situations as real, they are real in their consequences.' The underlying causes of the moral panic described here can be traced to a widespread belief in the existence of secret, criminal satanic cults among some segments of the population. Some authorities charged with detecting social deviance gave credibility to the rumor stories. Satanic cult rumors about evil, destructive forces are a metaphor for very real and increasing sources of stress in everyday life. Just as in past moral panics, the people most affected needed scapegoat evils to blame. Examples from the past include anti-Jewish pogroms in Europe and racist lynchings in the U.S. Satanic cult rumors were triggered by local anxieties about economic decline and the breakdown of stable family life.

RED HERRINGS: PROBLEMS IN CRIMINAL INVESTIGATIONS

Criminal investigators can be easily misled by false clues about a crime, unless they are familiar with what can happen during a moral panic. The following are some of the strange social and psychological phenomena that occurred, and continue to occur, during the moral panic about satanic cults that provided false clues to a crime.

Widespread Rumors

Rumours about satanic cult crimes led many authorities to conclude: 'Where there is smoke, there is fire.' The rumors were actually based upon stories from an historic and persistent legend that can be traced back to the middle ages and even to ancient times (Victor, 1993). These rumors were international in scope, so it was all too easy to conclude that there were international criminal organizations at work.

In reality, the rumors began in the United States and spread rapidly by various communication channels to Europe, particularly to those countries where English is the primary or secondary language, and where there are sizable fundamentalist Protestant groups (Victor, 1998a). The communication channels were the usual ones that convey new ideas across borders; newspapers, magazines, books, and even international conferences.

False Accusations

False accusations became common, because many authorities believed the rumors. Such accusations were a product of improper interviewing techniques with easily suggestible children, depressed patients in psychotherapy, and frightened people in police interrogations (Victor, 1996; Victor, 1998b). Many false accusations were given credibility by phony satanic cult 'experts' in identifying the signs of satanism. Many of these people, police, clergymen or psychotherapists, were believed to have special knowledge. In reality, they had well-publicized, money-making campaigns. In the United States alone, there were thousands of cases of false accusations, drawn from false memories.

False Memories

Perhaps the strangest false accusations are those that arise from false memories. False memories most commonly are prompted by incompetent techniques employed by psychotherapists, such as priming a suggestive patient, or by hypnosis or the use of 'truth' drugs (Victor, 1998b). False memories are also prompted by incompetent child care interviewers, especially in cases of alleged sexual abuse in child care centers. According to the records of the American False Memory Syndrome Foundation, a few cases of false memories of satanic cult ritual abuse prompted by incompetent psychotherapists continue to 2012 (available from www.fmsfonline.org). Many of these therapists have been sued in courts, have lost their licenses to practice and were required to pay millions of dollars in damages.

False Testimonials

During the satanic cult panic, many people came forth publically and testified, in books and on television talk shows, that they were members of satanic cults, or were ritually abused by satanic cults. Their claims expressed the stereotyped stories embedded in satanic cult rumors. Most likely, they were motivated by getting a moment of fame in the mass media, and in the hope of gaining lucrative book contracts. Some of these people have been noted in my book (Victor, 1993).

False Confessions

Psychological research has shown that false confessions can be elicited by intensive, rapid-fire interrogations, and that the false confessions may even come to be regarded by a subject as memories (Kassin and Kiechel, 1996). False confessions of satanic cult crimes occurred due to improper police interrogations, after lengthy and exhausting interviews, when frightened and suggestible people incriminated themselves. The most famous example is the case of Paul Ingram (Ofshe, 1992; Wright, 1994). In 1988, Ingram's two daughters and a son accused him and several other men of sexually abusing them in satanic cult rituals. After intensive interrogations, Ingram confessed to the sexual abuse, while following orders by Satan. Eventually, Ingram spent 14 years in prison.

Imitation of Rumors

This occurs when the actual criminals use supposed satanic cult symbols to distract police attention from them. This is a deliberate 'red herring.' The deliberate imitation of rumor stories to distract police is most likely to take place in locations where satanic cult rumors are in circulation and are widely believed. An example of a murder alleged to be committed by a satanic cult to distract police attention is offered by Ellis (2001).

The imitation of rumor stories is not unusual. Folklore scholars are well aware of the imitation of scary rumor stories by teenagers, who deliberately act out folklore legends or place false evidence, for pranks and entertainment. Folklorists call this behavior 'ostension.' It is not uncommon for teenagers to fabricate false evidence of satanic cult ritual sacrifices, as a hoax to scare local people in rural areas (Fine and Victor, 1994).

Teenage Group Delinquency

Teenage group delinquency occurs when groups of teenagers imitate satanic cult rumors and commit petty crimes, such as vandalism and defacing property with graffiti with supposed satanic symbolism (Fine and Victor, 1994; Victor, 1993, chapter 7). A few teenagers may even label themselves satanists, after cursory reading about the topic. As a result, local authorities may believe that there are satanic cults in the area.

Stereotyping

When rumors are circulating, local authorities sometimes stereotype unpopular, unconventional people, as being criminal satanists. Nothing in particular may get a person labeled as such. It could be wearing countercultural clothing (punk, Goth), or being a homosexual, or being a 'loner' in a rural area, or practicing an unusual religion. This is the danger of incompetent criminal profiling.

APPLICATION: THE CASE OF THE WEST MEMPHIS THREE

The case of the West Memphis Three provides an excellent illustration of how innocent people can be convicted of crimes during a moral panic. In 1994, three teenagers were convicted of the murders of three eight-year-old boys in West Memphis, Arkansas. The teenagers were Damien Echols (age 18), Jason Baldwin (age 16), and Jessie Misskelly (age 17). The case resulted in heated controversy and became the basis of several documentary films and books. Unfortunately, there is not enough space here to review all the details. (See Leveritt, 2002; Wikipedia, 2012a.)

The Social Demographics of West Memphis

West Memphis is a small town in a largely rural area, located across the Mississippi River from Memphis, Tennessee. According to a 2010 census data, the town had a population of 26,000 people; a very low average level of education, and a high proportion of people living below the poverty line. The area is solidly in the Bible Belt, a region of the U.S. dominated by fundamentalist Protestants and a socially conservative culture. (The Bible Belt is in huge area covering the Southern states across to Oklahoma in the west.) The relevance is that religious fundamentalists are particularly prone to believe in satanic cult rumors (Victor, 1994). Small town people also tend to be highly suspicious of non-conformists, as 'bad' people.

The Crime

The three murdered boys were found naked, hogtied hands to feet and stabbed with a knife numerous times. One boy was castrated. There was no evidence of anal rape. They were found in a stream bed in a wooded area.

Red Herrings

Allegations of Satanic Cult Crime

Immediately after the discovery of the murdered boys, the police concluded that the crime was committed by a satanic cult, even though there were no symbols marked on corpses, nor any graffiti symbols in the woods.

The police leaked allegations to the media asserting the crime was a satanic cult murder, inflaming local fears. Satanic cult rumors were circulating over nearby areas of the Bible Belt for many years. The tiny police department may have believed that they had a 'big' case on their hands.

Their preconception was confirmed by a pseudo-expert. At the trial, a well-known 'cult cop,' Dale Griffis, offered testimony that the crime was committed by a satanic cult. Griffis had testified in many cases as an expert in identifying signs of satanic cult activity. He has a phony doctorate from an unaccredited 'diploma mill' (Ricks, 1985) which was closed down in 2000 by the state of California for engaging in consumer fraud (Wikipedia, 2012b).

Stereotyping

When there are worries about dangerous criminals in an area, the people who are most likely to be prime suspects are those people stigmatized as social deviants, often for reasons totally unrelated to the crimes. That was certainly the situation for Damien Echols. He was previously arrested for shoplifting. He had been diagnosed with depression and spent several months in a psychiatric institution. He was a high school drop-out. He dressed in black and wore T-shirts showing weird-looking rock singers (heavy metal bands). He was the target of a wide variety of other malicious gossip. He was alleged to be interested in occult religion. His demeanor was arrogant and provocative in response to his unpopularity, like many unpopular teenagers. It was easy for police to believe that Echols was the ringleader of a satanic cult, as was alleged by the prosecutors at the trial.

Coerced Confession

After a long interrogation, perhaps 12 hours, Misskelly confessed to having committed the murder. He was a teenager with an IQ of 72, borderline retarded. Then, he quickly recanted his confession, claiming that he did so due to fear and intimidation. Eight months later, he confessed again, and implicated Echols and Baldwin as his accomplices. He claimed that Echols and Baldwin were members of a satanic cult. He was not a close friend of either one.

During the trial, Dr. Richard Ofshe, a social psychologist expert on interviewing techniques, testified that the confession was coerced, based upon hearing a tape of the interrogation.

False Accusations

A crucial false accusation came from Vicki Hutcheson, who testified under oath, that with police encouragement, she had attended a meeting of a witches' coven with Echols, where he bragged about killing the boys. Eleven years later, she told a reporter that her testimony was a 'total fabrication'; saying that it was made under police duress, after police threatened to take away her son (Hackler, 2004).

Eventual Release from Prison

There was a lack of any direct evidence against the three accused teenagers. There was no DNA evidence that they were at the scene of the murder. However, there was suppressed DNA evidence of someone else. The three were released in 2011. In an unusual legal agreement called an Alford plea, they asserted that they were innocent of the crime, but agreed that the prosecutors had enough evidence to convict them. The agreement enabled the prosecutors to avoid a civil lawsuit against them. They had spent 18 years in prison.

REFERENCES AND FURTHER READING

Bottoms, B. L., Shaver, P. R., and Goodman, G. S. (1996) 'An Analysis of Ritualistic and Religion-Related Child Abuse Allegations,' *Law and Human Behavior* 20:1, 1–34.

Caron, C. (2011) 'Therapist Brainwashed Woman into Believing She Was in Satanic Cult, Attorney Says,' *ABC News* (November 28).

Cohen, S. (1972) *Folk Devils and Moral Panics*. New York: St. Martin's Press.

Ellis, B. (2001) *Aliens, Ghosts, and Cults: Legends We Live By*. Jackson: University Press of Mississippi.

False Memory Syndrome Foundation (1996) personal communication.

——(1998) 'Data Excerpted from the FMSF Legal Survey, January 1998: Sample of Reports of Lawsuits Brought Against Mental Health Care Workers Alleging Creation of False Memory Syndrome Through the Use of Repressed Memory Therapy,' printed report.

Fine, G. A. and Victor, J. (1994) 'Satanic Tourism,' *Phi Delta Kappan* 76:1 (September), 70–72.

Goode, E. and Ben-Yehuda, N. (1994) *Moral Panics: The Social Construction of Deviance*. Cambridge: Blackwell.

Goodman, G., Qin, J., Bottoms, B., and Shaver, P. R. (1995) *Characteristics and Sources of Allegations of Ritualistic Child Abuse: Final Report to the National Center on Child Abuse and Neglect*. Washington, DC: National Center on Child Abuse and Neglect.

Hackler, T. (2004) 'Complete fabrication,' *Arkansas Times* (October 7).

Kassin, S. M. and Kiechel, K. L. (1996) 'The Social Psychology of False Confessions: Compliance, Internalization, and Confabulation,' *Psychological Science* 7:3, 125–28.

La Fontaine, J. S. (1994) *The Extent and Nature of Organized and Ritual Abuse: Research Findings*. United Kingdom Department of Health Report. London: HMSO Publications.

Lanning, K. V. (1992) *Investigator's Guide to Allegations of 'Ritual' Child Abuse*. National Center for the Analysis of Violent Crime, Quantico, VA: Federal Bureau of Investigation.

Leveritt, M. (2002) *Devil's Knot: The True Story of the West Memphis Three*. New York: Atria Books.

Michigan State Police (1990) *Michigan State Police Occult Survey*. East Lansing, MI: Michigan State Police Investigative Services Unit.

Netherlands Ministry of Justice (1994) *Report of the Working Group on Ritual Abuse*, trans. J. W. Nienhuys. Den Haag: Direction of Constitutional and Criminal Law.

Ofshe, R. (1992) 'Inadvertent Hypnosis During Interrogation: False Confession Due to Dissociative State; Mis-Identified Multiple Personality and the Satanic Cult Hypothesis,' *International Journal of Clinical and Experimental Hypnosis* 40:3 (July), 125–56.

Parr, L. E. (1996) *Repressed Memory Claims in the Crime Victims Compensation Program*. Olympia, WA: Department of Labor and Industries.

Ricks, S. (1985) 'Tiffin's 1-man Satan Squad Draws Fire,' *Cleveland Plain Dealer* (August 4), A6–A8.

Victor, J. S. (1993) *Satanic Panic: The Creation of a Contemporary Legend*. Chicago, IL: Open Court Press.

——(1994) 'Fundamentalist Religion and the Moral Crusade Against Satanism: The Social Construction of Deviance,' *Deviant Behavior* 15:3 (July), 305–34.

——(1996) 'How Should Stories of Satanic Cults be Understood?' *Harvard Mental Health Letter* 12:6 (Feb.), 8.

——(1998a) 'Moral Panics and the Social Construction of Deviant Behavior: A Theory and Application to the Case of Ritual Child Abuse,' *Sociological Perspectives* 41:3, 541–66.

——(1998b) 'Social Construction of Satanic Ritual Abuse and The Creation of False Memories,' in J. De Rivera & T. Sarbin, eds., *Believed-in Imaginings: The Narrative Construction of Reality*. Washington, DC: American Psychological Association, 191–216.

Virginia State Crime Commission Task Force (1991) *Final Report of the Task Force Studying Ritual Crime*. Richmond, VA: Virginia State Crime Commission.

Wikipedia (2012a) 'West Memphis Three'. Last modified on November 2, 2012.

——(2012b) 'Columbia Pacific University'. Last modified on October 16, 2012.

Wright, L. (1994) *Remembering Satan: A Case of Recovered Memory and the Shattering of an American Family*. Knopf: New York.

CHAPTER SIXTY-NINE

CONSPIRACY THEORIES AND THE OCCULT

Michael Barkun

It should be no surprise that occultism and conspiracy theories have connections and overlaps. Both, after all, deal with knowledge that believers think has been concealed and that they alone understand. There are differences, of course, in the type of knowledge; whether its concealment has been willful; and what benefits the possession of the knowledge confers on the possessor. Occult and esoteric knowledge is likely to concern basic issues that deal with human nature and the character of the universe. Concealment is unlikely to have been intentional and possession of the knowledge can often produce clear benefits in terms of either power or enlightenment. Conspiracy theories, on the other hand, are likely to deal with more mundane issues concerning the distribution of power and the nature of decision-making. In this case, the knowledge is often believed to have been intentionally hidden or withheld, and it is often unclear whether knowing it will prove beneficial. This is because believers in conspiracy theories may see themselves in an adversarial relationship with the evil power the theories describe. The theories may be seen as a means to awaken a slumbering public to danger, but it is not certain that the result will be victory over the enemy.

In addition to the comparisons just described, however, occultism and conspiracy theories do interact. Some examples have generated substantial literatures, such as the case of Nazism. That said, although one needs to treat the numerous melodramatic and sketchily documented accounts with some caution; it is clear, of course, that occultists did figure in the movement's antecedents and among clusters of its followers. However, it can be argued that esoteric Nazism is, generally speaking, a post–World War II creation, one of the products of which has been a myth projected back upon events of the 1930s and 1940s. The Nazis themselves, as scholars have demonstrated, were not quite the magicians, astrologers, or occultists that later mythmakers made them out to be (Goodrick-Clarke 2002; Strube 2012). In order to find substantial real world instances where the two forms of concealed knowledge actually interacted, it is useful first to construct a simple typology of interactions.

TYPES OF OCCULTIST–CONSPIRACIST INTERACTIONS

I want to begin by describing two pure types. In each there is an interaction between conspiracy theories and occultism, but they differ in the extent to which one or the other dominates. In one type, conspiracy believers are dominant and view occultism and occultists as part of the external world that they fear. In the other type, occultists are dominant and have, as it were, 'colonized' the domain of conspiracism.

The first kind of relationship – which I shall call Type I – occurs where adherents to a conspiracy theory believe that the evil power they seek to expose is occultist in whole or in part. Thus the evil cabal may be an alleged circle of witches, magicians, or other denizens of the occult realm who will supposedly use esoteric knowledge for malign ends. Alternatively, in a more moderate version, such figures may simply be part of a coalition through which a number of conspirators, some of whom may not be occultists, seek to gain power. Clearly, in this type, conspiracists dominate, since it is their worldview that identifies occultists as evil.

The second type of relationship – which I shall call Type II – occurs when those who hold a conspiracy theory are themselves believers in some form of occultism, whether or not they also attribute occultism to their putatively evil enemy. In the purest form of this type, the conspiracy theorist would be an occultist, while his/her imagined enemy would not be. In a less pure form, both the conspiracy theorists and the enemy would share attributes of occultism. Occultism dominates in this type, since it significantly defines the nature of the conspiracy theory involved.

One can never find cases in the real world that wholly reflect ideal types. However, in this instance, there are two real world instances that very closely approximate the two types just described. Type I was closely mirrored by the evangelical conspiracy theorist John Todd (1950–2007), whose bizarre campaign against an alleged occult conspiracy in the 1970s made him a minor celebrity among conservative Protestants, especially in the Midwest and lower Mississippi Valley. Todd was an obscure figure. The second person for examination is less so. For Type II, we need look no farther than David Icke (1952–), the prolific British conspiracy writer, whose views have metamorphosed to the point where he now espouses ideas of the sort described above.

TYPE I: THE STRANGE CAREER OF JOHN TODD

The man known variously as Kris Sarayn Kollyns, Kristopher S. Kollins, John Wayne Todd, and Johnnie W. Todd, will be referred to here as John Todd both for simplicity and because this appears to be the name he used most frequently during his days as a conspiracy theorist. Because of Todd's penchant for self-invention, if not outright deception, it is difficult to precisely trace his early life. He appears to have had his first contact with evangelicals in Phoenix, Arizona, in 1968, either through baptism or, as he often claimed, as someone seeking to escape from a life of 'witchcraft' (Noble 2010: 302). However, even after giving himself to Christ, he sometimes returned to Wiccan practice. This pattern of commitment and backsliding was to recur throughout much of his life. As he successively re-emerged from covens, the management of occult bookstores, and related activities, he regaled evangelical audiences with increasingly lurid tales of the world he had left behind. In churches from California to Maryland, Todd told shocked audiences that as someone who had seen witchcraft from the inside, he could now reveal the plans that the forces of evil were ready to implement (Rivera 2012; Barkun 2003: 55–57). In addition to his personal appearances in churches, he circulated audio cassettes of his lectures as well as an illustrated comic book-like pamphlet.

Todd's presentations began with what he claimed to be his family history, which he traced back to the witches of Salem, Massachusetts. He then told a remarkable story of his advance through the ranks of witchcraft until he was made a member of the 'Grand Druid Council of Thirteen' who 'only take orders from the Rothschilds.' This was part of an international hierarchy, he claimed, in which witchcraft overlapped the Illuminati. Indeed, he learned that 'we [i.e., witches] were the religion of a political organization called the Illuminati.' When a crime he committed during his army service threatened to earn him a long prison sentence, the intervention of 'a Senator, a Congressman, [and] a couple of Generals' earned him release and an honorable discharge. The witchcraft/Illuminati minions had infiltrated and taken control of a bewildering array of organizations – major banks, large corporations, non-governmental organizations (NGOs), even many Christian denominations, not to mention such obvious suspects as the Masons and the Anti-Defamation League (ADL). Despite Todd's inclusion of the ADL and the Rothschilds in his conspiracy, he staunchly denied any anti-Semitism (Collins 1977). By the time his presentation ended, his audience might well have felt that only they and he lay outside the conspiracy, so widely did its tentacles reach.

In addition to Todd's witchcraft/Illuminati conspiracy theory, he added a strange literary side note that has diffused widely on the radical right: namely, the claim that 'in the mid-1950's Philippe Rothschild ordered one of his mistresses...to undertake the writing of [a] code to the witches of the world' (Todd 2011). The alleged mistress was none other than the now fashionable Ayn Rand, and the supposed code was her doorstop of a novel, *Atlas Shrugged*. According to Todd, *Atlas Shrugged* 'is a step by step plan to take over the whole world by taking over the United States' (Todd 2012). Its intended readership was to be 'the occult and...the Illuminati,' and the latter were supposedly 'extremely mad' at the book's large sales to others. The intended readership allegedly tried to end publication but acquiesced in the novel's continued printing because it remained so lucrative (Todd 2012).

Todd claimed that there was a literally Satanic and occult hierarchy of incalculable power that reached into the highest levels of American politics, economics, and finance. It was also an international force with seemingly limitless ambitions. This cabal of witches and Druids had an eight-year plan 'for world takeover, ending in the December month of 1980.' At that time the Son of Lucifer would become ruler of the world (Collins 1977). For reasons that appear less than compelling, this prediction of imminent victory led Todd to exit the conspiracy. He ended his presentation by pleading for money in order to build a retreat on the West Coast of the United States for witches seeking to leave witchcraft (Collins 1977).

The electrifying effect of Todd's preaching can best be judged by the example of the community first called the 'Zarephath-Horeb' and later renamed the 'Covenant, Sword and Arm of the Lord.' Located in the Ozark Mountains of northern Arkansas, it was to become arguably the most heavily armed communal settlement in American history. Begun by evangelical Christians, the community eventually switched to the anti-Semitic theology of Christian Identity under its charismatic leader, James Ellison (Noble 2010; Barkun 1997: 192–93). However, early in its history, in the summer of 1978, the community anticipated an imminent day of destruction when God would visit his wrath on a sinful world. One of the community's principal teachers, Kerry Noble, who had secured a John Todd audiotape, played it when the promised destruction failed to take place. He listened to Todd's story of a looming occult conspiracy and shared the recording with others: 'our group embraced everything Todd preached. He seemed to confirm all that we felt was wrong in this country, as well as what we believed would happen in the future. He explained the source of our problems' (Noble 2010: 77). Noble bought and read Rand's *Atlas Shrugged*, since Todd told him it was the coded message of the Illuminati. He bought all the rest of Todd's tapes as well. Most importantly, between August 1978 and December 1979, 'we spent $52,000 on weapons, ammunition, and military equipment' (Noble 2010: 81) to defend against the conspiracy. As Noble ruefully admitted many years later, 'had we never learned of John Todd, it is safe to say that Zarephath-Horeb would never had [*sic*] purchased so many guns, would never have become Christian survivalists, and would never have become a paramilitary organization' (Noble 2010: 304). It would take a major FBI operation in 1985 to finally disarm the community.

Not surprisingly, after Todd stopped preaching, a variety of rumors circulated about his whereabouts and fate, some claiming that he was a recluse in Montana and others insisting that he had been shot and killed. The reality was far more bizarre. Todd's project for a retreat to house former witches seems particularly odd in view of the final trajectory of his life. In 1984 he was convicted of incest in Kentucky, for which he was placed on probation. In 1988, he was sentenced to 30 years in prison in South Carolina for rape (Hook 1988). Apparently, at the completion of his prison sentence, he was civilly committed to a Behavioral Disorders Treatment Program as a sexually violent predator. While incarcerated, he brought a civil suit, arguing that his constitutional rights were being violated, among them the failure to allow him to practice Wicca (Kollyns 2006). Thus the crusader against a witchcraft conspiracy had come full circle, back to the religion of witchcraft he claimed to have fled. He died in 2007.

TYPE II: DAVID ICKE: THE CONSPIRACY THEORIST AS OCCULTIST

David Icke has become one of the most visible conspiracy theorists in the English-speaking world. His visibility is a function of his international speaking tours, his elaborate website, and his publications. The latter emerge as a seemingly endless stream of self-published books, abundantly illustrated and written in a sprightly style. Indeed, Icke has become a conspiracy entrepreneur rivaled only by the American, Alex Jones. Icke's early volumes were difficult to distinguish from much of the other conspiracist literature that was generated in the 1980s and 1990s. Thus in *The Robots' Rebellion* (1994) Icke spoke of an amorphous cabal he called 'the Brotherhood' whose tentacles spanned the world and encompassed such organizations frequently cited by conspiracists as the Trilateral Commission, the Council on Foreign Relations, and international banks. While he was unsure whether or not the Brotherhood had connections with extraterrestrials, he was convinced that it had created the Illuminati and sought to bring about the dreaded 'New World Order,' the ubiquitous phrase used by conspiracy theorists to denote the coming global dictatorship (Icke 1994). A more detailed description of the Brotherhood appeared the following year in *...and the Truth Shall Set You Free* (1995), in which the conspiracy was portrayed as a pyramid of nested secret societies. None of the material in either volume was especially novel, and they were distinguished only by Icke's glib style, scarcely surprising for someone who had been a BBC sportscaster and the spokesperson for the Green Party.

Icke's conspiracism, however, began to acquire a special character with *The Biggest Secret* (1999), whose jacket proclaimed it to be 'the book that will change the world.' While it included much of the material already set out in its predecessors, *The Biggest Secret* also introduced what was to become the signature element in Icke's system: the claim that at the top of the conspiracist hierarchy was a non-human species, 'a reptilian race from another dimension [that] has been controlling the planet for thousands of years' (Icke 1999: 29). Sometimes by their capacity for shape-shifting, sometimes in the form of reptilian–human crossbreeds, these sinister creatures managed to insinuate themselves into positions of power, masquerading as human beings. This motif of reptilians who speak and walk erect actually originated in the fantasy and science fiction literature of the 1920s and 1930s prior to gradually emerging as factual assertions in works such as those of Icke (Barkun 2003: 121). He then proceeded to elaborate on and embellish this remarkable claim through successive books, such as *Children of the Matrix* (2001) and *Tales from the Time Loop* (2003). While the reptilian thesis was not in itself occult, it placed Icke in a curious position. His marketing ability allowed him to promulgate this strange theory in a way that few conspiracists could. By the same token, it placed him at the outer limits of conspiracism itself, for bizarre as some New World Order plots were, they seemed tame and conventional by comparison. Another implication of Icke's reptilian ideas was that once he had taken that leap, moving into occultism itself seemed a fairly small step.

As Icke's investment in the reptilian thesis increased, he began to provide it with a back-story in *Tales from the Time Loop* (2003). While his initial presentation gave no indication of where the reptilians had come from, he now presented a myth of origins. The back-story had markedly occult overtones. In seeking to explain where the reptilians came from, he reached to the occult astronomy of Zechariah Sitchin. Sitchin's argument derived from the obscure passage in Genesis 6:4, which speaks of the Nephilim who 'were on the earth in those days...when the sons of God went to the daughters of humans and had children by them.' He asserted that these creature were actually extraterrestrials who came from a mysterious 'twelfth planet' of the solar system (Icke 2003: 231–32; Sitchin 1978). For Icke, the Nephilim had to have been the reptilians, arriving on Earth from the twelfth planet. He went on to argue that the remote history of the reptilians could be found in the occult text, the Emerald Tablets, a text attributed to Thoth, a priest-king of the sunken realm of Atlantis (Icke 2003: 304–5). The Tablets had supposedly been 'translated' by Maurice Doreal (born Claude Doggins – 1898–1963), who claimed to have gotten them from the Great Pyramid in Egypt in 1925. Doreal also allegedly met two Atlanteans in Los Angeles in 1931, who transported him to a cavern 12 miles below Mount Shasta (Barkun 2003: 115, 120). According to Icke, the reptilians are also vampires, who can assume human appearance only if they continue to consume human blood. They do so, he claims, in establishment-sanctioned rituals of human sacrifice and blood-drinking at venues such as the Bohemian Grove in California and Montauk Point, Long Island (Icke 2003: 306–10).

Icke has absorbed other occult motifs of lesser importance to his overall scheme that nevertheless indicate his receptivity to an occult worldview. For example, he makes passing reference to 'Freemasonic imagery [that] adorn[s] the Denver airport' (Icke 2003: 275). The idea that a major air terminal has murals with encoded Masonic messages has had a lively existence on the Internet among conspiracists despite a striking absence of proof and denials by the artist, Leo Tanguma. Icke spends more time on another, more bizarre idea, namely, that the street plan of Washington and the placement of its major buildings and monuments conceal hidden occult meanings: 'Washington is a mass of esoteric and Babylonian/Roman symbolism in its street plan and architecture...' (Icke 2007: 138) Thus, the goddess Freedom on the top of the Capitol dome is really the Babylonian goddess Semiramis, according to Icke, and the flame on the grave of President John F. Kennedy in Arlington Cemetery is actually her consort Nimrod (Icke 2007: 244).

It should now be clear that by the early 2000s, David Icke's conspiracy theory had assumed a different character. Originally it differed little from the plots described by others in the conspiracist subculture, envisioning a plan concocted by a coalition of evil secret organizations, mostly of the super-rich, under some central leadership. However, with the introduction of the reptilians, Icke swung in a different direction, although initially not clearly occultist. Indeed, he first portrayed the reptilians almost as a kind of interest group, the master manipulators of the conspiracy by virtue of their superior cunning and their total absence of moral scruples. However, as he came to fill in the picture, the reptilian thesis took on an increasingly occult character. Their attributes, for example, included not only great intelligence and ruthlessness, but also a continual need for human blood, satisfied in gruesome rituals. Their control over religion and politics, through the Illuminati, allowed them to encode their licentious beliefs into ecclesiastical structures, city planning, and public monuments, although the true meaning of these symbols was known only to initiates.

THE MERGING OF FRINGE AND MAINSTREAM

Occultists and conspiracists used to share at least one thing in common, namely, that both were part of what might be termed the 'fringe.' That is, both were marginalized, segregated from that other vague category, the 'mainstream.' What differentiated the two was the latter's access to large audiences and the imprimatur of important validating institutions. Like some other segments of the fringe, both conspiracism and occultism are examples of what I have elsewhere called 'stigmatized knowledge' – knowledge claims that have failed to meet the tests or standards of universities, the scientific community, government, and similar organizations to which people look for judgments of approval (Barkun 2003: 26–28). Their character as stigmatized knowledge, variously rejected, ignored, and demeaned by those who provide a societal stamp of approval, has thus consigned them to the fringe.

In recent years, however, the formerly clear boundary between mainstream and fringe no longer exists. Its erosion is, in part, a function of changes in communications technology and of changes in popular culture. The former includes, of course, pre-eminently the Internet, which gives to marginalized and despised ideas a mode of dissemination that allows them to break out of their traditional isolation. They can do so without such barriers as high capital costs or gatekeepers. The mainstream, which feeds upon the fringe, utilizes the esoteric and conspiracist as raw material for films, television programs, and other modes of entertainment. Stigmatized knowledge now turns up frequently in mainstream venues, where former fringe status gives it novelty and the excitement of the forbidden. Consequently, one can no longer speak definitively of a fringe idea, for such an idea can at any moment pass into what was once deemed the mainstream through new communication channels. It may go from blog to blog, each with a larger and/or higher status audience, until it is eventually picked up by a cable news channel, a wire service, or a large newspaper, signifying that it has been, as it were, 'sanitized.'

Of course, this process operates within limits. The fringe–mainstream boundary has been eroded; it has not been erased. Although some ideas that once would have remained part of the fringe now pass into the mainstream, others still remain on the far side of the now-weakened boundary. It is difficult to imagine the ideas of either John Todd or David Icke making the transition to mainstream status at the present time. Nonetheless, they press on both acceptability and larger audiences in ways that would have been inconceivable thirty years ago. Icke clearly has the advantage in this regard, since, as a living conspiracy exponent, he can exercise some control over the content and channels for the dissemination of his ideas. Todd, on the other hand, ended his period of activity in the late 1970s, well before the advent of the Internet, although much by and about him was later transferred to it.

The foregoing begs the question concerning whether any limits on the acceptability of ideas will remain, or whether those limits have acquired an elasticity which will eventually permit virtually any beliefs once consigned to the fringe, to migrate to the mainstream, thereby effectively merging the one with the other. Should that occur, both the occult and the conspiracist would take their place along with the commonplace products of both high and popular culture, accessible to and recognized by mass audiences. Obviously, elements of both have occasionally made mainstream appearances. Neither has been completely sealed off. Thus, mediums, extra-sensory perception, and astrology, for example, have sometimes appeared both in popular culture and in news venues, just as some conspiracy theories, such as those that dealt with the assassination of President John F. Kennedy, have sometimes done so.

By way of an example, the general awareness of end-time prophecies about December 21, 2012, associated with the ancient Mayan calendar seems qualitatively new. Between 1975 and about 2006, Mayan calendar predictions were matters virtually entirely within the New Age subculture. However, the volume of publications about them suggests that, by 2006, the theme emerged into the mainstream, where it has been ever since. The fact that it became the subject of a major motion picture in 2009 (Roland Emmerich's *2012*) confirms the occurrence of such a shift (Austin 2011). The rapidity with which ideas that had previously appeared within a circumscribed sub-culture suddenly became part of the everyday awareness of urban populations is a phenomenon of fringe–mainstream migration that could not have occurred several decades earlier.

This example, as well as those of Todd and Icke, suggests that the occultism–conspiracism relationship is subject to two factors. First, occultism and conspiracism may interact in either of two principal ways, designated above as Type I and Type II and illustrated respectively by the real world examples of John Todd and David Icke. Second, both occultism and conspiracism have increasingly entered the cultural mainstream in ways that could not have been anticipated a quarter of a century ago and, as this continues, their status as stigmatized knowledge will decline. It is reasonable to assume that with the gradual reduction in their fringe status, the linkages between them that have been evident up to now will also be reduced. For the relationship between occultism and conspiracism has depended significantly upon the fact that both have been forms of stigmatized knowledge. Should the degree of stigmatization be reduced, the connection between the two is bound to diminish as well. To what extent this will occur is difficult to know. It is reasonable to suppose that some core of both occultism and conspiracism will remain part of the fringe and therefore never lose its stigmatized character, even if this core will in the future be much smaller than the body of stigmatized knowledge was in the recent past.

It is also possible, indeed likely, that the reception of elements of stigmatized knowledge into the mainstream will stir resentments among former believers, who cherished occultism and conspiracism precisely *because* they were disdained by authoritative institutions. This is so because those who make up fringe subcultures often have an anti-authoritarian bias and continue to believe in ideas that are rejected – whether of Atlantis, spirit visitations, or Bigfoot – not in spite of opposition, but because of it. For them, rejection by the mainstream is a badge of honor. People attracted to stigmatized knowledge therefore adhere to it in part as an act of revolt against the conventions around them. Consequently, the fact that some elements of either occultism or conspiracism enter the mainstream will not be perceived by them as victory. Rather, it will be perceived as the devaluation of those elements, their degradation through association with the hated institutions of mainstream society. Those for whom rejection is a mark of both honor and validation will consequently seek new forms of stigmatized knowledge to take the place of those that have entered the mainstream.

This suggests that the process of fringe-to-mainstream migration may be the catalyst for another process, namely, the creation of new elements of stigmatized knowledge. For new stigmatized knowledge must be found to replace those parts of occultism and conspiracism that have been received into the mainstream. Thus, in a paradoxical way, even though the boundary dividing the fringe from the mainstream is manifestly weaker as a result of factors already described, the very weakening will give rise to at least a partial regrowth of the fringe. Hence, in ways that cannot yet be seen, the fringe will eventually both contract and expand as a function of the dynamics of boundary change.

REFERENCES AND FURTHER READING

Austin, A. (2011) 'Roland Emmerich's *2012*: A Simple Truth,' in Joseph Gelfer, ed., *2012: Decoding the Countercultural Apocalypse*, Sheffield: Equinox, 108–22.

Barkun, M. (1997) *Religion and the Racist Right: The Origins of the Christian Identity Movement*, Chapel Hill, NC: University of North Carolina Press.

——(2003) *A Culture of Conspiracy: Apocalyptic Visions in Contemporary America*, Berkeley, CA: University of California Press.

Collins, J.T. (1977) 'The Testimony of John Todd Collins: The Conspiracy revealed by an Insider.' Online: http://www.textfiles.com/occult/jtc1.text (accessed October 18, 2012).

Goodrick-Clarke, N. (2002) *Black Sun: Aryan Cults, Esoteric Nazism and the Politics of Identity*, New York: New York University Press.

Hook, D-L.B. (1988) '"Survivalist" Protests Verdict,' *The State* (Columbia, SC), January 23. Online: http://nl.newsbank.com/nl-search/we/Archives?p_action = doc&p_docid = 0EB57 F8BC996 (accessed October 22, 2012).

Icke, D. (1994) *The Robots' Rebellion: The Story of the Spiritual Renaissance*, Bath, UK: Gateway Books.

——(1995)...*and the Truth Shall Set You Free*, Isle of Wight: Bridge of Love.

——(1999) *The Biggest Secret*, Scottsdale, AZ: Bridge of Love USA.

——(2001) *Children of the Matrix: How an Interdimensional Race has Controlled the World for Thousands of Years – and Still Does*, Wildwood, MO: Bridge of Love USA.

——(2003) *Tales from the Time Loop: The Most Comprehensive Expose of the Global Conspiracy Ever Written and all You Need to Know to be Truly Free*, Isle of Wight: David Icke Books.

——(2007) *The David Icke Guide to the Global Conspiracy (and How to End It)*, Isle of Wight: David Icke Books.

Kollyns, K.S. (Formerly #145461, AKA Kristopher S, Kollins, AKA John Wayne Todd, AKA Johnnie W. Todd), Plaintiff, vs. Dr. Russell Hughes; Brenda Young-Rice; Fred Pauer; Rev. Smith; Lt. Abney; Dr. Chavez, in their personal capacities; and South Carolina Department of Mental Health, for injunctive relief, Defendants. (2006) District Court, District of South Carolina, No. 3:05–0090-JFA-JRM.

Noble, K. (2010) *Tabernacle of Hate: Seduction Into Right-Wing Extremism*, Syracuse, NY: Syracuse University Press.

Rivera, D.A. (2012) 'The Rivera Report: The Story Behind John Todd.' Online: http://riverareport.blogspot.com/2012/05/story-behind-john-todd.html (accessed October 22, 2012).

Sitchin, Z. (1978) *The 12th Planet: Book One of The Earth Chronicles*, New York: Avon.

Strube, J. (2012) 'Die Erfindung des esoterischen Nationalsozialismus im Zeichen der Schwarzen Sonne,' *Zeitschrift für Religionswissenschaft*, 20:2, 223–68.

Todd, J. (2012) 'John Todd's introduction to Atlas Shrugged.' Online: http://www.kt70.com/~jamesjpn/articles/atlas_shrugged.htm (accessed October 18, 2012).

——(2011) 'Atlas Shrugged Outlines the Illuminati Purpose and Plan for World Takeover.' Online: http://truth11.com/2011/06/14/atlas-shrugged-outlines-the-illuminati-purpose-and-plan-for-world-takeover (accessed October 18, 2012).

CHAPTER SEVENTY

SCIENCE AND THE OCCULT

Egil Asprem

INTRODUCTION

Writing about 'science and the occult' is made difficult by the significant ambiguity both these terms represent. 'Science' may variably be defined in a *sociological* sense as a set of institutions, in a *substantial* sense as a certain body of facts, hypotheses, theories, and models, in an *epistemological* sense as a certain set of methods for building secure knowledge, or, indeed, in any combination of these three. Similarly, 'the occult', has been described variously as a certain set of doctrines, worldviews, or phenomena, as a certain 'mentality', way of thinking, or mental habit, or as a socially defined 'deviant' subculture. To discuss science and the occult it is therefore paramount to reflect on definitions and meanings of terms: results will vary depending on what one takes each to mean. For example, physical phenomena that have at some point in history been labeled 'occult', such as magnetism or gravity, have been important subjects for scientific inquiry and theorizing, but 'occult thought' defined as a cognitive habit of analogical thinking and associative linking has more typically been the enemy of 'scientific method' considered in a philosophical sense. On the social level things get even more complicated: on the one hand 'the occult' has been construed as 'rejected knowledge', the wastebasket of modern science and philosophy, and scientific professionals have relied on this notion for constructing their identity vis-à-vis 'pseudoscientific' and 'occult' Others; on the other, the 'occult worlds' of theosophical societies, esoteric orders, spiritualist séances and parapsychological experiments have been well visited and inhabited by people with at least one foot inside of the scientific establishment.

We shall chart some of these complexities in the present chapter. We must, however, start from the crucial recognition that historically, the very meanings of 'the occult' and 'science' are closely tied together: they are a troubled and often polemical pair that have evolved in tandem and thus share a common genealogy. Tracing the broad lines of this genealogy takes us through three stages: the pre-Enlightenment context of 'occult science' in natural philosophy; the explanation of occult qualities in terms of mechanistic philosophy during the so-called scientific revolution; and the post-Enlightenment context of rejected (pseudo)scientific knowledge and the subsequent creation of 'occultism' as a largely oppositional self-designation.

A GENEALOGY OF SCIENCE-AND-THE-OCCULT

'Occult qualities' in Pre-Enlightenment Natural Philosophy

The term 'occult' (from Latin *occultus*; 'hidden') has a long history in Western natural philosophy (for an overview, see Hanegraaff, 2005). In the medieval scholastic interpretation of Aristotle, the term 'occult qualities' (*qualitates occultae*) was used to describe the hidden qualities of material things, related to their 'form' rather than their 'substance', which could not be perceived directly but which nevertheless accounted for certain physical, observable *effects*. Thus, all physical properties that did not have a clearly discernable cause from the outside could be labeled occult: the property of attracting or repelling other objects was one such occult quality, but the curative or poisonous effects of herbs, mineral tonics, and 'magical' amulets were also included in the same natural–philosophical category. This was in fact the main meaning of the word 'occult' throughout the middle ages, and we find it used in this form among scholastic philosophers such as Thomas Aquinas.

Occult qualities remained an influential concept in renaissance natural philosophy. In extension, it became central for major representatives of Western esoteric thought. Occult qualities were at the foundations of 'natural magic' (*magia naturalis*), and central to the so-called 'occult sciences', particularly alchemy. Thus, Cornelius Agrippa's influential *De occulta philosophia* (1533) described a system of three worlds with three adjoining forms of magic: the terrestrial or sub-lunar world; the astral or supra-lunar world; and the spiritual and divine world beyond the fixed stars. Natural magic belonged to the lower sub-lunar world, and it worked by the skilled use of knowledge about the occult properties of things: metals, herbs, colours, and the occult correspondences between these and the entities of higher worlds, such as the planets.

The Mechanization of Occult Qualities during the Scientific Revolution

Occult properties were by no means separated from the legitimate science (or natural philosophy) of the early modern period; there was a continuum between natural *magic* and natural *philosophy*. This started to change during the scientific revolution, but not, as has often been contended, by an outright *rejection* of 'occult properties' (cf. Hanegraaff, 2012: 177–91). It is more correct to say that the emerging mathematical and mechanical paradigm in natural philosophy, associated with names such as Galileo, Descartes and Newton, found in mathematics a way to make the unobservable causes of 'occult qualities' subject to precise measurement, explanation and prediction – a possibility that had effectively been denied by scholastic philosophy. An example of these changing tides is found in Descartes' *Principia philosophiae* (1644): here we find a number of diagrams thought to explain the hidden mechanisms that govern previously 'occult' effects such as magnetism, now made explicable by an atomic theory of matter and the principles of mechanical motion.

An effect of the rise of the so-called mechanical philosophy, which by the eighteenth century had come to include mathematics, astronomy, physics and chemistry (with attempts to subsume biology, mental, moral and political philosophy as well, in the works of e.g. La Mettrie and Hobbes) was that research paradigms that had rested on the notion of occult qualities became increasingly marginalized. One example of this process was the separation of chemistry from alchemy by the end of the seventheenth century. This happened in the wake of Robert Boyle's work, sometimes labeled the 'father of chemistry', who is perhaps better described as a laboratory alchemist who embraced the mechanical philosophy and achieved explanatory success thereby (cf. Principe, 1998). What followed during the eighteenth-century Enlightenment was a grand-scale rejection of entire fields of superseded knowledge in natural philosophy, most notably of alchemy and astrology. This is the context in which notions of 'occult sciences' first started to take shape: alchemy, astrology and (natural) magic were all thought to share a foundation in occult qualities and correspondences, which had no place in Enlightenment epistemology.

The Post-Enlightenment 'Occult': Occult Forces and Rejected Knowledge

It is thus from the Enlightenment period onwards that we can truly speak of a notion of strict *separation* between science and the occult – a primarily polemical dichotomy created by the process of differentiation between modern science and other domains of thought, including philosophy and theology. This process continued in the nineteenth century, with the professionalization of the natural sciences, and the sociological differentiation of 'scientists' as a separate social class, the term 'scientist' having been coined by philosopher William Whewell as late as 1840.

In light of these very significant intellectual and social developments, notions of 'the occult' and of science were rapidly changing, and would come to take on quite different meanings. Two new developments must be mentioned here. First, the ascendency of the mechanistic philosophy led to a proliferation of pseudo-mechanical occult *forces*, typically formulated by people standing on the boundaries of the emerging modern sciences. Second, the Enlightenment project led to a view of the occult as pseudo-scientific and pseudo-religious 'rejected knowledge'; that is, as an undercurrent of ideas that were not 'scientific' because unacceptable from the standpoint of Enlightenment epistemology, and not 'religious' because unacceptable from the standpoint of established church doctrine (cf. Hanegraaff, 2012).

The notion of occult *forces* appears to have been invented during the Enlightenment under the influence of the mechanical philosophy. Occult forces were distinct from occult qualities in that they were conceived of in terms of pseudo-mechanistic 'laws', invisible 'fluids', or 'fields', modeled on the concepts proposed in the new physics. Indeed, where the prototypical examples of occult qualities were found in the Aristotelian doctrine of forms, the prototypical occult (i.e. hidden) force was found in Newtonian gravity. The notion of material bodies pulling each other from a distance, without any observable intermediary substance, triggered the imaginations of thinkers in other fields, and seemed to lend some legitimacy to postulating similar universal 'laws' and invisible 'forces' in other domains. In fact, a vast number of such forces, often connected to the notion of a subtle, invisible 'ether', were proposed by natural philosophers of the Enlightenment period (Asprem, 2011, 134–35). Most of these theories never made it to the status of scientific orthodoxy: Benjamin Franklin formulated an 'elastic ether' theory to account for electricity, for example, while George Le Sage's 'kinematic ether' was offered as explanation for a wide range of phenomena, including gravity, weight, and chemical affinity (cf. Laudan, 1981).

While most of these unsuccessful theories were simply forgotten, some of that which never became official science (at least not for any substantial period) would become highly influential in the emerging world of the post-Enlightenment 'occult'. A primary example of this is Franz Anton Mesmer's notion of 'animal magnetism', first conceptualized as a pseudo-mechanistic theory of subtle fluids, interpenetrating the cosmos and living beings, accounting for various physical and psychical ailments as well as special mental rapports between human beings (see the article on Mesmerism and Animal Magnetism). The different theories and practices associated with Mesmerism came to exert an enormous influence on nineteenth-century esoteric currents, notably occultism and spiritualism. It provided a science-like explanation of magic in Joseph Ennemoser's *Geschichte der Magie* (1844), which in turn became the single most important influence on H. P. Blavatsky's published works of Theosophy. Eliphas Levi's massively influential *Dogme et rituel de la haute magie* similarly looked to Mesmerism for its account of the magical agent, 'astral light'. Finally, the new interpretation of alchemy as *spiritual* alchemy, first outlined in Mary Anne Atwood's *Suggestive Inquiry into the Hermetic Mystery* (1850), used Mesmerism as the prism through which this physico-spiritual discipline was to be understood.

A number of other occult forces were proposed throughout the nineteenth century, modeled on concepts taken from physics. Among these we should mention the 'odic force' of the baron and industrialist Karl von Reichenbach, a form of vital energy named after the Norse god Odin, and the 'vril force', invented by the British author Edward Bulwer Lytton for his fantastical novel *The Coming Race* (cf. Strube, 2013). All these occult forces – animal magnetism, astral light, the odic force, vril – found their way into the synthetic doctrines of the Theosophical Society, and became central 'sciency' terms in occultism in the nineteenth and twentieth centuries. As forms of rejected scientific knowledge, they became important resources for occultists to *challenge* established science, typically perceived as 'materialistic' and 'dogmatic', while at the same time claiming a form of rational knowledge for themselves (cf. Hammer, 2001; Asprem, 2012, 446–59).

SCIENCE AND THE OCCULT IN THE TWENTIETH CENTURY: THREE RELATIONS

At the dawn of the twentieth century, both 'the occult' and 'science' had acquired meanings that are relatively close to those of our own days. Science referred to a privileged body of knowledge about the natural world, sanctioned by specialist institutions, supported by professional educational programs enjoying high prestige, and basing its epistemic claims on a set of increasingly sophisticated methods of inquiry. The 'occult', by contrast, was a residual category that included a great number of rejected knowledges, pursued on a social arena of secret lodges and occult societies, and disseminated through a number of periodicals and books provided by a flourishing occult publishing industry. 'The occult' thus included the theory and practice of ritual magic as taught by various Hermetic and Rosicrucian orders; it encompassed the arcane doctrines of Theosophy, the practice of astral travel, the Mesmeric trances, Spiritualist séances, and telepathic and clairvoyant communication; and a number of alternative histories of lost continents, hidden masters, and powerful secret societies were discussed in occult publications. While the contrast with professional science is evident, the invocation of reason and scientific legitimacy was seldom far away when such topics were discussed.

Thus, even when we limit our investigation of relations between science and the occult to a period in which these terms are relatively stable, that is, from about the start of the twentieth century until today, the picture remains complex. Recalling the words of caution that opened this chapter, I shall proceed to look at three different kinds of relations between science and the occult, namely: science *in* the occult, the occult *in* science, and science *of* the occult. Together, these three approaches reveal the most central aspects of the complex relationship between science and the occult in the modern world.

Science in the Occult

As we have already seen, there is a tight genealogical connection between the occult and the disciplines of science and natural philosophy. As a wastebasket category of rejected knowledge, the occult has thus come to include much that, from the perspective of contemporaneous scientists, would be associated simply with superseded or pseudo-scientific knowledge. It is hard to deny that the post-Enlightenment occult has typically been characterized by an *oppositional* ethos – sometimes revolutionary and utopian, other times 'reactionary' and counterrevolutionary – that brings an automatic fascination with all that is rejected by religious, political and scientific Establishments (cf. Webb, 1974). Thus references to occult forces bearing exotic, technical-sounding names only accrue over time, as we have seen.

The fascination for rejected and therefore 'forbidden' (and therefore powerful and subversive) scientific knowledge can thus be seen as a consequence of the *social form* and status acquired by the occult in the nineteenth century. However, this is not the whole story. The 'occult' of any given period (for it must always be seen as tied to historical contexts) shows an equal, if not even higher, interest for contemporary *established* science. Failing to recognize this comes at the risk of automatically assuming 'the occult' to represent simply a form of 'regressive' tendency of the human mind, a conception that has often been put forward (e.g. Adorno, 1994, 172: 'occultism is a symptom of the regression of consciousness') but which hardly squares with the historical evidence. Whether we are talking about Theosophy in the 1880s or 'New Age' in the 1970s, spokespersons of the occult are often deeply fascinated in what they consider to be the big scientific questions of their time. In the late nineteenth century, this included things like ether physics and controversies over Darwinian and non-Darwinian theories of evolution (e.g. Asprem, 2011; Asprem, 2013). There were genuine scientific controversies and uncertainties on these issues, and occult spokespersons were more than happy to share their own interpretations. A century later, the basic relation was the same, but now with quantum mechanics in the role previously occupied by ether physics.

How do we interpret occult interest in contemporary science? One aspect has to do with the air of *legitimacy* conferred by the appeal to science in modern society (Hammer, 2001). With the rise of prestige for the scientific project after the Enlightenment, science became a much sought-after commodity. Possessing it is to possess a form of cultural capital that may potentially elevate one's social status. The occult has thus found itself in a precarious situation where the legitimacy of science is very much desired, while the perceived worldview-implications of its most successful theories are something to be fiercely combated. The use of scientific knowledge in the occult is thus often part of an exercise in turning science against itself: the scientific Establishment got the basic facts right, but is led astray by materialistic and disenchanted dogma. An initiated, occult interpretation of science is needed to gain the higher insights that essentially *transcend* science, religion and philosophy alike. This type of fascination with 'higher knowledge' must be considered a major motivation for modern occult spokespersons to engage with current scientific thinking in the first place (cf. von Stuckrad, 2005; Asprem, 2014, 431–41).

Another aspect that must be mentioned here is the presence not only of scientific themes discussed by occultists, but of *individual scientists* contributing directly to occult discourse. Despite the occult's status as constituting a form of rejected, pseudo-scientific knowledge, a number of well-established and highly influential scientists have taken part in occult milieus, and willingly lent their credibility to support ideas circulated in them. We may think of the celebrated physicist and chemist Sir William Crookes, who was an ardent explorer of spiritualism and a supportive member of the Theosophical society in the late nineteenth century. The physicist Sir Oliver Lodge similarly spent the better half of his life defending spiritualism by aligning it with ether physics, lending credibility to the occult concept of the 'etheric body' (Asprem, 2011). In the second half of the twentieth century, all the most noteworthy authors of so-called 'New Age science' have been trained as scientists: Fritjof Capra, David Bohm, Rupert Sheldrake and Ilya Prigogine are only a few examples of more recent figures who are equally at home publishing technical scientific papers in peer-reviewed journals as writing popularizing, speculative interpretations of science mysticism for a broader pop-occultural audience (cf. Hanegraaff, 1996, 62–76).

Finally, we should consider the question of scientific *method* in the occult. It is true that, for the most part, the uses of science in occult discourses are *speculative* in nature. The aim is to squeeze out arcane secrets from a body of static knowledge borrowed from past and present sciences, and to harmonize these with religious, mythical and esoteric knowledge found elsewhere. In this process, science is just treated as a prestigious and hence desired body of knowledge, *not* as a set of methods or a system of organized scepticism actively concerned with *building* knowledge. In other words: despite criticizing the scientific establishment for being 'dogmatic', what occult spokespersons looking for higher knowledge in science actually do is to elevate certain pieces of knowledge to the status of unchallengeable dogma. This has created quite some problems for occult syntheses that have aligned their higher knowledge with the best science of a specific period only to see the scientific profession change their minds dramatically in light of new evidence and theory. This happened to the Theosophical Society, which faced major problems reconciling their old doctrines, harmonized with Victorian ether physics and pre-Mendelian biology, with the radical scientific changes of the early twentieth century (Asprem, 2013; Asprem, 2014, 471–80). The result is that, still today, references to quantum mechanics and relativity theory are simply patched onto a system that is still teeming with etheric bodies and vital forces.

While this appears to be a general trend, there are also a few examples of attempts to apply 'scientific methods' to the pursuit of esoteric knowledge. The *rhetoric* of scientific methodology was a central point for many spiritualists, basing itself on a rather unconvincing form of verificationism. Something similar is found in Annie Besant and Charles Webster Leadbeater's programme of 'occult chemistry'. Their project, begun in 1895 and continued in the early decades of the twentieth century, was to use clairvoyance to observe the chemical elements by direct vision – a method of observation that was claimed to be superior to the indirect and instrumentalized methods at the disposal of mundane chemists and physicists. While this represented a new way of engaging science from the perspective of the occult, emphasizing experiment and (occult) observations rather than the mere proclamation of esoteric doctrines, it was still far from recognizing the strictures of scientific methodology.

Aleister Crowley, whose magical system of 'Scientific Illuminism' was intended to make magic properly 'scientific', took a rather different approach (Asprem, 2008). Unlike most of his occult contemporaries, Crowley did not believe that using scientific nomenclature had anything to do with being 'scientific'; in fact, he frequently criticized other occultists for thinking so. Instead, Crowley sought to devise new methods of controlling and correcting magical practice. An important part of this was to construct magical rituals as experiments, taking measures to avoid subjective validation and confirmation bias by making the effects of magic intersubjectively available and subjected to a form of occult peer-review. This was done primarily through the use of a magical diary, which was to be written as a scientific protocol so that others could see what had actually been done and achieved. In addition to this, Crowley sought to recreate the hermeneutical tools of the kabbalah to work as ways to check the occult correspondences of magical *visions* – effectively inventing ways to falsify subjective experience. While Crowley's system hardly qualifies as science in its own right, a sincere attempt to incorporate scientific thinking in magical practice has to be recognized.

The Occult in Science

One of the lasting impacts of Frances Yates' much-read classic, *Giordano Bruno and the Hermetic Tradition* (1964), was the notion that 'the occult' (loosely understood as the 'Hermetic', 'esoteric' and 'mystical') had been a potent force in the establishment of the modern sciences. According to the Yates thesis, now generally dismissed, the fascination for the newly discovered Hermetic texts in the Italian Renaissance, and the attempted renovation of magic, constituted an important aspect of the first phase of the 'scientific revolution'. It was through a magical emphasis on 'man as operator' that the new experimentalism (later associated with the likes of Bacon, Boyle and Locke) found its original impetus, and it was the solar worship of the Hermeticists that gave heliocentrism its spiritual motivation. The Yates thesis thus gave some credit to identifying occult influences on actual scientific development. While the thesis is now generally dismissed, at least in its original form (cf. Hanegraaff, 2001), it remains the case that it is difficult to separate 'science' from 'the occult' in the medieval and early modern period, as we have discussed above. It is, however, problematic to ascribe a scientifically 'progressive' quality to Renaissance natural magic, or even to describe disciplines such as alchemy or astrology as 'proto-sciences'. Doing so means to abstract away everything in those broad fields that does not fit what we nowadays think of as science, keeping only the parts that, with hindsight of history, turned out to look a bit like predecessors for modern practices. By doing this one loses sight of the complexity of early modern natural philosophy, of which the so-called occult sciences were integral parts, while at the same time making an artificial link between our present concepts of 'the occult' and 'the sciences'.

Discussing the role of the occult *in* science we must therefore be more specific. One obvious place to start is by returning to the issue of scientific professionals who make the link between their scientific research and occult doctrines. Such individuals represent a form of *social* overlap between the *milieus* of the occult and of science; if we think in terms of Venn diagrams, it means that we can locate parts of the occult milieu within parts of scientific milieus. While this is in itself significant, it still remains a fact that there is little evidence of these occult-scientific threshold figures bringing occult concepts directly into their scientific work. The transaction is for the most part one-way, and it goes from science to the occult.

There are a few exceptions to this, but they remain rather superficial: When Francis Aston discovered the isotopes, for example, he first thought he had discovered a new element, which he named 'meta-neon' – after one of the elements 'clairvoyantly' descried by Besant and Leadbeater's occult chemistry. Aston had read the Theosophical literature with fascination, and found that his 'shadow element' had similar properties to those Besant and Leadbeater had described. However, it is revealing that Aston failed to mention this borrowing in his official publications at the time (Hughes, 2003). Similarly, there was a revived fascination for alchemy in early twentieth-century chemistry, revolving around the discovery that the elements of the periodic table were not stable and indivisible as previously thought, and that genuine transmutation of elements was not only possible, but happened spontaneously in nature through radioactive decay (cf. Morrisson, 2007). Once again the fascination was for the most part aesthetic, with scientists finding exciting metaphors and tropes in which to couch their narratives of scientific exploration when communicating it to a wider audience (cf. Asprem, 2014: 119–28). An influence of alchemical theories on actual scientific research is much harder to spot.

The role of the occult in science has been much more important as a resource for the *popularization* of science, and the attempted creation of worldviews based on scientific concepts. This brings us back to the genre of 'New Age science'. We should however also mention the more prestigious field of 'natural theology' – still very much alive today, supported by the economic muscles of institutions such as the Templeton Foundation. Natural theology was traditionally a theological branch of natural philosophy, concerned with the study of the divine through the application of reason and empirical investigation of nature. As a discipline, it lost credibility with the professionalization of the natural sciences after the Enlightenment, but it was revived in the late nineteenth and early twentieth century. Influential twentieth-century scientists and thinkers such as William James, Alfred North Whitehead, Henri Bergson, Arthur Eddington and James Jeans may be said to have contributed to the genre (see e.g. Witham, 2005; Bowler, 2001). Contrary to 'the occult', natural theology has mostly retained its status as a high-brow intellectual and respectable liberal-Christian discipline (e.g. Bowler 2001); nevertheless, its theological conceptions border very closely on the occult – whether in its reliance on forms of 'mysticism' and unmediated experience (as in the case of James and Eddington), in their views of a mathematical, Pythagorean godhead, graspable through pure reason (as in the case of Jeans), or in the immanent, panentheistic, evolutionary ways of conceiving the divine in e.g. Whitehead, Bergson, and a host of other 'emergentist' thinkers (cf.

Asprem, 2014, 232–46). While they have been able to keep a mantle of respectability, these theologies are about as heterodox as any occult doctrine, and very much for the same reasons: they break the separation between creator and creation, muddle the eternity and unchangeable nature of the divine, and hold higher, soteriological knowledge to be attainable outside of revelation, by the seeker's own initiative. Given such theological overlaps, it is reasonable to see the literature of natural theology as belonging to the broader occulture.

Science of the Occult

The final type of relation we shall consider in this chapter is that which occurs when science takes 'the occult' as its object of study. Here, all the meanings of 'science' are activated: professionals working in scientific institutions take the best methods of their disciplines and apply them in a study of what they consider 'occult phenomena', publishing their results in peer-reviewed journals. The reasons for undertaking such research are varied, oscillating between a wish to debunk and discredit and a wish to prove and legitimize specific occult phenomena. Spiritualism elicited such responses from the very beginning, and these would lead to the discipline of 'psychical research' – later developed into modern parapsychology while also providing a foundation for the organized 'Skeptics movement'.

We can thus divide 'science of the occult' into at least three camps based on *intentions*: (1) those who seek to justify occult phenomena, (2) those who seek to debunk them, and (3) those who study occult phenomena as interesting cases for the discipline they happen to belong to, whether this be psychology, sociology, or history. While the *intentions* differ, however, the *consequences* of all three types of research may in fact overlap in interesting ways. A historical study of occult movements may in practice have a legitimizing effect on occult practitioners, and a parapsychological study intended to demonstrate clairvoyance may in practice lead to a strengthening of the null-hypothesis of the sceptics.

While it will take us too far afield to discuss the full extent of such effects (examples may be gleaned from the articles on psychology and sociology of the occult in the present volume, as well as the one on the Society for Psychical Research), we should mention some notable contributions to science that have come about precisely from the scientific study of occult phenomena. The study of the occult has notably been an important experimental challenge, yielding significant methodological innovation in fields such as psychology, physiology, and statistical analysis. The 1784 investigation of Mesmer's animal magnetism by a commission of the French Royal Academy led to the development of the first blinded and controlled clinical trial, and the discovery of a placebo effect (cf. Herr, 2005). A century later, experimental studies in psychical research triggered much discussion about probability theory, with major figures such as C.S. Peirce contributing. It was also in the context of early experimental parapsychology that the full gamut of blinds, control and randomization was employed together in experimental trials for the first time (cf. Hacking, 1988). These may not have been quite the kind of contributions to science that most psychical researchers would have in mind, but they are nevertheless remarkable achievements of critical thinking. As these examples suggest, the scientific study of the occult is riddled with unintended consequences.

REFERENCES AND FURTHER READING

Adorno, Theodor (1994) 'Theses Against Occultism', in idem, *The Stars Down to Earth: And Other Essays on the Irrational in Culture*, London: Routledge, 172–80.

Asprem, Egil (2008) 'Magic Naturalized? Negotiating Science and Occult Experience in Aleister Crowley's "Scientific Illuminism"', *Aries* 8.2, 139–65.

——(2011) 'Pondering Imponderables: Occultism in the Mirror of Late Classical Physics', *Aries*, 11.2, 129–65.

——(2013) 'Theosophical Attitudes Toward Science: Past and Present', in Olav Hammer and Mikael Rothstein (eds.) *Brill Handbook of the Theosophical Current*, Leiden, Brill, 405–27.

——(2014) *The Problem of Disenchantment: Scientific Naturalism and Esoteric Discourse, 1900–1939*, Leiden and Boston: Brill.

Bowler, Peter J. (2001) *Reconciling Science and Religion: The Debate in Early Twentieth Century Britain*, Chicago: University of Chicago Press.

Hacking, Ian (1988) 'Telepathy: Origins of Randomization in Experimental Design', *Isis* 79, 427–51.

Hammer, Olav (2001) *Claiming Knowledge: Strategies of Epistemology from Theosophy to the New Age*, Leiden, Brill.

Hanegraaff, Wouter J. (1996) *New Age Religion and Western Culture: Western Esotericism in the Mirror of Secular Thought*, Leiden, Brill.

——(2001) 'Beyond the Yates Paradigm: The Study of Western Esotericism between Counterculture and New Complexity', *Aries* 1.1, 5–37.

——(2005) 'Occult/Occultism', in Hanegraaff et al. (eds.) *Dictionary of Gnosis and Western Esotericism*, 884–89, Leiden, Koninkleijke Brill.

——(2012) *Esotericism and the Academy: Rejected Knowledge in Western Culture*, Cambridge, Cambridge University Press.

Herr, H. W. (2005) 'Franklin, Lavoisier, and Mesmer: Origin of the Controlled Clinical Trial', *Urological Oncology*, 23.5, 346–51.

Hughes, Jeff (2003) 'Occultism and the Atom: The Curious Story of Isotopes', *Physics World*, September 2003, 31–35.

Laudan, Larry (1981) 'The Medium and Its Message: A Study of Some Philosophical Controversies About Ether', in G. Cantor and M. J. S. Hodge (eds.) *Conceptions of Ether: Studies in the History of Ether Theories, 1740–1900*, Cambridge, Cambridge University Press, 157–86.

Morrisson, Mark S. (2007) *Modern Alchemy: Occultism and the Emergence of Atomic Theory*, Oxford, Oxford University Press.

Principe, Lawrence (1998) *The Aspiring Adept: Robert Boyle and His Alchemical Quest*, Princeton, Princeton University Press.

Strube, Julian (2013) *Vril. Eine okkulte Naturkraft in Theosophie und esoterischem Neonazismus*, Paderborn, Wilhelm Fink.

Stuckrad, Kocku von (2005) 'Western Esotericism: Towards an Integrative Model of Interpretation', *Religion* 34.2, 78–97.

Webb, James (1974) *The Occult Underground*, London, Open Court Publishing.

Witham, Larry (2005) *The Measure of God: Our Century-Long Struggle to Reconcile Science & Religion*, New York, HarperCollins Publishers.

Yates, Frances (1964) *Giordano Bruno and the Hermetic Tradition*, London, Routledge & Kegan Paul.

CHAPTER SEVENTY-ONE

SOCIOLOGY AND THE OCCULT

Kennet Granholm

While the historical study of the occult has grown into its own discipline since the early 1990s, under labels such as 'the history of hermetic philosophy' and 'the history of Western esotericism,' no comparable developments exist for a sociology of the occult. Attempts were made in the early 1970s, but the work in this regard by pioneering researchers such as Edward Tiryakian has largely gone without notice in broader sociology. With historians of the occult neglecting or being uninterested in sociological perspectives, and with sociologists interested in the study of the occult rarely paying attention to existing historiographical work, we have a situation where incompatible definitions abound and misunderstandings are difficult to avoid.

A BRIEF (AND INCOMPLETE) HISTORY OF SOCIOLOGICAL APPROACHES TO THE OCCULT

The roots of the sociological study of what is today often termed the occult go as far back as to the early days of the discipline of sociology itself. In the early 1900s Ernst Troeltsch (1992) discussed 'mysticism' as a (Christian) religious orientation revolving around inner religious experience (Kippenberg 2009, 69), which is essentially individualistic and eschews social organization (Campbell 1972, 120; Partridge 2004, 20–21). Troeltsch's theories informed the study of cults as 'the organizational response associated with mystical religion' (Campbell 1972, 120), in effect implying loosely organized, inclusive, and doctrinally deviant religious groupings. Although having an origin in notions of 'mystical inner experience' studies of cult-type religiosity rarely employ the term 'occult' in any prominent way and have included many groups, practices, and philosophies that can hardly be recognized as occult. In the 1970s, however, studies that did just that emerged. Based on 'the worlds of the occult and the magical, of spiritualism and psychic phenomena, of mysticism and new thought, of alien intelligences and lost civilizations, of faith healing and nature cure' (1972, 122) having 'become a far more visible component of the total cultural system' (1972, 119), Colin Campbell formulated the notion of the cultic milieu as 'the cultural underground of society...[which] includes all deviant belief-systems and their associated practices' (1972, 122).

With Edward Tiryakian in the forefront, the 1970s also saw attempts to formulate a sociology of the occult. For Tiryakian (1974b, 265) occultism stood for:

> intentional practices, techniques, or procedures which *(a)* draw upon hidden or concealed forces in nature *or* the cosmos that cannot be measured or recognized by the instruments of modern science, and *(b)* which have as their desired or intended consequences empirical results, such as either obtaining knowledge of the empirical course of events or altering them from what they would have been without this intervention.

He also strongly focused on secrecy as a main ingredient in occult philosophies, writing that '[a]t the heart of esoteric knowledge is its concealment from public dissemination, from the gaze of the profane or uninitiated' (Tiryakian 1974b, 265–66). As with Campbell, and much sociological scholarship in the 1970s, Tiryakian contrasted 'occult culture' and 'normal' or 'exoteric' culture, seeking to highlight the deviant nature of the occult (Tiryakian 1974a, 1; 1974b, 267). This was also the case with another important sociologist of the occult in the 1970s, Marcello Truzzi (1974, 244–45), whose emphasis on the deviant and countercultural nature of the occult is even stronger than Tiryakian's. For Truzzi occultism is a 'wastebasket, for knowledge claims that are deviant in some way,' comprising of knowledge not accepted in mainstream religion, science, or culture (1974, 245). The major problem with these approaches is that esotericism/occultism becomes an empty category that can in essence include anything and everything, with the phenomena included ceasing to be occult when and if they cease to be deviant (for a critique of Truzzi, see Hanegraaff 1998, 40–42). This focus on deviance is problematic in marginalizing the occult and in making it dependent on other, more established categories of religion, science, philosophy, and culture. The focus on deviancy as constitutional is also unsustainable in light of the increased popularity of the occult, where the 'deviant alternatives' have become mainstream (Partridge 2004, 70).

Unfortunately, most sociologists have continued to employ the term 'occult' as a denominator for vaguely supernatural phenomena, beliefs, etc. that cannot easily be placed in other categories (see e.g. McGuire 2000, 121–22; Clark 2003). There are, however, indications that change might be occurring, much due to the research of Christopher Partridge since the early 2000s. Partridge's work builds on the theories of sociologists such as Max Weber, Troeltsch, and Campbell, but is set in an explicitly contemporary framework where mass media, popular culture, and consumerism play significant roles. The basic premise is that the contemporary West is undergoing significant religious transformations, that we are witnessing a *re-enchantment* in which 'alternative' forms of religiosity are flourishing. As he expresses it: 'Western culture is not becoming *less* religious, but rather that it is, for a variety of reasons, becoming *differently* religious' (Partridge 2013, 116). Closely influenced by Campbell's notion of the cultic milieu, Partridge presents *occulture* as 'the spiritual/mythic/paranormal background knowledge that informs the plausibility structures of Westerners' (2004, 187) that 'includes those often *hidden*, *rejected* and *oppositional* beliefs and practices associated with esotericism, theosophy, mysticism, New Age, Paganism, and a range of other subcultural beliefs and practices…' (2004, 68). This milieu 'is constantly feeding and being fed by popular culture', and is thus constantly updated with new material (Partridge 2013, 116). Indeed, as the title of Partridge's recent publication on the subject clearly states, 'occulture is ordinary.'

THE HISTORICAL STUDY OF WESTERN ESOTERICISM

Most research on the occult has been conducted by historians, since the early 1990s in the field of 'Western esotericism.' In this research a terminological distinction, which is actually of sociological significance, is usually made between occultism and esotericism, and I will therefore use the terms 'esoteric' and 'esotericism' when directly referring to historiographic studies. Whereas sociologists have defined the occult based on typological constituents, particularly a focus on 'deviance' and 'secrecy,' historians of esotericism have instead looked at the historical continuity of certain forms of philosophies and practices. There are approaches which seemingly build on typologies, such as Antoine Faivre's description of Western esotericism as 'an ensemble of spiritual currents in modern and contemporary Western history which share a certain *air de famille*, as well as the form of thought which is its common denominator' (Faivre 1998, 2), identifiable by the idea of invisible correspondences, the notion of a living nature imbued by divine forces, a focus on imagination as an 'organ of the soul' (Hanegraaff 1996, 398) and intermediary beings as central in the pursuit of hidden knowledge, and the experience of transmutation where the individual gradually purifies his/her soul or essence until a perfected state of being is reached (Faivre 1994, 10–14). This definition has been used as a 'check list' for determining if a phenomenon, practice, or philosophy is esoteric or not, but Faivre was in fact describing common denominators in a specific corpus of material. The description has been criticized for not taking the change over time into account (Hanegraaff 1998, 46–47; 2003), Renaissance and early modern material resulting in appearing more esoteric than later material.

An approach with typological inclination is Wouter Hanegraaff's discussion of reason, faith, and gnosis as three ideal typical modes of knowing in Western culture (2008. Cf. 1996, 518n5; 1998, 19–21). Reason-based claims, such as scientific ones, can be communicated easily and their validity can be checked by anyone with sufficient skills within the field the claim is made in. Faith-based claims, such as those found in religion, can be communicated to others but in no way checked for accuracy. Gnosis-based claims, however, relate to knowledge of an experiential nature that is essentially incommunicable and the validity of which cannot be checked by any conventional means.

Earlier historiographical studies proposed the existence of a more or less self-contained 'occult tradition' (see Yates 2002), but while still common among non-specialists (e.g. Katz 2005) and in insider accounts (e.g. Holman 2008), such notions have largely been abandoned in specialist scholarship. Prominent scholars in the field of Western esotericism are careful to emphasize that 'esotericism' is a scholarly tool used by researchers to analyze certain phenomena in Western cultural and religious history, something that is 'not "discovered" but *produced*' (Hanegraaff 1998, 11, 16). There is also a tendency towards staying clear of narrow definitions. For example, in Hanegraaff's most recent work the focus is on historically specific societal processes of exclusion, particularly linked to the Reformation and the 'scientific revolution,' in which a number of previously accepted and in many cases unrelated phenomena came to be deemed as either 'heresy' or 'flawed science' and marginalized as rejected knowledge (Hanegraaff 2012). The lumping together of these phenomena made it possible to regard them as constituting a single unified 'tradition.' Subsequently in the nineteenth-century 'occult revival,' they could be presented as a tradition which had unduly been persecuted and marginalized throughout Western cultural and religious history.

Kocku von Stuckrad has advocated a discursive approach in which the esoteric is regarded as a 'structural element of Western culture' consisting of '*claims* to "real" or absolute knowledge and the *means* of making this knowledge available' (2005b, 9–10). The approach also reintroduces the notion of secrecy, which was largely downplayed in earlier historical approaches due to the exaggerated focus on it in sociological studies. However, von Stuckrad is not interested in 'knowledge hidden from all but a select few' but in the '*dialectic of the hidden and revealed*' (2005b, 10), that is to say, a *rhetoric* of secrecy where the *revelation* of 'hidden knowledge' is in fact more elementary than keeping it secret. Esoteric discourse crosses boundaries of religious identities, and the very concept of the esoteric becomes an analytical tool through which interreligious connections and processes of identity formation are investigated.

A HISTORICAL-SOCIOLOGICAL APPROACH TO THE STUDY OF THE OCCULT

The historiographic study of Western esotericism, the sociology of the occult, and the study of contemporary religiosity with occult leanings, mainly in the fields of pagan studies and the study of new religions, have largely remained separate from each other. This means that even though the same phenomena may be discussed, the interpretation of them can vary to the degree that misunderstandings are impossible to avoid. In part this is due to different definitions informed by different research questions, as in the uncovering of historical connections in historical studies and the examination of typological similarities in sociological studies. Some scholars have suggested that keeping these foci separate is satisfactory (Hammer 2004, 448–49), but I disagree. If fruitful dialogue and cooperation is considered desirable and is to be achieved, sociological approaches to the occult need to be compatible with historical ones (Hanegraaff 1998, 41). As sustained research into the occult has primarily been conducted by historians of Western esotericism it is prudent to start the search for common ground there.

As with recent approaches in the field of Western esotericism, it might be best to avoid strict and narrow definitions of the occult. As von Stuckrad puts it, 'instead of asking what esotericism is and what currents belong to it, it is more fruitful to ask what insights into the dynamics of Western history we might gain by applying the etic concept of esotericism' (2005a, 80). This also highlights the major benefits of the esoteric/occult as an analytical tool, namely the possibility to investigate the often neglected and seemingly discrepant territories between religious and secular-scientific traditions, institutions, and identities (von Stuckrad 2005a, 90–91; 2013). Three approaches discussed above, those of Hanegraaff, von Stuckrad, and Partridge, in many ways complement each other, and in combining elements from each a potential for a viable historical-sociological approach emerges. Hanegraaff's approach and studies shed light on historical processes whereby certain phenomena have been lumped together, come to be seen as related to each other, and deemed to be both topics unworthy of serious scholarly investigation and practices and philosophies to be ridiculed and/or forbidden – while providing solid research on their actual historical roots and continuities, relations, and discrepancies. Partridge's approach and studies shed light on the processes and mechanisms whereby these practices are popularized, while providing theoretical tools for sociological investigation of the occult. Von Stuckrad's approach and studies provide means to examine typological qualities and similarities of use for sociologically inclined scholars while maintaining a solid historical grounding. By drawing on all three approaches it is possible to construct an overarching framework in which sociological topics and themes can be examined in ways that are historically sound.

Von Stuckrad (2005b, 6–11) presents a perspective of an esoteric field of discourse which crosses the boundaries of different religious identities and traditions as well as those of religious and secular-scientific institutions. In a sociological study focused on societal relations and responses it is of use to talk of 'the field of discourse on the esoteric,' i.e. all engagement with the occult, including pro-, contra-, and scholarly discourse (Granholm 2013b, 51). This added dimension introduces new potentials for the study of the occult that are overlooked in strict focus on only 'that which is occult,' further strengthening the relevance of the study of the occult for both historians and sociologists. Furthermore, in order to recognize both historical relations and continuities and new developments it is conducive to look for both uses of conventional occult notions and symbols and occurrences of '*claims* to "real" or absolute knowledge and the *means* of making this knowledge available' (Von Stuckrad 2005b, 9–10).

Naturally, introducing sociological perspectives to the study of the occult presents both new potentials and problems. Sociological studies introduce methodological tools such as ethnography and interviews, shedding light on the real life-contexts of lived occult practices and philosophies. This presents perspectives and may problematize ingrained assumptions in ways that a reliance on only textual material cannot. A questioning of the common propensity among historians to perceive the occult as a concern for elites rather than 'commoners' springs to mind. Historical perspectives on continuities and disruptions may challenge the perspectives on and overestimations of 'the new' that sociologists are often preoccupied with.

SOCIOLOGICAL DIMENSIONS OF THE OCCULT

There are many dimensions of the occult that are more or less neglected in the historiographic study of Western esotericism but lend themselves well to sociological research. I will briefly discuss a small number of these, presenting examples for future research rather than providing research findings (see Granholm 2011).

The idea of 'belief' as the core of religion is deeply influenced by Protestant theology and should be problematized, but at the same time it cannot be denied that the intellectual dimension is an important aspect of religion. 'Beliefs' as expressed in ritual manuals and occult treaties have been discussed to great extent in the historical study of the occult, however, how these beliefs are actually realized in ritual practices and the lives and of believers has received relatively little attention. If looking at discourse and rhetoric (e.g. Hammer 2001), it is possible to examine how communicative strategies influence and direct the lived lives and social contexts of occult practitioners. For example, I have suggested a model of investigating occult currents as discursive complexes, i.e. the interplay of specific discourses in specific combinations that inform ritual practice, teachings, rhetoric, social organization, and so on (Granholm 2013b). In this model the key discourses constituting a specific occult current – for example the primacy of nature and the goal to revive pre-Christian religion and culture in neopaganism – are fluidic and ever-changing, and in their interaction with broader societal discourses – e.g. those of secularism, feminism, or racialism – each manifestation of an occult current takes on unique forms, which then affects the lives and actions of the people involved in different ways. Just to give a couple of examples: Anthropologist Galina Lindquist (1997, vii–x) has discussed how members of the Swedish neoshamanic community actively opposed a construction project that would have leveled large areas of forest. The Swedish neoshamans' strong focus on the sacredness of nature resulted in direct social action. Conversely, Nordic Heathen communities often have to deal with accusations of fostering racist convictions, partly due to Nordic Heathenism being seen as closely linked to the rise of Nazism in 1930s' Germany and partly due to the focus on Old Norse *culture* that is common in many groups today. For some groups this has been resolved by maintaining a focus on race and culture, but recasting race as a spiritual quality, meaning that there is no conflict in non-Scandinavians being involved. What we see here is an interaction between the neopagan discourse of reviving pre-Christian religion and culture, an opposition to racist discourses, and an alignment with pluralist-multiculturalist discourses.

Ritual is an important element of many occult groupings, particularly initiatory magic orders and fraternities. This dimension has been researched to a certain degree, but the focus has largely been on ritual texts rather than ritual practice in real-life contexts (e.g. Bogdan 2007; for anthropological studies see Granholm 2012b; Luhrman 1989). In stark contrast, for sociologists the primary focus in looking at ritual is not on the content of the act but on the symbolic meaning attached to it by participants (McGuire 2000, 17–18). While ritual in and by itself would constitute an interesting subject for sociological study, it is the social context of initiatory practices that is of most interest. Through initiations the participant links his/her self-identity and spiritual progress to the group itself as well as to other members involved in the same initiatory processes. As higher degrees are commonly linked to increased organizational influence, the dynamics involved in initiation are central in the investigation of the interaction and interpersonal relations between members in a particular occult group.

Ritual connects to community, another dimension that is not really touched upon in historiographic studies. The shared experience in ritual reproduces and transmits a collective sense of identity and belonging among group members (McGuire 2000, 20–22). This sense of community often exists even in groups that have their membership spread across great geographical distances. A member may not have direct contact with other members, but has a sense of community in his/her identity as a group member. A certain sense of community can exist in settings that are much more loosely organized than those in initiatory societies, as for example in therapeutic or spiritualistic practices. In these cases the sense of community may be connected to a sense of spiritual kinship or to an extended family consisting of both living and deceased relatives. In addition, another sense of community, that of a cross-cultural and historical community of occultists joined in their pursuit of the same hidden knowledge. This imagined community grants the occultist a feeling of belonging, even though he/she might be the only one involved in the occult in his/her community, lacking any contacts with other living practitioners.

Demography is a dimension of interest for sociologists, and often a matter of quantitative research. If approaching the occult as an analytical tool rather than a 'religious tradition' expressed in self-identities, institutional affiliations, etc., conventional demographic research is made difficult. Counting members of conventionally identifiable occult groups, participants at mind, body, spirit-fairs, and subscribers to occult journals is possible to some extent, but such an approach hardly includes all of the people who are in some way engaged in and with the occult. Finding suitable parameters to secure that all or most of these people are included is difficult, and may even be impossible.

Finally, secrecy, while downplayed by historians of Western esotericism, is a dimension of considerable sociological significance. Earlier sociologists of the occult approached the subject as the literal keeping of secrets, but a more fruitful approach is to look at the rhetoric of uncovering hidden truth. The dialectic of the hidden and revealed informs the perceptions and relation to the world of individuals inclined towards the occult, as it will make the person perceive an inherent meaning in events and experiences that another person would consider insignificant. This may in turn direct that person to act and relate to other people, social life in general, nature, professional life, and so on, according to the hidden meaning which has been discovered. In initiatory societies the social context is directly informed by the revelation of hidden knowledge. Occult knowledge – the key form of social capital in initiatory orders – cannot be mediated by linguistic means, it must be experienced. Claiming such knowledge suggests shared experiences and creates bonds between members. Occult knowledge also structure hierarchies and group dynamics as novices must commonly follow specific pre-established practices before they can lay claim to it.

In addition themes such as gender balance and relation, connection to and enactment of political ideologies, individual identity-construction, and relation to the surrounding society constitute subjects of sociological interest which have not been sufficiently addressed in historiographic studies of the occult.

MODERNITY AND THE OCCULT

As sociological studies commonly revolve around modernity as a series of large-scale social, cultural, and political transformations, starting in the post-Enlightenment West but with far-ranging global implications (Giddens 1990, 1–4, 14; Wittrock 2002, 48; Crook, Pakulski and Waters 1992, 18–19), let us look at what some key theories on modernity might imply for the occult.

Modernity, in its western European forms,[1] is ideologically dominated by secularism, which, in simplification, posits a rationalist-scientific frameset as preferable to a religious one (Wittrock 2002, 54). Secularism is the driving force behind secularization, a process that is often regarded as the most elementary expression of modernization. Rather than forming a single theory detailing a more or less straightforward process, 'secularization theory' forms an overarching meta-theoretical framework, or even paradigm, containing several distinct and at times conflicting theories, which in turn deal with a number of intertwined processes. At the core of most secularization theories is the differentiation of societal institutions and functions where religion becomes its own sphere no longer integrated into others, which then results in the privatization and decline of religion (Casanova 1994, 19–39; Granholm 2013a). If the occult is regarded as phenomena that transgress the seemingly inviolable borders between the scientific-secular and the religious, the question arises to what degree the decline of religion, if taken as a matter of fact, also means the decline of occultism. The simple answer is that some forms of occultism decline, namely those with a strong religious ethos, whereas other forms might be unaffected or even flourish. New expressions of the occult were crafted under the impact of secularism, and this relates to the distinction between esotericism and occultism which is of significance in the historical study of Western esotericism, as mentioned earlier. For Hanegraaff, occultism signifies 'all attempts by esotericists to come to terms with a disenchanted world' (1996, 422). Occultists actively engaged with, and often adapted to, the new rationalist-scientific worldview, resulting in, among other things, the emergence of an evolutionary paradigm in discourses of spiritual progress and 'the psychologization of religion and sacralization of psychology' (Hanegraaff 1996, 411–513; 2003). This meant that occultists were more inclined to perceive impersonal, causal laws of nature, and to manipulate occult *mechanisms*, whereas the pre-Enlightenment esotericist would have seen the world as organic and imbued by divine forces, and also to describe mystical experience and encounters with spiritual beings as occurring in the psyche rather than on objectively existing astral planes. In short, occultism involved both the 'scientification of religion' and the 'religionization of science.'

It should also be noted that secularization theory commonly relies on strictly substantive definitions of religion and is concerned with specific institutionalized forms of Christianity, and 'the decline of religion' thus mainly implies 'the decline of (some) Christianity.' This de-Christianization, in turn, meant that the possibilities for unorthodox and eclectic religious expressions were greatly enhanced. Increasingly, inspiration was drawn from non-Western cultures and non-Christian religions, much influenced by (as well as partly inspiring) the new comparative study of religions (Hanegraaff 1996, 442–62). Another result was that phenomena that had been marginalized in the boundary work-processes of the Reformation and the scientific revolution came to be regarded as a semi-independent and persecuted wisdom tradition, which spawned 'the occult revival' and the creation of an occult cultural sphere in the form of initiatory orders and societies.

As for the privatization of religion (a notion that is criticized by e.g. Casanova 1994), it is certainly true that some phenomena conventionally included under the label the occult, such as astrology, had a far greater role to play in pre-Enlightenment European political life (see e.g. von Stuckrad 2010, 136–134). However, if the understanding of 'the public sphere' is broadened to not only include political life but also mass media and popular culture, we instead see an increased visibility and massive popularization of the occult in the post-Enlightenment West. Subject matter that had previously been reserved for elites became available for the larger masses.

Turning to more recent times, to what sociologists have variously termed late, accentuated, liquid, or post-modernity, the processes set in motion in earlier phases of modernity have accelerated. The drive towards the differentiation of societal institutions and functions has progressed to the degree where the ever-smaller fragments are no longer self-sustaining enough to maintain themselves and therefore flow into each other in new constellations that are constantly formed, broken up, and reformed (Crook, Pakulski and Waters 1992, 16, 36–37). In the modern individualist ethos, accompanied by a decreased trust in religious and secular authorities and the benefits of technological progress (Giddens 1990, 10; Bauman 1992, viii–x, xvii–xxii), increased pluralism and plurality brought on by greater immigration and multiculturalism, fluidic and often temporary occult approaches where elements of a diverse range of religious source material are dis-embedded from their original contexts and re-embedded in new constellations are formed to suit the needs and preferences of individual practitioners. Modernity, and particularly late modernity, thus inspires a more conscious, extensive, and accentuated eclecticism than what was common in pre-Enlightenment occultism, all in the desire to find increasingly distant exotic others[2] as the world shrinks due to globalization.

Along with the critique of many other hegemonic truths of earlier phases of modernity, secularism is put into question. Guided by 'post-secular' discourses,[3] people are more prone to both assess religion as beneficial for society and to perceive new functions and arenas for it. This applies primarily to non-institutionalized religiosity, and opportunities for the occult to thrive are ample. Post-secular discourses may be critical towards an overreliance on secularism, but they are also deeply dependent on the awareness of the precious hegemonic situation of the same, and the end result is thus not a return to pre-Enlightenment values and modes of life. Instead, the faculties of rationality, scientific findings, and offerings of contemporary society coexist with a renewed appreciation of the religious, meaning that the occult in late modernity moves away from the secular-religious divide of earlier phases of modernity. Metaphysical and scientific explanatory models exist side by side, relating to different but not opposed layers of reality.

In an increasingly globalized and transnational world, nation states and national identity experience devaluation at the expense of a revaluation of the regional. Translocal connections and interdependencies develop between various localities in transnational networks, and the distinctive is universally appraised in a 'universalization of particularism' at the same time as local and regional variations of global phenomena are forged in a 'particularization of universalism' (Friedman 1995, 72). The interconnectedness of different localities and the shrinking of the world also problematizes the view of the occult as a distinctly Western phenomenon, which is the dominant perspective in the historiographical study of esotericism (Granholm 2013c).

The increasing treatment of occult themes and subject matter in popular culture plays an important role in the popularization of the occult (see e.g. Granholm 2012c), which in turn makes the inclusion of occult themes a more compelling prospect for economically motivated producers of popular culture (Cf. Partridge 2004; 2005). Increasingly, the identity-construction of people is informed by popular culture (Clark 2003; Partridge 2004; 2005; Lynch 2006), and it has even been suggested that popular culture helps drive the development away from a Christian culture to one informed more by the occult (Partridge 2004; 2005; 2013). New media and communication technologies, in particular the Internet, not only make the maintenance of transnational networks possible (Friedman 1995, 70), but also result in a relative democratization of the occult where anyone in possession of the necessary technology and skills can market their own particular brand of occultism. Furthermore, the new media climate also introduces new possibilities, gives rise to changed forms, functions, and premises of communication. Mediatization, implying a development where social or cultural activities are 'to a greater or lesser degree, performed through interaction with a medium' and where these activities become dependent upon the media they operate through, is increasingly a central social factor (Hjarvard 2008, 13). For many small groups it becomes possible to have their membership spread throughout the world, while still being able to communicate effectively. Many occult groups also operate solely over the Internet (see Arthur 2002; Lövheim 2003).

CONCLUSION

This essay has briefly discussed sociological perspectives on the occult, focusing more on potentials and possibilities than on providing any definite answers. While the historical study of the occult is well established, its sociological equivalent has barely seen the light of day. Much work remains to be done, and indeed needs to be done, but combining historical and sociological perspectives offers great opportunities, particularly for the study of the occult in the present day.

NOTES

1 Modernity assumes many different and culturally specific forms and shapes (Eisenstadt 2003).

2 A common view in occultism is that hidden wisdom resides with exotic others (see Granholm 2012a; 2013c).

3 This use of the term post-secular differs from the one used by Jürgen Habermas. For Habermas, a society being post-secular refers to '*a change in consciousness*' in relation to religion within it (2008, 20), implying not religion 'returned to a position of renewed public prominence,' but more 'a revision of a previously over-confidently secularist outlook' (Harrington 2007, 547). For an outline of the scholarly debate concerning the post-secular, as well as an introduction to the more common interpretations based on Habermas' work, see Granholm, 2013a; Moberg, Granholm and Nynäs 2012, 3–8.

REFERENCES AND FURTHER READING

Arthur, S. (2002) 'Technophilia and Nature Religion: the Growth of a Paradox,' *Religion* 32(4), 303–14.

Bauman, Z. (1992) *Intimations of Postmodernity*, London: Routledge.

Bogdan, H. (2007) *Western Esotericism and Rituals of Initiation*, Albany, NY: State University of New York Press.

Campbell, C. (1972) 'The Cult, the Cultic Milieu and Secularization,' *A Sociological Yearbook of Religion in Britain* 5, 119–36.

Casanova, J., 1994. *Public Religions in the Modern World*. Chicago, IL: University of Chicago Press.

Clark, L. S. (2003) *From Angels to Aliens: Teenagers, the Media, and the Supernatural*, New York, NY: Oxford University Press.
Crook, S., Pakulski, J. and Waters, M. (1992) *Postmodernization: Change in Advanced Society*, London: Sage.
Eisenstadt, S. N. (2003) *Comparative Civilizations & Multiple Modernities*, 2 vols, Leiden: Brill.
Faivre, A. (1994) *Access to Western Esotericism*, Albany, NY: State University of New York Press.
——(1998) 'Questions of Terminology Proper to the Study of Esoteric Currents in Modern and Contemporary Europe,' in A. Faivre and W. J. Hanegraaff, eds. *Western Esotericism and the Science of Religion*, Leuven: Peeters, 1–10.
Friedman, J. (1995) 'Global System, Globalization and the Parameters of Modernity,' in M. Featherstone, S. Lash and R. Robertson, eds., *Global Modernities*, London: Sage, 69–90.
Giddens, A. (1990) *The Consequences of Modernity*, Cambridge: Polity Press.
Granholm, K. (2011) 'The Sociology of Esotericism,' in P. B. Clarke, ed. *The Oxford Handbook of the Sociology of Religion*, revised paperback edition, Oxford: Oxford University Press, 783–800.
——(2012a) 'The Serpent Rises in the West: Positive Orientalism and the Reinterpretation of Tantra in the Western Left-Hand Path,' in I. Keul, ed., *Transformation and Transfer of Tantra in Asia and Beyond*, Berlin: De Gruyter, 479–503.
——(2012b) 'Dragon Rouge: Left-Hand Path Magic with a Neopagan Flavour,' *Aries* 12(1), 131–56.
——(2012c) 'Metal and Magic: The Intricate Relationship Between the Metal Band *Therion* and the Magic Order *Dragon Rouge*,' in C. M. Cusack and A. Norman, eds., *Handbook of New Religions and Cultural Production*, Leiden: Brill, 553–81.
——(2013a) 'The Secular, the Post-Secular, and the Esoteric in the Public Sphere,' in E. Asprem and K. Granholm, eds., *Contemporary Esotericism*, London: Equinox Publishing, 309–29.
——(2013b) 'Esoteric Currents as Discursive Complexes,' *Religion* 43(1), 46–69.
——(2013c) 'Locating the West: Problematizing the *Western* in Western Esotericism and Occultism,' in H. Bogdan and G. Djurdjevic, eds., *Occultism in Global Perspective*, London: Equinox Publishing, 17–36.
Habermas, J. (2008) 'Notes on Post-Secular Society,' *New Perspectives Quarterly* 25(4), 17–29.
Hammer, O. (2001) *Claiming Knowledge: Strategies of Epistemology from Theosophy to the New Age*, Leiden: Brill.
——(2004) 'Esotericism in New Religious Movements,' J. R. Lewis, ed., *Oxford Handbook of New Religious Movements*, Oxford: Oxford University Press, 445–65.
Hanegraaff, W. J. (1996) *New Age Religion and Western Culture: Esotericism in the Mirror of Secular Thought*, Leiden: Brill.
——(1998) 'On the Construction of "Esoteric Traditions",' in A. Faivre and W. J. Hanegraaff, eds., *Western Esotericism and the Science of Religion*, Leuven: Peeters, 11–61.
——(2003) 'How Magic Survived the Disenchantment of the World,' *Religion* 33(4), 357–80.
——(2008) 'Reason, Faith, and Gnosis: Potentials and Problematics of a Typological Construct,' in P. Meusburger, M. Welker and E. Wunder, eds., *Clashes of Knowledge: Orthodoxies and Heterodoxies in Science and Religion*, Dordrecht: Springer Science & Business Media, 133–44.
——(2012) *Esotericism and the Academy: Rejected Knowledge in Western Culture*, Cambridge: Cambridge University Press.
Harrington, A. (2007) 'Habermas and the "Post-Secular Society",' *European Journal of Social Theory* 10(4), 543–60.

Hjarvard, S. (2008) 'The Mediatization of Religion: A Theory of Media as Agents of Religious Change,' *Northern Lights* 6, 9–26.

Holman, J. (2008) *The Return of the Perennial Philosophy: The Supreme Wisdom of Western Esotericism*, London: Watkins.

Katz, D. S. (2005) *The Occult Tradition: From the Renaissance to the Present Day*, London: Jonathan Cape.

Kippenberg, H. G. (2009) 'Max Weber: Religion and Modernization,' in P. B. Clarke, ed., *The Oxford Handbook of the Sociology of Religion*, revised edition, Oxford: Oxford University Press, 63–78.

Lindquist, G. (1997) *Shamanic Performances on the Urban Scene: Neo-Shamanism in Contemporary Sweden*, Stockholm: Stockholm University Press.

Luhrman, T. M. (1989) *Persuasions of the Witch's Craft: Ritual Magic in Contemporary England*, Cambridge, MA: Harvard University Press.

Lynch, G. (2006) 'The Role of Popular Music in the Construction of Alternative Religious Identities and Ideologies,' *Journal for the Scientific Study of Religion* 45(4), 481–88.

Lövheim, M. (2003) 'Religiös identitet på Internet,' in G. Larson, ed., *Talande tro: Ungdomar, religion och identitet*, Lund: Studentlitteratur, 119–41.

McGuire, M. B. (2000) *Religion: The Social Context*, fifth edition, Belmont, CA: Wadsworth Thomson Learning.

Moberg, M., Granholm, K. and Nynäs, P. (2012) 'Trajectories of Post-Secular Complexity: An Introduction,' in P. Nynäs, T. Utriainen and M. Lassander, eds., *Post-Secular Society*, New Brunswick, NJ: Transaction Publishers, 1–25.

Partridge, C., (2004, 2005) *The Re-Enchantment of the West: Alternative Spiritualities, Sacralization, Popular Culture, and Occulture*, 2 vols., London: T & T Clark International.

——(2013) 'Occulture is Ordinary,' in E. Asprem and K. Granholm, eds., *Contemporary Esotericism*, London: Equinox Publishing, 113–33.

Robertson, R. (1992) *Globalization: Social Theory and Global Culture*, London: Sage.

von Stuckrad, K. (2005a) 'Western Esotericism: Towards an Integrative Model of Interpretation,' *Religion* 35(2), 78–97.

——(2005b) *Western Esotericism: A Brief History of Secret Knowledge*, London: Equinox.

——(2010) *Locations of Knowledge in Medieval and Early Modern Europe: Esoteric Discourse and Western Identities*, Leiden: Brill.

——(2013) 'Discursive Transfers and Reconfigurations: Tracing the Religious and the Esoteric in Secular Culture,' in E. Asprem & K. Granholm, eds., *Contemporary Esotericism*, London: Equinox Publishing, 226–43.

Tiryakian, E. A. (1974a) 'Preliminary Considerations,' in E. A. Tiryakian, ed., *On the Margin of the Visible: Sociology, the Esoteric, and the Occult*, New York, NY: John Wiley & Sons, 1–15.

——(1974b) 'Towards the Sociology of Esoteric Culture,' in E. A. Tiryakian, ed., *On the Margin of the Visible: Sociology, the Esoteric, and the Occult*, New York, NY: John Wiley & Sons, 257–80.

Troeltsch, E. (1992 [1931]) *The Social Teaching of the Christian Churches*, 2 vols., Louisville, KY: Westminster John Know Press – originally published as *Die Soziallehren der christlichen kirchen und gruppen* in 1911/1912.

Truzzi, M. (1974) 'Definition and Dimensions of the Occult: Towards a Sociological Perspective,' in E. A. Tiryakian, ed., *On the Margin of the Visible: Sociology, the Esoteric, and the Occult*, New York, NY: John Wiley & Sons, 243–55.

Wittrock, B. (2002) 'Rethinking Modernity,' in E. Ben-Rafael and Y. Sternberg, eds., *Identity, Culture and Globalization*, Leiden: Brill, 49–73.

Yates, F. A. (2002 [1964]) *Giordano Bruno and the Hermetic Tradition*, London: Routledge.

CHAPTER SEVENTY-TWO

PSYCHOLOGY AND THE OCCULT
Dialectics of Disenchantment and Re-Enchantment in the Modern Self

Roderick Main

INTRODUCTION

At first glance, psychology and the occult might seem to be very far removed from each other. The one, predominantly empirical and rational, is well integrated and highly esteemed within mainstream modern cultures, while the other, predominantly speculative and seemingly irrational, is marginalized and viewed with disdain, for the most part tolerated only as a source of fantasy material within the field of popular entertainment. Yet if, as this chapter attempts, we look more closely at both psychology and the occult, we find that each is inherently complex and within its complexity is deeply and multiply involved with the other.

The fields of both psychology and the occult are vast, and a comprehensive account of their interactions would span most of human history. The focus in the present chapter is inevitably quite narrow. First, I shall note some features of specifically modern, scientific psychology which may have primed it for engagement with the occult. I shall then similarly note characterizations of nineteenth-century and later occultism in the light of which one can, in turn, understand occultists' interest in the newly emerging scientific psychology. Next, I shall illustrate some of the actual complex engagements of psychology with the occult and of occultism with psychology that have taken place from the late nineteenth to the early twenty-first century. Finally, I shall reflect further on some of the reasons why, despite their profound differences, modern psychology and occultism have had, and continue to have, so many interactions – with a central role ascribed to the cultural processes of disenchantment and re-enchantment.

SECULARIZATION AND THE EMERGENCE OF SCIENTIFIC PSYCHOLOGY

Psychology in the broad sense of providing a rational account (*logos*) of the soul (*psyche*) has existed since ancient times (MacDonald 2003, 2007), but modern, scientific (as distinct from philosophical and theological) psychology emerged only in the course of the nineteenth century. A crucial driver in its emergence was the process of secularization and the new conceptualizations of subjectivity to which secularization gave rise. As one important facet of this process, widespread industrialization and urbanization created a situation where identities could no longer so easily be sustained by traditional communities but, in ever more alienated mass societies, had to be sought instead in an intensified individuality and inwardness, with the result that the psychological subject was thrust into the foreground (Homans 1979, 1–5). Moreover, whereas traditionally subjectivity had been conceptualized in terms of the soul with its implications of the sacred, in the modern period, under the influence of Enlightenment thought, subjectivity was instead increasingly conceptualized in more rational, secular terms as mind and consciousness (Owen 2004, 115). This new conceptualization led to the hope that it might be possible to submit the psychological subject, the self, to natural scientific methods of empirical investigation and rational control (ibid.; Shamdasani 2003, 4–6).

However, attempts to establish psychology as a natural science remained fraught with difficulties. Above all, the intangible subject matter of psychology – the mind and its processes – meant that it was in large part not amenable to study by the kind of experimental, quantitative methods that had been having such inspiring success in physics and chemistry. Furthermore, because in psychology the mind was studying the mind, the dilemma of attempting to find an objective standpoint, one influenced as little as possible by the subjective preconceptions of the psychologists, was especially acute (Shamdasani 2003, 34). As a result, the efforts to separate psychology from philosophy and theology, as well as from physiology, literature, and other disciplines, were only partially successful (Owen 2004, 140). Psychology continued to lack a clear scientific identity, and as a result a multiplicity of diverse practices, both academic and clinical, developed in its name, including, for example, Wilhelm Wundt's (1832–1920) experimentalism, the same thinker's cultural psychology (*Völkerpsychologie*), Edward Titchener's (1867–1927) structuralism, William James's (1842–1910) functionalism (Schultz & Schultz 2008, 89–219), and the various depth psychologies of Pierre Janet (1859–1947), Théodore Flournoy (1854–1920), Frederic Myers (1843–1901), Sigmund Freud (1856–1939), and others (Ellenberger 1970), as well as a range of more popular 'practical' psychologies (Thomson 2006, 17–53). At the end of the nineteenth century, in James's view, psychology as a natural science remained 'particularly fragile,' allowing 'the waters of metaphysical criticism' to 'leak [into it] at every joint' (cited in Shamdasani 2003, 5; cf. Owen 2004, 140).

THE ENLIGHTENMENT'S DARK OTHER

Against the background of this scientific aspiration but insecure scientific status of psychology in the late nineteenth century, one can begin to appreciate the concurrent interest in the occult on the part of some early psychologists. For the nineteenth-century pioneers of scientific psychology, 'the occult' would primarily have been understood to refer to the beliefs and practices of spiritualists and their mediums and to the various somnambulistic phenomena associated with the latter: dissociation, multiple personalities, and heightened unconscious performance, including such putative paranormal phenomena as clairvoyance, telepathy, precognition, and even materializations – some of these seemingly replicable through hypnosis (Ellenberger

1970, 112–20). Putting aside the spiritualists' beliefs – for example, in the spirit's survival of bodily death and ability, through mediums, to communicate with the living – the early psychologists found in the mediums' practices and the phenomena they evoked a rich source of insight into the workings and structures of the mind, especially of what came to be conceptualized as the unconscious (ibid., 53–181; Shamdasani 1994).

However, as at least some of the psychologists will have known, spiritualism, widespread though it was, represented only the tip of an iceberg. Concurrently with the development of scientific psychology in the late nineteenth and early twentieth century, there was a burgeoning in Europe and beyond of a whole range of occult practices and movements. Among some of the better known and most influential of these are the Theosophical Society, the Hermetic Order of the Golden Dawn, and the 'Fourth Way' of George Ivanovich Gurdjieff (1866?–1949); and an important later twentieth-century instance is the New Age Movement. The Theosophical Society was founded in 1875 by Colonel Henry Steel Olcott (1832–1907) and Helena Blavatsky (1831–91). Drawing on both Eastern and Western religious and esoteric traditions, its members sought to explore and learn how magically to utilize the laws governing the 'unseen universe' (Santucci 2006; Hanegraaff 1998, 443–55, 470–82). The Hermetic Order of the Golden Dawn, established in 1888, was a widely proliferating ceremonial magical order with an elaborate series of initiatory grades and rituals based especially on freemasonry and Rosicrucianism but also drawing on other occult sciences and esoteric traditions, such as Tarot, alchemy, and Kabbalah (Gilbert 2006). Gurdjieff's 'Fourth Way' flourished in France, England, and America from the early 1920s. With sources in Middle Eastern and Central Asian as well as Western traditions, it sought to transform individual consciousness through exercises in 'self-remembering,' including mystical dance, set against the background of a complex esoteric cosmology (Moore 2006). Influenced by each of the preceding, as well as by much else, the New Age Movement can be seen as an eclectic milieu of essentially esoteric beliefs and practices which has been diffusing through popular culture especially in the West from about the 1970s to the present (Hanegraaff 1998). In addition to these movements there were many others, all of which more or less self-consciously drew, in various ways, on currents of heterodox religious thought reaching back, via the Renaissance, into the ancient pagan world: currents that included Illuminism, Christian theosophy, Rosicrucianism, Paracelsianism, alchemy, Christian Kabbalah, Medieval occult sciences and magical currents, Neoplatonic theurgy, Hermetism, and Gnosticism (for introductions to all of these, see Hanegraaff et al. 2006, as well as various chapters in the present volume; see also MacDonald 2007).

Under the general label of 'Western esotericism,' these currents of thought have recently begun to come under scholarly scrutiny. Antoine Faivre influentially defined them as a 'form of thought' (Faivre 1994, 10) exhibiting a set of four intrinsic and two non-intrinsic characteristics. Intrinsically, in Faivre's view, Western esoteric currents of thought connect events not primarily by cause and effect but through patterns of correspondences; they view nature not as mechanical but as living, suffering, and in need of redemption; they use imagination as a means of mediating (through symbolic images, intermediary spirits, what Henry Corbin [1903–78] called a *mundus imaginalis*, or imaginal world) between the visible world of Nature and the invisible divine world; and the knowledge to which they aspire requires that the knower not just reasons and speculates but undergoes an experience of transmutation (ibid., 10–13). Non-intrinsically esotericism also, in Faivre's view, frequently attempts to establish common denominators among different traditions (the 'praxis of concordance') and to transmit its knowledge by means of secret initiations from master to disciple (ibid., 14–15). Faivre's definition has had an immense, predominantly positive influence in orienting scholarship on Western esotericism – even if, inevitably, it has some limitations, such as its being arguably biased by Faivre's specific interests in Christian theosophy and German romantic *Naturphilosophie* (Hanegraaff 2012, 352–55).

Importantly for the topic of this chapter, Wouter Hanegraaff has refined Faivre's definition to take account of how esotericism has had to adapt to the modern, secular world dominated by science, and has accordingly been 'reflected' in what Hanegraaff calls 'the four "mirrors of secular thought",' which he lists as 'the new worldview of "causality", the new study of religions, the new evolutionism, and the new psychologies' (Hanegraaff 1998, 518). The impact of these secularizing factors was particularly marked on nineteenth- and twentieth-century currents of esotericism, the preferred scholarly term for which has become 'occultism,' a word seemingly first used in France in the mid-nineteenth century (Hanegraaff 2006, 888). In line with this, Hanegraaff has proposed that 'occultism,' used in an analytical and typological sense, might designate 'all attempts by esotericists to come to terms with a disenchanted world or, alternatively, by people in general to make sense of esotericism from the perspective of a disenchanted world' (Hanegraaff 1998, 422). Of course, occultists themselves have continued to be concerned with enchantment (Partridge 2004, 40), but the overall context in which this concern has had to be pursued has inevitably been that of an increasingly secularized, disenchanted culture (Hanegraaff 2012, 251 n. 369; 2003). Even when some secularizing features, such as the focus on causality, have been resisted, as in certain Romantic currents of esotericism which maintained a form of correspondence theory, other secularizing characteristics, such as evolutionism, religious comparativism, or – most relevant to the present chapter – preoccupation with psychology, have been pronounced (Hanegraaff 1998, 411–513).

Hanegraaff has suggested that all Western esoteric currents of thought, both pre-modern and modern (i.e. occultist), are structurally linked in that they involve a panentheistic (or 'cosmotheistic') understanding of God as permeating and giving structure and meaning to the world, including to humans, who therefore have an inborn capacity for obtaining direct, experiential, salvific knowledge of the divine ('gnosis') (Hanegraaff 2012, 370–73). Such an outlook, Hanegraaff notes, is in fundamental tension both with biblical monotheism, in which God is seen as separate from the creation and knowledge is obtainable only through faith and reason, and with Enlightenment science, in which the world is viewed independently of God and knowledge is obtainable only through empiricism and reason. Hence, especially since the Enlightenment, esotericism and occultism have been progressively suppressed by mainstream Western culture.

In the following, because my focus is on developments within a period when secularization and disenchantment had become culturally prevalent, I shall refer to occultism and the occult unless I am specifically discussing pre-nineteenth-century currents of esotericism or later developments that for explicit reasons do not fit the designation of occultism.

PSYCHOLOGY AND THE OCCULT

Engagements of Psychology with the Occult

The actual engagements of psychology with the occult have been diverse. In some cases psychology has been more or less directly influenced by esotericism and occultism; in other cases psychology has been used as a perspective from which to explain or interpret esoteric and occult beliefs, practices, and experiences; and in yet other cases the same psychological model has been both influenced by and used as an explanatory or interpretive perspective on esoteric and occult phenomena.

Of course, many, perhaps most, psychologists, past and present, have taken no interest whatsoever in the occult, or, if they have noted it, have done so only in order to dismiss it: 'No man of science, truly independent and without *parti pris*, could be interested in occult phenomena,' declared Wundt in the nineteenth century (cited, via Flournoy, in Shamdasani 1994, xiv). However, many psychologists did take an interest, and among their number were some of the most influential shapers of the discipline. James, Myers, Janet, Flournoy, and Freud, as well as Granville Stanley Hall (1844–1924), Eugen Bleuler (1957–1939), and Carl Gustav Jung (1875–1961), for example, all attended spiritualistic séances on multiple occasions (ibid., xi). Several of these same figures were also members of the Society for Psychical Research, which had been founded in 1882 in order to subject the claims of spiritualists and Theosophists to scientific scrutiny (Owen 2004, 120–21, 170–71).

However, even among psychologists who were deeply interested in occult phenomena various opinions were held about the status of these phenomena. For instance, Myers, not professionally a psychologist but the originator of ideas about the 'subliminal' consciousness which James expected to become the most important psychological ideas of the twentieth century (Shamdasani 1994, xv), ended up believing in the reality of spirits (Owen 2004, 171–82). By contrast, Flournoy, despite being deeply influenced by Myers's subliminal psychology, deployed and developed that psychology to prove that the origin of mediumistic phenomena was psychic rather than supernatural (Shamdasani 1994, xv, xxiv). Nevertheless, for Flournoy mediumistic trance phenomena were compatible with and might even promote good health, a view which in turn set him apart from other investigators, such as Janet, who considered the states of dissociation cultivated by mediums to be for the most part pathological (ibid., xvii–xviii).

There is hardly more of a consensus when we turn to the early history of psychoanalysis. Freud famously urged Jung to make the theory of sexuality 'a dogma […], an unshakeable bulwark[…]against the black tide of mud[…]of occultism' (Jung 1963, 173). And on one occasion, when an apparent poltergeist phenomenon occurred while Freud and Jung were discussing parapsychology, Freud wrote to Jung shortly afterwards with a thoroughgoing rational and naturalistic explanation of the event (ibid., 397). Yet Freud was also clearly fascinated by these phenomena: he wrote several papers on premonitions, telepathy, and the occult significance of dreams (collected in Devereux 1953), visited mediums with Sandor Ferenczi (1873–1933), performed telepathic experiments with his daughter Anna (1895–1982) (Totton 2003, 8), became a member of the Society for Psychical Research (Owen 2004, 120), and stated to one correspondent that were he able to begin his career again he would possibly choose 'so-called occult psychic phenomena' as his field of research (Charet 1993, 210–13, quoting Freud). As his biographer Ernst Jones wrote of Freud, 'it is possible to quote just as many pieces of evidence in support of his doubt concerning occult beliefs as of his adherence to them' (quoted in ibid., 210). A significant subgroup of later psychoanalysts has continued Freud's interest – and in some cases his ambivalence (Devereux 1953, Totton 2003). Such ambivalence, certainly in Freud's case, can be understood in the context of the wider situation described by Alex Owen where 'The struggle for scientific validation and recognition in the field of medical psychology was in part bound up with the effort to rid psychology of any taint of the occult arts' (Owen 2004, 142).

Jung, for his part, considered that what Freud rejected as 'occultism' included 'virtually everything that philosophy and religion, including the rising contemporary science of parapsychology, had learned about the psyche' (1963, 173–74). Jung's own interest in spiritualism, psychical research, parapsychology, Western esotericism, and just about everything that might be encompassed by the term 'occult' could scarcely have been greater than it was (Maillard 2006; Main 2010). He read and wrote substantially about mystery religions, astrology, Gnosticism, Kabbalah, and, most extensively of all, alchemy. While not uncritical in relation to this material, Jung accorded it a central place in his psychological thinking, and it deeply informed his concepts of the collective unconscious, archetypes, individuation, and synchronicity, among others. Moreover, as revealed especially by Jung's *Memories, Dreams, Reflections* (1963) and recently published *Red Book* (2009), his engagement with this material was as much practical as theoretical and as much personal as professional. Hanegraaff even goes so far as to characterize Jung himself as 'essentially a modern esotericist' (Hanegraaff 1998, 497; see also Main 2010).

The vicissitudes of some of the lesser known figures of early psychoanalysis also illustrate the complexity of engagements of psychology with the occult. Herbert Silberer (1882–1923), for instance, offered in his *Problems of Mysticism and Its Symbols* (1914) the first detailed psychoanalytic interpretation of alchemy and other Western esoteric traditions such as Hermeticism, Rosicrucianism, and Freemasonry. His anagogic (mystical and ethical) as well as psychoanalytic approach both was influenced by Jung's prior work on occult phenomena and myth, which Silberer cites, and in turn anticipated Jung's later work on alchemy, in which Jung cites Silberer. Silberer sought and seems to have expected Freud's approval for his work. But at a time when relations between Freud and Jung had deteriorated to the point of rupture, the affinity of Silberer's work with Jung's ensured Freud's cold dismissal of it. Indeed, Freud subsequently broke off personal relations with Silberer, criticized his ideas in print, and effectively ejected him from the psychoanalytic movement – shortly after which Silberer took his own life (Merkur 2000, 86–94).

At another level of engagement two British doctors who had trained under Jung, Maurice Nicoll (1884–1953) and James Young, attempted to further their esoteric interests by engaging, initially via A. R. Orage (1873–1934) and P. D. Ouspensky (1878–1947), in the Fourth Way work of Gurdjieff. Nicoll afterwards remained within this Gurdjieffian tradition and became one of its main exponents in Britain (Thomson 2006, 94–96). Young, however, while recognizing some value in Gurdjieff's approach, had sufficient misgivings about it to return to his former medical and psychotherapeutic work. He subsequently became a prominent spokesperson for the psychoanalytic approach pioneered by Alfred Adler (1870–1937), who, like Gurdjieff but unlike Jung, attached particular importance to the development of will (ibid., 85–86).

It was not only Jungians who felt the allure of occult groups. The Freudian Emilio Servadio (1904–95), as well as being one of the founders of the Italian Psychoanalytic Society in 1930 (and later its president from 1963 to 1969), was also for a period, anonymously, a member of the magical initiatory Group of Ur led by the Italian occultist Julius Evola (1898–1974) (Hakl 2006, 345).

As already noted, many early psychologists engaged with occult phenomena through the mediation of the new fields of psychical research and later parapsychology (J. B. Rhine's [1895–1980] parapsychology laboratory was founded in 1930). These fields allowed researchers to take occult phenomena seriously, while aligning themselves with an overall scientific agenda. Other, more obviously ideological agendas – religious, anti-religious, or occultist – can often be discerned in the background of work in psychical research, but a creditable body of scientific findings has nevertheless built up over the years (Radin 1997), and many psychical researchers and parapsychologists continue to operate from psychological bases of various kinds (Kakar & Kripal 2012). However, parapsychology remains an only partially tolerated and usually marginalized sub-field within psychology, with continual suspicions about its scientific status (Leahey & Leahey 1984). Most prospering at present, because most firmly aligned with mainstream psychology, is 'anomalistic psychology,' which specifically attempts to provide naturalistic explanations for putative occult phenomena in terms of established psychological knowledge (Zusne & Jones 1989).

Two other traditions of psychological work that have been explicitly influenced by esotericism are humanistic and transpersonal psychology – both often encompassed under the general rubric of the Human Potential Movement (Hammer 2006). The concern of these approaches with recognizing and developing latent human capacities, including paranormal abilities and access to altered states of consciousness, continues preoccupations of nineteenth-century mesmerists, hypnotists, and occultists. For example, one of the inspirational figures for humanistic and transpersonal psychology was James, whose functional psychology drew on the New Thought Movement, which in turn was influenced by the psychological reframing by the Marquis de Puységur (1750–1825), Charles Poyen (d. 1844), Phineas Quimby (1802–66), and others of Franz Anton Mesmer's (1734–1815) physical theory of a universal magnetic fluid, which had also been influential in the development of nineteenth-century spiritualism and occultism (Hanegraaff 1998, 483–96). Another inspirational figure, no less influenced by mesmerism, was Jung.

Finally, it is worth noting that psychology in an eclectic mix of approaches – cognitive psychology and philosophical psychology as well as psychoanalysis and psychotherapy – has also been found valuable as an ancillary discipline when researching esoteric groups, as in Tanya Luhrmann's use of psychological anthropology to study ritual magic in contemporary England (Luhrmann 1989).

Engagements of Occultism with Psychology

There have also been many implicit and explicit engagements of occultism with psychology. Mostly these have involved occultists either being influenced by specific psychological theories and practices or, more generally, looking to the mainstream discipline of psychology for validation of their own, in some ways comparable, theories and practices.

Just as some psychologists outright reject the occult, so some occultists outright reject modern psychology, but their proportion is undoubtedly much smaller. A conspicuous example is Traditionalist thinkers such as René Guénon (1886–1951) and Titus Burckhardt (1908–84), whose antipathy to modernity and science as a whole extends to both experimental and depth psychology (Burckhardt 2003).

Many other occultists, however, have been deeply interested in psychology. For instance, Annie Besant (1847–1933), President of the Theosophical Society from 1907 to 1933, was thoroughly informed about studies of multiple personality and trance states, took keen interest in the research of Janet during the 1890s, and herself wrote two books on psychology and Theosophy (Owen 2004, 126–27, 312). The teachings of the Hermetic Order of the Golden Dawn are also largely cast in psychological terms, at least as influentially presented by Israel Regardie (Hanegraaff 2003, 366). An important figure in the post–World War II popularization of occultism, Regardie (1907–85) was knowledgeable about both Freudian and Jungian approaches to depth psychology, became a lay analyst, and even subjected some of his former teacher Aleister Crowley's visions to oedipal interpretation (Owen 2004, 302n69). Crowley himself (1875–1947), perhaps the most influential of all twentieth-century occultists, accepted many of the conclusions of psychoanalysis and frequently referred to them in his writings, though he believed they had all been prefigured by magicians in previous centuries (ibid., 208–9, 302n70). Consistent with his appreciation of psychoanalysis, Crowley's work draws attention to the connection between sex and the occult, a connection that has only recently begun to receive serious scholarly attention (Hanegraaff & Kripal 2011). Another influential twentieth-century popularizer of occultism, Dion Fortune (ps. of Violet Firth, 1890–1946), by her own account came to occultism by way of psychology after suffering what she considered a psychic attack. She trained as a psychotherapist, wrote a popular psychology book, and continued to refer to psychology throughout her later occult writings (Fanger 2006, 377–78).

The esoteric system taught by Gurdjieff and Ouspensky does not appear to have drawn directly on mainstream psychological ideas or on psychoanalysis, though it was explicitly and successfully presented as a 'Psychology of man's inner development' (Owen 2004, 233). Concerned with realizing the potentialities of human consciousness and in particular one's real 'I,' Gurdjieff's 'psychological system' formed part of an important non-professional but intellectual engagement with psychology in the interwar years in Europe and America (ibid., 231–37; Thomson 2006, 76–105; Moore 2006).

Considerable similarities have been noted between the thought of Gurdjieff and Jung, but these are almost certainly not due to any direct influence. They are more likely a result of exposure to shared cultural milieux and common sources in ancient and modern occult literatures (Owen 2004, 235). However, many occultists since the 1960s explicitly have been influenced by Jung's psychology or have referred to it for support of their own ideas. In particular, modern neo-Pagans, magicians, and diviners often frame their practices in terms of Jung's concepts of the collective unconscious, archetypes, and synchronicity (Main 2004, 159, 168–69; Hanegraaff 1998, 90, 217, 228). Interpretations of spiritual alchemy and the notion of an esoteric counter-tradition in Western culture are also deeply indebted to Jung's psychology (Hanegraaff

2012, 277–95). Such influences and appeals for support are not surprising in view of the extent to which Jung's psychology itself drew on esoteric sources.

Finally, we can note that the New Age Movement, which Hanegraaff has convincingly presented as a contemporary manifestation of esotericism (Hanegraaff 1998), includes as one of the features that makes it a distinctively modern, secularized form of esotericism its transformation through a process of the 'psychologization of religion and sacralization of psychology' (ibid., 224–29). Hanegraaff highlights two psychological influences in particular: on the one hand, an American current encompassing New Thought, functionalist psychology, and harmonial religion; and on the other hand, again the psychology of Jung (ibid., 482–513).

DIALECTICS OF DISENCHANTMENT AND RE-ENCHANTMENT IN THE MODERN SELF

Underpinning most of the above engagements between modern psychology and occultism is the fact that the two fields share some important characteristics. Above all, both are primarily concerned with the inner rather than the outer world. More particularly, both focus on exploration of subjectivity or the self, and they tend to conceive of the self in terms of mind and consciousness rather than in terms of traditional theological concepts of the soul (Owen 2004, 114–16). Both also ascribe an important role to activities and products of the imagination as sources of data about the inner world (ibid., 151–56, 181–82). Again, psychology, at least in its depth psychological and clinical variants, resembles much occultism in its preoccupation with the development or transformation of the individual (ibid., 232–33). Furthermore, as highlighted by both Hanegraaff and Owen, psychology and occultism both attempt to apply rationality to the exploration of seemingly non-rational areas of experience (Hanegraaff 1998, 406–7; Owen 2004, 14, 248). In doing this, both are generally presented by their practitioners either as scientific or at least as compatible with science (Hanegraaff 2012, 286; Owen 2004, 238–39).

Nevertheless, there are very important differences between modern psychology and occultism in terms of the methodological, epistemological, and ontological assumptions on which they are based (Owen 2004, 142). Briefly put, psychology aims at a causal, scientific investigation of the self as an aspect of natural reality, while occultism, for all its attempts at accommodation with science and secularity and its eschewal of traditional theological language, ultimately aims to achieve participative, 'gnostic' illumination of the self as an aspect of spiritual reality (ibid., 114; Hanegraaff 2003). Even in the case of depth psychology, practitioners primarily aim to understand and heal human subjectivity, for which purpose they engage hermeneutically and therapeutically with an unconscious psyche. Occultists, by contrast, aim to explore occult 'planes of reality' by means of 'astral travel,' in order both to establish the reality of those planes and to gain control over them (Owen 2004, 144). The crucial difference of occultism from, despite its association with, psychology is aptly summarized by Owen: 'The occult account [of human consciousness and interiority],' she argues, on the one hand 'operated in dialogue with a concurrent innovative theorizing of the mind [i.e. the new psychology],' yet on the other hand 'refused a purely secularized formulation of human consciousness and sought to advance both the concept and experience of self as inherently spiritual and potentially divine' (ibid., 114).

Psychology, with its naturalistic assumptions, clearly fits more comfortably than occultism into a disenchanted worldview and for this reason has largely succeeded in becoming part of mainstream modern Western culture. Occultism, by contrast, with its aim of preserving or even proving an enchanted, magical world, carries at its core a deep underlying opposition to secular, disenchanted modernity, and hence tends to be marginalized. Hanegraff has noted that this marginalization is not necessarily a result of occultism's concern with enchantment and re-enchantment being demonstrably misguided. For, he argues, the prevalent disenchanted worldview and the ideology of instrumental causality underpinning it are the result of 'a complex series of contingent social and cultural developments' (Hanegraaff 2003, 375–76). There are, according to this view, no necessary reasons why an enchanted perspective based on 'participation' – which, no less than instrumental causality, may be 'a spontaneous tendency of the human mind' (ibid., 374) – should not co-exist with the perspective of instrumental causality, as it did before instrumental causality acquired its present ideological status and became the dominant narrative of Western culture (ibid., 378).

Recent scholarship tracing the processes by which occultism and esotericism in general have been polemically constructed as the other of both biblical monotheism and Enlightenment science – the two main sources of modern Western identities – has initiated a reconsideration of the status of the occult in Western culture. Hanegraaff, for example, has suggested that modern Western identities, especially intellectual and academic ones, may actually depend on 'an implicit rejection of [those identities'] reverse mirror image [in occultism]' (Hanegraaff 2012, 3). If this is so, then any revision of our understanding of occultism may necessitate a revision of our understanding of mainstream modern identities as well – and perhaps also of the intellectual and academic priorities associated with them.

Be that as it may, throughout the period from the late nineteenth to the early twenty-first century the dominant climate of disenchantment has contained significant counter-tendencies towards re-enchantment. In the case of the relationship between psychology and the occult, this has resulted in a complex dialectical tension between disenchantment and re-enchantment centered on the concept of the self. As Owen puts it:

> A distinctively modern Weberian disenchantment and converse aspiration to some kind of spiritual dimension of life emerged during this period as constitutive of a new dialectic of modernity. An oppositional contingent and transcendent self formulated through competing accounts of subjectivity operated at the heart of this dialectic. Indeed, that same dialectic could be intrinsic to both secularized and spiritualized accounts of the self.
>
> (Owen 2004, 146)

This dialectical tension has existed between the fields of psychology and the occult themselves. On the one hand, individuals such as Flournoy and approaches such as anomalistic psychology have attempted to explain putative occult phenomena in naturalistic ways that would advance the process of disenchantment. On the other hand, various occultists, such as Besant, Regardie, and Fortune, have co-opted psychology in support of their goal of ultimately presenting a re-enchanted, magical account of reality. But the dialectical tension has also existed among psychologists themselves, as between Flournoy and Myers or between Freud and Jung, and among occultists themselves, as between those like Besant, Regardie, and Fortune, who attempted to reach an accommodation with modernity, and those like Burckhardt, who outright rejected modernity. Finally, the dialectical tension between disenchantment and re-enchantment has existed, perhaps especially so, within the minds – some might claim souls – of individual psychologists and occultists. Among psychologists the ambivalence of Freud stands out (Owen 2004, 143), though we could also note the deep, lifelong tension within Jung between his commitments to both science and religion, on the one hand, and to both mainstream and esoteric thought, on the other (Main 2004, 2010). Among occultists, as we have seen, the tension, in varying degrees, is likely to have been almost ubiquitous, in view of their ultimate goal of seeking enchantment in a predominantly disenchanted culture.

REFERENCES AND FURTHER READING

Burckhardt, T. (2003) 'Modern Psychology,' in W. Stoddart (ed.) *The Essential Titus Burckhardt: Reflections on Sacred Art, Faiths, and Civilizations*, Bloomington, IN: World Wisdom.

Charet, F. X. (1993) *Spiritualism and the Foundations of C. G. Jung's Psychology*, Albany, NY: State University of New York Press.

Devereux, G. (1953) *Psychoanalysis and the Occult*, London: Souvenir, 1974.

Ellenberger, H. (1970) *The Discovery of the Unconscious: The History and Evolution of Dynamic Psychiatry*, London: Penguin.

Faivre, A. (1994) *Access to Western Esotericism*, Albany, NY: State University of New York Press.

Fanger, C. (2006) 'Fortune, Dion (ps. of Violet Mary Firth),' in W. Hanegraaff et al. (eds.) *Dictionary of Gnosis and Western Esotericism*, Leiden: Brill.

Gilbert, R. (2006) 'Hermetic Order of the Golden Dawn,' in W. Hanegraaff et al. (eds.) *Dictionary of Gnosis and Western Esotericism*, Leiden: Brill.

Hakl, H. (2006) 'Evola, Guilio Cesare (Julius or Jules),' in W. Hanegraaff et al. (eds.) *Dictionary of Gnosis and Western Esotericism*, Leiden: Brill.

Hammer, O. (2006) 'Human Potential Movement,' in W. Hanegraaff et al. (eds.) *Dictionary of Gnosis and Western Esotericism*, Leiden: Brill.

Hanegraaff, W. (1998) *New Age Religion and Western Culture: Esotericism in the Mirror of Secular Thought*, Albany, NY: State University of New York Press.

——(2003) 'How magic survived the disenchantment of the world,' *Religion* 33: 357–80.

——(2012) *Esotericism and the Academy: Rejected Knowledge in Western Culture*, Cambridge: Cambridge University Press.

Hanegraaff, W. & Kripal, J. (eds.) (2011) *Hidden Intercourse: Eros and Sexuality in the History of Western Esotericism*, New York: Fordham University Press.

Hanegraaff, W. (ed.) in collaboration with A. Faivre, R. van den Broek, & J.-P. Brach (2006) *Dictionary of Gnosis and Western Esotericism*, Leiden: Brill.

Homans, P. (1979) *Jung in Context: Modernity and the Making of a Psychology*, Chicago, IL: University of Chicago Press, 1995.

Jung, C. G. (1963) *Memories, Dreams, Reflections*, ed. A. Jaffé, trans. R. & C. Winston, London: Fontana, 1995.

——(2009) *The Red Book – Liber Novus*, ed. S. Shamdasani, New York: Norton.

Kakar, S. & Kripal, J. (eds.) (2012) *Seriously Strange: Thinking Anew about Psychic Experiences*, New Delhi: Penguin Viking.

Leahey, T. & Leahey, G. (1984) *Psychology's Occult Doubles: Psychology and the Problem of Pseudo-Science*, Chicago, IL: Nelson-Hall.

Luhrmann, T. (1989) *Persuasions of the Witch's Craft: Ritual Magic in Contemporary England*, Cambridge, MA: Harvard University Press.

MacDonald, P. (2003) *History of the Concept of Mind, Volume 1: Speculations about Soul, Mind and Spirit from Homer to Hume*, Aldershot, UK: Ashgate.

——(2007) *History of the Concept of Mind, Volume 2: The Heterodox and Occult Tradition*, Aldershot, UK: Ashgate.

Maillard, C. (2006) 'Jung, Carl Gustav', in W. Hanegraaff et al. (eds.) *Dictionary of Gnosis and Western Esotericism*, Leiden: Brill.

Main, R. (2004) *The Rupture of Time: Synchronicity and Jung's Critique of Modern Western Culture*, Hove and New York: Brunner-Routledge.

——(2010) 'Jung as a modern esotericist', in G. Heuer (ed.) *Sacral Revolutions*, London and New York: Routledge.

Merkur, D. (2000) *Psychoanalytic Approaches to Myth: Freud and the Freudians*, New York: Routledge, 2005.

Moore, J. (2006) 'Gurdjieff, George Ivanovich,' in W. Hanegraaff et al. (eds.) *Dictionary of Gnosis and Western Esotericism*, Leiden: Brill.

Owen, A. (2004) *The Place of Enchantment: British Occultism and the Culture of the Modern*, Chicago, IL: University of Chicago Press.

Partridge, C. (2004) *The Re-Enchantment of the West, Volume 1: Alternative Spiritualities, Sacralization, Popular Culture and Occulture*, Edinburgh: T & T Clark.

Radin, D. (1997) *The Conscious Universe: The Scientific Truth of Psychic Phenomena*, New York: HarperCollins.

Santucci, J. (2006) 'Theosophical Society,' in W. Hanegraaff et al. (eds.) *Dictionary of Gnosis and Western Esotericism*, Leiden: Brill.

Schultz, D. & Schultz, S. (2008) *A History of Modern Psychology*, 9th ed., Belmont, CA: Wadsworth.

Shamdasani, S. (1994) 'Encountering Hélène: Theodore Flournoy and the genesis of subliminal psychology,' introduction to T. Flournoy, *From India to the Planet Mars: A Case of Multiple Personality with Imaginary Languages*, trans. D. Vermilye, edited and introduced by S. Shamdasani, Princeton, NJ: Princeton University Press.

——(2003) *Jung and the Making of Modern Psychology: The Dream of a Science*, Cambridge: Cambridge University Press.

Silberer, H. (1914) *Problems of Mysticism and Its Symbols*, trans. S. E. Jelliffe, New York: Weiser, 1970.

Thomson, M. (2006) *Psychological Subjects: Identity, Culture, and Health in Twentieth-Century Britain*, Oxford: Oxford University Press.

Totton, N. (ed.) (2003) *Psychoanalysis and the Paranormal: Lands of Darkness*, London: Karnac.

Zusne, L. & Jones, W. (1989) *Anomalistic Psychology: A Study of Magical Thinking*, 2nd ed., Hillsdale, NJ: Lawrence Erlbaum Associates.

CHAPTER SEVENTY-THREE

OPPOSITION TO THE OCCULT

Douglas E. Cowan

CHEERLEADER EXORCISTS AND THE NEVERENDING CRISIS

Bob Larson has been fighting demons most of his life. Born in Nebraska in 1944 and converted to evangelical Christianity at the age of 19, since then he has waged a personal crusade against the forces of the occult wherever he finds them. And, for Larson, those forces are everywhere. Best known for his weekly call-in radio program, *'Talk Back' with Bob Larson*, which aired for two decades on Christian stations throughout the United States and Canada, he has also written more than two dozen books, ranging from *Larson's Book of Cults* (1982) to *Larson's Book of Spiritual Warfare* (1999), and from *Satanism: The Seduction of America's Youth* (1989) to *UFOs and the Alien Agenda* (1997). Over time, his ministry focused more on issues of demonic possession and he began performing exorcisms, not only on *'Talk Back'* but as part of a traveling evangelical road show. Currently, he is the leader of Spiritual Freedom Churches International, one of whose projects is to train exorcism teams for deployment around the world. At all points, Larson presents himself as 'the world's foremost expert on cults, the occult, and supernatural phenomena,' a stalwart defender standing in the breach against occult powers that swarm and writhe from under every rock.

In 1998, I attended what Larson advertised as 'Calgary's First Public Exorcism.' Held at a small hotel by the airport, Larson devotees filled the low-ceilinged conference room. A taped presentation preceded his appearance, warming up the crowd with rock video images of spiritual warfare, demonic possession, and the kind of fundamentalist triumphalism that has marked his ministry from its beginning. Once Larson himself took the stage, however, running from the back of the room to the pounding beat of the soundtrack, the evening took a turn toward the mundane. Larson recounted his many battles with the occult, a few people confessed minor sins, repented, and recommitted their lives to Christ, but there was nothing, well, demonic. Even what might have been called the evening's 'main event' turned out to be little more than an uncomfortable teenager trying to figure out who she was confronted by a belligerent preacher determined to prevent her from that. The young girl's goth dress, however, her facial piercings (which Larson identified as demonic entry points), as well as her ability to withstand his aggressive, almost abusive manner—for Larson, all these were clear evidence of the 'demon of teen rebellion.' More troubling, though, was Larson's insistence that he couldn't cast the demon out because the young woman 'has bipolar disorder, and that would have to be dealt with first' (see Cowan, 2003, 80–86; 2008, 181–83).

Off-the-cuff psychiatric diagnoses notwithstanding, wherever he goes and for as long has he has been in ministry, Bob Larson insists that occult danger and the need for spiritual intervention have never been greater. He points out how the Roman Catholic Church has reinstated exorcism classes for specially selected priests and lay theology students. Indeed, Father Gabriele Amorth (b. 1925), whom many consider the father of the modern Catholic exorcism movement, claims to have performed more than seventy thousand exorcisms—which, as *Times (London)* columnist Giles Coren puckishly notes, means something on the order of four exorcisms per day every day, with only Sundays off (2010). Larson, however, told British journalist Jeff Maysh that 'the Church just can't keep up with the demand' for exorcisms and, despite the claim that he has 'one hundred teams of trained exorcists working all over the world,' 'outbreaks of demonic possession are getting out of control' (Maysh, 2011). Of all these teams, the one that briefly caught the media's attention and was profiled by London's *Daily Mail* featured Larson's sixteen-year-old daughter Brynne and four of her friends. Pert and pretty, clutching Bibles and warding off evil with large, ornate pewter crosses, the five young women look like protagonists in a low-budget horror film. Think *Cheerleader Exorcists*. 'We have found,' Larson opines, 'that our female, teenage exorcists are particularly effective at curing the possessed' (Maysh, 2011).

CHRISTIAN OPPOSITION TO THE OCCULT

At first glance it may seem that Larson and his schoolgirl exorcists, Father Amorth and his seventy thousand exorcisms, C. Peter Wagner and his New Apostolic Reformation, which includes a program to spiritually map demonic hotspots in the United States (2012), or the prayers of controversial Kenyan pastor Thomas Muthee over then-gubernatorial candidate Sarah Palin for protection against witchcraft (Jamieson, 2008), are, as Giles Coren puts it, a bit of a 'woolly scarf' (2010). Christian opposition to what believers perceive as the occult, however—whether understood as demonic possession, witchcraft, satanism, or even alien abduction—has been an important component of Christian belief since the time of the early Church.

According to the Book of Acts, when Paul and Silas were in Philippi, they were confronted by 'a slave girl who had a spirit of divination' and from whom they cast the spirit out (Acts 16: 16–18). In Paul's letter to the Galatians, he warns them that 'sorcery' will be counted among 'the works of the flesh' and that 'those who do such things will not inherit the kingdom of God' (Gal. 6:16–21). Early Church Fathers from Augustine (d. 430 CE) to Gregory the Great (d. 604 CE) wrote and preached against involvement in witchcraft, the former, at least, because he simply could not believe that witches actually existed. Seven centuries later, Thomas Aquinas (d. 1274 CE) argued in the first part of his *Summa Theologica* that by leading them into sin demons participate in the sins of humankind. Two hundred years after that, at the behest of Pope Innocent VIII, two Dominican friars, Jacob Sprenger (d. 1495 CE) and

Heinrich Kramer (d. 1505 CE), produced the infamous *Malleus Maleficarum* ('The Hammer of Witches'), arguably the best-known witch-hunting manual of the day. Unlike Augustine, though, the *Malleus*'s very first question considers whether refusal to believe in witches—the mediaeval proxy for much of the occult world—was tantamount to heresy. The early nineteenth century saw the publication of Sir Walter Scott's *Letters on Demonology and Witchcraft* (1830), a collection of essays on belief in all manner of occult phenomena—witches, ghosts, fairies, and brownies—still abroad in the British Isles (Scott, [1830] 2001; cf. Evans-Wentz, 1911). At the same time, across the Atlantic, one of the principal complaints against Joseph Smith, the founder of the Mormon Church, was that he was a 'glass-looker,' a treasure hunter whose occult methods deeply informed the development of Mormonism (Quinn, 1987)—a charge that continues to haunt Latter-day Saints. With the rise of fundamentalist Protestantism in the early twentieth century, and especially the significant emergence of new religious movements following World War Two, identifying and countering the occult has never been far from Christian vogue.

Although often rubriced as 'the paranormal,' according to a 2005 Gallup study (Moore, 2005) belief in various aspects of the occult remains significant among Americans. Just over 40 percent, for example, believe that 'people on this earth are sometimes possessed by the devil'; this is down a bit from 1990, when that figure neared 50 percent. While less than 30 percent of Britons profess belief in the devil (Kiefer, 2004), among Americans that belief rose from 55 percent in 1990 to 70 percent in 2004 (Winseman, 2004). Nearly 40 percent believe 'that houses can be haunted,' a figure that has risen steadily since 1990, while about one-third of respondents indicated their belief 'that spirits of dead people can come back in certain places and situations.' Despite the enormous popularity of supernaturally oriented television programs such as *Beyond with James van Praagh*, *Crossing Over with John Edward*, *Medium*, and *The Ghost Whisperer*, only about one American in five actually believes 'that people can hear from or communicate mentally with someone who has died' (cf. Cowan, forthcoming). About one in four believe in 'the power of the mind to know the past and predict the future,' about the same as believe that 'the position of the stars or planets can affect people's lives.'

For millions of conservative Christians, however, these are alarming statistics. From belief in ghosts to spirit communication to demonic possession, all are considered aspects of the same Satanic plan for domination and Christians such as these have learned (and are socialized) to find the occult in almost every cultural nook and cranny. In *Jesus Camp*, for example, Rachel Grady and Heidi Ewing's 2006 documentary about a fundamentalist Christian summer camp, camp director Becky Fisher cautions the children and their parents about the dangers of the phenomenally popular *Harry Potter* series of novels and films. 'Let me say something about Harry Potter,' she warns them breathlessly. 'Warlocks are enemies of God. And I don't care what kind of hero they are, had it been in the Old Testament Harry Potter would have been put to death.' A few scattered 'Amens' greet her pronouncement. 'You don't make heroes out of warlocks,' Fisher declares. Although controversy generated by *Jesus Camp* prompted Fisher to cease operations shortly after the film's release, Christian opposition to *Harry Potter* remains strong (see Abanes, 2001; Matrisciana, 2001), while anti-*Potter* books appear regularly on religious bookstore shelves, Web sites, and blogs.

Indeed, in what I have called elsewhere 'the democratization of the countercult' (Cowan, 2003, 115–31), as for so many other interests and pursuits the Internet has spawned a number of Christian ministries contending against the darkness in its battle against the occult. Marcia Montenegro, for example, is a former astrologer and New Age devotee who converted to fundamentalist Christianity in 1990. Since then, she has produced 'Christian Answers for a New Age,' a Web site on which she posts brief articles related to all aspects of occult belief and comments on trends in popular culture. Almost anything that does not accord with her strict, conservative Christian beliefs is part of the occult worldview. From astrology to the Mayan 2012 'prophecies,' from Reiki to Elizabeth Wilson's phenomenally popular memoir, *Eat, Pray, Love*, and popular films ranging from *Avatar* to *The Matrix* to *Twilight*, Montenegro diligently points out where she believes these deviate from 'biblical Christianity,' exposing them as part of a Satanic conspiracy that began in the Garden of Eden and will only conclude with the Devil's ultimate defeat at the End of Days.

SKEPTICS: THE OTHER SIDE OF THE OCCULT COIN

For Bob Larson, Becky Fisher, and Marcia Montenegro, the world is cast in stark, Manichaean terms, a neverending battle between light and dark. For the tens of millions of Christians like them who are involved in this kind of spiritual warfare two things are never in doubt: (a) the occult in all its forms is a clear and present danger, and (b) because Satan will be defeated by God, Christians will prevail in the end.

A much smaller anti-occult movement, however, is based on significantly different premises and many of its members consider Christians such as Larson, Fisher, and Montenegro just as deluded as those who believe they are demon-possessed, in communication with the dead, or can predict the future by whatever means. These are the skeptics, represented most prominently in North America by the Skeptics Society (and its quarterly, *Skeptic Magazine*) and the Committee for the Scientific Investigation of Claims of the Paranormal (CSICOP, and its journal, *Skeptical Inquirer*). Taking a critical, though in many ways no less Manichaean stance toward all supernaturalist claims, whether from dominant religious traditions such as Christianity or fringe groups such as alien contactees, both the Skeptics Society and CSICOP work actively to investigate, falsify, and, in most instances, debunk claims of the occult and the paranormal.

One of the most enduring aspects of occult phenomena, for example, and one to which skeptics have devoted considerable resources for well over a century, is alleged communication with the dead, a practice many anthropologists and evolutionary psychologists locate at the origins of human religious consciousness. From late modern American mediums such as John Edward, James van Praagh, and Sylvia Browne to 'docu-soap' television programs such as *Ghost Hunters*, *Ghost Hunters International*, and, for younger viewers, *Ghost Hunters Academy*, the popularity of entertainment products dealing with aspects of the afterlife demonstrates how deeply embedded these beliefs remain in Western culture (see Hill, 2011). For skeptics, this is all the more reason to challenge these beliefs at every opportunity. In 'Talking Twaddle with the Dead,' *Skeptic* publisher Michael Shermer (1998) exposes the 'cold reading' and other fraudulent practices of James van Praagh, the principal means by which charlatans and supposed occultists prey on the grieving and the gullible.

Shermer carefully documents how, in claiming to speak with (and for) the dead, van Praagh is wrong far more often than he is right. Van Praagh focuses on his relatively few 'hits' while ignoring his 'misses,' and the willingness of people to believe fills in the rest. Viewers follow him because they are distraught and desperate for 'news' of their loved ones. Similarly, in 'Psychic Defective,' historian Ryan Shaffer investigates Sylvia Browne (d.2013), for many years a weekly guest on the popular *Montel Williams* talk show, and seen by many skeptics as the prima donna of a particularly odious occult choir (Shaffer and Jadwiszczok, 2010). In a 2003 *Montel* appearance, for instance, Browne told the parents of 11-year old Shawn Hornbeck—who had been missing four months—that their son was dead, and she gave detailed descriptions of who kidnapped him and where his body could be found. None of this was true. Four years later, Shawn was found alive, living a relatively short distance away from his still-grieving parents.

Outraged by this kind of emotional predation, since 1964 stage illusionist and arch-skeptic James Randi (b. 1928), has offered a cash prize—now valued at US $1 million—'to any person who demonstrates any psychic, supernatural, or paranormal ability under satisfactory observation.' Although more than one thousand people have applied for the prize, none has passed even the preliminary test, which 'is intended to determine if the Applicant is likely to perform as promised during the Formal Test' (James Randi Educational Foundation, 2012). In 2001, while a guest on CNN's *Larry King Live*, Sylvia Browne accepted the Randi Challenge but never attempted even the preliminary test.

In all this, two basic principles guide skeptical inquiry into the supernatural and the occult: (a) burden of proof, and (b) species of evidence. First, for skeptics, the burden of proof always lands on those making the claims to supernatural belief or occult experience. Thus, if Bob Larson claims to be locked in spiritual combat with a demon, the onus is not on the skeptic to prove he isn't, but on Larson to demonstrate his assertions. Otherwise, the skeptic is always in the untenable position of having to prove a negative. Second, as sociologist Marcello Truzzi (d. 2003) wrote in the first issue of the *Zetetic Scholar*, the forerunner to *Skeptical Inquirer*, 'an extraordinary claim requires extraordinary proof' (1978, 11). Reaching back both to Occam's Razor and to David Hume's famous essay, 'On Miracles,' if Bob Larson wants to prove the existence of demons, then skeptics will require something more robust, as it were, than personal anecdotes and faith-based reliance on a particular interpretation of the Bible. Before the occult even becomes a possibility, medical and psychiatric disorders must be excluded as explanations, and skeptical investigations must control for socialization and cultural expectations among participants. Only when all naturalistic explanations have been exhausted can the skeptic consider the supernatural. Indeed, as Thomas Huxley wrote in 1866, for those who would improve our understanding of the world, 'skepticism is the highest of duties, blind faith the one unpardonable sin.'

Scientific investigation, rational skepticism, and naturalistic explanation replace what many skeptics regard as anti-intellectual credulity, faith-based naïveté, and simple wishful thinking. Rather than attack by actual supernatural entities, for example, clinical psychologist Andew Reisner (2001) explains belief in demonic visitation (including its late modern variant, alien abduction) as examples of hypnagogic or hypnapompic hallucination. However real the events may seem to the experient, many of these phenomena are reported as we either descend into sleep (hypnagogia) or emerge from it (hypnapompia). That our brains simply confuse stimuli during these transitional states is a more realistic explanation than one requiring the existence of an entire supernatural order—the existence of which is itself in doubt. Similarly, in 2005, skeptic Lee Traynor found himself in Eagle Rock, California, attending an exorcism in a disused movie theater. In this case, the 'main event' was a married woman involved in an affair with another man—for the congregation a clear sign of occult activity, a demon of lust or adultery, or both. As the pastor tried repeatedly to get the demon to reveal itself—with no more success than Bob Larson had in Calgary—'his futile attempts at getting the spirit to speak up turned increasingly pathetic' (Traynor, 2005, 17). In this case, neither demonic possession nor the pastor's attempts at exorcism are seen as credible. According to Traynor, given the woman's ethnic heritage and the religious culture in which she was raised, as strange as it may seem, it was less traumatic for her to profess belief in demonic oppression and submit to an 'exorcism' than to admit to an extramarital affair.

While this incident may have been embarrassing for the woman and provided Traynor with material for an amusing column, skeptics point out that there is significantly more at stake than social discomfiture. That same year, only a month after Traynor witnessed the 'exorcism' in California, Maricica Cornici, a 23-year old Orthodox nun, died at a remote monastery in northeastern Romania. She had been chained to a cross for five days, gagged to prevent the so-called demon from speaking, beaten repeatedly, and denied food or water—all in an attempt to exorcise the demons by which the priest in charge believed she was possessed. Less than three months earlier, Cornici had been diagnosed with schizophrenia. From belief in demonic vistation to faith healing, from contact with the deceased to claims of psychic divination, at stake for skeptics is the intellectual and moral evolution of the human race.

A WORLD VERSUS *THE* WORLD

In his 'Letter to the Six Billionth Person,' Salman Rushdie, another skeptic who has felt the palpable wrath of religious believers, tells his unknown, utterly singular reader the basics of just a few creation stories: dancing sky gods, *creatio ex nihilo*, 'junior deities' and the 'cruel pantheons of the great polytheisms.' He then points out what he thinks should be obvious to everyone, but just as obviously isn't: 'As human knowledge has grown, it has also become plain that every religious story ever told about how we got here is quite simply wrong. This, finally, is what all religions have in common. They didn't get it right' (Rushdie, 1999). His point? If we cannot trust religion—whether dominant and socially approved, or marginal and stigmatized—with the most basic facts of our origin, why should we trust them with anything more significant than that?

In one important respect, though, for both Christian believers and secular skeptics the problem of the occult is the same, what Peter Berger and Thomas Luckmann identify as the sociological problem of '"*a* world", rather than "*the* world"' (1966, 192). Both see their battle against the occult as a contest for the real world. For many Christians, constant battle against the occult reinforces the plausibility, legitimacy, and presumed inevitability of their own worldview. It continually remakes their very identities *as* Christians. For skeptics, on the other hand, debunking the occult—whether its believers are part of the dominant religion or not—reinforces their conviction that humankind can put away the childish fears that have kept it mired in darkness for so long. Put differently, for believers such as Bob Larson or Marcia Montenegro, opposition to the occult is a question of ensuring that people back the right supernatural horse. For skeptics such as Michael Shermer or James Randi, it means continually pointing out not only that there are no supernatural horses in the race, but that there is no race.

REFERENCES AND FURTHER READING

Abanes, Richard (2001) *Harry Potter and the Bible: The Menace Behind the Magic*, Camp Hill, Penn.: Horizon Books.

Berger, Peter, and Thomas Luckmann (1966) *The Social Construction of Reality: A Treatise in the Sociology of Knowledge*, London: Penguin.

Coren, Giles (2010) 'Four exorcisms a day. Yes, it's a devil of a job', *The Times (London)* (13 March), 18.

Cowan, Douglas E. (2003) *Bearing False Witness: An Introduction to the Christian Countercult*, Westport, CT: Praeger Publishers.

——(2008) *Sacred Terror: Religion and Horror on the Silver Screen*, Waco, TX: Baylor University Press.

——(forthcoming) 'Psychics, Skeptics, and Popular Culture', in *The Brill Handbook of Spiritualism and Channeling*, ed., Cathy Gutierrez, Leiden: Brill.

Cuneo, Michael W. (2001) *American Exorcism: Expelling Demons in the Land of Plenty*, New York: Doubleday.

Evans-Wentz, W. Y. (1911) *The Fairy-faith in Celtic Countries*, London: Henry Frowde.

Frazier, Kendrick., ed. (1998) *Encounters with the Paranormal: Science, Knowledge, and Belief*, Amherst, NY: Prometheus Books.

Goode, Erich (2000) *Paranormal Beliefs: A Sociological Introduction*, Prospect Heights, Ill.: Waveland Press.

Hill, Annette (2011) *Paranormal Media: Audiences, Spirits and Magic in Popular Culture*, Oxford and New York.

James Randi Educational Foundation (2012) 'Challenge Application.' Online: www.randi.org/site/index.php/1m-challenge/challenge-application.html (accessed November 10, 2012).

Jamieson, Alastair (2008) 'Sarah Palin in witchcraft prayer on video clip', *Telegraph* (25 September). Online: www.telegraph.co.uk/news/worldnews/sarah-palin/3077964/Sarah-Palin-in-witchcraft-prayer-on-video-clip.html (accessed October 5, 2012).

Kiefer, Heather Mason (2004) 'Divine Subjects: Canadians Believe, Britons Skeptical', *Gallup®* (16 November). Online: www.gallup.com/poll/14083/Divine-Subjects-Canadians-Believe-Britons-Skeptical.aspx (accessed 3 November 2012).

Larson, Bob (1982) *Larson's Book of Cults*, Wheaton, Ill.: Tyndale House.

——(1989) *Satanism: The Seduction of America's Youth*, Nashville, Tenn.: Thomas Nelson.

——(1997) *UFOs and the Alien Agenda: Uncovering the Mystery behind UFOs and the Paranormal*, Nashville, Tenn.: Thomas Nelson.

——(1999) *Larson's Book of Spiritual Warfare*, Nashville, Tenn.: Thomas Nelson.

Maysh, Jeff (2011) 'Meet the exorcist schoolgirls who spend their time casting out demons around the world', *Daily Mail* (11 August). Online: www.dailymail.co.uk/ news/article-2024621 (accessed 2 October 2012).

Moore, David W. (2005) 'Three in Four Americans Believe in Paranormal' *Gallup®* (16 June). Online: www.gallup.com/poll/16915/Three-Four-Americans-Believe-Paranormal.aspx (accessed 3 November, 2012).
Quinn, D. Michael (1987) *Early Mormonism and the Magical Worldview*, Salt Lake City, UT: Signature Books.
Reisner, Andrew D. (2001) 'A Psychological Case Study of "Demon" and "Alien" Visitation.' *Skeptical Inquirer* 25, no. 2, 46–50.
Rushdie, Salman (1999) 'Imagine no heaven,' *Guardian* (16 October). Online: www.guardian.co.uk/books/1999/oct/16/salmanrushdie (accessed 13 November 2012).
Sagan, Carl (1996) *The Demon-Haunted World: Science as a Candle in the Dark*, New York: Ballantine.
Scott, Sir Walter (2001 [1830]) *Letters on Demonology and Witchcraft*, Ware, UK: Wordsworth.
Shaffer, Ryan, and Agatha Jadwiszczok (2010) 'Psychic Defective: Sylvia Browne's History of Failure,' *Skeptical Inquirer* 34, no. 2, 38–42.
Shermer, Michael(1998) 'Talking Twaddle with the Dead: The Tragedy of Death—The Farce of James van Praagh', *Skeptic* 6, no. 1, 48–53.
——(2002) *Why People Believe Weird Things: Pseudoscience, Superstition, and Other Confusions of Our Time*, rev. ed., New York: Henry Holt.
Traynor, Lee (2005) 'A Skeptic Goes to an Exorcism,' *Skeptic* 12, no. 1, 15–17.
Truzzi, Marcello (1978) 'On the Extraordinary: An Attempt at Clarification,' *Zetetic Scholar* 1, no. 1: 11–19.
Wagner, C. Peter, ed. (2012) *Territorial Spirits: Practical Strategies for How to Crush the Enemy Through Spiritual Warfare*, Shippensburg, Penn.: Destiny Image.
Winseman, Albert L. (2004) 'Eternal Destinations: Americans Believe in Heaven, Hell', *Gallup®* (25 May). Online: www.gallup.com/poll/11770/Eternal-Destinations-Americans-Believe-Heaven-Hell.aspx (accessed November 3, 2012).

Films

Grady, Rachel, and Heidi Ewing, dir. (2006) *Jesus Camp*, Magnolia Pictures.
Matrisciana, Caryl, dir. (2001) *Harry Potter: Witchcraft Repackaged*, Jeremiah Films.

INDEX

Note: Page numbers in *italic* refer to figures.

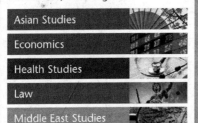